SCULPTURES FROM HARYANA
(Iconography and Style)

SCULPTURES FROM HARYANA
(Iconography and Style)

By
DEVENDRA HANDA

INDIAN INSTITUTE OF ADVANCED STUDY
Shimla

ARYAN BOOKS INTERNATIONAL
New Delhi

SCULPTURES FROM HARYANA

ISBN-81-7305-307-3

First published in **2006** by:

INDIAN INSTITUTE OF ADVANCED STUDY
Rashtrapati Nivas, Shimla - 171 005

and

ARYAN BOOKS INTERNATIONAL
Pooja Apartments, 4B, Ansari Road, Darya Ganj, New Delhi - 110 002
Tel. : 23287589, 23255799; Fax : 91-11-23270385; E-mail : aryanbooks@vsnl.com

Computer Typeset and Printed in India at
ABI Prints & Publishing Co., New Delhi

Dedicated to
the sacred memory of my parents

Preface

The present work embodies my Project Report on 'Sculptures From Haryana' submitted to the Indian Institute of Advanced Study, Shimla as a Fellow. I am thankful to the governing body, the Chairman and the Director of the Institute of Advanced Study, Shimla, for selecting me for the fellowship (May 2000 – May 2003) to work on the project which enabled me to put at one place what I had been studying almost all through my academic career till now. The Institute is a wonderful one to pursue higher studies and research.

My interest in sculptures goes back to 1964 when after my training in archaeology I happened to visit the famous pilgrim spot of Pehowa near Kurukshetra from where I acquired two fragments of a Vishṇu image showing *gadā* (mace) and *chakra* (discus) with attached steles carrying the representations of Brahmā-Sarasvatī and Śiva-Pārvatī respectively. These relics were deposited with Dr. Buddha Prakash, the then Director of the Institute of Indic Studies, Kurukshetra University, Kurukshetra. Since then I have sustained interest in the history and archaeology of the region and have also been bringing to light some of its important relics. Archaeologists and art historians in India were pained when the Śuṅga pillars from Amin near Kurukshetra were smuggled leaving their duplicates in the village. When the customs authorities at Bombay seized and put them under police custody, their duplicates there were again substituted for the originals. It was a matter of satisfaction that the original pillars were located in England and a case was filed. In the court again two sets were produced and India was asked to identify and get back the originals. Since Shri R.C. Agrawala had studied these pillars and published them in the *Lalit-Kala* (No. 14), he was deputed to do the needful. Ultimately the originals were brought back and are now displayed in the National Museum, New Delhi. The instance shows the importance of documentation.

Thefts have continued unabated even afterwards. A Vishṇu image was stolen from the Lal Dass Mandir from the village Kosli in district Rewari but was recovered and was examined by C. Sivaramamurti and P. Banerji in the office of the SSP, Rohtak on 6.7.1973. Vāmana and other sculptures from Mohanbari (Salhawas) in district Jhajjar were stolen on 18. 9. 1977. Sculptures from Jhanswa, Mohanbari, Jhadli, Goriya, Lulodh, Sudhrana, and Sundehri were also stolen as complained by the villagers. Many sculptures have been pilfered from Ahrwan in district Faridabad. Local people tell that Jaina sculptures obtained from the old mound at Binwa near Punahna in district Gurgaon were stolen. A raid at one of the posh houses in New Delhi many years ago resulted in the seizure of hundreds of art-pieces collected from the neighboring states including Haryana. The beautiful images of Mahishāsuramardinī and Sūrya from Gujjar Kheri in district Sonepat were smuggled but recovered with the help of the police in 1985. The Gurgaon police recovered sculptures stolen from Kira in district Faridabad and I had the opportunity to examine them in the police Malkhana there in 1990. The study and documentation of all known images has thus been a great desideratum.

Precious little was known from Haryana (then a part of Punjab) when S.K. Saraswati wrote *A Survey of Indian Sculpture* in 1957. When the prestigious art magazine *Mārg* brought out its Haryana Heritage Number in September 1974, it could illustrate only about a dozen sculptures in spite of the fact that the *Mārg* team toured the state for quite some time. When C. Sivaramamurti's *The Art of India* containing 1175 illustrations was published in 1977, it included only one piece from Haryana, that of a Śuṅga terracotta from Sugh, which too had been presented by the Panjab University to the National Museum, of which he was the Director at that time. In spite of a few pieces discovered till then, the state remained almost terra incognito for the known pieces remained either buried in not easily available books and journals or were not artistic enough to merit illustration in standard books. This inspired my quest and I have been pursuing the subject with great interest all through my career. A short stint as the Deputy Director of the Department of Archaeology and Museums, Haryana on deputation from the Panjab University during 1984-85 provided me the chance to make a first hand study of the collected material, see the different collections, public and private, and myself discover and collect a lot of material. The respective Directors of the Department of Archaeology and Museums, Haryana were kind enough to allow me to study and photograph the sculptures in the Department. All my colleagues in that Department, Sarvashri Madhav Acharya, D.S. Malik, J.S. Khatri, Dhoop Singh, Vinod Gupta and others, were quite helpful and made my work convenient. I am thankful to them all. I made occasional exploratory tours with friends and colleagues also; Prof. Ashvini Agrawal and Dr. Lalman of Panjab University, Dr. Mohinder Singh of Kurukshetra University, Dr. Manmohan Kumar of M.D. University, Rohtak to mention only a few. My friend Prof. Suraj Bhan put his collection of photographs of sculptures of the state at my disposal. Mr. Rajesh Purohit of Sri Krishna Museum, Kurukshetra sent me the photographs and details of some images recovered by him from Rasina and Thanesar. Photographs of the Govardhanadhara and Varāha images from Fatehabad now preserved in the Victoria and Albert Museum, London were kindly supplied by Dr. Guy, the then curator of the Museum. Prof. H.A. Phadke (since retired) of the Department of Ancient Indian History, Culture & Archaeology, Kurukshetra University, Kurukshetra kindly supplied the photographs of some sculptures in the departmental museum. The Government Museum & Art Gallery, Chandigarh also provided photographs of some sculptures and terracottas in its collection. The photograph of the Mehrauli Samkarshana image was obtained from the National Museum, New Delhi. Shri C. Dorje of the Chandigarh Circle of the Archaeological Survey of India (now Director, New Delhi) was always ready with any sort of help I required. He also provided some photographs included in this work. The magnanimous chief of the Asthal Bohr allowed me to photograph the sculptures in the Math. I have also copied some illustrations from the books and articles published earlier by Pratapaditya Pal, Joanna Williams, Yogananda Shastri, R.C. Agrawala and others. Taking help from what was published or even unpublished in the form of University dissertations that came to my notice, and the discoveries made by me and others have enabled me to list more than one hundred ninety sites which have yielded sculptural remains. Some of them have yielded unfinished sculptures also furnishing evidence of these sites being the centres of art in the medieval period.

I feel much beholden to the great polymath and renowned savant Prof. G.C. Pande, Chairman, and Prof. Bhuvan Chandel, the present Director, of the Institute of Advanced Study for including the work in the publication program of the Institute. The friendly Secretary and Deputy Secretary, the rich library with ever smiling staff, ever-accessible medical officer, the caring APO and PRO, the computer engineers, personnel in the estate, accounts, publication, store, etc. and of course every person in the Institute has been quite helpful and I thank them most cordially for all their help. I have benefited myself from the discussions with some of my learned colleagues at the Institute following this discipline and benefited from their views and discussions.

The late Prof. Ajay Mitra Shastri and Shri R.C. Agrawala have always been inspiring me and taking keen interest in my work. I have no words to thank them adequately.

I am, however, aware of my failings. Although I have visited most of the sites mentioned in this report, I could not visit every site yielding sculptural remains. Nor could I get all the desired photographs even though I was able to procure some from the Lahore Museum. I gratefully acknowledge the help of all those persons and institutions who have provided information and illustrative material.

I thank my son Tushar for spending many hours with me to scan the images and provide the technical help at the computer. To thank other members of my family who have always provided moral support will be mere formality. There may be some lapses here and there, for which I beg to be excused.

Chandigarh **Devendra Handa**

Contents

Transliteration Table

अ A, a	आ Ā, ā	इ I, i	ई Ī, ī	उ U, u
ऊ Ū, ū	ऋ Ṛi, ṛi	ऌ Ḷ, ḷ	ए E, e	ऐ Ai, ai
ओ O, o	औ Au, au	अँ Aṃ, aṃ	अः Aḥ, aḥ	
क् K, k	ख् Kh, kh	ग् G, g	घ् Gh, gh	ङ् Ṅ, ṅ
च् Ch, ch	छ् Chh, chh	ज् J, j	झ् Jh, jh	ञ् Ñ, ñ
ट् Ṭ, ṭ	ठ् Ṭh, ṭh	ड् Ḍ, ḍ	ढ् Ḍh, ḍh	ण् Ṇ, ṇ
त् T, t	थ् Th, th	द् D, d	ध् Dh, dh	न् N, n
प् P, p	फ् Ph, ph	ब् B, b	भ् Bh, bh	म् M, m
य् Y, y	र् R, r	ल् L, l	व् V, v	श् Ś, ś
ष् Sh, sh	स् S, s	ह् H, h	क्ष् ksh	त्र् tr
ज्ञ् jñ				

Jihvāmūlīya X

Upadhamānīya ≍

Common words and modern names are usually written without diacriticals. In the original titles and quotations, Ṛ/ṛ, C/c, Ṣ/ṣ, have also been used for ऋ, च्, ष्, *etc.*

Abbreviations

AI — *Ancient India*, Bulletin of the Archaeological Survey of India, New Delhi
AMB — *Aṃśumadbhedāgana*
ARASI — *Annual Report, Archaeological Survey of India*
ASI — *Archaeological Survey of India*
ASS — *Ānandāśrama Sanskrit Series*
AV — *Atharvaveda*
Ait. Br. — *Aitareya Brāhmaṇa*
BMA — *Bulletin of Archaeology and Museums in U.P.*
BS — *Bṛihatsaṃhitā*
c. — *circa*
CAGI — Cunningham's *Ancient Geography of India*
CASR — Cunnungham's *Archaeological Survey Reports*
CII — *Corpus Inscriptionum Indicarum*
DHI — *Development of Hindu Iconography* by J.N. Banerjea
DMT — *Devatāmūrtiprakaraṇa*
EHI — *Elements of Hindu Iconography* by T.A. Gopinath Rao
EI — *Epigraphia Indica*
EW — *East and West*
GOS — Gaikwad Oriental Series
HARDAM — Department of Archaeology and Museums, Haryana
IA — *Indian Antiquary*
IAR — *Indian Archaeology : A Review*
IHQ — *Indian Historical Quarterly*
IV — *Iconography of Viṣṇu* by Kalpana Desai
JA — *Journal Asiatique*
JASB — *Journal of the Asiatic Society, Bombay*
JIH — *Journal of Indian History*
JIM — *Journal of Indian Museums*
JISOA — *Journal of the Indian Society of Oriental Art*
JNSI — *Journal of the Numismatic Society of India*
JOI — *Journal of Oriental Institute*

JRAS	*Journal of the Royal Asiatic Society*
LK	*Lalit-Kalā*
MASI	*Memoir of the Archaeological Survey of India*
Mārk. P.	*Mārkaṇḍeya Purāṇa*
Mbh.	*Mahābhārata*
P	*Purāṇa*
PP	*Padma Purāṇa*
PS	*Pinjore Sculptures* by U.V. Singh.
PURBA	*Panjab University Research Bulletin (Arts),* Chandigarh
Rām.	*Rāmāyaṇa*
RL	*Roopa-Lekhā*
RM	*Rūpa-Maṇḍana*
RV	*Ṛigveda*
ŚB	*Śatapatha Brāhmaṇa*
SBE	*Sacred Books of the East Series*
SPB	*Suprabhedāgama*
SR	*Śilparatna*
TS	*Taittirīya Saṃhitā*
VDP	*Vishṇudharmottara Purāṇa*
VIJ	*Vishveshvaranand Indological Journal*
VSMRS	*Vaiṣṇavism, Śaivism and Minor Religious Systems* by R.G. Bhandarkar
YV	*Yajurveda*

List of Illustrations

FIGURES

PLATES

Chapter 1

Introduction

Though the present state of Haryana as a politico-administrative entity came into existence on November 1, 1966 as a result of the reorganization of Punjab (which had already been divided by the partition of the country in 1947) on linguistic basis, yet the territorial designations of Hariala,[1] Haritānaka,[2] Hariyānaka,[3] Haritāna,[4] Hariyāna,[5] etc.[6] found in literature and epigraphs bear ample evidence to the fact that this part of the country was known to the people as a distinct geographical-cultural unit for the last many centuries. Bounded by the Shiwaliks and the Yamunā on the east, the river Ghaggar on the northwest, the semi-arid tracts of northeastern Rajasthan on the western and south-western side and by the holy land of Kṛishṇa and Rādhā, Vraja-bhūmi, on the south, Haryana is now divided into nineteen districts of Ambala, Bhiwani, Faridabad, Fatehabad, Gurgaon, Hisar, Jhajjar, Jind, Kaithal, Karnal, Kurukshetra, Mahendragarh, Panchkula, Panipat, Rewari, Rohtak, Sirsa, Sonepat, and Yamunanagar. Delhi (ancient Ḍhillikā, Yoginīpura and Indraprastha) also formed part of it in ancient times. Wholly or partially, this territory formed part of and has also been known variously as Āryavarta,[7] Brahmarshideśa,[8] Brahmāvarta,[9] Kurukshetra,[10] Madhyadeśa,[11] Uttarāpatha,[12] etc.[13]

The discovery of 103 Pre-Harappan, 44 Harappan and 297 Late (or Post) Harappan sites in Haryana[14] indicates that the alluvial plains of the state were a great attraction for the Chalcolithic people. It thus formed part of the territory where the greatest of the civilizations of the old world evolved, developed and declined. It may rightly be designated as the cradle of the Indian civilization. The Aryans lit the sacred fires on the banks of the Sarasvatī, Dṛishadvatī and Āpayā rivers in Haryana[15] and the Great War was also fought here in the field of Kuru, i.e. Kurukshetra. It has seen the rise and fall of various dynasties, people, sects and many a decisive battle has been fought in its plains.[16]

Ever since the sages and the Bharatas kindled the holy sacrificial fire on the banks of its rivers, the entire region is regarded as sacred and is studded with pilgrimage centers. The association of such centers with certain heroes and deities and their development as centers of religious art in this holy land was thus a natural consequence. Ravages of time and clime, occasional battles and some iconoclastic conquerors have reduced many of those centers to mere mounds and consigned others to oblivion.

Not much was known about the sculptural heritage of the state till about the beginning of the last quarter of the last century. The monumental work of C. Sivaramamurti and M. Bussagli[17] that contains 396 illustrations does not include any specimen of sculpture or terracotta from Haryana. The Haryana Heritage Number of the well-known art journal *Mārg*[18] did not contain much valuable material except a few illustrations of sculptures from Rohtak, Kalayat and Pinjore. The attention of scholars was drawn to this region when two exquisitely carved Śuṅga pillars from Amin near Kurukshetra were stolen and seized by the custom authorities while they were being shipped abroad. They had earlier been published by R.C. Agrawala.[19] It was because of this fact that these pillars, which had been changed with duplicates while in the custody of the custom/police authorities and were shipped abroad, were located in London and ultimately brought back to India. Surprisingly enough, the voluminous and monumental work of C. Sivaramamurti on *The Art of India*[20] which contained 1175 illustrations, included only a Śuṅga terracotta figurine from Sugh, which too had been donated to the National Museum, of which he was the Director at that time, by the Panjab University, Chandigarh. The sculptures reported by Alexander Cunningham during the sixties and seventies of the nineteenth century,[21] Charles Jas. Rodgers during 1888-89,[22] the Śuṅga yakshī from Mehrauli and yaksha from Palwal discovered during 1912 and 1914 and published by Vasudeva Sharan Agrawala,[23] and sculptures recovered during the excavations at Agroha in 1939 by H.L. Srivastava,[24] some Jaina images from Rohtak noticed by B.C. Bhattacharya[25] and even the exquisite pieces discovered by the officers of the Archaeological Survey of India from Asthal Bohr, Rohtak,[26] sculptures and terracottas from the collection of the Gurukula Museum, Jhajjar,[27] and some images of Vishṇu and Hari-Hara explored from southern Haryana[28] remained buried in the reports of the survey, books and journals.

Archaeological explorations and excavations and some chance discoveries, however, have continued and brought to light some relics. I myself have been pursuing the search for relics of art in this state during the whole of my career extending over almost the last four decades now and have been fortunate in bringing to light some important sculptures and temples. The renowned art historian Shri R.C. Agrawala and some other scholars too have published some material, which came to their notice. Swami Omanand Saraswati of Jhajjar Gurukula has collected a good number of archaeological and art objects in the Gurukula where he has set up a museum. Unfortunately, however, the sculptural wealth amassed there has mostly remained unpublished except a few pieces. The Department of Archaeology and Museum, Haryana (now located at Panchkula, henceforth referred to as HARDAM) too possesses a large number of such remains, which again are not known to the outside world. Some sculptures from Haryana are preserved in the Department of Ancient Indian History, Culture and Archaeology, Panjab University, Chandigarh. Of these, I have published some important pieces. S.P. Shukla has fortunately published sculptures and terracottas collected by the Department of Ancient Indian History, Culture and Archaeology of the Kurukshetra University.[29] Being, however, a University publication, the catalogue of Shukla is not widely known. Sculptures of Haryana found in the pre-partition days and housed in the Lahore Museum were obtained as India's share and are now preserved in the Government Museum and Art Gallery at Chandigarh. These are included in a publication of the Museum.[30] This too has remained confined to sale on the museum counter and is hardly known to outsiders. A very important hoard of bronzes had come to light accidentally from Hansi in 1982. It lay buried in the vaults of HARDAM till 1990 and in the Pārśvanātha Digambara Jaina Atiśaya-kshetra at Hansi since then and has only recently been published by me.[31] Another hoard of Jaina bronzes from Charkhi Dadri lies preserved in HARDAM. As the Deputy Director of the State Department during 1984-85, I myself had an opportunity to locate, collect and study numerous art objects and even centers of art in Haryana and added nearly 150 pieces to the collection of the Deparment. Some iconographically interesting and exquisitely carved pieces were also saved from being smuggled out of the country. The researchers of the

Kurukshetra and M.D. University, Rohtak have also discovered valuable sculptures and have listed them in their dissertations and theses, which remain by and large unpublished. Many IAS officers of Haryana and certain individuals too possess some interesting sculptures from the state. Hundreds, probably thousands, of pieces belonging to Haryana have already been stolen, smuggled out and even broken. The rich material awaited proper study and publication.

A large number of sites yielding art remains are known to us now (Fig. 1). A collated list of important sites yielding art remains, visited and explored by others and me is given below.

1. **Ad Badri** at the foot of the Shiwalik hills about 15 km from Kapālamochana is regarded as the place where the Sarasvatī descends into the plains of Haryana. It is the last village on Haryana's border with Himachal. There is a medieval temple at Ad Badri with an image of Umā-Maheśvara. A broken head of Buddha has also been obtained from here.[32]
2. **Agroha**, identified with ancient Agrodaka, situated about 23 km north-northwest of Hisar on Delhi-Fazilka highway in district Hisar, is a well known archaeological site spread over more than 650 acres of land with a chain of mounds rising to more than 25 m above the surrounding fields. The Agrawal *banias* trace their origin from Agroha. The surface finds and the excavations conducted here by Rodgers (1888-89), H.L. Srivastava (1938-39) and HARDAM (1979-85) have brought to light very important coins, seals and sealings, structures, terracottas and sculptures which throw a flood of light on the history of the town and the region.[33]
3. **Ahirwan** about 20 km northeast of Fatehabad on road to Ratia has yielded many sculpted pieces. A Vishṇu head from this site is in the collection of HARDAM (Acc. No. 1/130).
4. **Ahrwan**, located about 12 km southwest of Palwal on road to Hathin, has a very extensive mound spread over about forty acres of land and nearly forty feet high. It has yielded PGW, early historic and medieval remains including copper coins of Śoḍāśa and Hagāmasha, inscribed clay sealings, bricks measuring 36 x 22 x 7 cm, sculptures and terracottas, Muslim glazed ware, and other relics. Some sculptured pieces of about 6th-7th century C.E. are lying in the temple of Lālā Dāsa to the south of the village. Some sculptures of the same period are piled up on the bank of a pool called Suraj Kund to the north of the village while many others are lying in the dilapidated Devī temple nearby. The local people inform that numerous sculptures from this site have been pilfered in the past.
5. **Ahir Majra** near Gujjar Kheri in district Sonepat has some sculptures.[34]
6. **Akbarpur-Barota** is located about 10 km east of Sonepat. The Gurukula Museum, Jhajjar has collected some sculptures from this site.
7. **Amin** (29° 54' N. and 76° 52' E.) is situated about 8 km southeast by south of Kurukshetra. It is associated with Abhimanyu and has a very huge mound measuring about a km by half and about sixty feet high, which yields antiquities from PGW onwards.[35] The red sandstone Śuṅga pillars were stolen from this site in the sixties of the last century and recovered from London in the next decade. They are now preserved in the National Museum, New Delhi. Spooner described a later Gupta stone slab from Amin bearing a four-armed figure of Gaṇapati with Śiva and Pārvatī seated on his proper left. The site has also yielded a stone Vishṇu head and some terracotta figurines.
8. **Anjanthali** in district Karnal has a temple of Añjanā, mother of Hanumān, located on the ancient mound and has yielded an image of *Pañchatapas* Pārvatī.

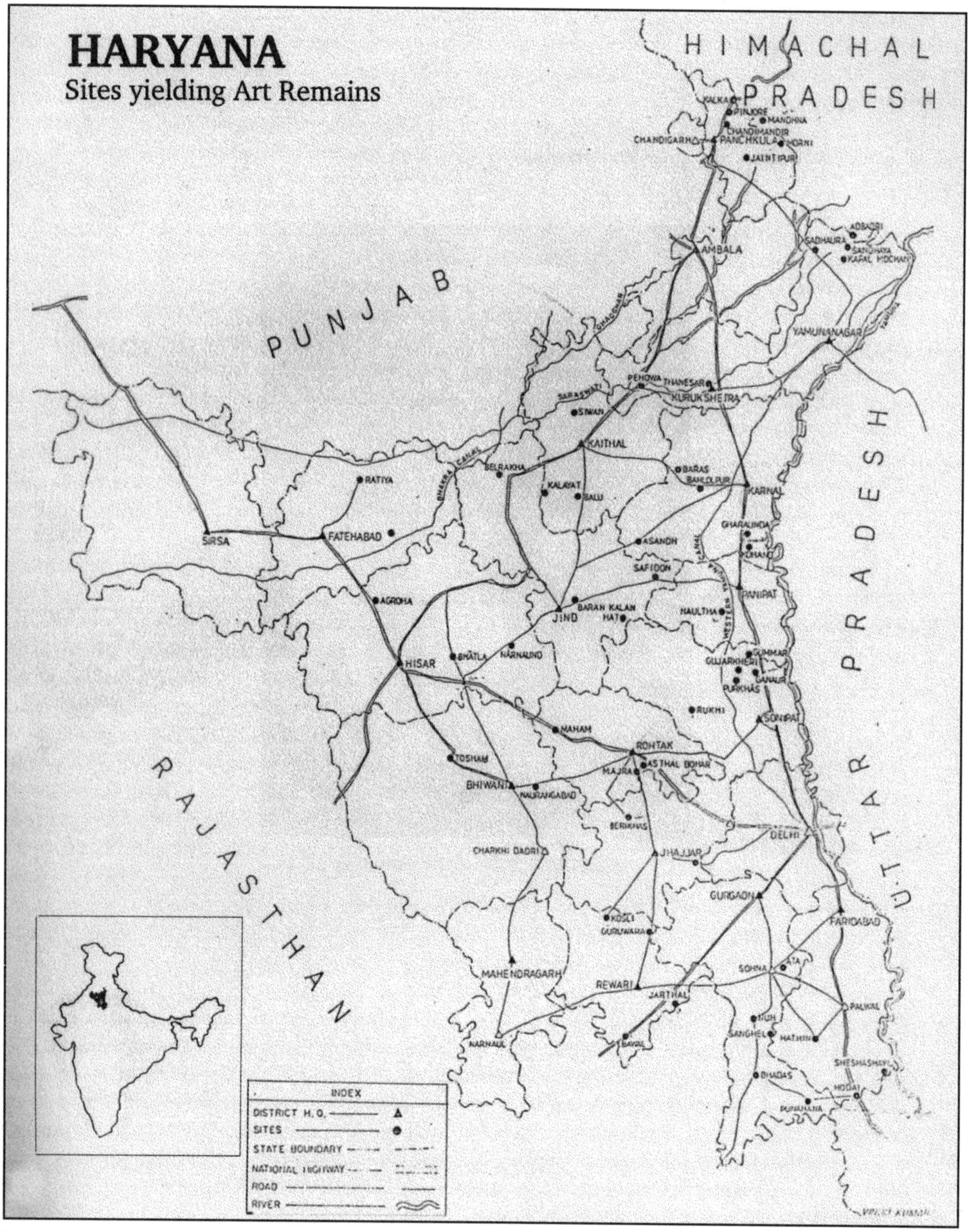

Fig. 1. Map of Haryana showing sites yielding art remains.

9. **Asandh** in tahsil and district Jhajjar has an extensive ten-acre and twenty feet high old mound yielding medieval remains. A medieval image of Vaikuṇṭha from this site is now housed in the Gurukula Museum at Jhajjar.
10. **Asiaki** is situated about 16 km north of Rewari and has four old mounds all yielding early medieval remains including broken images of Śeshaśāyī, Umā-Maheśvara, etc.[36]
11. **Ashrafgarh** is located about 7 km northeast of Jind. The mound here yields Late Harappan, PGW, early historic and medieval remains. An image of Mahishāsuramardinī is also known from this site.
12. **Asthal Bohr**, located about 4 km south of Rohtak on Delhi road, has become a part of Rohtak itself with the expansion of the city. More than a century back, Rodgers had noted that the nearby Bohr village "is full of remains, large and sculptured bricks, portions of sculptured stone temples and some beautiful stone images nearly perfect. In the chaupír or village meeting room is a large inscribed stone, 4 feet by 1 foot 9 inches, containing 22 lines. The images are in a small temple west of the village."[37] Nothing is known about the inscription and the images. The monastery called 'Jogion ka Math' at Asthal Bohr, however, has Hindu and Jaina sculptures. The old mound at Bohr yields early historic and medieval remains including beads, terracotta beads and balls, and sculptures. There is evidence that the site was an atelier of art during the medieval period.
13. **Ata** is located about 6 km from Sohna on road to Faridabad in district Gurgaon. In 1975, while constructing a road, some sculptures were recovered. Two of them are now placed in a temple and protected by the state government.
14. **Badali** (28° 30' N. and 76° 45' E.) on the Jhajjar-Najafgarh road has an old mound about 3 km south of the village. The village itself contains sculptures and fragments lying here and there obtained from an old well and elsewhere.
15. **Baghot** (28° 25' N. and 76° 16' E.) is situated about 12 km west of Kanina in district Mahendragarh. A medieval *pedyā* (lower oart of a doorjamb) showing Gaṅgā with an attendant has been found from here.
16. **Bahlolpur Mustarka** (29° 43' 44" N. 76° 50' 42" E.), situated about 16 km west of Karnal, has an old mound measuring 400 x 200 x 7 m, which has yielded late Harapan, early historic and medieval remains including terracotta beads and dabber, a copper coin of the Sultanate period and some sculptures including Gaṇeśa, doorsill, and architectural piece with *gandharvas*.
17. **Baholi** in district Panipat now in the area of the refinery has two mounds, which yield Late Harappan, PGW, early historic (mound I) and medieval (mound II) pottery. Small buff sandstone Vishṇu head of the medieval period was picked up from the surface by me and deposited in HARDAM.
18. **Bamni Khera** situated about 10 km south of Palwal in district Faridabad has yielded some relics of art.
19. **Banbhori** in district Hisar has yielded an image of Mahishamardinī.
20. **Banchari**, 4 km north of Hodal in district Faridabad, has a Śeshaśāyī Vishṇu.
21. **Bans** near Hansi is an old village. A figure of a lion from here has been collected by HARDAM (Acc. No. 1/107).
22. **Barah Kalan** is located about 11 km east of Jind. The old mound here yields PGW, early historic and medieval remains. The place is identified with Varāha-*tīrtha* of the *Mahābhārata* (III.83, 18-19) and has actually yielded a beautiful Varāha image of the early medieval period under worship in the Varāha temple by the side of a tank. Bathing

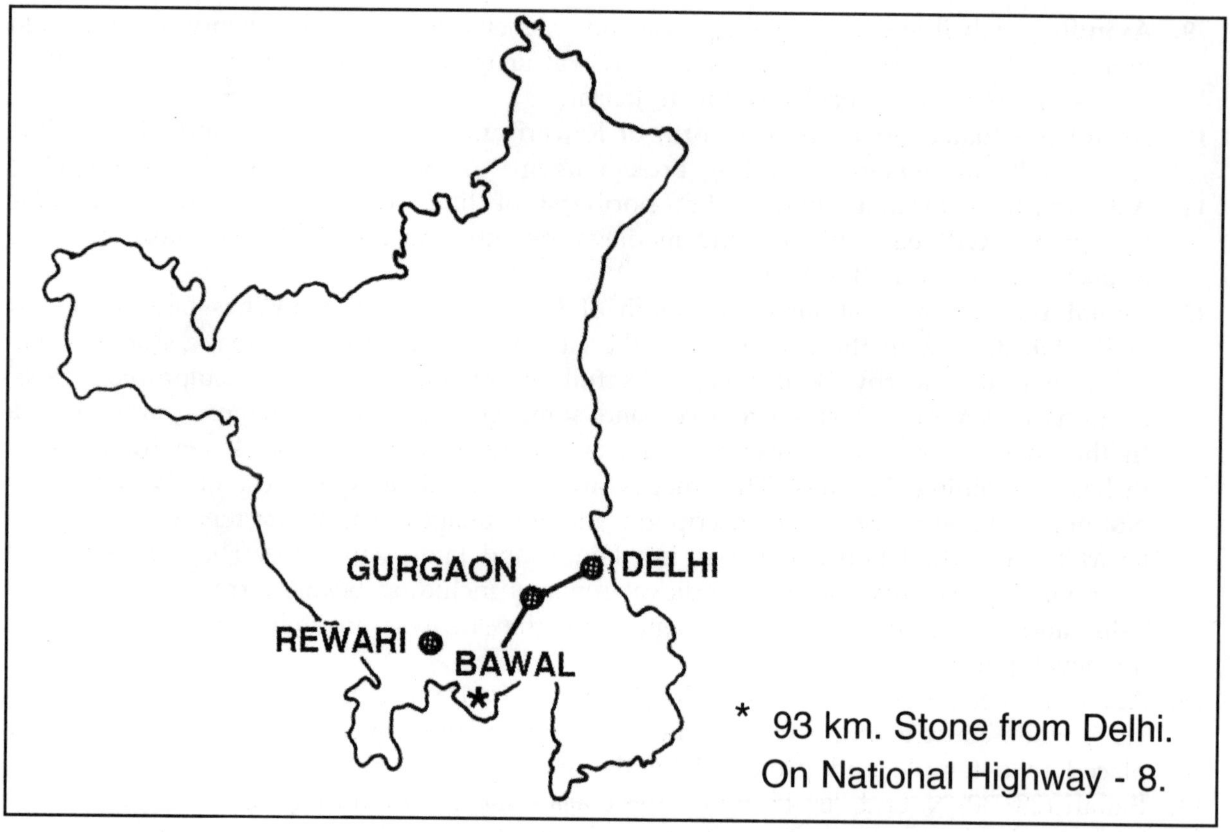

Fig. 2. Map showing the location of Bawal.

in the tank and worshipping god Varāha are believed to be meritorious deeds (*Vāmana Purāṇa* 34.32; *Padma Purāṇa* I.26, 15). The site has a Chandra-kūpa-tīrtha, Chandra-kuṇḍa, Sūrya-kuṇḍa, and Sapta-Ṛishi-kuṇḍa also.

23. **Baras** (29° 44' 16" N. 76° 45' 10" E.) located about 27 km west of Karnal has an old mound occupied by the village, which has yielded early historic and medieval pottery and a medieval image of Gaṇeśa.
24. **Bari Kohori** is situated about 6 km northwest of Naraingarh in district Ambala on the north bank of the Begna rivulet. The ancient mound here extends over an area of about fifteen acres and rises to nearly sixty-five feet. It yields early historic and medieval pottery, coins, terracottas and sculpted pieces.
25. **Baroli** in district Ambala has yielded an early medieval Maishamardinī figure.
26. **Barwala**, about 25 km east of Agroha on Hisar-Tohana road, has yielded an image of Gaṇeśa (Acc. No. 1/167) and the bust of a male deity (Acc. No. 1/164).
27. **Bawal** (28° 04' N. Lat. and 76° 35' E. Long.) lies about 16 km southeast of Rewari and 93 km southwest of Delhi on Delhi-Jaipur National Highway and Rewari-Alwar railway line (Fig. 2). The old mound here called Khera is about 2 m in height and yields early medieval relics.
28. **Belarkha** (29° 39' 45" N. and 76° 07' 43" E.) is situated about 6 km north of Narwana in tahsil Narwana, district Jind. There is a small old mound (100 x 100 x 0.5 m) near the village, which yields early medieval pottery, coins and other relics. More than sixty-five years back two Pratihāra images of Vishṇu and Umā-Maheśvara were recovered from near an old well near the village pond.

29. **Beri** (28° 10' N. and 76° 05' E.) on Jhajjar-Kalanaur road has an old mound extending over ten acres of land and nearly ten feet high, yielding early historic and medieval remains. HARDAM has collected some very beautiful sculptures from this site. An image of Vishṇu is enshrined in the Hathnor temple at Berikhera.
30. **Bhadas**, situated about 19 km north of Firozpur Jhirka in district Gurgaon, has yielded a Śuṅga railing pillar.
31. **Bhandin** in district Sirsa is known for its bust of a male deity now in HARDAM (Acc. No. 1/162).
32. **Bhatla** is situated about 8 km north of Hansi. A Jaina image of the shape of a wooden writing-pad (*takhti*) is enshrined in the village temple.
33. **Bhaund**, situated about 4 km from Firozpur Jhirka, has a temple called Dehra Mandira about a km west of the village at the foot of the hills, which is built of the old materials from Hindu temples. It once had an image of Mahādeva, which was taken away by the people and is now placed in the Jaina temple at Firozpur Jhirka.
34. **Bheron** village is situated about 5 km from Shahzadpur in the Naraingarh tahsil of district Ambala. A sandstone image of probably a Jaina tīrthaṅkara in meditative pose belonging to the Pratihāra period is enshrined in the village temple.[38]
35. **Bhoresaida** between Kurukshetra and Pehowa in district Kurukshetra is famous as the hermitage of sage Bhūriśravas. The old mound here has yielded some architectural pieces (Acc. Nos. 1/229-32) indicating the existence here of a huge medieval temple.[39]
36. **Bhuna** (29° 55' N. and 76° 15' E.), situated about 25 km east of Fatehabad on road to Tohana in district Fatehabad, is located on a huge old mound, more than eighty feet in height, which yields early historic and early medieval remains. Another mound lies about 3 km south of the town on road to Hisar. A Kushāṇa railing pillar was recovered from the site.
37. **Bhund** is located at a distance of about 3 km from Trilokpur on road to Raipur Rani in district Panchkula. There is a late medieval temple constructed near the junction of two *khuds* with material from old temples. On the top of a spur is situated the Kāsalā Devī Temple which must have once been a huge temple as can be guessed from a huge *āmalaka* of a diameter of 1.35 m. There are four Nandī bulls set up on the four corners of the present shrine. An image of Umā-Maheśvara, broken into two pieces, Śiva-*liṅgas*, dressed stones, moonstones, and worn out figures are strewn here and there.
38. **Binva**, situated about 12 km east of Firozpur Jhirka has an ancient mound, which sometimes yields medieval sculptures. Local people tell that Jaina images found from here were stolen.
39. **Bita** in district Ambala has yielded a head of Vishṇu.
40. **Bolni** (28° 07' N. Lat. and 76° 41' E. Long.) lies about 10 km south of Rewari and has yielded early medieval relics including an image of Umā-Maheśvara and five-faced Śiva-*liṅga*.
41. **Brahmanwas** in district Rohtak has yieded the folded legs (in *vajraparyaṅkāsana*) of a Kushāṇa Mathura mottled sandstone Buddhist image bearing the Brāhmī inscription 'Buddha-Kanaka-muni'.[40]
42. **Budauli** in district Mahendragarh has yielded a fragmentary Umā-Maheśvara (Acc. No. 1/308) relief of the medieval period.
43. **Bulandpur Mustarka** in district Karnal has yielded some *dikpāla* figures.
44. **Bulandpur Kheri** is a small village situated at a distance of about 25 km north of Sonepat and about 2 km west of Gujjar Kheri, and is linked with Ganaur by road. The Gujjar

Kheri mound extended up to this place and old relics including PGW, early historic and medieval remains including sculptures are still found here. Medieval sculptures obtained from the mound may be seen placed in the village temple and quite a few sculptures strewn here and there. Some important pieces are studded in the house of one Mr. Balbir.

45. **Chandimandir** near Chandigarh has yielded quite a few sculptures and sculptural fragments.
46. **Charkhi Dadri** (28° 35' N. and 76° 20' E.) is located on the Rewari-Hisar section of the Northern Railway about 28 km southeast of Bhiwani and 55 km northwest of Rewari. The site yields coins of the Yaudheyas and of Bhoja Pratihāra. Sometime back, a hoard of Jaina bronzes was discovered from here and acquired by HARDAM.
47. **Chhichhrana** in district Sonepat has yielded an image of Kubera.
48. **Chinat** near Hansi has also yielded a *dikpāla* figure.
49. **Chuliana** in the Sampla block of Rohtak has the auspicious triad of Gaṇeśa-Gajalakshmī-Kubera measuring 32 x 16 cm and datable to *circa* 10th century C.E.[41]
50. **Chulkana** near Samalkha on the Sonepat-Panipat border too has an early medieval auspicious triad showing Gaja-Lakshmī flanked by Gaṇeśa and Kubera.
51. **Darbi** in district Sirsa has yielded a stone male head now preserved in HARDAM (Acc. No. 1/157).
52. **Dhankot**, about 8 km southwest of Gurgaon on road to Sultanpur Lake, has two Hindu pillars used in the verandah of the mosque. The pillar shows the square *pūrṇaghaṭa* motif with ten sided shaft having human figures, hanging bell motif on the central facet, *kīrttimukha*, etc. datable to *circa* 10th century C.E.
53. **Dhurand Khera** has yielded a portable image of Sūrya.
54. **Dobh**, situated about 6 km south of Rohtak, has yielded a Pratihāra male head.[42]
55. **Durjanpura** (29° 27' 48" N. and 76° 01' 24" E.), situated about 15 km west of Uchana in tahsil Narwana of district Jind has a small (250 x 200 m) but 15 m high mound which yields early historic and medieval remains. One Veena Agrawal collected some sculptures from this site.
56. **Fatehabad**, the district headquarter on the Hisar-Sirsa road, is partially located on an old mound. The mosque here has an old sandstone pillar, probably originally Mauryan, bearing a Persian inscription now. HARDAM possesses a Jina head from this place (Acc. No. 1/142).
57. **Firozpur Jhirka** in district Gurgaon contains an image brought from Bhaund in the Panchayati Jaina Mandira outside the fort. Another image of Ādinātha is also housed in it.
58. **Gairatpur Bas**, located about 16 km from Gurgaon via Badshahpur has a lintel with Gaṇeśa as the *lalāṭa-bimba* and female deities on the sides, datable to *circa* 11th century C.E.
59. **Ganaur** has yielded medieval sculptures of Vishṇu and Brahmā in buff sandstone.[43]
60. **Garh Fazilpur** in district Sonepat has yielded a Śeshaśāyī image.
61. **Gharaunda** (29° 32' 02" N. 76° 58' 13" E.), situated 18 km south of Karnal on Sher Shah Suri Marg, has a low old mound measuring 150 x 60 m to the north of the town, which yields late Harappan pottery. Gharaunda is famous for its Mughal *serai* much of which has been occupied and demolished in the recent years. The Śiva temple here contains an interesting late Gupta Vaikuṇṭha and a medieval Mahishamardinī image.
62. **Ghasola** near Dadri in district Bhiwani has yielded a fragment of a Vishṇu image, a pilaster, an *āmalaka*, and a memorial stone (Acc. Nos. 1/435-38).

63. **Gujjar Kheri** is located on Ganaur-Ahulana road at a distance of about 25 km north-northwest of Sonepat. The present village covers only a small part of the extensive old mound, which is nearly 25 m high and whose circumference is more than 10 km. It lies on the western bank of the dry bed of what must have been once a mighty river, probably the ancient Yamunā, which now flows about 30 km east of it. The ancient sites of Ahir Majra and Bulandpur Kheri must have been the suburbs of the old town. Locally it is believed that the ancient town was known variously as Mayana, Kota, Satkumbha, and Jalallabad. Tradition connects it with king Chakwa Ben (*Chakravartī* Vena?). The site yields PGW, early historic plain red ware, and medieval relics including a very large number of sculptures,[44] even unfinished ones indicating it to have been an important center of medieval art. It may have been destroyed during an attack of Sultan Masud in C.E. 1036 when he defeated Dipal Har, the governor of Sonepat.[45]

64. **Gummar** is situated about 3 km northwest of Ganaur on road to Khubru on the dry bank of probably the Yamunā River. The mound here covers nearly six acres and is about six feet in height. It yields PG, Black Slipped, and medieval wares. An image of Vishṇu under the canopy of a snake and another figure of Brahmā is now installed in a temple in the village.

65. **Gurawara** (28° 23' N. Lat. and 76° 39' E. Long.) is situated about 20 km north of Rewari on road to Jhajjar and yields early medieval remains. Two inscriptions and several stone sculptures are reported from the site.

66. **Hansi** (29° 06' 19" N. and 76° 19' E.) is situated about 25 km east of Hisar on the Delhi-Sirsa road. To the north of the town lies the old fort on a huge mound from which has been found the PGW.[46] Yaudheya coins have been found from Hansi in considerable numbers.[47] A beautiful black stone image of Sūrya with shoes was recovered from the mound and installed in the local temple. Two other images of the Sun god and two of Mahishāsuramardinī, one of Narasiṃha, one *ekamukha-liṅga,* and various others belonging to the early medieval period throw welcome light on its religious history. A hoard of early medieval Jaina bronzes was incidentally discovered from the mound in 1982 and is now preserved in the Pārśvanātha Jaina temple. The site has yielded an important inscription of VS 1224 (C.E. 1167) and various other remains.[48]

67. **Harnol**, situated about 15 km north of Firozpur Jhirka and 23 km south of Nuh on the National Highway, has a huge mound spread over twelve acres of land and rising to about 12 m. It yields PGW and early historic relics. A broken head of Śiva is also known from Harnol.

68. **Hassangarh** in the Sampla block of Rohtak has yielded a medieval female figure and a *Chaturmukha-liṅga*.

69. **Hat** near Safidon in district Jind has the remains of an ancient city and an old image of Vishṇu now enshrined in the Hateshwar temple. Many pieces are studded in the walls of different houses of the village including a small beautiful image of Vaikuṇṭha.[49]

70. **Hathira** (29° 54' 16" N. and 76° 45' 12" E.), about 12 km southeast of Thanesar in district Kurukshetra has yielded an image of Umā-Maheśvara.

71. **Hisar** (29° 10' N. and 75° 44' E.) is the district headquarters situated about 102 km northwest of Delhi. In the Fort here is an Aśokan pillar having typical Mauryan polish and traces of Brāhmī letters and later inscriptions.[50] Some carved stones have been utilized in the construction of the fort and the palace. In the mosque near Gujri Mahal, there is a Gupta Brāhmī inscription and some early medieval epigraphs on the pillars. Firoz Tughlaq, who founded it, probably brought the old material from Agroha or Hansi.[51]

But the place has a mound also which yields Yaudheya and Kushāṇa coins. It has been identified with Aishukāri of the old days (Pāṇini IV.2, 54).[52]

72. **Jadthal** (28° 08' N. Lat. and 76° 43' E. Long.) is located about 14 km southeast of Rewari on the bank of the Sahibi River. It yields early medieval relics including sculptures.

73. **Jaintipur-Muradnagar** is the small twin-village situated about 6 km north of Raipur Rani in the shadow of the Shiwalik hills in tahsil Naraingarh of district Panchkula. Naraingarh is about 25 km southeast of this site and Chandigarh lies about 35 km to its northwest as the crow flies. The Tangri Nadi flows at a distance of about 1 km east of it taking southwesterly course. Jaintipur may be reached from Raipur Rani-Trilokpur metalled road with which it is connected by a link road. The name of the village seems to have derived from the goddess Jayantī whose temple also existed here. There is no mound at Jaintipur but a large heap of dressed and undressed stones now piled up near the Jaintidevi Temple outside the village amidst green fields indicates that once an elegant stone temple existed here. The present shrine, not an old one, too, seems to have been built of the old material. It now enshrines an image of Gaja-Lakshmī and some sculptures have been fixed in its outer walls also. In the heap of the crumbled material of the original temple may be seen architectural pieces, *chaitya* arches, pillars with vase and foliage, *kīrtimukhas* spewing chains and pieces of carved stones. Sculptures from Jaintipur seem to have been removed to the nearby village of Muradnagar also from where some of them were acquired by the Department of Ancient Indian History, Culture and Archaeology, Punjab University, Chandigarh in the mid-sixties. An image of Kārttikeya is enshrined in a temple at Muradnagar. An image of Devī and probably Rāvaṇānugraha-mūrti from here were collected by HARDAM.

74. **Jakhopur** is situated about 7 km south of Punahana in district Gurgaon and has yielded an image of Gaṇeśa of *circa* 12th century.[53]

75. **Jalmajri** in tahsil Naraingarh district Ambala has yielded some carved stone material.

76. **Jasat** (28° 19' 06" N. 76° 42' E.) is a small village situated about 40 km southwest of Gurgaon and is approachable via Pataudi, Inchapuri, Sherpur and Hakdarpur or via Patauda, Nurgarh and Chhilarki. The village is partly situated on the old mound, which is spread over more than thirty acres with a maximum height of about ten feet. It yields late Harappan, early historic and medieval remains. The site has yielded a large number of sculptures also.

77. **Jaurasi Khurd** in district Karnal has yielded medieval Brahmanical sculptures.[54]

78. **Jhansua** in district Jhajjar has yielded some sculptures including Mahishamardinī.

79. **Jind** (29° 19' 02"N. and 76° 18' 55" E.) is the district headquarters situated about 40 km west of Rohtak on the bank of the Chitang River. Its foundation is ascribed to the Pāṇḍavas who are said to have built the temple of Jayantīdevī, around which sprang up the town of Jayantīpurī, since corrupted into Jind. There are many temples and tanks at Jind.[55] It has got quite a good number of old mounds at or near it yielding remains from the pre-Harappan period onwards and has yielded some important images including an unfinished Jaina image indicating that it was an art-center during the medieval period.

80. **Jodhkan** near Sirsa must have been an important place during the Pratihāra period as known from Bhoja's inscription published by K.V. Ramesh and S.P. Tiwari.[56] A stone male head from this place is in the collection of HARDAM (Acc. No. 1/156).

81. **Kabri**, 6 km north of Panipat, has yielded an image of Mahishāsuramardinī.

82. **Kakrod** (District Jind) has yielded a fragmentary Gaṇeśa image.

83. **Kaithal** (29° 48' 07" N. 76° 26' 26" E.) is situated about 50 km southwest by south of Kurukshetra on the Kurukshetra-Narwana section of the Northern Railway and is the district headquarters now. The present name is derived from its ancient Sanskrit name Kapisthala which has been mentioned by Pāṇini (VIII.3, 91). Kapisthala means literally 'the abode of monkeys' and the place is connected by tradition with the monkey-god Hanumān and possesses a temple of Añjanā, his mother. It is also said to be the original home of the Kapishṭhalas known to us from very ancient times.[57] The author of the *Kāśikā* also seems to have known the place.[58] Varāhamihira also mentions it in his *Bṛihatsaṃhitā* (XIV.4). It was known as Kavital during the time of Alberuni.[59] The antiquity of the place is authenticated by the discovery of a small silver coin of Apollodotus.[60] Rodgers obtained from here coins of Sāmantadeva besides discovering old doorways, pillars, sculptures of goddess, etc.[61] An elegant Pratihāra image of Vishṇu is still under worship in the Kashipuri temple of Kaithal and a late Gupta image of Vaikuṇṭha and a broken image of Brahmā are preserved in the Hanumān temple. Kaithal is the only place where there were temples dedicated to the *Navagrahas* and Ekādaśa-Rudras. Timur found fire-worshippers amongst its inhabitants and halted here before attacking Delhi in C.E. 1398.[62]

84. **Kalanaur** in district Rohtak has the remains of a 10th century temple.

85. **Kalayat** (29° 40' 38" N. and 76° 15' 23" E.) is located about 20 km southwest of Kaithal on Ambala-Hisar road and Narwana-Kurukshetra section of the Northern Railway. It is famous for its Kapila-Muni Temple. According to a tradition, sage Kapila is said to have narrated Sāṅkhya to his mother here. A small 150 x 150 x 1 m mound here has yielded late Harappan pottery, a copper chisel and PGW and another one has yielded Late Harappan and early historic remains including Kuṇinda and Yaudheya coins of '*Yaudheya-gaṇasya jaya*' type.[63] Kalayat has the earliest and the only brick temples in the state still surviving. These temples are generally ascribed to the times of Harsha.[64] The Kapila-Muni temple and the Bhagavatī temple are located on the bank of the old tank and possess some beautiful old sculptures.[65]

86. **Kalka** is the tahsil headquarters of Panchkula and is the last town of Haryana towards its northeast on its border with Himachal Pradesh. It has the temple of Kālikā, Santoshī Mātā and Manasā Devī. The latter two have yielded medieval images of Umā-Maheśvara and Agni.[66]

87. **Kamoda** is the site of the Kāmya-*tīrtha* of Kurukshetra. A 9th century Mātṛikā (probably Māheśvarī) image holding a trident and supporting a child is known from here (Regn. No. HRN/KURU-46).

88. **Kanwari**, located about 26 km south of Hisar and nearly 15 km northwest of Tosham on Hisar-Tosham road, has two old mounds covering respectively one and ten acres of land. The smaller mound to the east of the village yields early historic pottery and the other, which has been leveled for cultivation, yields early medieval relics. Some sculptures were also recovered from this mound while ploughing.

89. **Kapālamochana**, situated about 15 km northeast of Jagadhari on the left bank of the Sarasvatī river in district Yamunanagar, is an ancient holy place which has yielded old relics comprising of Indo-Sassanian silver coins, Gupta carved bricks, fragmentary Gupta and late Gupta inscriptions, sculptures, Śiva-liṅgas, doorframes, ornamental stones and architectural pieces.[67]

90. **Kara Sahib** is located at a distance of nearly 12 km from Pehowa on road to Gulha. Devī Temple here is located on a mound that has yielded one dozen carved pieces.

They are now fixed in the southern wall of the temple near the well and include images of Umā-Maheśvara, Varāha, Kāli, etc.

91. **Kariwala** near Sirsa has yielded early historic and medieval pottery and inscribed Gupta terracotta of Gaṅgā.

92. **Karnal** (29° 41' N. and 76° 59' E.) is the district headquarters located on the Sher Shah Suri Marg and the Ambala-Delhi section of the Northern Railway, about 125 km north of Delhi. The place is traditionally connected with the *Mahābhārata* hero Karṇa. A part of the city is located on an old mound, which yields pottery, coins and other relics of different periods. Sten Konow published a Kharoshṭhī inscription from here.[68] Indo-Greek, Kuṇinda silver coin of Amoghabhūti, Kushāṇa and Yaudheya coins and seals are also known from Karnal.[69] Quite a good number of sculptures are housed in the Śiva temple of the Gaur Sabhā at Karnal.

93. **Karnoli** in district Hisar has yielded a broken human figure (Acc. No. 1/118).

94. **Karontha** in the Kalanaur block of Rohtak has a Pratihāra *pedyā.*

95. **Kasan** situated about 22 km from Delhi via Manesar on the Delhi-Jaipur Highway in district Gurgaon has the Puran Bhagat Temple, which contains some old images. Some pieces from this site have been acquired by HARDAM.

96. **Khajuraka**, 6 km east of Palwal in district Faridabad, has yielded art material.

97. **Khanpur** near Mohan Bari in district Rohtak has yielded forty medieval sculptures.[70]

98. **Kharawar** in the Sampla block of Rohtak has the *pedyā* of a doorframe and an architectural piece of *circa* 10th century C.E.

99. **Khatoli** in tahsil Naraingarh of district Ambala has yielded an image of Mahishāsuramardinī.

100. **Kherdi** in the Kalanaur block of Rohtak has yielded an early medieval Vishṇu image, measuring 42 x 23 cm, with hands disposed in *abhaya*, and holding *gadā, chakra*, and *śaṅkha*.

101. **Khubru** near Gujjar Kheri in district Sonepat has yielded some sculptures now set up in the village temple.

102. **Kiloi** (28° 55' N. and 76° 40' E.) about 10 km from Rohtak on road to Sonepat has two mounds yielding early historic and medieval remains. A Kushāṇa-Gupta *Ekamukha-liṅga* was recovered from the mound and has now been enshrined in a temple near the village. A fair is also held at the temple annually.

103. **Kira** is situated in tahsil Nuh, district Gurgaon. Six buff sandstone sculptures of Hindu and Jaina faiths belonging to about 10th century were examined by me in the Police Malkhana at Gurgaon on 8. 5. 1990.

104. **Kirmach** in district Karnal has yielded fragments of attendant figures.

105. **Kohand** (Lat. 29° 29' N. and Long. 76° 05' 18" E.) is situated about 20 km north of Panipat in district Karnal and is located on an ancient mound which yields early historic Red Polished ware and sprinklers ascribable to *circa* 1st-2nd century C.E. and medieval remains. Quite a good number of medieval stone images are known from this site,[71] many of which have been acquired by HARDAM but some are still preserved in the local temple.

106. **Korla Khera** situated about 5 km north of Hodal in district Faridabad has yielded some relics of art.

107. **Kosli**, located near the northern border of Rewari with Jhajjar, is the place from where police recovered a beautiful Vishṇu image (Acc. No. 1/351).

108. **Kot** situated about 16 km west of Hodal towards Punahana in district Gurgaon is also reported to have yielded some art remains.

109. **Kultajpur Khera**, situated nearly 8 km west of Narnaul in district Mahendragarh, is an old place yielding stone sculptures.

110. **Kurukshetra**, situated about 40 km south of Ambala on the Sher Shah Suri Marg and Ambala-Delhi section of the northern Railway is the famous holy place.[72] Quite a few sculptures have been found from Kurukshetra.

111. **Lalpura** near Rohtak was a Buddhist place as a *sūchi* (coping stone) with a *stūpa* is known from here (Acc. No. 1/127).

112. **Lulodh** is located about 8 km northwest of Kosli and 18 km southwest of Jhajjar. The ruined mound of Jhansua here has yielded sculptures, which are now housed in a temple. Some pieces have been acquired by the Gurukula Museum, Jhajjar.

113. **Madina** (28° 55' N. and 76° 25' E.) is located about 15 km west of Rohtak on Hisar road. A small mound to the west of the village yielding late Harappan, PG and Black Slipped pottery has almost been leveled for cultivation and the other to the southwest yielding PGW, Black and Red ware, Black Slipped, early historic and medieval wares is spread over twelve acres of land and is about ten feet high. The site has yielded sculptural remains also.

114. **Maham** (28° 53' N. and 76° 18' E.) is situated about 32 km west of Rohtak on road to Hansi and is located on a high mound about a mile long. Rodgers noted that though very few sculptured remains are found here yet they are sufficient to show that it had old stone sculptured temples.[73] It is identified with Mahettham[74] conquered by Nakula during his conquest of the western quarter, as described in the *Mahābhārata*.[75] The old mound here has yielded PGW, Indo-Greek, Yaudheya and Kushāṇa coins besides sculptures.[76] HARDAM too has some images from this site in its collection. Tradition alleges its destruction by Muhammad Ghori.[77]

115. **Mahmudpur** in district Rohtak has yielded a spotted red sandstone Bodhisattva head.[78]

116. **Majra**, a village close to the Asthal Bohr at Rohtak, accidentally yielded two inscribed images of Pārśvanātha while the laborers were digging a part of the old mound some years back. They are now enshrined on the site.

117. **Malab**, about 5 km south of Nuh on road to Firozpur Jhirka in district Gurgaon, has a huge mound, which yields art material also.

118. **Mandhna**, situated about 10 km upstream from Chandimandir on the left bank of the Ghaggar in tahsil Kalka of district Panchkula seems to have been a medieval temple site as a number of architectural pieces and dressed stones may still be seen in the local temple besides some important medieval images.

119. **Mansa Devi** near Mani Majra (Chandigarh) has yielded some stone sculptures from Bhainsa Tibba near here.

120. **Marhanwala**, about 8 km from Pinjore on road to Nalagarh, has yielded, besides the prehistoric stone tools, a good number of medieval sculptures[79] many of which are now preserved in HARDAM. An unfinished medieval Śiva-*liṅga* from this site furnishes evidence of its being a center of art.

121. **Mayan** (28° 13' N. Lat. and 76° 25' E. Long.) is situated about 25 km west of Rewari approachable via village Khol. A medieval lintel showing *Navagrahas* and *Ashṭavasus* indicates the existence of a temple here.

122. **Mehrauli** (38° 31' N. and 77° 14' E.) in Delhi, famous for Qutb Minar and the Iron Pillar, has yielded the remains of numerous temples and sculptures.[80] Of these, a buff sandstone Śuṅga yakshī image published by Vasudeva Sharan Agrawala[81] and the inscribed Vishṇu image published by B.N. Sharma[82] are of great interest.

123. **Meo Ali**, about 10 km northeast of Punahana, yields carved stone material.

124. **Mohan Bari** is located about 30 km southwest of Jhajjar and has the ruins of a large city. Stone idols and gold and silver coins were reported from this site long back by Rodgers.[83] Many pieces from Mohan Bari have been removed to the Gurukula Museum, Jhajjar.[84]

125. **Morni ka Tal** (30° 49' N. Lat. and 77° 5' E. Long.) is located 7 km down hill of the Tourist Resort of Morni in district Panchkula (Fig. 3). It contains the remains of 8th-9th century temples collected and built into a modern shrine. Quite a few sculptures from this place are preserved in the Depatment of Ancient Indian History, Culture & Archaeology, Panjab University, Chandigarh and the Department of Archaeology & Museums, Haryana at Kurukshetra.

126. **Mustafabad,** situated about 10 km north of Jagadhari in district Yamunanagar has yielded a Bodhisattva head in Gandhāra style.[85]

127. **Nachar Khera** in district Jind has an ancient mound which has yielded some Gupta terracottas depicting scenes from the *Rāmāyaṇa*, some of them bearing the inscribed *ślo*kas from Vālmīki's *Rāmāyaṇa*.[86]

128. **Narhera**, about 1 km from Pataudi in district Gurgaon, has an *uttaraṅga* with *navagraha* panel and a pillar, both obtained from a tank.

129. **Narnaul** (28° 03' N. Lat. and 76° 07' E. Long.) lies about 54 km south of Rewari and 26 km south of Mahendragarh, 160 km southwest of Delhi on Rewari-Ajmer section of the Northern Railway. Medieval copper coins and some Jaina sculptures are known from this place. A fragmentary 18th-19th century inscription names it as Nandigrāma.

130. **Narnaund** in district Hisar has yielded a stone lion and Nāga devotee figures (Acc. Nos. 1/140 and 1/155).

131. **Narwana** on Jind-Tohana road has a huge architectural piece placed in the bazaar.

132. **Naulatha** situated about 15 km southwest of Panipat has the image of a bearded sage placed in the local temple.

133. **Naurangabad-Bamla** (28° 45' N. and 76° 10' E.) is the twin village located about 8 km east of Bhiwani on Rohtak-Bhiwani road and is well known for its coin-molds. It has yielded some interesting terracottas also amongst which Gupta terracotta figurines of Vishṇu and Sūrya, now housed in the Gurukula Museum, Jhajjar, are worth mentioning.[87]

134. **Nilokheri** on the National Highway No. 1 about 25 km northwest by north of Karnal has an architectural piece just near the road.

135. **Nonod** in the Sampla block of Rohtak has a medieval Gaṇeśa image and another unidentified figure.

136. **Nyat** in district Jind is known for its image of Mahishamardinī.

137. **Paju Kalan** in tahsil Safidon, district Jind has yielded a medieval image of Mahishāsuramardinī.

138. **Palwal** (28° 09' N. and 77° 20' E.), about 63 km south of Delhi on Mathura road in district Faridabad, is located on one of the highest mounds extending over an area of about forty acres of land and about forty feet in height. It has yielded PGW.[88] The discovery of the head and bust of a colossal red sandstone yaksha image of Śuṅga yaksha in 1914 (now preserved in the State Museum, Lucknow),[89] the remains of walls of houses met with while excavating a well as deep as fifty feet below the surface[90] and other early historic remains bear evidence to its antiquity and long occupation. A local tradition connects it with the *Mahābhārata* story. The mosque at Palwal said to have been an accomplishment of the time of Iltutmish, having pillars bearing traces of defaced Hindu

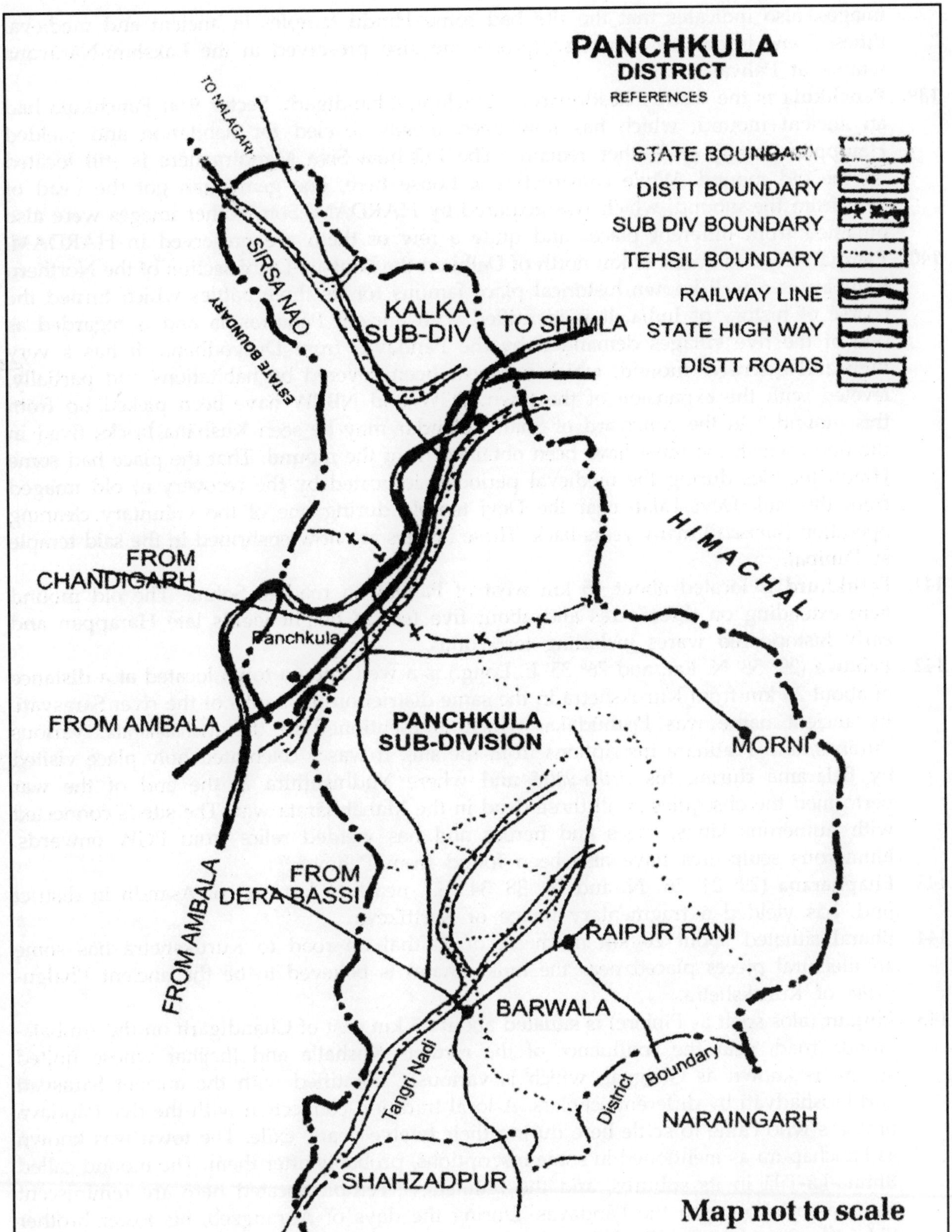

Fig. 3. Map showing the location of Morni.

images, also indicates that the site had some Hindu temples in ancient and medieval times. Some important Hindu sculptures are also preserved in the Lakshmī-Nārāyaṇa temple at Palwal.

139. Panchkula is the district headquarters touching Chandigarh. Sector 9 at Panchkula had an ancient mound, which has now been mostly leveled for habitation and yielded Harappan pottery and other remains. The Prāchīna Śiva Mandira here is still located on the old mound. While constructing a house here, one gentleman got the head of Śiva from the mound, which was acquired by HARDAM. Some other images were also obtained from different places and quite a few of them are preserved in HARDAM.

140. Panipat, situated about 90 km north of Delhi on the Ambala-Delhi section of the Northern Railway, is a well known historical place famous for its three battles which turned the coarse of history of India. It is identified with ancient Pāṇiprastha and is regarded as one of the five villages demanded by the Pāṇḍavas from Duryodhana. It has a very high and extensive mound, which has now been covered by habitations and partially, leveled with the expansion of the town. PGW and NBPW have been picked up from this mound.[91] In the courtyard of Shah Kalandar may be seen Kushāṇa bricks fixed in the floor, which too must have been obtained from the mound. That the place had some Hindu temples during the medieval period is indicated by the recovery of old imaged from the tank Devī Tālāb near the Devī temple during one of the voluntary cleaning operation (*kārasevā*) many years back. These images are now enshrined in the said temple at Panipat.

141. Patlikhurd is located about 15 km west of Palwal on road to Sohna. The old mound here extending on three acres and about five feet in height yields late Harappan and early historic red wares including terracottas.

142. Pehowa (29° 58' N. Lat. and 76° 35' E. Long.) is a well known town located at a distance of about 25 km from Kurukshetra in the same district on the banks of the river Sarasvatī. Its ancient name was Pṛithūdaka, which is mentioned in the *Mahābhārata*, various Purāṇas, and Pratihāra inscriptions from the site. It was a celebrated holy place visited by Balarāma during his *tīrtha-yātrā* and where Yudhishṭhira at the end of the war performed the obsequies of all those dead in the Mahābhārata war. The site is connected with numerous kings, sages and heroes and has yielded relics from PGW onwards. Numerous sculptures have also been found from Pehowa.[92]

143. Phapharana (29° 21' 26" N. and 76° 38' 34" E.), nearly 6 km east of Asandh in district Jind, has yielded a fragmentary image of Kārttikeya.

144. Pharal situated about 20 km northeast of Kaithal on road to Kurukshetra has some architectural pieces placed near the tank. Pharal is believed to be the ancient Phalgu-*tīrtha* of Kurukshetra.

145. Pinjaur (alos spelt as Pinjore) is situated about 25 km east of Chandigarh on the Ambala-Shimla road, near the confluence of the rivulets Koshalla and Jhajjhar whose united stream is known as Ghaggar, which is variously identified with the ancient Sarasvatī and Dṛishadvatī by different scholars. A local tradition connects it with the five Pāṇḍava brothers who came to settle here during their twelve years' exile. The town was known as Pañchapura as mentioned in some inscriptions, probably after them. The mound called Bhīma-kā-Ṭīlā in its suburbs, and the Bhīmādevī Temple located here are reminiscent of its association with the Pāṇḍavas. During the days of Aurangzeb, his foster brother Fidai Khan got laid the Mughal garden here whose fortification wall is built of the Hindu temple material as some sculptured pieces may still be seen studded into it. Numerous sculptures lie here and there, placed or fixed in the *baolis* or Ḍerās.[93] That it was a center of art is evidenced by unfinished sculptures from the site.

146. **Pugthala** in district Panipat has some very worn out images.

147. **Punahna** is located on the Haryana-Rajasthan border in district Faridabad. A small medieval mound to the west of the village yielded some Hindu and Jaina sculptures which were placed in a temple but were stolen and seized by the Gurgaon police.

148. **Purkhas** in district Sonepat has yielded an image of Hari-Brahmā.

149. **Raisina** in district Gurgaon has yielded a fragmentary Umā-Maheśvara, an architectural piece, and a *vyāla* figure (Acc. Nos. 1/399-401).

150. **Rājā Karṇa kā Kilā** near Thanesar-Kurukshetra has yielded some terracottas and images.[94]

151. **Ramhrada** near Barah Kalan in district Jind has yielded some medieval sculptures.[95] A female figure from Ram Rai forms part of the collection of HARDAM (Acc. No. 1/151).

152. **Rampur Jangi** near Pinjore has recently revealed the existence of the remains of a medieval Śiva temple evidenced by broken Śiva-*liṅgas*, architectural pieces and dressed stones.

153. **Ranila** situated about 27 km west of Bhiwani has yielded medieval buff sandstone images of Ādinātha and Chakreśvarī.[96]

154. **Rasidan** (29° 43' 14" N. 76° 01' 55" E.), situated about 19 km northwest of Narwana, has an old mound which yields early historic and early medieval remains including beads, terracotta animal figurines, copper coins and sculptured pieces. Fragmentary reliefs of Garuḍa and Gaṇapati are now enshrined in the nearby Maimond temple.

155. **Rasina** in district Kaithal has yielded two beautiful almost complete Pratihāra images of Vishṇu. They are now displayed in Śrī Kṛishṇa Museum at Kurukshetra.

156. **Ratia**, about 25 km northeast of Fatehabad, has yielded attendant figures of some deity (Acc. No. 1/145).

157. **Ratpur**, about 3 km from Pinjore on road to Nalagarh, has yielded a large number of images,[97] some in an unfinished condition, indicating the site to have been a center of medieval art. Many images and fragments from Ratpur have been collected by HARDAM.

158. **Ratta Khera** in district Hisar has yielded the stone figure of Sūrya's attendant Daṇḍa wearing a *kullah* cap (Acc. No. 1/141). The mound here contains historical and medieval remains.

159. **Rewari** (28° 12' N. Lat. and 76° 37' E. Long.) is the district headquarters located about 54 km east of Narnaul and 56 km west of Gurgaon. The old site near K.L.P. College yields early historic and medieval antiquities. Copper hoard tools have also been reported from Rewari. A Jaina stone sculpture is fixed in the wall of the Jaina *dharmaśālā* on Dharuhera road.

160. **Rithal** (28° 55' N. and 76° 40' E.) has two mounds known as Mājarewālā and Būḍhā kherā, the former yielding PGW and black slipped pottery and the latter yielding early medieval relics. A beautiful Kushāṇa head from Rithal is now preserved in the HARDAM.

161. **Rohtak** (28° 54′ N Lat. and 76° 35′ E. Long.), situated about 70 km northwest of Delhi on the Delhi-Bhatinda section of the Northern Railway, is the headquarters of the district and tahsil of the same name in Haryana. The antiquity of the site is witnessed by numerous literary references and a large number of antiquarian remains obtained from the old mound of Khokhrakot, which covers an extensive area on the northern side of the city. Another mound called Lalpura lies about 3 km west of it and yields stone

sculptures and other remains, and the third one, known as Rāmala ālā, located about 4 km northeast, is spread over three acres of land and yields PG, Black Slipped, and NBP wares. A Kushāṇa pillar capital from Khokhrakot is now preserved in the National Museum, New Delhi. The site was excavated jointly by the Department of History, M.D. University and HARDAM and a large number of stone images and fragments of railing pillars were recovered. About a century back, Rodgers had noticed Hindu material utilized in Adina and Kalan Masjids and some sculptures near Gokarṇa kā Tālāb at Rohtak, which may still be seen there.

162. Sadhaura (30° 23' N. and 77° 13' E.) is situated at the foot of the outlying range of the Himalayas on the left bank of the Nakti rivulet about 40 km east of Ambala in district Yamunanagar. It has a huge mound, a fort and some other ruins which yield PGW, old coins, sculptures, and other remains.[98]

163. Saga in district Karnal preserves a 10th century doorjamb showing a *mithuna* fixed in the village temple.

164. Safidon (29° 21' N. and 76° 42' E.) on Jind-Panipat road in district Jind is identified with ancient Sarpidamana-*tīrtha* (*Mbh.* III.81, 12). Amongst the relics of art a Pārvatī head, flying *gandharva*, and a female bust have been collected by HARDAM (Acc. Nos. 1/133-34 and 1/155) from here. An unfinished sculpture has also been obtained from Safidon (Acc. No. 1/139) indicating it to be a center of art during the medieval period.

165. Sagwan is situated nearly 5 km east of Tosham in district Bhiwani. The mound here yields early historic and medieval relics including medieval sculptures. According to a local tradition, it represents ancient Śālvamaṇi, the capital of the Śālva *janapada*.[99]

166. Salwan (29° 30' 44" N. and 76° 43' 12" E.) is situated about 25 km southwest of Karnal and nearly 13 km northeast of Safidon and has yielded a *Pañchāyatana-liṅga*, Gaṇeśa, and Surabhi figure (Acc. Nos. 1/135, 166, and 170).

167. Samchana in the Sampla block of Rohtak has a small Umā-Maheśvara figure.

168. Sampla on Rohtak-Delhi road has yielded a black stone fragment of a Vishṇu image representing Śrī and Balarāma.

169. Sandhaya is located at a distance of about 10 km north of Jagadhari and 3 km from Kapālamochana in district Yamunanagar and has a huge mound yielding Harappan, early historic and medieval remains.[100] A big hoard of Gupta gold coins is also said to have been discovered by some one and sold out. The mound has yielded a beautiful terracotta figurine of Rāma and some early medieval stone images including those of Lakulīśa and Naṭarāja.

170. Sanghan, situated at a distance of about 16 km west of Kaithal, has yielded an image of Vishṇu.

171. Sanghel, situated about 13 km east-southeast of Nuh and 4 km south of Ujina, on the bank of the Sahibi river has an old mound extending over sixteen acres of land and nearly 25 m in height, which yields PGW, Śuṅga-Kushāṇa pottery and sculptures as well as medieval remains. Some sculptures from this site were acquired by HARDAM.

172. Sanghi in district Rohtak has yielded an early medieval Buddha head.[101]

173. Satkumbha is an extension of the Gujjar Kheri mound and has a holy tank where a fair is held annually. It may be identified with the pilgrimage described in the *Mahābhārata*.[102]

174. Shahpur, about 18 km from Pinjore on road to Nalagarh, was the site of ancient temples. The plan of a small shrine is still surviving in the premises of the Gurudvārā here where many old sculptures obtained from the site have been utilized in the walls and the podium of the Nishan Sahib. Two fragments of Pratihāra inscriptions have also been procured from this site and preserved in HARDAM.

175. **Sheshashayi**, situated about 13 km east of Hodal via Khirbi and Bas in tahsil Palwal of district Faridabad contains an image of Śeshaśāyī Vishṇu in a temple said to have been built by Raja Ballu. The temple contains some beautiful murals also.

176. **Sikanderpur** (29° 12' N. and 75° 06' E.) is located about 8 km east of Sirsa and the old mound here yields Rangmahal and early medieval remains.[103] A medieval *Ekamukha-liṅga* and an image of Yama were also recovered from the site.

177. **Sirsa**, the ancient Śairīshaka, is the district headquarters of this name. It is located on the north bank of the dry bed of the Ghaggar, about 25 km south of Bathinda and 82 km northwest of Hisar on the Bathinda-Hisar section of the Northern Railway. A part of the town is located on a very lofty and extensive mound, which yields old relics from time to time. Kushāṇa and Yaudheya copper coins, a late Gupta inscription, early medieval sculptures and later remains testify its antiquity indicated by literary references to it in Pāṇini's *Ashṭādhyāyī, Mahābhārata, Divyāvadāna,* etc.[104]

178. **Siyana** (28° 27' N. Lat. and 76° 14' E. Long.) is situated at a distance of 18 km north of Kanina, approachable via Unhani on Kanina-Mahendragarh road. A medieval seated four-handed Gaṇeśa is known from here.

179. **Sondh** is located about 4 km west of Nuh in tahsil Palwal district Faraidabad. The old mound here covers approximately thirty acres and is 25 m in height. It yields PGW, Śuṅga-Kushāṇa pottery, bricks and terracottas, and medieval sculptures.

180. **Sonepat** (Lat. 28° 59' N. and Long. 70° 01' E.) situated about 44 km north of Delhi and nearly the same distance from Panipat towards its south on the Delhi-Ambala section of the Northern Railway is the district headquarters now. The river Yamunā is said to have once flowed near it but it now flows about 16 km east of this town. A part of the modern town is located on an ancient mound, which is fairly high and extensive. According to a local tradition, Sonepat was one of the five villages demanded by Yudhishṭhira from Duryodhana. Sherds of Northern Black Polished Ware have been picked up from the vertical sections of the mound.[105] V.S. Agrawala derives the present name from Śoṇāprastha of Pāṇini.[106] In 1866, a terracotta figure of sun in perfect preservation is said to have been found by the villagers from a depth of 70-80 feet while digging a well.[107] Graeco-Bactrian, Yaudheya and other coins and a copper seal of Harsha indicate its continuous occupation for many centuries.[108]

181. **Sugh** (30° North Latitude and 77° 23' East Longitude) lies about 4 km to the east of Jagadhari, a railway station on the Ambala-Saharanpur section of the Northern Railway in Yamunanagar district of Haryana. The West Yamunā Canal, which was dug by Firoz Shah Tughlaq on the old flood plain of river Yamunā, flows very close to the old mound though the river has now shifted about 10 km south of it. The huge mound forms a triangular spur covering an area of over 5 km in circumference and the present villages of Dayalgarh in the north, Sugh in the west and Amadalpur in the southeast actually lie over the ancient site. It has been identified with ancient Srughna. It was excavated by Suraj Bhan and has yielded some very interesting religious terracottas and other remains.[109]

182. **Sunderpura** near Kalka in district Panchkula has yielded an image of Brahmāṇī.

183. **Surehli** (28° 23' N. Lat. and 76° 26' E. Long.) about 5 km south of Kosli on road to Rewari yields early medieval relics.

184. **Thanesar** (29° 58' 30" N. and 76° 49' 40" E.) is the well-known ancient town because

of its association with king Harsha. It has been described very vividly by Bāṇa in his *Harshacharita* and by the Chinese pilgrim Hiuen Tsiang. Cunningham and others also surveyed it and brought to light its antiquarian remains.[110] The ancient site known as Harsha kā Ṭīlā was partially excavated by the Archaeological Survey of India during the eighties. A large number of antiquarian remains, including sculptures, are known from the site.[111]

185. Tandwal on the Ambala-Jagadhari section of the Northern Railway has a large mound, which yields PGW, early historic and medieval relics. In the Thakurdwara there is a beautiful Pratihāra Mahishamardinī image under worship.

186. Theh Polar about 10 km north of Kaithal towards Siwan is said to have yielded a Mahishāsuramardinī relief.

187. Tilpat near Delhi is a well-known place identified with ancient Tilaprastha. The local people have collected many sculptures lying in the fields to the south of the village at a place called 'Khera'. These include Gaṇeśa in grey sandstone, red sandstone Nandī, architectural pieces, and other fragmentary reliefs.

188. Tirkhu near village Seenk in district Karnal has a fragment of a Vishṇu image and a stele.

189. Tisimbli in district Kurukshetra contains some sculptural fragments.

190. Tosham (28° 54' N. and 75° 56' E.) is situated about 25 km south of Hansi and nearly 40 km southeast of Hisar. It is known for its Gupta rock inscription.[112] The epigraph throws considerable light on the religious history of the town, which have had some important temple/s also. Some sculptures have been obtained from the site.

191. Ujalmajra in district Ambala has yielded the fragmentary flying *gandharva* figure (Acc. No. 1/273).

192. Ujina, situated about 10 km east of Nuh on road to Hodal, has a huge mound covering about twelve acres and rising to about 15 m. It yields PGW, early historic and medieval relics. In the Chapar-Gamar temple outside the village there lay some mutilated old sculptures. A *maḍhī* of Bābā Paṭṭī in the middle of the village also contains some old pieces.

193. Vara in district Jind has yielded a Kushāṇa terracotta figurine of Mahishāsuramardinī.

There are many more sites which have also yielded art remains but they are either architectural pieces or worn out or unidentifiable insignificant pieces. We have listed above 193 sites and if we add to this the lesser significant sites also the number will swell further. It is for the first time that all these sites have been listed together. Many more may be lying unknown. This is by no means a mean number for any state, more so as the art remains of Haryana are not fully published and well known. The following chapters give thematic account of the sculptures from the state.

Notes and References

1. *Skanda Purāṇa*, Veṅkaṭeśvara Press, Bombay, V.S. 1965, ch. 39, vv. 127 ff. Also see A.B. Awasthi, *Studies in the Skanda-Purāṇa*, part I, Lucknow, 1965, p. 36.
2. Dasharatha Sharma, *Early Chauhan Dynasties*, Delhi, 1959, p. 59:

   *Vāshpa-vāriṇī Kālindī Haritānaka-yoshitām [/]**
   Satkrāntasya militā yatpramāṇe rajasvalā //

   (Ajmer Museum *Praśasti*)

3. *Abhoji Tomarairādau Chauhānaistadantaram /*
Hariyānakabhūreshā Śakendraiḥ śāsyate'dhunā //
(Boher-Palam Baoli Inscription, verse 3)
Rajendralal Mitra, "Note on the Palam Baoli Inscription", *Journal of the Asiatic Society of Bengal (New Series),* Vol. XLIII, Part I, Nos. 1-4 (1874), pp. 104-10. Also see S.R. Phogat, "Inscriptions of Haryana", *Journal Of Haryana Studies,* Kurukshetra, Vol. IX, Nos. 1-2(1977), pp. 37-38.
4. E. Eggelling, "Inscription in the Delhi Museum", *Epigraphia Indica,* Vol. I, pp. 93-95, verse 3 –
Deśo'sti Haritānākhyaḥ pṛithivyāṃ svarga-sannibhaḥ /
Ḍhillikākhyā purī tatra Tomarairasti nirmitā //
5. *Epigraphia Indica,* Vol. I, p. 64.
6. O.P. Bharadwaj (*Studies in the Historical Geography of Ancient India,* Delhi, 1986, p. 209) derives the name Haryana from the Vedic word Śarayāṇa or Śaryaṇā. Attempts have been made to derive the present name from Āryānā also [See *Hariyāṇā Śodha Patrikā,* Rewari, Vol. I, no. 2 (1966), p. 2].
7. *Manu Smṛiti* II. 22.
8. *Ibid.,* II. 19.
9. Nundo Lal Dey, *The Geographical Dictionary of Ancient and Medieval India,* New Delhi, 1971, 3rd ed., p. 40.
10. For details, see R.C. Agrawala, "Kurukṣetra in Early Sanskrit Literature", *Journal of Indian History,* Vol. XXXIII, part I, no. 97, April, 1955, pp. 85-90.
11. *Manu Smriti* II. 21. Also see B.C. Law, *Historical Geography of Ancient India,* Paris, 1954, p. 13.
12. V.S. Agrawala, *Vāmana-Purāṇa : A Study,* Varanasi, 1964, pp. 31-32.
13. Bahudhānyaka, Śrīkaṇṭha-*janapada,* Sārasvata-bhūmi, Vāgurī, etc. have also been mentioned as the divisions of Haryana in old literature.
14. B.B. Lal and S.P. Gupta (eds.), *Frontiers of the Indus Civilisation: Mortimer Wheeler Commemoration Volume),* New Delhi, 1984, pp. 519 ff. and maps.
15. *Ṛigveda* III. 23, 4 –
Ni tvā dadhe vara ā pṛithivyā Ilāspade sudinatve ahṇām /
Dṛishadvatyāṃ Mānushe Āpayāyāṃ Sarasvatyāṃ revadagne didīhi //
16. Buddha Prakash, *Haryana Through the Ages,* Kurukshetra (no date).
17. *5000 Years of the Art of India,* Harry N. Abrahams Inc. Publishers, New York, 1971.
18. *Mārg,* Vol. XXVII, no. 4, September 1974.
19. R.C. Agrawala, "Śuṅga Pillars from Amin, Near Kurukshetra," *Lalit-Kala,* no. 14, New Delhi, 1969, pp. 50-52, pls. XVI-XVIII.
20. Harry N. Abrahams Inc. Publishers, New York, 1977.
21. *Archaeological Survey Reports,* Vols. II and XIV.
22. *Report of the Panjab Circle of the Archaeological Survey For 1888-89,* Calcutta, 1891.
23. *JUPHS,* Vol. XXXIV-XXXV, 1951-52, pp. 188 ff, fig. 4.
24. "Excavations at Agroha, Punjab," *Memoirs of the Archaeological Survey of India,* no. 61.
25. B.C. Bhattacharya, *The Jaina Iconography,* Lahore, 1939, pl. VI.
26. *Indian Archaeology 1959-60 – A Review,* p. 74, pls. LX. D and LXI.
27. R.C. Agrawala, "Prāchīna Hariyānā," *Ājakala* (Hindi), Nov. 1968.
28. D.P.S. Punia, "Recently Explored Icons of Viṣṇu and Hari-Hara in southern Haryana," *Journal of the Oriental Institute,* Baroda, Vol. XXIX (1979), pp. 128-32.
29. S.P. Shukla, *Sculptures and Terracottas in the Archaeological Museum Kurukshetra University,* Kurukshetra, 1983.
30. D.C. Bhattacharyya, *Medieval Indian Sculpture (In the Government Museum and Art Gallery, Chandigarh),* Chandigarh, 1981.
31. Devendra Handa, *Jaina Bronzes From Hansi,* Shimla-New Delhi, 2002. This hoard was stolen from the Jaina Temple at Hansi on 26 October 2005 and a substantial part was recovered by the police in December 2005.
32. *IAR,* 1965-66, p. 82.

33. For details see J. Przyluski, *Ancient Peoples of the Punjab* (Eng. Tr. By Chitrabhanu Sen, Calcutta, 1962, p. 9; *Imperial Gazetteer of India*, Vol. I, p. 242; C.J. Rodgers, *Report of the Punjab Circle of the Archaeological Survey for 1888-89*, pp. 41-43 (henceforth *Report*); John Allan, *Catalogue of the Coins of Ancient India in the British Museum*, London, 1936 (henceforth *BMC*), pp. cliii-clviii; L.D. Barnett, *Bulletin of the School of Oriental and African Studies*, London, Vol. x (1940), pp. 277-84; P.L. Gupta, "Identification of Agācha on Agroha Coins," *Journal of the Numismatic Society of India*, Vol. IV, pp. 49 ff; H.L. Srivastava, *op. cit*; Swami Omanand Saraswati, *Ancient Seals of Haryana*, Jhajjar, VS 2031, pp. 76-80, Nos. 30-50; Devendra Handa, "Some Important Towns of Haryana: A Study of their Ancient Past," *Journal of Haryana Studies*, Kurukshetra, Vol. II (1970), pp. 4-6; "Agroha Revisited," in *Prācī-Prabhā: Perspectives in Indology (Essays in honour of Prof. B.N. Mukherjee)*, edited by D.C. Bhattacharyya and Devendra Handa, New Delhi, 1989, pp. 239-58; *IAR*, 1979-80 onwards; etc.
34. *IAR*, 1963-64, p. 90.
35. *CASR*, II, pp. 223-24; XIV, p. 97; CAGI, pp. 283-84; Rodgers, *Report*, pp. 14-15; *Annual Report of the Archaeological Survey of India*, 1921-22, p. 47; 1922-23, p. 89, pl. V. e; *Ancient India*, X-XI, p. 138.
36. *IAR*, 1979-80, pp. 29-30; see also Jagdish Singh Rahar, *Archaeological Settlement Pattern of Mahendragarh and Rewari Districts (Haryana)*, Unpublished Ph.D. Thesis, Maharshi Dayanand University, Rohtak, 2001, pp. 80-81.
37. C.J. Rodgers, *Revised List of Objects of Archaeological Interest in the Panjab, Lahore*, 1891 (henceforth *List*), pp. 75-76; *IAR*, 1959-60, p. 74, pls. LX-LXI.
38. Yogeshwar Kumar, *Archaeology of Naraingarh and Its Neighbourhood (District Ambala)*, Unpublished M.Phil. Dissertation, Kurukshetra University, Kurukshetra, 1987, p. 61, pl. XVIII. A.
39. Rodgers, *Report*, p. 14.
40. Silak Ram, *Archaeology of Rohtak and Hissar Districts (Haryana)*, Unpublished Ph.D. Thesis, Kurukshetra University, Kurukshetra, 1972, p. 222, pl. XXVI. A. This almost life-size piece is now preserved in the Gurukula Museum at Jhajjar. See also Devendra Handa, *Buddhist Remains from Haryana*, New Delhi, 2004, p. 34, Fig. 22.
41. *IAR*, 1960-61, p. 65.
42. Sneh Lata, *Archaeology and History of Sampla Block, District Rohtak (Haryana)*, Unpublished M.Phil. Dissertation, M.D. University, Rohtak, 1987-88, pp. 55-56, pl. VII. A. All sites from the Sampla block listed here are known from this dissertation.
43. Mani Ram Lamba, *Archaeology and History of Kalanaur Block, District Rohtak*, Unpublished M.Phil. Dissertation, M.D. University, Rohtak, 1987-88, p. 96, pl. XIII. B. Information about the sites of this block is collected from this dissertation.
44. *IAR*, 1963-64, p. 90.
45. *IAR, 1960-61*, p. 65; 1968-69, p. 9; Devendra Handa, "Some Unpublished Sculptures from Gujjar Kheri (Haryana)", *PURBA*, Vol. XXVII, no. 1 (April 1986), pp. 107 ff.
46. *IAR, 1963-64*, p. 90.
47. *CAGI*, p. 207; *BMC*, p. cli.
48. See for details Devendra Handa (2002), *op. cit.*, pp. 1-3.
49. *IAR, 1963-64*, p. 90; *1966-67*, p. 65.
50. B.Ch. Chhabra, "Aśokan Pillar at Hissar, Panjab," *Vishveshvaranand Indological Journal*, Hoshiarpur, Vol. II, part ii (September 1964), pp. 319-22.
51. *CASR*, V, pp. 140-42; Rodgers, *List*, pp. 65-67.
52. V.S. Agrawala, *India As Known To Pāṇini*, Varanasi, 1963, map 2; Y.D. Sharma, "Exploration of Historical Sites," *Ancient India*, no. IX (1953), p. 131. It may be the Isuyāra or Usuyāra of the *Uttarādhyayana Sūtra* (XIV.1-3) described as an "ancient, wealthy and famous town beautiful like heaven" situated in the Kuru country (*Sacred Books of the East Series*, Vol. XLV, p. 62 n).
53. D.P.S. Punia, *Archaeology of Mahendragarh and Gurgaon Districts (Haryana)*, Unpublished Ph.D. Thesis, Kurukshetra University, Kurukshetra, 1976, p. 223, pl. XXXIII.C.
54. *IAR*, 1966-67, p. 65.

55. *Imperial Gazetteer of India*, II, pp. 324-25; H.A. Rose, "A Note on Kurukshetra," *Indian Antiquary*, Vol. XXXIII (1904), pp. 299-300.
56. K.V. Ramesh and S.P. Tewari, "An Inscription of Pratihāra Vatsarāja, Śaka 717," *Epigraphia Indica*, Vol. XCI (1975-76), New Delhi, 1989, pp. 49-57. Though the editors of this inscription have not taken pains to ascertain the provenance of this important record, yet it is a matter of satisfaction that years ago, it had been noticed in a thesis which records its provenance as Jodhkan (Sirsa). For details, see Silak Ram, *op. cit.*, pp. 237 ff.
57. Dr. Raghuvir, *Kapishṭhala-Kaṭha Saṃhitā*, Lahore, 11932, Introduction.
58. *Ibid.*, p. 2.
59. Edward Sachau, *Alberuni's India*, p. 206.
60. James Prinsep, *Essays on Indian Antiquities* (edited by Edward Thomas), London, 1858, p. 46.
61. Rodgers, *List*, pp. 18-21.
62. H.M. Elliot and J. Dowson, *History of India as told by its own Historians*, Vol. II, pp. 317 and 353.
63. *Jana Sāhitya*, Patiala, Vol. IV, Nos. 10-11 (Oct.-Nov. 1965), p. 347.
64. Rodgers, *Report*, p. 42; *The Sunday Tribune*, Chandigarh, Oct. 16, 1966.
65. *IAR*, 1963-64, p. 90.
66. See also *IAR*, 1971-72, p. 23.
67. Devendra Handa, "Kapāla-Mocana: An Ancient Holy Place," *Purāṇa*, Vol. X, no. 2 (July 1968), pp. 148-53; "Late Gupta Sculptures and Epigraphs from Kapāla-Mochana," *Purāvṛitta*, Lucknow, no. I (2000-2001), p. 95 ff; "A Survey of Inscriptions from Haryana", in *Revealing India's Past-Recent Trends in Art and Archaeology: Prof. Ajay Mitra Shastri Commemoration Volume* (Eds. R.K. Sharma & Devendra Handa), 2 vols., New Delhi, 2004, Vol. II, pp. 259-83.
68. S. Sten Konow, *Corpus Inscriptionum Indicarum*, Vol. II (I), Calcutta, 1929, p. 179.
69. James Prinsep, *Essays on Indian Antiquities* (ed. Edwards Thomas), London, 1858, p. 24; *Journal of the Asiatic Society of Bengal*, XLIV, p. 82; *Proceedings of the Asiatic Society of Bengal*, 1875, p. 85; Vincent A. Smith, *Indian Museum Catalogue*, I, Oxford, 1906, p. xxi; *BMC*, p. ciii; Svāmi Omānanda Sarasvatī (VS 2031), *op. cit.*, p. 86, nos. 56-57.
70. *IAR*, 1965-66, p. 82.
71. *IAR*, 1960-61, p. 65; B.M. Pande, "Sculptures from Kohand, District Karnal, Panjab," *VIJ*, VI (1968), pp. 125-29.
72. R.C. Agrawala (April 1955), *op. cit.*, pp. 85-90; "Kurukṣetra in the Later Sanskrit Literature," *Indian Historical Quarterly*, Vol. XXXI, no. 1 (March 1955), pp. 3-31; "Early History and Archaeology of Kurukṣetra and Ambala Division," *IHQ*, Vol. XXXI, no. 4 (Dec. 1955), pp. 193-222 and Vol. XXXII, no. 1 (March 1956), pp. 15-35.
73. Rodgers, *List*, p. 76.
74. Jaya Chandra Vidyalankara, "Nakula kā Paśchima Digvijaya," in *Ojha Commemoration Volume*, Section VIII, pp. 3-4.
75. Sabhā Parva, ch.32.v:

    Śairīshakaṃ Mahetthaṃ cha vaśe chakre mahādyuti/
    Ākrośaṃ chaiva rājarshistena yuddhamabhūnmahat //
76. *Jana Sāhitya*, Patiala, Vol. IV, Nos. 10-11 (Oct.-Nov. 1965), p. 344; Suraj Bhan, "Excavations at Mitathal (Hissar) 1968," *Journal of Haryana History*, Kurukshetra, Vo. I, no. 1 (Jan. 1969), p. 1.
77. *Imperial Gazetteer of India*, Vol. I, p. 262.
78. Sheela Devī, *Art Traditions in Haryana*, Unpublished Ph.D. Thesis, Kurukshetra University, Kurukshetra, 1975, p. 208, P. XXXII.E.
79. *IAR*, 1971-72, p. 23.
80. *IAR*, 1961-62, p. 97, pls. CXXXIX and CXL.
81. "A New Yakshī Image From Mehrauli," *JUPHS*, Vol. XXIV-XXV (1951-52), pp. 191-92.
82. B.N. Sharma, "An Inscribed Image of Viṣṇu-Saṃkarṣaṇa from Mehrauli," *Journal of the Indian Society of Oriental Art, New Series*, Calcutta, Vol. VI, pp. 67-71. Earlier it had been noticed in *IAR*, 1958-59, p. 71, pl. XXXIV.A.
83. Rogders, *List*, p. 80.

84. Acharya Bhagwan Dev, *Vīra-bhūmi Hariyānā* (Hindi), p. 141.
85. *IAR*, 1965-66, p. 82.
86. *Bulletin of Museums and Archaeology, U.P.*, Lucknow, Nos. 5-6 (June-Dec. 1970), pp. 5-7. For a detailed account and illustrations of the different brick-panels from Nachar Khera and Jind see Yoganand Shastri, *Prāchīna Bhārata meṃ Yaudheya Gaṇarājya* (Hindi), New Delhi, 1999, pp. 192-95, pls. 91-96.
87. *Ājakala* (Hindi), Nov. 1969, p. 27 and figs.; Shukla (1983), *op. cit.*, pp. 73-74, pls. LVII.3-4 and Lviii.1-3.
88. *Ancient India*, no. X-XI, pp. 140-41.
89. V.S. Agrawala, *JUPHS*, XXIV-XXV, p. 188 and fig. 4.
90. *Gazetteer of the Gurgaon District* (Lahore, 1884), pp. 144-45; *Imperial Gazetteer of India*, I, p. 278.
91. *Ancient India*, Nos. X-XI, pp. 141-45.
92. Devendra Handa, *Holiest of the Holy – Pehowa: The Ancient Pṛithūdaka*, New Delhi, 2004.
93. See for details *CASR*, XIV, pp. 70 ff; IAR, 1959-60, p. 74; Devendra Handa, "Some Unpublished Sculptures from Pinjaur," *Vishveshvaranand Indological Journal*, Hoshiarpur, Vol. XIV, part I (March 1976), pp. 112-19, pls. I-XI; "Some Sculptures from Panjab and Haryana," *Panjab University Research Bulletin (Arts)*, Vol. VII, no. I (April 1976), pp. 95-96, figs. 6-8; "Some Interesting Medieval Sculptures From Pinjaur," *Ibid.*, Vol. XIII, no. 2 (October 1982), pp. 83-86, figs. 1-4; Udai Vir Singh, *Pinjore Sculptures*, Kurukshetra, 1977, pp. 1-52, pls. I-XXIV; D.C. Bhattacharyya (1981), *op. cit.*; Shukla (1983), *op. cit.*; etc.
94. *IAR*, 1970-71, p. 16; 1971-72, p. 24, pl. XXXIV. A; *Kurukshetra University Research Journal*, Vol. x (1976), pp. 25-27.
95. *IAR*, 1963-64, p. 90.
96. *Indian Express*, Wednesday December 11, 1991, p. 4.
97. *IAR*, 1971-72, p. 23.
98. *CASR*, XIV, pp. 72-75; Rodgers, *List*, pp. 51-52; *IAR*, 1963-64, p. 23.
99. Buddha Prakash, *Glimpses of Ancient Punjab*, Patiala, 1966, p. 35.
100. *IAR*, 1965-66, p. IV.7; Yoganand (1999), *op. cit.*, pp. 196-98, pls. 97-98.
101. Silak Ram, *op. cit.*, p. 223, pl. XXVI.B. It is now housed in the Jhajjar museum.
102. *Mbh.*, Gita Press edition, Vana Parva, Ch. 84, v. 10 and *Padma Purāṇa* I.28, 11.
103. *IAR*, 1967-68, pp. 20-22.
104. Devendra Handa, "Some Important Towns of Haryana: A Study of their Ancient Past – 3," *Journal of Haryana Studies*, Vol. III, part 2 (1971), pp. 4-5.
105. *Ancient India* (1954-55), pp. 23 and 145.
106. *India as Known to Pāṇini*, p. 69.
107. *Gazetteer Delhi District*, 1883-84, p. 209.
108. *CAGI*, p. 207; *BMC*, p. cli; *CII*, III, pp. 231-32.
109. Suraj Bhan, "Excavations at Sugh (1964 and 1965)," *Journal of Haryana Studies*, Vol. IX (1977), pp. 1-49; *Roopa-Lekhā*, Vol. LV (1984), pp. 90-91.
110. *CASR*, II, pp. 21-23; *CAGI*, pp. 276-83; Rodgers, *Report*, pp. 9-14; *ARASI* 1921-22, pp. 46-49; 1922-23, p. 90.
111. Shukla (1983), *op. cit.*
112. *CASR*, V, pp. 136 ff., pl. XL.5; XXIII, pp. 19-24, pl. XXVIII; Fleet, *CII*, III, pp. 269-71.

Chapter 2

Gaṇeśa

Gaṇapati[1], the lord of the Gaṇas, popularly known as Gaṇeśa, and also by various other names like Gajānana, Gajamukha, Guharāja, Ekadanta, Heramba, Lambodara, Vakratuṇḍa, Vināyaka, Vighneśa, Vighneśvara, Vighnapati, Guhyāgraja, etc. is the god of wisdom and success. Though the most popular deity from the medieval period onwards, yet his name is not found anywhere in the early literature.[2] It is in the *Baudhāyana Dharmasūtra*[3] (II.5, 6) that we get his first unmistakable reference. Probably initially, he was connected with Yaksha and Nāga cults of folk divinities.[4] Dr. Sampurnananda assigned him a non-Aryan origin.[5] His very name and epithets like Gaṇeśvara, Vināyaka, etc. suggest that he represented a group of divinities and stood at the head of that.[6] In the early phase of his worship he was the deity who created obstacles (*vighnas*) but by a natural opposite corollary, he became the 'destroyer of obstacles' (*vighna-vināśana*) and the 'bestower of success' (*siddhi-dātā*).[7] In the *Mahābhārata* (Ādi Parva I.75-79), Gaṇeśa is described as the scribe of the epic. Gaṇapati's reputation for wisdom seems to originate from the term Gaṇapati used for Bṛihaspati in the *Ṛigveda* (II.23, 1). Bṛihaspati is the Vedic god of wisdom and is called the sage of the sages. Head is the repository of brain and wisdom. The big head of the elephant perhaps symbolizes the highest wisdom. In the *Yājñavalkya Saṃhitā* (I.271 ff) for the first time, Vināyaka is described as the son of Ambikā. Various Purāṇas narrate the stories of his birth and life,[8] and the *Gaṇeśa Purāṇa*[9] elevates him to the status of the Supreme God – the creator, protector, and destroyer of the universe. A Kushāṇa coin bears the figure of Śiva with the legend 'Gaṇeśa', apparently for Śiva. The earliest epigraphic reference to Gaṇapati, the name of a Nāga ruler, is found in the Prayāga *Praśasti* of Samudragupta. A cult seems to have developed round Gaṇapati soon after, if not before or during the Gupta period[10], and spread far and wide in the old world during the medieval period.[11] He is worshipped by all classes of the Hindus (except Śrī-Vaishṇavas) at the commencement of any religious ceremony. Though the *Amarakosha* gives '*ekadanta*' (having one tooth or tusk), '*gajamukha*' (elephant-faced) and '*lambodara*' (having long paunch or pot belly) as the synonyms of Gaṇapati,[12] which have their iconographic connotations and significance, yet the *Bṛihatsaṃhitā* (LVII.58) contains the first iconographic description of the deity.[13] It states that Gaṇeśa should have an elephant's face with a single tusk and a bulging belly and should carry a *kuṭhāra* (hatchet) and a *mūlakanda* (turnip of dark foliage root) in his hands. No such image has come to light as yet. Even otherwise also, it is believed by scholars that two-handed Gaṇeśa is a rarity.[14] The *Vighneśvara Pratishṭhā Vidhi* and the *Gaṇeśa Purāṇa*, which refer to two-handed Gaṇeśa, indicate that the two-handed images existed.[15] According to the *Gaṇeśa Purāṇa* (I.18, 21), Mahotkaṭa Gaṇapati has a lion as his *vāhana* (*siṃhārūḍhaḥ*) in the Kṛitayuga, Mayūragaṇapati has peacock as his *vāhana* in the Tretā, Gajānana in the Dvāpara has rat as his vehicle and Dhūmraketugaṇapati in the Kali has horse. This Purāṇa also explains in a legend the circumstances in which the rat became the vehicle of the god. The *Brahmavaivarta Purāṇa* (III.13, 12), however, tells us that Vasundharā, the goddess of earth, gave mouse to Gaṇeśa as a vehicle. The *Vishṇudharmottara Purāṇa* (III.71, 13-16) describes Gaṇeśa image as having an elephantine face with one tusk and a bulging belly, wearing tiger-skin (*vyāghra-charma*) and serpentine sacred thread (*sarpa-yajñopavīta*), carrying trident and rosary in his right hands and *paraśu* (axe) and *modaka-pātra* (bowl of sweet-balls) in his left seated in *lalitāsana*. The *Matsya Purāṇa* prescribes that the image of Gaṇapati should have an elephantine face, large belly, large extended three eyes, big trunk, one tusk, strong arms, feet and shoulders, and should carry a tusk and a lotus flower in the right hands and battle-axe and pot of ambrosia in the left ones. He should also be accompanied by his consorts Ṛiddhi and Buddhi, and the mount Mūshaka, the rat.[16] The *Agni Purāṇa* (L.23-26), *Aparājitapṛichchhā* (12.35-37), *Rūpa-Maṇḍana*[17] and some Āgamas also describe four and more handed images of the god similarly or with slight differences.[18] Also a variety of his images are described in various texts and found actually.[19] He is the most universally adorned of all the Hindu gods and his images are found practically in every part of India. His popularity transcended the borders and extended to Nepal, Tibet, China, Burma, Siam, Indo-China, Korea, Japan, Java, Bali, Borneo, Afghanistan and Central Asia.

It was in 1955 that a Pakistani numismatist Agha Inayat Ali Shah published a silver drachmae issued in the name of Hermaios and averred that the Greek god Zeus on the reverse has been Indianized by wearing an elephant trunk like the Hindu deity Gaṇeśa.[20] Probably unaware of this publication, A.K. Narain presented similar idea in 1973 in his paper presented at the Paris session of the International Congress of Orientalists and in his presidential address at the Diamond Jubilee Conference of the Numismatic Society of India, 1973.[21] In 1978, following the same argument, he said that "The Pi-lo-sho-lo mountain in Kapisi was so called after its presiding deity who had the Greek god Zeus of the Indo-Greeks and the elephant deity of the local population of a part of Afghanistan".[22] Joe Cribb contested this view and showed that the photograph of the same coin, lit from a different angle, gives a different picture. He argued that what Narain took as the trunk of an elephant is a badly copied Zeus-Mithra's nose, beard and a fold in his gown.[23] Without caring for Cribb's criticism, Narain repeated the same argument in 1984[24] and 1988[25] declaring the so-called "elephant-headed" divinity on Hermaios' coins as a well established fact.[26] In two of his articles, Bopearachchi has shown the un-tenability of this view saying that the illusory "elephant-trunk" effect is the result of the engraver's hand and that other coins with the same monogram and showing the enthroned deity do not carry this effect.[27]

There is a tradition that the worship of Gaṇeśa was taken to Nepal from India by the daughter of Aśoka in the 3rd century B.C.E.[28] The tradition cannot be relied upon in the absence of any definite evidence. The elephant-faced figure crouching under the weight of a long serpent-shaped garland, which is upheld at intervals by other *gaṇas* (*māla-vāhakas*) on one of the Amaravati railings said to be not later than the beginning of the current era, is regarded as a transitional form of Gaṇeśa.[29] Some scholars regard clay figurines from Veṅgīpura, Kondapura, Kolhapura, Ter, Nagarjunakonda, Veerapuram, etc. as representations of Gaṇeśa belonging to late Sātavāhana and Mahārathī period (*circa* 2nd to 4th century C.E.).[30] The first epigraphic reference to a shrine of Gaṇapati comes from a pillar inscription of Velpuru (near Sattenapalli, district Guntur, Andhra Pradesh) which states that Mādhavavarman II during his 33rd regnal year (corresponding to C.E. 489) consecrated an image of Dantimukha Svāmī.[31] There is, however, no trace of Gaṇeśa worship in northern India before the 5th century C.E. as no images of the god belonging to an earlier date have been discovered from anywhere.[32]

Haryana has yielded quite a good number of images of Gaṇeśa belonging to the post-Gupta period, some of rare beauty (Pl. 1). They show the god as seated, standing or dancing. Two-handed images are rare and four-handed variety is the commonest. Seated images outnumber the standing and dancing ones. Gaṇeśa is shown alone or accompanying Umā-Maheśvara or Pārvatī; on the auspicious triads with Lakshmī or Mahishāsuramardinī and Kubera; carved independently or as the *lalāṭa-bimba* on a doorframe; in a *rathikā* or on *vedibandha* molding; etc. We describe below some of his important images from Haryana.

The earliest representation of Gaṇeśa from Haryana is a small molded clay figure, 4 x 3 cm, shown as seated on a pedestal in *sukhāsana* (Pl. 2) from Thanesar. It is four-handed. Probably the left hand had a bowl of sweets while the right hand is holding an object, which is difficult to identify because of the indifferent state of preservation of the piece. The back left hand is broken; the trunk is turned to left taking possibly sweet balls from the bowl. The elephant-head has fan-shaped ears. The left ear is damaged. The god is pot-bellied (*lambodara*). This is the first and the only known terracotta figure found from any site in Haryana. Similar figurines have been discovered from Ahichchhatra (*circa* C.E. 650 to 750).[33] No image of Gaṇeśa in metal is known from Haryana.

SEATED IMAGES

Two-handed Image

Two-handed images of Gaṇeśa are very rare not only in Haryana but in the whole of India as pointed out above. Only one specimen is known from the state. Made of buff sandstone and measuring 44 x 28 cm (Pl. 3), it is preserved in the Bansivat Behari Temple near Bhadra Talab at Sirsa registered in the name of the priest Sita Ram Shastri (Regn. No. SRS/HRN-70). The god is shown as seated in *sukhāsana* holding a bowl of sweet balls in his left hand and probably the broken tusk in the right. Not in a good state of preservation and with trunk broken, he wears a small coronet with a central jewel, necklace, serpent thread and anklets. The folded left leg rests on a cushion with the foot touching the earth with the toe. A lozenge-shaped *śrīvatsa* has been carved in the center of the chest. The rounded part of the back slab behind the head seems to serve as halo. The god is slightly pot-bellied. The ears have been carved as simulating palm leaves. Stylistically, the image may belong to the 10th century C.E.

Four-handed Images

Most of the images found from Haryana belong to the four-handed variety. A late Gupta red sandstone image of Gaṇeśa of *circa* 6th-7th century was noticed at Sondh, located nearly 6 km west of Nuh in tahsil Palwal, district Faridabad, but disappeared subsequently. No other details are available. Another piece in buff sandstone measuring 69 x 49 cm from the same site is preserved in HARDAM (Acc. No. 1/393). One of the early medieval images of Gaṇeśa of *circa* 8th century made of sandstone and measuring 19 x 11.5 cm is now preserved in the Gaur Sabhā Śiva Mandira at Karnal (Regn. No. HRN/KAR-102). This beautiful image shows the god seated in *sukhāsana*, holding the bowl of sweet balls in his proper left hand, radish (?) in the additional left and a lotus in the rear right. The normal right hand is broken but may have carried the broken tusk. The elephant-head is carved with right tusk only with the lower trunk turning almost horizontal to take the sweet ball from the bowl in the left hand. The god is pot-bellied and wears a serpent sacred-thread. The image has been whitewashed concealing other details.

Depicted on a rectangular blackish grey granite slab with Mahishāsuramardinī on the proper left (and Kubera on the proper right but missing now, and thus forming part of an auspicious triad), Gaṇeśa from the Bhagavatī Temple at Kalayat is undoubtedly the most beautifully executed image of the god from Haryana (Pl. 1). The elephant-headed (*gaja-mukhaḥ*) god is seated in *lalitāsana* on a double petalled lotus seat wearing a tiara bedecked with jewels, pearl necklace, *kaṅkaṇas*, finger rings, anklets and toe-rings. Flourishes of the *dhotī* flutter on the sides. The ears simulate winnowing baskets. The muscular body betrays potbelly (*pralamba-jaṭhara*) with double protuberance, about to burst and tied with a snake, which also serves as the sacred thread. As usual, the left tusk is broken and only the right one is there (*eka-vishāṇaḥ*). The broken tusk (or perhaps a blue lotus) is held in the proper right hand. The back right holds the *kuṭhāra* (axe) and the back left the *mūlaka*. The normal left holds the bowl of sweet balls from which the trunk has picked up one piece taking a twirl. Behind the head is a plain gloriole pointed at the top. Garland-bearing *vidyādharas* are shown on the top corners of the slab as hovering in the clouds. The mouse is missing. The care with which it has been carved bestows it a speciality and makes it an exquisite relief. Stylistically, it may be dated to *circa* 8th century C.E.[34] A very crudely carved auspicious triad from Khokhrakot (Rohtak)[35] datable to *circa* 9th century also shows Gaṇeśa as seated in *sukhāsana* on the proper right of Gaja-Lakshmī with Kubera occupying her left side (Pl. 4). A similar triad exists at Chuliana in the Sampla block of Rohtak and also at Chulkana village near Panipat and is still under worship. These very deities seem to have been carved in pillared and pedimented niches of *circa* 10th century on architectural fragments of a temple at Kasan near Gurgaon. The trunk of the four-armed Gaṇeśa falls vertically and takes a twirl to its right here (Pl. 5). Probably a similar triad existed at Sondh but only the Gaja-Lakshmī and Kubera have survived. Even these two are very badly mutilated.

A buff sandstone rectangular slab measuring 47 x 30 cm from Jadthal (Acc. No. 04/83) shows Gaṇeśa seated in *sukhāsana*, wearing a beaded band on the forehead with one string going backwards from over the head (Pl. 6). There is a small round *tilaka* (or third eye) on the forehead. The left tusk is broken. The trunk rises prominently and takes a horizontal turn to his left to pick up the sweet ball from the bowl held in the normal left hand. The natural right hand holds the broken tusk and the rear pair seems to hold a lotus and the rosary. Serpent forms the sacred thread with the head facing on the potbelly. The ears are fanned outwards and there is no halo. The rectangular slab has a small projection in front and its top corners are rounded. Compositionally, it is one of the simplest forms. It can be dated to about 8th century C.E.

A very beautiful image of Gaṇeśa comes from Pehowa. Now preserved in HARDAM (Acc. No. 1/354), it is made of buff sandstone and measures 33 x 20 cm. It was discovered from the Prāchī Śiva Temple complex at Pehowa. It shows the god seated on a cushion in *sukhāsana* holding a full-blown lotus and an axe in the rear pair of hands and a *mūlaka* and the bowl of sweet-balls in the proper right and left hands (Pl. 7). Gaṇeśa wears a small crown adorned with pearl strings and jewels, necklace, snake thread, beaded wristlets and anklets. The left tusk is broken and the trunk takes a turn to the left and twirls to pick up a sweet-ball. The mount of the god, mouse, is also shown near the right foot. There is a plain gloriole with beaded rim behind the head and the top corners show garland-bearing *vidyādharas*. A *tilaka* mark simulating a vertical third eye adorns the forehead. The god is slightly pot-bellied. A pleasing composition, sparse ornamentation and exquisite chisel work add grace to the image, which may have originally adorned a mature Pratihāra shrine.[36]

A sandstone image of Gaṇeśa with similar arrangement of the attributes in the four-hands was once studded in the back wall of the Faridkot Gurudvārā at Kurukshetra (Pl. 8) along with Umā-Maheśvara and a broken part of a Vishṇu image (showing the Narasiṃha incarnation in a panel and the lower part of some other figure above). Gaṇeśa here is wearing head ornament of beaded strings, necklet, *sarpa-yajñopavīta*, bracelets, and the nether garment. He is *Eka-danta* and *lambodara*, seated in *sukhāsana*. A *yoni-pīṭha* carved in front of the image indicates that some people used to worship it even as studded in the wall. Since the legs are damaged and some part of the image is buried in the ground, we are not sure whether his vehicle accompanied the god or not. Like the preceding example, this image too belongs to the Pratihāra period.

Amongst the other images of Gaṇeśa from Pehowa, mention may be made of small icons of red sandstone measuring 14.5 x 7.5 cm in the Dasanāmī Akhārā and 8 x 5 cm piece in the Bālā Sundarī Temple. Another representation, 21.5 x 14 cm, depicting the deity with two female attendants, is preserved on the Sarasvatī ghat in a small shrine. All these images may be assigned to the Pratihāra period. It is notable that Gaṇapati festival is still celebrated at Pehowa on the fourth day of the bright half of Bhādra and the fourth day of the dark fortnight of Māgha.[37]

Gaṇeśa from Kohand (Acc. No. 1/579), 36 x 26 cm, has beaded ornaments including the sacred thread, holds in his four-hands in the *pradakshiṇā* order a radish, lotus, axe and *modaka-pātra*, has cushions under both the legs and has a prominent halo behind the head flanked by garland-bearing *vidyādharas* (Pl. 9). The vehicle of the god is missing. It may also be dated to the Pratihāra period. A small black stone beautifully executed Pratihāra image from Hansi also shows the slightly potbellied god wearing a diadem, bracelets, armlets, etc. and having large ears with similar attributes in the four-hands. Mouse is missing in this case also.

Gaṇeśa image from Allawala in district Karnal is similar in conception but shows the top of the rectangular slab rounded in the center (Pl. 10). The god wears a three-stringed beaded band with a jewel in the center on the forehead, necklace, beaded bracelets, and waistband to secure the lower garment on the potbelly. The snake serving as the sacred thread comes down from the left shoulder and takes a turn to his right on the paunch. The trunk has been depicted to take a sweet ball. The normal right hand is raised in fear-allaying posture (*abhaya*) and the rear right holds a radish. The back and proper left hands support an axe and bowl of sweet balls. An outward moving mouse is shown near the right foot of the god. The execution is rather rough. The variety of the necklace depicted here did not evolve before the 10th century. An image with similar attributes and datable to the same period lay fixed in the back wall of the Faridkot Gurdwara at Kurukshetra but is missing now. A niched image of Gaṇeśa on the *vedibandha* molding of a temple now fixed in the wall near the door of the Kapila-Muni shrine in the Bhagavatī Temple complex at Kalayat shows the god with proper right hand displayed in *abhaya*, back right holding the *kuṭhāra*, rear left supporting a lotus by its stalk and the normal left holding the bowl of sweet balls as usual. The attributes in the four-hands of Gaṇeśa from Badali are similar with the exception of the proper right, which perhaps held the tusk, now damaged. The attributes in all the four-hands of the god from Basaula near Pinjaur cannot be made out clearly. Four-armed Gaṇeśa, 26 x 19 cm, installed in the Parāśara *tīrtha* in village Bahlolpur Mustarka in district Karnal has only the normal left hand surviving, holding the bowl of sweet balls. All these images are datable to the 10th century C.E. It seems that the tenth through twelfth centuries were the period of the construction of a large number of temples in the area. The ruling families during these centuries were the Pratihāras, Tomaras, and Chāhamānas. It seems that by this time the worship of Gaṇeśa at the beginning of any good work had become very popular as some epigraphs of this period also open with a salutation to him.

Pinjaur has yielded quite a few images of Gaṇeśa. An image which once lay fixed in the wall of the Kabir Chaurā temple is an exquisite piece (Pl. 11) showing the god wearing a *karaṇḍa-mukuṭa* bedecked with pearl strings and almond-shaped jewels, with normal right hand broken and others holding a lotus or goad, axe and *modaka-pātra*. It measures 46 x 33 cm.[38] Another image from the same site preserved in HARDAM (Acc. No. 1/24) measures 26 x 20 cm and shows the mouse near the right foot but is broken above the chest. A 10th century four-armed seated sandstone image of the god from Pinjore measuring 41 x 39.5 cm now adorns the Haryana Raj Bhawan at Chandigarh. A colossal 108 x 51 cm sandstone image from Pinjore is now preserved in the Department of Ancient Indian History, Culture and Archaeology of the Kurukshetra University, Kurukshetra showing the god seated in *sukhāsana* on a decorated cushion with his right foot placed on a lotus. The image is very badly mutilated with both the normal hands gone and holding a rosary and perhaps a radish in the damaged extra back right and left hands. The pot-bellied (*lambodara*) elephant-headed god with fan-shaped ears (*sūrpa-karṇa*) wears a torque, the *kaṅkaṇas, nūpuras, nāga-yajñopavīta* and *dhotī*. It is dated to *circa* 11th century C.E.[39] An *uttaraṅga* with Gaṇeśa and a rectangular architectural piece showing four-armed seated Gaṇeśa, both from Pinjore, are also housed in the same museum.[40] A gigantic image from the site, 134 cm in height, now displayed outside the Government Museum & Art Gallery, Chandigarh (Serial No. 122), though slightly mutilated, shows the god seated in *mahārājalīlāsana* holding the tusk in the normal right hand and a rosary in the back right (Pl. 12). The rear left, which may have carried the *kuṭhāra* or *aṅkuśa* (goad), is broken and the proper left is holding as usual the *modaka-pātra*. The realistic head of the elephant is adorned with a pearl string having lotus-shaped spacers and an elaborate decorative motif in front. There is a third vertical eye carved on the top of the trunk. One end of the *dhotī* is flourishing in the front on the pedestal with multiple folds. The upper part of the image, particularly the trunk of the elephantine face, shows sensitive plastic quality but the lower part of the body seems to be carved rather crudely. An interesting feature of the image is the depiction of two lions forming the seat on which the god is seated.[41] Such an arrangement of the attributes and the depiction of lions as the vehicle are not met with in the iconographical texts. The image belongs to *circa* 10th-11th century C.E. Two more figures of Gaṇeśa from Pinjore are housed in the Chandigarh museum. One is merely the head portion and the other one seems to be unfinished.[42]

A buff sandstone image of Gaṇeśa from Gurawara in district Rewari, broken below the big paunch, measuring 49 x 35 cm in its extant form, however, is of unusual interest as the trunk of the god turns to the right and a sword is shown in his upper right hand (Pl. 13).[43] The other hands carry the broken tusk, radish and pot of ambrosia perhaps (not very clear). The god has small elephantine eyes. The elephant head has two big bulging roundels and is adorned with a blossomed lotus at its top and a pearl string around. The sacred thread is also made of the pearl string instead of the usual snake. The round potbelly is stringed probably by a snake. The figure seems to have been portrayed in a fighting posture, a rare depiction in Indian iconography. It is, however, difficult to ascertain whether it represnts his fight with Kārttikeya or some other divinity. This 10th century relief is thus interesting from the iconographical viewpoint.

Yogāsana Gaṇeśa

An image from Pinjaur carved on an architectural piece of a temple (now detached) is, however, very interesting from the iconographical viewpoint. Gaṇeśa is seated in *padmāsana* (Pl. 14). The normal hands seem to be placed on the respective knees while the additional hands are raised above. The relief is so much worn out that it is difficult to make out the objects held by them. The elephant head with long frontally suspended trunk, *śūrpa-karṇas*, broken left tusk, and slight potbelly, however, are quite clear. No such image is known from the whole region. Stylistically it seems to belong to *circa* 10th-11th century C.E.

Four-armed Gaṇeśa on the *uttaraṅga* of the doorframe at Kapālamochana is an early example of the deity as the *lalāṭa-bimba*. Some doorframes from Pinjaur and Ratpur (Acc. No. 1/100) belonging to *circa* 12th century also show four-armed Gaṇeśa with usual attributes as the *lalāṭa-bimba*. A very crude figure of Gaṇeśa as the *lalāṭa-bimba* datable to the same period exists at Gairatbas in district Gurgaon. The light red sandstone image of Gaṇeśa in a temple at Maimond, a small hamlet near Rasidan in district Karnal shows the deity seated in *sukhāsana* carrying an *akshamālā* in the fear-allaying proper right hand while the additional ones on the right and left carry *kamala* and *kuṭhāra*. The proper left holds the *modaka-pātra* from which the twirled trunk picks up the sweet ball. It may also be dated to the 12th century C.E.[44]

The most beautiful specimen of this century, however, is preserved in the Asthal Bohr near Rohtak (Pl. 15).[45] This huge image of Gaṇeśa shows developed ornamentation. Even the long right tusk of the god is ornamented. The four-armed god seated in *sukhāsana* with a cushion below the folded left leg carries the broken tusk, rosary, axe or goad, and the *modaka-pātra* in the four-hands in the *pradakshiṇā* order. The serpent with a raised head serves as the sacred thread over the potbelly. A waistband secures the *dhotī*. A small circlet serves as the *tilaka* mark at the beginning of the trunk near the forehead. The vehicle of the god is shown under his folded right leg.

Gaṇeśa with Gaṇeśāṇī

A sandstone pillar from Sirsa bears a medallion carrying the figure of Gaṇeśa with Gaṇeśāṇī (Pl. 16). The god is shown as seated in *sukhāsana* as usual. He wears a small crown with a jewel in front, bracelets, and anklets and the *dhotī* secured by a waistband. The snake serves the dual purpose of the sacred thread and the belt around the paunch. The normal right hand of the god seems to support a radish and rear right a lotus. The proper left hand embraces Gaṇeśāṇī seated on his folded left leg while the raised back left hand is depicted as carrying the bowl of sweet balls. Unfortunately the face of Gaṇeśāṇī has suffered mutilation. She too is embracing her lord with her right hand. The other hand is broken. She wears *karṇa-kuṇḍalas*, necklace and lower garment held in position by a girdle. A big *dhammilla* coiffure may be seen on her head. Though the face is damaged, the stance clearly indicates her to be looking fondly towards her spouse. Gaṇeśa too is looking at her. This is the only depiction of Gaṇeśa with his spouse from the state. Stylistically, it may be dated to *circa* 10th century C.E.

STANDING IMAGE

Images of standing Gaṇeśa are very rare in Haryana. Only one specimen from Pinjaur is known so far. Slightly potbellied god is shown as standing in *dvibhaṅga* in a double-ribbed *rathikā* on an architectural piece (Pl. 17). There is a small crown on the elephant head and the left tusk is broken. The trunk turns to left to pick up a sweet ball from the bowl held in the normal left hand. The upper left hand seems to hold *śakti* (spear). The upper right hand is raised to the level of the shoulder but the attribute held in it is not clear. The proper right hand is in a suspended position and placed on the upper end of some staff-like object, difficult to be identified properly. Mouse leaping outwards and looking backwards is shown near the left foot of the god. The image is carved on an architectural piece of the ruins of the Bhīmā Devī temple at Pinjaur. The foundational relics, some other images and inscriptions from the ruins at this place suggest that there once existed a grandiose shrine dedicated to the deity during *circa* 11th century C.E., to which the present piece may also be dated.

Dancing Images

There are not many images of dancing Gaṇeśa. A very crudely carved two-handed dancing Gaṇeśa is known from Pinjaur (Pl. 18). Bereft of ornamentation, the elephant-headed god with an elongated torso and stumpy legs is shown in the dancing posture with its head and trunk swaying to left. The object held in the right hand is not clear and the left hand is broken. The right tusk is there and the left one missing. Another dancing figure of Gaṇeśa (Pl. 19) is still fixed in the wall of the *baoli* at Pinjaur and often remains submerged in water.[46] This image, too, is not in a good state of preservation but shares the elongated body and stumpy legs with the preceding example. The god bears a bejeweled band on the forehead, wristlets, *sarpa-yajñopavīta*, and nether garment held in position by a girdle. The small curved eyes and long snozzle evoke a sense of inebriation. The lower right hand supports the handle of an attribute, which looks like a sword while the upper right hand, is held in *lola-mudrā*. The object in the upper left hand is not clear and the normal one carries the bowl of sweet balls as usual. The dancing posture is distinctly marked by the bends of the legs and raised heels with only the toes touching the ground. Stylistically both these images from Pinjaur may be ascribed to *circa* 10th century C.E.

Badali has also yielded an image of dancing Gaṇeśa. The god is depicted in a dancing pose on a lotus seat placed on a *pañcharatha* pedestal accompanied on his proper right by a monkey-faced human figure (Nandikeśvara?) playing on the vertically placed long drum and a male figure beating cymbals and by a male figure playing the flute and another beating the drum with both hands (Pl. 20). Of the eight hands of the god only one right hand in a dancing posture with the thumb and the pointing finger touching each other as in the *vyākhyāna-mudrā* and one left hand holding the bowl of sweet balls has survived and all others are broken. The god has the elephant head with ears like the winnowing baskets, one tusk on the proper right and wears a diadem, necklace, armlets, bracelets, *sarpa-yajñopavīta* and *dhotī* secured by a girdle and sash on the thighs. A small mouse is shown near the left foot of the god. The waist is swinging slightly towards the left and the right foot is slightly raised over the ground in the dancing posture. The trunk is turned to left to pick up a sweet ball and takes a twirl near its tip. The upper portions of the back slab are broken. Stylistically, the image belongs to *circa* 10th century C.E.

The fragmentary head of Gaṇeśa found from Punahna[47] with its head slightly turned to its right and the trunk also swaying in the same direction may have originally belonged to a dancing figure of about the same period. A Pratihāra buff sandstone bust of Gaṇeśa measuring 50 x 31 cm from Thanesar wearing beaded *yajñopavīta* has the extant rear right hand holding some unidentifiable object raised up to the level of the head and the next right bent downwards in dancing posture and the trunk twirled on the right shoulder. It is now preserved in Śrī Kṛishṇa Museum at Kurukshetra. Bābā Baṅgālī kā Ḍerā at Trilokpur in district Panchkula has a dancing Gaṇeśa figure measuring 28 x 27 cm. Another example is known from Gujjar Kheri wherein Gaṇeśa is shown standing to front in a *rathikā*, measuring 38 x

18.5 cm (Regn. No. HRN/AMB-619). The dancing posture can be made out from the splayed out feet and bent legs of the god. The four-armed god shows the usual attributes of hatchet, goad and a bowl of sweet balls in his three hands with the normal right disposed in the gesture of reassuring. The trunk of the god falls down vertically and then turns slightly to its right. Such disposition of the trunk in this part of the country is rare. Outside the pillars of the *rathikā* are the *vyāla* decorations and above the cornice is an elaborate pediment with double *chaitya-gavāksha* motif. Leonine figures are discernible near the top portion. Obviously it is an architectural piece. It may also be dated to the 10th century C.E.[48]

Fragmentary Reliefs

An 8th century grey sandstone image broken waist upwards lies in the heap of carved stones in the courtyard of the temple at Morni-ka-Tal (district Panchkula). The extant fragment measures 64 x 50 cm. The original image must have been a huge one.[49] A small black stone figure measuring 6.5 x 7.5 cm from Hansi shows a beautifully executed slightly pot-bellied Gaṇeśa having large ears and wearing a diadem, bracelets, anklets, etc. seated in *sukhāsana* holding tusk, lotus, axe and bowl of sweet balls in his four-hands. Left tusk is broken. The trunk takes a twirl at its tip hanging in front. The mouse is conspicuous by its absence. Stylistically, it may be dated to *circa* 9th-10th century C.E. Fragmentary head and bust of Gaṇeśa from Gujjar Kheri, measuring 28 x 20 cm and ascribable to *circa* 10th century wears a small tiara, has long drawn face with hanging cheeks with the lower portion, left tusk and hands broken (Regn. No. HRN/SON-350). Gaṇeśa head from Ahir Majra, sandstone, 27.5 x 17.5 cm, *circa* 12th century (Regn. No. HRN/SON-55) is a lovely piece. A 113 x 33 cm, 11th century lintel from Gairatpur Bas in tehsil and district Gurgaon shows Gaṇeśa as the *lalāṭa-bimba* with female divinities on the sides. Images of Gaṇeśa or their fragments belonging to tenth through twelfth centuries are known from Chandimandir (Acc. No. 34/84), Panchkula (1/283), Ratpur (1/96), Mandhna, Barwala (1/167), Raipur Rani, Trilokpur (all in district Panchkula), Sadhaura, Kapālamochana and Ad Badri (district Yamunanagar),[50] Kakrod and Khokhri (Jind), Kurukshetra, Gharaunda, Baras (Karnal), Panipat, Ahir Majra (district Sonepat), Chuliana and Nonod (Rohtak),[51] Hisar region (53/84), Siyana (Rewari),[52] Sirsa (1/150), Tilpat (near Delhi), Sondh and Jakhopur (Gurgaon), and many other places indicating the widespread popularity of the worship of Gaṇeśa in the region during the medieval period.[53] A beautifully carved piece showing the hand of Gaṇeśa holding a bowl full of the sweetballs was recovered from Hisar. Crudely carved on a slab with un-proportionate limbs, the image of seated Gaṇeśa in the Chandigarh museum, furnishes evidence of the existence of a sculptors' studio or workshop in and around the region before its devastation at the hands of the iconoclasts.[54]

Notes and References

1. Cf. *Ṛigveda* II.23, 1: *Gaṇānāṃ tvā Gaṇpatiṃ havāmahe.*
2. *Vājasaneyī Saṃhitā* XIX.25; *Mādhyandina Saṃhitā* XVI.25; XXIII.19; *Aitareya Brāhmaṇa* I.21; *Tittirīya Āraṇyaka* IX.15; etc.
3. A.K. Coomaraswamy, *Yakṣas*, part I, Delhi, 1971, pp. 7 and 42, pl. XXIII.1.
4. Dr. Sampurnananda, *Hindu Deva Parivāra kā Vikāsa* (Hindi), Allahabad, 1964, p. 147.
5. Cf. R.G. Bhandarkar, *Vaiṣṇavism, Śaivism and Minor Religious Systems*, Poona, 1928 (henceforth *VSMRS*), p. 147. The *Yājñavalkya Smṛiti* refers to six Vināyakas such as Mita, Sammita, Śāla, Kaṭaṅkaṭa, Kūshmāṇḍa and Rājaputra.

6. Banerjea, *Development of Hindu Iconography*, Calcutta, 1956 (henceforth *DHI*), p. 355.
7. I.271 ff.
8. See for details, T.A. Gopinath Rao, *Elements of Hindu Iconography*, Madras, 1916 (Reprint, Indological Book House, Delhi-Varanasi, 1971), Vol. I, pp. 33 ff and Dr. Sampurnananda, *Gaṇeśa* (Hindi), Varanasi, VS 2001, pp. 6-10.
9. S.B. Singh, *Brahmanical Icons in Northern India*, New Delhi, 1977, p. 134.
10. Cf. R.G. Bhandarkar, *VSMRS*, pp. 149-50.
11. Alice Getty, *Gaṇeśa*, Oxford, 1936; M.K. Dhavalikar, "Gaṇeśa Beyond the Indian Frontiers," in *India's Contribution to World Thought and Culture*, Madras, 1970, pp. 1-16; P. Banerjee, "Hindu Deities in Central Asia," *Ibid.*, pp. 281-88; Amarendra Nath, "Gaṇeśa in Central Asian Art: An identification," *Journal of the Indian Society of Oriental Art*, New Series, Calcutta, Vol. VI, 1974-75, pp. 1-4; etc.
12. *Amarakosha* I.1, 38: *Vināyaka-Vighnarāja-Dvaimātura-Gaṇādhipaḥ/ Apyekadanto-Heramba-Lmbodara-Gajānanaḥ//*
13. *Pramathādhipo gajamukhaḥ pralambajaṭharaḥ kuṭhāradhārī syāt / Ekaviṣāṇobibhranmūlakandaṃ sunīladalakamalam //* R.G. Bhandarkar (*loc. cit.*) had doubted the authenticity of this verse but Banerjea (*DHI*, p. 357) differs from him.
14. Cf. *EHI*, I, Appendix C, pp. 1-13; *VSMRS*, *loc. cit.*, *Bhāratīya Vidyā* XIII, pp. 29-50; XXXIX (i), pp. 14-19, pls. I-II.
15. *Bhāratīya Vidyā* XXXIX (i), p. 18. See also S.B. Singh, *op. cit.*, pp. 138-40.
16. *Matsya Purāṇa* 260.52-55. The Āgamas refer to Bhāratī, Śrī, Siddhi, Vighneśvarī, Kshudhi, etc. also as his consorts.
17. See for details *EHI*, Vol. I, pp. 48 ff and Appendix C.
18. D.N. Shukla, *Bhāratīya Vāstuśāstra* (*Pratimā Vijñāna*), Vol. IV, pp. 280-81. The *Śāradātilaka* describes fifty-one forms of Gaṇeśa, each with its own attributes. See for details H.K. Sashtry, *South Indian Images of Gods and Goddesses*, New Delhi, 1986 (reprint), p. 173.
19. *Bhāratīya Vidyā* XIII. 19-50; Getty, *op. cit.*
20. Agha Inayat Ali Shah, "A Notable Numismatic Discovery," *The Museums Journal, Organ of the Museums Association of Pakistan*, August 1955, pp. 16-17.
21. *JNSI*, XXXVI (1974), pp. 180-91.
22. A.K. Narain, "On the Earliest Gaṇeśa," *Senerat Paranavitana Commemoration Volume*, Leiden, 1978, pp. 142-44. The coin, which Narain illustrated, belonged to the British Museum and was donated in 1961 by A.D.H. Bivar (no. 1961.3.2.1).
23. Joe Cribb, "The Earliest Gaṇeśa: a Case of Mistaken Identity," *Numismatic Digest*, 1982, pp. 30-32.
24. A.K. Narain, "Some Brahmanical Divinities on the Indo-Greek Coinage revisited," *Inaugural Seminar, Indian Institute of Research in Numismatic Studies*, January 8-10, 1984, Nasik, pp. 9-14.
25. A.K. Narain, "Iconographic Origins of Gaṇeśa and the Evidence of the Indo-Greek Coinage," in *Orientalia Iosephi Tucci Memoriae Dicta*, edited by G. Gnoli and L. Lanciotti, *Serie Orientale Roma*, LVI, 3 (1988), pp. 1007-1019.
26. A.K. Narain, "Gaṇeśa: A Protohistory of the Idea and the Icon," in *Ganesh: Studies of an Asian God*, edited by R.L. Brown, New York, 1991, pp. 19-48.
27. Osmund Bopearachchi, "Elephant-Headed Gaṇeśa or Zeus-Mithra," *Yavanika*, Vol. 2, 1992, and *Topoi*, Vol. 3/2(1993), *op. cit.*, pp. 425-53. Bopearachchi (1999), p. 123.
28. Sashtry, *op. cit.*, p. 168.
29. James Burgess, *Amaravati*, pl. 30, no. 1. See also I.K. Sarma, "A Unique Ushnisha (Coping Stone) from Amaravati," *Journal of Andhra Historical Research Society*, Hyderabad, Vol. XXXVI (1975), pp. 279-84.
30. I.K. Sarma, "Worship of Gaṇeśa at Veṅgipura," in *Essays on Indology, Polity and Administration in honour of Padmabhushan Sh. R.K. Trivedi*, edited by Dr. S.D. Trivedi, Vol. I, New Delhi, 1989, pp. 125-28.

31. *Epigraphia Indica*, Vol. XXXVIII, pp. 128-29; I.K. Sarma, *The Development of Early Śaiva Art and Architecture*, New Delhi, 1982, pp. 145-46.
32. For a comprehensive survey of all the extant literature and sculptural representations one may look beneficially to some recent writings on the subject: Nirmala Yadav, *Gaṇeśa in Indian Art and Literature*, Jaipur, 1997; Paul Martin Dubost, *Ganeśa the Enchanter of the Three Worlds*, Mumbai, 1997; etc.
33. Mohinder Singh, "Terracottas from Thanesar," in *Ajaya-Śrī: Recent Studies in Indology (Prof. Ajay Mitra Shastri Felicitation Volume*, 2, Delhi, 1989, p. 404, pl. 57.
34. Cf. *Mārg*, Haryana Heritage No., Vol. XXVII, no. 4 (Sept. 1974), p. 14.
35. Sheela Devi, *Art Tradition of Haryana*, Unpublished Ph. D. Thesis, Kurukshetra University, Kurukshetra, 1975, pp. 140, 169, 201 and pl. XVI.C.
36. Devendra Handa, *Pehowa*, pp. 105-06, pl. 43.
37. *Ibid.*, p. 106.
38. Devendra Handa, "Some Unpublished Sculptures From Pinjaur," *Vishveshvaranand Indological Journal*, Hosharpur, Vol. XIX, part I (March, 1976), pp. 112-13, pl. II.
39. U.V. Singh, *Pinjore Sculptures*, Kurukshetra University, Kurukshetra, 1977 (henceforth *PS*), pp. 32-33, pl. XII A and S.P. Shukla, *Sculptures and Terracottas in the Archaeological Museum Kurukshetra Unuversity*, Kurukshetra, 1981, pp. 17-18, pl. IX.2 (Acc. no. 72.9).
40. *PS*, p. 32, pl. IX A and B; Shukla, *op. cit.*, p. 17, pls. VIII.3 and IX.1 respectively.
41. D.C. Bhattacharya (*Medieval Indian Sculpture in the Governement Museum and Art Gallery Chandigarh*, Chandigarh, 1981, p. 81, fig. 39) regards the crudely represented animal figure under the seat of the god as rat. A very careful examination of the image, however, reveals the depiction of two lion faces on both ends of the seat.
42. *Ibid.*, p. 82.
43. Jagdish Singh Rahar, *Archaeological Settlement Pattern of Mahendragarh and Rewari Districts (Haryana)*, Unpublished Ph. D Thesis, M.D. University, Rohtak, 2001, pp. 193-94, pl. XVI B. For the disposition of the trunk to right, a characteristic of south Indian images of Gaṇeśa, see C. Sivaramamurti, "Geographical and Chronological Factors in Indian Iconography," *Ancient India*, Bulletin of the Archaeological Survey of India, New Delhi, no. 6 (1950), p. 30.
44. Amar Singh, *op. cit.*, pp. 196-97, pl. XXVII.A.
45. *Indian Archaeology, 1959-60: A Review*, p. 74.
46. *Mārg*, Haryana Heritage Number, Vol. XXVII, no. 4 (Sept. 1974), p. 15.
47. Dharampal Singh Punia, *Archaeology of Mahendragarh and Gurgaon Districts [Haryana]*, Unpublished Ph. D. Thesis, Kurukshetra University, Kurukshetra, 1976, p. 223, pl. XXXIII.B.
48. Devendra Handa, "Some Unpublished Sculptures from Gujjar Kheri (Haryana)," *Panjab University Reasearch Bulletin (Arts)*, Vol. XVIII, no. 1 (April 1986), p. 117, fig. 15.
49. Ashvini Agrawal, "Saiva Sculptures from Morni ka Tal," *Roopa-Lekhā*, Vols. LXVII-LXXI (January 2001), p. 83, fig. 15.
50. Manmohan Kumar, *Archaeology of Ambala and Kurukshetra Districts (Haryana)*, Unpublished Ph. D. Thesis, Kurukshetra University, Kurukshetra, 1976, pp. 148-50, pls. IX A and XII B (Kapālamochana and x D and XII A (Ad Badri).
51. Sneh Lata, *Arcaeology and History of Sampla Block, District Rohtak (Haryana)*, Unpublished M. Phil. Dissertation, M.D. University, 1987-88, pp. 56-57, pl. VII. B.
52. Rahar, *op. cit.*, p. 194, pl. XVII A.
53. Some inscriptions from Haryana also open with a salutation to Gaṇapati and bear out the popularity of the god during the medieval period. See for details, Alexander Cunningham, *Archaeological Survey Report*, Vol. XIV, p. 72; Jagannath Agrawal, *Inscriptions of Haryana, Punjab, Himachal & Kashmir*, New Delhi, 2001, nos. 14, 16 and 17.
54. B.C. Bhattacharyya, *op. cit.*, p. 82.

Chapter 3

Vishṇu

Yasmādvishṭamidaṃ viśvaṃ tasya śaktyā mahātmanaḥ /
Tasmātsā prochyate Vishṇurviśerdhātoḥ praveśanāt //

(*Vishṇu Purāṇa* III.1, 45)

Vishṇu has been invoked in five whole hymns and partially in another in the *Ṛigveda.*[1] His epithets *urukrama, vikrama* and *urugāya* meaning wide going and wide traversing, led Macdonell[2], Keith[3] and others[4] to ascribe him the solar origin. Gonda[5] has, however, tried to prove that Vishṇu also represented a fertility and vegetation god. In the *Brāhmaṇas,* Vishṇu is identified with sacrifice (*yajño vai Vishṇuḥ*) and since sacrifice was the highest form of religious expression, he gained ascendancy and achieved a higher status.[6] With the development of the concept of devotion during the Upanishadic period, a cult seems to have developed round the five Vṛishṇi heroes *(Vṛishṇi-pañchavīrāḥ)* of which Vāsudeva-Vishṇu was the main figure besides Saṃkarshaṇa, Pradyumna, Aniruddha and Sāmba.[7] According to the *Mahābhārata,* Vāsudeva is the Supreme Creator and Saṃkarshaṇa, representing all living beings, is only a form of Vāsudeva. From Saṃkarshaṇa sprang Pradyumna (mind) and from him came forth Aniruddha (self-consciousness). Vāsudeva describes the other four as his own *mūrtis* 'forms' produced from one another.[8] These four forms *(vyūhas)* are sometimes combined together and we get *chaturvyūhamūrtis* of Vishṇu, also called Vaikuṇṭha-*Chaturmūrti.*[9] Later the number of *vyūhas* increased to twenty-four under the *Pāñcharātra* impact and the only difference amongst the twenty-four forms *(Chaturviṃśatimūrtis)*[10] of Vishṇu was the order of attributes in their hands. It is interesting to note that the number of Jaina tīrthaṅkaras is also twenty-four and this number may have influenced the *vyūha* forms.

Bhandarkar has adduced sufficient evidence to establish that a religious cult centering on Vāsudeva had come into existence as early as the 4th-3rd century B.C.E.[11] Ghosundi[12] and Vidiśā[13] inscriptions, an inscribed image of four-handed Vishṇu holding conch, discus, mace and sword belonging to 2nd century B.C. found from Malhar (Madhya Pradesh)[14] and square copper coins of Agathocles (171-160 B.C.E.) depicting Vishṇu and Balarāma found from Ai Khanoum in Afghanistan[15] bear evidence to Vishṇu worship at an early date. *Vibhavavāda* 'incarnation theory' as well as some folk cults may have further contributed to the evolution of Vishṇu cult. Vishṇu worship seems to have flourished in the Gupta age and got further popularity in the early medieval period. Ultimately, the cult of Vishṇu gained ascendancy over others and became the most important of the Brahmanical cults.

Haryana, which formed part of the ancient Āryavarta,[16] Brahmarshideśa,[17] Madhyadeśa,[18] Uttarāpatha[19] etc., had its early association with Vāsudeva-Vishṇu. According to the

Mahābhārata, Vishṇu was worshipped at numerous holy places of Kurukshetra, viz., Vishṇuhrada, Vishṇupada, Garuḍa *tīrtha*, Chakra *tīrtha*, Chakrapāṇi *tīrtha*, Satata *tīrtha*, Padmanābha kūpa, Nābhikamala *tīrtha*, Vāmanaka, Varāha *tīrtha*, Narasiṃha *tīrtha*, Śaṅkhinī *tīrtha*, Brahmodumbara *tīrtha*, Devī *tīrtha*, Dattātreya *tīrtha*, Hayagrīva *tīrtha*, etc.[20] The Garuḍa-dhvaja Pillar Inscription of Vidiśā[21] tells us that Heliodoros, a Greek ambassador, who was the son of Diya (Dion), a resident of Taxila, installed the Garuḍa standard in honor of Vāsudeva at Vidiśā. Evidently, Vaishṇavism had spread to and was very popular in the Taxila region during the 2nd century B.C.E. Agathocles' coins depicting Vāsudeva and Saṃkarshaṇa found from Ai Khanoum[22] corroborate the evidence further. A unique Vṛishṇi coin,[23] a Kharoshṭi sealing,[24] numerous seals and sealings with Brāhmī legends or typical Vṛishṇi emblems[25] and the copper coins of Vṛishṇi rulers found from Sunet and elsewhere[26] acquaint us of the relevance of Vaishṇavism in the Punjab-Haryana region during the 1st century B.C.E./C.E. to 3rd century C.E. Numerous clay seals and sealings from Sunet,[27] a sealing of Harivara from Naurangabad, a seal of Harideva from Sugh[28] and of Nārāyaṇadeva from Agroha,[29] another sealing from the same site with the legend '*namo Vishṇo*' in 3rd-4th century Brāhmī characters, etc. also provide evidence of popularity of the cult in this region during the Gupta period. The Indianization of the Kushāṇas and the adoption of the name Vāsudeva also points to the popularity of Vaishṇavism in north India during the early centuries of the current era.[30]

Tosham Rock Inscription (district Bhiwani), assignable palaeographically to the end of the fourth or the beginning of the 5th century C.E., records the construction of two reservoirs and a house for the use of god Vishṇu (under the name of Bhagavat or the Divine One) by *Āchārya* Somatrāta.[31] The record begins with an invocation of Vishṇu and also refers to the donor's father, grandfather and great grandfather who were all devout Vaishṇavas. The epigraph thus enumerates four generations of Vaishṇava ā*chāryas* in this region. Also engraved on the same rock are a wheel (Sudarśana *chakra*) and a shorter inscription '*Jitaṃ bhagavatā bhagavat-pāda-deśe*' meaning, "victory has been achieved by the Divine One, in (this) Vishṇu-pada region".[32] The popularity of Vaishṇavism in the region during the Gupta period is thus attested to by the inscriptions.[33] Of the various small records on the Aśokan pillar at Hisar, '*Bhagavadbhaktaḥ*' in the Gupta characters[34] is also important from the viewpoint of the history of Vaishṇavism in Haryana. Bāṇabhaṭṭa's mention of the Pauranic legends in his *Harsha-Charita* indicates that the cult continued to flourish in the post-Gupta period in Haryana.[35] Pehowa *praśasti* of Bhojadeva engraved in VS 882 (=C.E. 825) also provides important evidence regarding the growing popularity of Vaishṇavism in this region. It refers to the donations made by horse-traders to a temple of Yajñavarāha built by Bhūvaka, son of Nāgarabhaṭṭa Prabhākara.[36] Another inscription from the same place assignable to the last quarter of the ninth or the beginning of the 10th century C.E., opens with an invocation to Mādhava (Vishṇu) and refers to a triple shrine of the god erected by three brothers Gogga, Pūrṇarāja and Devarāja, of a local Tomara clan, during the reign of the Pratihāra king Mahendrapāla.[37] A stone inscription of the time of Bhojadeva from Sirsa also mentions a brick and stone temple of Yogīśvara (Śiva), which was adorned with the images of Murāri along with that of Lakshmī.[38] A fragmentary stone inscription from Mohanbari ascribable to *circa* 9th century C.E. on palaeographic grounds, invokes "Lord Vishṇu who carries on his eye-lashes pearl-like drops rising from the foamy sea at the fall of a rock of Mahendrāchala..."[39] Two commemorative inscriptions from Gurawara (district Gurgaon) corroborate the growing popularity of Vaishṇavism in Haryana during the medieval period. One of these, dated VS 953 (=C.E. 896) mentions Vīrachandra 'who died after having remembered Vishṇu'[40] while the other commemorates Vishṇuhari who died next year, i.e. VS 954 (=C.E. 897) 'after remembering

Vishṇu'.[41] Hansi Stone Inscription of Pṛithvīrāja II (VS 1224=C.E. 1167) also invokes the god Murāri (Kṛishṇa) and compares king Pṛithvīrāja II to Rāma.[42] The Muslim historians refer to the existence of a temple of Chakrasvāmi at Thanesar in C.E. 1014 when Mahmud Ghaznavi attacked and plundered it. The idol of Chakrasvāmi was taken away to Ghazna by the Sultan, placed in a public square and desecrated.[43]

The foregoing evidence indicates great popularity of Vaishṇavism in Haryana particularly during the medieval period. Curiously enough, however, the hitherto found images are not commensurate with literary and epigraphic data. The paucity perhaps may be explained in the historic-geographical background of the region that has borne the brunt of repeated attacks of aliens and has been the venue of many a battle. The iconoclastic zeal of the foreign invaders resulted in the spoliation of ancient monuments and disappearance of images.[44] There are no standing temples existing in Haryana (and even in Punjab) except the brick temples at Kalayat, which too are bereft of sculptures. We, however, feel that improper explorations and lack of proper documentation and publication are also partially responsible for the meagerness of the known material. Our study and investigations have brought to our notice a large number of sites yielding remains of art in Haryana. The following Vaishṇava reliefs from the region have come to our notice.

EARLY IMAGES

A Kushāṇa Ekānaṃśā Relief

It was in 1962 that R.C. Agrawala published an interesting relief showing 'Ekānaṃśā flanked by Baladeva and Vāsudeva' from Mathurā, now in an individual collection in Pakistan.[45] Carved on red Mathurā sandstone, it measures 47 x 25.4 x 5.7 cm.[46] Later N.P. Joshi published three more Kushāṇa reliefs from Mathurā.[47] All of them are small spotted red sandstone plaques (7 to 7.5 inches) and are very much worn out. Separate Kushāṇa statues representing Saṃkarshaṇa-Balarāma, Ekānaṃśā and Vāsudeva-Kṛishṇa are known from district Gayā (Bihar) also.[48] The Gayā trio is thought to be inspired from the Mathurā School.[49] It shows certain similarities and differences with the Mathurā series[50] which, however, seems to be uniform in character and delineation. Though we also know some later kinship reliefs yet they are quite rare.[51]

To the early Mathurā examples we may add another relief, which is now preserved in the Department of Archaeology and Museums, Haryana (HARDAM) at Kurukshetra (Acc. No. 1/395). It measures 24.5 x 24 cm and the material used is mottled Mathurā sandstone (Pl. 21). It has been obtained from village Sanghel, tehsil Nuh in district Gurgaon of Haryana. Like the published reliefs, it shows the triad - Saṃkarshaṇa-Balarāma, Ekānaṃśā and Vāsudeva-Kṛishṇa - standing to front. Ekānaṃśā, the sister of Balarāma and Kṛishṇa,[52] is standing between them as per the iconographic injunctions. Standing on the proper right of Ekānaṃśā is quadrimanous Saṃkarshaṇa-Balarāma wearing a typical early-foliated *mukuṭa*,[53] earring in the left ear only, necklet, armlets and bracelets. He also wears a nether garment. His normal right hand is raised to the level of shoulder in fear-allaying gesture and the left one is akimbo, holding perhaps a flask. The rear right and left hand, not very clearly discernible in the relief,[54] carry a mace and a plough surmounted by a lion. Ekānaṃśā is two-handed. Her right hand is held in *abhaya-mudrā* and the left rests on the waist. But for the lower garment other items of drapery and jewelry on her person are not clear. The arch like canopy over her head, however, is quite conspicuous. Also, she is of comparatively short stature than the flanking figures. On her proper left stands Vāsudeva-Kṛishṇa with head broken. His normal right hand is disposed in *abhaya-mudrā* like Saṃkarshaṇa and Ekānaṃśā and the proper left is *kaṭyavalambita*, holding perhaps a conch, which looks very much like the *amṛita-ghaṭa*.[55] A part of the extra hand on the left indicates that the figure was four-handed originally. The broken backhands may have held mace and disc.

The triad thus resembles almost exactly to the known reliefs of Ekānaṃśā and comes from the neighboring region of Mathurā, the legendary ancestral home of the Vṛishṇis, indicating that the cult of Ekānaṃśā was popular not only at Mathurā but also in the surrounding regions. The present reliefs is, however, much better preserved than those published earlier.[56]

Garuḍavāhī Vishṇu from Khokhrakot, Rohtak

Prepared from the typical Mathura red sandstone used during the Kushāṇa period, this image (Pl. 22), unfortunately with head and arms broken, comes from Khokhrakot Rohtak and is now housed in the Gurukula Museum, Jhajjar. It shows the god as seated astride on his *vāhana* Garuḍa.[57] The figure is carved in the round (Pl. 23) like many other Kushāṇa sculptures. The extant relief, however, clearly reveals that it was a four-armed figure. The only surviving arm, though this too has suffered mutilation, is the normal left hand of the god which, to judge from the mutilated portion, may have held a conch. A part of the octagonal shaft of the mace has also survived. It may have been held in the rear right hand vertically. The normal right hand may have been disposed in *abhaya*, or less probably, in the *varada* pose. The upper left hand may thus be assumed to have held the discus.

The god wears a pearl necklet and the *vanamālā* (floral necklace) consisting of lotus and Aśoka or Kadamba flowers with a palm leaf serving as the pendent. Such floral necklaces were a peculiarity of the Kushāṇa images of Vishṇu.[58] The back view of the surviving parts of the left arms clearly shows that the god wore *keyūras* also. The end of the *dhotī* having been folded and falling beautifully from under the waistband may also be seen at the back.[59] Garuḍa is depicted with goggle eyes and plumes spread beautifully to symbolize the flying posture. The broad chest, the thin waist, and the spinal groove of the god have been carved very exquisitely and realistically. The overall impression of the relief is a pleasing one. When complete, it must have been a very exquisite and graceful creation.[60]

What, however, seems to be really a Kushāṇa Vishṇu image has wrongly been described and illustrated as Indra (in the illustration and Indrāṇī in the text) of an unpublished thesis.[61] The illustration clearly reveals the typical Kushāṇa foliated *mukuṭa*, the simple mace (in the rear right hand) looking like a round top-heavy rod, normal right hand raised to the level of the shoulder in *abhaya-mudrā* (slightly turned inwards), short bust and sparse ornamentation. Both the left hands and the portion below the belly are completely lost. The figure is comparable to a Vishṇu image in the Mathura Museum[62] and may belong to the 3rd century C.E. This, thus, is the earliest known Vishṇu image from Haryana.

Vishṇu from Agroha

An image of Vishṇu in mottled red sandstone from Agroha is now housed in the Gurukula Museum, Jhajjar.[63] It is nearly 1.35 m high. Unfortunately, the feet are missing. The god stands in contraposto wearing a typical Gupta crown, ear ornaments, armlets and lower garment (Pl. 24). *Vamamālā* may also be seen on the arms. The god seems to have possessed two arms but both are broken below the elbows. The face is round and serene with half-closed eyes, plump cheeks and full lips. One only wishes the figure to have been a complete image to give us an exact idea of its true form. The mottled red sandstone indicates that pieces of Mathura art were imported to Agroha during the Kushāṇa period though later it may have itself developed as a center of art.

Vishṇu from Mohanbari

Similarly, the so-called bust of a Kushāṇa Bodhisattva from Mohanbari,[64] is also is a Gupta icon of Vishṇu (Pl. 25). Not only the typical Gupta crown but also a part of the surviving *vaijayantīmālā* coming from behind the two shoulders, leaves little doubt to its being a Vishṇu image.

Vishṇu from Naurangabad

A terracotta image of Vishṇu from Naurangabad is housed in the Gurukula Museum, Jhajjar. The four-armed god stands in contraposto holding lotus and conch in the normal hands and mace and discus in the rear pair of hands (Fig. 4). The attributes in the *pralamba* 'hanging' back hands seem to have been placed on the *āyudha-purushas*, Gadādevī on the proper right, and Chakra-purusha on the proper left. The god wears a low crown, ear ornaments, torque, bracelets, *dhotī* reaching up to the knees, and the long garland. There is a simple halo behind the head.[65]

Vishṇu from Jind

Jind is an ancient holy place and a well-known district headquarters of Haryana. A male figure, probably Vishṇu (Pl. 26), found from Jind is now in a private collection.[66] The head, arms and legs below knees are missing. The sinewy body, the torque, the thickness of the twisted rope-like sash, groove to mark the navel, the pleats of the *dhotī* on the pubic region[67] and the free ends of the simple girdle falling on the side of the left thigh leave little doubt to its bearing a Gupta relief.

Vishṇu from Sondh

A headless red sandstone image (Pl. 27) measuring 44.45 x 29.20 cm from Sondh represents Vishṇu in contraposto wearing ear ornaments, torque, armlets, bracelets, *vanamālā* and *dhotī* secured by a girdle. The figure is quadrumanous. The front hands are placed over now mutilated and unidentifiable figures, which in all probability may have been the *āyudhapurushas*. What remains of them indicate that the figures stood slightly turned towards their Lord. The rear right hand of the god holds the mace placed vertically with its thicker end resting on the ground. The corresponding left hand supports a disc whose spokes look like lotus petals. This feature together with the bifurcation of the arms and their downward disposition, thick rope-like torque, sparse jewelry etc. point to the figure as belonging to the Gupta art tradition.[68]

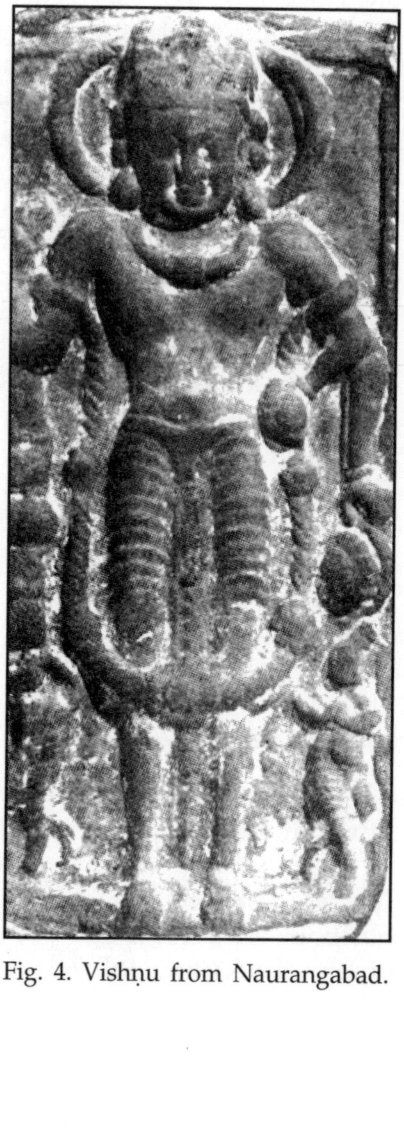

Fig. 4. Vishṇu from Naurangabad.

Vishṇu Head from Kapāla-Mochana

HARDAM has procured a small and worn out head of Vishṇu from Kapāla-Mochana measuring 27.5 x 20 cm (Acc. No. 1/102), which shows a disc or rosette in the center of the crown with loops of pearls issuing from its hub, and joined to the side rosettes (Pl. 28). This type of crown is a characteristic feature of the late Gupta period.[69] The serene face and physiognomy corroborate the date.

Chakra-purusha from Pehowa

A fragmentary panel representing Chakra-purusha slightly turned to his left holding the disc with spokes simulating lotus petals was recovered from Prāchī Śiva Temple at Pehowa and is now preserved in HARDAM (Acc. No. 1/357). A part of the long floral garland is also visible on the proper right hand side of the personified attribute whose frizzled locks, large earrings, *ekāvali*, armlets, bracelets and the typical Gupta *dhotī* are notable. The relief may belong to late Gupta period.

We thus see that the number of early images of Vishṇu from Haryana is not much. Nevertheless, the images or their fragments do indicate that images of Vishṇu started to be carved in the region from the Kushāṇa period.

MEDIEVAL IMAGES

Medieval images of Vishṇu, complete or fragmentary, have been found from a large number of places in Haryana. We describe below these figures.

STHĀNAKA-MŪRTIS (STANDING FIGURES)

Vishṇu from Meham

A small plaque of greenish talc measuring 16 x 8 x 2.5 cm (Acc. No. 1/165), said to have been obtained from Meham in district Rohtak, was purchased by HARDAM some years back from an antique dealer of Sirsa. Four-handed Vishṇu (Pl. 29) is represented in *samapādasthānaka* pose wearing a flat cylindrical crown, earrings, torque, sacred, thread, double armlets, bracelets, *dhotī* secured by a simple girdle and a *vaijayantīmālā*. The back slab shows faint lines of the halo. The front right hand is raised to the shoulder with palm slightly inwards in protection affording pose and the normal left hand bent downwards from the elbow holds a conch by its groove. The rear right and left hold the mace and disc respectively. Near the feet are carved rough and very small figures, the one on the proper left of the god may be recognized as Gaṇeśa and the other on the right side may perhaps be Kārttikeya. The folds of the *dhotī* and jewelry may also be seen indicated by engraved lines on the back of the figure. Such small plaques are a characteristic of the post Gupta and early medieval period, from seventh to tenth centuries C.E. The low crown, sparse ornamentation, simple composition, etc. indicate it to have been carved in the seventh or early 8th century C.E. The depiction of Gaṇeśa and Kārttikeya as the attendants of Vishṇu, however, is a unique feature of this plaque.

Two-armed Vishṇu from Pinjore

A very interesting Vishṇu image (Pl. 30) has been noticed at Pinjore. The two-handed god is shown as standing on a lotus seat in *samapāda-sthānaka-mudrā* (contraposto), placing his suspended hands on the *āyudha-purushas*, Gadādevī on the right and Chakra-purusha on the left. Gadādevī is depicted as holding the mace by its lower end in her right hand. Chakra-purusha is badly mutilated but seems to have a discus behind the head. Vishṇu bears a three-tiered crown indicating Pahari impact. There is a simple halo behind his head. Locks of hair may be seen on his forehead coming out of the crown as also falling at the back of the shoulders. He wears ear ornaments, a necklace, armlets, bracelets, an *ardhoruk*-like *dhotī* secured by a girdle with its free ends falling stylistically in front, and the long garland. The top corners of the back slab show semi-celestials. Stylistically, the image may be assigned to the 8th century C.E. The depiction of Vishṇu as two handed is an early feature and rare in the medieval period. Even in the early period, two-handed images are not very common.

Vishṇu from Belarkha

Belarkha is situated about 7 km north of Narwana on road to Patiala in district Jind. Enshrined in a temple of the village is a four-armed Vishṇu standing on a lotus pedestal in contraposto. The god wears *kirīṭa-mukuṭa,* ear ornaments, torque, armlets, bracelets, *vanamālā* and lower garment secured by a simple waist-girdle. The proper right hand is raised to the level of the shoulder in *abhaya* and the corresponding left hand holds the conch by its groove in the suspended position. The rear right and left hands hold the mace and disc respectively. A lotiform halo exists behind the head of the god. He is flanked by Śaṅkha-purusha and Śrī on his proper right on the receding projections of the *pañcharatha* pedestal and by Chakra-purusha and Sarasvatī (or Bhūdevī) on his left. The image measures 30 x 23 cm and is not in a good state of preservation. The placid expression may, however, be discerned clearly. Stylistically, it may be assigned to *circa* 8th century C.E.[70]

Vishṇu images from Kurukshetra

Some time back some images were acquired by us from Śrī Sthāneśvara Mahādeva Temple, Thanesar (Kurukshetra) for HARDAM (Acc. No. 1/512). The present image (Pl. 31) is one of those. It measure 61 x 40 cm and represents the god in *samapāda-sthānka* pose on a plain pedestal. The god wears all usual ornaments including flower in front between the two legs. The free end of the lower garment falls between the legs forming a zigzag line. The halo behind the head shows lotus pattern and has a beaded border. Garland-bearing *vidyādharas* are carved in the top corners in flying postures. Śaṅkha-purusha and Śrī stand on the proper right of the god while the left is occupied by Chakra-purusha and Garuḍa. The *āyudhapurushas* stand in symmetrical poses flexioned at the waist and looking at their Lord, holding the respective attributes they represent in both their hands. Śrī stands in a very graceful *tribhaṅga* pose holding probably a lotus in her raised left hand, resting the other on her right knee. She bears a beautiful *dhammilla* coiffure. The scarf worn by her is indicated by its free end dangling down gracefully from over her right arm. Garuḍa wears a *kullah* like triangular cap which is rather unusual for him.[71] The whole figure presents a balanced composition and is in a good state of preservation. Stylistically, it may also be assigned to the 8th century C.E.

Amongst the sculptures acquired from Śrī Sthāneśvara Mahādeva Temple, Thanesar is another very much worn out image of quadrimanous Vishṇu standing to front, holding the mace in the back right hand, disc in the back left and conch in the normal left. Proper right hand seems to have been disposed in *abhaya*. An aureole behind the head, usual ornaments including *vanamālā, āyudhapurushas* (Śaṅkha and Chakra) followed by Śrī and Bhūdevī on proper right and left of the god can still be made out in spite of the mutilation the image has suffered. The panel is broken below the knees. In its extant form, it measures 27 x 18 cm. Because of mutilation and wearing out, all details are lost. Stylistically, however, it does not seem to be far removed in date from the image from the same temple described above.[72]

A fragmentary panel measuring 15 x 9 cm, which appears to have been a part of the pedestal of a Vishṇu image showing two very much worn and hence unidentifiable figures standing on the receding *rathas*, was also acquired by us along with some other sculptures for HARDAM from Śrī Sthāneśvara Mahādeva Temple, Thanesar. Chronologically, this panel seems to be medieval.[73] There may have been an important medieval temple at the site of or near the present Sthāneśvara Mahādeva Temple whose sculptures were preserved in the present shrine.

A part of a pedestal depicting Chakra-purusha and Garuḍa, who must have occupied the proper left side of Vishṇu, was noticed by us in the mid-sixties at Jyotisar near Thanesar. The face and left arm of the former are lost. He is shown as standing with a great flexion at the waist holding the disc in his right hand near the shoulder. Earring in the right ear, bracelets and *dhotī* with a sash on the thigh can still be seen on his person. Garuḍa stands to front in *tribhaṅga*, with splayed feet, holding a snake in his left hand while the right is raised to the head in salutation. He bears *dhammilla* coiffure, earrings, pearl necklace, *dhotī* with a simple girdle and sash, bracelets etc. A part of the *vanamālā* of Vishṇu may be seen on the left side near the right hand of Chakra-purusha. On the basis of style, it may be assigned to *circa* 9th century C.E.

A fragmentary panel representing the proper left hand side of a Vishṇu image depicting Chakra-purusha, Bhūdevī and Garuḍa standing successively on the receding projections of the pedestal was also noticed at the same place. All the attendant figures stood gracefully slightly turned towards their Lord. A part of the *vanamālā* could be seen to the right of Chakra-purusha. All the figures bore *dhammilla* coiffure (Bhūdevī with a slightly higher pod), earrings, *ekāvalis*, armlets, bracelets, lower garments secured by pearl girdles etc. Bhūdevī, an elongated figure, held a lotus by its long stalk in her right hand and the scarf in the suspended left. Garuḍa saluted with his right hand and held a snake in the left. Both the male figures wore sacred threads also. All the three attendants were broken below the knees. On stylistic grounds, the panel could be placed in *circa* 10th century C.E. An elegant figure of Padma-purusha with head broken was also found from Thanesar. The *āyudhapurusha* stands elegantly holding a lotus in his right hand with left akimbo, wearing usual ornaments including *vanamālā*.

Vishṇu from Suderpura (Kalka)

A small Vishṇu image of greenish black sandstone from Suderpura (Kalka) measuring 21.0 x 10.5 cm (Acc. No. 1/215) is now housed in HARDAM. The god standing to front wears a squattish cylindrical crown, earrings, rope-like torque, *vanamālā* etc. Both the right hands are damaged, the back left holds a *chakra* and the normal left probably a conch. There is an attendant on either side. The image is so much worn out that the details are not discernible. It may belong to *circa* 8th-9th century C.E.

Vishṇu images from Agroha

The most beautiful image recovered from Agroha, received from Lahore as a share of India after the partition and now preserved in the Government Museum & Art Gallery, Chandigarh (Acc. No. 37), is a representation of an almost life-size Vishṇu (Ht. 145 cm) standing in contraposto with an exquisitely carved aureole at the back of the head (Pl. 32). The principal hands are broken below the elbows. The additional left is shown as holding a discus that also serves as the gloriole of the male attendant figure, presumably Chakra-purusha. The corresponding right hand of the god holds the thicker end of the mace placed vertically on the ground behind the head of the female attendant, the Gadā-devī. The *āyudha-purushas* stand gracefully flanking the god who wears usual but very exquisitely carved ornaments and jewelry including the lozenge-shaped *śrīvatsa* on the chest and the *vaijayantīmālā*. D.C. Bhattacharyya sees certain similarities between this image and the figure of Śiva in the Kalyāṇasundara panel from Kanauj and assigns it to *circa* 9th century C.E. on stylistic grounds.[74] Comparing the image of Vishṇu under discussion and Śiva of the Kalyāṇasundara-mūrti from Kanauj, D.C. Bhattacharyya observes that "There is a striking similarity between the types of the necklace, armlets, and diagonally hanging ends of the wavy girdle-scarve (sic. scarf) of the abovementioned image of Shiva and those of the present image of Vishnu." So he feels that "Agroha being situated on an ancient trade route.., one cannot perhaps rule out the possibility of some of the sculptures discovered from Agroha having been actually made somewhere else and imported to Agroha for transportation to other places in accordance with the exigency of the transactions of the trade. In that case, the present sculpture of Vishṇu could have come from Kanauj which was an important center of sculptural art in the Ganga-Yamuna valley, particularly in the period to which the present sculpture presumably belongs."[75] We, however, feel that similarities of certain motifs should not always be interpreted to mean imports. They may just be accidental or even influences. There are so many sculptures in Haryana, which show similarities of conception, composition, motifs, and so on. All of them cannot be interpreted to have been imported from elsewhere. Bhattacharyya himself has determined the provenance of the Vishṇu image described below as Agroha and not Kashmir on the basis of the similarity of the crown with that of the Lakshmī-Nārāyaṇa image from Agroha.[76] This type of crown, as noted below, is common to many other images found from Haryana. All of them cannot be believed to have been imports. Agroha has also yielded numerous terracottas and sculptures belonging to the Gupta and post-Gupta periods. The large number of terracottas found from the site and the excavations conducted there indicate the existence of a temple or temples at Agroha for which those terracottas and sculptures were meant. They must have been prepared at the site itself, which was an important town or city at that time. To us, however, this image reminds of the figure of Vishṇu recovered from Kankali Tila, Mathura, now preserved in the State Museum, Lucknow (Acc. No. H 111).[77] In Haryana, the Gupta traits lingered on for some time. We, therefore, feel inclined to assign this image to *circa* 8th century C.E.[78]

Another standing Vishṇu, recorded to be from Kashmir in the Register of the Chandigarh Museum, broken below the thighs and holding a conch in the only surviving principal left hand (Pl. 33) has rightly been ascribed to Agroha on stylistic grounds by D.C. Bhattacharyya who compares its facial type, the form of the crown, the plastic treatment of the torso, and the style of the conch in the lower left hand of Vishṇu in the Lakshmī-Nārāyaṇa image from Agroha in the same museum described below (Pl. 73).[79] We appreciate Bhattacharyya's stylistic analysis as we can now corroborate this ascription of provenance by another fragmentary relief of Vishṇu found recently and betraying similar treatment of the torso, the scared thread, the multifold sash on the thighs, and exactly the same mode of supporting the conch horizontally[80] in the lower left hand with the middle three fingers inserted in the groove, the *kanishṭhikā* 'small finger' providing a firm support and the thumb stretched along the spiral head (Pl. 34). Both the figures are assignable to *circa* 10th century C.E. The facial expression, the hairdo and the crown of Vishṇu (Pl. 33) may also be compared to many images illustrated here.

A small panel measuring 12 x 7 cm found from trench WAL-13, layer 1 in the excavations at Agroha, though badly mutilated, shows Balarāma holding wine-cup in his left hand with right akimbo, preceded by Śrī and Śaṅkha-purusha whose upper portions are lost. The graceful poses and sparse ornamentation suggests a 9th century date for this fragment of the pedestal of a Vishṇu image.[81] A discus[82] and a conch, both measuring 9.5 x 9.5 cm from trench XF-8, layer 1 from the same site, the latter showing patially preserved fingers holding it, betray the existence of another image of almost the same period at Agroha.

Vishṇu head from Jind

A life-size Vishṇu head of buff sandstone (Pl. 35) measuring 27 x 17 cm obtained from Jind is now housed in HARDAM (Acc. No. 1/1). The quasi-closed eyes, plump cheeks, full lower lip etc. are reminiscent of the Gupta art tradition still lingering on in the early medieval period to which this head may be assigned on stylistic grounds. The triple fold at the neck, which was a characteristic feature of the Gupta and later Gupta figures of western India, is also visible indicating a continuity and impact of the style that prevailed in the west and reached Haryana through Rajasthan. The elongate ears of the god are bedecked by beaded earrings. The cylindrical crown also bears beaded decorations. A hole in the center above the forehead may have been used to insert a flower or some ornament. The life-size head may have belonged to a standing Vishṇu image belonging to the early 9th century C.E.

A white quartzite piece of 12 x 10 cm from Jind (HARDAM, Acc. No. 1/152) shows the crowned head wearing earrings, pearl necklace, sacred thread etc. holding a mace in one of the right hands. It is broken below the chest. Hands are also broken. Halo, however, may be seen behind the head.

Vishṇu images from Rasina

Some time back two buff sandstone images of Vishṇu were exhumed from village Rasina in district Kaithal. The larger of the two measures 44.5 x 24.0 cm and shows the god standing to front on a lotus seat placed in the center of a *pañcha-ratha* pedestal (Pl. 36). He wears a *kirīṭa-mukuṭa* adorned with pearl strings and a jewel; earrings; necklet, torque and necklace; sacred thread; armlets; bracelets; diamond-shaped *śrīvatsa* on the chest; *vaijayantīmālā*; lower garment secured by a girdle whose free ends fall on the thighs; a sash; and anklets. The front right hand is raised to the level of the shoulder in the posture of reassurance while the rear right holds the mace with its thicker end upwards. The back left hand holds the discus while the proper left, now damaged, seems to have held the conch. Flanking him and standing on the receding projections of the pedestal are Śaṅkha-purusha and Śrī on his right and Chakra-purusha and Garuḍa on his left, standing almost symmetrically. The *āyudhas-purushas* stand in *dvibhaṅga* wearing *karaṇḍa-mukuṭa* and the usual ornaments including the sacred thread, holding the attributes they represent in the hand towards the Lord with the other on the respective thigh. Śrī bears a *dhammilla* coiffure with a prominent bun and usual ornaments holding the free end of the *uttarīya* in her suspended right hand. Garuḍa on the other extreme holds a snake in his left hand and also wears a long garland. His hair is raised in horrification. Behind the head of Vishṇu may be seen the round gloriole with lotus petals. The top corners carry stele showing tri-cephalous bearded Brahmā with four-hands disposed in *abhaya*, and carrying ladle, book, and water pot, seated in *sukhāsana* on the proper right and Śiva on the other side seated similarly and holding trident and snake in the back hands, the front right disposed in *abhaya*. The object in the normal left hand is not clear but looks like a water pot. The back slab is left plain. The use of pearls in ornamentation is a characteristic feature of the image. Stylistically, the image may be dated to *circa* 9th century C.E.

The second image from Rasina is more elaborate (Pl. 37). Made of chlorite schist of blackish green color and measuring 37 x 36 x 10 cm, it shows the god as standing on a lotus seat in the center of a *sapta-ratha* pedestal. The posture, dress and ornaments, attributes, etc. are similar to the preceding example with slight variations. The god is accompanied by three attendant figures on each side with diminutive Gaṇa-like *āyudha-purushas* standing in front of the figures immediately flanking the Lord. The attendant on his immediate right is Garuḍa holding a snake in his left hand, followed by Balarāma holding a cup in his right hand. The third figure holds the shaft of some attribute. Each of these figure bears *karaṇḍa-mukuṭa,* earrings, pearl necklet, bracelet, *dhotī* secured by a girdle, etc. Śaṅkha-purusha stands in front of Garuḍa. On the left side, the god is flanked by Śrī holding a lotus in her left hand, followed by two male attendants which cannot be recognized properly in the absence of any attributes of identification. Chakra-purusha stands in front of Śrī. The back slab shows mythical animal heads with leogryphs in the center above which may be seen crocodile faces at the back of which are Brahmā and Śiva as in the preceding image. These two gods are shown here as seated in *padmāsana.* The front right hand of Brahmā is disposed in *varada,* and so also perhaps of Śiva. The water pot in Śiva's hand is, however, very clear in this image. Ornamentation even in this image is characterized by the use of pearls. It probably represents a stage when gold ornaments and necklaces had not become very popular. Elaborate necklaces and other ornaments are generall seen on images belonging to a period after the mid 10th century and afterwards. The image may thus be placed stylistically to a slightly later period than the preceding example, i.e. early 10th century C.E.

Vishṇu from Madina

Madina is district Sonepat has yielded a part of a Vishṇu image (Pl. 38) which in its extant form measures 32 x 30 x 24 cm (Regn. No. HRN/AMB-872).[83] But for the beaded *vanamālā* and the feet of the deity, the main figure is completely lost now. The extant feet wearing anklets, placed on a lotus *pīṭha* in *sama* pose, however, make it clear that the god stood facing. Flanking the deity on the central facet of the *triratha* pedestal are Śaṅkha-purusha and Chakra-purusha, followed by Śrī and Bhūdevī on the receding projections on the proper right and left respectively. The face of Śaṅkha-purusha is damaged but he may not have been different in look from Chakra-purusha The ā*yudhapurushas* show matted locks held backwards, stringed like a sheaf and then piled up on the crown of the head in the form of a large puff. They wear earrings, *ekāvalis,* bracelets, and anklets, lower garments secured by beaded waist girdles and with sashes covering a part of the thighs. They hold the attributes they represent with both their hands near the chest and stand with their waists turned towards the god. Their facial expression, to judge from that of the Chakra-purusha, seems to have been serene. Śrī and Bhūdevī, too, stand in symmetrical postures parallel to the *āyudhapurushas.* They wear usual ornaments and hold lotus flower in the hand nearer to the god while the other hand dangles down gracefully in each case. The central jewels in their *dhammilla* coiffures are noteworthy. When complete, the figure must have been an elegant one. Stylistically, it seems to belong to the 9th century C.E.

Vishṇu from Mandhna

An image of standing Vishṇu also exists at Mandhna (Dist. Panchkula). Made of the typical dark greyish sandstone, it measures 24 x 21 cm. It is not in a good state of preservation.

Stylistically, it may be placed in *circa* 9th century C.E. Also known from Mandhna is a part of a pedestal, 32 x 17.5 cm, showing Chakra-purusha, Bhūdevī and Garuḍa belonging to the same period. The size of the pedestal indicates that the image may have originally been considerably big, but unfortunately it is lost to us now. It is notable that local material has been utilized for the images.

Vishṇu standing under the serpent hood from Gummar

Gummar is situated about 3 km northwest of Ganaur on road to Khubru. An ancient mound which is about six feet high and spread over six acres lies about a furlong to the east of the village and yields Painted Grey Ware, Black Slipped Ware and medieval relics.

A sandstone image of Vishṇu standing in contraposto is now enshrined in a temple in Baba Shankar Nath Ki Samadhi. It measures 31 x 28 cm. The quadrumanous god shows mace and discus in the upper right and left hands while the normal right, now slightly mutilated, is disposed in boon giving pose. The front left hand is broken but it probably held the conch. The god stands on the central offset of the *saptaratha* pedestal and is flanked on the successive projections by Śaṅkha-purusha, Śrī and another figure (Balarāma?) on the proper right and Chakra-purusha, Bhūdevī and probably Garuḍa on the left. There are two kneeling devotees near the feet of the god. The stele on the proper right probably depicted Brahmā (now mutilated) and on the left Śiva is seated in *lalitāsana*, holding trident and snake in the rear hands, water pot in the normal left with the proper right in protection affording pose. The extreme portions show *vyāla* figures and *makara-mukhas*. The most interesting feature, however, is the snake-canopy over Vishnu's head. The snake, though mutilated, seems to have been nine hooded. The figure may be assigned to *circa* 9th century C.E. Similar snake-hooded Vishṇu images are known from Deogarh and Kolkata also.[84]

Vishṇu from Kaithal

In the Kashipuri Temple at Kaithal is now enshrined a beautiful sandstone image of Vishṇu (Pl. 39) stated to have been brought from Siwan,[85] an ancient site situated about 10 km north of Kaithal. Unfortunately, this sculpture has now been painted with white paint concealing many of the minute details. It measures 128 x 58 cm. The main figure is almost similar to that of Vishṇu from Kanwari but some sophistication distinguishes it from the latter. The cylindrical crown is not as high as in Kanwari Vishṇu described below. Ornamentation, too, is moderate. Chakra-purusha here stands on the proper right of the god and Śaṅkha-purusha on his left (Pl. 40). The postures of Śrī and Bhūdevī are more graceful. The *āyudhapurushas* and the Lord's spouses show *dhammilla* type of hair coiffures. Balarāma on the extreme right of the god stands canopied by a five-hooded cobra and Garuḍa turned towards the god is partially obscured by Bhūdevī. The facial expression of Vishṇu is much more serene and placid than that of the god from Kanwari. The halo is more elaborate but graceful. The back-slab shows *gaja-śārdūla* figures covering the space between the stele with Brahmā and Śiva and the attendant figures on either side of the god. Just above the head of the god are carved in a panel seven seated figures in identical poses in a row (Pl. 41). They have wrongly been identified as Saptarshis as the first figure with lotus flower in either hand can easily be recognized as that of Sūrya. All other figures have their right hand raised in *abhaya* and the left ones holding water-pots. Obviously they represent Soma, Maṅgala, Budha, Bṛihaspati, Śukra and Śani, the planetary divinities (with Rāhu and Ketu missing). Just above Brahmā and Śiva are carved elephants in profile facing inwards with riders. One of these has been recognized as Indra riding on the elephant—his *vāhana*. This identification, too, does not seem to be probable as the riders on both the elephants are similar and are shown with folded hands. None of them carries *vajra*, the attribute of Indra. Balarāma and Garuḍa, too, have erroneously been identified as Nāga and Nāgī.[86] A comparison with the attendant figures of Vishṇu from Kanwari bears it out very well. Yoganārāyaṇa adorns the *tilaka* at the apex of our figure. This almost complete and elaborately but beautifully carved image is a masterpiece of the Pratihāra art of Haryana. Stylistically, it may be placed in the late ninth or early 10th century C.E.

Vishṇu from Kanwari

An exquisitely carved icon of Vishṇu from Kanwari (Pl. 42), now under worship, was discovered some time back. Measuring 90 x 58 cm, it shows the god standing in contraposto on a lotus seat on the central offset of a *saptaratha* pedestal. He wears a high cylindrical crown, ear ornaments, necklet, multi-stringed pearl necklace, sacred thread, beaded and jeweled armlets, beaded double bracelets, anklets, lower garment secured by an elaborate waist-band, *vanamālā* and a lozenge shaped *śrīvatsa* on the chest. There is a round eight-petalled gloriole behind the head. The proper right hand of the god is raised in *abhaya* with a rosary on the palm. A ring may also be noted around the thumb. The back right hand holds the *gadā* vertically in a stylish manner. The discus in the upper left hand, too, is held stylistically. It is sixteen-spoked and a tassel is shown as coming out of its hub. The suspended normal left hand holds the conch with three fingers in its groove, thumb towards its spiral portion and the little finger gripping it. The three successively receding projections are occupied by Śaṅkha-purusha, Śrī and Balarāma on the proper right and Chakra-purusha, Bhūdevī and Garuḍa on the left. The *āyudhapurushas* bear *karaṇḍa-mukuṭa*, ear ornaments, pearl necklets and necklaces, beaded armlets, bracelets, anklets and lower garment secured by an elaborate girdle. They hold the conch and disc in their left and right hand respectively, the other being akimbo. They stand slightly turned towards the god in *dvibhaṅga*. The spouses of the Lord too stand gracefully in *tribhaṅga*, wearing pearl earrings, necklet with a pendent string falling down from between the breasts, lower garments with waistband whose free ends fall on the thighs and a scarf with gracefully fluttering and dangling ends. They bear high pods on their heads adorned with jewels and beaded strings. The hand nearer to the god holds a lotus by its long stalk while the other is akimbo. Balarāma on the extreme *ratha* bears a *karaṇḍa-mukuṭa* and wears usual ornaments. He is shown with a cup in his right hand and a plough in the left. Garuḍa on the other extremity has his hair frizzled in horrification and holds the snake in his left hand with the right raised to the head in salutation. On either side of the head of Vishṇu are shown Brahmā and Śiva seated on lotuses. Tri-cephalous Brahmā bears matted locks, double stringed pearl necklace, bracelets, a long floral wreath (seen on the proper arms) and a lower garment. The central face is bearded. The proper right hand is held in *varada* pose with a rosary on the palm and the left holds a water-pot. *Sruk* 'ladle' and book are held in the upper right and left hands respectively. A similar figure on the other side represents (uni-cephalous) Śiva holding a trident in the back right hand. The upper left hand may have held a snake, but it is broken now. The normal hands are similar to those of Brahmā. The sides of the back slab have been left plain.

We thus see that elaboration in ornaments and subsidiary figures makes its appearance but has not reached its culmination as the back slab is left plain. The minute care bestowed even to the attendant figures is noteworthy. Stylistically, the image may be assigned to the 10th century C.E.

Vishṇu images from Pinjore

The head of Vishṇu (height 17 cm, Acc. No. 49)) bearing the cylindrical crown adorned with pearl strings and jewels, comparable to that of Vishṇu from Rasina (Pl. 16) described above, is now preserved in the Government Museum & Art Gallery at Chandigarh (Pl. 43). A perfectly round eight-petalled aureole behind the head indicates the divinity of the figure. Below the crown may be seen the hair combed backwards in a wavy fashion with curls on the sides. The eyebrows simulate a bow, the eyes are quasi-closed, the nose is sturdy and slightly damaged, and the face is round with plump cheeks. The semi-circular end of the back slab shows stele at the ends carrying the figures of Brahmā and Śiva, the latter very much mutilated. Brahmā on the proper right is tri-cephalous, having juvenile faces, bearing *jaṭā-mukuṭa*, wearing pearl necklet and the sacred thread, seated in *sukhāsana*, and holding the ladle in his additional right hand and a water pot in the normal left. The proper right hand seems to be in *abhaya*. The object in the back left hand, looking similar to that of the back right, is not very clear. Śiva on the other side is recognized from the trident in his upper right hand, the corresponding left probably held the snake. The relief represents standing Vishṇu. D.C. Bhattacharyya dates it to 12th century,[87] which is too late a date for it. The figures on the stele, the gloriole, the crown, and the facial features indicate it to be a work of the 10th century.

Another detached piece showing Vishṇu's hand holding a conch (height 17 cm, Acc. No. 183) from Pinjore is also housed in the above-mentioned museum. The hand with a bangle in the wrist is shown as holding the conch by its socket in a distinctive way with three fingers inserted in the groove, the index finger straightened and the thumb placed outside. D.C. Bhattacharyya dates it to the same period as the preceding figure[88] but the same material indicates it to have been a part of that figure and should be dated to about two centuries or more earlier as noted above.

From the relics of the Bhīmā Devī Temple at Pinjore comes a relief showing quadrimanous Vishṇu (Pl. 44) standing facing wearing usual but simple ornaments and holding mace and discus in the rear right and left hands respectively. The *pralamba* normal hands are damaged but the right hand seems to have been disposed in *varada* pose while the left probably held a conch. Near the feet stand male attendants, one on either side, representing probably *āyudhapurushas*. In pillared niches on the sides stand Śrī and Bhūdevī in *tribhaṅga* poses holding a lotus in the hand near to the god. The other suspended hand holds the dangling scarf. The relief is worn out to conceal minute details. The whole composition, however, reveals an attractive poise and simplicity. It belongs to *circa* 10th century C.E. The female figures in pillared niches flanking the god may have been independent of this image. Their placement, however, indicates that it was a part of the wall of a temple.

Another mutilated relief (Pl. 45) in the same temple at Pinjore shows the god flanked by Śaṅkha and Chakra-purusha on his right and left and holding a conch in his back right hand. Face and other hands are damaged. Still another small but very badly mutilated frieze lies in a private premises at Pinjore and can be recognized as that of standing Vishṇu only from the cylindrical crown and the *vaijayantīmālā*.

A detached head, probably of a Vishṇu image, bearing a high elaborate *kirīṭa-mukuṭa* adorned with arch-shaped and looped wreaths of pearl strings and jewels, datable to *circa* 10th-11th century (Pl. 46), has also been recovered from Pinjore. The god is depicted in an abstract mood with almost closed eyes. The nose and chin are slightly damaged.[89]

Another head in greenish sandstone, measuring 24 x 15 cm (Acc. No. 1/238), shows beautifully combed hair forming end curls with a crown bedecked with jewels and pearl strings. The arched eyebrows and semi-closed eyes add a charming grace to the face, which unfortunately is mutilated on the right side.

The third head from the same site and in the same material measures 15 x 9.5 cm (Acc. No. 1/242). It shows a crown resembling the Vishṇu head from Rohtak (Pl. 58) and face showing affinity to the preceding example.

A part of the *saptaratha* pedestal of an image of Vishṇu from Pinjore is now in a private collection at Kalka.[90] It measures 28 x 13 cm. Vishṇu seems to have stood in the center on a lotus *pīṭha* as can be judged by his extant right foot wearing an anklet, placed in *sama* pose. Śaṅkha-purusha, Śrī and another male attendant stood to his right on the successive recesses of the pedestal. A part of the *vanamālā* is also visible to the left of Śaṅkha-purusha. He wears a *karaṇḍa-mukuṭa* with a central jewel, earrings, *ekāvali*, sacred thread, beaded armlets, bracelets and *antarvāsaka*. Conch is held in his left hand near the chest and right hand is akimbo. His left foot rests in *sama* pose while the right is splayed out. He seems to be somewhat corpulent. Next to him, Śrī stands in *tribhaṅga* with lotus in her left hand and the suspended right hand holding the free end of the dangling scarf. Attractive coiffure, *karṇaphūla*, pearl necklet, armlets, bracelets, *sārī* secured by a beaded girdle, full breasts, a placid facial expression and a plain round halo behind her head are notable. The last figure with head gone stands cross-legged holding the staff of some attribute in his two hands. He wears ear ornaments, pearl necklace, bandolier, *antarvāsaka*, scarf, bracelets and v*anamālā*. The figure may be identified with Balarāma. The material used is typical sandstone of Pinjore. Stylistically, it may be placed in the 9th-10th century C.E.

Vishṇu from Ratpur

Amongst the ruins at Ratpur near Pinjore are the part of a doorjamb depicting Balarāma, a hand of Vishṇu placed on the head of an *āyudhapurusha*, indicating the existence here of a Vishṇu temple of about 10th century. Important evidence from the site, however, is preserved in HARDAM in the form of an unfinished image of the god (Pl. 47) holding the mace in the right hand and *chakra* in the left (Acc. No. 1/4). There are chisel marks over the arms and the image has not been finished. Only the upper part of the image has been recovered. The god is shown as wearing a torque, bracelets, elaborate but only partially preserved crown, and the sacred thread. The image seems to belong to *circa* 9th century C.E. and furnishes the coveted evidence of Ratpur being an art center where such images were carved.

Vishṇu from Hat

In a temple at Hat (district Jind) is under worship an image of four-armed Vishṇu standing facing, holding a conch in the normal left hand while the right is disposed in *varada-mudrā* (Pl. 48). The rear right hand holds a mace and the back left is broken. It probably held a disc. The god wearing usual ornaments is flanked by Chakra-purusha, Śrī and Balarāma on his proper right and Śaṅkha-purusha, Bhūdevī and Garuḍa on his left on the receding recesses of the *saptaratha* pedestal.[91] Balarāma is holding a cup in his right hand near his chest and Garuḍa is depicted in *añjali-mudrā*. Brahmā sitting in *lalitāsana* with hands disposed in *varada*, holding ladle, book and water-pot in the *pradakshiṇā* order may be seen on the top corner to the right of the god. Śiva on the other side is lost now. The image, measuring 94 x 49 cm, has been placed in a niche secured by iron bars in front so as to frustrate any effort to photograph the image properly. It, however, seems to be a typical Pratihāra image of *circa* 10th century C.E.

Vishṇu from Khubru

A sandstone image of Vishṇu measuring 27 x 14 cm from Khubru in district Karnal shows the deity standing to front holding mace and discus in the rear right and left hands, conch in the normal left and the proper right disposed in *abhaya*. The god wears usual dress and ornaments and is flanked on either side by male attendants, perhaps personified attributes, but difficult to be identified because of the weathering the image has suffered. Stylistically, it may be placed in *circa* 10th century C.E.

Vishṇu from Bulandpur

In the Śiva Temple at Bulandpur Kheri near Gujjar Kheri in district Sonepat is placed a small Vishṇu image of sandstone, measuring 22 x 15 cm, with two attendants on either side. The god wears usual dress and ornaments. His normal right hand is disposed in *abhaya* and the rear right holds the mace. The normal and back left hands hold conch and discus. It is a Pratihāra image.

A detached Vishṇu head in buff sandstone measuring 22 x 11 cm (Acc. No. 1/120) from Bulandpur Kheri shows an exquisitely carved crown with a *kīrttimukha* spewing golden chains and lotus-shaped jewel of leaf-like decor which is repeated on the sides also (Pl. 49).

Vishṇu images from Jaintipur

Manmohan Kumar[92] has described a Vishṇu image from Jaintipur, which is now missing. The image with the upper parts lost, represented the deity in contraposto, wearing a long garland, sacred thread, girdle and a lower garment. One of the right hands was held in *varada-mudrā.* On the proper right hand side of the god stood Śaṅkha-purusha and on his left Chakra-purusha holding the attributes they represented. On the recessed corner were depicted female figures on either side, standing in *tribhaṅga* with delicate body and rhythmic movement. On the further corner were shown two male attendants bearing long *vanamālā,* lower garment and *karaṇḍa-mukuṭa*. Over the top of the left recessed corner appeared a male figure probably holding a lotus. The donor couple was carved at the feet of Vishṇu on either side with folded hands, the male on the proper right and the female on the left. The image belonged to *circa* 9th-10th century C.E.

Another frieze found at Jaintipur had the central figure broken. Chakra-purusha with a discus in his right hand near the chest with left akimbo followed by Garuḍa saluting with one hand and holding a cobra in the other indicate the relief to have been the proper left hand side of the pedestal of a Vishṇu image, datable almost to the same period.

The sandstone relief acquired by the Kurukshetra University from Jaintipur also represents the lower part of a Vishṇu image showing the god as standing in *sama-bhaṅga* on a lotus seat, wearing *vanamālā* and flanked by *āyudha-purushas* and other attendant figures. It has been dated to *circa* 10th-11th century C.E.[93]

Attendant figures of Vishṇu, Jhajjar

A part of the pedestal of a Vishṇu image is now housed in the Gurukula Museum, Jhajjar (Rohtak).[94] Representing the proper right hand side of the pedestal, it shows Śaṅkha-purusha slightly turned to his left, followed by Śrī and Balarāma. Śaṅkha-purusha, with feet broken, bears a *karaṇḍa-mukuṭa* and other usual ornaments. He holds a conch in his left hand near the chest while his right hand is akimbo. Śrī is shown with a lotus in left hand and the free end of the scarf in her suspended right hand. Balarāma wears a cylindrical crown and holds a plough in the left hand and a wine cup in the right. All the three figures show a tendency towards growing ornamentation and have been carved with minute care and details. They have, however, not lost their grace as yet. Stylistically, the image may have belonged to *circa* 10th century C.E.

Attendant figures from Pehowa

A very elegantly carved panel of buff sandstone measuring 46 x 20 cm (Acc. No. 1/549) in its extant form found from Pehowa depicts Garuḍa, following Bhūdevī bearing beautifully combed hair with two tiers of frizzled curls at the crown of the head tied with a twisted band and adorned with a *chūḍāmaṇi*. The fleshy cheeks, semi-closed fish-like eyes with bow-like eye brows, smiling face, triple fold of the neck, serpentine earrings, necklace and sacred thread; *dhotī* secured by a simple waist band; jeweled armlets and wings behind the shoulders of Garuḍa are the notable features. His right hand raised above is broken and the left one akimbo seems to have held a snake also. Equally graceful is the figure of Bhūdevī though its head and right arm are lost. Both these figures are broken below the knees. The image of Vishṇu whose part this panel is must have been a gigantic and very elegant icon of the Pratihāra period.

Bust of Vishṇu from Gujjar Kheri

From Gujjar Kheri comes a badly mutilated piece, which measures 28 x 21 cm in its extant form, and shows the bust and head of Vishṇu with long cylindrical crown placed over curly hair combed backwards (Pl. 50). The crown is adorned with a central jewel; a face of glory *(kīrtimukha)* spewing beaded festoons and lively retrorse animal figurines filling the space between the looped tassels.[95] The aureole behind the head must have been lotiform as can be made out from the still surviving petal on the proper left of the crown. The god bears an expression of beatitude with quasi-closed long fish-like eyes, sturdy nose, thick lower lip, plump cheeks and prominent chin. He wears a *patra-kuṇḍala* in his left ear (right one gone), pearl necklet and beaded *graiveyaka*, beaded sacred thread and armlet (on the extant left arm). *Śrīvatsa* on the chest and *vaijayantīmālā* on the left shoulder and arm may also be made out. All the four-hands are broken but the disposition of the back left hand may easily be guessed as rising above the elbow from the broken portion. The hands, however, must have possessed the usual attributes. The complete image in its original form must have been an elegant piece of about the 10th century C.E. It bears Registration No. HRN/AMB-630.

Gujjar Kheri has also yielded a *parikara* of a Vishṇu image (Pl. 51) measuring 44 x 27 cm. This ornamental arch shows two armed seated Sūrya in a pillared niche in the *tilaka* (apex) flanked by garland bearing *vidyādharas* with the incarnatory forms of Vishṇu depicted below in a row. Beginning from the proper right, we have Fish surmounted on a post, Tortoise between the legs of the following two human figures which probably symbolically represent gods and demons churning the ocean, Rāma holding a bow in the left hand with right akimbo, Balarāma with a similar posture but supporting perhaps a mace in his left hand, therianthropic Varāha and Nṛisiṃha, Vāmana and Paraśurāma. In the *nāgara-kūṭas* on the two sides are carved Brahmā and Śiva with *makara-mukhas* facing out and supporting perhaps the *apasarases* on their snouts on the extremities.

The depiction of Fish on a post is interesting.[96] Also the incarnatory forms do not follow the fixed order. No image from Haryana shows the incarnatory forms in this way.

Also recovered from the site is a Vishṇu's hand with mace (Pl. 52). The 16-cm high broken piece showing the forearm and the upper right hand stylistically holding the fluted shaft of the mace with its thicker end pointed downwards is obviously a part of some Vishṇu sculpture. The wrist bears a beaded bracelet. Vishṇu's hand with lotus (Pl. 53) from the same site may have belonged to the same image. The beautiful realistic hand holding a *nīlotpala* (6.5 cm high) seems to have been the proper right hand of the same image of Vishṇu whose detached upper right holding the mace has been described above. The treatment of the nails in both the examples is noteworthy. The buff color of the sandstone is also common to both.

Fragmentary relief from Sagwan

Sagwan is an ancient village nearly 5 km east of Tosham in district Bhiwani. It has an old mound, which is nearly fifty feet in height. A fragmentary sculpture from this site is now preserveded in HARDAM. Consisting of greenish stand stone, it measures 48.5 x 26 cm (Acc. No. 1/103). The extant frieze (Pl. 54) shows a kneeling devotee in profile, a female holding the shaft of a flywhisk perhaps and seated Buddha just behind her. Rāma and Vāmana are carved one over the other on the extreme portion of the slab. As such, it seems to be a part of a large Vishṇu image with the depiction of his ten incarnatory forms on the back slab. Besides the kneeling devotee and the female fly-whisker, the three incarnatory figures are those of Vāmana, Rāma and Buddha. Vāmana is shown as seated in *lalitāsana* wearing earrings, *ekāvali*, sacred thread, etc. and holding a parasol in his left hand. The object in his right hand is mutilated. Rāma just below him is seated similarly bearing *jaṭā-mukuṭa* with central jewel and other usual ornaments. To his left and behind the fly-whisker is Buddha in *padmāsana* bearing *jaṭā-jūṭa* 'a high topknot' and wearing a *saṃghāṭī*. He has placed his left hand on his right foot and the right hand holds a roundish object, which may be a water pot. The unimpressive facial expressions and profuse ornamentation seen on the person of the fly-whisker indicate a decline, which had set in the sculptural art of the region. The sculpture may be assigned to *circa* 11th century C.E. on stylistic grounds.

Vishṇu from Berikhera

A slightly later image, 46 x 25 cm in size, is now enshrined in the Hathnor Temple at Berikhera in district Jind (Pl. 55).[97] The deity stands in contraposto on a lotus *pīṭha*. The attributes in the four-hands of the god in the *pradakshiṇā* order are *abhaya*, the mace, discus and conch. The attendants, however, are reduced in number to four - Śaṅkhapurusha and Śrī (or a fly-whisker) on his right and Chakrapurusha and Garuḍa (or devotee) on his left. On the top corners may be seen Brahmā and Śiva while *vyāla* figures fill up the space on the sides. Another exactly similar but better-preserved figure exists at Panipat. This and the Berikhera image seem to have a common provenance and it will be wonder even if the same sculptor carved them.

Vishṇu from Badali

In the outer wall of Chaudhary Randhir Singh's *haveli* at Badali (28° 36' N and 76° 45' E) are fixed many old sculptures, which have a thick coat of whitewash. Amongst these sculptures is a head of Vishṇu with a lotiform gloriole behind the head, discus to the left of the face, which must have been held in the left hand and the stele depicting Śiva (Pl. 56). The thick coat of whitewash has concealed the details but a high cylindrical crown and the discus leave absolutely no doubt to the identification. This elegant standing image of the god must have been worshipped at Badali in about the 11th century C.E.

A part of the proper left hand side pedestal of another Vishṇu image, probably of about 9th century, showing a very much mutilated figure with equally badly damaged Chakra-purusha following that has also been noticed at Badali (Pl. 57). A pedestal, probably of an image of Vishṇu, also lies at Badali. It shows four-handed Pṛithvī seated in *padmāsana* on an inverted lotus seat in *añjali-mudrā* and supporting the *viśva-padma* which rises at her back and serves as the lotus seat of the principal deity with her back hands raised up. She wears *karṇa-kuṇḍalas*, necklace, armlets, bracelets, a scarf and the nether garment and is flanked by a female (probably fly-whisker) and a hybrid half-human half-serpent figure in adoration on either side. All the figures are carved with care and are bedecked with beautiful ornaments. The central panel showing Pṛithvī is flanked on either side by crocodile faces, beautifully executed male and female figures, *udadhi-kumāras* and outward moving lions.

Vishṇu's hand with mace from Rohtak

The upper right hand holding a mace, 23 cm in height and a part of an imposing image of Vishṇu from Rohtak, forms part of the sculptural collection of the Chandigarh Museum.[98] The mace has an imposing knob and ribbed body. The stele of the proper right hand side of the god showing Brahmā with usual iconographic features has also survived on the right of the mace. The image when complete must have been an interesting figure belonging to the 10th century or so.

The tendency towards over-ornamentation to the neglect of physical beauty may be seen in a head bearing an extraordinary long cylindrical crown (Pl. 58) coming probably from Rohtak (Regn. No. HRN/SON-368). It may have been carved in *circa* 12th century C.E.

Unfinished Vishṇu from Asthal Bohr

An unfinished Vishṇu image (Pl. 59) bearing chisel marks all over and with un-carved gloriole, stele and details is known from Asthal Bohr (Rohtak). It is important as it indicates that sculptures were carved at this place and were not imported here ready made from elsewhere. Standing in contraposto, Vishṇu has his front right hand raised in protection affording pose, the back right holds mace; back left disc and the suspended normal left conch. Śaṅkhapurusha and Śrī stand on his right and Chakrapurusha and Bhūdevī on the left. This image may be placed in the 10th century C.E. Rohtak has been an important place located on the highway, which connected Pāṭaliputra with Takshaśilā in the ancient times. Excavations and explorations have yielded Kushāṇa and Gupta relics but it seems to have developed as a center of art during the medieval times.

Vishṇu from Kasan

An image of Vishṇu with head and whole portion of the back slab gone is now displayed in HARDAM. It was obtained from Puran Bhagat Temple, Kasan (district Gurgaon) and measures 78 x 64 cm (Acc. No. 1/309). The god standing in contraposto on a lotus *pīṭha* placed on the central portion of the *saptaratha* pedestal flanked by the same attendant figures as the Kanwari and Kaithal Vishṇu images also shows devotees seated on lotus flowers in profile on either side. The back slab shows the *gaja-śārdūla* figures as well like the Kaithal image. The head of Śaṅkhapurusha is broken. He holds conch in his left hand while the right one is akimbo. Śrī holds a lotus in the left hand and her right hand is *pralamba*. Balarāma holds the plough in the left hand while the suspended right hand is placed on the thigh. The face of Chakrapurusha is mutilated and so also of Bhūdevī. Garuḍa bears frizzled locks on his head and wears *vaijayantīmālā*. His right hand is held in *abhaya* and left is akimbo. All these attendant figures wear usual ornaments and are haloed. Stylistically, the image may be assigned to *circa* 11th century C.E.

A two-tiered cylindrical crown showing a decor of jewels and pearl strings adorns the head of Vishṇu obtained from Puran Bhagat Temple, Kasan. The head bears beatific expression, beautifully combed hair and almond shaped elongated eyes. It consists of buff sandstone and measures 11 x 8 cm (Acc. No. 1/311).

A small blackish sandstone panel measuring 15 x 9 cm from Puran Bhagat Temple at Kasan (Acc. No. 1/152) shows the deity with crown, earrings, torque, *śrīvatsa*, *dhotī*, and *vaijayantīmālā*, and holding a disc in the back left hand. Feet and all other hands are gone.

Vishṇu images from Beri

Beri in district Rohtak has yielded a rich harvest of sculptural wealth of the state.[99] That it must have been an important center of religion and art is obvious from the icons, which have been acquired from the place by the Directorate of Archaeology and Museums of Haryana. Amongst these, there are three images of Vishṇu.

The first image measuring 40 x 25 cm (Acc. No. 1/234) shows the god as standing to front in contraposto (*sampāda-sthānaka-mudrā*) on a round lotus *pīṭha* placed on a *pañcharatha* pedestal (Pl. 60). He wears a *kirīṭa-mukuṭa*, earrings, mutli-stringed pearl necklets, *yajñopavīta*, *aṅgadas*, beaded writlets and anklets. *Śrīvatsa* adorns the chest of the god and the *vaijayantīmālā* hangs gracefully to the knees encircling the back and running inward from over the arms. A waistband whose free ends fall on the thighs touching the knees secures the lower garment. The proper right hand holds a rosary and is held in *abhaya* while the back right hand holds the *gadā* by its fluted shaft. The back left hand holds the *chakra* with a tassel issuing forth from its hub. In the front left hand is held the *śaṅkha* from its groove. The conch is placed horizontally and the god has put the middle three fingers in its groove, the small finger above it and the thumb towards its spire. Behind the head is the round eight-petalled aureole.

Flanking the god on his proper right are Śaṅkha-purusha, Śrī and a female acolyte while Chakra-purusha, Bhūmi and Garuḍa occupy the other side on the receding *rathas* of the pedestal respectively. All these figures are standing in graceful symmetrical poses. Both the *āyudha-purushas* stand in *dvibhaṅga* turned towards their lord and wear *karaṇḍa-mukuṭas* adorned with pearl strings and central jewels, earrings, *ekāvalis*, *yajñopavīta*, *keyūras*, *valayas*, *nūpuras*, and the garments fastened with *mekhalās*. Śaṅkha-purusha holds the conch near the chest with left hand and rests the other on the respective knee while Chakra-purusa holds the discus with the right hand and places the left on the left knee. Śrī and Bhūmi stand in asymmetrical *tribhaṅga* posture wearing *dhammilla* hair-coiffure and *ekāvalis*, each with a pearl string dangling down from between the breasts. They hold a lotus each in one hand and support the free end of the lower garment with the other. They both wear the usual ornaments also. The female devotee with similar dress and jewelry stands on the extreme proper right hand projection cross-legged in *gopāla-mudrā* with folded hands. Garuḍa on the other extreme with usual dress and ornaments and in analogous pose holds a snake in the left hand. His right hand is not visible. On the upper corners are shown Brahmā and Śiva on the proper right and left of Vishṇu respectively. Both bear matted locks, wear *ekāvalis*, *yajñopavīta*, *karṇa-kuṇḍalas*, *kaṅkaṇas*, etc. and are seated on inverted lotus-petalled seats in *lalitāasana*. Both are quadrumanous. Tricephalous Brahmā bears a beard and his front right hand is held in *abhaya* (with probably a rosary). The rear right hand supports the ladle while the back left holds a manuscript. The proper left holds a water-pot. The juvenile Śiva holds a trident and a snake in the rear right and left hands while the proper pair of hands is dispensed in the same way as that of Brahmā. The space between these and the subsidiary figures below in filled by *gaja-śārdūla* motifs. Vishṇu has half-closed eyes and a beatitudinous smile. The arrangement of the attributes suggests the image to be of Trivikrama form of Vishṇu. The halo, attributes, and *āyudha-purushas* remind us of an image of Lakshmī-Nārāyaṇa found from Agroha.

The second image measuring 54 x 31 cm (Acc. No. 1/227) is almost an exact copy of the preceding example with the only difference that the pedestal here is *saptaratha* and that the extreme bands on either side show a *śārdūla*, *makara-mukha*, and devotees with folded hands - male on the proper right and female on the left. Some of the subsidiary figures are damaged (Pl. 61).

The third image (Pl. 62), 65 x 36 cm (Acc. No. 1/232), too, is similar in conception with the difference that the god's proper right hand is held in *varada* pose (with a rosary) and the corresponding other holds the conch vertically with its spire downwards. Vishṇu from Kosli described above also holds the conch in this fashion. Dress and ornaments and the aureole show more elaboration. A touch of sophistication is also ubiquitous. Brahmā, though tri-cephalous, is juvenile; the *pañcharatha* pedestal is bedecked with a row of pellets. The *śārdūla* figure on the extreme *rathas* is lonely. The minute care devoted to all the figures is noteworthy.

Vishṇu from Jasat

The Vishṇu image from Jasat is made of reddish sandstone and measures 49 x 35 cm.[100] The head of the god lay detached near it when we visited the site on 7.5.1990. However, it was placed on the figure before taking the photograph (Pl. 63). All the four-hands of the god and the faces of some subsidiary figures have suffered damage. At places, mud and white wash is also sticking to the image. The villagers sometimes apply oil and vermilion also to it and even worship it by offering wheat grains and coins.

The god stands to front in *samapāda-sthānaka-mudrā*. He bears a long cylindrical crown over the hair combed backward. It is studded with a central jewel and pearl strings. The other ornaments include a torque, a long multi-stranded necklace, *keyūras*, and elaborate waistband with free ends falling on the thighs, a sash and an *adhovastra* the end pleats of which may be seen between the thighs. The long floral garland, *vanamālā*, may also be seen. There is a round lotus-petalled gloriole behind the head. The god is flanked by Śaṅkha-purusha, female (Śrīdevī), a male in the dress of a cowherd, and another male figure with a long bow held in his right hand, on the proper right hand side, and by Chakra-purusha, a female (Sarasvatī), a male with frizzled locks followed by another male figure holding a bow from the middle in his left hand on the corresponding left hand side. In front of the *āyudha-purushas* are seated in profile the donor couple, the male one before Śaṅkha-purusha and the female before Chakra-purusha. They are seated in half-kneeing posture with folded hands. Their faces are damaged and so also are those of the female and the extreme male figure on the proper left of the god.

Flanking the halo are the stele showing quadrimanous Brahmā and Śiva. At the waist level are depicted two sages, one on either side, seated in profile in kneeling posture and in *añjali-mudrā*. The extremities of the back slab show *gaja*-śārdūla motifs in the middle and human figures emerging from *makara-mukhas* on the top corners.

The attendant figures deserve greater attention. While the *āyudha-purusha* and the two females may easily be identified as Śaṅkha- and Chakra-purusha and the two spouses of the lord, Śrī and Sarasvatī, it is somewhat difficult to identify the extreme two male figures on either side with certainty at the first glance. Two, four or six attendants usually accompany Vishṇu in the images from the Punjab-Haryana region. When two, they are the *āyudha-purushas*, when four, the *āyudha-purushas* are generally accompanied by the two spouses of Vishṇu, often shown as holding lotuses in their hands. When there are six attendants, one is generally Garuḍa, the vehicle of Vishṇu, often shown with frizzled locks. The other (sixth) figure is that of Balarāma, quite often depicted with a plough or a pestle and/or with a serpent hood. Garuḍa, too, is shown with a serpent hood in an image of the god from Kaithal, and generally as holding a serpent in one hand. The third attendant figures flanking the god here may thus be recognized as Balarāma in the *gopa-veśa* on the proper right hand side, and Garuḍa with frizzled locks on the left. Both wear *vanamālā* because of their Vaishṇava association. The extreme figures of the males, wearing conical crowns and slightly turned towards the main figure, holding bows in their hands may be identified with Rāma and Lakshmaṇa. Though Balarāma has popularly been shown as an attendant figure in many medieval images of Vishṇu from Punjab and Haryana, the depiction of Rāma and Lakshmaṇa is a very interesting iconographic feature seen here.

We know of only one such example where Rāma has been shown as an attendant figure of Vishṇu. The *chaturbhuja* image belongs to the Paramāra period and is preserved in the Birla Museum, Bhopal. The god, in this relief, is flanked by Śaṅkha-purusha, Garuḍa and Paraśurāma with battle-axe on his proper right and by Chakra-purusha, Lakshmī and Rāma with bow on his proper left. This image, however, shows other incarnatory forms also and is a Daśāvatāra relief, but our image is not. And hence the uniqueness of our image which may be assigned to the 11th century on stylistic grounds.

Vishṇu from Kosli

A blackish sandstone image of Vishṇu was recovered by the police at Kosli near Jhajjar. Measuring 94 x 54 cm (Acc. No. 1/351), it shows the god standing to front on a round *pīṭha* placed in the center of a *pañcha-ratha* pedestal (Pl. 64). He wears a double-tiered cylindrical crown adorned with pearl strings and a *stūpikā* finial, circular ear ornaments, an elaborate torque and double-stringed pearl necklace, sacred thread, armlets, bracelets, anklets, *dhotī* held in position by an elaborate girdle with two pearl strings knotted in front with free ends having leaf-shaped pendants falling on the thighs, the long garland bedecked with spacer shaped jewels at the lower end going across the legs between the knees and the feet, and holding conch, lotus, mace and discus in the four-hands in *pradaksiṇā* order. There is a stylized halo behind the head flanked by stele showing diminutive seated figures of Brahmā and Śiva on the proper right and left, and a similar niche at the apex probably with Sūrya. The back slab carries the figures of the incarnatory forms; Matsya and Kūrma (simple fish and tortoise) at the top of the extreme projections, Varāha and Narasiṃha flanking the apex, pot-bellied Vāmana and Paraśurāma holding the axe in his right hand seated in *sukhāsana* at the level of the suspended normal hands of the god carrying discus and conch on the left and right, standing Rāma holding the bow in his left hand and Balarāma holding the shaft of the plough or the pesle in his right below Paraśurāma and Vāmana respectively, and Buddha in *bhūmisparśa-mudrā* at the lower extreme on the viewer's left and Kalki carrying the sword in his right hand seated on the horseback on the other side. Just below the fish and tortoise on the extreme projections are the crocodile faces and leogryphs in profile covering the space between the incarnatory forms. Flanking the Lord on his right and left are the double-flexioned figures of Garuḍa holding the snake in his left hand and Śrī holding the lotus by its long stalk in her right hand, the other hand being akimbo. At their feet are the figures of the donor couple in adoration, the bearded male sitting in front of Garuḍa and the female at the feet of Śrī. Stylization, profuse ornamentation, and crowded composition render this image to be dated to 12th century C.E.

The form of Vishṇu with the above-mentioned attributes is named as Madhusūdana in the *Padma Purāṇa* (IV.79), and Nārāyaṇa according to the *Rūpa-maṇḍana* (V) and *Ahirbudhnya Saṃhitā* (26.33-46).

Vishṇu from Mehrauli

A black stone image of Vishṇu (Pl. 65) was discovered by the Archaeological Survey of India to the southeast of the Qutab-Minar at Mehrauli, Delhi that was transferred to the National Museum, New Delhi (Acc. No. L.39).[101] This 105 cm high image shows the deity standing between two profusely decorated pillars supporting an ornamental arch *'toraṇa'*; holding in his four-hands *gadā, śaṅkha, padma,* and *chakra* in the *pradakshiṇā* order; wearing a high bejeweled crown, ear ornaments, necklaces, long garland, armlets, bracelets, the lower garment secured by an elaborate girdle, and anklets; and also bearing a *śrīvatsa* on the chest. An ornamental lotus halo with stylized *gaja-mukha* decorations on either side is caved behind the head. The god has curly hair and pointed nails of the fingers betraying the labor spent on carving the image. On the right and left sides of the crowned head of the god are seated figures of Brahmā and Śiva respectively. The lower right hand of Brahmā is displayed in *abhaya* while the corresponding left holds the *kamaṇḍalu,* the additional hands hold the ladle and the book. Śiva on the other side holds a trident and a cobra in the rear hands while the normal ones are shown as in case of Brahmā. Near the feet of Vishṇu are shown on the right Chakra-purusha with his right hand placed on the waist and the left holding the discus, followed by Śrī and Balarāma, the latter under the canopy of a three-headed serpent and carrying a ploughshare in his left and resting the right on his thigh. On the proper left of the deity are depicted Śaṅkha-purusha holding a conch in his right hand and resting the left on his waist, followed by another consort of the god and winged Garuḍa with his right hand raised above the head and the left holding a cobra. Flanking the central projection of the pedestal is shown the donor couple in *añjali-mudrā* seated in profile.

The elaborately carved *prabhā-torana* illustrates in a row the ten incarnatory forms of Vishṇu, viz. Matsya, Kūrma, Varāha, Nṛisiṃha, Vāmana, Rāma, Paraśurāma, Balarāma, and Kalki holding usual attributes in their hands. The toraṇa depicts at the top in a semi-circular row the figures of the *Navagrahas,* i.e. Sūrya, Soma, Maṅgala, Budha, Bṛihaspati, Śukra, Śani, Rāhu and Ketu. The profusely carved pillars and the *toraṇa* illustrate in separate niches the images of the various forms of Vishṇu which can be identified variously on the basis of the attributes held in their hands as given in different texts; identified here by B.N. Sharma as Keśava, Nārāyaṇa, Aniruddha (with a standing Gaṇeśa holding battle-axe and a bowl of sweet-balls), Govinda, Vishṇu, Trivikrama, Purushottama, Hari (in the niche at the apex), Janārdana, Adhokshaja, Pradyumna, Śrīdhara, Hṛishīkeśa, Padmanābha, and Dāmodara beginning from the bottom right to the bottom left. These images are also flanked by their consorts and show the image of four-armed Sarasvatī with her normal right hand disposed in the *varada-mudrā* and the remaining ones carrying lotus, manuscript, and waterpot. *Gajaśārdūla* motifs have also been depicted. The pedestal bears a five-line inscription on the central projection of the pedestal recording that this image of Saṅkarshaṇa was installed by Tīsara Sāhu, the grandson of

Govinda Sāhu belonging to the Rohitaka family, on Friday in the Māgha month of (Vikrama) Saṃvat 1204 (=C.E. 1147).

It seems that with the advent of Islam and the iconoclastic zeal of the rulers, the existing temples were razed and the sculptures damaged. Construction of temples and carving of images stopped till the time of the Marathas during the late Mughal period. If any stray images were created they are far from being artistic. The worship of Vishṇu, however, seems to have continued in the form of Śāligrāma. The weakening of the Mughal power led to the recreation of images but the use of marble seems to have become popular. The centers for making images of marble developed in the areas where marble was available. In the case of Haryana, probably Rajasthan catered to the needs. Marble images of Vishṇu in modern temples, however, indicate a continuity of the cult. Vishṇu from a village Banbhori in district Hisar showing a *chakra* on the crown (Pl. 66) is an interesting example of modern marble images.

ĀSANA-MŪRTIS (SEATED IMAGES)

Garuḍavāhī Vishṇu

Seated images of Vishṇu are rare not only in Haryana but in the whole of the country. We have, however, already noted above the Kushāṇa *Garuḍavāhī* image of Vishṇu from Khokhrakot, Rohtak (Pls. 22-23). Besides this, one other image of *Garuḍāsana* Vishṇu is known from Gujjar Kheri. This small 15 x 19 cm piece (Reg. No. HRN/AMB-625) shows anthropomorphous Garuḍa in flying pose bearing on his back the god Vishṇu whose folded left leg supported by Garuḍa on his left arm and the lower left hand holding the conch only have survived (Pl. 67). Garuḍa has his hair combed backwards with probably a *karaṇḍa-mukuṭa* over it. His facial expression indicates the vigor with which he is carrying his lord. He wears ear ornaments, a serpentine necklace, sacred thread, armlets, and bracelets. The portion below the waist is broken. The conch in Vishṇu's hand has been held horizontally and is carved prominently. The general workmanship is not of a high standard.[102]

Garuḍvāhī Vishṇu is shown as the *lalāṭa-bimba* on an unfinished door-surround in the Prāchī Śiva Temple at Pehowa also (Fig. 5). Preserved in the Hanumān Temple at Kaithal now is a small sandstone Pratihāra piece (16 x 9 cm) which also shows Vishṇu riding the celestial bird.

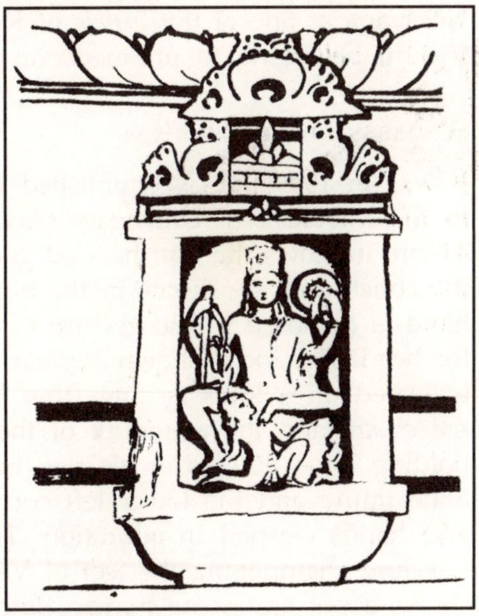

Fig. 5. *Garuḍāsana* Vishṇu on the unfinished doorway, Pehowa.

Yogāsana Vishṇu

The other form of seated Vishṇu in Haryana is represented by the *Yogāsana-mūrtis*, also called Yoga-Nārāyaṇa. A roughly carved yet beautiful image of Yoga-Nārāyaṇa was recovered from Sirsa (Pl. 68) and housed in HARDAM (Acc. No 1/105). Measuring 30.5 x 24 cm, it has been carved out of light buff sandstone. The god is seated on a lotus *pīṭha* in a pillared niche in meditation with his front hands resting one over the other in the lap upon the upturned soles of the feet. The back right hand holds the mace vertically and the corresponding left hand holds the lotus by its long stalk.

The cylindrical crown on the head is not very high. Facial features and details of ornaments except the armlets and bracelets are not visible. Winding side stems can be seen on either side of stalk of the lotus over which sits the god. The pillars of the *rathikā* show ribbed divisions. The bases and vase-like abacuses of the pillars are notable. Lozenge-shaped *ratnas* 'diamonds' within squares surmount the abacuses. An ornamental arch showing scrollwork connects the squares. Obviously, this is a subsidiary image of some 11th century temple, probably representing the Buddha incarnation.

Another Yoga-Nārāyaṇa image (Pl. 69) is now fixed in the outer wall of a Śiva temple at Lalru on Chandigarh-Ambala road.[103] It was brought here by a local contractor from Pinjore. The image measures 60 x 27.5 cm. The god bearing a cylindrical crown adorned with the diamond motif, large circular earrings, necklets and necklace, lozenge shaped *śrīvatsa* on the chest, armlets, wristlets, long garland, *dhotī*, etc. is seated in *dhyāna-mudrā* with both the lower hands placed one over the other in the lap over the folded legs. A semi-circular loop of the long garland is shown on the seat. The god holds a discus in the upper right and an *ūrdhva-śaṅkha* in the back left hand. What is remarkable is that the image is unfinished and chisel marks may still be seen all over the figure, indicating Pinjore to be the center of art where this image was being carved but left unfinished because of some reason unknown to us. Stylistically, the image may be dated to *circa* 10th century C.E.

Some scholars think that Yoga-Nārāyaṇa may be the representation of the Buddha incarnation of Vishṇu.[104]

The rarity of Yoga-Nārāyaṇa images in Haryana, however bestows these figures a great importance.

ŚAYANA-MŪRTIS (Reclining Images)

Śeshaśāyī Vishṇu

The worship of Vishṇu as Śeshaśāyī has a long history in Haryana. In the Tīrthayātrāparva of the *Mahābhārata* is recorded an exhortation that pilgrims should worship Padmanābha-Nārāyaṇa at one of the *tīrthas* of Kurukshetra.[105] Strangely, however, no images of Śeshaśāyī Vishṇu belonging to pre-medieval period are known from the state as yet.

Śeshaśāyī from Thanesar

It was in 1969 that we published the first Śeshaśāyī image from Thanesar (now preserved in the Kurukshetra University (Acc. No. 75.419).[106] Made of sandstone and measuring 55 x 44 cm, it shows the four-handed god lying on the coils of the seven-hooded serpent, holding the conch and the discus in the normal and additional left hands (Pl. 70). The normal right hand is disposed in the gesture of reassurance while the extra right arm is bent to support the head. The god is shown as wearing the usual ornaments. The mace lies to his right. Brahmā is seated on a lotus issuing from the navel of Vishṇu just above the conch-shell. Between the *chakra* and the extremity of the rectangular slab may be seen the upper part of Sūrya holding lotus flowers in his two hands and Umā-Maheśvara. Below the latter is a dancing male figure and the lower left corner is occupied by a male donee figure with folded legs and hands clasped in adoration. The right hand side of the slab which may have shown Lakshmī shampooing the feet of Vishṇu is broken. The space below the coils of the serpent shows a pot and some human figures carrying weapons and betraying postures of fighting, probably depicting the fight with Madhu and Kaiṭabha. Stylistically, the relief may be dated to *circa* 10th century C.E.

Śeshaśāyī from Mandhna

We discovered a beautiful image of dark grey sandstone, measuring 44 x 31.5 cm, from Mandhna in district Panchkula (Pl. 71). The god is reclining on a crescent-shaped couch over which faint traces of the coils of the great serpent are still visible. The head of the god is supported by the rear right hand, which is raised from the elbow almost vertically. The proper right hand is shown with a lotus near the chest. The back left hand holds the disc while the normal left is shown with a conch. Mace is placed behind the rear right hand. The god wears a not very high cylindrical crown, ear ornaments, torque, bracelets, *vanamālā, dhotī* secured by a simple girdle with a sash on the thighs. The left leg is slightly raised at knee. The right leg is stretched to reach Lakshmī who is shown as shampooing it. Only traces of the lotus with Brahmā are left now. The extant traces, however, indicate that the lotus issued not from the navel of the god but perhaps from behind the left arms. Madhu and Kaiṭabha are shown as fighting with clubs in the space between conch and Lakshmī. The back wall depicts the planetary divinities in a row. The serpentine Ketu and the prominent head of Rāhu are to be distinguished from others who seem to be seated in *lalitāsana* with right hand disposed in *abhaya* and left placed on knee (or holding water pot). The top left corner is broken. Probably Sūrya was depicted here as holding a lotus in either hand. An unidentifiable female figure is seen behind the conch and just below the thicker end of the mace on the extreme left. Lakshmī's face is mutilated. The whole composition is marked by a harmonious balance and simplicity. Stylistically, it may be assigned to *circa* 9th century C.E.

Śeshaśāyī from Sanghan

Not in a good state of preservation, this image measuring 21.5 x 16 cm, comes from Sanghan, 16 km west of Kaithal.[107] The attributes in the four hands of the god are similar to those of Śeshaśāyī from Mandhna but the lotus with Brahmā atop is issuing forth from the navel of the god here. Lakshmī is pressing Vishṇu's slightly raised right foot. A male figure holding a long club-like object in his left hand with right akimbo is shown as standing near Lakshmī.[108] No details are discernible because of the indifferent state of preservation of the image, which seems to belong to the same century as the preceding one.

Śeshaśāyī Vishṇu from Garh Fazilpur

A similar but much better preserved image, measuring about 45 x 30 cm, in red sandstone, is known from Garh Fazilpur in district Sonepat (Pl. 72). It shows the god sleeping on a couch upon the bedstead of the coils of the Śesha who also canopies his head. The ocean is indicated by a lotus bud and perhaps some other aquatic plants one of which looks just like a small mushroom. The standing male figure near Lakshmī is replaced by a seated unidentifiable figure. There is no lotus issuing from the navel, nor Brahmā is shown. The upper portion of the panel, however, shows the *navagrahas* seated in a row in *lalitāsana* except Rāhu and Ketu who are represented by a head and colubrine figure. Sūrya holds the lotus flowers in both his hands and the other *grahas* are shown with *abhaya* and water pot in their right and left hands respectively. The image may belong to *circa* 9th-10th century C.E. (Regn. No. HRN/SON-21).

Śeshaśāyī from Thanesar

A small fragment of buff sandstone, measuring 15.0 x 15.5 cm, from Thanesar shows the god lying on the couch with his head towards the left. With a *kirīṭa-mukuṭa* on the head and with usual other ornaments, Vishṇu is shown as lying on a couch below which are depicted the figures of crocodile and tortoise to symbolize the sea. The coils of the snake, which served as his pillow, are damaged. He is holding a mace in the right hand and a flywhisk is also visible near his head. A fly whisker stands in profile behind the main figure. The figure is dated to *circa* 9th century C.E.[109] Unfortunately this relief is much damaged to furnish us other details of the figure. Its small size indicates it to have been a subsidiary image adorning some niche of a 9th century Vaishṇava shrine at Thanesar.

Śeshaśāyī from Gurawara

Further development may be noticed in a much-damaged relief from Gurawara, about 20 km north of Rewari (Pl. 73).[110] It measures 64.75 x 33 cm. The whole of the upper portion is lost but it may not have been much different from those described above. It is interesting to note that the god sleeps on the couch, which seems to have been decked with an ornamental bed sheet only. There are no traces of the coils of the snake nor is the couch curved. Ocean, however, seems to have been indicated by certain aquatic plants (?), a fish, a *kalaśa* and perhaps horse.[111] Lakshmī is seated on a stool. The relief may be placed in *circa* 11th century C.E.

Another image measuring 91.5 x 64.75 cm from the same place is now housed in the Gurukula Museum, Jhajjar. The god lies on the coils of the serpent as usual but Lakshmī is shown as seated kneeling shampooing the right foot of her Lord. Vishṇu holds a small mace in his lower right hand and conch in the corresponding left. The back right hand supports the head and the left may have held a discus now mutilated. A lotus, however, is shown as rising from his navel and Brahmā is seated on it. On the upper register are the planetary divinities. Being not in a good state of preservation, details are difficult to be discerned properly. Two figures with clubs near Lakshmī may be identified with Madhu and Kaiṭabha.

Another fragmentary sandstone relief from Guruwara in the same museum shows the god on the coils of the serpent supporting his head with the back right hand and holding the mace in the normal right. Both the left hands and the upper part of the frieze are lost. Lakshmī, interestingly seated on a wooden *chowki*, but with the head gone is depicted at the feet of the Lord. There seems to be the head of an elephant below her seat. Very small adoring figures may also be seen below the couch under the feet of Vishṇu. Stylistically, however, it seems to be much later than the figures described above and may be ascribed to *circa* 12th century C.E. An unfinished and badly mutilated figure of white spotted grayish sandstone, datable almost to the same period as the preceding example, lies in the village temple at Asiaki, nearly 5 km south of Guruwara in district Rewari.

Śeshaśāyī from Banchari

Śeshaśāyī image from Banchari near Hodal is also preserved in the same museum. Measuring 110.5 x 70 cm, it consists of black stone. The god is depicted with his head on the right supported by the back left hand. The proper left perhaps holds a lotus near the navel from which also rises a stalk to support Brahmā seated on the lotus. The other hands are not clear. Lord's spouse may faintly be seen shampooing his foot but the frieze is too much worn out to yield more details. A large lotiform aureole may, however, be seen at her back. Madhu and Kaiṭabha fighting with clubs may also be guessed from what remains of their figures now near Lakshmī. The upper register shows the *navagrahas*.[112]

A small elegant Śeshaśāyī image is still under worship at the village Sheshashayi, about 13 km east of Hodal. Another small piece lies in the Dehra Temple at Gurgaon. Still another small panel depicting Śeshaśāyī Vishṇu is studded in the wall of a temple on the Saraswati Ghat at Pehowa.

All these reliefs of Śeshaśāyī Vishṇu indicate the popularity of this form of the god during the medieval period in Haryana.

LAKSHMĪ-NĀRĀYAṆA

Standing Images

Only two specimens of standing Lakshmī-Nārāyaṇa images are known so far. They come from Agroha and Pinjore and are described below.

Lakshmī-Nārāyaṇa from Agroha

Obtained as a part of India's share and now housed in the Chandigarh Museum is a beautiful buff sandstone image of Lakshmī-Nārāyaṇa from Agroha (Museum Register No. 47), 50 cm in height (Pl. 74), shown as standing on a *pañcha-ratha* pedestal.[113] The back slab has a semi-circular upper end decorated with a beautiful eight-petalled perfectly round lotiform aureole with beaded border round the pericarp in the center behind the heads of the divine couple. The principal right hand of the god is badly damaged. Originally, it may have held a lotus or may have been disposed in *abhaya* or *varada-mudrā*. The normal left hand holding the conch is thrown across the shoulder of Lakshmī. The remaining right and left hands hold the mace and the discus respectively. Lakshmī's right hand is also thrown across the shoulder of her Lord. Her other hand is broken at the elbow. D.C. Bhattacharyya has wrongly identified the attendant figure standing near the right foot of the god as Gadānārī.[114] The figure is a male attendant standing gracefully holding a conch vertically in both of his hands near the chest. There is thus absolutely no doubt to its being the Śaṅkha-purusha, the figure on the corresponding side being that of Chakra-purusha. The two figures following these *āyudhapurushas* are both females and may represent the *parivāradevatās* of Vishṇu. *Vidyādhara* figures hovering in the sky may be seen on the top corners of the back slab.

Vishṇu is shown as wearing a cylindrical crown adorned with pearl strings as also seen in the Vishṇu images described above. His nose is slightly damaged. The bow shaped eyebrows, quasi-closed eyes, round face with plump cheeks, sturdy chin, etc. bestow distinctiveness to this figure. The god also wears ear ornaments, torque and necklace of beads, sacred thread, armlets, bracelets, anklets, an elaborate girdle to keep the under garment in position, sash covering part of the thighs, and a long garland as ordained in the iconographic texts. Pearl strings characterize the ornaments. Lakshmī bears a high bun bedecked with a *kīrtimukha* in the pod and stringed beads. A torque, a necklace with beaded strings falling from between the breasts and the third one falling gracefully over the breasts are all made of pearl strings. Her *dhotī*, girdle, and sash are similar to those of Vishṇu. It has been rightly observed " It is a beautiful piece of sculpture showing fair amount of sensitivity of the plastic surface and rotundity of the form. The contours are characterized by smoothly gliding lines. The faces of the figures are sensitively rounded and they show the liveliness of the flesh. The torso, particularly of Vishṇu, is modeled with subtle grace."[115] But to ignore its known provenance and regard it as an import from Kanauj in the Gaṅgā-Yamunā valley and date it to the 12th century[116] does not seem to be logical as we have seen above that such crowns and images exist at several places in Haryana and the ornaments characterized by the use of pearl strings were prevalent here before the latter part of the 10th century.

Lakshmī-Nārāyaṇa from Pinjore

A rectangular slab with semi-circular upper end, 63 cm in height, carrying a crude representation of Vishṇu and his spouse Lakshmī, is known from Pinjore also (Pl. 75).[117] Vishṇu stands in *ābhaṅga* (slight flexion of the body), with hands holding lotus, mace, discus and conch in the four-hands, wearing usual dress and ornaments, accompanied by Lakshmī standing independently on his left. Lakshmī is two handed, holding a lotus in her right hand with the suspended left. A circular halo is shown over the head of Vishṇu. Surprisingly, this halo is not carved behind the head of Lakshmī who is shown with a cylindrical crown[118] on her head and wears a *vanamālā* like Vishṇu. Near the right foot of Vishṇu is seated a dwarfish figure with folded hands representing Garuḍa.

D.C. Bhattacharyya has observed that "Stylistically the sculpture is an example of a complete exhaustion of the repertoire of medieval idiom of artistic expression. The low relief carving with a flattened effect, the rigidity of the form, particularly of the figure of Lakshmi, a complete circular form of faces of all the figures, and the angularity of the lower edges of the garments of both Vishṇu and Lakshmi characterize the sculpture as an example of workmanship of debased nature. The sculpture, although follows the medieval Indian iconographic conventions, is a blatant testimony of the decadence of medieval Indian style, particularly in respect of the visual vocabulary."[119] He dates the image to *circa* 13th century C.E.[120] We, however, feel that it is a work of an un-experienced and untrained artist who was not fully conversant with the tradition of carving Lakshmī-Nārāyaṇa images as he has carved the two figures not as the *āliṅgaṇa-mūrtis* but as standing independently.

Seated Images

Very few icons of Lakshmī-Nārāyaṇa in sitting posture are known from Haryana. The following representations of the divine couple in a seated posture, however, still remain unpublished.

Lakshmī-Nārāyaṇa from Pinjore

Quadrimanous Vishṇu holding lotus, mace, discus and conch in his four-hands is shown in a pedimented *rathikā* seated on anthropomorphic Garuḍa in *lalitāsana* with Lakshmī on his left lap. He wears a simple crown, *ekāvali* and other usual ornaments. The normal left hand of the god, which holds the conch, is put round the waist of the goddess from the back to embrace her. Lakshmī too embraces the god with her right hand while her left hand rests on her right knee. Fly-whiskers flank the couple on the recessed *rathikās* and *gaja-śārdūlas* appear on the extreme panels. The figure is quite worn out. It may be assigned to *circa* 10th century C.E.

Lakshmī-Nārāyaṇa from Panipat

Now enshrined in the Devī Temple at Panipat, this image is said to have been found from the temple-tank during its clearance (Pl. 76). Measuring 17 x 14 cm and made of dark greyish fine-grained stone it gives a metallic look. Vishṇu is seated in *lalitāsana* with Lakshmī on his left lap on anthropomorphic Garuḍa. The two hands of Garuḍa, who is depicted in a flying posture, support the right foot and left knee of the god who is wearing all usual ornaments including *śrīvatsa* and *vanamālā* and holds a conch (placed horizontally) in his *varada* normal right hand, lotus in the rear right, mace in the back left and disc in the normal left hand. Lakshmī is embracing her spouse with her right hand while her left hand is held in *varada-mudrā*. She also wears all usual ornaments. Her right leg is folded while the left hangs down. A very notable feature of this image is that she has placed her left foot on the head of an elephant carved in profile to its left. This thus is a unique image, as we know no such example from anywhere else. The back slab shows lotus petals behind the heads of the deities. The style of holding the conch is also rare. Stylistically, the image does not seem to be earlier than the 12th century.

In the Department of AIHC & Archaeology, Panjab University, Chandigarh, is preserved another fragmentary relief from Marhanwala which shows the lower half of a female figure seated on the folded left leg of a god. The female wears a nether garment, which is secured by a waist-hand. She also wears anklets. The heads of two subsidiary figures, one below the right foot of the goddess and the other below the folded knee of the god may also be seen. A leogryph jumping to right has also survived on the extreme projection of the panel behind and above the folded left leg of the goddess. Much more important, however, is the hand which has survived below the folded left leg of the god. This may have been the hand of anthropomorphic Garuḍa and the whole relief may have represented Lakshmī-Nārāyaṇa supported by Garuḍa.

That an image of Lakshmī-Nārāyaṇa existed at Marhanwala is definitely proved by another fragmentary relief measuring 23 x 17 cm showing the head and bust of Lakshmī with the left hand of Vishṇu holding the discus above her left shoulder. The goddess bears a massive bun on her head, wears *karṇa-kuṇḍalas*, *evkāvali* and a necklace, which falls on her slender belly from over the globular breasts. Vishṇu's hand shows a bracelet. A tassel comes out from the hub of the discus. The execution of the relief is rather crude. Stylistically, this as also most other reliefs discussed above may be place in *circa* 10th century C.E.

We do not know whether the paucity of Lakshmī-Nārāyaṇa images in Haryana is because of inadequate discoveries or the worship of the couple was not very popular in the region.

Vaikuṇṭha

Vaikuṇṭha is one of the thousand names of Vishṇu according to the *Mahābhārata*[121] and the Purāṇas.[122] In the realm of plastic art, Vaikuṇṭha is a unitary multiple image which symbolically represents Vaikuṇṭha (i. e. Vāsudeva Vishṇu) as the Highest Being along with his three emanations[123] – Saṃkarshaṇa, Pradyumna, and Aniruddha – or incarnations, i. e., Nṛisiṃha, Varāha and Kapila.[124] The *Mahābhārata* refers to this esoteric form of Vishṇu as *Mūrtichatushṭaya*[125] but does not give any details. The first iconographical description of the Vaikuṇṭha image occurs in a *dhyāna* 'meditation' of the Pāñcharātra text *Jayākhya Saṃhitā* of the late or post Gupta period where it has been described as having four faces of Vaikuṇṭha, Nṛisiṃha, Varāha and Kapila and four arms holding a conch, a discus, a mace, and a lotus, and mounted on a white Garuḍa.[126] The *Vishṇudharmottara Purāṇa*, another text of the late Gupta period, states that the joint image of Vāsudeva (human), Saṃkarshaṇa (lion), Pradyumna (boar) and Aniruddha (terrific face) is called Vaikuṇṭha which should be quadricephalous (*Chaturmukha, Chaturmūrti*), having the main eastern face as placid representing strength (*bala*), southern leonine face representing knowledge (*jñāna*), northern boar face representing affluence (*aiśvarya*), and western terrific (*raudra*) face as representing energy (*śakti*).[127] Elsewhere, this very text lays down that it should have placid, Nṛisiṃha, Kapila, and Varāha faces on the east, south, west, and north sides respectively.[128] The octomanous deity should hold an arrow, a rosary, a pestle, etc. in the right hands and a shield, a plough, a bow, and a discus in the left ones.[129] Also, the god should ride the mount Garuḍa (*Garuḍa-sthitam*). Later texts like the *Aparājitapṛichchhā*,[130] *Rūpamaṇḍana*[131] and *Devatāmūrtiprakaraṇa*[132] also describe Vaikuṇṭhamūrti similarly as four-faced, eight-handed and riding the mount Garuḍa. The attributes, according to these texts, should be a mace, a sword, a discus and an arrow in the right hands[133] and a conch, a scutum, a bow and a lotus in the left ones. Some scholars hold that the multi-headed (*bhūyishṭhavaktra*) images of Vishṇu were the central object of worship by the followers of the Tantrāntara sub-sect, which was popular during the medieval period with other Vaishṇava sub-sects like the Mantra, Āgama, and Tantra.[134] The *Pādma*[135] and *Paushkara*[136] *saṃhitās* also describe Vishṇu, the chief deity of the Tantrātara sub-sect, as having the placid, leonine, and other faces.

Yaśovarmmadeva's Khajuraho inscription of VS 1011 (=C.E. 954) tells us a very interesting story about the four-faced Vaikuṇṭha form of Vishṇu. It states that Kapila and two other demons had obtained a boon from Brahmā that they should be killed only by one who would assume their forms. In order to kill the demons, Vishṇu assumed the syncretistic form of Vaikuṇṭha with the faces of lion, boar and Kapila.[137] This mythological story, however, is not met with anywhere else.[138]

Very few temples of Vaikuṇṭha have survived the vicissitudes of nature and human vandalism. Yaśovarman had installed the four-faced Vaikuṇṭha image in the Lakshmaṇa Temple at Khajuraho, which he constructed for this very purpose. This image was brought by Bhoṭanātha from the Kailāśa region and presented to the Sāhi king of Kīra (Kangra region) as a token of friendship. Herambapāla took this image forcibly from the Sāhi king and the Chandella king Yaśovarman took this image from Herambapāla's son Hayapati Devapāla. The *bhadra* (cardinal, main) niches of the sanctum of this temple contain images of Varāha, Narasiṃha, and Hayagrīva indicating the association with and importance of these incarnatory forms for Vaikuṇṭha. The present image of the Lakshmaṇa Temple, however, is about 150 years later.[139] The other Vaikuṇṭha temple known to us is the larger Sās (of the Sās-Bahu) temple at Gwalior built in C.E. 1093 by the Kachchhapaghāta king Mahīpāla.

Four-faced Vaikuṇṭha images are characteristic of the Kashmir region which were popularly worshipped by the followers of the Pāñcharātra of the Kāśmīrāgama, also called Tantrāntara Siddhānta.[140] This sect worshipped multi-headed (*bhūyishṭha-mukha*) Vishṇu. Numerous images of Vaikuṇṭha were installed in Kashmir from 8th century onwards. Queen Diddā, wife of Kshemagupta and grand-daughter of the Sāhi king Bhīma, installed Vaikuṇṭha images and founded Diddāsvāmin shrine in C.E. 972[141] and Queen Ratnādevī constructed a Vaikuṇṭha-maṭha in mid-12th century C.E.[142]

A unique four-faced Yaksha image from Bhita, now exhibited in the State Museum, Lucknow,[143] showing small figures of lion and boar below the badly mutilated side faces at the waist level, is regarded by some scholars to represent the earliest attempt at carving the Vaikuṇṭha form in the 2nd century B.C.E.[144] The existence of the Vaikuṇṭha form at such an early age, however, seems to be historically impossible as the earliest Vaikuṇṭha images showing the lion and boar heads may be traced to only the Gupta period.[145] Most of the scholars, however, regard Vaikuṇṭha image of the Kushāṇa period from Mathura which shows three busts attached to it, one on the top and two near the shoulders, as the earliest representation of this deity.[146] Vaikuṇṭha images showing lion and boar faces, however, seem to have come into existence during the Gupta period.[147] During the early medieval period, Vaikuṇṭha worship had grown quite popular in the hill region of Kashmir and Himachal Pradesh. Vaikuṇṭha-mūrtis continued to be carved during this period from Kashmir to Madhya Pradesh and from Uttar Pradesh to Gujarat.[148] The Vaikuṇṭha form seems to have traveled from the north even to Karnataka as indicated by an inscribed medieval *makara-toraṇa* from Huli in district Belgaum which shows the four-armed Vaikuṇṭha, seated on a *padma-pīṭha* in *mahārājalīlāsana*. The only independent sculptural representation of Vaikuṇṭha, assignable to *circa* 12th-13th century, however, comes from Banashankari Temple, Basavakalyāṇa, district Bijapur, Karnataka. It is a relief sculpture executed on a rectangular sandstone slab, depicting Lakshmī-Vaikuṇṭha seated on Garuḍa in *ardhapadmāsana*, holding discus and mace in the upper hands, lotus in the normal right hand and embracing the goddess Lakshmī with the lower left hand. Gadā is shown in a minuscule fashion on the extreme left. Garuḍa has fluttering wings and holds *amṛita-kalaśa* in his two hands.[149] There is evidence that Vaikuṇṭha worship was prevalent in the Gandhāra region also.[150]

The early Brahmanical Vaikuṇṭha figures may be regarded the visual images of the cosmogonic theory. Their anthropomorphic figures are emanatory, they issue from a central figure and represent, not a group of figures, but a process of cosmic becoming in its continuity. The assemblage of emerging anthropomorphic figures emanating from one central body betrays the sculptural rendering of a process, representing an ongoing progression in its three-dimensional form. The multiple sculptural form presents the virtual correspondence to a theological thought-structure created in the Pāñcharātra system to celebrate Vishṇu as the universe.[151]

In Bhāgavata theology,[152] the principal cult-figures were the five Vṛishṇi heroes.[153] The Pāñcharātra system transformed four of them (except Sāmba) into symbols of the stages in a new formulation of the cosmogonic process. Sāmba, the fifth member and the other son of Kṛishṇa besides Pradyumna, was left out for having disgraced himself for he had dressed as a woman and taunted the sages who cursed him to give birth to an iron club from which came the swords which destroyed the Yādavas, Kṛishṇa's clan in Dvārakā.[154] The unitary multiple image gradually lost its inherent emanatory, cosmogonic character and the full-bodied figures issuing laterally and apically from their source, became reduced to their heads only, inaugurating the subsequent multi-headed images of gods.[155]

The *Jayākhya Saṃhitā* (VI. 73) describes Vaikuṇṭha as *anādinidhana*, without beginning and end, and *jagatsrashṭā īśvara*, God who created the Universe. According to the *Bhāgavata Purāṇa* (X.6, 26), Vaikuṇṭha is beseeched for the protection of children from various evil spirits.

More than a dozen Vaikuṇṭha images have been brought to light, mostly by us, from Haryana. Ranging in date from *circa* 6th to 11th-12th centuries, they have been found from Kapāla-Mochana, Gharaunda, Kaithal, Agroha, Pinjaur, Sirsa, Hat, Chandimandir, Kurukshetra, Asandh and Jasat.

The earliest representation of Vaikuṇṭha from Haryana comes from Kapāla-Mochana[156] a holy place near Jagadhari in district Yamunanagar, and belongs to the late Gupta period (Pl. 77). The extant piece, measuring 23 x 16 cm and broken below the chest, seems to have originally been carved on a rectangular sandstone slab and is in a poor state of preservation. It is now preserved in HARDAM and bears Acc. No. 1/264. The central human face with a *kirīṭamukuṭa* and placid expression, the boar face on proper left and the stylized and humanized leonine face on the right are very clear and leave little doubt to its being a Vaikuṇṭha-mūrti. There is no nimbus behind the head and we do not know the number of hands the god may have possessed as the figure is badly mutilated. Another Vaikuṇṭha image (Pl. 78), assignable to *circa* 6th century C.E., comes from Gharaunda, located on the Sher Shah Suri Marg (National Highway No. 1) between Panipat and Karnal in district Karnal. Measuring 22.5 x 12 cm, this greyish sandstone image is now installed in a Śiva temple. It shows the god standing with a prominent gloriole behind the head. Its border is bedecked by a floral scroll. The god bears a flat cylindrical crown over the central human head and wears earrings, *ekāvali, aṅgadas, valayas, vaijayantīmālā,* and a lower garment. The boar head emerging diagonally above the left shoulder may be seen but the lion face on the right is damaged. The god holds a conch in the proper left hand and an indistinct object (perhaps a fruit) in the normal right. The rear arms are broken but seem to have been disposed in a suspended position and bifurcated from the front ones at the elbow level like the Gupta examples. On the proper left of the god stands a female figure holding a lotus in the right hand. Her left hand is akimbo. She may be Lakshmī. The male figure on the other side is perhaps an *āyudha-purusha.* Because of an indifferent state of preservation, it is not possible to discern all details and identify these attendant figures properly.

Vaikuṇṭha from Kaithal is comparatively a better-preserved image though all details cannot be made out even here (Pl. 79). Carved out of coarse-grained dark greyish sandstone and measuring 65 x 40 cm, it shows the god standing to front with slightly splayed out feet. There is a protrusion between the feet but it cannot be said with certainty if there was any figure carved here. A bold plain halo exists behind the head. A not very high *kirīṭa-mukuṭa, kuṇḍalas,* torque, sacred thread, bracelets, *vanamālā,* lower garment secured by a simple girdle, etc. can be seen on the person of the god. The lion face on the proper right and boar face on the left are also quite clear. The normal right hand of the god holds a lotus and the left a conch. The rear hands are placed over personified mace and disc respectively. Gadādevī stands holding a lotus in her right hand with left akimbo. Round thick upper end of the mace, however, seems to have been carved behind her head over which is placed the back right hand of the god. Chakra-purusha stands with his right hand raised to the level of the shoulder and left akimbo. A spoked wheel (*chakra*) behind his head serves as his nimbus. Stylistically, this image may be placed in *circa* 7th century C.E.

The period of seventh through 9th century saw the evolution of small portable plaques of deities. Such plaques have been recovered from various parts of the country. Probably because of more mobility, people wanted to carry small portable representations of their deities with them when they moved away from their places. Small portable plaques therefore became a necessity. These plaques were generally not very sophisticated and fine in execution. A small figure measuring 14 x 6 cm, probably of schist but badly besmeared by paint, is fixed on the lintel of the doorway of the main entrance of Shri Darya Singh's house at Hat in district Jind. Most of the details have been concealed by the paint but the heads of lion and boar attached to the placid human face wearing a crown with a lotiform gloriole behind the head leaves little doubt to its being a Vaikuṇṭha image. The *vaijayantīmālā* and the lower left hand placed on enface discus (probably on the head of the Chakra-purusha) may also be discerned. The other details can be known only after cleaning the image properly. Stylistically, this figure may also be dated to *circa* 7th century C.E.

Agroha, located about 22 km from Hisar on the highway to Sirsa, has yielded three small plaques. Only one of these is complete (Pl. 80). It shows Vaikuṇṭha carved in low relief standing frontally wearing a two-tiered flat crown, probably holding a lotus and conch in the normal right and left hands and touching the club and the disc placed on the pedestals with his extra hands. The rear arms seem to bifurcate from the elbows in the tradition of the Gupta style. The god wears the *dhotī* and the long garland. A roundish halo carved with lotus petals exists behind the head. The lion and the boar faces, however, are indicated on the proper right and left of the crown by squarish and triangular projections. Another plaque, broken below the knees and on the viewer's right behind the head, with a plain halo, is rather crude in execution, but seems to be similar in concept and composition. Still a third one may only be guessed to have been similar as it has suffered mutilation in its upper half and proper right side (Pl. 81). Carved crudely, yet these plaques betray the popularity of Vaikuṇṭha worship by the masses during the early medieval period.

Another small plaque obtained from Sirsa is now preserved in HARDAM (Index No. 1/165). Carved on slate stone and measuring 7 x 7 cm, it shows engraved lines simulating the lion and boar faces on the sides of the central human face of the god. The artist may have made an attempt to carve out the Vaikuṇṭha form.

A crudely executed Vaikuṇṭha image of coarse-grained greyish sandstone measuring 25 x 20 cm, obtained from Pinjaur,[157] also shows the deity wearing a flat cylindrical crown, torque, sacred thread, earrings, bracelets, *vaijayantīmālā*, etc. standing in a frontal pose (Pl. 82). A part of the central human face below the right eye and the boar face on proper left are slightly damaged. The normal right hand, too, is mutilated. The rear right hand holds the mace and the left disc. Conch is held in the normal left hand. A very roughly carved attendant figure may be seen on the left of the god and another probably existed on the corresponding right side. The image is broken below the knees of the god and is marked by crudity, frontality and squatness. Stylistically, the image may be placed in *circa* 8th century C.E. A Vaikuṇṭha-head (along with lion and boar faces) in a *śukanāsa* assignable to *circa* 9th century is also known from Pinjaur.[158]

A medieval *Chaturvyūha* image was recovered during 1922-23 from Rājā Karṇa kā Kilā near Kurukshetra. The image, bearing the additional faces of a boar and a lion, showed the god holding the mace, the lotus, the conch and the wheel in the four-hands in the *pradakshiṇā* order.[159] Nothing, however, is known about the whereabouts of this image now.

The most beautiful of all the Vaikuṇṭha images from Haryana, however, comes from Prāchī Śiva temple, Pehowa (Pl. 83) now preserved in HARDAM (Acc. No. 1/533).[160] The buff-colored sandstone sculpture measuring 52 x 29 cm shows the tricephalous octomanous deity standing gracefully in *dvibhaṅga* wearing a *kirīṭamukuṭa*, ear ornaments, *graiveyaka*, sacred thread, armlets, beaded *kaṅkaṇas*, anklets and an *ardhoruka* tied firmly with a waist-band having *muktā-dāmas* dangling down on the thighs and knees. There is a *tilaka* mark on the forehead. A beautiful long garland adorned with lotus flowers at intervals hangs down from behind the back of the god gracefully. On the proper right of the placid human face, which bears a beatific expression, is the lion face and on the other side the boar face. The fourth face at the back may only be presumed. The front right hand is held in the gesture of reassurance and the others hold a discus, a sword and an arrow respectively. The proper left hand holds a conch, the second hand is placed on the thicker end of the mace, the third holds a scutum and the fourth one is broken but can be presumed to have held a bow. This arrangement of the attributes is unique and is not found in any known iconographical text. Near the feet of the deity, stand in a symmetrical posture the *āyudha-purushas* (Śaṅkha-purusha and Chakra-purusha) accompanied by female attendants or the Lord's consorts Śrī and Bhūdevī on the receding projections of the pedestal. Above in the corners are shown the garland-bearing *vidyādharas*. The absence of *Kaustubha-maṇi* and the *śrīvatsa* symbol on the chest, the gloriole at the back and the mount Garuḍa is noteworthy.[161]

Sparing use of jewelry, graceful curves and contours, pleasing composition, detailed care given even to the incidental figures and delicacy of chisel work bestow a distinctive character to this one of the loveliest reliefs from Haryana. Stylistically, it bears great affinity to the Pratihāra idiom and may be assigned to the first half of the 10th century C.E. Verily this image is one of the masterpieces of the medieval art of Haryana and bespeaks highly of the artistic accomplishment of the region.

Chandimandir near Chandigarh has also yielded a Vaikuṇṭha image (Pl. 84). Measuring 53 x 39 cm, it is preserved in HARDAM (Acc. No. 15/84). Unfortunately, the image is broken below the neck portion. The placid human face with a three-peaked beaded crown and earrings, lion and boar faces on the proper right and left and a beautiful eight-petalled halo with beaded rim behind the head give us an idea as to how the original image looked like. We cannot have any idea of the number of hands and their attributes as well as the attendant figures but the backslab represents the ten incarnatory forms. Matsya and Kūrma may be seen on the proper right and left of the celestial figures in the flying pose bearing a high cylindrical crown at the apex of the lotiform gloriole. Varāha and Narasiṃha have been carved on stele to the left and right of the halo, Vāmana and Buddha just above Varāha, and Paraśurāma and Kalki (with sword in his right hand) above Nṛisiṃha. The standing figures on the extreme upper corners may represent Rāma and Balarāma though their attributes are absent. The depiction of the ten incarnatory forms as subsidiary figures indicates that the Vaikuṇṭha was considered as the Supreme Being by the worshippers. The extreme ends show *makara* and *gaja-vyāla* motifs. The image may be assigned to *circa* 10th century C.E. on stylistic grounds.

An 11th century Vaikuṇṭha image (Pl. 85), now housed in the Gurukula Museum, Jhajjar,[162] probably comes from Asandh in district Panipat.[163] The god stands to front on a lotus seat placed on a *pañcha-ratha* 'quincunx' pedestal with a slight flexion at the waist. The right foot of the god is in *sama* pose whereas the left one is splayed out. The central placid human face bears a beaded and bejeweled *kirīṭamukuṭa* adorned with a *kīrtimukha*. As usual, the lion face exists on the proper right and the boar face on left. A beautiful eight-petalled lotus halo is carved behind the head. Earrings, necklet and necklace, *śrīvatsa, yajñopavīta,* armlets, double beaded bracelets, lower garment secured by an elaborate girdle, *vaijayantīmālā,* etc. are all indicative of the profuse ornamentation which is a characteristic feature of almost all contemporary images from the region. The four-armed god holds a lotus and a conch (with spiral head pointing upwards) in the normal hands while the rear ones are placed on the heads of the *āyudha-purushas* – that of Gadādevī on the proper right and Chakra-purusha on the corresponding left, both standing in *atibhaṅga* and looking at their Lord. On the extreme receding projections of the pedestal stand Śrī and Sarasvatī (?). The diminutive female figure seated between the feet of the god may be identified with Pṛithvī. Near the additional lion and boar faces appear Brahmā and Śiva respectively. Both are seated in *lalitāsana* on lotus seats and are quadrimanous. Their front hands are disposed in *abhaya* and holding waterpot while the rear pair supports ladle and book in case of Brahmā and trident and snake in case of Śiva. At the level of the waist are shown on lotus seats devotees in profile with folded hands. The main as well as the accessory figures are carved with great care.

Vaikuṇṭha-Lakshmī

Pinjaur has yielded two Vaiuṇṭha-Lakshmī images also. One is now housed in HARDAM. Almost complete, it shows the four-handed Vaikuṇṭha with placid human face in the center to which are attached the lion and boar faces on the proper right and left of the god, standing in a little flexion (*ābhaṅga*). The god is shown as holding a conch in his normal left hand. The proper right hand, which seems to have been disposed in the posture of reassurance (*abhaya*), is damaged slightly. The *pralamba* 'suspended' left hand is placed on a disc while the right is placed on the mace. Below these attributes are shown kneeling human figures in profile at the feet, probably the *āyudha-purushas,* who are seldom depicted in such a posture, or the devotees. The god wears the usual ornaments including the long garland. To the proper left of the god stands Lakshmī flexioned slightly towards her spouse. Her right hand and head have suffered mutilation. She is wearing an elegant *ekāvali* 'pearl string' and necklace. Her suspended left hand holds the scarf which is winding down from the left shoulder to her knee. A waistband secures her undergarment. The backslab, which is common to both, is rounded behind the heads of the divine couple and is engraved with round halos. The plain halos, the rounded backslab, sparse ornamentation, single projection of the pedestal, proportionate figures, etc. make it a work of about 7th century C.E.

The second image of Vaikuṇṭha-Lakshmī (Pl. 86), measuring 72.5 x 40 cm, is now indiscriminately fixed in the wall of a Śiva temple at Lalru, a small village 33 km from Chandigarh on the main road to Ambala, where it is said to have been brought from Pinjaur by a local contractor. Encrusted with whitewash, oil, dust and vermilion, it is not in a good state of preservation. The god bears a long cylindrical crown over the human head to which is appended the lion and boar faces. He also wears *karṇa-kuṇḍalas* 'earrings', necklet with a pendent, sacred thread, armlets, *vaijayantīmālā*, undergarment, elaborate waistband, sash on the thighs, etc. The quadrimanous god supports the mace in the back right hand and the discus in the upper left. The normal left hand holds the conch. The proper right hand, which is lost completely, can be visualized to have been disposed in *abhaya*. Between the feet seems to be the figure of Pṛithvī. An acolyte holding a discus in his left hand and placing the right on the respective thigh is shown standing near the right foot while the hybrid Garuḍa, with upper half human body and lower half avian, occupies the corresponding position on the other side. The vehicle of the Lord is shown in *añjali-mudrā* (with folded hands). To the left of the god stands Lakshmī, slightly turned to her lord, holding a lotus flower in her right hand and a *kuṇḍikā* (nectar flask) in the suspended left. She also wears a jeweled crown, *karṇa-kuṇḍalas*, necklet with a pendent string falling down to the left waist from between her breasts, armlets, wristlets, undergarment secured by a waistband with sash on the thighs and pendent strings falling on the knees, and the long garland. There are chisel marks on the body of the god as if the image was left unfinished due to some reason. That Pinjaur was a center of art is borne out by other unfinished images also. On stylistic grounds, this image may be dated to *circa* 9th century.

It is notable that from nowhere in India has any image of standing quadrimanous Vaikuṇṭha accompanied by Lakshmī and attended by four-armed avianthropomorphic Garuḍa and Chakra-purusha been found. This, thus, is a unique image in the whole realm of plastic art in India.

Vaikuṇṭha-Viśvarūpa

Jasat (76° 42' N. Lat. and 28° 19' 06" E. Long.) is a small village situated about 40 km southwest of Gurgaon which has yielded the only known image of Vaikuṇṭha-Viśvarūpa from Haryana.[164] This image (Pl. 87) is made of greyish sandstone and measures 62 x 38 cm. It has now been fixed indiscriminately along side an image of Pārvatī in the outer wall of the house of Shri Ram Kumar Singh, the *nambardar* of the village. The image is badly mutilated and bears small holes all over. It shows the god standing gracefully in a slight flexion flanked on either side by three attendant figures and with twenty-four small standing figures carved on the backslab in four registers. The central human face of the god is mutilated but the cylindrical crown on the head can be made out clearly. To the central face are appended two animal faces in profile on the right and left of the god. Though these faces have been carved in somewhat stylized way without much difference in their appearance, yet they may be recognized as lion and boar faces as seen in other Vaikuṇṭha images. There may have been two more faces just above these but it is difficult to to make out anything certain because of the mutilated and worn out condition of the relief. Just behind the central face of the god is depicted Brahmā, with central bearded face and juvenile side faces, seated probably in *lalitāsana* and holding his usual attributes of rosary, ladle, book and waterpot in his four hands in the *pradakshiṇā* order. The four panels on the backslab show four figures each flanking the god in the uppermost panel, with three each in the next two panels, and two each in the lowermost panel. The figures are so small that it is difficult to make out their details, more so because of the indifferent state of preservation of the relief. The total number of these figures is twenty-four and since all of them are shown as wearing long garlands, they may be recognized as the twenty-four *vibhavas* of Vishṇu.

The quadrimanous god rests his normal right hand on his right thigh. This is very unusual feature not met with anywhere else. His back right hand is shown as taking an arrow from a quiver, which is placed vertically on the ground behind the *āyudha-purusha*. Such depiction of the hand and quiver in a Viśvarūpa image is also quite interesting. In the extra left hand, the god supports a bow from its middle, damaged slightly, and the principal left hand holds the conch horizontally. Such a configuration of the attributes has not been prescribed by any iconographical text nor seen in any other image. It thus seems to be the innovation of the artist.

Besides the tall cylindrical crown on the central human head, anguine ear ornaments, armlets, wristlets, long garland, *dhotī* secured by a waistband, etc. may also be seen on the person of the god. The whole figure was carved on a *pañcha-ratha* (having five projections) pedestal. The main figure occupies the central projection and two *āyudha-purushas* too have been shown near the feet. They may be identified with Śaṅkha-purusha and Padma-purusha. The next projections on both the sides are occupied by two female figures, Śrīdevī and Sarasvatī. The extreme projection on the proper right shows another male figure wearing a cylindrical crown and holding a staff in his left hand, probably Balarāma. The corresponding left projection, lost now, may have represented Garuḍa.

The image has suffered considerable mutilation. In its original form, it must have been an elegant piece. It may be dated to *circa* 10th century C.E. on stylistic grounds. The depiction of the four-hands and their attributes, the depiction of twenty-four *vibhava* forms and the six attendant figures are interesting iconographical features. This is the first and the only Viśvarūpa figure from Haryana known as yet.

We thus see that a total of sixteen images of Vaikuṇṭha have come down to us. Two of these represent Lakshmī also and one is the Viśvarūpa form. No *Garuḍa-vāhī* Vaikuṇṭha has, however, been discovered from Haryana as yet. This form was quite popular in Himachal Pradesh.

Of the complete images, none except the Jhajjar example shows clearly the earth goddess depicted between the feet of the god or on the pedestal. Showing Pṛithvī between the feet of Vaikuṇṭha and the fourth face at the back (optionally of course) were the characteristics of the images from Kashmir and Himachal.[165] The complete absence of the fourth face indicates that the people of Haryana were adherents of the Bhāgavata-Sāttvata school and not the Pāñcharātra of the Kāśmīrāgama. A specimen from Baijnath in Uttaranchal shows the earth goddess between the feet on the coils of snake.[166] The Earth goddess was depicted below the feet on the pedestal of the Vaikuṇṭha images in central India.[167] Mathurā Vaikuṇṭha images did not carry the figure of Pṛithvī and the fourth terrific face at the back at all. Being close to Mathurā, Haryana seems to have followed the Mathurā tradition but the Pahari influence does seem to have percolated as seen in the Jhajjar example. Vaikuṇṭha from Pehowa shows some affinity with the Jhalawar specimen.[168] Vaikuṇṭha Viśvarūpa from Jasat has the subsidiary figures in four rows on the back-slab, a feature that is noticeable on the 10th century Vaikuṇṭha Viśvarūpa image in the Gwalior Museum[169] and the 12th century Vaikuṇṭha-paṭṭa from Khajuraho.[170] The tradition of depicting the subsidiary figures on the upper half part of the back slab in four registers may have traveled from Haryana towards the south. Vaikuṇṭha Viśvarūpa images from Mathura, Deogarh, Kanauj, Bhuili, etc. show busts or heads on the fringe of the halo[171] but this feature is not to be seen in Jasat image. Hayagrīva, equated with Kapila and Pradyumna in the Pāñcharātra texts,[172] and seen in some of the Vaikuṇṭha Viśvarūpa images (Baijnath, Deogarh, Kannauj, Śamalājī, etc.) is also completely absent in Haryana.

Haryana artists thus seem to have been affected by the winds blowing from various directions. They, however, did not follow the Pahari, Rajasthani, Uttaranchal or Uttar Pradesh traditions blindly and made use of their own creative genius as is evidenced by the examples described above. In their turn they probably influenced the central Indian depictions.

Fragments of Vishṇu Images

Besides the images described above, a large number of medieval images of Vishṇu and their fragments have been obtained from Haryana. Those bearing Acc. Nos. are preserved in the Department of Archaeology and Museums, Haryana. Important amongst them are the following.

1. Vishṇu from village Kherdi (Tahsil Kalanaur, District Rohtak), 42 x 23 cm, showing *abhaya*, mace, discus, and conch in the four-hands, datable to *circa* 8th century C.E.[173]
2. Part of an architrave with Vaishṇava attendant from village Kharawar (Tahsil Sampla, Dt. Rohtak), 22 x 20 cm, 9th-10th century.[174]
3. A hand from Marhanwala holding a horizontally placed conch (9.5 x 6.5 cm).
4. The uppermost part of an image from Marhanwala showing the flying *vidyādharas* supporting a cylindrical crown above the gloriole.
5. A part of a sculpture from Marhanwala represents only a hand with a conch (11.5 x 5.5 cm), greenish black sandstone, Acc. No. 1/12.
6. A very fragmentary relief of brownish sandstone from Marhanwala, 24.5 x 20 cm, showing a hand holding the mace and the other disposed in *abhaya*. Acc. No. 1/13.
7. Attendant figure of Śrī from Marhanwala, 23 x 10 cm, black sandstone, Acc. No. 1/197.
8. Attendant figure of Garuḍa in black sandstone from Marhanwala, 22 x 20 cm (Acc. No. 1/196).
9. Śaṅkha-purusha from Bhīmā Devī Temple, Pinjore, 9 x 8 cm, greenish sandstone, Acc. No. 1/43.
10. Bust with *śrīvatsa* and sacred thread, same place and material, 18 x 13 cm, Acc. No. 1/45.
11. Proper left hand side fragment of the pedestal of a Vishṇu image (Pl. 88) once fixed in the wall of the Kabir Chaurā temple at Pinjore, 30 x 25 cm, showing three attendant figures with conch held in Vishṇu's lower left hand (partly visisble). The three figures may be identified as those of Śaṅkha-purusha, Chakra-purusha, and Garuḍa, all having beautiful coiffures and wearing ear ornaments, necklaces, armlets, wristlets, and elegant habiliments. The first two figures hold the respective attributes in their right hands near the chest with left resting on the thighs. Garuḍa holds a snake in his left hand near

the chest and salutes with his right, raising it above his head. At the feet of the Śaṅkha-purusha is a seated female figure in three-fourths profile with hands clasped in adoration. The fragment may be dated to *circa* 9th century C.E.[175]

12. Fragment of a colossal sandstone Vishṇu image showing Padma-purusha holding a lotus flower in his right hand held near the chest. The piece measures 43 cm in height and is dated to *circa* 9th century C.E. It is now preserved in the Museum of the Department of Ancient Indian History, Culture and Archaeology, Kurukshetra University, Kurukshetra (Acc. No. 72.3).[176]
13. A 9th century sandstone fragment from Pinjore (ht. 14 cm) showing the right hand of Vishṇu holding a blossomed lotus flower is also preserved at the same place (Acc. No. 72.52).[177]
14. In the same museum is preserved another sandstone fragment of Vishṇu image from the same site and datable to the same period, 37 cm in height (Acc. No. 72.4), showing Śaṅkha-purusha standing in *tribhaṅga*, holding a conch in his right hand with left placed on the respective thigh. Bearing *dhammilla* type of coiffure, he wears *karṇa-kuṇḍalas*, neck ornaments, armlets, *kaṅkaṇas*, and *muktā-yajñopavīta*. A part of the *vaijayantīmālā* is also visible. Above the head of this *āyudha-purusha* may also be seen the hand of Vishṇu wearing a bracelet holding the conch.[178]
15. Another sandstone piece representing the lower portion of a Vishṇu image of *circa* 10th century from Pinjore measuring 42 x 33 cm is also housed at the same place (Acc. No. 72.12). It shows the feet of the deity in the center flanked by Śaṅkha and Padma-purushas on the left and right side respectively, followed by badly mutilated female figures on the receding recesses of the *pañcha-ratha* pedestal.[179]
16. The same museum houses another sandstone fragment of a Vishṇu image from Pinjore measuring 27 x 18 cm (Acc. No. 72.115) showing a crocodile face surmounted by a *vidyādhara* couple.[180]
17. Attendant figure with a *vanamālā*, Pinjore, 29 x 25 cm, greenish sandstone, Acc. No. 1/72.
18. Vishṇu's upper right hand holding the mace with *gajamukha* and *śārdūla-vyāla* in the Bhīmādevī Temple complex at Pinjore.
19. Black sandstone stele with Brahmā from the same site, 14 x 9 cm, probably a part of a Vishṇu image.
20. Attendant figures, Ratpur (Kalka), 27 x 17 cm, black sandstone, Acc. No. 1/88.
21. A stele (14 x 9 cm) in black sandstone showing Brahmā from Ratpur (Acc. No. 1/91) also seems to be a part of some Vishṇu image.
22. Chakra-purusha and Śrī (?), Ratpur, 18.5 x 12 cm, black sandstone, Acc. No. 1/94.
23. Lower part of a Vishṇu image from Chandimandir, 10 x 9 cm, greenish sandstone, Acc. No. 20/84.
24. Vishṇu's mace, Chandimandir, 6.5 x 5.2 cm, greenish sandstone, Acc. No. 27/84.
25. Vishṇu's discus, Chandimandir, 22 x 17 cm, greenish sandstone, Acc. No. 22/84.
26. Vishṇu's thighs showing a girdle, sash, sacred thread and left hand holding the conch horizontally, Chandimandir, sandstone, 10 x 9 cm, Acc. No. 1/466.
27. Part of Vishṇu's pedestal with male and female attendants, Mansa Devi, Panchkula, 28.5 x 21.5 cm, Acc. No. 1/467.
28. A stele showing Brahmā, probably a part of some Vishṇu image, from Panchkula, brownish sandstone, 23 x 18 cm (Acc. No. 1/280).

29. Śaṅkhapurusha, Panchkula, 24 x 9 cm, greenish sandstone, Acc. No. 1/281.
30. A small 15 x 10 cm brownish buff sandstone Vishṇu head from Bita (Acc. No. 1/259) in district Ambala shows an intricately bedecked crown placed over the frizzled locks.
31. Bust of Vishṇu with *śrīvatsa* and lotus in one of the right hands, Jalmajri (Naraingarh, Ambala), 11 x 11 cm, greenish black sandstone, Acc. No. 1/271.
32. Chakrapurusha and a female attendant, Kurukshetra, 12 x 7 cm, white spotted red sandstone, Acc. No. 1/276.
33. A Vishṇu head wearing a cylindrical crown and a part of the left shoulder intact is known from Tisimbli in district Kurukshetra. The crown is adorned by diamond and disc motif with ornamental chains coming out of the hub of the latter.
34. A buff sandstone lower part of a Vishṇu image from Pehowa, 33 x 30 cm, belonging to *circa* 10th-11th century C.E. is now preserved in the Dept. of AIHC & Archaeology of the Kurukshetra University (Acc. No. 75.275). It shows the legs of the god below the knees along with a part of the long garland resting on the lotus seat in the center of a *pañcha-ratha* pedestal, flanked by Śaṅkha and Chakra-purushas on his right and left. The figures on the receding recesses are mutilated beyond recognition.[181]
35. Vishṇu's hand with mace and stele, buff sandstone, Pehowa.
36. Vishṇu's hand with discus and stele, buff sandstone, Pehowa.
37. Vishṇu's hand holding a conch from Amin near Kurukhetra, buff sandstone, 12 x 5 cm
38. Vishṇu head from Amin, sandstone, 12 x 10 cm, beautiful face with crown.
39. Vishṇu head from Pehowa, buff sandstone, 15.5 x 7.5 cm.
40. Pedestal with Chakra-purusha from Pehowa, buff sandstone, 22 x 15 cm, broken into two parts, Acc. Nos. 1/351-52.
41. Chakra-purusha and Bhūdevī, Pehowa, 22 x 15 cm, buff sandstone, Acc. No. 1/358 (very elegantly carved Pratihāra piece).
42. *Pedyā* with Gaṅgā and Śaṅkha-purusha, Pehowa, height 25 cm, buff sandstone.
43. A doorjamb with Yamunā and attendant figure on the *pedyā* and amorous couples in the panels above (Fig. 6).
44. A small buff sandstone piece (height 15 cm) with Kalki

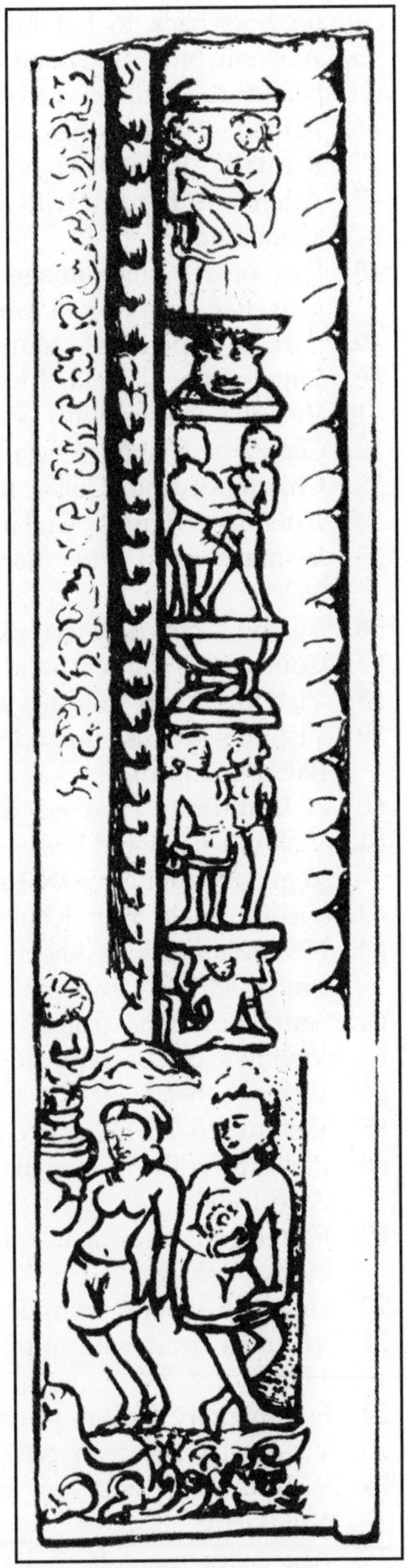

Fig. 6. Doorjamb of a Vishṇu temple, Pehowa.

on horseback to left holding sword in right hand above the head, Pehowa.

45. A small buff sandstone head measuring 9 x 4 cm from Baholi in district Karnal is a beautiful Pratihāra piece.
46. Attendant figures (probably *āyudhapurushas,* Śrī and Balarāma, all very much mutilated, Kirmach (Karnal), 26 x 16 cm, sandstone.
47. Attendant figures with a part of Vishṇu's *vanamālā,* Kohand (Karnal), 38 x 17 cm, sandstone.
48. Part of a Vishṇu image pedestal showing two small attendant figures from a village near Panipat, 11 x 5 cm, buff sandstone (now housed in HARDAM).
49. Part of a pedestal, Muradnagar.
50. Lintel with Garuḍa, Muradnagar.
51. Vishṇu's discus with Śiva from Jaintipur.
52. *Chakra* of Vishṇu, Gujjar Kheri, 9 x 11 cm, white marble, Acc. No. 1/171.
53. Chakrapurusha, Gujjar Kheri, 9 x 11.5 cm, buff sandstone, Acc. No. 1/178.
54. Attendant figures, Gujjar Kheri, 32 x 22 cm, buff sandstone, Acc. No. 1/185.
55. Vishṇu's hand with discus, Gujjar Kheri, 10.5 x 4.5 cm, buff sandstone, Acc. No. 1/382.
56. Vishṇu's conch, Gujjar Kheri, 8 x 3.5 cm, buff sandstone, Acc. No. 1/384.
57. Conch in Vishṇu's hand, Gujjar Kheri, 9 x 7 cm, buff sandstone, Acc. No. 1/159.
58. Vishṇu's hand holding a conch, Gujjar Kheri, 7 x 5 cm, buff sandstone.
59. Vishṇu's discus, Bulandpur Kheri (Gujjar Kheri complex, studded in the wall of Mr. Balbir's house).
60. A beautifully crowned Vishṇu head, Bulandpur Kheri, 14 x 7 cm, schist.
61. Vishṇu's head and bust, Ganaur (probably from Gujjar Kheri, now in a private possession, Regn. No. HRN/SON-10).
62. Vishṇu head from Khubru, 17 x 10 cm.
63. Headless image of kneeling Garuḍa with folded hands, wearing a snake thread, Rasidan (Jind), 48 x 31 cm, pink sandstone.
64. Śaṅkha-purusha from Jind, buff sandstone, 18 x 9 cm (Acc. No. 1/386).
65. Vishṇu's discus with stele showing Umā-Maheśvara, Hat, sandstone.
66. Vishṇu's head, 19 x 6 cm, fixed in the wall of Pt. Parsanna's house at Hat.
67. Vishṇu's head, 10 x 6 cm, fixed in the wall of Ram Krishna Prajapat's house at Hat.
68. Pedestal with Śrī and Balarāma from Sampla, 25 x 20 cm, black marble, Acc. No. 1/27 (pl. 89).
69. Part of an architrave with Vaishṇava figure, 22 x 20 cm, at Kherawar in the Sampla block, Rohtak.
70. Head of Vishṇu from Rohtak, buff sandstone, 21.5 x 15.5 cm (Acc. No. 1/255).
71. Vishṇu's head with aureole from Rohtak, brownish sandstone, 12.5 x 11 cm (Acc. No. 1/258).
72. Fragmentary Chakra-purusha from Jhansua, black marble, 12.5 x 9 cm (Acc. No. 1/301).
73. Vishṇu's hand with *gadā,* Kasan, 9.5 x 4 cm, buff sandstone, Acc. No. 1/314.
74. Vishṇu image with feet and left arm broken, Kasan, 15 x 9 cm, blackish sandstone, Acc No. 1/310.
75. Arm with mace from Kasan, 9 x 8 cm, buff sandstone, Acc. No. 1/322.
76. A broken image of Vishṇu of the late Gupta idiom from Ahrwan (district Faridabad), 69 x 24 cm, on the bank of Suraj Kund to the north of the village.

77. A small plaque of Vishṇu at the same place at Ahrwan.
78. A broken image of Vishṇu of the late Gupta style housed in the dilapidated Devī Temple near Suraj Kund at Ahrwan in district Gurgaon.
79. Śaṅkhapurusha, Jind, 18 x 9 cm, buff sandstone, Acc. No. 1/386.
80. Attendant figures, Safidon (Jind), 11.5 x 5.5 cm, brownish black sandstone, Acc. No. 1/137.
81. Vishṇu head from Uchana (Jind), buff sandstone, 19.5 x 9.5 cm, face badly damaged (Acc. No. 1/562).
82. A brown sandstone piece, 9 x 8 cm, from Ghasola near Dadri in district Bhiwani (Acc. No. 1/435), depicts the deity standing on a lotus placed on the central offset of a *triratha* pedestal, flanked by *āyudhapurushas* (probably Gadādevī on his proper right and Chakrapurusha on left and wearing a *vanamālā*. The figure is broken above the thighs.
83. Vishṇu's hand with conch, exact provenance not known (collected by Registering Officer, Hisar), 6 x 4 cm, buff sandstone, Acc. No. 48/84.
84. *Nāga-śākhā* of a doorjamb, Agroha, 13 x 8cm, from trench No. XF-1 (1979-80).
85. Nāga attendant with folded hands, Agroha, 7 x 4.5 cm, trench No. XD-8 (1979-80).
86. Legs of Vishṇu, Agroha, 22 x 15.5 cm, trench No. XA-9, layer 3 (1979-80).
87. Nāga attendant, Agroha, 12 x 5 cm, surface find.
88. Vishṇu, Agroha, 17 x 9 cm, trench No. XE-6, layer 7 (1979-80).
89. Upper portion of Vishṇu, Agroha, 9 x 6.5 cm, trench No. XG-8, layer 1 (1979-80).
90. Legs of Vishṇu, Agroha, 7 x 5 cm, trench No. XG-7, layer 5 (1979-80).
91. Vishṇu head from Hansi, buff sandstone, 24 x 13 cm (HSR/HRN-57).
92. Vishṇu head from Ahirwan (Fatehabad), buff sandstone, 13 x 13 cm, Acc. No. 1/130.
93. Vishṇu head from Hisar division, buff sandstone, Hisar division (exact provenance not known), 9 x 4 cm, Acc. No. 50/84.
94. A buff sandstone head measuring 17.5 x 8 cm from Sirsa (Acc. No. 1/109) shows a very high and elaborate crown placed over the combed hair of the god with beatific expression and having a *tilaka* mark on the forehead, which simulates the vertical third eye of Śiva.
95. Proper right hand side pedestal of a Vishṇu image representing an *āyudha-purusha*, Śrī and Balarāma holding the plough in his left hand, Sirsa, 11.5 x 8 cm, coarse grained red sandstone.
96. Crown resembling the spire of a medieval temple, Sikanderpura (Sirsa), 17.5 x 13.5 cm, buff sandstone, Acc. No. 1/116.
97. Vishṇu's hand with conch, Hisar Division, sandstone, 6 x 4 cm, Acc. No. 1/490.
98. Vishṇu's discus and *vidyādhara*, Hisar Division, sandstone, 25 x 24 cm.
99. Vishṇu in an arched niche, brownish red sandstone, 38 x 27 cm, from Kanwari (Acc. No. 1/246).
100. Śrī (?) and Balarāma as attendants, Kalayat, 48 x 27.5 cm, schist.
101. Also from Kalayat, fixed in the outer wall of the Kapila Muni Temple, is a schist pedestal of Vishṇu showing two feet in *sama* pose on a lotus *pīṭha* borne by a female figure (Pṛithvī?) on her upraised hands. She is depicted in flying posture. Lotus buds and calyxes are shown with stalks as if issuing from her back. Two nāga-female figures with serpentine lower parts are shown as adoring her with folded hands. On the receding projection on the proper left are the feet of another figure, probably attendant. Stylistically, the figure may be assigned to *circa* 10th century C.E.
102. The part of the pedestal illustrated by Punia[182] and described as Ardhanārīśvara is actually a fragment of a Vishṇu image showing on the proper left hand side attendant

figures of Balarāma with a plough in his right hand and left akimbo, followed on the receding projection by a female figure (Bhūdevī) with a devotee in a kneeling pose in profile at the feet of Balarāma facing towards the deity. The immediate figure of an *āyudha-purusha* near the god on his left seems to have been broken. It measures 19 x 12.7 cm and is datable to *circa* 12th century C.E.

103. Four-armed standing Vishṇu is shown as *lalāṭa-bimba* on the *uttaraṅga* of a 12th century doorframe found at village Mayan in district Rewari.[183]

This is no way to be taken as a complete and comprehensive list as many fragments of Vishṇu images still lie unknown and unrecognized in many collections, museums and temples at different places in Haryana.

GARUḌA

Garuḍa, the vehicle of Vishṇu, is generally identified by scholars with divine bird Tārakshya (*Ṛigveda* X.178, 1) and Garutmān having beautiful wings (*Divyaḥ sa suparṇo Garutmān* - *ṚV* I.164, 64; *AV* IV.6, 3).[184] It is, however, in the *Mahābhārata*[185] that we get details of the story of his birth and the events connected therewith. He is described in the epic as the son of sage Kaśyapa and Vinatā. Being the son of Vinatā, he is known as Vainateya also. One of the major achievements of Garuḍa was the release of his mother from the deceitful captivity of his stepmother Kadrū by forcibly snatching away the pitcher of nectar (*amṛita-ghaṭa*) from Indra for the Nāgas, the sons of Kadrū (Ādi Parva 34.8-20). An interesting episode of his agreeing to be the vehicle of Vishṇu has also been narrated in the epic (Ādi Parva 33.13-16). The *Brahma Purāṇa* (III.95) describes Garuḍa as the brother of Aruṇa (*Vinatāyāstu dvau putrau vikhyātau Garuḍāruṇau*), the charioteer of Sūrya.

The *Vishṇudharmottara*[186] describes Garuḍa as having the body of a bird with powerful wings, round eyes and face, owl-like nose and legs like that of a kite, and four-arms holding an umbrella and pot of ambrosia with the remaining two hands folded. When, however, he is shown as carrying Vishṇu, two of his hands should be engaged in supporting the feet of the Lord. He should have a potbelly and wear all ornaments. *Śrītattvanidhi*[187] prescribes for him human body and face, raised nose, two wings and two hands in *añjali-mudrā,* left knee resting on the earth, flabby thighs, and head bedecked with snakes. *Mānasāra* provides for Garuḍa a *karaṇḍa-mukuṭa* (*mukuṭaṃ sakaṇḍakam*) and two hands in *añjali-mudrā*. The *Śilparatna,*[188] however, prescribes two or eight arms for Garuḍa. In the former case one should be disposed in *abhaya*, and in the latter case he should hold mace, conch, discus, sword and snake. The *Agni Purāṇa* and the *Aparājitapṛichchhā* provides human body for Garuḍa, and the latter text says that he should have a raise pointed nose (*Nara-rūpa samākāraḥ tuṅga-tīkshaṇ=ogra-nāsikā*).[189]

We have described above the figures of Vishṇu with Garuḍa as the vehicle where the latter is generally shown as holding a snake with one hand and the other raised above the head in salutation. Another feature of these figures has been the hair raised in horrification. Sometimes Garuḍa is shown having a snake canopy also. Some fragmentary and independent figures of Garuḍa are described below.

A small figure from Narnaund, broken below the legs and much worn out, shows Garuḍa with folded hands and probably having a snakehood (Pl. 90). The fragmentary figure from Marhanwala, 22 x 20 cm (Acc. No. 1/196), depicts him with a beautiful coiffure and in *añjali-mudrā* (Pl. 91). Garuḍa from Sagwan (Tosham) measuring 35 x 19 cm and made of buff sandstone (Acc. No. 1/73), though very much worn out and damaged, shows Garuḍa in *ālīḍhāsana,* holding a snake in the right hand, bearing a spread out hair-coiffure and wearing all ornaments (Pl. 92). A lintel with Garuḍa is fixed in the Jaintidevi Temple at Jaintipur indicating the existence of a Vaishṇava shrine. We have two figures of Garuḍa from Pehowa. One is an architectural piece but the other seems to have been an independent image. It shows Garuḍa in *vīrāsana* on a pedestal with right knee placed on the ground and folded and the left foot placed firmly on the ground (Pl. 93). Unfortunately the head is broken. Garuḍa is shown as wearing a snake necklace, a snake girdle and also holding a snake in his surviving left hand. The broken right hand seems to have been raised above. This image probably stood independently in a Vishṇu temple.

The most interesting example, however, comes from Gujjar Kheri (Regn. No. HRN/AMB-624). Made of buff sandstone, it is 24 cm high in its extant form. Garuḍa is shown here in human form wearing *patra-kuṇḍalas*, *ekāvali*, *keyūras*, *valayas*, and a tight fit short (*ardhoruk*) secured with a twisted rope-like girdle (Pl. 94). He is holding a vase in both of his hands near his left shoulder. Important, however, is the fact that on the upper right arm (Pl. 95) there are marks of a wing, now lost. The wing on the left shoulder may partially be seen behind the vase, which is decorated very tastefully and seems to represent the *pūrṇa-ghaṭa* or the *amṛita-kalaśa*. The hair coiffure, however, is of some interest as it betrays *udīchya* style. Garuḍa is standing slightly turned to his left. The legs are broken below the thighs. The general features and style of this figure may very well be compared with Garuḍa carrying Lord Vishṇu from Gujjar Kheri (Pl. 47) described above. Stylistically this figure may be assigned to *circa* 9th century C.E. It may be pointed out that figures of Garuḍa carrying the nectar pot are very rare. So this figure from Haryana is of considerable importance.

The foregoing account makes it amply clear that there is no scarcity of Vaishṇava images in Haryana. Like many other parts of the country, Vaishṇava images began to be carved here from Kushāṇa period onwards. There, however, seems to be a sudden efflorescence during the medieval period, particularly the Pratihāra period. The largest number of standing icons indicates that it was the most popular form. In spite of the similarity of posture, these images show variety within the same type. Depiction of two, four or six attendant figures is a characteristic feature. Most of the images show Vishṇu as holding the mace in the upper right hand and discus and conch in the rear and normal left hands, which conforms to the Nārāyaṇa form of Vishṇu according to the *Padma Purāṇa* and Trivikrama according to the *Rūpa-Maṇḍana*. Since the latter text actually belongs to a period later than the images in question, we feel that it was the Nārāyaṇa form, which was popular in the region during the Pratihāra period. These subsidiary figures invariably represent personified attributes, of which Śaṅkha and Chakra purusha are the commonest, Padma-purusha is rare and Gadādevī is almost absent. Vishṇu's spouses holding lotuses are also almost invariable when the accessory figures increase to four or more. Garuḍa and Balarāma are the additional attendants in the most developed images. Garuḍa is always represented in anthropomorphic form. Some icons show the depiction of the incarnatory forms on the back slab. Of the four-hands of Vishṇu, the normal right is shown either in *abhaya* or in *varada*, the rear right and left hold the mace and disc while the normal left is shown with a conch. The mace is generally depicted with thicker end upward, the disc is sometimes depicted with a fillet issuing forth from its hub and the conch is held vertically or horizontally or even slantingly. Kosli Vishṇu, however, varies and represents the Nārāyaṇa form as it shows conch, lotus, mace and disc in the four hands in the *pradakshiṇā* order. The much-damaged image with conch in the rear right hand from Pinjore, too, might have represented another form but the other broken hands render any certitudinous conclusion impossibility.

The depiction of Brahmā and Śiva on the stele in most of the medieval images indicates the importance given to the Hindu Trinity by the devotees of Vishṇu. Only the Kaithal *sthānaka* Vishṇu shows the depiction of the planetary divinities. *Navagrahas* were, however, popularly depicted on the Śeshaśāyī reliefs.

Yoga-Nārāyaṇa images are rather rare. Lakshmī-Nārāyaṇa image from Panipat reveals the novel feature of the depiction of an elephant under the foot of Lakshmī. Images of Vaikuṇṭha, with Lakshmī and in Viśvarūpa form also, were quite popular. They show impact from the hilly region of Kashmir and Himachal Pradesh on the one hand and from Mathura on the other, but the artists were not mere imitators and made certain innovations also.

The images and their fragments enumerated above represent the largest number of the icons of any single deity in Haryana. Evidently, there were numerous temples dedicated to Vishṇu in early and medieval Haryana but unfortunately time and iconoclastic zeal of some of the invaders have wiped them out completely. Their number may only be guessed from the foregoing account, which is in no way all comprehensive and complete.

Notes and References

1. A.A. Macdonell, *Vedic Mythology*, Varanasi, 1963, pp. 37-39.
2. *Ibid.*
3. A. B. Keith, *Indian Mythology*, New York, 1964, p. 29.
4. E.W. Hopkins, *The Religion of India*, Boston, 1895, p. 56.
5. J. Gonda, *Aspects of Early Viṣṇuism*, Utrecht, 1954, pp.1-11.
6. *Śatapatha Brāhmaṇa* XIV. 1,1; *Aitareya Brāhmaṇa* I.1; etc.
7. These Vṛishṇi heroes were later deified and identified with *parama, mahat* or *jīva, manas* and *ahaṃkāra*—the first four creative principles of the Sāṅkhya system. The Purāṇas attach some allegorical meanings also to these names. For details, see *VSMRS*, pp. 4ff.; Kalpana Desai, *Iconography of Viṣṇu*, New Delhi, 1973, pp. 3 and 37 ff.; N.P. Joshi, *Iconography of Balarāma*, New Delhi, 1979, pp. 10-15; etc.
8. *VSMRS*, p. 5.
9. *Mahābhārata* XIII, Vishṇu-Sahasranāma Stotra, verse 28: *Chaturātmā chaturvyūhaśchaturdaṃshṭraśchatur-bhujaḥ.*
10. Kalpana Desai, *loc. cit.*
11. *VSMRS*, p. 4.
12. *Epigraphia Indica* XVI, pp. 25 ff.; D.C. Sircar, *Select Inscriptions*, Vol. I, Calcutta, 1965, pp. 90-91.
13. Sircar, *op. cit.*, pp. 88-89.
14. Prof. K.D. Bajpai and S.K. Pandey, *Malhar*, Sagar, 1978, pl. X.
15. *Journal of the Numismatic Society of India*, Vol. XXXV, pp. 73-75.
16. *Manusmṛiti* II. 23.
17. *Ibid.*, II. 19.
18. *Ibid.*, II. 21.
19. V.S. Agrawala, *Vāmana Purāṇa: A Study*, Varanasi, 1964, pp. 31-32.
20. For details, see *Mahābhārata*, Vana Parva, Tīrthayātrāparvan. Also see V.S. Agrawala, *Mahābhārata kī Nāmānukramaṇikā* (Hindi), Gorakhpur, V.S. 2016; *Kurukshetra Māhātmya*, Kurukshetra, 1973; etc.
21. Sircar, *loc. cit.* The discovery of some uninscribed square copper coins of 2nd century B.C.E. from Taxila (*BMC*, p. 229) containing the representation of pillar surmounted by a fan-palm capital which symbolically represents Saṃkarshaṇa [*DHI*, p. 385] also indicates the popularity of Vaishṇavism in the north-west India during the 2nd century B.C.E. See for details Brajesh Krishna, "The Development of Vaishnavism in Ancient Punjab", *Proceedings, Punjab History Conference, 17th Session*, Patiala, 1983, pp. 48 ff.

22. *Journal of the Numismatic Society of India*, Vol. XXXV, pp. 73-75.
23. Allan, *op. cit.*, p. 281, pl. XVI. 5.
24. Swami Omanand Sarasvati, *Ancient Seals of Haryana*, Jhajjar, V.S. 2031, no. 189.
25. *Ibid.*, Nos. 187-94; *JNSI*, XXXV, pp. 95-97; etc.
26. Devendra Handa, "Vṛishni Copper Coins From Punjab", *Numismatic Digest*, Vol. VII, parts I & II, 1983, pp. 11-21.
27. Devendra Handa, "Seals and Sealings from Punjab—A Study", *Panjab University Research Bulletin (Arts)*, Vol. XV, no. 1, April, 1984, pp. 163-64.
28. Sarasvati, *op. cit.*, Nos. 30 and 60.
29. Devendra Handa, "Agroha Revisited," in *Prācī-Prabhā: Perspectives in Indology (Essays in honour of Professor B.N. Mukherjee)*, ed. D.C. Bhattacharyya & Devendra Handa, New Delhi, 1989, p. 244, pl. 34.b.
30. It is, however, notable that Vishṇu has been represented on a gold coin of Kushāṇa Vāsudeva I.
31. J.F. Fleet, *Inscriptions of the Early Gupta Kinga and their Successors*, Corpus Inscriptionum Indicarum, Vol. III, Varanasi, 1970, pp. 269-70, pl. XL. A.
32. *Ibid.*
33. Suvira Jayaswal, *The Origin and Development of Vaiṣṇavism*, Delhi 1967, p. 180.
34. Alexander Cunningham, *Archaeological Survey Report*, Vol. V, p. 141; B.Ch. Chhabra (September 1964), *op. cit.*, pp. 319-22, pls. III-V.
35. V.S. Agrawala, *Harshacharita: Eka Sāṃskṛitika Adhyayana* (Hindi), 2nd ed., Patna, 1964, p. 206.
36. *Epigraphia Indica* I, pp. 184-90.
37. *Ibid.*, p. 242.
38. *Ibid.*, XXI, p. 295.
39. S.R. Phogat, "Inscriptions of Haryana", *Journal of Haryana Studies*, Kurukshetra, Vol. IX, 1977, p. 21.
40. *Ibid.*, p. 22 ... *dhyātvā Vishṇum suroge tu viśvamupagata(ḥ) Vīrachandraḥ sukarmmā.*
41. *Ibid.*, p. 21 ... *vichintya Vishṇum Vishṇuharirito gataḥ svarggam 954.*
42. D.R. Bhandarkar, "Hansi Stone Inscription of Pṛthvīrāja, (Vikrama) Samvat 1224", *Indian Antiquary*, Vol. XLI (1912), pp. 17-19.
43. M. Nazim, *The Life and Times of Sultan Mahmud of Ghazna*, Delhi, 1971, pp. 103-04. Also see Edward Sachau, *Albearni's India*, Vol. I, p. 117.
44. Brajesh Krishna, *op. cit.*, p. 50.
45. R.C. Agrawal, "Krishna-Balarama as Attendant Figures", *Indian Historical Quarterly*, Vol. XXXVIII, no. 1 (March, 1962), pp. 86-87.
46. Doris Srinivasan, "Early Krṣna Icons: The Case at Mathura", *Bulletin of Museums & Archaeology in U.P.* (henceforth *BMA*), Nos. 21-24 (June 1978-Dec. 1979), p. 15, fn. 59.
47. N.P. Joshi, "Ekānaṃśā in Early Kuṣāṇa Art", *Journal of the Indian Society of Oriental Art*, N.S., Vol. II (1967-68), pp. 34-36, and "Devī Ekānaṃśā in Kuṣāṇa-Kālīna Mūrtiyāṃ", *BMA*, no. 1 (March, 1968), pp. 24-29. Also see P.L. Gupta, "Ekānaṃśā and her Images", *Journal of the Bihar Research Society*, Vol. LIV (1969), pp. 229-44. These reliefs have also been discussed and illustrated recently by D. Srinivasan. For details see *BMA*, Nos. 21-24, pp. 6 ff., figs. 1-3.
48. C.R.P. Sinha, "Some Important Sculptural Acquisitions of the Patna Museum", *JBRS*, Vol. LIII (1967), pp. 165-70 and "The Kuṣāṇa Art of Bihar", *Ibid.*, Vol. LI (1973), pp. 65-74.
49. Srinivasan, *op. cit.*, p. 7.
50. *Ibid.*
51. N.P. Joshi, *op. cit.*, p. 28 fn. Krishna Kumar, "An Ekānaṃśā relief of Ellora", *Journal of Indian History*, Vol. XLIV, pt. III, S. no. 132 (Dec., 1966), pp. 831-38; Kalpana Desai, *Iconography of Viṣṇu*, New Delhi, 1973, p. 138, fig. 102 etc.
52. *Mahābhārata* (Gita Press ed.), Sabhā Parva, Ch. 38, pp. 820-21, compares Ekānaṃśā flanked by Kṛishṇa and Baladeva with Lakshmī between the two elephants. Gaja-Lakshmī images have remained very popular in India from *circa* 3rd-2nd century B.C.E. to the medieval period. It seems that these Gaja-Lakshmī images appropriated the Ekānaṃśā concept and that is why the images of Ekānaṃśā become rare after the Kushāṇa period.

53. Cf. Kalpana Desai, *op. cit.*, fig. 3.
54. The Karachi Museum specimen too may have been four-handed of which the rear hands are not clear because of the indifferent state of preservation.
55. The feature of the depiction of the conch like an *amṛita-ghaṭa* in early Vishṇu images of Mathurā has already been noted by V.S. Agrawala in his article "Brahmā, Viṣṇu and Śiva in the Muthurā Art," *Journal of the U. P. Historical Society*, Vol. XXII, p. 105.
56. Incorporated from Devendra Handa, "A Kuṣāṇa Ekānaṃśā Relief from Haryana", *Bulletin of Museums & Archaeology in U.P.*, no. 29-30, pp. 41-43.
57. Cf. N.P. Joshi, *Mathurā kī Kalā* (Hindi), Mathura, 1965, fig. 63.
58. *Ibid.*, figs. 60-61; Kalpana Desai, *op. cit.*, figs. 1-3, 31 and 59.
59. Cf. N.P. Joshi (1965), *op. cit.*, Fig 62.
60. For details see Devendra Handa, "A Kushāṇa Image of Garuḍavāhī-Vishṇu from Haryana," in *Aspects of History and Culture*, edited by R.D. Choudhary and Shri Bhagwan Singh, Delhi, 1991, pp. 175-79, figs. 1-2.
61. Sheela Devi, *Art Tradition in Haryana (upto 1200 A.D.)*, Unpublished Thesis, Kurukshetra University, Kurukshetra, 1975, pp. 128, 200, 252, pl. XXV.B.
62. Kalpana Desai, *op. cit.*, p. 8, fig. 3.
63. Silak Ram (*Archaeology of Rohtak and Hissar Districts, Haryana*, Unpublished Thesis, Kurukshetra University, Kurukshetra, 1972, p. 214, pl. XXII. B) describes it as belonging to Śaka-Kushāṇa times.
64. Sheela Devi, *op. cit.*, 208, 250-51, pl. XXXIII. B.
65. R.C. Agrawala, "Prāchīna Hariyānā," *Ājakala*, Nov. 1968.
66. It belongs to Mr. Gulshan Bharadwaj of Jind.
67. For pleats of the lower garment on the raised pubic region carved in a similar fashion see J.C. Harle, *Gupta Sculpture*, Oxford, 1974, pls. 87 (Vishṇu from Bhinmal) and 112 (Narasiṃha from near Mathura).
68. Dharmpal Singh Punia, *Archaeology of Mahendragarh and Gurgaon Districts (Haryana)*, Unpublished Thesis, Kurukshetra University, Kurukshetra, 1976, p. 188, pl. XXIII.B. Punia regarded it as Kushāṇa image. It has, however, to be noted that Kushāṇa images are carved in the round and generally show a mace in the rear right hand. Both these features are absent in the present image. The conch-blowing pose, too, is not seen in any of the known Kushāṇa Vishṇu images. The figures may be compared with Vishṇu blowing the conch, datable to the 8th century C.E. now in the Nalanda Museum (Kalpana Desai, *op. cit.*, fig. 12).
69. Harle, *op. cit.*, p. 18 and pls. 8, 18, 61, 62, etc.
70. Devendra Handa, "Vaishṇava Icons from Haryana," *Panjab University Research Bulletin (Arts)*, Chandigarh, Vol. XVI, no. 2 (October 1985), p. 130, fig. 5. Earlier, it was noticed by Amar Singh [*Archaeology of Karnal and Jind Districts (Haryana)*, Unpublished Thesis, Kurukshetra University, Kurukshetra, 1981, pp. 180-181 pl. XIX.A].
71. It was first noticed by S.P. Shukla, "Thanesar: Past Revealed", *Haryana Review*, August 1977, pp. 6-9. Also see V.N. Datta & H.A. Phadke, *History of Kurukshetra*, Kurukshetra, 1984, p. 92 and pl. III.
72. Handa (1985), *op. cit.*, pp. 133-34, fig. 10.
73. *Ibid*, p. 145, fig. 30.
74. D.C. Bhattacharyya (1981), *op. cit.*, pp. 43-45.
75. *Ibid.*, p. 45.
76. *Ibid.*, p. 42.
77. N.P. Joshi, *Catalogue of the Brahmanical Sculptures in the State Museum, Lucknow*, part I, Lucknow, 1972, pp. 82-83, pl. 2, figs. 4-5.
78. Devendra Handa (1989), *op. cit.*, p. 245.
79. D.C. Bhattacharyya (1981), *op. cit.*, pp. 41-43, fig. 13. V.C. Ohri, *Sculpture of Western Himalayas*, Delhi, 1991, pl. 5.48 assigns it to Jammu and dates it to 11th century.
80. This seems to have been a popular style of depiction of the conch and may also be seen in many other sculptures. For details see Handa (1985), *op. cit.*, figs 5, 6, 8, 9, 14, 15, etc.

81. Handa (1985), *op. cit.*, p. 144, fig. 29.
82. 81a. *Ibid.*, fig. 31.
83. Now in the private collection of Mrs. Raj Kumari Malik, it bears Regn. no. HRN/AMB-872.
84. Kalpana Desai, *op. cit.*, figs. 18-20.
85. J.N. Banerjee in *The Age of Imperial Kanauj* (ed. R.C. Majumdar and A.D. Pusalkar) Bombay, 1955, p. 335. See also R.C. Agrawala, "Early History and Archaeology of Kurukshetra and Ambala Division", *The Indian Historical Quarterly*, Vol. XXXI, No. 4 (Dec. 1955), p. 21. The present priest of the temple, Shri Dinesh Kumar Shastri, however, does not know that this sculpture was ever brought from Siwan.
86. *Ibid.*
87. D.C. Bhattacharyya (1981), *op. cit.*, pp. 62-63.
88. *Ibid.*, p. 63.
89. It is now in a private collection. It bears Regn. no. HRN/KAR-410.
90. It belongs to Mr. Pawan Kumar Mittal of Kalka.
91. The image was first noticed by Amar Singh (*op. cit.*, p. 182, pl. XX.A) but he wrongly described the attendant figures on the extreme recesses as devotees.
92. Manmohan Kumar, *Archaeology of Ambala and Kurukshetra Districts (Haryana)*, Kurukhetra University, Kurukhetra, Unpublished Ph. D. Thesis, 1978, p. 140, pl. VI.B.
93. Shukla (1983), *op. cit.*, p. 40, pl. XXXI, 5.
94. Handa (1985), *op. cit.*, p. 141, fig. 28.
95. Devendra Handa, "Some Unpublished Sculptures from Gujjar Kheri (Haryana)," *Panjab University Research Bulletin (Arts)*, Vol. XVII, no. 1 (April 1986), p. 110, fig. 1.
96. *Ibid.*, p. 111, fig. 4. Cf. Matsya in the Udaipur Museum (Kalpana Desai, *op. cit.*, Fig.56).
97. Amar Singh, *op. cit.*, p. 181, pl. XX.B.
98. D.C. Bhattacharyya (1981), *op. cit.*, p. 63.
99. Devendra Handa, "Sculptures from Beri," *Roopa-Lekha*, Vol. LIII (march 1982), pp. 36-46.
100. Devendra Handa, "An Interesting Vishṇu Image from Jasat," *Pañchāla*, Kanpur, Vol VIII (1995), pp. 135-37.
101. *IAR*, 1958-59, p. 71, pl. XXXIV.A; B.N. Sharma, "An Inscribed Image of Viṣṇu-Saṃkarṣaṇa from Mehrauli," *Journal of the Indian Society of Oriental Art, New Series*, Calcutta, Vol. VI, pp. 67-71.
102. Handa (1986), *op. cit.*, p. 110, fig. 2.
103. Devendra Handa, "Medieval Brahmanical Stone Sculptures from Punjab," *Roopa-Lekha*, Vol. LIV (March 1983), p. 26, Fig.7.
104. Kalpana Desai, *op. cit.*, p. 141.
105. *Mahābhārata* III. 81,150:
    Nārāyaṇaṃ chābhigamya Padmanābhamarindram/
    Śobhamāno mahārāja Vishṇulokaṃ prapadyate//
106. Devendra Handa, "A Vishnu Sculpture From Kurukshetra", *Journal of Haryana Studies*, Vol. I, no. 2, 1969, pp. 1-2 & fig. See also Shukla (1983), *op. cit.*, p. 47, pl. XL.1.
107. Amar Singh, *op. cit.*, pp. 183-84, pl. XX. C.
108. Amar Singh (*Ibid.*) had identified this figure as Madhu or Kaiṭabha.
109. Shukla (1983), *op. cit.*, p. 41, pl. XXIV.1.
110. Punia, *op. cit.*, pp. 212 ff., Pl XXX. B.
111. For explanation, see Ratan Parimoo, "Sculptures of Sheshashayin Vishnu: Some Iconographical Problems", in *India Studies (Essays Presented in Memory or Prof. Niharranjan Ray*, ed. Amita Ray et al) Delhi, 1984, p. 152.
112. Punia, *op. cit.*, p. 214; Sheela Devi, *op. cit.*, pp. 129 and 179, pl. XIX. A.
113. D.C. Bhattacharyya (1981), *op. cit.*, pp. 52-54, fig. 19.
114. *Ibid.*, p. 52.
115. *Ibid.*, p. 53.
116. *Ibid.*, pp. 53-54.
117. *Ibid.*,pp. 51-52, fig. 18.

118. Bhattacharyya (*Ibid.*) regards the halo as covering partially Lakshmī's head also and the crown as *karaṇḍa-mukuṭa.*
119. *Ibid.*, p. 52.
120. *Ibid.*, p. 51.
121. *Mahābhārata* (Gita Press edition) VI. 775, 15.
122. *Bhāgavata Purāṇa* III. 16, 6 and VIII. 5, 4; *Vishṇu Purāṇa* III.1, 41.
123. The concept of devotion perhaps owes its origin to the practice of hero worship. Vāsudeva, Saṃkarshaṇa, Aniruddha, Pradyumna and Sāmba were the five heroes of the Vṛishṇi clan whose rule in Punjab is evidenced by their coins, seals and sealings (See for details, John Allan, *BMC*, pp. clv-clvii and 281, pl. XVI.5; Swami Omanand Sarasvati, *Ancient Seals of Haryana*, Jhajjar, VS 2031, Nos. 187 ff; Devendra Handa, *Studies in Indian Coins and Seals*, Delhi, 1985, pp. 66-74 etc.). Later on, the Vṛishṇi heroes were deified and incorporated in the cosmological speculations of the Sāṅkhya system. The *Mbh.* (BORI ed. XII. 326, 38-39) tells us that "The principal heroes of the cult were identified with the four creative principles of the Sāṅkhya system – *parama, mahat* or *jīva, manas* and *ahaṃkāra*. Vāsudeva is the highest *nirguṇātmaka*, from him emanates Saṃkarshaṇa in the form of *jīva* or individual soul, from him emanates Pradyumna in the form of *manas* and lastly comes Aniruddha identified as *ahaṃkāra*" (Vide Kalpana Desai, *op. cit.*, p. 3).
124. Regarding various incarnatory forms of Vishṇu mentioned in different texts see *DHI*, pp. 388-92. The *Mahābhārata* identifies Kapila with Sūrya (III.3, 181), Agni and the founder of the Sāṅkhya philosophy (III, 211, 21: *Agni sa Kapilo Sāṅkhyayoga-pravartakaḥ*) and as a form of Vāsudeva (III, 106, 2). The *Bhāgavata Purāṇa* (I. 3, 10) and the *Rāmāyaṇa* (ed. G. H. Bhaṭt, Oriental Institute, Baroda, I.39, 26-28) regard Kapila to be an incarnation of Vishṇu. See also Cf. S.N. Chaturvedi, "The Vaikuṇṭha Images and the Khajuraho Inscription of Yaśovarmmadeva," *Journal of the Indian Society of Oriental Art*, New Series, Calcutta, Vol. XIV (1984-85), pp. 47 ff.
125. *Mbh.* XIII.326, 43.
126. *Jayākhya Saṃhitā* (GOS, Baroda, 1931) VI. 73-76:
    Anādinidhanaṃ devaṃ jagatsrashṭāramīśvaram /
    Dhyāyechchaturbhujaṃ vipre śaṅkhachakragadādharam //
    Chaturvaktraṃ sunayanaṃ sukāntaṃ padmapāṇinam /
    Vaikuṇṭhaṃ Narasiṃhāsyaṃ Vārāhaṃ Kapilānanam //
    Śuklaṃ khageśvarārūḍhaṃ sarvābharaṇabhūshitam /
    Sarvalakshaṇasampannaṃ mālyāmbaradharaṃ vibhum //
    Kirīṭakaustubhadharaṃ karpūrāliptavigraham /
    Sūryāyutasahasrābhaṃ sarvadevanamaskṛitam //
127. *Vishṇudharmottara Purāṇa* (GOS, Baroda, 1958) III. 44, 43-45:
    Ekamūrtidharaḥ kāryā[o] Vaikuṇṭhetyābhiśabditaḥ /
    Chaturmukhaḥ saḥ karttavyaḥ prāguktavadānanaḥ prabhuḥ //
    Chaturmūrtiḥ sa bhavati kṛite mukhachatushṭaye /
    Pūrvaṃ saumyamukhaṃ kāryaṃ yattu mukhyatamaṃ viduḥ //
    Karttavyaṃ siṃhavaktrābhaṃ tu dakshiṇam /
    Paśchimaṃ vadanaṃ raudraṃ yattadaiśvaryamuchyate //
128. *Ibid.*, III. 44, 11-12:
    Saumyaṃ tu vadanaṃ pūrvaṃ Nārasiṃhaṃtu dakshiṇam /
    Kāpilaṃ paśchimaṃ vaktraṃ tahtā Vārāhamuttaram //
129. *Ibid.*, III. 44, 12-13 as suggested by Kalpana Desai, *op. cit.*, p. 39, and fn. 21.
130. *Aparājitapṛichchhā* 219, vv. 25-27:
    Pravachmyatha Vaikuṇṭhaṃ so'ashṭabāhurmahābalaḥ /
    Garuḍasthaśchaturvaktraḥ karttavyaḥ śāntimichchhitā //
    Gadākhaḍgau bāṇachakre dakshiṇe'strachatushṭayam /
    Śaṅkhaṃ kheṭo dhanuḥ padmaṃ vāme chāstra chatushṭayam //
    Pūrvataḥ purushākāro Narasiṃhaścha dakshiṇe /
    Apare Śrīmukhākāro Vārāhāsyastathottare //

131. *Rūpamaṇḍana III.* 52-54:
Vaikuṇṭhaṃ cha pravakshyāmi so'shṭabāhurmahābalaḥ /
Tārkshyāsanaśchaturvaktraḥ karttavyaḥ śāntimichchhitā //
Gadāṃ khaḍgaṃ śaraṃ chakraṃ dakshiṇe syāachchatushṭayam /
Śaṅkhaṃ kheṭaṃ dhanuḥ padmaṃ vāme dadyāchchatushṭayam //
Agrataḥ pururshākāraṃ Nārasiṃhaṃ cha dakshiṇe /
Aparaṃ strīmukhākāraṃ Vārāhasya tathottare //
132. *Devatāmūrtiprakaraṇa* V. 91-93.
133. *Vāṅachakre* of the *Aparājitapṛichchhā* has been changed to *'śaraṃ chakraṃ'* in the *Rūpamaṇḍana.* Also *'śrīmukhaṃ'* of the former becomes *'strīmukhaṃ'* in the latter.
134. Pratapaditya Pal, *Vaiṣṇava Iconology in Nepal – A Study in Art and Religion,* Calcutta, 1985, p. 108.
135. *Saumyasiṃhādibhūyishṭhavaktrabhrdaiśchaturmukha /*
Dvitrimukhabhedā vā mūrtirekaiva pūjyate //
Samvṛitā parivāraiḥ svairvinā vā sarvakāmadā /
Yatra tantrāntaraṃ tatsyāchchaturtha chaturānana //
As quoted by Pal, *loc. cit.,* p. 176.
136. *Mukhyānuvṛittibhedena yatra siṃhādayastu vai /*
Chatustridvayādkenaiva yogenābhyarchite tu vai (natu) //
Saṃvṛitāḥ parivāreṇa svena svenonvi(sthi)tāstu vā /
Yachchhaktyārādhitaṃ sarvaṃ viddhi tantrāntarṃ tu tat //
(Paushkarasaṃhitā 38, 300-02)
137. *Epigraphia Indica,* Vol. I, p. 124:
Dadhānānekāṃ yaḥ kiripurushasiṃhobhayajusham /
Tadākārochchhedyāṃ tanumsuramukhyānajavarāt //
Jaghāna trīnugrān jagati Kapilādīnavatu vaḥ /
Sa Vaikuṇṭhaḥ kaṇṭhadhvanichakitaniḥśeshabhuvanaḥ //
Dr. L.K. Tripathi has rightly amended the last compound word of the first line to *'Kiripurushasiṃhānanajushaṃ'* ("Restoration of the First Verse of the Yaśovarman Stone Inscription," *Bhāratī,* Varanasi, No. 4, 1960-61, pp. 115 ff.). This has further been amended to *'Kiripurushasiṃhāravajusham'* recently (For details see, Devangana Desai, *The Religious Imagery Of Khajuraho,* Mumbai, 1996, Appendix B, p. 212).
138. V.S. Pathak, "Vaikuṇṭha at Khajuraho and Kāśmīrāgama School," *Journal of the Madhya Pradesh Itihāsa Parishad,* Bhopal, no. 2, 1960, pp. 9 ff. and "Vaikuṇṭha kā Vikāsa," in *Rāshṭrakavi Maithilīśaraṇa Gupta Abhinandana Grantha,* Calcutta, 1959, pp. 532 ff.
139. Devangana Desai, *op. cit.,* pp. 211-17.
140. *Ibid,* p. 53. Pathak, *op. cit.,* p. 11; H. Daniel Smith, *A Descriptive Bibliography of the Pāñcharātrāgama,* 2 Vols., GOS Nos. 25 and 168, Baroda, 1975 & 1980 respectively.
141. *Rājataraṅgiṇī* of Kalhaṇa, Eng. tr. by R. S. Pandit, Sahitya Academi, New Delhi, 1977 (reprint), VI, 300, 305.
142. *Ibid.,* VIII, 2433.
143. N.P. Joshi, *Catalogue of the Brahmanical Sculptures in the State Museum, Lucknow,* part I, Lucknow, 1972, pp. 116-16. Also see *East and West,* New Series, Vol. 22, Nos. 1-2 (March-June 1972), pp. 41-43, figs. 1-4; Debala Mitra, "Vishṇu Chaturmūrti Images in Hari Rai Temple at Chamba," in *Arts of Himachal Pradesh* (ed. V.C. Ohri), State Museum, Simla, 1975, pp. 2-3. She, however, assigns the image to 1st century B.C.E. See also Chaturvedi, *op. cit.,* pp. 48-49.
144. T.S. Maxwell, *Viśvarūpa,* Delhi (OUP), 1988, pp. 125ff.
145. N.P. Joshi, *Mathurā kī Mūrtuikalā* (Hindi), Mathura, 1965, pl. 38. There are examples even of *Chaturvyūha Śakti* (Kushāṇa, Mathurā), Śiva (Kushāṇa, Musanagar, U. P.) and other deities showing emanatory busts coming out of the shoulders. For details and illustrations see T.S. Maxwell, *op. cit.*
146. Kalpana Desai, *op. cit.,* pp. 40- 41.

147. *Ibid.*, pp. 40-47.
148. Maxwell, *op. cit.*, p. 31.
149. K.P. Poonacha, M.V. Visweswara and T.M. Kesava, "An Interesting Inscribed Makara Torana From Huli, District Belgaum," in *Facets of Indian Civilization: Recent Perspectives – Essays I Honour of Prof. B.B. Lal* (Chief Editor Jagat Pati Joshi) Vol. II, Aryan Books International, New Delhi, 1997, pp. 448-53 and pls. 55.9 & 10.
150. Information from Dr. Deen Bandhu Pandey, BHU, Varanasi.
151. If the main central figure with a club, *vanamālā* and *kirīṭa-mukuṭa* may be identified with Vāsudeva-Kṛishṇa and the figure emanating from his right shoulder holding a wine-cup in his left hand and probably also a canopy of serpent hoods as Saṃkarshaṇa, then the identification of the complete original image as a plastic representation of the Pāñcharātra *chatur-vyūha* cosmogonic metaphor seems to be quite certain.
152. R.G. Bhandarkar, *op. cit.*, pp. 1-41.
153. Mora Well Inscription of Śoḍāsa refers to the five Vṛishṇi heroes – *Bhagavatāṃ Vṛishṇīnāṃ pañchavīrāṇāṃ pratimāḥ*. (*Epigraphia Indica*, Vol. XXIV, p. 194 ff). Some Vṛishṇi seals/sealings and copper coins have also been discovered from Sunet near Ludhiana in Punjab (Swami Omanand Sarasvati, *Ancient Seals of Haryana*, Jhajjar, VS 2031, no. 189; *Journal of the Numismatic Society of India*, XI, pp. 87-91; Devendra Handa, *Studies in Indian Coins and Seals*, Delhi, 1985, pp. 66-74 and 99 ff). So far only one sculptural representation of the five Vṛishṇi heroes has been known from Kondamotu in Andhra Pradesh. For details see Abdul Wahid Khan, *An Early Sculpture of Nṛsiṃha*, Hyderabad, 1964, pl. I.
154. The connection between the Bhāgavata and Pāñcharātra systems has been discussed by various scholars. See *DHI*, pp. 386-87; Kalpana Desai, *op. cit.*, pp. 2-4; W.E. Begley, *Viṣṇu's Flaming Wheel: The Iconography of the Sudarśana Cakra*, New York, 1973, pp. 17-18, 37-40 etc.
155. Maxwell, *op. cit.*, pp. x-xi.
156. For details see Devendra Handa, "Kapāla-Mocana; An Ancient Holy Place," *Purāṇa*, Vol. X, no. 2 (July 1968), pp. 148-53.
157. Now in a private collection, it bears Registration no. HRN/AMB-411.
158. Devendra Handa, "Some Unpublished Sculptures From Pinjaur," *Vishveshvaranand Indological Journal*, Vol. XIV, pt. I (March 1976), p. 115, pl. V. Like many other sculptures, this piece was subsequently shifted to Kurukshetra at the behest of the then Governor Shri B.N. Chakravarty. See S.P. Shukla (1983), *op. cit.*, p. 12, pl. III.1.
159. *Annual Report, Archaeological Survey of India, 1922-23*, p. 89, pl. V. d.
160. Devendra Handa, "Some Interesting Sculptures From Pehowa," *PURBA*, Vol. XVI, no. 1 (April 1985), pp. 130-31, fig. 3; *Pehowa*, p. 110, pl. 54.
161. All the iconographical texts invariably refer to the mount of Vaikuṇṭha.
162. Kalpana Desai, *op. cit.*, p. 42, fig. 34.
163. Sheela Devi, *op. cit.*, p. 148, pl. XIX.D.
164. For other relics from this site, see Devendra Handa, "An Interesting Vishṇu Image From Jasat (Haryana)," *Pañchāla*, Kanpur, Vol. 8 (1995), pp. 135-37 and "A Newly Discovered Viśvarūpa Image From Haryana," in *Facets of A Marwar Historian* (ed. B.L. Bhadani and Dwijendra Tripathi), Jaipur, 1996, pp. 134-37.
165. Kalpana Desai, *op. cit.*, pp. 37ff.
166. *Ibid.*, fig. 42.
167. Devangana Desai, *op. cit.*, p. 55.
168. Kalpana Desai, *op. cit.*, p. 44, fig. 39.
169. *Ibid.*, p. 46, fig. 44.
170. Devengana Desai, *op. cit.*, p. 62, fig. 61.
171. Maxwell, *op. cit.*, pls. 49, 55, 63, 69 and 70. Even the Vaikuṇṭha-Viśvarūpa from Bajaura (Kullu) shows this feature (V.C. Ohri, *Sculpture of Western Himalayas*, Delhi, 1991, Plate 2.8).
172. Devangana Desai, *op. cit.*, p. 113.

173. Mani Ram Lamba, Archaeology and History of Kalanaur Block, Dt. Rohtak, Unpublished M. Phil. Disseratation, M.D. University, Rohtak, 1987-88, p. 95, pl. XII.A.
174. Sneh Lata, Archaeology and History of Sampla Block, District Rohtak (Haryana), Unpublished M. Phil. Dissertation, M.D. University, Rohtak, 1987-88, pp. 54-55, pl. VI.D.
175. Devendra Handa (1976), *op. cit.*, p. 96, fig. 8.
176. Shukla (1983), *op. cit.*, p. 11, pl. I.1.
177. *Ibid.*, p. 12, pl. II.2.
178. *Ibid.*, p. 11, pl. I.2.
179. *Ibid.*, pl. I.3.
180. *Ibid.*, p. 12, pl. II.1.
181. *Ibid., p. 50, pl. XLIII.3.*
182. Punia (1976), *op. cit.*, pl. XXXII.A.
183. Jagdish Singh Rahar, *Archaeological Settlement Pattern of Mahendragarh and Rewari Districts (Haryana)*, Unpublished Ph. D. Thesis, M.D. University, Rohtak, 2001, p. 197, pl. XXI A).
184. Shanti Lal Nagar, *Garuḍa - the Celestial Bird*, New Delhi, 1992.
185. Ādi Parva 23.12; 31.34-35; 35.1-25.
186. *VDP*, III. 54, 2-6a:

    Tārakshyo marakataprakhyaḥ kauśikākāranāsikaḥ /
    Chaturbhujaḥ kartavyo vṛittanetramukhastathā //
    Gṛidhrorujānucharaṇaḥ pakshadvayavibhūshitaḥ /
    Prabhāsaṃsthānasovarṇkalāpena virājitaḥ //
    Chhattraṃ tu pūrṇakumbhaṃ cha karayoratāsya kārayet /
    Karadvayaṃ tu karttavyaṃ thatā virachitñjali //
    Yadāsya bhagavānpṛishṭhe chhattrakumbhadharau karau /
    Na karttavyau tu karttavyau devapādadharau śubhau //
    Kiṃchillambodaraḥ kāryasarvābharaṇabhūshitaḥ /

187. *EHI*, Vol. 1, part 2, Appendix C, p. 73:

    Upendrasyāgrataḥ pakshī guḍākeśaḥ kṛitāñjaliḥ /
    Savyajāugato bhūmau mūrdhnā cha phaṇimaṇḍtaḥ //
    Sthūlajaṅgho naragrīvastuṅganāso narāṅgakaḥ /
    Dvibāhuḥ pakshayuktaścha karttavyo Vinatāsutaḥ //

188. *Ibid.*, p. 74 – *Garutmānamṛitaghaṭagadāśaṅkhachakrāsināgānbibhrāṇaḥ.*
189. See for details Shanti Lal Nagar (1992), *op. cit.*, pp. 63 ff.

Chapter 4

Vishṇu's Incarnatory Forms

Among the Hindu deities Vishṇu has the unique quality of being credited with *avatāras* (incarnations). The term *avatāra* is applied to the act of the god coming down in the form of a man or an animal to the earth and living there till the purpose for which he had descended in the universe was fulfilled. It also sometimes denotes the assumption of different forms by the god for the attainment of particular objectives.[1] Though the earliest exposition of the theory of incarnation (*avatāra-vāda* or *vibhāva-vāda*) occurs in the *Bhagavadgītā*,[2] the origins of the concept of divine multiform, metamorphosis, transformation, and reincarnation may be traced to the time of the *Ṛigveda* and later Vedic literature where we find the pre-figuration of several later stories particularly pertaining to the Vāmana 'Dwarf',[3] Matsya 'Fish',[4] Kūrma 'Tortoise',[5] and Varāha 'Boar'[6] forms, the last three being originally connected with Prajāpati. The great epic, however, attributes the functions of the Fish, Tortoise and Boar forms to Vishṇu and contains different lists with varying numbers of the *avatāras*. Of the varied lists,[7] however, the one occurring in the Nārāyaṇīya section gives for the first time the total number of incarnations as ten mentioning Haṃsa, Kūrma, Matsya, Varāha, Narasiṃha, Vāmana, Bhārgava Rāma, Dāśarathī Rāma, Sāttvata (i.e., Vāsudeva/Balarāma), and Kalkin.[8] The *Vāyu Purāṇa*[9] also mentions the ten incarnations of Vishṇu: Yajña, Narasiṃha, Vāmana, Dattātreya, unnamed fifth belonging to Tretā-yuga, Jāmadagnya Rāma, Dāśarathī Rāma, Vedavyāsa, Vāsudeva-Kṛishṇa, and Kalkin, the future incarnation. We thus see that Buddha does not find place even in this list and Matsya, Kūrma, and Varāha are replaced by Yajña, Dattātreya, and Vedavyāsa. The first three *avatāras* (Yajña, Narasiṃha, and Vāmana) are considered as celestial, and the rest are human incarnations. *Vibhāva-vāda* seems to have undergone several stages of evolution and the Buddhist conception of the former Buddhas may have influenced the development of the conception.[10] So Buddha too was included in the list soon. The *Matsya Purāṇa* enumerates the ten *avatāras* as the three divine incarnations of Nārāyaṇa, Narasiṃha, and Vāman, besides the seven human incarnations of Dattātreya, Māndhātṛi, Rāma Jāmadagnya, Rāma Dāśarathī, Vedavyāsa, Buddha, and Kalki.[11] The *Bhāgavata Purāṇa* refers to innumerable incarnations of Vishṇu[12] but mentions twenty-two, twenty-three, and sixteen at different places.[13] The first list contains the names of (1) Purusha representing Sanaka, Sanandana, Sanātana, Sanatkumāra, etc., (2) Śaṅkara or Varāha, (3) Nārada, (4) Nara-Nārāyaṇa, (5) Kapila, (6) Dattātreya, (7) Yajña, (8) Ṛishabha, (9) Pṛithu, (10) Matsya, (11) Kūrma, (12) Dhanvantari, (13) Mohinī, (14) Narasiṃha, (15) Vāmana, (16) Paraśurāma, (17) Parāśara, i.e., Vedavyāsa, (18) Dāśarathī Rāma, (19) Balarāma, (20) Kṛishṇa, (21) Buddha, and (22) Kalkin.

The second list omits Nārada and Mohinī and adds Hayagrīva, Trivikrama, and Haṃsa. The last list omits Nos. 1, 3-7, 9, 12-13, 17 and 19-20 from the first list and Trivikrama from the second but adds the four *vyūha* forms, i.e., Vāsudeva, Saṃkarshaṇa, Pradyumna, and Aniruddha.

The *Sāttvata Saṃhitā*, an early Pāñcharātra work of *circa* 8th century C.E., enumerates the following thirty-nine incarnations of Vishṇu: (1) Padmanābha, (2) Dhruva, (3) Ananta, (4) Śaktyātman, (5) Madhusūdana, (6) Vidyādhideva, (7) Kapila, (8) Viśvarūpa, (9) Vihaṅgama, (10) Kroḍātman, (11) Baḍavāvaktra, (12) Dharma, (13) Vāgīśvara, (14) Ekārṇavaśāyin, (15) Kamaṭheśvara, (16) Varāha, (17) Narasiṃha, (18) Pīyūshaharaṇa, (19) Śrīpati, (20) Kāntātman, (21) Rāhujit, (22) Kālanemighna, (23) Pārijātahara, (24) Lokanātha, (25) Śāntātman, i.e., Buddha, (26) Dattātreya, (27) Nyagrodhaśāyin, (28) Ekaśṛiṅgatanu, (29) Vāmanadeha, (30) Trivikrama, (31) Nara, (32) Nārāyaṇa, (33) Hari, (34) Kṛishṇa, (35) Paraśurāma, (36) Rāmadhanurdhara, (37) Vedavid, (38) Kalkin, (39) Pātālaśayana.[14] This list has been copied almost verbatim in the *Ahirbudhnya Saṃhitā*.[15] The *Garuḍa Purāṇa* refers to the following twenty-two *avatāras* at one place: (1) Kumāra, (2) Yajñeśa, (3) Varāha, (4) Nārada, (5) Nara-Nārāyaṇa, (6) Kapila, (7) Dattātreya, (8) Yajña, (9) Urukrama, (10) Ṛishabhadeva, (11) Matsya, (12) Kamaṭha, (13) Dhanvantari, (14) Mohinī, (15) Nṛisiṃha, (16) Vāmana, (17) Paraśurāma, (18) Vyāsa, (19) Dāśarathī Rāma, (20) Kṛishṇa, (21) Buddha, and (22) Kalkin.[16] Elsewhere, however, this very Purāṇa[17] accepts the following order of the ten incarnations:

Matsyaḥ Kūrmo Varāhaścha Nṛisiṃho'tha Vāmanaḥ /
Rāmau Rāmaścha Kṛishṇaścha Buddhaḥ Kalki tathaiva cha //

The *Agni Purāṇa*,[18] while stating that the past and future incarnations of Vishṇu are really innumerable, also describes the ten *avatāras* including Buddha and Kalki. *Varāha Purāṇa*, too, gives the stereotyped list of the ten incarnations as mentioned by the *Garuḍa Purāṇa*, and elsewhere in the following order: (1) Matsya, (2) Kūrma, (3) Varāha, (4) Narasiṃha, (5) Vāmana, (6) Paraśurāma, (7) Dāśarathī Rāma, (8) Sāttvata, i.e., Vāsudeva/Balarāma, (9) Buddha, and (10) Kalki.[19] This order of incarnatory forms has been accepted by Pusalkar[20] and Hopkins[21] also. That this order had come to be generally accepted in about the 7th century C.E. is also proved by the Pallava Grantha inscription of the Ādivarāha Cave Temple, Māmallpuram.[22]

We thus see that though individual incarnations find mention in early literature, yet, collectively the generally accepted list may not have been finalized before the 7th century C.E. It is also notable that though individually some incarnatory forms find representation in Indian art from about the Kushāṇa period, yet, collectively the ten *avatāras* do not seem to have been represented anywhere before C.E. 1000. Huntington has tried to show that the *avatāra* theory assumed an evolutionary pattern. She states that the first three *avatāras*, viz. Fish, Tortoise, and Boar, are concerned with rescuing Manu, the Vedas, and the Earth from the waters and symbolize the emergence of life. The theri-anthropomorphic Narasiṃha is symbolic of nascent humanity. Vāmana, the dwarf, is physically underdeveloped man while Paraśurāma, Dāśarathī Rāma, Kṛishṇa-Balarāma, and Buddha represent the full potential of human qualities. Kalki, the future incarnation, may represent purity and plenitude.[23] It has, however, been rightly observed that this "pattern of evolution is purely interpretational and neither historical nor chronological in its association with Vishṇu."[24]

We now take up the history and iconography of these incarnatory forms and their representation in the art of Haryana, if any.

MATSYA

The origin of the association of fish with Vishṇu is clouded in mystery. A creature of water, the fish stands for the water of life and symbolizes the power of fertility.[25] Vishṇu was also a god of fertility,[26] and as Nārāyaṇa, he had his abode in the waters. Fecundity and association with water thus seem to be the common factors and may have provided the nexus.

The concept of the Fish incarnation seems to have originated from the legends of the great deluge of which the earliest account occurs in the *Śatapatha Brāhmaṇa*. It tells us of the story of the fish which sought Manu's protection and saved him from the great deluge of which it had forewarned him.[27] The *Mahābhārata* describes the legend in some details but the Fish here represents Prajāpati-Brahmā.[28] The Purāṇas, however, transfer the myth to Vishṇu and contain more detailed accounts which sometimes vary in minutiae.[29] The main story goes as follows. One day towards the close of the Chākshusha Manvantara, when Manu was bathing (performing rites for his manes on a river) a small fish got into the hollow of his hands and sought his protection. As foretold, Manu put her in a jar, in a pond, and finally in the ocean as she grew bigger and bigger. The great Fish forewarned Manu of the imminent great deluge because of the demon Hayagrīva stealing and destroying the Vedas fallen from the mouths of Brahmā. She also instructed Manu to take with him the necessary provisions of life, the seeds of creation, and the seven sages, and board the ship, which would appear before him. As forewarned, the deluge occurred. Manu did all as instructed and tied the ship (representing the Earth) to the horn (*śṛiṅga*) of the great Fish who steered it to a safe spot on a mountain. Also, Hayagrīva was killed and the Vedas were retrieved by the Fish.[30] Vaivasvata Manu being the only one to survive the great flood, became the progenitor of the human species for the next cycle.

According to the *Vishṇudharmottara Purāṇa*, the images of the Fish incarnation should be made in the form of a horned fish: *Śṛiṅgī Matsyastu karttavyo devadevo Janārdanaḥ*.[31] At another place it says *Matsyāvatāriṇaṃ devaṃ matsyākāraṃ prakalpayet*[32] i.e., the Matsya incarnation should be represented in the form of a fish. The *Merutantra*, however, recommends that this incarnation should be represented in a therianthropomorphic form having piscine lower half and human upper part showing four-armed Vishṇu wearing a *kirīṭa-mukuṭa* and other usual ornaments, with front hands disposed in *varada* and *abhaya* and the rear ones holding conch and disc.[33]

Kalpana Desai has noted that "Not many images of the fish incarnation have been found, and those that are available belong to the post-Gupta period."[34] Important images known so far include those of Chamba (Himachal Pradesh); Ramnagar (Jammu); Gyaraspur, Sohagpur, Garhwa, and Khajurao (Madhya Pradesh), Udaipur (Rajasthan), and Bajrayogini (Bangladesh).[35] Iconographically, however, they hardly show any peculiarity or variation.

The complete absence of any shrine dedicated to the Matsyāvatāra and the paucity of its independent images indicate the relatively lesser significant and subsidiary character of this form. Its representation in the *avatāra* panels, however, reveals that by the medieval period the Fish, and also the Tortoise incarnation, was invariably included in the stereotyped list of the ten incarnations.

Haryana has yielded a terracotta figurine of fish without any horns or Vaishṇava attributes (Pl. 96). Does it represent the Fish incarnation in the form of a simple fish as recommended by the *Vishṇudharmottara*? If it does, then it becomes the earliest representation of this *avatāra* in Haryana. It comes from Thanesar and may be stylistically assigned to the Gupta period.[36] In stone, however, the earliest representation of the Fish incarnation may be seen on the *parikara* of a (Vishṇu) image of *circa* 9th century from Gujjar Kheri showing the fish on a pillar along with other incarnatory forms (Pl. 51). The simple representation of fish may also be seen on the Vaikuṇṭha image from Chandimandir, Vishṇu image from Kosli, and a fragmentary pedestal from Musepur in district Rewari.

KŪRMA

Kūrma, the tortoise, also called Kaśyapa, is extolled in the *Atharvaveda* not only as the regulator of the sun but also as the sun itself.[37] The *Taittirīya Āraṇyaka* also refers to Kaśyapa as the eighth sun.[38] The *Śatapatha Brāhmaṇa* deals with the origin, importance, symbolism, etc. of the tortoise in some details. When Prajāpati desired to create the Earth, he compassed the Primeval Egg and the juice, which flowed from it, became a tortoise.[39] It is said that Prajāpati created the living beings having assumed the form of tortoise. The Kūrma being the same as Kaśyapa, all the creatures are said to have descended from Kaśyapa. He is thus the Lord of the Creation.[40] He is also identified with the universe of which he is the creator. The lower shell of the tortoise is compared with this world, the upper shell with the sky, and the space in between with air. The tortoise thus represents these worlds.[41] The quality of the reptile to draw all its limbs has also led to its identification with the sun (who withdraws his rays) and the Universal Soul.[42] The *Śatapatha Brāhmaṇa*[43] and the *Vājasaneyī Saṃhitā*[44] also call Kaśyapa as the Lord of the Waters. It is, therefore, clear that the tortoise symbolizes the sun and the waters and is considered to be the Lord of Creation. His connection with the sun and the waters led to the identification of Vishṇu with Kūrma in the Purāṇas.[45]

Kūrma plays an important role in the cosmogonic, cosmographic, and genealogical conceptions of Indian peoples.[46] As an incarnation of Vishṇu, however, the only important part played by it was to serve as a support of the mountain Mandara or Meru, or Śiva-*liṅga*, all of them representing the axis of the world, in the churning of the ocean a detailed account of which occurs in the two epics, with some differences of course. According to the *Rāmāyaṇa*[47], the sons of Kaśyapa from Diti and Aditi, i.e., the *Daityas* (*Dānavas*, the demons) and the *Ādityas* (*Devas*, the gods), churned the ocean to obtain nectar and the riches of the nether world using the Mandara mountain and the serpent Ananta (Vāsuki) as the churning staff and rope. The partners quarreled amongst themselves over the distribution of ambrosia and other objects that came out from the ocean. The *daityas* were ultimately defeated and killed or banished. In the *Mahābhārata*,[48] we find the gods approaching the tortoise-king (*Kūrma-rāja*) to lend his back or shell as a support to Mandara. In the Purāṇas, however, the myth is completely Vishṇnuized.

According to the *Vishṇu Purāṇa*,[49] when Indra, the king of gods, was rendered weak and inglorious as a result of Durvāsā's curse, the demons defeated the gods. Led by Agni, Indra and other gods he approached Brahmā who in turn took them to Vishṇu and implored him for help. Vishṇu advised the gods to invite the demons to churn the ocean promising them a share of nectar and other objects to be obtained from the ocean. As advised, putting various medicines (*oshadhis*) into the ocean, the gods churned the ocean with the help of the demons using Mandara Mountain as the churning staff and the serpent Vāsuki as the rope. Vishṇu supported the Mandara Mountain on his back as a tortoise. Amongst the fourteen precious objects obtained as a result of the churning were the moon, Lakshmī, Vāruṇī (wine), Kaustubha-jewel, Pārijāta (coral tree, *erythrina indica*), Surabhi (cow of plenty), Airāvata elephant, Uchchaiśśravas (the white horse), umbrella, etc. Dhanvantari came out with a vase of nectar which Vishṇu distributed only amongst the gods in the form of the enchantress Mohinī, deceiving the demons. The *Bhāgavata Purāṇa* also contains this legend.[50]

According to the *Vishṇudharmottara*[51] and the *Agni Purāṇa*,[52] the image of Kūrma is to be created exactly in the form of a tortoise. Later iconographic texts, however, describe the anthropomorphous images of the Kūrma. The *Sāttvata Saṃhitā*[53] and the *Merutantra*[54] describe Kūrma as holding conch, disc, mace, and plough in the four-hands while *Śrī-tattva-nidhi*[55] suggests that two hands of the god should be shown as holding disc and conch and the other two should be held in *abhaya* and *varada* pose.

As in the case of Matsyāvatāra, images of Kūrma incarnation are also rare. Bharat Kala Bhawan, Varanasi has an interesting 9th century image of tortoise with four-handed Vishṇu holding his usual attributes, on the neck of the tortoise.[56] In the circumambulatory of the Lakshmaṇa Temple at Khajuraho, Vishṇu with disc and mace in the rear hands is shown as seated in *yogāsana* on a tortoise.[57] The churning of the ocean scene, however, is popularly depicted in Indian art. In Haryana, no independent image of this incarnation has come out as yet but the *parikara* from Gujjar Kheri depicts the rod on the back of a tortoise being churned by two figures representing the gods and demons (Pl. 51). *Samudra-manthana* scene with Airāvata coming out of the ocean has been depicted in a mural of the Prāchī Śiva Temple at Pehowa also. It may be dated to the 19th century C.E.

VARĀHA

The antiquity of Varāha has been traced back to the *Ṛigveda*.[58] The use of the word Varāha in most of the passages, including the one in which Rudra has been described as the 'boar of the sky',[59] however, seems to be figurative (*lākshaṇika*) only.[60] U.P. Shah[61] seeks to identify Varāha with the Vṛishākapi of the *Ṛigveda*[62], but here, too, we cannot be very sure of the identification.[63] References to Varāha occur in the later Vedic literature also.[64] It is, however, in the *Śatapatha Brāhmaṇa*[65] that we get a clear reference to the assumption of the Varāha form by Prajāpati for the creation of the earth. As a boar called Emusha, Prajāpati raised up the earth and became her lord. The *Taittirīya Brāhmaṇa*[66] also refers to this myth of creation. It is said that in the beginning, nothing was to be seen except water, with a lotus-leaf standing out above it. Prajāpati, having resolved to create firm ground, thought of giving the lotus-stalk a resting-place. He then assumed the form of a boar and dived deep into the water and brought out some earth which he spread out (*prath*) on the lotus-leaf, whence originated this earth (*pṛithvī* 'that which has been spread out'), which was fastened down by him by means of pebbles.

Later, when Vishṇu, more appropriately called Nārāyaṇa, became the supreme God, the creator and ruler of the universe and upholder not only of the cosmic but also of the moral order of the world, and the doctrine of *avatāravāda* developed under the Pāñcharātra school,[67] the concept of the Boar-incarnation was transferred to Vishṇu and we get several references to this incarnation in the *Rāmāyaṇa*[68], the *Mahābhārata*[69] and the Purāṇas.[70]

The symbolism of Yajña-Varāha is associated with the Vedic-Purāṇic ideology of cosmology and different parts of the body of the Boar are compared to parts of the Vedic sacrifice (*Yajña*).[71] The *Agni Purāṇa* (49. 3) states that the installation of Varāha helps the donor to secure a kingdom and to cross the *bhava-sāgara*, the ocean of mundane existence. In the medieval period the concept of royalty or regal power was linked with the Boar.[72]

Rao[73] has given detailed account of the Bhū-varāha or Ādi-varāha and Pralaya-varāha images as enunciated in the *āgamas* and *tantras*. In the realm of art, however, though the Varāha incarnation has been represented in several forms, yet two of them are the principal modes of representation - pure theriomorphic (Varāha or Śūkara) and hybrid,[74] (i.e., therianthropomorphic, called Ādi-Varāha or Nṛi-varāha). Of these, the earliest example found so far is therianthropomorphic, a 1' 2" x 1' buff stone inscribed image discovered from Mathurā City and datable to the Kushāṇa period, in the 2nd century C.E.[75] In the Gupta period, however, it appears that both the forms became popular and quite a few images, both in the zoomorphic and hybrid forms, were executed at different places in the Gupta dominions.[76] The colossal and gigantic therianthropomorphic representation at Udaigiri[77] near Vidiśā and zoomorphic form at Eran[78] in the Sagar district, both *in situ*, and in Madhya Pradesh, are the superb examples of the boar-incarnation of Vishṇu. The other classical examples in the former form come from Mahābalipuram,[79] Belur,[80] Badami[81] and Nāgalapuram[82] in Southern India,[83] and from Kadvar,[84] Kasara,[85] and Than[86] in Gujarat; Rajim[87] and Khajuraho[88] in Madhya Pradesh; Amjhara,[89] Atru,[90] Krishna Vilas,[91] Kanyadah,[92] Arna,[93] Phalodi,[94] Phalodi (Merta),[95] Osian,[96] Kiradu,[97] Sadadi[98] and in Jhalawar, Kota[99] and Udaipur[100] Museums in Rajasthan; Mathurā[101] and Kanauj[102] in U.P., and from various other places and Museums in Gujarat, Maharashtra, Orissa, Bengal and Bihar.[103] Zoomorphic representations of the deity are confined to the north only and are comparatively rarer.[104]

The boar-form has been referred to in the inscriptions also. The Eran Stone Inscription of the time of Toramāṇa (*circa* C.E. 500-515)[105] refers to the Varāhamūrti as the pillar of victory of the great house of the three worlds.[106] The Varāha-incarnation, along with Nṛisiṃha and Trivikrama (in the Vaikuṇṭha form), has been mentioned in Yaśovarman's Khajuraho inscription also.[107] The Garibnath Temple inscription of Bhoja I's reign at Pehowa[108] refers to a temple and image of Yajña-varāha[109] set by the Nāgara-Bhaṭṭa-Bhūvaka. A fragmentary inscription of the reign of Bhartṛipaṭṭa of the Guhila dynasty of Mewar, found at Ahar and dated VS 1000, described the construction of a temple of Ādi-varāha at Gaṅgodbheda.[110] The Sāraṇeśvara Temple Inscriptions of VS 1010 also records the construction of a Vishṇu temple in his Varāha form during the reign of his son Allaṭṭa.[111] The Aḍhai-din-kā-Jhomprā (Ajmer) inscription eulogizes Vishṇu and his ten incarnations including Varāha.[112]

The Varāha-cult thus seems to have become quite popular during the medieval period. It is well known that the Pratihāra rulers were great devotees of this form of Vishṇu and Bhoja I struck coins bearing the figure of the Varāha incarnation and the legend *'Śrīmad-Ādi-varāha'* on his coins.[113]

According to the *Mahābhārata*,[114] it was at a place in the Kurukshetra region that Vishṇu appeared in his Boar form. This place came to be known as Varāha *tīrtha*. It has also been mentioned in the *Vāmana Purāṇa*[115] and is identified with the modern Barah Kalan, a village situated about 11 km east of Jind. Interestingly enough, an image of Varāha, measuring 67 x 38 cm, is still under worship in this village. The god in his therianthropomorphic form (Pl. 97) stands in *ālīḍha* pose resting his left foot on a lotus *pīṭha* placed on the coils of the Nāga couple. The upper halves of the Nāga couple are anthropomorphic. Both, the Nāga and his spouse, are shown with folded hands adoring the Lord. A triple hooded cobra canopies the Nāga while a unicephalous cobra is shown over the head of the Nāgī. Varāha is eight handed. He wears an *ekāvali* and a necklace, beaded armlets and bracelets, *vaijayantīmālā* and *dhotī* secured by a pearl girdle. The central part of the *vaijayantīmālā* between the legs is shown as resting on a full-blossomed lotus on a stalk. The proper right hand, now slightly mutilated, probably held a lotus near the chest. The second hand (in the *pradakshiṇā* order) is holding the tail of the snake at the back of the thigh; the third holds the upper end of the mace placed on the ground and the back fourth supports a disc behind the head of the god. The proper left hand is placed on the left thigh, the second left is placed on the serpent hoods over the Nāga figure, the third holds a conch and the uppermost supports the goddess Earth on its bent elbow. The goddess is shown as seated in *lalitāsana* resting her right foot on a lotus and holding a fang of the god with her right hand. She is slightly turned towards the god and gazing at him. Garland bearing *vidyādharas* are depicted on the top corners. The image is fixed in a wall and even whitewashed. Stylistically, it may be assigned to *circa* 8th century C.E.

A part of a temple doorframe (Pl. 98) is preserved in the Government Museum & Art Gallery, Chandigarh (Museum Register No. 89).[116] Three of its sides are carved with figures of divinities and decorative designs and the fourth side, which was fixed in the wall of the temple, is un-carved. Each side of the frame is divided by a number of sections demarcated by decorative horizontal bands. Each such section shows a figure sculpture depicting a divinity. In the extant part of the doorframe, however, only the lower sections have survived and the others on the top are lost. The frontal section representing the river goddess Yamunā on her vehicle kūrma (tortoise), betrays clearly that this is a part of the proper left hand side of the doorframe of a temple. The panel to the left of Yamunā depicts the boar incarnation of Vishṇu in the act of rescuing the earth goddess Pṛithvī. The panel on the third side carries the representation of Rāma holding the bow in his left hand. Presumably the doorframe carried the depiction of the ten incarnatory forms of Vishṇu besides the river goddesses. The depiction of the Nṛi-varāha under consideration is one of the earliest from Haryana showing the god standing on a full-blown lotus slightly turned to his left supporting the female figure of the earth-goddess on his left elbow raised to the level of the face. The graceful modeling, well-proportioned figure, the meandering vine scroll below the lotus-seat of the god, the looped flower garlands above, the diaper decoration in the upper part are all reminiscent of the Gupta idiom which seems to have lingered on in the region till about the 7th century to which this figure may be assigned.[117]

Therianthropomorphic representation of the god may also be seen in a pedimented niche obtained from Sthāneśvara Mahādeva Temple, Thanesar.[118] It measures 41.5 x 32 cm and consists of sandstone. The four-handed god stands in *ālīḍha* pose with left leg bent and foot placed on a full-blown lotus (Pl. 99). The right foot is firmly placed on the ground. The god holds the mace in his rear right hand while the proper right rests on the respective thigh. The principal left hand rests on the left knee and holds a conch. Goddess Pṛithvī seems to have been supported by the rear left hand of the god. She is depicted as standing on the left thigh of the god keeping her balance by holding the snout of the boar. A full-blown lotus canopies the god. Stylistically it may also be placed in the same period as the preceding image.

Almost similar in conception is a small figure obtained from Gujjar Kheri in district Sonepat.[119] Its left portion is completely gone but the boar head on the human body with a full blown lotus halo behind, Pṛithvī on the elbow of the upper left hand which also holds a disc and the lower left hand placed on the knee of the bent left leg have survived. A horn at the back of the slantingly carved boar head, necklace, sacred thread, beaded bracelets, pearl girdle and the long garland are the noteworthy features. On the top of the back slab on the right is quadrimanous figure seated in *sukhāsana*. The rough execution makes it difficult to identify it with certitude. It seems to have originally formed a part of some Vishṇu image of 9th century C.E.

Another elegant image of Nṛi-varāha (Pl. 100) obtained from Bhīmā Devī Temple, Pinjore is now displayed in the Museum of the Department of Archaeology and Museums, Haryana, Kurukshetra.[120] Made of greenish sandstone and measuring 42 x 19 cm, it depicts the god in the usual *ālīḍha* pose with left leg raised and bent at the knee. The image is badly mutilated and all the hands, snout, lower portion of legs, etc. are completely lost. The lotiform halo behind the crowned head, triple-stranded beaded torque, *śrīvatsa* on the chest, floral sacred thread, beaded *vaijayantīmālā* and dagger slantingly tucked up in the waistband at the right, however, are clear. When complete, it must have been a very exquisite image. This again is a typical Pratihāra icon of 9th-10th century C.E.

More than a century back, Alexander Cunningham[121] had brought to light two Pratihāra inscriptions from Pehowa.[122] One of them, still fixed in the wall of Garibnath ki Haveli is dated in Saṃvat 276 (of the Harsha era of C.E. 606) and refers to a horse fair held at Pṛithūdaka (Pehowa) and the construction of a temple of Yajñavarāha here for which the traders voluntarily agreed to contribute a cess.[123] The date of the inscription falls in Bhoja's reign who is well known to have issued coins of Ādi-varāha type.[124] The temple of Yajña-varāha referred to in this inscription of Bhoja's time must have been a magnificent fane but unfortunately it has not survived. Some fragmentary reliefs, however, further corroborate the popularity of Varāha worship at Pehowa. Two pieces of buff colored sandstone found from the Prāchī Śiva Temple at Pehowa are the fragments of a Varāha image. One of these, measuring 30 x 12 cm, represents the pedestal with the Nāga couple supporting a lotus on which is placed the left foot of the God and the right foot splayed out on the left projection of the *triratha* pedestal. Both the feet wear anklets. The other piece, measuring 20 x 10 cm, shows the torso of the God with left leg raised and bent in *ālīḍha* pose. The head, arms, lower parts of the leg are all broken but a pearl *yajñopavīta*, waist-band with a dagger tucked to it slantingly on the right, a sash on the thigh and lower garment with folds indicated by two parallel incised wavy lines are clearly visible. Stylistically, these pieces may also be assigned to the Pratihāra period.

The most beautiful and life-size image of therianthropomorphic Varāha (Pl. 101) is now enshrined in the Gokarṇa kā Mandira at Rohtak. It measures 98 x 60 cm and consists of buff sandstone. Unfortunately, however, the Temple authorities to make it more attractive have painted it now forgetting of course that the paint would mar the real beauty of this elegant icon.

As usual, the god stands in *ālīḍha* pose placing his left foot on the coil of the seven-hooded Śesha. This coil just encircles his anthropomorphic upper half. The quadrimanous Śesha is shown with folded proper hands. His back left hand is concealed behind his body but the right one holds a long staff. Behind the god is a vine scroll from which different branches issue forth stylistically, some with buds at their ends. The main branch rises from behind his figure and canopies of the boar-head of the god with an inverted full-blown lotus at its pinnacle. The right foot of the god is placed on a lotus. Behind this foot stands Śrī in graceful *tribhaṅga* pose holding a lotus by its stalk in the left hand with suspended right supporting the loose dangling end of the scarf. On the left of the god stands Garuḍa to front in double flexion slightly turned towards his Lord. His coiffure shows frizzled locks spread like a fan on the head. His ornaments include *vaijayantīmālā* also. His right hand is raised to the shoulder in *abhaya* while the *pralamba* left placed on the respective thigh seems to hold a cobra. Both, Śrī and Garuḍa, bear beautiful expression and have been carved minutely.

Varāha wears a small tiara, necklet, necklace, sacred thread, lozenge-shaped *śrīvatsa*, *vaijayantīmālā*, armlets, bracelets, anklets and lower garment held in position by the girdle. The dagger is tucked up in the waistband horizontally. With his normal right hand placed on the thigh, the god also holds the tail of the serpent. Mace with its thicker end upward is held vertically in the suspended rear right hand. The front left hand holds a conch and also supports on the bent elbow the Earth Goddess who sits in *ardha-paryaṅkāsana* with folded hands. The back left hand of the god holds the disc. Behind his head is carved a round gloriole. Steles on the top corners show Brahmā and Śiva. The image ascribable to the 10th century C.E. is a masterpiece of the medieval art of Haryana.[125]

A broken relief preserved in the Asthal Bohr at Rohtak (Pl. 102) shows the left foot of the god placed on an inverted lotus supported on the hoods of the great serpent and his spouse, who are seated slightly turned to each other poising the weight of their bodies on their right and left arm respectively, placed on the ground. Their hair is combed backwards and the heads are canopied by multiple snake-hoods. They wear beaded earrings, necklet, armlets, bracelets, a scarf and a lower garment. The lower halves of the couple are serpentine and intercoiled. Both the feet of the god show anklets and toe-rings. A small part of the *vaijayantīmālā* is visible near the left foot. The placement of the two feet is clearly indicative of the *ālīḍha* posture of the god. A diminutive figure of Chakra-purusha standing gracefully in *dvibhaṅga* on a slightly raised pedestal, holding a disc in his right hand near the chest with left hand akimbo, and wearing usual dress and ornaments is carved just behind the Nāgī. On the receding portion on the right stands very gracefully Śrīdevī holding a lotus by its stalk in her right hand and the dropping scarf in the suspended left. She bears a beautiful hair-coiffure, which consists of a lotus pod encompassed by high ribbons edged with pearls. She also wears earrings, pearl necklet and necklace, the latter with a pendent falling down on the belly slightly left of the navel. Armlets, wristlets, rings on the fingers, anklets, scarf and a lower garment secured by a pearl waist-band forming loops on the thighs and with free ends falling on the knees can also be seen on the person of the goddess who has a plum face with a beatific smile and massive rotund breast. Elegant ornamentation, graceful curves and contours, pleasing composition and detailed care given even to the incidental figures bestows a distinctive character to this image which unfortunately is broken. Nevertheless, it is representative of the artistic excellence of the Pratihāra sculptors of the region.

A beautiful small sculpture, 38 cm in height, found in the neighborhood of Fatehabad, in blackened carboniferous shale depicting the Ādi-Varāha, belonging to *circa* 9th century C.E. (Pl. 103), is preserved in the Victoria & Albert Museum (I.M. 307-1921).[126] The god in this relief stands facing to the right, with his raised left leg resting on an open lotus-plant symbolizing cosmic waters from which it mythically grows. The stem of the lotus-plant is supported by male and female water snakes. The right leg is planted firmly on the back of a partly submerged turtle, also symbolizing the cosmic waters or the ocean. The anthropomorphized god has four human arms, the hand of the proper right arm resting on the right thigh, and the back right holding the mace vertically. The front left arm is bent at the elbow raised to the shoulder-height supporting the seated figure of Bhū-devī in *añjali-mudrā* with conch in the hand and the hand of the back left arm is shown as holding the discus. An inverted lotus flower above the god's head forms an umbrella-like canopy. Flanking the lotus-halo behind the head of the god are carved in high relief against the stele four-armed figures of Brahmā on the left and Śiva on the right. Half-way down on each side are the adoring figures seated on lotus flowers and on the base at each side are the two *āyudha-purushas*, Śaṅkha-purusha holding a conch on the left and Chakra-purusha holding a disc on the other. The whole group, thus, seems to "symbolize the Deliverance of the world from the Deluge of Sin by Viṣṇu, as the Power of the Supreme Being."[127]

A contemporary pedestal of the Nṛi-varāha may be seen at Ahir Majra in district Sonepat. Measuring 24 x 92 cm, it consists of schist and shows the left foot of the god placed on a lotus borne by the Nāga couple. The right foot of the god is also visible indicating the deity to have stood in the *ālīḍha* pose. On the receding projection on the proper left is Śaṅkha-purusha and another figure (Garuḍa?) broken above the waist. The fragment seems to have belonged to the nearby ancient site of Gujjar Kheri, which has yielded a large number of old sculptures and other relics.[128]

Small fragmentary Nṛi-varāha reliefs have been seen at Pinjore[129] and Kara Sahib[130] near Pehowa also but they are only subsidiary representations forming part of Daśāvatāra Vishṇu images. A fragmentary Daśāvatāra panel of *circa* 10th century is known from Ujina, about 10 km east of Nuh in southern Haryana. The extant frieze, 28 x 30.5 cm, shows Nṛi-Varāha and Nṛi-siṃha.[131] A late medieval Daśāvatāra panel is still under worship at Humayunpur-Tisimbali on the Punjab-Haryana border near Lalru.

A Nṛi-varāha image, excavated during 1938-39 from Agroha (ancient Agrodaka)[132] in the present Haryana state, has, however, escaped the notice of the scholars. The excavator has given its description as "One sculpture pieced together found in 7L/4 at a depth of 9' 4" represents an image standing on lotus supported by Nāgas (1' 7", pl. X.1)."[133]

This therianthropomorphic a-cephalous figure (Pl. 104) shows the four-handed deity standing in the *ālīḍhāsana*, slightly turned to left, resting his upper right hand on his hip and supporting the Earth-Goddess on the elbow of his upper left arm as laid down in the *Śilparatna*. The ease with which Pṛithvī is held on the bent left arm of the god indicates the vigor and prowess of Varāha. The backhands are shown supporting the club and the discus respectively. The Varāha face is mutilated but for the extremity of the snout on which the Earth-Goddess has placed her right hand. Wearing *dhammilla-mukuṭa*, earrings, necklace, armlets and bracelets, she seems to be holding a flower in her left hand. She is shown as looking at the Varāha gratefully. The extent portion of the snout also indicates that Varāha's face was tilted slightly upwards and the god was looking at Bhūdevī, lovingly perhaps.

The serrated aureole behind the broken head of the deity is also damaged. It has the lotus-petal pattern carved on it. On the top left corner near the halo and above the thicker end of the club, is a *vidyādhara* in the flying attitude, wearing ornaments and holding the peduncle in the right hand. The god is shown as wearing a four-stringed pearl necklace with a small central pendant attached to the lowermost string, armlets and wristlets, anklets, the sacred thread and a *vaijayantīmālā* which encircles his back running inward from over both the arms and hangs down to the right knee of the figure. It is broken at places. The loincloth is fastened securely to the waist with a *kaṭi-bandha*, the free end of which hangs beautifully on the right thigh. On the right side, a dagger is tucked to the waistband.

The right foot of the deity is firmly planted on the ground while the left one has been slightly raised and placed on the lotus-cushion held by the serpent Ādiśesha. It is worth noting that that there is no serpent-hood over his head but only a coil of his lower portion. Ādiśesha has been represented here, as usual, in therianthropomorphic form, having the human body above the thighs and serpentine and annular coils representing the legs. The facial expression betrays tranquility and quietism. The image is broken near the lower right corner and we are not sure if Ādiśesha's consort was also shown. The serpent-god, however, wears beautiful hair-coiffure, earrings, necklace and bracelets.

On the true extremities of the pedestal are shown, in very graceful and identical *tribhaṅga* postures, two female figures flanking the deity, each wearing *karaṇḍa-mukuṭa*, earrings, necklace with a central pendant hanging down from between the breasts to almost the naval, armlets and bracelets, the lower garment tied with a waistband whose free ends hang gracefully on the thighs. The upper garment is seen on the arms in the form of folds. The female figure on the proper right, slightly behind the right leg of the deity, is holding a flower (?) in her left hand which is held up above the corresponding shoulder, while the right hand is shown as hanging up to and touching the right knee. Both the hands of the figure on the left are broken. It is difficult to identify these female figures with certainly, but they may be the river-goddesses Gaṅgā and Yamunā, shown also on some other Varāha figures.

The whole composition is somewhat compact but balanced and, though badly damaged, it deserves attention for the vigor and dynamism it reveals, the detailed care given even to the subsidiary figures, the absence of the serpent-hood over Ādiśesha, as also probably his consort, and the presence of the river-goddesses Gaṅgā and Yamunā, a feature reminiscent of the Gupta tradition. The whole image, the main figure in particular, has been carved out very exquisitely and the expression is one of dynamism and quietude, but there is inherent in it a certain primitive rigidity. The placement of the club with its thicker end above and the handle below, the flat discus with a tassel (or tongue of flame) issuing forth from its hub and darting down leftwards, habiliments and ornaments etc. are typical medieval features. So the sculpture may be ascribed to *circa* 9th-10th century C.E. It may have been carved by some Pratihāra craftsman during the reign of Bhoja I or his successor Mahendrapāla I, more probably of the former during whose reign a temple of Yajña-varāha was also got constructed by Nāgara-Bhaṭṭa Bhūvaka at Pehowa. It is also distinctive from other medieval images for the absence of the serpent-hood over Ādiśesha's head and the presence of the river-goddesses Gaṅgā and Yamunā.

The most elaborate and tastefully ornamented therianthropomorphic icon of Varāha, however, comes from Hansi (Pl. 105). Conceptually similar to the Rohtak and Agroha images, it shows a very naturalistic boar-head on the human body. The anthropomorphic upper half of the serpent, whose tail is held by the God in his natural suspended right hand, is shown in *añjali-mudrā* and is canopied by cobra hoods. Śrī stands behind the serpent on the extremity of the black slab. Pṛithvī is also shown turned to her right in adoration. Steles show *vidyādhara* figures. A beautiful calyx serves as canopy over the head of the God. It may not be far removed in age from the Rohtak Nṛi-varāha image.

A very small 8 x 8 cm buff sandstone Pratihāra detached piece from Devī temple at Kara Sahib shows the figure broken below the waist holding a disc in the left hand on whose elbow is seated Pṛithvī touching the snout of the god. Other arms are broken. There is a beautifully carved halo behind the head.

As far as zoomorphic representations are concerned, one image is known from Pinjore.[134] Belonging to *circa* 12th century C.E., this relief depicts the god in simple boar form without the representation of different deities except a male figure entwined with its tail unlike most other zoomorphic images of the god known from other sites. A window-screen from Pehowa contains within a circle a small figure of boar standing on a stemmed lotus flower. It may also be the representation of the boar form of Vishṇu.[135] Quite in consonance to these simple zoomorphic representation is another one (Pl. 106) from southern Haryana (exact provenance unknown) which shows the boar wearing a golden necklace. It may also be assigned to the Pratihāra period.

The foregoing account makes it amply clear that Varāha worship started in about the 7th century and became quite popular in Haryana during the Pratihāra period. An earlier representation from the state will be looked forward eagerly. But for the Barah Kalan image, which shows the god as octomanous, all other representations are of the quadrimanous type. Nṛi-varāha is invariably depicted in the *ālīḍha* pose. Pṛithvī is shown in standing, half standing and seated postures gazing at the god, holding his snout or fang or in *añjali-mudrā*. The subsidiary figures, if present, are of Śrīdevī, Garuḍa and *āyudha-purushas*. With the exception of early images from Barah Kalan, Kurukshetra, etc. others show a dagger tucked up in the waist-belt of the god. A full-blown lotus or the calyx of the vine scroll serves as the gloriole or the canopy behind or over the boar head of the god. It seems that the zoomorphic representations of the god were simple in form and did not bear the figures of other deities on the body of the animal. The zoomorphic figure extends the area of such representations to Haryana also.

The *Agni Purāṇa* (49.3) states that the installation of Varāha secures for the donor a kingdom and facilitates him to cross the ocean of mundane existence. From the Gupta period onwards the Boar became a metaphor of political power. In the religious and court literature of medieval India the concept of royalty or regal power (*rājya-śakti*) was linked with the Boar. The *Aparājitapṛichchhā* (121.14), *Rūpamaṇḍana* (III.66) and the *Kūrma Purāṇa* (I.16, 82) prescribes a Boar containing all divinities (*sarvadevamaya*), to be placed in front of a Vishṇu temple. In the *Bhāgavata Purāṇa* (III.13, 41) the Yajña-Varāha represents the three Vedas, *Veda-trayī*, In the *Agni Purāṇa* (31.12) also Yajña-Varāha is invoked in the form of *Veda-trayī*. The Varāha images from Haryana thus indicate the Vedic-Purāṇic religious constituent and a tendency towards orthodox Brahmanical religion.

NARASIṂHA

The story of the Lord appearing from a pillar in the from of Man-Lion (Narasiṃha/Nṛisiṃha) and killing the demon Hiraṇyakaśipu in order to protect his devotee Prahlāda, son of the demon, is very well known. Though Narasiṃha, possessing sharp claws and keen fangs, had been invoked in the *Taittirīiya Āraṇyaka*[136] and *Mahānārāyaṇa Upanishad*,[137] yet the myth of Narasiṃha as an incarnation of Vishṇu appears in the *Mahābhārata*[138] for the first time. The complete exposition of the myth of Narasiṃha incarnation is, however, found in the *Harivaṃśa*,[139] *Padma*,[140] *Kūrma*,[141] *Vāmana*[142] and *Bhāgavata*[143] Purāṇas. *Vishṇu Purāṇa*[144] also makes a passing reference to the legend. The all powerful demon Hiraṇyakaśipu, who after having performed severe penance for thousand years had acquired a boon which assured him protection against all beings, remained unaffected by weather in heaven and the nether world as he could be killed by neither a man nor an animal, neither by weapon nor by hands, neither inside any building nor outside in the open, neither during the day nor during the night. The demon thus became a veritable terror to the gods who made repeated prayers to Vishṇu for his destruction. Vishṇu assumed the form of a Man-Lion and appearing from a column, which was burnt red hot to be hugged by Prahlāda, tore out the entrails of the demon by his sharp claws.[145]

Images of Narasiṃha tear opening the entrails of the demon have been described in the *Harivaṃśa*, *Vishṇudharmottara*, *Agni* and *Matsya* Purāṇas as well as in the iconographical texts like *Rūpamaṇḍana*, *Śilparatna*, *Devatāmūrtiprakaraṇa*, etc.[146] *Jayākhya Saṃhitā*, an early Pāñcharātara text, also contains *Nṛisiṃha - mantra* and *dhyāna*.[147]

Though the antiquity of Vaikuṇṭha images showing lion and boar aspects has been traced back to an early period[148] yet it seems that Narasiṃha worship became popular only in the Gupta period.[149] During the medieval period, however, this incarnatory form had a very wide prevalence in the country. Though the early images do not necessarily show Narasiṃha as killing the demon yet in the post-Gupta period it was the most popular form.[150] These images, according to the Āgamas, are called Sthauṇa-Narasiṃha images while those depicting the deity in *padmāsana*, *lalitāsana*, *sthānaka-mudrā*, etc. are called Girija or Kevala-Narasiṃha. The latter type is earlier, though not invariably, and shows the god with two or four-hands whereas the former type depicts him as having four, six, eight, twelve or even sixteen hands. In the four-armed Kevala-Narasiṃha images, two hands are generally shown as holding Vaishṇava emblems.

The tradition of Vishṇu's worship in Haryana seems to have become well established during the age of the *Mahābhārata*. There are many places of pilgrimage in the state connected with Vishṇu and his different incarnations[151] and a large number of images of the god have also been obtained from the region.[152] Kṛitaśaucha-*tīrtha*,[153] traditionally located at village Barah Kalan in district Jind,[154] in regarded as the place where Vishṇu, in the form of Nṛisiṃha, killed Hiraṇyakaśipu.[155] Village Dhundhu in the same district also has a Narasiṃha-*tīrtha*.[156] During the course of our investigations we have come across some important images of the deity as well as his female energy, Nārasiṃhī, from the region which we describe below.

The earliest images of Narasiṃha in India, as indicated above, seem to have been carved during the Gupta period.[157] The Department of Archaeology and Museum, Haryana (HARDAM) exhumed some time back from Agroha, a small fragmentary terracotta piece which originally seems to have been a part of some Gupta image of Narasiṃha. Only the lion-face and the human hand (with a dagger?) near the left shoulder have survived. The human hand is indicative of the therianthropomorphic nature of the depiction of Narasiṃha. Though fragmentary, this piece in common man's art indicates the popularity of the theme in Haryana during the Gupta period.[158]

In stone, the earliest Nṛisiṃha figure known so far, was preserved in a private collection at Sirsa.[159] Found from Haryana, this sandstone image is unfortunately broken below the chest (Pl. 107). The extant portion shows the god tearing open the stomach of Hiraṇyakaśipu with his claws.[160] The demon and the lower portion of the figure are missing as indicated above. The god has round bulging eyes, long lolling out tongue and ferocious face with sharp fangs. Long manes falling on both the shoulders add to the ferocity of the figure. The god also wears a bandolier (*chhannavīra*) consisting of triple-stringed cross-band fastened with a small circular clasp at the chest. An armlet on the left arm is also visible. Reminiscent of the Gupta art tradition, the image may be assigned to the early medieval period.[161]

A very interesting image of Narasiṃha, however, comes from Morni Ka Tal in district Panchkula (Pl. 108). Morni is a small tourist-spot of northeastern Haryana. It is connected with Chandigarh by road. A large number of old sculptures from this site are preserved in the Department of Ancient Indian History, Culture and Archaeology of the Panjab University, Chandigarh[162]; the Government Museum and Art Gallery, Chandigarh[163] and HARDAM.[164] The image under reference belongs to the first institution.

The sandstone sculpture measuring 50 x 30 cm shows Narasiṃha with lion-face and human body, standing against a column in contraposto. The face unfortunately is somewhat damaged but the manes spread on the chest like an acanthus fan leave little doubt to the face having been leonine. The claws of hands and feet are also leonine. The suspended left hand touches the waist and right one is raised to the level of the chest. Between and outside the feet are carved small posts, which indicate his emergence from a pillar. The feature of carving a small pillar in the feet may also be seen in the Gupta images of the deity found from Besnagar (Vidiśā) and the one preserved in the Gwalior Museum,[165] but the present image does not show a *vanamālā* like them. There is a chronological gap also between the creations of these images. Stylistically, the image from Morni may be ascribed to *circa* 10th century C.E. or slightly earlier.

Though we know the images of Kevala-Narasiṃha belonging to the Gupta period from Besnagar, Pahlejpur (near Eran), Deograh (all in M.P.) and Basarh (Bihar)[166] yet the image from Morni differs from them and is unique. It also indicates the persistence of the Gupta art tradition in the mountainous region of Haryana till the medieval period. Be it as it is, the icon from Morni is an important piece iconographically and presents a beautiful and interesting specimen of the medieval art of Haryana.

Another very interesting image of Narasiṃha comes from Hansi (Pl. 109).[167] Roughly executed on a small plaque measuring 19 x 14 cm, it shows the quadrimanous god tearing open the entrails of the demon with his normal hands. His right foot is placed on the lotus. The god wears beaded necklet and wristlets. The *triśikhaṇḍaka* manes fall on the shoulders. Incised triple lines on the back slab indicate halo. Very interesting, however, is the fact that the god is shown as holding in his back hands what looks like a scarf or a stylized *vanamālā*.[168] This feature is comparable to Yoga-Nārāyaṇa images from Didwana[169] and Osian[170] in Rajasthan in which the god is depicted as supporting the long garland in the upper two hands in a similar fashion. For a Narasiṃha image, however, it is unique feature.

Hat near Safidon (district Jind) has a mutilated and worn out figure of Nṛisiṃha in grey sandstone measuring 26 x 13 cm fixed in the wall of a temple.[171] It shows the god in *ālīḍha* pose. The left hand rests on the left knee and the right one is broken. The feet are also gone. In spite of the mutilation it has suffered and the indifferent state of its preservation, lion face placed on a human body is quite clear. Interestingly, we do not see the demon, nor does the extant left hand indicate the act of tearing open the entrails of the demon as is usually seen in medieval images.

HARDAM possesses fragmentary Nṛisiṃha head from Jind,[172] Gujjar Kheri,[173] Chandimandir[174] and Manas,[175] all assignable to the medieval period, indicating the popularity of Narasiṃha worship in Haryana during the period. Small detached pieces showing Narasiṃha are known from Manas (14 x 13 cm) and Ujina also.

Quite a few years back, we had seen an image of Nṛisiṃha, along with those of Umā-Maheśvara and Gaṇeśa, fixed in the wall of a Gurudwara at Kuruskehtra with a Śiva-*liṅga* in front.[176] It showed the therianthropomorphic god standing in *ālīḍhāasana* tearing open the demon Hiraṇyakaśipu with his normal two hands while the back hands were raised above holding some indistinct objects. Human legs just above this panel indicated that it formed a part of a large image, which probably depicted the ten incarnatory forms. Nṛisiṃha may also be seen on the *parikara* of Vishṇu images from Pehowa,[177] Baras[178] and Gujjar Kheri (Pl. 52)[179] and the Vaikuṇṭha image from Chandimandir.[180] Nṛisiṃha seems to have been depicted on the doorjambs also. One such doorjamb is now preserved in the Gurukula Museum, Jhajjar[181] and another from Pehowa in HARDAM.[182] The former depicts the god in *ālīḍha* pose, supporting the demon on the bent left leg, tearing open his entrails with his normal hands. The backhands are raised above the head. The god wears *karṇa-kuṇḍalas, ekāvali*, bracelets and an under garment. Ears standing erect on the sides of the forehead indicate the leonine head. Above may be seen a lotus seat in the extant fragmentary piece probably for another figure. The fragment of the door surround from Pehowa shows only the head of Nṛisiṃha. A doorjamb from Lulodh in district Rohtak,[183] measuring 142 x 45 cm is the best preserved of all such pieces as show the incarnatory forms. From bottom upwards, it depicts the Kūrma (actually churning of the Ocean), Nṛisiṃha, Paraśurāma and Balarāma in beautiful *rathikās*, outside which stand two female attendants on the proper left. The topmost panel has one female and the *gaja-śārdūla* motif clearly indicating this doorjamb to have been the proper left hand side of the door surround. The other doorjamb to right may have shown the incarnatory forms of Matsya, Varāha, etc. Nṛisiṃha in the present panel stands in a frontal pose which looks very much like the dancing pose with the legs bent at knees which go outwards, right foot slightly splayed outwards while the left one is placed on the back of a demon. The god wears *ekāvali*, armlets and a long garland. The two ears on the leonine head stand erect. The god is shown as killing Hiraṇyakaśipu with his principal hands, the back right hand is broken and the back left hand is held towards the chest with thumb touching the mouth. This again is an interesting feature. The doorjamb under reference may have belonged to a Vishṇu temple of *circa* 11th-12th century C.E.

A fragmentary panel of sandstone, 28 x 30.5 cm, found from Ujina, about 10 km east of Nuh, represents Varāha and Nṛisiṃha. The panel is broken on both sides. When complete, it probably represented all the ten incarnatory forms in a row. The extant piece is in a very indifferent state of preservation and belongs stylistically to about the 10th century C.E.[184] We may also refer here to another Daśāvatāra panel of a late medieval date now enshrined in a modern temple in the village Tisimbli (Humayunpur) on the Haryana-Punjab border in district Patiala (Punjab) which shows the incarnatory forms in a row.

The foregoing account reveals that Nṛisiṃha worship has continued since the Gupta period in Haryana and some iconographically very interesting images were also produced here, Nārasiṃhī, the female energy of Narasiṃha, was also worshipped here and her images, too, have been obtained from Agroha, Pehowa, Asthal Majra (near Rohtak) and Gujjar Kheri.[185]

VĀMANA-TRIVIKRAMA

The Vāmana myth has its germ in the 'three steps' of Vishṇu, with which he traversed the universe as referred to in the *Ṛigveda*.[186] In the *Śatapatha Brāhmaṇa*,[187] the myth develops slightly. The demons got ascendancy in the struggle for supremacy and decided to divide the world amongst them. The gods wanted their own share and approached them accompanied by Vishṇu in the form of sacrifice. The demons agreed to give them "as much as Vishṇu lies upon and no more." Vishṇu being dwarf was laid by the gods on all the three directions. They thus obtained the entire earth. The *Taittirīya Saṃhitā*[188] and the *Taittirīya Brāhmaṇa*[189] also relate this legend wherein Vishṇu is described as taking possession of the whole earth with his three steps. It is, however, in the *Rāmāyaṇa*[190] that we come across the evolved form of the myth for the first time. When the demon king Bali was performing sacrifice for being the overlord of the three worlds, Vishṇu approached him in the form of a dwarf and asked for the gift of land measuring the size of his three steps. Śukrāchārya, the preceptor of the demon king, suspected deception and tried to prevent Bali, in vain of course, from granting the boon. When the demon king poured the water of ablution in accepting the demand of the dwarf, the latter enlarged himself into a wonderfully giant form and measured the entire earth and the heaven with his two steps. Asked as to where he should place his foot after taking the third step, Bali offered his head for that and was consequently sent to the nether world (*Pātālaloka*), as the king of all the *asuras*. Purāṇas like the *Harivaṃśa*,[191] *Matsya*,[192] *Agni*,[193] *Padma*,[194] *Vāmana*,[195] *Bhāgavata*,[196] etc. also narrate the story with almost the same details.

The plastic representations of Vishṇu in this incarnation depict him either in the form of Vāmana (dwarf) or as Trivikrama, the dwarf growing into gigantic dimensions and measuring the three worlds with his three steps. Both the forms are described in details in iconographical texts.[197] Extant examples, however, show that images of the former type are comparatively rare.[198]

The holy land of Haryana has its association with the Vāmana incarnation. There is a Vāmana *kuṇḍa* at Amin and a pilgrimage dedicated to this god (Vāmana-*tīrtha*) exists at the village Vānapura (also called Ujjaḍa Kheḍā) in Kurukshetra.[199] Till date, however, Haryana has yielded only one icon of Vāmana. It comes from Bawal in district Mahendragarh. It is now preserved in the Museum of the Department of Archaeology and Museums Haryana at Kurukshetra.

This sandstone relief measuring 64 x 40 cm shows the quadrimanous pot-bellied dwarfish figure standing in *samabhaṅga* (contraposto) on a lotus seat (Pl. 110). The god bears curled locks on the head and wears necklet, necklace, sacred thread, wristlets, bracelets, *makara-kuṇḍalas* (earrings of the shape of a crocodile), anklets, *śrīvatsa* (an auspicious symbol) on the chest, a long *vanamālā* and a lion-cloth. The legs are stumpy and disproportionate to the body. The god holds mace and discus in the rear right and left hands and a conch in the proper left. The conch is placed vertically with spiral-top below. The normal right hand is held in boon-conferring pose with a rosary. Behind the head is a round halo with eight petals carved on it. Brahmā and Śiva occupy the top corners. Both sit in *lalitāsana* and are four-handed, holding a water-pot in the normal left hand with proper right in protection-affording pose. The bearded Brahmā on the proper right holds a ladle and a book in the rear pair of hands while Śiva on the other side carries a trident and a snake in those. Near the feet of the god are carved diminutive figures of *āyudha-purushas* and the spouses of the Lord on the receding projections of the pedestal. On the proper right is Śaṅkha-purusha with conch in the left hand and on the left is Chakra-purusha holding the disc in his right hand. The other hands rest on their respective knees. Śrīdevī and Sarasvatī stand gracefully on the extreme corners probably holding a lotus by stalk in one hand (towards the god) with other suspended beautifully. Stylistically, the image belongs to the Mathura art-tradition[200] and can be assigned to *circa* 12th century C.E.

A four-handed Vāmana image (Pl. 111) from Mohanbari (Salhawas, in district Jhajjar) was unfortunately stolen on 18. 09. 1977. This image, measuring about 42 x 30 cm, resembled the one described above except the depiction of the flying *vidyādharas* on the top corners of the back slab, which was semicircular at the top. The depiction of the main figure on the central offset of the *pañcharatha* pedestal, its dress and ornamentation, the style of holding and the position of the attributes in the four-hands, and the subsidiary figures on the side recesses are so similar to those of the image described above that it seems to have been prepared from a common model. It, however, suffered some mutilation and does not seem to have been executed as exquisitely as the former. It may have belonged to the same period.

A very small similar image but with a parasol above the head and without the attendant figures is known from Chulkana in district Karnal. An architectural piece in the Jhajjar Museum also carries the depiction of standing Vāmana in a *rathikā*. The two-handed god standing in *dvibhaṅga* 'double-flexion' is shown as holding the parasol in his left hand and wearing the usual ornaments including the long garland (Pl. 112). Another similar piece with a *Nāgarakūṭa* above from Hisar region depicts the two-handed Vāmana as seated in *sukhāsana* under the parasol held in his left hand (Pl. 113). Both these architectural pieces seem to have been part of the doorframe of some Vishṇu temple. The depiction of Vāmana bearing boyish looks and wearing earrings, pearl necklet, sacred thread, *dhotī*, etc., seated in *sukhāsana* holding a parasol in his left hand with right in *abhaya,* on the fragmentary pedestal of the Vishṇu image from Sagwan and other incarnatory figures on the back slabs or *parikaras* of Vishṇu images has already been noted above and need not be repeated here.

TRIVIKRAMA

Depiction of Vishṇu in his Vāmana-Trivikrama form is very rare in Haryana. We know the only example from Gujjar Kheri (Pl. 114). The quadrimanous god holding a mace horizontally over the head with his upper right hand, a lotus in the proper right near the chest and the discus in his back left hand is shown as taking a stride with his right leg stretched aloft at the end of which is seen a bearded demon head which typifies the Brahmāṇḍa or Rāhu.

The image is broken bellow the waist and the normal left hand of the god is also broken. The god bears a not very high crown, ear ornaments, pearl necklet, armlets, bracelets, and *vanamālā.* The disc in the back left hand shows petal-like spokes around a prominent hub. The refined workmanship is missing.

The image in its extant form measures 19 x 16 cm. It bears Reg. No. HRN/AMB-626. Being, however, the first Trivikrama Vishṇu from Haryana, it is important.[201]

PARAŚURĀMA

The five *avatāras* discussed above probably represent the stages of the evolution of life on this earth from the earliest form to manhood, the latter only partially developed and not full-stature human being. Paraśurāma, perhaps a real historical figure, but one who did not have full control over his senses and could get incensed immediately, represents the next stage. He may have been a great warrior of some tribe, probably the people mentioned as Paraśus by Pāṇini (V.3, 119), because of using axe (*paraśu*) as their main weapon. His proper name was Rāma, belonging to the family of Bhṛigu (therefore Bhārgava), and son of Jamadagni (so known as Jāmadagneya also), but became famous as Paraśurāma for his association with his favorite weapon *Paraśu* (axe).

The *Mahābhārata* (III.116) relates the story of Paraśurāma in details. He was the fifth son of sage Jamadagni from Reṇukā. Once she went to the riverside to fetch fruits for the sacrifice and felt infatuated for king Chitraratha whom she saw sporting merrily in the river. Jamadagni got enraged over it and ordered his sons, one by one, to kill her. The four sons refused to carry out father's orders and were cursed to death by Jamadagni. Paraśurāma killed his mother. Jamadagni was very much pleased with him and asked him for a boon. Paraśrāma asked for the resurrection of his mother and brothers.

Another famous story related to him is also found in the epic (I.64, 4; III. 116-17). When king Kārtavīrya forcibly took away the cows from Jamadagni's hermitage which he happened to visit, Paraśurāma killed him. Kārtavīrya's son avenged the death of his father by killing Paraśurāma's father in his absence. Paraśurāma took the oath of destroying all the kshatriyas and undertook his campaign of destroying the race twenty-one times. It was at Kurukshetra (also called Samanta-pañchaka) in Haryana that Bhārgava Rāma, after extirpating the kshatriya race during the interval between the Tretā and Dvāpara Yugas, made five tanks of blood with which he satiated his manes and received a boon from them (I.2, 5-7). The southwest corner of Samanta-pañchaka is placed at Rāma-hrada (modern Ramray, 8 km southwest of Jind). V.S. Agrawala identified Rāmahrada with the Vedic Śaryaṇāvat, which was also called Brahmasara after some time and is located at Kurukshetra.[202]

Paraśurāma received his axe from Śiva by pleasing him through his austerities. He taught the use of various weapons to Droṇa (I.129, 66) and also gave him the Brahmāstra (I.165, 13). In the *Rāmāyaṇa*, however, Paraśurāma has been portrayed as very emotional and wrathful, defeated by Rāma (*Rām.* I.71).

The *Vishṇnudharmottara* prescribes that Paraśurāma should have *jaṭā* on his head, wear the skin of the black antelope, and hold axe in his hand.[203] The *Agni Purāṇa* describes his four-handed form as holding the bow, arrow, axe, and sword.[204] The *Vaikhānasāgama*, however, describes both the two-handed and four-handed varieties, the former holding axe in the right hand and the other in pointing posture, the latter as holding the usual attributes of Vishṇu.[205]

As an incarnation of Vishṇu, Paraśurāma did not attain much importance and his images are few and far between. Very few temples were dedicated to him.[206] In spite of his association with the Kurukshetra region as noted above, no independent image of Paraśurāma has been discovered from Haryana. He is shown as one of the incarnations in the Daśāvatāra reliefs only. The *parikara* of a Vishṇu image found from Gujjar Kheri (Pl. 52, last figure), and the back slab of the Vishṇu image from Kosli shows Paraśurāma along with other incarnatory forms. The latter shows Paraśurāma as seated in *sukhāsana* holding the axe in his right hand over the respective shoulder and supporting what looks like a pitcher in the left hand resting on the bent knee.

RĀMA-DĀŚARATHĪ

The story of Rāma is too well known to be retold. Strangely, however, he does not figure in the literature before the *Rāmāyaṇa* of Vālmīki, of which he is the hero. Fr. Camel Bulcke, who has studied the evolution of the Rāma legend very thoroughly, has concluded that Rāma was originally a hero who was deified and identified with Vishṇu later.[207]

Recent archaeological evidence based on the excavations of the important sites like Ayodhyā, Nandigrāma, Śṛiṅgaverapura, Bharadvāja Āśrama connected with the story of Rāma indicate that the Rāmāyaṇa episode may not have been older than the 7th century B.C.E.,[208] a date which was suggested by H.C. Raychaudhary also on quite independent literary evidence.[209] The *Rāmāyaṇa*, however, wielded immense impact not only on the life of the Indians through the ages but also became very popular outside India – from central Asia to southeast Asia.[210]

Rāma was a great archer *'dhanurdhara'* and throughout in Indian iconography he is characterized by this chief attribute of bow. According to the *Vishṇudharmottara*, he should be depicted as a royal personage, but his brothers, though carved similarly, should not be shown with the tiara.[211] The *Agni Purāṇa*, however, describes his two-handed and quadrimanous forms, the former as holding bow and arrow, and the latter as holding bow, arrow, sword, and conch.[212] The *Bhāgavata Purāṇa* (IX.109) also describes him as *Koṇḍapāṇi*. Though some scholars hold the depiction of scenes of *Rāmāyaṇa* as going back to the pre-Christian era[213] yet there is absolutely no doubt to the earliest sculptural representations of *Rāmāyaṇa* scenes coming from Nagarjunakonda on the Krishna river in Andhra Pradesh, datable to *circa* 3rd century C.E. Longhurst had published these reliefs, one showing Hanumān carrying on his back Rāma (with a huge bow) and Lakshmaṇa followed by another figure, and the other depicting Rāma and Sītā in ascetic garb taking leave of king Daśaratha, but thought that these illustrated the episodes from the Daśaratha Jātaka.[214] P.K. Agrawala,[215] however, has rightly identified the former as belonging to the *Rāmāyaṇa*. P. Banerjee[216] has published the other relief from Nagarjunakonda (published earlier by Longhurst) which seems to represent the episode from the Daśaratha Jātaka. Depiction of the *Rāmāyaṇa* scenes, however, seems to have become popular from the Gupta period onwards.[217] Rāma is generally shown wearing *chhannavīra* (cross-band) with the *tūṇīra* (quiver) sticking out from behind his shoulders, holding the bow (and sometimes arrow also).

Haryana has some places connected with Rāma – Daśaratha-kuṇḍa at village Agondh; Daśaratha-*tīrtha* at Dashayan; Pañchavaṭī-*tīrtha* at Thanesar; Lava-Kuśa-*tīrtha* at Mundhari; and Rāma-*tīrtha*[218] at Pehowa. One would thus naturally look for some images of Rāma or representations of the *Rāmāyaṇa* scenes from the region.

Sugh near Jagadhari in district Yamunanagar is a very important ancient site of Haryana. It has been mentioned about half a dozen times in the *Mahābhāshya* of Patañjali who was probably a contemporary of Pushyamitra Śuṅga. It seems that Sugh was in a very flourishing state during the Śuṅga period, a fact vouched by numerous Śuṅga terracotta figurines found from the site. Amongst these is a molded piece measuring 12.0 x 9.6 cm and baked red (Pl.

115). The hair are coiled on the left and supported by a flowery wreath.[219] The figure is shown as wearing triple earrings and a torque composed of tiny rosettes. Small rosette-like marks exist on the chest and left shoulder also. A projecting ridge indicates that he wore a *dhotī*. A very conspicuous feature, however, is the presence of a quiver full of arrows behind the left shoulder. The left arm is broken but it seems to have been extended to left. The right hand seems to have been raised above the shoulder with a deep groove indicating that it was meant for insertion of some object, probably the upper end of a bow made of wood or bamboo stick. The face is oval with round open eyes, long nose, plump cheeks and a small mouth with thick lower lip. The strokes of the use of a fibrous brush are visible on the bust. Unfortunately the piece is broken below the abdomen. The coiled hair supported by flowery wreath, sparse ornamentation, bare bust, quiver on the back and the groove in the right hand probably for holding a bow indicate that the terracotta represents Rāma.[220] Another similar but badly mutilated piece measuring 9.0 x 7.0 cm in its extant form,[221] probably prepared from the same mould, indicates the popularity of such pieces at Sugh. Stylistically these pieces may be assigned to *circa* 2nd-1st century B.C.E. If the proposed identification is accepted, this terracotta will be the earliest evidence of the depiction of Rāma in art.

Kala had observed, "Rāmāyaṇa subjects in Indian sculpture are unknown in the pre-Christian era."[222] A terracotta showing a 'man carrying a woman in his arms' belonging to the Allahabad Museum and assignable to the 2nd century B.C. described and illustrated by Kala himself[223] has been identified by Sengupta[224] and Sivaramamurti[225] as Rāvaṇa abducting Sītā. Our terracottas too indicate that the *Rāmāyaṇa* story was popular during the 2nd-1st century B.C. and provided inspiration to the artists to depict its hero and various episodes in the medium of clay. As such, these terracottas may be regarded as the earliest depiction of Rāma in Indian art.

Sandhaya, another village located about 3 km northeast of Kapāla-Mochana, an ancient and well known pilgrim center, and about 25 km northwest of Sugh, in the same district, has also yielded a terracotta figurine measuring 18 x 11 cm, which is now displayed in the Government Museum and Art Gallery, Chandigarh. It is baked red and represents a male figure whose head, left arm and legs are completely lost (Pl. 116). A quiver at the back of the right shoulder and bandolier (*chhannavīra*, cross-band), however, indicates the figure to have been that of a warrior. In Gupta art, Rāma is generally depicted with a *chhannavīra* and holding a bow as we have noted above. The presence of the quiver indicates that the bow may have been held in the left hand, now broken. The right hand held near the chest may have held an arrow. The comparatively larger size of the figure also indicates that it adorned some religious establishment. It may be added here that bricks carved in the typical Gupta style indicating the existence of a Gupta temple have also been found from this place. Stylistically, this terracotta may be dated to *circa* 5th century C.E.

A large square panel from Sandhaya which originally measured 55 x 55 cm when complete but is unfortunately broken on the left depicts a very rare and interesting scene of the fight between Rāma and the demon Makarāksha from the *Rāmāyaṇa* (Pl. 117). Makarāksha (literally meaning 'having eyes like a crocodile') was the son of the demon Khara (literally meaning 'ass'). It is well known that to avenge the ignominy of the cutting of the nose of his sister Śūrpanakhā, the demon king Rāvaṇa had sent his brothers Khara and Dūshaṇa to the Daṇḍakāraṇya (Daṇḍaka forest) to kill Rāma and Lakshmaṇa. They were, however, themselves killed along with other demons by the two brothers. To avenge his father's assassination, Makarāksha got the opportunity to fight against Rāma during the final battle of Laṅkā. Makarāksha had not only the eyes but also the face of a crocodile and the body of an ass. When Makarāksha could not succeed to harm Rāma with his weapons in a horrible fight he ultimately attacked and held his left arm in his jaws. It is this scene which has been depicted in the panel. The force with which Rāma combated the demon is indicated by his kicking the demon with his left foot and trying to inflict a severe blow with his right hand which is extended backwards to be struck vehemently. The right forearm of Rāma is, however, unfortunately broken and so also his right leg below the knee which, to judge from the stance, was planted very firmly on the ground in *ālīḍha* pose. Rāma is shown as a young sturdy warrior wearing a head-guard with tresses of his long locks coming out from the back of the ears. He wears beaded wristlets, circular earrings and a necklace with twelve-spoke pendent. The under garment shows multiple folds and is twisted like a rope and knotted at the back of the right hip. The *Rāmāyaṇa* describes that Rāma had killed the horses and destroyed the chariot of Makarāksha. A dead horse lying in the foreground indicates the sequence of the fight. The intensity with which the demon charged at Rāma is indicated by his vertical stance with tail raised upwards towards the head and fully open mouth to grab the whole folded arm of Rāma.

Another partially preserved panel from Sandhaya (Pl. 118) shows Rāma desperately trying to liberate himself from the fetters of *nāga-pāśa* (serpent-noose). Five hoods of the snake are shown behind Rāma's head and one concealed by his broken right arm. Some other badly mutilated parts of this panel showed even the feet also fettered by the serpentine noose. The helplessness of Rāma is indicated by his facial expression. The panel may have depicted Lakshmaṇa too in the same condition as described in the epic. The *nāga-pāśa* was ultimately cut by Garuḍa and the two brothers were liberated to continue the fight.

Still another piece from this site is said to have depicted the scene of the cutting of the nose of Śūrpanakhā by Lakshmaṇa with his sword, but it has been completely lost now. All these panels are, however, definite evidence of the existence here of a temple bedecked with the panels depicting scenes from the *Rāmāyaṇa*.[226]

Ten sculpted terracotta bricks depicting scenes from the *Rāmāyaṇa*, some of which bear descriptive verses from the epic engraved in Brāhmī characters of the Gupta period, have been obtained from the village Nachar Khera, about 15 km from Tohana in district Jind. They are housed in the Gurukula Museum, Jhajjar and described by Yogānanda. Almost all of them have suffered mutilation, partial or substantial. One of them, originally nearly one and a half foot square but now broken more than half of it, depicts Rāma, Lakshmaṇa and Sītā going to Pañchavaṭī (Pl. 119). The figure of Rāma is completely lost but that of Sītā above the navel and of Laksmaṇa above the knees have survived. Sītā wears large *karṇa-kuṇḍalas* and has a beautiful coiffure bedecked with flowers. She has large almond-shaped eyes, sturdy nose, plump cheeks and thick lips bearing an expression of contentment. Lakshmaṇa walking behind her has a bandolier on the chest, holds the bow in his left hand with right hand raised to the level of the shoulder as if explaining something to her. The quiver is tucked slantingly at the back of his right shoulder. The hair has been assembled and tied with a string forming a bun above. The lower garment is tight fit on the extant part of the legs with parallel horizontal folds. A part of the scarf is visible as falling on the left thigh from over the left arm. The damaged inscription in Gupta Brāhmī characters reads '*- - n antarā Raghunandana āsasāda mahāgṛidhraiḥ*' which seems to be an abbreviated version of the following verse from the Vālmīki *Rāmāyaṇa* (Araṇyakāṇḍa XIV.1) –

Atha Pañchavaṭīṃ gachhan antarā Raghunandanaḥ /
Āsasāda mahākāyaṃ gṛidhraṃ bhīmaparākramam //

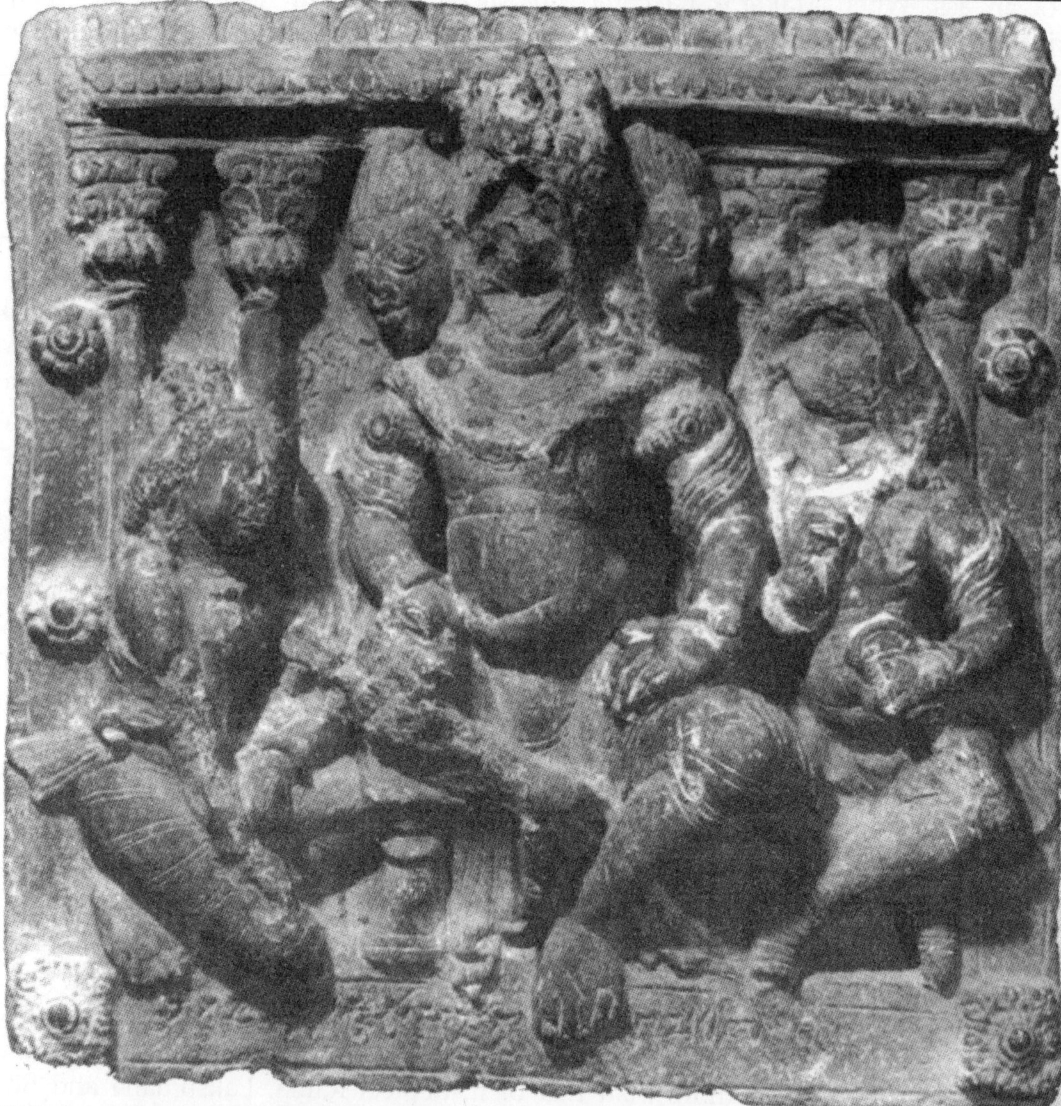

Fig. 7. Demon Triśira with two soldiers, Nachar Khera.

The broken portion obviously carried the depiction of Rāma and the great bird. What has survived gives us an insight into the real beauty of this Gupta panel.

Another brick (Fig. 7) shows a tri-cephalous demon (with his name Tṛiśira = Triśira 'having three heads' written near his right face) being informed by two soldiers sitting flanking him that the fourteen demons sent by Rāvaṇa have been defeated by Rāma as indicated by the engraved part of the verse at the bottom of the panel: *Chaturdaśa rākshasā sujitvā Rāmadhe yaśaḥ*. Triśira, perhaps a commander in the army of Rāvaṇa, is shown as seated in a pillared room or pavilion on a wooden couch in *sukhāsana* resting his left hand on the thigh and right on the respective knee listening to the soldiers. His central face is damaged as also of the soldier on his left who is depicted as holding a sword in his left hand and wearing long boots which remind us of the Kushāṇa figures wearing such shoes. The third panel shows three-headed six-handed Triśira demon seated in *padmāsana* on a chariot fighting his foes (Fig. 8). Two heads are lost and the third one is depicted as about to fall having been cut

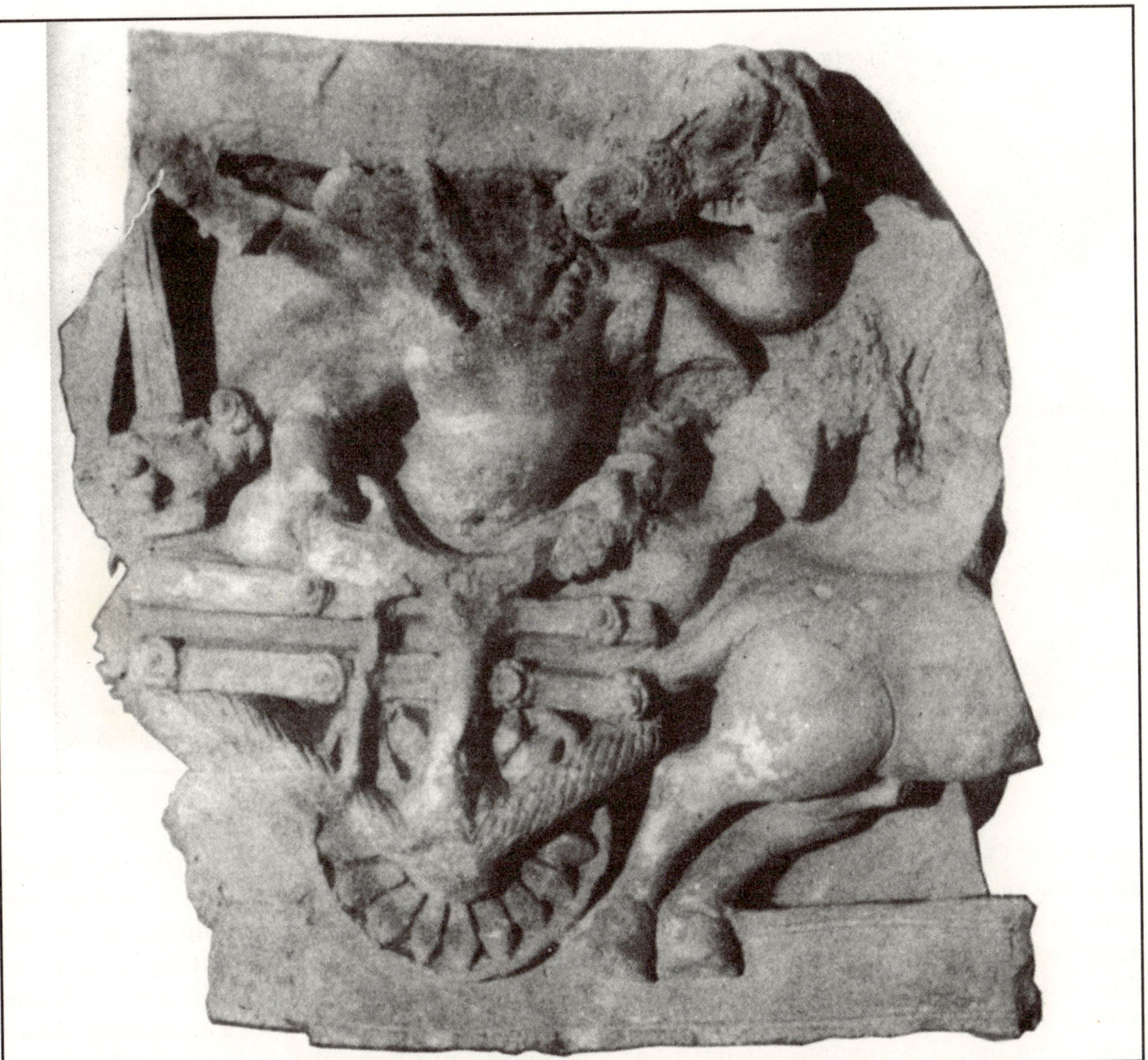

Fig. 8. Triśira fighting on his chariot, Nachar Khera.

by an arrow. The demon has also lost four of his hands and holds a sword and a discus in the surviving two. The panel has suffered mutilation on both ends but the central part showing the chariot with demon sitting on it has survived. One badly damaged panel depicts Rāvaṇa's son Meghanāda engaged in fighting, recognized as such by the Brāhmī inscription '*Indrajit*' on the upper border. Another shows the scene of the 'golden deer' (Pl. 120). The panel is broken on the top left corner taking away the head portion of Lakshmaṇa but preserves a substantial part of the scene showing Sītā seated to the left of Rāma insisting to catch the golden deer who is taking a leap looking backwards. Rāma has matted locks and like Lakshmaṇa holds his bow in his left hand with a quiver on the back and right hand disposed in the act of reassurance. Sītā has bedecked her coiffure with flowers and wears large circular earrings.

Most of the other panels are too broken to give us an exact idea of the depicted scenes. We must also refer here to some similar and elegant terracotta panels from Jind and

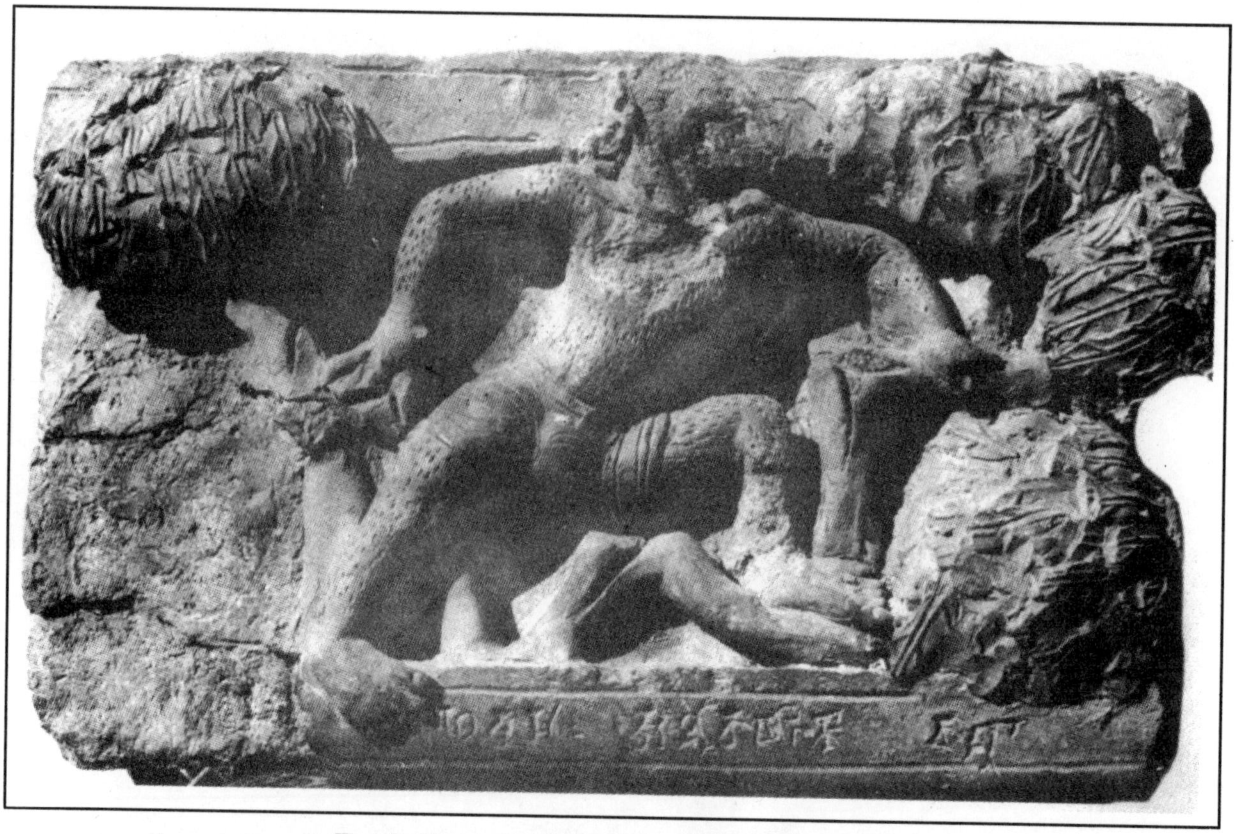

Fig. 9. Hanumān destroying Aśoka-vāṭikā, Jind.

elsewhere. One of the panel from Jind is inscribed like the Nachar Khera panels and shows the scene of the devastation of the Aśoka-vāṭikā (Fig. 9). Hanumān, whose head and tail are unfortunately badly mutilated, has uprooted many of the trees and plants while some others have been slanted and damaged. The monkey-god has been depicted as having thick hairy skin and wearing an *ardhoruk*. The inscription in Gupta Brāhmī letters on the bottom frame reads '*Aśokavāṭikā hantā Hanumān*', i.e., Hanumān, the destroyer of the Aśoka-vāṭikā. Another panel from Jind is simply marvelous. It has not suffered much mutilation but is not inscribed. There was perhaps no need to label it as the scene depicted is very well known. It shows the duel between Sugrīva and Bālī (Pl. 121). Both are monkey-faced and wear small beaded diadems, wristlets, waist-guards and nether garments. Sugrīva is shown almost diagonally in *pratyālīḍha* posture with both hands raised above the head to attack Bālī who stands turned towards him with right hand raised above the head and left akimbo, pushing Sugrīva with his right foot placed on his left thigh. The figures are proportionate and whole scene looks very natural and exudes dynamism of depiction. It is to be noted that the two terracotta panels from Jind described above actually come from two different spots in Jind, one km apart from each other, thus indicating the existence of different temples to which they belong. The clay used for them is also different.

One inscribed *Rāmāyaṇa* panel from Sirsa shows a demon holding a sword in his right hand with a broken chariot and two dead horses, a headless big bird with long feathers on his knees and some similar object below his right hand. The head of the demon had detached but has been joined to the body very crudely affecting the beauty of the panel. The inscription is engraved on the top frame and reads '*Tṛiśiravadhe* (*namaḥ*) *kṛitihantā . . . raṇasya*'.

A terracotta representing the god Rāma (Pl. 122), 47 cm in height and fired brown, from Nachar Khera, was gifted by Marilyn Walter Grounds to the Los Angeles County Museum of Art Collection (Acc. No. M.83.221.6), and has been published by Pratapaditya Pal.[227] It also bears the identificatory inscription '*Rāma*' in Gupta Brāhmī letters near the left thigh of the god. Large, open eyes, obliquely sweeping eyebrows, and elongated ears characterize the face. The face is expressive of his strong personality. Here also Rāma is dressed like a warrior in a tunic resembling those of the Gupta monarchs on their coins. Also vividly depicted are the cross-belt (*chhannavīra*), the bow in the left hand and a quiver full of arrows, behind the right shoulder. The right hand is raised in the gesture of reassurance. The figure is detached from a larger composition. It seems that all these bricks adorned some Vaishṇava temple at Nachar Khera during the Gupta period.

No independent image of Rāma in stone has come down to us in Haryana. An elegant depiction of Rāma, however, exists on a doorframe from Pinjore now preserved in the Government Museum & Art Gallery at Chandigarh. The extant portion of the doorframe is 73 cm in height and has three of its sides carved with decorative designs and figures of divinities. The backside, which was fixed on the wall of the temple, is plain. The carved sides are divided into different sections by decorative horizontal bands. In the panel on the right side of the river goddess Gaṅgā, there stands Rāma with a bow in the left hand, while the right hand is placed on the hip (Pl. 123).[228] Rāma dons a *dhotī.* There seems to be a quiver also at the back of the right shoulder. The figure is carved very sensitively showing the lingering on of the Gupta idiom in the region. The doorframe may stylistically be assigned to *circa* 7th century C.E. This, however, seems to have been the depiction of the incarnatory forms of Vishṇu as there exists the figure of the Varāha form also on another facet of this doorframe as noted above. Rāma has been depicted in some Vishṇu images also showing the Daśāvatāras. He is shown with an elaborate *karaṇḍa-mukuṭa*, earrings, pearl necklet and necklace, wristlets, etc. holding the bow in his left hand and resting the right on the respective thigh on the back slab of the Kosli Vishṇu image.

HANUMĀN

Hanumān, son of the wind-god Mārūti[229] and Añjanā according to popular Hindu belief, got this name because his chin was broken by Indra who hurled his *vajra* at him[230] as the monkey child, after his birth, took the glittering sun as an object of food, jumped at it but finding Rāhu to be bigger, diverted to him. On seeing Airāvata (Indra's elephant), he tried to eat it but was hit by Indra with his thunderbolt. The *Champū Rāmāyaṇa* (IV.10) also supports this view but the *Padma Purāṇa* says that he got this name as he was born at a place known as Hanuruha.[231] In the Vālmīki *Rāmāyaṇa* and most other texts, he is described as a monkey. The Rudra Saṃhitā of the *Śiva Purāṇa* describe him as an incarnation of Rudra, who appeared in the form of monkey to render assistance to Rāma.[232] Some scholars consider him to be of non-Aryan origin. On the advice of his guru Sūrya, he accepted the minister-ship and companionship of Sugrīva (Sūrya's son). The *Gheruṇḍa Saṃhitā* records a tradition that Hanumān learnt the secrets of breath control from his mother Añjanā, who had learnt it from Vāyu. He was unequalled in bravery, courage and competence and observed strict celibacy. He possessed the power of reducing (*Aṇimā*) or expanding (*Mahimā*) his size and could assume any form. The *Padma Purāṇa* endows him with all the knowledge of arts and letters, besides being a literary genius.[233] His devotion and obedience to Rāma is unprecedented. The *Brahma Purāṇa* identifies the Vṛishākapi of the *Ṛigveda* with Mahākapi Hanumān of the epic and Puranic literature.

The earliest definite representations of Hanumān in the plastic art known so far go back to the Ikshvāku and Gupta periods. But Sugh has yielded some terracottas, which indicate the popularity of Hanumān at an early period in Haryana. One small figure (Pl. 124), 5.0 x 3.5 cm, representing only the molded head shows round eyes with prominent eyeballs, protruding prognathism with heavy upper and thin lower lip and negligible chin. A conical crown with a crest is placed on his head. It is the crown, which distinguishes it from ordinary monkey figurines and help us to identify it as the head of Hanumān. Stylistically, it may be placed in *circa* 2nd-3rd century C.E.

Another head (Pl. 125), which measures 9.5 x 3.0 cm, is similar in conception though crude in execution. A tenon below it indicates that it was meant to be attached to a modeled body. On stylistic grounds it seems to be slightly later than the preceding example. A small terracotta moulded head of Hanumān with a typical conical headdress and a tenon below at the neck is known from Thanesar also (Pl. 126).[234]

Still another molded head of Hanumān from Sugh measuring 5.25 x 2.75 cm (Pl. 127) betrays the popularity of the god in the region. The hair are drawn upwards and held by a fillet on the forehead and fan outward above (Pl. 128). Oblique lines on the sides going up to the ears separate the head and the face. The facial features show a decline in the terracotta art. Stylistically, it may be assigned to *circa* 5th-6th century C.E.

Numerous large-sized Gupta terracotta bricks and figurines discovered from Agroha indicate the existence there of temples adorned with these figures. Amongst them is what seems to be the broken figurine of a demon (Pl. 129).[235] Some figurines from this site represent Kṛishṇa-*līlā* scenes described below. It is not surprising if the broken demon figure from Agroha represents some scene from the *Rāmāyaṇa* but one cannot be very certain about it unless some more or corroborative evidence comes forth from the site.

All these figurines in clay show the popularity of Hanumān amongst the common folk. The molded heads further indicate that such figurines were produced on a large scale to cater to the demand of the masses.

BALARĀMA

Balarāma, the elder brother of Kṛishṇa, is believed to be a form of Vishṇu and an incarnation of the cosmic serpent Ananta.[236] As such, he is endowed with many attributes of Vishṇu and Ananta.[237] He was expert in club-fighting *gadā-yuddha-viśeshajño gadā-yuddha-viśāradaḥ*[238] and had trained Bhīma and Duryodhana in this art.[239] The appearance of a club in his hand in some of his early images is thus quite natural.[240] Snake-hood, *hala*, and *mūshala*, the two original attributes of Ananta,[241] however, are the usual features of the iconography of Balarāma almost from the beginning.[242] His addiction to wine,[243] so popularly known to ancient authors,[244] is responsible for the depiction of a wine flask or cup in most of his images from the Kushāṇa period onwards.[245]

The veteran scholar N.P. Joshi, who studied a large number of images of the god from northern India and has produced an excellent monograph on the Iconography of Balarāma, has described and illustrated an interesting Kushāṇa piece from Mathura which shows a small crocodile, with face turned upwards, near the left foot of the god.[246] Since this was the only example of the type known to the author, he was not sure whether the reptile's appearance was intentional or casual.[247] He, however, explained the presence of the crocodile near the feet of Balarāma as symbolic of the ocean.[248]

More than four decades back, a gigantic image of Balarāma was found at Asthal Bohr, Rohtak[249] but has remained neglected so far. It is preserved along with other sculptures in the premises of the Asthal Bohr, which is a *maṭha* of the *Kanaphaṭā Jogīs*, on Rohtak-Delhi road. This more than the life-size image of buff sandstone, 2.10 m in height, shows the god standing on a *padma-pīṭha* on the central projection of a *triratha* pedestal (Pl. 130). The two-handed god stands in a double flexion pose[250] holding a long scepter-like hexagonal pestle in the right hand and a plough in the left. The lower one-third portion of the shaft of the plough, held vertically, is also hexagonal and its top shows a lion (with head broken) on it. The hair of the god is combed backwards and is tied in a high bun[251] held in position by pearl strings and adorned by a crest-jewel in front.[252] The plump oval face bears quasi-closed intoxicated eyes (*mada-vibhrama-lochana*) with *chāpākāra* 'bow-like' eyebrows, a prominent nose, and full lips. His ears are long and bear ornaments.[253] He wears a beautiful torque and a multi-stranded necklace with lotus-shaped spacers. There is a diamond shaped *śrīvatsa* carved on the chest. He wears a sacred thread, armlets, bracelets, *hatha-phūla*, finger-rings, scarf, *adhovastra* held in position by a beautiful girdle, anklets and the long garland.[254] Near the left foot of the deity is carved the forepart of a crocodile with its snout turned upwards,[255] seemingly supporting the lower end of the plough in its mouth. The image thus reveals that the depiction of the crocodile with Balarāma is not casual but intentional and that the tradition may have continued from the Kushāṇa period onwards to the 11th century C.E. to which date it may be assigned on stylistic grounds.

We have already referred to Balarāma as an incarnation of Ananta above. The association of Ananta with ocean/water, which is symbolically represented by crocodile[256] also, is well established. Hence the presence of crocodile in Balarāma's image is not surprising. Obliquely, the crocodile may symbolize the serpent Ananta also.[257] The absence of snake-hood over Balarāma's head is perhaps compensated by the depiction of the crocodile near his feet in the present image.[258] The gigantic size indicates it to have been an independent image. A temple dedicated to Balarāma may have existed at Asthal Bohr. Being, however, the singular independent image of the god found so far in Haryana, and also showing the presence of the crocodile, it is all the more important.

A small, detached frieze is also housed in the Asthal Bohr monastery at Rohtak (Pl. 131). It shows two-handed Balarāma holding a pestle in his right hand and a plough in the left, standing in a somewhat unusually flexional posture with both the feet turned slightly towards the left. The lower end of the plough rests on the ground. Balarāma wears the *karaṇḍa-mukuṭa* with a bun of hair on the top, usual ornaments including the *vaijayantīmālā*, and stands probably under the serpent-canopy and is accompanied by two diminutive acolyte figures. The figure may be dated to 10th century.

Balarāma has been depicted as an attendant of Vishṇu also as we have seen above. Balarāma figures on the medieval doorframes also. He is shown as standing in *dvibhaṅga* in a *rathikā* on the *pedyā*, holding a plough in his right hand and a pestle with a long shaft in the left hand, at Ratpur near Pinjore (Pl. 132). The lower hands are broken. On the top proper right hand corner of a doorframe from Hat, Balarāma is shown as standing in *dvibhaṅga* in a pedimented *rathikā* having triple ribbed pilasters, bearing a *karaṇḍa-mukuṭa,* earrings, *ekāvali*, armlets, wristlets, lower garment secured by a girdle, long garland, etc. and holding the plough from the lower end of the shaft in his left hand, resting the right one on the respective thigh (Pl. 133). It may be dated to *circa* 10th century C.E. On an architectural piece in the Jhajjar Museum, Balarāma is wearing a cylindrical crown and sacred thread, besides the usual ornaments and dress, holding the plough in his right hand and resting the other on the left thigh (Pl. 134). Two-handed Balarāma standing in *tribhaṅga*, wearing *kirīṭa-mukuṭa,* long garland and other usual ornaments, holding a plough in the right hand with left akimbo, may be seen in a niched panel of a doorjamb from Lulodh (Pl. 135) also.

KṚISHṆA

In the absence of any definite historical evidence, it is difficult to ascertain exactly the origin and antiquity of the Kṛishṇa-cult.[259] Mentioned as a renowned seer in the *Ṛigveda*,[260] Kṛishṇa Āṅgirasa finds a reference in the *Kauśītaki Brāhmaṇa*[261] also but has been alluded to as Devakīputra and a disciple of the solar priest Ghora Āṅgirasa in the *Chhāndogya Upanishad*.[262] The *Mahābhārata*, the earliest and most important work to give details of the life of Kṛishṇa, repeatedly refers to his mother Devakī [263] and father Vasudeva. He belonged to the Vṛishṇi family, a branch of the Yādavas. Being the son of Vasudeva, Kṛishṇa is well known as Vāsudeva also. Many passages in the *Mahābhārata*, and subsequently the Purāṇas, represent Vāsudeva-Kṛishṇa as the Supreme Soul, the Absolute Being and an incarnation of Nārāyaṇa-Vishṇu. These works also relate in details various myths and stories about the life of the god as also of his feats and exploits.[264]

Pāṇini (5th century B.C.E.) provides the definite evidence of the worship of Kṛishṇa as a god through his grammatical formula '*Vāsudevārjunābhyāṃ vuñ*'[265] to explain the formulation of the word Vāsudeva in the sense of an object or subject of devotion. The association of the word Arjuna is also significant here. Patañjali (2nd century B.C.E.), while commencing on Pāṇini's *sūtras* III. 1, 26 and IV.3, 98 makes it very clear that during his period Vāsudeva-Kṛishṇa was regarded as both, a hero and a god.[266] That Kṛishṇa worship was quite popular in northwest India in the 4th century B.C.E. is revealed by the Roman historian Curtius who records the fact that the army of king Porus carried an image of Heracles (=Kṛishṇa) in front of them during its fight against Alexander.[267] Megasthenes also refers to the prevalence of the worship of 'Indian Heracles' among the Sourasenoi who inhabited Methora (Mathura) and Cleisobora (Kṛishnapura?).[268] The depiction of Vāsudeva and Saṃkarshaṇa on the square bronze coins of Agathocles (171-160 B.C.E.) found from Afghanistan[269] further corroborate the popularity of the worship of Vāsudeva and Saṃkarshaṇa in northwest India and beyond during the 2nd century B.C.E. Ghosundi inscription (2nd century B.C.E.) from Rajasthan also refers to the shrine of Vāsudeva and Saṃkarshaṇa called Nārāyaṇa-vāṭikā.[270]

With the development of the concept of devotion during the Upanishadic period, a cult seems to have developed around the five Vṛishṇi heroes (*Vṛishṇipañcha-vīrāḥ*) of which Vāsudeva was the main figure besides Saṃkarshaṇa Pradymna, Anirddha and Sāmba.[271] The Mora well inscription (*circa* C.E. 10-25), found about 10 km west of Mathura, records the existence of a stone shrine housing the images of the five Vṛishṇi heroes.[272] Vṛishṇi coins, seals and sealings found from Sunet and elsewhere in the present day Punjab provide evidence of the habitation of the region by the Vṛishṇis during the early centuries of the current era.[273]

There is ample evidence of the prevalence of Vaishṇavism in Haryana during the early historic and medieval periods[274] but not much is known about the popularity of the cult of Kṛishṇa. Kṛishṇa themes in the art of the region are also wanting. Clay sealings bearing the names of Balabhadra from Sanghol; Krishnadatta, Nandisoma and Kṛishṇaghosha from Sunet (Punjab);[275] Sirsa stone Inscription of Bhojadeva referring to a brick and stone temple of Yogīśvara (Śiva) adorned with the images of Murāri and other deities,[276] and the Hansi Stone Inscription of Pṛithvīrāja II (VS 1224= C.E. 1167) invoking the god Murāri (Kṛishṇa),[277] however, do indicate that Kṛishṇa has remained known in the region and his worship has also continued through the ages.

As is well known, the Mahābharata war, in which Kṛishṇa played a very prominent role, was fought at Kurukshetra in Haryana. Also, it was at Kurukshetra that Kṛishṇa enlightened Arjuna with the exhortations of the *Gītā*. There are many spots in the region of Kurukshetra that are associated with the characters or events of the *Mahābhārata* but those related to Kṛishṇa are very few.[278] No independent image of Kṛishṇa, nor any panel depicting

Kṛishṇa-*līlā* scenes, has yet been found from Haryana. This almost complete paucity of the Kṛishṇa theme in the plastic art of Haryana is rather intriguing. In the following lines, we put before the scholars some relics, which may probably be associated with the god.

Sugh has yielded, among others, a large number of terracottas. Interesting and noteworthy amongst them is a plaque with a child, seated in a natural pose with a wooden board, *takhtī*, between his legs.[279] The head of the boy is gone. He is shown as naked but has anklets. The *takhtī* shows four lines of letters, all vowels.[280] The boy points out at the letters with the pointing finger of his right hand while the left hand holds the *takhtī* firmly (Pl. 136). The form of the Brāhmī letters written on the *takhtī* indicate 2nd century B.C.E. as the date of the terracotta.

B. Ch. Chhabra, on a suggestion of Sivaramamurti, thinks that the terracotta depicts Kṛishṇa receiving education in the hermitage of Sandīpani at Avantipura.[281] In the absence of any definitive identificatory mark, however, it is difficult to certainly identify the boy with Kṛishṇa.

Some years back, D.S. Punia published a Kushāṇa red sandstone image, measuring 38 x 32 cm, from Sondh in southern Haryana. Unfortunately it is very much mutilated. It shows only the bust of a four-armed deity holding a discus in the back left hand while the corresponding right is damaged. The principal hands hold a conch shell near the chest so as to blow it. The face of the god is badly mutilated beyond recognition but traces of typical Kushāṇa triangular necklace and bracelets on his person may still be made out. Punia has recognized the deity as Vishṇu (Pl. 137).[282]

More than three decades back, N.P. Joshi had listed a large number of references from various texts like the *Mahābhārata, Vishṇu Purāṇa, Matsya Purāṇa, Liṅga Purāṇa, Brahma Purāṇa, Padma Purāṇa*, etc. where Vāsudeva Kṛishṇa has been described as holding *śaṅkha, chakra* and *gadā* only, rarely a sword or a bow also, the absence of *padma* being notable. So he advocates that the early Mathura Vishṇu images showing only the above-mentioned attributes should be recognized as those of Vāsudeva Kṛishṇa.[283] It is to be noted that Sondh is located near Mathura and the image under discussion does not show the lotus. The posture of blowing the conch, we think, provides an important clue for its identification with Kṛishṇa who has been described as such at various places in the *Mahābhārata*.[284] So we feel that the Sondh image represents Vāsudeva-Kṛishṇa rather than Vishṇu.

The earliest definite representation of the deity however comes from Sanghel in the Nuh tehsil of district Gurgaon in the form of an Ekānaṃśā relief described above (Pl. 21). It shows the triad - Saṃkarshaṇa-Balarāma, Ekānaṃśā and Vāsudeva-Kṛishṇa - standing to front. The normal right hand of Vāsudeva-Kṛishṇa is raised to the level of the shoulder in fear-allaying gesture and the left one is akimbo. Unfortunately, the head and the additional hands are broken. The triad, however, resembles almost exactly the known reliefs of Ekānaṃśā and comes from the neighboring region of Mathura, the legendary ancestral home of the Vṛishṇis.

Agroha has got very extensive mounds, which have even partially been excavated. Rodgers' excavations during 1888-89 brought to light a very large number of carved bricks and sculptured stones, which clearly indicated the existence of a brick temple.[285] Srivastava's excavations during 1938-39 and the recent excavations (1979-85) by the Department of Archaeology & Museums, Haryana,[286] too, have corroborated the evidence of Gupta brick temples at Agroha. The temple/s seem/s to have been adorned by panels depicting probably the *Rāmāyaṇa* and Kṛishṇa-*līlā* scenes. A fragmentary brick panel measuring 21.5 x 15 cm recovered during the excavations,[287] shows the head, neck and one of the forelegs of a horse (Plate 138). Unfortunately, the rest of the figure is broken. The ferociousness of the equine, however, is evident from the sharp teeth, swollen nostrils, wide-open eye and mouth, erect manes and the upraised foreleg. Obviously, the animal has been depicted in the posture of attacking. As such, it seems to have been a representation of the demon Keśī who rushed to attack Kṛishṇa on his chest with his front legs and attempted to kill him but was done to death by the god.

Another fragmentary panel from the same site, measuring 21.5 x 19 cm, shows a wrestling scene (Pl. 139).[288] But for the left leg, the figure of the wrestler on the left has survived completely but the other one has survived in the form of his firmly planted left leg and a small portion of the belly only. There is no definite identification mark but the robust bodies of the wrestlers, the gracefully depicted garment and the elegance with which the panel has been carved endow it with a speciality. The panel, when complete, may have depicted the scene of Śāla-vadha or a wrestling match between Bhīma and Jarāsandha watched by Kṛishṇa or a scene of the wrestling arena of Mathura.

Stylistically assignable to the post-Gupta period are some relics from Gujjar Kheri, which may have belonged to some Vaishṇava temple depicting Kṛishṇa-*līlā* scenes. To judge from its very extensive mound and the large number of antiquarian remains it has yielded, Gujjar Kheri may have remained a very important town of Haryana during the early historic and medieval times.[289] A square pilaster showing *ardhapadma* and beautiful vine-scroll motifs provides evidence of the existence of a stone temple at Gujjar Kheri in about C.E. 700. A doorjamb (Pl. 140), probably belonging to the same temple, contains two vertical and two horizontal panels, alternatively placed. In the lowermost panel is shown a beautifully carved male figure wearing *ardhoruk*, *ekāvali* and *vanamālā*, standing in *pratyālīḍha* posture, uprooting or breaking something with both his hands. The hairstyle is very exquisite and the facial expression very serene. The *vanamālā* here certainly suggests the figure to have been that of Kṛishṇa.[290] The upper vertical panel shows the god in the posture of Kāliya-damana with anthropomorphic Kāliya standing before him with folded hands. The horizontal panels, which are much smaller in size, depict two equestrians and elephant riders respectively facing each other.

Gujjar Kheri has yielded another small figure, broken below the waist, which may be recognized as Veṇu-Gopāla (Pl. 141).[291] The execution is somewhat crude. The cowherd-god is shown as playing on his flute held stylistically in both of his hands. The hair is combed backward, and bedecked with a jewel at the apex. *Ekāvali*, armlets and bracelets may also be seen on the person of the god. The bend of the body in the extant portion indicates that the god must have stood gracefully playing on his flute. Stylistically, it may be assigned to *circa* 8th century C.E.

A small but beautiful sandstone relief from Fatehabad (No. IM 309-1921) is preserved in the Victoria & Albert Museum, London (Pl. 142).[292] It shows on the central offset of a *triratha* pedestal a calf suckling the mother-cow who has turned back her head to lick the calf at its back. There is a foliated canopy over the cow that is bedecked with pearl-strings on the head, a necklace around the neck and ornamental chains covering the body. The calf also has a necklace. Both the figures are very lively and animated with their tails taking a circular upward curl. In front of the cow is a pedestalled vase full of sweet-balls. More important, however, is the figure on the left offset of the pedestal showing a graceful human figure in *tribhaṅga*, clad in a *dhotī* with a sash on the knees, and wearing an *uttarīya*, sacred thread, necklet, *keyūras*, *valayas*, etc. and supporting on his raised left hand the stylized mountain. The right hand rests on the right knee. At the back of the cow is another human figure, wearing similar clothes and ornaments, with a six-petalled halo behind the head, holding some unidentifiable rod-like object in his upraised right hand. This thus is the depiction of Kṛishṇa uplifting the Govardhana Mountain to protect Gokula from the wrath of Indra who caused excessive rain to punish the inhabitants who had worshipped Kṛishṇa instead of the rain-god. The relief is carved very exquisitely and may be dated to the 9th century on stylistic grounds. The relief resembles very much a grey sandstone sculpture of child Kṛishṇa lifting the Mount Govardhana found from the village Govardhana in the Mathura district.[293]

The foregoing account reveals that though Kṛishṇa was not unknown in Haryana yet his plastic representations are not commensurate with his importance as a Hindu god and an incarnation of Vishṇu. The reason is not far to seek, however. Right from the earliest representations of Kṛishṇa belonging to the Kushāṇa period, where his *Ārādhya* or incarnatory form was to be emphasized, he is depicted as having four-hands and carrying the same emblems as Vāsudeva-Vishṇu. Since the Sāttvat Pañcharātra sect was dominant at Mathura and in the surrounding region including Haryana, Kṛishṇa was depicted in his *Ārādhya* form as Vāsudeva-Kṛishṇa, hardly distinguishable from Vāsudeva-Vishṇu.[294] Arjuna and Kṛishṇa are regarded as the incarnations of Nara and Nārāyaṇa, i.e. the four-handed Vāsudeva holding *śaṅkha, chakra, gadā* and *padma*.[295]

BUDDHA

Buddha, as we have seen above, is mentioned in some of the Purāṇas like the *Agni*, *Bhāgavata*, *Matsya*, etc. as an incarnation of Vishṇu. The *Agni* (49.8) prescribes him to be seated on an *ūrdhva-padma* 'high lotus seat', bearing a very benign and calm appearance, long ears and a halo, with hands in the gesture of protection and reassurance, without any other Vaishṇava emblem. *Ūrdhva-padma* is the characteristic of Buddhist images and sometimes Yoga-Nārāyaṇa is also shown as seated on a high pedestal; so it is believed that the sculptors may have tried to represent Buddha incarnation through the image of Yoga-Nārāyaṇa.[296] Yoga-Nārāyaṇa images from Sirsa (Pl. 68) and Pinjore (Pl. 69) have already been described above.

KALKI

Kalki, the future incarnation of Vishṇu to appear at the end of the Kali age according to the *Bhāgavata Purāṇa* (I.3, 26), will be holding the sword, the conch, the disc, and the mace according to the *Agni Purāṇa* (49.9). Kalki is generally represented in the Daśāvatāra panels as seated on the horseback and holding the sword as on the back slab of the Kosli Vishṇu image (Pl. 64). No independent image of Kalki is known from Haryana nor is there any *tīrtha* in the region associated with him.

Though no images of the lesser known incarnatory forms of Vishṇu have been found from anywhere in Haryana yet some of them are associated with some *tīrthas* in the Kurukshetra region. Haṃsa is associated with Haṃsa-*tīrtha* at village Salwan and Eka-haṃsa at village Ikkas. Hayagrīva-*tīrtha* occurs at Awatpur. At Bahadurpur is located Dhanvantari-*tīrtha* and Dattātreya-*tīrtha* is pointed out at village Ittal.

Notes and References

1. *DHI*, p. 388.
2. *Bhagavadgītā* IV.7-8.
3. *ṚV* I.154, 1-2; *Ś. Br.* I.2, 5.
4. *Ś.Br.* I.8, 1, 1-6.
5. *Tait. Saṃ.* VII.1, 5;*Tait. Br.* I.1, 3.
6. *Ś. Br.* XIV.1, 2, 11; *Tait. Ār.* VI.3, 5, 8; and X.1, 6.

7. *Mbh.* XII.349, 37; 389, 77-90 etc. The *HV* (I.41) quotes a list of ten incarnations, which omits Matsya, Kūrma, one Rāma and includes Paushkaraka, Datta, Keśava, and Vyāsa. Cf. *Brahma P.*, ch. 213.
8. *Mbh.* XII.389, 104.
9. Ch. 98, vv. 71 ff.
10. D.C. Sircar, *Studies in the Religious Life of Ancient and Medieval India*, Delhi, 1971, p. 42.
11. *Matsya P.* LVII.237-48.
12. *Bhāg. P.* I.3, 26:
    Avatārā hyasaṃkhyeyā Hareḥ sattvanidherdvijāḥ /
    Yathāvidāsinaḥ kulyāḥ sarasaḥ syuḥ sahasraśaḥ //
13. *Ibid.*, I.3, 6-22; II.7, 1 ff and XI.4, 3ff respectively.
14. As quoted by Banerjea, *DHI*, pp. 391-92.
15. Otto E. Schrader, *Introduction to the Pañcarātra and the Ahirbudhnya Saṃhitā*, Madras, 1916, pp. 42 ff.
16. *Garuḍa P.* I.1, 13-15.
17. *Ibid.*, II.20, 31.
18. *Agni P.* Chs. 2-16. Cf. *Varāha P.* chs. 39-48.
19. *Varāha P.* IV.2.
20. A.D. Pusalkar, *Studies in the Epics and Puranas*, Bombay, 1955, p. 10.
21. E.W. Hopkins, *Epic Mythology*, p. 217.
22. See R. Champakalakshmi, *Vaiṣṇava Iconography in the Tamil Country*, New Delhi, 1981, p. 81.
23. Ronald M. Huntington, "Avatāras and Yugas: An Essay in Puranic Cosmology," *Purāṇam*, Vol. VI, no. 1 (Jan. 1964), pp. 33-37.
24. Champakalakshmi, *op. cit.*, p. 28.
25. Kalpana Desai, *Iconography of Viṣṇu*, p. 63.
26. J. Gonda, *Aspects of Early Viṣṇuism*, Utrecht, 1954, pp. 11-21.
27. *Ś. Br.* I.8, 1-9.
28. *Mbh.* III.185, 48:
    Ahaṃ Prajāpati Brahmā matparaṃ ṇādhigamyate /
    Matsyarūpeṇa yūyaṃ cha mayāsmānmokshitā bhayāt //
29. Compare the accounts in the *Bhāg.* and *Matsya P.*
30. Hopkins, *op. cit.*, p. 218. Cf. Kennedy, *Hindu Mythology*, p. 432.
31. *VDP* 65.59. Cf. *Mbh.* III.185, 31: *Āgamishyāmyahṃ śriṅgī vijñetena tāpasa/*
32. *VDP* 85.60.
33. *Merutantra*, Bombay, 1904, p. 127.
34. Kalpana Desai, *op. cit.*, p. 63.
35. *Ibid.*, pp. 63-64, figs. 53 and 56. See also B.C. Bhattacharyya, *Indian Images*, Calcutta, 1954, p. 19, and N.K. Bhattasali, *Iconography of Buddhist and Brahmanical Sculptures in the Dacca Museum*, p. 105.
36. Mohinder Singh, "Terracottas from Thanesar," in *Ajaya-Śrī*, Vol. 2, p. 408, pl. 67.
37. *AV* IV.20, 7;XIII.3, 10;XVII.1, 28;XIX.53, 10 etc. Also *Ś. Br.* VII.5, 6.
38. *Tait. Ār.* I.7, 1: *Kaśyapaḥ ārogabhrājādi saptasūryāpekshayā ashṭamaḥ sūryaḥ /*
39. *Ś. Br.* VI.1. 1, 12.
40. *Ibid.* VII.5, 5-6.
41. *Ibid.* VII.5, 1, 2.
42. *Ibid.*
43. Ibid.
44. *Vāj. Saṃ.* XIII.31.
45. *Kalpana Desai, op. cit.*, p. 66.
46. Gonda (1954), *op. cit.*, p. 126.
47. *Rām.* I.41.
48. *Mbh.* I.16 ff.
49. *Vishṇu P.* I.9.

50. *Bhāg. P.* VIII.6-7.
51. *VDP* III.85, 59.
52. Agni P.
53. XII.69-70.
54. *Merutantra*, pp. 26-27.
55. *Śrī-Tattva-nidhi*, Veṅkaṭeśvara Press, Bombay, *dhyāna* 215 (p. 40):
Kāñchanasannibhaḥ abhaya-chakra-śaṅkhaṃ-varada-hastaḥ /
Pītāmbaradharaḥ sarvālaṅkārabhūshitaḥ //
56. Kalpana Desai, *op. cit.*, fig. 55.
57. Urmila Agrawal, *Khajuraho Sculptures and Their Significance*, Delhi, 1964, p. 36; Ramashray Awasthi, *Khajurāho kī Deva Pratimāyeṃ*, Agra, 1967.
58. *Cf.* (i). *Asyedu mātuḥ savaneshu sadyo mahaḥ pituṃ papivāñchārvannā /*
Mushāyad Vishṇnuḥ pachataṃ sahīyān vidhyadvarāhaṃ tiro adrimastā //
(*ṚV* I. 61, 7)
(ii). *Viśvet tā Vishṇurābharaurukramastveshitaḥ /*
Śataṃ mahishān kshīrapākamodanaṃ Varāhamindra Emusham//
(*ṚV* VIII.77, 10)
(iii). *Prakāvyamuśeva bruvāṇo devo devānāṃ janimā vivakti /*
Mahivrataḥ śuchibandhuḥ pāvakaḥ padā Varāho abhyeti rebhana//
(*ṚV* IX. 97, 7)
(iv). *Idaṃ su me jaritarā chikiddhi pratīpaṃ śāpaṃ nadyo vahanti /*
Lopāshaḥ siṃhaṃ pratyañchmatsāḥ kroshṭā Varāhaṃ niratakta kakshāt //
(*ṚV* X. 28, 4)
(V). *Yamimaṃ tvaṃ Vṛishākapiṃ priyamindrābhirakshasi /*
Śvā nvasya jambhiyadapi karṇe Varāhayurviśvasmādindra uttaraḥ//
(*ṚV* X. 86, 4)
59. *Divo Varāhamarushaṃ kapardinaṃ tveshaṃ rūpaṃ namasā ni hvayāmahe/*
Haste bibhrad bheshajā vāryāṇI śarma varmachchhardirasmabhyaṃ yaṃsat// (*ṚV* I. 114, 5)
60. See also *ṚV* I.88, 5; 121, 11; *Tait.Ār.* 1.9.4; etc.
61. U.P. Shah, *Journal of the Oriental Institute*, 7 (1957-58), 41 ff. Also see *IV*, pp. 71-83.
62. *ṚV* X.86, 4.
63. E.W. Hopkins, *Journal of the American Oriental Society*, 17 (1865), 67.
64. *AV*, VIII.7.23; 12.1.48; *Kāṭhaka Saṃhitā*, 8.2; 25.2; *Tait.Saṃ.*VI.2.4.2; VII.1.5.1; etc.
65. *Śat. Br.* II.1.1.10; XIV.1.2.11; *Sacred Books of the East*, Vol. XII, p. 280; Vol. XLIV, p. 451. cf., *ṚV* 8.77.10. Suvira Jaiswal holds the view that Boar was originally a totemic deity of some powerful non-Aryan tribe undergoing Brahmanization and it got associated with the Creator god Brahmā (Prajāpati), and later with Vishṇu (*The Origin and Development of Vaiṣṇavism*, 2nd ed., New Delhi, 1981, pp. 131-32).
66. *T. Br.*, 1.1.3.5. Cf., *Tait. Ār.*(I.10.8) where the earth is described to have been uplifted by a black boar with a hundred arms:
Varāheva Kṛishṇena śatabāhunā uddhṛitā /
67. We get some references regarding the existence of the *avatāra-vāda* in the later Vedic texts, but the ideology finds its consummate exposition in the *Bhagavad Gītā*. Cf.
Yadā yadā hi dharmasya glānirbhavati Bhārata /
Abhyutthānamadharmasya tadātmānaṃ sṛijāmyaham//
Paritrāṇāya sādhunāṃ vināśāya cha dushkṛitām/
Dharmasaṃsthāpanārthāya sambhavāmi yuge yuge // (IV. 7-8)
68. *Rām.*, Ayodhyā-kāṇḍa, 110.3; Araṇya-kāṇḍa, 31.24; and Yuddha-kāṇḍa, 117-13.
69. *Mbh.* (Gita Press ed.), Sabhā-parva, 39.29 ff, (pp. 784-85).
70. *Vishṇu Purāṇa*, 3.1.36-44; *Bhāgvata Purāṇa*, 1.3.6-22; *Padma Purāṇa*, (Bareli, 1970), vv. 1-171; *Skanda Purāṇa*, (Bareli 1972, Vol. II, pp. 416.28) vv. 1-61: *Matsya Purāṇa*, (Bareli, 1970, Vol. II, pp. 350-62), vv. 1-79; *Kūrma Purāṇa*, (Bareli 1971, pp. 91-95) vv. 1-25; etc. Besides these detailed accounts

brief references are found in the *Agni Purāṇa*, (Chowkhamba, 1966), 4.1-3; *Liṅga Purāṇa* (Bareli, 1959), Vol. I, p. 152; *Garuḍa Purāṇa*, (Bareli, 1970), Vol. I, p. 500; etc.

71. V.S. Agrawala, *Solar Symbolism of the Boar (Yajña-Varāha, An Interpretation)*, Banaras, 1963.
72. Devangana Desai, *The Religious Imagery of Khajuraho*, Mumbai, 1996, p. 64.
73. *EHI*, Vol. I, pt. I, (Rpt. Delhi, 1971), pp. 132-37.
74. *DHI*, p. 413. The hybridism in these forms lies in the head only and the rest of the body is shown as fully human. See also C. Sivaramamurti, 'Geographical and chronological and chronological factors in Indian iconography', *Ancient India*, New Delhi 6 (1950) 42.
75. N.P. Joshi, 'Kuṣāṇa Varāha Sculpture', *Arts Asiatique*, 12 (1965) 113-19, figs; *Lalit Kala*, no. 12 pp. 46-47, pl. XXX A; and *Bulletin of Museums and Archaeology in U.P.*, no. 11-12 (June-Dec., 1973), p. 52, no. 86.
76. B.N. Sharma, 'A Rare image of Varāha in the National Museum, New Delhi', *Vishveshvaranand Indological Journal*, 7 (1969), 131.
77. Alexander Cunningham, *Archaeological Survey Report*, Vol. X, pl. XVIII; A.K. Coomaraswamy, *History of Indian and Indonesian Art*, fig. 174; R.K. Mookerji, *The Gupta Empire*, (Bombay, 1959), pl. XVII.
78. C. Sivaramamurti (1950), *op. cit.*, pl. XIV. C; K.D. Bajpai, *Sagar through the Ages*, Sagar, 1964, p. 36, pl. IV.
79. K.R. Srinivasan, *Cave Temples of the Pallavas*, New Delhi, 1964, p. 146, pl. XLI.
80. *EHI*, pl. XLI, fig. 2.
81. R.D. Banerji, *Memoirs of the Archaeological Survey of India*, no. 25, pls. IX. b and XVII. b.
82. *EHI*, pl. XXXIX, fig. 1.
83. Varāha served as an emblem of the Western Chālukyas, the Kākatīyas and the Vijayanagara rulers (See C. Sivaramamurti, *Indian Epigraphy and South Indian Scripts*, Madras, 1966, p. 22). Rao (*EHI, op. cit.*) has also described and illustrated some Varāha images in the Madras Museum.
84. H. Cousens, *Somanatha and other Medieval temples in Kathiavad*, p. XXXV.
85. J. Burgess, *Archaeological Survey of Western India*, VIII (NIS), pt. ii, 1905, pls. XC-XCI.
86. Cousens, *op. cit.*, pl. I.
87. *EHI*, pl. XXXVIII
88. R.A. Awasthy, *op. cit.*, pls. XXX-XXXI.
89. *Sculptures: Udaipur Museum* (Jaipur, 1960), pls. XXXI.
90. *The Researcher*, 5-6 (1964-65) 97.
91. *Ibid.*
92. *Ibid.*
93. G.H. Ojha, *History of the Jodhpur State*, part I, Ajmer, 1938, p. 28.
94. *EHI*, pl. XXXIX, fig. 2.
95. Ojha, *op. cit.*, p. 37.
96. Kalpana Desai, *op. cit.*, fig. 60.
97. Ojha, *op. cit.*, p. 46.
98. *Ibid.*, p. 65.
99. *Catalogue Govt. Museum, Kota*, (Jaipur, 1960-61), p. 26.
100. *Sculptures: Udaipur Museum*, pls. XXI and XXV.
101. *Bulletin of Museums and Archaeology in U.P.*, no. 11-12, p. 52, no. 87.
102. R.K. Dikshit, *Kannauj*, Lucknow, 1955, pl. II. Here the spirited image of Vishṇu as Varāha has been shown as rescuing the earth from the clutches of the demon Hiraṇyakaśyapa.
103. *EHI*, pp. 137ff., Sivaramamurti (1950), *op. cit.*, p. 42; B.N. Sharma, 'Unpublished Pala and Sena sculptures in the National Museum, New Delhi', *East and West*, New Series, Vo. 19 (1969) 415-16, fig. 4.
104. Sivaramamurti, (*loc. cit.*), refers to the famous boars from Eran and in the Gwalior and Lucknow Museums and observes that "the normal area of the zoomorphic representation is Uttar Pradesh, Central India and the other parts of Orissa bordering on Madhya Pradesh". The Śūkara Varāha in the Udaipur Museum (*Supra*, fn. 41), however, extends this area to Rajasthan also. A beautiful

Śūkara Varāha image from Harda (Dt. Hoshangabad), ascribable to the 11th century, is exhibited in the Nagpur Museum.

105. This inscription has been inscribed on the Śūkara-Varāha itself.
106. J.F. Fleet, *Corpus Inscriptionum Indicarum*, III, p. 159.
107. *Epigraphia Indica*, I (1892), 121 ff.
108. *Ibid.*, pp. 184 ff.
109. This image corresponds to the Yajña-varāha form described by Rao (*EHI*, p. 135-36) as having "four arms, two of which are carry the *śaṅkha* and the *chakra*, the figure should be seated upon a siṃhāsana, with the right leg hanging down and the left resting upon the seat. On the right side should be seated the figure of Lakshmī on the left should be seated Bhūdevī ". Unfortunately no such image has been found from Pehowa though some sculptures and temple-remains have been notices there. See for details, Devendra Handa, "Pehoa-The Ancient Pṛthūdaka," *Purāṇa*, 9 (1967), 297-306.
110. *Report of the Rajputana Museum, 1913-14*, p. 2. Also see *Journal of Indian History*, 25 (1947), 355 ff.
111. *Indian Antiquary*, 58 (1929), 161.
112. Dasharatha Sharma (Gen. ed.), *Rajasthan through the Ages*, Vol. I, pp. 232-33 and 241.
113. Vincent A. Smith, *Catalogue of the coins in the Indian Museum, Calcutta*, Vol. I, Oxford, 1906, pp. 232-33 and 241.
114. Vana Parva, 83, 18-19.
115. *Vāmana P.* (Veṅkaṭeśvara Press), p. 62.
116. D.C. Bhattacharyya, *Medieval Indian Sculpture in the Government Museum and Art Gallery Chandigarh*, Chandigarh, 1981, pp. 92-93, fig. 46.
117. D.C. Bhattacharyya (*loc. cit.*) puts it in 8th century.
118. It was acquired by us for the Department of Archaeology and Museums, Haryana while serving as its Deputy Director during 1984-85. It is now preserved in the said department.
119. Devendra Handa, "Varāha Images from Haryana," in *Researches in Indian History, Archaeology, Art and Religion (Prof. Upendra Thakur Felicitation Volume)*, edited by G. Kuppuram and Kumudmani, Delhi, 1990, Vol. I, p.
120. It bears Index no. 1/81.
121. *CASR*, XIV, p. 101.
122. Handa (1967), *loc. cit.*
123. *Epigraphia Indica*, Vol. I, pp. 184-90.
124. *Supra* fn. 54.
125. An unfinished Vishṇu image from Asthal Bohr near Rohtak bears evidence to the fact that Rohtak was a center of art during the medieval period. For details see Devendra Handa (October 1985), p. 136, fig. 14.
126. John Irwin, "Viṣṇu in the archaic cosmogony," in *Indian Art & Connoisseurship Essays in Honour of Douglas Barret*, edited by John Guy, Indira Gandhi National Center for the Arts in association with Mapin Publishing Pvt. Ltd., New Delhi and Ahmedabad, 1995, pp. 75-85, fig. 1. An unfinished doorway now fitted in the Prāchī Śiva Temple at Pehowa [S.P. Shukla, "Relics of Ancient Art from Pehowa", *Research Bulletin (Arts) Panjab University*, Chandigarh, Vol. XI, 1980, pp. 76-77, fig. 10] indicates that sculptures were carved at Pehowa itself.
127. *Ibid.*, p. 78.
128. Devendra Handa (April 1986), *op. cit.*, pp. 107-21, figs. 1-20.
129. *Summaries of Papers, All India Oriental Conference*, 27th Session, 1974, Kurukshetra, p. 221. Also see S.P. Shukla, *Sculptures and Terracottas in the Archaeology Museum Kurukshetra University*, Kurukshetra, 1983, p. 12, pl. II.3.
130. Kara Sahib is located about 12 km from Pehowa on road to Gulha. There is an ancient mound here on which is located the Devī Temple. in the southern wall of this temple are fixed numerous small and fragmentary reliefs found from the old mound. One of these depicts a small Varāha figure, 8 x 8 cm, broken below the waist. The God holds a disc in his left hand. The Earth Goddess

is also seated on the elbow of the bent left arm. She touches the snout of the boar face. A finely carved halo behind the head has also survived. The piece may be dated to *circa* 10th-11th century C.E.

131. Dharampal Singh Punia (1976), pp. 215-16, pl. XXX.C. Punia has wrongly dated it to 11th-12th century C.E.
132. For a historical sketch of Agroha, see Devendra Handa, "Some Important Towns of Haryana: A study of their ancient past", *Journal of Haryana Studies*, II (Jan-Dec. 1970), 4ff.
133. H.L. Srivastava, *Excavation at Agroha, Punjab*, MASI no. 61, Delhi, 1952, p. 3, pl. X.1.
134. Udai Vir Singh, *Pinjore Sculptures*, Kurukshetra, 1977, p. 31. See also Shukla (1983), *op. cit.*, p. 50, pl. XLIII.2.
135. Shukla (1980), *op. cit.*, p. 75, fig. 9.
136. X.1.
137. III.17.
138. *Mahābhārata* (BORI, Poona) XII, 337, 34-36.
139. *Harivaṃśa* (Gita Press ed.), Bhavishya Parva, Chapters 41-47.
140. As quoted in *EHI*, Vol. I., part I, pp. 145 ff.
141. *Kūrma Purāṇa* (ed. M.R. Mor, Calcutta 1962) II, 36, 38-39.
142. *Vāmana Purāṇa* 63.5.
143. *Bhāgavata Purāṇa* (Gita Press ed.) VII.3, 35-37; 8, 18-33.
144. *Vishṇu Purāṇa* (Gita Press ed.) I.16-20.
145. For details, *EHI*, *loc. cit.*, Kalpana Desai, *op. cit.*, pp. 84 ff.
146. *EHI.*, Vol. I, part II, Appendix C, pp. 32-36.
147. *Jayākhya Saṃhitā* (GOS, Baroda, 1967), Paṭala VI. 135ff and XIII, 142-44.
148. An image from Bhita now in the State Museum, Lucknow showing small lion and boar figures on the sides, belonging to *circa* 2nd-1st century B.C.E., is generally regarded to be the earliest attempt to render the form of *Chaturmūrti*. For details see N.P. Joshi, *Catalogue of the Brahmanical Sculptures in the State Museum, Lucknow*, Part I, Lucknow, 1972, pp. 115-16. Also see *East and West*, New Series, Vol. 22, Nos.1-2, March-June, 1972, pp. 41-43, and Debala Mitra, "Vishnu Chaturmurti Image in Hari Rai Temple at Chamba", in *Art of Himachal* (ed. V.C. Ohri), State Museum, Simla, 1975, pp. 2-3.
149. Desai, *op. cit.*, pp. 86-88.
150. *Ibid.*, pp. 88 ff; *EHI*, Vol. I, part I, pp. 145ff; 145ff; *DHI*, pp. 415-17.
151. Barah Kalan near Jind is connected with the Boar incarnation, Vāmana Kuṇḍa (Amin) and Vāmana *tīrtha* (Banpura) with Vāmana, Ekahaṃsa (Ikkas) with Kṛishṇa, etc. Other notable *tīrthas* connected with various forms of Vishṇu are Paraśurāma *tīrtha* (Pehowa), Dattātreya (Ittal), Hayagrīva (Awatpur), Vishṇu-Pada (Gharaisi), Vishṇu-hrada (Bhaur Shyam), Chakra (Thanesar), Chakrapāṇi (Shardha), Nābhi-Kamala (Thanesar), Padmanābha (Narakatari), etc. all in the Kurukshetra region.
152. Devendra Handa (October, 1985), pp. 125-57 and figs.1-40.
153. *Mbh.* (Gita Press ed.), Vana Parva 83-21.
154. Silak Ram, "Tirthas of Kuruskehtra as Enumerated in the Mahabharata and Vamana Purana", *Journal of Haryana Studies*, Kurukshetra, Vol.VIII, Nos.1-2 (1976), p. 18.
155. *Kūrma Purāṇa* II.36, 38-39; *Vāmana Purāṇa* 63.5.
156. Hṛidaya Nārāyaṇa Jhā Sarasa, *Saṃkshipta Kurukshetra-Māhātmya* (Hindi), Kurukshetra, 1973, p. 10.
157. Kalpana Desai, *op. cit.*, pp. 86-88.
158. We had seen this terracotta in HARDAM some years back but it could not be located when we wanted to check it up again.
159. It belonged to Shri L.D. Sharma of Sirsa. We are thankful to his son who allowed us to photograph it for publication.
160. The right hand is broken but traces of the broken arm, however, may still be seen near the chest in the extant relief.
161. See also Devendra Handa, "Gupta Reliefs from Haryana," *Bulletin of Museums and Archaeology in U.P. Indira Gandhi Commenoration Volume*, no. 35-36, June-December, 1985, pp. 18-19, fig. 8.

162. *Indian Archaeology 1963-64-A Review*, p. 90.
163. These sculptures were donated to the Museum and Art Gallery by the Panjab University on Dr. M.S. Randhawa's request. They have been published by D.C. Bhattacharyya (1981), pp. 28-30 and 102, figs. 7-9 and 51.
164. Index Nos.1/29-30.
165. A.K. Coomaraswamy, *History of Indian and Indonesian Art*, London, 1927, p. 170.
166. Desai, *op. cit.*, pp. 86-87.
167. It was acquire by us for HARDAM on 2/3/1985 while serving as Deputy Director of the Department.
168. Its lower portion is not visible. Incised lines near its ends probably indicate the folds of the scarf and rule out the possibility of its being the *vanamālā*.
169. *Marg*, Vol. XII, no. 2 (March, 1959), p. 22, fig. 20.
170. Devendra Handa, *Osian: History, Archaeology, Art & Architecture*, Delhi, 1984, p. 83.
171. *Indian Archaeology 1963-64 - A Review*, p. 91.
172. Acc. no. 1/108. Measuring 19 x 12 cm, this piece was purchased by the Department from Shri L.D. Sharma of Sirsa. It shows the Narasiṃha head with a conical coiffure.
173. Measuring 19 x 15 cm, this brown-banded buff sandstone head was procured by us for HARDAM from Shri Krishan Karwal of Ganaur who had obtained it from Gujjar Kheri.
174. Measuring 14 x 14 cm, this much-mutilated Nṛisiṃha head was obtained from Ram Mandir, Chandimandir and is now preserved in HARDAM.
175. Manas, situated about 5 km northwest of Kaithal, is identified with Mānusha of the *Ṛigveda* (I.128, 7, III, 23, 4), *Mbh.* (III, 83, 65-67), etc. The small sandstone Nṛisiṃha head obtained from here measure 14 x 13 cm and shows a small *ardha-padma* tiara over a slightly damaged face. Erect ears and *triśikhaṇḍaka* manes falling on the shoulders and the back are the notable features of this piece. It is preserved in HARDAM.
176. All these sculptures have disappeared now.
177. Now preserved in HARDAM.
178. Amar Singh, *Archaeology of Karnal and Jind Districts (Haryana)*, Unpublished Thesis, Kurukshetra University, Kurukshetra, 1981, p. 185, pl. XXI. B.
179. Devendra Handa (April 1986), *op. cit.*, p. 111, fig. 4. It forms part of the collection of Mrs. Raj Kumari Malik of Panchkula.
180. Devendra Handa, "Vaikuṇṭha Images from Haryana", *Journal of the India Society of Oriental Art*, Calcutta, New Series, Vol. XIV (1984-85), p. 56, pl. VIII.2.
181. Sheela Devi, *Art Tradition in Haryana (up to 1200 A.D.)*, Unpublished Thesis, Kurukshetra University, Kurukshetra, 1975, p. 183, pl. XX.A.
182. Shri D.S. Malik, the then Deputy Director, procured it for HARDAM in July 1985.
183. Silak Ram, *Archaeology of Rohtak and Hissar Districts (Haryana)*, Unpublished Thesis, Kurukshetra University, Kurukshetra, 1972, p. 208, pl. XVIII.B.
184. D.P.S. Punia (1976), *op. cit.*, pp. 77 and 215-16, however, dated it to *c.* 11th-12th century C.E.
185. Devendra Handa (1986), *op. cit.*, p. 113 and fig. 8.
186. *Ṛigveda* I. 22, 17; 54, 2-4 and 55. 6.
187. *Śatapatha Brāhmaṇa* I.35. Also see *Aitareya Brāhmaṇa* VI.3, 7.
188. *Taittirīya Saṃhitā* II.1, 3.
189. *Taittirīya Brāhmaṇa* I.6, 1.
190. *Rāmāyaṇa* I.27, 12-14.
191. *Harivaṃśa Purāṇa* III. 58-68.
192. *Matsya Purāṇa*, Chapters 161-67.
193. *Agni Purāṇa*, Ch. 5.
194. *Padma Purāṇa*, Chs. 266-67.
195. *Vāmana Purāṇa*, Chs. 23-31.
196. *Bhāgavata Purāṇa* VIII.15, 30-34.
197. *Agni Purāṇa* 49, 5; *Aparājitapṛichchhā* III.219; *Bhāgavata Purāṇa* VIII. 18, 23-24; *Devatāmūrti- Prakaraṇa* V.71; *Gāndharva Tantra* XIX.6-7; *Kālikā Purāṇa* 83.16-21; *Mānasollāsa* III.1, 697-98 and 712-14; Meru-

Tantra 26.341-42; *Paurāṇa-karṇa* III.3; *Rūpa-maṇḍana* III.26; *Śāradātilaka* XV.56-60; *Śilparatna* XXV.111-12; *Vaikhānasāgama,* Paṭala 58; *Vishṇudharmottara Purāṇa* III.85, 54-56; etc.

199. Kalpana Desai, *op. cit.*, pp. 99-107; *DHI*, p. 419.

199. *Mahābhārata,* Vana Parva 83, 103; 84, 130; *Agni Purāṇa* 109.20; *Padma Purāṇa* I.26, 96 and 38, 47. It is located at the modern Barsana village near Pundri in district Kurukshetra. A tank of the name of Vāmana Sara exists at the Hat village near Kalayat in district Jind.

200. Cf. Vāmana in the Mathura Museum, Acc. no. 78.1 (vide *BMA*, no. 19-20, p. 78).

201. Devendra Handa (April 1986), *op. cit.*, pp. 107 ff.

202. *Hindi Hindustan Weekly*, New Delhi, April 18, 1954, p. 19. Tradition, however, places Rāmahrada and Paraśurāma-kuṇḍa (mentioned in the *Padma Purāṇa* III.83, 17 and *Garuḍa Purāṇa* 83.24) at Ramrai, Jamadagni-kuṇḍa at village Jājanapura, Reṇukā-tīrtha at Arnaycha, and Paraśurāma-tīrtha at Pehowa, all in the Kurukshetra region.

203. *VDP* III.85, 61-61:

Kāryastu Bhārgavo Rāmo jaṭāmaṇḍaladurdaśaḥ /
Haste'sya paraśuḥ kāryaḥ kṛishṇājinadharasya tu //

204. *Agni Purāṇa* 49.5: *Rāmaśchāpeshuhastaḥ syātkhaḍgī paraśunānvitaḥ / /*

205. *Vaikhānasāgama* (Trivandrum Sanskrit Series, Trivandrum, 1935), Paṭala 59, p. 200.

206. Kalpana Desai, *op. cit.*, pp. 112-13.

207. Camel Bulcke, *Rāma-kathā* (Hindi), Prayag, 1962, pp. 129-37.

208. B.B. Lal, 'Key-Note Address,' in B.P. Sinha (ed.), *Śrī Rāma in Art, Archaeology & Literature*, Patna, 1989, pp. 1-11.

209. H.C. Raychaudhary, *Political History of Ancient India*, Calcutta.

210. H.K. Chaturvedi, "Rāmāyaṇa in Asia," in Lokesh Chandra and S.P. Gupta (eds.), *India's Contribution to World Thought and Culture*, Madras, 1970, pp. 181-88; Kapila Vatsyayana, *Rāmāyaṇa in the Arts of Asia*, Teheran, 1975; V. Raghavan (ed.), *The Ramayana Tradition in Asia*, Madras, 1980; B. N. Puri, "Rāma and Rāma Legend in Central Asia," in Sinha, *op. cit.*, pp. 87-93; V.C. Srivastava, "Rāma-Tradition in South-east Asia: A Historical Perspective," *Ibid.*, pp. 99-105; etc.

211. III.85, 62-63: *Rāmo Dāśarathiḥ kāryo rājalakshaṇalakshitaḥ //*
Bharato Lakshmaṇaśchaiva Śatrughnaścha mahāyaśāḥ /
Tathaiva sarve kartavyāḥ kintu maulivivarjitāḥ //

212. *Agni Purāṇa* 49.6: *Rāmaśchāpī śarī khaḍgī śaṅkhī vā dvibhujaḥ smṛitaḥ /*

213. R. Sengupta, "Scenes of Rāmāyaṇa on two Terracottas of Pre-Christian date," *Journal of the Andhra Historical Research Society*, Vol. XXXII (1971-72), pl. 1.

214. A.H. Longhurst, The Buddhist Antiquities of Nagarjunakonda Madras Presidency, MASI no. 54, Delhi, 1938, pp. 49-50, pl. XLV.a. It was illustrated in *Marg* ('Nagarjunakoṇḍā Sculptures,' *Marg*, Vol. XVIII, no. 2, March 1965, fig. 14 on plates facing p. 16) also and captioned as 'Close-up of a jumping monkey with riders.'

215. P.K. Agrawala, "Identification of Hanumān and Rāma on a Nagarjunakonda Relief," *Journal of Oriental Institute*, Baroda, Vol. XXX (1980-81), pp. 105-11; reprinted in P.K. Agrawala, *Studies in Indian Iconography*, Jaipur, 1994, pp. 93-95, pl. III.72.

216. P. Banerjee, *Rāma in Indian Literature Art and Thought*, Delhi, 1986, Vol. II, fig. 59.

217. Krishna Deva, "Gupta Ramayana Panels from Nachna," *Chhavi 2*, Varanasi, 1981, pp. 10-12. M.S. Vats, *The Gupta Temple at Devagarh*, MASI no. 70, pp. 16-18 and pls. XV-XVII. See also Krishna Deva, "Sculptural Representations of Some Rāmāyaṇa Episodes – Regional Variations," in B.P. Sinha, *op. cit.*, pp. 65-69.

218. It has been mentioned in the *Bṛihannāradīya Purāṇa*, Uttara-khaṇḍa, adhyāya 64, verse 14 and *Garuḍa Purāṇa* 83.24 and 33.

219. Cf. *AI*, no. 4, pl. XXXII. 13-14.

220. Cf. S.C. Kala, *Terracottas in the Allahabad Museum*, New Delhi, 1980, fig. 298.

221. AIHCA, Panjab University, Chandigarh, Acc. no. 1278. See Devendra Handa and Satya Vrat, "Some Religious Terracottas From Sugh," *Haryana Sahitya Akademi Journal of Indological Studies*, Vol. I, no. 1, fig. 12.

222. Kala, *op. cit.*, p. 58.
223. *Ibid.*, pp. 57-58, fig. 145.
224. Sengupta, *op. cit.*, p. 104.
225. Kala, *op. cit.*, Foreword, p. ix.
226. Yogānanda, *op. cit.*, pp. 196-98, Pls. 97-98. See also his description and illustrations of the *Rāmāyana* panels from Nachar Khera and elsewhere (*Ibid.*, pp. 192ff and Pls. 91-96 & 99); and "Vālmīki śloka se aṃkita Ishṭikā Phalaka," *Bulletin of Archaeology and Museums in U.P.*, Nos. 5-6 (1970), p. 6. Silak Ram also described some of these bricks in his thesis "*Archaeology of Rohtak and Hissar Districts (Haryana)*," Ph. D. Thesis (Unpublished), Kurukshetra University, Kurukshetra, 1972, p. 203.
227. *Indian Sculpture, A Catalogue of the Los Angeles County Museum of Art Collection*, Vol. I, University of California Press, Berkeley, Los Angeles, and London, 1986, p. 232, S 107.
228. D.C. Bhattacharyya (1981), *op. cit.*, pp. 92-93, fig. 46.
229. Different texts, however, describe him as the son of Śiva, Rāma (according to the Indonesian version of the *Rāmāyaṇa*), incarnation of Brahmā or even of the Hindu trinity, incarnation of Nandī (Śiva's bull), an *aṃśa* (part) of Nārāyaṇa, and born of milk from Daśaratha's *yajña* (sacrifice) consumed by Añjanā.
230. *Tadā śailāgra-śikhare vāmo hanurabhajyata / Tato hi nāmadheyaṃ te Hanumāniti kīrtitam //* Vālmīki *Rāmāyaṇa* IV.66, 24.
231. For details see Shanti Lal Nagar, *Hanumān in Art, Culture, Thought and Literature*, New Delhi: Intellectual Publishing House, 1995.
232. Ch. 20, vv. 4-6 and 9.
233. Nagar, *op. cit.*, pp. 3ff.
234. Mohinder Singh, *op. cit.*, p. 408, pl. 64.8.
235. Devendra Handa, "Agroha Revisited," in *Prācī-Prabhā: Perspectives in Indology (Essays in honour of Professor B.N. Mukherjee)*, ed. D.C. Bhattacharyya & Devendra Handa, New Delhi, 1989, p. 242, pl. 27.
236. *Mbh.* (Gita Press, Gorakhpur), Anuśāsana Parva CXLVII.60:
    Ya eva Vishṇuḥ so'nanto bhagavān vasudhādharaḥ /
    Yo rāmaḥ sa hṛishīkeśo yo'chyutaḥ sa dharādharaḥ //
    Also Ādi Parva LXVII.152: *Śeshasyāṃśaścha nāgasya Baladevo mahābalaḥ /*
    Balarāma is also considered to be one of the ten well-known incarnations of Vishṇu. For details, see *DHI*, pp. 388 ff.
237. *Agni Purāṇa* (CSS, Varanasi, 1966) II.6-7; 12:
    Gadālāṅgaladhārī cha rāmo vātha chaturbhujaḥ //
    Vāmordhve lāṅgalaṃ dadyadatha śaṅkhaṃ suśobhanam /
    Mushalaṃ dakshiṇordhve tu chakrañchādhaḥ suśobhanam //
    Lāṅgalī mushalī rāmo gadāpadmadharaḥ smṛitaḥ /
    At Osian, two images show Balarāma holding, among others, a *chakra* and a *śaṅkha* and as seated on Garuḍa in one case. For details, see Devendra Handa (1984), *op. cit.*, pp. 94-95, pl. 58 and pp. 57-58, pl. 36.
238. *Mbh.*, Śalya Parva LX.2. in one of the earliest representations of Balarāma on a rectangular bronze coin of the Indo-Greek ruler Agathocles (*circa* 180-165 B.C.E.) found from Ai-Khanum along the border of Russia with Afghanistan, the god is shown as carrying a plough and a club in his rear hands. For details, see *JNSI*, XXXV (1973), pp. 73-77, pl. VII.
239. N.P. Joshi, *Iconography of Balarāma*, New Delhi, 1979, p. 45.
240. *Ibid. Brahma Purāṇa* (L.50) also describes him as *gadāmuśaladhāriṇam.*
241. *Harivaṃśa Purāṇa* II.26, 49.
242. Joshi, *op. cit.*, pp. 58 ff.
243. The story of his tasting of wine for the first time just before the *chakra-mushala* war on the Gomanta Mountain is narrated in details in the *Harivaṃśa* II.41, 6 ff.
244. There are ample literary sources, which corroborate his addiction. For details, see Joshi, *op. cit.*, pp. 48 f.

245. *Ibid.*, pp. 59 ff.
246. *Ibid.*, p. 50, pl. 16.
247. *Ibid.*
248. *Ibid.*
249. *Indian Archaeology 1959-60, A Review*, p. 74.
250. *Cf. Trinata* pose as prescribed in the *Vikhānasāgama*. See *EHI*, Vol. I, pt. 2, Appendix B, p. 44.
251. *Udbaddha-kuntala* of the *Vaikhānasāgama* (*Ibid.*).
252. It may be compared to the *hema-chūli*, gold crest, mentioned in the *Harivaṃśa* II.26, 52.
253. *Harivaṃśa* (II.26, 50; 41.32; 42.48; 46.25; 89.3), *Vishṇu Purāṇa* (V.18, 38; 25.15), *Brahma Purāṇa* (L.50), *Bṛihatsaṃhitā* (LVII.36), *Bhāgavata Purāṇa* (X.65, 22), etc. refer to him as wearing only one earring. in medieval sculptures, however, Balarāma is generally shown as putting on ear ornaments in both the ears (Joshi, *op. cit.*, p. 40).
254. For the meaning and type of *vanamālā* worn by Balarāma, see *Ibid.*, pp. 40 ff.
255. The snout of the crocodile simulates the trunk of an elephant. Similar representation of crocodile may be seen in the images of Varuṇa in Topnāth kā Mandira and Bhīmādevī temple at Pinjore.
256. As the vehicle of Varuṇa and Gaṅgā for example.
257. It will not be irrelevant here to mention that the attributes of *hala* and *mushala*, originally belonging to Ananta (*Harivaṃśa* II.26, 49), were given to Balarāma before his fight with Jarāsandha (*Ibid.*, II.35, 57-60). These attributes are associated with agriculture also. Crocodile, symbolic of water and fertility, is quite in consonance with plough and pestle.
258. The Mathura Museum image of Balarāma showing crocodile is unfortunately headless and we do not know whether it had the snake canopy or not.
259. E.J. Mackay had discovered a steatite tablet in his excavations at Mohenjodaro, which depicts a young boy uprooting two trees from which emerge two human figures. Mackay (*Further Excavations at Mohenjodaro*, 1938, p. 355, fig. 90/23-24, pl. XC.23b-24b) compared the scene with the uprooting of the twin trees Yamala and Arjuna by child Kṛishṇa as mentioned in the Bhāgavata Purāṇa. V.S. Agrawala (*Poddāra Abhinandana Grantha*, p. 781) also accepted this identification. The long gap between this and the subsequent depictions of the concerned scene, however, does not render Mackay's comparison as plausible. See also H.D. Sankalia, "Kṛishṇa in Historical Perspective – Contribution of Kṛishṇa Saga and Indian Culture," *Journal of the Asiatic Society of Bombay*, nos. 54-55 (1979-80), pp. 153-57; K.D. Bajpai, "Vāudeva-Kṛishṇa Cult – The Early Phase," *Dinesh Chandrika*, New Delhi, 1983, pp. 149-51.
260. *Ṛigveda* VIII 84-3-4.
261. *Kauśītaki Brāhmaṇa* XXX 9.
262. *Chhāndogya Upanishad* III 17.6. It is interesting to note that in the *Mahābhārata* (Karṇa Parva) Kṛishṇa alleges the superiority of the teachings of Aṅgirasa (*Aṅgirasa-śruti*) over others.
263. S. Sorensen, *An Index to the Names in the Mahābhārata*, Delhi, 1963, (reprint), p. 237.
264. For details, see P. Banerji, *Life of Krishna in Indian Art*, New Delhi, 1978; *Blue God*, New Delhi, 1981; A.L. Dallapiccola et al. (ed.), *Krishna-the Divine Lover: Myth and Legend through Indian Art*, Bombay, 1982; Milton Singer (ed.), *Krishna Myths, Rites and Attitudes*, Honolulu, 1966: D.C. Bhattacharyya, *Lord Krishna: The Light Through Darkness*, Chandigarh, 1988; etc.
265. *Ashṭādhyāyī* IV.3. 98. See also VI.3, 38.
266. *DHI*, p. 85. See also R.G. Bhandarkar, "Allusions to Krishna in Patanjali's Mahabhashya", *Indian Antiquary*, Vol. III, 1874, pp. 14ff.
267. R.G. Bhandarkar, *Vaiṣṇavism, Śaivism and Minor Religious Systems*, Pune, 1929, p. 26; R.C. Majumdar, *The Classical Accounts of India*, p. 119.
268. Majumdar, *op. cit.*, pp. 221-22.
269. *Journal of the Numismatic Society of India*, Vol. XXV, pp. 73-75.
270. *Epigraphia Indica* XVI, pp. 25ff; D.C. Sircar, *Select Inscriptions*, Vol. I, Calcutta, 1942, p. 92.
271. These Vṛishṇi heroes were later apotheosized and identified with *parama*, *mahat* or *jīva*, *manas* and *ahaṃkāra* - the first four creative principles of the Sāṅkhya system. The Purāṇas attach some allegorical meanings also to these names. For details see Bhandarkar (1929), *op. cit.*, pp. 4ff; Kalpana

Desai, *op. cit.*, pp. 3 and 37ff; N.P. Joshi (1979), pp. 10-15; etc.
272. Banerjea, *op. cit.*, pp. 114-15.
273. Devendra Handa (October 1985), pp. 125ff.
274. *Ibid.*
275. Handa (1985), *op. cit.*, pp. 96, 104 and 108.
276. *Epigraphia Indica* I, p. 295.
277. D.R. Bhandarkar, "Hansi Stone Inscription of Pṛthvīrāja, (Vikrama) Samvat 1224," *Indian Antiquary*, Vol. XLI (1912), pp.17-19.
278. The Eka-haṃsa *tīrtha* at Ikkas in district Jind, Ekarātri and Jyotisara near Thanesar are the only places, which can be connected with Kṛishṇa traditionally. But even these places have not yielded any archaeological relics, which could be associated with the god.
279. It was presented to the National Museum, New Delhi by the Vice-Chancellor of the Panjab University, Chandigarh in December, 1968 and is exhibited there as No.68. 193 in the Early Indian Sculpture Gallery.
280. Some more plaques showing both the vowels and the consonants have also been recovered from Sugh and are preserved in the Gurukula Museum at Jhajjar (Rohtak) and with some individuals. See also *Indian Archaeology 1968-69 - A Review*, p. 80, pl. LVIII.
281. *The Hindustan Times*, dated 19.12.1968: B.Ch. Chhabra, "Sugh Terracotta with Brahmi Barakhadi," *Bulletin National Museum*, New Delhi, no. 2, pp. 14-16. See also R.C. Agrawala, "Learning The Alphabets," *Journal of the Oriental Institute*, Baroda, Vol. XVIII, no. 4 (June 1969), pp. 358-59 & pl.
282. D.S. Punia, "Recently Explored Icons of Viṣṇu and Hari-Hara in South Haryana," *Journal of the Oriental Institute*, Baroda, Vol. XIX, nos. 1-2 (Sept.-Dec.1979), pp. 128-29, fig.1. The accompanying plate is after Punia's fig. 1.
283. N.P. Joshi, "Prārambhika Vishṇu-mūrtiyoṃ kā eka Adhyayana," *Bulletin of Museums and Archaeology in U.P.*, No.2 (Dec. 1968), pp. 6-26 and figs.
284. *Mahābhārata*, Bhīshma Parva 25.15: Droṇa Parva 88.21; *Śrī-mad-bhagavad-Gītā* 1. 14-15; etc.
285. Rodgers, *op. cit.*, p. 42.
286. *Indian Archaeology 1979-80 - A Review* onwards. See also R.C. Agrawala, "Prāchīna Hariyānā," *Ājakala*, Nov. 1968, p. 28.
287. It was obtained from Trench no. XD-7, Quadrant III, at a depth of 50 cm from layer 1.
288. Trench No.XG-8, Quadrant IV, layer 2, and depth 2.05 m.
289. Devendra Handa (April 1986), pp. 107-22 and fig. 20.
290. I showed the photographs of the Gujjar Kheri relics to Sh. R.C. Agrawala and Prof. D.C. Bhattacharyya and discussed with them the possibility of the figure being that of Kṛishṇa. They concurred with my view.
291. All the relics from Gujjar Kheri described here are preserved in the Department of Archaeology and Museums, Haryana.
292. *In the Image of Man* (a catalogue published by Art Council of Great Britain on the occasion of exhibition at Hayward Gallery, London, 25 March – 13 June 1982), p. 101.
293. *Annual Report of the Archaeological Survey of India*, 1921-22, pp. 103-04, pl. XXXVI, fig. E.
294. N.P. Joshi, "Kṛṣṇa in Art - Whether Two-Armed Or Multi-Armed," *Bulletin of Museums and Archaeology in U.P.*, no. 21-24 (June 78-Dec. 79), pp. 19ff.
295. *Ibid.*, p. 20. A large number of Vishṇu images from Haryana and Punjab show Balarāma as an attendant of the god. We feel that all these images are the result of the identity of Vishṇu and Kṛishṇa in the minds of the people of the region. For details see our paper "Balarāma as an attendant of Vishṇu," *Gleanings of Indian Archaeology History & Culture - Prof. Dr. R. N. Mehta Felicitation Volume* (eds. K.D. Bajpai et al.), Vol. II, Jaipur, 2000, pp. 87-91.
296. Kalpana Desai, *op. cit.*, p. 141.

Chapter 5

Śiva

An important god of the Hindu Trinity, Śiva as Paśupati is regarded to be a proto-historic deity.[1] The terrific god Rudra associated with hills and animals in the *Ṛigveda*[2] came to be looked upon as the lord of all creatures (Paśupati) and a Mahāyogī, an originator and exponent of various arts and accomplishments like music, dancing, etc., thus becoming Śiva 'the auspicious.'[3] The *Atharvaveda* presupposes his ascendancy to the supreme position[4] and assigns him various epithets such as Bhava, Śarva, Paśupati, Ugra, Mahādeva and Īśāna, to which the *Śatapatha* (IV.1, 3, 7) and the *Kauśītaki Brāhmaṇa* (VI.1, 9) added Aśani and typified his terrific and peaceful aspects – *ghora* and *saumya* respectively.[5] It is, however, of interest that in the *Ṛigveda* (II.33, 6-8) one of Rudra's epithets is Vṛishabha and in the *Taittirīya Saṃhitā* of the *Yajurveda* (I.8, 6) he is associated with Ambikā as his sister. The *Mahābhārata* (VII.74, 56) describes Śiva as the creator, omnipresent, and omniscient and the *Rāmāyaṇa* (I.36, 9-10) accords him the rank and status of the highest god. The latter also mentions Nandī (VII.16, 8). The sectarian Purāṇas accord Śiva the supreme status.

Though there is ample literary evidence regarding the continuation and development of the cult of Rudra-Śiva from the Ṛigvedic to the early historic and later times, yet there is an utter lack of archaeological data from the decline of the Harappan civilization to about 3rd-2nd century B.C.E.[6] Patañjali's reference to Śiva-Bhāgavatas[7] proves beyond cavil the existence of a Pāśupata sect in India during the 2nd century B.C.E. Bull, the vehicle of Śiva, also regarded as the zoomorphic representation of Śiva, is depicted on punch-marked, local and tribal coinages.[8] Punch-marked coins are generally believed to have appeared in about the 5th century B.C.E.[9] Prof. Ajay Mitra Shastri considers the figure on Kāḍa coins to be the earliest anthropomorphic representation of Śiva.[10] These coins are datable to *circa* 3rd-2nd century B.C.E. and the largest number of definitely known provenance of these coins suggests that their provenance is Sugh near Jagadhari in Haryana.[11] Irrefragable evidence of the anthropomorphic representation of Śiva on coins, however, is presented by the coins of Wema Kadphises and Gondophernes, belonging to the 1st century B.C.E./C.E.[12] The Gudimallam Liṅgodbhavamūrti[13] and the Bhita *Pañchamukha* Śiva-*liṅga*,[14] dated by some scholars to *circa* 3rd-2nd century B.C.E., are not considered to be much later.[15] A mutilated terracotta plaque of late Śuṅga period, now in the Bharat Kala Bhawan, Banaras, is regarded by Biswas to represent Śiva riding on his mount Nandī.[16] But the absence of any definite Śaiva emblems in the hands of or on the person of the rider renders the identification to be quite doubtful. There is, however, no denying the fact that the images of Śiva, both in stone and clay, began to be created popularly during the Kushāṇa period. From then onwards, we see an ascendancy and profusion of the iconic forms and representation of not only Śiva, but also of other deities. Early images of Śiva are rare in Haryana but his worship seems to have remained quite popular in the *Liṅga* form through the centuries as is evidenced from some specimens found from different places.

MUKHA-LIṄGAS

The worship of Śiva in the form of a *Liṅga*[17] 'Phallus', the pillar supporting the universe, has been practiced in India since ancient times.[18] The *Rāmāyaṇa* refers to Rāma worshipping Śiva in the form of a sand *Liṅga* at Rāmeśvaram before the construction of the bridge to Laṅkā (*setu-bandha*).[19] The *Mahābhārata*, too, contains numerous references to the worship of Śiva-*liṅga*. Arjuna is described to have worshipped Śiva by making a clay image of the great god.[20] The early Śiva-*liṅgas* may, thus, have been made of perishable materials and have therefore not survived. The earliest known examples, generally believed to go back to the 2nd century B.C.E., are from Gudimallam[21] and Bhita.[22]

The *Liṅga Purāṇa* (99.8) refers to the eternal creative power of the *Liṅga* by stating that all beings merge in it at the time of the great Destruction and emerge from it at the time of the Creation of the universe –

Layaṃ gachchhanti bhūtāni saṃhāre nikhilaṃ yataḥ /
Sṛishṭikāle punaḥ sṛishṭastasmālliṅgamudāhṛitam //

Daily worship of the *Liṅga* was enjoined upon all the people and it is said that failing this the *dvijas* 'twice-born' will become *chaṇḍālas* 'low-born depraved' and a *śūdra* 'low-born' will be born as a boar in his next life.[23] The *Śiva Purāṇa* gives details of various types of Śiva-*liṅgas* and the religious ceremonies associated with their installation and worship.[24] The *Agni* (LIV.33-34), *Matsya* (262.10-11), and *Vishṇudharmottara Purāṇa* (III.74), *Samarāṅgaṇa-sūtradhāra* (ch. 70), *Rūpa-Maṇḍana* (IV.37-84), *Aparājitapṛichchhā* (chs. 197-203), and various other texts[25] describe different types of Śiva-*liṅgas* and their parts. Broadly speaking, the Śiva-*liṅgas* may be grouped under two broad categories: (1) *Nishkala* (*Sthāṇu*) or plain, and (2) *Sakala* or those which bear human faces or full iconic representations of Śiva or even other deities.

Liṅgas bearing one or more faces are known as *Mukha-liṅgas*.[26] A *mukha-liṅga* with turbaned base in the Bharatpur Museum[27], and another with curls in the Philadelphia Museum are regarded to be the earliest *mukha-liṅgas* belonging to *circa* 2nd century B.C.E. It was, however, in the Kushāṇa period that the *mukha-liṅgas*, particularly the *eka-mukha liṅgas*, became quite popular. Many of them are preserved in various museums and even *in situ*.

Joanna Williams has published an interesting Kushāṇa piece from Agroha in the Gurukula Museum, Jhajjar showing an Ardhanārīśvara figure "standing against what appears to be a *liṅga*."[28] The back slab is flat at the back and not round as in case of Śiva-*liṅgas*. We, therefore, have our reservations about its being a Śiva-*liṅga*. Perhaps the author herself was not sure of this as is evident from her wording. It is, however, surprising that besides this above-mentioned piece, no early *mukha-liṅgas* are known from Haryana, a state in very close proximity of Mathura, which has yielded numerous superb examples of early *mukha-liṅgas*. During the course of our explorations and researches, however, we have noticed the following pieces, which may be of interest to the readers.

Mukha-Liṅga from Gujjar Kheri

Gujjar Kheri in district Sonepat is very rich in archaeological relics.[29] Smugglers, collectors, and dealers have taken away hundreds of sculptures, architectural pieces, terracottas, and other remains from this site. HARDAM, too, has acquired a large number of relics from this place, which include a *mukha- liṅga* (Pl. 143). Made of buff colored sandstone, it measures 15.5 x 11.0 cm (Acc. No. 1/87). Broken at the back and detached from the *Liṅga*, it shows the face with plump cheeks, thick lower lip, mustached upper lip, roundish eyes with a *tilaka* mark between the eyebrows and a horizontally placed third eye on the forehead. The nose has suffered some damage. The matted hair is worn in smooth bulging locks pulled up like a sheaf and stringed. The *tilaka* mark reminds us of the *ūrṇā* of the Buddhist images, and the face with moustaches betrays the impact of the Gandhāra school.[30] It may well be compared with the face of Śiva in the Calmann galleries, London,[31] *Ekamukhaliṅga* in the State Museum, Lucknow[32] and *Ekamukhaliṅga* in the Baroda Museum.[33] The horizontally placed third eye which is the peculiarity of the Kushāṇa period is noteworthy. We do not know for certain whether the original Śiva-*liṅga* had only one or more faces.

Eka-mukha Liṅga from Sondh

Sondh in tehsil Palwal of district Faridabad has an extensive mound spread over more than thirty acres of land, as high as 25 m, yielding remains from Painted Grey Ware onwards. It has also yielded a Śiva-*liṅga* with a face protruding on one side of its shaft (Pl. 144). Unfortunately, however, it is very much worn out and no details could be discerned clearly but the protrusion of the face only on one side leaves absolutely no doubt to its being an early *eka-mukha liṅga* only, assignable probably to the Gupta period, as also indicated by a Gupta Vishṇu image from this site noted above. Nothing is known about the present whereabouts of this *liṅga*.

Eka-mukha Liṅga from Kiloi

Kiloi is a small village at a distance of about 10 km east of Rohtak via Bhalaut on road to Sonepat. It yields early historic remains including Yaudheya copper coins bearing the *Yaudheya-gaṇasya-jaya* legends. An old *eka-mukha liṅga* obtained from the ancient site is now enshrined in a temple at some distance from the village. It is 94 cm in height and 36 cm square at the base. According to a *bahī* (old traditional account-book) of Lala Pyare Lal of M/s Lala Bishambar Dass Kapur Chand, Commission Agents, Anaj Mandi, Rohtak, this *liṅga* was discovered by a farmer while ploughing his field and was set up in the present shrine in C.E. 1734. Made of typical Mathura mottled red sandstone, the round shaft bears a single face on one side (Pls. 145-46). Being in an indifferent state of preservation and under worship, the details of the facial features are not very clear. The round face with chubby cheeks, eyes with drooping eyelids, bow-like eyebrows, long drawn mouth, matted locks stringed at the top forming a bun-like topknot, long ears, and an *ekāvali* on the neck can, however, be made out easily. Unfortunately, the third eye on the forehead has vanished leaving only traces to make out that like the Gujar Kheri example it was placed horizontally. It may be assigned to the Kushāṇa-Gupta transitional phase.

Chaturmukha-Liṅga from Rohtak

More than a century back, Rodgers had noticed Hindu material in the Adina and Kalan Masjid and some old sculptures near Gokarṇa kā Tālāb at Rohtak.[34] During a visit to this temple some years back, we found a *Chaturmukha-liṅga*, measuring 30 x 26 cm in its sanctum (Pls. 147-48). The faces protrude out of the cylindrical column and are depicted with matted locks.

Being under worship and in an indifferent state of preservation, the expression of the faces cannot be discerned very clearly. The workmanship is rather crude and the relief may be assigned to the Gupta period marked by a decadent style. In the sanctum of the same temple there were many other Śiva-*liṅgas* installed around this *chaturmukha-liṅga* and worshipped by the people.

A clay sealing of about 3rd-4th century C.E. from Achchheja reading *'Karavīreśvarasya'* and bearing a trident may have belonged either to an individual named Karavīreśvara or to a temple of this name which may have had a Śiva-*liṅga* named after Karavīra as generally *īśvara*-ending names indicate the existence of Śiva-*liṅgas* named after the donors or patrons. Similarly the late Gupta clay sealing from Daulatpur near Thanesar with the legend *'Sthāneśvarasya'* may have belonged to a temple of the god. It, however, cannot be ascertained whether these Śiva-*liṅgas* were plain or the *Mukha-liṅgas*. If the fragmentary Śāradā inscription from Morni and the actual recovery of a *Chaturmukha-liṅga* from there described below is any indicator, these *Liṅgas* may have actually been the *Mukha-liṅgas*. This, however, remains only a hunch in the absence of corroborative evidence.

Mukha-liṅga from Ahrwan

Once a late Gupta *mukha-liṅga* with *yoni-pīṭha*, measuring 74 cm in diameter and 63 cm in height, of about 6th-7th century C.E., lay amongst the ruins piled up near a pool called Suraj Kund to the north of the village Ahrwan, located about 7 km southwest of Palwal on road to Hathin in district Faridabad. Nothing, however, is known of its whereabouts now.

Ekamukha-liṅga from Hansi

A white spotted red sandstone *ekamukha-liṅga* measuring 22 x 17 x 13.5 cm was obtained from Hansi and is now housed in HARDAM. The big face protrudes out of the long shaft on one side. The shaft has un-hewn thicker lower portion as it was probably meant to be buried in the ground. The nose and the *mukuṭa* portion are damaged. The execution is very rough and betrays decadent Gupta idiom. The piece may be dated to *circa* 8th century C.E.

Chaturmukha-liṅga from Palwal

A *chaturmukha-liṅga* of buff sandstone showing four-faces around the round shaft near its flat top is installed in the Lakshmī-Nārāyaṇa Temple at Palwal. All the faces have been carved with great care and represent as usual Sadyojāta, Vāmadeva, Aghora and Tatpurusha. They bear matted locks on the heads and wear *sarpa-kuṇḍalas* in the elongated earlobes. The faces are oval with half-closed eyes and a vertical third eye on the forehead. The Vāmadeva head bears a *dhammilla* type of coiffure. The bearded and mustached Aghora face is marked with a *kapāla* in the matted locks, has a wide-open mouth with long teeth, and wears a *sarpa-hāra*. This *chaturmukha-liṅga* is a beautiful specimen of the Pratihāra period.[35]

Chaturmukha-liṅga from Morni

A Śiva-*liṅga* in the Chandigarh Museum (Catalogue No. A. 18) is carved with four seated human figures, which along with the top section of the *Liṅga* may be taken to represent five primal elements (Pañchabhūta) like the earth, water, air, fire, and ether, which in their turn are generally identified with the five faces (Pañchānana) of Śiva, viz. Sadyojāta or Mahādeva (east face), Vāmadeva or Umāvaktra (north face), Aghora or Bhairava (south face), Tatpurusha or Nandivaktra (west face), and Sadāśiva or Īśāna (at the top). This Śiva-*liṅga* thus belongs to the general category of *chaturmukha-liṅgas* but has the uniqueness of the Sadyojāta, Vāmadeva, Aghora and Tatpurusha aspects to have been represented in full bodily forms around the central Śiva-*liṅga*. There are examples of four figures shown on the four sides of a *Liṅga* but they generally represent the four different cults other than that of Śiva. But here in the Śiva-*liṅga* under discussion, the four figures represent the four forms of the same deity, i.e. Śiva. This thus is a unique example of the aniconic-iconic form of Śiva.[36]

The probable provenance of this sculpture is mentioned in the Catalogue as Naraingarh. It is, however, one of the sculptures collected from Morni-ka-Tal (Lat. 30° 49' N. and Long. 77° 5' E.) in district Panchkula and donated by the Department of Ancient Indian History Culture and Archaeology, Panjab University, Chandigarh to the Chandigarh Museum at the instance of Dr. M.S. Randhawa. The sculpture (Pl. 149) shows the Śiva-*liṅga* on an imposing lotus placed on a square molded pedestal. The four figures are carved as seated in *svastikāsana* on the four sides. Two of the four figures have four hands but their number in the other two cannot be ascertained with definiteness because of the indifferent state of preservation. Even in the case of hands the attributes cannot always be recognized properly. In one figure the right hand holds a staff (*daṇḍa*) while another figure shows the right hand drawn near the chest holding an *akshamālā*. These are the attributes respectively of Aghora and Sadyojāta forms of Śiva according to the *Vishṇudharmottara Purāṇa* (III.48, 1 ff.). Since they represent the southern and eastern faces of Śiva, their opposite faces may be taken to be Vāmadeva and Tatpurusha respectively. The top of the *liṅga* should be taken to represent the fifth face known as Īśāna or Sadāśiva. Another notable feature of this image is the presence of small seated figures in the laps of Sadyojāta and Vāmadeva forms at least if not of others. It is difficult to be certain about the exact nature of these diminutive figures. If they are female figures as seems likely, they may be the *śaktis* of the different forms of Śiva, but one cannot be sure about this.

The four figures seem to be wearing *karṇa-kuṇḍalas*. Other ornaments cannot be made out. In spite of crude carving the plasticity of modeling is fairly sensitive. The image has been dated to *circa* 9th century C.E.[37] This Śiva-*liṅga* may have been got installed by the queen of king Upendradeva and named –khikeśvara as mentioned in the 9th century fragmentary Śāradā inscription reading '- - - *Upendradevasya rājñī Śrī - - - / - - -khikeśvaramidaṃ - - -*,' studded in the wall of the Śiva temple erected near the Tal (pool) at Morni out of the relics of the old temple/s.

Mukha-liṅga from Sikanderpura

A sandstone *mukha-liṅga* is known from Sikanderpura, about 10 km east of Sirsa. Its lower half portion is square and the upper half grows round with a beautifully carved human face on one side (Pl. 150). There is a long crown of matted hair in three tiers adorned with jewels on the head and the oval face, broken at the chin and with damaged nose, looks placid and serene with half-closed long-drawn eyes and plump cheeks. On stylistic grounds, it may be dated to *circa* 11th century C.E.

Chaturmukha-liṅga from Pehowa

Paśupatinātha Temple at Pehowa has in its sanctum now a huge *chaturmukha-liṅga* of touchstone, the equivalent of which is pointed out to be there in the Paśupatinātha Temple of Kathmandu in Nepal. It may be dated to the Maratha period[38] Installation of a *chaturmukha-*

liṅga at such a late period, however, points to the continuity of the tradition of worshipping such *liṅgas* in the region.

ARDHANĀRĪŚVARA-*LIṄGA* FROM AGROHA

Our account of the Śiva-*liṅgas* bearing faces or figures will not be complete without a reference to the Ardhanārīśvara-*Liṅga* from Agroha preserved in the Gurukula at Jhajjar and published by Joanna Williams as referred to above. This 31 cm high fine-grained mottled reddish Sikri sandstone piece of Mathura idiom shows the male and female halves differentiated by their hairstyle, moustache lightly carved on the left, earrings, single breast, bisection of the erect phallus, fleshy female waist on the proper left, and even in the contours of the two shoulders and legs (Pl. 151).[39] It may be dated to the Kushāṇa-Gupta transitional phase ascribable to the Yaudheyas in Haryana.

PLAIN ŚIVA-*LIṄGAS*

The discovery of two Śiva-*liṅgas* from Marhanwala[40] indicates the existence of Śiva temples at the site. The bigger of the two measures 46 x 20 cm, and is unfinished (Pl. 152). It thus provides us the important evidence of the sculptures having been carved at Marhanwala itself. The other Śiva-*liṅga* measures 42 x 14 cm and has been prepared according to the canonical injunction dividing it into the square Brahma-*bhāga,* octagonal Vishṇu-*bhāga* and roundish Śiva-*bhāga* of equal dimensions (Pl. 153). In the early medieval period, plain Śiva-*liṅgas* also began to be carved. A 36-cm high sandstone Śiva-*liṅga* belonging to *circa* 11th-12th century from Pinjore in the collection of the Kurukshetra University also shows the upper part as cylindrical but the lower one showing octagonal and square parts is not finished properly.[41] A temple of Jayantīdevī at Jayantipur has a Śiva-*liṅga* in the heap of stone pieces, relics of an old temple of about 10th century. It is 150 cm in height divided equally into the square Brahma-*bhāga* with 25 cm side, octagonal Vishṇu-*bhāga* and rounded Śiva-*bhāga*.[42] A similar Śiva-*liṅga* is known from Bulandpur Kheri near Gujjar Kheri in district Sonepat. A medieval Śiva-*liṅga* from Hat (Regn. No. HRN/AMB-878) has been set up in a square *yoni-pīṭha.* A Śiva-*liṅga*, a broken head of Nandī, *āmalakas*, and other remains near a *samādhi* at Kathgarh between Kapālamochana and Ad Badri indicate the existence of a medieval Śaiva temple there. Special mention should be made here of an Ekādaśa-Rudrīya Śiva-*liṅga* lying uncared for in the premises of the Devī Tālāb Temple at Panipat. There are ten round holes around the central Śiva-*liṅga* fixed in a *yoni-pīṭha*. Like other sculptures now set up in this temple, it was recovered from the tank adjoining this temple during its cleaning by voluntary service (*kara-sevā*) many years back. These 12th century images seem to have been immersed in the tank during one of the Muslim attacks at Panipat. This is the only Ekādaśa-Rudrīya Śiva-*liṅga* to have come to light from the state. A late medieval temple dedicated to Ekādaśa-Rudras, however, exists at Kaithal.

Plain Śiva-*liṅgas*, simple cylindrical columns or fluted ones or divided into the Brahma, Vishṇu and Śiva-*bhāga*, may be seen at many old places like Pinjaur, Morni-ka-Tal, Kapālamochana, Rohtak, Sanghel, Ata, Pehowa, etc.

The very name of Haryana is connected with Hara, i.e. Śiva. A Kushāṇa inscription in Brāhmī script from Chiḍiyā refers to a priest (name lost) son of Śivaśarman of Kauśika *gotra* which indicates that people in this region named even their children after the name of this god.[43] A Gupta inscription on he Aśokan pillar in the Gujri Mahal at Hisar refers to goldsmith named Nandila who was the son of Rudra. Another person named Umādāsa has also been mentioned. Seals and sealings found from different places belonging to early centuries mentioning Śaivite names like Śrī-Rudra (Thanesar), Rudravarma (Rohtak), Śaṅkaramala (Agroha), Pāvaneśa (Agroha), Kāśīśvara (Theh Polar), etc. and depicting trident and Nandī bull indicate that Śaivism was well established here during that period. The Hūṇa ruler Mihirakula issued coins with the legend *'Jayatu Vṛishaḥ.'* Śaivism enjoyed a pre-eminent position at Sthāṇvīśvara (Thanesar) during the 7th century C.E. as indicated by Bāṇa who records in his *Harshacharita* that Śiva was worshipped in every house and that his shrine resounded with the murmur of the *Rudra-stotra.* Fasts were kept for appeasing the Lord. So much so, considering the sanctity of the place, a Śaivite ascetic like Bhairavāchārya came here to perform *vetāla-sādhanā* (*Harshacharita* III). Harsha himself was a great devotee of Śiva and bore the title of *Parama-māheśvara.* His gold coins bear the figure of Umā-Maheśvara.

ICONIC FORMS

Trinetra Śiva

The story of the appearance of a third eye on Śiva's forehead is stated in the *Mahābhārata.*[44] It is said that when Śiva, seated on the Himālaya mountain, was engaged in austerities, Umā, dressed as an ascetic, came behind him and playfully put her hands over his eyes. As a sudden and tremendous effect, a great flame burst from his forehead, in which a third eye, luminous as the sun, was formed. The fire from his third eye scorched the mountain and everything upon it. Umā stood bewildered and submissive before Śiva, who, however, restored Himavat to his former condition.[45] The episode of Śiva destroying Madana with his third eye is so well known to need any elucidation. The *Mahābhārata* refers to Śiva as Lalāṭāksha, Trilochana, Trinayana, Trinetra, etc.[46] clearly indicating the popularity of the episode of Śiva's third eye. The *Vishṇudharmottara Purāṇa* (III, 50, 7), one of the earliest iconographical texts available to us, also refers to the third eye of Śiva.[47] The carving of stone and terracotta images of Śiva with third eye seems to have begun during the Kushāṇa period and continued later.[48]

The earliest three-eyed terracotta head of Śiva, however, has been obtained from the excavations at Śṛiṅgaverapura near Allahabad (U.P.). It belongs to the 1st century C.E.[49] That Haryana did not lag behind is evidenced by a fragmentary terracotta head obtained from Agroha (ancient Agrodaka), situated at a distance of about 23 km from Hisar on Delhi – Fazilka road.[50] Broken below the neck, this fragmentary head shows the god as having an oval face with fish like eyes. The pupils are perforated. The arched eyebrows shaped like a bow (*Chāpākaram*) are marked by an incised line. The nose is slightly damaged but still prominent. The lower lip is thicker than the upper one. The vertical third eye is carved prominently on the forehead. The hair seems to have been marked with schematic lines. The elongated ears are adorned with rings. Stylistically, this head resembles Indo-Scythian pieces[581] and may be assigned to *circa* 1st-2nd century C.E.

Another fragmentary head of white-specked red sandstone, measuring nearly 9 x 9 cm in its extant form, has been discovered from Harnol, situated about 15 km north of Ferozpur Jhirka in district Faridabad. The site has an old mound spread over about twenty-five acres and rising to a height of nearly thirty feet. It yields Painted Grey Ware, early historic and medieval relics including sculptures and terracottas.[52] The fragmentary head of Śiva, broken below the eyebrows, shows the vertical third eye on the forehead. The hair on the head is rendered by short semicircular incisions. Just below the *chāpākara* eyebrow, the drooping eyelid of the right eye of the god indicates his meditative pose. Stylistically, the piece may be assigned to the Kushāṇa-Gupta transitional phase.[53]

That Śiva images with three eyes were popularly created during the Kushāṇa and Gupta periods is indicated by some examples in the Mathura Museum,[54] Bharat Kala Bhawan, Varanasi[55] and elsewhere.[56] The tradition continued even in the medieval period.

Naṭarāja

Images of dancing Śiva, popularly known as Naṭarāja (literally 'King of dancers'), are known from various parts of India from the Gupta period onwards.[57] The complex symbolism and the philosophic implications of Śiva's dance have been discussed and explained by various scholars.[58] Naṭarāja images were perhaps not popular in the region north of Mathura as in its south and east.[59] Kashmir has been one of the greatest seats of Śiva worship but has yielded only one Naṭarāja image.[60] No images have been found from Himachal Pradesh and Punjab.[61] In spite of its early association with Hara (Śiva),[62] no Naṭarāja image is known from the present state of Haryana. This extreme scarcity in the northern region lends importance to any new discoveries even though the examples may not be artistically superb or unique. Our survey of the relics of art in the state of Haryana has resulted in the discovery of four images of Naṭarāja, which are described below.

Quite some time back, one Naṭarāja image (Pl. 154) was found on an old mound near the village Sandhaya, situated to the north-east of the ancient pilgrimage center of Kapālamochana[63] on the Sarasvatī river, nearly 18 km north-northwest of Jagadhari in district Yamunanagar. The mound, though disturbed, is very extensive and probably represents the town that developed near the pilgrimage center during the ancient times. The whole mound is littered with pottery and brickbats belonging to late Harappan, early historic and medieval periods. Large square bricks, some of them carved, Gupta inscriptions, terracottas and sculptures found from the site indicate that a brick temple stood here during the Gupta period.[64] The Naṭrāja image under discussion, when photographed, was preserved in a *ḍerā* at Sandhaya. It is almost life-size. This eight-handed image has suffered some mutilation and three of the left arms are lost. The main figure, however, is intact. The partly preserved square pilaster with vase-and-foliage base on the right indicates that the image was carved in a *rathikā*, which perhaps adorned one of the walls of an 8th century shrine of Śiva at the site. This is indicated by other relics also now preserved in the said *ḍerā* which include, besides *āmalakas* and architectural pieces, images of Lakulīśa and Śiva. The right foot of the dancing god is in *sama* pose and the left one in the *agratalasañchāra* with the heel lifted and the tip of the big toe touching the ground. Śiva's main left arm is in *gajahasta* and the right arm holds *patākāhasta* beside the face. A round object seems to have been held in the main left hand. The second right hand holds a *ḍamaru*, the third perhaps a trident (its upper portion is broken) and the rearmost is mutilated but what remains of it indicates that it held above the head a snake which was supported on the other side by the uppermost left hand also. The attributes of the second and third left hands are only to be guessed. The god bears matted locks on the head and wears large earrings, *ekāvali,* beaded wristlets and lower garment of animal skin secured by a waistband which shows a flower–shaped clasp in the center with loops on the sides. The hip of the god is deflected to the right side while the torso is raised in the opposite side. The facial expression betrays beatitude. A male drummer slightly turned to his left is depicted in the lower right corner.

The second image (Pl. 155) comes from Śītalā Mātā Temple, Rohtak.[65] Made of brownish sandstone, this small image measuring 24 x 17.5 cm, shows the four-handed god holding a trident in the upper right hand and the snake in the back left. The tail of the snake comes from behind the head of the god and winds the shaft of the trident held in the rear right hand. The main right hand is disposed in *abhaya,* slightly turned inwards, beside the face. The principal left arm is in *gajahasta,* almost touching the ankle of the upraised right foot. The thigh is raised slantingly upwards and the leg is folded at the knee. The left foot is slightly splayed out. The toe touches the ground and the heel has been raised up slightly. The god bears matted locks tied up in the form of a crown. He wears ear ornaments, wristlets, diaphanous lower garment and a long garland whose lower end forms a loop around the left thigh and knee of the god indicating the swaying movement of the body. The relief, unfortunately, is not in a good state of preservation. The face of the god is mutilated. Nandī, the bull, however, is depicted beautifully in profile in the lower right corner seated on his hind legs with his head, tilted upwards, probably to emphasize Śiva's ithyphallic nature. Interesting iconographically is the fact that the bull is playing on the drum (slightly mutilated) with its forelegs. Though anthropomorphic Nandī is shown as playing a drum in some Naṭarāja images[66] yet it is the bull here which performs this act. This perhaps is the unique feature of our image. On the other side of the pedestal may be seen a lute-player slightly turned to the left. Stylistically, this image may be placed in *circa* 9th century C.E.

Two images of Naṭarāja come from Morni-ka-Tal. One of these two is better preserved. The panel containing this image (Pl. 156) measures 57 x 37 cm and shows an *ardha-padma* motif in the center of the horizontal band at the top. The eight-armed god is shown dancing with his right leg bent and raised parallel to the *kaṭi-sūtra* and the left one carved gracefully bearing the weight of the whole body, with only the toe touching the ground. Apasmāra-purusha is missing. Śiva is wearing a tiger-skin around the waist with folds hanging in front as per the specifications of the iconographic texts. The god wears *jaṭā-mukuṭa,* necklace and bracelets in all the hands. The front right arm is in *gajahasta* with hand drooping in the posture of dance. The second right hand holds the trident. The third is in the *pralamba* pose and touches the head of a female figure seated on the corner of the pedestal to the proper right of the deity. The uppermost pair of hands holds the snake from two sides. The normal left hand is disposed in the gesture of reassurance while the other two support a *khaṭvāṅga* and a water-pot. Nandī is shown in the background facing left, wearing a bell around its neck. The small figure on the proper left of the god is depicted as playing on the drums. Ashvini Agrawal has identified it with Vishṇu[67] but because of the smallness of size and the details having gone away it is difficult to be very definite about it. The image is devoid of heavy ornamentation and is marked by simplicity. It is dated to *circa* 8th-9th century C.E. It seems to be a copy of the Naṭarāja figure found from Lakhamandal in Uttaranchal[68] and may have been inspired by that.

The other image, slightly larger in size (67 x 55 cm), is very badly mutilated but seems to have been similar to the preceding example. The front having been chiseled off, the details have been lost. The god, however, is shown as holding a kettledrum in the upraised rearmost right hand. On the proper left of the god are depicted two figures, one seated and the other standing, probably of the *gaṇas.* The figure on the other end is damaged beyond recognition. The image, however, seems to belong to the same period as the preceding one.[69]

These Naṭarāja images from Haryana show the common attributes of trident and the snake. Another notable characteristic is the absence of the Apasmāra-purusha. These images conform to Types A. III ad B of the northern region, Period 2 (C.E. 800-1100) described and illustrated by Gaston.[70] The discovery of these images, however, shows that Haryana was not completely devoid of Naṭarāja images and that the Haryanavi artist was not a blind follower of tradition.

Andhakāsuravadha-mūrti

One of the terrific forms of Śiva is represented by his Andhakavadha-mūrtis. Gopinath Rao has given the story of the destruction of the demon Andhaka, as narrated in the Purāṇas.[71] When Prahlāda, son of Hiraṇyakaśipu who was killed by Vishṇu assuming the Narasiṃha form, renounced the world, Andhaka began to rule over the demons. By performing severe austerities, he obtained several boons from Brahmā and grew very powerful. Andhaka tormented the gods and tried even to carry away Pārvatī. Śiva fought against him with his trident making the well known snakes Vāsuki, Takshaka and Dhanañjaya as his belt and bracelets and wearing the elephant skin, given to him by Vīrabhadra after killing the inimical demon Nīla in elephant form, as upper garment. When drops of blood falling from the body of Andhaka assumed the shape of similar demons, Śiva created a *śakti* called Yogeśvarī out of the flame that was issuing forth from his mouth. Other gods like Vishṇu, Brahmā, Kumāra, Indra, Yama, etc. also created similar *śaktis* to help Śiva. During the final assault, Śiva killed Andhaka as the drops of blood falling from his body were collected by these *śaktis* before falling on the ground. Vishṇu killed with his discus the secondary demons produced from the blood-drops. Indian sculptors have picked up the theme.

No image of Andhakāsuravadha is known from Haryana as yet. From Mohanbari near Rohtak comes a much-mutilated relief depicting this episode, now housed in the Gurukula Museum at Jhajjar (Pl. 157). Śiva is shown as charging on the demon in *pratyālīḍha* posture thrusting the trident in the body of the demon in order to kill him. He has pierced the body of the demon and held it aloft to the level of his left shoulder with the pokes of his trident held in his normal right hand and perhaps one left hand. The natural left hand holds a *kapāla* (skull-cup) to collect the drops of blood falling from the body of the demon. One of the additional left hands seems to support a bow but the other additional right and left hands are damaged beyond recognition. The total number of hands was probably eight. Snakes serving as necklace, armlet and girdle are partially visible in the extant image. The one in front of the Apasmāra-purusha is carved as raising its hood. His left leg is folded with foot placed on the back of the Apasmāra-purusha and the right leg is stretched diagonally with foot placed firmly on the ground. Unfortunately the head of Śiva is damaged. He is wearing a long garland of skulls and the elephant skin is stretched by his uppermost pair of hands to serve as the gloriole. The elephant-head with long tusked trunk is clearly visible in the uppermost left hand of the god. An emaciated female figure identifiable with Yogeśvarī or Kāli is shown as standing on the pedestal on the viewer's right with a cup in her right hand raised above to collect drops of blood of the demon. A diminutive figure probably with a trident in his right hand and left akimbo is standing turned to the god looking at him. Another human figure (or figures) standing behind Śiva are mutilated beyond recognition. Though badly damaged, the figure exudes dynamism and force. Being the first specimen of an Andhakavadha-mūrti to come to light from this region, it is important. Conceptually, this image is so similar to the Andhakāsuravadha-mūrti from Lakhamandal in Uttaranchal[72] that the latter seems to have served as its model. Stylistically, it may be dated to *circa* 9th century C.E.

SO-CALLED ŚIVA-KĀMĀNTAKA

A badly mutilated rectangular stone slab of 32 cm height from Morni in the collection of the Chandigarh Museum depicting a male figure seated in *lalitāsana* on a bull, holding a water pot in the normal left hand with the principal right in *varada* pose, with additional hands damaged, flanked by female figures in pilastered niches on the receding projections (Pl. 158) has been identified with Śiva-Kāmāntaka by D.C. Bhattacharyya.[73] The face of the figure is very badly mutilated but the high *jaṭā-jūṭa* rising conically has survived partially. The elongated straight and rigid torso with thin waist and sturdy chest is suggestive of the meditative posture. The neck bears *trivali* (triple fold). There was probably a *sarpa-hāra* around it, now badly damaged. There are traces of armlets, *yajñopavīta*, and *dhotī* secured by a girdle. The long thin floral garland, however, has survived well. The head of Nandī is also lost.

Though there remains little doubt to the figure being that of Śiva, its identification with Kāmāntaka is very doubtful. Bhattacharyya identified one of the female figure on Śiva's left as Pārvatī and he mistook the other as that of a male, which he thought was Madana or Kāma. The other figure too is certainly female bearing a *dhammilla* coiffure on the head and with breasts mutilated. We have many sculptures from Pinjore where gods are shown similarly flanked by female attendants in the niches on the receding projections. An almost identical figure from Pinjore holding a trident in the additional right and a snake in the rear left hand, and holding a water pot in the principal right (Pl. 159) has been obtained from the Bhīmādevī Temple complex. Still another exact copy, marred by successive whitewashing, is fixed in the wall of the *baoli* in the bazar at Pinjore. Bhattacharyya himself was not very sure of his identification and did not regard it as final. He dated the image to *circa* 13th century, which is too late a date for it. The double-ribbed pillars of the *rathikā*, the dress and ornamentation of the female figures and stylistic considerations render it to be a piece of *circa* tenth or at the latest 11th century C.E.

A fragmentary part of a door-surround from Morni-ka-Tal in the Chandigarh Museum identified by D.C. Bhattacharyya as Śiva-Gaṅgādhara[74] is actually the representation of the river-goddess Gaṅgā with attendant on the proper right of the doorway of a temple (probably dedicated to Vishṇu as indicated by the long garland worn by the male attendant or of Śiva as suggested by the diminutive emaciated figure near Gaṅgā's left foot) and should also belong like the preceding relief to the eleventh rather than the 13th century C.E.

RĀVAṆĀNUGRAHAMŪRTI

While returning to Laṅkā after having defeated Kubera, the Pushpaka-*vimāna* of Rāvaṇa stopped suddenly near the Śaravaṇa. On being enquired, a monkey-faced powerful dwarf Nandikeśvara (an adherent and form of Śiva) told him that his car stopped as Mahādeva was sporting with his spouse Umā on the mountain and had prohibited all from crossing that way. When Rāvaṇa laughed at Nandikeśvara contemptuously, the latter cursed him that monkeys like him shall destroy him. In anger and disdain, Rāvaṇa started shaking the mountain to lift and throw it away. At the shaking of the mountain Umā clung to her spouse out of fear. Śiva, knowing the real cause, pressed the mountain with the toe of his foot and pinned down Rāvaṇa beneath it. Helpless, Rāvaṇa cried (*Rautīti Rāvaṇaḥ*) and propitiated Śiva who ultimately became compassionate and let him go. This theme is depicted in some Indian sculptures known as Rāvaṇānugraha-mūrtis.

The theme of Rāvaṇānugraha has been more common to the south and the Deccan and comparatively rare in the north. A specimen of Rāvaṇānugraha-mūrti, 48 x 30.5 cm in size, stylistically belonging to southern Haryana and probably coming from Ata in district Gurgaon and now in a private collection (Regn. No. HRN/MGD-19), is, however, published here for the first time. The image, when photographed, was badly spoiled by whitewash (Pl. 160). The broad details may, however, be made out distinctly. Śiva is shown as seated in *sukhāsana* with Umā seated on his folded left leg. The god bears a *jaṭā-jūṭa* on the head and wears ear ornaments, a thick necklace, broad armlets, bracelets, nether garment, a long garland and perhaps anklets also. There seems to be a *yoga-paṭṭa* around the legs. Slightly turned towards Umā, he is embracing her with his normal left hand. The natural right hand is held in *abhaya*. The upper left hand carries a trident and the additional right holds a *nīlotpala* (blue lily). He is looking fondly at the face of his spouse who too is having a similar stance. She has thrown her right hand around the neck of Śiva and touching his right hand lovingly with her left hand. Having a *dhammilla* coiffure on her head, she is wearing prominent circular discs and perhaps flower ornaments also in her ears. Her necklace is similar to that of her spouse. She also wears bracelets, an *uttarīya* (upper garment), and lower garment held in position by a girdle. Her rotund breasts represent her youth. Two celestials are shown as inverting a pitcher on the head of Śiva. Brahmā occupies the top corner on the proper right and perhaps Vishṇu on the other. Nandī finds representation in the form of bull's head licking the left foot of Śiva. Gaṇeśa and Kārttikeya are shown on the extreme lower corners of the pedestal. Śiva's right foot is placed on a lotus emanating from the ground. Multi-headed Rāvaṇa is depicted below as being crushed trying to bear the load by resting his palms on the ground and supporting the weight with his upraised feet and soles. There is perhaps a human figure holding an umbrella to indicate the royalty of Rāvaṇa. Though the relief is badly marred by whitewash yet basic features of the image are clear to date it to *circa* 10th century C.E. on stylistic grounds. The scarcity of Rāvaṇānugraha-mūrtis in the region endows this specimen with great importance.[75]

LAKULĪŚA

The *Vāyu Purāṇa* (ch. 23) and the *Liṅga Purāṇa* (ch. 24) represent Maheśvara to have told Brahmadeva that he would incarnate himself as a *Brahmachārin* named Lakulin (variant Nakulin) after entering a dead body thrown into a cemetery at Kāyāvarohaṇa in the Lāṭa country (Karvan in Gujarat) as a contemporary of Vāsudeva Krishṇa during the twenty-eighth repetition of the Yugas (aeons) and would have four disciples Kuśika, Garga, Mitra, and Kaurushya who would propagate his views with their bodies sprinkled with ashes, and resorting to the Yoga of Maheśvara, and would ultimately go to the world of Rudra.[76] Mādhava calls the Pāśupata system that he explains in his *Sarvadarśanasaṅgraha* as Nakulīśa-Pāśupata, and quotes some words from a work attributed to him. It thus appears that Lakulin (the holder of a Lakula, Lakuṭa, or Laguḍa, i.e., a club) was a historical figure that founded a Pāśupata system. Many inscriptions of Gujarat and other places also refer to him.[77] *Pañchārthī-bhāshya* of Rāśikara furnishes interesting details of Lakulīśa-Pāśupata system during the Gupta period.[78] The *Harshacharita* of Bāṇa gives interesting details of the popularity of Śaivism at Sthāṇvīśvara. Bāṇa refers to the region around Sthāṇvīśvara as Śrīkaṇṭha-*janapada*, a term that is not met with anywhere else. Śrīkaṇṭha is one of the names and forms of Śiva. The name Śrīkaṇṭha may have been given to the region because of the popularity of Śaivism here to which Bāṇa alludes time and again. The Chinese pilgrim Hiuen Tsiang also refers to the Pāśupatas twelve times in his work. He says that there were temples of Maheśvara where Pāśupatas worshipped, and in a few of them they also resided. Another great center of Pāśupata sect was the monastery of Mattamayūras near Rohtak. An inscription of the time of king Bhojadeva, the Pratihāra ruler, from Sirsa refers to the construction of a magnificent temple of Yogīśvara (Śiva) embellished with the images of Vishṇu, Lakshmī, other gods, *daityas*, *gandharvas*, yakshas, *gaṇas*, *kinnaras*, *siddhas*, etc. by Nīlakaṇṭha, who was a fifth generation ascetic of Ratnarāśi, a champion of the Pāśupata sect.[79] The Pāśupata system flourished in the form of various sects and sub-sects later. Quite a good number of images of Lakulīśa have come down to us from various parts of India[80] but they are quite scarce in the Punjab-Haryana region. The system, however, seems to have been quite popular in the Morni hills of Panchkula which have yielded important evidence in this connection. Two images of Lakulīśa from this site are now housed in the Government Museum & Art Gallery at Chandigarh.[81] The better preserved image (Pl. 161) shows the ithyphallic god seated cross-legged on a lotus seat in a niche formed by two bracketed pilasters, holding the club from the middle in his left and with right, now damaged, probably held in *abhaya* and also holding a rosary. Interestingly enough, the god wears a flat *kirīṭa-mukuṭa* and not the matted hair on his head. The relief is so worn out that no details of the facial features can be made out except the long earlobes, which touch the shoulders. Obviously, the image was put as an adornment on the wall of some 9th century temple. The second image in the collection of the Chandigarh Museum is similar but debased. The face is flattened and the body parts show angular treatment. Both these images may have formed part of the exterior decoration of a Śiva temple at the site. Another image of Lakulīśa is still under worship in the sanctum sanctorum of the temple at Morni-ka-Tal. It shows Lakulīśa seated cross-legged on a lotus-seat in *svastikāsana*, has matted locks of hair and elongated earlobes with *kuṇḍalas* (Pl. 162). His eyes are almost closed in meditation. The two-armed deity holds a club in the left hand and the right hand, which is raised in the gesture of reassurance, also holds a rosary in it. The *ūrdhva-liṅga* is a prominent feature of this ithyphallic image. The image, datable to *circa* 8th-9th century C.E., may have adorned the outer wall of the temple as indicated by the horizontal moldings with an *ardha-padma* motif in the center.[82] Iconographically very interesting piece comes from Sandhaya near Kapālamochana. Unfortunately, however, it is very much worn out (Pl. 163) to give us the details. The four-armed god sits in *padmāsana* with the proper right hand in the gesture of reassurance and the back right hand holding the club. The rear left hand holds a snake while the normal left seems to rest on the respective knee. The matted hair and ear ornaments may be guessed. The god is not shown as ithyphallic. There, however, is carved an animal looking like an ass moving to left with its head near the club held in the right hand and tail near the left hands of the god. The square relief may have stylistically belonged to *circa* 8th-9th century C.E.

BHAIRAVA

Bhairava, *pūrṇarūpa* or the full form of Śiva according to the *Śiva Purāṇa*,[83] is described in the *Vishṇudharmottara Purāṇa* (III.59, 1-7) as a terrific god possessing a flabby belly, round tawny eyes, side tusks, wide nostrils, adorned with snakes and *muṇḍamālā*, holding many weapons in his numerous arms. Once a beautiful image of Bhairava lay fixed in the wall of the Kabir Chaurā temple at Pinjore showing the nude god standing gracefully in a triple-flexion posture, wearing a *jaṭā-jūṭa* bedecked with a skull, a long garland with a *kapāla* as an ornament at its lower end, *sarpa-hāra*, etc. and holding a sword in his proper right hand, skull in the suspended natural left hand, horn in the back left, and unidentified object in the rear right (Pl. 164). Because of the indifferent state of preservation and some mutilation besides having been whitewashed, the presence of the dog as the vehicle and other details could not be ascertained. This beautifully executed and gracefully standing figure may have adorned some 9th century shrine at Pinjore.[84] A black stone image of Bhairava wearing a turban with skull as the *chūḍāmaṇi*, ear ornaments, three-stringed necklet with a pendent, a necklace and girdle of big beads simulating skulls, holding a dagger and sword in his right hands and trident and dumb-bell in the left hands, seated in *lalitāsana* on his vehicle dog, enshrined in the Bhairava Temple belonging to the Maratha period is still under worship at Pehowa (Pl. 165). An equestrian very much mutilated figure carved on a 10th century architectural piece is under worship as Bhairomjī at Jasat in district Gurgaon.

No complete stone image of anthropomorphic Śiva of an early period has been found from Haryana so far. A fragmentary terracotta head from Agroha (Pl. 166) belonging to the Gupta period may be identified as that of Śiva. It shows a very serene face expressing beatitude. The matted hair on the head has a small vertical slit, probably for flowers. As such, it may have been an object of worship. A divine grace exudes from the face and the eyes.[85]

It must be confessed that independent anthropomorphic images of Śiva are few and far between in Haryana. Mention must be made of a niched image of the god from the ruins of the Bhīmādevī Temple at Pinjore shown as standing in *sama-bhaṅga* (contraposto) bearing an elaborate high *jaṭā-jūṭa*, ear ornaments, *ekāvali*, sacred thread, armlets, wristlets, long garland, *dhotī* secured by an elaborate girdle, etc. holding the handle of a trident with its upper portion damaged in the rear right hand and snake in the back left (Pl. 167). The proper right hand of the god is suspended in *varada-mudrā* touching the head of a small human figure standing in *tribhaṅga* standing behind the bull at the right foot of the god holding a club-like object in the right arm but with hands clasped in *namaskāra-mudrā*. The *pralamba* (suspended) left hand of the god also touches the head of a standing male attendant in adoration, perhaps Triśūla-purusha as indicated by the prongs of the trident on his head. The figure is badly marred by a coating of *chunam* (lime), which has concealed the finer details. This 10th century relief, however, is one of the few complete figures of the deity that have come down to us. A similar piece of the same date measuring 50 x 23 cm has been set up in the Haryana Raj Bhawan at Chandigarh. A 10th century sandstone bust measuring 20 x 15 cm was discovered from Jind. The god bears matted locks having a gem with a *kīrttimukha* in the center spewing beaded strings, third eye on the forehead, wearing a *sarpa-kuṇḍala* in the right ear, sacred thread, etc., with all the hands broken.[86] A beautiful 12th century image, probably of Śiva, having an elaborate *jaṭā-jūṭa* adorned with jewels, wearing *sarpa-kuṇḍalas*, a thick rope-like necklace, sacred thread, a bejeweled girdle, etc. is fixed in a wall of the Śītalā Mātā Temple at Rohtak. Heads with matted locks, presumably belonging to Śiva images, are known from Morni, Badali, Chandimandira (Acc. No. 16/84), Pinjore (Acc. Nos. 1/38, 1/290, 1/293), Sirsa (Acc. No. 1/112), Jhansua (Acc. No. 1/299), Kasan (Acc. No. 1/316), etc.

That three-headed Śiva-Mahādeva was also depicted in Haryana sculptures is indicated by a beautiful surviving fragment from Kohand. The extant piece shows a very serene central face with an elaborate *jaṭā-jūṭa* adorned with almond-shaped *chūḍāmaṇi* and pearl-strings flanked by side faces in three quarters profile with a part of the lotus-petalled gloriole carved behind. When complete, the relief must have been a masterpiece of Pratihāra art. Depiction of three heads of Śiva with different expressions indicating the deity to be Pañchānana, sometimes up to the bust (with two heads at the back being not visible), in the *bhadra-mukhas* was very common at Pinjore (Pl. 168),[87] Morni, and Kapālamochana from where we have quite a few specimens. Śiva, two-handed or four-handed, single or with Pārvatī, is generally depicted in the stele on the images of Vishṇu and Sūrya. Some of the steles betray the care bestowed to the figures whereas some have been carved rather crudely. The attributes in the hands are generally *abhaya* or *varada*, trident, serpent, and water pot.

UMĀ-MAHEŚVARA

It was, however, the worship of the couple as Umā-Maheśvara, which was very popular in Haryana. Quite a large number of Umā-Maheśvara images have come down to us. Though the images of Umā-Maheśvara came into vogue during the Kushāṇa period, the earliest piece known from Haryana is a very much weathered and mutilated late Gupta slate stone representation measuring 32.5 x 30 cm preserved in the Radha Krishna Temple at Kapālamochana (Regn. No. HRN/AMB-125) showing the god with Umā on his folded left leg (Pl. 169).[88] It is difficult to discern the details but Śiva, wearing an *ekāvali,* seems to hold a trident in his left hand with the river Gaṅgā flowing from his matted locks. The right hand of the god near his right knee is broken.

A rectangular greenish sandstone slab measuring 45 x 33 cm from Bhīmādevī Temple, Pinjore (Acc. No. 1/294), however, is a beautiful specimen showing the deity seated on the enface Nandī bull to left (Pl. 170). The god bears finely arrayed matted locks and wears floral ear ornaments, double-stringed pearl necklace, *yajñopavīta,* and *dhotī* held in position by a simple girdle. There is a plain halo behind the head pointed at the top. Both the legs of the god are gone but the principal right hand in *varada-mudrā* holds a rosary and the left hand a *mātuliṅga.* The additional right hand holds a trident and the left embraces Umā holding a mirror (?). Śiva's facial expression betrays quietude. Umā is seated on the left lap of her spouse slightly turned towards and embracing him with her right arm and holding a lily in her left. The curled locks on her head are adorned with a double peaked crown having lotus-shaped jewel in the center. The ring in her right ear is circular whereas the one in the left ear is floral. The pearl necklace has a pendent between the breasts from which the pearl string falls down. She wears armlets, *dhotī* and an *uttarīya.* There is a nimbus behind her head like that of her lord. The head of Nandī is also adorned with a crown and there is a bell hanging from his neck. The composition is very pleasing and balanced though the relief seems to have been left unfinished. It reminds us of the representation of Umā-Maheśvara on the gold coin of Harsha.[89] The image may be dated to *circa* 8th century C.E.

An image of Umā-Maheśvara, measuring 46 x 26 cm, comes from Belarkha in tehsil Narwana, district Jind.[90] Śiva is shown as seated in ease on Nandī. He is wearing high matted locks, pendent ear ornaments, *ekāvali,* pearl bracelets, long garland, etc. holding a blue lotus in the principal right hand and trident in the additional one, snake in the upper left hand and embracing the goddess with the normal left. Umā is seated on his left thigh as usual and bears a *dhammilla* coiffure with a central jewel in front, earrings, *ekāvali,* etc. Nandī is seated to right below. Bhṛiṅgī is carved just below the left foot of Śiva. It is a good specimen of Pratihāra art but unfortunately very badly spoiled by a thick coat of oil, dust and vermilion. The figure, along with another one of Vishṇu, is now fixed inside the niche of a modern Śiva temple, which has an octagonal plan and faces north. The sculptures were obtained from near an old well at the southeast corner of the village pond. An ancient mound lies about 2 km further east from the pond.

Almost similar in conception and form is the image of the couple from Durjanpur in district Jind, 24 x 12 cm, executed somewhat crudely with the difference that the bull is seated to left, Bhṛiṅgī is absent and the right foot of Śiva is placed on a lotus seat (Pl. 171). Umā-Maheśvara figures from Kalka, Morni-kā-Tāl, Nigadu, Jaintipur, etc. seem to have been similar in conception. The image from Santoshi Mata Temple, Kalka is too worn out to be detailed. The image from Jaintipur is broken above the legs but shows Gaṇeśa on the proper right hand side and Mahishāsuramardinī on the proper left of the pedestal.[91] This is an interesting iconographic feature. Umā-Maheśvara from Nigadu too has survived only in its lower part but is beautifully executed and shows Gaṇeśa on the proper right and Kārttikeya seated in *sukhāsana* on his vehicle peacock to left. The head of Bhṛiṅgī too has survived. It must have been a good example of *circa* 9th century C.E. The image from Morni is preserved in the Chandigarh Museum and is very much worn out though almost complete. Gaṇeśa and

Kārttikeya are there but Bhṛiṅgī is missing. Another carefully carved Pratihāra image is obtained from Pehowa showing the couple seated on the Nandī to right with Śiva's right foot placed on a lotus held on its head by a *gaṇa* and another *gaṇa* standing holding sweet balls to the bull (Pl. 172). Bhṛiṅgī was there originally as indicated by his surviving feet in the center of the pedestal. There is a *yoga-paṭṭa* around the right knee of Śiva going to the left shank. The god holds *mātuliṅga* in the natural suspended right hand and the corresponding left embraces Umā. His additional right hand carried the trident now surviving only in the form of its lower end and the back left hand holds the snake as usual. Umā's left hand holding the mirror is broken and she has put her right hand around Śiva's neck. Gaṇeśa and Kārttikeya seated at ease on his peacock and holding the lance in his left hand are carved on the receding projections of the pedestal followed by standing figures of Kāla and Mahākāla behind them. Minute care has been bestowed even to the subsidiary figures to make the relief an elegant one.[92]

Two beautiful Umā-Maheśvara images come from Beri. One of these (Acc. No. 1/229) measures 55 x 34 cm and shows Śiva seated on caparisoned Nandī to left in *sukhāsana* with left leg folded and right one dangling down (Pl. 173). The right foot is placed on a double lotus *pīṭha*. Śiva bears an elaborate *jaṭā-jūṭa* adorned with a crescent (Chandra-śekhara) and wears beaded circular ear ornaments, a double *ekāvali* and pearl necklace, beaded armlets and bracelets, an *uttarīya*, nether garment secured by beaded *netra-sūtra*, anklets, and *yajñopavīta*. There is the vertical third eye on the forehead and lozenge-shaped *śrīvatsa* on the chest. The plump round face bears semi-closed eyes giving an abstract expression. His head is slightly turned towards Umā who is looking at him fondly. Śiva holds a flower in the normal right hand and the trident in the rear. The principal left hand embraces Umā and the additional left holds the snake. The semi-circular top of the back slab bears the lotus-shaped aureole. Śiva's folded left leg serves as the cushion for Umā who is having a full plump face with a *dhammilla* hair coiffure and throwing her right arm on the right shoulder of her lord from behind the neck and holds a *līlā-kamala* in her left hand. The prominent circular earrings, *ekāvali*, pearl necklace falling on the belly from between the round rotund breasts, *sārī* secured by a waist band having pearl strings forming loops on the thighs and free ends falling touching the knees, *trivali* on the neck and anklets on feet characterize her person. Nandī has turned his head backward to look towards her. Bhṛiṅgī in a dancing pose and *añjali-mudrā* is carved in the center of the *triratha* pedestal while Gaṇeśa standing near the right foot of Śiva and Kāla holding a *khaṭvaṅga* in his left hand stand on the receding recesses of the pedestal. The corners of the back slab before it turns semi-circular are occupied by garland-bearing *vidyādharas* hovering in the sky. The relief is a happy blending of the classical and medieval traits and is amongst the superb carvings of the Pratihāra period.[93]

The second image from Beri (Pl. 174), though similar in conception and composition, is more elaborately carved. Measuring 65 x 36 cm (Acc. No. 1/233), it betrays dominant and developed dress and ornamentation of the figures. The snake in the additional left hand of Śiva is three-hooded and Umā holds the mirror in her left hand. The principal left hand of Śiva cuddles the left breast of his spouse. The top of the semi-circular back slab shows semi-celestial male figures holding a *jaṭā-jūṭa* followed by garland-bearing *vidyādharas* hovering in the sky. The top corners of the back slab carry stela showing four-handed Brahmā and Vishṇu with their usual attributes on the proper right and left sides. Gaṇeśa and Kārttikeya are seated on the extreme recesses with Kāla and Mahākāla standing behind them. A vessel of sweet balls is placed below the head of Nandī who is looking up with head turned towards the divine couple. Diminutive emaciated Bhṛiṅgī is carved as dancing as usual in front. The elaborate jewelry, compactness of composition, and minute care provided even to the subsidiary figures render this figure to be later than the preceding one by a few years.[94]

A different style and mode of presentation may, however, be witnessed in the Umā-Maheśvara image from Ata (Pl. 175).[95] The rectangular buff sandstone slab measuring 158 x 89 cm depicts Śiva in *lalitāsana* on Nandī to front with Umā seated on his folded left leg. The branches of a tree with long leaves and fruits or flowers over his head indicate the venue to have been a pleasure garden. Śiva bears beautiful bejeweled matted locks on his head, some of them falling gracefully on his shoulders also. The *keyūras* seem to have been of snake. There is a *yoga-paṭṭa* around his right dangling leg. His right foot is placed on a lotus *pīṭha* arising from the ground. All hands except the upper left holding the trident above the level of the head from between the faces of the couple are broken. The upper right hand, though damaged, seems to have held the snake, the long rope-like body of which still survives behind the heads of the couple. Below the garland-bearing *vidyādhara* couples on the top corners are depicted three-headed Brahmā on the proper right and Vishṇu on the other side. Mutilated female figures occupy the middle portions of the back slab whereas Gaṇeśa, Kārttikeya, Bhṛiṅgī and probably Kāla and Mahākāla occupy the pedestal. This arrangement of this tenth-century composition is totally different from other examples and the style of holding of trident in the left hand above the head as seen in the image of Umā-Maheśvara from Nand Chand, Panna indicating influence from Madhya Pradesh.[96] An image of Umā-Maheśvara from Jadthal also shows Śiva holding the trident in the upper left hand in the same way but Umā is seated on his left leg with both the legs hanging down. It is the only example to show the goddess in this stance and is thus an interesting specimen (Pl. 176).

The image of Umā-Maheśvara from Asthal Bohr is a superb example of carving in sandstone and gives a frontal view of the couple seated on couchant caparisoned Nandī to left. The right legs of both Śiva and Umā dangle down with feet placed on lotuses. A small female figure is shown as holding a bowl of sweet balls near the mouth of the bull. Gaṇeśa and Kārttikeya are standing on the right and left. The top right hand side corner of the back slab is lost but it seems to have carried Brahmā in the stele. Vishṇu on the other side is intact. The only surviving hands are Uma's right placed on Śiva's right shoulder and Śiva's lower left touching Uma's left breast from behind her back. The elaborate dress and jewelry and the style of carving are reminiscent of the chisel work of Khajuraho of the 10th-11th century C.E.[97]

Gujjar Kheri has yielded quite a few images of the divine couple. One of these, measuring 57 x 42 cm and now housed in the Chandigarh Museum bearing Acc. No. 4289 (Pl. 177) shows Śiva seated in *lalitāsana* on the mount bull to right with its head raised upwards to gaze at his lord, and Umā sitting in rather an awkward posture on the left thigh of Śiva with her bust turned towards him and legs turned to her left. The high elaborate matted locks bedecked with jewels, ear ornaments, necklaces, armlets, wristlets, anklets, under garment secured by a waist band, a long beaded garland and *yoga-paṭṭa* wound around the right leg of Śiva and equally elaborate dress and ornamentation of Umā bespeak of the medieval traits at their zenith. The upper proper right hand side of the back slab is lost. It may have carried the lotus aureole behind the head of the god and the stele depicting Brahmā on the right top corner. The long shaft of the trident held in the upper right hand of the god has survived though the hand is damaged. The corresponding additional left hand carries the snake and the normal right holds the *līlākamala* while the proper left hand cuddles Umā's left breast. Pārvatī's left hand is broken and the right goes to the right shoulder of her lord from behind the neck. The surviving top corner on the proper left hand side of the rectangular slab shows four-armed Vishṇu seated in *lalitāsana* with hands disposed in *abhaya*, holding mace, discus and conch. There is a gracefully standing female figure behind Vishṇu holding probably the long shaft of the umbrella, which she held over the god. Interestingly enough there is a nimbus behind her head also betraying her divinity. On the *tri-ratha* pedestal are depicted four-armed Gaṇeśa seated in *lalitāsana*, a garland-bearing female behind him and a male figure standing on the extreme projection of the pedestal holding a cup in his right and a long shafted club in the left hand (Kāla) on the proper right of Śiva. The left side shows Kārttikeya seated in *lalitāsana* on his mount peacock, garland-bearing female figure behind and a mutilated male figure holding probably a lance (Mahākāla) on the extreme projection. The surviving back slab above shows *vyāla* and *makara-mukha*. Bhṛiṅgī, now slightly mutilated, is carved in the center in a dancing pose on the pedestal. The image may be dated stylistically to about 11th century C.E.[98] A similar image from Gujjar Kheri is housed in the National Museum, New Delhi (Acc. No. L. 40),[99] but more care seems to have been provided to carve it (Pl. 178). The couple here is seated on the bull to left with head turned backwards. The back slab contains figures and stele lost in the preceding piece but the hands of Śiva and Umā's left hand are broken, Bhṛiṅgī is guessed only by one of his surviving foot on the pedestal, and Kārttikeya's upper part is also lost. A third figure from Gujjar Kheri (55 x 32 cm) of about the same period is very badly mutilated.[100]

Pinjore has yielded quite a few images of the couple. One (Acc. No. 1/55) is very badly mutilated. The image in the Chandigarh Museum (Acc. No. 3293) is carved on a *tri-ratha* rectangular slab and is completely preserved but for minor mutilations (Pl. 179). Interestingly the god is depicted as seated on a well bedecked high stool and the small figure of bull is shown as seated to left behind the right foot of Śiva which dangles down slantingly with foot splayed out. The left leg is folded to seat Umā whose left foot is placed on a double-petalled lotus. On the face of the pedestal is also carved the lotus pattern while a lion has been carved below the double-petalled lotus under Umā's left foot. Bhattacharyya has rightly observed that it seems to be a later interpolation.[101] The normal right hand of Śiva is shown in *varada-mudrā* and the left embracing the goddess is damaged. The rear pair of hands holds a trident and the snake. The god bears an extraordinarily high *jaṭā-jūṭa* decorated with jewels and pearl strings. He has also the vertical third eye on the forehead and wears a torque, a beaded necklace, circular ear ornaments, armlets, double beaded wristlets, the *dhotī* held in position by a beaded girdle and anklet in the right foot. A round lotus-petalled halo has been carved behind the head. I don't know why Bhattacharyya missed it.[102] Umā too bears a high *dhammilla* coiffure on the head and wears beaded earrings, torque and beaded necklace falling down from over the two robust breasts, *keyūras* and wristlets similar to those of her spouse, a scarf and the under garment secured by the waistband. The anklet is visible only in her left foot. She embraces her lord with her right hand and holds the convex mirror in her left hand near the corresponding knee. Her bust is leaning towards Śiva whose head is turned towards Umā. On the receding projections of the pedestal are shown probably Gaṇeśa and Kārttikeya, the former in a strange side pose but to be recognized by the hanging trunk. Bhattacharyya identifies them with devotees.[103] The middle portions of the back slab are decorated with leogryphs while the top corners show unidentified divinities. Bhattacharyya did not take cognizance of these figures.[104] The dress and ornaments, emphatic flexions and mechanical treatment of the figures renders this image to be a work of the 11th century C.E.

A 12th century, 52 cm high Umā-Maheśvara image from Agroha (Pl. 180), now in the Chandigarh Museum, is similar in conception to the preceding one but shows the dangling right and left foot of Śiva and Pārvatī placed on their respective vehicles, the bull and the lion, depicted on the central facet of the *pañcharatha* pedestal. The bull has drawn his face unusually vertically to look towards his master. In between these vehicles is the dancing figure of Bhṛiṅgī. The attendant *gaṇa* figures on the extreme projections of the pedestal are almost lost and Brahmā and Vishṇu on the stele, too, have suffered mutilation. And so also the upper right hand of Śiva holding the trident and the normal left hand of Umā, which may have held the mirror or the lotus. The normal left hand of the god touches the left breast of his spouse from behind the back and Umā has thrown her right hand on the right shoulder of Śiva from around the neck. As in the preceding piece, the normal right hand of Śiva is held in *varada* pose and the upper left holds the snake. Both Śiva and Umā bear elaborate hair coiffure, *jaṭā-jūṭa* adorned with jewels and *dhammilla* with a high pod respectively. The rotundity of the breasts of Umā is in keeping with the medieval tradition. The full round faces however betray an expression of selflessness. The third eye on Śiva's forehead is conspicuously absent.[105] Another fragmentary relief from Agroha showing a headless female figure with the surviving left hand in the posture of reassurance, standing gracefully turned towards her right and with her left breast cuddled by a hand coming from behind may also have been a part of some Umā-Maheśvara image. It is now preserved in HARDAM.

Quite a good number of medieval images of Umā-Maheśvara or their fragments are preserved in HARDAM from Belarkha (Acc. No. 1/55), Bohr Majra (Acc. Nos. 1/439-40), Budauli (Acc. No. 1/308), Hat (Acc. Nos. 1/306, 379), Hisar region (Acc. No. 45/84), Jadthal (Acc. No. 1/83), Jhansua (Acc. Nos. 1/298, 302), Kalka (Acc. Nos. 1/205, 209), Panchkula (Acc. Nos. 1/284, 481), Pinjore (Acc. Nos. 1/55, 76), Raisina (Acc. No. 1/399), Ratpur (Acc. Nos. 1/90, 250), Thanesar (Acc. No. 1/444), Tirkhu (Acc. No. 39/84), etc. Some images or fragments are fixed in the walls of houses or placed in shrines at Asiaki,[106] Bolni,[107] Hat, Gujjar Kheri, Samchana,[108] etc. while the Kurukshetra University museum too has a few pieces from Pinjore and Thanesar.[109]

NANDĪ

Vṛishabha was originally an epithet of Rudra. The *Mbh.* (XIII. 225, 25) refers to Nandikeśvara as the mount of Śiva. Several other texts like the *Rāmāyaṇa, Śiva Mahāpurāṇa, Liṅga Purāṇa,* and the *Bhāgavata Purāṇa* also narrate the stories of his origin.[110] In art, Nandī is represented in anthropomorphic form as a duplicate of Śiva, in therianthropomorphic (bull-faced human) form, or more often as a bull. The earliest evidence of Nandikeśvara comes from Sirsa in the form of typical Kushāṇa terracotta showing a monkey-faced human playing on the *tabla* (Pl. 181).[111] Two Gupta terracotta figurines, one representing the forepart (Pl. 182) and the other only the face of bull (Pl. 183), are known from Agroha.[112] An 8th-9th century buff sandstone headless seated image of the bull on a plain pedestal from Sirsa bears a garland around the neck with a series of human skulls as decorations.[113] A humped Nandī bull from Kohand, seated to left on a pedestal with decorative golden chains adorning the head, neck, and body with a vessel full of sweet balls in front (Pl. 184) is a beautiful creation of the Pratihāra period. The chain around the neck shows lotus and diamond patterns. A bell is also shown suspended from the middle of the back with two beaded strings on its two sides. The existence of Śaiva temples is corroborated by three Nandī (bull) figures from Pinjore, which measure 60 x 31.5 cm, 49 x 39 cm and 42 x 38 cm. An 11th-12th century unfinished Nandī bull from Pinjore (Pl. 185)[114] provides evidence of the site being a center of art during the early medieval period. Bhainsa Tibba near Mansa Devi Temple, Mani Majra has yielded two Nandī bulls – 38 x 26 cm, broken above the bust (Acc. No. 1/22) and 49 x 39 x 25 cm (Acc. No. 1/23) in greenish sandstone with decorative belts and straps to right. Jadthal has yielded grey sandstone seated Nandī with a prominent hump of *circa* 10th century. Two medieval bull figures are known from Ata. Four old images of Nandī bulls have been set up on the four corners of a Śaiva shrine constructed with the old material of the temples at Bhund in district Panchkula. One bull figure lies in the Devī Temple at Panipat. One red sandstone Nandī with head broken and wearing ornamental belt is known from Kasan. Numerous other sites have also yielded such figures.

Notes and References

1. Sir John Marshall, *Mohenjodaro and the Indus Civilization*, Vol. I, London, 1931, pp. 48 ff and pls. VII-XII.
2. Macdonell, *op. cit.*, pp. 74 ff.
3. J.N. Banerjea, *The Development of Hindu Iconography*, Calcutta, 1956 (*DHI*), pp. 446-47.
4. R.G. Bhandarkar, *Vaiṣṇavism, Śaivism, and Minor Religious Systems*, Poona, 1929 (*VSMRS*), pp. 145 ff.
5. *DHI*, p. 448; *VSMRS*, pp. 145 ff.
6. T.A. Gopinath Rao, *Elements of Hindu Iconography* (Reprint, Delhi 1971), Vol. II, Pt. 1, pp. 39 ff; *VSMRS*, pp.145ff; V.S. Agrawala, *Śiva-Mahādeva*, Varanasi, 1966; Pranabanand Jash, *History of Śaivism*, Calcutta, 1974; R.K. Siddhantashastree, *Śaivism Through the Ages*, Delhi, 1975; Mahadev Chakravarti, *The Concept of Rudra-Śiva Through the Ages*, Delhi, 1986; etc.
7. Commenting on Pāṇini's *sūtra* V.2, 76. Also see Bhandarkar, *op. cit.*, p. 165.
8. John Allan, *Catalogue of the Coins of Ancient India in the British Museum*, London, 1936.
9. P.L. Gupta and T.R. Hardarkar, *Ancient Indian Silver Punchmarked Coins of the Magadha-Maurya Karshapana Series*, Anjaneri, 1985, p. 1 ff.
10. Ajay Mitra Shastri, "Symbols on Tribal coins: An Interpretative study" in *Seminar papers on Tribal coins of Ancient India (C.200 B.C. to 400 A.D.)*, edited by Jai Prakash Singh and Nisar Ahmad, Varanasi, 1977, pp. 88-89.
11. Allan, *op. cit.*, pp. xciii and 145; Devendra Handa, "Kada Coins From Sugh," *Numismatic Digest*, Vol. 20 (1996), pp. 25-32.
12. Percy Gardner, *The Coins of the Greek and Scythic Kings of Bactria and India in the British Museum*, Chicago, 1966, pp. 104 (Gondophernes) and 124-128 (Kadphises II).
13. I.K. Sarma, *The Development of Early Saiva Art and Architecture (with special reference to Andhra Pradesh)*, Delhi, 1982, pp. 61-62 has suggested a date of 3rd-2nd century B.C.E. while D.R. Bhandarkar (*Carmichael Lectures on Ancient Indian Numismatics*, Calcutta 1921, pp. 19-20) assigns it to the 4th century C.E. For a discussion of these and various other views see H. Sarkar, 'Beginnings of Śaivism in South India with special Reference to Date of Gudimallam Liṅga' in *Rupanjali in memory of O.C. Gangoly* (ed. By K.K. Ganguli and S.S. Biswas), Calcutta, 1986, pp. 115ff.
14. The Bhita *Pañchamukha* Śiva-*liṅga* has been assigned to *circa* 3rd-2nd century B.C.E. by Marshall (*Annual Report of the Archaeological Survey of India*, 1911-12, p. 49, pl. XI.8) and N.P. Joshi (*Catalogue of the Brahmanical Sculpture in the State Museum, Lucknow*, part I, Lucknow, 1972, pp. 99-101, figs. 24-27. Rao (*op. cit.*, pp. 63-65) considered it to be of the pre-Christian period and J.N. Banerjea (*DHI*, pp. 464-65) dates it to the 1st century B.C.E. D.R. Bhandarkar (*loc. cit.*) has suggested for it a date in the Kushāṇa period. For a detailed discussion see Sarkar (*loc. cit*).
15. Sarkar, *loc .cit.*
16. T.K. Biswas, "Early Śaivite Terracottas in Bharat Kala Bhavan", in *Dimensions of Indian Art (Pupul Jayakar Seventy)*, edited by Lokesh Chandra and Jyotindra Jain, Delhi, 1986, Vol. I (Text), p. 45, Vol. II (plates), p. 10, fig. 1.
17. *Liṅga* is a Sanskrit word meaning a sign, symbol, mark, or even an image.
18. Westropp and C.S. Wake, *Symbol Worship: Influence of the Phallic Ideas in the Religions of Antiquity*, New Delhi, 1979.

19. *Rāmāyaṇa*, Yuddha-kāṇḍa, 123.20.
20. *Mahābhārata* III.39, 65:
    Sa ramyaṃ śaraṇaṃ gatvā bhagavantaṃ Pinākinam/
    Mṛinmayaṃ sthaṇḍilaṃ kṛitvā mālyenāpūjayad Bhavam//
21. A.K. Coomaraswamy, *Introduction to Indian Art*, Delhi, 1969, fig. 16.
22. R.D. Banerji, "Three Sculptures in the Lucknow Museum," *ARASI, 1909-10*, pp. 147-48, pl. LIV, figs. C, d, and e.
23. *Liṅgārchanatantra* and *Prāṇatoshṇītantra* as quoted by R.K. Bhattacharyya, "Popularity of Śiva Worship in India," *VIJ*, x (I-ii), p. 82.
24. *Śiva Purāṇa*, Prathama Vidyeśvara Saṃhitā, ch. XI; *Vāyu Saṃhitā*, Uttara Bhāga, ch. XXIV, etc.
25. *EHI*, II, Appedix B.
26. *Rūpa-Maṇḍana* describes *mukha-liṅgas* with one, three, and four-faces –
    Mukha-liṅgaṃ trivaktraṃ syādekavaktraṃ chaturmukham /
    Shaṇmukhaṃ chaikavaktraṃ syāt trivaktre pṛishṭhake na hi //
27. *Catalogue & Guide To State Museum, Bharatpur (Rajasthan)*, Jaipur, 1960- 61, p. 9, pl. II.
28. *Kusumāñjali*, II, pp. 299-305, pls. 1-3; see also Yogānanda Shastri (1999), *op. cit.*, p. 189, Pl. 79.
29. Devendra Handa, "Some Unpublished Sculptures from Gujjar Kheri (Haryana)," *Panjab University Research Bulletin (Arts)*, Chandigarh, Vol. VII, No.1 (April, 1986), pp. 107-21 and figs. 1-20.
30. Cf. Harle, *Gupta Sculpture*, pl. 27; V.S. Agrawala, *Gupta Art*, figs. 8 & 10.
31. *Journal of the Indian Society of Oriental Art*, Vol. VI, p. 202, pl. XLIV. Also see S.K. Saraswati, *A Survey of Indian Sculpture*, Calcutta, 1957, fig. 89.
32. N.P. Joshi (1972), *op. cit.*, fig. 30.
33. *Indian Archaeology 1967-68 – A Review*, pl. XXVIII. A.
34. C.J. Rodgers, *Revised List of Objects of Archaeological Interest in the Punjab*, p. 74. A small (8 x 7 cm) early medieval *Trimukha-liṅga* showing the Bhairava, Vāmadeva and Tatpurusha faces of Śiva is reported to have been installed in a temple near the Gharaunda College in district Karnal (Amar Singh, *Archaeology of Karnal and Jind Districts [Haryana]*, Kurukshetra University, Kurukshetra, 1981, p. 191, pl. XXIV A). Actually it is not a round Śiva-*liṅga* but a rectangular slab showing Mahādeva with three faces. Similarly the five-headed figure from Bolni village in district Rewari described as 11th-12th century *Pañchamukha* Śiva-*liṅga* is very doubtful. Rising from the waist level with two arms, one held in *abhaya* (?) and the other akimbo, with five very crudely carved elongated human faces in a single row, it seems to be very late depiction and one cannot be sure of its being a five-faced Śiva-*liṅga*. The black stone six-headed Śiva-liṅga from Rewari dated to 10th-11th century and described by him, however, is interesting with five faces around the shaft and one placed above (For details see Rahar, *op. cit.*, p. 191, pls. XIII B and XIV A respectively).
35. Ranbir Singh, *History and Archaeology of Tehsil Palwal (District Faridabad), Haryana*, Unpublished Ph. D. Thesis, Kurukshetra University, Kurukshetra, 1995, p. 42, pls. VII-VIII. A small 20 x 15 cm *chaturmukha-liṅga* also exists at Hassangarh in the Sampla block of Rohtak. Sneh Lata (*op. cit.*, p. 57, pl. VII. C) has wrongly identified it as a female figure. A *Pañchāyatana-Liṅga* from Salwan in district Karnal is preserved in HARDAM also (Acc. no. 1/135).
36. D.C. Bhattacharyya, *op. cit.*, pp. 36-38, fig. 11. See also D.C. Bhattacharyya, 'The Caturmūrti-Liṅga of Śiva," *Journal of the Varendra Research Museum*, Dhaka, Vol. 6, pp. 33-38, pl. I.
37. *Ibid.*
38. Devendra Handa, *Pehowa*, p. 113, pl. 61.
39. Joanna Williams, "An Ardhanarisvara-Linga," in *Kusumāñjali: New Interpretation of Indian Art & Culture – Sh. C. Sivaramamurti Commemoration Volume*, ed. M.S. Nagaraja Rao, Vol. II, Delhi, 1987, pp. 299-305, pls. I-III.
40. Devendra Handa, "Relics of Art from Marhanwala," *PURBA*, Vol. XX, no. 2 (October 1989), pp. 165-69, figs. 1-9.
41. Shukla (1981), *op. cit.*, p. 14, pl. IV.2.
42. Devendra Handa, "Art Remains from Jaintipur," *Haryana Sahitya Akademi Journal of Indological Studies*, Chandigarh, Vol. III (1988), pp. 279-80.

43. *Epigraphia Indica*, XLI, no. 23, pp. 206-10.
44. *Mahābhārata* (Gita Press), Anuśāsana Parva, ch.140, vv. 33-38.
45. W.J. Wilkins, *Hindu Mythology: Vedic and Puranic* (Indian reprint, 1972), pp. 276-77. Also see E.W. Hopkins, *Epic Mythology* (Indian reprint, 1968), p. 216.
46. Vasudeva Sharan Agrawala, *Mahābhārata Kī Nāmānukramaṇikā* (Hindi), Gita Press, Gorakhpur, V.S. 2036, p. 351.
47. *Vishṇudharmottara Purāṇa* (GOS), p.169. Also see B.N. Sharma, *Iconography of Sadāśiva*, Delhi, 1976, p. 1.
48. The Mathura Museum possesses some Kushāṇa Śiva heads with a third eye. See also T.K. Biswas, *op. cit.*, pp. 45ff. and figs. 2-5: J.C. Harle, *Gupta Sculpture*, Oxford, 1974, pls. 9, 50, 54, 128, etc. in the Kushāṇa and Kushāṇa-Gupta transitional phase the third eye was carved horizontally but subsequently it was put vertically on the forehead.
49. Prof. B.B. Lal illustrated this piece in one of his Tagore Lectures in the Panjab University, Chandigarh, on February 18, 1987. See also the jacket design on *Facets of Indian Civilization – Recent Perspectives (Essays in Honour of Prof. B.B. Lal)*, Chief editor Jagat Pati Joshi, 3 Vols., New Delhi, 1997.
50. Devendra Handa, " Trinetra Śiva from Haryana," *Indologica Jaipurensia*, Vol. II (1988-95), pp. 74-79, pl. X.
51. Cf. J.M. Rosenfield, *The Dynastic Arts of the Kushans*, University of California Press, Barkeley and Los Angles, 1967, fig. 19.
52. Dharmpal Singh Punia, *Archaeology of Mahendragarh and Gurgaon Distircts (Haryana)*, Unpublished Thesis, Kurukshetra, University, Kurukshetra, 1976, p. 61.
53. Handa (1988-95), *loc. cit.*, pl. X. Punia (loc. cit.) ascribed it to the Gupta period.
54. N.P. Joshi, *Mathurā Kī Mūrttikalā* (Hindi), State Museum, Mathura, 1965, p. 73; *Catalogue of the Brahmanical Sculptures in the State Museum, Lucknow*, part-I. The State Museum, Lucknow, 1972, figs. 9 and 30 and pl. 5; Mahadev Chakravarti, *op. cit.*, pls. 3-4; *Indian Archaeology1960-61 – A Review*, pl. LXXIX.C; *Ancient India*, no. 6 (Jan, 1950), pp.54 ff and pl. XIX.
55. Biswas, *loc. cit*.
56. V.S. Srivastava, *Catalogue and Guide to Ganga Golden Jubilee Museum, Bikaner*, Jaipur, 1960-61, pl. I; *Catalogue and Guide to Rajputana Museum, Ajmer*, Jaipur, 1960-61, pl. IV; S.C. Kala, *Terracottas in the Allahabad Museum*, Delhi, 1980, pp.104-5, Nos. 626-30, figs. 293-95.
57. C. Sivaramamurti, *Naṭarāja in Art, Thought and Literature*, New Delhi, 1975; A-M Gaston, *Śiva in Dance, Myth and Iconography*, Delhi, 1982.
58. A.K. Coomaraswamy, *The Dance of Siva*, Bombay, 1948; Jose Pereira, "The Naṭarāja Theme, a new interpretation", *Journal of the Royal Asiatic Society of Bombay*, vol. XXX (1), 1955, pp. 71-86; J.M. Somasudaram Pillai, *Śiva Naṭarāja – The Cosmic Dancer in Cidambaram*, Chidambaram, 1970; Sivaramamurti, *op. cit.*, pp. 23-41; etc.
59. Gaston, *op. cit.*, p. 213 (map).
60. Sivaramamurti, *op. cit.*, p. 306, fig. 184.
61. An image of dancing Śiva from Bhatinda (Punjab) probably holds a *vīṇā* and represents Vīṇādharadakshiṇā-mūrti. See for details Devendra Handa, "Medieval Brahmanical Stone Sculputure from Punjab," *Roopa-Lekha*, LIV, 1983, pp. 28-29, fig. 8.
62. Some scholars derive the very name of the present state from *Hara-yāna*. Thanesar (Kurukshetra), which is one of the oldest cities of Haryana, derives its name from Sthāṇvīśvara. There are many other *tīrthas* in Haryana associated with Śiva, e.g., Rudrasara (Thanesar), Hāṭakeśvara (Hat), Bhuteśvara (Jind), Ekādaśa-Rudra (Kaithal), Rudrapada (Nigadu), Tripurāri (Tighri), Rudra-kūpa (Narakatari), etc.
63. Devendra Handa, "Kapāla-Mocana: An Ancient Holy Place," *Purāṇa*, x 2, July 1968, pp. 148-53.
64. Devendra Handa, "Some Unpublished Terracottas From Haryana," *Prāchya-Pratibhā*, Vol. XII, no. 1-2 (1984), p. 29, Fig.4; "Gupta Reliefs From Haryana," *Bulletin of Museums & Archaeology in U. P.*, no. 35-36 (June-Dec. 1985), p. 17, figs. 4 & 5. "Late Gupta Relics From Kapāla-Mocana," *PURBA*, Vol. XXII, no. 2 (October 1991), pp. 147-50, Figs 7.

65. It is now preserved in the Department of Archaeology and Museums, Haryana, Panchkula (Index no. 1/252).
66. Gaston, *op. cit.*, Pl, 40. Also see Sivaramamurti, *op. cit.*, figs. 137, 154; E. Bhavnani, *The Dance in India*, Bombay, 1965, pl. 33, fig. 8.
67. Ashvini Agrawal, "Saiva Sculptures from Morni-Ka-Tal," *Roopa-Lekha*, Vol. Nos. LXVII-LXXI (January 2001), pp. 83-84, fig. 16.
68. See for illustration Brajesh Krishna, *The Art under the Gurjara-Pratihāras*, New Delhi, 1989, pl. 55.
69. Ashvini Agrawal, *loc. cit.*, fig. 17. A very much-mutilated four-handed image in a *rathikā* in Chhattā Rai Balmukund Dasa at Narnaul described as dancing Śiva by Rahar (*op. cit.*, pp. 191-92, pl. XIV B) is that of Īśāna as a *dikpāla* and not Naṭarāja.
70. Gaston, *op. cit.*, pp. 46 ff., pls. 39-48.
71. *EHI*, Vol. I, part II, pp. 379-83.
72. Brajesh Krishna, *op. cit.*, pl. 56.
73. D.C. Bhattacharyya, *op. cit.*, pp. 28-29.
74. *Ibid.*, pp. 33-34, fig. 9.
75. A very fragmentary 10th century relief in HARDAM (Acc. no. 1/272), 17 x 15 cm, in grey sandstone from Jaintipur also seems to be a part of Rāvaṇānugraha-mūrti.
76. *VSMRS*, p. 165.
77. *Ibid.*, pp. 165 ff.
78. V.S. Pathak, *Śaiva Cult in Northern India*, Varanasi, 1960, pp. 9 ff.
79. *Epigraphia Indica*, XXI, p. 295 ff. See also Sheo Bahadur Singh, "Pāśupata-Śaivism in Haryana," *Journal of Haryana Studies*, Kurukshetra, Vol. XVIII (1986), pp. 1-6.
80. K.C. Panigrahi, "Sculptural Representations of Lakulīśa and other Pāśupata Teachers," *Journal of Indian History*, Vol. XXXVIII, part III, pp. 635 ff.
81. D.C. Bhattacharyya, *op. cit.*, pp. 30-31. Bhattacharyya, however, wrongly dates the two Lakulīśa images from Morni to 13th century C.E. They should belong to ninth or 10th century as is also indicated by various other sculptures and architectural pieces obtained from the site.
82. Ashvini Agrawal, *op. cit.*, p. 86, fig. 21. The figure here is printed as reversed, i.e. the right hand shown as the left and vice versa.
83. *EHI*, Vol. II, part I, p. 176.
84. Sheela Nagar ["A Note on the Sculptures from Pinjore (Haryana)," *Journal of Oriental Institute*, Baroda, Vol. 36, Nos. 1-4, Sept. 1986-June 1987, p. 279, fig. 4] wrongly dates it to the 12th century C.E. A 9th-10th century *śukanāsa* with the head of Bhairava with grinning face from Pinjore is now preserved in the Kurukshetra University museum. For details see U.V. Singh, *Pinjore Sculptures*, Kurukshetra, 1977 (henceforth *PS*), p. 27, pl. IV B and Shukla (1981), *op. cit.*, p. 14, pl. V, 1.
85. Devendra Handa, "Agroha Revisited," in *Prācī-Prabhā: Perspectives in Indology (Essays in honour of Professor B.N. Mukherjee)*, edited by D.C. Bhattacharyya and Devendra Handa, New Delhi, 1989, p. 242, pl. 26.
86. Amar Singh, *op. cit.*, pp. 191-92, pl. XXIV B.
87. Devendra Handa (1976), *op. cit.*, p. 95, fig. 5; *PS*, p. 26, pl. III; Shukla (1981), *op. cit.*, pp. 13-14, pls. IV.1 and 3.
88. Manmohan Kumar, *Archaeology of Ambala and Kurukshetra Districts (Haryana)*, Unpublished Ph. D. Thesis, Kurukshetra University, Kurukshetra, 1976, p. 146, pl. IX.C.
89. *JNSI*, XXVII, pp. 103-06.
90. Amar Singh, *op. cit.*, pp. 192-93, pl. XXV A.
91. Devendra Handa, "Art Remains From Jaintipur," *Haryana Sahitya Akademi Journal of Indological Studies*, Chandigarh, Vol. III (1988), p. 280, fig. 4.
92. Devendra Handa, *Pehowa*, pp. 112-13, pl. 59.
93. Devendra Handa, "Some Medieval Sculpture From Beri – Haryana," *Roopa-Lekhā*, Vol. LIII (March 1982), pp. 36-46.

94. *Ibid.*
95. Punia (1976), *op. cit.*, pp. 197-200, pl. XXVII.A.
96. Brajesh Krishna, *op. cit.*, pl. 53.
97. *Marg*, Haryana Heritage Number, Vol. XXVII, no. 4 (Sept. 1974), p. 17, fig. 15.
98. V.N. Singh, "Govt. Museum & Art Gallery, Chandigarh (Recent Acquisitions 1983-84)," *Journal of Indian Museums*, New Delhi, Vol. XXXIX (1983), pp. 194-95.
99. Brajesh Krishna, *op. cit.*, pl. 54.
100. Devendra Handa, "Some Unpublished Sculptures from Gujjar Kheri (Haryana)," *PURBA*, Vol. XVII, no. 1 (April, 1986), pp. 115-16, fig. 12.
101. D.C. Bhattacharyya (1981), *op. cit.*, pp. 21-22.
102. *Ibid.*
103. *Ibid.*
104. *Ibid.*
105. *Ibid.*, pp. 20-21, fig. 2; Devendra Handa, "Agroha Revisited," in *Prācī-Prabhā*, pp. 246-47, pl. 41.
106. Rahar, *op. cit.*, p. 192, pl. XV.A.
107. *Ibid.*, pl. XV.B.
108. Sneh Lata, *op. cit.*, p. 54, pl. VI.C.
109. Shukla (1983), *op. cit.*, p. 13, no. 8, pl. III.2; p. 41, no. 117, pl. XXXIII.2; pp. 48-49, no. 147, pl. XLI.2.
110. *EHI*, II, pp. 455-59.
111. Devendra Handa, "The Antiquity of Tabla," *Journal of the Asiatic Society of Bombay*, New Series, Vol. 73, 1998, pp. 47-49 and Plate.
112. Devendra Handa, "Agroha Revisited," in *Prācī-Prabhā*, p. 242, pls. 28-29.
113. Shukla (1983), *op. cit.*, p.51, pl. XLIV.2.
114. *PS*, p. 28; Shukla (1983), *op. cit.*, p. 15, pl. V.3.

Chapter 6

Śakti

Man has ever been a worshipper of Śakti – the universal energy. Śakti worship can be traced back in India, as in many other parts of the world, to a very remote past. The prehistoric rock paintings and terracotta mother-goddess figurines, the Vedic invocation to Vāk and other female deities, their identification with primeval energy and depiction as the creator of universe, the mothers of gods, the spouses of supreme deities, and the various names and epithets like Umā-Haimavatī, Rudrānī, Bhavānī, Īśānī, Ambikā, Āryā, Durgā, Kālī, Kauśikī, Kātyāyaṇī, Aparṇā, Nārāyaṇī, Śivā, Jagadambā, etc. in literary works down the Ṛigvedic period are not only indicative of her continued worship but also of different Aryan, non-Aryan and other multifarious strands which contributed to the formation of the concept of her composite character. The culmination is reached in the Devī-Māhātmya of the *Mārkaṇḍeya Purāṇa* which characterizes Devī as symbolizing supreme energy, highest knowledge and absolute truth.[1] Representative of the three *guṇas* ('qualities', *sattva, rajas,* and *tamas*) and the malign and benign aspects, Śakti has been conceived of in various forms – as the inherent energy of different deities and as the primeval, supreme, universal energy itself. As such, we find her represented as the counterpart of the various gods or assuming different forms to redress the gods and men of their woes and miseries and punish the wicked.[2] We describe below her various manifestations as encountered in Haryana.

PĀRVATĪ

Pārvatī,[3] the daughter of the great snow-clad mountain Himavān and Menā, occupies an important place in the galaxy of female divinities described in literature and *śilpa* texts and represented in art. Symbolizing primordial power, she is the source of various *Śaktis* 'energies'[4] and is known by multiple names such as Umā, Aparṇā, Gaurī, etc. In order to obtain Śiva, who was absorbed in meditation, as her spouse she prepared to undertake penance. Seeing her tender age, Menā discouraged her to do so by the words *'U mā'* 'Oh, No'. She thus came to be known as Umā.[5] During her austerities, she discarded even the fallen leaves of trees and plants for subsistence and became Aparṇā, i.e., one (living) without leaves.[6] The austerity of penance continued and ultimately she observed *pañchāgnitapas* placing her in the middle of the four fires with sun as the fifth source of heat. It is this incidence, which has popularly been depicted in sculptures from the Kushāṇa period onwards[7] in different parts of India. As yet no such image belonging to the Gupta period is known but copious literary references, the depiction of *pañchatapas* Pārvatī in the 6th century Cave No.1 at Badami[8] and Cave No.21

at Ellora datable to *circa* C.E. 600[9] indicate the continuity of the tradition. Four-armed Pārvatī holding *varada* 'boon giving pose', rosary, *kuśa* 'grass' and water flask in her hands, with lion and deer at the feet from Muṇḍeśvarī (Bihar), assignable to 7th century C.E.,[10] is another important early image. In the Pratihāra period, the popularity of this form seems to have increased much and a large number of images of *tapasvinī* Pārvatī have been found from Uttar Pradesh, Madhya Pradesh and Rajasthan.[11] Images datable to the eighth and ninth centuries C.E. are very simple in nature and direct in appeal. They show the goddess as seated or standing amidst four fires flanked by lion and deer near her feet.[12] During the following two centuries the goddess is invariably depicted as standing on a *godhā* 'alligator' accompanied by a number of attendants. These images are lavishly ornamented.[13] Madhya Pradesh, Uttar Pradesh and Rajasthan remained the nucleus zone of *pañchatapas* Pārvatī images and four-handed form was the most popular, rather the invariable type. The popularity of this form, however, seems to have waned considerably after the 11th-12th centuries.

Though Śakti worship has remained popular, and still continues to be so in the whole of northern India, as in other parts of the country, from very early times, yet it is strange that no image of *tapasvinī* Pārvatī is known from the region comprising the present day states of Haryana, Punjab, Himachal Pradesh, and Jammu and Kashmir. The reason lies perhaps not in the complete paucity of such images but in inadequate search as our survey of art remains in Haryana indicates.

Pinjore is a well-known archaeological site. Though Cunningham found 'few traces of antiquity'[14] yet the remains of two dilapidated temples of Bhīmādevī and Baijnāth, numerous sculptural and architectural relics as well as some inscriptions found from the site indicate that it was an important town during the medieval period. When Rodgers visited the place during 1888-89, he recorded a large number of remains.[15] He noticed, among others, "gods and goddesses seated and standing, scraps of ornamentation, groups of subsidiary images, heads of idols, hands of others, trunks of more, Buddhist heads all curled, and small images, Ganesh, lions from some image pedestal, half lotuses, diaper bands, heads on wrong trunks, etc., etc.," built into an outer wall of a *dharmaśālā* called Kabir Chaurā by a Kabir Panthi Lehna Singh.[16] This wall stood as described by Rodgers when we surveyed the site in 1965 and photographed it (Pl. 186).[17] Later, most of the sculptures and architectural pieces from Kabir Chaurā as well as other places were removed to Kurukshetra University[18] and scores of others to Chandigarh and other places. Some sculptures were obtained probably at the instance of Mr. B. N. Chakravarty, the then Governor of Haryana, to adorn the lawns and lobbies of the Haryana Raj Bhawan at Chandigarh in the early seventies.[19] A few pieces were acquired by the Government Museum and Art Gallery, Chandigarh also.[20] Still, some of the sculptures seen by us in 1965, are not traceable anywhere. One of these was a rare piece of *tapasvinī* Pārvatī which once stood fixed indiscriminately in the wall of the Kabir Chaurā.

The sandstone image measuring 37 x 22 cm (Pl. 187), though badly mutilated, shows the goddess standing to front on a lotus pedestal, holding a *sruk* (ladle) in her rear right hand and an object looking like a manuscript in the back left. The front hands are broken but the principal right seems to have been disposed in *abhaya* and the suspended normal left hand may have carried a *kamaṇḍalu*. Generally, the main right hand of such images is shown in the *varada* pose with an *akshamālā*.[21] The association of ladle and water vessel with *tapasvinī* Pārvatī is suggested in the *Kumārasambhava*[22] by the words *'kṛitābhishekāṃ hutajātavedasām'* i.e., 'one who has purified herself with water and has offered incense in the scared fire.'[23] The goddess bears matted locks on the head, partially damaged. She wears ear ornaments, necklet, *yajñopavīta*, and undergarment. The sacred thread and the book emphasize her celibate aspect while performing penance. Two female attendants flank the goddess. The one on the proper right is badly mutilated. These maids, however, seem to have stood in graceful poses, slightly turned towards the goddess, resting one hand on the waist and holding an indistinct object (lotus?) in the hand towards the goddess. Near the left foot of the deity is to be seen an animal to left in profile, probably a deer, with face partially damaged. The corresponding right hand side of the pedestal is broken and may have carried a lion as seen in similar images from Naresar, Batesar, Amrol (all in Madhya Pradesh) and in the Allahabad Museum.[24] Important, however, is the depiction of four *agni-kuṇḍas* (pots of fire), two just above the heads of the attendant figures at the waist level of the goddess and two above, one on either side of her head. The Sun served as the fifth fire. These fire pots leave little doubt to the figure being identified as Pārvatī performing *pañchāgnitapas*. Stylistically, the image may be dated to *circa* 8th century C.E.

Sruk in the upper right hand in place of the upper left[25] that holds a book[26] and the *varada* pose of the main hand, as can be presumed from the broken arm, are the characteristic features of this image.

The Department of Ancient Indian History, Culture and Archaeology, Panjab University, Chandigarh obtained from the village Jaintipur in tahsil Naraingarh, district Ambala, in the sixties, the lower part of an image which doubtlessly represents Pārvatī in penance (Pl. 188). Measuring 60 x 46.5 cm this sandstone icon shows the goddess standing in *samabhaṅga* (contraposto) on a lotus *pīṭha* ('base') flanked by a female attendant on either side. The heads of both the maids are mutilated. They, however, stand gracefully with their middle portions inclined towards the goddess. The maid on the proper right seems to have held in her right hand the handle of an attribute, which may have either been a trident or a ladle. Her left hand raised to the level of the head is damaged and so also is the right hand of the maid on the left. She holds in her left hand a drinking bowl, which perhaps is the result of some tantric influence on the image. Both the maids, however, are beautifully poised, have round breasts, wear long fluttering scarves and loin clothes. The main figure, too, wore a long lower garment reaching the ankles, represented by elegantly dangling hems and zigzag pleats between the legs, The shanks may well be compared with the plantain trunks. Iconographically important, however, is the depiction of the lion on her right and two deer[27] on the left which provide the desired evidence for the proper identification of the deity as *tapasvinī* Pārvatī. The animals have been carved with care. The image may be placed in *circa* 9th century C.E. on stylistic grounds. When complete, it must have been a veritable masterpiece.

A rectangular slab with a tenon above, depicting Pārvatī standing in contraposto (Pl. 189) is also preserved in the Department of Ancient India History, Culture and Archaeology, Panjab University, Chandigarh. It was obtained from Morni in the mid-sixties of the last century. The figure is very much worn out and badly mutilated. The features of the face and the breasts are lost. The undergarment reaching the ankles, the attenuated waist and the broad hips, however, clearly indicate that the figure is that of a female. She seems to have had a *dhammilla* coiffure with locks falling on the shoulders. The four-armed goddess holds a Śiva-*liṅga* placed on the top of an attribute having a long shaft in her rear right hand while the normal one seems to have been held in *varada-mudrā*. The object in the additional left hand cannot be identified properly. It may have been a lotus with a stalk. The suspended normal left hand seems to have been placed on the head of an attendant figure standing near her left foot. There may have been another attendant figure on the right also but that is completely lost now. If the acolyte figure on the left was a male, it may have been that of Skanda, if female, the attendant figures may have been that of Jayā and Vijayā. Stylistically, the figure may be dated to about the 9th century C.E.

No figure of *tapasvinī* Pārvatī with such an arrangement of attributes is known from anywhere else. This figure, thus, reflects the creativity and novelty of the anonymous Haryanavi artist.

Our next figure is now fixed in the wall of a Vishṇu Temple at Sagwan in district Hisar. Measuring 50 x 25 cm, it shows the goddess standing to front between two pillars (Pl. 190). The image is coated with a thick layer of whitewash, which has concealed some of its finer features. The goddess bearing matted locks on her head wears ear ornaments, a necklace with a pendent string falling to the left of her navel from between her breasts, armlets, bracelets, undergarment secured by a waist-band, and a long garland. Her normal right hand is held in *varada* pose. The attributes in the upper two hands are not clear nor is the object in the suspended left hand identifiable. There is a round gloriole behind the head. The unquestionable evidence to identify her as Pārvatī performing the penance has survived in the form of a small fire-altar on either side of her feet. The image may be dated to *circa* 10th century C.E.

Dr. N.P. Joshi has made a special study of the images of Pārvatī performing penance and distinguished two types – pre-marriage and post-marriage penance.[28] The Sagwan image represents the latter type.

One image lies fixed in the outer wall of the house of Shri Ram Kumar Singh (Nambardar) in village Jasat, located about 40 km southwest of Gurgaon and approachable via Pataude and Nurgarh. Jasat has an extensive mound spread over thirty acres, nearly ten feet in height, now partly under habitation. Medieval images of Vishṇu, Brahmā, Nandī, *vidyādharas*, architectural piece with a later carving of Gogā on it now preserved in the Śiva Temple, Bhairon ji ka Temple, and fixed in the walls of private buildings indicate the existence of Vaishṇava and Śaiva temples at Jasat. The image under consideration, fixed alongside a Viśvarūpa image, in the outer wall of the Nambardar's house, is made of blackish grey sandstone and measures 61 x 44 cm. The goddess stands to front with a slight bend in the upper part of her body, holding Śiva-*liṅga* and Gaṇeśa (?) on lotuses in her rear right and left hands (Pl. 191). Both the front hands are broken. She bears matted locks on her head, circular rings in ears, multi-stringed necklace, *keyūras*, *valayas*, *vanamālā*, *dhotī* secured by *netra-sūtra*, *nūpuras*, etc. Garland-bearing *vidyādharas* in flying postures are depicted on the top corners of the rectangular slab. At the waist level may be seen fire-altars on both the sides. Two attendant figures, one on either side, flank the goddess near her feet. There is a round lotiform halo behind the head of the goddess. Her face, breasts, normal hands, the *vidyādhara* and the attendant figures have suffered mutilation. The image may be assigned to the 10th century C.E. on stylistic grounds.

The next image comes from Gujjar Kheri, situated about 25 km north-northwest of Sonepat. What again must have been an elegant image survives only as a part of the *pañcharatha* (five recessed) pedestal showing the feet of Pārvatī on lotus seat under which is depicted a *godhā* (iguana), the vehicle of the goddess, flanked by an inward facing lion on the proper right and an artistically and tastefully carved deer with its head turned backwards to scratch its hind left leg on the other side (Pl. 192). Behind the deer is a garland bearing female turned slightly towards the goddess, standing gracefully with a triple bend in her body. Unfortunately, the face of the female figure is mutilated but the hair with a round bun at the back, large earrings, necklet, an *ekāvali* with a pendent string falling down from between the breasts, armlets, bracelets, *uttarīya* (upper garment), and *dhotī* (lower garment) secured by a girdle have all been carved very exquisitely. A part of Pārvatī's long garland is visible above the right hand of this attendant figure. Also notable is the small fire pot, partly damaged, carved just above her head. On the receding recesses behind her are to be seen a fly-whisker and a male attendant. The chowrie-bearer stands gracefully wearing ornaments similar to those of the garland-bearer, holding a lotus by its stalk in her right hand raised to the level of and touching her left breast while the suspended right hand supports the flywhisk by its shaft. Her coiffure and lower garment, however, differ slightly from the preceding figure. Her elongate figure with a pleasant smile, full breasts, thin waist, broad sciatic portion, and slender legs bestow her distinctiveness and make her attractive. The male figure on the extreme recess holds a trident in his left hand with right one in protection giving pose. He bears matted locks in two conical tiers over hair combed backwards. The bow-like eyebrows, long quasi-closed eyes, sturdy nose, oval face with smiling expression resemble the fly-whisker. Large earrings are also similar. He wears beaded necklace and long garland. Wristlets may also be seen. His lower garment carved with double-lined wavy patterns goes down only up to the knees. In its treatment, sash and the thighs, a loose end of the girdle falling vertically on the shank, however, it looks similar to the fly-whisker. Anklet may also be seen in the right foot of the male attendant. The necks of all the three attendant figures are marked by *trivali* (three lines), symbolic of beauty. Above the heads of the two figures is partially visible the twirling trunk of the elephant (*gaja-muṇḍa*), which was carved to adorn the back slab. It may be presumed that the corresponding right hand side of the image also carried similar attendant figures and decorations. The extant relief measures 40 x 38 cm and has been carved out of buff sandstone.

The attendant with trident indicates the Śaivite nature of the main image. The depiction of *godhā* is characteristic of the images of Gaurī[29] which is one of the different appellations of Pārvatī.[30] The presence of the lion and deer and *agni-kuṇḍa* in the extant image make sure of its identification with Pārvatī performing the austere penance of five fires. Though icons of the goddess in *pañchatapas* on alligator or with lion and deer are known yet those with all the three are rare.[31]

This elaborately carved and profusely ornamented image may be assigned to *circa* 11th century C.E. on stylistic grounds.

An image of *Pañchatapas* Pārvatī is registered in the name of Smt. Krishna Bai, Durga Temple, Hansi (HSR/HRN-46) also. Another very small (14.5 x 10.5 cm) black stone mutilated relief of Pārvatī is under worship in a temple at Anjanthali in district Karnal. The four-handed goddess bearing *jaṭā-jūṭa* and wearing usual dress and ornaments like *ekāvali*, wristlets, etc. is seated cross-legged holding *abhaya*, trident, *śakti*, and *kamaṇḍalu* in the four-hands in *pradakshiṇā* order. Stylistically, it seems to belong to *circa* 12th century C.E.[32]

We thus see that the region north of Mathura was not completely devoid of the images of *tapasivinī* Pārvatī in the early medieval period.

Complete independent images of Pārvatī, not in penance, are very rare in Haryana. It is, however, difficult to identify some pieces because of their very fragmentary nature. A red sandstone beautiful almost life-size (26 x 23.5 cm) Kushāṇa female head from Rithal (Acc. No. 1/28) having an oval face with fish-like eyes and bow-like eyebrows, thick lower lip, sturdy chin and bearing hair combed backward with frontal wavy locks and a round bun on the head wearing massive circular earrings must have belonged to some very important figure as indicated by its features and the round lotus-bun adorned with loops and free ends of the pearl strings and the lotus-shaped frontal forehead ornament (Pls. 193-94). The imposing hairdo with beautiful bun, the serenity and grace of the face pose the likelihood of this head belonging to that of Pārvatī, the consort of Śiva, but one cannot be very sure of it in the absence of any definitive evidence. Similarly, the broken 23 cm high head of a female from Agroha in the Chandigarh Museum (Acc. No. 7.38) having a beautiful crest studded with pearls and gems with imposing hairdo in the form of a huge bun representing the *dhammilla* coiffure (Pl. 195) is thought likely to be the head of Pārvatī. It has an ear ornament studded with pearls, the eyes carved slightly diagonally with drooping eyelids betraying an inward expression, full and fleshy lips, pointed chin with its sensitively modeled cusp adding to its liveliness. It has been dated to *circa* 7th century C.E. on stylistic grounds.[33] A few female heads from Pinjore and elsewhere cannot be identified with certainty. A female bust with massive breasts and *dhammilla* coiffure adorned with a lion-face spewing pearl strings from Pinjore (Pl. 196) and another similar fragment probably from the same site in Chandigarh Museum with the indication of the existence of a halo behind the head (Pl. 197),[34] both belonging to the medieval period, are also likely to have belonged originally to Pārvatī images. HARDAM possesses some pieces from Anjanthali (Acc. No. 1/70), Hisar region (Acc. No. 47/84), Gujjar Kheri (Acc. No. 1/114), Ratpur (Acc. Nos. 1/98-99), etc. recorded as belonging to Durgā/ Pārvatī.

DURGĀ

Scholars believe that a number of deities worshipped by hill tribes are traceable in Durgā.[35] As a synonym of Ambikā who is described in the *Vājasaneyī Saṃhitā* (III.57) and the *Taittirīya Brāhmaṇa* (I.6, 10, 4-5) as Rudra's sister, the name of Durgā Vairochanī appears along with Kātyāyanī and Kanyā-Kumārī for the first time in the *Taittirīya Āraṇyaka* (X.1, 7) as Rudra's consort. The Āgamas and the Purāṇas refer to her nine manifestations (Nava Durgā) and describe her iconographic features in details.[36]

Rao has described different forms of Durgā as having four, eight or more hands, three eyes, beautiful look with a well developed bust, stout thighs and big hips, clad in garments, adorned with *karaṇḍa-mukuṭa* and wearing various ornaments.[37] Standing in *samabhaṅga*, *dvibhaṅga* or *tribhaṅga* upon a lotus, head of a buffalo or a lion, she should carry a trident and noose, or a parrot or mirror and a blue lily[38] if two-handed; a noose and a goad with the other two hands disposed in *abhaya* and *varada* poses in four-handed variety or carrying in addition a conch, discus, bow, arrows, sword, shield, etc. if multi-handed.

Images of Durgā are very rare in Haryana. A very much worn out and mutilated image, marred by paint, in a square frame fixed near the tank at Kapālamochana shows the four-handed goddess sitting in *sukhāsana* on a couchant lion to right holding sword and shield in the back pair of hands with normal right in *abhaya* and principal left holding some unidentifiable object (Pl. 198). The finer details of the body and ornaments have been concealed by the paint but the image may be dated to *circa* 7th century on stylistic grounds. Another worn out image measuring 71 x 44 cm from Mandhna in HARDAM shows the goddess seated at ease, probably on a lion, holding a trident and sword in the right hands and citron or water-pot in the normal left and probably a shield in the back left (Pl. 199). The back slab has been rounded on the top to serve as the halo behind the goddess. She bears a *dhammilla* hair coiffure adorned with a jewel in front. The details cannot be discerned even in this case but the piece seems to belong stylistically to *circa* 8th century C.E.

A sandstone image measuring 41 x 37 cm from Jaintipur, now preserved in the Department of Ancient Indian History, Culture and Archaeology, Panjab University, Chandigarh, shows a female deity seated in *lalitāsana* on a lotus seat. Her right leg is folded and the left one hangs down with the splayed out foot placed on a lotus. Unfortunately, the head of the goddess is lost and hands too are broken. The disposition of the damaged hands, however, indicates that the right one was raised to the level of the shoulder perhaps in *abhaya-mudrā* and the left one held some roundish object (citrus?), now broken. The extant portion left now indicates that the goddess bore *dhammilla* coiffure and had a gloriole behind the head. An *uttarīya*, lower garment, armlets, wristlets, and earrings may also be seen on her person. The goddess is flanked by two female figures on either side, one shown in *añjali-mudrā* facing towards her and the other holding some long unidentifiable object in one hand and the other akimbo. The heads of both the upper attendant figures are broken. The relief is quite worn out and mutilated and it is not possible to identify the deity properly, but a worn out leonine face under the lotus-seat on the proper right hand side of the relief indicates the goddess to have been Durgā. On the proper left also there is a damaged portion similar to that of the lion face on the right. If there were actually two lions, the deity may have been Kshemaṅkarī. Stylistically, the figure may belong to the 9th century C.E.[39]

KSHEMAṄKARĪ

A small portable image, barely 10.5 cm in height, probably from Rohtak, now in the Chandigarh Museum (Acc. No. 143) shows the goddess standing in *samapāda* on a *tri-ratha* pedestal holding trident and lotus or arrows in the rear hands with principal right in *varada* and the normal left holding a water-pot flanked by two lions seated on the receding projections of the pedestal (Pl. 200). It has been identified by D.C. Bhattacharyya with Durgā.[40] The image betrays archaic simplicity and a naturalistic treatment of the plastic surface, although apparently showing crude expression and drab frontality, and has been dated to *circa* 8th century C.E. Goddess showing two lions is sometimes identified as Kshemaṅkarī by some scholars.

Kshemaṅkarī is one of the nine forms of Durgā.[41] In the *Devī Purāṇa* (39.121 ff), she is identified with primeval energy. She appeared before the gods, when requested to kill the demon Subala, who had troubled the gods. She is described a having terrific form, appearing as an old emaciated lady whose veins were visible, with open mouth, trampling, frightening the world and equipped with hundreds of weapons. She is called Kshemaṅkarī because she always protects the gods and the worshippers.[43]

According to the *Padma Purāṇa*,[44] Kshemaṅkarī is the most powerful *sāttvikā śakti* who has a face like a white lotus and large good eyes resembling blue lotuses. Divine maidservants and friends surround her. Mounted on a throne, the young maiden with blossoming breasts, decorated with various types of flowers, is worshipped by the people. Main support of the world, she is a Vaishṇavī *śakti* having twenty-four-hands which hold weapons like the bow, sword, *śakti* (lance), arrows, trident, mace, discus, pestle, gun, hatchet, dumb-bell, bell, *śataghnī, mudgara, bhushuṇḍī*, noose, banner, lotus, etc. She rides a lion to fight with the demon Mahisha. She is called Kshemā or Kshemaṅkarī for she provides protection and fulfills the desires of the devotees.[45]

The *Bhavishya Purāṇa*[45] describes her as nude, having a loathsome face, filling the quarters with unrestrained shrieks, having a frightful body with a fierce expression. The *Aparājitapṛichchhā*[46] and the *Rūpamaṇḍana*[47] describe the goddess as capable of giving health, carrying trident, lotus and a drinking vessel in three hands with fourth disposed in the *varada mudrā*. In art, she is generally recognizes by two lions depicted on her pedestal or as her vehicles. So the image described above may be identified with Kshamaṅkarī.

A sandstone image from Sondh (Pl. 201), measuring about 100 x 74 cm, represents a female deity seated in *lalitāsana* on a lotus seat under which are shown two lions, back to back. The hanging right foot of the goddess rests on a circular lotus leaf placed on the back of one of the lions. Unfortunately, the face of the goddess, most part of the halo, all the hands except the lowermost left and a part of the proper right hand side of the back slab are damaged and mutilated. What, however, remains, is sufficient to reveal the identity of the goddess. She bears a beautiful *dhammilla* coiffure bedecked with pearl strings and wears large circular discs in the ears, a necklet and a necklace, the latter with a pendent string falling from between the breasts to the left of the navel, armlets and perhaps wristlets and anklets also. A girdle secures the lower garment. Important, however is a long garland, *vanamālā,* worn by her. It comes from over the shoulders and the arms of the goddess and forms a semi-circular loop over the legs. The only extant lowermost left hand holds a water pot and one of the right hands, to judge from the disposition of the damaged part, may have been held in the *varada* pose. The damaged arms indicate that the goddess bore eight hands. The lotiform halo behind the head is only partially preserved. On a stele to the left of the head of the goddess is shown a *Mātṛikā.* She is seated in *lalitāsana.* Other details are mutilated. On the successive recesses of the *pañcha-ratha* pedestal, are depicted garland-bearing and fly-whisker females. Just above the fly whiskers are carved the slab shows a *makara-mukha* surmounted by a female standing with a lute in her two hands. The proper right hand side, too, may have shown similar decorative motifs. The pedestal bears a finely executed band of scroll decoration on front.

The figures has been identified with *Mahishāsuramardinī* by Punia and described as six-armed with one of the right hands piercing a trident in the neck of Mahisha from whose decapitated head the demon is coming out in human form. There are also many other features of the image, which have been wrongly described. The two lions seated back to back under the *padmapīṭha* over which sits the goddess certainly indicate the image to have been that of *Kshemaṅkarī.* Since the proper right hand side of the sculpture is damaged, the head of the lion on that side is gone. The body, the hind legs and the forepaw are, however, clear. As such the image may certainly be identified as that of *Kshemaṅkarī.* Stylistically, it may be placed in *circa* 10th century C.E.

The Prāchī Śiva Temple at Pehowa has also yielded the lower portion of an image which shows the main deity seated on a lotus seat in *lalitāsana*, resting her right foot on a lotus *pīṭha*. The deity may be recognized as Kshemaṅkarī from the two lions carved under the lotus seat and the female attendants. The image belongs to the mature Pratihāra phase.[48]

MAHISHĀSURAMARDINĪ

Mahishāsuramardinī, literally meaning 'the crusher of the buffalo demon', is one of the earliest and most important manifestations of Durgā in her ferocious form. The *Vāmana Purāṇa* (chs. 17-20) gives a detailed account of the destruction of Mahishāsura[49] at the hands of Devī. Gods, having been defeated by the demon Mahisha, approached Vishṇu under the leadership of Brahmā, for protection. Śaṅkara was also present there. On hearing the grievances of the gods, Vishṇu, and at his command Brahmā, Śiva and all other gods emitted flames of anger from their eyes and faces as a result of which a mountain of effulgence was formed. From this mountain came forth profusely resplendent eighteen-armed goddess Kātyāyanī whom Śiva gave a trident, Vishṇu a disc, Varuṇa a conch, Agni a dart, Yama an iron rod, Vāyu a bow, Sūrya a quiver and arrows, Indra a thunderbolt, Kubera a mace, Brahmā a rosary and a water-pot, Kāla sword and a shield, Viśvakarma a battle-axe and other weapons, Himavān a lion, etc. Other gods also gave her various arms and ornaments. Kātyāyanī then proceeded to the Vindhya mountain where Chaṇḍa and Muṇḍa saw her and reported about her beauty to their king Mahishāsura. Having heard high encomiums of her splendid and beautiful form the demon king determined to obtain her and marched with his army to the vicinity of the mountain from where he sent Dundubhi, his grandson, as messenger. Devī told him that she would marry the demon Mahisha if he vanquished her in combat. A severe battle ensued in which the whole army was routed and killed but the demon-king, because of a boon granted by Śiva, had been rendered invulnerable. Seeing that the army had been destroyed, the demon advanced for a personal combat.[50] Ultimately, during the terrible duel, Durgā dismounted from her lion and jumped upon the back of Mahisha and pierced his neck with the trident by the right hand while trampling on his back with her right leg.[51] It is this incident of the combat which is very popular in Indian art.[52] Her victory over the demon Mahisha is regarded as symbolic of the triumph of virtue over evil.[53] Rao thinks that the story indicates the substitution of the buffalo totem worship by a form of Devī worship among some early primitive tribes in the country.[54] The *Mahābhārata* and several Purāṇas, especially the *Mārkaṇḍeya*, also narrate the exploits of Devī.[55]

Though the antiquity of her images has been traced back to the pre-Kushāṇa times[56], yet her cult seems to have become popular in north India during the Kushāṇa period as evidenced by quite a few terracotta and stone plaques and statuettes found from the Mathura region.[57] It is interesting to note that in the earliest reliefs the goddess has only two or four-hands and is shown as subduing the buffalo demon by sheer physical force - by compressing the throat of the animal or pulling out its tongue by one hand and pressing its back by the other. Stunted spear or trident is her principal weapon which she holds in one or two of her additional hands.[58] Six or more handed varieties of the Kushāṇa images of Mahishamardinī are also known.[59] Lion as the vehicle of the goddess, though absent initially, makes its appearance in the late Kushāṇa period[60] but does not become an essential adjunct of her images till the early medieval period. If present, it was depicted as a docile animal. During the Gupta period, the goddess in generally shown as pressing the back of the buffalo with her right or left foot and piercing it with a long handled spear or trident held in her principal right hand. The next stage of development of the Mahishāsuramardinī images in northern India is beautifully described in the Devī-Māhātmya of the *Mārkaṇḍeya Purāṇa*[61] assignable to the 7th century C.E. if not earlier[62] -

> *Evamuktvā samutapatya sārūḍhā taṃ mahāsuram /*
> *Pādenākramya kaṇṭhe cha śūlenainamatāḍayat //*
> *Tataḥ so'pi pādākrāntastayā nijamukhāttataḥ /*
> *Arddhanishkrānta eveti devyā vīryyena saṃvṛitaḥ //*
> *Arddhanishkrānta evāsau yudhyamāno mahāsuraḥ /*
> *Tayā mahāsinā devyā śiraśchhittvā nipātitaḥ //*

When the demon emerged in anthropomorphic form out of the severed neck of the buffalo, the goddess slew him with her sword. This form of the goddess has been very popular with the artists from *circa* 8th century C.E. onwards.[63]

Being contiguous to the Mathura region, one may expect some early images of Mahishāsuramardinī from Haryana also. The expectation is fulfilled by the discovery of a small plaque measuring 21 x 12 cm from a village Vara in district Jind. It is now preserved in HARDAM (Acc. No. C.15). The lower portion of the rectangular plaque is broken. The four-handed goddess is shown as standing to front holding the buffalo with her normal hands and piercing his back with a spear or trident held in or thrust by her rear right hand now broken. The additional left hand, raised up to the level of the head, supports a disc (Pl. 202). The hair of the goddess, damaged in front, is arranged in a broad flat crown of the *dhammilla* type. She has protruding wide open eyes with irises indicated by pinpricking. She wears earrings, multiple bracelets and an *adhovastra* marked by incised parallel lines indicating the folds. The upper part is bare. She has slit mouth and round rotund breasts. The waist is attenuated and arms and legs seem to be elongate. The figure lacks proportion and perspective. The buffalo seems to have been uplifted in the air by the goddess without any strenuous effort as is indicated by a calm and relaxed expression. The buffalo looks like a toy. Hard pressed between the two hands, the animal has raised its head upward in agony and helplessness. The utter absence of irresistible dynamism in subduing the demon so well illustrated in the Kushāṇa icons[64] is discernible in this figure also. Though the plaque is partly damaged from below yet it seems that the lion was not depicted at all. Frontality, simplicity, lack of proportion and perspective, elongation and crudity are the noticeable features, which indicate that the plaque may be assigned to the beginning of our era.

In all the known early specimens of Mahishāsuramardinī figures where a spear or trident is shown, it is always short-handled. Being pierced in the back of the animal, the weapon in the present example cannot be certainly identified but may be a trident in all probability. The shaft of the trident is not visible above the arms. Unfortunately, the upper right hand, too, is damaged. It had a long handle and the goddess held its hilt in her rear right hand, the traces of the shaft should have been there on and above the front right arm. But it is not so. Even if we presume that it came from between the two arms, which of course is not logical, it must have left its traces above the arms. Was it then a short-handled trident struck with force into the back of the animal with the upper right hand of the goddess? It is probable, though not very logical. This, however, is an interesting feature, which, we hope, will provoke the imagination of many a savant to come forward with their explanations and suggestions.

The disc held in the upper left hand of the goddess is also interesting. If the corresponding right hand held the trident, this wheel may represent the wheel of Vishṇu given to the goddess. A Mahishāsuramardinī plaque of 3rd-4th century C.E. in the Gurukula Museum, Jhajjar also holds wheel and conch.[65] Some late Kushāṇa Mahishamardinī figures show solar and lunar discs in the two upper hands. If the disc in the Vara plaque represents either of these luminaries, it is the earliest example to show this feature.

A very badly mutilated image of Mahishāsuramardinī of mottled red sandstone is now enshrined in a recently constructed Rukhiyā Dādī kā Mandira at Rukhi, about 10 km south of Gohana on the metalled road to Rohtak. The part of the relief below the knees of the goddess is now embedded in the cement pedestal from which the top of the slab on which it is carved rises about 57 cm in height. It is 45 cm in width. The image may have been about 90 cm high when complete. The face is very badly mutilated but ornaments like ear discs, necklace and multiple bracelets may still be made out (Pl. 203). The upper part of the body is bare but the goddess wears a *dhotī*. But for slight mutilation, all the eight arms of the goddess have survived. Slightly turned to her left, probably because of the onrush of the buffalo, she overwhelms the animal, rearing up in her front, by pressing its back emphatically as if to crush its spine by her normal right hand and receiving the onslaught of the assailant with her upper left hand wound around its neck to strangulate it. The pressure she exerts to break the spine of the animal with her right hand can easily be guessed from the bulbous bulge of the shoulder and the stiffness of the right arm. The body of the buffalo is for the most part horizontal but for the forepart which is lifted up. It is still not diagonal as we see in some Kushāṇa reliefs. The head of the animal does not reach the level of the shoulder of the goddess. The forelegs are bent double. The face of the buffalo is worn out, but it may have been half-opened with tongue sticking out.[66] The uppermost fourth pair of hands seems to have held a short-handled trident as if before an impending action, as is also seen in a terracotta plaque obtained from Sonkh excavations.[67] The third pair holds the solar and lunar discs.[68] The second pair of arms, also raised up like the preceding pair, probably held a small scimitar in the now broken right hand and probably a small shield in the left. We do not know if the lion was depicted on the lower part of the relief now embedded in the pedestal and thus not visible. We, thus, see that this figure combines in it the features of the early and typical Kushāṇa images.[69] It has also got the distinction of being the biggest stone relief of the representation of the goddess during the Kushāṇa period.

A highly worn out small figure of Mahishamardinī in red sandstone, measuring 11.5 x 9 cm, is known from Sanghel, situated about 13 km south-east of Nuh on the bank of the Sahibi in district Faridabad.[70] An extensive mound at Sanghel, nearly 25 m high and spread over sixteen acres of land, yields Painted Grey Ware, early historic and medieval remains. The goddess, probably six-armed, is represented almost in the same posture as the preceding example but the buffalo here lurches forward and upward in a diagonal form as if its onrush had been suddenly halted. Its head is almost level with the left shoulder of the goddess, the mouth is half open and the forelegs are double bent in agony (Pl. 204). The middle right hand holds some indistinct object, probably a sword[71] and the uppermost right hand is held upwards at the back with its attribute not clearly identifiable. The additional hands on the left are gone. The relief is so much worn out and mutilated that it is difficult to discern the details. It, however, seems to be similar to some Kushāṇa statuettes of the goddess from Mathura.[72] The presence or absence of lion in this fragmentary relief cannot be ascertained with certitude. The discovery of this frieze, however, makes it quite clear that almost the same tradition of iconographic representations of Mahishamardinī as prevailed in the Mathura region was followed in Haryana also.

A plaque from Naurangabad in the Gurukula Museum, Jhajjar[73] shows a development over the preceding examples. The goddess is depicted as containing the onrushing animal in the same manner as in almost all typical Kushāṇa reliefs but has a trident with a comparatively longer handle in one of her additional right hands with which she pierces the back of the buffalo. She carries the Vaishṇavite emblems *śaṅkha* and *chakra* in another pair of hands. The garland (also identified variously as serpent, towel, iguana, drum, basket, etc. by different scholars) is held in the uppermost pair of upraised arms (Pl. 205) as seen in some other Kushāṇa and Gupta reliefs.[74] The lion and a *gaṇa* figure are also conspicuous by their presence in this 22.5 cm high plaque which has tentatively been dated to *circa* 3rd-4th century C.E.[75]

We are yet to find a complete Gupta specimen from Haryana. The fragmentary frieze showing the lower portion of a Mahishamardinī image from Sanghel, now preserved in HARDAM, depicts the goddess as pressing the face of the buffalo with her right foot and lifting it by the tail with her left hand (Pl. 206). Bearing Acc. no. 1/394, the extant relief measures 24 x 21 cm. Standing in *pratyālīḍha* pose, the goddess is thrusting the trident into the back of the buffalo with her right hand, now broken. The left foot of the deity rests on the ground in *sama* pose. The goddess may have worn a *dhotī* from waist to ankles as its traces may still be seen on the right leg. The left hand holding the tail of the buffalo shows a bracelet also. The helplessness of the animal has been delineated very beautifully in the relief. Lion, the mount of the goddess, is conspicuous by its absence. The number of hands and their attributes are matters of mere guess only. Stylistically, it belongs to the Gupta art tradition. The upper part of a rectangular terracotta plaque measuring 11 x 10 cm in its extant form found from Patlikhurd in tahsil Palwal depicts the goddess as lifting the animal with her right hand and strangulating it with the left (Pl. 207). She holds a long-handled trident in her rear right hand and a shield in the additional left. The facial expression is that of quietude and serenity. She bears *jaṭā-jūṭa* on the head, circular earrings, a broad torque, a triangular necklace, and multiple bangles. The terracotta belongs to the Gupta idiom.[76] A similar broken piece in terracotta, crudely hand-modeled, is known from Naurangabad showing the buffalo demon being trampled by right foot of the goddess whose figure is completely gone. The foot trampling the buffalo wears an anklet and the figure is assigned to *circa* 5h-6th century C.E.[77]

Slightly later in date is a small sandstone plaque acquired by the state department from village Baroli near the confluence of the Mārkaṇḍā and Sarasvatī rivers in district Kurukshetra. The four-handed deity is shown as standing in *pratyālīḍha* pose pressing the back of the buffalo with her right foot and thrusting the trident held in her principal right hand in its back (Pl. 208). She is twisting the neck of the animal by pulling one of its horns and then pressing it forcefully. The utter helplessness of the demon is evident from its elongated folded neck. The rear right hand seems to have held the animal by its tail while the upraised back left holds what looks like the uprooted horn of the buffalo. Her vehicle, the lion, does not figure in the extant relief. The goddess wears a flat crown with a horn-like projection on the proper left-hand side, the one on the right side being broken. We know of images where the demon is depicted in a hybrid form having human body with a buffalo-head[78] and with human body and horns on the head[79] but no example of the goddess having horns on her head is known to us. This specimen from Baroli provides a parallel to the demon with human body and having horns on the head. An undercurrent may have existed in the pre-medieval period that the goddess assumed similar form to meet the challenge of the demon, as is also seen in the Vaikuṇṭha form of Vishṇu to kill a demon.[80] This is illustrated by another image from Gujjar Kheri, which has yielded a very interesting small buff sandstone image showing the goddess standing in *pratyālīḍha* pose, pressing the back of the buffalo with her right foot (Pl. 209). She is piercing the back of the anthropomorphic demon which is emerging from the severed buffalo head with a long-handled trident held in her principal right hand while the normal left hand holds the demon by the neck. In her rear right and left hands she holds a sword and a bell respectively. The most unusual feature, however, is the animal (buffalo or boar) head of the goddess herself. Though the face has not been carved very realistically yet the long horns on the head leave little doubt to his being the head of an animal. The goddess wears a small tiara, beaded necklace, bracelets and a girdle to secure the lower garment. The execution lacks refined chisel work. The lion is absent. Stylistically the image may be placed in the 8th century C.E. The small size (14.5 x 8 cm) and the portability of the image indicate that it was required by some devotee for his personal use. Another similar piece from the same site, in blackish grey sandstone, is preserved in the Gurukula Museum, Jhajjar (Rohtak). An image of Mahiushāsuramardinī from Bangladesh also shows the goddess with a buffalo head.[81] Another small sandstone broken figure (18 x 15 cm) of about 10th century from Pinjore showing the bust of a female figure with small horn on the surviving one side of the damaged head and thrusting probably a long-handled trident into the body of the buffalo demon, too, represents the animal-headed goddess killing the *asura*, and has rightly been identified as a part of Durgā Mahishāsuramardinī image.[82]

Medieval images of the goddess are known from the following sites in Haryana.

1. Agroha (Dt. Hisar)[83]
2. Ashrafgarh (Dt. Jind)
3. Badali (Dt. Jhajjar)
4. Banbhori (Dt. Hisar)[84]

5. Bohr (Dt. Rohtak)
6. Chandimandir (Dt. Panchkula)
7. Gharaunda (Dt. Karnal)
8. Gujjar Kheri (Dt. Sonepat)
9. Gurawara (Dt. Gurgaon)[85]
10. Hansi (Dt. Hisar)[86]
11. Hat (Dt. Jind)
12. Jadthal (Dt. Rewari)
13. Jhansua (Dt. Rohtak)
14. Kabri (Dt. Karnal)
15. Kalayat (Dt. Jind)[87]
16. Kanwari (Dt. Bhiwani)
17. Khatoli (Dt. Ambala)
18. Khokhrakot (Dt. Rohtak)
19. Mandhna (Dt. Panchkula)
20. Marhanwala (Dt. Panchkula)[88]
21. Mohanbari (Dt. Rohtak)
22. Morni-ka-Tal (Dt. Panchkula)[89]
23. Nyat (Dt. Jind)
24. Pehowa (Dt. Kurukshetra)[90]
25. Pinjore (Dt. Panchkula)[91]
26. Ratpur (Dt. Panchkula)
27. Sadhaura (Dt. Yamunanagar)
28. Sanghel (Dt. Faridabad)
29. Satkumbha (Dt. Sonepat)
30. Shahpur (Dt. Panchkula)
31. Sirsa (Dt. Sirsa)
32. Sondh (Dt. Gurgaon)
33. Tandwal (Dt. Yamunanagar)
34. Thanesar (Dt. Kurukshetra)[92]
35. Theh Polar (Dt. Kaithal)[93]

The list is not an unimpressive one and some of the sites have yielded more than one figure. Sirsa has yielded a large number of terracotta moulds for preparing the figures of Mahishamardinī. Though many of the images found from Haryana are fragmentary, yet some complete and beautiful icons, too, have been recovered. Some of these images are important iconographically also.

The Gurukula Museum at Jhajjar houses a plaque, a complete and a fragmentary image of Mahishamardinī from Satkumbha, a village adjacent to Gujjar Kheri. The plaque shows the same attributes in the hands of the goddess as noted above but a lion is shown here as attacking the buffalo from behind. The goddess stands pressing the back of the buffalo with her right foot and holding the anthropomorphic demon emerging from the severed head of the animal from the neck. The fragmentary image shows only the lower part of the relief, the figure above the thighs having been lost. The complete image from the site is similar in form and conception to the plaque described above.

A plaque from Mohanbari also shows the lion attacking the buffalo from behind. The proper left-hand side of the plaque is broken. A fragment from the same site shows the back of the buffalo being pierced by a trident and attacked by a lion from behind. Both are preserved in the Gurukula Museum, Jhajjar.

A small plaque (13 x 10.5 cm) from Jadthal (Acc. No. 1/453), in district Rewari, though crudely carved, shows the goddess in *pratyālīḍha* holding trident and the neck of the demon in her two hands. The lion, as usual, attacks the buffalo from the back. The plaque indicates the popularity of the cult of the Mahishamardinī in southern Haryana during the 9th century C.E.

The fragment from Guruwara depicts the buffalo realistically and the lion, with head broken, pouncing upon it from the back holding its tail between the forepaws.[94]

The lower part of a Mahishamardinī figure recovered from the Bhīmā Devī Temple, Pinjore measures 23 x 17 cm and is made of greenish sandstone (Acc. No. 1/69). It is badly mutilated.

A small fragment obtained from Khatoli in the Naraingarh tehsil of Ambala by the Department of Ancient Indian History, Culture and Archaeology, Panjab University, Chandigarh shows the trident being thrust into the neck of the buffalo. The back of the buffalo is bedecked with a checkered cover. A bead-necklace is also seen round its neck. The lion in its mouth catches the tail of the buffalo demon from behind. The firmly planted left foot of the deity on the ground and the right foot on the back of the buffalo may also be seen in this 9th century relief.

At the ancient temple site of village Shahpur, about 18 km from Pinjore on Nalagarh road, a broken image of Mahishamardinī, 32 x 29 cm, lies embedded in the wall of the residence of the priest of the Gurudwara. It is broken above the waist of the goddess and is thickly coated with whitewash. The helpless buffalo lies couchant, with legs folded, attacked by the lion from behind. From the severed head emerges the demon in his human form holding a sword in his right hand. His left hand is firmly held and pressed against the left shoulder by the left hand of the goddess. With right hand she is thrusting the trident into the back of the buffalo. The complete image must have been an elegant piece of the Pratihāra art.

Slightly earlier in date and more elegantly carved is the similar lower portion of a Mahishāsuramardinī figure from Rohtak (Pl. 210). A broad beaded waistband and a multi-fold sash on the things add greatly to the charm of the figure. The goddess holds the anthropomorphic demon by the hair with her left hand effortlessly. The lion attacking the buffalo from behind, however, is bigger than the normal size. Another Pratihāra image of Mahishāsuramardinī from Asthal Bohr, Rohtak was taken to the Central (now Government) Museum, Lahore and is preserved there.[95] Mahishamardinī image from Sadhaura also shows the goddess in *ālīḍha* pose pressing the neck of the buffalo with her right foot and lifting it by the tail with her left hand. The right hand is thrusting the trident into its body and the goddess is ready to severe its neck with the sword held in her additional right hand (Pl. 211). The lion is attacking the head of the buffalo.

The red sandstone broken image fixed in the wall of a shrine of Buā Kuṃbhārā at Kanwari, nearly 26 km south of Hisar on road to Tosham, measures 68 x 58 cm and is damaged above the waist of the goddess. The left leg of the goddess is placed firmly on a lotus *pīṭha* and the right one is folded with the foot placed on the back of the buffalo. This leg seems to be quite disproportionate to the left one. The buffalo bears an ornamental belt and a bell is hung round its neck. The lion is pouncing upon it from the back. The snout of the buffalo has been cut vertically and the small anthropomorphic demon is being held by the goddess with her left arm (? it looks like the foot). A discus has been half thrust in the body of the buffalo, which, being attacked by the lion from the back, is falling forward with forelegs folded.

Pehowa has yielded quite a few fragments of Mahishamardinī images. One of these from Garībanātha kā Ḍerā is similar to the pieces described above with upper part of the goddess broken. Measuring 60 x 45 cm, it shows the goddess in *ālīḍha* posture putting her left foot on the back of the buffalo. The anthropomorphic demon emerging from the decapitated neck of the animal wears earrings, a necklet and a snake necklace, bracelets, *ardhoruk*, etc. and is holding a sword with both of his hands. The goddess is shown twisting his face with her right hand.

Another fragmentary relief from the same site in buff sandstone is very badly mutilated but betrays refined execution. What is interesting here is the depiction of perhaps another figure of a buffalo at the back of the main figure.

A fragmentary hand with a bell found form Prāchī Śiva Temple at Pehowa probably represents the upper left hand of Mahishāsuramardinī (Ac. No. 1/422).

The image from Jhansua in district Ambala, too, is badly damaged. It shows additional human figures, perhaps the attendants.

The image from Badali near Jhajjar must have been the most elaborate of all the images of Mahishāsuramardinī from Haryana. The main figure of the goddess, however, is lost and only the lower portion of the relief has survived. The buffalo to right is a beautiful realistic creation. It is shown wearing an elegant necklace around its neck. The discus thrown at the demon has pierced the side. The lion is attacking the buffalo from behind clasping its back with the forepaws. The buffalo has also charged with the full might as is indicated by the curled tail of the animal and a soldier being crushed by it under its hind right leg. The goddess, however, has rendered the buffalo immobile by pressing its back with her right foot which is placed on a lotus *pīṭha* on the back of the buffalo. The left foot of the goddess, wearing an anklet, is planted firmly on the lotus *pīṭha* placed on the ground in front of the demon. After having immobilized the buffalo, the goddess has cut its neck and the anthropomorphic figure is coming out of the severed head, holding a sword and in a fighting pose. The figure on the extreme right is mutilated beyond recognition. Standing on a lotus-seat, however, it may have represented an attendant of the goddess. Her face is badly damaged but her graceful posture, coiled earrings, pearl necklet, robust and round breasts, pearl armlets and wristlets, long scarf and the *sārī* reaching the ankles render her to be an interesting and elegant figure. Just before her was perhaps another acolyte in half-kneeling posture, but it has suffered considerable mutilation. The facet of the pedestal is beautifully bedecked by an exquisitely carved vine motif.

Another panel lying near a well at Badali from which it is said to have been extracted depicts the four handed goddess holding trident, sword, bell and the tuft of the demon in her four hands in the usual *pratyālīḍha* posture. The face of the goddess is mutilated.

The popularity of Mahishāsuramardinī at Agroha, already evidenced by small figurines published by Srivastava, is corroborated by a fragment excavated from the site, showing only the two right hands of the goddess, one holding the shaft of the trident and the other a *kapāla* indicating that the figure may not have been different in conception from that of Morni-ka-Tal, now preserved in the Chandigarh Museum (Acc. No. 557).[96] The same museum houses another image of the goddess from Pinjore which depicts her as holding sword and shield in the rear hands and is broken below the waist.

Ratpur near Pinjore, too, may have remained an important center of her worship. Though a part of a rectangular slab depicting the haloed bust of a female may probably, but not very certainly, represent Mahishāsuramardinī yet a stone slab still under worship at the site shows her popularity in the region. In attributes and composition, this figure resembles those of Pinjore and Morni described above. Marhanwala, about 15 km northwest of Pinjore, has also yielded a crudely carved image of the goddess.[97]

Hansi[98] has yielded two complete icons of Mahishāsuramardinī. One of these is a four-handed figure and the other eight handed. The former, carved on a rectangular slab (Pl. 212), is a typically early medieval form showing the goddess subduing the demon by pressing its back with her right foot and severing its neck with a trident held in her front right hand. She holds the anthropomorphic demon coming out of the decapitated head of the buffalo, from the tuft with her normal left hand. The rear right holds a sword and the left a shield. The lion is attacking the buffalo from behind. There is a lotus-petalled gloriole behind the head of the goddess and the top corners show stylized acanthus-leaf decorations. The goddess, standing in the *ālīḍha-mudrā*, is a disproportionate figure. The whole relief betrays poor workmanship. The second relief, carved more sharply but still showing lack of proportions, is similar in composition but for the fact that the goddess holds arrow, discus and sword in the extra right hands and shield, bell and bow in the left ones (Pl. 213). The pedestal is *tri-ratha* and the top of the slab is curved.

It seems that in the 7th-8th century C.E. eight-armed images of Mahishāsuramardinī had become characteristic in Haryana. A rectangular relief of blackish grey granite preserved in the Bhagavatī Temple at Kalayat is a beautiful specimen of the early eight-handed images of Mashishāsuramardinī from Haryana (Pl. 214). It shows the goddess trampling the buffalo by putting her left foot on its head and pressing its head and back with her right foot. The crouching position of the buffalo indicates its helplessness, which seems to be further aggravated by the attack of the lion from behind and the trident being thrust into its back by the goddess. The goddess bears an expression of beatitude indicating that she has subdued the animal almost effortlessly. The robust anthropomorphic demon coming out of the decapitated head of the buffalo is being strangulated by the goddess with a serpent-noose held in one of her left hands.[99] The normal right hand of the goddess holds the sword vertically while the extra hands support an arrow and a discus besides the trident already mentioned above. The principal left hand holds a wine-cup and the additional ones a bell and a bow in addition to the serpent-noose in the lowermost left. She wears a bejeweled three-peaked crown, circular earrings, torque, and pearl necklace with pendent strings falling from between the breasts, *keyūras, valayas, nūpuras, uttarīya, adhovastra* and *vanamālā*. There is an arch-shaped halo behind her head and the top corners show *vidyādharas* in flying postures, carrying flowers in their hands. Sensitively chiseled with remarkable care for the details, it is one of the exquisite examples of the art of Haryana. The three-peaked tiara, facial expression and elongation are reminiscent of the hilly style of Himachal Pradesh.[100]

The best-preserved image of Mahishāsuramardinī and a masterpiece of the Pratihāra art of Haryana, however, comes from Sirsa (Pl. 215). Made of red sandstone, this pedestalled rectangular relief shows the life-like figure of Mahishāsuramardinī in *pratyālīḍha* pose occupying the available space diagonally and holding in her eight hands in the *pradaskshiṇā* order trident, taking out an arrow from a quiver placed vertically on the ground, discus, sword, shield, bell, bow and the bust of the anthropomorphic demon emerging from the severed neck of the buffalo. Wearing all the usual ornaments and *adhovastra*, the goddess seems to be the ideal of the feminine form. She bears a beautiful *dhammilla* coiffure. The locks on the forehead are exquisitely arched and the hair above bedecked with bejeweled clasps. There is a vertical eye on the forehead. The eyebrows simulate a bow. The long eyes are only half-open. Sturdy nose, plump cheeks, thick lower lip and the prominent chin endow the benign form with an unmatched charm. Lion, the vehicle of the goddess, attacks the buffalo from behind as usual. The discus hurled by the goddess at the animal has pierced his hind part. The head of the buffalo has been cut completely and separated from the neck. The right leg of the demon is still emerging from the neck of the buffalo. As per the śāstric injunction, the demon is holding a sword in his right hand.[101]

Exquisite ornamentation, graceful lines and contours, balanced composition and refined chisel work make this image to be one of the most elegant icons found from Haryana. The find-spot of the image (Sirsa) indicates that it may have been the *mūla-bera* of a temple dedicated to the goddess Chaṇḍikā (Mahishamardinī) constructed by one Gallaka in the Śaka year 717 (= C.E. 795) as known from an inscription of Pratihāra Vatsarāja.[102]

The goddess in invoked in the second verse of this epigraph -

> *Proddāma-śyāma-dhā'mno virachita-mahisha-chchhadmanā dānavasya*
> *vyāsakto mūrdhni mūrchchāvaśam-iva gatavān=niḥpatat=tāṭakasya* [/]
> *pāyād-vaḥ paṅka-pūrād=aravikara-bhay=āmbhoruhahāra-dhārī*
> *Yādor-vāla-pravāla-dyutir=Aditi-sut=ā(na)nda-kṛich=Chaṇḍikāyāḥ* [//]

If our surmise is correct, this image may be precisely dated to C.E. 795.

An equally elegant image comes from Pehowa and is still under worship in a temple. The image has unfortunately been badly painted (Pl. 216). The attributes in the right hands are similar to the preceding examples with the only difference that rather than taking out an arrow from a quiver, one of the right hand holds a bunch of them. The top corners show garland-bearing *vidyādharas* and the top is rounded and carved with lotus petals to serve as the gloriole behind the hand. The *dhammilla* on the head is more elaborate and an attendant of the *asura* on the extreme right has been added in the composition. Verily, it is a superb example of the Pratihāra art.[103]

Another Pratihāra masterpiece is under worship in a Ṭhākuradvārā at Tandwal in district Ambala. The face of the goddess is slightly mutilated and like the preceding example, this image too is unfortunately painted (Pl. 217). Chronologically, it may be placed between the Sirsa and Pehowa images. The right hands hold a *kapāla*, trident, and sword, with one drawing an arrow from the quiver at the back of her right shoulder. It is said that the image was originally brought here from Siwan near Kaithal.

Mahishāsuramardinī image preserved in the Chandimandir near Chandigarh (Pl. 218) reveals that there was no dearth of her superb icons in Haryana even during the subsequent centuries. Carved out of the local greyish shale, this 75 x 52 cm figure shows the same attributes in her eight hands as the Tandwal figure. The trident is pierced in the neck of the buffalo with a backward stroke and the *kapāla* is held sideways. The bearded human-shaped *asura* is grabbed by the tuft. An arrow and a discus still peep out of one side of the buffalo. The goddess bears beautifully combed hair with a high *jaṭā-jūṭa* in the center of which is tucked a *kīrtimukha* clasp. Behind the head is lotus-shaped aureole. The elaboration of jewelry is obviously discernible. The stele on the sides carry *mātṛikās*, Vaishṇavī on her proper left and perhaps Brahmāṇī on her right. This latter figure being concealed by the upraised uppermost right hand holding the hilt of the sword cannot be made out clearly. The semi-circular top shows a panel of semi-celestial figures - musicians, garland-bearers and the like. The side extremities show *gaja-śārdūla* and *makara-mukha* motifs.

A very late image of the goddess is now enshrined in the sanctum of the Chandimandir and worshipped.

About 10 km south of Chandimandir lies in the village Mandhna a temple of Chaṇḍi-devī which also houses a 100 x 60 cm image of Mahishāsuramardinī. In an indifferent state of preservation, it has a thick coat of oil and dust and even whitewash at places. The dark dungy cell in which it has been enshrined and the mutilation it has suffered make it difficult to see the details.[104] The image, however, seems to be analogous to Chandimandir example in conception and composition. Elaboration of ornamentation and intricate carving, however, indicate that it may have belonged to 11th-12th century C.E.

Our account of the medieval images of Mahishāsuramardinī from Haryana will not be complete without a reference to the image preserved in the Śivālaya (Śiva Temple) at Gharaunda in district Karnal. Though late and crudely carved (Pl. 219) it is an interesting image iconographically. The goddess standing in the *pratyālīḍha* pose is shown as killing the buffalo with the trident held in both of her front hands. The extra right hands support clockwise arrows, discus and sword and the left ones shield, bow and the crest of the demon that is hybrid, having a human body but the head of an animal (buffalo?). The lion, as usual, is there but not in an attacking posture. The face of the goddess is worn out.

The foregoing account, thus, makes it clear that not only Mahishamardinī was popularly worshipped in Haryana from the Kushāṇa period onwards but also the Haryanavi artists created many of her superb and iconographically interest images during that period.

SAPTA-MĀTṚIKĀS

The concept of the Seven Mothers goes back perhaps to the Vedic times yet it is strange that the Purāṇas vary in giving their numbers and names.[105] The usually accepted list, supported by iconographic data, however, comprises the names of Brahmāṇī, Maheśvarī, Kaumārī, Vaishṇavī, Vārāhī, Indrāṇī, and Chāmuṇḍā. The *Bṛihatsaṃhitā*, *Vishṇudharmottara Purāṇa* (III.73), and some Āgamas state that the Mātṛikās should be sculptured in accordance with their respective gods and should have similar emblems. The *Agni Purāṇa* (XX.18-22), Āgamas, *Rūpa-Maṇḍana*, etc., however, detail out their iconographic features thus: four-faced fair complexioned Brahmāṇī should ride a swan and hold *kuṇḍa*, *akshapātra*, *akshamālā* and *sruk* in her four-hands; Maheśvarī should be seated on a bull and carry a bow and arrow in her right hands and a discus in the left; Kaumārī should ride a peacock and wield a spear; seated on Garuḍa, Vaishṇavī should carry *śaṅkha*, *chakra*, *gadā*, and *padma*; Vārāhī seated on a buffalo should have a boar's face and hold a staff and bowl or plough and *śakti* or *ghaṇṭā*, *chāmara*, *gadā* and *chakra*. Indrāṇī should be seated on the elephant with a thunderbolt in her left hand; Chāmuṇḍā should ride a corpse, have three eyes, erect hair, emaciated body, wear tiger-skin and hold in her hands a bowl and trident with others in *abhaya* and *varada mudrā* or a goad, sword, shield, noose, bow, staff and hatchet.

The images of the Mātṛikās are carved in a group or individually, in the panels of the lintels of the doorways or on other architectural parts. The earliest evidence comes from Gokarṇa-kā-Tālāb, Rohtak where five of the seven Mātṛikās have survived sitting in European style[106] on a loose piece measuring 26 x 16 cm (Pl. 220).[107] Even the fifth figure is broken indicating the original panel to have carried all the seven Mothers. The extant figures show somewhat bulky bellies with right hand raised in *abhaya* and the left placed on the knee. The third figure may have been Vārāhī as it seems to have a sow-face. The extant relief indicates that some of the Mātṛikās had other than human faces, animal or even avian. It may very well be compared with the five seated mother goddess figurine with animal and bird faces preserved in the Mathura Museum belonging to the early Kushāṇa period.[108] The position of the right hand held up in *abhaya* turned sideways is an early feature. The absence of the cognizances is notable. After a long gap of time we find a broken Pratihāra panel at Palwal showing Indrāṇī and Chāmuṇḍā seated at ease.[109] This obviously is the end part of the panel as is also indicated by the vertical edge of the back slab. Perhaps the Mātṛikā figures were carved in twos or so and then put together as the edge on the Indrāṇī side also suggests. The figures were executed beautifully with a nimbus behind the head. Two-handed Indrānī wears circular earrings, pearl necklace with a looped pendant string falling from between the massive round breasts, bracelets, *dhotī* secured by multi-stringed pearl girdle. The bun on the head is adorned with jewels. The plump face with drooping eyelids gives a meditative expression. The thunderbolt in the right hand is only partially preserved. She supports a child with her left hand. Chāmuṇḍā on her left is an emaciated figure seated on a corpse. Her head is broken. The original must have been an elegant panel. The Pratihāra doorframe now fitted in the Sarasvatī temple at Pehowa also shows Saptamātṛikās on the surlintel (Pl. 221).

A small 32.5 x 25 cm very much mutilated red sandstone broken panel of *circa* 10th century from Gusaion ki Samadh, Gujjar Kheri (Regn. No. HRN/SON-82) shows three of the seven Mothers in a dancing posture. The attributes to identify them properly are not clear.

BRAHMĀṆĪ

There are a few reliefs depicting Brahmāṇī. A small unfinished image from Gujjar Kheri measuring 19 x 12.5 cm is now in a private collection (Regn No. HRN/AMB-631). It shows the goddess standing in *samapāda-sthānaka* pose on a lotus seat wearing a *jaṭā-mukuṭa, ekāvali,* earrings, bracelets, lower garment with a sash on the thighs, and a long garland (Pl. 222). There is a plain round gloriole behind the head. The suspended normal right hand is disposed in *varada-mudrā* while the other three hold ladle, book, and water-pot in the *pradakshiṇā* order. Near the feet on either side are carved attendant figures – a female and a male, but they are so crude that it is difficult to identify them properly. The details of the main as well as subsidiary figures and the back slab have not been carved and the image has been left unfinished for some unknown reason. The evidence, however, indicates that Gujjar Kheri was a great center of art during the 10th century.

An early medieval badly mutilated image in HARDAM (Acc. No. 1/458) shows a female figure standing between two pillars in contraposto with lower right hand suspended in boon giving posture and the corresponding left holding the water-pot. The upper pair of hands seems to support *sruk* and book. As such, it may be the representation of Brahmāṇī. Other coeval crude figures are known from Sunderpura near Kalka (Acc. No. 1/212), Ratpur (1/369) and Jagadhari (12/84).

A small sandstone image of tri-cephalous Brahmāṇī of unknown provenance from Haryana shows the goddess seated at ease in a pillared *rathikā* with simple dormer-*chaitya* pediment, the goddess holds a rosary in her suspended *varada* right hand and a water-pot in the left (Pl. 223). The central face is damaged and the proper left hand side one is completely lost but the additional face on her proper right leaves little cavil to the figure having been three-faced. She wears an *ekāvali* with a pendent string falling in front from between the breasts and a pearl necklace forming a loop from over the breasts. The armlets too are made of pearl beads. A simple girdle holds the nether garment in position. This image seems to have originally adorned some tenth-century temple.

Another small buff sandstone image measuring 15 x 10 cm is fixed in the outer wall of the godown of Shri Jagdish Singh Chauhan, former Sarpanch of Jasat. The three-headed goddess is seated in *sukhāsana* on a cushion with right leg folded and left suspended slantingly holding a rosary in the fear-allaying principal right hand, *sruk* in the back right, book in the additional left and water vessel in the normal left hand. All the three faces are intact. The goddess bears a *jaṭā-mukuṭa* and usual dress and ornaments. There is, however, no vehicle depicted. Like the former example, this small image too must have decorated some 10th-century temple at Jasat.

Housed in the Maṭha at Rohtak is a beautiful image of a four-armed goddess seated in *padmāsana* on a *viśvapadma*, holding a *kamaṇḍalu* in her normal left hand and an *akshamālā* in the *varada* right (Pl. 224). The upper two hands are broken. She wears a high bun bedecked with pearl strings, ear ornaments, necklet and pearl necklace, *vaikakshyaka*, armlets, multiple beaded bracelets, *dhotī* secured with a waist-band, anklets and rings in her thumbs and some other fingers. A long garland coming from behind her shoulders forms a semi-circle in front on the lotus seat. The goddess has a broad plump face with long drawn meditative eyes. The nose is damaged. The breasts are round and rotund. There is a small and simple eight-petalled halo incised behind her heand on the semi-circular top of the rectangular back slab. The donor couple is depicted on the pedestal in adoration. There are two female fly-whiskers on the sides. On the pilasters on either side of the main figure are small female figures holding a lotus in the right and a water-vessel in the left hand. The extreme projections of the back slab show *gaja-mukhas* and *vyālas*. Dr. Y.D. Sharma identified her with Chakreśvarī.[110] But there is absolutely no evidence to identify the image as such. In the absence of a miniature Jina figure on her head or on top of the figure, and the existence of wheels in her hands which is a characteristic feature of Chakreśvarī, it is difficult to regard this image as belonging to a Jaina deity and agree to Dr. Y.D. Sharma's identification. The presence of the rosary in the *varada* right hand and the water vessel in the left are indications enough to identify the image as that of Brahmāṇī. The minute and detailed carving of every figure and feature, and the dress and ornamentation indicates it to have been a creation of the mature Chauhan period.

A greenish sandstone image of Brahmāṇī standing in *samapāda-sthānaka-mudrā* in a pedimented niche from Pinjore has suffered the effect of time, clime and perhaps vandalism also, and shows her bearing a conical *jaṭā-mukuṭa*, usual dress and ornaments including a long garland, holding rosary in the suspended boon-granting principal right hand, ladle in the back right, manuscript in the additional left and water-pot in the *pralamba* normal left hand. The image belongs to the early 12th century C.E.[111] The double-ribbed pillars of the niche and the pediment above are sure indications of its having been a decorative image on the wall of a temple.

VĀRĀHĪ

A broken rectangular sandstone slab from Pinjore shows goddess Vārāhī seated in *sukhāsana* on her vehicle buffalo (*mahishopari saṃsthitā*) bearing a decorative chain on the head and wearing a necklace with a beaded pendent string falling to the left of the belly from between the breasts. She also wears bracelets, long garland, and the nether garment (Pl. 225). The snout is slightly damaged and there seems to have been a fang on the left side of her face (*Varāha-vaktrī*). She is looking to her right. Her right breast is broken and so also are her right hands. The upper left hand, also damaged, holds the discus and the normal left holds the conch. Only the upper part of the head of the buffalo showing the left eye, forehead and horns has survived as the slab is broken below. The right leg of the goddess below the knee is also gone. A part of the proper right hand side upper corner of the back slab too is lost but it did not contain anything except the decorative leaves. Stylistically the image may be dated to *circa* 9th century C.E.

A Vārāhī image is preserved in the Jhajjar Museum also (Pl. 226). The boar-faced (*śūkarāsyā*) goddess is shown as seated at ease on her vehicle, which looks like a boar, depicted under her folded left leg, supporting a child on her left lap. The whole of the rectangular slab on the proper left side is broken slantingly. The right side shows a long sword and discus in two of her right hands and at least two more hands seem to be broken. There is a lotus-shaped halo behind the head and the top corners of the back slab are occupied by garland-bearing *vidyādharas*, one being visible on the proper right side. On the receding recesses of the *tri-ratha* pedestal are shown small female attendant or Mātṛikā figures. The front of the pedestal is bedecked with lotus leaves. The relief is in an indifferent state of preservation. It may be dated to *circa* 10th century C.E.

What must have been a masterpiece of the Pratihāra art of Haryana has survived only in the form of the lower part of the image of Vārāhī, now preserved in the Asthal Bohr, Rohtak (Pl. 227). Broken above the belly, the extant part shows the goddess wearing rippled nether garment secured by an elaborate triple-stringed beaded *netra-sūtra* with a rectangular clasp in the center and floral anklets. A beaded circular pendent with a double beaded string falls very gracefully towards the left side of the belly. The buffalo below is covered with lion-skin and has anklets in the feet. The care bestowed in carving the limbs and details even up to the nails of the feet of the goddess and features of the buffalo render it a remarkable creation datable to *circa* 10th century C.E. When complete, it must have been a remarkable and matchless image.

CHĀMUṆḌĀ

Chāmuṇḍā, so named for having killed the demon brothers Chaṇḍa and Muṇḍa, is the counterpart of Bhairava and represents the terrific aspect of Śakti. She also killed Raktabīja. The *Vishṇudharmottara Purāṇa*, as quoted by Rao, describes her as terrific, having an emaciated body, pit-eyes, sharp teeth, open mouthed, riding a corpse and wearing snake ornaments.[112] She is generally depicted with four, six and eight hands but sometimes with as many as sixty-four hands also.

A very badly mutilated 9th century sandstone image of Chāmuṇḍā, broken below the belly, showing the emaciated body with hanging breasts, holding a *ḍamaru*, a trident-like object and sword in the extant right hands, wearing snake ornaments and having a *muṇḍa-mālā* on the head, which once lay studded in the wall of the Kabir Chaurā temple at Pinjore was published by me in 1976.[113] It was removed to the Kurukshetra University museum later.[114] A fragment from Pinjore, 25 x 15 cm (Acc. No. 1/54), showing the head and four right hands of a female deity holding wine-cup, severed human head (*kapāla*), bell and discus, belonging to about 10th century C.E., may also belong to Chāmuṇḍā. Bulandpur Kheri too has yielded a small head (Acc. No. 1/163) of Chāmuṇḍā of about the same period. A medieval fragment from Mohanbari is preserved in the Gurukula museum at Jhajjar (Pl. 228) showing the emaciated deity wearing an *ekāvali* and holding trident in the right hand and a noose in the left with a part of the round halo behind the head.[115]

A bigger, but unfortunately again broken and showing only the lower portion of an image of Chāmuṇḍā, is known from Gujjar Kheri (Regn. No. HRN/AMB-622). The extant part measures 34 x 25 cm. The goddess is shown as dancing with her right foot in *sama* pose and the left one in *kuñchita-mudrā* (Pl. 229). Both the knees are bent outwards. The anklets in the feet are clearly visible. Carved lines on the legs and thighs indicate the lower garment, which must have been secured by a waistband whose loop can still be seen on the right thigh of the goddess. The long garland of bones and skulls represented as long and round pieces is swinging to the right of the goddess indicating the movement of the body in the dance. The goddess is dancing on a lotus held by a goblin (*preta*) lying prostrate below with the torso lifted sideways and right hand supporting the head looking upwards. This figure is bedecked with a beautiful coiffure, large discs in the ears, beaded *graiveyaka*, bracelets and lower garment tightened with a girdle. Behind the feet of the goddess is a jackal to right with a beaded band round its neck (Pl. 230). On the proper right may be seen a female attendant standing in graceful triple-flexion pose, holding a wine-cup and a trident in her right and left hands respectively. Near the left foot of the goddess is another female attendant having a jackal-head on a human body. As such she may be Śivadūti. Turned slightly towards the goddess in *tribhaṅga* pose, she holds a cup in her right hand and a spear in the left. She is licking blood from the cup. Behind her is a male figure but it cannot be identified with certitude. Probably a similar figure stood behind the other attendant also. On the extreme recesses of the *tri-ratha* pedestal stand the female fly-whiskers. The whole composition gives a very pleasing look and bespeaks volumes for the Pratihāra artist who carved it. As we have noted above, Gujjar Kheri served as an atelier during the Pratihāra period and catered to the needs of the people in the region.

Mention must be made here of an elegant grey sandstone sculpture (40.5 x 28 cm) from Muradnagar collected by us for HARDAM. The ten-armed goddess sits in *lalitāsana* over a supine human figure resting his head on his right palm (Pl. 231). There is a lion to right sitting on its haunches with right forepaw raised up and the tail twirled at its back below the folded left leg of the goddess. Here thus we see a mingling of the features of Durgā and Chāmuṇḍā. A male attendant is shown on either side of the pedestal and the one behind the head of the supine figure is putting one of his fingers in the mouth of the goblin. The right foot of the goddess is placed slightly splayed out on a lotus placed on the pedestal. The goddess bears a very serene expression. She has a long sharp nose, pointed chin, thick lower lip, plump cheeks, quasi-closed long fish-like eyes and bow-shaped eyebrows. The hair, beautifully combed backwards and twisted to form a bun, is adorned with pearl strings and a leonine clasp, which spews a pearl string covering the parting of the hair. There is a round gloriole behind the head having a beaded rim and eight lotus petals in the center. The goddess holds a cup, a sword, and an arrow in three of the extant right hands and the other two, one of which may have held a hammer, are broken. The left hands hold a *ṭaṅka*, a trident, a bell, a bow (in the broken hand) with its upper end visible on the shield in the uppermost left hand. The ornaments of the goddess include serpentine earrings, necklace with the pendent string falling downwards from between the breasts, another necklace forming a loop from over the breasts, multiple armlets, beaded bracelets and anklets. A twisted *mekhalā* secures the *sārī* indicated by double incised wavy lines on the legs and thighs. The image may be dated to *circa* 9th century C.E.[116]

A fragment from Pehowa shows the left hands of a female deity holding a *kapāla*, a drinking bowl and a snake. It may have been a part of a Pratihāra image of Chāmuṇḍā.[117] Fixed in the southern wall of the Devī Temple at Kara Sahib is a small late Pratihāra sandstone piece measuring 25 x 18 cm showing a foot placed on a lotus on the back of a demon lying supine. Probably Chāmuṇḍā was worshipped at this place also. Rodgers[118] noticed an image of Kāli broken into two pieces in the Śītalapurī Temple at Kaithal but nothing is known about it now.

NĀRASIṂHĪ/NṚISIṂHĪ

A 13 x 10 cm buff sandstone small image of Nārasiṃhī from Gujjar Kheri is preserved in a private collection (Regn. No. HRN/AMB-634). The goddess is seated on a cushion in *lalitāsana* (Pl. 232). Unfortunately, the face of the goddess is slightly damaged but the manes arranged in two braids falling on the shoulders and the extant portion of the face leave little doubt to its being Nārasiṃhī. The four-handed goddess holds a wine-cup and *Śrīphala* (wood-apple) in her principal right and left hands and a sword and a bell in the corresponding additional ones. She is wearing an *ekāvali*, another single stringed pearl necklace falling on the belly fom over the rotund breasts, bracelets and the *adhovastra*. Part of a lotus is carved on the pedestal just below the feet of the goddess. The back slab bears lotus petals carved behind the head of the goddess and its upper part has been rounded off with a central depression. The simplicity of dress and ornamentation and the modeling of the contours of the body suggest an 8th century date for it.[119]

A buff sandstone image of Nārasiṃhī was excavated from Agroha during 1983-84. Measuring 44 x 30 cm, it depicts the goddess as seated in *lalitāsana* on a full-blown lotus flower under which are shown two lions seated back-to-back (Pl. 233). The four-armed goddess holds a wine-cup and a sword, both attributes being slightly damaged, in her principal and back right hands, the additional left is broken, and the normal left, touching the folded left leg, holds a fruit or *bījapuraka*. The lower tip of the shaft of the attribute in the broken upper left hand may be seen resting on the left thigh of the goddess. The face of the deity has also suffered some damage but the erect ears and long manes clearly betray her identity. The goddess bears a round beaded ornament on the head, pearl necklace with pendent string falling from between the breasts, beaded armlets, bracelets, *dhotī* secured by a girdle, and anklets. The upper part of the back slab has been rounded off and its border beaded to serve as the halo. Stylistically, it may be not be far removed from the preceding example.[120]

Rodgers had noticed an interesting fragmentary relief in the wall of the Garībnātha Temple at Pehowa: "It is that of a seated female feeding a child, but both child and mother have the head of a dog or a monkey."[121] This relief may still be seen fixed up high in a wall of the said temple (Pl. 234). Shukla (Fig. 10) has identified the figure as a "boar-headed goddess seated on a lion."[122] A careful examination would reveal that the goddess sits on her vehicle lion in *sukhāsana* with right foot placed on the ground. On the folded left leg is seated a child fondling with the left breast of the goddess. The upper left and lower right arms of the goddess are irretrievably lost. The upper right arm is folded upwards. The wrist touches the right breast but the hand is broken. The face of the goddess and the child, too, have suffered mutilation. The goddess wears a beaded necklace whose pendent string falls to the left of her navel from between her breasts. *Valayas*, *dhotī*, the long garland and a beautiful round lotiform gloriole behind the head are also there. On the top corners are the divine garland-bearing *vidyādharas*. Behind the lion is a small female figure with *pralamba* right hand touching the thigh and holding some indistinct object in her upraised left hand. The middle portion of the back slab above her shows stylized *makara-mukha* decoration. On seeing this relief very carefully many a time we feel convinced that it is not 'boar-headed Siṃhavāhinī' but Nārasiṃhī as can be made out from the braided manes falling on her shoulders, her lion mount and the *vanamālā* which is usually though not exclusively associated with Vaishṇavite deities. The relief may be dated to *circa* 9th century C.E.[123] Another Mātṛikā relief

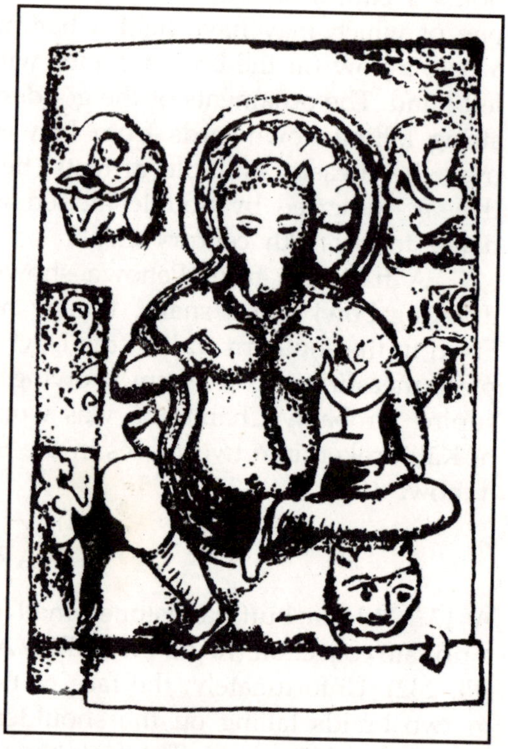

Fig. 10. Nārasiṃhī, Pehowa.

from Prāchī Śiva Temple at Pehowa, of about the same period, shows seven animal-headed female figures on the pedestal.[124]

LAKSHMĪ

She symbolizes luck and good fortune. As such, she has come to be respected and worshipped alike by the Hindus, Buddhists and Jainas.[125] The antiquity of the concept of Lakshmī has been traced to the Chalcolithic times.[126] Probably folk elements were instrumental in shaping her ideology and form. Even though the word Śrī, which later became a synonym of Lakshmī, occurs in the *Ṛigveda* (I.87, 6) yet the concrete concept about her person can only be traced from the later Vedic period onwards. In the epic and Paurāṇic period, she came to be recognized as the Śakti of Vāsudeva Vishṇu.[127] As the goddess of wealth, she became naturall associated with Kubera, also the god of wealth.[128] Still later, she formed a triad with Kubera and Gaṇeśa. Lakshmī has been represented on seals and coins from about the 2nd century B.C.E.[129] In Indian art, Śrī-Lakshmī is associated with lotus flowers – she stands on a lotus amid lotuses and even herself holding lotus(es). Another popular form of her depiction is the Gaja-Lakshmī (or Abhisheka-Lakshmī) showing the deity being anointed by elephants inverting pitchers of water over her.[130]

A clay sealing of about 2nd-1st century B.C.E. from Agroha[131] and coins of the Agra *janapada* of Agācha (Agroha)[132] indicate the popularity of the worship of Lakshmī in Haryana during the early centuries before and after the inception of C.E. The evidence of the stone images, however, is much later and it must also be admitted, much sparse.

We have already referred to triads of Gaṇeśa, Gaja-Lakshmī and Kubera from Khokhrakot, Rohtak (Pl. 4), Kasan, Chuliana and Chulkana above. Gaja-Lakshmī is shown as occupying the central position seated in *sukhāsana* holding lotus flowers in both of her hands on which stand the elephants inverting pitchers of water on her. Sondh too has yielded a similar triad (with Gaṇeśa completely lost), which unfortunately is very badly mutilated. But the graceful figure of Gaja-Lakshmī seated at ease holding lotus flower by its long stalk and accompanied by a seated male and standing female attendant on either side may clearly be discerned. It seems that these three auspicious deities were worshipped at the time of Diwali. These auspicious triads thus seem to give evidence of the celebration of Diwali in different parts of the country from which they have been found.

A four-handed Pratihāra image of Gaja-Lakshmī enshrined in a small fane at Kapālamochana and painted by the priest to make it more attractive and still under worship shows the goddess seated in *sukhāsana* on a fully blossomed double-petalled lotus seat with proper right hand in the gesture of reassurance and the principal left holding a conch (?), with additional hands supporting the lotuses from which the elephants pour water on her (Pl. 235). A fly-whisker stands on either side and interestingly enough there are two lions on the sides of the pedestal which emphasize her Kshemaṅkarī aspect. The goddess wears usual ornaments details of which have been concealed by the paint. But the *dhammilla* coiffure, thin waist and expression of beatitude on her face are very clear.

An image of Gaja-Lakshmī measuring 80 x 48 cm has indiscriminately been fixed in a temple at Jaintipur (Pl. 236). The goddess is seated in *lalitāsana* with right leg tucked up and the left dangling down. The left foot, splayed outwards, is placed on a full-blown lotus. The face of the lion, the vehicle of the goddess, may be seen below her right knee.[133] As noted above, it is an interesting iconographic feature. The goddess holds a full-blown lotus in her right hand. The attribute in the left hand is not clear. It seems to have been another lotus with a bud. The goddess wears a cylindrical crown on her head and circular earrings.

She wears a *dhotī* and perhaps armlets and bracelets too. Caparisoned elephants in profile inverting pitchers of water on her head are shown on the sides. Stylistically, it may be dated to *circa* 9th century C.E. This image is fixed over another broken image of which the folded right leg and the face of a jackal may be seen. The deity may thus have been Śivadūti or some other form of Devī.

SARASVATĪ

As the goddess of learning and fine arts, Sarasvatī commands equal respect from the Hindus, Buddhists and Jainas. She is shown in art as seated or standing and among others, lotus and *Vīṇā* are her distinctive attributes.

That Sarasvatī was very popularly worshipped by the Jainas is evidenced by the occurrence of four of her figures out of about sixty in the Hansi bronze hoard where she is always shown as standing holding a lotus and book in her two hands.[134] As far as stone is concerned we have only some possible evidence of her depiction. A light buff sandstone image from Rohtak (Acc. No. 1/160) measuring 41 x 27.5 cm shows a female deity wearing a torque, a pearl necklace with pendent string falling vertically to the abdomen from between the breasts (*hāramuktābharaṇabhūshitām*), ear ornaments, *keyūras*, beaded bracelets, anklets, etc. (*sarvābharaṇabhūshitā*), bearing a bejeweled bun of matted locks (*jaṭāmakuṭasaṃyuktā*), seated in *lalitāsana* on a damaged white lotus seat (*śvetapadmāsanāsīnā*), with a lotiform gloriole behind the head (*prabhāmaṇḍalasaṃyuktā*), attended by female fly-whiskers on both the sides but unfortunately with both the hands damaged (Pl. 237) may have been a representation of Sarasvatī for there is a possibility of there being a lotus (a part of the stalk of which is still visible) in the right hand and a *vīṇā* in the left. Garland-bearing *vidyādharas* are shown hovering in the sky as usual on the upper corners of the back slab. The relief may be placed in the 9th century on stylistic grounds.

The second possible representation of the same period comes from Uchana (Pl. 238). The extant 40 x 30 cm rectangular slab on which it is carved is unfortunately broken below the waist of the goddess who bears a more elaborate *dhammilla* coiffure with a *chūḍāmaṇṇi* and pearl strings, and other usual ornaments and holds a fully blossomed lotus in her right hand. The attribute in the left hand is damaged but the long shaft held from the waist to the left shoulder indicated that it was the *vīṇā*. The face is also damaged but the relief appears to be pleasing to the eyes.

GAṄGĀ AND YAMUNĀ

Gaṅgā riding on the crocodile and Yamunā on the tortoise are invariably shown on the doorframes from early medieval period. In the Gupta period they occupied the T-shaped frames on the top corners of the door-surrounds. That the depiction of the river-goddesses was quite popular during the Gupta period is indicated by Gupta gold coins and the famous terracotta representations from Ahichchhatra, now in the National Museum, New Delhi. The river goddesses are shown as carrying a *ghaṭa* or simply a lotus.

The earliest representation of Gaṅgā in Haryana is in the form of a terracotta from Kariwala in district Sirsa (Pl. 239). The river goddess attended by two female figures stands in the center in *dvibhaṅga* holding with her left hand the branch of the Śāla tree which covers her back and also canopies her. The right hand is broken. The plaque is not in a good state of preservation. Discular ear ornament bearing lotus petal motif (simulating a spoked wheel) and the lower garment with multiple pleats indicated by sharp incised lines can, however, be seen on her person clearly. She bears *dhammilla* type of hair-coiffure and an oval plain gloriole is carved behind her head. The breasts are damaged but their rotundity can still be made out from what remains. The slender waist, slightly expanding pelvis and long tapering legs add to the grace of the figure. It must have borne a beautiful facial expression, which can only be guessed now because of the indifferent state of preservation. The right foot of the goddess is placed in *sama* pose while the left is slightly splayed out. *Makara*, the vehicle of the goddess, can be seen behind her feet with a swirling tail but in a much-mutilated condition.

On the proper right of the goddess stands a female, wearing similar dress and ornaments, slightly turned towards her, with both hands damaged and all details lost. The other female figure to the left of the river goddess, however, is comparatively better preserved though even she has lost her hands. Her face, too, is mutilated. The *dhammilla* coiffure, circular ornament in the left ear, and lower garment with incised folds match well with the dress and ornamentation of the river goddess. A beautifully bedecked pot probably hung by a string in her left hand, round rotund breasts, slightly enlarged belly (as if she be pregnant) and knees bent outwards provide distinctiveness to this figure. Do the accompanying figures represent Yamunā and Sarasvatī? We are not sure, but there is little doubt that the central figure imitating a Śālabhañjikā is that of Gaṅgā. The aureole and the crocodile behind her head and feet provide the desired evidence for proper identification, which is also confirmed by the much-mutilated inscription on the pedestal of which *'Gaṅgā-pratimā kāritā'* can still be made out. Both, the style of the image and the palaeography of the extant letters, indicate it to be a work of the Gupta period. Baked red, this large sized terracotta image measures 46 x 29 cm and may have adorned, as can be judged from its size, some Gupta brick temple at Kariwala which unfortunately is completely lost now.[135]

A pillar from Kapālamochana, 41 cm in height in its extant form (Acc. No. 1/307), with Gaṅgā standing facing holding a water pot in her right hand raised to the level of the shoulder and *pralamba* left hand betrays late Gupta features (Pl. 240).[136] A late Gupta pillar from Akbarpur Barota near Sonepat also bears a *tribhaṅga* figure of the river goddess carrying the pitcher on her right shoulder.

An early medieval jamb of a doorframe of about seventh or 8th century from Pinjore in the Chandigarh Museum carries a beautiful representation of Yamunā standing gracefully in *dvibhaṅga* on the tortoise (Pl. 241). The *dukūla* worn from over the head with free ends dangling down gracefully to the knees, the sparse ornamentation, proportionate physiognomy and high relief give it distinctiveness, which is but rare in this region.

As mentioned above, all medieval temples carried the figures of the river-goddesses on the lower parts of the doorframes. It will be futile to describe all the numerous pieces from Haryana but mention must be made of the river-goddess figurines on the doorframe fitted in the Sarasvatī temple at Pehowa for the grace and elaboration achieved during the Pratihāra period (Pls. 242-43).

Notes and References

1. V.S. Agrawala, "The Devī-Māhātmya," *Journal of Indian History*, Vol. 43, no. 3 (1964), pp. 823-32.
2. Cf. *Mārkaṇḍeya Purāṇa* (ed. Panchanan Tarkaratna, Calcutta, Śaka 1812), Nārāyaṇī-Stuti, Ch. 91, v. 51 –

Ittham̩ yadā yadā bādhā dānavotthā bhavishyati /
Tadā tadāvatīryāham̩ karishyamyarisam̩kshayam//

3. *'Pārvatī parvatodbhavā'*, *Aparājitapṛichchhā* (GOS, Baroda, 1950) 222.9; *Rūpamaṇḍana* V, 3. Also *Kumārasambhava* I. 26: *Pārvatītyabhijanena nāmnā.*
4. *Mārkaṇḍeya Purāṇa*, Ch. 85, v. 40: *Śarīrakoshādyattasyāḥ Pārvattya niḥsṛitāmbikā/Kauśikīti samasteshu tato gīyate.*
5. *Kumārasambhava* I. 26; *Brahma Purāṇa* 34.86.
6. R.D. Trivedi, *Iconography of Pārvatī*, Delhi 1981, pp. 22-23. Cf. J.N. Banerjea (*DHI*, p. 492) who explains Aparṇā as 'nude'. See also *Brahma Purāṇa* 34,85.
7. S.B. Singh, *Brahmanical Icons in Northern India*, New Delhi, 1977, p. 149.
8. R.D. Banerji, *Bas Reliefs of Badami*, Memoirs of the Archaeological Survey of India, no. 25, 1928, p. 10, PI. VI. a.
9. R. Sen Gupta, "The Panels of Kalyāṇasundaramūrti at Ellora", *Lalit Kala*, no. 7 1960, p. 14.
10. K. Deva, "Iconography of Pārvatī as Tapasvinī", *Bharati*, Varanasi, N.S., No.1, 1968, p.2.
11. S.B. Singh, *op. cit.*, pp. 149-51; Trivedi, *op. cit.*, pp. 35 ff.
12. Lion as the vehicle of Durgā (Pārvatī as the consort of Śiva) is well known. The myth of its creation from the wrath of Pārvatī against Śiva is given in details in the *Matsya* (Ch. 153, pp. 124ff) and *Padma Purāṇa* (Sṛishṭikhaṇḍa, 45.54-65, p. 423). It is interesting to note that deer is also depicted as her mount in some Pallava sculptures. See R. Nagaswami, *Tantric Cult of South India*, Delhi, 1982, pls. 35 and 40. The depiction of both of animals, however, seems to suggest the sylvan environment in which Pārvatī performed the *pañchatapas*, as pointed out by Trivedi (*op. cit.*, pp. 37-39). The depiction of two deer in some of the images further supports this view.
13. Trivedi, *op. cit.*, p. 60.
14. Alexander Cunningham, *Archaeological Survey Report*, Vol. XIV, p. 71.
15. Rodgers, *Report*, pp. 28-32.
16. *Ibid.*
17. Devendra Handa, "Some Unpublished Sculptures from Pinjaur," *VIJ*, XIV (i), March 1976, pp. 112-19, pls. I-XI.
18. *PS*, pp. 1-52, pls. I-XXXIV. Subsequently all these sculptures with many other acquisitions were published by S.P. Shukla (1983), *op. cit.*, Nos. 1-112, pp. 11-39, pls. I-XXXI.4.
19. These include images of Śiva, Gaṇeśa, Kārttikeya, pillars, doorjambs, and architectural pieces.
20. D.C. Bhattacharyya (1981), *op. cit.*, pp. 21-22, 31-32, 51-52, 62-64, 81-82, 85-86, 90, 95, and 108, figs. 18, 25, 39, 44, and 51.
21. Trivedi, *op. cit.*, pls. V, XVI, XVII, XIX-XXIII, etc.
22. *Kumārasambhava* V.16.
23. Trivedi, *op. cit.*, p. 37.
24. *Ibid.*, pp. 36ff.
25. *Ibid.*, pls. III-XI.
26. The occurrence of a book in the hand of *tapasvinī* Pārvatī is a rare phenomenon. Book and *sruk* are the characteristic attributes of Brahmāṇī. The images may have been influenced by Brahmāṇī figures or perhaps the book, like the sacred thread, emphasizes the celibate aspect.
27. Two deer may also be noticed in the image from Naresar Temple no. 2 (Trivedi, *op. cit.*, pl. III).
28. N.P. Joshi, *Tapasvinī Pārvatī - Iconographic Study of Pārvatī in Penance*, New Delhi, 1996, pp. 2-7.
29. *'Godhāsanā bhaved Gaurī,' Aparājitapṛichchhā* 222.37; *Rūpa-maṇḍana* V.38.
30. Banerjea, *op. cit.*, p. 502.
31. Menal image of Pārvatī performing *pañchatapas* (Trivedi, *op. cit.*, pp. 58-60, pl. XVIII) is the only one known to us showing the *godhā*, the lion, and the deer together.
32. Amar Singh, *op. cit.*, pp. 200-01, pl. XXVIII.A. A fragment from Pehowa too may have originally belonged to a *Pañchatapas* Pārvatī image of the late 9th century C.E. (*Pehowa*, pp. 115-16, pl. 65).
33. D.C. Bhattacharyya (1981), *op. cit.*, p. 69, fig. 28.

34. *Ibid.*, p. 108 (Acc. no. 3236). A *śukanāsa* with the face of Pārvatī (Acc. no. 72.51), a badly mutilated Mātṛikā holding a child on her left lap with the figure of Gaṇeśa on a pillar on her right (Acc. no. 72.7) and another haloed head with face completely gone and having a sword in one of the right hand (Acc. no. 72.13), all from Pinjore and belonging to *circa* 10th century C.E., now in the Kurukshetra University museum, were published by Udai Vir Singh (*PS*, p. 29, pl. VII.A; p. 28, pl. VI.A and p. 29, pl. VI.B respectively) and Shukla (1983), *op. cit.*, pp. 15-16, pls. VI.1-2 and VII.B respectively.
35. *DHI*, pp. 489 ff.
36. *EHI*, I, pp. 356 ff.
37. *Ibid.*, *PP. 341-42.*
38. S.B. Singh, *op. cit.*, p. 154.
39. Devendra Handa (1988), *op. cit.*, pp. 277-78, fig. 2.
40. D.C. Bhattacharyya (1981), *op. cit.*, p. 68, fig. 27. Bhattacharyya, however, identifies the attribute in the lower left hand as *mātuluṅga*, which is not held in a suspended hand in the way shown here. The attribute here, therefore, should be regarded as water-pot.
41. *EHI*, I, p. 342.
42. *Devī Purāṇa* 39.166.
43. *Padma Purāṇa* V.30, 2 ff.
44. *Ibid.*, V.30, 186.
45. *Bhavishya Purāṇa*, Uttara Parva, 61.15:
    Digvasanā vikṛitamukhā pheṭkāroddāmapūritadiśaughā /
    Jayati vikarāladehā Kshemaṅkarī raudrabhāvasthā //
46. *Aparājitapṛichchhā* 222.32.
47. *Rūpamaṇḍana* V.36:
    Varaṃ triśūlaṃ kheṭañcha pānapātrañcha bibhratī /
    Kshemaṅkarī tadā nāmā kshemārogya-pradāyinī //
48. Devendra Handa, *Pehowa*, p. 116, pl. 66.
49. For an account of his birth and exploits see *Agni Purāṇa*, chs. 17-20; *Brahmāṇḍa Purāṇa* II.19, 40-41; *Matsya Purāṇa* 122.59-60; *Vāyu Purāṇa* 49.37; *Vishṇu Purāṇa* II.4, 27; etc.
50. *EHI*, I, p. 366.
51. Cf. *Mārkaṇḍeya Purāṇa*, Devī-Māhātmya (III.37).
52. *DHI*, p. 498.
53. *East and West*, New Series, Vol. XIX, Nos. 3-4, p. 420; Cf. *Padma Purāṇa* I.35.
54. *EHI*, I, p. 354.
55. *Ibid.*, pp. 348 ff.
56. R.C. Agrawala, "Some Sculptures of Durga Mahishasuramardini from Rajasthan," *Brahma Vidya*, New Series, Adyar, Vol. 19, Nos.1-2, pp. 37-46; "A Terracotta plaque of Mahishamardini from Nagar," *Lalit Kala*, Nos. 1-2, 1955-56, p.73; "The Goddess Mahisasuramardini in Early Indian Art," *Artibus Asiae*, Vol. XXI, no.2, pp. 124-27, figs. 1-2; H. Hartel, "Some Results of the Excavation at Sonkh; A Preliminary Report," in *German Scholars on India*, Vol. II, Bombay, 1976, pp. 74-78 and 92, figs. 10-36; Gourishankar De, "The Earliest Mahishamardini Image of India," paper presented at the 42nd Annual Session of the Indian History Congress, Bodh Gaya, 1981; B.N. Mukherjee, "Foreign Elements in Iconograph of Mahishasuramardini. - The War Goddess of India," *Zeitschrift der Deutschen Morgenlandischen Gesellschaft*, Supplement VI, Vom 21, Bis 25, Marz 1983, pp. 406-08 etc.
57. J. Ph. Vogel, *Catalogue of the Archaeological Museum at Mathura*, Allahabad, 1910, p. 97; V.S. Agrawal, "Mathura Terracottas," *The Journal of the United Provinces Historical Society*, Lucknow, Vol. IX, part II, pp. 32 ff., Fig.47 and 53; "A Catalogue of the Brahmanical Images in Mathura Art," *Ibid.*, Vol. XXII, 1949, p. 158; Odette Viennot, "The Goddess Mahishasuramardini in Kushana Art," *Artibus Asiae*, Vol. XIX, nos. 3-4, 1956, pp.368-73, fig. 1; R.C. Agrawala (1958), *op. cit*, pp. 124-27; "Mahisamardini Plaque in the Gurukul Museum at Jhajjar, Haryana" in *Ajaya-Sri: Recent Studies in Indology (Prof. Ajay Mitra Shastri Felicitation Volume)*, Vol. II, Delhi, 1989, pp. 397-98, pl. 52;

Hartel (1956), *op. cit*, p. 92, fig. 36; Gritli Von Mitterwallner, "The Kusana Type of the Goddess Mahisasuramardini As Compared to the Gupta and Medieval Types" in *German Scholars on India*, Vol. II, fig. 1-3; S. Czuma, *Kushana Sculpture - Images from Early India*, Cleveland, 1985, pp. 105-06; Mukherjee (1983), *op. cit.*, figs. 3-9.

58. Hartel (1976), *op. cit.*, fig. 36; Mitterwallner, *op. cit.*, figs. 1-3; Mukherjee, *op. cit.*, p. 406, figs. 3-7.
59. R.C. Agrawala (1958), *op. cit.*, p.123; (1989), *op. cit.*, pp.397-98, pl.52; Mukherjee, *op. cit.*, fig. 7.
60. Mitterwallner, *op. cit.*, p. 205.
61. *Mārkaṇḍeya Purāṇa*, Vaṅgavāsī Steam Press, Calcutta, Ch.83, vv, 37-39.
62. Nileshvari Y. Desai, *Ancient Indian Society, Reliogion and Mythology as depicted in the Markandeya Purana: A Critical Study*, Baroda, 1968, pp. 3-4.
63. M. Seshadri, "Mahishasuramardini", *Half-Yearly Journal of the Mysore University, Mysore,* Section A - Art, Vol. XXII, no.2, pp. 1-28 & pls. 1-43.
64. Vogel (1910), *op. cit.*, p. 97; Viennot, *op. cit.*, pp. 368-72; R.C. Agrawala (1958), pp. 123-30 etc.
65. R.C. Agrawala (1989), p. 398, pl. 52.
66. Cf. Viennot, p. 371, fig. 1.
67. Hartel (1976), *op. cit.*, fig. 36.
68. Cf. Hartel (1980), p. 68, no. 28; Mukherjee, *op. cit.*, fig. 7.
69. Mitterwallner, *op. cit.*, figs. 1-3; Hartel (1976), fig. 36; (1988), p. 68, no. 28.
70. D.P.S. Punia, "Recently Explored Icons of Mahisasurardini from South Haryana", *Vishveshvaranad Indological Journal*, Hoshiarpur, Vol. XIX (1981), p. 239, fig. 1.
71. Cf. Punia, *loc. cit.*
72. Cf. Viennot, *op. cit.*, fig. 1; Mitterwallner, *op. cit.*, figs. 1 and 3.
73. R.C. Agrawala (1989), pp. 397-98, pl. 52.
74. Harle (1969), pp. 147-54; (1971-72), pp. 44-48, pls. V-VII; Hartel (1980), p. 68, no. 28; Mukherjee, *op. cit.*, fig. 7.
75. R.C. Agrawala (1989), p. 398.
76. Ranbir Singh, *History and Archaeology of Tehsil Palwal (District Faridabad) Haryana*, Unpublished M. Phil. Dissertation, Kurukshetra University, Kurukshetra, pp. 44-45, pl. IX B. Cf. Harle (1971-72), pl. V; Viennot, pl. XII.4.
77. S.P. Shukla (1983), *op. cit.*, p. 74, pl. LVIII.2.
78. K.M. Munshi, *Saga of Indian Sculpture*, Bombay, 1957, pls. 84 & 146.
79. R.C. Agrawala (1966), p. 109, figs. 1-2.
80. Handa (1988), pp. 313-14.
81. Mukhlas-ur-Rahman, "Three Mahishamardini Images From Bangladesh," *Journal of the Asiatic Society of Bangladesh*, Dhaka, Vol. XVIII, no. 3, pp. 156-57, pl. XII.
82. Shukla (1983), *op. cit.*, p. 16, pl. VII.1.
83. H.L. Srivastava, *Excavations at Agroha (Punjab)*, MASI, no. 61, Delhi, 1952, p. 3. pl. X. 4, 8.
84. *Report of the Working of the Central Museum of Lahore*, 1930-31, p.4, pl. I.
85. D.P.S. Punia, "Recently Explored Icons of Mahisasurardini from South Haryana", *Vishveshvaranad Indological Journal*, Hoshiarpur, Vol. XIX (1981), pp. 237 ff.
86. *Annual Report of the Archaeological Survey of India, 1922-23*, p. 92.
87. *Marg*, Haryana Heritage Number, Vol. XXVII, no. 4 (Sept.1974), p. 14, fig. 10.
88. Devendra Handa, "Relics of Art from Marhanwala," *Panjab University Research Bulletin (Arts)* [henceforth *PURBA*], Chandigarh, Vol. XX, no. 2 (Oct. 1989), pp. 166-67, fig. 5.
89. D.C. Bhattacharya (1981), p. 65, fig. 26.
90. Devendra Handa "Some Interesting Sculptures from Pehowa", *PURBA*, Vol. XVI, No.1 (April 1985), p. 130, fig. 1.
91. Bhattacharyya, *op. cit.*, p. 64, fig. 25.
92. Shukla, *op. cit.*, p. 49, pl. XLI. 3.
93. Information from Dr. Manmohan Kumar, Rohtak. Dhup Singh Dhattarwal [*Archaeology of Safidon Tehsil (Dist. Jind)*, M. Phil, Dissertation (Ms.) K.U., Kurukshetra, 1978, pp. 88-89] has reported a Mahishamardinī image from Paju Kalan also.

94. Many of the fragmentary pieces described here are illustrated in our article "Mahishāsuramardinī in the Medieval Art of Haryana" in *Researches in Indian Archaeology, Art, Architecture, Culture and Tradition (Vijayakanta Mishra Commemoration Volume)*, edited by Phanikanta Mishra, Delhi, 1995, Vol. 1, pp. 279-89 and Plates (73-96) in Vol. 2.
95. *Report of the Working of the Central Museum of Lahore, 1930-31*, p. 4, pl. I.
96. Bhattacharyya (1983), *op. cit.*, p. 65, fig. 26. See also *Himachal Art & Archaeology*, State Museum, Simla, 1980, pl. IV.7.
97. *PURBA*, Vol. XX, no. 2, October, 1979, pp. 165-69.
98. For details see *Annual Report of the Archaeological Survey of India, 1922-23*, p.92, pl. V; Devendra Handa, "Some Important Towns of Haryana, A Study of their Past -3," *Journal of Haryana Studies*, Kurukshetra, Vol. III, part 2 (1971), pp. 3-4; Aditya Lohan, *A Historical Cultural Study of the Hansi Region (From the Earliest Times to A.D. 1526)*, Unpublished Ph. D. Thesis, K.U., Kurukshetra, 1988.
99. Cf. *Mārkaṇḍeya Purāṇa* 83. 28:
Sa kshiptvā tasya vai pāśaṃ taṃ babandha mahāsuram /
Tatyaja mahishaṃ rūpaṃ so'pi baddho mahāmṛidhe //
100. Cf. *Marg*, Vol. XXVII, no. 4 (September 1974), p. 14.
101. *Mārkaṇḍeya Purāṇa* 83 29:
Tataḥ siṃho'bbhavat sadyo yāvat tasyāmbikā śitaḥ /
Chhinatti tāvat purushaḥ khaḍgapāṇi iva dṛiśyata //
102. K.V. Ramesh and S.P. Tewari, "An Inscription of Pratihāra Vatsarāja, Śaka 717," *Epigraphia Indica*, Vol. XCI (1975-76), New Delhi, 1989, pp. 49-57.
103. S.P. Shukla, "Relics of Ancient Art from Pehowa," *PURBA*, Vol. XI, no. 1-2, April-October 1980, pp. 72-73; Devendra Handa, *Pehowa*, pp. 113-14, Pl. 62.
104. See for illustration Devendra Handa (1995), *op. cit.*, pl. 95. It is not illustrated here because the poor quality of the photograph.
105. *DHI*, p. 383.
106. Cf. Harle, *op. cit.*, pl. 27.
107. Devendra Handa, "Gupta Reliefs From Haryana," *BMA*, no. 35-36 (1985), p. 16, fig. 2.
108. V.S. Agrawala, *A Catalogue of the Brahmanical Images in Mathura Art*, Lucknow, 1951, p. 59; Shivaji K. Panikkar, *Sapta Mātṛkā Worship and Sculptures*, New Delhi, 1997, pl. 6; O.P. Misra, *Iconography of the Saptamātrikā*, Delhi, 1989, pl. 6.
109. Brajesh Krishna, *op. cit.*, p. 165, pl. 71.
110. *Indian Archaeology, 1959-60: A Review*, p. 74.
111. *Heritage of Haryana-1- Sculptures of Hindu Divinities*, Chandigarh, no date, p. 20.
112. *EHI*, I, Appendix C, p. 152. Cf. *Mārkaṇḍeya Purāṇa* 261.33-37; *Agni Purāṇa* 50.21-22.
113. Devendra Handa (1976), *op. cit.*, p. 117, pl. VIII.
114. *PS*, p. 29, pl. VII.B; Shukla (1983), *op. cit.*, p. 16, pl. VII.3.
115. Sheela Devi (*op. cit.*, p. 199, pl. XXIV.F) regarded it to have come from Lalkot near Rohtak.
116. Devendra Handa (1988), *op. cit.*, pp. 281-82, fig. 9.
117. Devendra Handa, *Pehowa*, p. 115, pl. 64.
118. Rodgers, *Report*, p. 20.
119. Devendra Handa, "Some Unpublished Sculptures from Gujjar Kheri (Haryana)," *PURBA*, Vol. XVII, no. 1 (April 1986), p. 113, fig. 8.
120. Devendra Handa, "Agroha Revisited," in *Prācī-Prabhā*, p. 247, pl. 42.
121. Rodgers, *Report*, p. 16.
122. Shukla (1980), *op. cit.*, p. 73, fig. 5.
123. Devendra Handa, *Pehowa*, p. 115, pl. 63.
124. *Ibid.*, p. 116, pl. 67.
125. *DHI*, P. 370. See also Rai Govinda Chandra, *Prāchīna Bhārata meṃ Lakshmī Pratimā - Eka Adhyayana*, Varanasi, 1964.
126. B. Chatterjee, "Antiquity of the Concept of Lakṣmī," in *Foreigners in Ancient India and Lakṣmī and Sarasvatī in Art and Literature* (ed. D.C. Sircar), Calcutta, 1970, p. 152-57.

127. *DHI*, p. 370.
128. Cf. *Mahābhārata* II.10, 19; III.168, 3; etc.
129. *DHI*, pp. 133 ff.; Sircar (1970), *op. cit.*, pp. 112-31.
130. Cf.*Padmasthā padmahastā cha gajotkshiptaghaṭaplutā* /
     Śrīḥ padmamālinī chaiva Kālikākṛitireva cha //
131. Devendra Handa, "Some More Sealings From Haryana," *PURBA*, Vol. XXIII, no. 1 (April 1992), p. 112, pl. I.b.
132. *BMC*, p. 283, pl. XLV.24.
133. Lion is shown as the vehicle of Lakshmī on Gupta coins also (*JNSI*, XXVI, 1964, pp. 103-04).
134. Devendra Handa, *Jaina Bronze Hoard From Hansi*, Shimla-New Delhi, 2002, pp. 30-31, pls. 45-48.
135. Devendra Handa, "A Gupta Terracotta of Gaṅgā From Haryana," *Journal of the Ganganatha Jha Kendriya Sanskrit Vidyapeetha*, Allahabad, Vol. XL (1984), pp. 165-68 and pl.
136. Devendra Handa, "Late Gupta Sculptures and Epigraphs from Kapāla-Mochana," *Purāvṛitta*, Lucknow, no. I (2000-2001), p. 99, fig. 6.

Chapter 7

Sūrya

Sūrya, the brightest amongst the visible celestial luminous bodies and the 'one who animates or arouses (the world)' has been worshipped by mankind since time immemorial in an aniconic form initially and iconic form later on.[1] The world over there seems to have existed the tendency to deify natural phenomena. Described in the *Ṛigveda* (I.164, 46) as 'the beautiful-winged celestial bird Garutmān,' 'a little white brilliant steed brought by Ushas' (*ṚV* VII.73, 3) and 'moving on a car driven by one, several or seven fleet and ruddy steeds' (*ṚV* I.115, 3-4; VII.60, 3; 63, 2), etc., he is shown later as riding on a one-wheeled (*eka-chakra*) chariot drawn by four, five or seven horses with Aruṇa, a brother of Garutmān, as his charioteer, attended on either side by arrow-shooting Ushā and Pratyushā personifying the different aspects of 'dawn' and signifying the driving away of darkness. Lotus, symbolic of the presence of sun in which it blossoms, became his attribute in both the hands to show ubiquity. Lotus also symbolizes the beauty of creation,[2] which can only be realized in the light provided by sun. His name Aryaman, Vivasvān and Mitra have their foreign parallels.[3] In the early centuries of the current era, the import of the Maga (Bhojaka)[4] priests from Iran gave a new turn to Sun worship in India. Scythian impact brought for Sūrya long boots, *avyaṅga*,[5] acolytes wearing typical northern dress (*udīchya-veśa*), and sometimes a dagger also, thus causing a reorientation in the creation of his images, in north India in particular, and the Paurāṇic mythology played its part in providing him wives and sons, which too are sometimes shown on his images. Described as 'the soul of the movable and the immovable things' in the *Ṛigveda* (I.115, 1), Sūrya did not take much time to become 'the lord of the gods' (*deveśvara* – *Mbh.* II.50, 16). The lord of light became the embodiment of the Hindu trinity in the Gupta period and various cults vied with each other in identifying their Supreme deities with Sūrya. 'Supreme Godhead' of Sūrya became established[6] and Sun worship spread far and wide, in every direction, like his rays.

Literary evidence furnishes evidence of the continuity of the worship of the Sun throughout from the period of the *Ṛigveda* onwards. The ubiquity of the sun symbol on the coins of the punch-marked series (except the latest examples), the coins issued by rulers with their names ending in Mitra found from various parts of the country, and Kushāṇa coins with the figure of Miiro (Mihira = Sun), Helios, etc. shows that Sun-worship has remained popular throughout the early centuries before and after the current era.[7] A terracotta sealing bearing the Brāhmī legend '*Bhadramitra*' in the characters of 2nd century B.C.E. is known from Khokhrakot, Rohtak. Amin near Kurukshetra, traditionally connected with Aditi and Abhimanyu, still has a Sūrya-kuṇḍa. A clay sealing of *circa* 3rd century C.E. excavated from

Agroha (Trench XC-7, Qd. II, layer 2) shows the sun symbol in its upper half. The names of Ādityavardhana, Prabhākaravardhana, etc. indicate the respect which this luminous deity commanded during the reign of the Pushpabhūti rulers.

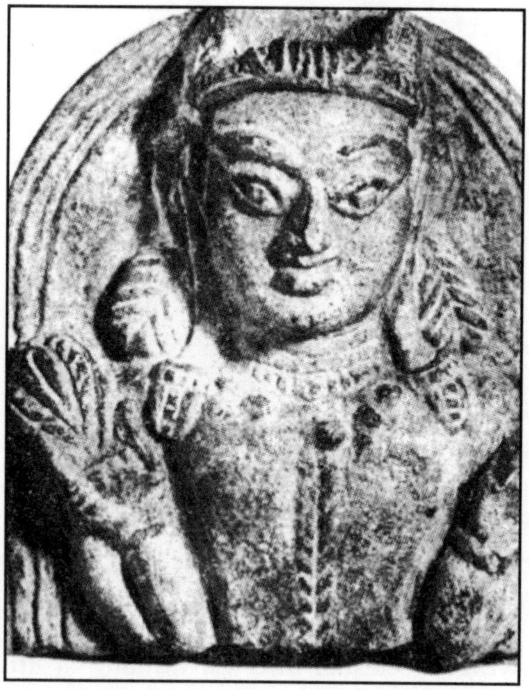

Fig. 11. Sūrya from Naurangabad.

It was in 1886 that a terracottas figure of Sun in perfect preservation was discovered from Sonepat.[8] Nothing, however, is known about its date and disposal now. A terracotta figurine of Sūrya from Naurangabad-Bamla, now preserved in the Jhajjar Gurukula (Fig. 11), was published by R.C. Agrawala in the late sixties.[9] It shows the bust of Sūrya wearing Sassanian buttoned dress holding two lotus flowers in his two hands. The terracotta belongs to the Kushāṇa-Gupta transitional phase. Surprisingly and interestingly, no image of the Sun god belonging to the Gupta period has been found from Haryana as yet. A very much worn out square relief from Kapālamochana (Pl. 244) in such an indifferent state of preservation rendering its identification as mere guess has been regarded as 'Sapta-Mātṛikās' by Manmohan Kumar and dated to *circa* 10th-11th century.[10] We, however, feel that it represents Sūrya holding lotuses in his two hands and sitting in the *utkuṭikāsana* on a chariot drawn by four or five horses as in the Kushāṇa figures. Like many other reliefs found from Kapālamochana, it may belong to the late Gupta or early medieval period.

Prāchī Śiva Temple at Pehowa has yielded a red sandstone fragmentary relief measuring 34 x 32 cm showing the feet of Sūrya wearing high boots and the typical long *cholaka* with sharp edges in the center. Sūrya is accompanied by Piṅgala on his proper right and Daṇḍa on his left. The latter has churbish looks. Piṅgala is badly mutilated. Both stand slightly turned towards their master, resting their outer hands on their respective thighs. The others probably held their respective attributes. The feet of Sūrya in *sama* pose indicate that the figure was contraposto. A scarf, which may have been held by him in simulation of *vanamālā*, can be seen partially over the feet. On stylistic grounds the figure may be attributed to the late Gupta period. At least three more images of Pratihāra period are known from Pehowa. Two of them, one seated and the other standing, are very small in size and are fixed in a wall near Bhairava temple. The former is depicted in a pedimented niche and shows the god seated alone. The standing Sūrya has Āśvins and two spouses as the subsidiary figures. One very elegant image was in a private collection,[11] subsequently probably handed over to the state department.

A small buff sandstone 19 x 12 cm figure of Sūrya with the god bearing moustaches and standing wearing usual dress and ornaments holding lotuses in his two hands accompanied by Daṇḍa and Piṅgala obtained from Jind has been assigned to *circa* 7th-8th century C.E. on stylistic grounds.[12] The upper part of an image of Sūrya broken below the waist belonging to the same period is fixed in the wall of the Śītalā Mātā Temple at Rohtak. The god, wearing a flat cylindrical crown, floral ear ornaments, *avyaṅga*, and girdle to keep the nether garment in position holds full-blown lotus flowers in his two hands. The upper ends of the scarf may also be seen on his arms. There is a halo behind the head and very crude and small garland-bearing *vidyādharas* are shown on either side of the head. The back slab below them is plain. The image is badly painted with oil and vermilion.

A very crude unfinished 8th century figure (Acc. No. 1/454) standing in contraposto with lotuses in two hands and wearing a small flat crown, long garland, and stone-blocks left uncarved for the attendants comes from Jadthal and provides evidence of the site to have been a center of art in the early medieval period. Another small grey sandstone crude figure (20 x 13.5 cm) of Sūrya from the same site, thickly coated with oil and dust, is preserved in HARDAM (Acc. No. 06/83).

A small 23 x 13 cm image of 8th century is preserved in the Gaur Sabhā Śiva Mandira at Karnal. The god stands in contraposto with lotuses in his two hands and wears a crown, ear ornaments, bracelets, *dhotī*, sash, boots, scarf like the *vanamālā*, etc. *Avyaṅga* is not very clear, may be because the image has been whitewashed. Daṇḍa and Piṅgala are shown standing on his left and right. A small 22.5 x 14 cm portable early medieval plaque from Dhurand Khera (Acc. No. 1/126) shows Sūrya standing to front holding lotuses in his two hands and wearing usual ornaments including *avyaṅga*, a *vanamālā*-like scarf, boots, etc. (Pl. 245). Instead of the crown, however, he bears matted hair on his head. A halo with lotus petals is carved behind the head. Flanking the deity are two diminutive attendants, which are difficult to be recognized properly for their summary treatment.

The most beautifully executed portable sandstone image measuring 21.5 x 14 cm comes from Gujjar Kheri. It was smuggled but was retrieved with the help of the police and is now preserved in HARDAM (Acc. No. 1/571). The rectangular frieze (Pl. 246) shows the main figure of Sūrya standing on a lotus *pīṭha* placed on the central offset of the *pañcharatha* pedestal in *udīchyaveśa* – wearing *kirīṭa-mukuṭa*, *karṇa-kuṇḍalas*, pearl necklet, sacred·thread, *avyaṅga*, coat of mail, nether garland secured by a girdle with pendent bead strings falling vertically on the thighs, a sash going around the thighs, wristlets, a scarf simulating a long garland held on the two forearms, long boots with Mahāśvetā standing between the feet, and holding lotus flowers by their long stalks in the two hands. Behind the head is a round eight-petalled glorìole with garland-bearing *vidyādharas* on the top corners. At the waist level are shown Ushā and Pratyushā while Daṇḍa, and Piṅgala followed by Chhāyā and Suvarchā occupy the receding recesses near the left and right feet of the god. Stylistically it belongs to *circa* 9th century C.E.

An almost similar piece datable to the same period carved in rough *kankar* (lime) stone comes from Khokhrakot but the rectangular slab on which it is carved is bigger and measures 52 x 30 cm. There is, however, no halo behind the head, the back slab is plain except the figures of bearded Brahmā and Vishṇu near the top corners, Piṅgala near the right foot of the god is bearded, Chhāyā and Suvarchā are substituted by horse-headed Aśvins, the diminutive figure at the feet of Sūrya being half seems to be that of Aruṇa, and the god bears a lozenge-shaped *śrīvatsa* on the chest (Pl. 247). The figure is not in a very good state of preservation and has suffered some mutilation here and there.

A buff sandstone torso found from Thanesar, measuring 59 cm in height in its extant form, belonging almost to the same period, is now preserved in the Kurukshetra University museum. The original image must have been a colossal one. The extant piece shows that the god stood in *samabhaṅga* wearing a *dhotī* tied with a girdle having festoon hanging downwards. There are traces of the chest-plate, scarf below the thighs.[13] The broken image of Revanta in the same stone and belonging to the same date found from Thanesar corroborates the existence of a Sun temple at Thanesar. This place has also yielded an image of headless Sūrya of *circa* 10th-11th century C.E. showing the two-armed god as holding a water-pot in the left hand and a rosary in the right seated on a chariot in profile driven by Aruṇa who sits on his front holding the reigns of the seven horses (Pl. 248). The extra arms projecting from the shoulders are missing. The extant piece measures 31 x 30 cm.[14] On the basis of the *Viśvakarmā-śāstra,* S.B. Singh has identified the image as that of Āditya-Sūrya.[15]

A small 15 x 8 cm sandstone architectural piece from Sirsa datable to the same period shows four-armed figure of Sūrya seated in *dhyāna-mudrā* in a pillared niche holding lotus flowers by their stalks in the extra hands. The god wears a crown, *ekāvali, kaṅkaṇas,* etc. and is now housed in the Kurukshetra University museum.[16] The same museum possesses a 12th-century head from Pinjore wearing an elaborate and high *kirīṭa-mukuṭa* which has been identified as that of Sūrya[17] but may as well be that of Vishṇu. In the *baoli* in the main bazar at Pinjore may still be seen fixed in the wall a *śukanāsikā* with the bust of Sūrya, wearing a *kirīṭa-mukuṭa, karṇa-kuṇḍalas, hāra* and holding lotus buds in his two hands. There is a diamond-shaped *śrīvatsa* also on the chest and traces of *avyaṅga* also seem to be there. An architectural member is also fixed in the wall of this *baoli.* It shows the god wearing a very long *cholaka,* boots, *avyaṅga* and other usual ornaments, accompanied by Daṇḍa and Piṅgala, standing in a pilastered niche. The triple-folded scarf simulating the *vanamālā* is adorned with a small lotus flower. The head of the god is damaged. Both these pieces may have belonged to a temple of the god during the 11th-12th century C.E. The Chandigarh Museum also possesses an image of the god from Pinjore. It is 56 cm in height and shows the deity standing in the center flanked by Daṇḍa and Piṅgala, who, instead of their usual attributes, hold a staff and a lotus in their two hands. The hand with the lotus is towards the god in both the cases. The sun also holds the lotus flowers as usual and there is a crudely carved floriated halo behind the head. Iconographically interesting feature is that the god wears a long garland like the *vanamālā* of Vishṇu images. The *ekāvali* and the short crown are graceful but the figure has not been carved with much of the iconographic details as the boots are there but the *avyaṅga* is missing. On the face of the pedestal are shown seven prancing horses. The sculpture bears the crudity of execution. The upper registers of the stele have remained vacant and were intended presumably to be filled in with various other forms. Seemingly, therefore, the sculpture is an unfinished example. D.C. Bhattacharyya has dated it to *circa* 15th century[18] but we feel that it represents that phase when sculptures started to be made again during the rule of Akbar in the 16th century C.E. Chandigarh Museum has another similar image of Sūrya from Morni but the upper part of the sculpture is missing. Sūrya stands on a lotus placed on the *pañcharatha* pedestal wearing boots and *avyaṅga,* and is accompanied by Daṇḍa and Piṅgala followed by Chhāyā and Suvarchā. D.C. Bhattacharyya dates it to *circa* 13th century C.E.[19] Like all other images obtained from Morni it may also belong to *circa* 10th century C.E. The most graceful image of Sūrya in the Chandigarh Museum is, however, the piece from Agroha obtained as India's share from the Lahore Museum. This 56 cm high image (Acc. No. 41) depicts the god as standing to front on a *pañcharatha* pedestal with his acolytes Daṇḍa and Piṅgala and spouses Chhāyā and Suvarchā (Pl. 249). Both the hands of the god holding lotus flowers originally are broken from the elbows. The face is also mutilated. The god wears a *kirīṭa-mukuṭa*[20] bedecked with pearls and jewels, a pearl necklace, *avyaṅga, dhotī* secured by a waist-band having golden chain forming loops on the outer sides of the thighs and then falling vertically with the pendants touching the knees, long boots and a scarf simulating Vishṇu's *vanamālā.* The lotiform halo behind the head of the god has the outer frame as if emitting the radiance of the Sun god. Hovering on either side of his head are the celestial *Gandharva* couples mutilated considerably. The females are shown as seated on the legs of the male *Gandharvas* stretched backwards. The *Gandharva* male on the proper right hand side of the god is shown as holding a bow in both his hands. The corresponding figure on the other side too may have held some object but is not clear because of the mutilation the figure has suffered. Bhattacharyya[21] has wrongly identified these figures with Ushā and Pratyushā. He dates the image to *circa* 12th century C.E. but we feel that it should be revised to the 10th century.[22] Excavations at Agroha during 1979-85 have yielded a medieval fragment showing the legs of Sūrya wearing the long *cholaka*.

Beri has yielded two magnificent images of Sūrya. One measuring 60.5 x 35 cm (Acc. No. 1/231) shows the god standing to front in contraposto on a lotus *pīṭha* placed on *pañcharatha* pedestal (Pl. 250). He holds two lotuses, one each in the two hands. Sūrya wears *kirīṭa-mukuṭa* and usual ornaments, an *avyaṅga*, long boots, a typical lower garment with sharp flourishes and a scarf simulating Vishṇu's *vanamālā*. A diminutive standing figure of Mahāśvetā is carved between Sūrya's feet. Flanking the god are Daṇḍa and Piṅgala on the proper left and right followed by Rājñī and Nikshubhā and the horse-faced Aśvini-kumāras on the receding *rathas* of the pedestal. The juvenile Daṇḍī and bearded Kuṇḍī bear typical conical headdress (*udīchyaveśa*) and wear *ekāvalis, karṇa-kuṇḍalas, aṅgadas,* beaded *valayas,* lower garments secured by waistbands, etc. Both stand in asymmetrical *dvibhaṅga* postures turned towards their lord. Daṇḍī holds a staff in his right hand with left hand akimbo and Piṅgala holding the manuscript and stylus in his left and right hands. Dasra and Nāsatya, the Aśvini-kumāras, occupy the extremities and are each shown as standing cross-legged holding a water-pot in the left hand near the chest with right in the gesture of reassurance.

Behind the head of the god is the round eight-petalled halo. The steles on the two sides show on lotus seats in *lalitāsana* four-handed Vishṇu and Brahmā on the proper right and left respectively. Vishṇu is shown as wearing a crown and the usual ornaments with four hands disposed in *abhaya,* and holding mace, discus and conch in the *pradakshiṇā order*. Tri-cephalous bearded Brahmā holds a ladle in the back right hand and some ring-like round object in the left hand while the attributes of the proper hands are rosary and water-vessel. Ushā and Pratyushā shooting arrows fill the space between the steles and the subsidiary figures below.

The other image of Sūrya from Beri (Acc. No. 1/228) measures 55 x 31 cm and is almost exactly similar to the preceding example but does not show Ushā and Pratushā and *gaja-śārdūla* motifs occupy the middle portions of the extremities of the back slab (Pl. 251). Brahmā on the stele holds manuscript in his back left hand with normal right disposed in protection-giving posture. The top of the back slab is rounded and does not bear the ring with half diamonds around the halo as in the preceding example.

Both these images of Sūrya are the masterpieces of the Pratihāra art of Haryana remarkable for their minute care endowed even to the subsidiary figures and delicacy of carving. They may be dated to *circa* 10th century C.E.[23]

Badali has also yielded three representations of Sūrya, two of them on architectural members and one independent. One of the former shows the god seated in *utkaṭikāsana* in a niche, wearing a cylindrical crown adorned with a central jewel, circular earrings, thick rope-like necklace, coat of mail, bracelets, boots, nether garment tied with a *netra-sūtra,* and holding lotus flowers in his two hands. The second figure shows the god standing in a similar niche with usual dress and ornaments and supporting the attributes in his two hands. But the independent image, retrieved from a well, is a beautifully and elaborately carved one (Pl. 252). The god wears a very high cylindrical crown adorned with jewels, earrings, necklet and necklace, sacred-thread, *śrīvatsa,* finger-rings, nether garment secured by an elaborate girdle, boots, etc. and stands on a lotus-seat in *samapāda-sthānaka-mudrā,* holding the lotus flowers by their stalks in his two hands. The scarf as usual is carved like a long garland with its free upper ends supported on the arms. The god bears a vertical third eye on the forehead. His eyes are half-closed. All the limbs are sturdy and attractive. Mahāśvetā stands at his feet gracefully. Ushā and Pratyushā shooting arrows to dispel darkness are carved at the waist level. Daṇḍa and Piṅgala followed by horse-faced Āśvins serve as acolytes and four-armed bearded Brahmā and Vishṇu seated in *sukhāsana* with their usual attributes occupy the stele. *Gaja-śārdūla* figures adorn the extremities of the back slab, which is rounded at the top. A plain round gloriole is marked behind the head of the god. The whole relief including even the attendant figures are so delicately and carefully carved that one wonders as to why have the necklet and necklace, the sash and the scarf, the lotus flowers in the hands of the god and the halo behind his head not been treated so delicately and left as plain bands giving a drab look. Stylistically, however, the image, along with the small figures described above, may be dated to *circa* 12th century C.E. representing the Chauhan art at its acme.

Hansi seems to have been a stronghold of the sun cult during the medieval period as it has yielded quite a few images of the god. An image similar to the Badali example with round gloriole engraved with lotus petals but completely featureless rounded top of the back slab was procured from Hansi during 1984-85 and is now preserved in HARDAM (Acc. No. 1/496). But here Sūrya is shown with *avyaṅga* and Aśvini-kumāras are substituted by the spouses of Sun. The back slab does not show the *gaja-śārdūla* motifs and Mahāśvetā is depicted as sitting between the feet of the god (Pl. 250). The execution is quite rough. Another medieval Sūrya image of black stone (48 x 28 cm) is still under worship with Shri Ram Chandra Sharma of Dhanvantari Aushadhalaya, Barsi Gate, Hansi (HSR/HRN-12). The most remarkable, however, is the black stone image of Sūrya recovered from the mound and enshrined in the temple in the main bazar of Hansi (Pl. 254). It is now covered with clothes and modern jewelry and even painted. The god is accompanied by his acolytes Daṇḍa and Piṅgala, spouses Rājñī and Nikshubhā and sons the Āśvins. Mahāśvetā stands at the feet and arrow-shooting Ushā and Pratyushā have been carved at the waist level. Above them are the small unidentifiable male figures with Brahmā and Vishṇu occupying the top corners as usual. The top of the back slab has been rounded but it is not plain and carries the depiction of the *navagrahas* and Brahma-śāstā Sūrya as the *tilaka* (Pl. 255). The image shows some affinity of crown and other ornaments with the Kosli Vishṇu image (Pl. 64) described above in chapter 3. Some elongation marks the figure. It is masterpiece of the Chauhan art of the region.

A Sūrya image from Jind shows the deity standing in *samabhaṅga* on a lotus wearing a *kirīṭa-mukuṭa*, ear ornaments, necklet and necklace, *śrīvatsa*, *avyaṅga*, elaborate girdle to secure the lower garment, long boots and *vanamālā*-like scarf on the forearms. In his two hands he holds lotus flowers by their stalks and there is a lotiform halo behind the head. Brahmā and Vishṇu occupy the stele near his shoulders while Ushā and Pratyushā shooting arrows are depicted at the waist-level. Daṇḍa and Piṅgala followed by Chhāyā and Suvarchā are standing near the feet on the receding recesses of the pedestal. Aruṇa sits at the feet depicted as usual in only the upper half part of the body. Stylistically, it may be dated to *circa* 12th century C.E.[24]

Medieval fragments of the images of the Sun god have been found from various places. HARDAM possesses a buff sandstone image (40 x 25 cm) obtained from the office of the Registering Officer, Hisar (HRN/HSR-40). A 38 x 17 cm fragmentary piece of *circa* 9th-10th century C.E. showing Daṇḍa and Piṅgala is known from Kohand.[25] The bust with a plain round halo showing lotus flowers in the two hands and feet with boots and *cholaka* showing a part of Piṅgala holding a stylus in his right hand, probably belonging to some 10th century image, are known from village Majra near Asthal Bohr, Rohtak. A fragment of the pedestal of a Sun image showing Piṅgala, Rājñī and Aśvini-kumāra from Rohtak are in a private collection

(Regn. No. HRN/ROH-481). Another very badly mutilated piece with these three figures of the pedestal is housed in the temple of village Chinat near Hansi. A third such piece from Asandh is preserved in HARDAM (Acc. No. 1/448). A fragment depicting a garland-bearing *vidyādhara* with a big lotus below from Hat is the proper left hand side piece of a 10th century image of Sūrya. An almost coeval architectural piece showing Sūrya seated in a pedimented *rathikā* with a *makara-mukha* on the outer side is preserved in the Jhajjar Gurukula.

We thus see that images of Sūrya from Haryana start from the Kushāṇa-Gupta period and continue to the medieval period. All images show the god with two hands holding the lotus flowers. The scarf of the god is generally shown like the *vanamālā* of Vishṇu. The god is depicted invariably in the *udīchya-veśa*, northern dress, wearing coat of mail, sometimes a long *cholaka* also, and long boots. In the main standing images of Sūrya Mahāśvetā or the Earth goddess is generally depicted as standing between his feet. The god is normally accompanied by Daṇḍa and Piṅgala and also with Aśvinīkumāras or with his spouses in addition in certain cases. Ushā and Pratyushā shooting arrows are shown on the sides in the developed images of the medieval period. The steles show Brahmā and Vishṇu or the flying celestials. *Sama-pāda-sthānaka-mudrā* and *utkuṭikāsana* are the usual postures for the standing and seated images. Depiction of the god in a *śuka-nāsikā* is an interesting feature. Sūrya seated with folded legs on a chariot drawn by seven horses and holding a rosary in the right and water pot in the left hand from Thanesar identified with Āditya by S.B. Singh as referred to above, is of unusual interest. Agroha, Asandh, Badali, Beri, Chinat, Dhurand Khera, Gujjar Kheri, Jadthal, Jind, Hansi, Hat, Kapālamochana, Karnal, Kohand, Kurukshetra, Majra, Morni, Pehowa, Pinjore, Rohtak, Sirsa and Sonepat were the important centres of sun worship in Haryana.

Notes and References

1. Lalta Prasad Pandey, *Sun-Worship in Ancient India*, Delhi-Patna-Varanasi, 1971, pp. 1 ff.; V.C. Srivastava, *Sun-Worship in Ancient India*, Delhi, 1971, pp. 122-26.
2. Chamanlal Gautam, *Devavāda kā Vaijñānika Svarūpa* (Hindi), I, Vishṇu-Rahasya, Bareilly, 1967, pp. 375-404.
3. Surya Kanta, *Vaidika Devaśāstra* (Hindi), Delhi, 1961, pp. 98-103.
4. Acccording to the *Bhavishya Purāṇa* (ch. 134), the Magas were brought from Śākadvīpa (Iran) to serve as the priests of a Sun temple erected on the bank of the river Chandrabhāgā by Sāmba, son of Kṛishṇa from Jāmbavatī.
5. It is the Indianized form of *Aiwiyaonghen*, the sacred waist-girdle of the Iranians. See *DHI*, p. 437.
6. H. Goetz, "Sūrya as the Supreme Godhead," in *Professor P.K. Gode Commemoration Volume*, Poona, 1960, pp. 113 ff and Fig.
7. For details see Shanti Lal Nagar, *Sūrya and Sun Cult*, New Delhi, 1995.
8. *Gazetteer of Delhi District*, 1883-84, p. 209.
9. *Ājakala* (Hindi), Nov. 1968.
10. Manmohan Kumar, *Archaeology of Ambala and Kurukshetra Districts (Haryana)*, Unpublished Ph. D. Thesis, Kurukshetra University, Kurukshetra, 1976, p.157, pl. XIV.C.
11. Devendra Handa, *Pehowa*, pp. 111-12, pls. 55-57.
12. Amar Singh, *op. cit.*, pp. 199-200, pl. XXVII.C.
13. Shukla (1983), *op. cit.*, p. 42, pl. XXXIV.3. Dr. Shukla thinks that the image was originally four-handed but it is difficult to accept it as all the medieval images of Sūrya from Haryana are only

two-handed.
14. *Ibid.*, p. 48, pl. XL.2.
15. S.B. Singh, "Āditya-Sūrya and his Rare Image," *JHS*, Vol. XIX (1981), pp. 220-25 and Plates.
16. Shukla (1983), *op. cit.*, pp. 53-54, pl. XLVIII.2.
17. *Ibid.*, p. 17, pl. VIII.2.
18. D.C. Bhattacharyya (1981), *op. cit.*, p. 84, Acc. no. 121 (i).
19. *Ibid.*, pp. 84-85, no accession number.
20. Bhattacharyya (*Ibid.*, p. 83, fig. 40) wrongly identifies it as *karaṇḍa-mukuṭa.*
21. *Ibid.*
22. Brajesh Krishna (*op. cit.*, p. 157) also places it in early 10th century.
23. Devendra Handa, "Sculptures from Beri," *Roopa-Lekha*, Vol. LIII (March 1982), pp. 36-46.
24. Sat Dev, *op. cit.*, pp. 80-81, pl. XV.A.
25. Amar Singh, *op. cit.*, p. 200, pl. XXVII.D.

Chapter 8

Syncretistic Images

The Vedic concept of *'sa esha eka eva vṛideka eva'* (He is One and the only One God)[1] and *'Ekaṃ sad viprā bahudhā vadanti'* (The wise call that One by various names),[2] etc.[3] reflect the way of thinking of the Hindus who, though divided later in a good number of sects, each having its own set of religious beliefs and observances, did not feel any religious acrimony amongst them and have emphasized through the ages the sentiment of the one eternally existing principle in different ways.[4] The Upanishads,[5] the *Bhagavadgītā*[6] and the Purāṇas[7] show the persistence of this sentiment and the influence it exercised on the people.

Though blatant examples of morbid sectarianism are not rare in the field of plastic art, particularly during the medieval period, yet attempts of reconciliation and rapprochement between rival sects and creeds outnumber the former. The Purāṇas, wherein we find the development, growth and expansion of Hindu mythology, show a general tenor and tendency of broad toleration between the various sects of Hinduism.[8] The process of synthesism seems to have been at work from a fairly early date and the mental attitude of the early foreign immigrants like the Śakas, the Pahlavas and the Kushāṇas may also have been an important contributory factor to the growth of cult-syncretism.[9] The Kushāṇa example of Harihara[10] and Ardhanārīśvara[11] indicate that Vaishṇavism, Śaivism and Śāktism were the great cults of that period. The Hindu concept of Trinity and the Smṛiti injunctions strengthened the concept of unity and the process of synthesis culminated in the *pañchopāsanā* that is well-represented in Pañchāyatana worship of the *smārtas* and by the *pañchāyatana* 'quincunx' temples, *Chaturmukha* Śiva-*liṅgas* depicting Gaṇapati, Vishṇu, Pārvatī and Sūrya on the four sides of the central Śaiva emblem and the Hariharahiraṇyagarbha (Sūrya-Hari-Hara-Pitāmaha) images during the early medieval period, combining almost all the prominent contemporary cults. Sometimes even the Buddhist and Jaina influence is also discernible on Hindu composite icons. The syncretistic tendency seems to have been fairly popular during the medieval period and is interestingly illustrated by a large number of images of that period.[12]

HARIHARA

The earliest literary reference to the composite form of Vishṇu and Śiva occurs in the *Mahābhārata*[13] wherein we find Arjuna addressing a hymn to Hari-Rudra after the completion of his penance. The *Vishṇu Purāṇa* also refers to the identity of Śiva and Vishṇu (*Śaṅkaro bhagavāñchhauriḥ).*[14] Elsewhere in the same text, Kṛishṇa, an incarnation or form of Hari (Vishṇu), talks of his identity with Śaṅkara.[15]

The composite image of Vishṇu and Śiva has been called variously as Harihara, Haryardha, Śiva-Nārāyaṇa, Śaṅkara-Nārāyaṇa, etc. in the epigraphs and iconographical texts. The *Matsya Purāṇa* prescribes that the left side of the image of Śiva-Nārāyaṇa should be occupied by *Mādhava* (Kṛishṇa = Vishṇu) and the right side by Śiva. Both the (left) arms of Kṛishṇa should be adorned with bejeweled bracelets and should hold conch shell and discus or mace. Kṛishṇa should have a calm expression; yellow garment and a bejeweled foot, (the right half representing Śiva) should wear necklets, sacred thread, and the serpents and show the right arm in *varada-mudrā*. He should wear the lower garment of skin and have the foot adorned with jewels and serpents.[16]

The *Vishṇudharmottara Purāṇa* also suggests the right half to belong to Śiva and the other half to Hṛishīkeśa but prescribes *vara*, trident, *chakra* and lotus in the four hands with bull (Nandī) on the right side and Garuḍa on the left.[17] The *Devatāmūrtiprakaraṇa* repeats this description[18] as also of Śiva-Nārāyaṇa as found in the *Matsya Purāṇa* detailed above.[19] It also describes the image of Kṛishṇa-Śaṅkara which differs only in having a rosary instead of *varada-mudrā* in one of the hands of Śiva.[20]

The *Suprabhedāgama* says that Vishṇu should be shown with a *kirīṭa-mukuṭa* and Śaṅkara with matted locks.[21] The *Śilparatna*[22] and the *Pūrvakāraṇāgama*[23] not only prescribe similar treatment of the head but also mention crescent on Śiva's locks.

Though both Vaishṇavism[24] and Śaivism[25] were the prominent and popular cults in Haryana from quite early times yet no image of Harihara belonging to the Kushāṇa or Gupta periods has been found from the region so far. It is not surprising that like many other parts of India syncretistic tendency gained ascendancy here from the early medieval period. We describe below the Harihara images known from Haryana so far.

Pinjaur is a well-known archaeological site situated about 25 km east of Chandigarh on road to Shimla.[26] It has yielded a large number of sculptural and architectural remains.[27] About a quarter century back, the walls of the Kabir Chaurā Temple were studded with sculptures placed indiscriminately. Most of these pieces were later removed to the Kurukshetra University but some interesting examples are not traceable anywhere now. Amongst these is a head of Harihara (Pl. 256).[28] Broken below the neck this head had an elongate crown with flat top and was adorned with pearl festoons. The proper right hand side half, however, showed the matted locks as prescribed in the iconographic texts. An interesting feature of this *jaṭā-mukuṭa* was that it showed a human skull tucked up in it on the right side. The face had a smooth rounded appearance with slightly protruding lips and betrayed an expression of quietude. The long eyes arched by eyebrows were quasi-closed. The third eye was drawn vertically on the forehead. The image, when complete, must have been a beautiful piece of art. Stylistically the piece may be dated to *circa* 9th century C.E.

Another fragmentary head of Harihara has been recovered from Pehowa, an ancient holy place, located at a distance of about 25 km west of Kurukshetra on the bank of the sacred Sarasvatī river. Unfortunately, the Harihara head under discussion is mutilated below the tip of the nose. The long eyes with drooping eyelids and arched eyebrows, ears with long lobes, backward combed hair and the exquisite decorations of the coiffure, however, acquaint us with the care with which the artist carved this figure. The division of the coiffure, the right hand side showing matted locks with a crescent and the left hand side showing an exquisite bejeweled cylindrical crown, however, leave little doubt to the head being that of Harihara. This head, too, may be dated to the Pratihāra period on stylistic grounds.[29]

A 9th century Harihara head of buff stone from Thanesar was brought to light by Dr. S.P. Shukla in 1983.[30] Quite similar to the preceding example from Pehowa but comparatively cruder in workmanship, it shows a *kīrttimukha* adorning the crown in front.

About a decade back, D.S. Punia published a Harihara image from Punahna, now preserved in the Siddheśvara Temple at Gurgaon.[31] The sandstone relief measuring 81 x 70 cm shows the four-armed deity standing in *sama-bhaṅga*, the proper right hand being Śiva and the other half Vishṇu (Pl. 257). The hair-coiffure is divided into *jaṭā-mukuṭa* and *kirīṭa-mukuṭa* and the long garland also shows round beads (*kapālas*) on Śiva's side and *bakula* flowers on Vishṇu's side. The god also wears a beaded necklet with a lozenge (*Śrīvatsa*) shaped pendent, *ananta keyūras, valayas*, a beaded sacred thread,[32] a lower garment secured by a waist-band consisting of a golden chain forming loops on the thighs with free ends suspended in front and touching the knees. There is a beaded-bordered halo behind the head of the god. The normal hand on Śiva's side is suspended in *varada* pose while the rear right holds a trident. Vishṇu's upper hand supports the discus but the suspended front hand is mutilated. In all probability, it held an *ūrdhva-śaṅkha*. Near the right foot of the god may be seen retrorse Nandī bull looking up towards his lord while the extreme right shows a corpulent *gaṇa* holding a long shaft of some weapon. He may be the Triśūla-purusha. On Vishṇu's left are shown two figures, probably an *āyudha-purusha* or Garuḍa in anthropomorphic form, and Śrīdevī holding a lotus flower by its stalk.[33] On the top corners on both the sides are shown the garland-bearing *vidyādharas* in flying postures while the intermediary space on the extreme slabs is filled by *vyāla* figures. Stylistically, the image may be dated to *circa* 9th century C.E.

A small portable image measuring 17.5 x 12 cm was obtained from Gujjar Kheri and is now preserved in a private collection.[34] It is an unfinished piece still showing chisel marks on the back slab. As prescribed in the iconographical texts, we find the right half of the image representing Śiva and the left half Vishṇu. The god stands enfacing on the central off-set of the *pañcha-ratha* pedestal wearing circular discs in the ears, *graiveyaka*, *yajñopavīta*, armlets, bracelets, lower garment held in position by a waist-band and the long garland which comes down lower than the knees from over the arms and back of the god (Pl. 258). The coiffure is the combination of *jaṭā* and *kirīta-mukuṭa*. The normal right hand is broken and the rear right holds a trident with a long shaft vertically. A conch and a disc are held in the suspended proper left and uplifted back left hands. Near the right foot of the god is shown the front half of Nandī bull in profile with face turned to look at his master whereas on the corresponding other side is depicted Garuḍa having human torso and avian lower half. A very crudely carved figure, perhaps Śrī, may be seen on the extreme projection of the pedestal, standing next to Garuḍa.

This unfinished icon furnishes the evidence that images were carved at Gujjar Kheri itself. It may have belonged to the 9th century C.E.

Chandimandir (near Chandigarh) has also yielded, amongst others, a Harihara image, broken into parts,[35] similar in conception to the one described above, but giving better details (Pl. 259). The normal right hand is suspended in *varada* pose and has a rosary, the back hand holds the *triśūla* by its long shaft, the upper left may have held a discus and the suspended front left the conch-shell. All the hands and their attributes have suffered mutilation but the details may still be discerned. The round gloriole behind the head shows lotus petals. Triśūla-purusha and the forepart of bull may be seen on the receding projections on Śiva's side while the corresponding *rathas* on the other side show Chakra-purusha and anthropomorphic Garuḍa. The middle portions of the extreme projections are adorned with *śārdūla-vyālas* while the top corners bear as usual the garland-bearing *vidyādharas*. This figure, too, may be assigned to 9th century C.E. on stylistic grounds. Another similar figure from Pinjaur is preserved in HARDAM.[36]

A buff sandstone image of Harihara, 65 x 39 cm in size, is enshrined in the Mansa Temple in village Bass in district Bhiwani. The four-handed deity is shown as holding lotus and trident in the normal and rear right hands while the corresponding hands on the other side support conch and discus. As usual the right side shows matted locks and the left the *kirīṭa*. The accessory figures on the right hand side represent probably Bhṛiṅgī and Kāla and the left side is occupied by Chakrapurusha and Garuḍa. Brahmā and Sūrya occupy the stele on the right and left sides respectively and in the center are the adoring figures. Stylistically, the image may be dated to *circa* 10th century C.E.

The most beautiful Harihara image from Haryana, however, comes from Beri, about 30 km south of Rohtak.[37] Conforming to the canonical injunctions, this 55 x 37 cm relief shows the deity standing on a lotus *pīṭha* placed on a *pañcha-ratha* pedestal in *samapāda* pose (Pl. 260). There is a beautiful lotus-petalled halo behind the head. Matted locks are shown on the right side of the *kirīṭa-mukuṭa* and the third eye is carved on the forehead. The god wears *karṇa-kuṇḍalas, graiveyaka, yajñopavīta, aṅgada,* beaded *valayas,* finger rings, *adhovastra* secured by girdle, *nūpuras,* etc. A *vanamālā* also adorns the figure. The front and back right hands belonging to Śiva are shown as holding a lotus and a trident spiraled by a snake while the corresponding left hands support a conch and discus. Nandī, the bull, is shown on the proper right hand side as turning its neck upwards to gaze at his lord while on the other side is depicted semi-anthropomorphic Garuḍa with folded hands, having human body with wings at the back and the lower half avian portion. Garuḍa wears earrings, pearl necklets, armlets, wristlets, etc. Nandī and Garuḍa are followed by female figures each holding lotus flower in one and the flourish of the undergarment in the other hand. The extreme figure on the proper right seems to be that of a sage or acolyte of Śiva with matted locks and usual ornaments. The corresponding figure on the other side depicts probably Padma-purusha who holds lotus in the right hand near the chest and rests the other on the left thigh. The extreme figures on either side are surmounted respectively by *gaja-śārdūla* and *makara-mukhas* supporting the stele depicting Brahmā and Sūrya and unidentified male figures behind on the extremities. Brahmā is tri-cephalous, pot-bellied, wearing a belt-like sacred thread, seated in *lalitāsana* on the lotus seat, with proper right hand in *abhaya,* others holding *sruk,* book and water-pot. Sūrya on the other side holds lotuses in his two hands.

Stylistically, this image may be dated to *circa* 11th century C.E. In spite of profuse ornamentation, squatishness, rigidity and crowded composition this relief is a good specimen of the medieval art of Haryana.[38]

From Panipat comes the last of our relief in black stone (Pl. 261) giving a steel-like look.[39] In contrast to the preceding example, it shows elongation of figures. The concept, however, remains the same. Harihara is flanked by Triśūla-purusha and Chakra-purusha and a female figure holding a lotus by its long stalk. Nandī, the bull, is depicted in profile in front of Triśūla-purusha, and anthropomorphic Garuḍa, also in profile, in the *vīrāsana,* in front of Chakra-purusha. The top corners are occupied by Brahmā and Sūrya and the middle portions show sages or devotees in profile. There was originally an inscription on the central projection of the *pañcha-ratha* pedestal but it has chipped off leaving only traces of a few letters. The image is still under worship in a temple near the Devī Tālāb at Panipat. Being complete and well preserved, this image, datable to *circa* 12th century C.E. provides another good specimen of the medieval art of Haryana.

We thus see that Harihara was popularly worshipped in Haryana from *circa* ninth to 12th century C.E. and the state has yielded iconographically interesting and aesthetically beautiful images of the composite deity.

ARDHANĀRĪŚVARA

According to the *Śiva Purāṇa*,[40] Brahmā, the Hindu god of creation, begot a number of Prajāpatis and exhorted them to proceed with the creation of other beings. Brahmā felt discomforted at the slow progress and prayed to Śiva for succor. The latter appeared before him in the composite male-female form of which the former prayed for the female half to proceed with the task of creation. The request having been granted the work of creation continued satisfactorily. But this story does not represent the tendency of religious rapprochement and synthesis which may have truly been the causative factor for the Ardhanārīśvara images. Another story related by Rao, however, suggests the presence of the syncretistic tendency. Once, when the gods and sages circumambulated Śiva and Pārvatī at Kailāśa, the *Ṛishi* Bhṛiṅgī went round only the former for being Śiva's exclusive worshipper, Pārvatī grew angry at his insolence and reduced him to a skin-covered skeleton. Bhṛiṅgī, unable to stand erect on his two skinny legs, was provided with a third leg by Śiva who took pity on him. In order to save Pārvatī's honor, however, Śiva united his body with hers in order that Bhṛiṅgī would be compelled to pay homage to the goddess while worshipping him. Thus came into being the Ardhanārīśvara form.[41] While describing the Ardhanārīśvara (Gaurīśvara) images, the *Vishṇudharmottara Purāṇa*[42] states that it is the representation of Purusha and Prakṛiti (the male and female principles) in unison. We know that in Indian philosophy Purusha stands for, besides other things, the Supreme God and Prakṛiti represents the primeval energy, Śakti. It is this synthesis of the primeval parents of the universe, Śiva and Śakti, that has been delineated in the Ardhanārīśvara images, during the Kushāṇa period for the first time perhaps.[43] The *Bṛihatsaṃhitā*[44] prescribes that Śiva should be represented as having Pārvatī for his left half in the Ardhanārīśvara images. To this, the *Vishṇudharmottara*,[45] the *Matsya Purāṇa*,[46] and the Āgamas[47] add some further details.

Ardhanārīśvara images are very rare in Haryana. One figure which once stood studded in the wall of the Kabir Chaurā at Pinjore (Pl. 262),[48] but is not traceable now, shows Ardhanārīśvara standing on a double-petalled pedestal. The proper left hand side of the image represents Pārvatī with a *dhammilla* hair coiffure, *graiveyaka*, *uttarīya*, and *adhovastra* and the right half represents Śiva with matted hair and wearing what looks like a tiger skin. A long garland also adorns the body of the deity. The round lotus-petalled gloriole existed at the back. The backhand of Śiva holds a trident and the front one is broken. It probably held a *nīlotpala* near the chest. Both the left hands (of Pārvatī) are broken but it can be surmised that one of them probably held a mirror. The breast on Pārvatī's side and penis erect representative of the *ūrdhva-meḍhra* (ithyphallic) aspect of Śiva are interesting. The main figure is flanked by a beautiful female attendant (with head broken) in *tribhaṅga* pose on the proper left and a corpulent *gaṇa* figure on the right side near the feet. Stylistically, the image may be dated to *circa* 10th century C.E.

A buff sandstone image of Ardhanārīśvara measuring 98 x 72 cm in the main niche of the eastern wall of the Lakshmī-Nārāyaṇa Temple at Palwal shows the deity standing on the central offset of the *sapta-ratha* pedestal in *samabhaṅga* with a clear demarcation of matted hair and *dhammilla* coiffure, ear ornaments and single breast on the proper left, i.e. female side (Pl. 263). There is a round nimbus behind the head with six lotus petals. The necklet and the necklace, armlets, bracelets, the girdle with elaborate sash and pendent strings falling on the thighs, and the long garland worn by the syncretistic figure do not show any difference on the two sides nor is there any accentuation of the hip or sturdiness of the shoulder visible on any side. The rear right hand supports the trident and the left holds the mirror. The normal hands are broken but they were *pralamba* (suspended). The offsets on the proper right near the feet show the bull looking upwards towards his master, Kārttikeya and Gaṇeśa respectively while on the corresponding left are depicted a deer gazing upwards, a broken figure, and a Mātṛikā respectively. Just behind these small figures stand Triśūla-purusha with a trident in his left hand, Mahākāla with a *khaṭvāṅga* in the left hand, a female figure on the right hand side and a female holding a garland on the left with the following two figures broken. Flanking the main deity near the head are the niched figures of Brahmā and Vishṇu. The extreme slabs on the last projections show *vyāla* figures, *makara-mukhas*, and female figures. This thus is a very crowded composition. Due care, however, seems to have been bestowed even to the subsidiary figures and minutiae. Stylistically, the image may be dated to *circa* 12th century C.E.

We may also refer here to a small 31 cm high mottled red sandstone figure of Ardhanārīśvara standing against what appears to be a *liṅga*, obtained from Agroha and now preserved in the Gurukula Museum, Jhajjar (Pl. 151).[49] The hairstyle, earrings, single breast, and bisection of the erect phallus differentiate the two halves of the figure besides the subtle distinctions of mustache lightly incised on the left, the folds of flesh on the right side of the waist, and even in the contours of the shoulders and legs. The swag of drapery continuing in the line of the phallus accentuates the curve of Pārvatī's hip. Śiva's hand raised to the level of the right shoulder, and the continuity of the sacred thread give a balancing effect to the composition, which is further enriched by the softly rounded form of the top of the back slab. Joanna Williams thinks that the smallness of size indicates it to have been meant for domestic worship, rather than in any shrine, and that it may have been imported from Mathura by some prosperous businessman.[50]

In the medieval period the image of Ardhanārīśvara in the north may also be considered as a visual paradigm of Kashmir Śaivite epistemology the quintessence of which is *Trika* or *Advaita* (monism, non-duality). Śiva and Pārvatī stand in perfect harmony. Pārvatī holds a mirror in her left hand. It is not meant for her own use and is not an expression of her vanity, but is held up for Śiva to see his own face in it. When he sees himself in the mirror he feels wonderstruck. His lustful cognition and romance turn into amazement. According to Kashmir Śaivism, knowledge progresses by celebration and affirmation, arising from a sense of wonder and by repeated cognitions, and ends in the subjective realization of wonder, as it is in that moment of wonder (*adbhuta*) that the world appears one and undivided. Repeated cognitions on the part of Śiva remove all traces of duality from Śiva's cognition of Pārvatī. This is the essence of Pratyabhijñā system (philosophy of recognition of self) – cognition through re-cognition. Parama Śiva, according to Kashmir Śaivism, is not merely a passive mass of light (*prakāśa*), but also energy (*vimarśa*). Prakāśavimarśamaya Parama Śiva contains the entire universe pulsating within it just as the seed of the mighty *nyagrodha* (banyan) potentially contains the entire tree. At the lowest level of reality, one sees in the image of Ardhanārīśvara, Śiva and Śakti, the *aham* and *idam*, subject and object, split into two. This differentiation, however, is unified by the non-duality of consciousness, as Śiva and Śakti are never metaphysically divided. So at the immanent level, the transcendent 'Prakāśavimarśamaya' splits into *prakāśa* and *vimarśa*, Śiva and Śakti, held together in pulsating, dynamic harmony, best illustrated in the image of the Ardhanārīśvara. The images of Ardhanārīśvara in the north, thus, seem to have been the result of an attempt to explain the non-dualistic nature of Śiva and Pārvatī. Since the images described above are the only examples of Ardhanārīśvara, and that too perhaps subsidiary images, Kashmir Śaivism does not seem to have made any headway in Haryana.

ARDHANĀRĪ-VISHṆU

A badly mutilated bust of half-male half-female form from Jaintipur (Pl. 264) in district Panchkula is not traceable now. The image showed the figure up to the belly with hands broken. The smiling face with a low crown on the head, a circular halo behind the head, wearing circular earrings, a necklet and a necklace with pendant strings dangling down, may not have provided any clues to its exact identification but one breast on the proper left side and a lotus held by a long stalk on the left of the face betrays the syncretistic nature of the image. There, however, is no indication of its being the combination of Śiva and Pārvatī. The low flat crown on the head, and the lotus held in the left (female) hand would indicate it to be a combination of Vishṇu and Lakshmī. It may be called Ardhanārī-Vishṇu. This, however, seems to have evolved on the Śaivite pattern of Ardhanārīśvara, but is not the only composite image of Vishṇu and his spouse. Some scholars have noted such medieval figures elsewhere also.[51] What is notable is that this is the earliest composite image of Vishṇu and Lakshmī known so far which may be dated to *circa* 8th century C.E. on stylistic grounds. It seems that the innovation was made in Haryana first and followed later on in other parts of the country.

HARI-BRAHMĀ

Examples of composite images revealing multiple aspects of a deity, combining the iconographical characteristics of two or more deities belonging to different sects or cults, and those representing the concept of the emergence of multiple forms out of a principal image or vice versa are not lacking in Indian plastic art. These syncretistic images indicate a spirit of toleration or animosity and sometimes try to establish the supremacy of particular deity through its Supreme Form.[52] The largest amongst the composite images, however, are those, which represent dual forms combining two male (Hari-Hara), or one male and one female (Ardhanārīśvara), or both female deities (Pārvatī-Lakshmī). Enumerating the example of the first category Bhattacharya has referred to, described and discussed, besides Hari-Hara, the dual forms of Hari-Brahmā, Mārtāṇḍa-Bhairava, Śiva-Rāma, Kṛishṇa-Kārttikeya or Brahmaṇyadeva-Vishṇu, Śiva-Buddha, Śiva-lokeśvara, Vishṇu-lokeśvara, Sūrya-lokeśvara, Sūrya-Brahmā, Śiva-Sūrya, Hanu-bhairava, etc.[53] The identity of the first two gods of the Hindu triad is indicated by the following passage of the *Bradmāṇḍa-Purāṇa*:

> *Ko bhavān viśvamūrttistvaṃ karttavyaṃ kiñcha te mayā /*
> *Evaṃ bruvāṇaṃ vaikuṇṭhaṃ pratyuvācha pitāmahaḥ //*
> *Yathā bhavāṃstathā chāhamādikarttā prajāpatiḥ /*
> *Nārāyaṇa samākhyātaḥ sarve vai mayi tishṭhati //* [54]

As an example of the composite form of Vishṇu and Brahmā, Bhattacharyya has described and illustrated an image of the multi-handed god seated in *lalitāsana*, bearing a *kirīṭa-mukuṭa* on the head which is adorned by *jaṭājūṭa* also. The god carries a book and a water vessel in his upper right and lower left hands and a conch in the upper left hand. The pedestal shows birds or winged creatures, badly mutilated, two of which may have been swan and Garuḍa, the respective mounts of Brahmā and Vishṇu.[55] The image belongs to about the 10th century C.E. We know no other example of the composite form of Vishṇu and Brahmā.

A different type of image of Hari-Brahmā, however, has been obtained from Purkhas in district Sonepat. It is an addorsed image now housed in HARDAM.[56] Made of buff sandstone, the extant image measures 60 x 23 cm. Unfortunately all the hands of both the deities are broken. The portion below the knees is also gone as also the halo. Both the deities seem to be standing in contraposto. Vishṇu on one side (Pl. 265) is shown as wearing a high cylindrical crown placed on the curled locks combed backwards. The crown is adorned with a *kīrtimukha* spewing pearl strings which form ornamental open loops on the front facet of the *mukuṭa*. The side facets show *ardha-ratna* and *ardha-padma* decor. The god wears *ekāvali, graiveyaka, patra-kuṇḍalas,* sacred thread, armlet (on the extant part of the left arm), a lower garment secured by a beautiful waist-band the free ends of which after forming loops, fall gracefully on the thighs with floral pendants touching the knees. A multifold sash may also be seen on the thighs. The *vanamālā* consists of three strands of *bakula* flowers on the sides but is twisted like a rope in form where it is bedecked by other floral decorations. Fan-like projections of the coiffure may be seen a little above the back of the ears. The extant portion of the left arms almost to the elbow indicate that the image was originally quadrimanous. The high arched eyebrows, long drawn quasi-closed eyes, slightly mutilated but sharp nose, thick lower lip, and plump cheeks betray a beatitudinous expression. A very small part of the nimbus shows that it bore floral and half-diamond patterns. The mutilated part of the *vanamālā* and a slightly mutilated projection on the back slab just at its lower end indicate that the god probably held a conch in his lower left hand.

Brahmā on the other side (Pl. 266) bearing a *jaṭājūṭa* on the head wears dress and ornaments, including the *vanamālā*, similar to those of Vishṇu. The long hanging earlobes, however, are distinct. The central face bears a knotted beard while the side ones, which are comparatively smaller, are juvenile. A part of the back slab on the proper right of the god shows a small fire-altar, which leaves little doubt to the deity being Brahmā. The extant portion of the proper right hand shows that it was held in *abhayamudrā*. The expression and facial features resemble those of Vishṇu. Brahmā and Vishṇu are addorsed without much space for any sort of partition (Pl. 267).

The tradition of addorsed images has a long history in India though its examples are not numerous. 'Domukhī Devī' installed in a modern simple brick-built flat-roofed temple at Kumarahar (Patna) actually represents an addorsed Śālabhañjikā carved out on both the opposite sides of a railing pillar of the Śuṅga period.[57] From Mathura, an unusual Kushāṇa devotional image shows two identical male figures back to back, each holding a long, looped garland.[58] A Gandhāra Buddha-Bodhisattva addorsed image is known from Gai Collection.[59] Variously identified as Bodhisattva, Sūrya and Vishṇu, an addorsed figure of *circa* 4th century C.E. from atop a pillar now exists in the Archaeological Museum, Gwalior.[60] Another Gupta addorsed image of Śiva and Pārvatī is housed in the Mathura Museum.[61]

On stylistic grounds, our image may be placed in *circa* 10th century C.E. – the same date to which the Hari-Brahmā image referred to above belongs. It is, however, difficult to visualize precisely how it was erected in a sanctuary and what exactly was the purpose of creating such an image. The possibility of this image being an illustration of the concept of the identity of Brahmā with Vishṇu, however, cannot be ruled out. The uniqueness of the image is obvious and hence its importance.

VISHṆU-KUBERA

Once studded in the wall of the Kabir Chaurā temple at Pinjore but not traceable now, was a beautiful and interesting figure of the quadrimanous deity shown as standing in a triple-flexion pose in a small niche (Pl. 268).[62] The god holds the top-end of the mace in the upper right hand in between the thumb and the first finger, and an un-blossomed lotus by its long stalk in the back left. There is a round object held in the front right hand. It seems to have been a disc or bowl. The lower left hand is broken but it seems to have held a *nakulaka*, which is partially preserved. The god wears a *karaṇḍa-mukuṭa* with an almond-shaped jewel (*mukuṭa-maṇi*) in the center, *karṇa-kuṇḍalas*, *ekāvali*, wristlets, etc. He also wears a lower garment and the long garland. The feet are held sideways. Hair, combed backward in the *piṅgalordhva* fashion, has been partly shown below the crown. The god bears a churbish look and the potbelly. A couchant figure of some animal, evidently the vehicle of the deity, has been carved near the left foot. The attributes of mace and lotus are common to Vishṇu and Kubera, but the bowl and *nakulaka*, the *karaṇḍa-mukuṭa* and the potbelly, are the features of Kubera.

There is another somewhat similar figure preserved in the Gurukula Museum, Jhajjar showing the slightly potbellied deity seated in *sukhāsana*, holding citrus, mace, lotus and *nakulaka* in the four-hands in *pradakshiṇā* order, weaing *karaṇḍa-mukuṭa*, ear ornaments, pearl necklet and necklaces, bracelets, sacred thread, *uttarīya* and *adhovastra*, anklets, and the auspicious lozenge-shaped *śrīvatasa* mark on the chest (Pl. 269). Behind the head is an eight-petalled halo. The right foot of the god is placed on a cushion and below the right knee is a pitcher representing the treasure of Kubera. R.C. Agrawala has termed this figure as Vishṇu-Kubera.[63] Both the images seem to belong to the same deity and may be assigned to *circa* 10th century C.E.

SŪRYA-NĀRĀYAṆA

Syncretism is a characteristic feature of early medieval art in India. Syncretistic icons of Sūrya-Nārāyaṇa (i.e. Sūrya and Vishṇu combined together) hail from different parts of India but are comparatively rare north of Mathura.

An image of Sūrya-Nārāyaṇa recovered from the mound of Khokhrakot at Rohtak (Pl. 270) is now preserved in the Department of Archaeology and Museums, Haryana. Carved out of a crude block of kankar stone it measures 64 x 30 cm. The god stands to front in *samapādasthānakamudrā* wearing a *kirīṭa-mukuṭa*, earrings, *ekāvali*, *keyūras*, *valayas* and an undergarment with a sash running across the thighs. A beaded long garland coming from behind the shoulders and hanging down below the knees may also be seen on his person. The upper part of the back slab with a beaded border serves as the gloriole behind the head of the god. The facial expression is that of quietude. The normal right hand is raised in protection giving pose while the backhand holds the hilt of the mace whose thicker end is suspended downwards. The principal left hand supports the conch horizontally while the rear left hand holds the discus. Just above the hilt of the mace and the discus are carved *ashṭadala* lotus flowers on either side of the head. On the receding projections of the *pañcharatha* pedestal are shown the attendant figures near the feet of the god. The one of proper right hand side is a female holding a lotus in her left hand and resting the right on her respective thigh, bent at the middle towards the lord and gazing at him. She may be identified with Śrī. The corresponding figure on the other side wears a squat cylindrical crown and holds a lotus or discus in his right hand resting the other on his left thigh. He may, thus, be identified as Padma-purusha or Chakra-purusha.

But for the presence of the lotus flowers on either side of the head, the deity would have been identified as Vishṇu but the presence of the lotus flowers is indicative of the Saura aspect. In the known images of Sūrya-Nārāyaṇa the lotus flowers are shown in the two hands of the god. It seems that the concept of the identity of Vishṇu and Sūrya in the iconoplastic art was just emerging when this image was created. This is corroborated by the date of the image also which can be assigned to *circa* 7th century C.E. on stylistic grounds. The squat cylindrical crown, the serenity of the face, the depiction of the attendant figures, simplicity of form, sparse ornamentation and beaded rim of the gloriole are noteworthy features of the image. It seems to be a good example of the ingenuity of the artist who depicted the Vaishṇava and Saura attributes so imperceptibly as to suggest the identity of Vishṇu with Sūrya. The image is, thus, a unique one.

Nearly four decades back, an image of *yogāsana* Sūrya-Nārāyaṇa stood fixed indiscriminately in the wall of Kabir Chaurā Temple at Pinjaur. This image (Pl. 266), along with many others, has since been removed from the building and is not traceable now. Here the deity, bearing a beatific smile is sitting in *padmāsana* and *dhyāna-mudrā* like Yoga-Nārāyaṇa images.[64] The god wears a squat cylindrical crown, earrings, *ekāvali*, armlets and wristlets. The front hands, which rested one over the other beside the belly in *dhyāna-mudrā*, are broken but the still extant portion of the left arm on the right foot and the mutilated portion of the belly of the god indicate their existence in this posture. The back right hand holds the mace and the left, though mutilated, evidently held the discus, which can be seen above the left shoulder of the deity. The middle right hand holding a lotus is very clear and the existence of the corresponding left hand can be visualized by the traces of the lotus on the left also between the face and the discus. Partially preserved *prabhā-maṇḍala* on the left indicates that it covered the whole of the back of the deity above the waist. Also, it had a beaded border. The *pañcha-ratha* pedestal shows a diminutive figure of Aruṇa perhaps, in a niche over a solar *chakra* on the central face flanked on either side by an outward moving but facing lion with twirled tail forming a complete circle, and an upraised front paw. On the extreme recesses are depicted elephants holding some indistinct object (animal) in the trunk. Stylistically, this icon may be ascribed to *circa* 8th century C.E.

During 1959-60, Dr. Y.D. Sharma of the Archaeological Survey of India, discovered some sculptures at Asthal Bohr near Rohtak.[65] These included an icon which was identified by him as Vishṇu. The god seated in *yogāsana* on a full blown lotus with legs folded and palms of normal hands placed one over the other in the lap and holding lotuses by their stalks in his extra hands should actually be identified as Sūrya-Nārāyaṇa (Pl. 272).[66] The almost closed eyes of the god also indicate his meditative mood. He wears a long cylindrical crown bedecked with jewels, pearls and festoons, beaded ear ornaments, jeweled necklet and a beaded necklace, a lozenge-shaped *śrīvatsa* on the chest, three-stringed sacred-thread, jeweled *keyūras* double beaded *valayas,* undergarment and the long garland. On his either side stand the male fly-whiskers. At the level of the shoulders are carved adoring figures seated on lotus flowers (donor couple?) sprouting from the back slab while the top corners show *vidyādhara* couples holding floral garlands. Behind the head of the deity is carved a perfectly round halo with incised lotus petals in it. The image may be dated to *circa* 10th century C.E. on stylistic grounds.

In the Prāchī Śiva Temple complex at Pehowa is fixed a *pañcha-śākhā* doorway, 1.75 m high and 1.37 m broad with a door opening of 1.40 x 0.70 m. The *lalāṭa-bimba* shows a male figure seated on a lotus seat in *yogāsana* with two hands placed in the lap over the soles of the feet in a *rathikā* pedimented by a dormer window motif having an *ardha-ratna* in the center and *makara-mukhas* with rampant leogryphs outside the ribbed pillars. The attributes in the upper two hands of the *yogāsana* figure are the lotus flowers as rightly recognized by Rodgers[67] and not elephants anointing the god as described by Cunningham.[68] The god wears a cylindrical crown, ear ornaments, bracelets, long garland, etc. and may thus be identified as Sūrya-Nārāyaṇa. Rodgers, however, has wrongly described the deity to have been seated on two lions. The lotus stem with buds under the lotus seat seems to have been mistaken by Rodgers as two lions.[69]

We thus see that Haryana was not totally devoid of Sūrya-Nārāyaṇa images during the medieval period and has yielded some iconographically interesting specimens.

Notes and References

1. *Atharvaveda* XIII, 4, 20.
2. *Ṛigveda* I, 164, 46.
3. *Ibid*., II.1, 3-4; III.54, 17; VIII.I, 27, 58, 2; 114, 5; *Atharvaveda* XIII.4; *Vājasaneyī-Saṃhitā* XXXII.1; etc.
4. B.N. Sharma, "Puranic Message of Religious Tolerance and its Limitations", *Purāṇa*, Varanasi, Vol. XIII, no. 1 (Jan. 1971), p. 4.
5. *Aitareya Upanishad* X. 114, 5; *Nṛisiṃhatāpan Upanishad* I. 3, 9; etc.
6. VIII. 9; IX. 23, etc.
7. *Agni Purāṇa*, 1.1; *Vishṇu Purāṇa*, I.2, 66; *Śiva Purāṇa*, IX, 55-56; *Skanda Purāṇa* XXIII. 41; *Padma Purāṇa*, Sṛishṭi Khaṇḍa XXIII.60; Pātāla Khaṇḍa XVIII; *Harivaṃśa*, II.125, 26 ff; etc.
8. Sharma, *op. cit*., pp. 4-25.
9. J.N. Banerjea, *The Development of Hindu Iconography*, Calcutta, 1956, pp. 241-42.
10. D.B. Diskalkar, "Some Brahmanical Sculptures in the Mathura Museum", *Journal of the U.P. Historical Society*, Lucknow, Vol. V, part-I (Jan. 1932), p. 44, pl. 18; Banerjea, *op. cit*., pp. 123-24.
11. Banerjea, *op. cit*., pp. 181- 82.
12. *Ibid*., p. 544. See also Shanti Lal Nagar, *Composite Deities in Indian Art and Literature*, New Delhi, 1989. The following combinations seem to have remained popular -
    i) Vishṇu and Śiva - Harihara, Haryardha, Śiva-Nārāyaṇa or Śaṅkara-Nārāyaṇa.
    ii) Vishṇu and Sūrya – Vishṇu-Nārāyaṇa.
    iii) Vishṇu and Kārttikeya – Brahmaṇyadeva-Vishṇu,
    iv) Vishṇu and Buddha - Yoga-Nārāyaṇa, Yogeśvara-Vishṇu, Vishṇu-Lokeśvara.
    v) Vishṇu, Śiva and Brahmā - Hariharapitāmaha.
    vi) Vishṇu, Śiva, Brahmā and Sūrya – Hariharahiraṇyagarbha or Sūrya-Hari-Hara-Pitāmaha.
    vii) Vishṇu, Śiva, Sūrya and Buddha - Hari-Hara-Sūrya-Buddha.
    viii) Śiva and Buddha - Śiva-Lokeśvara
    ix) Śiva and Pārvatā - Ardhanārīśvara
    x) Śiva and Sūrya – Mārttaṇḍa-Bhairava
    xi) Sūrya and Brahmā.
13. *Mahābhārata* (BORI, Poona) III.40, 57.
14. *Vishṇu Purāṇa* (Gita Press, ed.) I.8, 23.
15. *Ibid*. V. 33, 47-49.
    Tvayā yadabhayaṃ dattaṃ taddattamkhilaṃ mayā /
    matto' vibhinnamātmānaṃ drashṭumarhasi Śaṅkara //
    Yo' haṃ sa tvaṃ jagachchedaṃ sadevāsuramānusham /
    matto nānyadaśeshaṃ yattattvaṃ jñātumihārhasi //
    Āvidyāmohitātmanaḥ purushā bhinnadarśinaḥ /
    vadanti bhedaṃ paśyanti chāvayorantaraṃ Hara //
16. *Matsya Purāṇa*, (Ānandāśrama Sanskrit Series, Poona, 1907) 260, vv. 22-27:
    Vāmārdhe mādhavaṃ vidyāddakshiṇe Śūlapāṇinam /
    Bāhudvayañcha Kṛishṇasya maṇikeyūrabhūshitam //
    Śaṅkhachakradharaṃ śāntamāraktāṅguliviprabham /
    chakrasthāne gadāṃ vāpi pāṇau dadyād gadābhṛitaḥ //
    Śaṅkhañchaivetare dadyāt kaṭyardhaḥ bhūshaṇojjvalam /
    pītavastraparidhānaṃ charaṇaṃ maṇibhūshitam //
    Bhujaṅgahāravalayaṃ varadaṃ dakshiṇam karam /
    vyālopavītasaṃyuktaṃ kaṭyardhaṃ kṛittivāsasam //
    Maṇiratnaiścha saṃyuktaṃ pādaṃ nāgavibhūshitam /
    Śivanārāyaṇasyaiva kalpayedrūpamuttamam //
17. *Vishṇudharmottara Purāṇa* (GOS, Baroda, 1958) III.
    Kāryam Hariharasyāpi dakshinārdham sadāśivah /
    vāmamardhaṃ Hṛishīkeśaśśvetanīlākṛitiḥ kramāt //

Varatriśūlachakrābjadhāriṇo bāhvaḥ kramāt /
dakshiṇe vṛishabhaḥ pārśve vāmabhāge vihaṅgarāṭ //

18. *Devatāmūrtiprakaraṇa* (Calcutta, 1936) VI. 56-57.
19. *Ibid.* VI. 35-41.
20. *Ibid.* VI. 33-34.
21. *Vishṇuṃ kirīṭasaṃyuktaṃ Śaṅkaraṃ tu jaṭānvitam.*
    For complete description see the text as given by T.A.G. Rao (*EHI,* Vol. II, Part II, Appendix B, p. 168).
22. *Ibid.*, pp. 170-71.
23. *Ibid.*
24. Devendra Handa (October 1985), *op. cit.*, pp. 125 ff.
25. Devendra Handa, "Trinetra Siva from Haryana," *Indologica Jaipurensia* (Mr. Karl Khandalwala Felicitation Volume), Vol. II (1988-1995), Agra, 1996, pp. 74-79, pls. X-XII.
26. *CASR*, Vol. XIV, pp. 70 ff.; C.J. Rodgers, *Report of the Punjab Circle of the Archaeological Survey for 1888-89*, pp. 28-32.
27. Devendra Handa (March, 1976), pp. 112-19, pls. I-XI; "Some Sculptures from Punjab and Haryana", *PURBA*, Vol. VII, no. I (April, 1976), pp. 95-96, figs. 6-8; "Some Interesting Medieval Sculptures From Pinjaur", *Ibid.* Vol. XIII, no. 2 (October, 1982), pp. 83-86, figs. 1-4; Udai Vir Singh, *Pinjaur Sculptures*, Kurukshetra, 1977, pp. 1-52, pls. I-XXIV; D.C. Bhattacharyya (1981); S.P. Shukla (1983); etc. Quite a good number of sculptures have been recovered by the Department of Archaeology and Museums, Haryana from the Bhīmā Devī Temple at Pinjaur. Some still lie scattered at various places in Pinjaur while many have been taken away by individuals. Many sculptures from the site are still unpublished.
28. Handa (Oct. 1982), *op. cit.*, p. 84, fig. 3. We took the photograph of this sculpture in 1964.
29. Devendra Handa, "Harihara Images from Haryana," in *Studies in Indian History and Culture (Kanaklal Barua Commemoration Volume)*, edited by R.D. Choudhary and Bhagwan Singh, Delhi, 1990, p. 102, Fig. 2.
30. Shukla (1983), p. 41, pl. XXXIV. 2.
31. D.S. Punia, "Recently Explored Icons of Viṣṇu and Harihara in South Haryana", *Journal of the Oriental, Institute*, Baroda, Vol. XXIX, nos. 1-2 (Sept.-Dec. 1979), pp. 131-32, fig. 5.
32. Punia (*Ibid.*) describes the right hand side of this *yajñopavīta* as anguine which is not correct.
33. Punia (*Ibid.*) regards both the figures on Vishṇu's side as females but does not identify them.
34. For details see Devendra Handa (April, 1986), pp. 107 ff.
35. It is now preserved in the Department of Archaeology and Museums, Haryana, Kurukshetra and bears Acc. no. 1/460.
36. Acc. no. 1/292. It was recovered from the Bhīmā Devī Temple complex.
37. See for details Devendra Handa, "Some Medieval Sculpture From Beri - Haryana", *Roopa-Lekha*, New Delhi, Vol. LIII, No.1 and 2 (March 1982), pp. 36 ff.
38. Acc. no. 1/230.
39. It is still under worship in Devī Mandira at Panipat.
40. Rao, *loc. cit.*, pp. 321ff.
41. *Ibid.*, pp. 322-23.
42. *VDP* III.55, 1-6.
43. Banerjea, *op. cit.*, p. 546.
44. *Bṛihatsaṃhitā* LVIII.53.
45. *VDP, loc. cit.*
46. *Matsya Purāṇa* 258.1-7.
47. *Rao, loc. cit.*, p. 323.
48. Devendra Handa (October 1982), pp. 83-6, fig. 2.
49. Joanna Williams, "An Ardhanarisvara-Linga," in M.S. Nagaraja Rao (ed.), *Kusumāñjali: New Interpretation of Indian Art & Culture (Sh C. Sivaramamurti Commemoration Volume)*, Vol. II, Delhi, 1987, pp. 299-305, pls. 1-3.

50. *Ibid.*, p. 299.
51. For similar blending of Vishṇu and Lakshmī in sculptures and literary references to such figures see Pratapaditya Pal, "Composite Form of Vāsudeva and Lakṣmī," *Journal of the Asiatic Society*, Calcutta, Vol. V, Nos. 3-4, 1963, pp. 73-79; "Notes on Five Sculptures from Nepal," *British Museum Quarterly*, Vol. XIX, 1964-65, pp. 29-34 and plates; *Bronzes of Kashmir*, New Delhi, 1975, p. 76, fig. 13; Dipakachandra Bhattacharyya, "The Composite Image of Vāsudeva and Lakṣmī," *Journal of the Asiatic Society*, Calcutta, Vol. VIII, no. 4, pp. 261 ff.; S.B. Deo, "Some Ardhanārī Forms of Viṣṇu," *Bhāratī*, Vols. X-XI, pp. 125 ff.; K.S. Desai, "Some Lakṣmī-Nārāyaṇa Images from Western India," *Journal of the Oriental Institute*, Baroda, Vol. XIV, pp. 292-96; R.C. Agrawala, "Unpublished Sculptures and Terracottas in the National Museum, New Delhi, and Some Allied Problems," *East and West*, New Series, Vol. 17, Nos. 3-3 (Sept.-Dec. 1967), pp. 278-79, fig. 10; D.C. Sircar, *Studies in the Religious Life of Ancient and Medieval India*, Delhi, 1971, pp. 221-28. Pal names these figures as Vāsudeva-Kamalajā. The *Śilparatna* (Trivandrum Sanskrit Series, no. 98, part II, XXV.74, p. 162) refers to even half-male half-female form of Gaṇeśa called Śakti-Gaṇapati, many examples of which have also been published. See for details B.N. Sharma, *Iconography of Vaināyakī*, New Delhi.
52. D.C. Bhattacharyya, *Iconology of Composite Images*, Delhi, p. 25.
53. *Ibid.*, pp. 10-26.
54. *Brahmāṇḍa Purāṇa* (Vaṅgavāsī ed.), Ch. XXII vv. 21-22 (as quoted by D.C. Bhattacharyya, *op. cit.*, pp. 19-20).
55. D.C. Bhattacharyya, *op. cit.*, p. 20, fig. 13. This image was originally published under the caption of Hari-Brahmā (central India, 10th-11th century, red sandstone, Ht. 23´inches, collection of Mr. and Mrs. Bob Willoughby) in J. Leroy Davidson, *Art of The Indian Subcontinent From Los Angeles Collections*, University of California, Los Angeles, 1968, p. 45, fig. 59.
56. Accession no. 1/350.
57. Udai Narain Roy, *Śālabhañjikā in Art, Philosophy and Literature*, Allahabad, 1979, p. 141, figs. 17-18.
58. J.M. Rosenfield, *The Dynastic Arts of the Kushans*, Berkeley, 1967, p. 219, fig. 21.
59. Herald Ingholt, *Gandharan Art in Pakistan*, New York, 1947, no. 276.
60. Stella Kramrisch, *Indian Sculpture*, Calcutta, 1933, pl. 45; P.K. Agrawal, "A Note on the so-called Surya Statue from Pawaya." *Bulletin of the Ancient Indian History and Archaeology*, no. 11 (1968); J.C. Harle, *Gupta Sculpture*, Oxford, 1974, p. 40, pl. 34.
61. D.B. Diskalkar, "Some Brahmanical Sculptures in the Mathura Museum", *Journal of the U.P. Historical Society*, Vol. V, part I, 1932, pp. 18-57.
62. Devendra Handa, "Some Interesting Medieval Sculptures From Pinjaur," *PURBA*, Vol. XIII, no. 2 (October 1982), pp. 84-85, fig. 4.
63. R.C. Agrawala, "Prāchīna Hariyānā," *Ājakala* (Hindi), November 1968, p. 28 and figure.
64. *Bhāratīya Vidyā*, Bombay, Vol. XLI, Nos. 3-4 (1981), pp. 26-28.
65. *IAR*, 1959-60, p. 74, pl.
66. This image was published again in the *Marg*, Vol. XXVII, no. 4 (September 1974), Haryana Heritage Number, p. 16, fig. 16 as Vishṇu.
67. C.J. Rodgers, *Report of the Panjab Circle of the Archaeological Survey for 1888-89*, p. 15.
68. *CASR*, XIV, p. 103.
69. For details see Devendra Handa, "A Pratihāra Doorway from Pehowa," *PURBA*, Vol. XVII, no. 2 (October 1986), pp. 151-55.

Chapter 9

Miscellaneous Icons

With the passage of time Hindu pantheon went on growing as a result of which the number of deities and their *parivāra* and *āvaraṇa-devatās* also grew substantially. Some of these gods had their own cults developed around them but others had limited following or even regional in character. Important deities representd by their images in Haryana are described below.

BRAHMĀ

Born in a golden egg (Hiraṇyagarbha) and the first deity of the orthodox Brahmanical triad, Brahmā could not gather importance comparable to the other members of the Trinity, not even others like Sūrya, Devī, and Gaṇapati. It was probably because the act of creation came to be associated with the followers of different cults with their own respective divinities.[1] Though his worship is enjoined upon all those who worship Vishṇu or Śiva and he figures as one of the most important of the *parivāva-devatās* of the first *prakaraṇa* of a temple dedicated to either of the above-mentioned deities,[2] yet there is no denying the fact that he enjoyed no success as a cult god and was reduced to the status of a titular deity only to find sometimes, not always as laid down in some scriptures, a niche here or there, in a Hindu shrine. Though even a late text like the *Rūpa-Maṇḍana* describes Brahmā's temple along with *parivāra-devatās*, *dvārapālas*, etc. yet there are very few temples dedicated to him.[3] Anyway, we find only subsidiary images of the god in the Hindu temples.

The earliest iconographic description of Brahmā occurs in the *Bṛihatsaṃhitā*. It says that the four-handed god holds a ritual water-pot (*kamanḍalu*) in one of his hands and is seated on a lotus.[4] Evidently his images in the early period were two-handed like those of other deities.[5] He is referred to as having four hands in all later texts. The *Āditya Purāna* refers to his four faces, lotus seat and Sāvitrī on his left lap.[6] The *Vishṇu Purāṇa* refers to Brahmā with eyes closed as in meditation and seated on a chariot drawn by seven swans (*Saptahaṃsarathasthitam*).[7]

By the time of the Āgamas, great elaboration had taken place in his iconic representations.[8] The *Aṃśumadbhedāgama* describes the four-handed god as having *jaṭā-mukuṭa*, wearing ornaments, *yajña-sūtra*, *kaṭi-sūtra*, rearing beard and holding water-vessel, ladle, etc. as also showing *abhaya* and *varada* poses. He may be seated or standing on a lotus seat and is also associated with Sarasvatī and Sāvitrī.[9] *Suprabhedāgama* refers to four-faced and four-armed Brahmā as wearing all ornaments, *jaṭā-mukuṭa*, holding *kamanḍalu* and *akshamālā* 'rosary' with Sāvitrī on his left.[10] The *Śilparatna* describes him as seated on a lotus seat (*kamalāsana*) or riding a swan (*haṃsārūḍham*), holding a ladle and *kamaṇḍalu*, with right hand in *varada* pose and the four Vedas in front. He should be flanked by Sarasvatī and Sāvitrī on his right and left.[11] The *Rūpa-Mandana* prescribes a rosary, ladle or lotus, book and water-vessel in hands, a beard and lotus seat for him.[12]

We do not agree with Banerjea who held that 'it is curious that in none of these elaborate accounts there is an explicit reference to his face or faces being bearded.'[13] The *Aṃśumadbhedāgama* clearly states that Brahmā should bear *kūrcha* (*kūrchcham chaiva tu dhārayet*).[14] Since *kūrcha*, which is also translated as 'a handful of *kuśa* grass'[15] is never depicted in Indian images, we would prefer its other meaning of 'beard'. Also we do not subscribe to the view of the learned savant 'that all the later images of Brahmā have bearded faces.'[16] We shall see presently that facts go against this view.

Brahmā from Agroha

The earliest representation of Brahmā from Haryana comes in the form of a terracotta figurine from Agroha (Pl. 273).[17] It shows the god as tricephalous but unfortunately the whole portion below the heads is badly mutilated. All the three heads are bearded. Incised lines mark the beard and the matted hair on the head. The eyeballs are pricked. The almond-shaped eyes are wide open, nose (damaged on the central face) is prominent, cheeks are plump and lips thick. The plain back portion indicates that the figure was molded in the form of a brick which probably originally adorned some temple. Stylistically, the figurine may belong to the late Gupta period. The depiction of Brahmā in terracotta is rather rare.

Brahmā from Sirsa

The most elegant and almost complete image of Brahmā comes from Sirsa (Pl. 274s). It forms part of a private collection and consists of buff sandstone. The image shows the god standing to front on a lotus seat placed on the central offset of a *pañcha-ratha* pedestal. The god bears three faces the central one of which is bearded with two knots in the beard. He has an elaborate matted hair coiffure adorned with jewels. There is a round lotus-petalled halo behind the head. Brahmā wears long hanging ear ornaments, a double necklace, broad *yajñopavīta*, *keyūras*, long garland, *dhotī* secured by a girdle with sash on the thighs, etc. The central face has an expression of beatitude with a serene smile, sturdy nose, plump cheeks, thick lower lip, and semi-closed eyes. The side faces in profile have almost closed eyes. The normal right hand of the god is held in *varada-mudrā* with the rosary on the palm. The extra right hand holds the ladle vertically and the additional left supports the manuscript while the *pralamba* normal left hand holds the water pot by its neck. The god is flanked near his feet by garland-bearing female figures standing slightly turned towards him. At the feet of these females may be seen the donor couple, male on the proper right and female on the left, seated in profile in *añjali-mudrā*. The extreme recesses on both the sides show male acolytes standing with crossed legs, bearing bejeweled matted hair, pearl necklet, sacred thread, *dhotī* held in position by the girdle, and with right hand disposed in the gesture of reassurance. Just above them are the *gaja* and *śārdūla* motifs topped by *makara-mukhas*. The stele on the two sides of the aureole show Śiva and Vishṇu seated in *sukhāsana* wearing usual ornaments and holding their respective attributes. The extreme upper corners show saluting male figures. The image may be assigned to the Pratihāra period on stylistic grounds.

Brahmā from Pinjore

A badly mutilated sandstone image of three-headed four-armed Brahmā standing in contraposto in a pillared niche is known from Pinjore. All the faces are shown as juvenile. The normal right hand (broken) was probably disposed in *varada* and the rear right seems to have held the ladle of which only the shaft has survived. The corresponding left probably supported a manuscript (now completely gone) and the lower left touches the long neck of the swan shown in profile to right behind the god. Brahmā wears a pearl necklace, sacred thread, long garland, *kaṅkaṇas* and an undergarment secured by an elaborately bedecked girdle. The figures at the feet are almost completely gone. When complete, it must have been a 9th-century masterpiece.

Pinjore has also yielded architectural pieces with the figures of Hindu Trinities. One of these (Pl. 275) shows two-handed Brahmā seated in *sukhāsana* in a pedimented niche with ribbed pillars. The god has only one face and bears matted hair, beard, sacred thread, holding the water-vessel in his left hand while the right one is disposed in the gesture of reassurance. Brahmā is flanked by Sūrya on his right and Vishṇu on his left. This thus is the representation of Hari-Hara-Sūrya.

The similar second triad comes from Panditon ka Tila at Thanesar. It measures 50 x 30 cm (Acc. No. 1/497) and shows Brahmā seated in the center in *sukhāsana* with left leg folded and resting on a cushion and the right one stretched outward and then turning inward and resting on the ground in a similar niche flanked by Vishṇu (?) on his right and Umā-Maheśvara on his left (Pl. 276). Brahmā here is uni-cephalous and juvenile bearing an elaborate and high *jaṭā-mukuṭa*, ear ornaments, pearl necklace, bracelets, etc. There are some traces of the sacred thread also and the lower garment may only be visualized through traces of the pearl girdle. The normal right hand of the god is disposed in *abhaya* while the proper left seems to have held the *bījapuraka*. The rear pair of hand supports the *sruvā* and the book. Stylistically this and the preceding triad may be assigned to *circa* 10th century C.E.

Pinjore has also yielded an independent standing image of Brahmā, also on an architectural piece in the same complex. Unfortunately, however, it is badly mutilated. The portion above the lower parts of the faces is completely lost, hands are broken and the accessory figures too are lost. However the surviving part clearly shows the three juvenile faces, ear ornaments, pearl necklace, sacred thread, elaborate girdle, and the long garland. The suspended lower right hand is broken and the extant part of the right rear hand seems to have held the ladle by its shaft. The upper left hand may have held a book, which is completely lost, but the suspended left hand touches the neck of the swan that has survived except some damage. Originally, it seems to have been an elegantly carved piece, which may be dated to the same period as the above-mentioned examples.

Another broken relief from Pinjore in greenish sandstone measuring 14 x 9 cm (Acc. No. 1/199) is a part of another image showing juvenile tri-cephalous Brahmā with Saraśvatī on the stele with *gaja-mukha*, *siṃha-vyāla*, a *nāgara-kūṭa* borne by a flying human figure, etc. but is very badly mutilated. A small, broken piece of a bigger image showing standing bearded Brahmā and Sarasvatī flanked by human figures riding mythical animals and with a *nāgara-kūṭa* above flanked by *makara-mukhas* is preserved in the Gurukula Museum at Jhajjar. All these pieces belong to the Pratihāra period. Still another almost coeval greenish sandstone piece, 25 x 20 cm, from Bhīmā Devī Temple at Pinjore (Acc. No. 1/159) carries the figure of the deity with head broken. A stele in the same material from the same site measuring 14 x 9 cm also depicts Brahmā in the usual posture and with usual traits and attributes.

Brahmā from Pehowa

Pehowa has yielded a standing and three seated images of Brahmā, all belonging to the Pratihāra period. The standing image (Pl. 277), though badly damaged, depicts the deity standing to front accompanied by an acolyte on either side of the feet.[18] The partially preserved right hands show *abhaya* with a rosary and holding the handle of the ladle. The left hands are damaged. The suspended normal left hand may have originally held a nectar-flask or a water-pot and the rear one the manuscript. Ear ornaments, pearl necklace, bracelets, armlets and a three-stringed sacred thread can be seen on the god's person. What is, however, interesting is the placement of the three heads of the god frontally in a single row. All the faces, of which only the left one is complete, are juvenile. The matted locks on the head are adorned with jewels. The image measures 53 x 29 cm.

The seated images are all tri-cephalous and four-handed. One piece (Pl. 278), 19 cm in height, shows the god with juvenile faces seated in *sukhāsana* on a lotus seat holding *sruvā* in the rear right hand, book in the extra left, water-pot in the normal left while the proper right is held in *abhaya*.[19] The god bears bejeweled matted locks, pearl necklace, sacred thread, wristlets, anklets, scarf, etc. The other example (Pl. 279) is almost similar but for the bearded central face and the pearl sacred thread. The third piece in buff sandstone measuring 24 x 16 cm was discovered from Viśvamitra kā Ṭīlā at Pehowa and is now preserved in HARDAM (Acc. No. 1/244). It shows three-headed Brahmā in a miniature temple niche. Another stele with a *makara-mukha* in the same material and from the same site, 21 x 21.5 cm (Acc. No. 1/253) also carries Brahmā as usual. A detached Pratihāra head of Brahmā from Pinjore (19 x 8 cm) shows bearded face, matted locks with central jewel.

Brahmā from Kaithal

A broken sandstone image of tri-cephalous Pratihāra Brahmā seated in *sukhāsana* on a lotus seat lies in the old Hanumān Temple at Kaithal also. The god has bearded central face and holds ladle and book in the rear pair of hands and water-pot in the normal left. The principal right hand is disposed in *abhaya*. A small Pratihāra sandstone image of tri-cephalous Brahmā studded in the wall of Mr. Balbir's house at Bulandpur Kheri shows the god seated in *padmāsana* holding rosary, *sruk*, book and the water pot in the four-hands.

Brahmā from Satkumbha

A beautiful but unfortunately badly mutilated image of Brahmā has been found from Satkumbha (Ahir Majra) near Gujjar Kheri. The three-faced Brahmā has bearded central face while the side faces are juvenile. The heads bear very elaborate *jaṭā-mukuṭa* adorned with jewels and pearl strings. There are long ear ornaments hanging from the ears of the central face. A broad beaded torque and a part of the sacred thread are also clear. The god is pot-bellied. All the hands and the portion below the belly is lost. Originally it must have been an elegant image adorning some Pratihāra temple.[20]

Brahmā from Morni

The most interesting image of Brahmā, however, comes from Morni (Acc. No. 1/330). Carved on an architectural piece which originally supported the superstructure as indicated by the still extent brackets on the top corners of the slab, this greenish sand stone relief measuring 48.5 x 41 cm shows the three-headed god standing in *samapāda-sthānaka* stance flanked by diminutive figures, two on either side (Pl. 280). The side faces have been shown in three-quarters profile. The god bears matted locks and all the faces are juvenile. The figure is clad only in a *dhotī* with a sash on the thighs. The right hand, though slightly damaged, is clearly disposed in the gesture of reassurance. The left hand seems to have held a water pot. The expression of the central face though mutilated seems to be that of abstraction while the right and left faces betray placidity and beatitude.

Very interesting, however, are the subsidiary figures flanking the god. They all stand gracefully holding probably a water pot in the left hand with right disposed in *abhaya-mudrā*. The one standing immediately to the right is noteworthy for having an animal head on a human body. Faces of other figure are worn out.

It is interesting to refer to a Kashmiri bronze image in the Museum für Indische Kunst, Berlin which shows similar standing five figures on a pedestal provided with a pouring lip.[21] The four-handed single-headed central figure is attended by dwarfish acolytes who have two hands each of which are disposed as in our relief. The attendant figure near the right foot of the god also has an animal head. The deity wears a long garland and an animal skin across his left shoulder. His normal hands show *abhaya-mudrā* and water-pot and the additional ones hold respectively a rosary and a staff. Unlike the relief from Morni, the attendant figures are provided with haloes. The ascetic nature of the principal figure emphasized by the animal skin in the Kashmiri bronze, however, is revealed by the absence of jewelry and simple drapery in our example. The attributes of the two hands are also in perfect conformity with those of the principal hands of the bronze image. Also, there cannot be any doubt that the attendant figures, though not provided with haloes in our relief, are identical as revealed by the animal headed figures standing near the right foot of the main deity in both the examples. There can be no doubt about the identical nature of the deities and their acolytes in the two reliefs.

The Kashmiri bronze figure has been identified as Śiva-Lokeśvara in the Berlin Catalogue. Long back, M.T. de Mallmann had aptly and quite convincingly demonstrated the non-tenability of such images as Śiva-Lokeśvara.[22] It has also rightly been observed by Pratapaditya Pal that "while in the others alleged images of Śiva-Lokeśvara the figure does display the erect phallus and the third eye, no such Śaiva signs are visible in the Berlin image."[23] The Morni image, too, does not show these Śaiva signs.

Pal has identified the Kashmiri bronze as that of Brahmā, as a member not of the Hindu but the Buddhist pantheon, as indicated by the dedicatory inscription on the pedestal beginning with the expression, *deya dharmeya*.[24] There is, however, absolutely no evidence to connect our image with Buddhism. Morni has yielded numerous sculptures and architectural remains that were parts of only the Hindu temples. Most of the iconographical texts mention Brahmā as four-faced and four-armed.[25] *Kamandalu* 'water-pot', *aksha-mālā* 'rosary', *sruk* 'ladle' and *pustaka* 'book' are the usual attributes. The four faces could be carved only if the image is in the round. So Brahmā's images are generally found with three faces as we have seen above, the fourth one at the back is to be presumed. He is sometime shown with single face also as noted above. His face/s could be bearded or youthful. Various medieval icons found from Sirsa, Ahir Majra, Sonepat, Kaithal, Pehowa, etc reveal that Haryana preserved the tradition of depicting the deity both as bearded and juvenile.

Pal identified the four attendant figures of the Berlin image as the personification of the four Vedas or simply four acolytes of Brahmā.[26] We may point out that they certainly are the Veda-*purushas*. The *Vishṇudharmottara Purāṇa* prescribes that the *Sāmaveda* should be depicted as horse-headed (*Sāmavedastu karttavyaḥ kintvaśvavadanaḥ prabhuḥ*).[27] The *Jayākhya-saṃhitā* (XII.10) also states that the four Vedas beginning with the *Ṛigveda* should be depicted as composite figures of horse and man-*Ṛigvedādyaṃ chatuśśākhaṃ tu pītaṃ haya-narākṛitim*. The

Chaturvarga-Chintāmaṇi (*circa* 13th century C.E.) lays down that the *Ṛigveda* should be depicted as of white color and having two hands and the face of an ass - *Ṛigvedaḥ śvetavarṇaḥ syād dvibhujo rāsabhānanaḥ* and the *Atharvaveda* should have the face of a monkey - *Ātharvaṇābhido Vedo dhavalo markaṭānanaḥ*.[28] So if one of the attendants have been carved with an animal (horse or ass) head it certainly represents a personified Veda, the *Ṛigveda* or the *Sāmaveda*. We may refer to four artistic sealings from Rajghat, two in the Bharat Kala Bhavan and two in the Allahabad Museum now, showing a central composite animal-headed and human-bodied two-handed figure in *dvibhaṅga* posture flanked by two small ones under a canopy of a tree and bearing the legend *Bahvṛicha-charaṇa* in Gupta Brāhmī characters. The composite figure has been identified by Thaplyal as that of *Ṛigveda* as the *Āśvalāyana* and *Śāṅkhāyana śākhās* of the *Ṛigveda* had a common *charaṇa* of Bahvṛicha.[29] It is thus clear that the four pursuant figures represent the four Vedas. Recently N.P. Joshi[30] has brought out ample evidence to show the association of horse with the Vedas, including the *Śrītattvanidhi*, a late medieval work, which describes the *Ṛigveda*, *Yajurveda*, *Sāmaveda*, and *Atharvaveda* as having heads respectively of an ass, goat, horse and monkey.[31] Joshi has endorsed Pratapaditya Pal's identification of the animal headed pursuant figure of the Berlin image of Brahmā with the *Sāmaveda*.[32] It is very difficult to ascertain whether the animal headed Veda-*purusha* in our image is ass-headed or horse-headed, i.e. whether it should be identified with the *Ṛigveda* or the *Sāmaveda*. Considering the serial number from the proper right hand side of the god in the *pradakshiṇā* 'circumambulatory' order, it may, however, be identified as that of the *Ṛigveda*.

Simple drapery, lack of ornamentation, simply matted hair, two-handedness, the style of depiction of the loop of the sash on the right thigh, incised floral pattern on the sides and the type of the extant brackets on the top corner indicate that the relief might have belonged to some 8th century Hindu temple. The importance of the image cannot be over stated for being the singular example of this type known so far.

We have already noted above that the stele in many of the Vishṇu images carry the figures of Brahmā and Śiva either alone or with their spouses. Some more detached stele and small subsidiary images of Brahmā, which have come to our notice, are listed below.

A stele near the image of Vishṇu in Baba Shankar Nath ki Samadhi at Gummar, measuring 16 x 20 cm, shows Brahmā with an additional female figure. Once a tri-cephalous bearded Brahmā existed at Theh Polar but is missing now. A 30 cm high image of Brahmā lies in a temple at Lulodh (Rohtak). A Pratihāra tri-cephalous juvenile Brahmā (19 x 14 cm) seated in *sukhāsana* is preserved in the Hanumān Temple at Kaithal with the normal right hand displaying *abhaya-mudrā* and holding *sruk* in the rear right, book in the back left and *kamaṇḍalu* in the proper left hand.

KĀRTTIKEYA

The history and antiquity of Kārttikeya, known variously as Skanda, Kumāra, Guha, Viśākha, Mahāsena, Shaṇmukha, Shaḍānana, Brahmaṇyadeva, Subrahmaṇya, Muruga, Murugan, etc., are shrouded in mystery. Father Heras identified the name Murugan adu which he read on a seal of Mohenjo-daro with Murugan.[33] Arvamuthan tried to identify Skanda on certain other seals.[34] Karmarkar[35] connected Muruga, the Tamilian name of the god, with Mūradevāḥ of the *Ṛigveda*.[36] All these, however, seem to be forced identifications and interpretations.[37]

Though the name Skanda or Kārttikeya does not occur in the *Rigveda*[38] yet Kumāra has been mentioned several times.[39] Kumāra stands for a boy, a child, a youth, a son or a descendant but at one place it appears as an independent deity in the *Ṛigveda*.[40] Sukumar Sen regards Kumāra of the *Ṛigveda* as the prototype of Skanda-Kārttikeya.[41] In the *Ṛigveda*,

Kumāra is associated with various gods but his association and collocation with Agni[42] and Rudra[43] are not insignificant as the later literature describes him as the son of these deities and he partakes of many of their characteristics and functions. The *Atharvaveda* mentions Kumāra as *agnibhūti.*[44] In the Vedic literature, Rudra has been called as Agni also[45] and the *Mahābhārata* mentions Dahana (Fire) as one of the names of the eleven Rudras.[46] Many of the epithets of Agni in the *Ṛigveda* have later been applied to Kumāra. The connection of Agni[47] and Rudra[48] with war seems to have stood at the root of the epic concept of Kumāra as the Generalissimo of the divine forces. The *Śatapatha Brāhmaṇa* presents an epitome of the various myths by referring to Kumāra as the son of Prajāpati, also named Rudra because he wept or cried (*rud*), Rudra being Agni and Kumāra being the ninth name of Agni (Rudra) and so on.[49] Kumāra's association with various gods in the Vedic literature, thus, seems to be the basis of the multiple aspects of his personality.

The multiple aspects of Skanda have also been highlighted in the *Skanda-yāga*, also called *Dhūrta-Kalpa*, a *pariśishṭa* 'appendix' of the *Atharvaveda.*[50] It refers to his various names like Viśakha, Kumāra, Shaḍānana or Shaḍāsya, Agniputra, Kārttikeya or Kṛittikāputra, Brahmaṇya, Svāmi, etc. and associates him with peacock (*yaṃ vahanti mayūrāḥ*), lance or spear (*yasyāmoghā sadā śakti nityaṃ ghaṇṭā-patākinī*), mothers (*Yaścha mātṛigaṇairnityaṃ parivṛito yuvā*) and refers to his multiple parentage-

> *Āgneyaṃ kṛittikāputramaindraṃ kechidadhīyate /*
> *Kechit pāśupataṃ Raudraṃ yo'si so' si namo'stu te iti //*

The *Dhūrta Kalpa* shows that Skanda was a maleficent deity worshipped by the people of the underworld, the primitive and criminal tribes and the *Vrātyas* earning their livelihood by the strength of arms (*āyudha-jīvī*).[51] His epithet Guha also points in the same direction. Skanda-Kārttikeya, however, seems to have been the ultimate amalgam of a number of strands and sub-currents of popular religious and folk beliefs which connected him with the pleiads, mothers, *grahas*, child birth, thieves, bandits, warriors, etc.[52] He was invoked by all those people who desired wealth, grains, herds, enjoyment, wisdom, slaves, status, jewels, offspring and honor –

> *Dhanadhānyakulān bhogān sa me vachanavedanam /*
> *Dāsidāsaṃ tathā sthānaṃ maṇiratnaṃ surañjanam //*
> *Ye bhaktyā bhajane Dhūrtam Brahmaṇyam cha yaśasvinam /*
> *Sarve te dhanavantāḥ syuḥ prajāvanto yaśasvinaḥ //* [53]

In the Sūtra period (600-200 B.C.E.), the status of Skanda seems to have been elevated to the level of the supreme gods. The *Hiraṇyakeśin Gṛihya Sūtra* (II.9, 19) mentions him along with Vishṇu, Rudra, etc. The *Baudhāyana Dharma Sūtra* identifies him with Sanatkumāra, Shaṇmukha, Viśākha, Mahāsena, etc. –

> *Om Sanat Kumāraṃ tarpayāmi, Skandaṃ tarpayāmi*
> *Indraṃ tarpayāmi, Shashṭhīṃ tarpayāmi,*
> *Shaṇmukhaṃ tarpayāmi, Viśākhaṃ tarpayāmi,*
> *Jayantaṃ tarpayāmi, Mahāsenaṃ tarpayāmi,*
> *Skandapārshadamaṃ tarpayāmi.*

The *Taittirīya Āraṇ*yaka (24.10, 15) also mentions Shaṇmukha and Mahāsena while the *Chhāndogya Upanishad* (VII.26, 2) identifies Skanda with Sanatkumāra like the *Baudhāyana*

Dharma Sūtra. It may have, however, been the child-giving quality, which made Skanda a very popular deity. Various Sūtras refer to the fact that Naigameya, an aspect of Skanda-Kārttikeya, mentioned as Nejamesha in a *Khila* of the *Ṛigveda* (IV.13, 1), was worshipped by those desirous of sons.[54]

The epics and the Purāṇas deal in details with the stories of the birth and deeds of Kārttikeya. The Śalyaparvan gives us an idea of the various myths of his parentage, which might have been floating in the society:

Kechidenaṃ vyavasyanti Pitāmaha-sutaṃ prabhum /
Sanat-kumāraṃ sarveshāṃ brahmayoniṃ tamagrajam //
Kechinmaheśvara-sutaṃ kechitputraṃ Vibhāvasoḥ /
Umāyāḥ Kṛittikānāṃ cha Gaṅgāyāścha vadantyuta // [55]

Some explain him as the son of Pitāmaha,
Sanatkumāra, the eldest born of Brahman,
Some say he is the son of Maheśvara,
Some say he is the son of Agni,
Some say he is the son of Umā,
Some say he is the son of the Kṛittikās (Pleiads),
Some say he is the son of Gaṅgā.[56]

The Vanaparvan (*Mbh.* III, 213-21) narrates the story of the birth of Skanda from Agni (*Mbh.* IX.43-465). It is said that having seen the wives of the Seven Sages (Saptarshi), Agni fell in live with them. Svāhā, the daughter of Daksha (Prajāpati), mated with Agni assuming successively forms of six of the wives of the Seven Ṛishis. Agni deposited a part of his seed, each time and Svāhā cast the seed on the top of the *Śveta* (white) mountain in Śaravana (forest of reeds) where it developed into Skanda, with six heads. The Śalyaparvan (*Mbh.* XIII.83-84), however, tells us that when at the sight of Umā the vital seed of Śiva fell into the blazing fire (Agni) and developed into a fetus, Agni, unable to bear it, deposited the fiery fetus in the river Gaṅgā on Brahmā's advice. Gaṅgā, too, unable to sustain it, abandoned it in the Śaravana on the Himalayas where the embryo developed into a lustrous child. The divine child was seen by the six Kṛittikās, who, out of motherly tenderness, suckled him at their breasts. The child suckled all the six Kṛittikās assuming six mouths. And hence his name Kārttikeya. Bṛihaspati, the preceptor of the gods, then performed the consecration ceremony of his birth. Gathered at that occasion were, amongst others, his parents and sustainers, in order to please whom he divided himself into four-forms - Skanda, Śākha, Viśākha and Naigameya, for the satisfaction of Rudra, Umā, Gaṅgā and Agni.

The Anuśāsanparvan presents a mixed version of these two stories (*Mbh.* XIII.86). Elsewhere, it is stated that Agni was united with the six Kṛittikās who all delivered simultaneously but the six kids united into one form. The story of the birth of Kārttikeya is told variously with some change here and there in the *Rāmāyaṇa* (*Rāmāyaṇa*, 1, 37-38) and the Purāṇas[57] also. Kālidāsa has given it perpetuity by composing the *Kumārasambhava*.

The *Mahābhārata* and the Purāṇas[58] acquaint us with the story of his appointment as the Generalissimo of the army of the gods. On that occasion, he was offered various gifts by different gods which included spear (*Śakti*) from Indra, large army from Śiva, *vaijayantī* from Vishṇu, peacock from Garuḍa, cock from Aruṇa (or Varuṇa or Agni), etc.[59] Skanda's consort is Devasenā also called Shashṭhī.[60]

We have already noted the elevation of status and popularity of Skanda during the Sūtra period. Kauṭilya refers to the construction of shrines of various gods like Aparājitā, Apratihata,

Jayanta, Vijayanta, Śiva, Vaiśravaṇa, Aśvins, Śrī and Madirā in various parts of the city – *Aparājitāpratihata-Jayanta-Vijayanta-koshṭhān Śiva-Vaiśravaṇāśvin Śrī-Madirā-grihaṃ cha.*[61] Commenting upon a *Sūtra* of Pāṇini, Patañjali refers to the images of Śiva, Skanda and Viśākha made for worship and the sale thereof by the Mauryas for making money: *Apaṇya ityuchyate tatredaṃ na sidhyati/ Śivaḥ Skandaḥ Viśākha iti/ Kiṃ kāraṇam/ Mauryairhiraṇyārthibhirarchāḥ prakalpitāḥ.*[62]

These and numerous other references, however, indicate that Skanda, Viśākha, Mahāsena, Jayanta, Vaijayanta, etc. were not yet one but different deities. Huvishka's coins with three standing figures named as 'Skando Komaro Bizago Maaceno'[63] clearly demonstrate it. The *Vishṇudharmottara* (III.71, 3) also describes the fourfold images of Kārttikeya:

> *Chaturmūrteḥ Kumārasya rūpaṃ te vachmi Yādava /*
> *Kumāraścha tathā Skando Viśākhaścha Guhastathā //*

The amalgamation, however, seems to have taken place immediately after the Kushāṇa period as we find Kārttikeya, Skanda, Kumāra, Shaṇmukha, Brahmaṇyadeva used for the same deity in later literature.

Kārttikeya is closely associated with Haryana. There are various *tīrthas* in Kurukshetra sacred to him – Auśanasa, Koṭi-*tīrtha*, Ojas or Taijas, Pṛithūdaka, Samantapañchaka, Somākhya-tīrtha, Sthāṇu-tīrtha, etc.[64] Pṛithūdaka is described to have been the venue of his consecration to the post of Generalissimo and has a temple dedicated to him.[65] Rohitaka is also described to be a city dear to him.[66] The *Mahāmāyūrī* also refers to his worship at Rohitaka.[67]

In the realm of art the earliest depiction of Kārttikeya is believed to be on the coins. Allan identified the anthropomorphic figure holding a pot and shaft in his two hands and a crest-like object on the head, occurring on some punch-marked coins, with Kārttikeya.[68] Some scholars have, however, identified it as Śiva.[69] A similar figure occurs on Ujjayinī coins also.[70] The shaft is not a trident, the attribute of Śiva. It is nearer to the depiction of a spear or javelin (*śakti)* and as such it is probable that the figure represents Kārttikeya. Punch-marked coins found from Sugh near Jagadhari show this figure.[71] These coins may be assigned to *circa* 3rd-2nd century B.C.E.[72]

A similar depiction occurs on some Kāḍa coins also.[73] The discovery of one Kāḍa coin in the excavations and about one and a dozen more from the surface at Sugh indicates that Kāḍa coins were the popular currency of this area during the 3rd-2nd century B.C.E.[74] The figure on Kāḍa coins has been identified with Kārttikeya by Allan but Ajay Mitra Shastri takes that to be Śiva.[75]

Numerous stone and bronze images of two-handed Kārttikeya holding a long spear in one of the hands found from the Mathura region[76] and the coins of Huvishka[77] indicate the popularity of the god in the region. The Yaudheyas, an *āyudha-jīvi saṅgha* mentioned by Pāṇini[78], worshipped Kārttikeya as their national god. They ruled from Rohtak which was their capital and mint-town, very dear to Kārttikeya as mentioned in the *Mahābhārata.*[79] Coins of Class 3 of the Yaudheyas[80] show not only six-headed *Kārttikeya* on the obverse but six-headed Shashṭhī also on the reverse. The god has been named as Brahmaṇyadeva-Kumāra in the coin-legend.[81] What is, however, important from the viewpoint of art is the arrangement of the six heads on these coins. The unique silver coin shows the god standing, facing, holding a long spear in his right hand with left akimbo, having two rows of three heads each. The top row clearly shows that the hair has been arranged with a topknot. The god stands on a lotus with feet splayed out, as seen in most of the Kushāṇa sculptures. The coin being small and worn out, the facial and other features are not distinct. The reverse shows the goddess on a lotus with right hand raised almost vertically from the elbow (and holding a lotus?) and *kaṭyavalambita* left. Her head is surrounded by perhaps four more heads, the fifth being hid by her raised right hand. She, thus, may obviously be identified with Shashṭhī, the spouse of Shaḍānana.[82]

The copper coins of this class, though generally very much worn out, show the god and the goddess with the following arrangements of heads[83] -

	Kārttikeya	*Shashṭhī*
1.	Parallel rows of heads	Circular heads
2.	Circular arrangement of heads	Parallel heads
3.	Parallel rows of heads	Parallel heads

Though the depictions of Kārttikeya in stone and his different aspects like Skando-Komaro, Bizago and Maaceno were popular in the Kushāṇa art of Mathura yet the absence of any six-headed specimen indicates that it was the Yaudheya innovation. The parallel and circular arrangements of the heads of the deity and his consort, too, were devised indigenously. Neither the stone nor the numismatic representations, however, reveal the presence of peacock, the vehicle of the god, till this period.

The legends on the Yaudheya coins of Class 3 refer to the god as Svāmi, Brahmaṇyadeva and Kumāra.[84] Jai Prakash Singh thinks that the epithet *Svāmi* was adopted by the Yaudheyas for their deity after their defeat at the hands of the Western Kshatrapas[85] as stated in Rudradāman's Girnar *Praśasti*.[86] This view, however, cannot be upheld as this epithet has been used for the god even in the *Dhūrtakalpa* (VI.5) - *Svamine namaḥ Śaṅkarāyāgni-putrāya Kṛittikā-putrāya* namaḥ.

Yaudheya coins of Class 6, however, depict the deity as uni-cephalous but accompanied by the peacock as his vehicle.[87] The god is shown as standing, facing, holding a long spear in his right hand, left hand resting on the hip, bearing a top-knot on the head, wearing *karṇa-kuṇḍalas, a thick graiveyaka,* puffed bracelets, *dhotī*, etc. with peacock near his left foot and the Brāhmī legend *Yaudheya-gaṇasya jaya(ḥ)*[88] around. The deity on the reverse, standing slightly turned to her right, wearing a flowing *sārī*, torque, earrings and probably a *lalāṭikā* also[89] is identified with Devasenā flanked sometimes by *kalaśa* 'pot' and *nandipada* or *Śaṅkha* 'conch' and *Śrīvatsa*. These coins are based on Kushāṇa module and are datable to the third and 4th century C.E.[90]

Kālidāsa's *Kumārasambhava* and the christening of the rulers of the Gupta dynasty as Kumāragupta (I and II) and Skandagupta, together with the depiction of the deity on the coins,[91] indicate the popularity of Kārttikeya during the Gupta period. It is, however, notable that during this period, the uni-cephalous form with peacock was more popular. That the tradition of six-headed form, too, may have continued, though no specimens belonging to the Gupta period have come down to us, is indicated by a unique bronze image of the god from the Punjab hills, showing six-headed Kārttikeya (with a circular arrangement of the heads) holding *Śakti-devī* in his left hand and the *mayūra-purusha* in the right. The image has been dated to 6th-7th century C.E.[92]

Kārttikeya from Rohtak

We have already noted above that Rohtak has been described in the *Mahābhārata* as a city dear to Kārttikeya and the *Mahāmāyūrī* also refers to the worship of Kārttikeya-Kumāra at this place. That Kārttikeya continued to be popularly worshipped at Rohtak is evidenced by a stone image of the god found from there (Pl. 281).[93] Unfortunately, however, it is not in a good state of preservation and the details of the round central face are completely lost. The god is seated on his vehicle in *lalitāsana* holding *śakti* in his right hand and *kukkuṭa* (cock) in his left. The depiction thus corresponds to the description of the *Agni Purāṇa*,[94] *Bṛihatsaṃhitā*[95], *Matsya Purāṇa*[96] and the *Aṃśumadbhedāgama*.[97] Two small faces have been carved on the two sides of the big central face and three small faces exist on the central head. The *jaṭā-jūṭa* protrudes behind the upper three heads. The god wears ear-ornaments, pearl necklet, sacred thread, armlets, bracelets, long garland and the nether garment. The semi-circular top of the back slab and a part of the pedestal below the peacock are lost. The execution is not very fine. Stylistically, the image may be dated to 8th century C.E.

An unfinished image from the same site shows the god seated similarly on the peacock to right, also holding the same attributes but is uni-cephalous and has an elaborate *jaṭā-jūṭa* on the head (Pl. 282). The top part of the back-slab is semi-circular, indicating an early date, around 9th century C.E. Earrings, necklet and *valayas* are clearly visible and the peacock seems to be pecking at the beaded bracelet.[104]

Kārttikeya from Gujjar Kheri

A small figure in sandstone, belonging stylistically to the same century, comes from Gujjar Kheri in district Sonepat (Pl. 283).[98] The god is seated in *lalitāsana* on the beautifully feathered peacock, broken below unfortunately. The folded left leg of the god, too, is damaged. The six-headed god has an exquisite and bigger central face with the other five arranged around that in a circular fashion. The head on the proper left of the god is gone. The god bears hair combed backwards on the main head. Of the ornaments, only the *ekāvali* is seen clearly. There is a plain round gloriole behind the heads and the god holds a long spear in his left hand while the right seems to have held a fruit or cock. This is a small portable image indicating it to be in an individual's possession that could carry it with him even during travel and sojourns.

Kārttikeya from Ratpur

A very fragmentary piece representing only the bust and the six heads arranged in the circular fashion is known from Ratpur near Pinjore (Pl. 284).[99] The bigger central face shows large ear discs and all the heads have locks of hair. A triple stringed necklace is visible on the chest. The image may be ascribed to *circa* 9th century C.E. It may not have been much different from the buff sandstone icon from Thanesar showing almost exactly similar heads arranged in the circular fashion. The lower part of this latter image is broken. It probably held the *śakti* in the right hand. The left hand is irretrievably lost.[100]

Kārttikeya from Muradnagar

Another image ascribable to almost the same period is now preserved in a temple at Muradnagar in district Ambala. It has, however, been very badly painted besides having suffered some mutilation (Pl. 285). The god sits facing on a retrorse peacock carved to left in profile. The left leg of the god is folded and the right hangs down with the foot placed on a lotus. The god is uni-cephalous with a high *jaṭā-jūṭa*, large circular earrings, *ekāvali*, armlets, wristlets, *vaijayantī-mālā* and lower garment secured by a *kaṭi-sūtra*. Of the four hands, only the rear right holding the *śakti* has survived. The back-slab is broken on the upper right corner but a beautifully carved lotus-petalled *prabhāmaṇḍala* behind the head may clearly be made out. The top corners carried flying *vidyādhara* figures. This is the largest image of Kārttikeya found so far. It has so badly been coated with paint that all details have been concealed but the perfect proportions of the limbs, the exquisiteness of ornamentation, the liveliness of the peacock turning its neck backwards and its beautiful plumage may still be discerned. When complete, it must have been a masterpiece of the Pratihāra art of the region.[101]

Kārttikeya from Morni-ka-Tal

Morni-ka-Tal in district Panchkula has yielded two images of Kārttikeya, one is completely broken with only the lower half left and the other, though complete, is very badly worn out. This latter image measures 102 x 48 cm and is made of grey sandstone. It shows six-headed Kārttikeya seated on a peacock in *ardhparyaṅkāsana*. The left leg of the god goes around the neck of the peacock. His front right hand, holding a rosary, is disposed in the gesture of reassurance (*abhaya*). The back right hand holds the *śakti* (lance). The front left hand rests on the left knee and the additional left hand holds an object, which is worn out beyond recognition. The image may be dated to the 9th century on stylistic grounds.[102]

Kārttikeya from Pinjore and Jind

A small broken 9th century image of Kārttikeya, 18 x 16 cm, from Pinjore was taken to adorn the lawn of the Haryana Raj Bhawan during the Governorship of Mr. B.N. Chakravarty. The god is shown as riding a peacock and both the hands are broken. A fragmentary head and bust from Jind may be recognized to have been that of Kārttikeya from the *tri-śikhaṇḍaka* hair-coiffure so typical of the deity (Pl. 286).[103] It may be dated to *circa* 10th century C.E.

Kārttikeya from Thanesar

Bust of hexcephalic buff sandstone Kārttikeya measuring 29 x 24 cm is known from Thanesar (Pl. 287).[104] The additional five heads form a semi-circle around the central head of the god. All the heads are decked with *jaṭā-jūṭa* and the *kuṇḍalas*. The god wears a beaded double necklace, armlets, sacred thread and probably the long garland also. All the four-hands are broken but the rear right hand seems to have supported the spear the upper part of which has survived. Garland bearing *vidyādharas* are shown hovering on the upper corners of the image which may be dated to the late ninth or early 10th century C.E.

Kārttikeya from Pinjore

A pedimented *rathikā* fixed in the wall of a *baoli* in the main bazar of Pinjore behind the *Dhārā-kshetra* also carries an image of four-handed and six-headed Kārttikeya now encrusted with a thick coat of whitewash (Pl. 288). The five heads have been arranged around the bigger central face. The god sits in *lalitāsana* on peacock to right. The normal right hand of the god is disposed in *varada-mudrā* while the corresponding left holds probably a fruit or *mātuliṅga.* The peacock is pecking at the beaded bracelet perhaps mistaking the beads for the seeds of the pomegranate. The rear pair of hands holds *śakti* and cock respectively. Stylistically, the image may be dated to 12th century C.E.

Kārttikeya finds representation in most of the Umā-Maheśvara images also and is generally shown with peacock and *śakti* in one of his hands.

We thus see that Haryana has yielded both uni-cephalic as well as poly-cephalic images of Kārttikeya, which belong to two-handed and four-handed varieties only. All extant images show the god as seated in *lalitāsana* on the peacock. *Śakti* and cock are almost invariable attributes. All these stone images date between eighth and twelfth centuries C.E.

The six-headed representation seems to have been evolved in the 2nd century C.E. by the Yaudheyas who initially experimented to arrange the six heads in two parallel rows or in a circular fashion, of which only the latter survived in this region and was adopted popularly in the early medieval period. The peacock, too, was carved for the first time by the Yaudheyas on their coins of Class 6 and has continued since then in all subsequent representations of the deity. The Guptas preferred seated images of Kārttikeya on peacock but the standing figures, too, were carved now and then. The god, however, was shown as uni-cephalous and having only two hands holding *Śakti* and the cock or some other object. In the early medieval Haryana, the characteristic Yaudheya Shaṇmukha figures with circular arrangement of heads but seated like the Gupta ones, were more popular though uni-cephalous representations were not totally forgotten. The characteristic attributes of *śakti* and *kukkuṭa* and the vehicle peacock were invariable features in all images of the god, which were two or four-handed only.

REVANTA

Revanta, the son of Sūrya and Sañjñā and the lord of the Guhyakas, is one of the lesser-known but important deities of Hinduism. The myth of his birth is narrated at some length in the *Vishṇu Purāṇa*.[105] It is said that Sañjñā,[106] the daughter of Viśvakarmā, bore to her spouse Sūrya three children – Manu (Vaivasvata), Yama and Yamī (Yamunā). However, being unable to endure the refulgence of her husband, she left her Chhāyā (literally meaning shadow, reflection) as his handmaid and herself repaired to the forests to practice devout austerities. The sun mistook Chhāyā to be his wife and begot by her three more children - Śanaiśchara (Saturn), another Manu (Sāvarṇi) and Tapatī (the Tapati river). Once being offended with Yama, Chhāyā denounced an imprecation upon him whereby Yama and Sūrya could know that she is not actual Sañjñā. Then having been informed by Chhāyā that Sañjñā had gone to the forests, the sun saw Sañjñā through his mental eyes as engaged in austerities in the form of a mare. Metamorphosing himself into a horse the sun rejoined her and begot three more children – the two Aśvins and Revanta and then brought her back to his own place.[107] The *Mārkaṇḍeya Purāṇa* also narrates this story though some of the details differ.[108]

The fact that the Vedic literature, the *Harivaṃśa Purāṇa* and the *Narasiṃha Purāṇa* give detailed descriptions of Sūrya and his family but do not mention Revanta clearly indicates that this deity is a later creation.[109] Sahai opines that probably when the horses became the most important element of war in the first few centuries of the current era, the worship of Revanta became popular.[110] Early literary references to Revanta may be found in the *Agni*[111] and *Vishṇudharmottara Purāṇa* (III.67, 9) and the *Bṛihatsaṃhitā* (LVII.56). All these texts may be ascribed to the Gupta and late Gupta period and it is interesting to note that the earliest image of Revanta discovered so far also belongs to the 5th-6th century C.E.[112]

While the *Agni Purāṇa* refers to Revanta as 'a horseman' the *Bṛihatsaṃhitā* describes him as riding a horseback with attendants in the sport of hunting.[113] The *Vishṇudharmottara*[114] and *Bhavishya Purāṇa*[115] as also the *Chaturvargachintāmaṇi*[16] emphasize his likeness to Sūrya. The god finds mention in the *Skanda Purāṇa*,[117] *Kālikā Purāṇa* (85.46-49), *Kuvalayamālā Kathā*,[118] Jayānaka's *Pṛithvīrāja Vijaya* (Canto I), *Śabda-kalpa-druma*, *Kalpataru* and various medieval epigraphs.[119]

Images of Revanta have been found from various parts of the country and have systematically been studied by B.N. Sharma.[120] The break up of the 43 images described and illustrated by him is as follows: Rajasthan 13, U.P. 10, Bihar 6, Gujarat 2, Haryana 1, Bengal 1, Orissa 1, Bangladesh 1, Maharashtra 1 and South India 1. Thus his worship seems to have been popular from Rajasthan and Gujarat in the west to Bangladesh in the east. Epigraphs indicate that Revanta had a following in the Deccan and South India also except Tamilnadu but the evidence of his worship north of Haryana is still wanting. Chronological considerations show that the worship of Revanta has been popular in Rajasthan, M.P., Bihar and U.P. from the Gupta period onwards and these states account for 33 images of the deity out of 43 mentioned above. In other parts, which together have yielded only nine images, the worship of Revanta started in or after the 10th century C.E. 33 images belong to the early medieval period (seventh to twelfth centuries C.E.), 6 are earlier and 4 later. However, recent discoveries show that Haryana too was a part of the nucleus zone of the worship of Revanta though it started there a bit later than Rajasthan, U.P., Bihar, etc.

Revanta from Gujjar Kheri

A fragmentary relief from Gujjar Kheri (Acc. No. 1/343), located at a distance of about 25 km north of Sonepat on Ganaur-Ahulana road, shows a badly mutilated figure of an equestrian to right with a full-blown lotus gloriole behind the head (Pl. 289). Made of buff sandstone and measuring 26 x 25 cm in its extant form, the relief represents Revanta on horseback with an attendant holding the shaft of an umbrella which canopied the head of the deity (Acc. No. 25/84). It is significant to note that most of the images of the god found from various parts of India show this feature. Unfortunately the head of the god, both his hands, the legs of the horse, the head of the *Chhatra-dhara* 'umbrella-bearer' and the upper part of the halo are irretrievably lost. There are traces of a female figure holding a pot of wine standing in front of the horse. Revanta is generally shown holding a wine-cup in one of his hands and even in this case he may have been originally depicted as holding one in his right hand. The left hand probably held the reins of the horse. The image, to judge from the style of the surviving parts, may have belonged to *circa* 8th century C.E.

Revanta from Thanesar

Thanesar (Kurukshetra) has also yielded a badly broken panel showing the equestrian figures of Piṅgala and Daṇḍa, preceding and following the central figure of Revanta, completely lost in the extant relief, moving to left hunting and trampling boars and deer with the help of a dog. The presence of a round lotus-petalled *prabhā-maṇḍala* 'halo' and an attendant holding the shaft of the *chhatra* 'umbrella' certainly indicate the central figure to have been that of Revanta. There are some other subsidiary figures also but they are mutilated beyond proper identification. This is a buff sandstone panel measuring 84 x 67 cm assignable to *circa* 8th-9th century C.E. (Acc. No. 13/84).[121]

Revanta from Chandimandir

A worn out fragmentary relief of Revanta has been recovered from the Hanumān Temple of Chandimandir cantonment area near Chandigarh (Acc. No. 25/84). Made of grey sandstone, it measures 46 x 36 cm and shows the horse-riding Revanta being canopied by an attendant (Pl. 290). A female figure, probably with a wine-pot, is also shown in the panel. The head of the attendant, the right leg of the god and the mouth of the steed are mutilated. This surviving part of the panel seems to be central part of the relief, which is broken on both sides. It is not found in good state of preservation and the details of even extant figures cannot be made out precisely. On stylistic grounds, it may be dated to *circa* 10th century.

Rāma Mandira in the same Chandimandir cantonment area has yielded a 30 x 20 cm greenish sandstone broken image of Piṅgala, the acolyte of Revanta (Pl. 291), seated on horseback, holding a pen in his right hand. His left hand, now mutilated, may have held the leaf for writing (Acc. No. 13/84). Piṅgala wears a typical conical hat reminiscent of his Iranian association, large circular earrings, necklet, *avyaṅga* 'chest cover' and bracelets. The caparisoned horse on which he sits is looking back. The panel is broken below the waist of Piṅgala. Stylistically it may have preceded the image recovered from the Hanumān Temple, Chandimandir by about a century.

Revanta from Kanwari

The best-preserved panel depicting Revanta is now fixed in the wall of the Brāhmaṇa *dharmaśālā* in the middle of the village of Kanwari located about 26 km south of Hisar on road to Tosham. It is a buff sandstone panel measuring about 23 x 20 cm (Pl. 292).[122] On the central projection of the *triratha* 'triple-projection' pedestal is shown Revanta wearing a cylindrical crown, earring, pearl necklace, bracelets, *dhotī* and boots, seated on a caparisoned horse, holding the reins in his left hand and a cup in his right. The hind left leg of the steed is trampling a boar. An attendant behind holds an umbrella over the god's head. Piṅgala who is turning backwards as if talking to or looking at Revanta precedes the latter. He wears a high beaded conical cap, ear ornaments, *ekāvali* 'single stringed necklace' and an undergarment. Both his hands are partly damaged. The horse, as usual, is caparisoned and trampling a boar under its hind left foot. An unidentifiable male head is visible behind and above the head of Piṅgala's steed and a female head, probably of the wine-pot bearer, between Revanta and Piṅgala. Revanta is followed by Daṇḍa who holds a staff in his right hand and the reins of the horse in his left hand. The horse tramples a deer. Stylistically, the relief may be assigned to *circa* 10th century C.E.

Revanta from Pehowa

In 1974, we had discovered the first relief of Revanta from Pehowa, 25 km west of Kurukshetra.[123] It showed Revanta and Piṅgala as usual but Daṇḍa was missing. Subsequently, however, we have discovered the detached panel depicting Daṇḍa also (Pl. 288).[124] The image is datable to the Tomara period, *circa* 12th century C.E. There is another buff sandstone panel, 15.5 x 10 cm, discovered from Prāchī Śiva Temple, Pehowa (Acc. No. 1/408) which shows an equestrian figure on an architectural piece and may represent Revanta. It may be dated to *circa* 10th century C.E.

We thus see that Haryana has yielded about half a dozen images of Revanta – two from Chandimandir, two from Pehowa (one piece being doubtful), one each from Thanesar, Gujjar Kheri and Kanwari. Considering the small size of the state it is a considerable number. While Thanesar (Kurukshetra) and Pehowa are ancient holy places, Gujjar Kheri was one of the great center of art.[125] Pehowa was also a famous trade-center for horses during the medieval period. It is also noteworthy that all these places have yielded images of Sūrya.[126] Chandimandir may be said to be extension of the well-known art center of Pinjaur which too has yielded images of sun.

The *Mārkaṇḍeya Purāṇa* (105.20-23) tells us that when Sūrya appointed Revanta to the lordship of the Guhyakas, he said that the latter will be worshipped by the whole world and that who shall call him to mind amid the terrors of forests and other lonely places, of great conflagrations, of enemies and robbers, shall be delivered out of great calamity. Sūrya also said that when worshipped and well satisfied, Revanta shall bestow on men comfort, intelligence, happiness, kingship, perfect health, renown and exalted position. The *Skanda Purāṇa* (164.1-4) says that a dedicated glance of the Rājyabhaṭṭāraka Revanta seated on horseback will free one from all evils and bestow upon him religious merit. Uddyotana Sūri[127] tells us that Revanta delivers people from the terrors of forests and other lonely places, of great conflagration, of enemies and robbers and bestows upon his worshippers comfort, intelligence, happiness, kingship, robust health, renown and exalted position. It, thus, repeats Sūrya's benediction to his son as narrated in the *Mārkaṇḍeya Purāṇa*. The *Śabda-kalpa-druma* enjoins upon kings or generals desirous of victory to worship Revanta.[128]

The sites, which have yielded images of Revanta in Haryana, were not the capital cities of any kings at the period when these images were carved. B.N. Sharma had observed that since Revanta was the divine master of the horses, his worship was specially done for the protection and care of one's own horses.[129] But for Pehowa, none of the above-mentioned sites is connected with horses though the possession of horses at these places by individuals cannot be denied. A generalization of B.N. Sharma's observation, however, would lead us to expect images of Revanta for protection against certain dangers and for certain gains as described in the *Mārkaṇḍeya Purāṇa* and the *Kuvalayamālā Kathā*. This worship, it is to be noted, was not independent but an adjunct of the worship of sun as all the images described above do not seem to have been independent images but the subsidiary ones.

DIKPĀLAS

The Hindu concept of *Dikpālas* or *Lokapālas*, the guardians of the quarters or of the world, owes its origin to the Atharvavedic description of the regents (*adhipati*) and wardens (*rakshitā*) of the six quarters which it recognized – the gods Agni, Indra, Varuṇa, Soma, Vishṇu and Bṛihaspati as the regents of the eastern, southern, western, northern, fixed and upwards quarters with the Nāgas, Asita, Tiraśchirāji, Pṛidāku, Svaja, Kalmāshagrīva and Śvitra as the wardens of those quarters respectively.[130] The *Taittirīya Saṃhitā* (V.5, 10) substitutes Vishṇu by Yama. The *Gobhila Gṛihyasūtra* (IV.7, 41), however, recognizes ten *dikpālas* of which eight, with some variations of course, seem to have been adopted ubiquitously later on as the protectors of the four main and four minor quarters. The said Gṛihyasūtra supplies the following list: Indra (East), Vāyu (Southeast), Yama (South), Pitaras (Southwest), Varuṇa (West), Mahārāja (Northwest), Soma (North), Mahendra (Northeast), Vāsuki (downwards), and Brahmā (upwards). The *Rāmāyaṇa* (II.16, 24) recognized Indra (E), Yama (S), Varuṇa (W), and Kubera (N) as the guardians of the main quarters. The *Mahābhārata* (I.74, 85; VII.70, 45 and 91, 3) also agrees with the above at one place while at another Agni replaces Kubera.[131] Hopkins thinks that 'the grouping Agni, Yama, Varuṇa and Indra seems older than when Kubera is substituted for Agni.'[132] That the worship of Yama, Varuṇa, Kubera and Vāsava (Indra) as *lokapālas* had been fairly well recognized by the 1st century B.C.E. is indicated clearly by the Nanaghat Inscription of Nāganikā. In the Buddhist literature, we find the Brahmanical conception of the four *dikpālas* or *lokapālas* represented by more elaborate and definite ideas of the four Mahārājas.[133] Later, the number of the *dikpālas* or *lokapālas* was raised to eight: Indra, Anila (Vāyu), Yama, Arka (Sūrya), Agni, Varuṇa, Chandra (Soma), and Vitteśa (Kubera) in the *Manusmṛiti* (VV.4-7) and Indra, Vahni (Agni), Pitṛipati (Yama), Nairṛita, Varuṇa, Marut

(Vāyu), Kubera and Īśa (Īśāna), beginning from the east to north-northeast in the *Amarakosha* (II.2, 6). This conception of the eight *dikpālas* grew traditional in the medieval period and sometimes Brahman in the zenith and Ananta in the nadir were also added to the list.[134] Since there are no early or even medieval standing temples in Haryana, we do not have the representation of the *dikpālas* at one place. That there existed such temples where the *dikpālas* occupied their fixed places is, however, indicated by the stray images of some of the *dikpāla*s found from Pinjore, Pehowa, Bulandpur Mustarka, Sikanderpur, etc. We describe below some of these important *dikpālas* whose images have been found from different places.

INDRA

The foremost god of Vedic mythology,[135] Indra was reduced to the position of a mere *dikpāla* of the eastern quarter later. In the *Ṛigveda*, we hear of a thunderbolt and goad (I.32, 2; VIII.33, 11), bow and arrow (VIII.45, 4; 66, 6-11; X.103, 2-3; *Mbh.* VIII.17, 92) as his weapons. Even a noose is associated with him (*AV* VIII.8, 5-7; *Mbh.* III.234, 17). The cutting of the wings of mountains with his thunderbolt (*ṚV* I.57, 6; *Mait. Saṃ.* I.10, 13), shattering Vṛitra with his weapons (ṚV I.35, 5; 61, 10; X.89, 7) and releasing of waters (V.32, 1-2; 33, 1; X.89, 7) are some of his feats especially lauded in the *Ṛigveda*. The last trait persists indirectly when we find him eulogized as a god of rain. His immoral and capricious traits, though referred to in the *Ṛigveda,*[136] do not show him sexually malpheasant as he is in the epics. Indra's car and steeds also find mention in the *Ṛigveda* (I.111, 1; V.31, 4), but the Samudramanthana episode acquaints us of the acquisition of the elephant Airāvata by him, which finds mention in literature as his mount (*Mbh.* I.60, 61; *Agni Purāṇa* 51.14). Indra's name occurs in the *Avesta*[137] and Boghaz Kui inscriptions[138] indicating his antiquity going back to the Indo-Iranian period.

The *Agni Purāṇa* (51.14 – *vajrī gajārūḍhaḥ*), *Matsya Purāṇa* (260. 66 ff), *Bṛihatsaṃhitā* (LVII.42), and *Abhilashitārthachintāmaṇi* (III.1, 811) describe Indra as having a thunderbolt as his attribute and elephant as his vehicle. The *Vishṇudharmottara* (III.50, 2-6) contains a detailed description of the deity as four-armed, three-eyed, having four-tusked elephant as his vehicle, holding the thunderbolt, elephant-goad and lotus in his hands and embracing his consort Śachī seated on his lap with the fourth. The *Aparājitapṛichchhā* (213.9) and *Rūpa-Maṇḍana* (II.31), too, describe him as seated on the elephant with the normal right hand in *varada* pose and others holding clockwise a thunderbolt, goad, and water-vessel. Some other texts[139] including the Jaina ones also describe the four-armed god with varying attributes, seated on the elephant.

At Bulandpur Mustarka in district Karnal must have existed a temple during *circa* 10th century C.E. as quite a few *dikpāla* images seated at ease on their respective mounts in pilastered niches have been obtained from there. The images, however, are not in a good state of preservation and have been marred by whitewash also. The image of Indra from this site shows the god seated on his vehicle elephant to left in profile. The god wears a cylindrical crown, scarf and *dhotī*. His left hand is placed on his left knee and the attribute in the right is not clear. The elephant has been depicted as walking. Below the niche is shown, as in other cases also from this site, a *vidyādhara* holding long winding garlands. There is another probable depiction of Indra from Sagwan near Tosham (Acc. No. 1/113) on a light brown sandstone pillar, 48 x 21 cm in its extant form, showing a beautully carved *dvibhaṅga* male deity holding probably a *vajra* (broken on one side) in his right hand with left akimbo (Pl. 294). Indra bears a *karaṇḍa-mukuṭa* decorated with jewels on his head and wears earrings, *ekāvali*, pearl *yajñopavīta*, *keyūras*, bracelets, long garland, *dhotī* secured by a pearl-girdle with pendent free ends falling on the thighs, sash, and anklets. There seems to be a diminutive depiction of the elephant near his right foot. The facet of the pillar on which Indra has been shown is decorated with an inverted lotus at the top with a beaded rim below. Lotus petals hang down from the top. There are golden chains with bells at their ends shown falling on the two sides. Diamond and vine scrolls decorate the sides of the pillar. The whole composition gives a very pleasing look. The image may be dated to *circa* 9th century C.E. on stylistic grounds.

AGNI

Agni, the chief terrestrial deity, is next only to Indra in importance in the Vedic pantheon. Agni is described variously in the *Ṛigveda* as having a burning head or three heads; one, three or seven tongues; an archer who sharpens his flames like a blade of iron.[140] The tongues obviously are the flames of Agni. His description as a priest and a seer (*ṚV* IX.66, 22; III.21, 3; VI.14, 2; etc.) probably led to his depiction with a beard. His description as one who protects his worshippers and takes them across calamities just like a ship in the ocean (*ṚV* VII.3, 7; III.20, 4; V.4, 9; VII.12, 2; etc.) seems to have provided the basis for his appointment as a protector of the quarter. The first detailed iconographic description of Agni is met with in the *Vishṇudharmottara* (III.56, 1-10), which says that the god should be bearded, four-armed, having three eyes, four-tusked, riding upon a chariot with smoke standard drawn by four parrots and driven by the wind, with his consort Svāhā on his left lap and holding flames, trident, and rosary in his hands. The *Agni* (51.15) and the *Matsya* (261.9-12) Purāṇa prescribe a halo of flames, sacred thread, long beard and goat (ram according to *Śilparatna*) as his vehicle for the two-armed Agni holding rosary and water-vessel. Other texts also describe Agni with more or less such features. In Indian art, Agni is represented from 1st century B.C.E. onwards.[141]

Besides a niched figure of juvenile Agni having an aureole of flames behind his head and seated on his vehicle goat to left in profile from Bulandpur Mustarka, we have a beautiful representation of the god from Pinjore (Pl. 295) showing the elongate figure of the deity standing in *ābhaṅga* in a pilastered *rathikā*, bearing a high *jaṭā-jūṭa* bedecked with jewels, knotted beard and lozenge-shaped *śrīvatsa* on the chest and wearing earrings, *ekāvali*, triple-stringed sacred-thread, *valayas*, *dhotī* secured by a *netra-sūtra*, sash on the thighs, a long garland and holding a rosary in the suspended normal right hand and water-vessel in the left, ladle and lotus in the additional right and left hands, accompanied by ram to left near his right foot. There is a leaf-shaped halo of flames behind his head. The *rathikās* on either side on the receding recesses show female figures. The one on his proper right is carved equally elegantly in *tribhaṅga*. She bears a topknot on her head and wears earrings, necklet with pendent string falling to the right of her belly from between her round breasts, armlets, four bangles on the wrist, nether garment held in position by beaded girdle, holding the free-end of her *uttarīya* in her suspended right hand. The female figure on his proper left is shown as turning her back with face to left. She is supporting a child in her left lap. She has very sharp facial features; her hair is combed backwards with a bun at the back. She is wearing a beautiful ear ornament, an *ekāvali*, armlets, an *uttarīya* wound from the back with free-ends coming over the shoulders, and the lower garment. It is difficult to identify these female figures with the spouses of Agni in the absence of any definite iconographic clue. They may just be *apasarases* adorning the temple walls. The image stylistically belongs to about 10th century C.E. There is another Agni image amongst the remains of the Bhīmādevī Temple at Pinjore but this figure is very badly mutilated. The god is shown as bearded with a halo of flames holding a ladle in his upraised right hand and water-vessel in the suspended left. A head from the same complex (Acc. No. 1/41) may also belong to Agni. Chandigarh Museum possesses another figure of Agni (Pl. 296), which D.C. Bhattacharyya has described as belonging to Central India (Acc. No. 9.147)[142] but actually it belongs to Rohtak. This bearded male deity characterized by slight obesity stands on a *tri-ratha* pedestal with a plain round aureole behind the head, holding a rosary in the right hand and a *kamaṇḍalu* in the left. The god has matted locks on the head and wears earrings, *ekāvali*, sacred-thread, *valayas*, *keyūras*, nether garment secured by a girdle, and a long garland. Near the feet are shown in profile the devotee couple in *añjali-mudrā*. The back slab is plain. Stylistically, it has been dated to 10th century C.E. In the absence of the vehicle, the identification is not certain though quite probable.

YAMA

Yama, the younger son of Vivasvant Mārtaṇḍa by Suraṇyu (*ṚV* X.14, 5), the daughter of Tvashṭri, was the first of the mortals who died (*AV* XVII.3, 13). In the *AV* (V.28, 31) Yama has been described as the lord of all men and manes and has been identified with death. He is described as cayying a rod of justice (*daṇḍa*) with which he himself is also often identified.[143] He also carries a noose to catch souls.[144] Chitragupta, Yama's scribe, keeps a record of the good and bad deeds of man and Yama passes the judgment accordingly.[145] The buffalo as his vehicle appears for the first time in the *Harivaṃśa* (52.30). The *Bṛihatsaṃhitā* describes Yama simply as holding a staff and riding a buffalo (LVII.57 – *Daṇḍī Yamo mahishago*). The *VDP* (III.51, 1-7), however, gives a detailed description of the four-armed god seated on a buffalo with his spouse Dhūmorṇā on his left lap, his right hand holding a *khaṭvāṅga* and a sword and the left ones a trident with flames and a rosary, accompanied on his right by Chitragupta dressed as a northerner (*udīchya-veśa*), holding a pen and a leaf in his hands, and by fierce-looking Kāla holding a noose in his hand, on his left. The *Aparājitapṛichchhā* (213.11) and the *Rūpa-Maṇḍana* (II.33) give a similar description of Yama riding a buffalo and holding a pen, a cock, and a staff in his hands.[146]

We have referred to the niched images of Indra and Agni from Bulandpur Mustarka. It has yielded the image of Yama also in the same style as riding on his vehicle buffalo to left. The relief is so mutilated that the details of the figure of Yama are difficult to be discerned. The buffalo, however, has been depicted very lively as turning its face to lick the hoof of one of its hind leg held forward. A lively image of Yama comes from Pehowa where the god is shown as seated at ease on the buffalo to right. It is made of red sandstone measuring 60 x 40 cm and is now preserved in the Dasanāmī Akhārā at Pehowa (Regn. No. HRN/ KURU-419). The god wears a flat cylindrical crown and an effort has been made to give him a fierce look by carving his wide-open eyes and moustaches on his face. He is holding his right hand raised to the level of his shoulder but the attribute in it is not clear. In his left hand, however, he holds a *khaṭvāṅga* (Pl. 297). This is a beautiful Pratihāra image.[147]

A very elaborately carved image of Yama is known from Sagwan (Pl. 298). Made of buff sandstone, it measures 71 x 44 cm (Acc. No. 1/172). The god is shown as standing in *dvibhaṅga* in an arched *rathikā* wearing matted locks on the head, big circular earrings, a pearl necklace, *yajñopavīta*, *dhotī* held in position by a girdle, sash on the thighs, and a long garland. The face is slightly mutilated by the oblique open eyes with curved eyebrows giving a frightful look to the deity, which is enhanced further by the *khaṭvāṅga* held by its long bone in his right hand. The left hand, now broken, may have been akimbo. The mutilated figure of buffalo to left may be noticed behind the legs of the god. Jumping leogryph figures have been carved outside the pillars of the niche. It must have formed part of a beautiful 10th-century shrine. A small fragment from Bhīmādevī Temple at Pinjore (Acc. No. 1/44) also shows the head and *khaṭvāṅga* in a pedimented *rathikā*. It may have been a part of a Yama figure. An image of Yama is lying in the compound of the Chandimandir also.

NIRṚITI

Nirṛiti (Decease), as the personification presiding over death, is the regent of the southwestern quarter and is often depicted in art as a terrific deity riding an ass or horse and holding a sword (*vājivāhana, khaḍga-hasta*). The only known image of Nirṛiti comes from Bulandpur Mustarka and shows the deity as seated in *lalitāsana* on a big lotus placed on the back of the ass, holding a sword in the right hand and a noose in the left (Pl. 299).

VARUṆA

Varuṇa is the regulator of waters and lord of sea. As such he is the regent of the western quarter. Most of the iconographic texts describe him as holding a noose (*pāśa*) and riding a swan or a crocodile. The Bhīmādevī Temple at Pinjore has yielded a beautiful image of Varuṇa standing in *dvibhaṅga* bearing a high *jaṭā-jūṭa* adorned with jewels and wearing the usual ornaments, with proper right hand suspended in *varada* pose, probably also with a rosary in the palm, holding a noose in the rear right hand (Pl. 300). The upper left hand is broken and water-vessel is shown in the suspended proper left hand. Crocodile appears near the left foot of the god. The part of the wall outside the *rathikā* carrying this image shows an erotic couple indicating clearly that the wall of this 10th-11th century shrine was not much different from those of the Khauraho temples.

Another image of Varuṇa is preserved in the Topanātha kā Mandira at Pinjore and shows the god as standing in *dvibhaṅga* in a pillared *raṭhikā*, wearing a *karaṇḍa-mukuṭa* and other usual ornaments including *yajñopavīta* and the long garland, and holding a beautiful lotus in his upper right hand with proper right suspended in *varada* and also holding a rosary. The normal and additional left hands show the water-vessel and the noose. Crocodile touching the water-vessel is depicted near the left foot of the god (Pl. 301). This too must have adorned a 10th-century shrine at Pinjore.

VĀYU

Vāyu, the divine personification of winds and the regent of the northwestern quarter, is verily depicted in art as having deer or stag as his vehicle. *Dhvaja* (flag or banner), *daṇḍa*, *kamaṇḍalu*, etc. are his usual attributes according to the iconographic texts. Vāyu is being represented sculpturally from the Kushāṇa period onwards and his images have been discovered from various parts of the country.[148] A good image of Vāyu is known from the Bhīmādevī Temple at Pinjore (Pl. 302) where the god is shown as standing in a niche with his vehicle the deer. Unfortunately all the hands are broken but the suspended principal hands may have been disposed in *varada* and holding a water-vessel and the additional ones may have held a banner and a staff.

KUBERA

Kubera, the god of wealth, is known by various names such as Dhanada, Dhaneśvara, Dhanapati, Gadādhara, Guhyakādhipati, Kailāśanilaya, Naravāhana, Rājarāja, Rākshaseśvara, Vaiśravaṇa, Yakshādhipa, etc. and is worshipped from very early times. These names are indicative of his lordship of the riches and treasures, *guhyakas* and the *rākshasas*, yakshas and *rājās*. The various iconographic texts describe Kubera as pot-bellied and having two, four or eight arms.[149] He holds a club, an axe, rosary or *śakti*, *nakulaka* (mongoose-purse), etc. with one of his hands in *varada* or *abhaya*. The mount of Kubera has variously been described as a man, sheep, elephant, ram or a buffalo. Śaṅkha and Padma, the personified treasures and his councilors are his iconographic traits also. He is united with Ṛiddhi (prosperity) and Bhadrā or Lakshmī (goddess of wealth) who are later described as his consorts also (*Mbh.* I.199, 6; III.136, 8; 168, 13, etc.). Kauṭilya lays emphasis on the installation of the images of Kubera.[150] Some very remarkable images of Kubera from the Śuṅga period onwards showing these traits and attributes are now known. The early images of Kubera are based on the existing statues of Yakshas, who appear in Buddhist art as attendants, guardians or *dvārapālas* holding either a bag of jewels or a mongoose vomiting gems.[151] Several Kushāṇa images of Kubera have been unearthed at Mathura which show him as pot-bellied, wearing a thick necklace, heavy rings and a sash tied around his shin and the waist. He has rolling eyes, wig-shaped curly locks, well trimmed moustaches, holding a wine-cup and *nakulaka*, sometimes accompanied by his consort Hārīti with a child on her lap.[152]

The popularity of the images of Kubera at an early period may be postulated from Gupta terracotta of the god from Agroha (Pl. 303). Seated in *utkaṭikāsana*, the pot-bellied Kubera is having locks of hair falling on his shoulders and holding a *chashaka* (wine-cup) in his right hand and a mongoose on his left arm.[153] Terracotta is common man's art and if a god is represented in this medium, it may just be guessed as to how much demand for his images even by the poor people must have been there.

A seated sandstone image of Kubera from Thanesar measuring 29 x 29 cm showing the god as seated in *utkuṭikāsana* holding in the left hand a mongoose purse and an indistinct object in the right hand, wearing a bejeweled *mukuṭa*, earrings, armlets, bracelets, ornamental girdle with *vidyādhara* figures on either side and the rounded back slab serving as the halo, datable to *circa* 6th-7th century C.E., is now preserved in the Kurukshetra University Museum (Fig. 12).[154] A standing image of Kubera (59 x 52 cm) as a *dikpāla* with Īśāna on the other facet, which once studded the wall of the Kabir Chaurā at Pinjore, is now housed in the Kurukshetra University museum. It may be dated to *circa* 9th-10th century C.E.[155]

A 29 x 25 cm sandstone upper part of an image of Kubera is known from Lalkot near Rohtak (Pl. 304). The face is unfortunately very badly mutilated but that the god wore earrings and an *ekāvali* can be made out from what has survived. The back slab behind the head bore the carvings of the lotus petals in the form of gloriole and there are two *vidyādharas* in profile on either side of the head. The god may have been slightly pot-bellied. The deity may be recognized by the wine-cup in his right hand. It may belong to the early medieval period.

A small 22 x 13 cm figure from Kheri Chhichhrana in district Sonepat showing the slightly pot-bellied deity seated in *lalitāsana* holding a purse in the damaged left hand and a wine-cup in the right, bearing a rounded crown of matted hair adorned with a jewel in front on the head and wearing ear ornaments, torque, armlets and a cloth-belt going around the right leg and the belly, datable to *circa* 8th century is also known (Pl. 305). Another small crudely carved figure of 14 x 9 cm made of buff sandstone from Sirsa is preserved in HARDAM

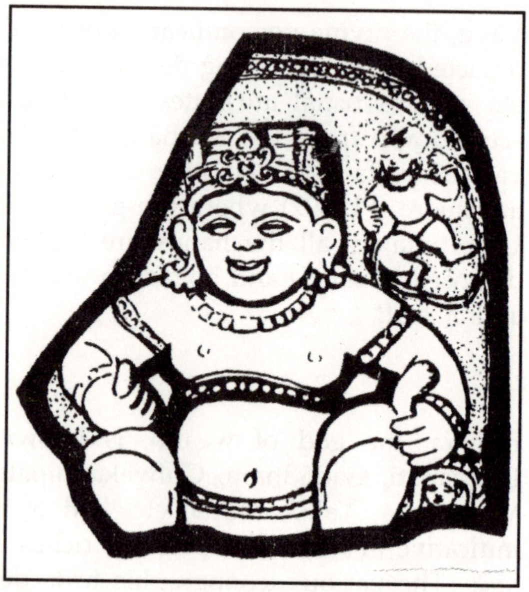

Fig. 12. Kubera, Kurukshetra University Museum.

(Acc. No. 1/132) and shows Kubera seated in *ardhaparyaṅkāsana*, holding the wine-cup in his right hand and *nakulaka* in his left, wearing a *karaṇḍa-mukuṭa*, ear ornaments, bracelets, necklace, etc. and having a thick rope-like loop behind the head to serve as the gloriole. It may be dated to *circa* 9th century C.E.

We have already referred to the auspicious triads showing Gaṇeśa, Gaja-Lakshmī or Mahishamardinī and Kubera found from Chuliana, Chulkana, Kalayat, Kasan, and Sondh. Kubera is depicted in these triads not as a *dikpāla* but as an auspicious and gracious deity with his usual iconographic features.

ĪŚĀNA

Īśāna, the regent of the northeastern quarter, represents a particular aspect of Śiva as his name indicates.[156] According to the *Matsya Purāṇa* (261.23), Īśāna should have three eyes and a trident and seated on a bull. *Pūrvakāraṇāgama* also describes him similarly. The *Aṃśumadbhedāgama* describes the two-handed Īśāna as placid, wearing all ornaments, *jaṭā-mukuṭa*, standing on a white lotus and holding trident and skull in his right and left hands.[157] The *Śilparatna* prescribes *jaṭā-maṇḍala*, a crescent, three eyes, *nāga-yajñopavīta*, *maṇi-kuṇḍalas*, tiger-skin, one hand in *varada* pose and *triśūla* in the other hand of the god riding a bull. According to the *Suprabhedāgama*, Īśāna should have matted locks, three eyes, four hands showing *varada* and *abhaya* and holding trident (fourth one left out unspecified), and riding a bull.[158] The *Aparājitapṛichchhā* (213.16) and *Rūpa-Maṇḍana* (II.38) describe Īśāna riding a bull and holding a trident, snake and *vījapūraka*, with one hand in the boon-conferring pose.

Quite a few images of Īśāna are known from Pinjore. One of them, carved on the other side of a corner stone with Kubera figure on the northern facet referred to above,[159] shows the four-armed deity standing gracefully wearing a *jaṭā-jūṭa*, *yajñopavīta*, long garland and other items of dress and ornaments holding a trident in his upraised back right hand. All other hands are damaged but the normal ones were shown as *pralamba*. The bull stands to left near the right foot of the *dikpāla*.

The most exquisite figure, however, belongs to the Bhīmādevī Temple, Pinjore showing Īśāna standing gracefully in the central niche with two *apasarases* flanking him in the niches on the receding *rathas* (Pl. 306) in the same style as seen in the image of Agni described above. Even the artist seems to have been the same as betrayed by expression, style, dress and ornamentation. The elongated figure shows the *dikpāla* wearing an elaborate and high *jaṭā-jūṭa* adorned with pearl strings and jewels, earrings, necklet and necklace of pearls, sacred-thread, *śrīvatsa* on the chest, long garland, *dhotī* tied with pearl girdle and sash on the thighs. The bull standing behind the god is holding its face up to have a look of his master. The four-handed regent holds a trident and a snake in the rear pair of hands, the principal right is suspended (now damaged) in *varada* and the corresponding normal left holds the water-pot. The relief measures 68 x 56 and is now preserved in HARDAM (Acc. No. 1/83). Two more equally beautiful reliefs from the same complex measure 68 x 35 cm (Acc. No. 1/80) and 58 x 52 cm (Acc. No. 1/291). They all furnish evidence of the existence of numerous temples in the same complex.

NAVAGRAHAS

In Hindu mythology, astronomy and astrology Sūrya, Soma (Chandra), Maṅgala (Bhauma), Budha, Bṛihaspati, Śukra, Śani, Rāhu and Ketu are regarded as '*grahas*'[160] and are collectively known as *Navagrahas* because of their number nine. Though Sūrya and Soma are referred to in literature individually from very early times, yet collectively they are first mentioned in the *Yājñavalkyasūtra*.[161] The *Vishṇudharmottara Purāṇa*, *Agni Purāṇa*, *Matsya Purāṇa*, *Aṃśumadbhedāgama*, *Śilparatna*, and some Buddhist texts like *Nishpannayogāvali*, *Kṛityasaṅgrahapañjikā*, *Dharaṇīsaṅgraha*, *Dharmakośasaṅgraha* and *Pūjā-vidhi*[162] describe them in detail. These texts sometimes differ and the extant reliefs too show variations.[163]

No independent images of the *Navagrahas* have been found from anywhere as yet from Haryana. Collectively, *navagrahas* have been depicted on the door-surrounds and even on individual images. The Pratihāra doorframes fitted in the Prāchī Śiva temple and the Sarasvatī temple at Pehowa show the *navagrahas* on the lintel. They are depicted on the Vishṇu image in the Kashipuri Temple at Kaithal, Śeshaśāyī from Mandhna and elsewhere as also on the *parikara* of the Sūrya image from Hansi. We have given details of the *navagraha* panels while describibg these images in the preceding pages. Mention, however, should also be made of a very much-mutilated 44 x 20 cm panel fitted into the wall of the house of Shri Dhanpat at Hat, which partly shows a *navagraha* panel with prominent head of Rāhu. A small 16 x 14 cm panel from Kurukshetra shows three of the nine standing planetary divinities – Sūrya holding the lotus flowers in both of his hands, followed on his proper left by Soma and Maṅgala, the former with right hand in *abhaya* and left holding the water-vessel (Pl. 307). An architectural piece, obviously a part of the lintel of some doorframe, from Rohtak also shows six of these divinities seated in *sukhāsana* holding a water-pot in the left hand with right disposed in *abhaya*.

GANDHARVAS, VIDYĀDHARAS, KINNARAS AND *APASARAS*

"The *gandharva* minstrels and the *vidyādhara* angels, the *kinnara* bird-men and the *apasaras* maidens add, by their presence, material meaning to the spiritual content of a medieval Indian temple."[164] They are classed as demigods and occupy subsidiary rungs on the ladder of celestial hierarchy. It has, however, been aptly remarked that "in terms of plastic expression, they, all the same, rival and occasionally excel their superiors, the higher gods."[165]

We have described above the *gandharvas*, alone or couples, as the adjuncts of various images. Mention, however, must be made here of an independent terracotta medallion depicting a *gandharva-yugala* from Sirsa (Pl. 308). Within a beaded border is shown the male celestial in a flying posture to his proper right with his spouse seated gracefully on his left leg. The face of the *gandharva* is unfortunately mutilated but his beautiful hair-coiffure, ear ornaments, necklace, bracelets, an ornamental belt with round spacers simulating the sacred thread and a *dhotī* with multiple pleats are very clear. The right leg is slightly folded at the knee but the left one extends backwards and provides a support to his spouse. The minstrel is shown as holding a sword in his right hand and embracing his wife with the other. The female, bearing a round puff at the back of her head, earrings, bracelets, anklets, *sārī*, etc. supports probably a lotus flower with a bud by its stalk by her right hand while the other one rests near her left calf. Lotus flowers bedeck the field with long stalks issuing from what seems to be similar to modern flowerpots. It is a beautiful specimen of the typical Gupta art.[166]

Gandharvas playing on the musical instruments, sometimes accompanied by their spouses, are shown on the top corners of some images or pillars, or even panels decorating the basement moldings or walls of the temples. A yawning beauty from Pinjore (Pl. 309) shows a *gandharva* playing on a flute with two females holding other musical instruments. A beautiful piece depicting a *gandharva* embracing a female on either side is fixed in a wall at Pinjore. Panels showing male and female figures playing on various musical instruments and dancing to their tunes (Pls. 310-11) are collected in the Bhīmādevī complex.

Vidyādharas, vidyādharīs or couples are generally shown as garland-bearing semi-celestials on the upper corners of the images flanking the head of the deities or occupying the rounded tops, sometimes accompanying figures holding crowns, or even on some other parts of the temple walls or ceilings. *Kinnaras* are sometimes shown on the *udumbaras* (Pl. 312) and screen walls, as at Pinjore. *Apasarases* are the personification of female beauty and sexual pleasure. They sing, dance, play on musical instruments, sport and seduce. They generally adorn the temple walls assuming various beauteous forms: slender, seductive, sensual; singing, dancing, coquetting, disrobing, revealing their physical charm, sporting with ball, yawning, pedicuring, binding anklets, bedecking themselves, rinsing water from the wet pleats of hair, removing thorn, fondling a baby, playing with pets, applying collyrium, etc. Some good specimens of such beauties occur in the remains of the Bhīmādevī temple complex. Specimens of *Kīchakas* or *Bhāraputras* may also be seen there (Pl. 313).

VYĀLAS, KĪRTIMUKHAS, ETC.

Some good specimens of *vyālas*, particularly of the *siṃha* and *gaja*, are sometimes shown on the back slabs of the images or on architectural elements. *Kīrtimukhas* occur on various parts of the temples: walls, pillars, pilasters, pedestals, doorways, *chaitya* apexes, etc. and present a good variety of forms. Sometimes very beautiful mythical bird (Fig. 13), animal and aquatic figures are met with on the basement moldings, doorframes, pillars, etc. A *kīrtimukha* carved on a brick of the late Gupta period from Kapālamochana (Pl. 314) is interesting. Examples of the depiction of bird-life also exist (Pl. 315). Evidence of snake worship has been found in the form of a Gupta Nāga figure in terracotta from Sugh (Pl. 316) and in stone from Ratpur

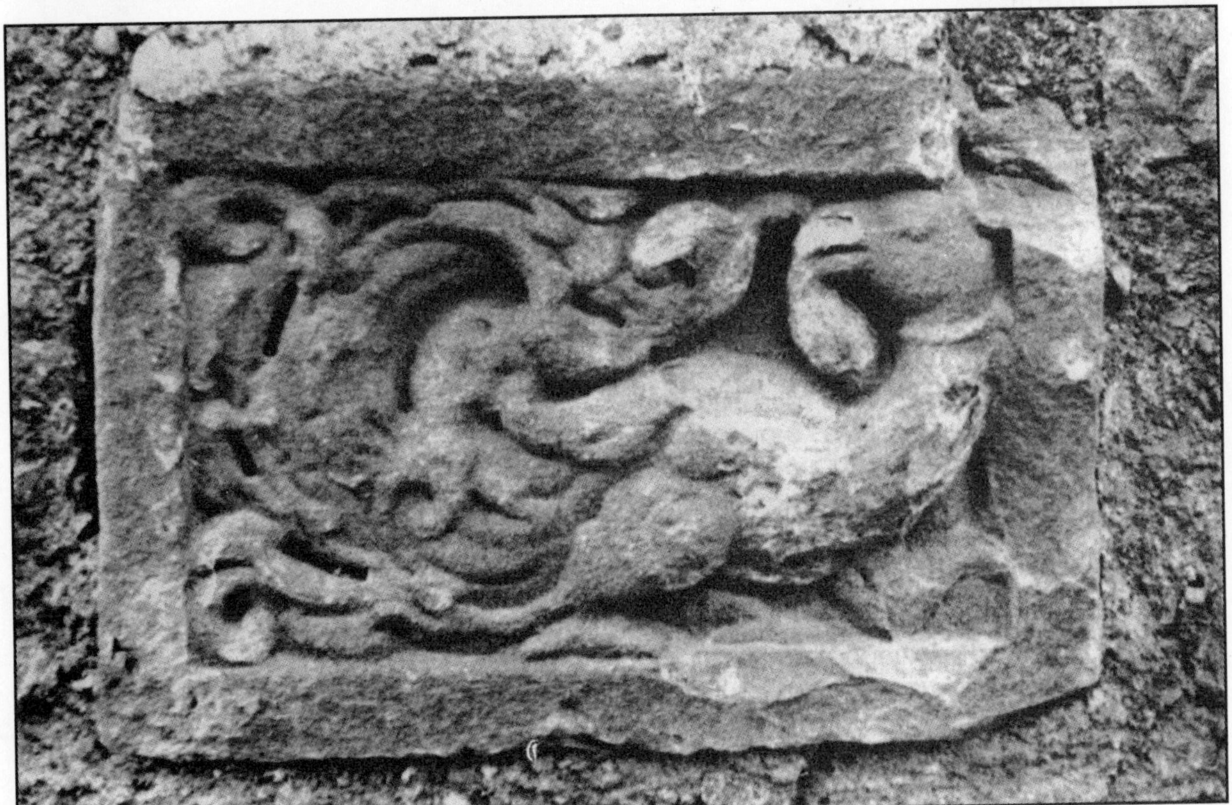

Fig. 13. Mythical bird with foliated tail, outer fortification wall, Pinjore.

(Pl. 317), the latter now preserved in HARDAM (Acc. No. 1/97). A Kushāṇa red sandstone image of a mythical lion from Ahrwan (Acc. No. 1/392; Pl. 318) and a medieval *charaṇa-pādukā* from Gujjar Kheri (Pl. 319) add to the variety of sculptural representations in Haryana.

EROTIC SCULPTURES

Erotic sculptures found on the temple walls of Khajuraho need no introduction.[167] It is interesting to note that such sculptures occur even at Pinjore. There are examples of mating with mutual consent (Pl. 320) and unnatural, plural and orgiastic sex (Pl. 321).[168]

There are many more interesting sculptures, which do not fall under the above-mentioned categories and betray the religious beliefs of the people of Haryana during the first millennium of our era. And many more await discovery.

Notes and References

1. *DHI*, p. 510.
2. *EHI*, II, pp. 502-03.
3. *Ibid.*; *DHI*, p. 515.
4. *Bṛihatsaṃhitā* LVII.41: *Brahmā kamaṇḍalu-karaśchaturmukhaḥ paṅkajāsanasaṃsthitaścha.*
5. C. Sivaramamurti,"Geographical and Chronological Factors in Indian Iconography," *Ancient India*, no. 6, p. 21.
6. *EHI*, II, Appendix B, p. 245.
7. As quoted by Rao (*Ibid.*). Cf. *VDP* III.44, 6.
8. *DHI*, p. 516.
9. *EHI*, II, Appendix B, pp. 243-44.
10. *Ibid.*, p. 244.
11. *Ibid.*
12. *Rūpa-Maṇḍana* II.7.
13. *DHI*, p. 516.
14. *EHI*, II, p. 243.
15. *V.S. Apte, Sanskrit-English Dictionary,* Delhi-Varanasi-Patna, 1959, p. 157.
16. *DHI*, p. 517. Sivaramamurti (*AI*, NO. 6, p. 35) also states that Brahmā in Rajasthan and Gujarat is represented with a beard like an old sage emphasizing the Pitāmaha (grandfather) aspect of the god. Cf. Devendra Handa, *Osian: History, Archaeology, Art & Architecture*, Delhi, 1984, pp. 134-37, pls. 97-98.
17. Devendra Handa, "Some Unpublished Terracottas From Haryana," *Prāchya-Pratibhā*, Bhopal, Vol. XII (1984), p. 30, fig. 6.
18. Devendra Handa, *Pehowa*, p. 116, Pl. 68.
19. *Ibid.*, pls. 69-70.
20. Bhagavāndeva Āchārya, *op. cit.*, p. 86.
21. H. Haertel, *Indische Sculpturen*, 1 (*Berlin Museum für Völkerkunde*), 1960, figs. 44-45; *Catalogue Museum für Indische Kunst Berlin*, Berlin, 1971, No. 101, fig. 22.
22. M.T. De Mallmann, "Divinities hindoues dans le tantrisme bouddhique", *Arts Asiatique*, X, 1, 1964; pp. 67 ff.
23. Pratapaditya Pal, "A Brahmanical Triad from Kashmir and some Related Icons", *Archives of Asian Art*, XXVII, 1973-74, pp. 33-45.
24. *Ibid.*, p. 35; *Bronzes of Kashmir*, 1975, p. 54, fig. 3.
25. *EHI*, II, Appendix B, pp. 243-47.
26. Pal (1973-74), *op. cit.*, p. 34; (1975), *loc. cit.*
27. P. Shah, (ed.), *Vishṇudharmottara Purāṇa*, Baroda, 1961, III, 73, 42; alternately, it states that the *Ṛigveda* should be depicted like Brahmā, *Yajurveda* like Indra, *Sāmaveda* like Vishṇu and *Atharvaveda*

like Śambhu-*Athavā devarūpeṇa vedāḥ kāryā vichakshaṇaiḥ Ṛigvedastu smṛito Brahmā Yajurvedastu Vāsavaḥ / Sāmavedastathā Vishṇuḥ Śambhuśchātharvaṇo bhavet //*. See also Bhattacharya, Gauriswar, "Deva Caturmukha-Pañcamukha: Brahmā and Śiva - Śilpa Texts and Art Objects," *Shastric Tradition in Indian Art*, Heidelberg, 1989, p. 53, fn. 16.

28. B.C. Siromani, (ed.), *Chaturvarga-Chintāmaṇi*, Vrata Khaṇḍa, Chapter I, p. 104.
29. K.K. Thaplyal, "Therianthropic representations of the Rigveda and its two Sakhas", *Bulletin of Museums and Archaeology in U.P.*, no. 7, 1971, pp.25-28, fig. 1.
30. N.P. Joshi, "Association of Horse with the Vedas," *Kalā*, Vol. V: 1998-99 *(Prof. G.N. Pant Commemration Volume)*, pp. 5-8.
31. *Śrītattvanidhi*, edited by Devanayakacharya, Silver Jubilee Proceedings of the Sāṅgavidyālaya, Varanasi, V.S. 2002 as quoted by Joshi.
32. Joshi, *op. cit.*, p. 7.
33. Father Heras, "The Seals of Mohenjo-daro," *New Indian Antiquary*, Vol. I, p. 52. See also his article "The Religion of Mohenjodaro People according to Inscriptions," in the *Journal of the University of Bombay* (*Sardesai Com. Vol.*), Vol. I, 1936, pp. 228 f.
34. T.G. Arvamuthan, "Gods of Harappa," *Journal of the Bihar Research Society*, Patna, 1948, pp. 30ff.
35. A.P. Karmarkar, The *Vrātya or Dravidian Systems*, Lonavala 1950, p. 128.
36. *Ṛigveda* VII.104, 24; x .87, 2 and 14.
37. Prithivi Kumar Agrawala, *Skanda-Kārttikeya*, Varanasi, 1967, p. xii.
38. The word Skanda is derived from the root *Skandir* which is used in words like *Chaskanda*, *Skanna*, etc., which occur in the *ṚV*. Nowhere, however, does the word Skanda occur in that text. It occurs for the first time in the *Chhāndogya Upanishad* (VII.26, 2). Kārttikeya occurs in the *Maitrāyaṇī Saṃhitā* for the first time.
39. Seventeen times. See for details P.K. Agrawala, *op. cit.*, p. 1 and Kachan Sinha, *Kārttikeya in Indian Art & Literature*, Delhi, 1979, p.1.
40. *ṚV* X. 135. in the *ṚV* IV. 15,7-10 *Kumāra* seems to occur as a proper name.
41. Sukumar Sen, "Iranian Sorasha and Indian Skanda," *Indo-Iranica*, Vol. IV, No.1 (July, 1950), p. 27.
42. *ṚV* I.66, 8; I.164, 46; X.79, 3 etc.
43. *ṚV* II.33, 12.
44. *Atharva Veda* VI.67, 2.
45. For detailed references, see P.K. Agrawala, *op. cit.*, pp. 1-11; Sinha, *op. cit.*, pp. 1-15; Asim Kumar Chatterjee, *The Cult of Skanda-Kārttikeya in Ancient India*, Calcutta, 1970, pp. 1-70; R. Navaratnam, *Kārttikeya – The Divine Child*, Bombay, 1973, pp. 1ff.
46. *Mahābhārata* I.103, 9.
47. *ṚV* VII.63, 1; X. 84, 2: *Kāṭhaka Saṃhitā* 36, 8; *Maitrāyaṇī Saṃhitā* I.10, 14; III.13, 14; *Śatapatha Brāhmaṇa* V, 3,1,1.
48. *AV* XI.2, 31; 1; *Vājasaneyī Saṃhitā* XVI.17; *Śatapatha Brāhmaṇa* IX.1,1, 18.
49. *Sacred Books of the East Series*, Vol. XLI (Pt. III, Eng. Tr. By Eggling), pp. 157ff.
50. For relevant portions and their English translation, see, P. K. Agrawala, *op. cit.*, Appendix II, pp. 104-10.
51. *Ibid.*, pp. 18-22.
52. *Ibid.*, p. 11. Cf. E.W. Hopkins, *Epic Mythology*, Strassburg, 1915, p. 229.
53. *Dhūrtakalpa* (as quoted by P.K. Agrawala) V.2-3.
54. *Dhūrtakalpa* V.1-5; *Vishṇudharmottara* III, 223, 18.
55. *Mbh.* IX.46, 98-99. Also Cf. *Mbh.*I.126, 13 –
    Āgneyaḥ Kṛittikā-putro Raudro Gāṅgeya ityapi /
    Śrūyate bhagavān devaḥ sarva-guhya-mayo Guhaḥ //
    Also *Dhūrtakalpa* VI.4.
56. P.K. Agrawala, *op. cit.*, p. 24.
57. *Bhavishya Purāṇa*, Brahmaparvan, Ch.39; *Brahma Purāṇa*, Ch.128; *Brahmāṇḍa Purāṇa* II.40; *Brahma-Vaivarta Purāṇa* III.1-2 & 14; *Liṅga* I.104, 105; *Matsya*, Chs.108-60; *Padma* VI.38; *Saura*, Chs.60-62; *Śiva* IX.19; *Skanda* I.1, 20-30; I.2, 20-32; VI.261; *Vāmana*, Ch.25 & 52; *Vāyu* LII, 20-50; *Vishṇudharmottara* 1.228, etc.

58. *Mbh.* IX.44, 1-12; *Skanda* VI. 264, 6; etc.
59. *Mbh.* XII. 86, 15ff.; III.218, 32; IX.45, 41-47; 86,15-25. *Tvashṭā* is also said to have presented Skanda a toy as *Kukkuṭa* and Vishṇu is said to have presented him a fowl and a peacock (Agrawala, *op. cit.*, pp. 56-57).
60. *Mbh.* III.213, 16ff. Cf. *Mbh.* III. 218,49. She is identified with Lakshmī also. For details see Hopkins, *op. cit.*, p. 229; J. Gonda, *Aspects of Early Viṣṇuism*, Utrecht, 1954, p.218. For the iconography of Shashṭhī see R.C. Agrawala, "Goddess Shasṭhī in Mathura Sculpture," *Bulletin of Museums & Archaeology in U.P.*, Lucknow, No.4 (Dec. 1969), pp.1-6 and N.P. Joshi, "Sasthi in Literature and Art," in *Ajaya-Śrī: Recent Studies in Indology (Prof. Ajay Mitra Shastri Felicitation Volume)*, ed. By Devendra Handa, Delhi, 1989, Vol.2, pp.391-95.
61. *Kauṭilīya Arthaśāstra* II.4, 17.
62. *Mahābhāshya* of Patañjali, ed. by F. Kielhorn, Vol. II, p. 429.
63. Percy Gardner, *The Coins of the Greek and Scythic Kings of Bactria and India in the British Museum*, London, 1886 (Reprint, New Delhi, 1967), pl. XXVIII 22-24.
64. P.K. Agrawala, *op. cit.*, p. 87; Chatterjee, *op. cit.*, pp. 82ff.
65. Devendra Handa, *Pehowa*, p. 44.
66. *Mbh.*, Sabhāparva, 29.4:
    Tato bahudhanaṃ ramyaṃ gavāḍhyaṃ dhanadhānyavat /
    Kārttikeyasya dayitaṃ Rohitakamupādravat //
67. *Mahāmāyūrī* (ed. Sylvan Levi, *Journal Asiatique*, 1915) verse 21 –
    Rohitake Kārttikeyaḥ Kumāro lokaviśrutaḥ.
68. John Allan, *Catalogue of The Coins of Ancient India*, London 1936 (Reprint, New Delhi, 1975), p. xxxvi.
69. Cf. Alexander Cunningham, *Coins of Ancient India*, pp.97-98; J.N. Banerjea, *The Development of Hindu Iconography*, Calcutta, 1956, pp. 117, 141; Moti Chandra, "Presidential Address", *Journal of the Numismatic Society of India*, XVI, p. 8.
70. Allan, *op. cit.*, p.245.
71. Devendra Handa, *Studies in Indian Coins and Seals*, Delhi, 1985, pp. 18-19.
72. P.L. Gupta and T.R. Hardarker, *Indian Silver Punchmarked Coins of the Magadha-Maurya Karshapana Series*, Anjaneri, 1985, p. 10.
73. Allan, *op. cit.*, pp. xciii and 146, pl. XIX.17-19.
74. Handa (1985), *op. cit.*, pp. 36 ff.
75. Allan, *loc. cit.*, Ajay Mitra Shastri, "Symbols on Tribal Coins: An Interpretative Study," in *Seminar Papers on the Tribal Coins of Ancient India (c. 200 B.C. to 400 A.D.)*, eds. Jai Prakash Singh & Nisar Ahmad, Varanasi, 1977, p. 89.
76. P.K. Agrawala, *op. cit.*, pp.46-52, pls. VII-XII; Chaterjee, *op. cit.*, pp. 114ff, figs. 1-4; Sinha, *op. cit.*, pp. 109-17.
77. Devendra Handa, *Early Indian Coins From Sugh*, New Delhi, 2006, pp. 72-85, Pls. XI-XIV.
78. For details see K.K. Dasgupta, *Tribal History of Ancient India – A Numismatic Approach*, Calcutta, 1974, pp.195ff.
79. *Mbh.* Sabhā Parva 29, 4.
80. Allan, *op. cit.*, pp.270-72, pls. XXIX.20-22 and XL.10-11.
81. The complete legend on the unique silver coin may be read as *Yaudheya bhagvata-svāmino brahmaṇyadevas(y)a* and on the copper coins as *Bhagavata-svāmino brahmaṇ(y)a devas(y)a Kumāras(y)a.*
82. V.S. Agrawala, *Prāchīna Bhāratīya Loka Dharma* (Hindi), Varanasi, 1964, (as quoted by Sinha, *op. cit.*, p.74, fn.11); "The Goddess Shashṭhī on the Yaudheya Coins," *Journal of the Numismatic Society of India*, Vol. V, pt. II, pp.1-4. See also Deenbandhu Pandey, "Six headed Kṛittikā on Yaudheya Coins," *Ibid.* XXIX, pp. 5-8 and R.C. Agrawala, "Six-headed Goddess on Yaudheya Coins," *Ibid.*, XXX, p. 182.
83. P.L. Gupta, Editorial Note, *Numismatic Digest*, Bombay, Vol. II, pt. II, p. 22.
84. Allan, *op. cit.*, pp. cxlix-cl, 270-72.
85. Jai Prakash, "Observations On the Tribal Coinages of Ancient India," *JNSI*, XXVII, pp.133-34.
86. *Epigraphia Indica* VII, pp. 42ff.

87. Allan, *op. cit.*, pp. cl-cli and 276-78, pl. Xl.1-9.
88. Two other varieties show the word *dvi* and *tri* at the end (*Ibid*).
89. K.D. Bajpai, *India Numismatic Studies*, New Delhi, 1976, p.32.
90. Allan, *op. cit.*, p. cl.
91. John Allan, *Catalogue of the Coins of the Gupta Dynasties and of Śaśāṅka, king of Gauḍa*, London, 1914, pp. 84ff, pl. XV.5-14; A.S. Altekar, *Coinage of the Gupta Empire*, Varanasi, 1957, pp. 165-275, pl. XIII.11-14.
92. R.C. Agrawala, "A Rare Bronze of Skanda Kumāra from the Punjab Hills," *Vishveshvaranand Indological Journal*, Hoshiarpur, Vol. V, pp. 206-08.
93. Acc. No. 1/385; 18 x 12.5 cm.
94. L.27: *Dakshe śaktiḥ kukkuṭastathā ekavaktrastathā shaṇmukhaḥ.*
95. LVII.41: *Skandaḥ Kumārarūpaśśaktidharo barhiketuścha.*
96. 260.50: *Dvibhujasya kare śaktirvāmaḥ syāt kukkuṭopari.*
97. *Dvibhuje kukkuṭam vāme śaktirdakshiṇahastake.*
98. For the history and some sculptural remains of this site see Devendra Handa, "Some Unpublished Sculptures from Gujjar Kheri (Haryana)," *Panjab University Research Bulletin (Arts)*, Chandigarh, Vol. XVII, No. 1 (April, 1986), pp. 107-21 and Fig.20; "A Unique *Mahishāsuramardin* Image from Haryana," *Annali*, Vol. 46, pp. 111-12, pl. 1.
99. Acc. no. 1/131. It is carved out of sandstone and measures 13 x 17 cm.
100. Brajesh Krishna, "Six-Headed Kārttikeya from Thanesar," *Journal of Haryana Studies*, Kurukshetra, Vol. XII, Nos.1-2 (1980), pp. 3-7. The image has been dated to the 10th century by the author here.
101. Manmohan Kumar, *Archaeology of Ambala and Kurukshetra Districts (Haryana)*, Unpublished Ph.D. Thesis, K.U., Kurukshetra, p. 151, pl. XII. C. He, however, dates it to 10th-11th century A.D.
102. Ashwini Agrawal, "Saiva Sculptures from Morni-Ka-Tal," *Roopa-Lekha*, New Delhi, Vol. Nos. LXVII to LXXI (Jan. 2001), p. 87, fig. 22.
103. The image is in a private collection at Jind.
104. Brajesh Krishna (1980), pp. 3-7; Shukla (1983), *op. cit.*, p. 48, pl. XLI.1. A very fragmentary image of the seated god (21 x 17 cm) from Jhanswa representing the lower part only (Acc.No.1/303) and another small piece (12 x 8 cm), also broken, from Pehowa are preserved in HARDAM. A fragmentary image exists at Phapharana in district Karnal also.
105. *Vishṇu Purāṇa* (Gita Press, ed.), III.2, 2-8:

    Sūryasya patnī Sañjñābhūttanayā Viśvakarmaṇaḥ /
    Manuryamo Yamī chaiva tadapatyāni vai mune //
    Asahantī tu sā Sūryastejaśchhāyāṃ yuyoja vai /
    Bhartṛiśuśrūshaṇe'raṇyaṃ svayaṃ cha tapase yayau //
    Sañjñeyamityathārkaścha Chhāyāyāmātmajatrayam /
    Śanaiścharaṃ Manuṃ chānyaṃ Tapatīṃ chāpyajījanat //
    Chhāyā-Sañjñā dadau śāpaṃ Yamāya kupitā yadā /
    Tadānyeyamasau buddhirityāsīdyamasūryayoḥ //
    Tato Vivasvānākhyāte tayaivāraṇyasaṃsthitām /
    Samādhidṛishṭyāṃ dadṛiśe tāmaśvāṃ tapasi sthitām //
    Vājirūpadharaḥ so'tha devāvathāśvinau /
    Janayāmāsa Revantaṃ retaso'nte cha Bhāskaraḥ //
    Āninye cha punaḥ Sañjñāṃ svasthānaṃ bhagavānraviḥ /
    Tejasaśśamanaṃ chāsya Viśvakarmā chakāra ha //

106. She is named as Sureṇu and Suraṇyu also. See Bhagwant Sahai, *Iconography of Some Important Minor Hindu Deities*, New Delhi, 1975, p. 89.
107. Viśvakarmā is said to have then reduced the splendour of the sun by one-eighth by putting him on the sharpening wheel and created Vishṇu's wheel, Śaṅkara's trident, Kubera's chariot, Kārttikeya's *śakti* 'energy, lance' etc. with the sun's splendour which fell down on the earth—

    Bhramamāropya Sūryaṃ tu tasya tejo niśātanam /

Kritavānashṭamaṃ bhāgaṃ sa vyaśātayadavyayam //
Yattasmādvaishṇavaṃ tejeśśātitaṃ Viśvakarmaṇā /
Jājvalyamānamapatattadbhūmau munisattam //
Tvashṭaiva tejasā tena Vishṇośchakramakalpayet /
Triśūlaṃ chaiva Śarvasya śibikāṃ Dhanadasya cha //
Śakti Guhyasya devānāmanyeshāṃ cha yadāyudham /
Tatsarvaṃ tejasā tena Viśvakarmā vyavardhayat //

Vishṇu Purāṇa, III.2, 9-12.

108. *Mārkaṇḍeya Purāṇa* (Vaṅgavāsī Steam Press, Calcutta, Śaka 1812), Ch.109, vv. 5-11:
Iti śātitatejāḥ sa śuśubhe nātitejasā /
Vapurdadhāra Mārttaṇḍaḥ sarvvāvayavaśobhanam //
Sa dadarśa samādhisthaḥ svāṃ bhāryāṃ vaḍavākṛitim /
Adhṛiśyāṃ sarvvabhūtānāṃ tapasā niyamena cha //
Uttarāṃścha Kurūn gatvā bhūtvā'śvo Bhānurāgaṃat /
Sā cha dṛishṭvā tamāyāntaṃ parapuṃso viśaṅkayā //
Jagāma sammukhaṃ tasya pṛishṭharakshaṇatatparā /
Tataścha nāsikāyogaṃ tayostatra sametayoḥ //
Vaḍavāyāñcha tattejo nāsikābhyāṃ Vivasvataḥ /
Devau tatra samutpannavaśvinau bhishajāṃ varau //
Nāsatya-Dasrau tanayāvaśvavaktrādvinirgatau /
Mārttaṇḍasya sutāvetāvaśvarūpadharasya hi //
Retaso'nte cha Revantaḥ khaḍgī tanvī tanutradhṛik /
Aśvārūḍhaḥ samudbhūto vāṇatūṇasamanvitaḥ //

109. B.N. Sharma, *Iconography of Revanta*, New Delhi, 1975, p. 26; Sahai, *loc. cit.*
110. Sahai, *loc. cit.*
111. See B.N. Sharma, *op. cit.*, p. 28.
112. *Ibid.*, p. 41.
113. *Bṛihatsaṃhitā* 57.56: *Revanto'śvārūḍho mṛigayākrīḍādiparivāraḥ /*
114. *VDP*, III 70, 5: *Pṛishṭhe'śve Sūryavatkāryo Revantaścha tathā prabhuḥ /*
115. *Bhavishya Purāṇa*, 79.78: *Revanto nāma yo'rkasya rūpeṇārkasamaḥ sutaḥ/*
116. Hemādri, *Chaturvargachintāmaṇi* (Calcutta, S.1934) Vrata-khaṇḍa, p. 137: *Pṛishṭhasthaḥ Sūryavatkāryo Revantaścha tathā prabhuḥ /*
117. *Skanda Purāṇa* (Veṅkaṭeśvara press, Bombay, 1909). Prabhāsa Khaṇḍa, 164, 1-4.
118. *Kuvalayamālā Kathā* (Bombay, 1959), p. 68.
119. For details see B.N. Sharma, *op. cit.*, pp. 29-40.
120. *Ibid.*, pp. 41-70 and figs. 1-46.
121. S.P. Shukala (1983), *op. cit.*, p. 42, PI. XXXV, 1.
122. Shri Dhup Singh (HARDAM) first brought it to my notice.
123. Devendra Handa, "Hariyānā meṃ Revanta pūjā," *Journal of Haryana Studies*, Kurukshetra, Vol. VI (1974), pp. 15-18; B.N. Sharma, *op. cit.*, pp. 48-49, Fig. 21.
124. Devendra Handa, "Some Interesting Sculptures from Pehowa," *Panjab University Research Bulletin (Arts)*, Chandigarh, Vol. XVI, no. 1 (April 1985), p. 130, Fig.2.
125. Devendra Handa, "Some Unpublished Sculptures from Gujjar Kheri (Haryana)," *Panjab University research Bulletin (Arts)*, Chandigarh, Vol. XVII, no. 1 (April 1986), pp. 107-21, figs. 20.
126. Shukla, *op. cit.*, p. 42, PI. XXXIV. 3 and p. 48, PI. XL. 2 (Thanesar); Handa (1985), *op. cit.*, p. 8, figs. 8-9.
127. *Kuvalayamālā Kathā*, p. 68.
128. B.N. Sharma, *op. cit.*, p. 29.
129. *Ibid.*, p. 31.
130. *DHI*, p. 521. See also *AV* III.26, 1-6 and III.231-36.
131. *Mbh.* VII.55, 6. The Karṇa Parva (VIII.45, 31-32) mentions Agni, Yama, Varuṇa and Soma as representing east, south, west and north and the Udyoga Parva mentions Kubera, Yama, Soma and Varuṇa (V.16, 27 ff.).

132. Hopkins, *op. cit.*, p. 149.
133. D.C. Sircar, *Studies in the Religious Life of Ancient and Medieval India*, Delhi-Varanasi-Patna, 1971, pp. 238-40.
134. *Ibid.*, p. 245.
135. A.A. Macdonell, *Vedic Mythology*, Varanasi (Reprint), 1963, pp. 54 ff.
136. *Ibid.*, p. 65.
137. *Ibid.*, p. 66.
138. O.R. Gurney, *The Hittites*, Pelican, 1961, p. 105.
139. Sahai, *op. cit.*, p. 13.
140. Macdonell, *op. cit.*, pp. 88-89.
141. Sahai, *op. cit.*, p. 29.
142. D.C. Bhattacharyya (1981), *op. cit.*, pp. 89-90, fig. 44.
143. W.J. Wilkins, *Hindu Mythology*, Varanasi-Delhi, 1972, pp. 82-83.
144. E. Max Muller (ed.), *Sacred Books of the East Series*, Vol. XIV, p. 135; Vol. XXV, p. 217.
145. Wilkins, *op. cit.*, p. 82; James Hastings (ed.), *Encyclopaedia of Religion and Ethics*, New York, Vol. II, 1967, p. 806 b.
146. *Lekhanīṃ pustakaṃ dhatte kakkuṭaṃ daṇḍameva cha / Mahishārūḍho Yamaḥ kṛishṇāṅga īritaḥ //*
147. Devendra Handa, *Pehowa*, p. 117, pl. 71.
148. Sahai, *op. cit.*, pp. 54, 58, etc.
149. Sahai, *op. cit.*, p. 59.
150. *Arthaśāstra*, translated by R. Shamasastry, Mysore, 1956, p. 54.
151. A.K. Coomaraswamy, *Yaksha*, Washington, part I, 1929, pp. 6-9; Arundhati Banerji, "Rare Icons of Kubera from Menal (Rajasthan)," in *Cultural Contours of India* (ed. Vijai Shankar Srivastava), New Delhi, 1981, pp. 204-06.
152. N.P. Joshi, *Mathura Sculpture*, Mathura, 1966, figs. 40, 46.
153. Devendra Handa, "Agroha Revisited," in *Prācī-Prabhā*. Yogānanda Shastri has published some small terracotta figures of Kubera belonging to the Kushāṇa period from Agroha and Naurangabad (*op. cit.*, Pls. 87-90).
154. Shukla (1983), *op. cit.*, p. 40, pl. XXXII.1.
155. *Ibid.*, p. 14, pl. V.2.
156. *DHI*, p. 529.
157. *EHI*, II, Appendix B, p. 265.
158. *Ibid.*
159. Shukla (1983), *op. cit.*, pp. 14-15, pl. V.2.
160. '*Graha*' literally means 'seizer.' The word was used to mean a planet because of the belief that the planets influence or seize the destinies of man. See Pratapaditya Pal and Dipak Bhattacharyya, *Astral Divinities of Nepal*, Varanasi, 1969, p. 29.
161. *DHI*, p. 443.
162. Pal and Bhattacharyya, *op. cit.*, pp. 29 ff.
163. Debala Mitra, "A Study of Some Graha Images of India," *Journal of Asiatic Society*, Calcutta, Vol. VII, no. 1, 1965; Saradha Srinivasan, "A Study of Navagraha Panels from Western India," *Haryana Sahitya Akademi Journal of Indological Studies*, Chandigarh, Vol. I, no. 1 (Spring 1986), pp. 209-216, Figs 1-17.
164. *Journal of Oriental Institute*, Baroda, Vol. XX, no. 2, p. 143.
165. *Ibid.*
166. Devendra Handa, "Some Unpublished Terracottas From Haryana," *Prāchya-Pratibhā*, Bhopal, Vol. XII (1984), PP. 28-29, fig. 3.
167. For details and their interpretation see Devangana Desai, *Erotic Sculpture of India*, New Delhi, 1975.
168. See also Devendra Handa, "Pinjore – The Archaeological Heritage," *Newsletter (Chandigarh Pinjore Kalka Regional Chapter)*, INTACH, March-1992, pp. 13-19, figs. 6, 11-14.

Chapter 10

Buddhist Images

In Buddha's times, Kuru was one of the sixteen major states "*soḷasa Mahājanapada.*" During the long span of slightly less than half a century after his enlightenment, Buddha himself had taken strenuous journeys from state to state, town to town and village to village to propagate the Faith. Though the heart of Madhyadeśa remained the main scene of activities, yet he is said to have traveled even to distant lands.[1]

If the Buddhist texts are to be relied upon, it may be said that Buddhism reached Haryana through the Buddha himself. The *Mahāvastu* and *Dīgha-Nikāya* state that the Buddha himself converted the people of the Kuru tribe.[2] The *Vinaya* of the Mūlasarvāstivādins refers to Buddha's long journey along with Ānanda from Hastināpura to Rohitaka via Mahānagara, Srughna, Brāhmaṇagrāma and Kālanagara[3] and from there to Gandhāra and Uḍḍiyāna and back with Yaksha Vajrapāṇi.[4] Frauwallner, however, regards the account of the journey of the Buddha with Yaksha Vajrapāṇi to be a later interpolation.[5] Of the places mentioned in the first leg of the journey, Rohitaka is doubtlessly modern Rohtak[6] and Srughna was rightly identified by Cunningham with Sugh near Jagadhari.[7] O.P. Bharadwaj, has identified Mahānagara with Indraprastha, Brāhmaṇagrāma with Tohana and Kālanagara with Kalanaur (32° N and 75° 10' E) near Rohtak.[8] No Buddhist remains have, however, been found from these places. The identifications, therefore, leave corroborative evidence as a desideratum.

Dīpavaṁsa refers to Buddha's visit to a city in the Kuru country where he received alms on the banks of the Anotatta lake which he crossed.[9] The city may have been Kurukshetra if the Anotatta lake is the Anyataḥplaksha of the *Śatapatha Brāhmaṇa* (IX. 5.1, 4).[10]

Thullakoṭṭhita and Kammāsadamma find repeated references in the Buddhist literature as the places where Buddha used to stay during his sojourns to the Kuru country. Buddha delivered numerous discourses at these places.[11] Thullakoṭṭhita was the seat of the contemporary Kuru king, Koravya, and had a beautiful garden called Migachīra nearby. Aśvaghosha gives us the Sanskrit version of the name as Sthūlakoshṭhaka and records the initiation of Rāshṭrapāla, a saint of a local Vaiśya family, by the Buddha.[12] His true spirit of self-abnegation and religious discussion with king Koravya have been narrated in the *Raṭṭhapālasutta.*[13] Raṭṭhapāla is described to have converted the Kuru king and his parents to Buddhism and as having contributed some verses to the *Theragāthā.*[14] The *Madhuratthavilāsinī* alternately spells the name of the town as Thullakaṭṭhika where the two Brāhmaṇas Bhadraśāla and Vijitamitra got initiation along with their families.[15] The Pāli version of the name which has popularly been used, however, is Thullakoṭṭhita. Buddhaghosha has explained that the town was a prosperous market-place surrounded by fertile and affluent country, plentiful in grains which always kept the stores of the inhabitants full.[16] D.C. Ahir identifies Thullakoṭṭhita with Sthāneśvara[17] and Bharadwaj with the twin village Thol-Kurri (30° 10' N and 76° 40' E) on the road from Ambala City to Kurukshetra via Jhansua.[18] Thol-Kurri has a huge mound which yields Painted Grey Ware, early historic and medieval pottery and other relics. It has thus a better claim to be identified with Thullakoṭṭhita, even philologically plausible but yet to be confirmed by the discovery of Buddhist relics from the site.[19]

During his visits to the Kuru country, the Buddha usually stayed at Kammāsadamma, which was a celebrated trade-center. Kammāsadamma has variously been identified with Kamaspur or Kumaspur (in Meerut district),[20] Kaithal[21] and Kamoda, about 15 km from Thanesar on road to Pehowa[22] but none of these sites has yielded any Buddhist remains or is traditionally connected with Buddhism.

During one of his journeys from Bhaddiyanagara to Sāvatthi, Buddha is said to have passed through Aṅguttarāpa, Āpaṇa, Kuśinārā and Ātumā.[23] Aṅguttarāpa has been equated with Aggalapura and is described to have fallen on Revata's way also during his journey at the time of the Second Council. This town also occurs in Tche Mang's journey from Śākala to Rohitaka. The Chinese version of the name *A-kia-lou-t'o* may be rendered as Sanskrit Agroda or Agrodaka, mentioned in the *Mahāmāyūrī*[24] and elsewhere also.[25] It has rightly been identified with modern Agroha, 22 km northwest of Hisar.[26] Przyluski has observed that "The Chullavagga proves that before the editing of the *Vinaya*, that is to say probably before the beginning of our era, the capital of the Udumbaras and the city of Aggalapura were recognized as the citadels of Buddhism in the northwestern regions".[27] We shall see subsequently that Agroha was an important Buddhist center of Haryana during the historical period. Rohitaka, too, occurs on Buddhist itineraries. Besides the *Vinaya* of the Mūlsarvāstivādins, it finds mention in the *Divyāvadāna* as a great and prosperous city.[28] The same text narrates the story of Buddha's visit to Srughna (modern Sugh near Jagadhari) where he won over the Brāhmaṇa Indra who boasted of having no equal in beauty, youth and learning.[29]

Aśoka is said to have collected relics from seven of the *śārīrika-stūpas* (Buddhist monuments or kind of Topes for keeping the corporeal remains)[30] and redistributed them into 84,000 *stūpas* which he built subsequently throughout the length and breadth of his empire. The Chinese pilgrim Yuan Chwang (Hsüan Tsang), however, makes specific references to Aśokan *stūpas*. Giving an account of Thanesar, he says: "To the north-west of the city, 4 or 5 *li* is a *stūpa* about 300 feet high which was built by Aśoka-rāja. All the bricks are of the yellow red color, very bright and shining; within is a peck-measure of the relics of Buddha. From the *stūpa* is frequently emitted a brilliant light and many spiritual prodigies exhibit themselves".[31] From Thanesar, the Chinese pilgrim 'went north-east for above 400 *li* and came to the country *Su-lo-kin-na*'. *Su-lo-kin-na* has been restored as Srughna, a name which occurs in literature.[32] It has rightly been identified with modern Sugh near Jagadhari on the right (west) bank of the Yamunā.[33] Yuan Chwang's account of the Buddhist remains here is noteworthy: "To the south-east of the capital and in the west side of the Jumna outside the east gate of a large monastery was an Aśoka tope at a place where the Ju-lai had preached and admitted men into his church. Beside this tope was one which had hair and nail-relics of the Ju-lai, and round about were some tens of topes with similar relics of Śāriputra, Mudgalaputra, and other great *arhats*".[34]

By the side of the *stūpas*, sacred structures and perhaps independently also, Aśoka raised monumental stone pillars called *dharma-stambhas*. Such a pillar, which once existed at Topra near Jagadhari, was shifted by Firoz Tughlaq to Delhi and is now placed on the top of the Firozshah Kotla monument near Delhi Gate. Firoz Tughlaq also perhaps shifted another

Aśokan pillar now installed near the Gujri Mahal in Hisar Fort from Agroha to its present place. The pillar in the *Idgah* at Fatehabad too may have originally been an Aśokan pillar.

Two red sandstone pillars were discovered by D.B. Spooner some eighty years ago from Amin.[35] They have been dated to 2nd-1st century B.C. on stylistic and palaeographic ground and bear close affinity with the contemporary pillars from Mathura, Sanchi, Bharhut, etc.[36] These pillars have been carved on all the four sides.

Pillar No. 1 is about 125 cm in height and 42.5 cm in width. On the main facet is carved a yaksha-yakshī couple standing in an amorous pose in a 67.5 cm niche (Pl. 322). The yakshī stands to the right of the yaksha clasping him with her left hand while the right hangs down (*pralamba*). The yaksha, too, is shown embracing the yakshī with his right hand and holding a wine cup (*madhu-pātra*) in his left, held near the left breast of his spouse. He wears a typical turban on his head in the Śuṅga style and a tight fitting *dhotī* is touching his knees. The pleats of the *dhotī* may be seen falling down between his legs from over his left thigh. The nether garment is held in position by a cloth-band knotted in front and with its two ends hanging down vertically in front, the proper left hand side being slightly longer. The yaksha wears in his ears *Prākāra-vapra-kuṇḍalas* (a kind of thick, strong earrings)[37] that may be seen in the art of Bharhut also and are never used in Kushāṇa sculptures. He also wears a four-stringed necklace of early style but no torque, bracelets on his forearms but no *keyūras* (armlets). The yakshī also wears similar *kuṇḍalas* (earrings), a three-stringed necklace of the Bharhut style, a beaded triple-stringed girdle round her waist and multiple bangles covering almost the entire forearm and lower portions of the legs like the present-day *Bhīla* (name of a tribe) ladies of Rajasthan.[38] A slender cloth band coming from behind the waist is tied on the right hand side with its free ends falling gracefully on the right thigh, one end being held in the *pralamba-hasta* (hanging arm) of the yakshī. She stands slightly turned towards the yaksha, bearing the whole weight of her body on her right leg with the left bent at the knee and crossing the former from behind with toe placed on a small pedestal in the lower corner of the niche.

The modeling of the figures is pleasing and the entire composition is devoid of flatness, which we notice in the Bharhut sculptures. All around the rectangular niche is a very elegant rosette border and below the niche we see the decorative motif of the railing with four uprights and an equal number of cross-bears.

The second pillar is as elegant as the first. It is 115 cm in height. The lower part is plain and simple and the upper part shows two stylized lotus flowers. The rectangular niche in between them represents a yaksha holding a lotus by its long stalk in his right hand near the chest and the left end of the waistband in his left hand. He wears four-stringed necklace, ear-ornaments[39], and bracelets in his right arm, typical turban and a scarf thrown on the forearms executed exquisitely (Pl. 323). This yaksha may be compared to one on the gateway of Sanchi.

Next in date are the railing pillars from Hathin and Bhadas in southern Haryana. Hathin is situated about 16 km southwest of Palwal in district Faridabad and has an ancient mound nearly thirty feet high and spread over thirty acres of land. It yields PGW, early historic and medieval relics.[40] The railing post found from Hathin[41] shows on its front face a yaksha standing facing in *samapāda-sthānaka-mudrā* (contraposto) on a pedestal supported by a fabulous figure having human face and animal horns and ears (Pl. 324).[42] The face of the yaksha is unfortunately mutilated beyond recognition. He wore earrings and probably had his head adorned with a diadem or a turban. A broad collar, many-stranded necklace looped stiffly on the chest, multiple beaded bangles, broad *chīvara* (rag, a kind of Buddhist-mendicant's dress)–like sacred thread, diaphanous lower garment going lower than the knees and forming zigzag pleats between the legs, a sash tied over the hip and knotted in front with loose ends falling over the pleats form the important items of dress and ornamentation. The arms hang down straight on the sides. The left hand seems to have held an Aśoka flower also suspended downwards by its stalk.[43] The feet are slightly splayed outwards. Frontally conceived, this slightly elongate figure in medium relief standing erect with weight equally distributed on both feet has a flat belly.

On the sides of the post, there are mortise holes for the reception of crossbars. There is absolutely no doubt to its being a railing post of a Buddhist *stūpa* as it shows queen Māyā's dream also in a medallion on the square abacus above the head of the yaksha (Pl. 325). The edges of the shaft above the shoulders of the yaksha are beveled and show bells (or perhaps bell-like tulip flowers) hanging down from the sides of the medallion. The shallow carving on the medallion shows queen Māyā sleeping on a couch, slightly turned to her proper left with her folded left arm serving as the pillow. The female fly-whisker seated on the ground towards her head, too, is dozing. A huge elephant is shown as descending from the heaven to enter the queen's womb as she saw it in her dream. The size of the elephant is conditioned by its importance in the story. In the top right corner may be seen a tenement with vaulted roof and arched *chaitya* (dormer) window indicative of the palace perhaps, the space on the left shows a pedestalled spouted vessel, an oval tray with small circular handles on the sides resembling five-arched *chaitya*-motif with a prominent lamp above.[44] The lamp indicates night and the female fly-whisker leaning against the cot suggests the late hours of the night when the queen was fast asleep and the attendant had started dozing. These accessory details are important from the architectural and socio-cultural viewpoints.

This spotted red sandstone post[45] may be assigned to *circa* 2nd century B.C.E. on stylistic grounds. This date is corroborated by the traces of a few Brāhmī letters (*pa da pi ki ni u*) which may still be seen on one of its sides.[46] The worn out lower part of this post clearly indicates that it must have once been buried in the ground, pointing to the actual use of this post in the railing around a *stūpa*. A tenon to hold the coping in place still survives. The back is plain.

The other railing post comes from Bhadas situated about 19 km north-northeast of Firozpur Jhirka on road to Nuh. The front face of this pillar shows a yaksha standing on a (fabulous?) animal with a mythical creature in the demi-medallion above (Pl. 326). Unfortunately the head of the yaksha is mutilated. A part of the oval turban plaque may, however, still be seen. The square block-shaped earrings with spiral loops seem to have been the *prākāra-vapra-kuṇḍalas*.[47] A broad collar, a five-stranded necklace stiffly looped on the chest and bedecked with large beads, seven-stringed *keyūra* with rosettes, multiple bangles, diaphanous *dhotī* secured by a sash knotted in front with one free end held by the right hand and another dangling on the right thigh may also be seen worn by the yaksha. It is interesting to note that the tail of the animal, on which the yaksha stands, is tied with the hem of his lower garment. The left arm of the yaksha is irretrievably lost. The demi-medallion above shows a mythical animal having the forepart of the body of a deer and the fin-like twirled hind part. The medallion shows lotus motif with flowers hanging on the sides and falling on the beveled edges of the shaft of the pillar. There are mortises on the sides to receive crossbars. Stylistically, this pillar seems to be slightly later than that of Hathin and may be assigned to the 2nd century B.C.[48]

That Buddhism continued to flourish in Haryana during the early period is evidenced by a fragmentary railing pillar depicting some story in two surviving sunk niches,[49] a

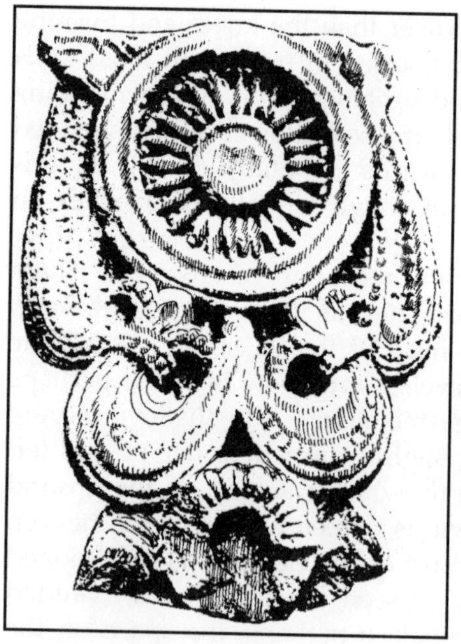

Fig. 14. *Triratna* in Gurukula Museum, Jhajjar.

fragmentary frieze which may be part of an architrave (Pl. 327)[50] and *triratna* ('three-jewels', an auspicious symbol in Buddhism representing the Buddha, *Dhamma*, and *Saṅgha*) (Fig. 14),[51] all found from southern Haryana and now housed in the Gurukula Museum, Jhajjar. The railing pillar with two rectangular panels shows four human figures in different postures representing some narrative/s in a lively way. The carving is in low relief showing elongate figures resembling those of the early Buddhist rock temples like Bhaja, Kondane, etc.[52] from which they may not be far removed in age. The panels show balustrades below and *chaitya* motifs carved above with pillars having animals on capitals on the sides. The tenon has also survived. Two of the four human figures in both the panels are smaller in size and probably represent two children of the couple. The fragmentary frieze which we regard to be a part of the architrave of a *toraṇa* (an ornamental arched doorway) shows a prominent retrorse lion on one end and three human figures of which the central one is a female holding a garland in two hands raised to the level of the shoulders. The male figure between her and the lion is holding some object that looks like an ornamented vase. He has a beautifully fluttering scarf around his shoulders. All the three figures bear exquisite coiffures and jewelry of which only the ear-ornaments, *ekāvalis* ('single-stringed', pearl necklet) and *valayas* (bracelets) are visible in the extant frieze whose lower portion (below the busts of the figures) is completely lost. The physiognomy of the male figure next to the lion and his hair-coiffure betray alien impact. It may, thus, have been a creation of the Indo-Greek or Kushāṇa period. The depiction of lion is reminiscent of Buddha, a lion among men. It is also to be noted that lion occupies a proud place in the Buddhist art of Aśokan and even later periods.

Triratna is a sacred symbol of the Buddhists. Also called *Nandipada* and *Nandyāvarta*, it has been very popular in India from the Harappan period and is found on punch-marked, tribal and other early coins in varied forms. It is common knowledge that before the evolution of Buddha/Bodhisattva image, Tathāgata was worshipped in the form of a symbol – *stūpa*, *chakra*, Bodhi-tree, etc. Here we see that the *triratna* supports a wheel. So this symbol cannot be taken to represent the Buddha, the *Dhamma*, and the *Saṅgha* as is generally believed, for in that case there will be a duplication of Buddha's representation. It is only a sacred and an auspicious symbol supporting Buddha in an aniconic form.

The symbol consists of a circular base having sixteen lotus petals (partly mutilated) around a prominent hole (hub). It was probably flanked on either side by a slantingly placed conch with spiral head inclined towards the circular lotus base that supports the three prongs of the symbol formed by two jeweled garlands. The central prong is pointed while the side prongs with loops in the center and slightly curved free-ends of the garlands on its sides resemble fish-tails.[53] Placed gracefully on the three prongs is an elaborate and exquisitely carved wheel having a very prominent circular hub out of which converge elongated diamond shaped spokes placed in position by triple ringed rim. Beaded garlands hang gracefully from the horizontal support visibly placed behind the wheel and adorned with a lotus petal on the surviving top portion on the left side. These garlands may well be compared with the common motif of a calyx yielding cloth, necklaces, etc. found on Bharhut railing posts.[54] This well-preserved *triratna* symbol supporting a wheel furnishes evidence of aniconic Buddhist worship in Haryana about two thousand years ago.

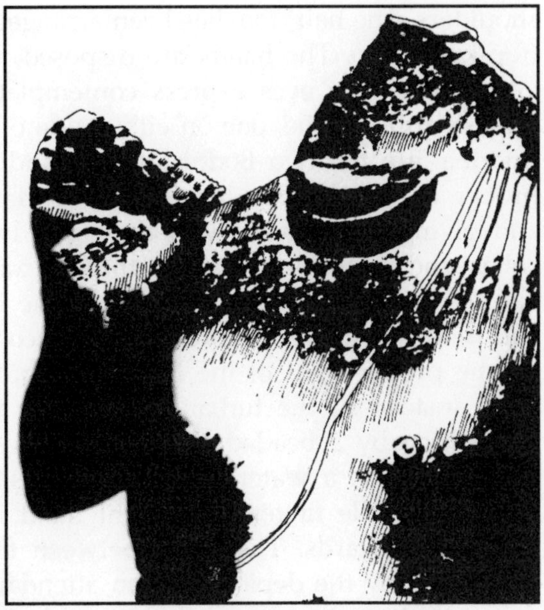

Fig. 15. Budhha's torso, Jhajjar Museum.

A few Kushāṇa images of Buddha/ Bodhisattva have been found from Haryana but unfortunately they are generally broken or have suffered mutilation. The one recovered from village Brahmanwas in Rohtak district shows only the folded legs in *vajraparyaṅkāsana* (a typical posture of sitting) in mottled Mathura sandstone. It is identifiable only because of the Brāhmī inscription in early Kushāṇa characters which reads '.. *Buddha Kanaka-muni..*'. *Padma* and *Chakra* have been carved on the soles of Buddha Kanaka-muni.[55] Kanaka-muni is one of the Mānushī or Mortal Buddhas of the Mahayanists.[56] Brahmanwas, as we have seen above, may be identified with the Brāhmaṇagrāma of the Buddhist texts. Another image preserved in the Gurukula Museum, Jhajjar survives only in the form of a torso with the head and legs lost completely (Fig. 15).[57] Buddha is shown having broad shoulders and attenuated waist. He is clad in *saṅghāṭī* (a type of shawl worn by the Buddha) which passes over the left shoulder. Its folds are visible on the left shoulder. The left nipple covered by it is clearly visible because of the diaphanous nature of the *saṅghāṭī*. The deep navel accentuates the softness of the belly. The right hand is raised to the level of the shoulder in *abhaya*. The palm is marked by a beautiful *chakra*. The thumb, too, seems to have some auspicious mark. The webbed fingers are also to be noted. It is a characteristic of the greatness (*Mahāpurusha-lakshaṇa*).[58] The fleshy modeling of the torso, the broad square shoulders and the typical Mathura red sandstone render it a creation of the early phase of the Kushāṇa school of Mathura.

Joanna Williams has referred to one broken Kushāṇa Buddha figure recovered from Agroha and now preserved in the Gurukula Jhajjar, which like the preceding example, is also a product of the Mathura school of art.[59]

A Bodhisattva head from Mahmudpur (Pl. 328)[60] in spotted red sandstone shows oval face with plump cheeks, round chin, thick lips, prominent nose, quasi-closed eyes, and bow-like eyebrows with a small, incised circlet representing the *ūrṇā* (a circle of hair between the eyebrows). The coiffure is interesting. The prominent circular ornament bearing petal decorations[61] emits beaded strings three of which take a turn to enter similar circular ornaments on the either side and two central bead strings are attached to the two sides of reel-like ornament on the forehead. The long ears, too, bear ornaments. Placidity is a characteristic feature of the face. It betrays some alien impact also. Another Bodhisattva head of Gandhāra style was recovered from Mustafabad in district Ambala during 1965-66.[62]

The best-preserved Buddhist image found from Haryana is the Gandhāra Buddha recovered from Jhajjar (Pl. 329).[63] This beautiful relief shows Buddha seated in *padmāsana* ('Lotus seat', a particular posture in religious meditation) on a lotus-seat with his knees projecting beyond it. The lotus-seat has a double row of drooping petals. The *saṅghāṭī* covers both his shoulders and the folds form schematically disposed incised parallel lines across the shoulders. The hair, too, has been arranged symmetrically and the curves run over the *ūshṇīsha* (top-knot) also. The hands are disposed in the pose of preaching. The facial features are not very sharp. The eyes express contemplation. Diminutive figures with folded hands and in three-fourths profile, one on either side of the lotus seat, represent the donor couple. Flanking Buddha, are the two Bodhisattvas, standing on lotus pedestals.[64] Of these, the figure on the proper left of the Buddha is that of Maitreya, shown with a water-vessel in the left hand and giving benediction with the right. He is wearing a bejeweled turban, ear ornaments, a collar and a necklace, sacred thread, *valayas, uttarīya* (upper garment) and a heavy lower garment and perhaps sandals also. The dress and ornamentation, thus, combines the royal and monastic features representing the concept of *sambhogakāya* (carnal body). The Bodhisattva on the proper right of the Buddha wears similar ornaments but the dress differs except for *dhotī*. Instead of the turban, his hair is arranged in the form of a hemi-spherical pile kept in position by a beaded string. The *saṅghāṭī* covers the left shoulder and upper part of the arm. He holds a water bottle in his suspended left hand by its neck between the pointing and the middle fingers. The right hand is raised to the level of the shoulder but the palm is turned inwards. The space between the heads of the Buddha and the Bodhisattvas has been filled by the depiction of an attendant wearing a mendicant's dress and perhaps a royal devotee who wears a peculiar crown but usual dress and ornaments. The top portion shows three *apasarases* 'celestial damsels' seated over lotus buds. Calyxes of four other flowers are emitting necklaces. The face of the pedestal bears lotus rhizome. This theophany relief[65] betraying the concept of the simultaneous plurality of Buddhas and Bodhisattvas is thus arranged in three tiers compositionally and tapers like a tower as if to lead the worshipper upwards to heaven.

Bhuna (29° 55' N and 76° 15' E) near Fatehabad has a very large and lofty mound more than 25 m high, and the present town is partially located on the ancient site. A railing pillar of spotted red sandstone measuring 96 x 23 cm has been found from this site.[66] It was carved on both the sides. The caved faces are compartmented from bottom upwards into a succession of panels, separated from one another by a railing-motif. The subject matter of the panels seems to be mundane, showing a couple in love postures. In this pillar, there were three compartments, the lowermost is almost gone but for its top portion. The middle one shows a male seated on a high stool in *sukhāsana* (posture of ease) trying to loosen the girdle of his spouse who is standing gracefully putting her left arm around his neck (Pl. 330). The venue of the scene is a pillared pavilion with open sides. The pillars supporting the roof are having *ghaṭa* (pitcher) bases placed over square moldings, tapering octagonal shafts over which are slightly projecting members of the shape of inverted *ghaṭas*, supporting round abacuses on which rest lions. Above the lions are gradually expanding slabs in a corbelled fashion supporting check-patterned eaves. These are characteristically Kushāṇa pillars betraying the admirable skill of the artists. The topmost panel has been chiseled off and a rectangular hole has been made in it for its reuse at a later period. There are mortises on both the sides for the reception of the crossbars. They measure 27.5 cm. in height and 7.5 cm in width. Some of the holes between the mortises and the sculpted panels may have been made later to reuse the pillar. The central panel of the other side shows the male standing akimbo, holding his right hand near the chest. The female with her back towards the viewers but with retrorse face is putting her left arm around the neck of her spouse and touching the protuberance of his turban with her right hand. The scene is depicted in a similar pillared pavilion.

A Kushāṇa pillar capital of white spotted red sandstone, measuring 94 x 43.5 cm, dug out from the Khokhrakot mound at Rohtak, was acquired by the National Museum, New Delhi in 1967 (Acc. No. 67.617). In an excellent state of preservation, it shows beautifully carved addorsed lions, winged on one side, and with a female and a male rider on the other, the latter offering a wine-cup to his spouse (seated on the lion behind). Between them is depicted a wine-jar (*madhu-kalaśa*) placed on a typical stand.[67] A very charming lion-capital though, yet being detached off its proper context, its association with a Buddhist establishment could not be recognized. The Department of History, Maharshi Dayanand University, Rohtak has recovered some railing pillars with lenticular eyes, cross bars and coping stones from near the same spot indicating the existence of a *stūpa* at the site.

A beautiful molded plaque depicting an equine-headed figure from Sugh is, however, an interesting find (Pl. 331).[68] It measures 7 x 5 cm. Unfortunately it is broken below the neck but the presence of a human hand with a puffed bracelet on the right of the extant figure indicates that it was connected to a human body. The horse-head is bedecked with a double band on the forehead. Both the bands bear small rosette marks. A plain band passes through the mouth and is connected on the side with the lower band of the forehead. The small ear stands erect. The crest manes are beautifully depicted. Bell-shaped flowers or ornaments hang from the ears. The neck is also adorned with a bell-shaped necklace. There is a round holed projection on the left extreme near the head, maybe for inserting flower or incense stick. The plaque is broken on the right side. What was depicted here is only a matter of guess. Suraj Bhan has dated this terracotta to the Gupta period[69] but we feel inclined to place it in the 1st century C.E. on stylistic grounds. The exact significance of this terracotta figurine has not been ascertained as yet. A similar plaque from Sugh exists in the collection of the Gurukula Museum, Jhajjar also.

This horse-faced figure may be identified as a *Kinnarī*. The *Vishṇudharmottara Purāṇa* refers to two types of *Kinnaras*: one with human head joined to an equestrian body, and the other with horse-head joined to a human body.[70] The plastic representations of the first type are found in the sculptural art of Sanchi and Mathura and in the terracotta art of Ahichchhatrā, Kauśāmbī and Rajghat while those of the second type are found in the bas reliefs of Bhaja, Sanchi, Mathura, Bodh Gaya, on a medallion from Patna now in the Indian Museum, Kolkata, on a stone *toraṇa* pillar showing Kṛishṇa-*līlā* scenes at Mandor (Rajasthan), in the Malegatti Temple at Badami, and also on a terracotta plaque in the Vadodara Museum, belonging to the 1st century B.C.[71] The *Rāmāyaṇa* refers to *aśvamukhī* women. While on his way back to Ayodhyā at the time of the coronation of Rāma (and the death of Daśaratha), Bharata saw a horse-faced *rākshasī* (female demon) in his dream.[72] A similar *rākshasī* is described as seducing Lakshmaṇa in the hermitage of the sage Mātaṅga.[73] Horse-headed women lived also on the Maināka mountain in the north.[74]

The *Kumārasambhava* (I.11) also mentions *Aśvamukhī*. The *aśvamukhī* figures in Indian art have generally been identified by scholars with the yakshī /yakshiṇī of the 'Aśvamukhī Jātaka'.[75] The Jātaka story tells us of an *aśvamukhī* yakshī living in a forest that would capture the passers by, take them to her cave and kill them. Once she caught hold a handsome Brāhmaṇa but developed a liking for him, espoused him and provided him all comforts in the cave. The depiction of a male turbaned figure being forcibly caught and led by a horse-faced yakshī in the Buddhist cave at Bhaja, the equine-faced yakshī carrying a similar turbaned male on the *Stūpa* No. 2 at Sanchi, the yakshī shown with a male figure on the lower architrave of *Stūpa* No. 3 at the same place, the stone sculpture from Mathura showing the horse-faced yakshī standing putting her left hand on the right shoulder of the turbaned male figure, similar yakshī holding and leading a male on the ground railing pillar of Bodh Gaya as well as the equine-headed bejeweled yakshī holding the right hand of the male as depicted on the Baroda Museum terracotta may all be the representations of the 'Aśvamukhī Jātaka' for almost all of them have Buddhist association. In the light of all these examples, the terracotta horse-headed figure of Sugh too may be identified with the *Aśvamukhī* yakshī as Sugh also is associated with Buddhism, as we have seen above. One may object to this identification on the basis of the bridled face of the *yakshī* but it may be pointed out that the *Mahāvaṃsa,* a Buddhist text of Śrī Laṅkā, too, refers to an *aśvamukhī* yakshī who was controlled by prince Pāṇḍukābhaya on the mountain Dhumarakkha by using bridle in her mouth.[76]

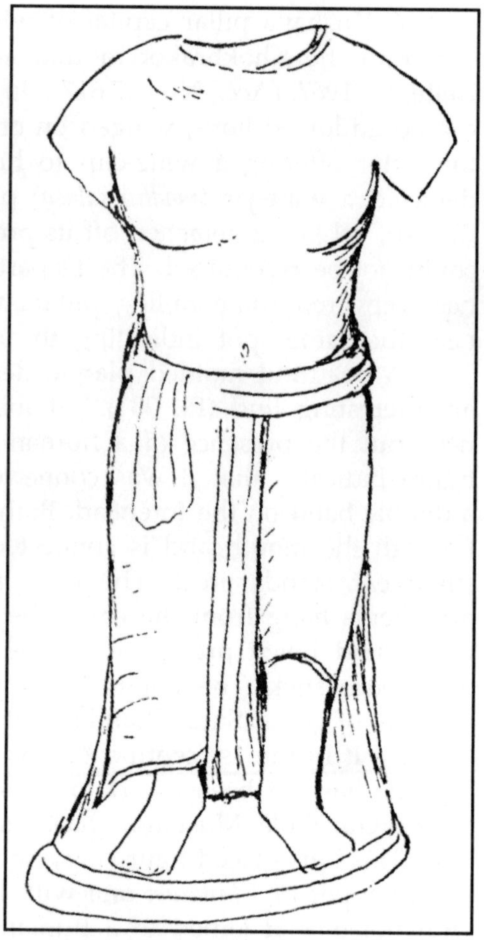

Fig. 16. Bodhisattva from Sirsa.

Sirsa, the ancient Śairīshaka,[77] has yielded a small terracotta figurine whose head and arms are unfortunately irretrievably lost.[78] The pedestalled plaque, however, shows a male standing to left, wearing a *dhotī* (Fig. 16). A loose end of the undergarment dangles down on the right thigh from the waist while in between the two legs may be seen its pleated fall. The right foot of the figure is in *sama* pose while the left one is slightly splayed out. The disposition of the hands may have revealed the identity of the figure in the absence of the head, but they are lost. So any endeavor to specifically identify the figure will only be a conjecture. Nevertheless, the general appearance, the frontal pose, absence of the sacred thread, two-handedness and typical style of wearing the *dhotī* indicate that the figure may have been that of Buddha or Bodhisattva.[79] This possibility gets further strengthened when we find that Sirsa was an important town in ancient times which finds mention in the *Divyāvadāna*[80] and various other texts.[81]

Another Kushāṇa terracotta figurine of Bodhisattva obtained from mid levels of Period II at Sugh (Pl. 332)[82] betrays the popularity of Buddhism with the masses. This is a fairly executed head and bust wearing a high cylindrical crown, thick double earrings and an upper garment whose vertical folds indicate that both the shoulders were covered. The crown bears four tiers of *ardha-padma* (half-lotus) or semi-circular decorations, which remind us of the Vaikuṇṭha-Vishṇu image in the Mathura Museum (Acc. No. 14.392-95).[83] The face is roundish having open eyes, plump cheeks and a large mouth. The nose is slightly damaged. Both the arms are also gone. The figure bears a serene facial expression. It measures 9.5 x 5 cm and may be dated to the 2nd-3rd century A.D on stylistic grounds.

A badly mutilated and ill-preserved image of a female with a child on her left thigh touching her left breast, found from Mohanbari in district Rohtak and now preserved in the Gurukula Museum, Jhajjar, may be identified with Hārīti (Pl. 333). Originally it probably formed part of a larger slab which showed the auspicious triad of Kubera-Lakshmī-Hārīti or simply Kubera-Hārīti, as known from Mathurā. This fragmentary relief may be dated to the post-Kushāṇa or Gupta period on stylistic grounds. Hārīti is believed to have been the yakshī of Rājagṛha converted by Buddha.

A small rectangular tablet obtained from Sugh depicts a beautiful figure of Buddha unfortunately broken below the bust (Pl. 334). The head with top-knot, oval face, elongate ears and *saṅghāṭī* on the left shoulder with multiple folds, however, are very clear. Flanking the Buddha are two standing attendant figures, probably Bodhisattvas. The arms bend inwards from the elbows and though the hands are broken now yet it can be legitimately presumed that they were placed one over the other in the lap on the inverted soles of the feet. A lined frame at the back of the figure of the Buddha seems to indicate a niche of a *stūpa*. Rising from the back of the *ushṇīsha* is a tall multiple umbrella which is generally depicted as surmounting the *stūpas*. This molded piece may be assigned to the Gupta period. Some more pieces, probably prepared from the same mould, but in varying states of preservation and preserving the lower parts of the rectangular plaque have also been discovered from Sugh and form part of some private collections. One such piece shows traces of a Brāhmī legend which being very much worn out could not be deciphered properly. That Buddhism continued to be popular with the masses during the Gupta period is also evidenced by a Bodhisattva head in the common man's art obtained from the excavations at Agroha.

Rodgers had discovered the lower portion of an image that he thought to be of standing Buddha lying on the bank of the tank of Kurukshetra. It showed three figures on either side of the legs and two central *nāgas* with folded hands clasped in devotion below.[84] The image has not been illustrated but from the description it seems to have been a representation of the Jaina tīrthaṅkara Pārśvanātha, probably of the medieval period.

A relief from Rohtak[85] representing a couple on a common platform, tentatively identified as Jaina tutelary couple or Pañchika and Hārītī, shows the female supporting two children in the two arms (Pl. 335). The right hand of the male figure is disposed in *abhaya* (protection-giving posture) while in his *pralamba* left hand he holds a water vessel. The divine character of the couple is indicated by plain round haloes behind their heads. The absence of the diminutive Jina figure and the presence of two children in the arms of the female negate the Jaina affiliation of the image and the water vessel in the hand of the male figure poses the difficulty of its identification with Pañchika. The relief is in a very indifferent state of preservation but the simplicity of depiction; drapery, ornamentation and the curled locks falling on the sides are reminiscent of the classical tradition, which seems to have lingered on in this region. The image may thus be dated to *circa* 8th century C.E. If its identification with Pañchika-Hārītī is accepted, it would indicate the continuation of Buddhism in Haryana in the 8th century C.E.[86]

It is generally believed, perhaps erroneously, that Buddhism disappeared from the land of its birth because of the hostility of the Hindus. Post-Harsha relics are rare but not totally absent. In 1982, hoard of fifty-seven bronzes was discovered from Hansi.[87] Most of the bronzes in it are Jaina but two are definitely Buddhist. One of these shows Buddha in *bhūmisparśa-mudrā* (Pl. 336), symbolizing the Great enlightenment of the Śākya prince under the Bodhi tree at Bodh–Gaya.[88] Seated straight in *vajraparyaṅkāsana* on the pericarp of an ovalish lotus with the left hand placed on the lap with palms upwards and the right one resting against his right knee and pointing downwards, he looks to be a calm and serene figure. The pedestal below the lotus is completely gone. The bronze is badly mutilated and corroded concealing the details. The hair with schematic curls and the topknot may still be made out. The oval face is badly mutilated and a part of it below the nose has gone off leaving a depression. The plump cheeks and eyes with drooping lids and thick eyebrows, however, may still be discerned. There was probably an *ūrṇā* also on the forehead. The extant left earlobe hangs down almost touching the left shoulder. A thick line across the chest running from over the left shoulder to the right armpit indicates the diaphanous *uttarāsaṅga* (Buddhist upper garment). The figure was probably clad in an *antarvāsa* (lower garment) also, as there are faint traces of its portion spread on the seat. At the back is a big horseshoe-shaped hale, broken on the proper right hand side. A part of the edge on the other side is also lost. The halo consists of three plain moldings enclosed within a border bedecked with a continuous row of flames. Between these three plain moldings and probably another set of similar moldings there is a four-dot lotus decoration. The apex is crowned with an indistinct projecting finial.

Like all other bronzes of Hansi, it is a small, light and easily portable image. Evidently, the icon was under prolonged religious use and underwent repeated applications of sandal-paste and the like. Presented in full frontality, as most of the images of this type are, it is not accompanied by any Bodhisattvas, attendants or devotees. The oval serene face, broad chest with round shoulders, long arms and tall body, attenuated waist and sensitively modeled limbs, the beautifully bedecked long elliptical halo covering the whole of the back portion and rising above the head bestow this figure a distinctive grace. When complete and fresh, it must have been a masterpiece.

The thick fold of drapery across the chest may be compared with that of the bronze Buddha from Amaravati dated to *circa* 6th century C.E.[89] The long elliptical halo may be compared with the bronze images from Achutrajpur[90] and Kurkihar,[91] datable to a period from eighth to tenth centuries C.E. The absence of any inscription and the badly rubbed off face make it slightly difficult to date this image precisely. However, on the basis of fairly good modeling, simplicity of composition and stylistic consideration it may be attributed to *circa* 8th century C.E.

It may be noted that Buddhist images are not as abundant in western and northern India, particularly north of Delhi, as in eastern India during the early medieval period. Bronze Buddhist figures are still more rare.

The second figure from Hansi represents Bodhisattva Padmapāṇi (Pl. 337),[92] also called Avalokiteśvara, the most important of the Mahāyāna Buddhist divinities. Avalokiteśvara Padmapāṇi, the all-seeing Lord holding the lotus in his hand, not only saves the sentient beings from the impending perils but also watches over the world until the appearance of the future Buddha, Maitreya. The Bodhisattva is seated beautifully in *lalitāsana* (sitting posture with one leg folded and the other hanging down) on the pericarp of a finely executed *viśva-padma* ('World-lotus') having two rows of petals. His right leg is folded and the left hangs down with foot placed on a roundish footrest attached to the bottom of the lotus-pedestal. The folds of the *uttarīya* (upper garment) have been carved with care and grace. The Lokeśvara wears a beaded crown with three ornate triangular projections, the central one of which bears a tiny, seated figure of Amitābha in *dhyāna-mudrā* (meditative posture). The eyes and the circular mark on the forehead are inlaid with silver. Several coiled locks of hair may be seen falling gracefully on the shoulders. The Bodhisattva bears ear ornaments of a cluster of round flowers and has auspicious lines around the neck. He wears an *ekāvali* of big pearls, the sacred thread, beaded armlets and *valayas.* He holds a lotus by its long stem in his left hand, placed on the corresponding thigh. The right hand is disposed in a strange way raised to the level of the shoulder with palm inwards, thumb and the middle two fingers bent, probably to touch each other, and the index finger pointing to the face. This posture is quite different from that seen in the conventional figures of Bodhisattva Padmapāṇi. It may, however, be seen in some bronze figures of Bodhisattva Padmapāṇi of the 7th-8th century from Kashmir and is regarded as symbolizing pensiveness.[93] The Bodhisattva is the compassionate savior and may have thus been shown engaged appropriately in contemplating ways to save the human race. There is a circular halo with flamboyant edge behind the head and a small figure of a devotee with folded hands has been attached to the pedestal to the right of the Bodhisattva.

Eyes guild with silver look like wide-open eyes but this is only the effect of guilding. The quasi-closed eyes are an almost ubiquitous feature of such figures. The face is placid. The image is covered with sandal-paste indicating prolonged religious worship. Being better preserved, however, it shows sharp features. The modeling appears to have been fairly good. On an overall consideration, this small icon measuring 11 x 5.5 cm, may be attributed to the early 8 century C.E.

A sandstone Buddha head from Sanghi in district Rohtak (Pl. 338) with a top-knot of curled hair,[94] ascribable to the same period, a broken Buddha head from Rohtak,[95] another one from Ad Badri in district Yamunanagar (Pl. 339)[96] datable to *circa* 9th-10th centuries, however, indicate that Buddhism did not disappear altogether from this part of the country. That it continued to live later in Haryana is proved by a late medieval image recovered from a temple at the historic site of Taraori in district Karnal showing Buddha seated on a lotus pedestal in *bhūmisparśa-mudrā* (Pl. 340).

We thus see that though efforts were made during the very lifetime Buddha yet Buddhism could flourish in Haryana only during the reign of Aśoka. It continued to be an important religion during the Śuṅga, Indo-Greek and Śaka rule and touched its all time high in the region during the Kushāṇa period. Thereafter, though it received good impetus by Harsha during the 7th century C.E., yet it could not regain its old glory and importance. It, however, continued to be a living religion during the medieval period and did not disappear completely. Rohtak, Agroha, Sugh and Thanesar have been the most important centers of Buddhism in Haryana during the ancient period.

Geographically, Haryana is located between Mathura and Gandhāra. The trade route which connected Gandhāra with Pāṭaliputra (Uttarāpatha) and the south (Dakshiṇāpatha), passed through Haryana. As noted above, Haryana has yielded not only relics belonging to the Mathura and Gandhāra schools but also those showing traits of both the schools. As such, this region seems to have been the melting pot of influences from both the sides, particularly during the Kushāṇa period, and this is well reflected in the Buddhist remains of Haryana and Punjab, as known from Sanghol.

Notes and References

1. D.C. Ahir, *Buddhism in the Punjab, Haryana and Himachal Pradesh*, New Delhi, 1971, pp. 11ff.; Devendra Handa, *Buddhist Remains from Haryana*, New Delhi, 2004, pp. 1ff.
2. *Mahāvāstu*, Calcutta ed., Vol. II, p. 564; *Dīgha Nikāya*, II.55ff. Also see *Aṅgutta Nikāya*, V.29-32; *Majjhima Nikāya*, I. 55ff.; II.54 ff., 261 ff.; *Sutta Nipāta* II, 92-93, 107ff.; *Therīgāthā*, vv. 769-93; B.C. Law, 'Kurukshetra in Ancient India', *S K. Belvalkar Felicitation Volume*, p. 259.
3. M. Winternitz, *A History of Indian Literature*, Vol. II, Calcutta, 1933, p. 232.
4. E. Frauwallner, *The Earliest Vinaya and the Beginnings of Buddhist Literature*, Rome, 1956, pp. 31ff.
5. *Ibid*.
6. Devendra Handa, "Some Important Towns of Haryana: A Study of their past," *Jounal of Haryana Studies*, Kurukshetra, Vol. II (1970), pp. 4-12.
7. Alexander Cunningham, *Archaeological Survey Report*, Vol. II, pp. 226 ff.
8. Bharadwaj, *op. cit.*, p. 39.
9. *Dīpavaṃsa* (ed. H. Oldenberg, London, 1879), vv. 43-44.
10. Datta and Phadke, *op. cit.*, p. 39.
11. Ahir, *op. cit.*, pp. 12-15. We owe much to Bharadwaj regarding the details of these two places.
12. *Buddhacharita* (ed. with Hindi tr. S.N. Chaudhuri, Purnea, 1955) XXI. 26. In the *Avadānaśataka* (ed.

P.L. Vaidya, Darbhanga, 1958, p. 227), however, Raṭṭhapāla has been described as Kuru king's nephew.
13. *Majjhima Nikāya*, no. 82.
14. B.C. Law, *Tribes in Ancient India*, 2nd ed., Poona, 1973, p. 22; 46; *Majjhima Nikāya* (ed. Jagdish Kashyap, Nalanda, 1952), Vol. II, pp. 281ff.
15. Bharadwaj, *op. cit.*, p. 157.
16. Chaudhuri, *op. cit.*, p. 31.
17. Ahir, *op. cit.*, p. 15.
18. Bharadwaj, *op. cit.*, p. 157.
19. Silak Ram (*Archaeology of Rohtak and Hissar Districts*, Unpublished Thesis, Kurukshetra University, 1972, p. 107 fn. 1) identified Thullahoṭṭhita with Dhankot in District Gurgaon but without any evidence. Upadhyaya, *op. cit.*, p. 410.
20. Upadhyaya, *op. cit.*, p. 410.
21. Ahir, *op. cit.*, p. 14.
22. Bharadwaj, *op. cit.*, p. 159. There is another place known as Kamash now, located on the Barara-Shahbad road, about 5 km from the former, in district Ambala. The mound here, measuring 250 x 200 x 8 m, is partly under habitation and yields Painted Grey Ware, early historic red ware, coins, and other relics (Manmohan Kumar, *Archaeology of Ambala and Kurukshetra Districts [Haryana]*, Unpublished Thesis, Kurukshetra University, Kurukshetra, 1978, p. 37), but the definite Buddhist association or Buddhist relics from this site are still awaited.
23. For details see J. Przyluski, *Ancient Peoples of The Punjab*, Indian Studies, Calcutta, 1960, pp. 9 ff.
24. *Agrodake Mālyadharaḥ* (line 8) and *Agrodake Muñjakeśaḥ* (line 70) of *Mahāmāyūrī* edited by Sylvain Levi in *Journal Asiatique*, 1915, pp. 19-138.
25. Handa (1970), *loc. cit.*
26. Przyluski, *op. cit.*, p. 11.
27. *Ibid.*, p. 12.
28. *Divyāvadāna*, pp. 77 ff. Also see Handa (1970), *loc. cit.*
29. *Ibid.*, p. 47.
30. He could not reopen the *stūpa* of Rāmagrāma because of the opposition of the Koliyas. There is, however, another tradition that Aśoka obtained the corporeal relics of Buddha from an underground chamber of Rājagṛiha where Ajātaśatru had secretly deposited the relics of seven of the original *śārīrika stūpas.*
31. Samuel Beal, *Si-Yu-Ki: Buddhist Records of the Western World*, Vol. I, London, 1906, p. 186. See also Thomas Watters, *On Yuang Chwang's Travels in India*, Delhi, 1961 (First Indian ed.), p. 316.
32. Pāṇini, *Ashṭādhyāyī*, I.3, 25; Patañjali, *Mahābhāshya*, III.2, 15; *Divyāvadāna*, 74. 17, 22; *Mahāmāyūrī*, 11.23 & 60; *Bṛihatsaṃhitā* XVI. 21 etc.
33. Cunningham, *Archaeological Survey Report*, Vol. II, pp. 226-27; *The Ancient Geography of India*, Varanasi, 1963 (reprint), pp. 290-91.
34. Watters, *op. cit.*, p. 319.
35. *Annual Report, Archaeological Survey of India 1921-22*, p. 47; *Ibid*, 1922-23, pl. V.E.
36. R.C. Agrawala, "Sunga Pillars From Amin, Near Kurukshetra," *Lalit Kala*, Number 14 (New Delhi, 1969), pp. 50-52, pls. XVI-XVIII. Also see his "Early History and Archeology of Kurukshetra Region," *Indian Historical Quarterly*, Calcutta XXXI (4), 1955, pp. 204-06. These pillars were smuggled from Amin to London but were brought back to India and are now displayed in the National Museum, New Delhi. The duplicates of these pillars were left by the smugglers in the Ṭhākurajī kā Mandira on the bank of Suraj Kund at Amin.
37. Cf. Alexander Cunningham, *Stūpa of Bharhut*, Varanasi, 1962 (Reprint), pl. 49.13-14, V.S. Agrawala, *Studies in Indian Art*, Varanasi, 1965, pls. 95-96, fig. 57 on p. 95.
38. R.C. Agrawala (1969), *op. cit.*, p. 51.
39. The ornament in the right ear is circular but the one in the left ear seems to be a *patra-kuṇḍala.*
40. Dharmpal Singh Punia, *Archaeology of Mahendragarh and Gurgaon Districts [Haryana]*, Unpublished Ph. D. Thesis, Kurukshetra University, Kurukshetra, 1976, Chapter II, no. 36.
41. *Indian Archaeology 1979-80 A Review*, pp. 95-96. *Ibid.*, p. 183, pl. XXII. See also D.S. Punia, "New

Evidence of Pre-Kushan Sculpture from Gurgaon District (Haryana)," *East and West*, New Series, Vol. 31 (1981), pp. 133-4, figs. 1-2.

42. For details see Prem Goswamy, "Two Early Kuṣāṇa (?) Railing Pillars from Haryānā," *Journal of the Indian Society of Oriented Art*, New Series, Volume XV (1985-86), pp. 1ff. & pl. I.
43. *Ibid.*, pl. I.4.
44. Cf. Bharhut relief medallion illustrating the dream of Māyā. For illustration see Coomaraswamy, *op. cit.*, pl. XXIV, fig. 61 and Niharranjan Ray, *Maurya and Post-Maurya Art*, New Delhi, 1975, fig. 30.
45. Punia gave its measurements as 142.50 x 25.5. Prem Goswamy (*loc._cit.*) says that "The total height of the Hathin pillar inclusive of the boss of 5 cm is 154 cm and the width is 26 cm."
46. Devendra Handa, (2004), *op. cit.*, p. 25; "A survey of Inscriptions from Haryana", in *Revealing India's Past*, Vol. II, p. 261, Fig. 39.2. Cf. Prem Goswamy, *op. cit.*, p. 5 referring to Shri Krishna Deva's reading *'PADAYIKINI'*.
47. Cf. Similar earrings in the ears of a yakshī on a Bharhut railing post vide Pramod Chandra, *Stone Sculpture in the Allahabad Museum*, Poona, 1970, p. 41, pl. VII.
48. This post, too, was first noticed by Punia (1976, *op. cit.*, p. 182, pl. XX and 1981, *loc. cit.*, figs. 3-4). Punia gives it dimensions as 190 x 26.27 cm whereas HARDAM records rightly show them to be 149 x 24 cm. Prem Goswamy (*op. cit*, p. 3) has also followed the dimensions of HARDAM.
49. Sheela Devi, *Art Traditions in Haryana*, Unpublished Thesis, Kurukshetra University, 1975, pl. XXVII. A. The author, however, thinks that it depicts some 'Toilet Scene' and belongs to the Kushāṇa period (*Ibid.*, p. 129).
50. *Ibid.*, p. 129. pl. XXXIV. A. Sheela Devi, however, thinks that the panel depicts flying figures.
51. *Ibid.*, p. 131, l. XXX. F.
52. Cf. Vidya Dehejia, *Early Buddhist Rock Temples*, London, 1972, figs. 9-13, 31 etc.
53. Cf. Bharhut railing post fragment with *triratna* vide Pramod Chandra, *op. cit.*, fig. 20 b.
54. *Ibid.* figs. 59, 62, 63, 65, 66, etc.
55. Silak Ram, *Archaeology of Rohtak and Hissar Districts [Haryana]*, Unpublished Thesis, Kurukshetra University, 1972, p. 222, pl. XXVI. A. This life-size image in now housed in the Gurukul Museum, Jhajjar.
56. Benoytosh Bhattacharyya, *The Indian Buddhist Iconography*, Calcutta, 1968 (reprint), p. 76.
57. Handa, (2004), *op. cit.*, p. 34, Fig. 23.
58. The *Chitrasūtra* says, "Universal monarchs are to be portrayed with webbed fingers and toes. The auspicious curl of hair between the brows is to be shown in its place." C. Sivaramamurti, *Chitrasūtra of the Vishṇudharmottara*, New Delhi, 1978, p. 171).
59. Joanna Gottfried Williams, "An Ardhnarisvara-Linga," in *Kusumāñjali: New Interpretation of Indian Art & Culture (Sh. C. Sivaramamurti Commemoration Volume)*, edited by M.S. Nagaraja Rao, Vol. II, Delhi, 1987, p. 299.
60. Handa, (2004), *op. cit.*, p. 35, Fig. 24. It is also preserved in the Gurukula Museum, Jhajjar.
61. It is similar to the circular base of the *triratna* symbol described above.
62. *Indian Archeology 1965-66 – A Review*, p. 82.
63. The police from Jhajjar seized it in November 1972 while investigating the theft of three Gandhāra images from a temple near Jhajjar.
64. Exactly similar arrangement may be seen in a relief from Jamalgarhi (in Pakistan), now in the British Museum, Illustrated by John M. Rosenfield in his book *The Dynastic Arts of The Kushans*, California, 1967, Fig 92.
65. Made of fragile *kankar* stone, it measures 39 x 32 cm, and is now preserved in HARDAM.
66. It bears Index no. 1/352. It was procured by us for HARDAM while serving as Deputy Director during 1984-85.
67. R.C. Agrawala, "Some Kuṣāṇa Sculptures in the National Museum, New Delhi and Allied Problems," *Bulletin of Museums and Archeology in U.P.*, no. 3, June 1969, p. 19-20 and figs. 10-11; Handa (2004), *op. cit.*, p. 44, Figs. 31-32.
68. Devendra Handa & Satya Vrat, "Some Religious Terracottas from Sugh," *Haryana Sahitya Akademi*

Journal of Indological Studies, Vol. I, no. 1, Chandigarh, Spring 1985, pp. 96-97, fig. 15.

69. Suraj Bhan (1977), *loc. cit.*
70. III.42, 13-14:
    Kinnarāḥ dvividhāḥ proktā nṛivaktrā hayavigrhāḥ/
    Nṛidehāśchāśvavaktrāścha thatānye parikīrtitāḥ //
71. A.L. Srivastava, "Kinnara Kinnarī in Indian Art and their allied Problems," in *India's Cultural Contacts with Greek World (In the memory of Demetrius Galanose, 1760-1833, A Greek Sanskritist of Benaras)*, edited by U.P. Arora, Delhi, 1991, pp. 14-24 and figs. 1-20. See also Gourisankar De, "Aśva-mukhī Yakṣī", in Sharma and Handa, *Revealing India's Past*, Vol. I, pp. 153-55, Pl. 20.1.
72. *Rāmāyaṇa* (Gita Press, edition) II. 69, 16.
73. *Ibid.*, III.69, 15.
74. *Ibid.*, IV.43, 31.
75. Fausboll, *op. cit.*, no. 432.
76. *Mahāvaṃśa* X.53-61 (tr. Bhadant Anand Kausalyayan, Prayag, VS 2014, p. 53.
77. V.S. Agrawala (1963), *op. cit.*, p. 74.
78. Vidya Sagar Shukla, "Some Terracotta Figures from Sirsa (Haryana)", in *Indological Studies (in memory of S.P. Singhal)*, ed. Devendra Handa, Delhi, 1987, p. 81, fig. 3.
79. Cf. The early Kushāṇa Bodhisattva on a railing pillar in the Lucknow Museum vide Ananda K. Coomaraswamy, *History of Indian & Indonesian Art*, New York, 1965, pls. XXXI.78 & XXII.83 respectively.
80. *Divyāvadāna* (ed. P.L. Vaidya, Darbhanga, 1959), 256:
    Śairīshakaṃ ye pravare vimāne putrā vadatāṃ varasya /
    Anugrahārthaṃ mama te viśokā hyāyāntu kāruṇyanivishṭabhāvāḥ//
81. See for details Devendra Handa, "Some important Towns of Haryana: A study of their past-3", *Journal of Haryana Studies*, Vol. III, part 2, 1971, pp. 4-5.
82. Handa (2004), *op. cit.*, p. 48, Fig. 35.
83. N.P. Joshi, *Mathurā kī Mūrti-Kalā* (Hindi), Mathura, 1965, pl. 38.
84. Rodgers, *op. cit.*, p. 9.
85. D.C. Bhattacharyya, *Medieval Indian Sculpture in the Government Museum and Art Gallery Chandigarh*, Chandigarh, 1981, pp. 96-99, fig. 48; Handa (2004), *op. cit.*, p. 59, Fig. 46.
86. Bhattacharyya (*loc. cit.*), however, dates it to the 8th century.
87. Devendra Handa, *Jaina Bronzes From Hansi*, Shimla-New Delhi, 2002.
88. *Ibid.*, pp. 32-33, pl. 59.
89. D.R. Thapar, *Icons in Bronze*, Bombay, 1961, pl. XXIV. A.
90. Debala Mitra, *Bronzes From Achutrajpur, Orissa*, Delhi, 1978, pls. 31, 38-40, 42, 44, 47, etc.
91. Thapar, *op. cit.*, pls. XXVIII and XXXI.
92. Handa (2002), *op. cit.*, pp. 33-34, pl. 60.a-b.
93. Cf. P. Pal, *Bronzes of Kashmir*, New Delhi, 1975, pp. 134-7, figs. 45-46.
94. Handa (2004), *op. cit.*, p. 64, Fig. 49. It is now preserved in Gurukula Museum, Jhajjar. It measures 25 x 17.5 cm.
95. HARDAM. Index no. 1/115. A Buddha image is said to have been found from here in the last century (*Journal of the Asiatic Society of Bengal*, 1881, p. 72). Rodgers had also seen an image of Buddha near the tank of Gokarṇa (Rodgers' *Report*, p. 74.). A Buddha head is enshrined in the Śītalā Mātā Mandira near Gokarṇa kā Tālāb and worshipped as Śiva now.
96. Handa (2004), *op. cit.*, p. 64, Fig. 50. It is now preserved in the Department of Ancient Indian History, Culture and Archaeology, Panjab University, Chandigarh. Buddha in *padmāsana* and *dharma-chakra-pravartana-mudrā* datable to *circa* 11th-12th centuries from this site have also been noticed by Manmohan Kumar (1978), *op. cit.*, pp. 148, 163 and 288, pl. XVI. C and B respectively.

Chapter 11

Jaina Images

Jainism is a religion of hoary antiquity. The Jainas believe it to be eternal having been revealed repeatedly by twenty-four Tīrthaṅkaras, of which the last two are certainly historical figures. Pārśva, the penultimate pontiff, lived between 877 - 777 B.C.E., and the last tīrthaṅkara Mahāvīra died two hundred and fifty years after him, i.e., in 527 B.C.E.[1]

Jaina traditions regarding the first tīrthaṅkara Ṛishabhanātha turning the wheel of the Jaina faith at Takshaśilā, his visit to the Yavana country, etc. are not compatible with historical and archaeological evidence.[2] An atheistic religion like Buddhism initially, Jainism later adopted paradoxically like the latter, image-worship and the twenty-four tīrthaṅkaras came to be worshiped as Supreme Deities along with their attendant Yakshas and Yakshīs. Severe discipline, self-control, renunciation and austerity, characteristic of the Jainas did not allow much embellishments to be introduced in their sculptural representation, still some superb examples do exist amongst the numerous Jina images found from different parts of the country. These images are generally found carved either in *kāyotsarga* (also called *khaḍgāsana*)[3] or *padmāsana* (also called *paryaṅkāsana*).[4] Śrutadevīs or Vidyādevīs are other important but secondary deities of Jainism represented in art. Since converts could not dissociate themselves from their former faith completely, we find many Hindu deities like Śrī-Lakshmī, Gaṇeśa, etc. included in the fold of Jainism. *Dikpālas, Navagrahas, Apasarases, Gandharvas, Vidyādharas, Kinnaras*, etc. too came to be adopted as the sculptural embellishments on religious edifices.

Chhattra-traya or *Chhattrāvali* (triple umbrella); *lāñchhana* (cognizance); *Chaumukhī* or *Sarvatobhadrikā*,[5] a type of shrine-model with openings on all the four sides; *Chaubīsī* or *Chaturviṃśatikā*, a stele frieze or image with the twenty-four tīrthaṅkara figures, *tri-* and *pañcha-tīrthikās*, images with three or five Jina figures, etc., absent in Kushāṇa and Gupta sculptures, make their appearance later. Decorated glorioles and *śrīvatsa*-mark on the chest of the Jina figures, however, continued throughout from the early period.[6]

Carved in purely human form in *kāyotsarga* or *dhyāna-mudrā*, the Jina images, shown as sky-clad in Digambara tradition and wearing (white) garments in Śvetāmbara tradition, are depicted as young and beautiful in appearance, with a tranquil expression, arms reaching down to the knees, and *śrīvatsa* on the chest.[7] Iconographical texts[8] refer to the eight *Prātihāryas* which should be seen in a complete image of a tīrthaṅkara: (1) divine (Aśoka) tree, (2) shower of celestial blossoms, (3) drum, (4) fly-whisks, (5) throne seat (a lion throne), (6) aureole, (7) trilinear umbrella, and (8) heavenly music. Jina images can be recognized by their emblems, yakshas and yakshīs, acolytes, *Kevala-vṛikshas* (trees under which they got enlightenment), etc.

Jainism, however, seems to have been in a flourishing state at Mathurā during the 2nd century B.C.E.[9] A baked clay seal with a hole on one side for passing a string, found from Ahrwan, 12 km southwest of Palwal, has the Brāhmī legend *Śamaṇasa* in the characters of the later half of the 2nd century B.C.E. The old mound at Ahrwan spread over forty acres of land and 12 m in height has yielded Painted Grey Ware, early historic and medieval relics including sculptures, terracottas, silver and copper coins indicating here the existence of an important settlement in the early historic and medieval times.[10] If the word Śramaṇa was not a proper name, the seal may be interpreted to have belonged to a Jaina monk. But the Jaina monks cannot be expected to run commercial activities to use such seals, though its use by a monk to send some confidential messages to other or higher monks or teachers cannot be ruled out altogether. Even if we accept that the word does not signify a Jaina monk but a personal name still the adoption of such a personal name indicates the proclivity towards Jainism. Corroborative evidence, however, will remain a desideratum to be fulfilled by future discoveries.[11] A Jaina patriarch Lohāchārya is said to have propagated Jainism amongst the mercantile tribe of Agroha (i.e., Agrodaka *Janapada*) during the 1st century C.E.[12] *Therīgāthā*, which forms part of the *Khuddakanikāya*, contains stanzas of Nanduttarā and Mittakali (five each) of Kururaṭṭha. The traditional mention of names with the lives of the *Bhikshuṇīs* 'nuns' is preserved in the commentary of Dhammapāla known as the *Parmatthadīpinī*, ascribable to the 5th century C.E. Both the *therīs* (nuns) belonged to the Brāhmaṇa families of Kammāsadamma *nigama* 'corporation' in the Kuru country. Nanduttarā had earlier been initiated to Jainism.[13] There is, however, complete paucity of archaeological evidence regarding the prevalence of Jainism in Haryana during the Kushāṇa and even Gupta period as no Jaina inscription, icon or *āyāga-paṭa* has so far been discovered from the region. Jaina relics of Gupta art tradition found from Murti in district Jhelum of Pakistan[14] and the presence of the Jainas in the Gandhāra region as recorded by Hiuen Tsiang,[15] however, reveal that Jainism must have spread to those areas after having traversed the present day Haryana and Punjab states of India.

BRONZE IMAGES

The earliest archaeological evidence of the spread of Jainism in Haryana, however, comes from Hansi in the form of a hoard of bronze images containing four figures of Ādinātha (Ṛishabhanātha), two each of Mallinātha and Chandraprabha, twenty of Pārśvanātha, six of Mahāvīra, five unidentified Jinas, three *Sarvatobhadrikās,* one representing the Parents of the Jina, one of a Jaina *Āchārya* (?), two of Achchhuptā, and four of Sarasvatī, besides two Buddhist images and some others. A detailed account of this hoard, which contained some beautiful and exquisitely wrought images, has been published elsewhere[16] and need not be repeated here.

The Lahore Museum possesses a bronze figure of a Jaina tīrthaṅkara from some site in the Punjab.[17] Since the acquisition was made in the pre-partition days when Punjab included Haryana also, it is quite likely that the image was acquired from somewhere in Haryana as most of other acquisitions in the Lahore Museum were made from Hansi, Agroha (Hisar), Rohtak, Pehowa, etc. So Hansi or Rohtak seems to be more likely place of its acquisition. The bronze figure represents the Jina standing in *khaḍgāsana* on a simple round pedestal (Pl. 341). Since the figure is nude, it belongs to the Digambara sect. This elongate figure in a frontal pose seems to have been cast by the *cire perdue* or 'lost wax' method. The Jina bears schematic frizzled circlets of locks, long ear lobes, long arms hanging up to the knees, and has almost open staring eyes. The plump oval face does not bear the usual tranquility and beatitude, which generally characterizes such images. Except the three lines on the neck (*kambu-grīvā*) no care has been taken to represent the body-muscles realistically or even ideally. Even the *śrīvatsa* on the chest is not clear. Stylistically, it may be assigned to *circa* 9th century C.E.

This bronze piece has remained neglected all these years though it could be regarded as the earliest and the only bronze from the region before the discovery of the Hansi hoard.

Some years back, the Department of Archaeology and Museums, Haryana (HARDAM) acquired a hoard of fifteen Jaina bronzes from Charkhi Dadri. All the bronzes are inscribed but the corrosion has concealed some epigraphs and the chemical treatment has resulted only in their traces on some of them.

Seven of the bronzes belong to Pārśvanātha, others to Mahāvīra, etc. They belong to Saṃvat 1055, 1102, 13—, etc. The eyes are generally gilded with silver. The bronzes are not hollow cast like the Hansi bronzes or show different parts assembled together. None of them shows *navagrahas* and the *lāñchhanas*. Chowrie-bearers, Yaksha-Yakshī, lion-thrones, triple-umbrellas, etc. are generally present. One piece represents the *Tri-tīrthikā* of Pārśva. Many of the bronzes refer to the Subrahmāṇa-gachha in their inscriptions.[18]

HARDAM also possesses bronzes acquired from village Badhara in district Bhiwani. One of these represents Pārśvanātha (Pl. 342) seated in *padmāsana* on a cushioned seat under the canopy of seven-hooded snake over which rises the multi-foil umbrella flanked on either side by two very crude male celestial figures, one holding the garland and the other holding some unidentifiable objects. The image has suffered slight damage here and there. There is a depression in the center of the chest probably to insert some jewel to mark the *śrīvatsa*. Two paneled pillars with rounded tops flank the Jina. Outside these pillars are the fanners standing on lotus blossoms slightly turned towards the pontiff. The yaksha and yakshī are seated in *lalitāsana* on the proper right and left of the pedestal but in the absence of the usual snake-hoods on their heads there is nothing to be definite that they are Dharaṇendra and Padmāvatī. The pedestal seems to carry the small figure of snake, the cognizance of Pārśvanātha. On the extreme corners of the *triratha* pedestal are the diminutive figures of the donor couple in *añjali-mudrā*, seated kneeling in three-quarters profile. There are nine very crude figures on the pedestal, which seem to represent the *navagrahas*. A beaded fringe and other carvings bedeck the oval back slab with a *stūpikā* finial rising from between two beaded flower-shaped motifs. Stylistically, it may be dated to *circa* 16th century C.E.

Another figure, similar in conception and composition but slightly different in details of decoration, represents a tīrthaṅkara which is difficult to be identified with certainty in the absence of any definitive clue like the cognizance, the yaksha and yakshī figure, locks of hair on shoulders or snake-hoods.[19] Similarity of conception and composition with the image of Pārśvanātha indicates the same date for this figure also.

Three octo-alloy (*ashṭa-dhātu*) images of Pārśvanātha under the seven-hooded snake-canopy, and one of Naminātha, all inscribed and bearing the *lāñchhanas* on the pedestal, seated in *padmāsana* and having muscular bodies bearing *śrīvatsa* symbol on the chest, executed beautifully by *cire perdue* technique, are housed in the Supārśvanātha Jaina Śvetāmbara Temple at Ambala City and are under worship. The inscriptions have not been read because of certain religious restrictions. Stylistically, however, they seem to belong to the late 16th century.

STONE IMAGES

Ādinātha

The Panchayati Jaina Mandira (also called Bābā Haridāsa kā Mandira) outside the fort (Garh) at Firozpur Jhirka contains a red sandstone image measuring 75 x 75 x 22 cm assignable to *circa* 7th-8th century representing Ādinātha or Ṛishabhanātha, the first tīrthaṅkara. Being covered all over, its details could not be ascertained. A buff sandstone image of Ādinātha, which was once studded in the wall of a school building at Jind, is now preserved in HARDAM. The Jina is seated on a lion throne bedecked with a sheet bearing the lotus design in *padmāsana* with a lotus halo behind the head (Pl. 343). The hands are broken but they were certainly placed one over the other in the lap over the soles in meditative posture. The pontiff has a slender body with thin waist and elongated limbs. Locks of hair fall on both the shoulders. The expression is that of inward looking. He bears a topknot above which may be seen the stem of the tree or the *chhattrāvali* canopying the head. On either side of the halo toward the top are shown acanthus-like leaves with rectangular stele carrying the *vidyādhara* couples in flying postures, the male members holding the long garlands and facing towards the tīrthaṅkara. The couples are wearing lower garments, pearl necklets (males)/ necklaces with a pendent string dangling down from between the breasts to the navel (females), earrings, armlets, bracelets, etc. Above the *vidyādhara* couples are shown elephants with riders, broken at the top. Just below the *vidyādharīs* are shown on either side additional small figures of *vidyādharas* holding big flowers from their long stalks. Near the knees of the pontiff are shown the yaksha and yakshī. On the left hand side of the tīrthaṅkara is the four-armed Chakreśvarī seated in *lalitāsana,* supported by anthropomorphic Garuḍa. The yakshī holds discs in all the four-hands and bears a crown on the head. On the corresponding other side is the yaksha Sarvānubhūti holding a longish *nakulaka* in his left hand and an unidentified object in the other placed on the knee. The yaksha is seated in *bhadrāsana* and the vehicle is missing. He wears a *karaṇḍa-mukuṭa,* ear ornaments, necklace, *dhotī,* etc. Just above the yaksha and yakshī are depicted the fanners, Bharata and Bāhubali, in *tribhaṅga* postures, holding the flywhisks in their hands towards the Jina and resting the other on their respective thighs. Both these figures bear regal dresses and ornaments, including the *karaṇḍa-mukuṭa* and the long garland. On the face of the pedestal in the center is a disc in profile with two outward moving lions, facing, raising their one paw as usual, and with tails twirled at their backs. A couchant bull, the cognizance of the tīrthaṅkara, is carved in shallow relief in the center of the pedestal which also bears an inscription of Saṃvat 918 (=C.E. 861) on one side of the pedestal in five lines.[20] Another tīrthaṅkara image found from the Jind region shows the Jina in *padmāsana,* bearing curly hair, *śrīvatsa* on the chest, and half-closed eyes. There is no cognizance. The image is unfinished furnishing evidence of the creation of such images at the site itself and not having been imported from outside in their finished form.[21]

A buff sandstone image of Ādinātha is known from Narnaul (Pl. 344).[22] The Jina is seated cross-legged in meditation on a lion-throne on the upper facet of which may be seen lotus petals indicating *padma-pīṭha.* Two rampant lions are depicted on the pedestal. They are enfacing and there is a discus in profile between their backs in the center. The Jina bears curled top-knot, a *śrīvatsa* on the chest, elongated earlobes touching the shoulders on which fall the locks of hair also to give the Jina its distinction of being recognized as the first pontiff. There is engraved a very shallow gloriole marked with lotus petals separated from one another by a dividing line. Bow-shaped eyebrows, a sturdy nose, a strong chin and plump cheeks with semi-closed eyes give an expression of beatitude. The Jina is attended by two fanners who can be recognized as Bharata and Bāhubali by their *kirīṭa-mukuṭas.* They hold the flywhisk in the right hand and the left is akimbo. Above the head of the Jina is the triple umbrella with garland-bearing *vidyādharas* hovering on either side. The space above the heads of the fanners on both sides is filled up with unrecognizable human figures. This 10th century relief betrays the popularity of Jainism in the Narnaul region.

Some images from Pinjore, which were subsequently removed to the Department of Ancient Indian History, Culture and Archaeology, Kurukshetra University, Kurukshetra, represent Ādinātha. Two of them are unfortunately badly damaged and show the headless pontiff as seated in *padmāsana* with the fanner on his proper left. In one of them, made of sandstone and 46 x 40 cm in size, the lion throne has survived (Pl. 345), showing as usual the *chakra* in profile in the center with outward moving facing lions between triple-ribbed pilasters. A plain sheet spread on the seat falls down and covers the pedestal. Udai Vir Singh,[23] and following him S.P. Shukla[24] also, have wrongly identified this figure as that of Neminātha and date it to *circa* 12th century C.E. The Jina can be recognized from the locks of hair falling on his shoulders. Lozenge-shaped *śrīvatsa* on the chest is very clear. The male fanner with both the hands broken has hair combed backwards and piled up above. He wears pearl necklet, ear ornaments, sacred thread, nether garment secured by a girdle, etc. He may have carried the flywhisk in his right hand and the left may have rested on the thigh. Care has, however, not been taken to carve the hands, placed in the lap, and the fingers proportionately and realistically.

In the other figure (Pl. 346), 51 x 68 cm, the hands are damaged and the lion throne is missing.[25] The seat, however, shows the covering sheet marked with lotus design in the center. The *śrīvatsa* on the chest is carved with care and two roundels with a dot in the center mark the nipples on the chest. The fanner on his proper left, too, has been carved very carefully, bearing a *karaṇḍa-mukuṭa* adorned with a central jewel on the head, earrings, pearl necklet, *yajñopavīta*, bracelets, *dhotī* with a sash on the thighs, a long garland going down below the knees, etc. The facial expression is that of quietude and serenity. He is holding the flywhisk in his right hand raised to the shoulder and resting his left hand on the thigh. The image has been dated to *circa* 11th-12th century by Singh and Shukla but seems to belong to the 9th century C.E. along with the preceding image. A white marble headless image from this site, measuring 43.5 x 48 cm, bearing a *śrīvatsa* on the chest and seated on an ornamental cushion in *dhyāna-mudrā*, with the figure of the cognizance bull on the pedestal,[26] however, is definitely an image of Ādinātha belonging to *circa* 11th-12th century C.E.

From the same site comes another fragment (43 x 38 cm) which was once fixed indiscriminately over another headless figure of a Jaina tīrthaṅkara in a wall of the Kabir Chaurā temple (Pl. 347)[27] and was subsequently removed to the Kurukshetra University.[28] The locks falling on the shoulders help us identify the figure as that of Ādinātha. The head shows schematic curls and the topknot, round face with quasi-closed eyes, slightly damaged nose, thick lower lip, double chin, plump cheeks, hanging earlobes, and *kambu-grīvā*. There is a simple round aureole around the head with a *chhattrāvali* above, surmounted by the divine drummer. On either side of the drummer are elephants in kneeling postures inverting pitches of water indicating ablution. On both the sides of the head of the main Jina are small figures of meditating Jinas indicating that the relief originally represented probably a *tri-* or *pañcha-tīrthikā* of Ādinātha. This image from Pinjore, too, may be dated to *circa* 9th century on stylistic grounds.

Another upper part of an image from the same site, 43 x 35 cm in size, showing the bust of the Jina below the parasol with the figure of *devadundubhi* flanked by caparisoned elephants inverting the pitchers of water on the Jina, also shows a lock of hair on the left shoulder and may, thus, be identified as Ādinātha. The disposition of the arms indicated the meditative posture though the arms below the elbows are lost now. There is a simple round halo behind the head on either side of which may be seen miniature figures of meditating Jinas. The proper left hand side shows another figure of *kāyotsarga* Jina on Ādinātha's left.

Originally the relief was a *pañcha-tīrthikā* of Ādinātha. Singh and Shukla have left it unidentified and date it to *circa* 12th century C.E. like other images[29] but it also seems to belong to *circa* 9th century C.E.

A fragmentary sculpture of buff sandstone measuring 86.5 x 68.5 cm was discovered from the village Binwa, 12 km east of Firozpur Jhirka, in district Gurgaon. The tīrthaṅkara is shown as standing in *khaḍgāsana*. His arms and head are broken. *Śrīvatsa* mark is seen very distinctly in the center of the chest. An almost mutilated halo may be seen behind the head. The pontiff is clad in a loin-girdle with schematic folds falling between the legs. The cognizance, seated bull, is carved on the pedestal below the feet. On either side near the feet, a seated devotee is shown with folded hands. On the recessed corners of the panel stand two female figures, now mutilated, in *dvibhaṅga*. Besides the central Jina figure, twenty-three miniature Jina figures seem to have been carved around as is indicated by some of the extant figures on the proper left hand side of the main figure. This, thus, was actually a *chaturviṃśati* of Ādinātha. There is an un-deciphered inscription also on the pedestal. The execution and style make it a piece of *circa* 9th century C.E.[30]

Another sandstone *chaturviṃśati* Jina image with Ādinātha in the center as the main figure was found from Narnaul (Pl. 348). Measuring 51 x 32 cm, it shows Ādinātha sitting in *padmāsana* under a triple umbrella with the branches and leaves (of the *nyagrodha*) falling on either side of the head. Garland-bearing *vidyādharas* hovering in the sky are depicted on either side of the umbrella. Long locks of hair fall on his shoulders. A lozenge-shaped *śrīvatsa* is carved on the chest. The Jina sits on a lion throne adorned with a sheet. On the face of the pedestal is depicted a wheel in profile in the center and a lion on either side back to back, with one fore-paw resting on the ground and the other raised up. The lions look to front. From the level of the knees to the top of the triple umbrella are four panels showing two *padmāsana* Jinas each on either side while the top row carries the figures of seven such Jinas, making the total number, including the main figure, as twenty-four. The receding recesses of the pedestal show the yaksha and yakshī, the latter with a child in her lap. This yakshī may thus be identified with Ambikā. It is to be noted that before the yakshas and yakshīs belonging to a particular tīrthaṅkara came to be essentially depicted with that tīrthaṅkara, Ambikā was usually shown as accompanying the different tīrthaṅkaras. The image thus seems to belong to *circa* 9th century C.E. Another similar frieze is also preserved in the Jaina temple at Narnaul but here Gaṇeśa is shown on the extreme lower proper right hand projection of the pedestal and the parents of the Jina, king Nābhi and queen Marudevī, are depicted below the pedestal with adoring celestials and couples in small panels on either side. *Vidyādhara* couples with divine elephants above are also shown on either side of the Jina near his head (Pl. 349).[31]

A buff sandstone *chaturviṃśati* frieze of Ādinātha was accidentally discovered at the village Ranila near Charkhi Dadri, about 27 km from Bhiwani on 18 October 1991.[32] Ādinātha sits in *padmāsana* on the lion throne under triple umbrella, flanked by Bharata and Bāhubali as fanners, on the central projection of the *triratha* pedestal (Fig. 17). Garland-

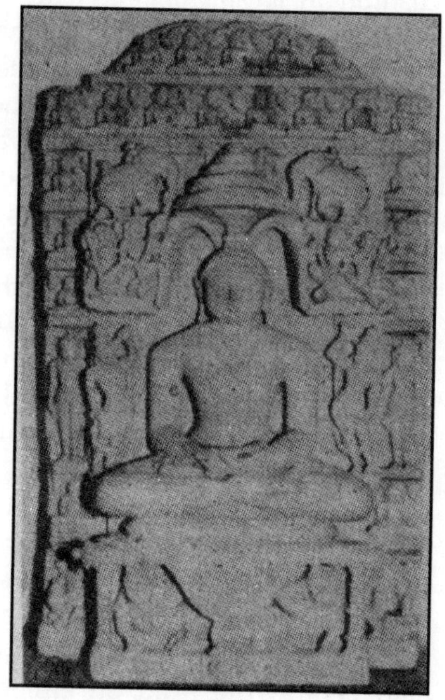

Fig. 17. Ādinātha, Ranila.

bearing *vidyādhara* couples and elephant riders are shown on either side of the head of the pontiff and the umbrella above. Bull, the cognizance of the tīrthaṅkara, is carved on the lower edge of the pedestal in the center making the identification easier. The recesses on either side carry the figures of the yaksha and the yakshī at the lower ends while above them are shown five Jinas in successive panels from bottom upwards. The second Jina on either side stands in *khaḍgāsana* while all others are seated in meditation. The top two rows carry the figures of eight and five seated Jinas respectively. The image was discovered by a villager while removing sand to raise the level of the street before being brick-lined. It is one of the rarely found complete images and seems to have been buried for the fear of being desecrated at the time of some attack. Stylistically it may be placed in *circa* 10th century C.E.

An almost human-sized red sandstone headless nude *khaḍgāsana* image of Ādinātha was found from a field near Naraingarh and acquired by HARDAM. The pontiff stands on a pedestal with a cloth hanging, with wheel in the center flanked by deer and lions moving outwards as usual. Flanking the Jina are Bharata and Bāhubali, his fanners, and the top corners show the *vidyādharas*. The yaksha seems to be Sarvānubhūti and yakshī Ambikā. Stylistically, it may belong to 10th century C.E.

CHANDRAPRABHA

Only two images of the eighth tīrthaṅkara Chandraprabhu are known from Haryana. The first one is a very badly mutilated figure from Ratpur near Pinjore (Pl. 350). It is headless and almost half of its proper left is also gone. What survives shows that the tīrthaṅkara is seated in meditation. There is a *śrīvatsa* on the chest and a faint crescent mark on the pedestal indicating the identity of the Jina. Stylistically, it may have belonged to *circa* 9th century C.E.

The second figure is still under worship not as a tīrthaṅkara but as some deity placed in a niche of the Topanātha kā Mandira at Pinjore. It is carved out of grayish coarse-grained sandstone and measures 61 x 49 cm. The Jina is seated in *dhyāna-mudrā* with a stylistic and prominent *śrīvatsa* on the chest (Pl. 351). He bears schematic curls on the head, an oval face, eyes closed in meditation, long sturdy nose, and plump cheeks. The depiction of the crescent in the center of the cushioned seat reveals the identity of the tīrthaṅkara. The figure has been painted with ultramarine and vermilion. The image may be dated to *circa* 10th century C.E.[33]

ŚREYĀṂSANĀTHA

A 12th century buff sandstone image of Śreyāṃsanātha is preserved in the Jaina *dharmaśālā* at Rewari. The Jina is seated in *padmāsana* under the Tumbara (or Tinduka) tree attended by fanners (Pl. 352). The top-knot and the face is stylized and there is a prominent lozenge-shaped *śrīvatsa* on the chest. Divine elephants below which are shown the garland-bearing *vidyādharas* followed by their spouses holding musical instruments flank *Chhattrāvali* above the head. The Jina is recognized by a small rhinoceros carved on the center of the pedestal.[34]

ŚĀNTINĀTHA

Rohtak seems to have been an important center of Jainism in the early medieval period. The Asthal Bohr monastery at Rohtak houses a good number of Jaina and Hindu images. Amongst these is a Jina figure, which has unfortunately been spoiled by indiscriminate strokes of the black paint on the chest and belly (Pl. 353). It shares most of the physical features with other Jaina images of the site and shows the pontiff seated in *padmāsana* under the triple umbrella, which is surmounted by the divine drummer. The Jina is seated on a lion throne on the pedestal of which are depicted as usual the outward moving lions and inward looking deer, badly damaged, flanking a wheel in profile in the center. An exquisitely carved round lotus-petalled halo may be seen behind the head of the pontiff. Leaves of the *chaitya-vṛiksha* hang down stylistically from above and below the umbrella. The back slab shows on either side elephants in profile facing outwards, leogryphs, garland bearing, *vidyādhara* couples, and elephants with riders from bottom upward from about the middle of the torso of the Jina. The trunks of the elephants are broken, so it is difficult to say with certainty whether they were inverting pitchers of water and anointing the Jina or not. On the proper right hand side top corner may be seen female parasol holder. There was probably another one on the corresponding side. The face, topknot, left arm, elephants and their riders and the pedestal have suffered mutilation. There is no *lāñchhana* on the pedestal. Made of the same type of sandstone, the image measures 109 x 69 cm. The figure may be dated to *circa* 10th century C.E. on stylistic grounds. The Jina may be identified as Śāntinātha.

Another pedestal showing two lions and two deer flanking a wheel is fixed in a wall of the Jogion kā Maṭha at Asthal Bohr (Pl. 354). The cloth hanging contains three *kīrtimukhas* spewing pearl strings, which form loops and three pendants, carved on it. The lions are shown with their backs towards the center and have been carved facing as usual with one paw raised. The wheel in the center is 14-spoked with fillet coming out of its hub. Two miniature figures of deer flank the wheel facing towards it. This pedestal, too, may have belonged to an image of Śāntinātha as no other cognizance is carved on the pedestal. Stylistically, it may be assigned to the same age as the above-mentioned figure.

A small piece showing the corpulent yaksha Sarvānubhūti is fixed along with the pedestal described above, but on the wrong side. The yaksha may be recognized from the *nakulaka* held in his left hand.

An image of Śāntinātha from Rohtak is now preserved in the Lahore Museum, Pakistan (Pl. 355).[35] The Jina is seated in *padmāsana* on a cushioned seat placed on a lion throne. There is an elegant eight-petalled halo behind his head. The right arm and a part of his folded right leg are gone. The schematic curls and top-knot, long earlobes touching the shoulders, broad, serene face with elongated meditative eyes, conch-like neck (*kambugrīva)*, rounded shoulders, broad chest with *śrīvatsa* mark, attenuated waist with a deep groove representing the navel etc. are the features which very much resemble the Jina figures described above. The nose, as in other images, is broken. A flourish of the *dhoti* at the crossing point of the legs is visible on the cushioned seat.

Just behind the head of the tīrthaṅkara may be seen a ribbed staff supporting the trefoil umbrella above. On the top of this *chhattra* is the drummer as seen in other images also. Flanking the Jina are the male fly-whiskers standing on lotuses emanating from below the pedestal. They stand facing in triple flexion posture holding the *chāmara* in one hand towards the pontiff and other resting on the respective thigh. Each of them bears a beautiful *karaṇḍa-mukuṭa*, ear ornaments, pearl necklet, sacred thread, armlets, bracelets, anklets, nether garment and a long garland. Just above them are carved the celestial musician couples against the background of clouds. On either side of the trefoil umbrella may be seen an elephant with usual trappings and howdah on the back. The cloth hanging on the pedestal is bedecked with two *kīrtimukhas* spewing pearl strings which form four loops and two pendants. The two outward moving lions and the wheel flanked by two deer are the usual features of the pedestals. On the extreme projections of the pedestal are depicted the yaksha and the yakshī, Sarvānubhūti and Ambikā, as noted in the Śāntinātha image described above. Sarvānubhūti sits in ease with a cushion under his folded left leg, wearing ear ornaments, pearl necklet, armlets, *dhotī* and anklets, holding *nakulaka* in the left and *bījapuraka* in the right hand. Ambikā holds an *āmralumbī* in her right hand and supports a child with her left. Interestingly, her vehicle, lion, is also carved under her folded left leg. The simplicity of the halo and ornamentation indicates this image to be a creation of the 10th century C.E.

A 10th century buff sandstone *padmāsana* image of Śāntinātha from Tosham is preserved in HARDAM. The Jina is identified only on the basis of the pedestal, which shows deer flanking the wheel and back-to-back lions as usual on the pedestal.

MALLINĀTHA

An exquisitely carved buff sandstone Digambara image of Mallinātha (Pl. 356) was recovered from the bed of the river Krishnavati near Narnaul. Obviously it seems to have been immersed there for fear of some imminent attack and desecration of the image. It is now preserved in HARDAM and bears accession no. 1/366. The Jina bears schematic curls with a topknot on the head, long hanging earlobes, quasi-close eyes, plump round face with nose and chin slightly damaged, lozenge shaped *śrīvatsa* on the chest, navel marked by a shallow hole, palms of the hands placed one over the other in the lap, soles of the feet facing upwards with toes pointing downwards, and is shown seated on the lion throne in *padmāsana* on a cushioned seat bearing floral and other designs. A part of the sheet hangs down from the lion throne. It bears decorations like the lotus flanked by diamond shaped motifs, wavy panels, etc. The facet of the pedestal between two triple-ribbed pilasters depicts two outward moving facing lions with forepaws raised up. On the central offset of the pedestal are shown deer flanking a facing *chakra* with *ghaṭa* (pitcher) below. The extreme projections of the pedestal bear the figure of Kubera yaksha on the proper right and Aparājitā yakshī on the left. Kubera is depicted as four-faced (the fourth face at the back) but two-handed, seated in *lalitāsana*. He wears pearl necklet, ear ornaments, sacred thread, *dhotī*, etc. and holds a fruit (citrus?) in his right hand. The left hand is concealed. There is no vehicle depicted under him. Aparājitā also sits gracefully in *lalitāsana* holding a pitcher in her left hand with right placed on the respective knee. She bears an exquisite *karaṇḍa-mukuṭa*, earrings, necklace with a pendant suspended from between the round rotund breasts, and the lower garment. Canonical injunctions do not seem to have been followed in the depiction of the yaksha and the yakshī. There are diminutive unidentified figures near the knees of the pontiff. The fanners flanking him are carved with care. They stand gracefully in *tribhaṅga* turned slightly towards the Jina, wearing regal dress and ornaments, holding the flywhisk in the hand towards the pontiff and resting the other on the thigh.

The image has suffered a crack above the bust of the pontiff and the heads of the fanners and a portion of the proper right hand top corner have been lost. What survives, however, gives us a complete picture of what it would originally have been. Above the fanners are steles showing the *vidyādhara* couples on either side. The *vidyādharas* are depicted as carrying long garlands and their female counterparts, seated on their long stretched legs are holding the *vīṇa* in one hand with other raised up in the posture of singing. Elephants with riders are shown just above the *vidyādhara* stele. At the back of the elephants are shown in pedimented niches toping the pilasters on the extreme projections of the back slab Jina figures in *dhyāna-mudrā* under a canopy and two branches of the sacred tree looped downwards. The apex too has similar miniature Jina figure flanked by *khaḍgāsana* Jinas in pedimented niches. Between the apex and the side pilasters are shown semi-celestials bearing long garlands and musical instruments, three on each side. Just above the pinnacle of the umbrella is the half bust of a conch-blower, Dundubhi. Stylistically, this elaborately but exquisitely carved image may be dated to *circa* 12th century C.E. HARDAM possesses another image of Mallinātha in buff sandstone measuring 54 x 57 x 18.5 cm obtained from Tosham (Acc. No. 59/84) but its details or the photograph could not be obtained from the Department.

NEMINĀTHA

A sandstone headless image from Ratpur (Pl. 357) shows the figure of the pontiff seated on a lion-throne in meditation. The hands placed in the lap and the right knee has suffered damage. The throne-blanket covers the central portion of the pedestal, which carries a vertically placed conch in the center, flanked by outward moving lions in profile. The lions are robust, having up curled tails and have been carved with care. The depiction of the conch on the pedestal helps us to identify the figure as that of Neminātha. On the proper right of the main figure is a headless Jina figure in *kāyotsarga*. Another similar figure may be presumed to have been there on the corresponding other side. It, however, cannot be ascertained definitely whether it was a *tri-tīrthikā* or a *pañcha-tīrthikā*, probably the latter to judge from the size of the extant *kāyotsarga* Jina. Stylistically, the image may be dated to *circa* 9th century C.E.

A white marble pedestal, 28 x 41 cm, broken on the proper right, from Pinjore, shows a four-handed female holding perhaps lotus flowers in the upper pair of hands, standing gracefully under an ornamental arch in the center below which we have the usual motif of *dharma-chakra* flanked by two deer. On the proper left of the female figure is carved the outward moving facing lion with one paw raised up, followed by an unidentified figure, and standing Ambikā supporting the child with her left hand. The image may be identified with Neminātha on the basis of yakshī Ambikā, but *śaṅkha* (conch), the *lāñchhana* of the Jina, is not there even at this late stage of *circa* 12th century to which this pedestal may be dated on stylistic grounds.[36]

A schist pedestal representing a figure seated in the middle in *lalitāsana* flanked by lions in opposite directions with a wheel with deer in profile in the center, a horizontal band containing miniature *lalitāsana* figures of the *navagrahas* holding lotus flowers, etc. has been found from Sirsa. It measures 69 x 33 cm and is now displayed in the museum of the Kurukshetra University. A conch placed above the central figure provides the clue to the identification of the main figure. The cognizance indicates the original image to have belonged to Neminātha. The image, dated to *circa* 10th-11th century C.E., is badly obliterated but provides important evidence.[37]

PĀRŚVANĀTHA

A sandstone image of Pārśvanātha, measuring 101.5 x 68.5 cm, is placed in a recently built shrine at Ata (Āṭā), situated about 5 km east of Sohna and 26 km south of Gurgaon. The pontiff is seated in *padmāsana* with legs crossed and palms placed over the soles turned upwards in the posture of meditation (Pl. 358). The *padma-pīṭha* is supported by two lions walking sideways with a *dharma-chakra* placed between them. The *śrīvatsa* symbol is very distinct on the chest. The tīrthaṅkara has locks of hair falling on his shoulders. This feature is seen in the bronze image of Chandraprabhu from Hansi and some other figures also. A *chhattrāvali* is seen above his head. It appears that there are some branches of a (*Nyagrodha*, banyan) tree above the parasol. A halo is marked behind the head. A careful examination betrays the existence of seven hoods of the snake, now badly damaged, canopying the head of the pontiff. On either side are the garland-bearing *vidyādharas* hovering in the sky. Flanking the tīrthaṅkara in the center of the panel are male figures standing in *tribhaṅga* pose. Below these figures may be seen a pot-bellied male figure on the proper right and a mutilated female figure on the corresponding left. These figures represent probably yaksha Sarvānubhūti and yakshī Ambikā. The figure thus represents the stage when the particular yaksha and yakshī were not stereotyped and the pontiffs were shown with locks of hair falling on their shoulders like that of Ādinātha. If we miss to see the serpent hood the Jina may be recognized as the first tīrthaṅkara. The absence of the vehicle, the presence of the triple umbrella, outward moving lions on the pedestal, the hair-knot on the head of the pontiff, the subsidiary figures with simple drapery and sparse jewelry indicate an 8th century date for this image.

A sandstone image (40.5 x 25.5 cm) of Pārśvanātha was discovered from Narnaul (Pl. 359). It shows the pontiff seated in meditation on a lotus seat placed on the lion throne showing a discus in profile in the center flanked by outward moving facing lions with one paw raised. A part of the sheet of the lion throne with schematic folds covers the pedestal. The Jina has broad shoulders and somewhat muscular body. He bears schematically curled locks with a pod on the head, which is encircled by a lined and beaded halo with seven hoods of the serpent all around. Two acolyte figures may be seen flanking Pārśvanātha. This simple figure without any cognizance and prescribed yaksha and yakshī bears the lingering classical effect and may be dated to *circa* 8th century C.E.

More than a century back, Rodgers had seen some very fine Jaina images in the monastery of the Nātha sect at Asthal Jogian in the vicinity of Rohtak.[38] In 1939, B.C. Bhattacharya referred to and illustrated an image of standing Pārśva from the Jogion kā Maṭha.[39] In 1959, Dr. Y.D. Sharma also noticed some Brahmanical and Jaina images in the Asthal Bohr monastery.[40] But for some casual references to one or two of these images by the subsequent writers and scholars of Jaina art they have remained neglected.[41]

As far as Jaina literature is concerned, Rohtak finds mention in the *Vipākasūtra*. According to the Jaina tradition accepted by the Śvetāmbaras, *Vipākasūtra* is the eleventh of the total twelve Aṅgas, which are regarded as the core of the Jaina canonical literature. R.N. Mehta ascribes *Vipākasūtra* to the later part of the 9th century C.E.[42] The *Vipākasūtra* refers to Vesamanadatta (Vaiśramaṇadatta) and Pusanandi (Pushya Nandi) who ruled from Rohidiya (Rohitaka = Rohtak).[43] The same text refers to the shrine of Dharaṇa-Jakkha in the Pudhavivadamsa (Pṛithvyavataṃsa) Udyāna of Rohida (Rohtak).[44] Dharaṇa is the yaksha of Pārśvanātha. The *Vipākasūtra,* thus, indicates the popularity of the worship of Pārśva at Rohtak in the 9th century C.E. if not earlier. References to the lay worshippers (*śrāvakas)* of Rohada (=Rohtak) in the *Kharatara-Gachchha-Bṛihad-Gurvāvali*[45] indicate that Jainism continued to flourish at Rohtak during the Chāhamāna and the subsequent periods and the city had a substantial population of enthusiastic lay Jaina worshippers. The *Gurvāvali* also refers to the foundation of *vidhichaityas* at Hansi as well as at Māyaḍa, and Tosham near it by Jinavallabha Sūri.

The image of Pārśvanātha from Asthal Bohr, Rohtak referred to and illustrated by B.C. Bhattacharya (Pl. 360) is made of buff sandstone and measures 132 x 40 cm. The Jina stands in the *kāyotsarga* posture on a lotus seat placed in the center of the middle projection of the *triratha* pedestal. The right arm of the Jina is broken just below the shoulder. Pārśva stands under the canopy of the seven-hooded snake but all the hoods are unfortunately broken. Five coils of the snake behind the body of the pontiff may be seen clearly. The tīrthaṅkara wears a diaphanous *dhotī* which is held in position by a cord with a central knot shaped like an arch from which fall the central folds in a wavy pattern. There are beautiful semi-circular *valli*-shaped folds on the left thigh.

The face is broad, the nose is damaged and the eyes are elongated. The upper eyelids are drooping indicating blissful meditation (Pl. 361). The lower lip is thicker and the double chin is pointed. The cheeks are plump. The elongated earlobes touch the shoulders. The torso is modeled beautifully having broad shoulders and a well-developed chest adorned with a lozenge-shaped *śrīvatsa*. The waist is attenuated and the navel is marked by a deep groove. The hair on the head is arranged in schematic curls with an *ushṇīsha* on top. The extant left arm hangs down up to the knee (*ājānulambabāhu).* The Jina seems young and energetic having a pleasing countenance as prescribed by Varāhamihira.[46] He is flanked by male fly-whiskers, female figures and yaksha and yakshī (Pl. 362). The *Chāmaradharas* bear beautiful *karaṇḍa-mukuṭas* adorned with jewels. They wear ear ornaments, bejeweled necklets, pearl necklace, sacred threads, beaded bracelets, long garlands and undergarments. Standing in graceful triple-flexion poses they hold a flywhisk in the hand towards the pontiff, resting the other on the respective thigh.

Two female figures are shown standing before them.[47] Both of them wear exquisite dress and ornaments. The one on the proper right hand side of the Jina holds a snake each in her two hands and the other on the left hand side holds a sword in her right hand and a water-vessel in the left. They may thus be identified with the *vidyādevīs* Vairoṭyā and Mahāmānasī respectively.[48] Seated in front of them are the pot-bellied yaksha Sarvāubhūti holding a *nakulaka* in his left hand and the yakshī Ambikā holding mango-twig in her right hand and supporting a child on her left lap.

On the two sides of the serpent canopy are shown the divine musicians (the proper right hand side figure being broken), the garland-bearers and elephants with full trappings and rider couples, inverting pitchers of water held in their trunks to perform the *abhisheka*. The divine drumbeater is depicted on the top of the triple umbrella in the center.

Shah felt inclined to place this image of Pārśva from Rohtak slightly later than an inscribed bronze dated Saṃvat 744 (C.E. 687) and another undated one from Vasantgarh on the basis of the style of the *dhotī*.[49] Tiwari has dated it to *circa* 7th century C.E.[50] Later, Shah assigned it to *circa* 8th-9th century C.E.[51] The Rohtak image has got a short *dhotī* hardly reaching the knees whereas that of Vasantgarh has got a long one reaching the ankles. Also there is no zigzag pattern of the central fold between the legs in the former. If at all the style of the *dhotī* can be compared with other images they are those of Nemināthа from Narhad (Rajasthan) in the National Museum, New Delhi[52] and Muni Suvrata now preserved in the Jaipur Museum,[53] which may be dated to the 12th century C.E. We may also point out that the type of the *graiveyaka* shown around the necks of the fly-whiskers in the Rohtak image did not appear popularly in the sculptures of the region before the 9th century. The girdle of our image is simpler than that of the Narhad image and the facial expression too is that of beatitude, not stiff and stylized as in the above-mentioned Neminātha and Suvrata images. So we feel inclined to date our image from Rohtak to the 9th century C.E.

B.C. Bhattacharya had observed "A clear representation of Pārśva Yakṣa's figure may be seen in the statue of Pārśvanātha from Jogion kā Maṭha, near Rohtak town".[54] Referring to this image, M.C. Joshi has noted, "An icon of the elephant-headed yakṣa Pārśva, who is the nearest parallel to Gaṇeśa in Jainism, has been noticed at Rohtak". [55] There is, however, no image of the elephant-headed yaksha Pārśva in the said *maṭha*, or even anywhere else in Rohtak now.

The Asthal Bohr monastery possesses an image (Pl. 363) of buff sandstone, 136 x 39 cm, which differs from the image of Pārśvanātha referred to above only in the manner of mutilation and the number of the hoods of the serpent canopying the Jina. Instead of seven, five hoods have been shown and unfortunately all of them are broken. The triple umbrella, the divine musician near the left shoulder of the pontiff, his nose and left arm, the heads of the *vidyādevī* Mahāmānsī and yakshī Ambikā have also suffered mutilation. The style of carving and the details of even the subsidiary figures resemble so much that it seems to have been carved simultaneously, if not by the same artist, with the Pārśva image described above. No *lāñchhana* has been represented on the pedestal.

Shah had rightly observed that "Pārśvanātha, the twenty-third Tīrthaṅkara, is also represented with a canopy of snake-hoods overhead which often renders it difficult to differentiate between images of Pārśva and Supārśva in the absence of an inscription or the cognizance on the pedestal. Usually Pārśva is shown with coils of snake behind his body, while in the case of Supārśva only the snake-hoods overhead are carved or painted". [56] The conception of the two images, carving of five coils behind the body, the depiction of the divine musicians, garland-bearers, elephants anointing the Jina, the drum-beater on the top and the fly-whiskers, *vidyādevīs* and yaksha-yakshī are so similar that one feels tempted to identify even this second image as that of Pārśvanātha but the number of snake-hoods is five which is prescribed for Supārśvanātha, the seventh tīrthaṅkara.[57] It may, however, be pointed out that images of Pārśva with five snake-foods are also known from Aihole, Badami, Rajgir, etc.[58] Revising his earlier conviction that "in northern, eastern and western India Pārśva was always shown with seven and not five snake-hoods"[59] Shah lately observed that "With Klaus Bruhn I also feel that where the Jina has coils of a snake at his back the Jina is to be identified as Pārśvanātha, irrespective of the number of snake-hoods held over his head".[60] We also feel that Pārśva was the most popular tīrthaṅkara in Haryana and was depicted with five snake-hoods also though seven was the conventional number. The image under discussion, and some of the other pieces described below showing the Jina under the canopy of five hoods may, therefore, be identified as those of Pārśva.

Shah has referred to another image of Pārśvanātha from Rohtak.[61] Preserved in the Jogion kā Maṭha at Asthal Bohr, it is made of buff sandstone and measures 119 x 68 cm. It shows Pārśva seated in *padmāsana* on a lion throne (Pl. 364). Behind his head is a very exquisitely carved halo. The hair of the Jina has been arranged in schematic curls with a topknot. He has elongated quasi-closed eyes with arch-shaped eyebrows. Left eye, nose, mouth and chin are damaged but the serenity of the broad face may still be made out. The conch-like neck, the broad round shoulders, robust chest with *śrīvatsa* mark, slim waist, deep round hole of the navel and long arms are the notable physical features. Both the hands placed one over the other in the lap and the right leg of the pontiff are also damaged. A flourish of the *dhotī* is seen in the center of the seat clearly indicating it to be a Śvetāmbara image. The Jina is flanked on either side by well-dressed and ornamented elongated male *chāmaradharas* (Pl. 365) standing on lotuses while the extreme projections behind them show female figures, elephant heads and leogryphs leaping outwards. On either side of the head of the Jina are the *vidyādhara* couples in flying postures, the male ones holding long garlands. The uppermost register shows elephants anointing the pontiff by inverting pitchers of water held in their trunks. Two Jina figures in *kāyotsarga* posture, wearing *dhotīs* and having round glorioles behind their damaged heads may be seen behind the elephants on the extreme top corners. In the center just above the serpent hoods is that triple umbrella with a divine drummer upon it. Leaves of Dhātakī tree (*Grislea tomentosa*) may be seen at the back of the trefoil umbrella. The space between the raised elephant trunks and the *prabhāvalis* of the standing Jinas is filled with celestial musicians and dancers. A throne-blanket on the pedestal shows small half-human figures of Dharaṇa yaksha and his queen in profile in *añjali-mudrā,* flanking a beautiful *kīrtimukha* spewing strings of pearls, which form an exquisite pattern of loops and pendants on the cloth hanging (Pl. 366). The pedestal shows outward moving facing lions, with one paw raised up, and two deer in profile flanking a *chakra* in the center. On the extreme projections of the pedestal are carved the yaksha and the yakshī. The pot-bellied Sarvānubhūti holding a *nakulaka* in his left hand (right hand is broken) has a beautiful roundish hairdo serving as his glorìole (Pl. 367). Ambikā, whose head and left arm are unfortunately badly broken, on the other side holding an *āmralumbī* in her right hand, too, has been carved carefully (Pl. 368). Just above the yaksha and the yakshī are shown the donor couple in profile in adoration. The image may be dated to the late 9th century C.E. on stylistic grounds.

The Jaina temple at Narnaul houses another beautiful *Pañchatīrthikā* of Pārśvanātha seated in *padmāsana* under the canopy of a five-hooded serpent. The top corners of the rectangular slab show diminutive meditating Jinas whereas flanking the main figure are *khaḍgāsana* pontiffs wearing *dhotīs*. The pedestal shows an enface wheel with two outward moving lions with the depiction of the *navagrahas* in the lower register (Pl. 369). Stylistically, it may be dated to *circa* 9th-10th century C.E.[62]

A very badly mutilated fragment from Jind also shows *padmāsana* Jina seated on a lion throne in a pedimented *rathikā* canopied by five-hooded snake. Another small *padmāsana* Jina figure on its side indicates it to have been a fragment of a larger *chaturviṃśatikā* or a *pañchatīrthikā* of *circa* 10th century C.E. A buff sandstone tympanum, measuring 75 x 45 cm, from Durjanpur in Jind district, also shows five-hooded snake canopying the Jina seated in meditative pose on the lion throne. The coils of the snake have been depicted at the back of the pontiff.

Two very exquisitely carved Pārśvanātha images (Pl. 370) were discovered accidentally sometime back from village Majra near Asthal Bohr. These rectangular friezes are almost identical and the inscription on their pedestals refers to their installation together (*Jina-yugalaṃ*) in (Vikrama) Saṃvat 1016 (= C.E. 959). Pārśvanātha stands in *khaḍgāsana* on a lotus below which is carved the plant from which it rises stylistically. The Digambara nature of the images is evident from their nudity. The seven-hooded serpent Kamaṭha rises forming five coils at the back to canopy the pontiff. Above the snake-hoods is the trefoil umbrella flanked by anointing elephants and perhaps topped by the divine drummer. On the proper right and left of the Jina stand gracefully slightly turned towards the pontiff Padmāvatī and Dharaṇendra, the yaksha and yakshī, also canopied by triple snake-hoods, holding lotus flowers in their hands disposed towards the pontiff and resting the other on the thighs. Above them are carved on the extremities of the back slab leogryphs, *makara-mukhas*, and garland-bearing *vidyādharīs* from bottom upward. At the feet of Dharaṇendra is shown a small kneeling female figure in profile in *añjali-mudrā*, probably the donor of the images. Both the images betray the care provided to even the carving of the subsidiary figures and minutiae. The images have been enshrined in an improvised shrine at the site now.

Long back, we had published the broken head of an image of Pārśvanātha fixed indiscriminately in the wall of Kabir Chaurā temple at Pinjore. Measuring 42 x 44 cm, this unidentified fragment has been dated to *circa* 11th-12th century by Singh and Shukla.[63] The round face with schematic curls and topknot, almost closed contemplative eyes, multifoil umbrella and the canopy of seven hoods over it (Pl. 371) furnish the coveted evidence of its definite identification and the popularity of the worship of Pārśvanātha at Pinjore. There are two diminutive meditating Jina figures on the proper right hand side of the halo indicating that originally it may have been a *chaturviṃśatikā* of Pārśvanātha belonging to *circa* 9th or 10th century C.E.

Rodgers had discovered the lower portion of an image that he thought to be of standing Buddha lying on the bank of the tank of Kurukshetra. It showed three figures on either side of the legs and two central *nāgas* with folded hands clasped in devotion below.[64] The image has not been illustrated but from the description it seems to have been a representation of the Jaina tīrthaṅkara Pārśvanātha, probably of the medieval period. A very badly mutilated dark grey sandstone piece measuring 16 x 14 cm from Ratpur now in HARDAM (Acc. No. 1/93) shows a head under the canopy of seven hoods. It can be identified as the head of Pārśvanātha and may belong to *circa* 10th century C.E.

YAKSHA DHARAṆENDRA

That Badali (28° 36′ N and 76° 45′ E), situated on the Jhajjar-Najafgarh road, about 40 km west of Delhi in district Jhajjar, was an important village with Jaina population is indicated by its references in the *Kharataragachchha-Bṛihadgurvāvali*, which gives an authentic account of the Jaina *āchāryas* of Kharataragachchha from the 11th to the 14th century C.E. It is said that having obtained the permission of *Āchārya* Jinachandra, his disciple Vardhamāna came to Delhi and Badali - *Tato guroḥ sammatyā nirgatya katichinmunisameto. Ḍhillī-Vādalī-prabhṛiti-deśeshu samāyātaḥ Āchārya.*[65] Jinachandra himself also visited this place in VS 1222(= C.E. 1165) to set up golden *kalaśas* in the temple of Pārśvanātha – *Saṃ 1222 Vādalī-nagare Śrī-Pārsvanāthā=pyambikā-śikhara-yogyaṃ sauvarṇa-kalaśaṃ cha pratishṭhāpya, Rudrapallyāṃ vihṛitāḥ.*[66] Reference to the temple of Pārśvanātha shows the popularity of this Tīrthaṅkara at Badali.

Some carved pieces are fixed in the outer wall of Chaudhary Randhir Singh's *havelī* and have thickly been coated with whitewash. They include, among others, an image of Dharaṇendra, the yaksha of the penultimate Jaina tīrthaṅkara.

We have already noted above that Dharaṇa was quite popular in the 9th century as referred to in the *Vipākasūtra* and a shrine dedicated to him existed at Rohtak also. Unfortunately, however, no image of Dharaṇendra from Rohtak or anywhere else even, has been discovered.

The image under reference shows Dharaṇendra as a hybrid figure, half-human, half-snake (Pl. 372). The yaksha sits on a *triratha* pedestal under the canopy of nine-hooded snake with serpentine legs entwined artistically with tapering tails falling outwards. Dharaṇendra, the Lord of the *Nāga-Kumāra* class of semi-divine beings,[67] is appropriately endowed with a cylindrical crown. His right hand, raised to the level of the shoulder, is broken but seems to have been originally disposed in the protection affording pose. The left hand holds a *kalaśa*, water-pot. On his proper right is a diminutive half-human, half-snake female (?) figure in *añjalimudrā* in profile. She may be identified with Padmāvatī, the spouse of the yaksha, as indicated by the snake-hood over her head. On the corresponding left side is another hybrid figure in profile with folded hands. At the level of the chest are two small figures, one on either side, holding some musical instrument in their two hands across the chest. On the top corners of the back-slab are shows *vidyādharas,* holding long garlands and hovering in the sky. The two sides of the back-slab are slightly concaved but the top in convex. Since the image has been whitewashed repeatedly, the whole image bears a thick encrustation concealing the details of the yaksha and other subsidiary figures.

The yaksha is two-handed like the early images known from Osian, Gyaraspur, and the Deccan. The attributes in the two hands are similar to those of Digambara figure from the Māládevī Temple. This image, too, is obviously a Digambara one. It, however, betrays the peculiarity of having a nine-hooded canopy and being hybrid, half-human, half-serpent. Stylistically, it may be dated to *circa* 10th century C.E. The importance of this image of Dharaṇendra, unique in form and the first to be discovered from Haryana, cannot be overstated.

MAHĀVĪRA

A beautiful sandstone image of the early medieval period assignable to the Gurjara-Pratihāra reign representing Mahāvīra seated in the meditative pose in *padmāsana* with the *lāñchchhana* lion carved on the pedestal is placed in a temple of Bheron village which is situated about one and a half km from Kakar Majra, 3 km from Shahzadpur on road to Chandigarh.[68]

A fragmentary sculpture of a very crude workmanship in the Chandigarh Museum representing a male figure in *dhyāna-mudrā* seated in *vajraparyaṅkāsana* in the center, flanked by a male and a female (Museum Register No. 02817/115), has been identified by D.C. Bhattacharyya with the twenty-fourth tīrthaṅkara Mahāvīra with his yaksha Mātaṅga and *śāsanadevī* Siddhāyikā (Pl. 373).[69] Nearly a foot in height and found probably from Pinjore, the head of the main figure is now lost, but that it had a nimbus behind it is evident from the frontal designs partially visible on one side. In the frontal register of the pedestal there is an ornamental design, *nandyāvarta* symbol according to D.C. Bhattacharyya, flanked by two lions and other animal figures.

Since the composition is conventional and stereotyped and the treatment of the central figure is flattened, besides the crude workmanship, the image has been dated to *circa* 13th century C.E.[70] An interesting feature of this image missed by D.C. Bhattacharyya has been highlighted by Nagar that the Jina is adorned with armlets and the necklace and as such he observes that the image "could be presumed to represent the Jīvantasvāmī aspect of the Jina".[71]

We may point out that since *nandyāvarta* is the *lāñchhana* of Śvetāmbara Supārśvanātha or Digambara Aranātha (the eighteenth tīrthaṅkara), the image cannot be identified as that of Mahāvīra. Since five or nine hooded snake does not canopy the Jina, it cannot represent Supārśvanātha either. So the image may represent Aranātha if the *lāñchhana* has rightly been recognized as *nandyāvarta*. Nagar does not mention the *nandyāvarta* symbol on the pedestal. We, too, have not been able to see the said symbol on the actual examination of the image in the Chandigarh Museum. No doubt that the arms seem to have the armlets (the necklace is not clear), yet the figure does not seem to us to be that of Jīvantasvāmī because of the absence of other ornaments including the crown and the posture of sitting which is typical of the Jina figures. Also, our study shows that Pinjore was destroyed in the late 12th century and all art activity stopped there, at least for some time. The image, therefore, cannot be as late as the 13th century C.E., it should be earlier.

A red granite image of Mahāvīra of 18th century with a Devanāgarī inscription on the pedestal and a lion with up curled tail in the center of the pedestal is wrongly dated to 11th-12th century and identified with Ādinātha by Rahar.[72]

UNIDENTIFIED JINAS

We have already noted above the head of Ādinātha fixed indiscriminately on another Jina figure in the wall of the Kabir Chaurā temple at Pinjore (Pl. 347). The fragment studded on the proper left of the Jina seems to belong to the same Ādinātha figure but the rest of the relief showing the pontiff in meditative mood on a lion throne and an acolyte figure on his right represents an unidentified Jina. There is neither the *lāñchana* on the pedestal nor any other clue to help us to identify it definitely. Stylistically, however, it may be dated to the 9th century like other images described above.

Another headless *padmāsana* Jina figure, made of sandstone and measuring 47 x 59 cm, removed from the wall of the *baoli* at Pinjore to the Kurukshetra University, is an exquisitely carved figure (Pl. 374).[73] Not only the upper portion but also the pedestal below the cushion seat is missing. The *tribhaṅga* fanners wearing *ekāvalis*, bracelets, nether garments, and long garlands with one hand placed on the thigh flank the Jina. The heads and the hands of the fanners holding the flywhisks are gone. There is a lozenge shaped *śrīvatsa* on the chest of the pontiff.

A figure of a Jaina tīrthaṅkara in *khaḍgāsana* (Pl. 375), 62 x 34 cm, removed from the wall of the *baoli* at Pinjore to the Kurukshetra University[74] shows the diamond shaped *śrīvatsa* on the chest, round nipples of the chest, deep navel, embroidered *dhotī* going down to the knees and tied gracefully with free ends falling on the thighs and the fold between the legs. The waistband with a floral pattern gives us an idea of the beauty the original image may have possessed. Unfortunately, however, the head, both the arms, and legs below the knees are irretrievably lost.

Two white marble headless images and one pedestal of a Jina image from Pinjore, now housed in the Kurukshetra University, deserve mention. The better preserved figure, 51 x 66 cm, shows the sky-clad tīrthaṅkara in *dhyāna-mudrā* seated in *padmāsana* on an ornamental cushion. *Śrīvatsa* on the chest is clear. The flat space below the cross-legged Jina contains a three-lined Sanskrit inscription in the characters of *circa* 12th century. It refers to Saṃvat 551, probably of Harsha Era (= C.E. 1157), and to one Paṇḍita Sūryakīrti, perhaps the donor of the image[75] or the Jaina teacher who installed it. The second image, 24 x 25 cm, shows the portion below the belly. The meditating Jina on the ornamental cushion contains a short inscription in similar characters referring to Paṇḍita Somakīrti.[76] A marble image of a Jaina tīrthaṅkara from Dadri (23 x 18 cm) and inscribed Jaina–*Pādukā* (Feet), 8.3 cm square (Acc Nos. 1/444-5), are also preserved in HARDAM.

An upper part of a Jina image, a *Parikara*, and a pedestal from Pinjore,[77] and fragments here and there, indicate that Pinjore was an important center of Jainism from the 9th to 12th century C.E.

A buff sandstone head with curled locks and topknot (28 x 17 cm) found from Thanesar (Pl. 376)[78] betrays that during the 10th-11th century C.E., Thanesar-Kurukshetra region was not only a prominent Hindu pilgrimage but had a substantial Jaina population also. Though the Chinese pilgrim Yuan Chwang who visited Thanesar does not refer to anything related to Jainism (which actually may not have been there at that time), this Jina head indicates the existence of a temple at the site. A 10th century fragmentary sandstone head from Surehli in district Rewari may also have been that of some tīrthaṅkara.[79]

CHAKREŚVARĪ

An almost complete image of light brown sandstone was accidentally recovered by a villager at Ranila village near Charkhi Dadri in October 1991. Almost a foot in height, it shows the yakshī of the first tīrthaṅkara seated in *lalitāsana* (Fig. 18). Her folded left leg is supported by anthropomorphic Garuḍa. Her splayed right foot touches the *triratha* pedestal by the forepart and the heel is raised slantingly. The twelve-armed yakshī bears a high bun on the head adorned in the center with a discus-like motif. She wears an *ekāvali*, armlets, wristlets, undergarment secured by an elaborate waistband, etc. She supports *chakras* on the pointing fingers of the uppermost pair of hands in a horizontal fashion while the additional left hands hold the *chakras* almost en face except in the lowermost left hand which carries a citrus. One of the backhand on either side

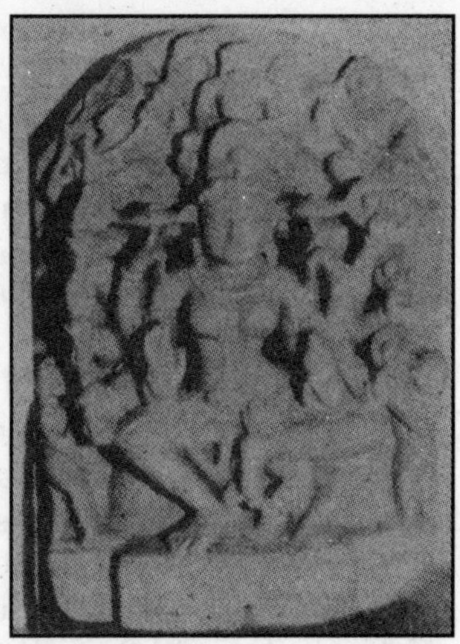

Fig. 18. Chakreśvarī, Ranila.

probably carried thunderbolt as per the Digambara Jaina tradition. The normal right hand is held in *abhaya* and the next additional is disposed in *varada-mudrā*. One hand carries the thunderbolt as pointed out above and other additional right hands seem to support the wheels. Just above her head is depicted a miniature Jina figure in meditation. Garland-bearing *vidyādharas* are hovering on either side of her head and two small figures are shown in *añjali-mudrā* standing in profile on the receding recesses of the pedestal. This beautiful 9th-century image is the only example of Chakreśvarī found so far from Haryana. Ranila seems to have been an important Digambara center during the Pratihāra period.

AMBIKĀ

We have already referred to two inscribed images of Pārśvanātha found from Majra near Asthal Bohr (Rohtak). A very badly damaged brownish banded sandstone image of a female deity seated in *lalitāsana* on a lion holding a child on her folded left leg (Pl. 377) was also obtained along with the above-mentioned and some other sculptures by the villagers while excavating the old mound for ballast and bricks. The head of the female as well as the child are lost. The right arm and leg have also suffered mutilation. The female deity is shown as wearing necklaces. One of these curves from over the breasts and the pendent of the other falls from between the breasts. The hand supporting the child wears a bracelet. The child is shown with his right arm going around the neck of the goddess while the other hand and legs are broken. On the proper left hand top corner may be seen the legs of a *vidyādhara* indicating the divinity of the female. The female seated on a lion and supporting a child in her left lap may be identified with the Jaina yakshī Ambikā. The type of the necklaces worn by her indicate a 10th century date which goes very well with the Pārśvanātha images referred to above. It may be stated here that this is the only image of Ambikā in stone from Haryana known as yet.

MISCELLANEOUS REMAINS

Of unusual interest, however, is a *takhtī* (wring board) shaped 50 x 33.5 cm buff sandstone relief from Go(va)rdhana Nāthajī kā Ḍerā at village Bhatla near Hansi (Pl. 378) showing the main figure of a meditating Jina in a pedimented niche in the center borne by a four-armed semi-celestial (*bhāraputra*?) with his upper pair of hands. Two *padmāsana* Jina figures flank this semi-celestial in the lower panel, two similar figures are shown on either side of the central Jina figure, and two such diminutive images exist in the top corners, making the total number of Jinas seven. This, thus, appears to be a *sapta-tīrthikā*, something rare in Jaina art. Stylistically, it may be dated to *circa* 9th century C.E.

A small relief, 28 cm in height, now in the Chandigarh Museum and Art Gallery (Muṣeum Register No. 62), has been identified as 'Jaina tutelary couple' (Pl. 335).[80] Its probable source has been mentioned as Murti (now in Pakistan) but Suwarcha Paul and Poonam Khanna (the former and present Curator of the Museum) have described it as coming from Rohtak,[81] which seem to be more probable. The relief shows a nimbate couple standing on a common platform. The right hand of the male figure is disposed in *abhaya-mudrā* and the left holds a water vessel. He wears an *ekāvali*, a beaded bracelet, and *dhotī* with central fold depicted prominently. D.C. Bhattacharyya has mistaken this fold with a sword. Never in Indian sculpture has a sword been depicted in this fashion anywhere. The wig-like hair reminds us of the Gupta art tradition. The female figure with a child in her left lap stands to his left, holding probably a lotus in her right hand. Since D.C. Bhattacharyya regards the image to have come from

Murti, which is well known for its Jaina temple remains, he identifies it with the depiction of a Jaina tutelary couple, though he discusses some other possibilities also. We have noted above that the likely provenance of this image is Rohtak, which was a well-known center of Jainism during the early medieval period. So the possibility of this image, dated to *circa* 8th century C.E. by D.C. Bhattacharyya (which is too late for Murti Jaina images), being the Jaina tutelary couple, cannot be ruled out though one would have expected the figure of a miniature Jina somewhere in the relief.

A lintel in the Gurukula Museum at Jhajjar, obtained from Rohtak (where still exists a fragmentary lintel with similar decorative pattern) shows a *khaḍgāsana* Jina in a full-blown lotus, flanked by female fly whiskers, and meditating Jina figures in half lotuses on the lintel-ends, assignable to *circa* 10th century C.E. (Pl. 379), indicating the existence of a 10th century Jaina temple at the site.

Bari Kohori, about 6 km northwest of Naraingarh in district Ambala, has yielded a *nāgara-kūṭa* with a small meditating Jina in it which is now preserved in an improvised small shrine in Shri Ravi Dass Mandira on the top of the huge old mound at the site. A small 9th century buff sandstone head of a tīrthaṅkara with curled locks from Sikanderpur near Sirsa;[82] a sandstone architectural piece of 10th-11th century (15 x 9 cm) with a meditating Jina, a white marble miniature Jina figure in a pedimented niche; etc. from Sirsa indicate that Sirsa too had a considerable Jaina population during the tenth-eleventh centuries.[83] Six buff sandstone sculptures were stolen from village Kira on the southern border of Haryana with Rajasthan in tehsil Nuh, district Gurgaon (now Faridabad). We examined these sculptures in the Police Malkhana (Sadar Police Station), Gurgaon on 8. 5. 1990 with Shri (now late Dr.) Mohinder Singh of Kurukshetra University. One of these pieces showed a Jaina tīrthaṅkara in *kāyotsarga-mudrā* with vertical panels of *padmāsana* Jinas on the sides. This seemed to be an architectural pillar belonging to some Jaina temple at Kira datable to *circa* 10th century C.E. A Jaina *parikara* of sandstone measuring 34 x 15 cm is preserved in the Śiva Mandira (Kumhari Kuan inside Jundla Gate) at Karnal. At the same place lies a Jaina tīrthaṅkara in *padmāsana* in a pedimented niche at the apex and another figure (perhaps a Yakshī) in *lalitāsana* on the right datable to *circa* 10th-11th century C.E. A small sandstone figure of a Jina in a pedimented *rathikā* obtained from Kanwari and assignable to *circa* 11th century C.E. is now preserved in HARDAM (Acc, No. 1/503). Fragments of Jaina images or architectural fragments have been obtained from Ahrwan, Narhet, Nagram, Somerwala (all in Hisar district) as well as from Agroha, Gharoda, Jadthal, etc., all belonging to the medieval period (*circa* 9th-10th century) betraying the popularity of Jainism in Haryana. Like Hinduism, Jainism too seems to have suffered at the hands of the Muslim invaders in the eleventh and following centuries, but images were worshipped here and there, particularly from 16th century onwards as evidenced by the marble, schist and octo-alloy images in the Jaina temple at Ambala (Pl. 380). It may also be mentioned here that four octo-alloy images were stolen from village Bichhor near Jhajjar in 1979 and many others were stolen from the Digambar Jaina Temple at Banchari in August 1983 and an FIR was lodged at Hodal, but no recovery was made.[84]

The foregoing account makes it amply clear that Pinjore, Jind, Hansi, Narnaul, Badali, and Rohtak were important centers of Jainism in the medieval period. The images described above reveal that Supārśva was popularly worshipped in the *kāyotsarga mudrā, Ś*āntinātha in *padmāsana* and Pārśva in both. Iconographically important is the fact that even Pārśvanātha was depicted under the canopy of five-hooded snake. Also Sarvānubhūti and Ambikā were the yaksha and yakshī carved on all the images at Rohtak up to the 10th century C.E. The cognizance was not generally carved on the pedestals.

We find that the faces, noses in particular, and arms of most of these figures, some of which otherwise seem to be quite fresh, have been mutilated. They may have suffered this damage during the attacks of the Muslim invaders during the eleventh and the following centuries and a revival of image worship took place during the reign of Akbar in the 16th century C.E.

Notes and References

1. Some scholars prefer 467 B.C.E. as the date of Mahāvīra's *nirvāṇa*.
2. A. Ghosh (ed.), *Jaina Art and Architecture* (*JAA*), Vol. I, New Delhi, 1974, p. 51.
3. It is described as 'the standing posture with feet at a distance of about two inches from each other, the hands resting naturally by the sides, but not so as to touch the body' (B.C. Bhattacharya, *Jaina Iconography*, 2nd revised edition, Delhi-Varanasi-Patna, 1974, pp. 139-40). It is enjoined that Ajitanātha, Sambhavanātha, and Abhinandana should be especially sculptured in this posture.
4. It has been prescribed for Mahāvīra, Ṛishabha, and Neminātha:
   Vīraḥ Ṛishabhaḥ Nemiḥ eteshāṃ Jinānāṃ paryaṅkāsanam /
   Śesha Jinānāmutsargāsanam //
5. *Sarvatobhadra* (four-fold) tīrthaṅkara images were also carved from the late Kushāṇa period.
6. *JAA*, I, PP. 114-16.
7. *Bṛihatsaṃhitā* LVII.45:
   Ājānulambabāhuḥ śrīvatsāṅkaḥ praśāntamūrtiścha/
   Digvāsastaruṇo rūpavāṃścha kāryyo'rhataṃ devaḥ//
8. *Aśokavṛikshaḥsurapushpavṛishṭirdivyadhvaniśchāmaramāsanañcha/*
   Bhāmaṇḍalaṃdundubhirātapatraṃshaṭ pratihāryāni Jineśvarānām//
   As quoted by D.R. Bhandarkar, "Jaina Iconography," *Indian Antiquary*, 1911. Cf. *Jaina Iconograpgy*, p. 20, fn. 1 :
   Divyatarusurapushpavṛishṭidundubhirāsanayojanaghoshau/
   Ātapavāraṇachāmarayugame yasya vibhāti chāmaṇḍalatejaḥ//
   See also *Rūpa-Maṇḍana* VI.33-34.
9. *JAA*, I, p. 51.
10. Punia, *op. cit.*, pp. 157 ff.
11. A systematic survey of southern Haryana is a great desideratum to ascertain its connection with Mathurā.
12. Jyoti Prasad Jain, *The Jaina Sources Of The History of Ancient India*, Delhi, 1964, p. 106.
13. *Therīgāthā*, which forms part of the *Khuddaka-nikāya*, contains stanzas of Nanduttarā and Mittakālī (five each), of Kururaṭṭha. The traditional mention of the names with the lives of the Bhikshuṇīs 'nuns' is preserved in the commentary of Dhammapāla known as the *Paramatthadīpanī*, ascribable to the 5th century C.E. Both the *therīs* 'female recluses' belonged to the Kammāsadamma *nigama* 'corporation' in the Kuru country. Kammāsadamma is identified with village Kamaspur in Haryana by Bharadwaj (*op. cit.*, pp. 157-58). Nanduttarā had earlier been initiated to Jainism – *Imasmiṃ buddhuppāde Kururaṭṭhe Kammāsadamma-nigame brāhmaṇa-kule nibbattitvā ekachchānaṃ vijjāṭṭhānāni sippāyatanāni cha ugga-hetvā nigaṇṭhapabbajjaṃ upagaṃtvā vādasutā jambusākhaṃ gahetvā bhaddā.*(*Therīgāthā*, ed. N.K. Bhagwat, Bombay, 1956, p. 63).
14. Aurel Stein and Fred H. Andrews discovered Murti in 1889. Stein and Fabri revisited it in 1931. Yuan Chwang had also seen a Jaina temple there (Thomas Watters, *On Yuan Chwang's Travels in India*, Delhi, 1961, 1st Indian ed., pp. 250 ff). The remains of this and other fanes recovered by Stein were removed to the Central Museum, Lahore. For details see *Punjab District Gazetteer: Jhelum District*, Lahore, 1907, p. 45; M.A. Stein, *Archaeological Reconnaissances in North-Western India and South-Eastern Iran*, London, 1937, pp. 52-57, pls. 20-21; Charles Fabri, 'Archaeology in the Punjab,' *Marg*, X (2), March 1957, p. 13; etc.
15. Watters, *op. cit.*, pp. 250 ff.

16. Devendra Handa, *Jaina Bronzes From Hansi*, Shimla - New Delhi, 2002.
17. We are thankful to the Director, Government Museum, Lahore for the photograph published here.
18. It is regretted that in spite of repeated requests I was not allowed to study these images nor were the photographs supplied to me.
19. The figure has been named as Mahāvīra and dated to 11th-12th century C.E. on a picture-postcard published by HARDAM, like the preceding figure of Pārśvanātha.
20. Jagannath Agrawal, *Inscriptions of Haryana, Himachal Pradesh, Punjab, Kashmir & Adjoining Hilly Tracts*, New Delhi, 2001, p. 94.
21. Amar Singh, *Archaeology of Karnal and Jind Districts [Haryana]*, Unpublished Ph. D. Thesis, Kurukshetra University, Kurukshetra, 1981, p. 212, pl. XXXII.B.
22. Rahar, *op. cit.*, pp. 200-201, pl. XXIV B.
23. *Pinjore Sculptures*, Kurukshetra, 1977 (*PS*), p. 35, pl. XV.B.
24. Shukla (1983), *op. cit.*, p. 19, pl. XII.2.
25. *PS*, p. 34; Shukla (1983), *op. cit.*, p. 18, pl. XI.2.
26. *PS*, p. 34; Shukla (1983), *op. cit.*, p. 19, no. 28.
27. Devendra, Handa, "Some Unpublished Sculptures from Pinjaur," *VIJ*, XIV (i), 1976, pp. 118-19, pl. XI.
28. *PS*, p. 34, pl. XV.A; Shukla (1983), *op. cit.*, p. 18, pl. XI.1.
29. *PS*, P. 36, pl. XVIII.B; Shukla (1983), *op. cit.*, p. 19, pl. XII.1.
30. Punia (*op. cit.*, pp. 207-08, pl. XXIX) has wrongly described this image and dates it to 10th-11th century.
31. Rahar (*op. cit.*, p. 202, pl. XXVI A) wrongly identifies the parents as additional yaksha and yakshi and wrongly dates this 10th century image to 13th-14th century.
32. *Indian Express*, Wednesday December 11, 1991.
33. Devendra Handa, "Some Sculptures from Panjab and Haryana," *PURBA*, Vol. VII, no. 1 (April 1976), pp. 95-96, fig. 7.
34. Rahar (*op. cit.*, pp. 202-03, pl. XXVI B) dates the image to *circa* 10th-11th century and identifies the Jina as Ajitanātha.
35. We are thankful to the Director, Lahore Museum, for information and photograph of this image.
36. *PS*, p. 35, pl. XVI.A; Shukla (1983), *op. cit.*, p. 20, pl. XII.3 date it to *circa* 11th century C.E.
37. Shukla (1983), *op. cit.*, p. 55, pl. L.1. Rahar (*op. cit.*, p. 203, pl. XXVII A) has wrongly dated a black stone 19th century image under worship in the Jaina temple at Narnaul as belonging to *circa* 12th century C.E.
38. *Imperial Gazetteer of India*, London, 1908, Vol. XXI, pp. 310-22; *Gazetteer Rohtak District, 1883-84*, p. 16; Rodgers, *op. cit.*, pp. 74-76; *Annual Progress Report, Northern Circle, 1918-19* (published 1920), p. 13; J. Przyluski, *Ancient Peoples of the Panjab* (translated into English by Chitrabhanu en), Calcutta, 1960, pp. 2ff; Birbal Sahni, *The Technique of Casting Coins in Ancient India*, Bombay, 1945, pp. 4ff; Devendra Handa, "Some Important Towns of Haryana: a Study of their Ancient Past", *Journal of Haryana Studies*, Kurukshetra, Vol. 11(1970), pp. 6 ff; O.P. Bharadwaj, "The Romance of Ancient Rohtak", *VIJ*, Vol. XIII, Nos. I-II (1975), pp. 17-28.
39. B.C. Bhattacharya, *The Jaina Iconography*, Lahore, 1939, pl. VI.
40. *Indian Archaeology, 1959-60: A Review*, p. 74, pls. LX.D. & LXI.
41. Umakant P. Shah, *Studies in Jaina Art*, Banaras, 1955, p. 17; *Jaina Rūpa-Maṇḍana*, Vol. I, New Delhi, 1987, p. 180; M.A. Dhaky, "Some Early Jaina Temples in Western India", *Mahavira Jaina Vidyalaya Golden Jubilee Volume*, Bombay, 1968, p. 293; M.N.P. Tiwari, *Jaina Pratimāvijñāna*, Varanasi, 1981, pp. 52 and 126.
42. *Summaries of Papers of the All India Seminar on Jaina Canonical Literature*, Ahmedabad, 1986, p. 14.
43. Rasesh Jamindar, "Political Conditions as Narrated in the *Vipakasutra*", in Devendra Handa (ed.), *Ajaya-Śrī: Recent Studies in Indology (Prof. Ajay Mitra Shastri Felicitation Volume)*, Vol. I, Delhi, 1989, p. 102.
44. Shah (1987), *op. cit.*, p. 209. 9.
45. Acharya Jina Vijaya Muni, *Kharatara-Gachchha-Bṛihad-Gurvāvali*, Bombay, 1956, pp. 66 and 68 (text): *Rohada-Śrī-Yoginīpura-Dhamaina-Yamunāpāra-nānā-sthāna-vāstavya-prabhūta-susrāvaka-*

mahāmelāpakena prārambhite Śrī-Hastināgapure-Śrī-Mathurā-mahātīrtha-yātrotsave.. and *Tato mārge Dhamaina-Rohada-pramukha-nānā-sthāna-suśrāvaka-lokān vandāpayantaḥ Śrī-Kanyānayane Śrī-Mahāvīraṃ devaṃ namaśchakruḥ.*

46. *Bṛihatsaṃhitā* 58, 45 (supra fn 7).
47. Shah (1987, *op. cit.*, p. 180) has referred to a lotus and a sword in the hands of these two female figures respectively and has left them unidentified.
48. The depiction of the *vidyādevīs* with *Pārśvanātha* may be seen in an image from Pindwada also. See Umakant P. Shah, *Akota Bronzes*, Bombay, 1959, fig. 49.
49. Shah (1955), *op. cit.*, pp. 16-17.
50. Tiwari, *op. cit.*, p. 52.
51. Shah (1987), *op. cit.*, p. 180.
52. *JAA*, III, pl. 336 B.
53. *Ibid.*, vol. II, pl. 152.
54. B.C. Bhattacharya, *op. cit.*, p. 83.
55. *JAA*, II, p. 253.
56. Shah (1987), *op. cit.*, p. 139.
57. B.C. Bhattacharya, *op. cit.*, p. 60.
58. Umakant P. Shah, "Some Interesting Images of Pārśvanātha," *Indologica Taurinensia*, Vol. XXI-XXII (1995-96), pp. 285-89, figs. 8, 10-16.
59. *Ibid.*, p. 140.
60. Shah (1995-96), *op. cit.*, p. 289.
61. Shah (1987), *op. cit.*, p. 180.
62. Rahar (*op. cit.*, pp. 203-04, pl. XXVIII A) describes the *khaḍgāsana* Jinas as attendants and *padmāsana* diminutive figures as yogis and dates the relief to *circa* 12th-13th century.
63. *PS*, p. 36, pl. XVIII.A; Shukla (1983), *op. cit.*, p. 21, pl. XV.1.
64. Rodgers, *op. cit.*, p. 9.
65. *Kharataragachchha-Bṛihadgurvāvali*, p. 1.
66. *Ibid.*, p. 20.
67. Umakant P. Shah, *Jaina-Rūpa-Maṇḍana*, Vol. I, New Delhi, 1987, p. 3.
68. Yogeshwar Kumar, *Archaeology of Naraingarh and its Neighbourhood (Distt. Ambala)*, M. Phil. Dissertation (Unpublished), Kurukshetra University, 1987, p. 61.
69. D.C. Bhattacharyya, *op. cit.*, p. 95. Suwarcha Paul and Poonam Khanna ("Some Brahmanical Sculptures of Chandigarh Museum – A Reappraisal," *PURBA*, Vol. XXI, no. 1, April 1990, pp. 186-87, fig. 15), however, state that this image belongs to Kangra.
70. *Ibid.*
71. Shanti Lal Nagar, *Jaina Sculptures in Indian and world Museums*, New Delhi, 2000, p. 75, pl. 42.
72. Rahar, *op. cit.*, p. 201, pl. XXV A.
73. *PS*, p. 35, pl. XVI.B; Shukla (1983), *op. cit.*, p. 20, pl. XIII.1. See also Shanti Lal Nagar, *loc. cit.*, pl. 43.
74. *PS*, pp. 33-34, pl. XIV; Shukla (1983), *op. cit.*, p. 18, pl. X.
75. *PS*, p. 36, pl. XVII.B; Shukla (1983), *op. cit.*, p. 21, pl. XIV.1.
76. *PS*, p. 37; Shukla (1983), *op. cit.*, p. 21, pl. XIV.2.
77. *PS*, pp. 36-38, pl. XVII.A, XIX; Shukla (1983), *op. cit.*, pp. 20-22, pl. XIII.2, XVI and XV.3 respectively.
78. Shukla (1983), *op. cit.*, p. 46, pl. XLII.2.
79. Rahar, *op. cit.*, p. 204, pl. XXVIII B]
80. D.C. Bhattacharyya, *op. cit.*, pp. 96-98, fig. 48.
81. Suwarcha Pal and Poonam Khanna, *op. cit.*, p. 182, fig. 4. They have, however, referred to it as Kubera and Hārītī.
82. Shukla (1983), *op. cit.*, p. 53, pl. XLVII.3.
83. *Ibid.*, pp. 54-55, pls. XLIX.1 & 3.
84. *Navabhārata Times*, August 8, 1983.

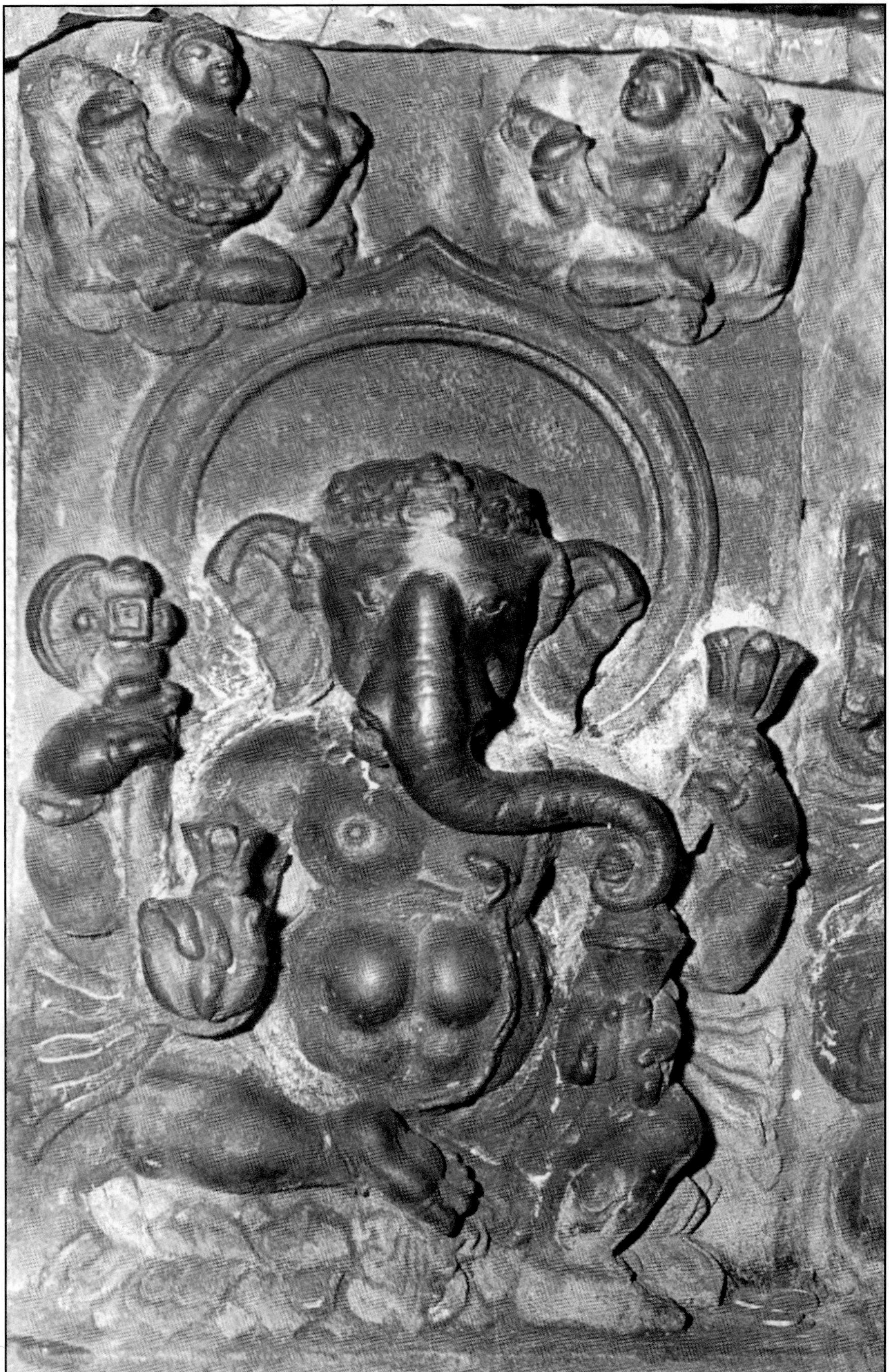

Pl. 1. Four-handed Gaṇeśa, Kalayat.

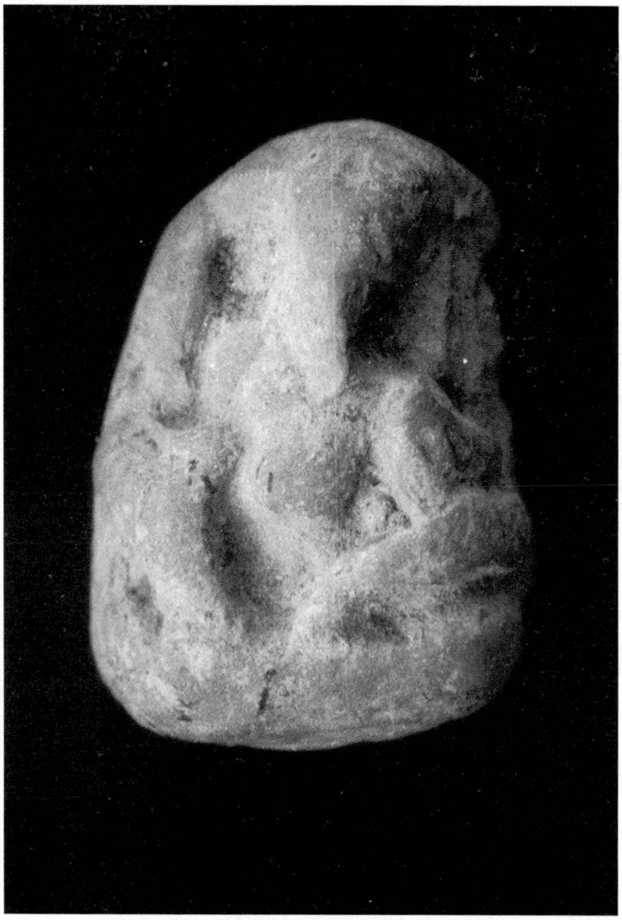

Pl. 2. Gaṇeśa, terracotta, Thanesar.

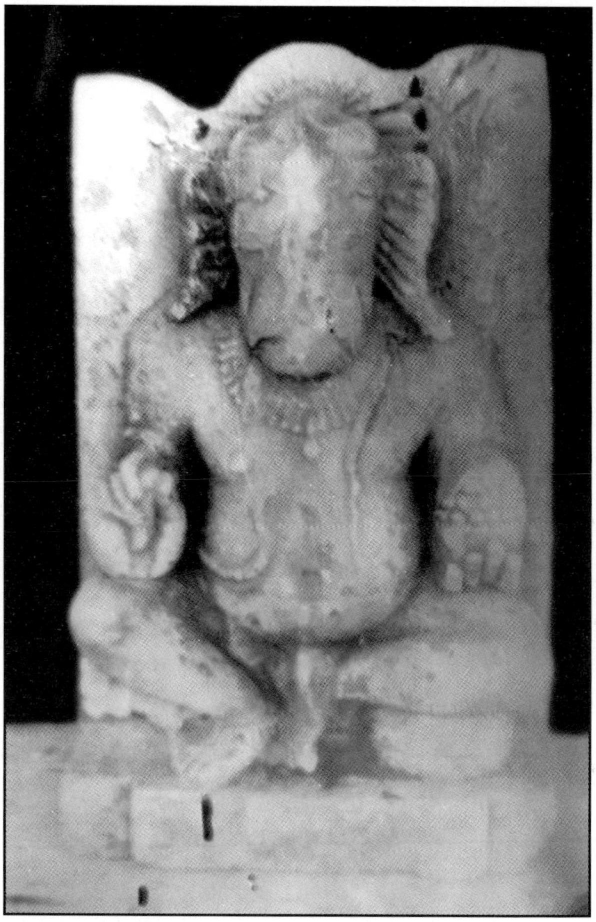

Pl. 3. Two-handed Gaṇeśa, Sirsa.

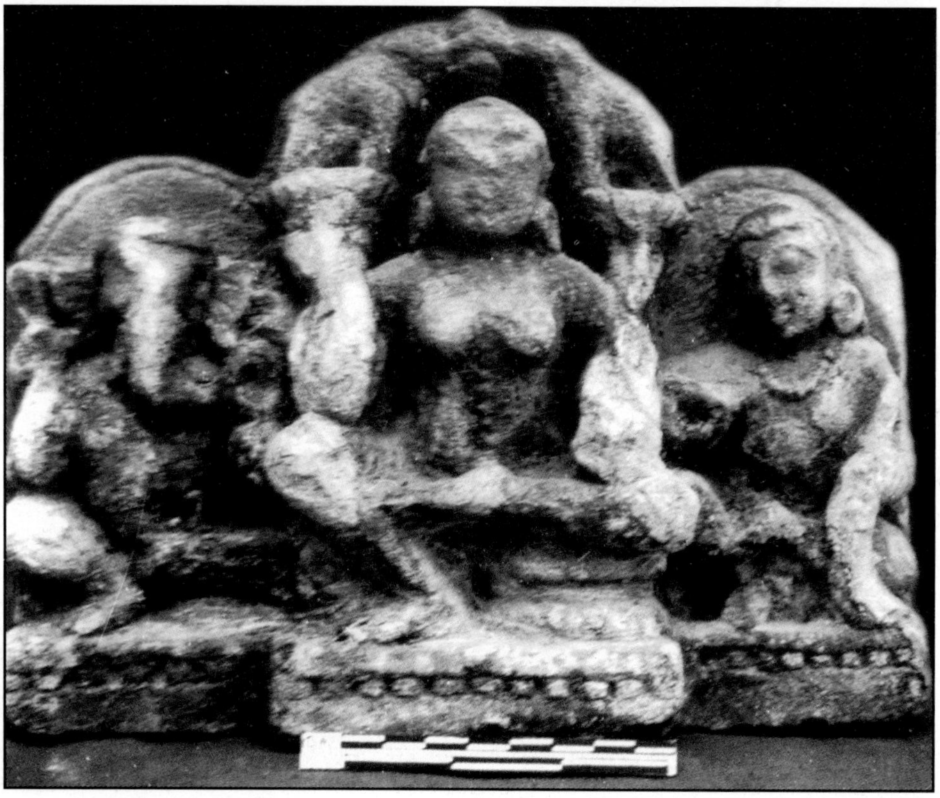

Pl. 4. Gaṇeśa in the auspicious triad, Khokhrakot, Rohtak.

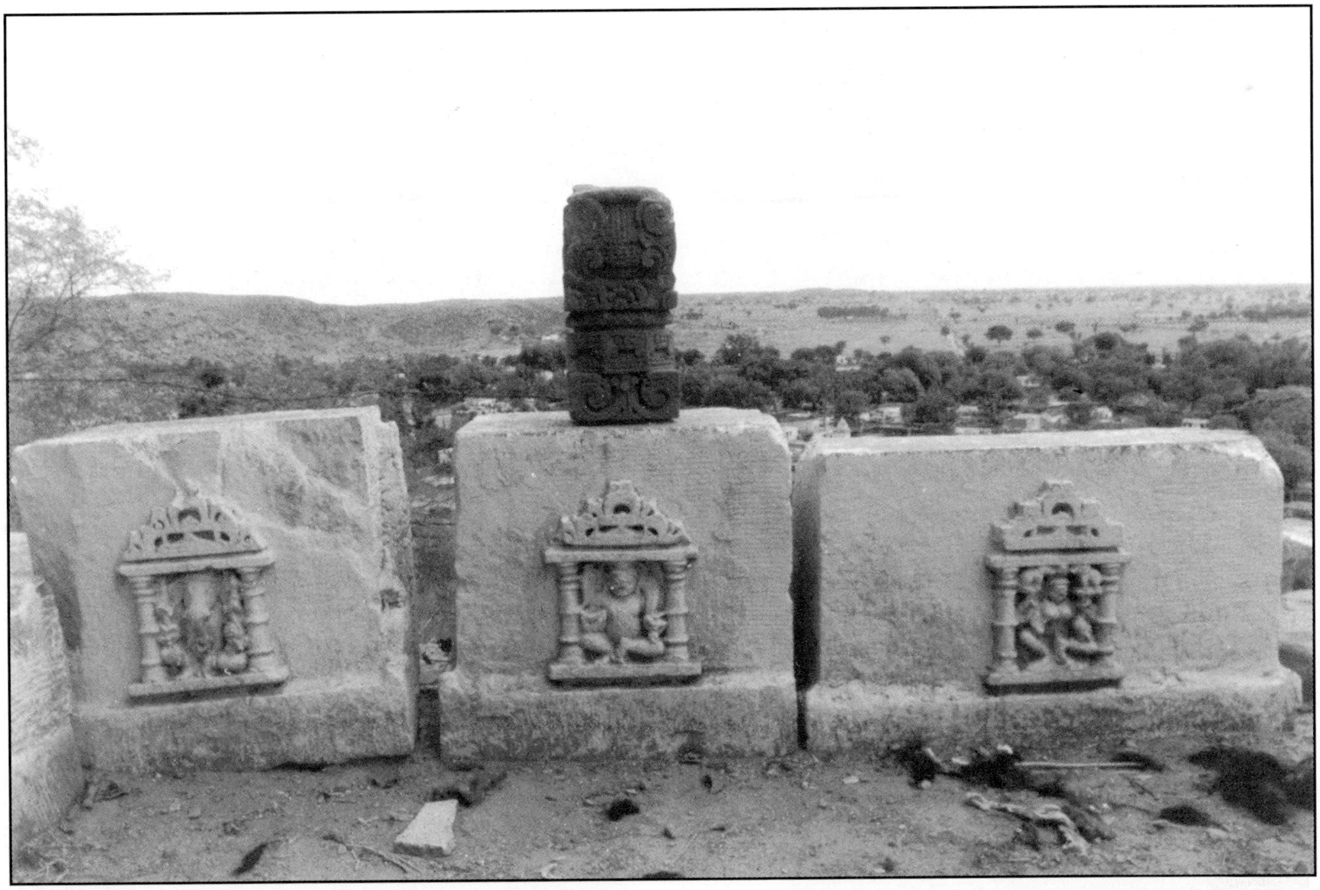

Pl. 5. Gaṇeśa in the auspicious triad, Kasan.

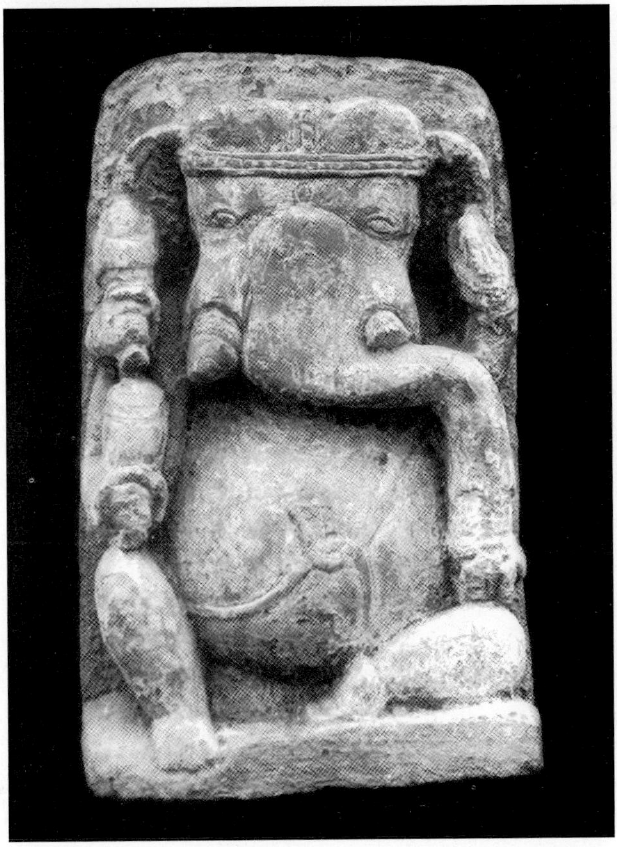

Pl. 6. Gaṇeśa, Jadthal.

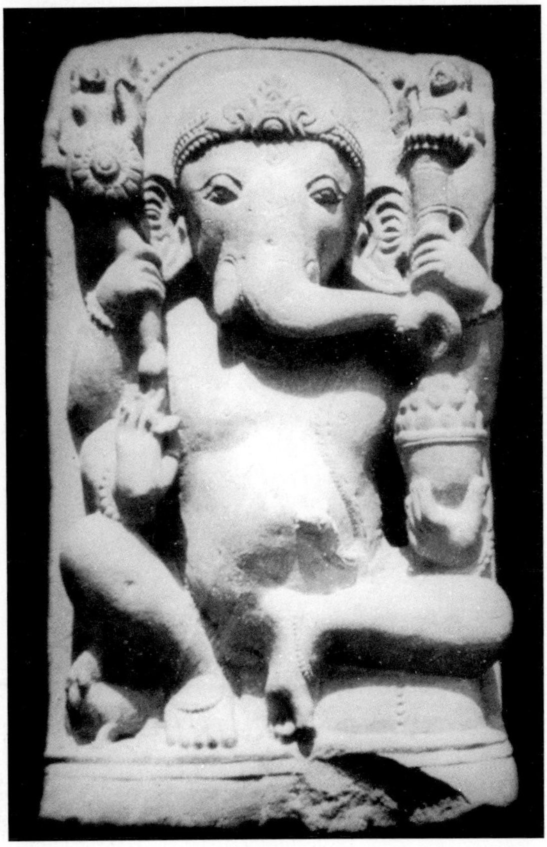

Pl. 7. Gaṇeśa, Pehowa.

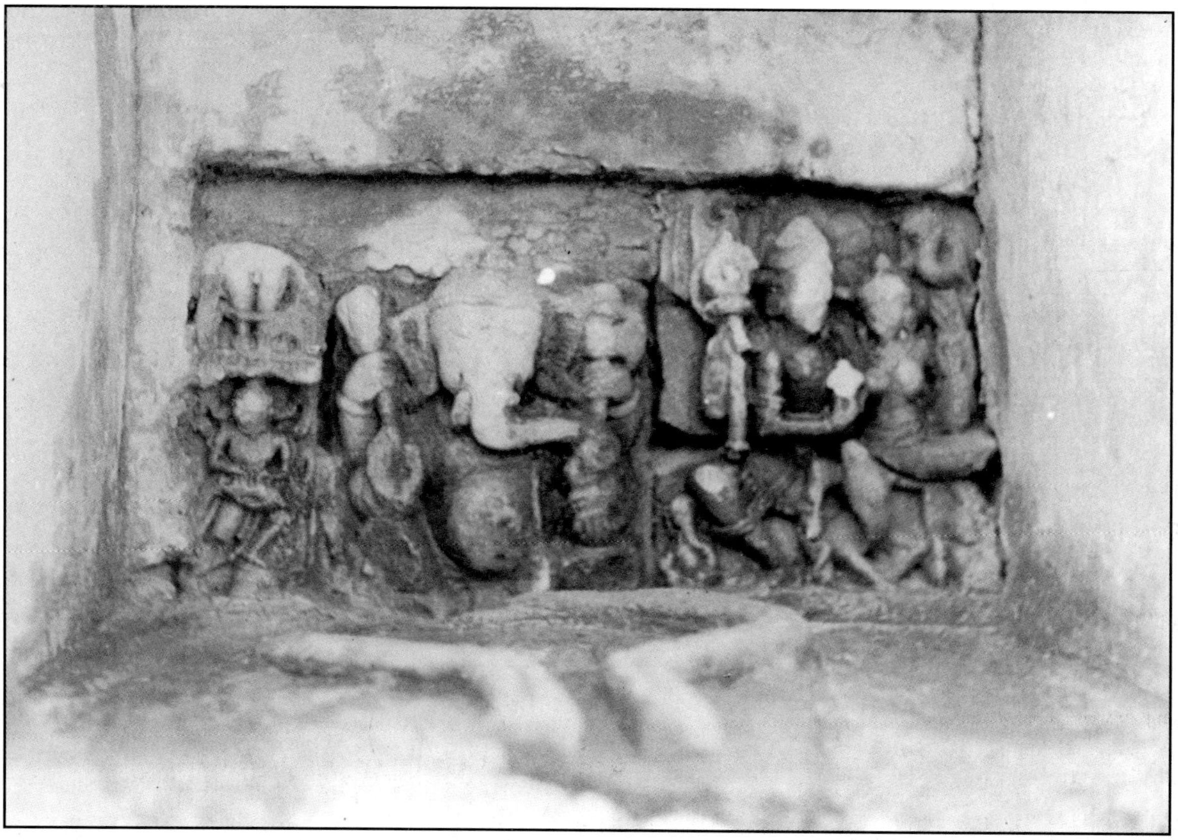

Pl. 8. Gaṇeśa, Kurukshetra.

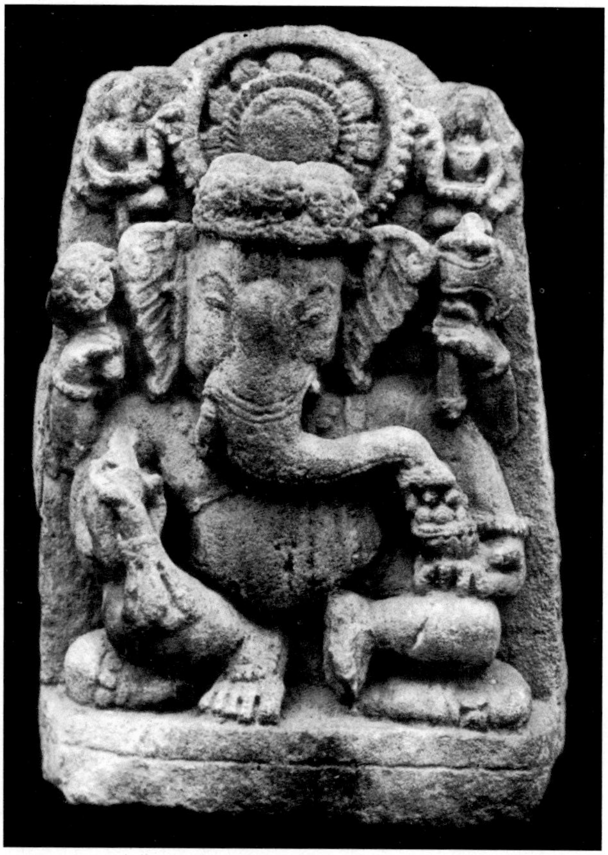

Pl. 9. Gaṇeśa, Kohand.

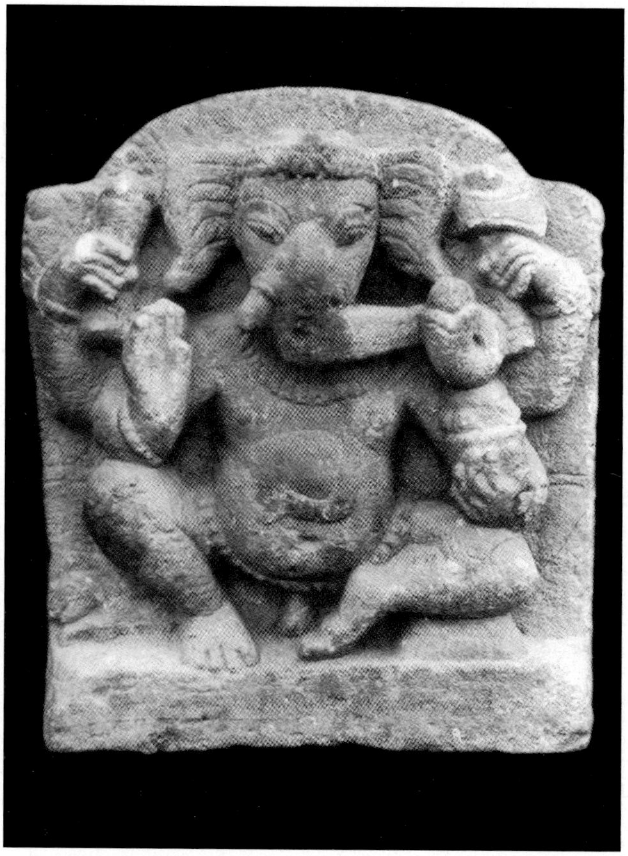

Pl. 10. Gaṇeśa, Allawala.

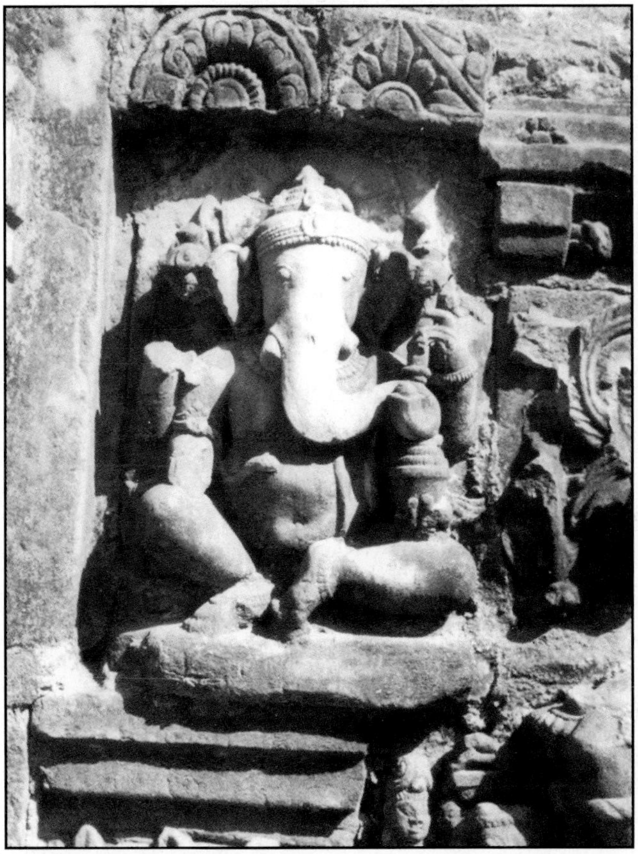

Pl. 11. Gaṇeśa, Pinjore.

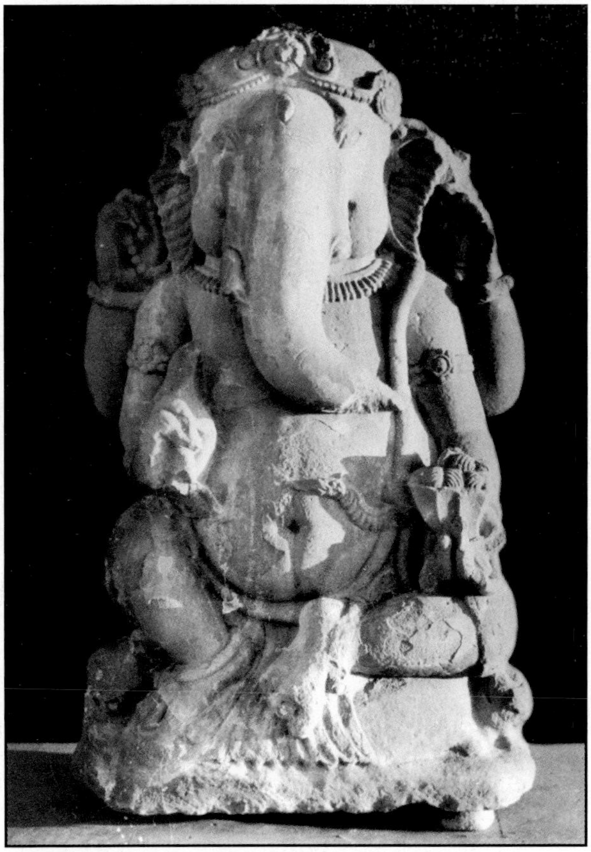

Pl. 12. Gaṇeśa, Pinjore.

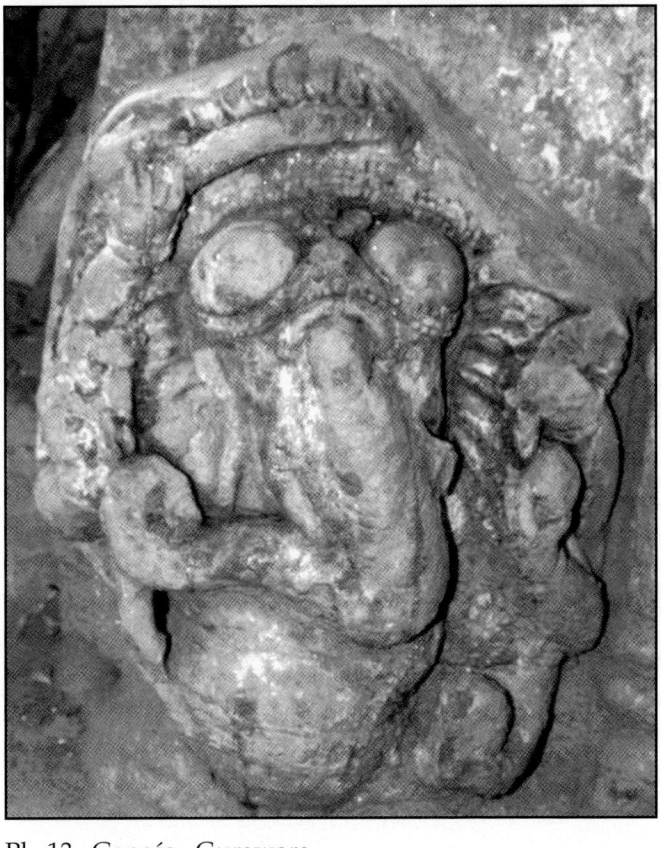

Pl. 13. Gaṇeśa, Gurawara.

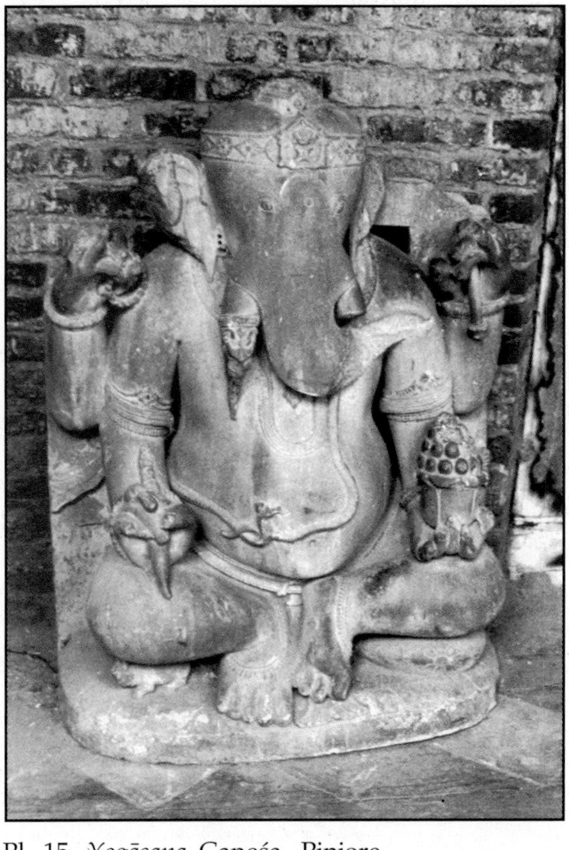

Pl. 15. *Yogāsana* Gaṇeśa, Pinjore.

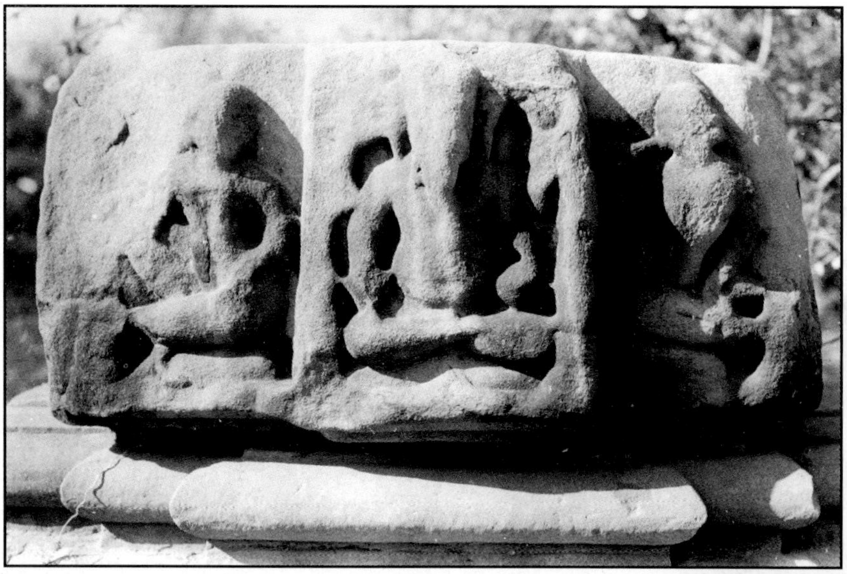

Pl. 14. Gaṇeśa, Asthal Bohr, Rohtak.

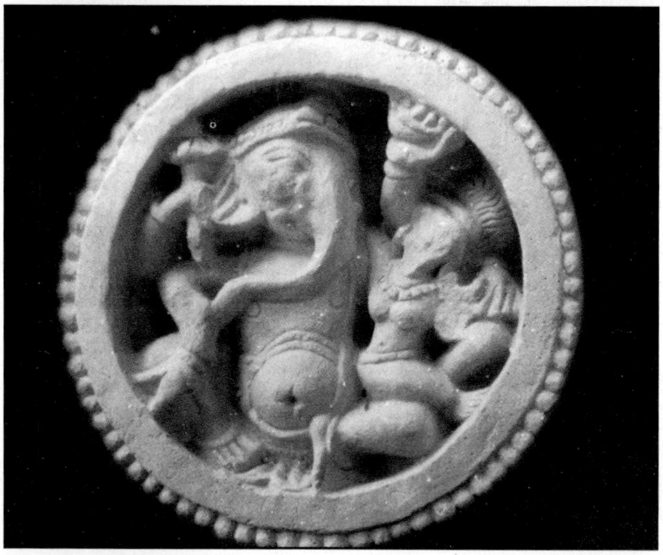

Pl. 16. Gaṇeśa and Gaṇeśānī, Sirsa.

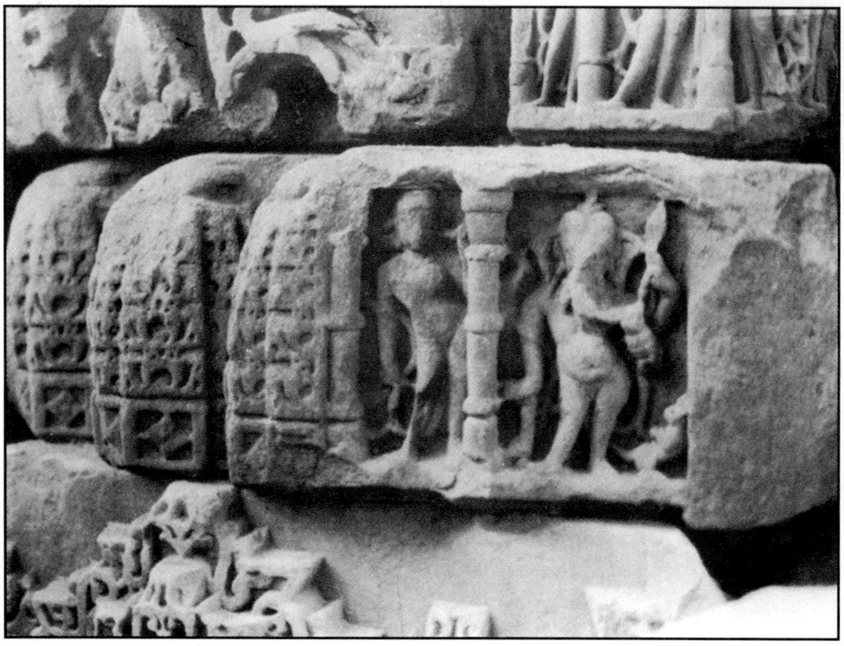

Pl. 17. Standing Gaṇeśa, Pinjore.

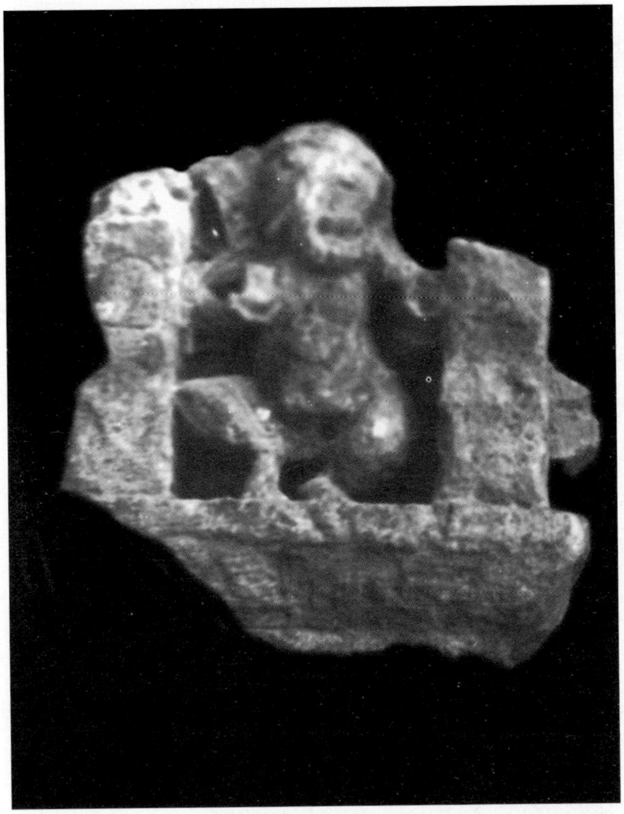

Pl. 18. Dancing Gaṇeśa, Pinjore.

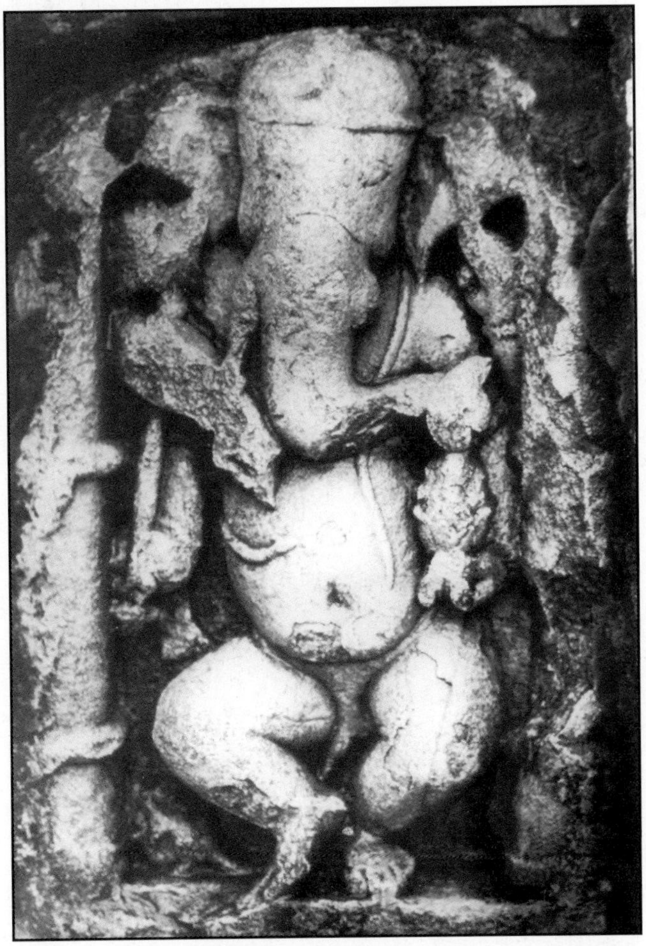

Pl. 19. Dancing Gaṇeśa, Pinjore.

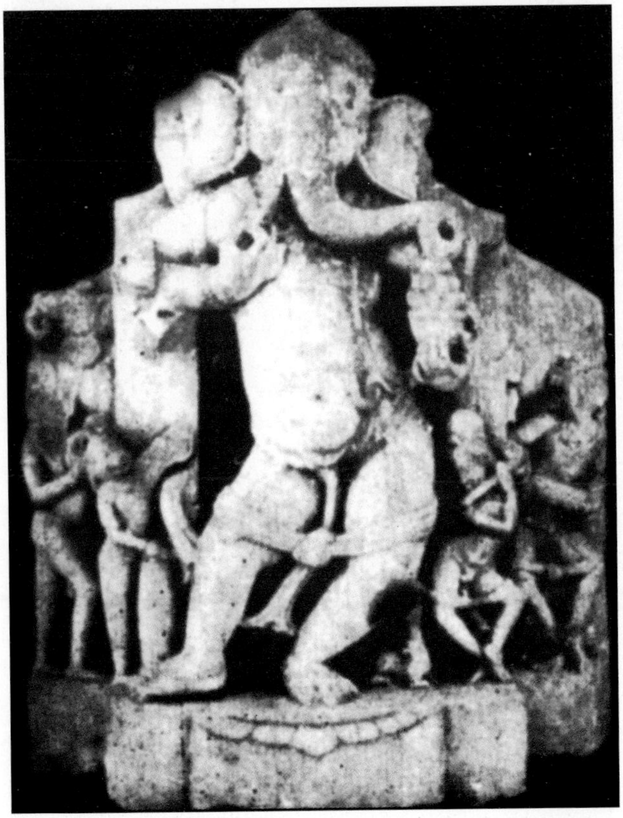

Pl. 20. Dancing Gaṇeśa, Badali.

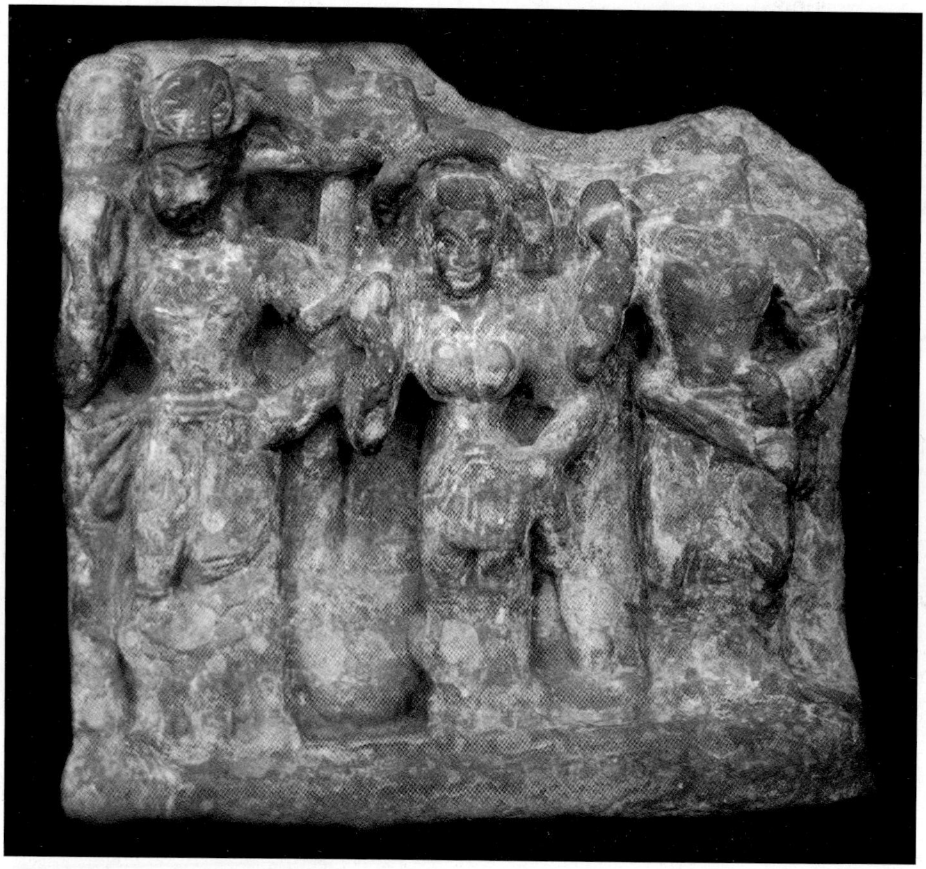

Pl. 21. Ekānaṃśā, Sanghel.

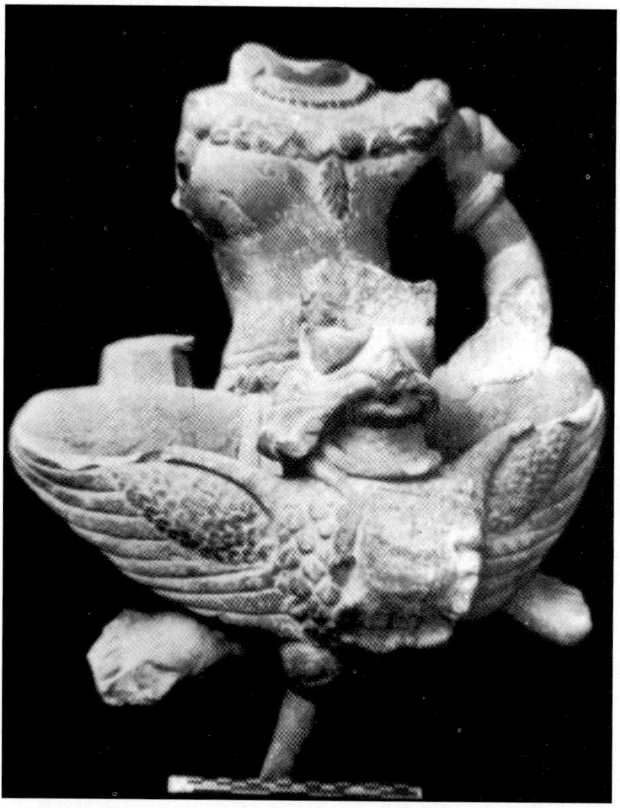

Pl. 22. *Garuḍavāhī* Vishṇu, Rohtak.

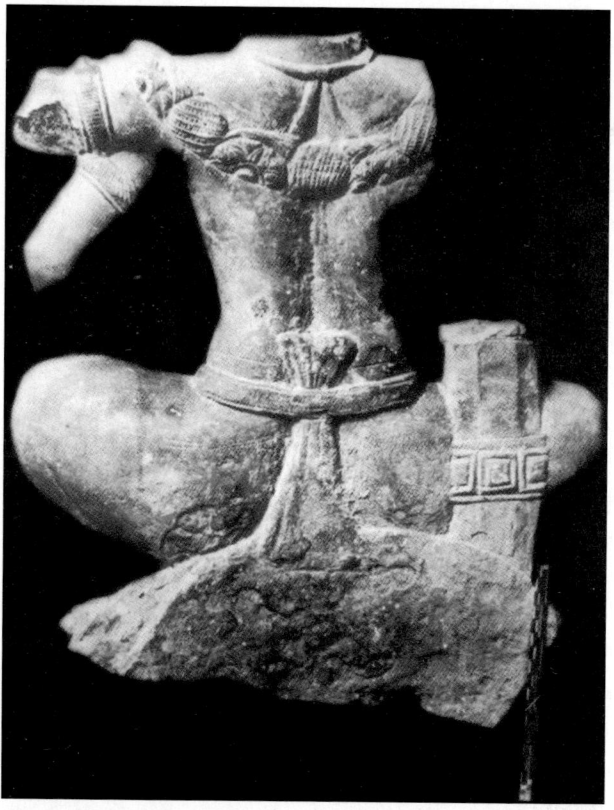

Pl. 23. *Garuḍavāhī* Vishṇu, Rohtak (back view).

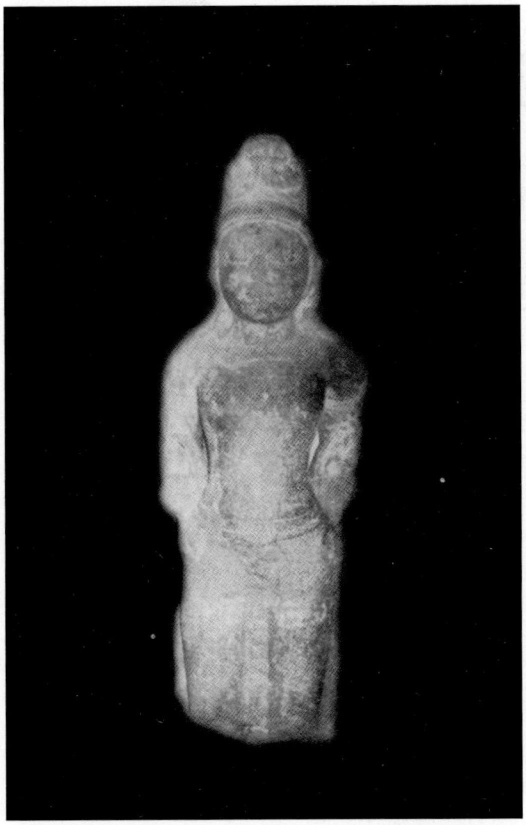

Pl. 24. Vishṇu, Agroha.

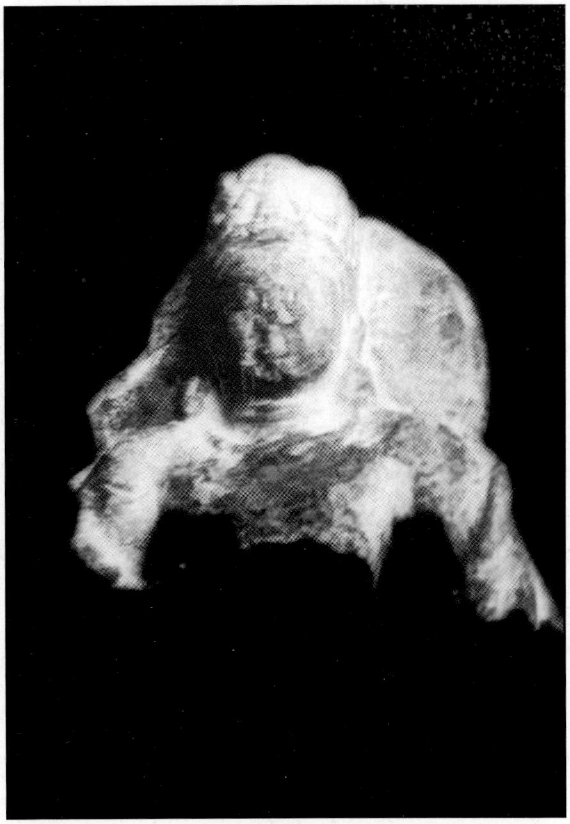

Pl. 25. Vishṇu, Mohanbari.

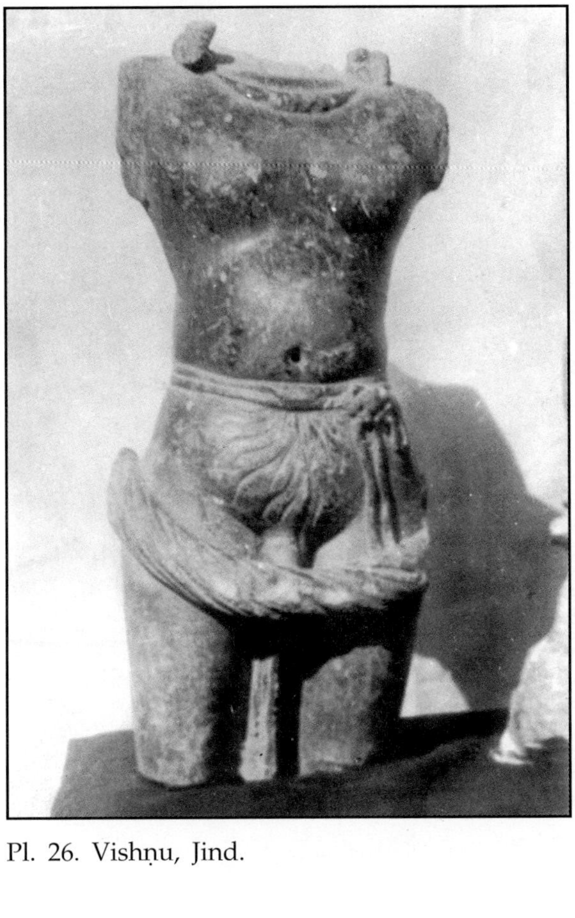

Pl. 26. Vishṇu, Jind.

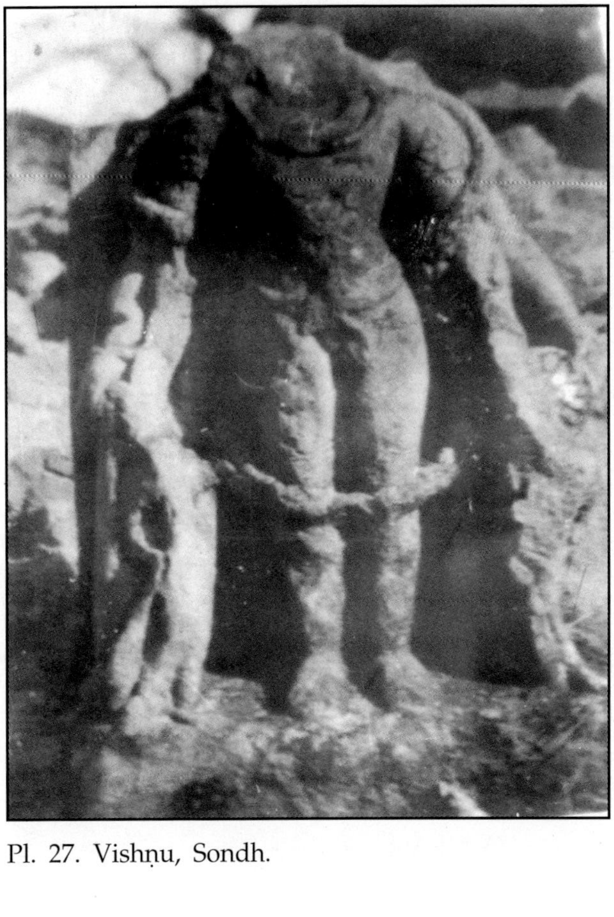

Pl. 27. Vishṇu, Sondh.

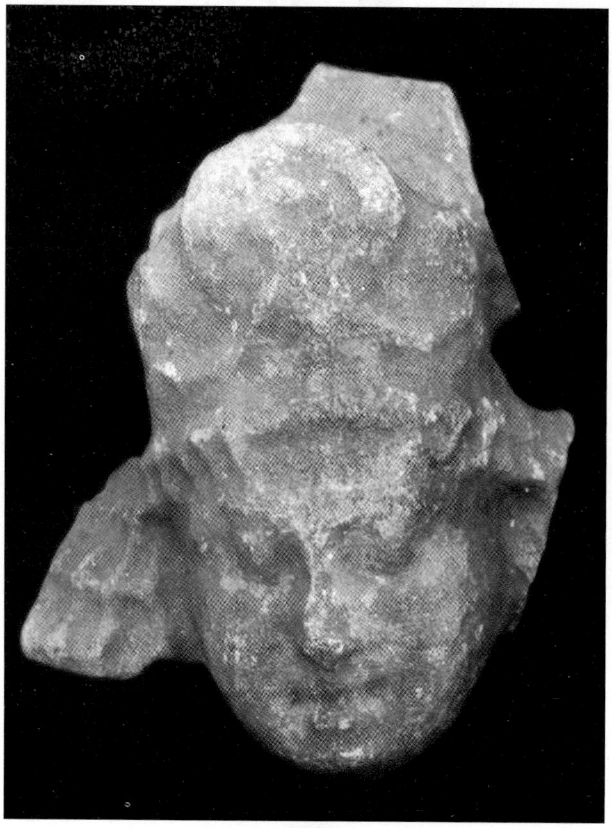

Pl. 28. Vishṇu head, Kapālamochana.

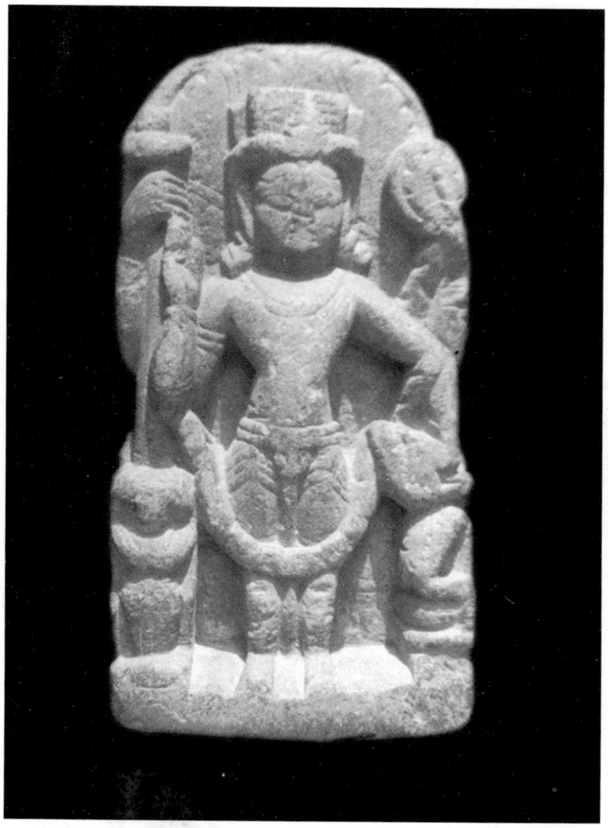

Pl. 29. Vishṇu, Meham.

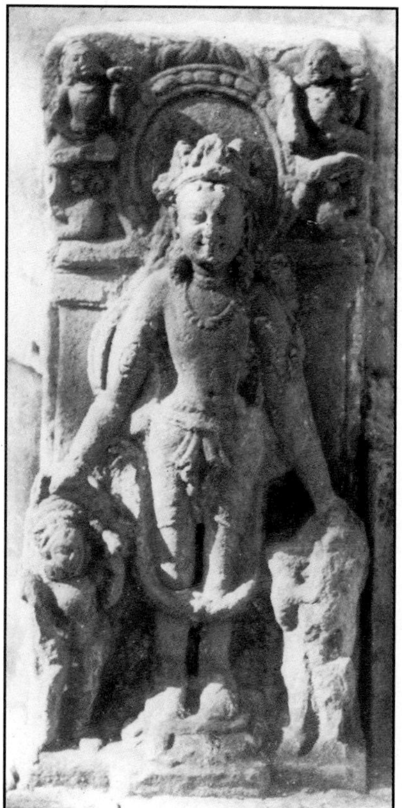

Pl. 30. Vishṇu, Pinjore.

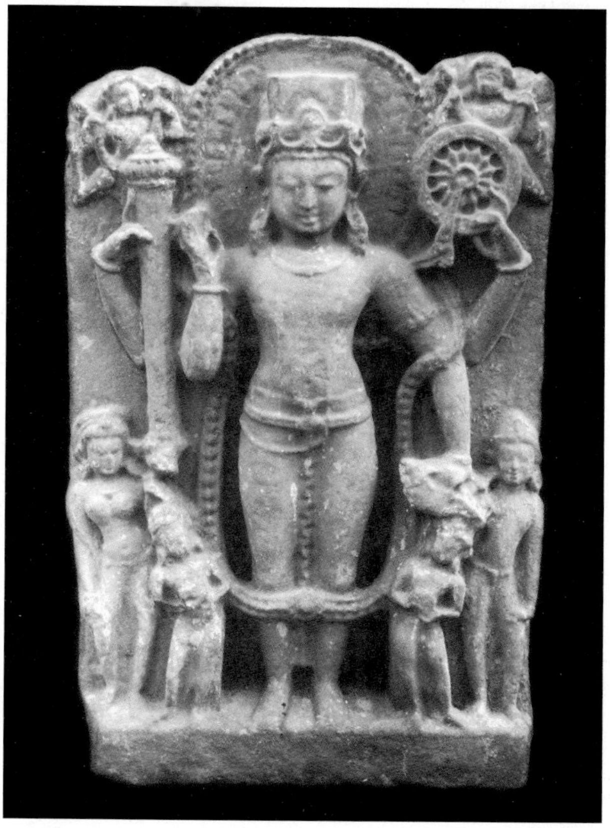

Pl. 31. Vishṇu, Kurukshetra.

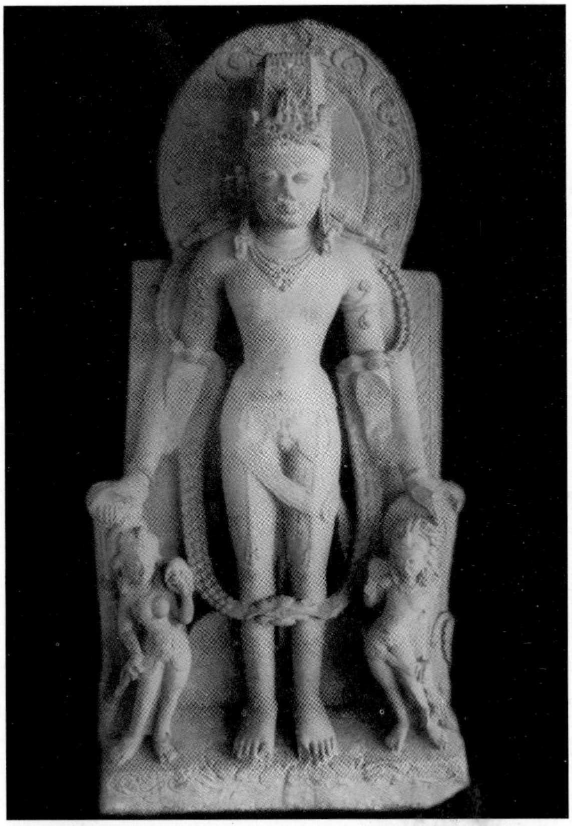

Pl. 32. Vishṇu, Agroha.

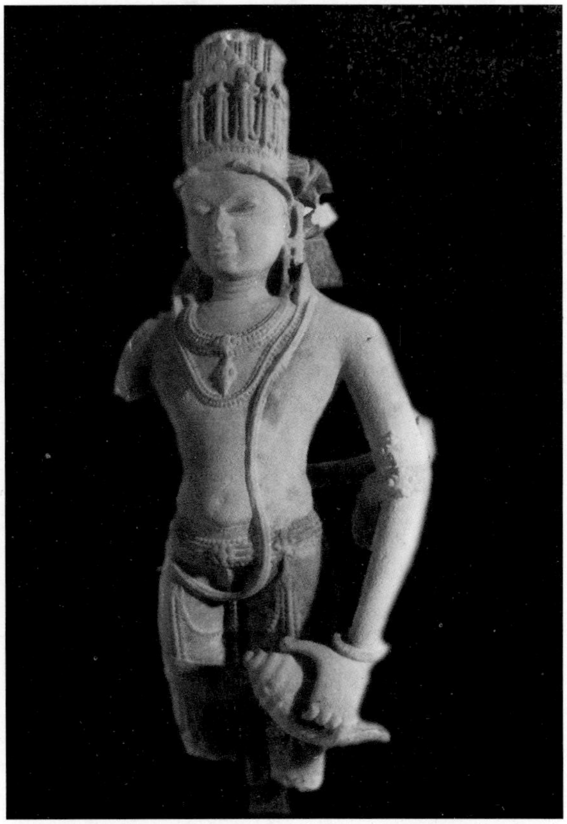

Pl. 33. Vishṇu, Agroha.

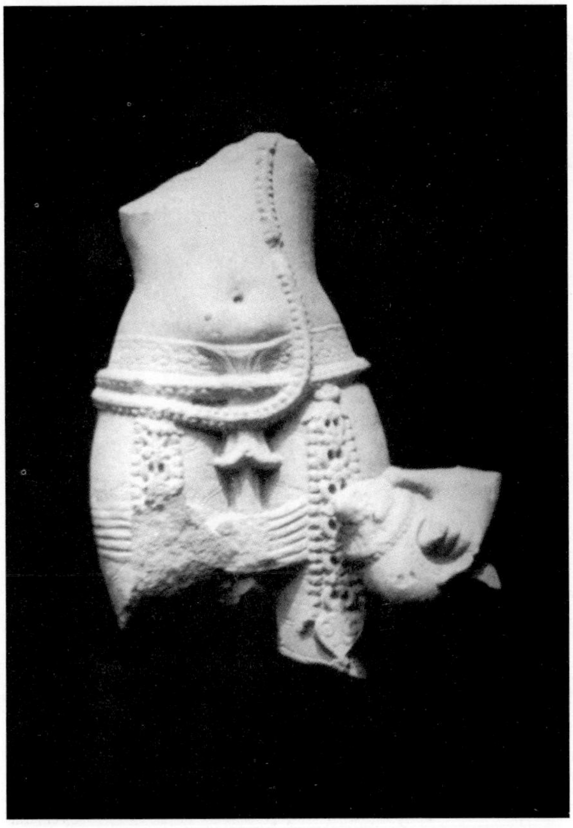

Pl. 34. Vishnu, Agroha.

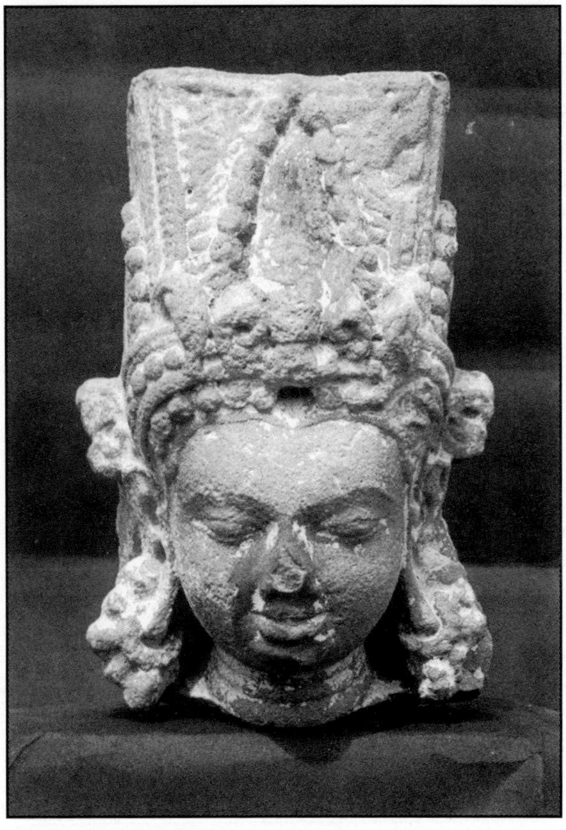

Pl. 35. Vishṇu head, Jind.

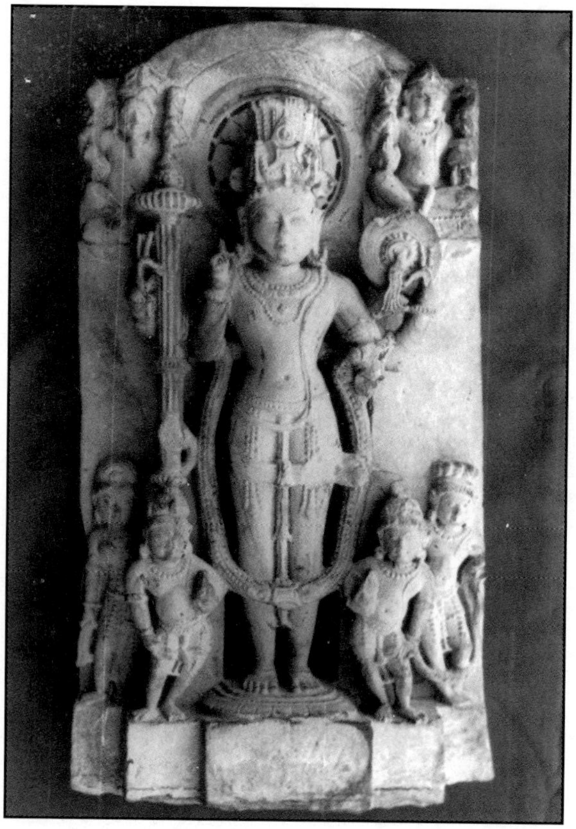

Pl. 36. Vishṇu, Rasina.

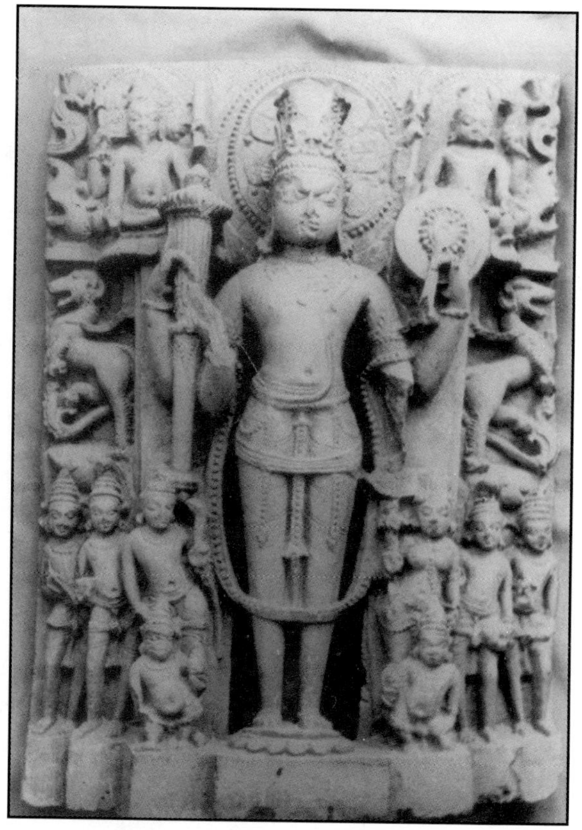

Pl. 37. Vishṇu, Rasina.

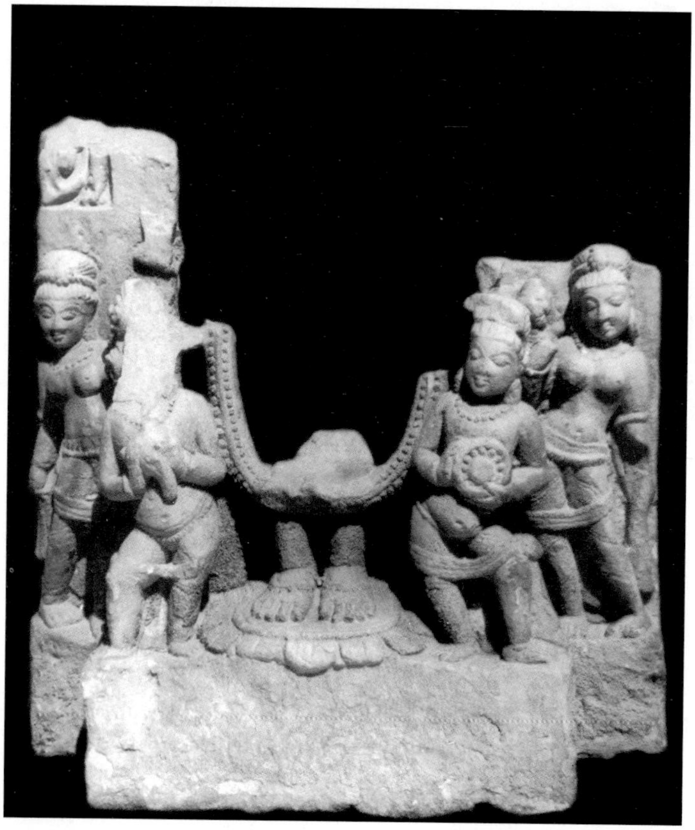

Pl. 38. Vishṇu, Madina.

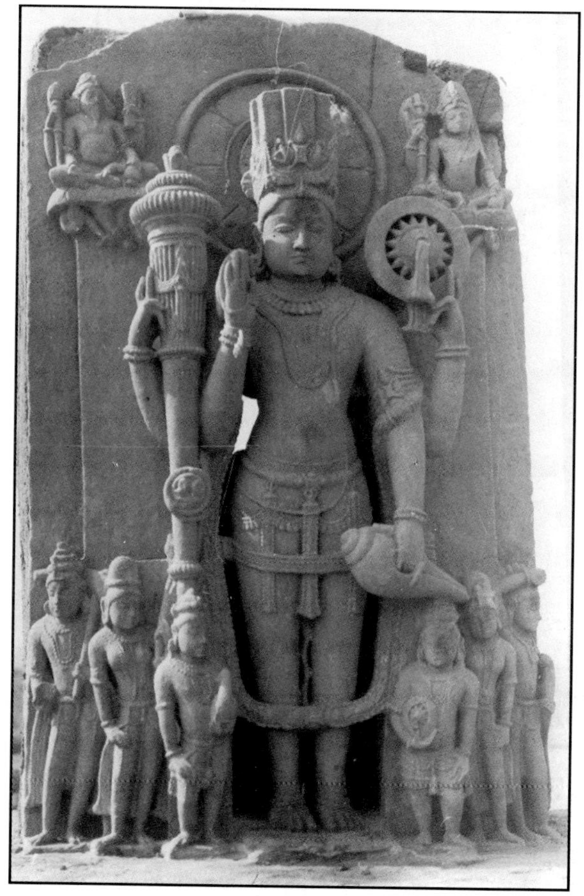

Pl. 42. Vishṇu, Kanwari.

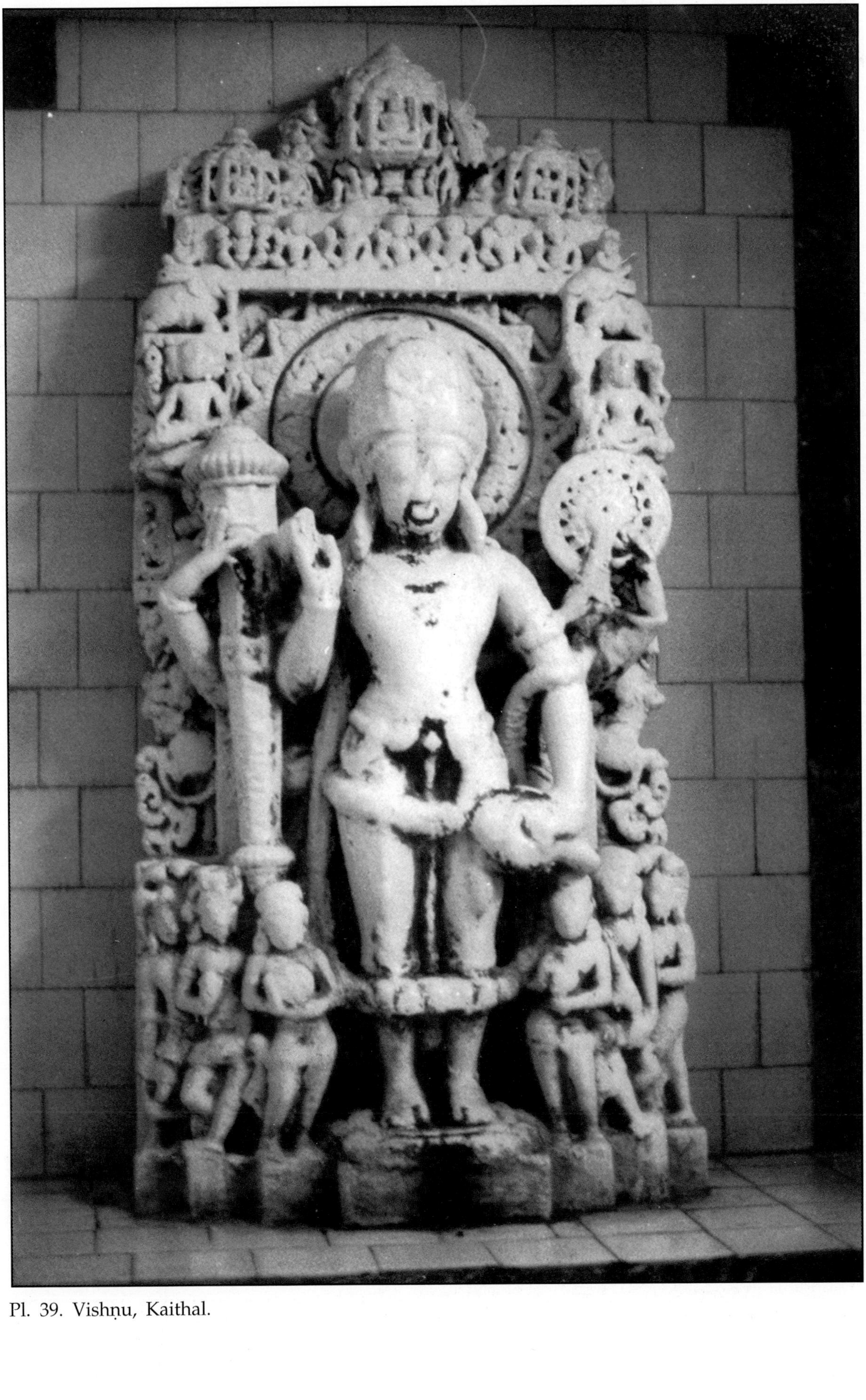

Pl. 39. Vishṇu, Kaithal.

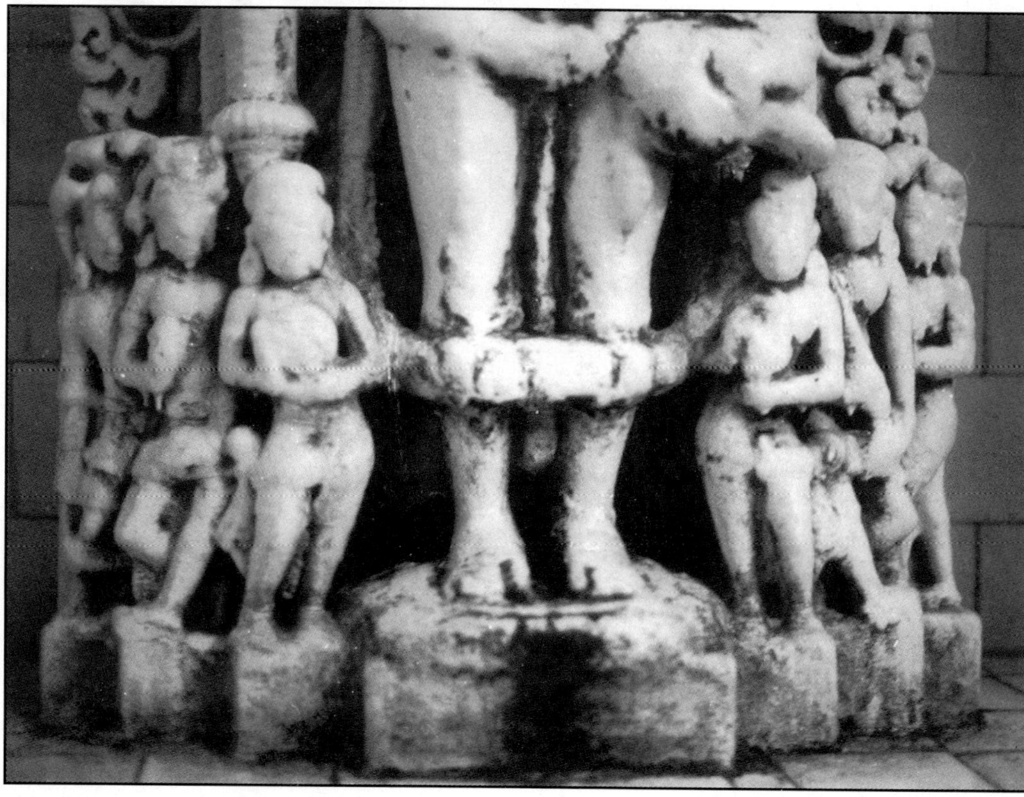

Pl. 40. Vishṇu, Kaithal, details of the pedestal.

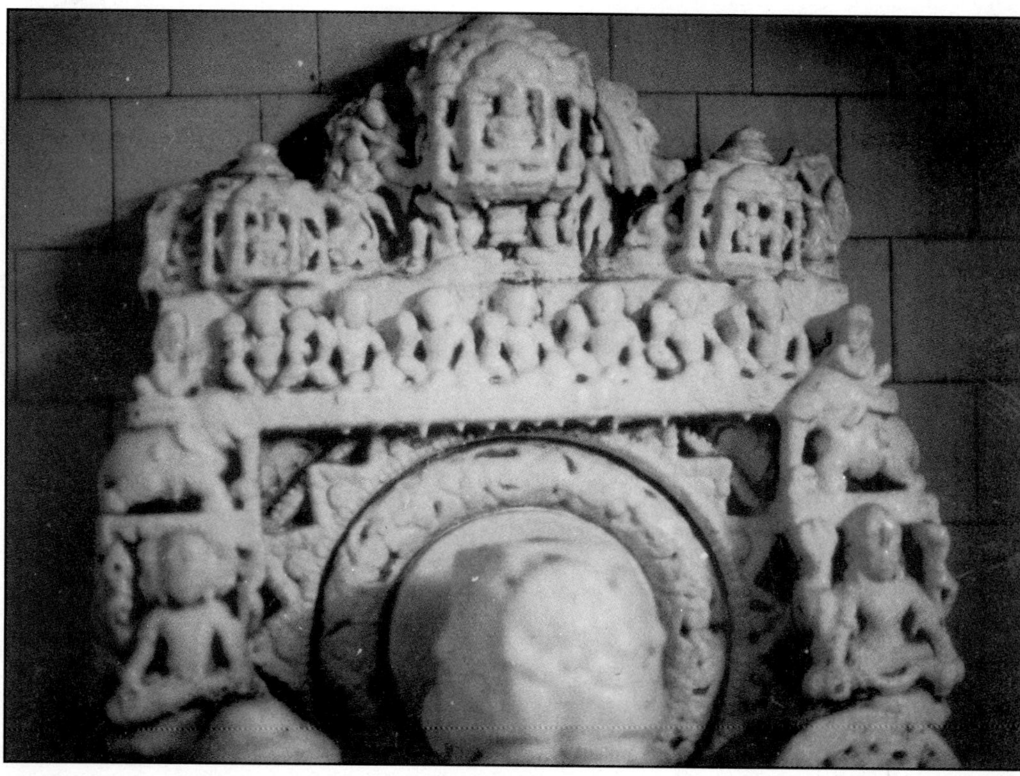

Pl. 41. Vishṇu, Kaithal, details of the *parikara*.

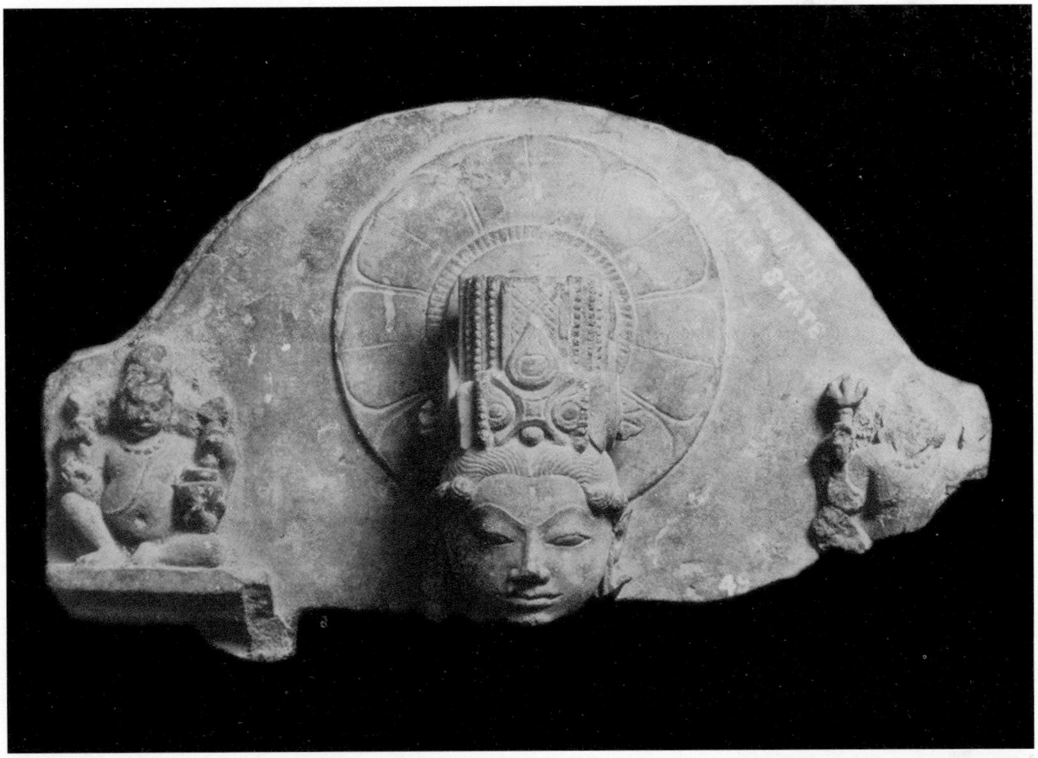

Pl. 43. Vishṇu head, Pinjore.

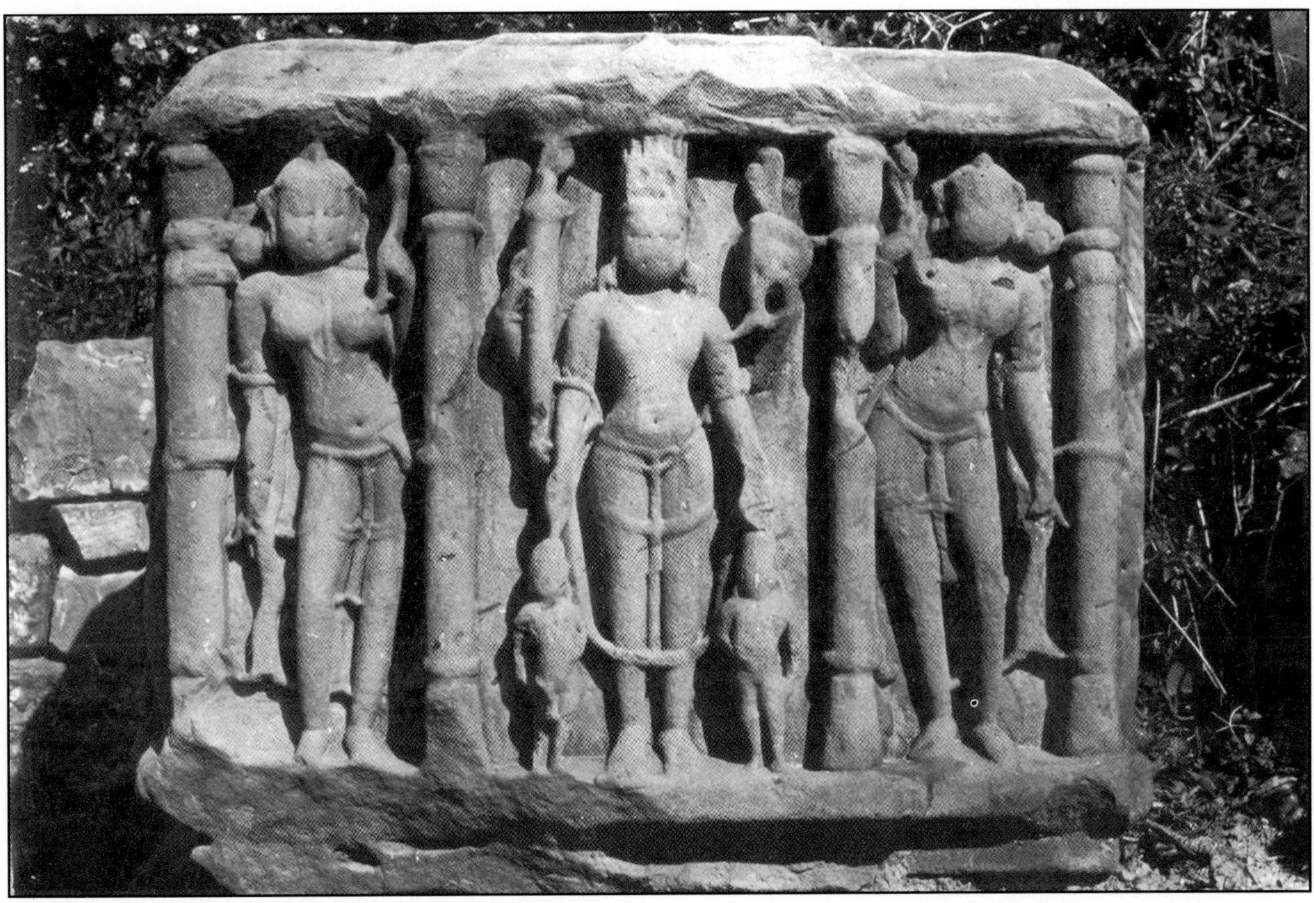

Pl. 44. Vishṇu, Pinjore.

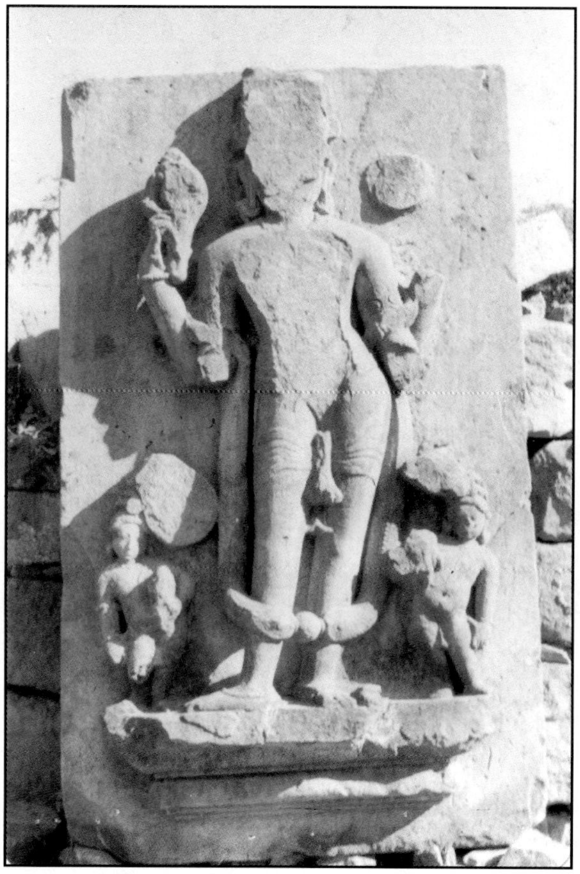

Pl. 45. Vishṇu, Pinjore.

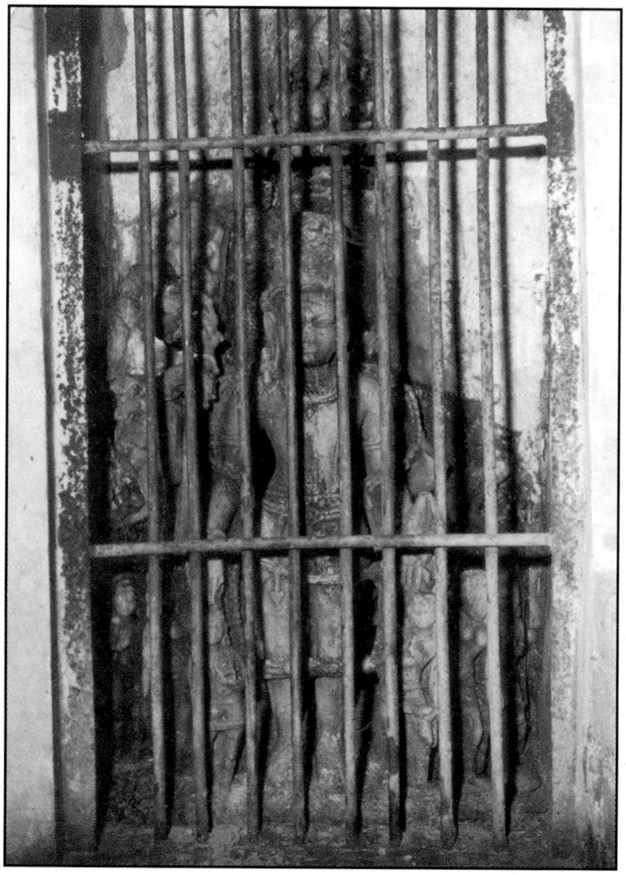

Pl. 48. Vishṇu, Hat.

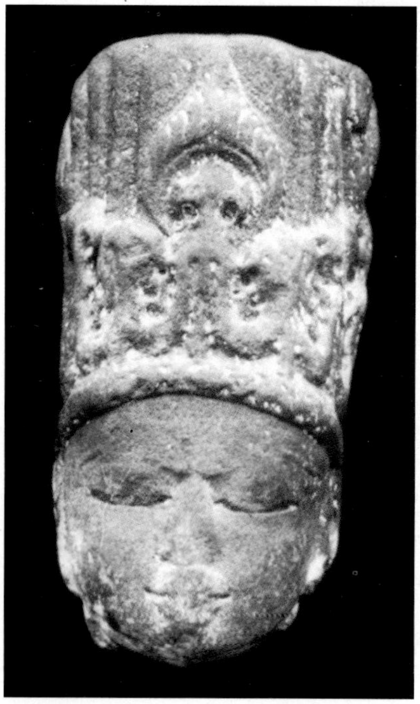

Pl. 46. Vishṇu head, Pinjore.

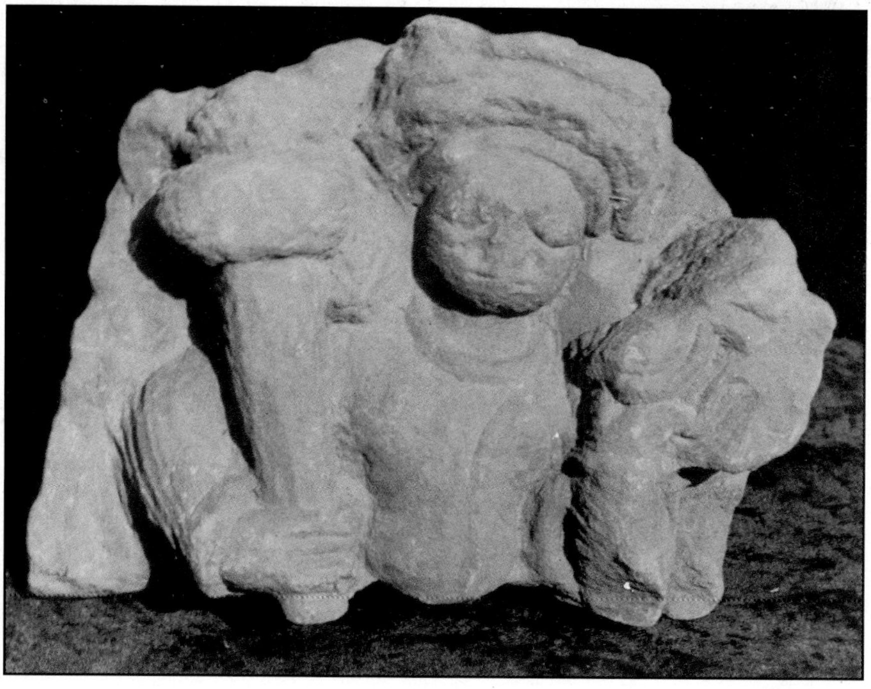

Pl. 47. Vishṇu, Ratpur.

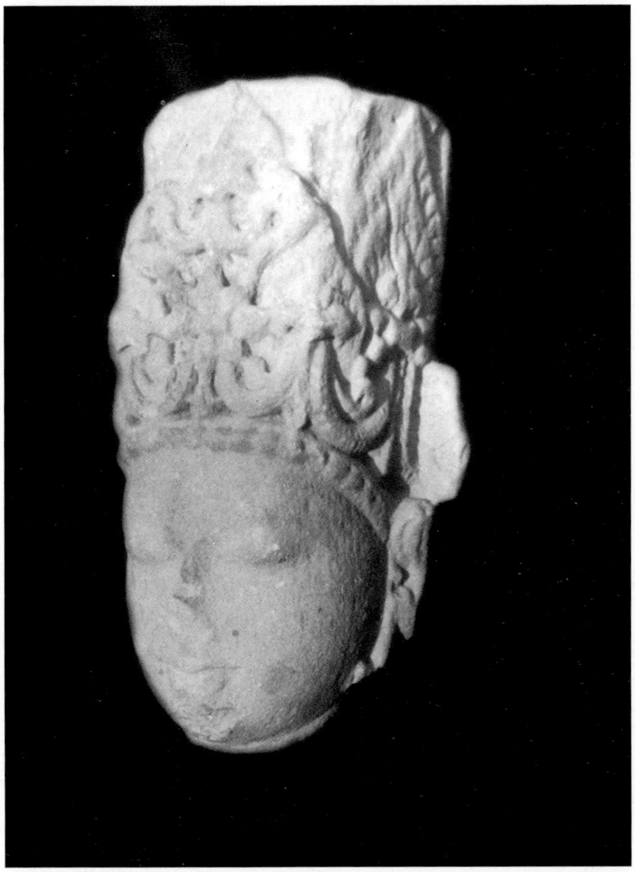

Pl. 49. Vishṇu head, Bulandpur Kheri.

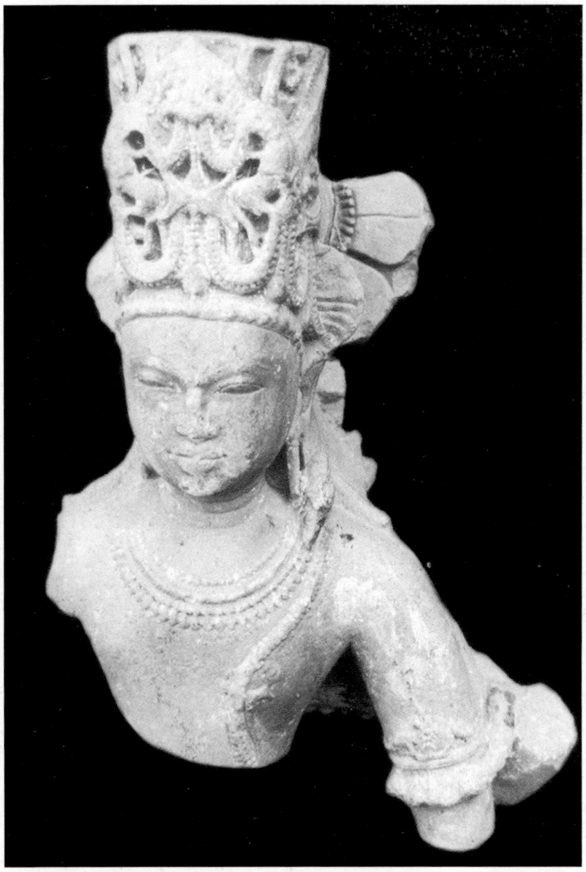

Pl. 50. Bust of Vishṇu, Gujjar Kheri.

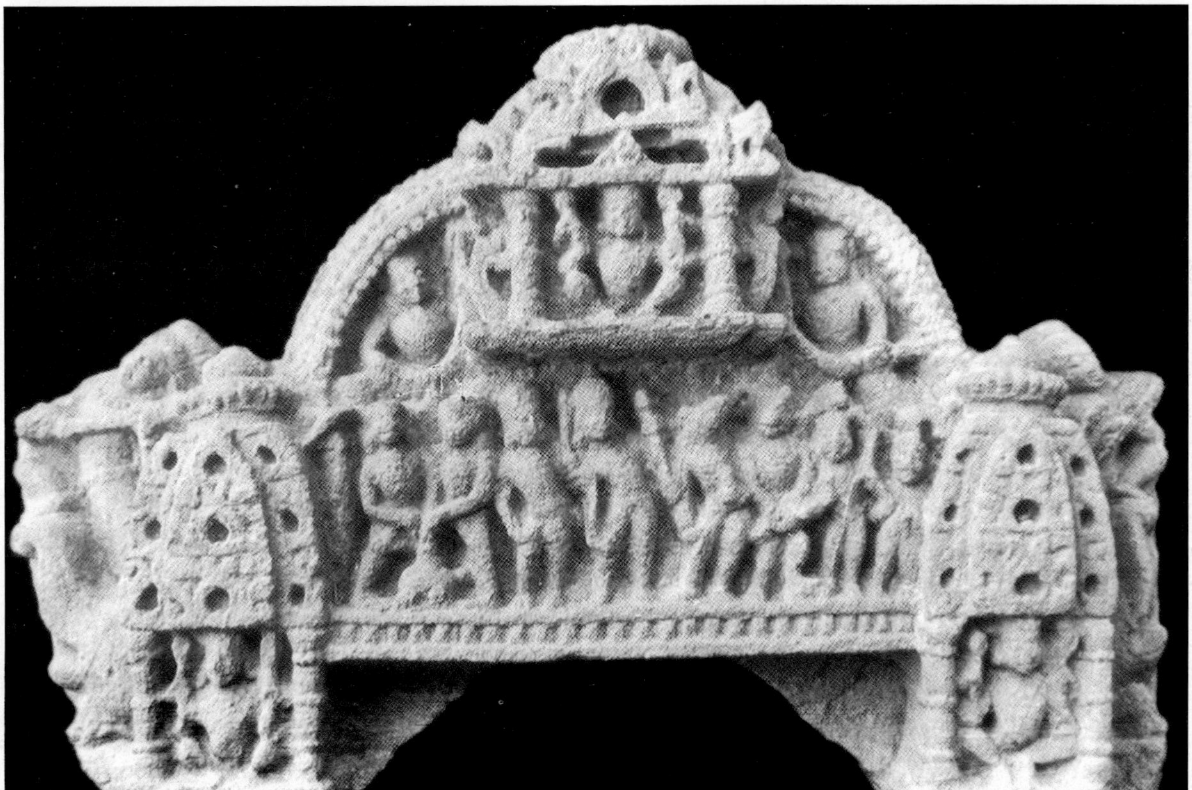

Pl. 51. *Parikara* of Vishṇu, Gujjar Kheri.

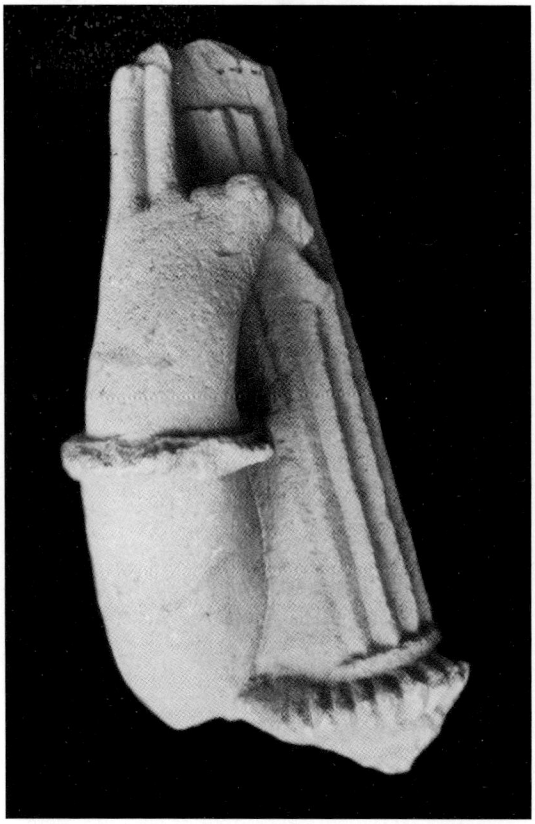

Pl. 52. Vishṇu's hand with mace, Gujjar Kheri.

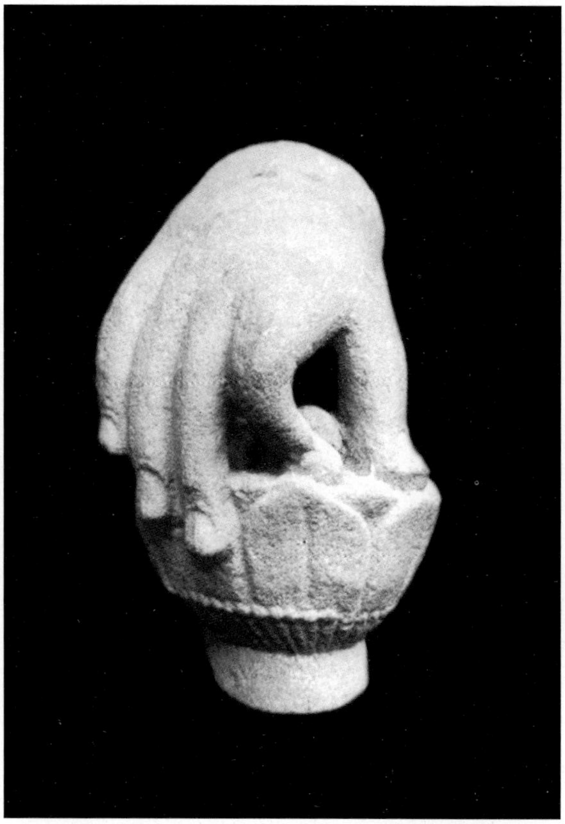

Pl. 53. Vishṇu's hand with lotus, Gujjar Kheri.

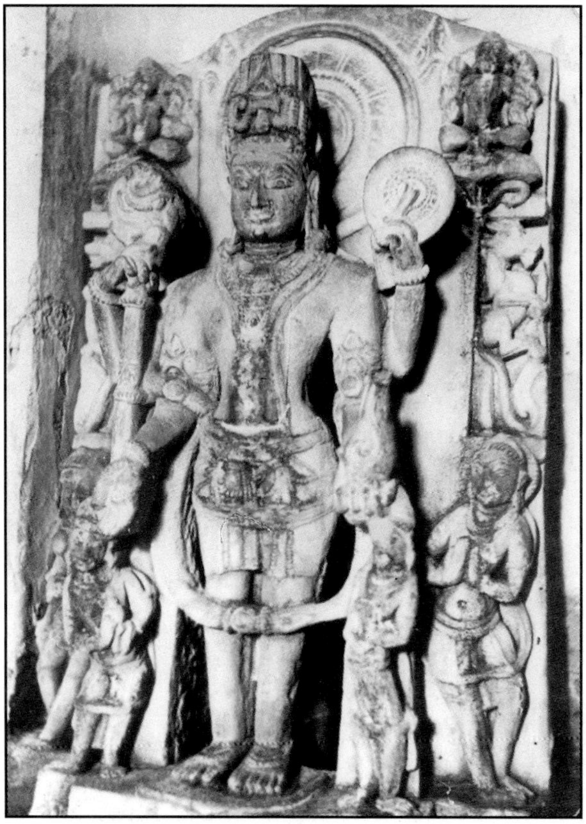

Pl. 55. Vishṇu, Beri Khera.

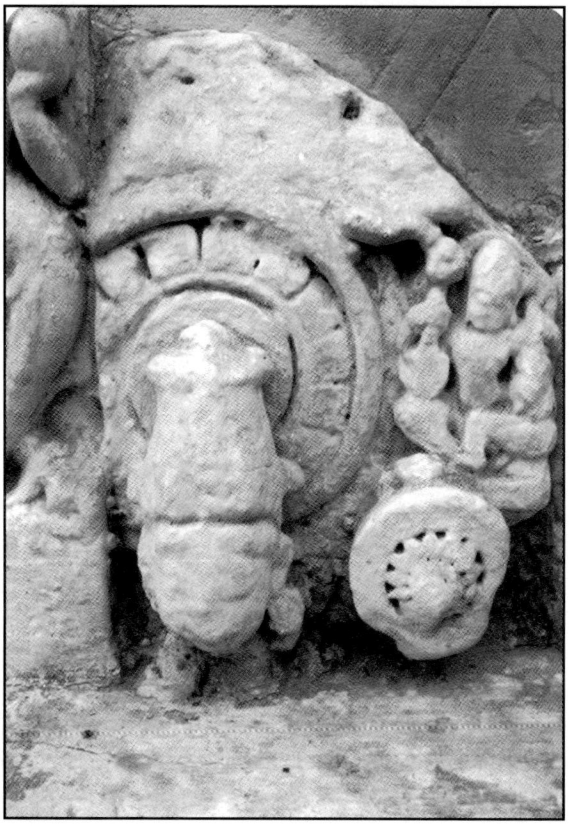

Pl. 56. Bust of Vishṇu, Badali.

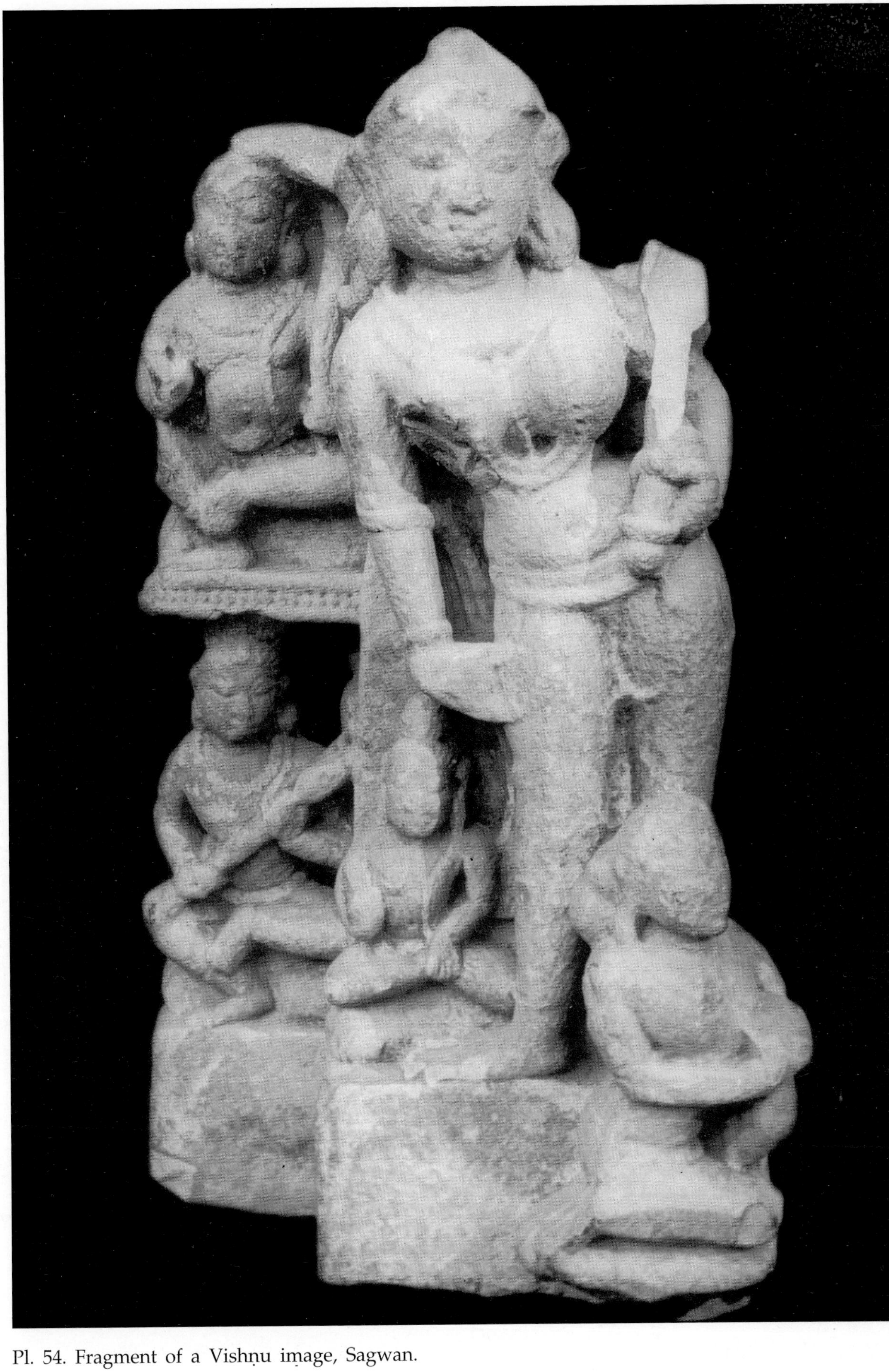

Pl. 54. Fragment of a Vishṇu image, Sagwan.

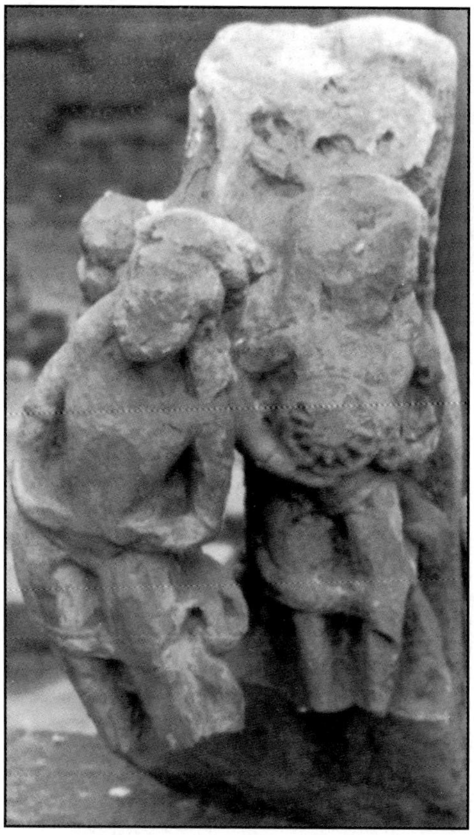

Pl. 57. Chakra-purusha, Badali.

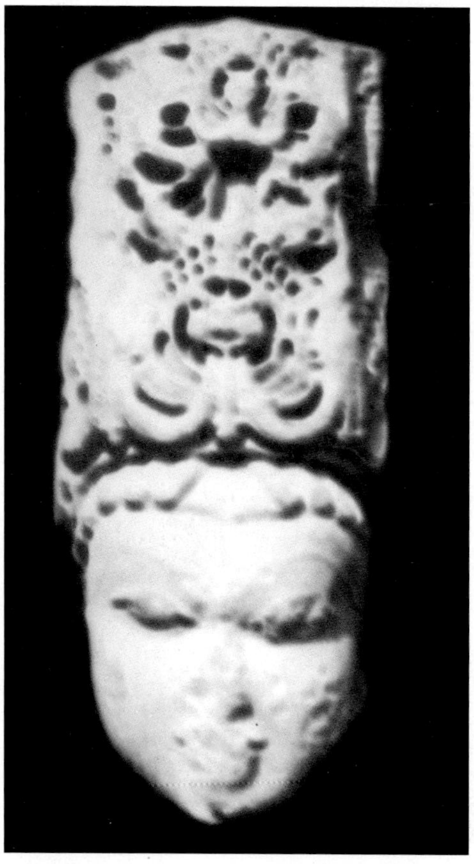

Pl. 58. Vishṇu head, Rohtak.

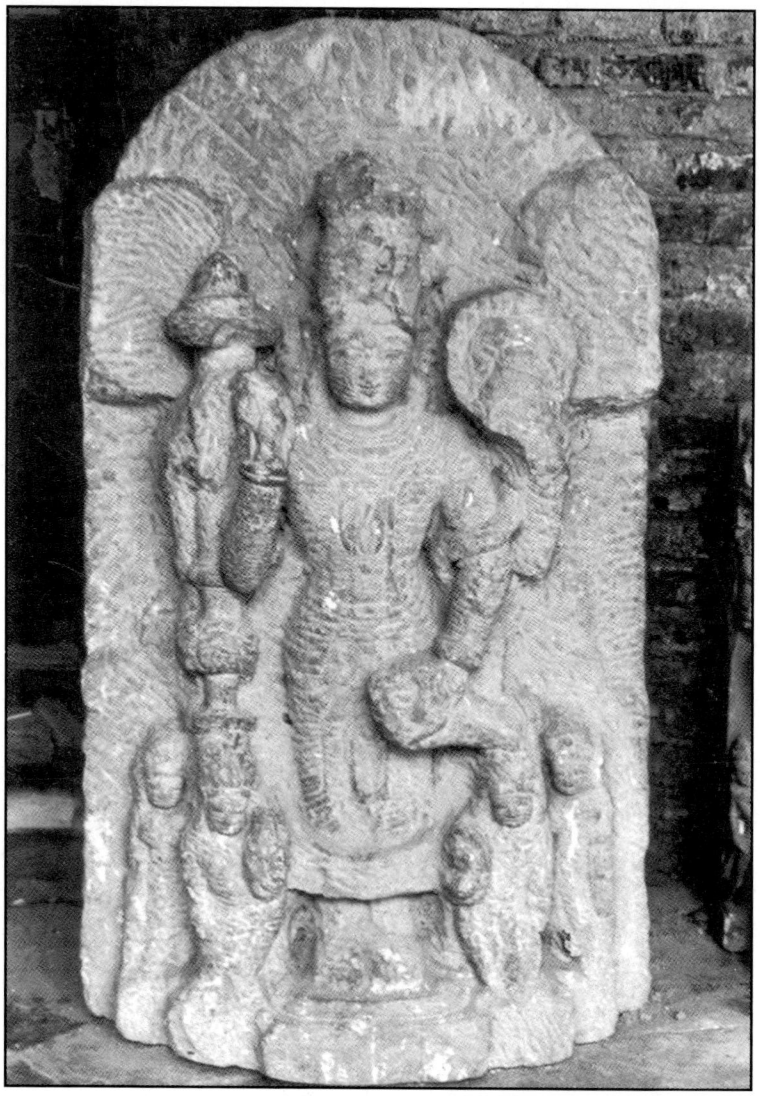

Pl. 59. Unfinished Vishṇu, Asthal Bohr, Rohtak.

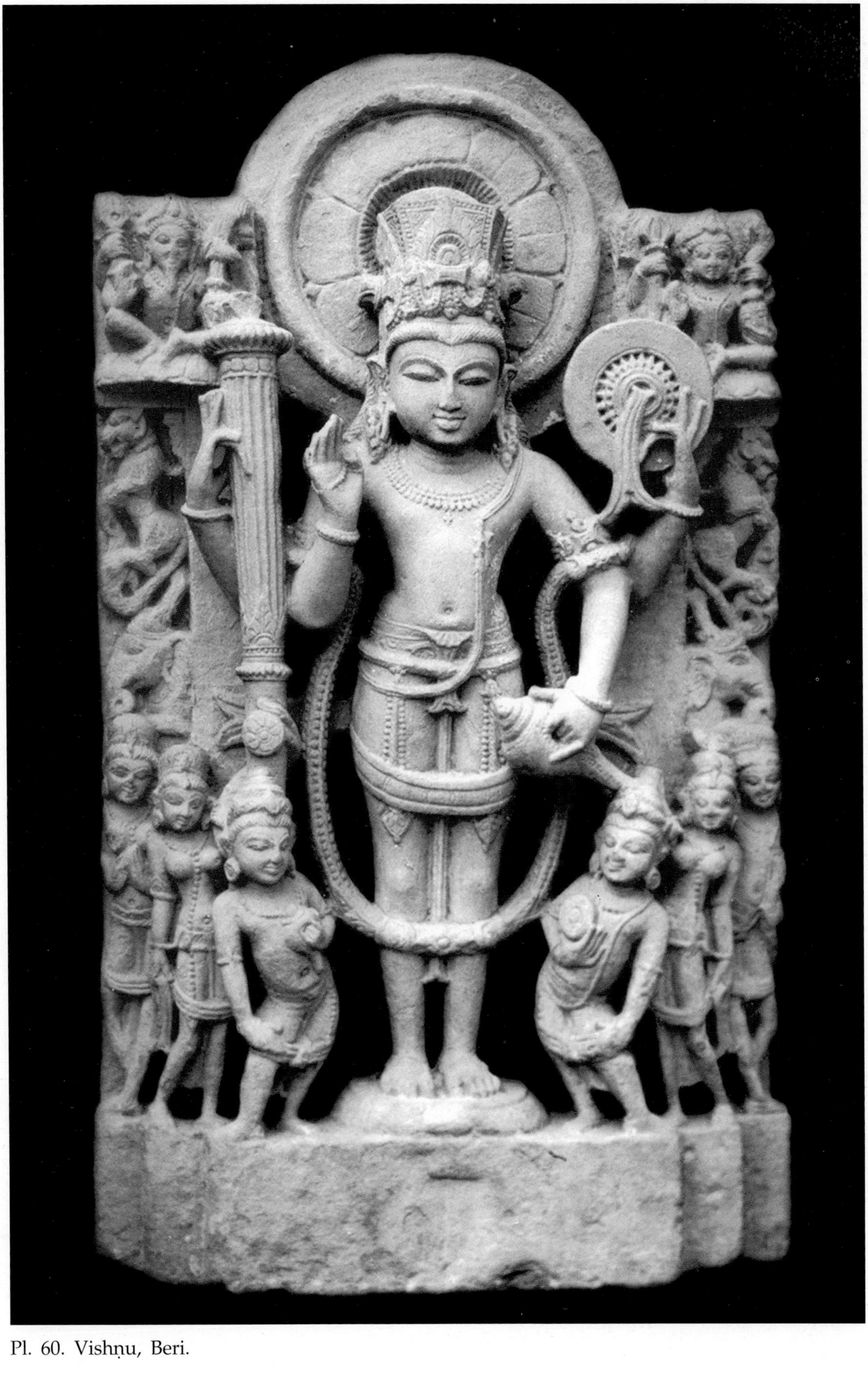

Pl. 60. Vishṇu, Beri.

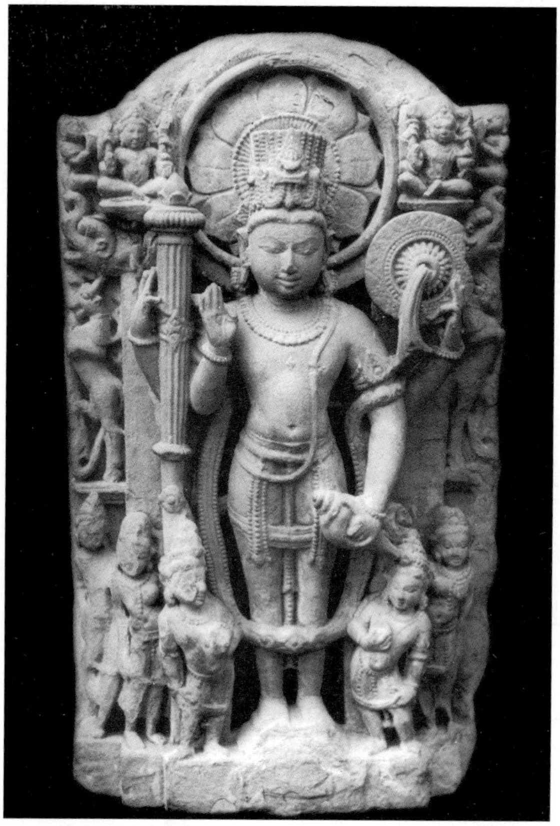

Pl. 61. Vishṇu, Beri.

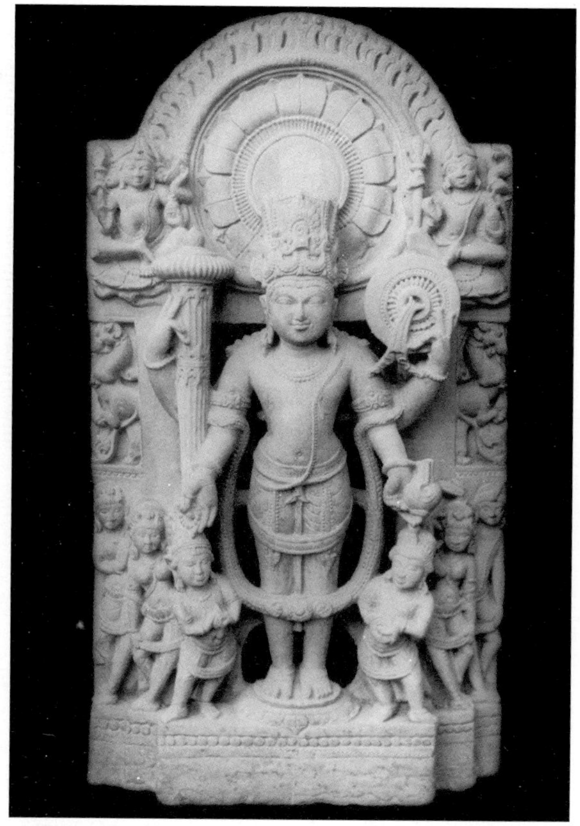

Pl. 62. Vishṇu, Beri.

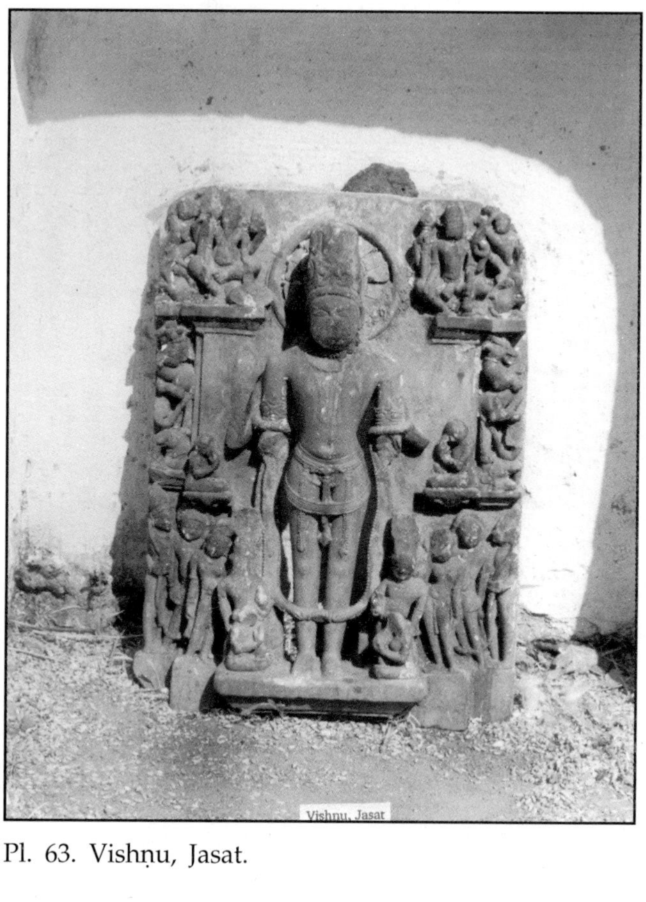

Pl. 63. Vishṇu, Jasat.

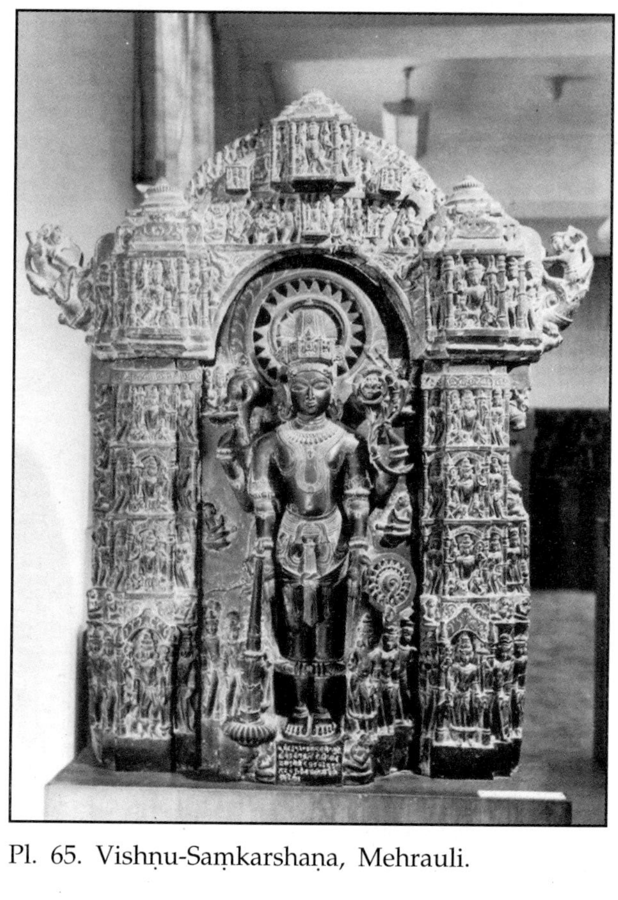

Pl. 65. Vishṇu-Saṃkarshaṇa, Mehrauli.

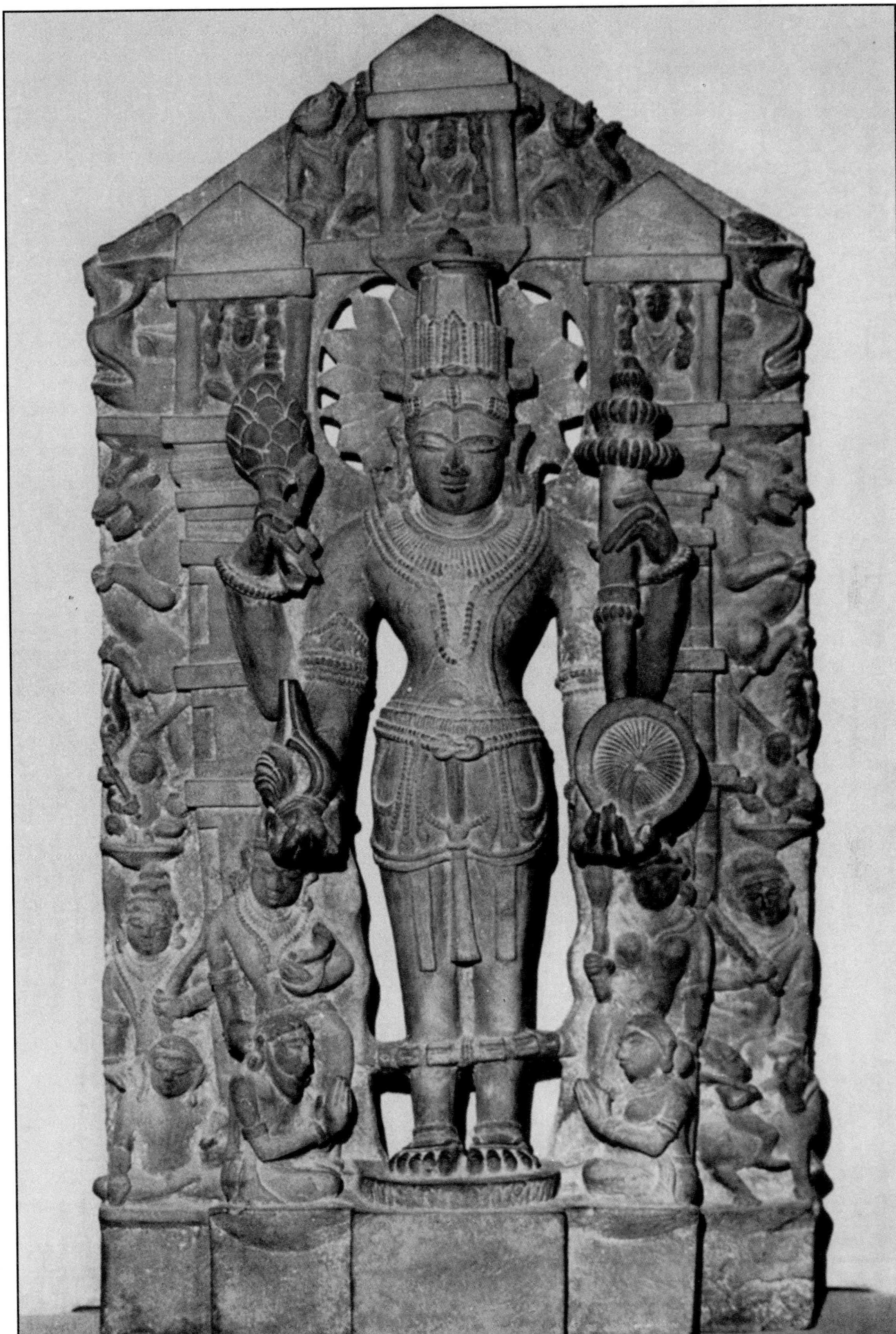

Pl. 64. Vishṇu, Kosli.

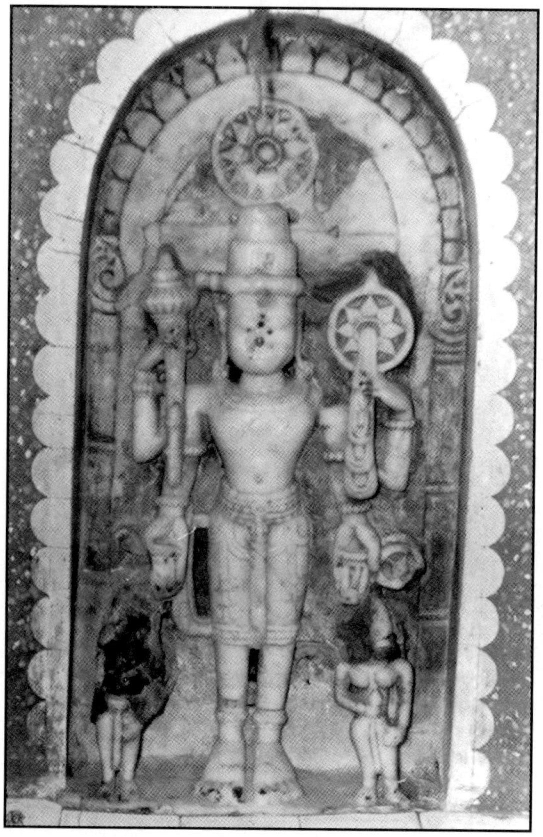

Pl. 66. Vishṇu, Banbhori (Hisar), modern.

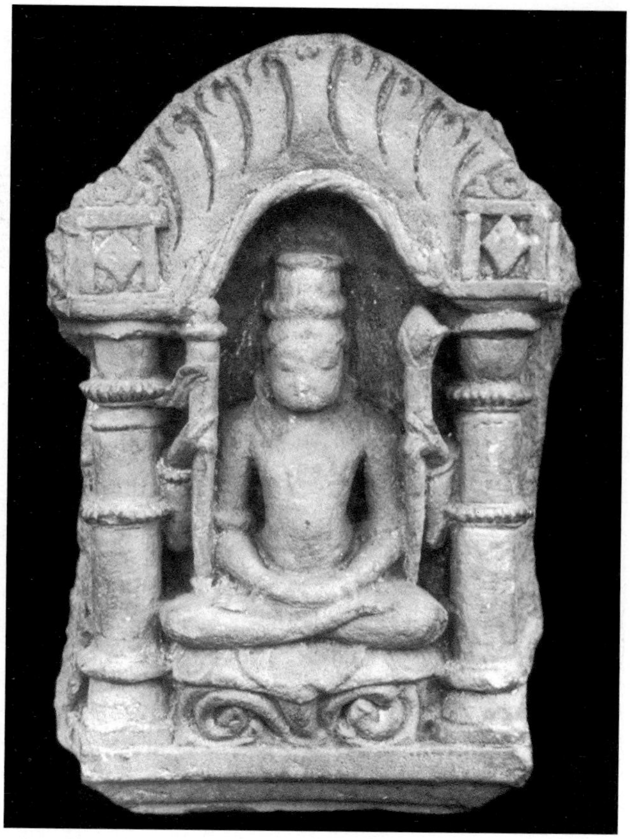

Pl. 68. *Yogāsana* Vishṇu, Sirsa.

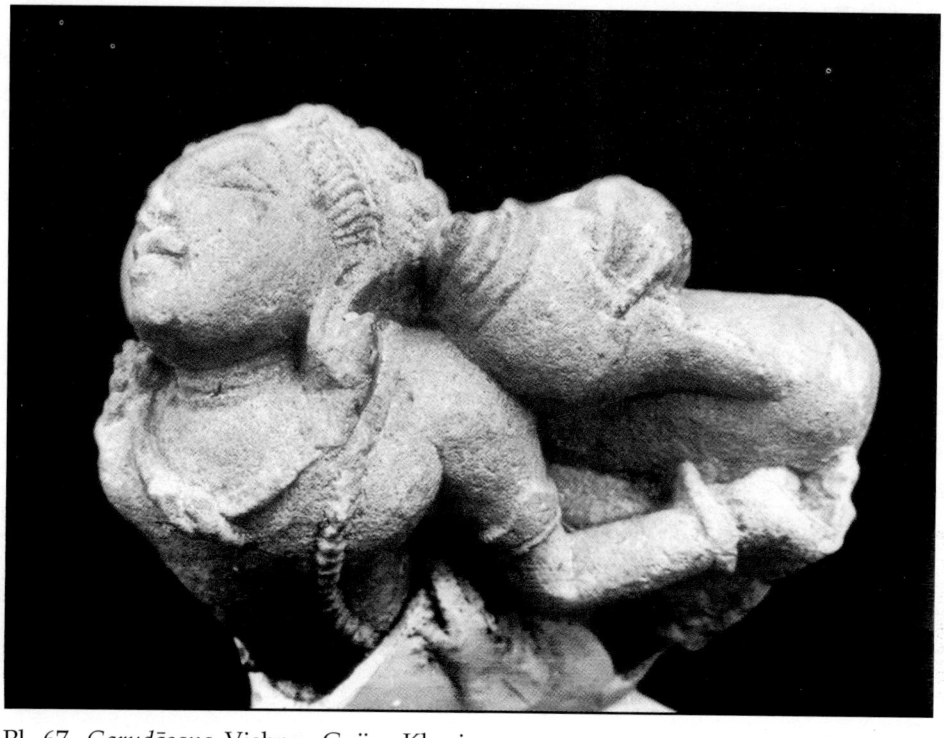

Pl. 67. *Garuḍāsana* Vishṇu, Gujjar Kheri.

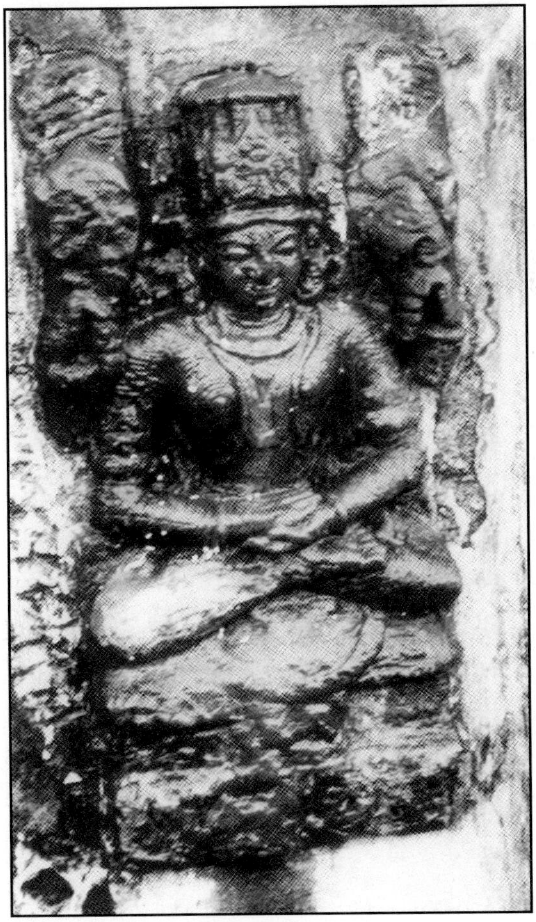

Pl. 69. *Yogāsana* Vishṇu, Lalru.

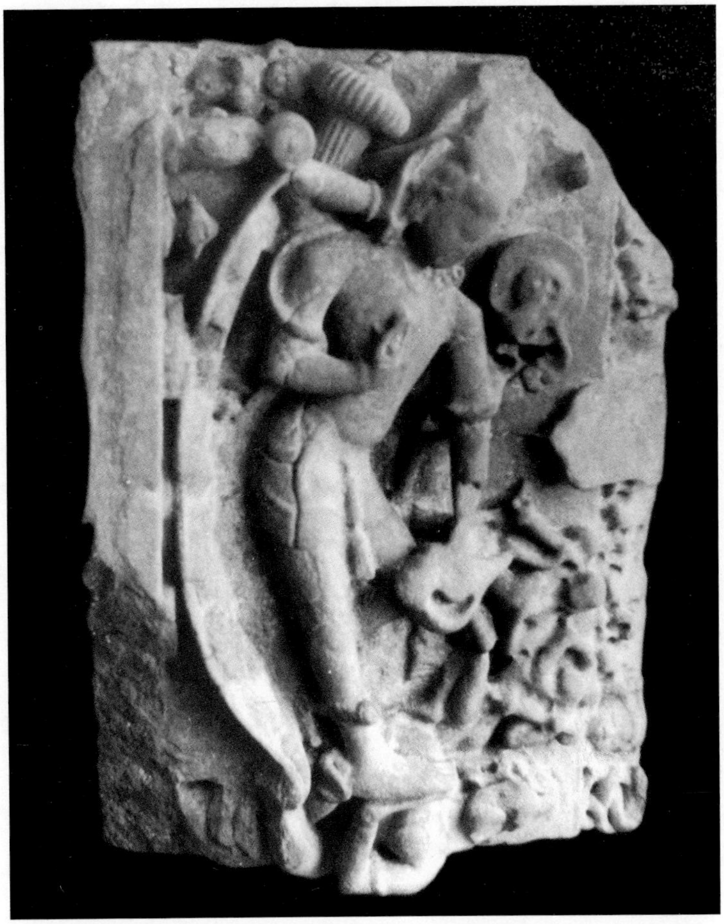

Pl. 70. Śeshaśāyī Vishṇu, Kurukshetra.

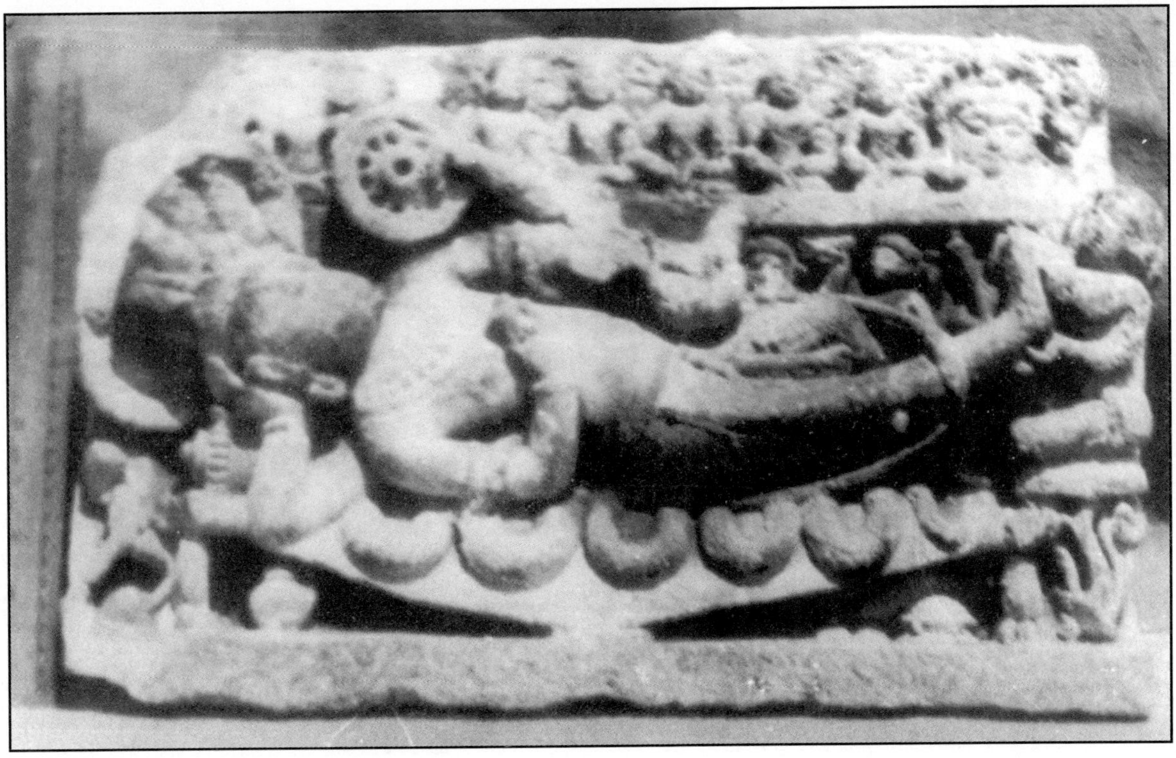

Pl. 71. Śeshaśāyī Vishṇu, Mandhna.

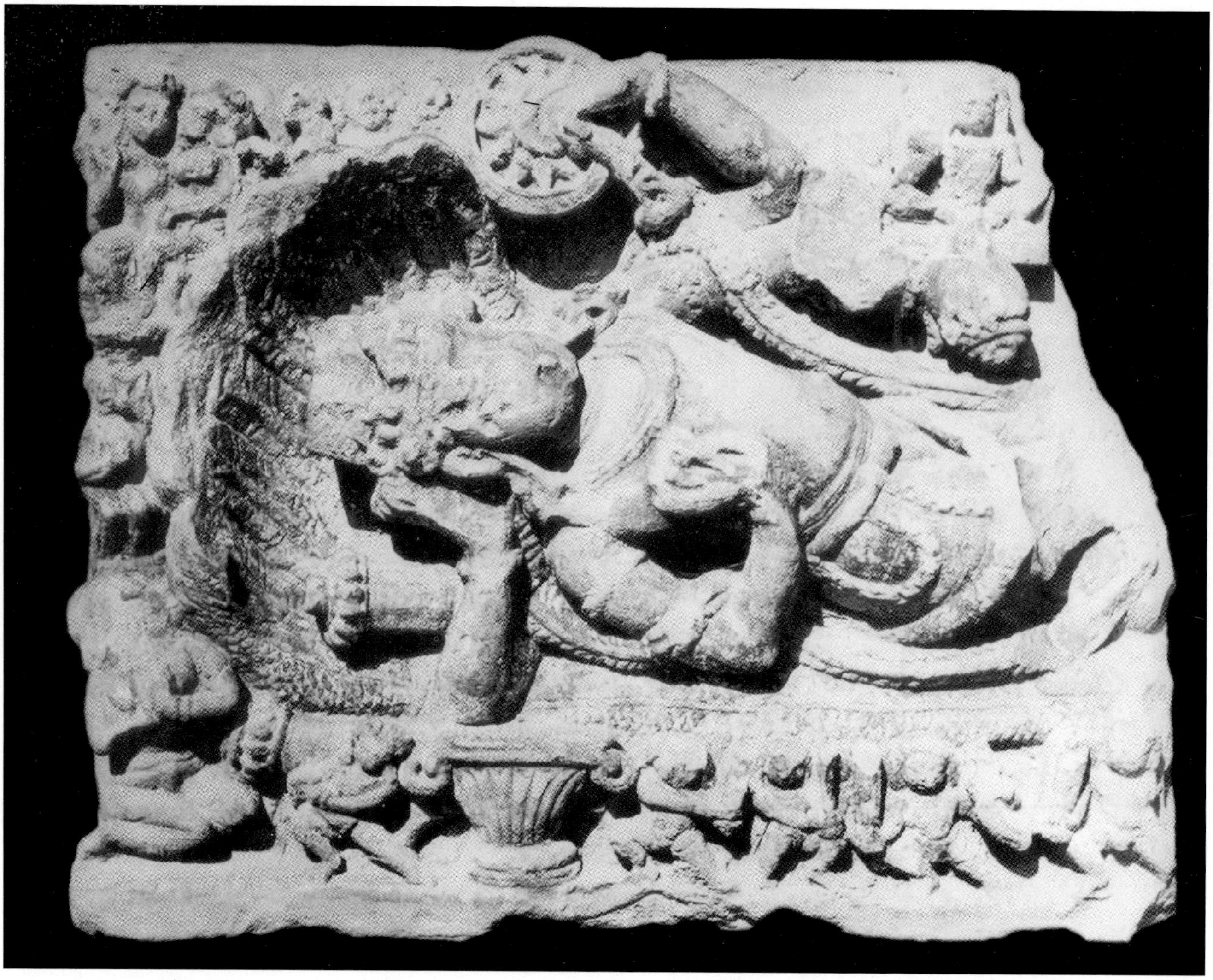

Pl. 72. Śeshaśāyī Vishṇu, Garh Fazilpur.

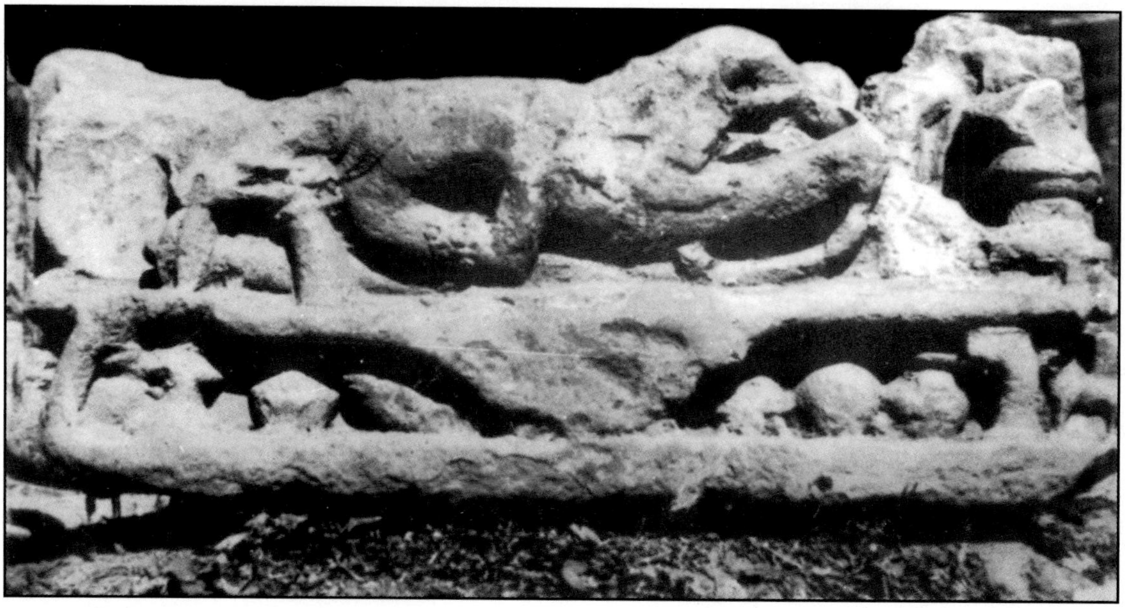

Pl. 73. Śeshaśāyī Vishṇu, Guruwara.

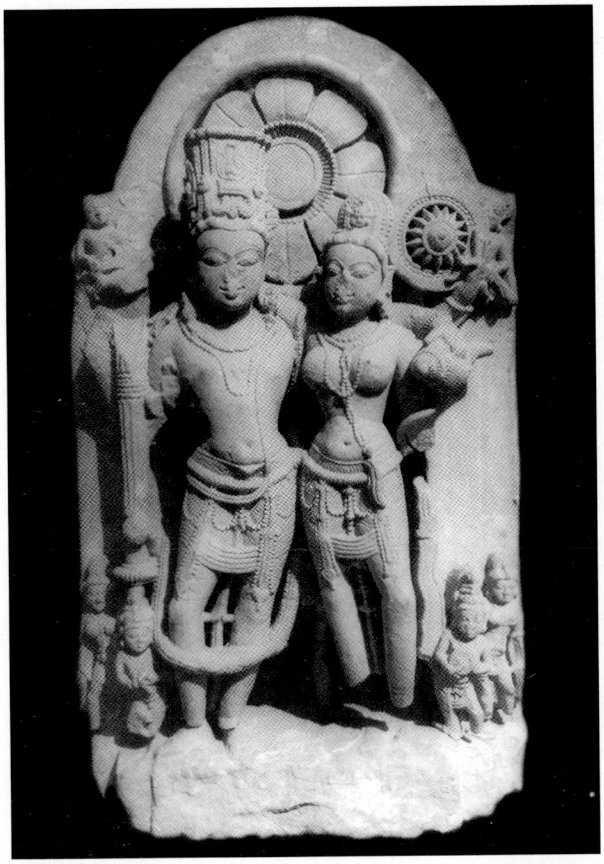

Pl. 74. Lakshmī-Nārāyaṇa, Agroha.

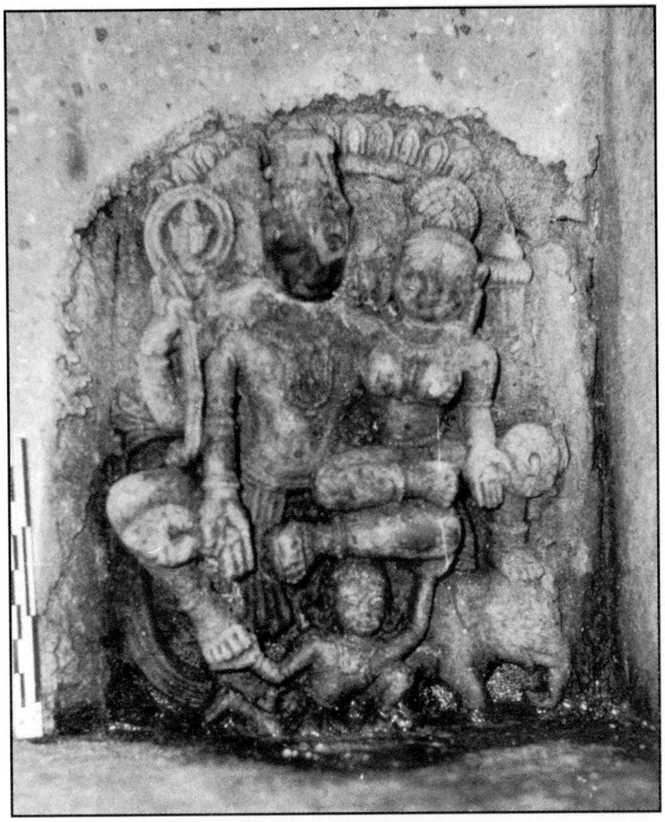

Pl. 76. Lakshmī-Nārāyaṇa, Panipat.

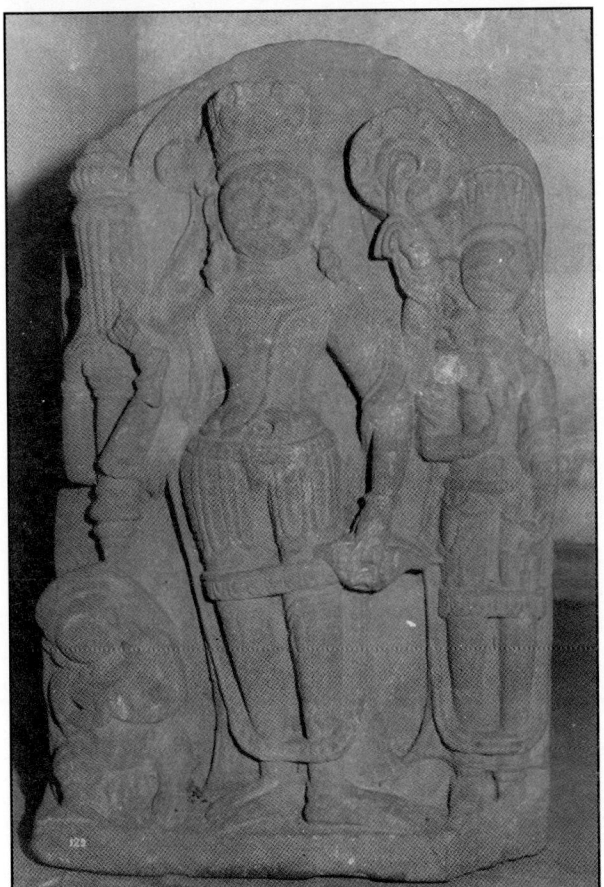

Pl. 75. Lakshmī-Nārāyaṇa, Pinjore.

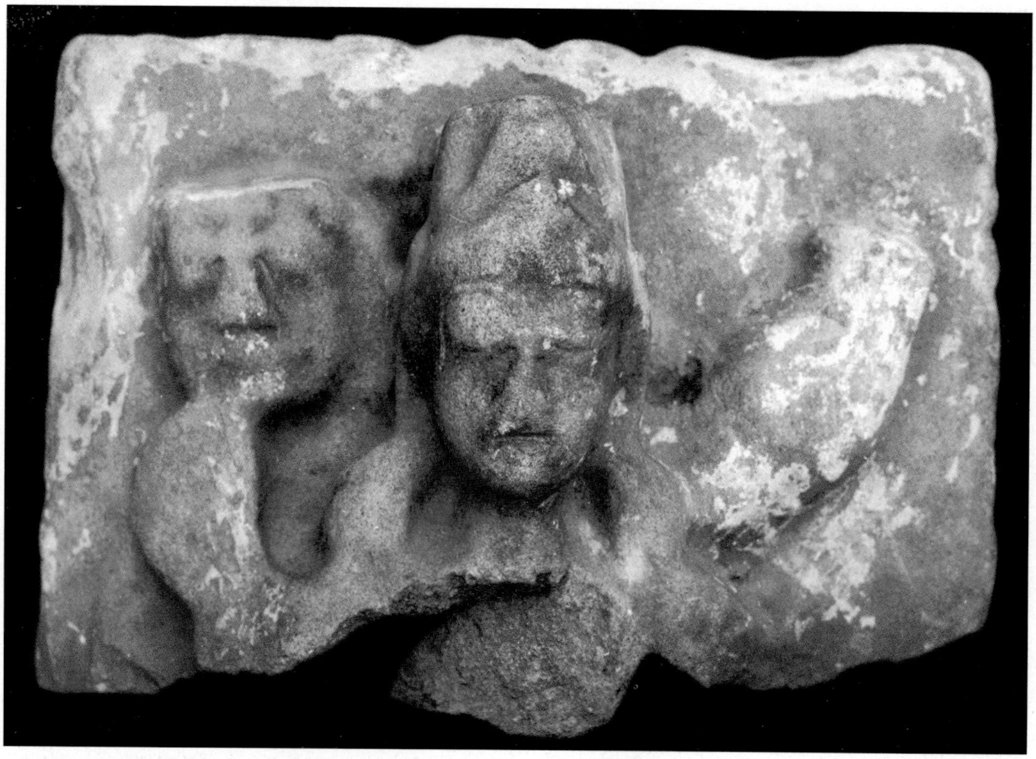

Pl. 77. Vaikuṇṭha, Kapālamochana.

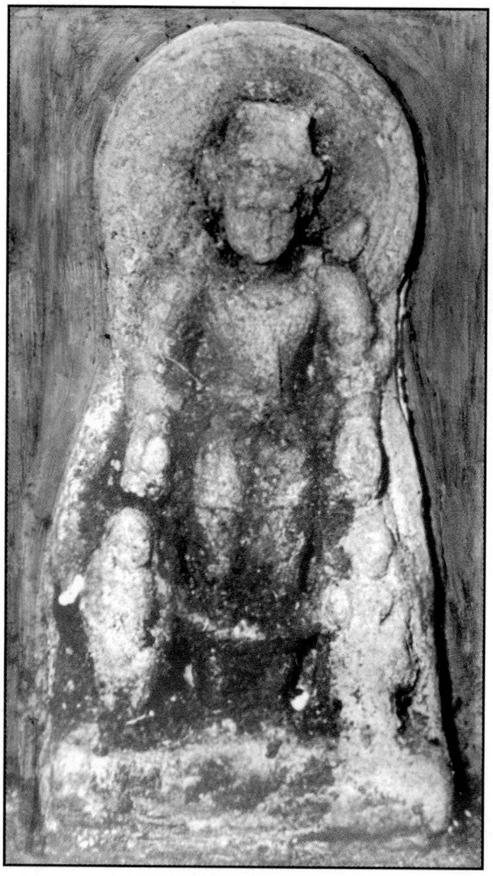

Pl. 78. Vaikuṇṭha, Gharaunda.

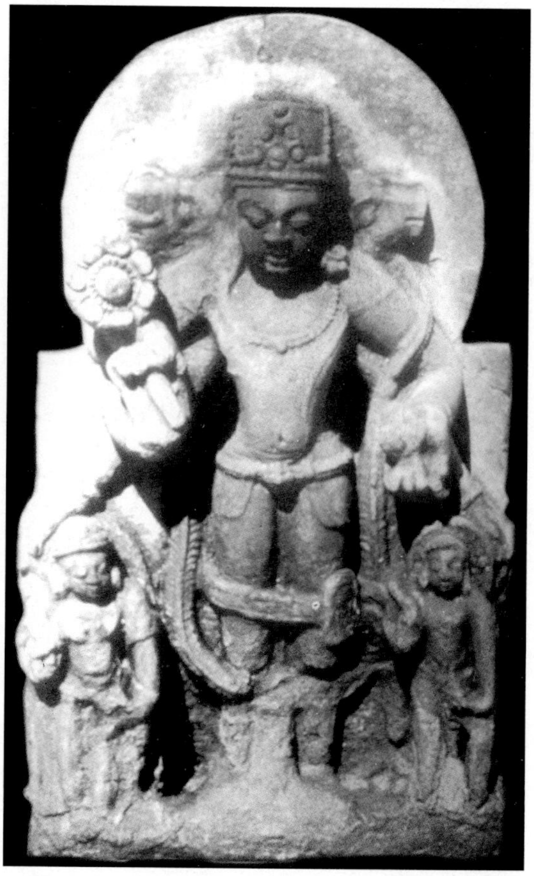

Pl. 79. Vaikuṇṭha, Kaithal.

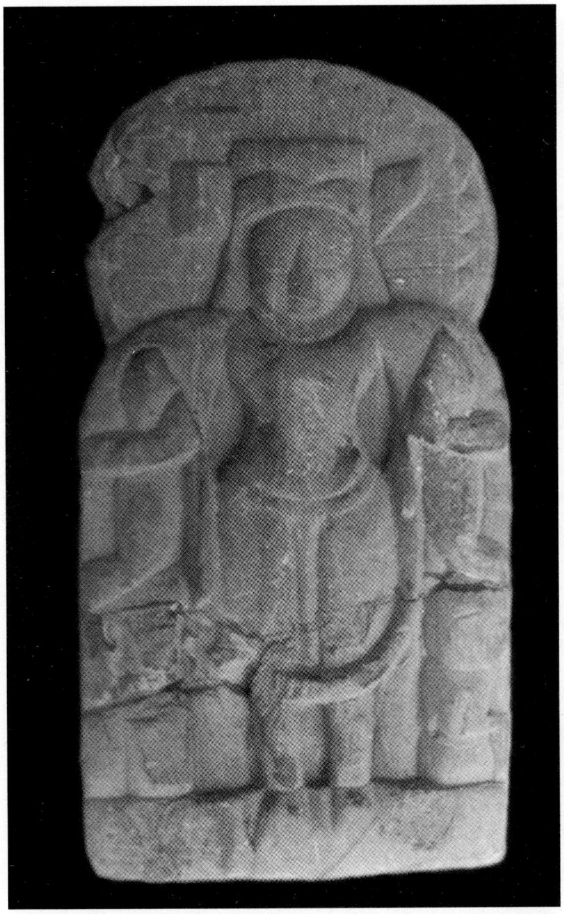

Pl. 80. Vaikuṇṭha plaque, Agroha.

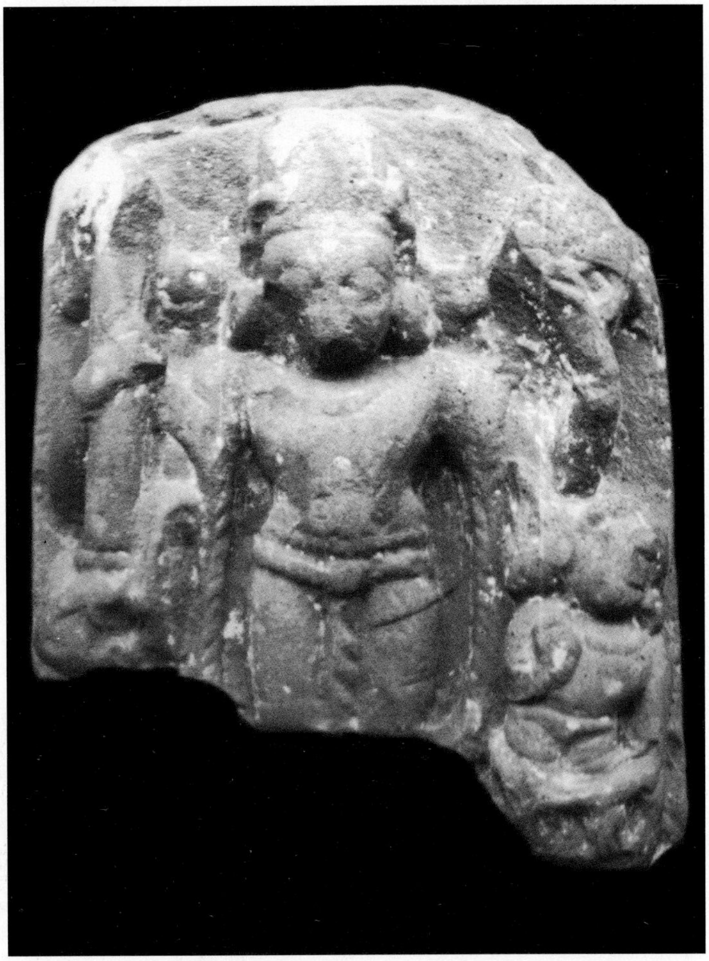

Pl. 82. Vaikuṇṭha, Pinjore.

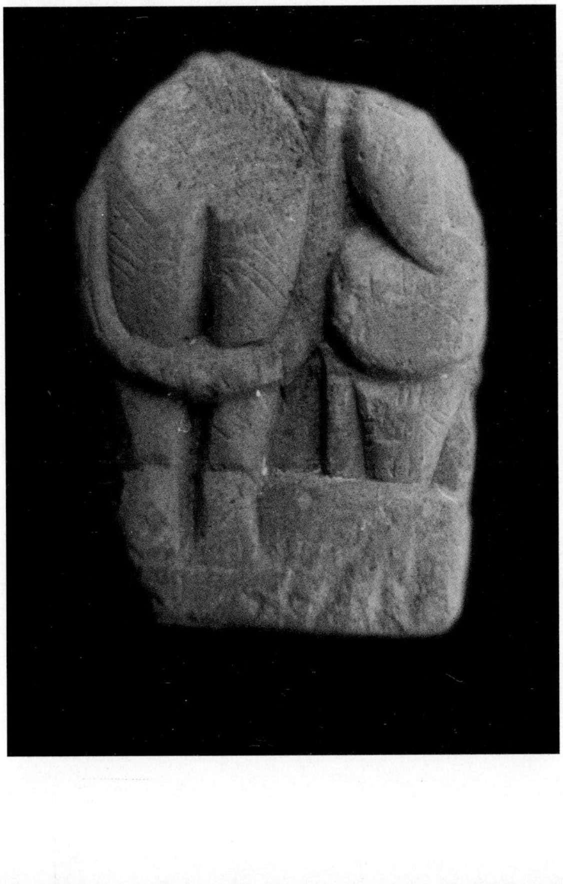

Pl. 81. Vaikuṇṭha plaque, Agroha.

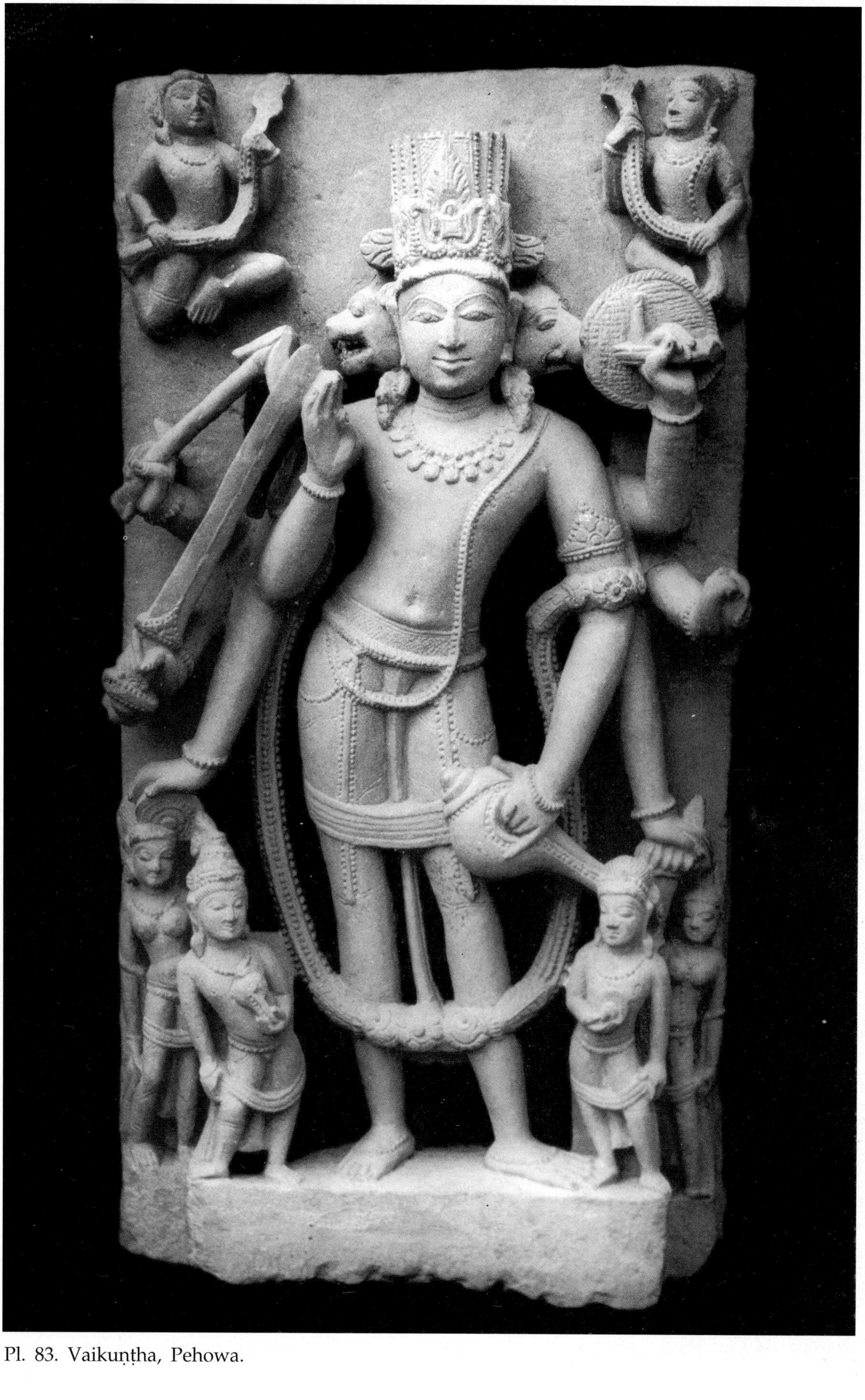

Pl. 83. Vaikuṇṭha, Pehowa.

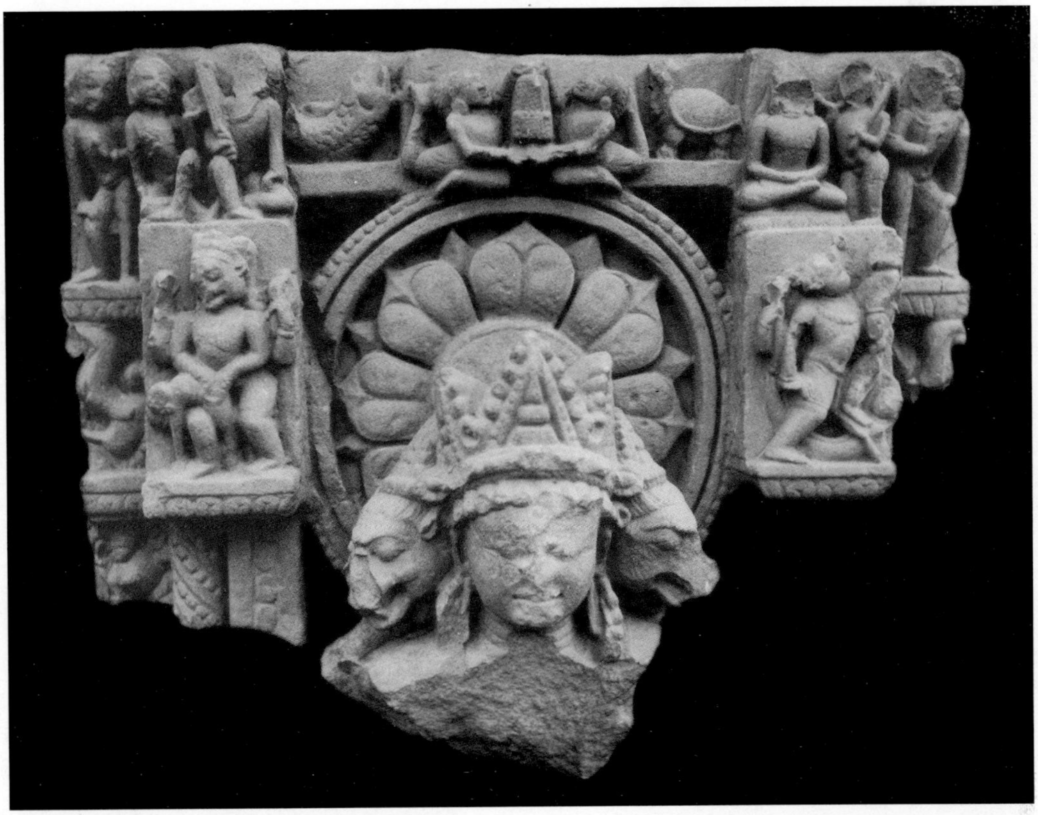

Pl. 84. Vaikuṇṭha, Chandimandir.

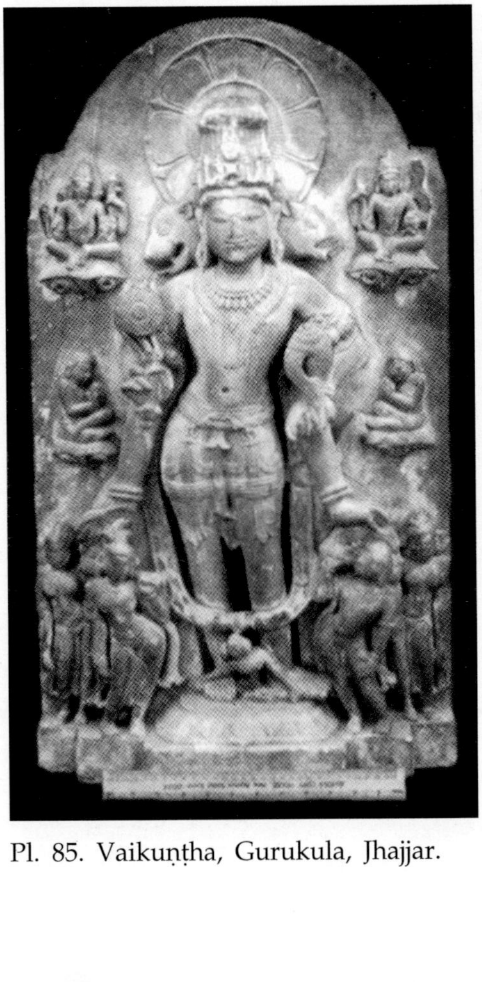

Pl. 85. Vaikuṇṭha, Gurukula, Jhajjar.

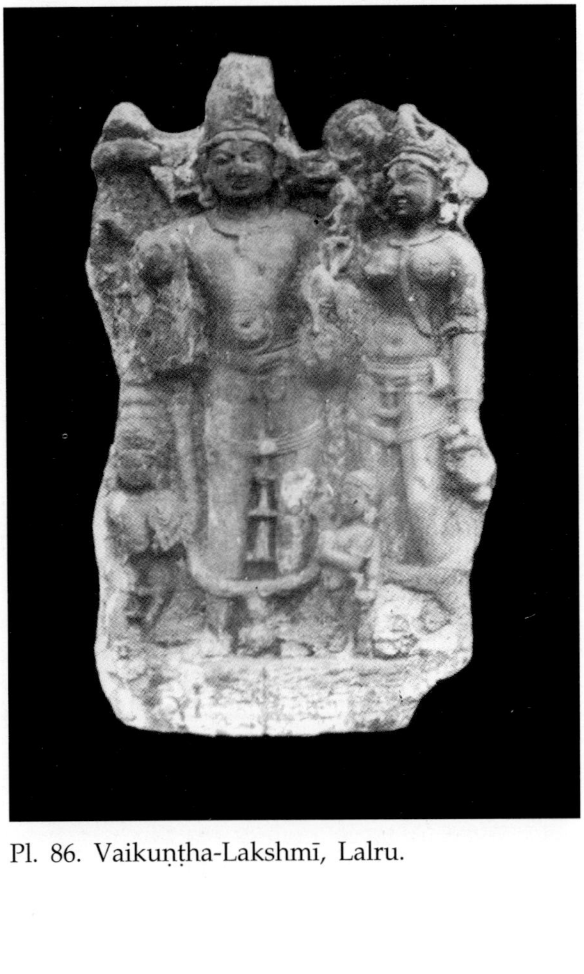

Pl. 86. Vaikuṇṭha-Lakshmī, Lalru.

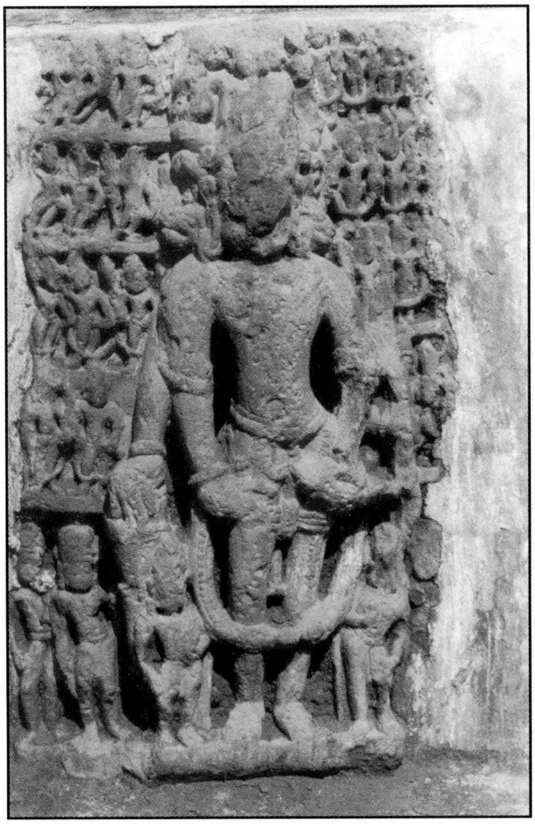

Pl. 87. Vaikuṇṭha-Viśvarūpa, Jasat.

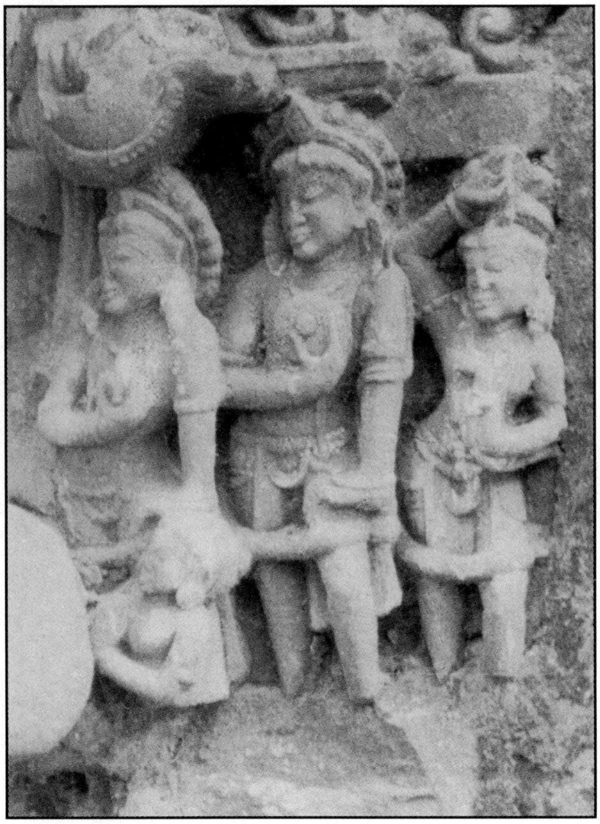

Pl. 88. Vishṇu's pedestal, Pinjore.

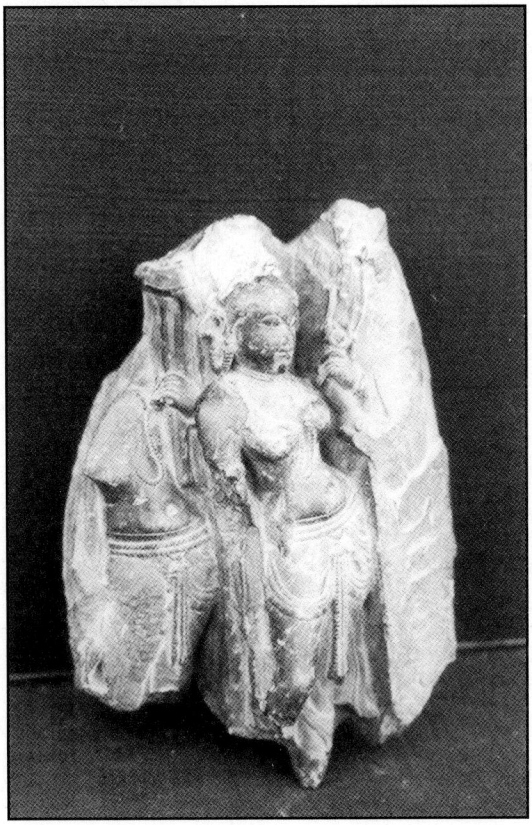

Pl. 89. Vishṇu's pedestal, Sampla.

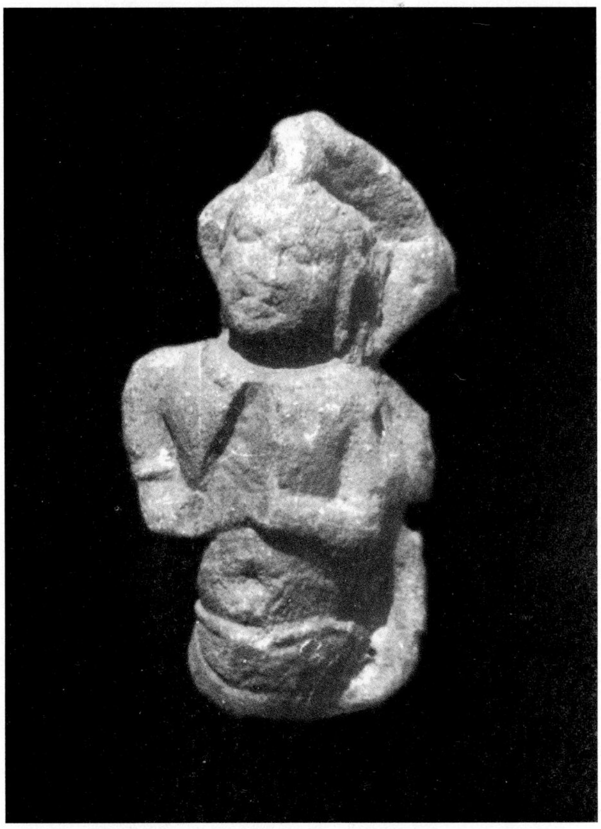

Pl. 90. Garuḍa, Narnaund.

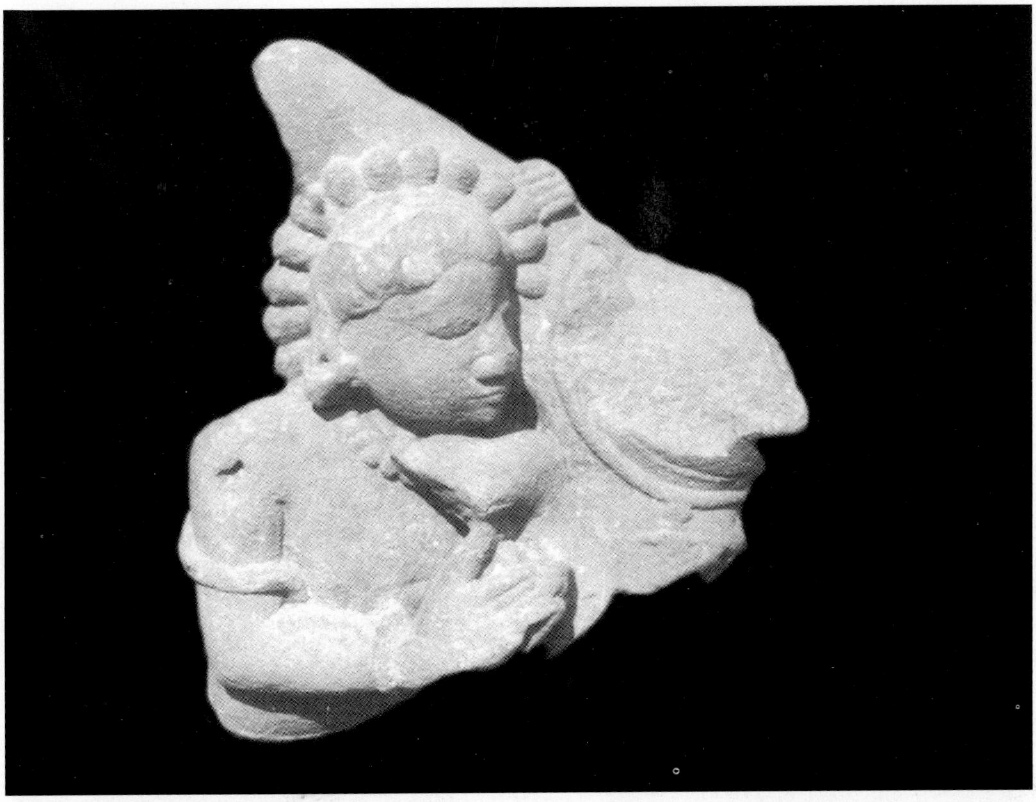
Pl. 91. Garuḍa, Marhanwala.

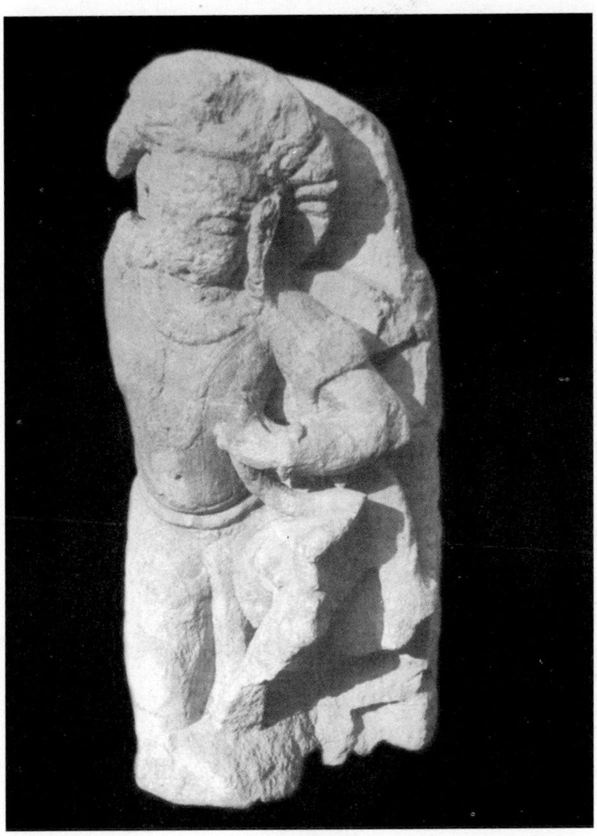
Pl. 92. Garuḍa, Sagwan.

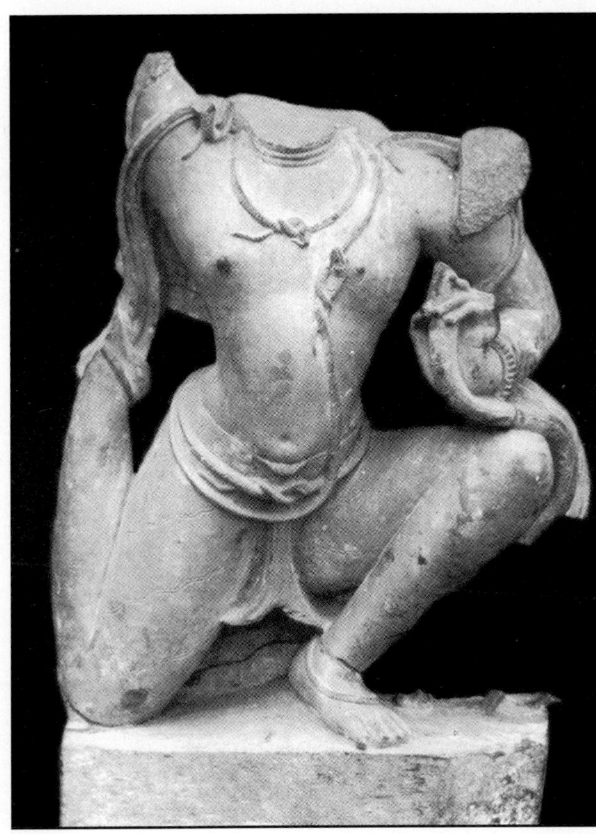
Pl. 93. Garuḍa, Pehowa.

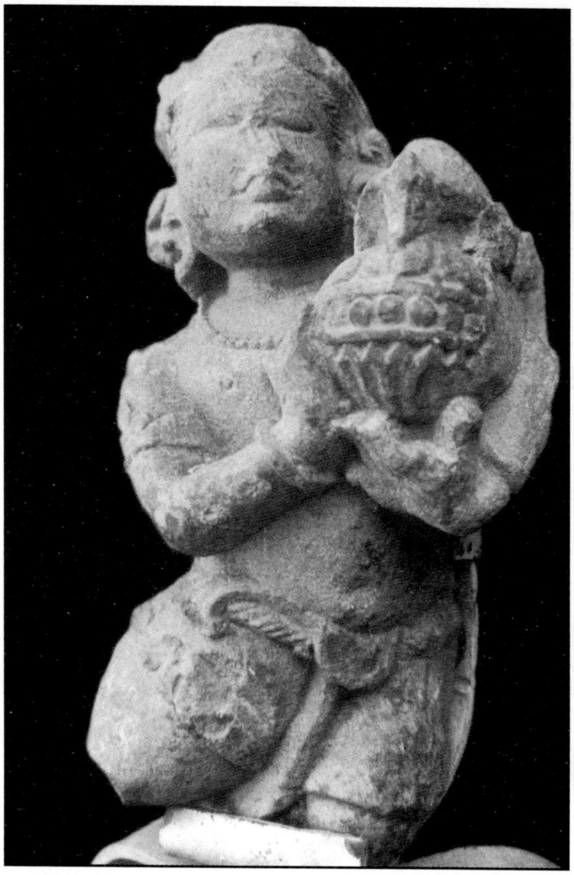

Pl. 94. Garuḍa, Gujjar Khei.

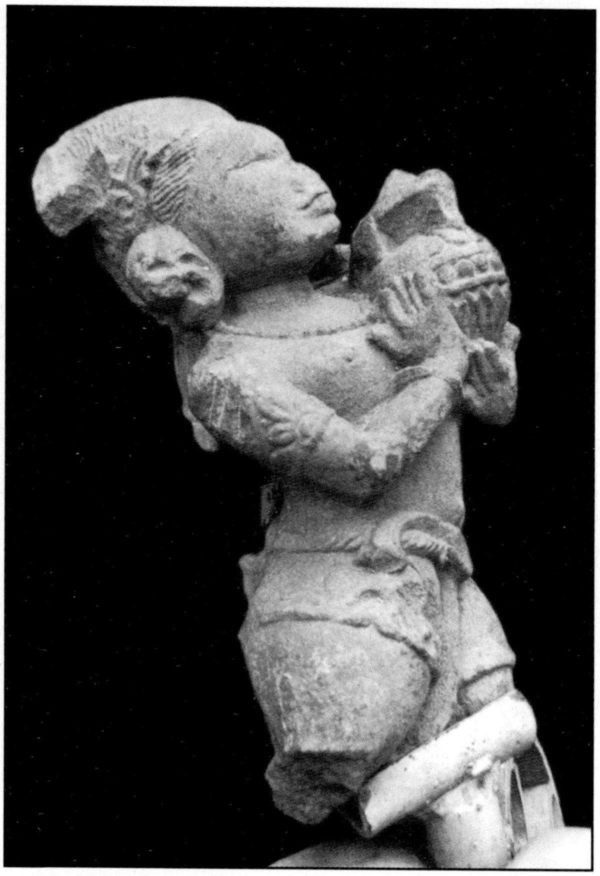

Pl. 95. Garuḍa, Gujjar Kheri (side view).

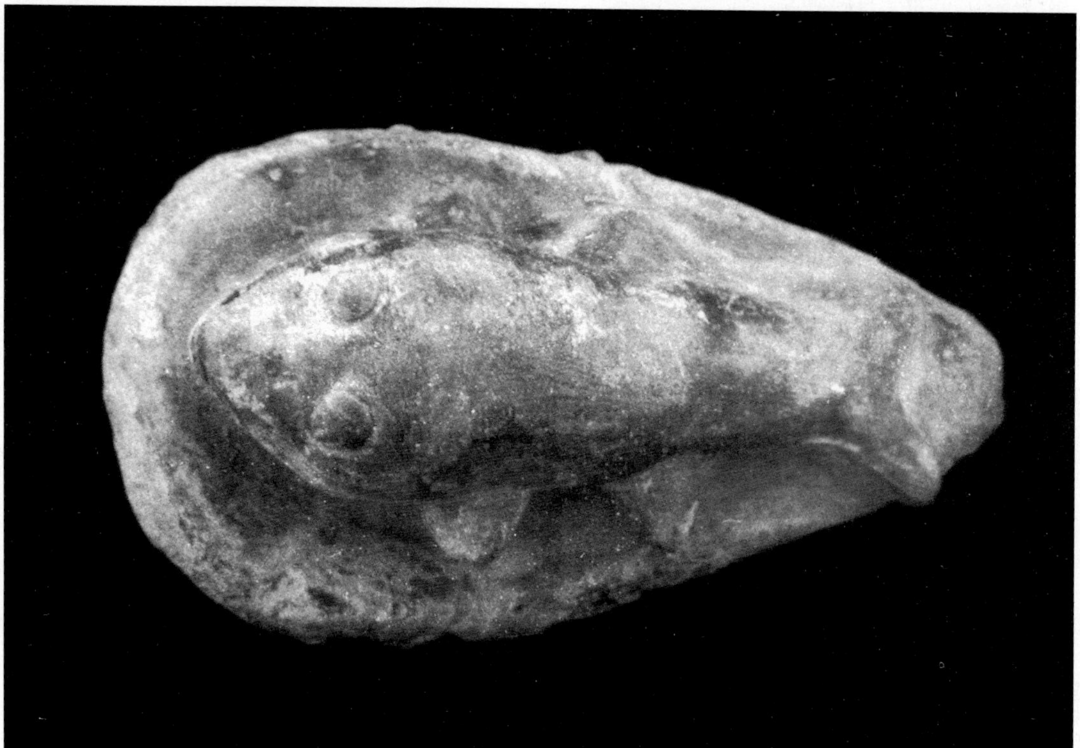

Pl. 96. Fish, terracotta, Thanesar.

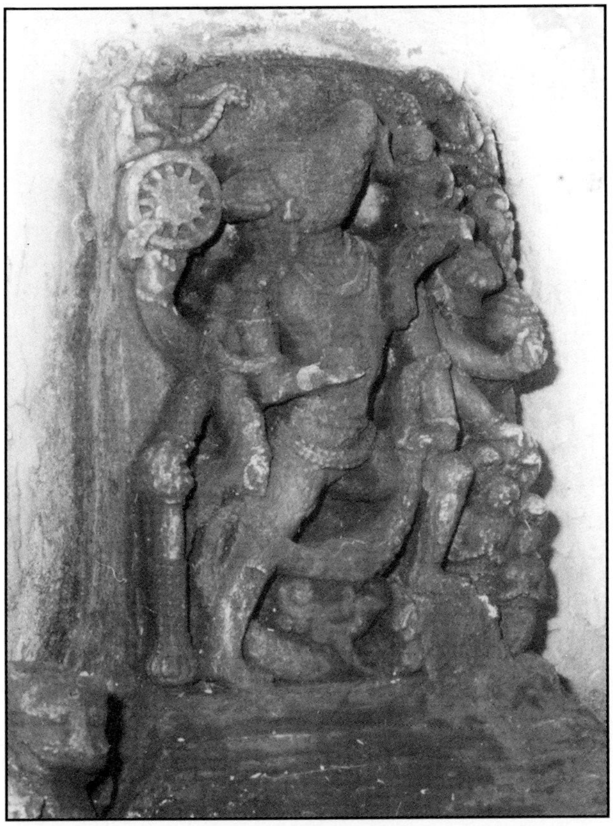

Pl. 97. Nṛi-Varāha, Barah Kalan.

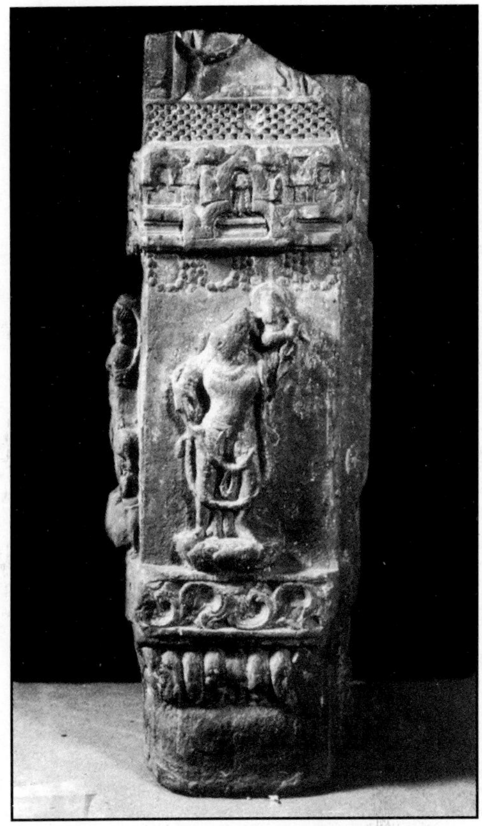

Pl. 98. Nṛi-Varāha on a doorframe, Pinjore.

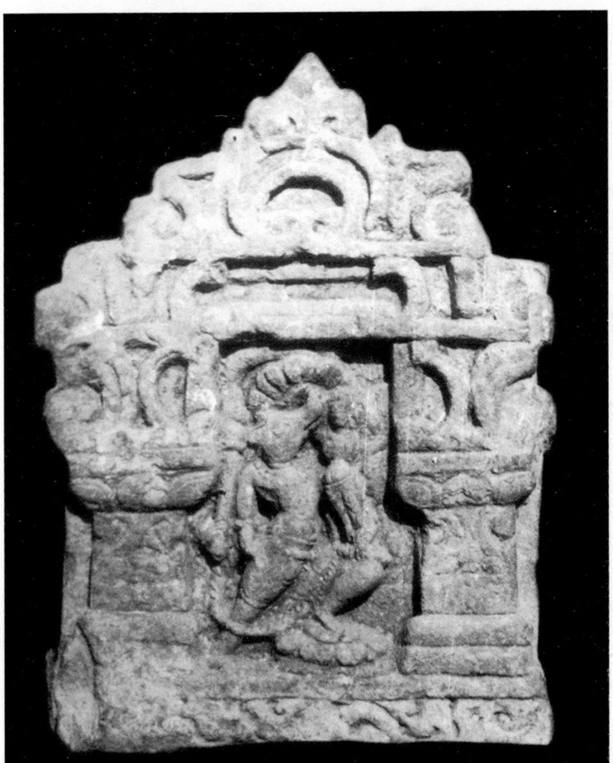

Pl. 99. Nṛi-Varāha, Kurukshetra.

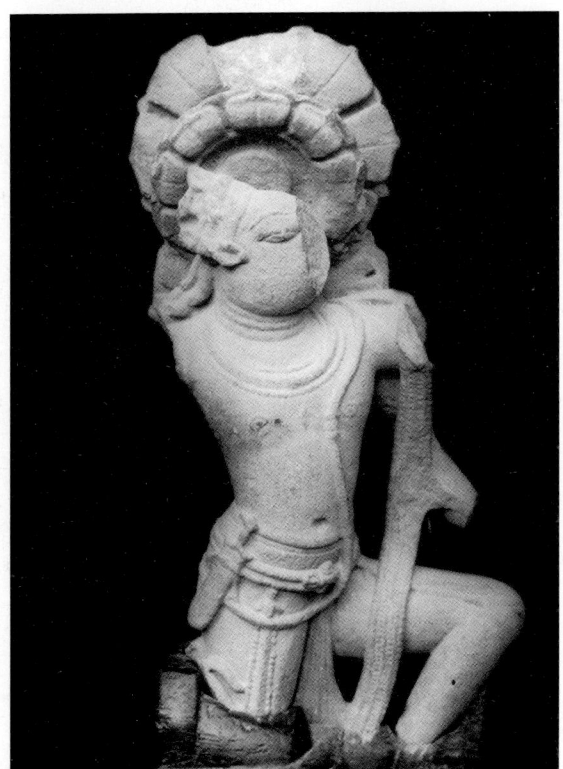

Pl. 100. Nṛi-Varāha, Pinjore.

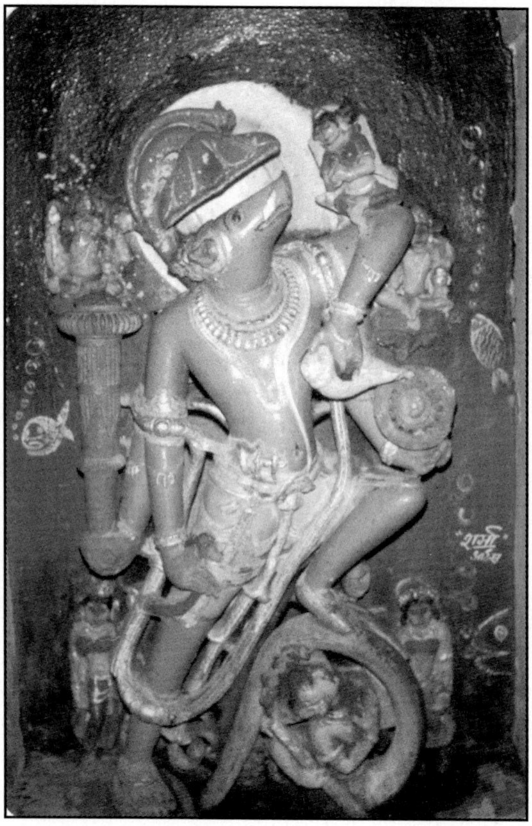

Pl. 101. Nṛi-Varāha, Gokarṇa kā Tālāb, Rohtak.

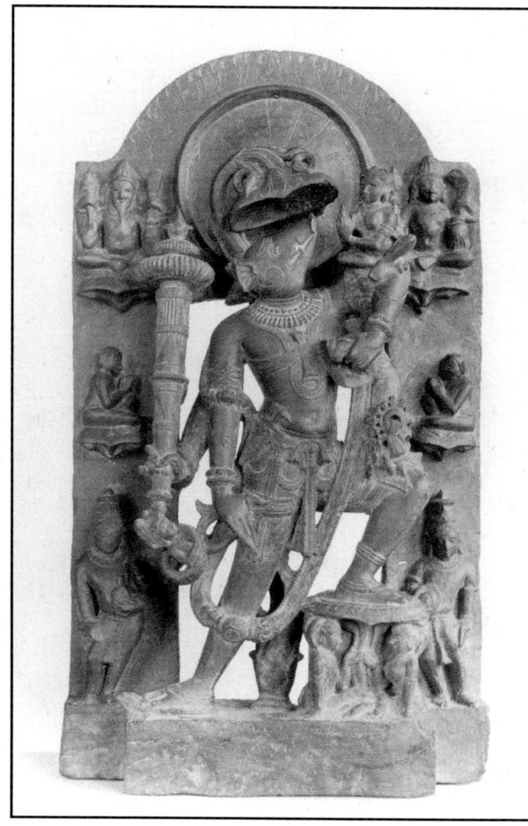

Pl. 103. Nṛi-Varāha, Fatehabad.

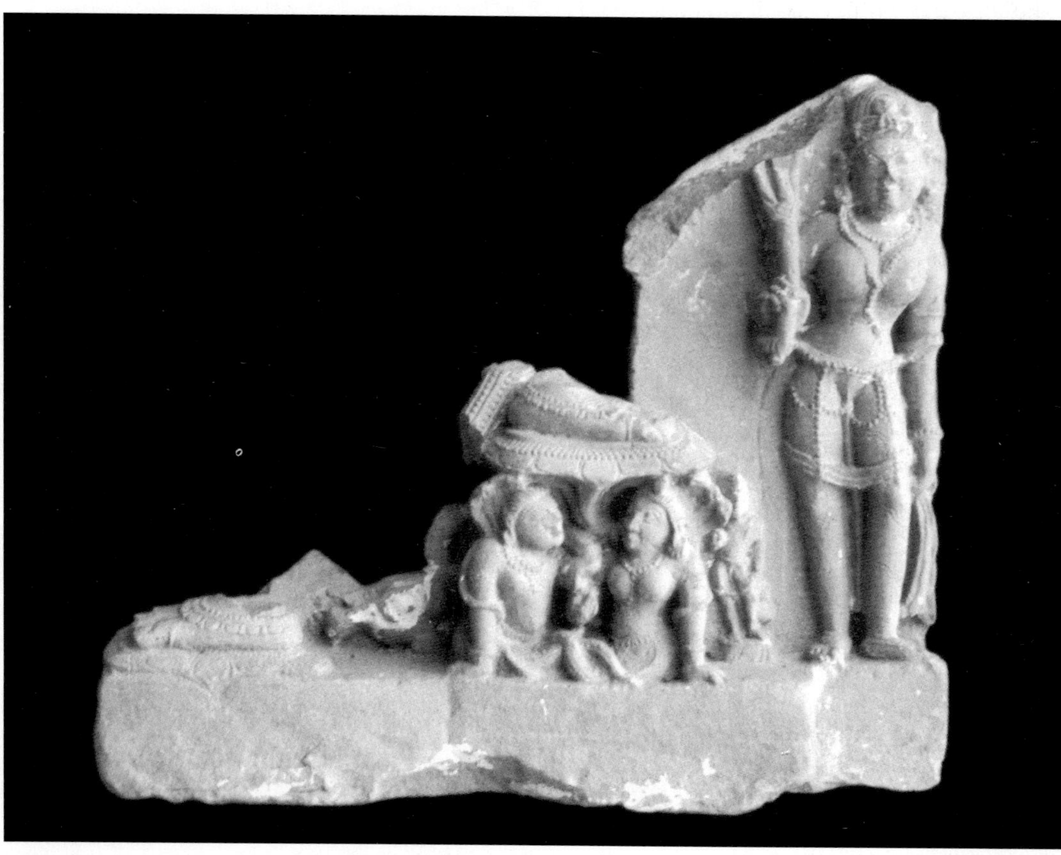

Pl. 102. Nṛi-Varāha, Asthal Bohr, Rohtak.

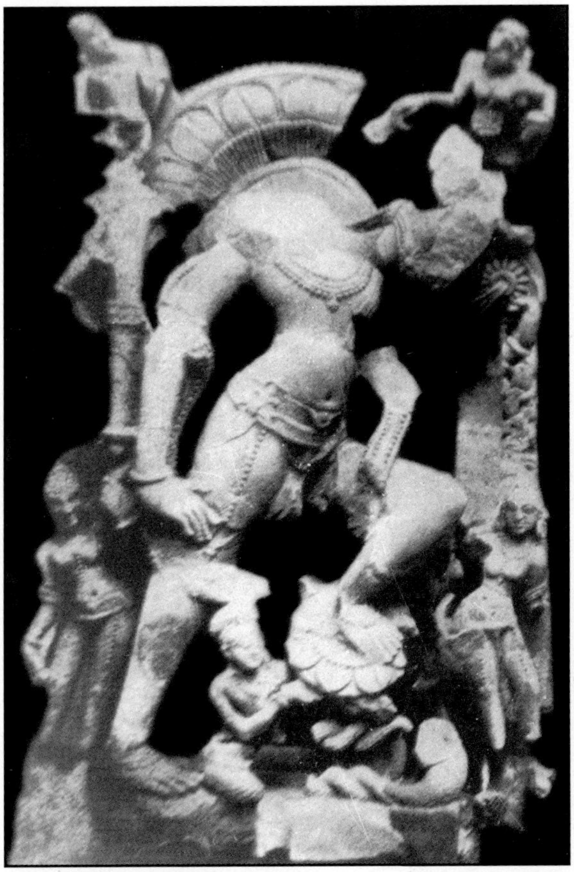

Pl. 104. Nṛi-Varāha, Agroha.

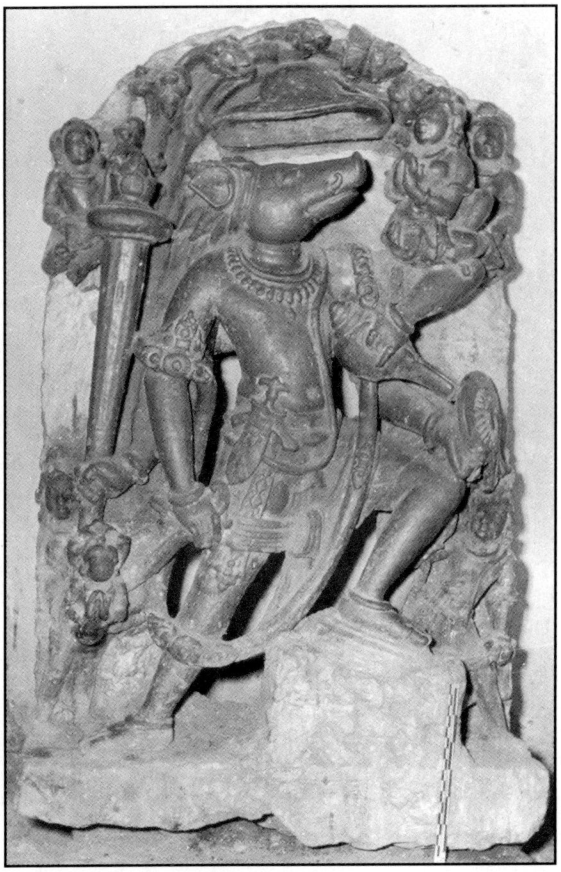

Pl. 105. Nṛi-Varāha, Hansi.

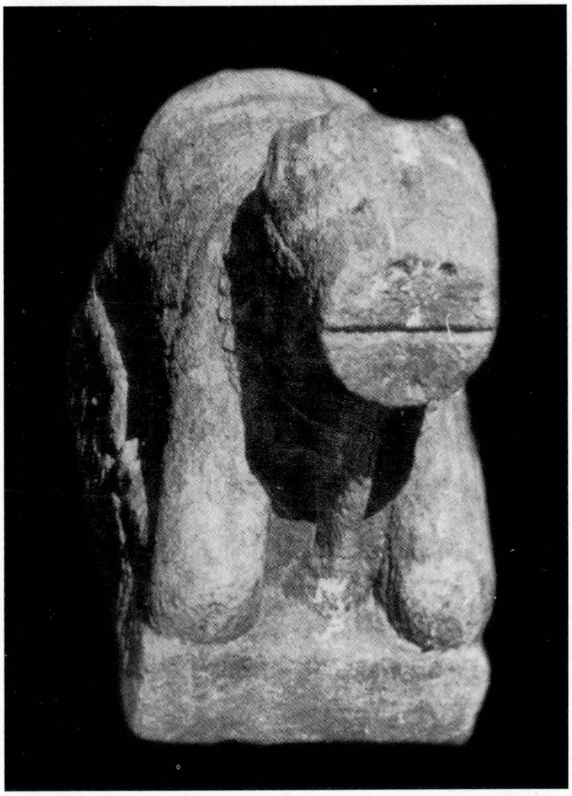

Pl. 106. Zoomorphic Varāha, Southern Haryana.

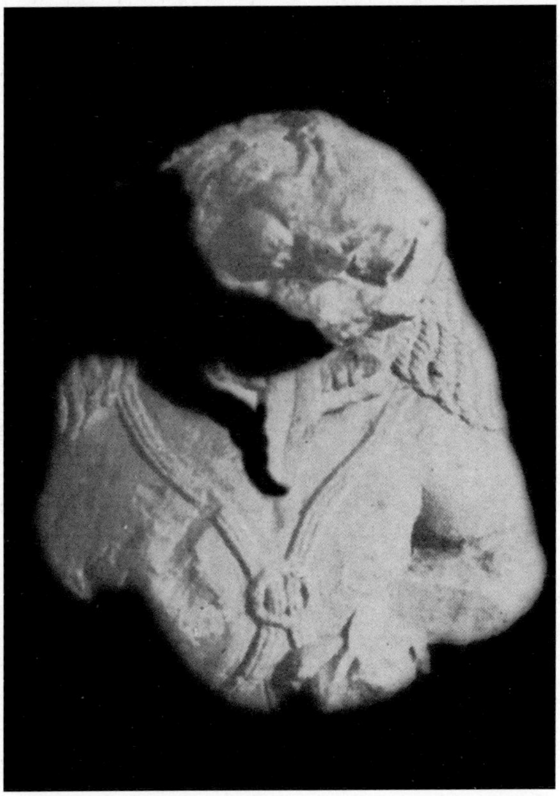

Pl. 107. Nṛisiṃha, Sirsa.

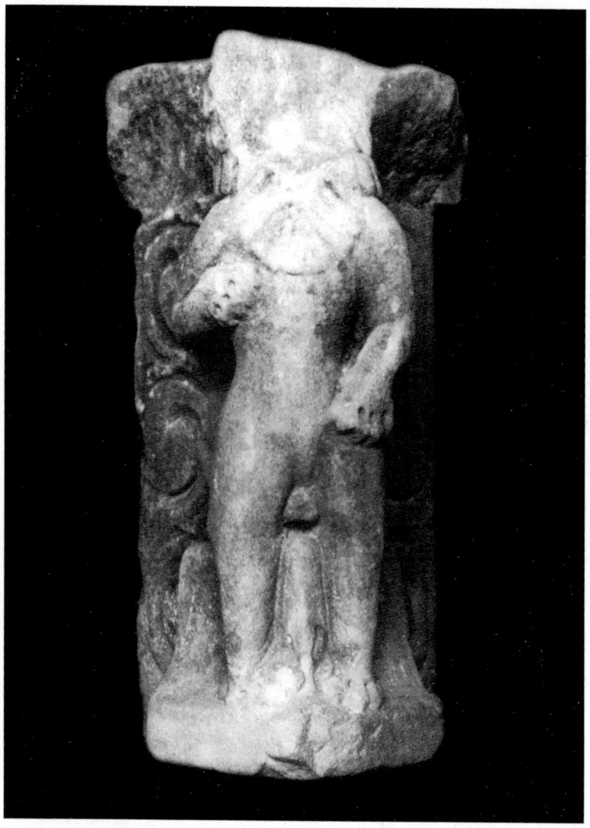

Pl. 108. Nṛisiṃha, Morni-ka-Tal.

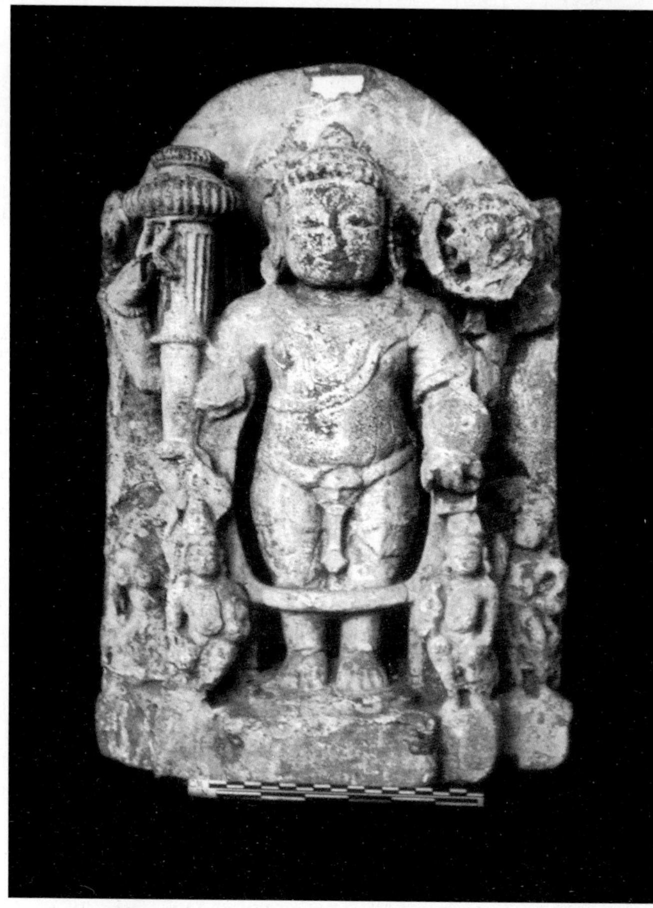

Pl. 111. Vāmana, Mohanbari.

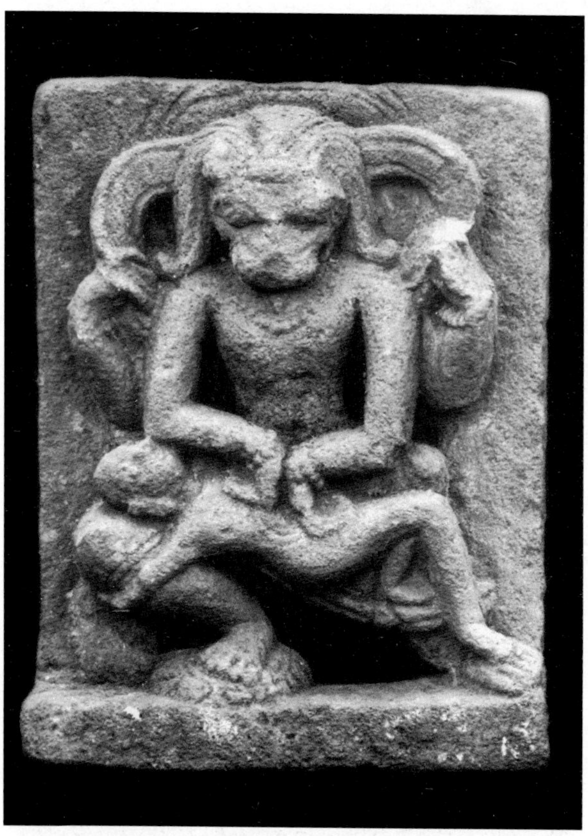

Pl. 109. Nṛisiṃha, Hansi.

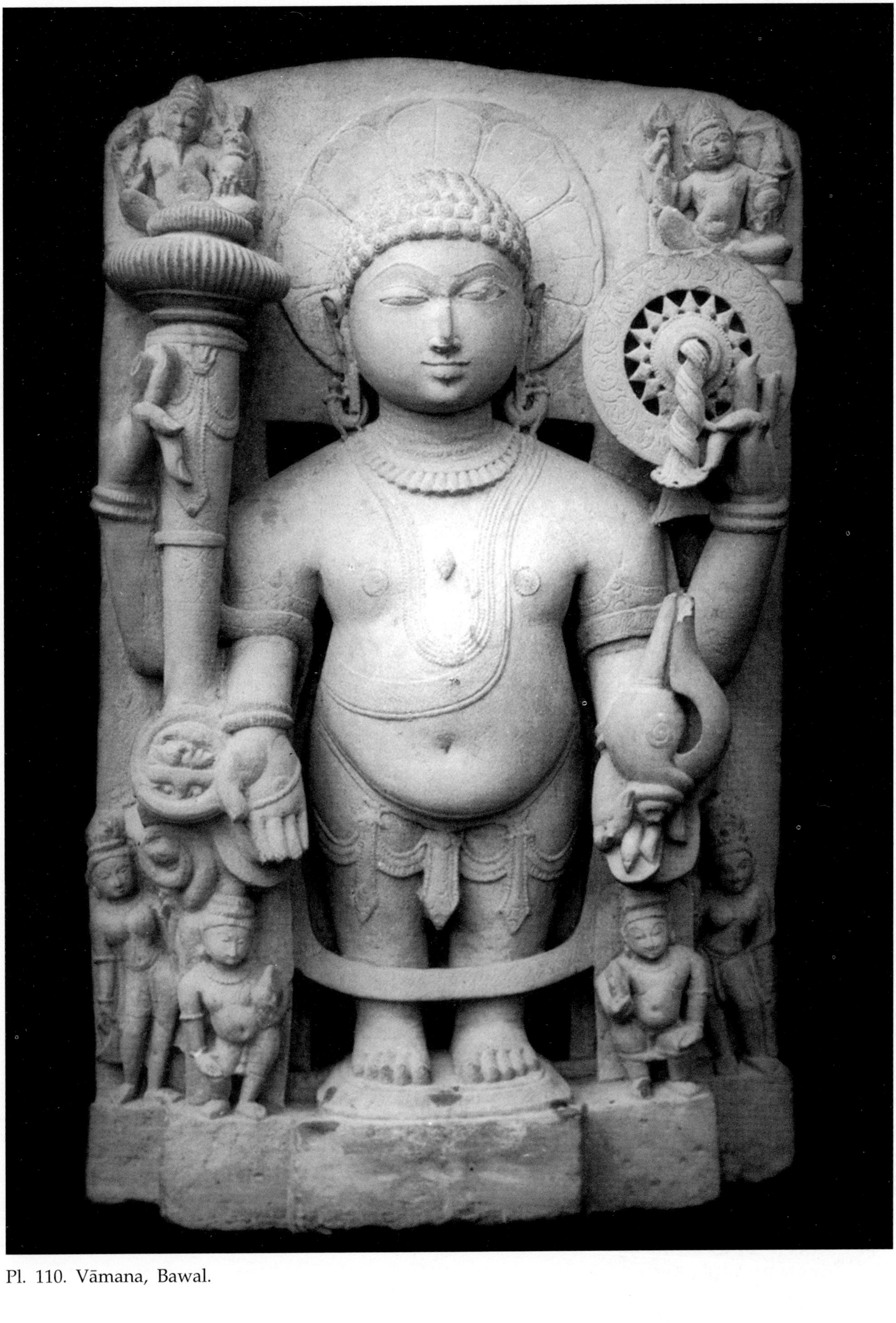

Pl. 110. Vāmana, Bawal.

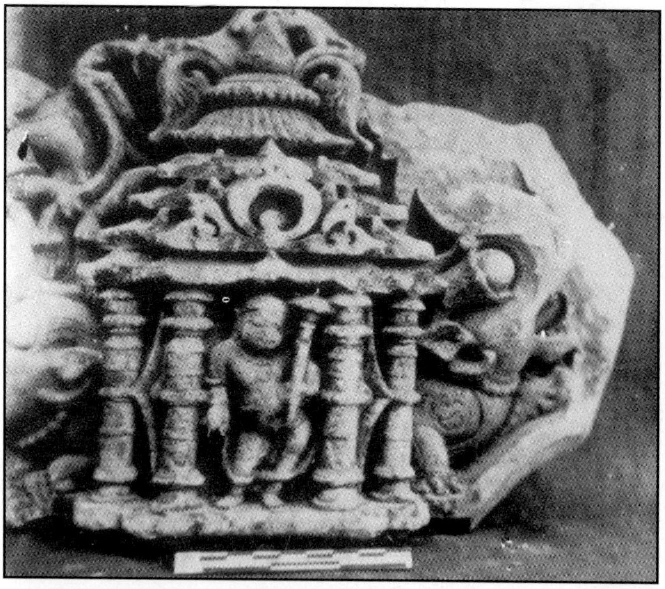

Pl. 112. Vāmana on an architectural piece, Gurukula, Jhajjar.

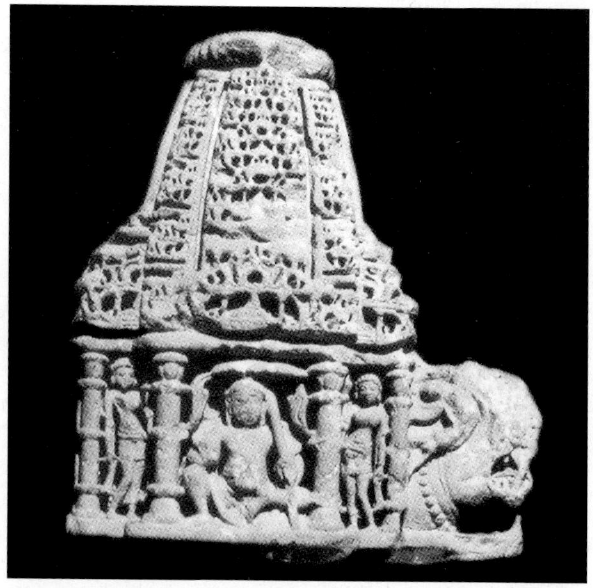

Pl. 113. Vāmana on a *nāgarakūṭa*, Hisar.

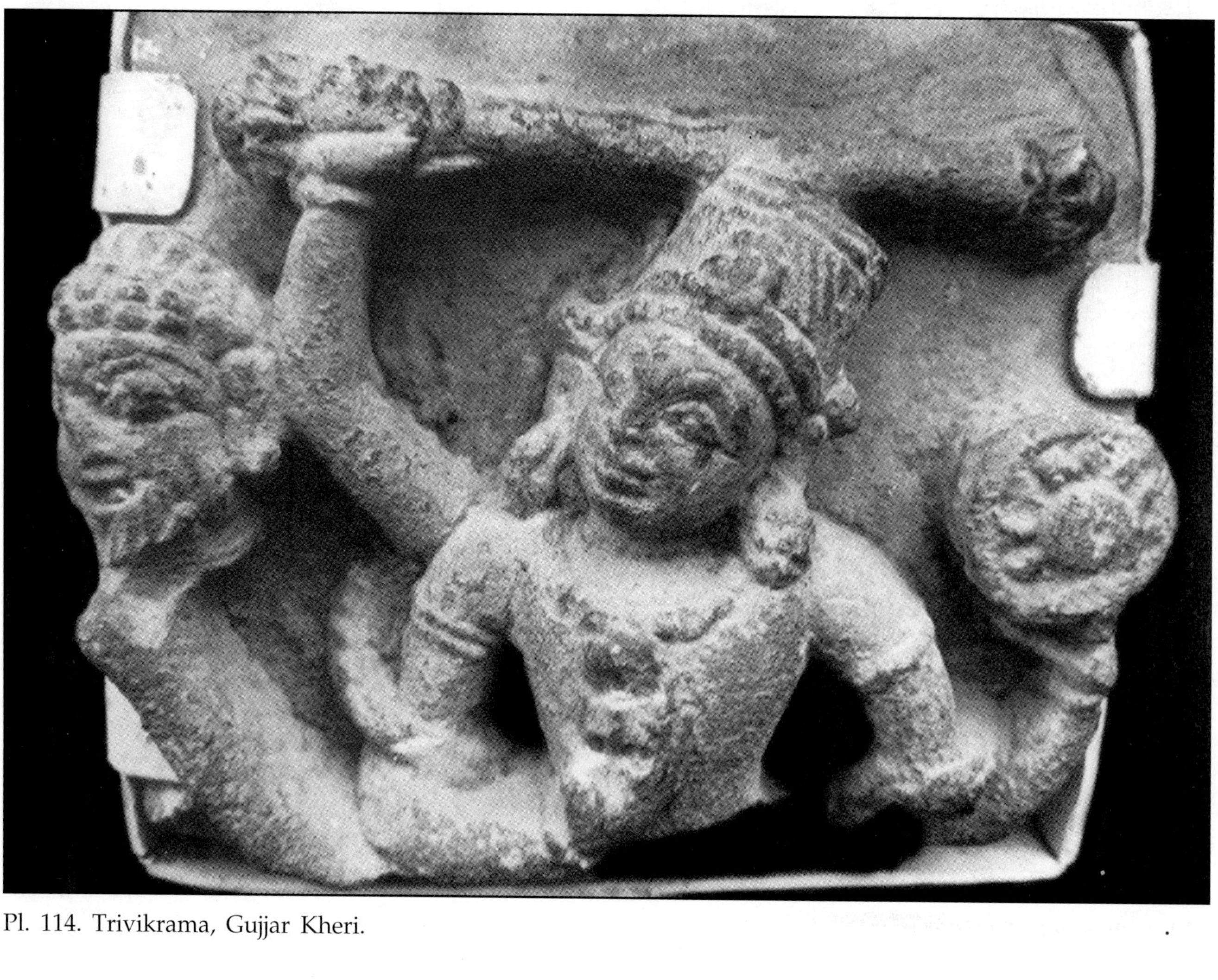

Pl. 114. Trivikrama, Gujjar Kheri.

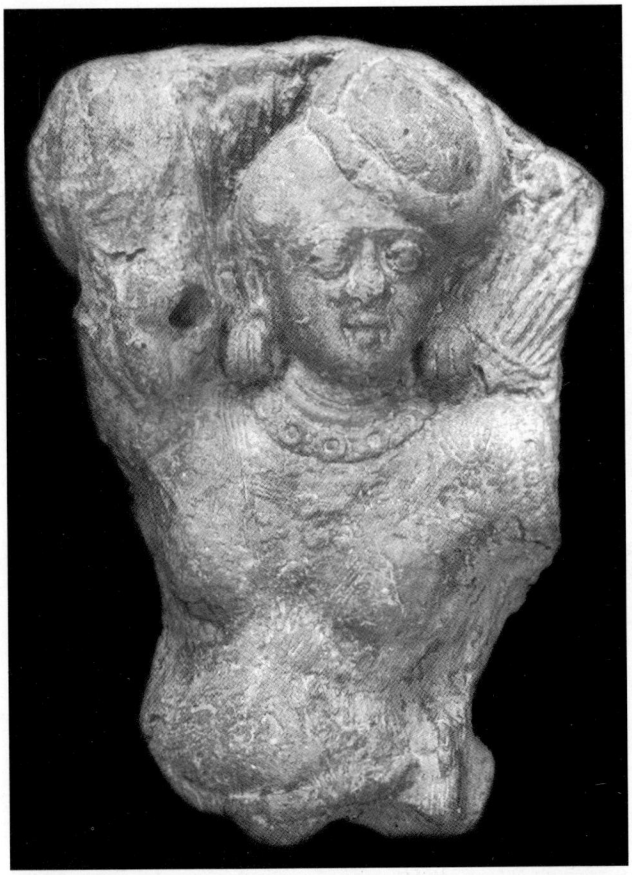

Pl. 115. Rāma, terracotta, Sugh.

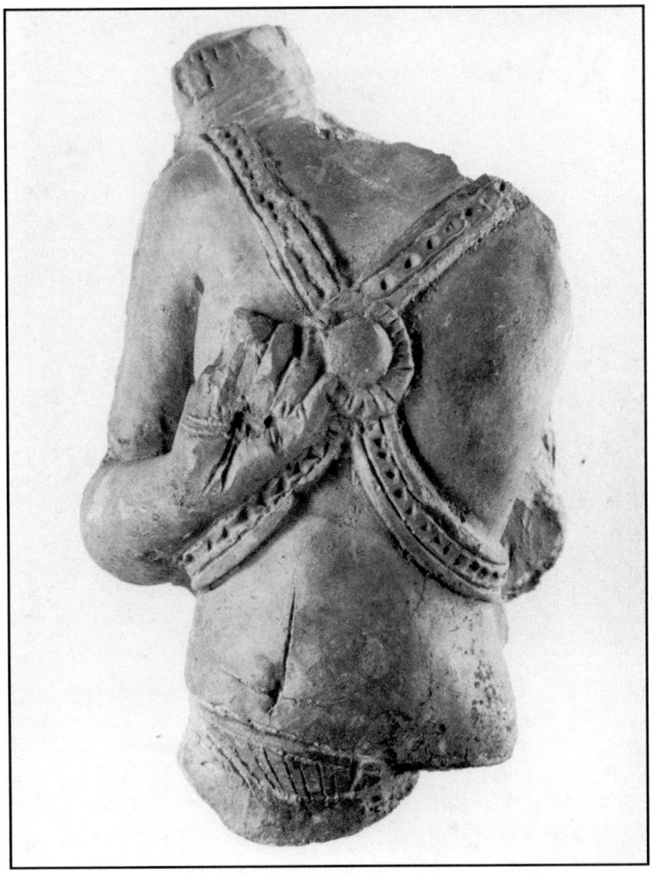

Pl. 116. Rāma, terracotta, Sandhaya.

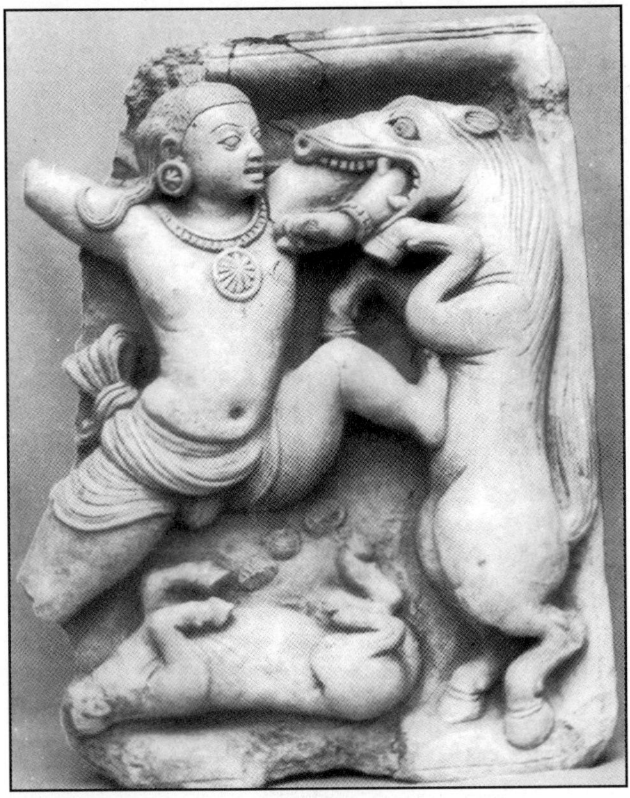

Pl. 117. Fight between Rāma and demon Makarāksha, Sandhaya.

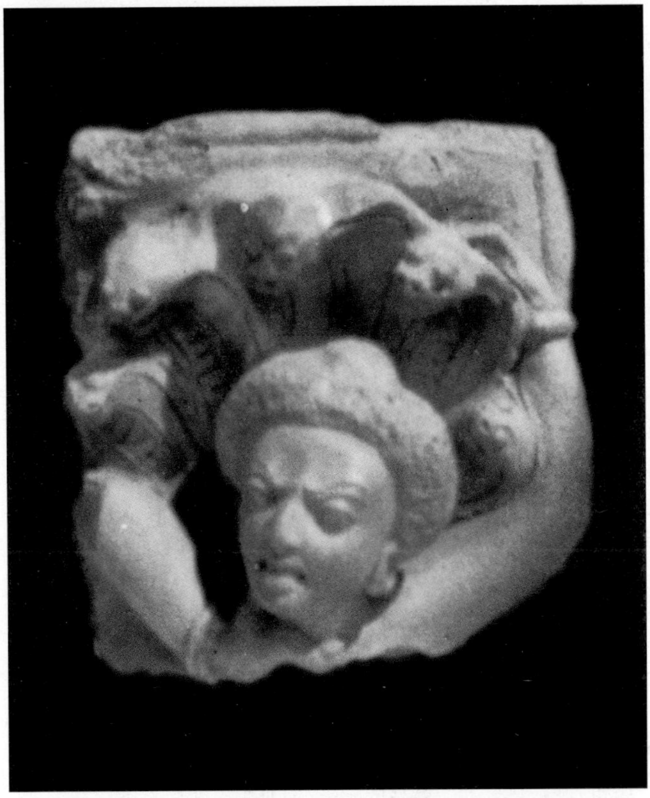

Pl. 118. Rāma fettered in *nāga-pāśa*, Sandhaya.

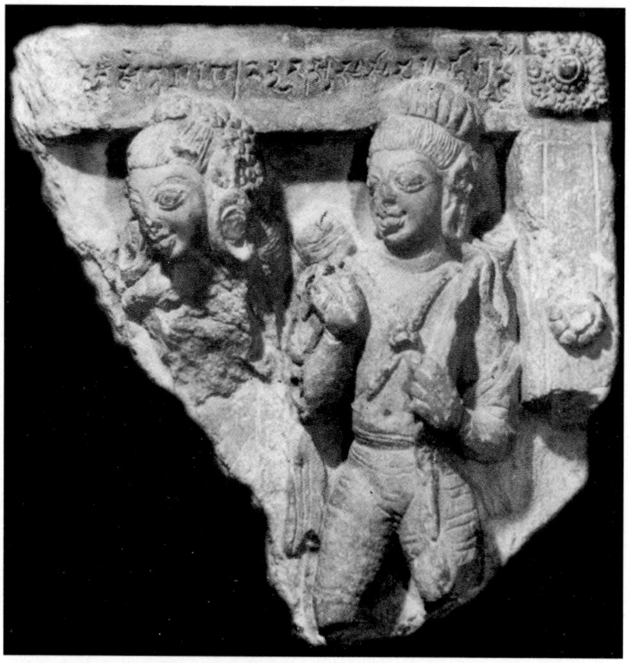

Pl. 119. Rāma, Lakshmaṇa and Sītā going to Pañchavaṭī, Nachar Khera.

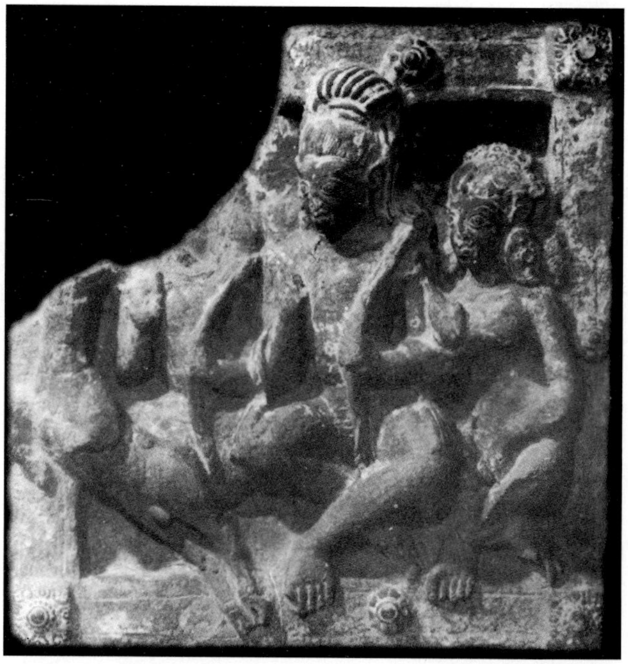

Pl. 120. The golden deer near Pañchavaṭī, Nachar Khera.

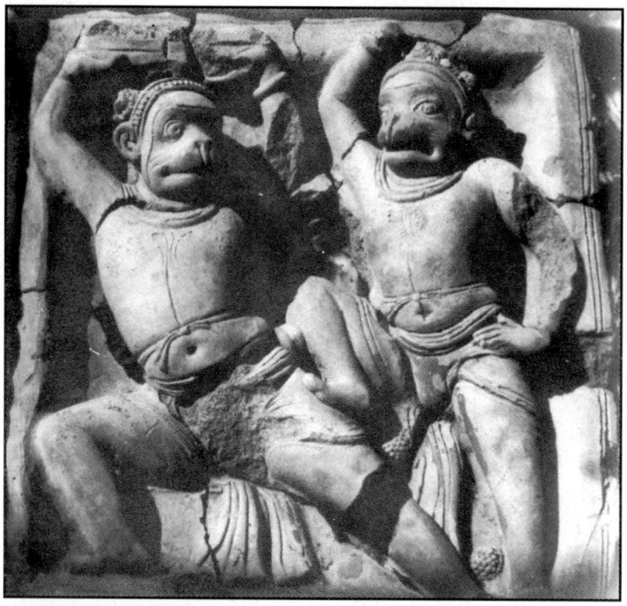

Pl. 121. Bālī-Sugrīva duel, Jind.

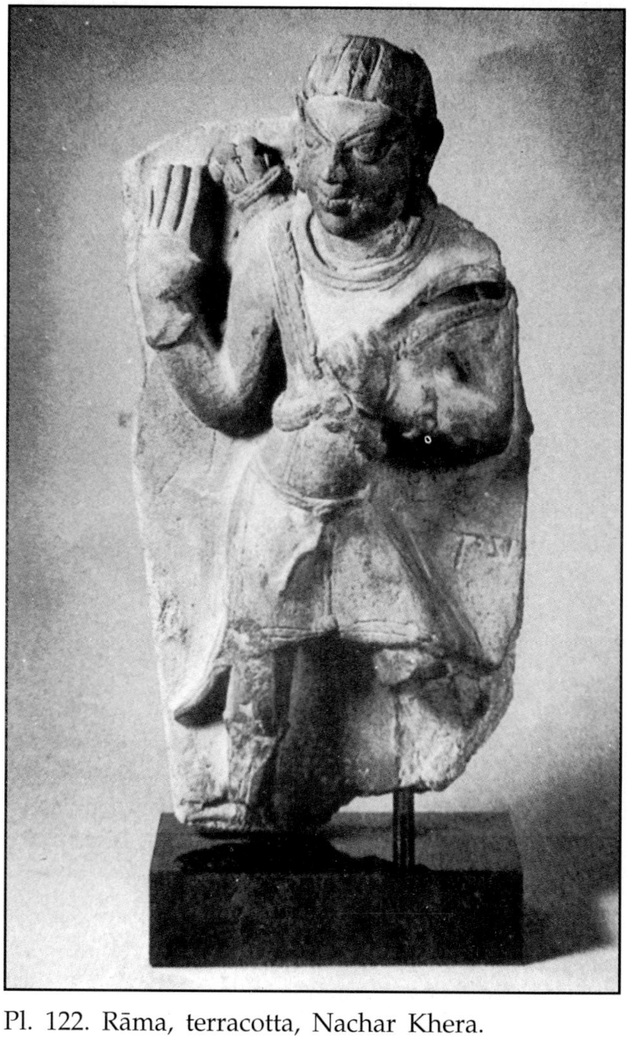

Pl. 122. Rāma, terracotta, Nachar Khera.

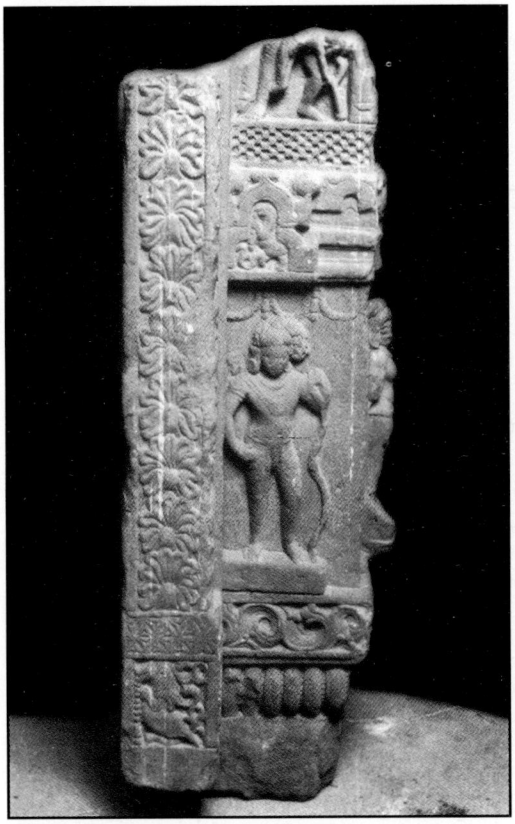

Pl. 123. Rāma on a doorframe, Pinjore.

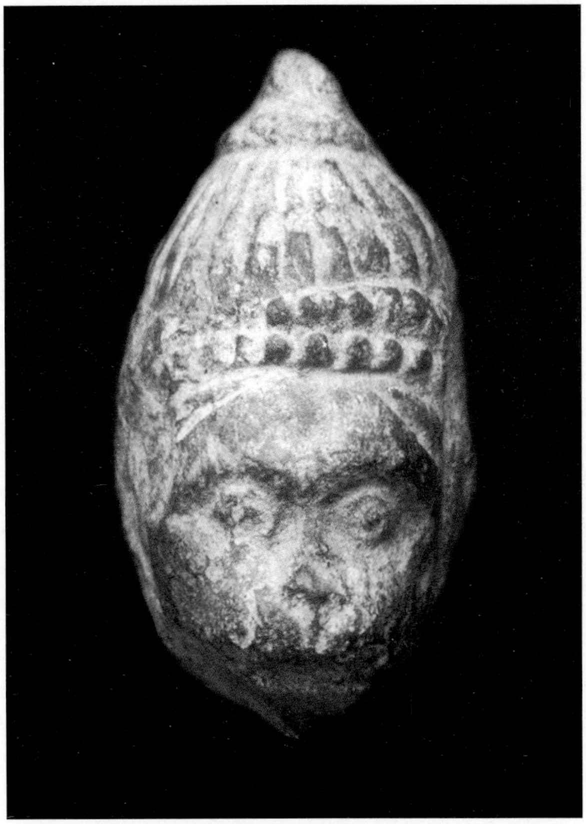

Pl. 124. Hanumān, terracotta, Sugh.

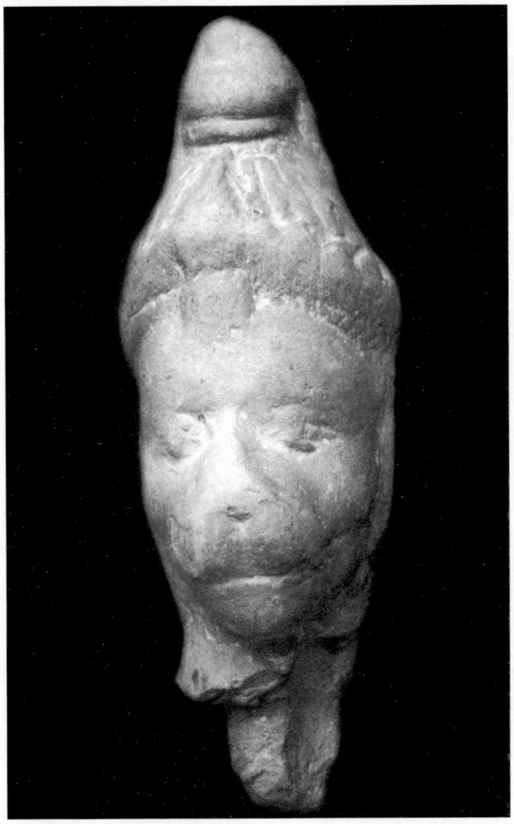

Pl. 125. Hanumān, terracotta, Sugh.

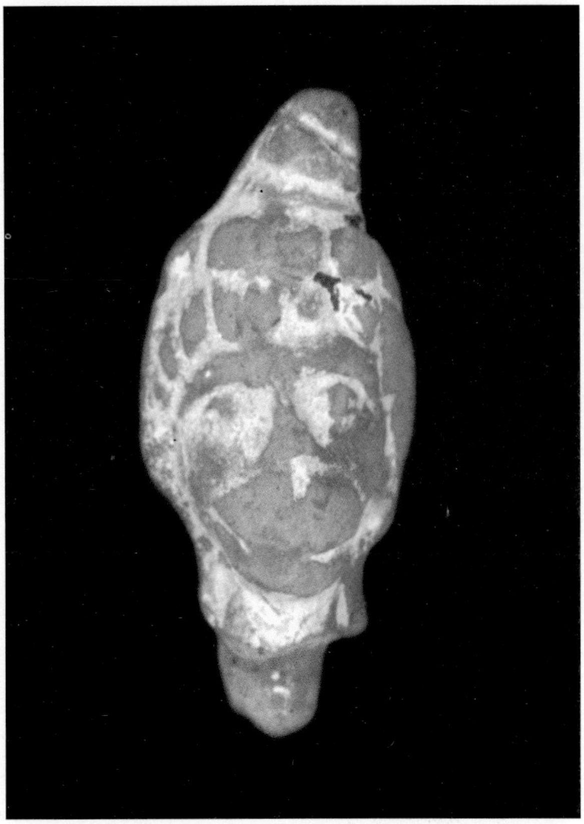

Pl. 126. Hanumān, terracotta, Thānesar.

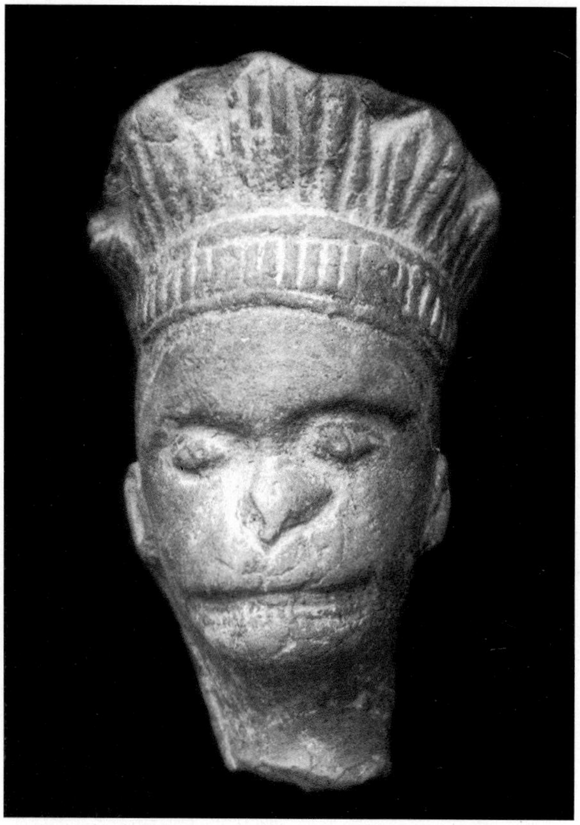

Pl. 127. Hanumān, terracotta, Sugh.

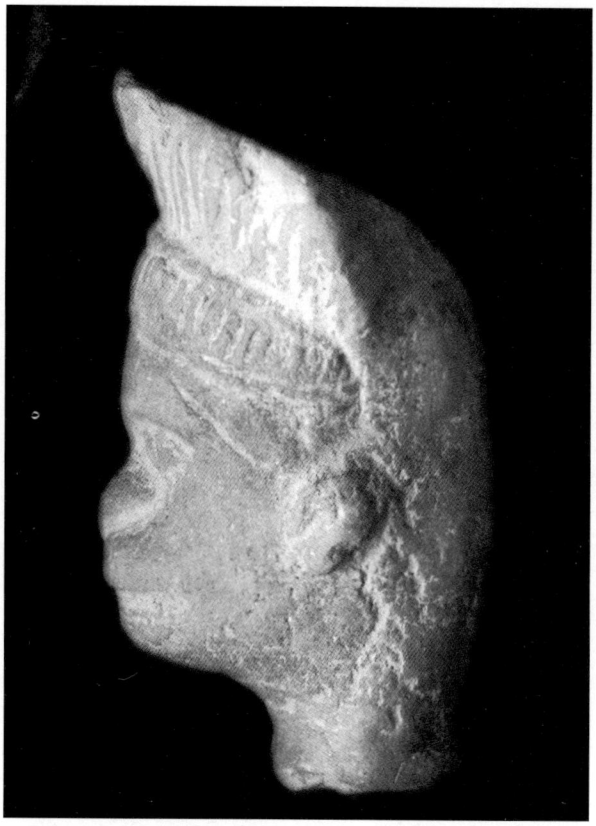

Pl. 128. Hanumān, terracotta, Sugh (another view).

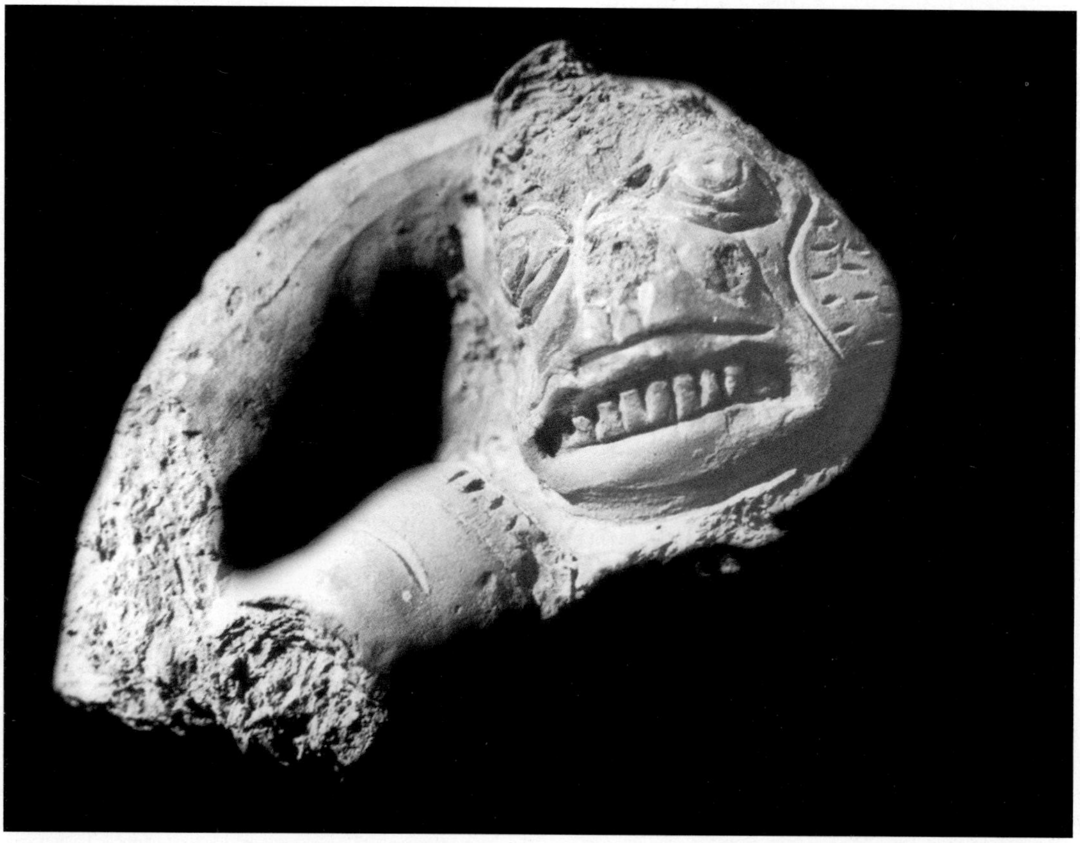

Pl. 129. Demon, terracotta brick, Agroha.

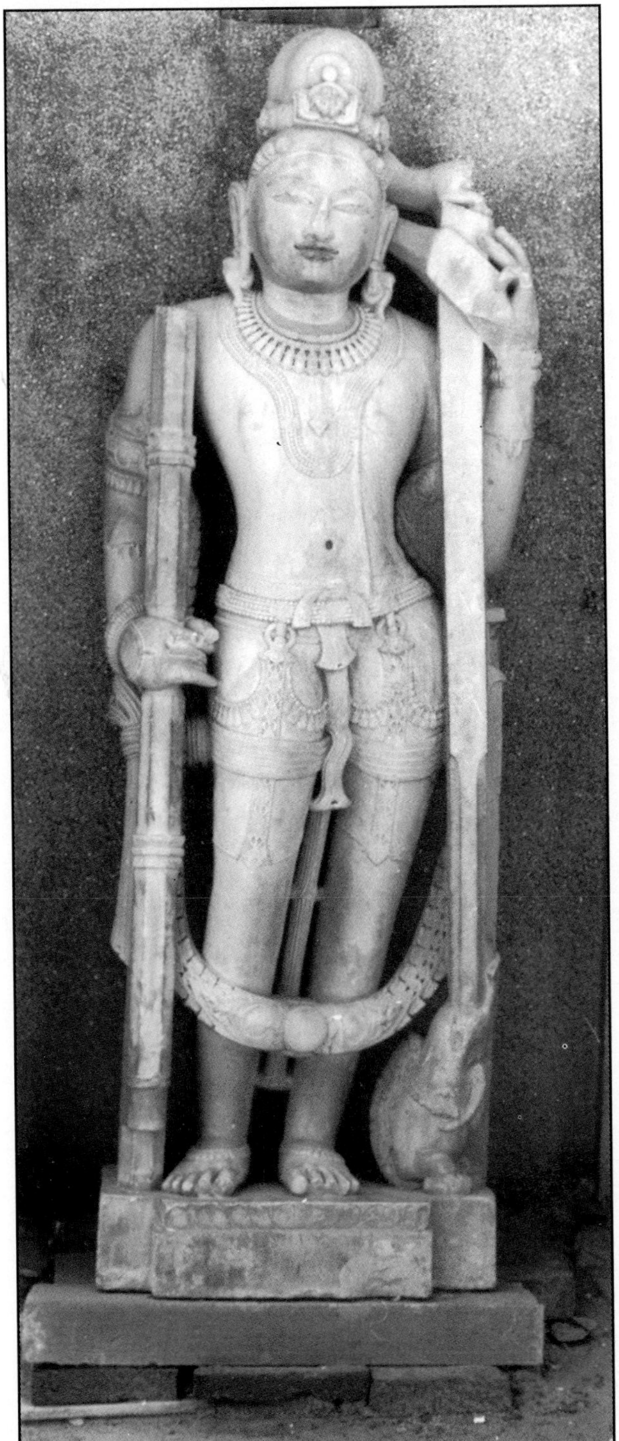

Pl. 130. Balarāma, Asthal Bohr, Rohtak.

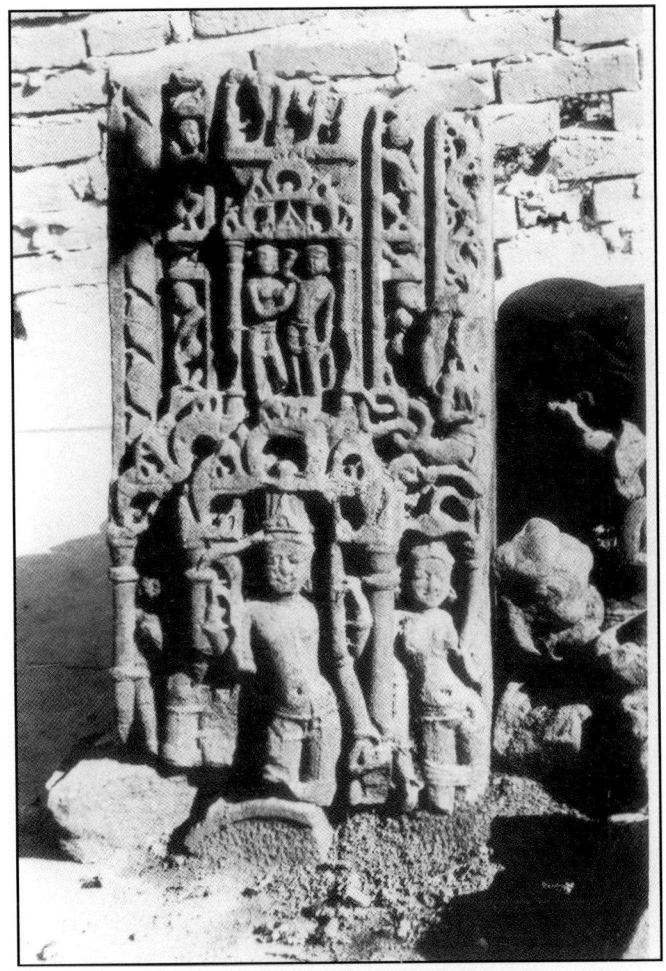

Pl. 132. Balarāma on a doorframe, Ratpur.

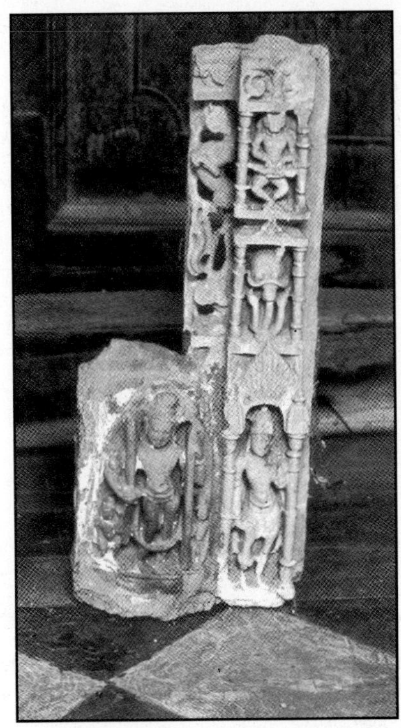

Pl. 131. Balarāma on a detached frieze, Asthal Bohr, Rohtak.

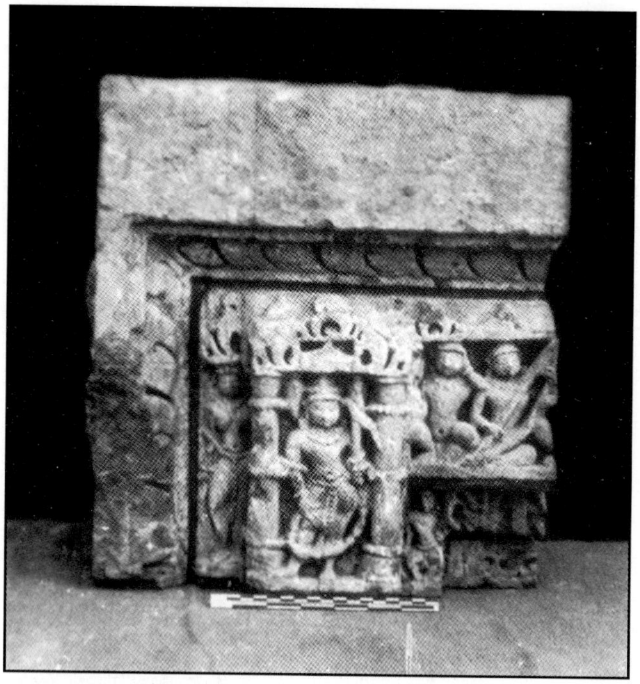

Pl. 133. Balarāma, Hat.

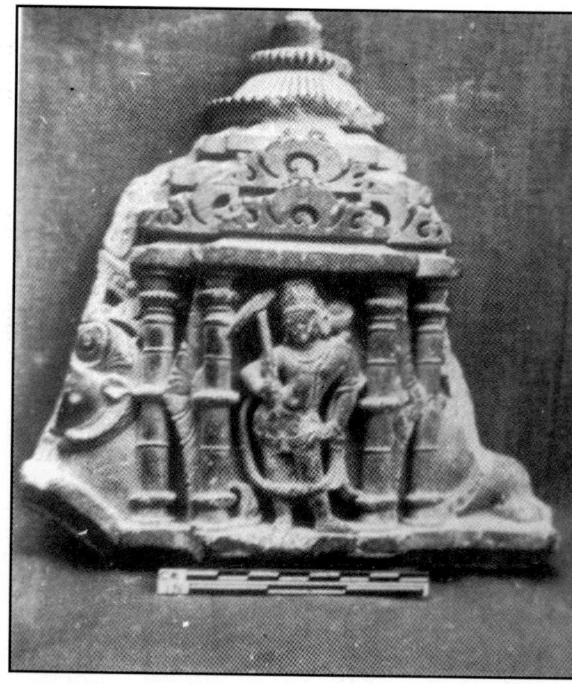

Pl. 134. Balarāma on an architectural piece, Gurukula, Jhajjar.

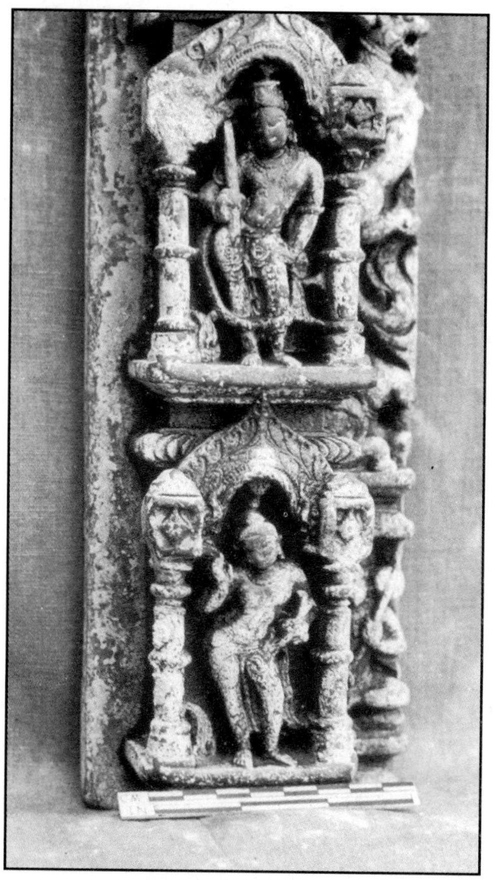

Pl. 135. Balarāma on a doorjamb, Lulodh.

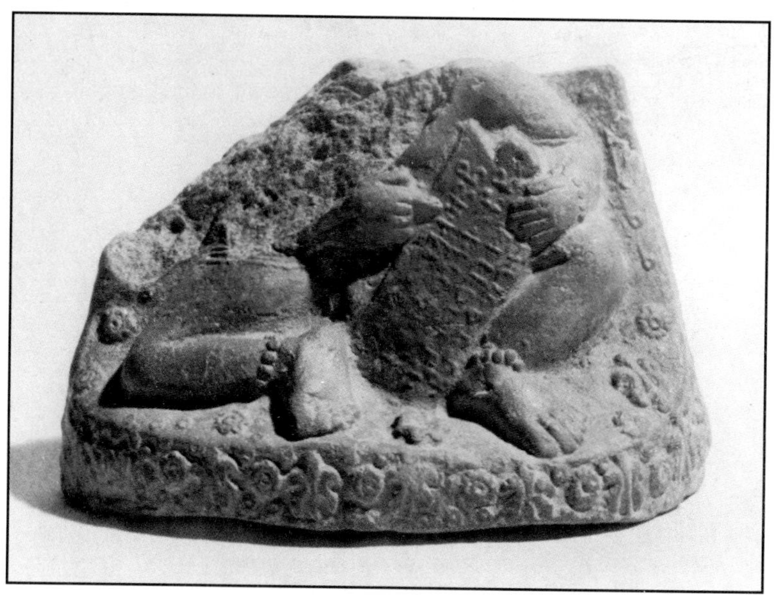

Pl. 136. Kṛishṇa learning the alphabets, terracotta, Sugh.

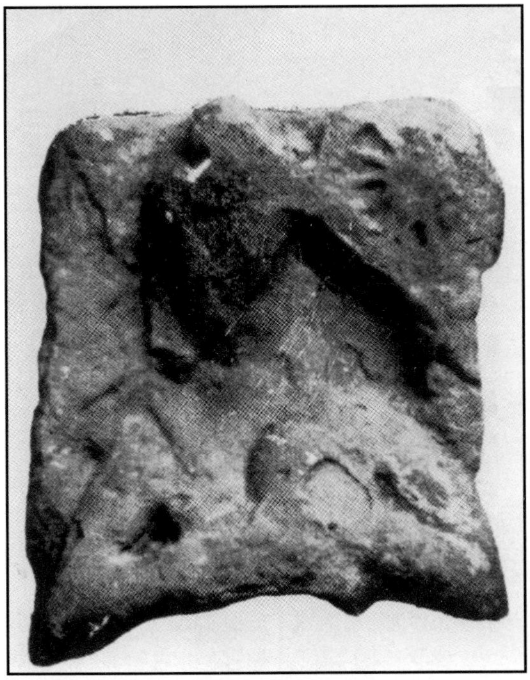

Pl. 137. Bust of Kṛishṇa, Sondh.

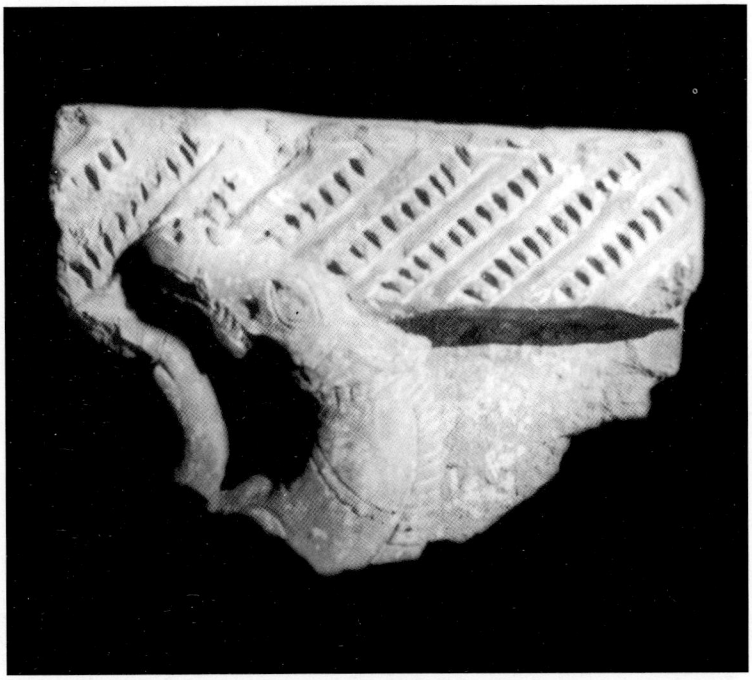

Pl. 138. Keśī, terracotta, Agroha.

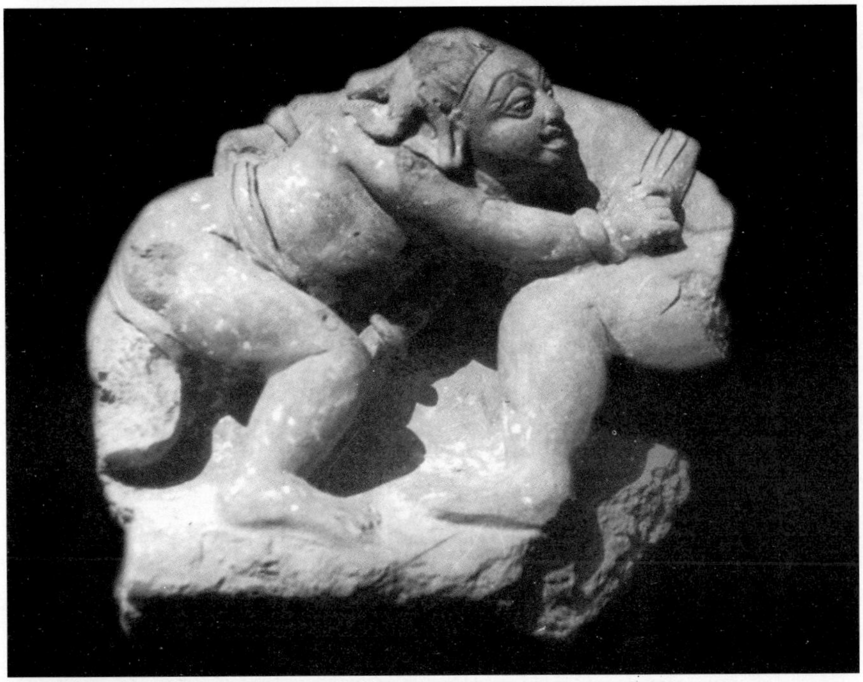

Pl. 139. Wrestling scene, terracotta, Agroha.

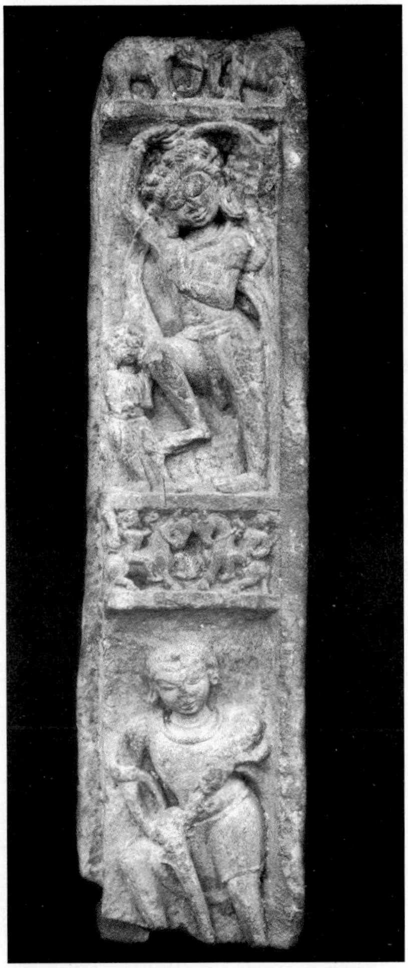

Pl. 140. Kāliya-damana on a pilaster, Gujjar Kheri.

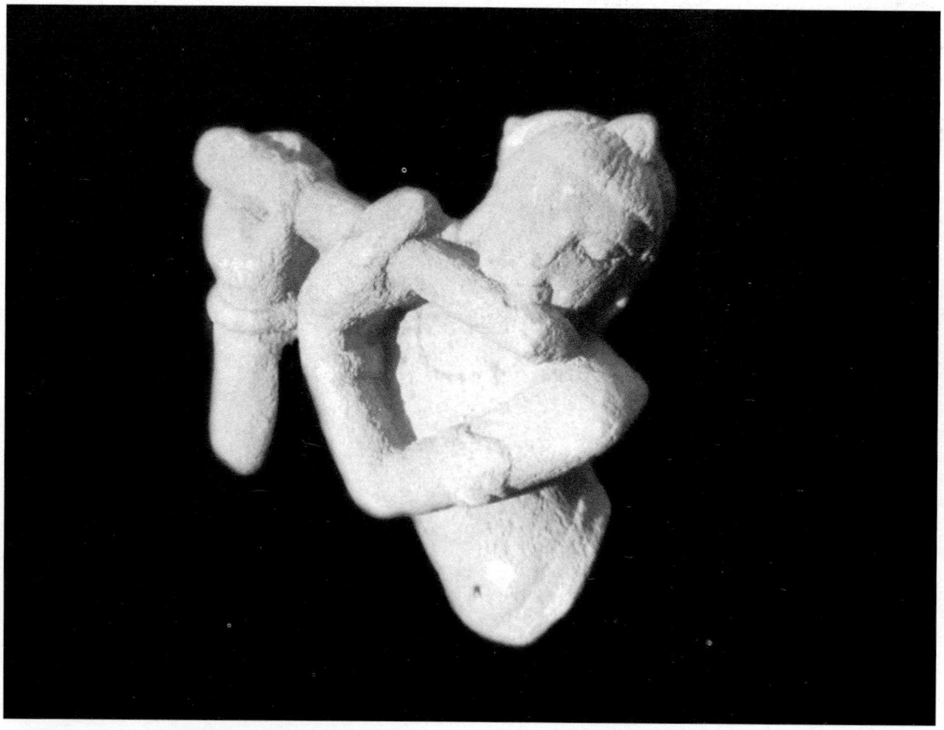

Pl. 141. Veṇu-Gopāla, Gujjar Kheri.

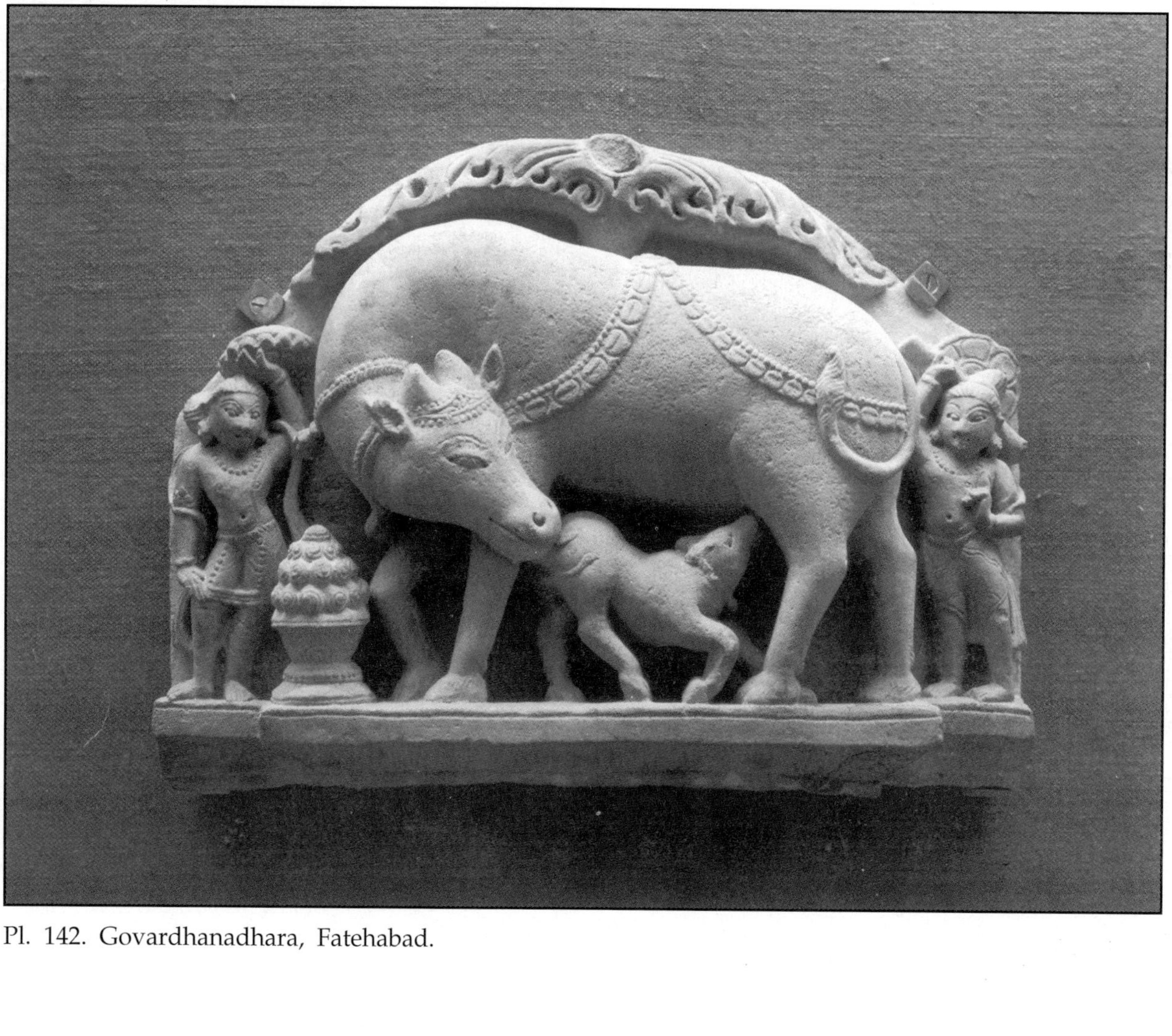

Pl. 142. Govardhanadhara, Fatehabad.

Pl. 144. *Mukha-liṅga*, front view, Kiloi.

Pl. 145. Same, side view.

Pl. 146. Same, view from the other side.

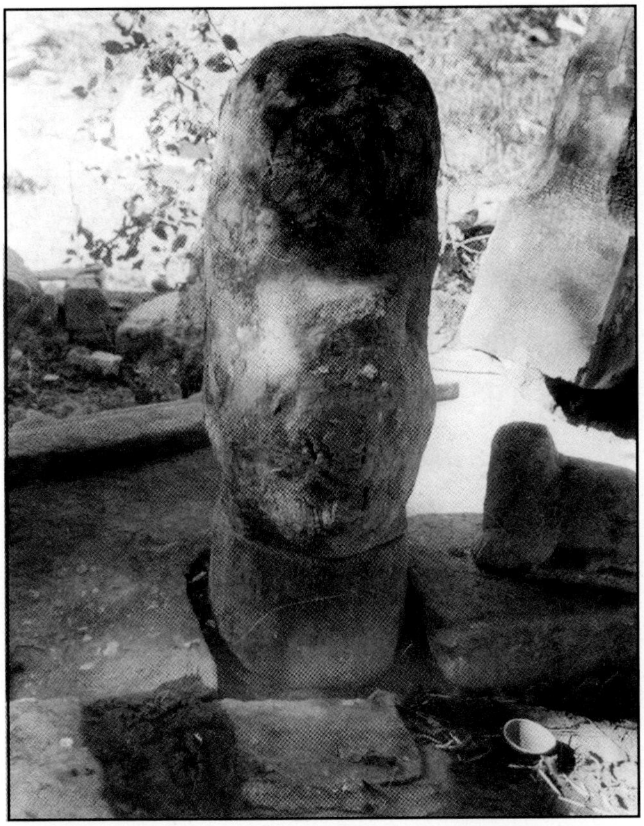

Pl. 144.

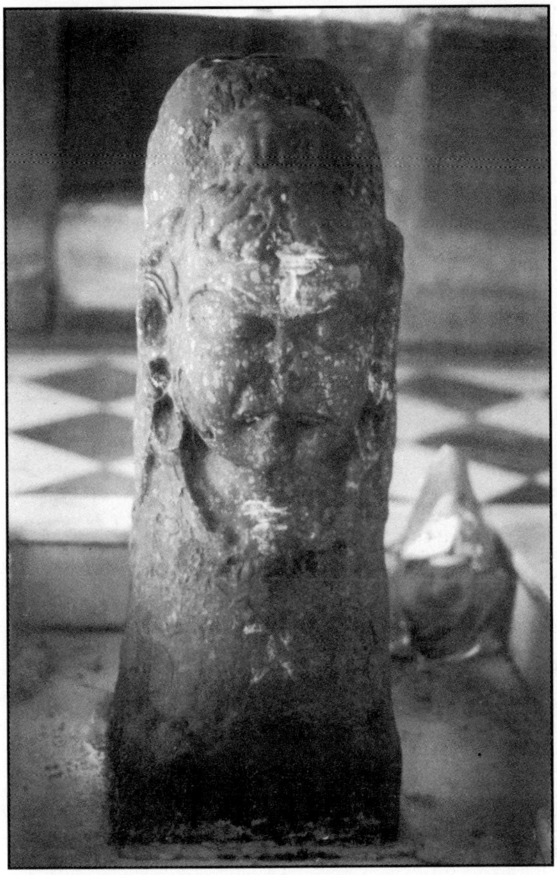

Pl. 145.

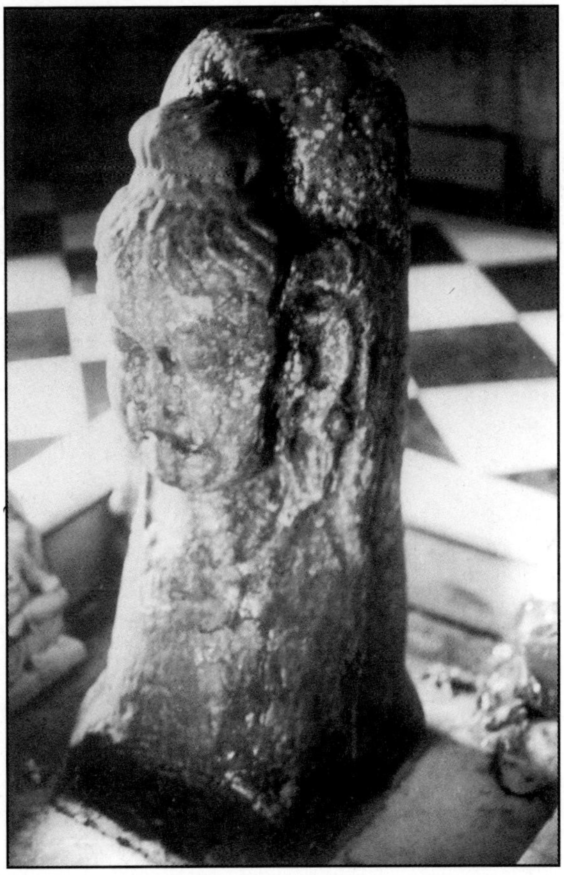

Pl. 146.

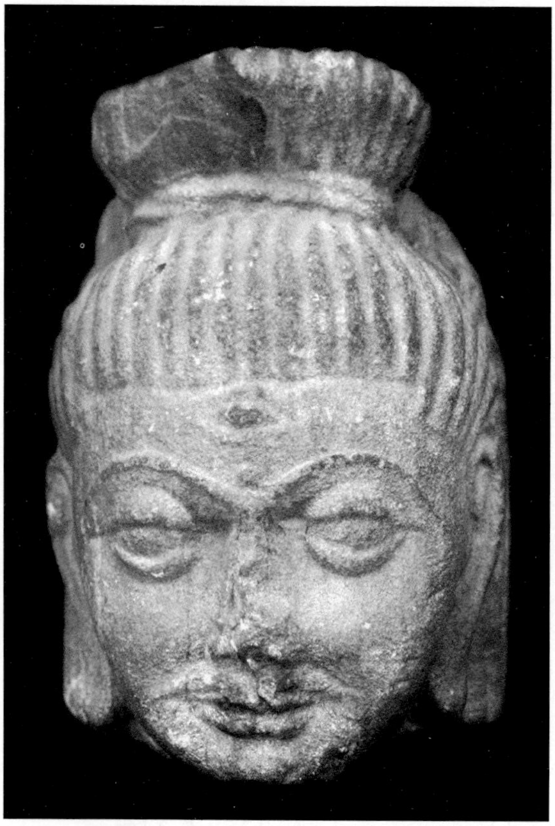

Pl. 143.

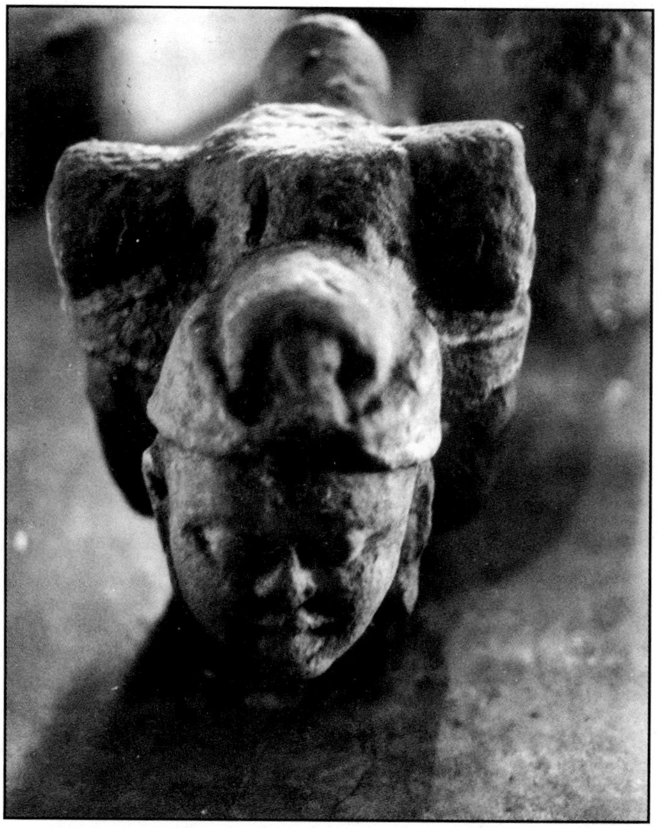

Pl. 147.

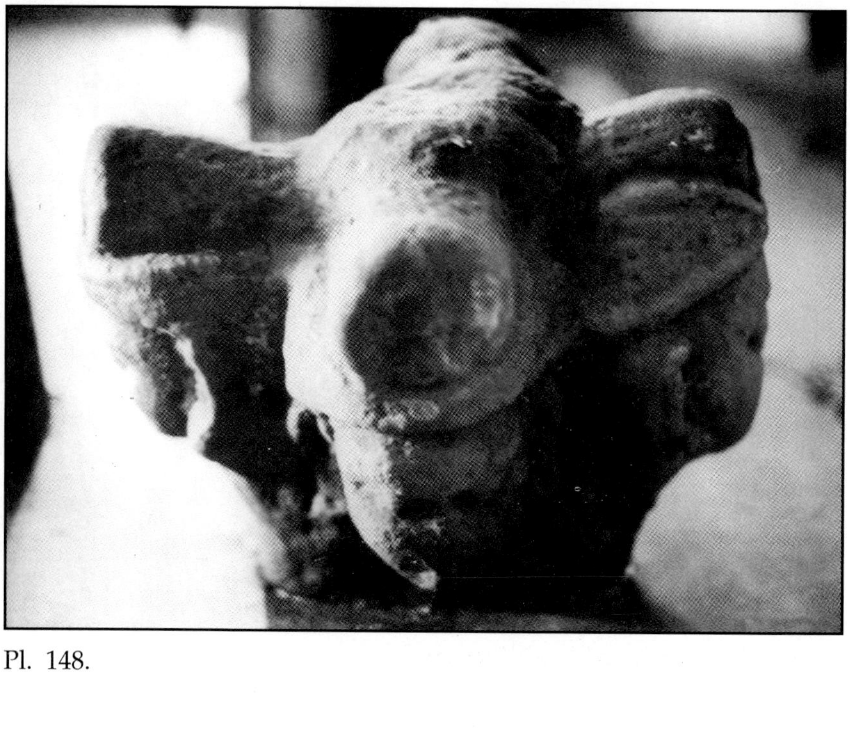

Pl. 143. *Mukha-liṅga*, Gujjar Kheri.

Pl. 147. *Chaturmukha-liṅga*, Rohtak.

Pl. 148. Same, another view.

Pl. 148.

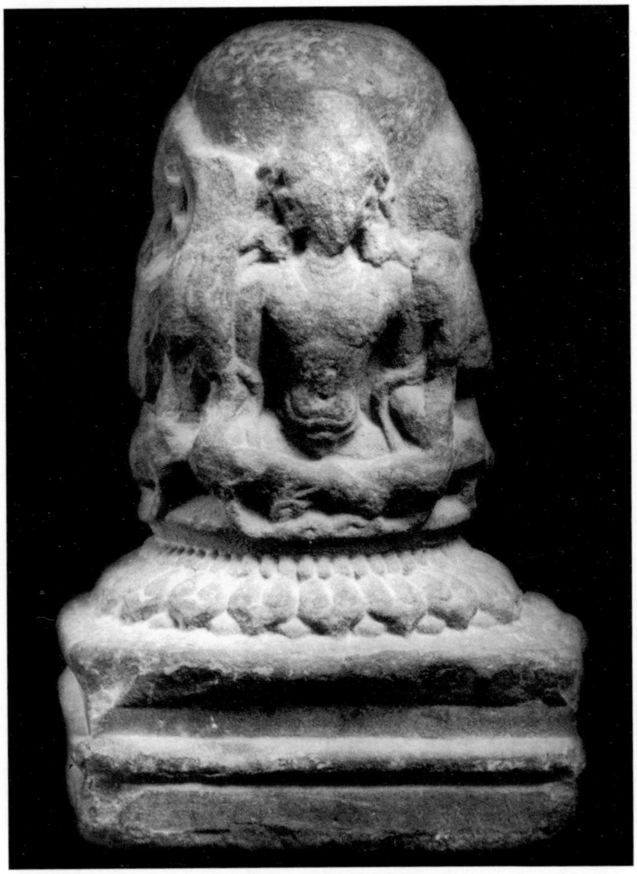

Pl. 149. *Chaturmukha-liṅga*, Morni-ka-Tal.

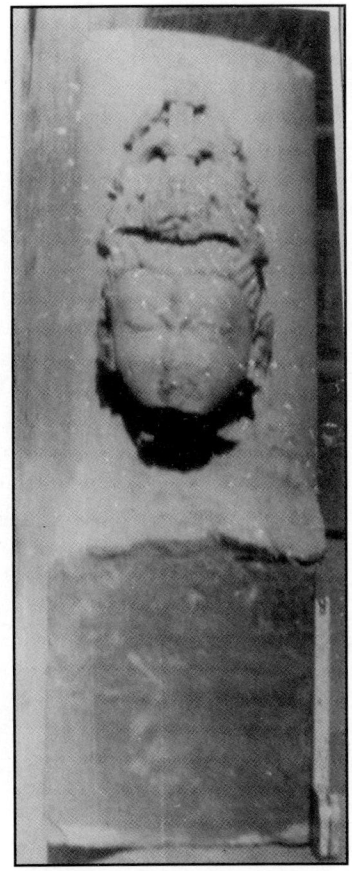

Pl. 150. *Mukha-liṅga*, Sikanderpura.

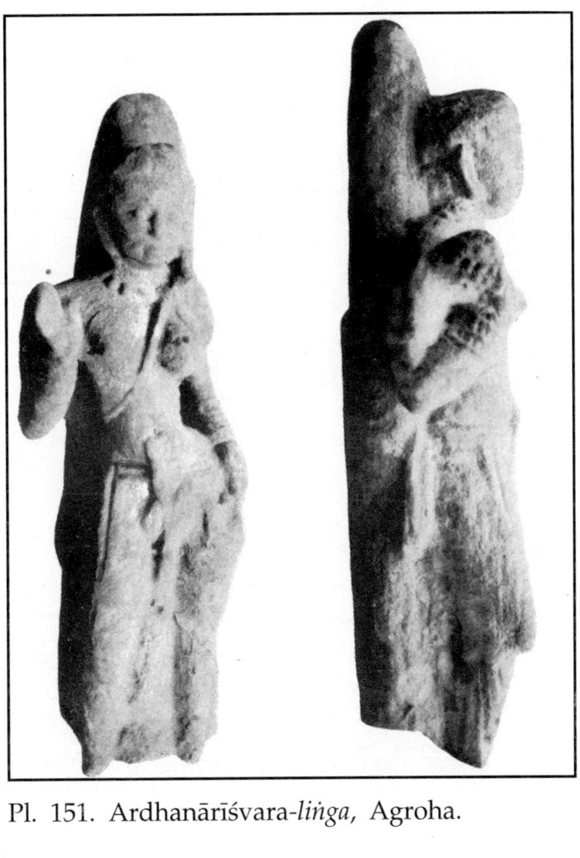

Pl. 151. Ardhanārīśvara-*liṅga*, Agroha.

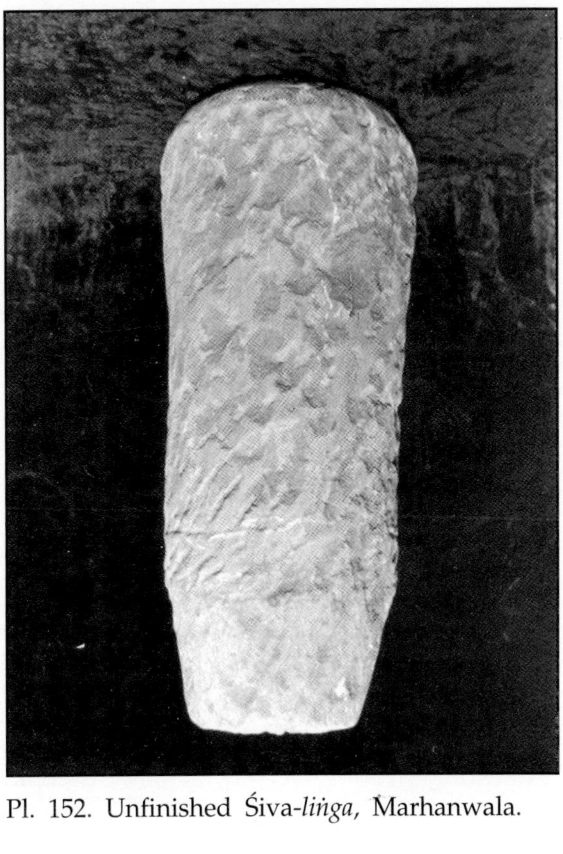

Pl. 152. Unfinished Śiva-*liṅga*, Marhanwala.

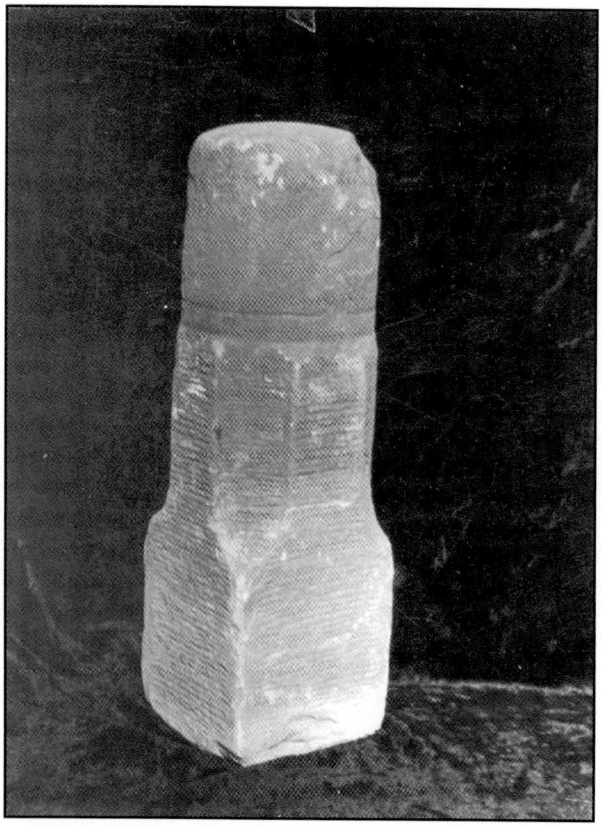

Pl. 153. Śiva-*liṅga*, Marhanwala.

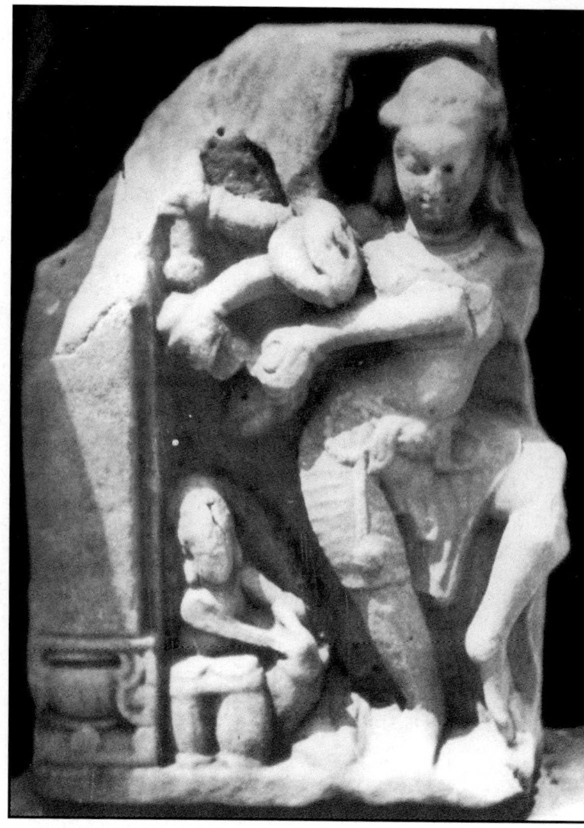

Pl. 154. Naṭarāja, Sandhaya.

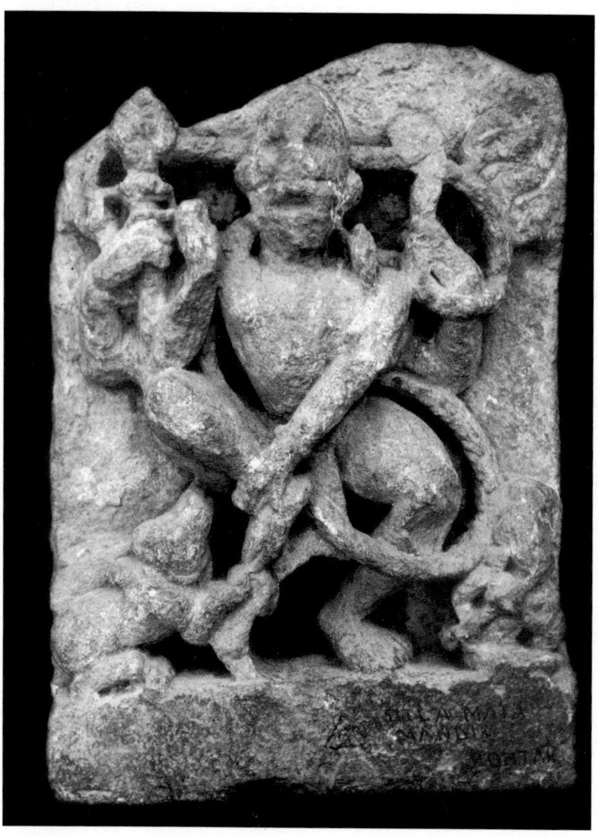

Pl. 155. Naṭarāja, Rohtak.

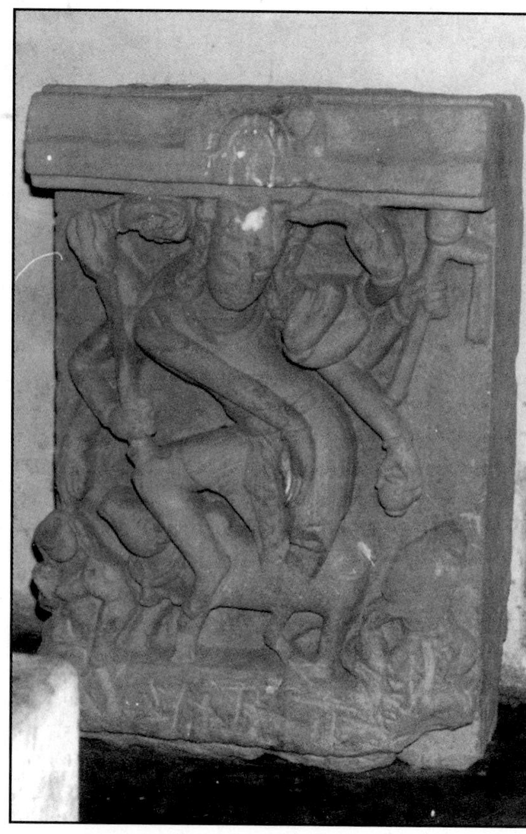

Pl. 156. Naṭarāja, Morni-ka-Tal.

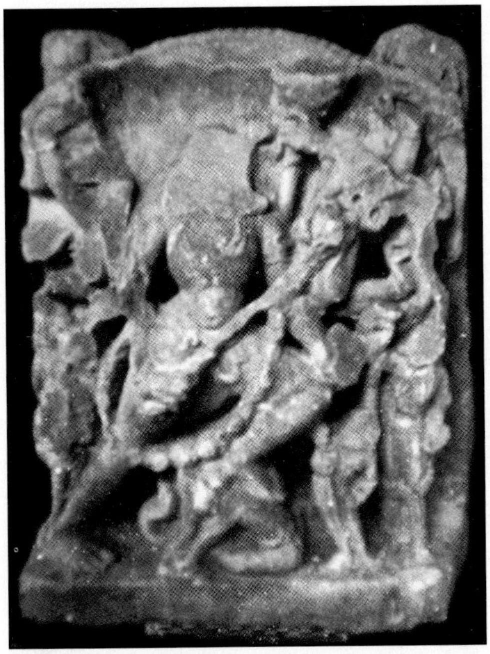

Pl. 157. Andhakāsuravadha-mūrti, Mohanbari.

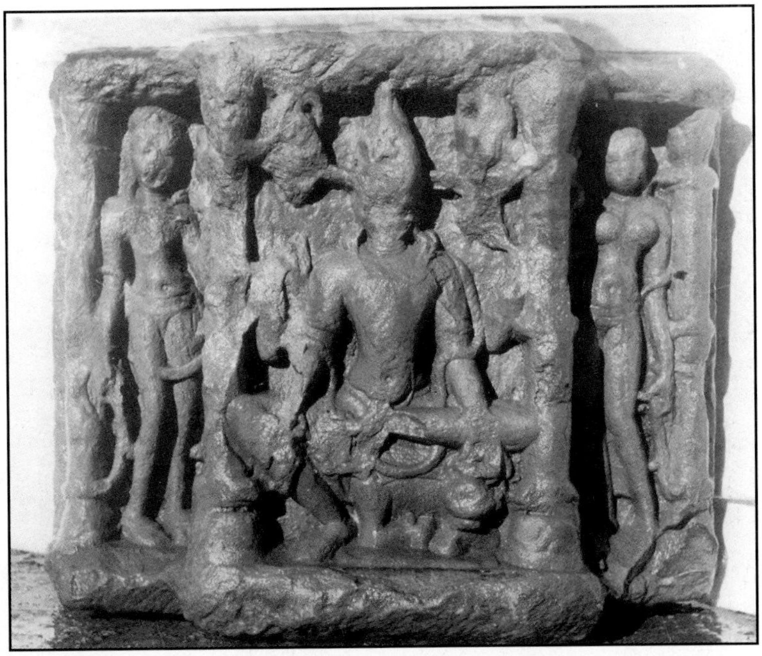

Pl. 158. So-called Śiva-Kāmāntaka, Morni-ka-Tal.

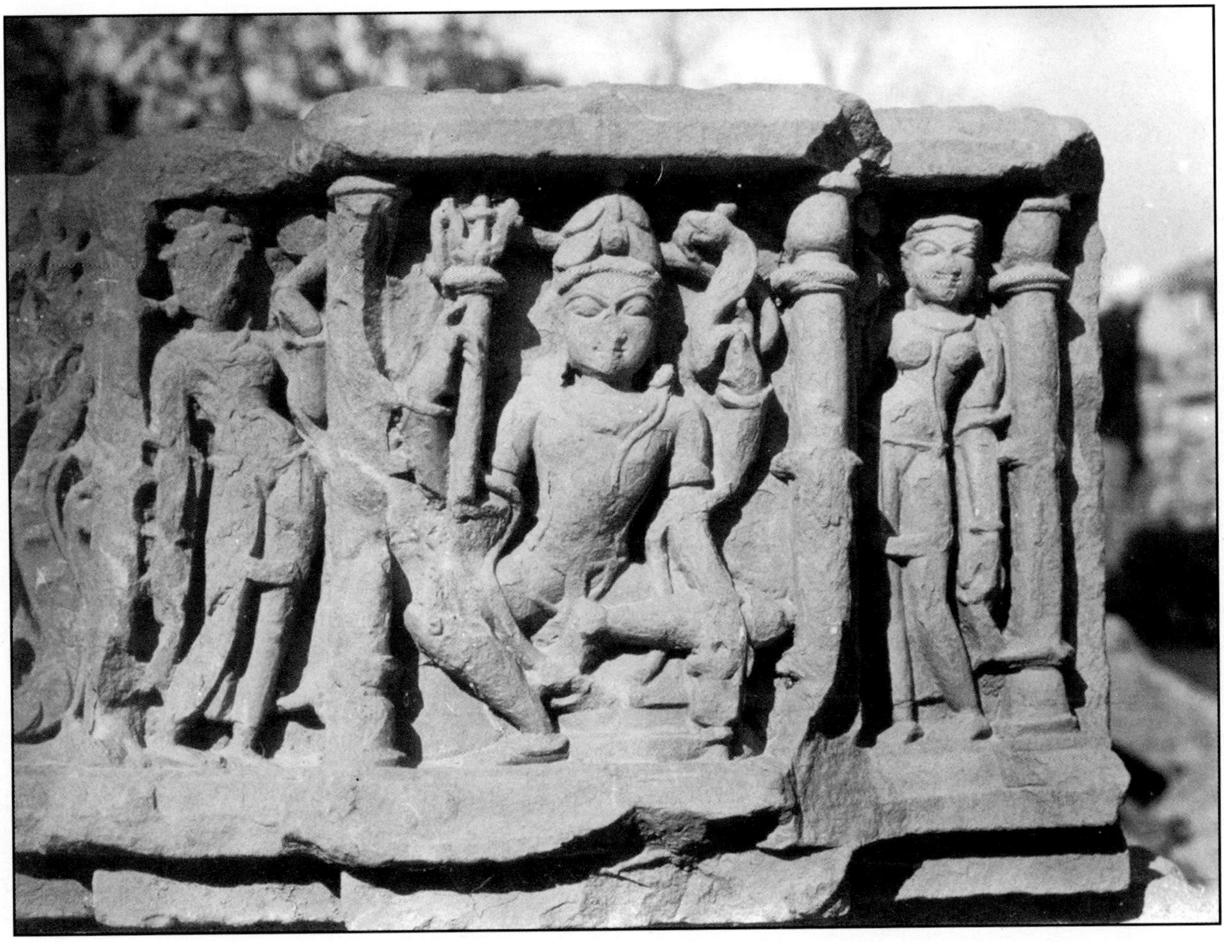

Pl. 159. Śiva, Pinjore.

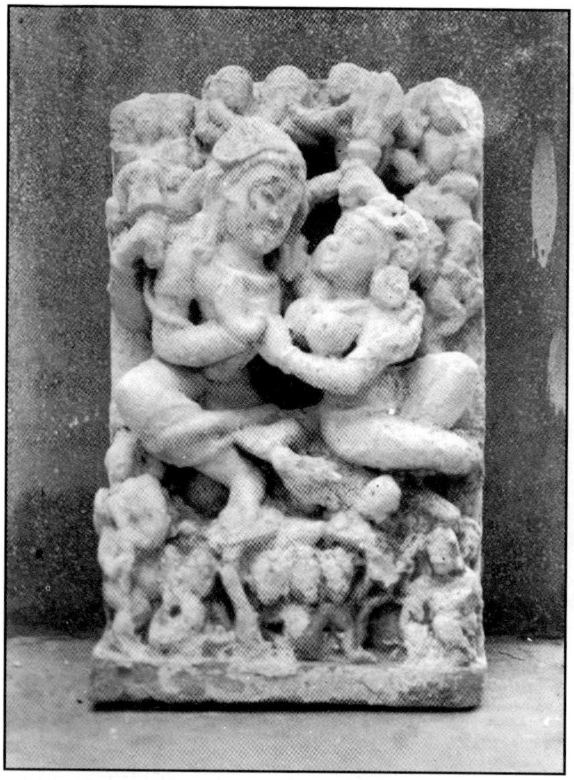

Pl. 160. Rāvaṇānugraha-mūrti, Southern Haryana.

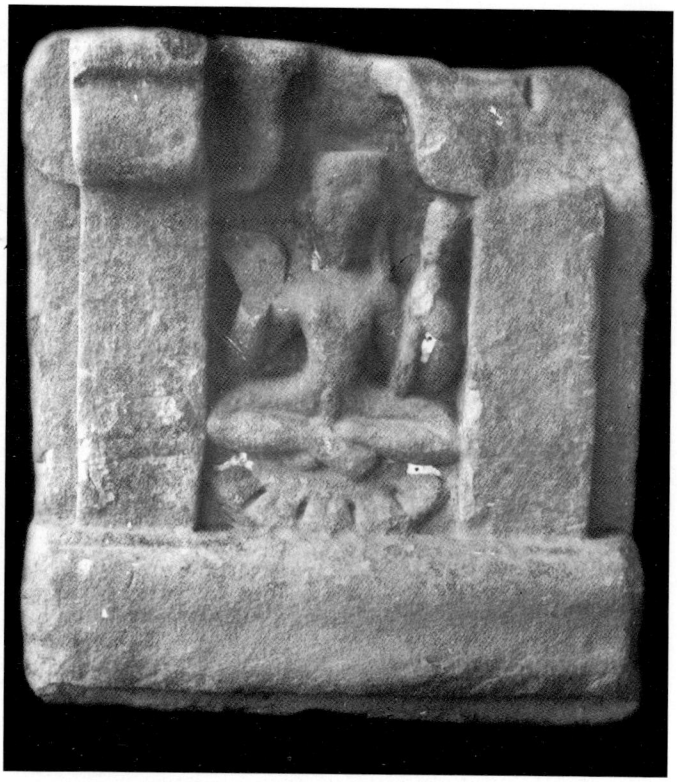

Pl. 161. Lakulīśa, Morni-ka-Tal.

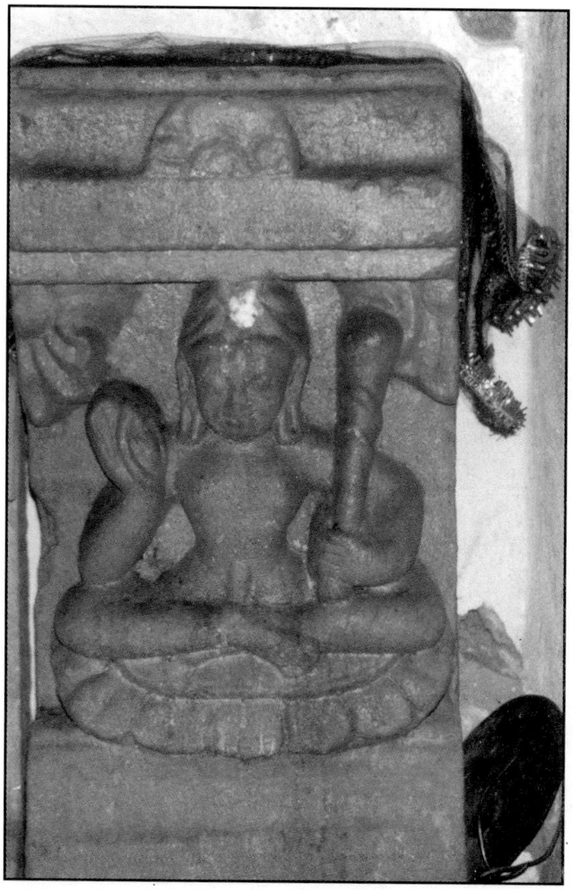

Pl. 162. Lakulīśa, Morni-ka-Tal.

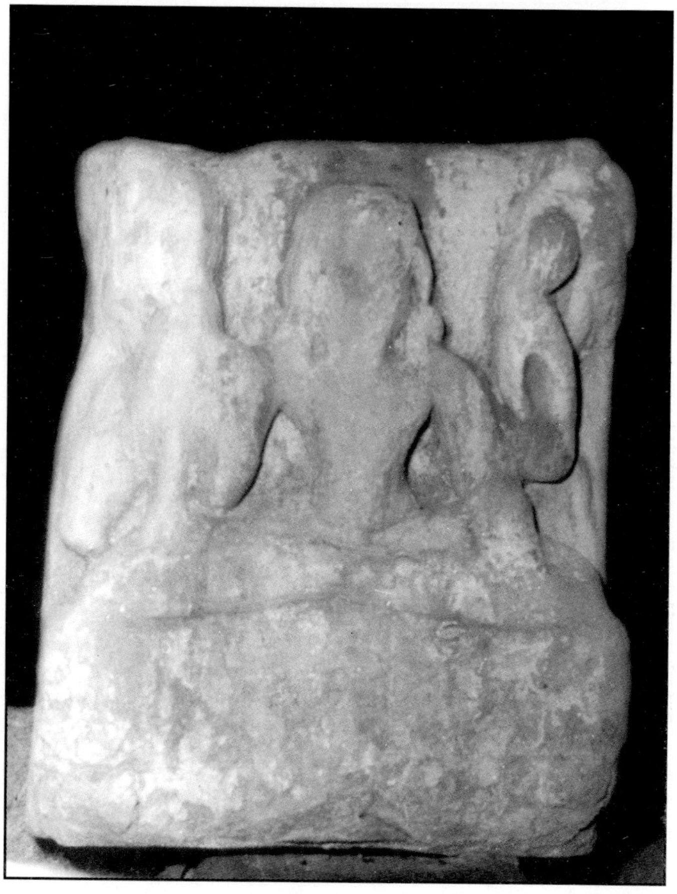

Pl. 163. Lakulīśa, Kapālamochana.

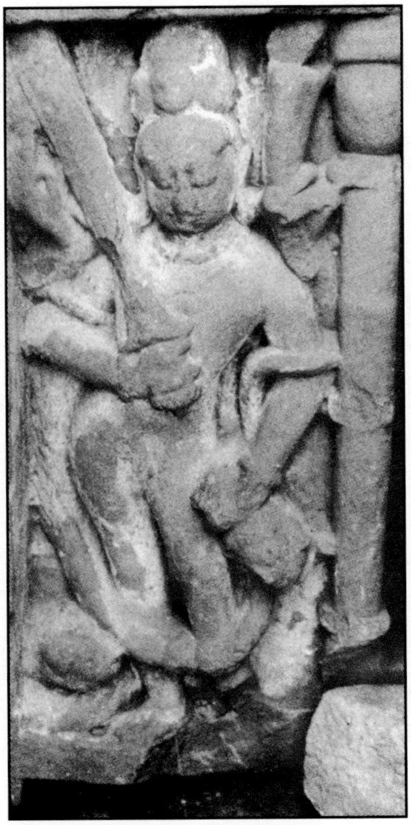

Pl. 164. Bhairava, Pinjore.

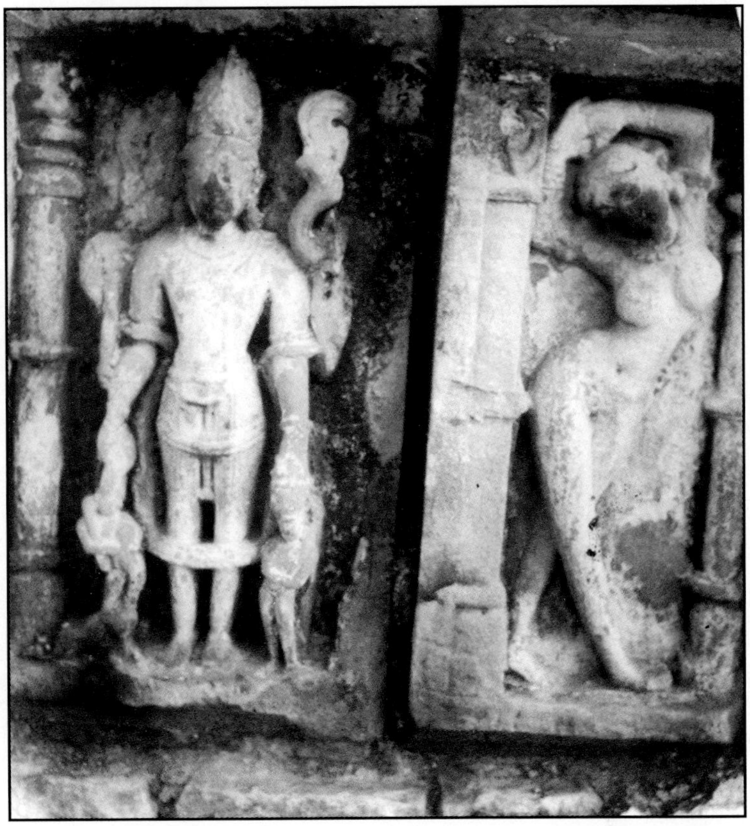

Pl. 167. Śiva, Pinjore.

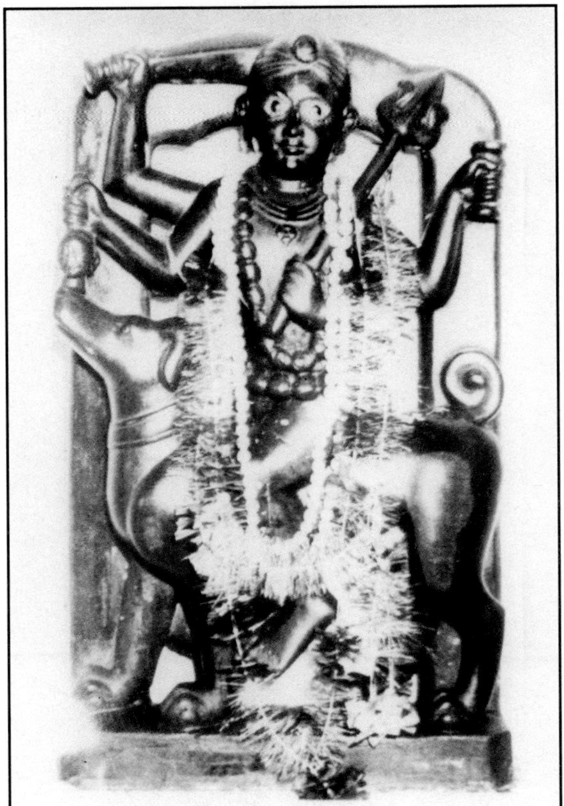

Pl. 165. Bhairava, Pehowa.

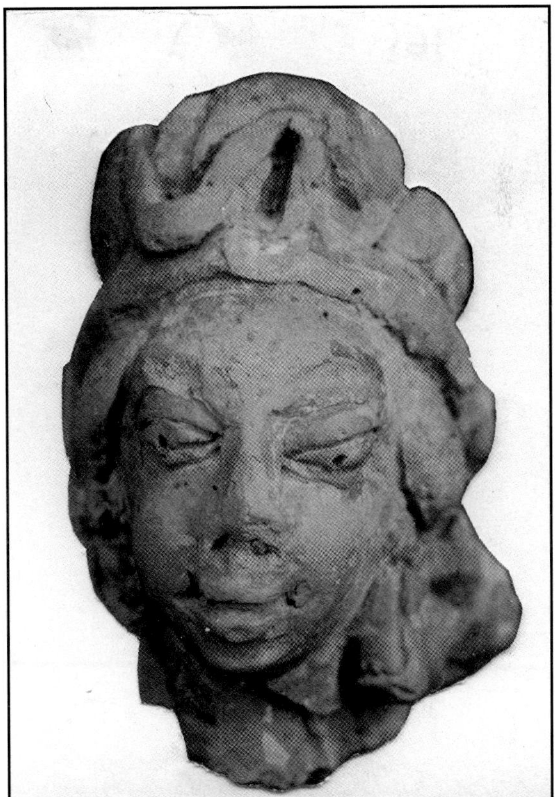

Pl. 166. Head of Śiva, terracotta, Agroha.

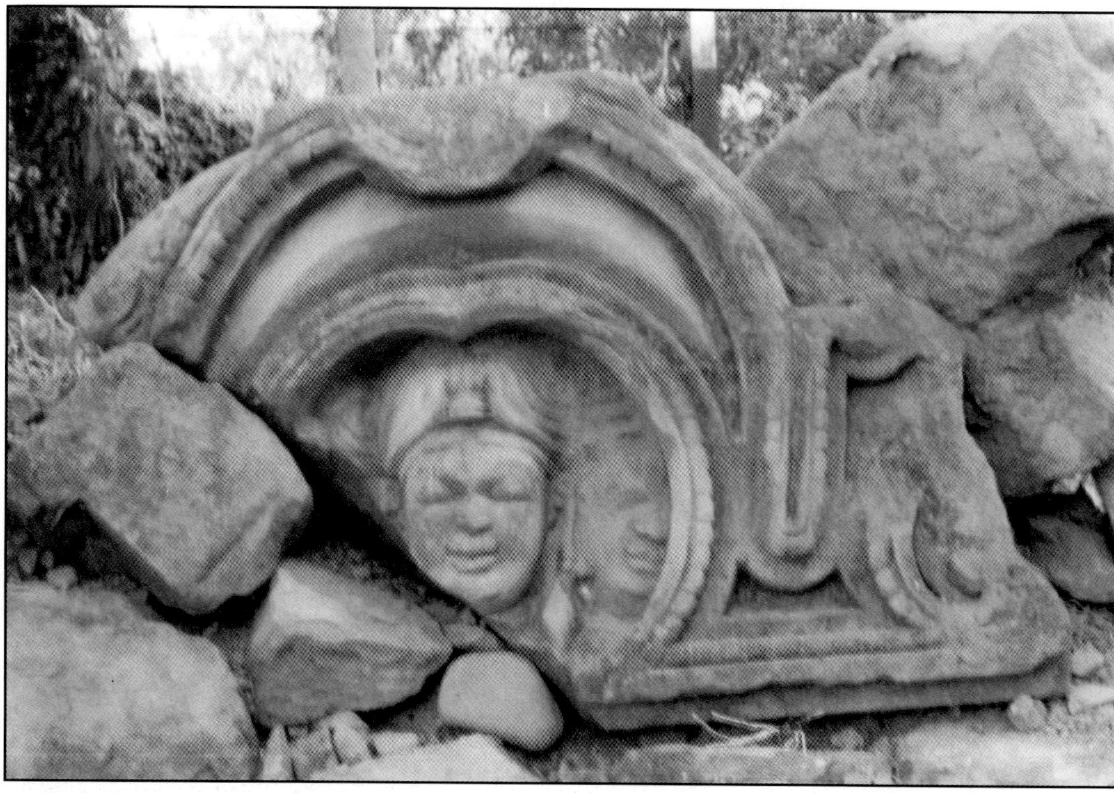

Pl. 168. Śiva in *bhadramukha*, Pinjore.

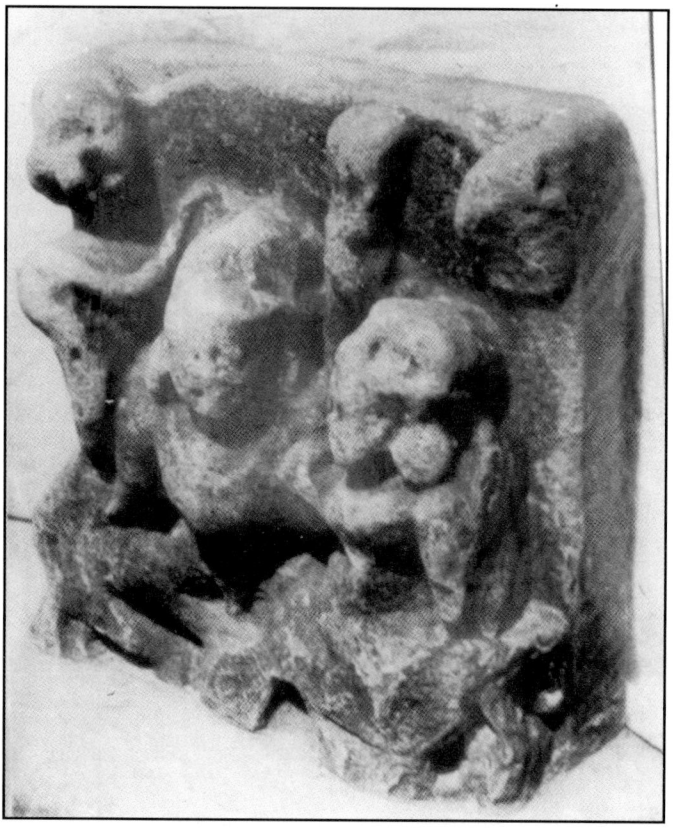

Pl. 169. Fragmentary Umā-Maheśvara, Kapālamochana.

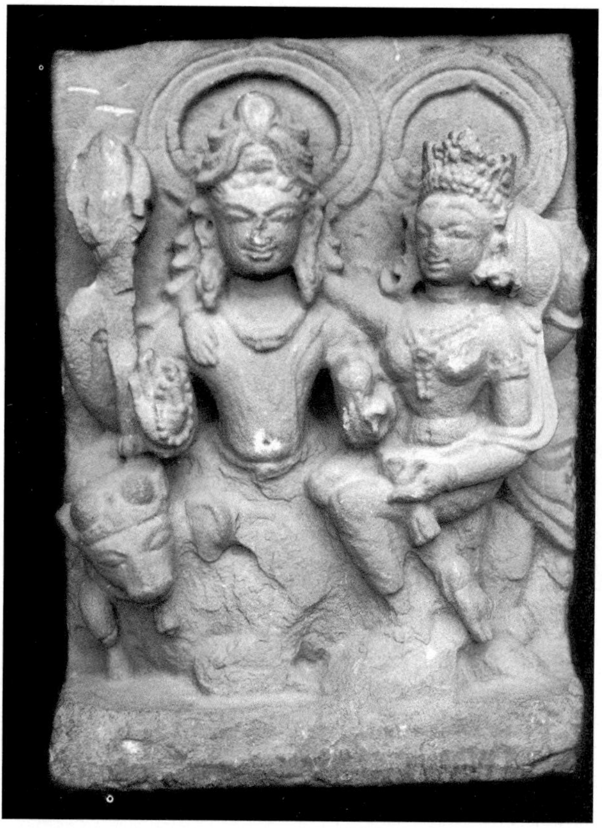

Pl. 170. Umā-Maheśvara, Pinjore.

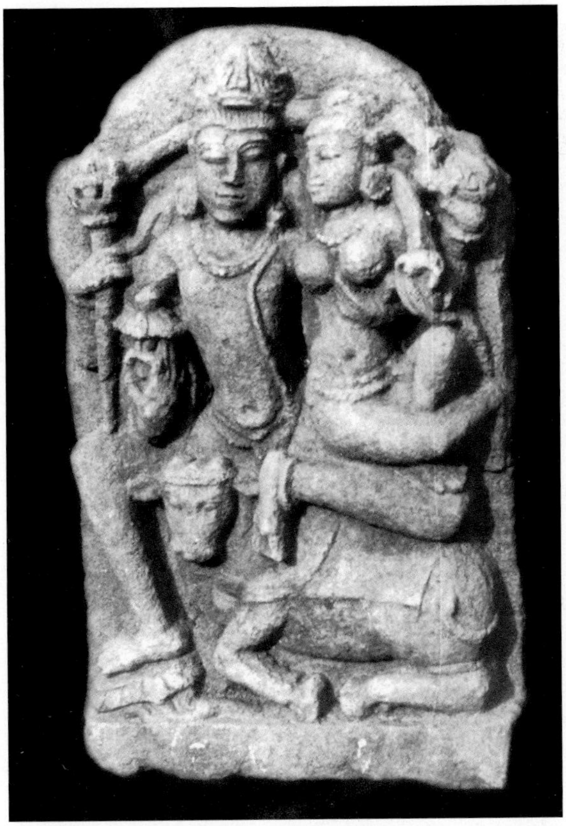

Pl. 171. Umā-Maheśvara, Durjanpura.

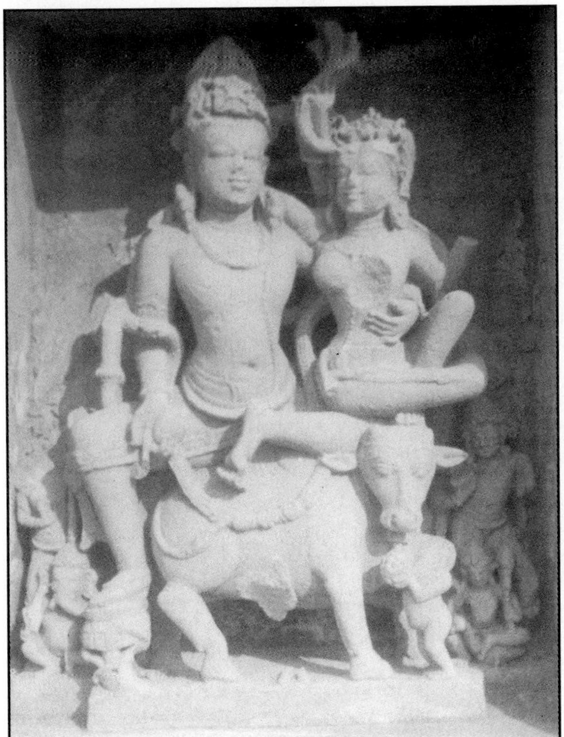

Pl. 172. Umā-Maheśvara, Pehowa.

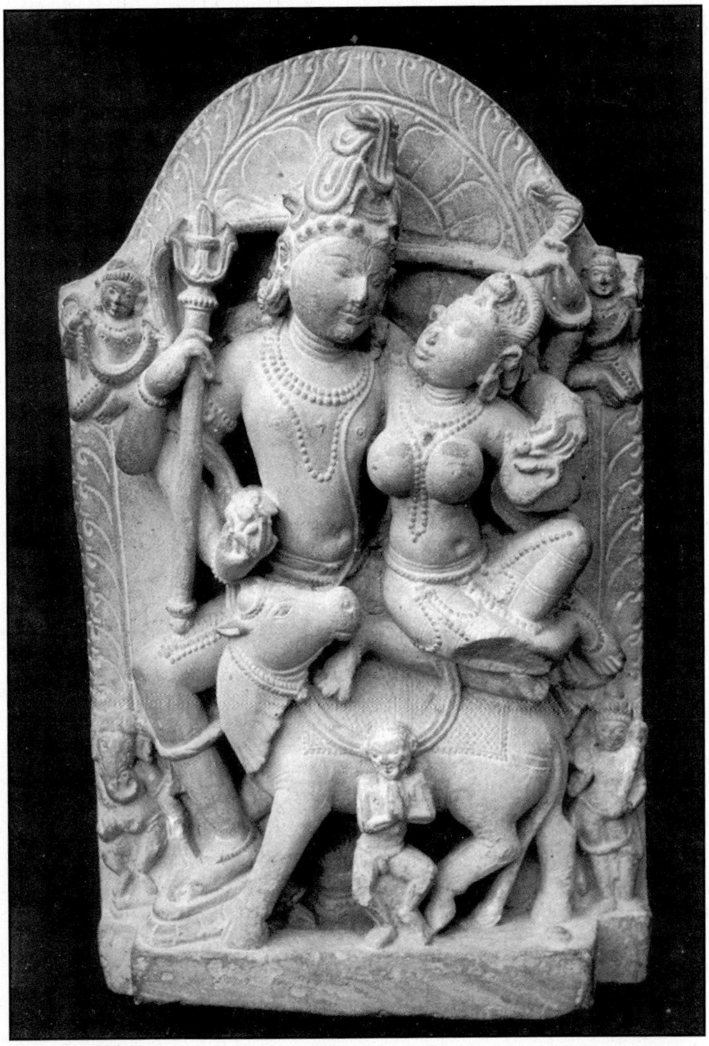

Pl. 173. Umā-Maheśvara, Beri.

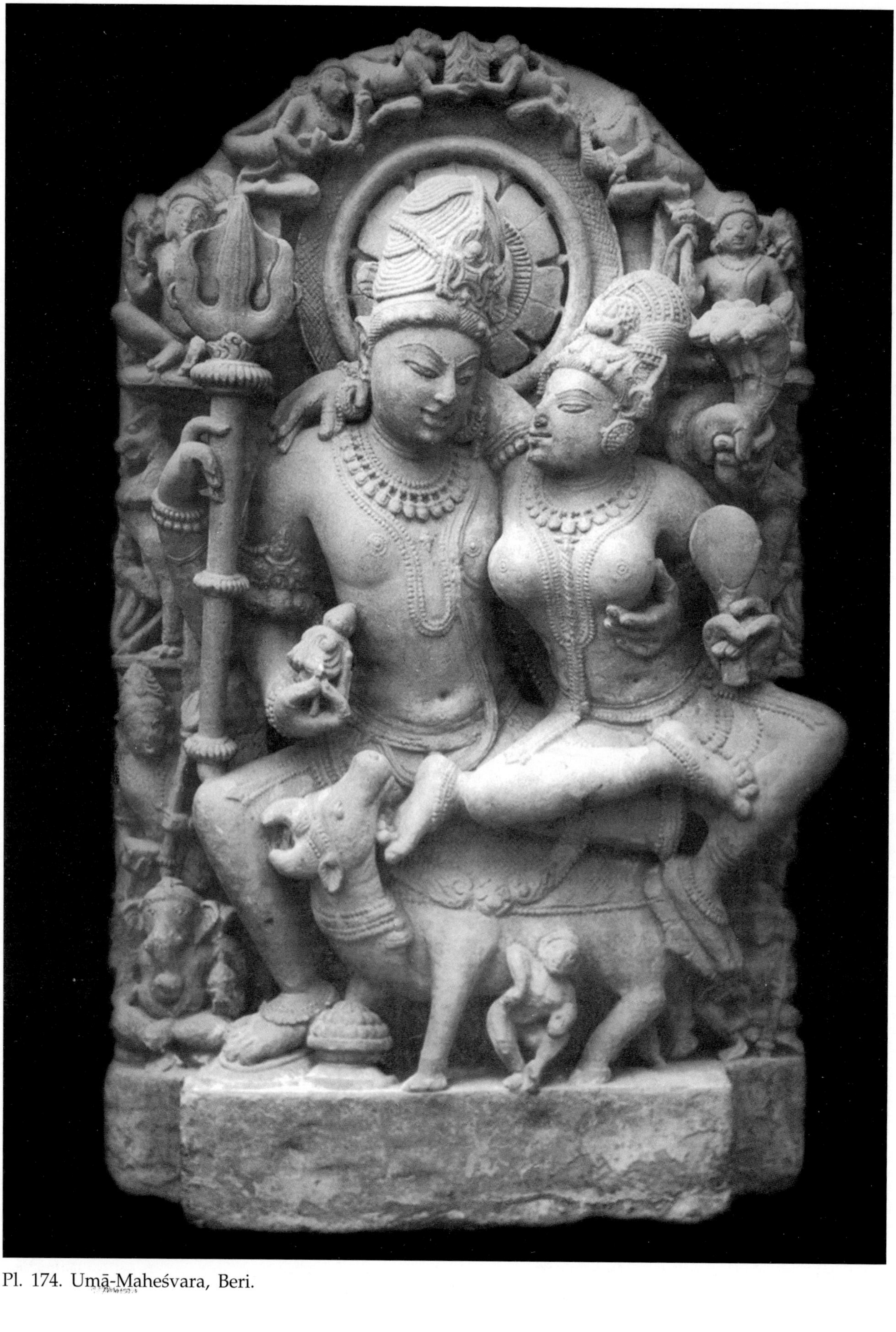

Pl. 174. Umā-Maheśvara, Beri.

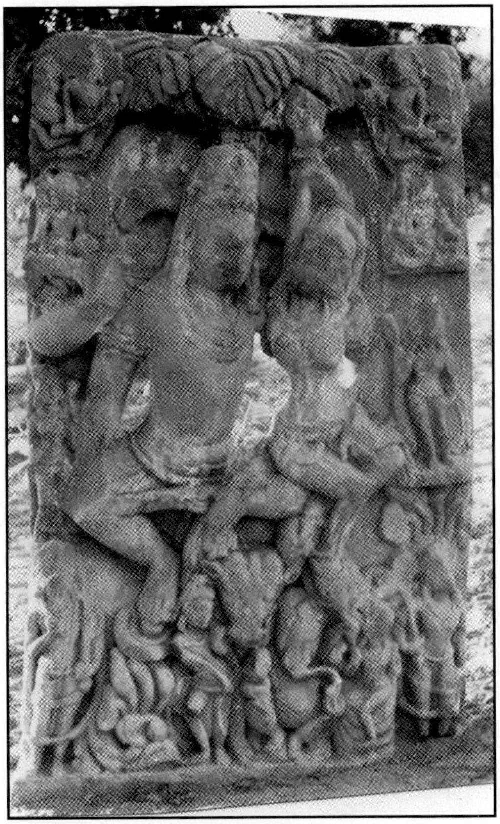

Pl. 175. Umā-Maheśvara, Ata.

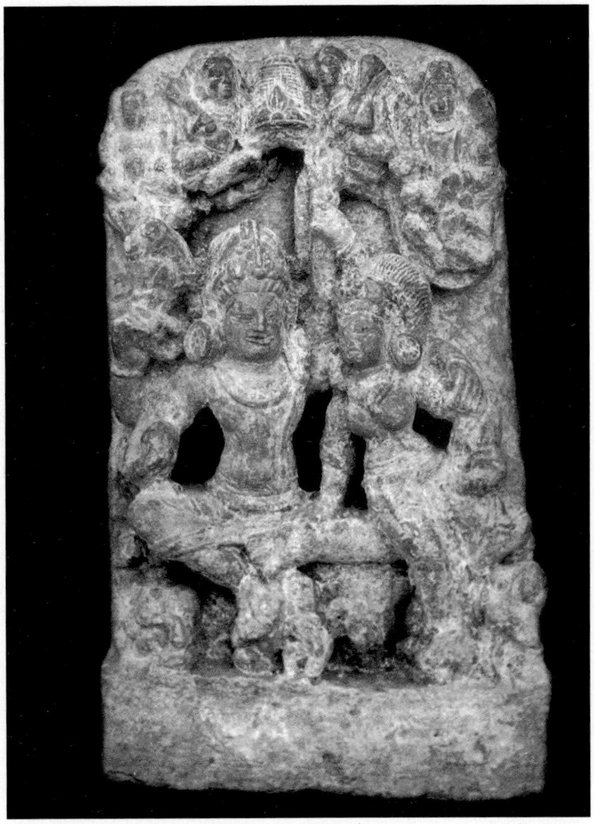

Pl. 176. Uma-Maheśvara, Jadthal.

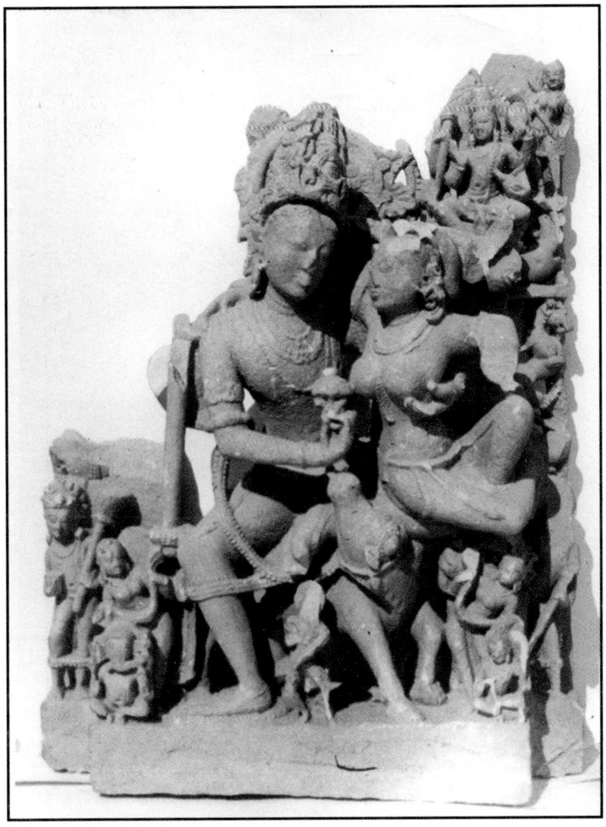

Pl. 177. Umā-Maheśvara, Gujjar Kheri.

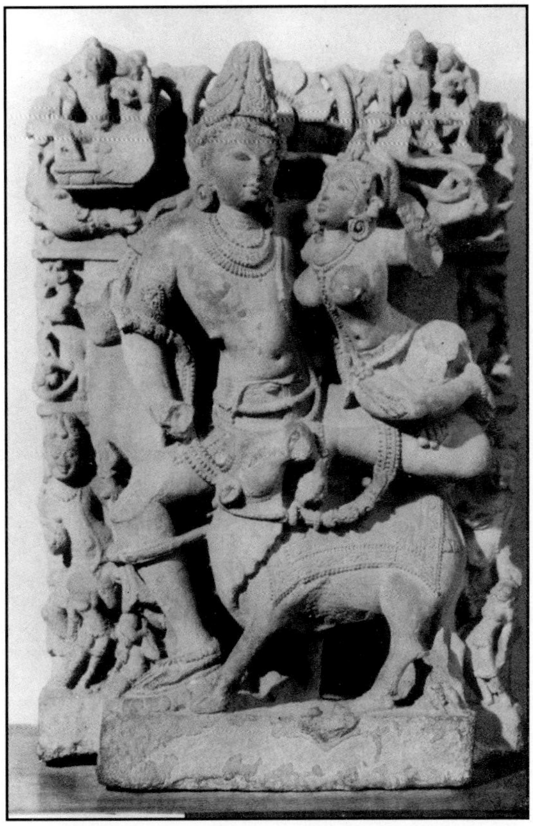

Pl. 178. Umā-Maheśvara, Gujjar Kheri.

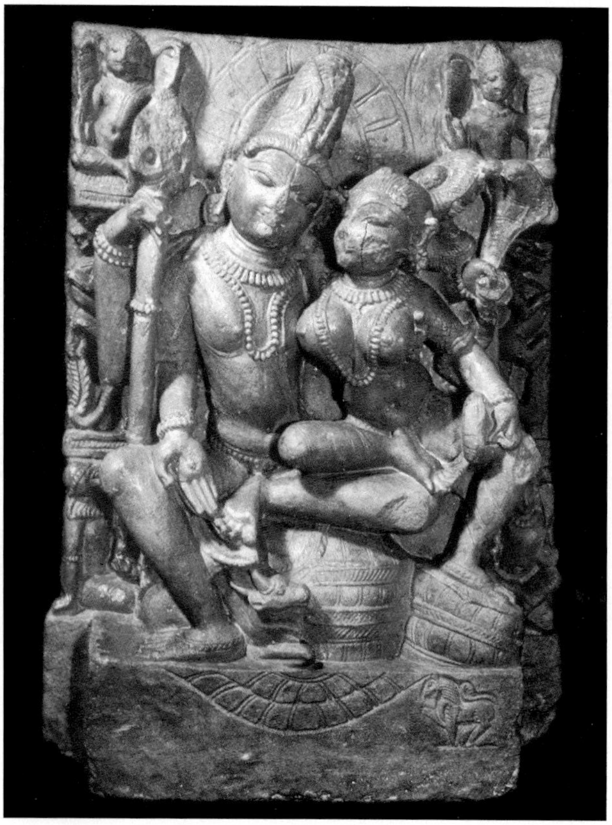

Pl. 179. Umā-Maheśvara, Pinjore.

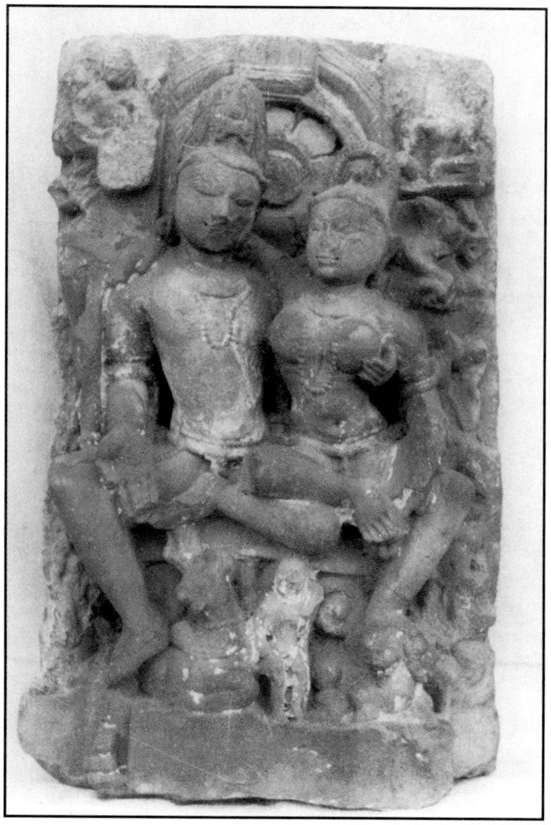

Pl. 180. Umā-Maheśvara, Agroha.

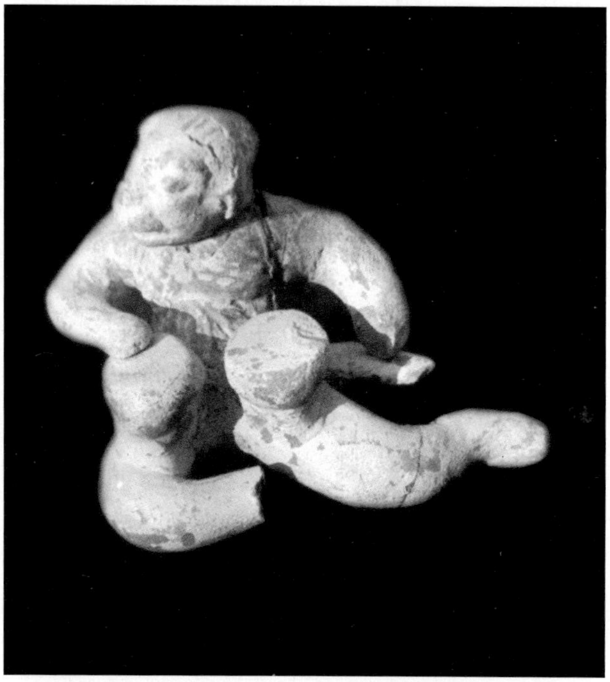

Pl. 181. Nandikeśvara, terracotta, Sirsa.

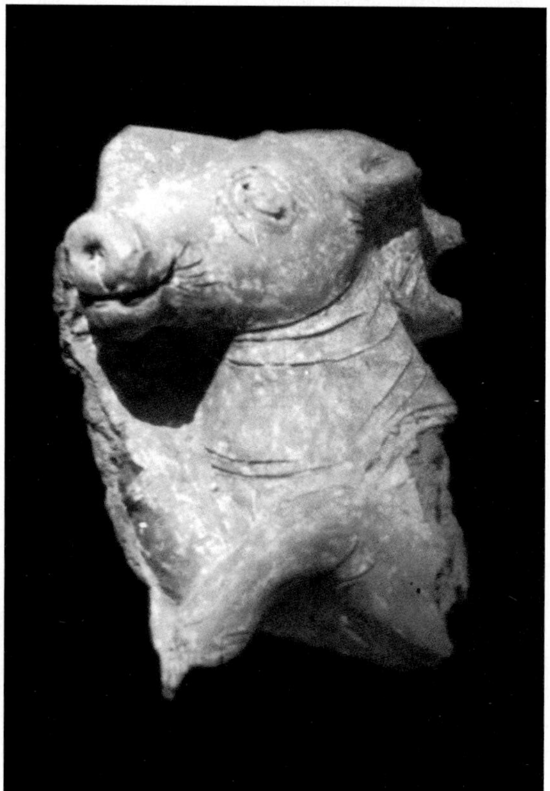

Pl. 182. Forepart of Nandī, terracotta, Agroha.

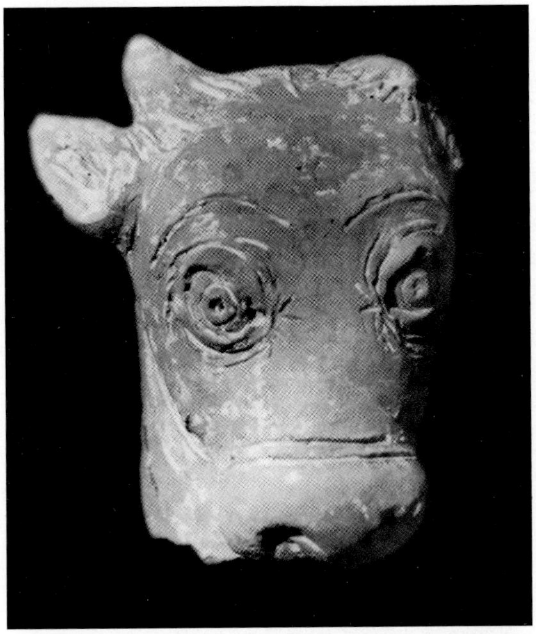

Pl. 183. Head of Nandī, terracotta, Agroha.

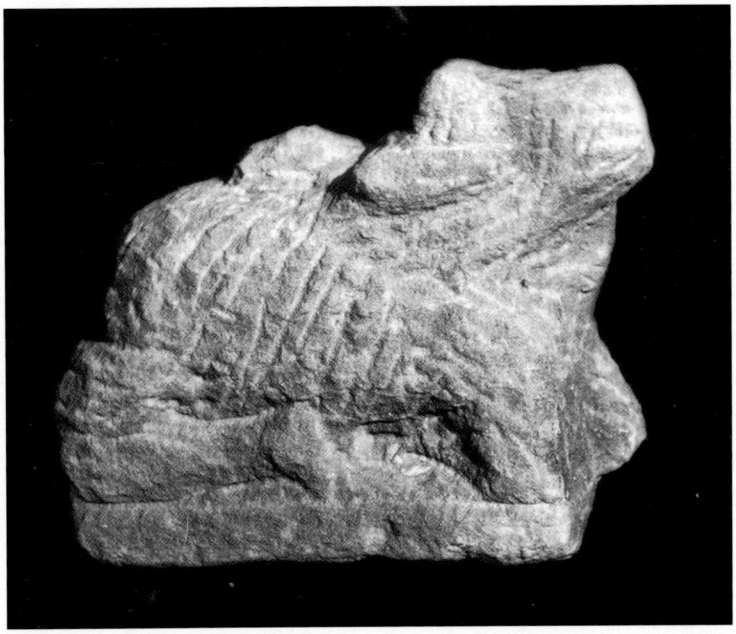

Pl. 185. Nandī bull, Pinjore.

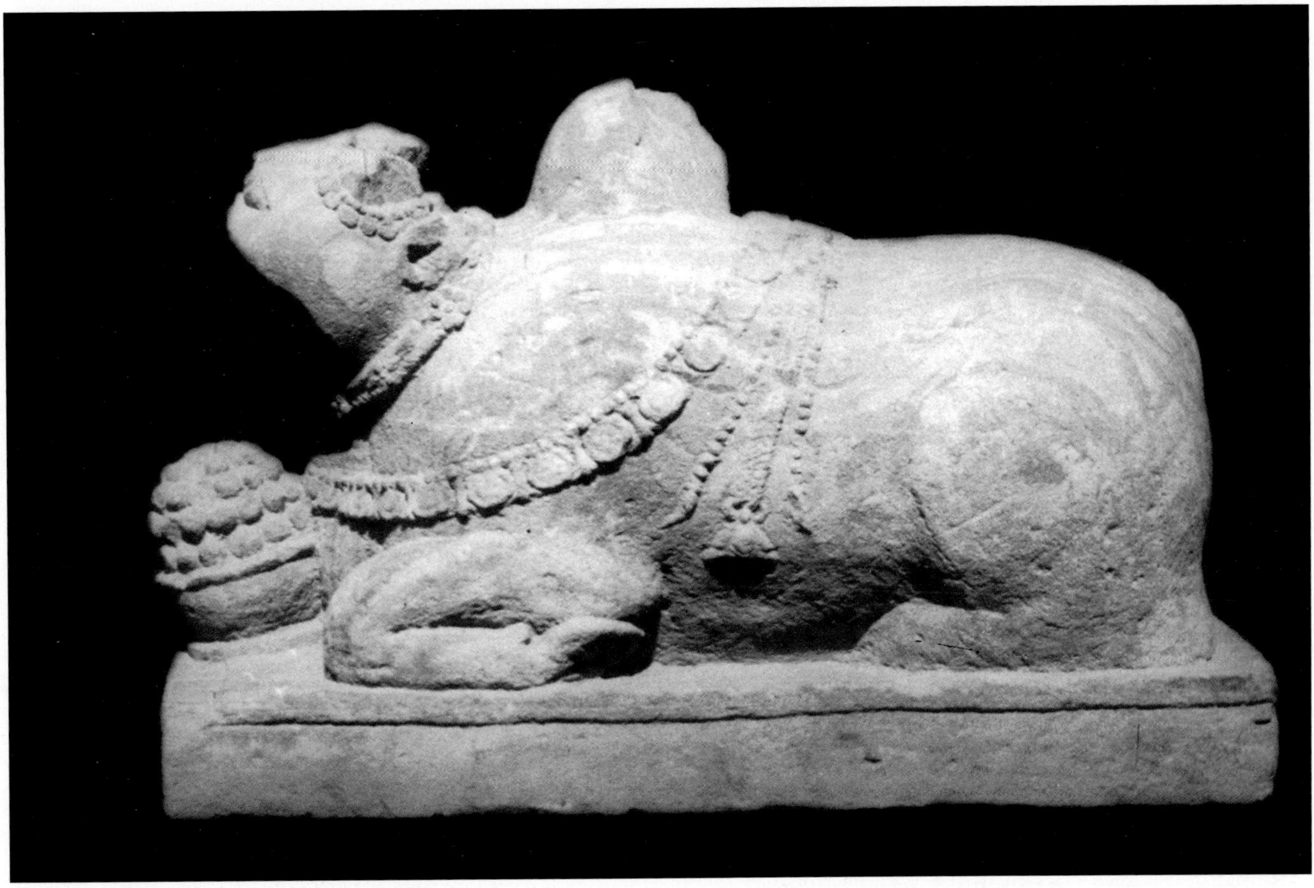

Pl. 184. Humped Nandī bull, Kohand.

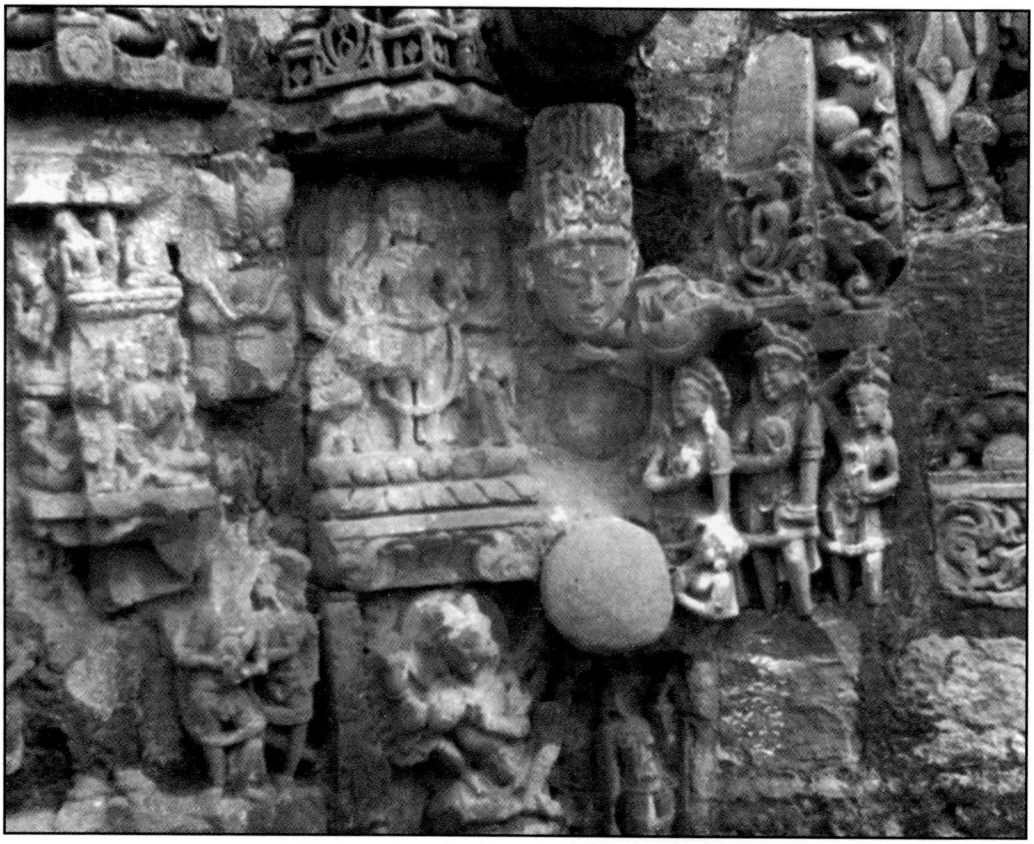

Pl. 186. Wall of Kabir Chaurā at Pinjore studded with sculptures.

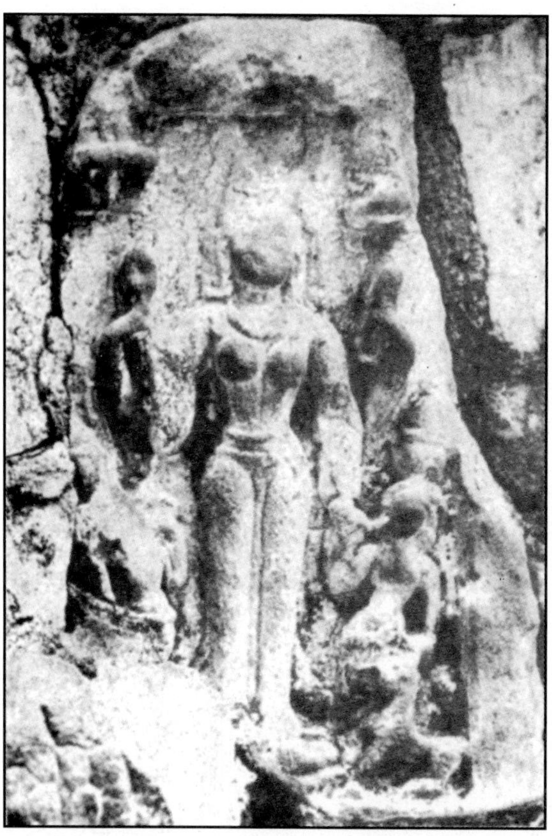

Pl. 187. *Pañchatapas* Pārvatī in the wall of Kabir Chaurā, Pinjore.

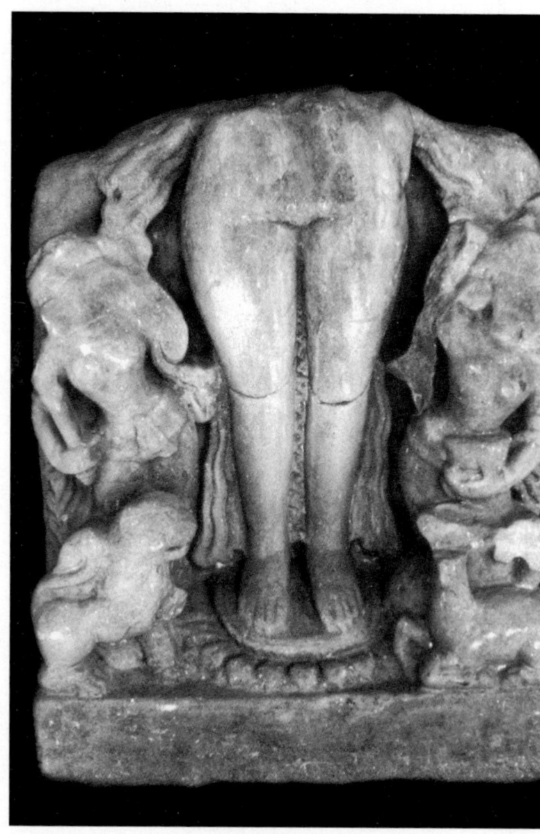

Pl. 188. *Pañchatapas* Pārvatī, Jaintipur.

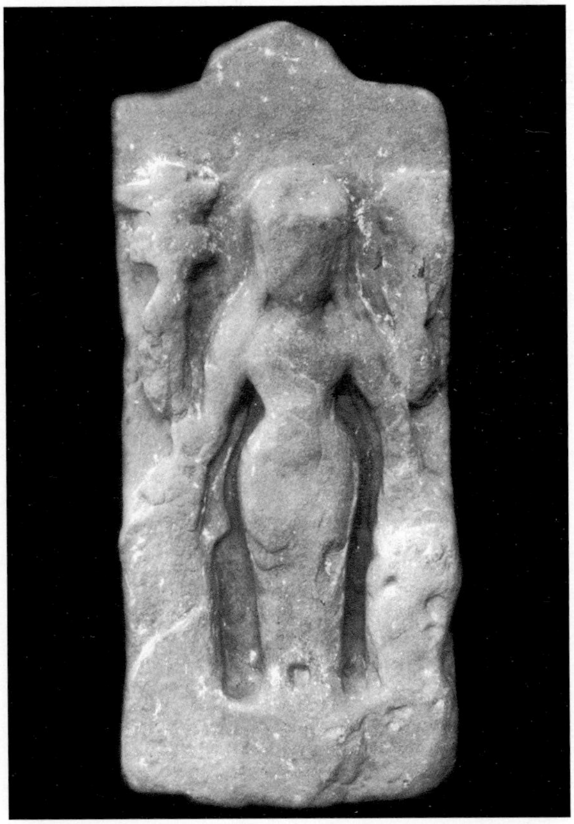

Pl. 189. *Pañchatapas* Pārvatī, Morni-ka-Tal.

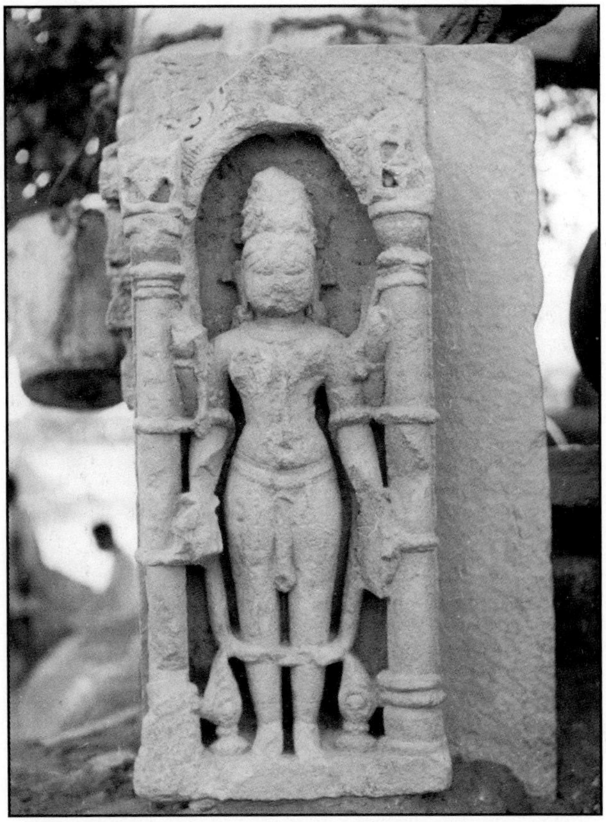

Pl. 190. *Pañchatapas* Pārvatī, Sagwan.

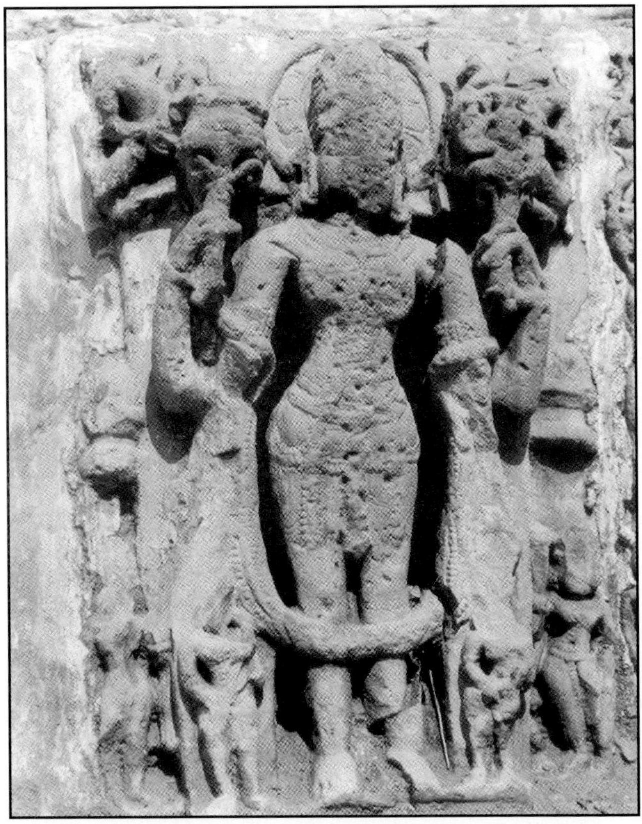

Pl. 191. *Pañchatapas* Pārvatī, Jasat.

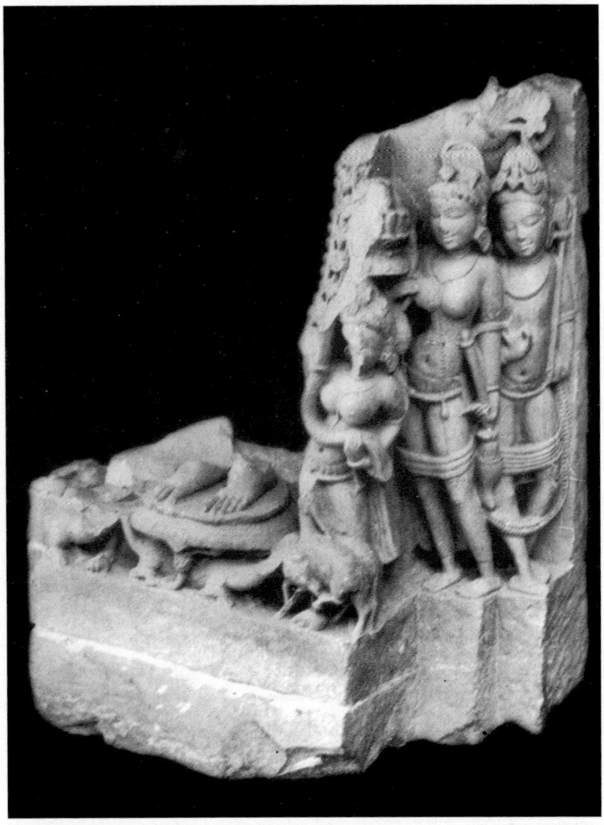

Pl. 192. Lower portion of *Pañchatapas* Pārvatī, Gujjar Kheri.

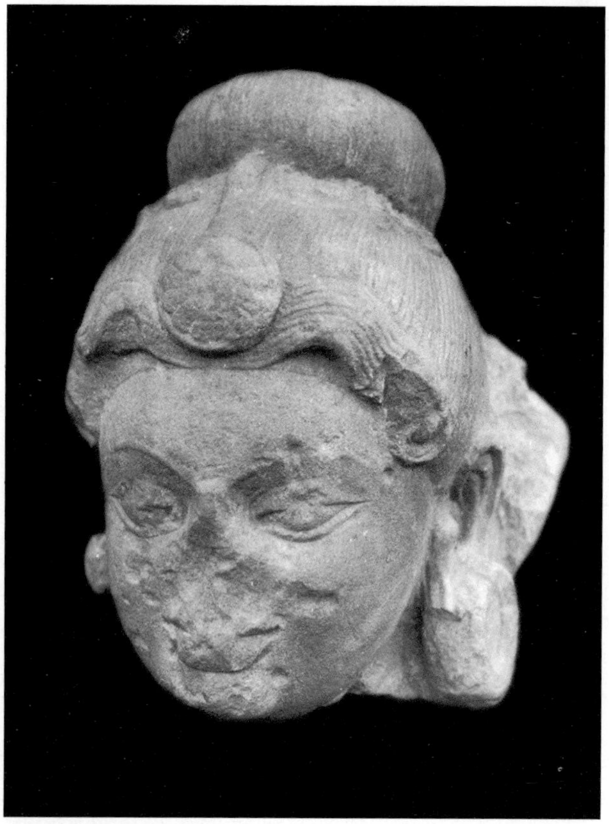

Pl. 193. Pārvatī head, Rithal.

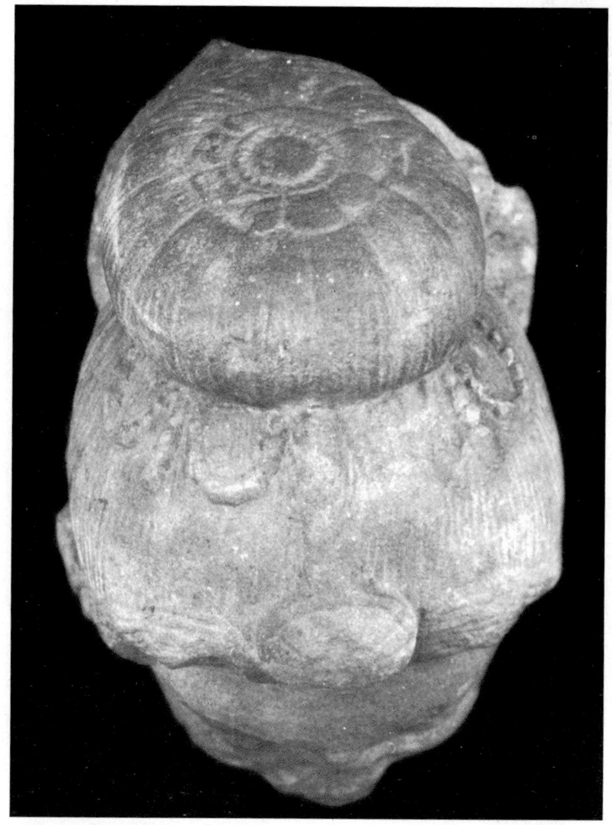

Pl. 194. Same, top view.

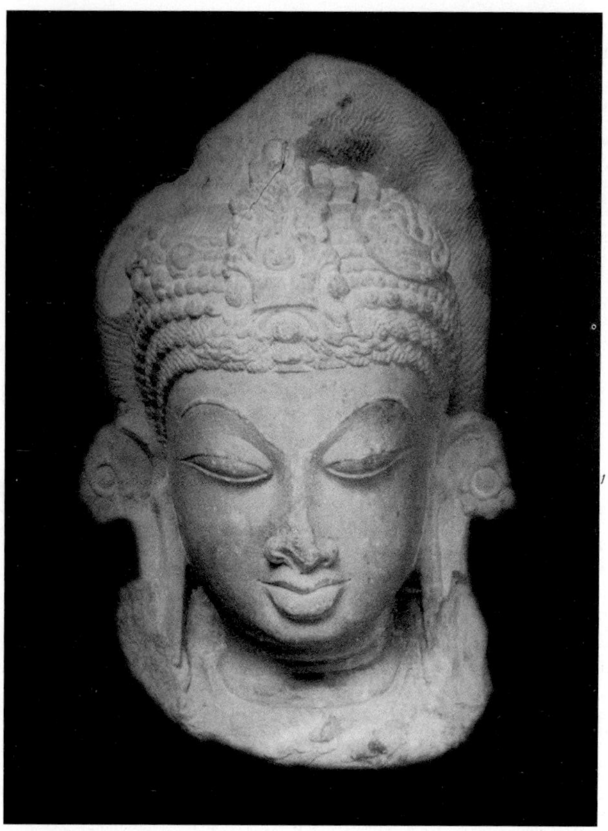

Pl. 195. Pārvatī head, Agroha.

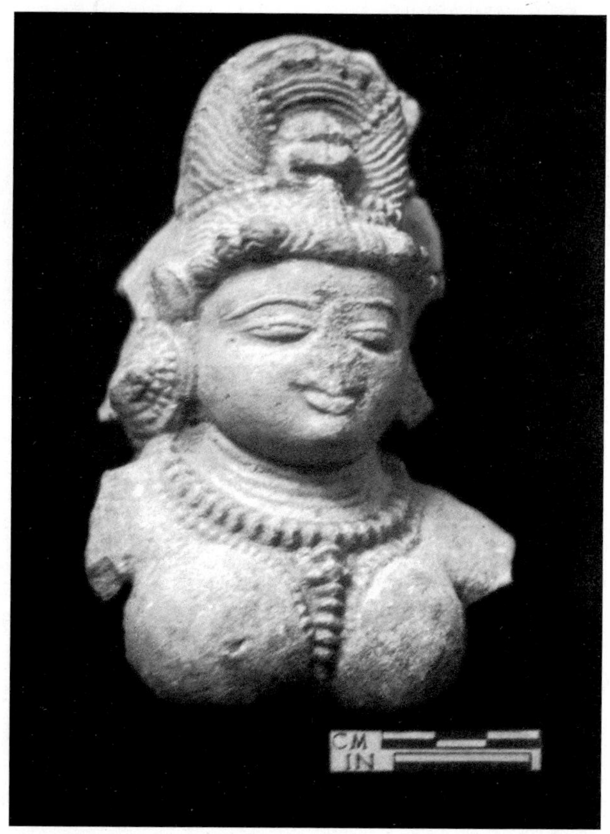

Pl. 196. Bust of Pārvatī, Pinjore.

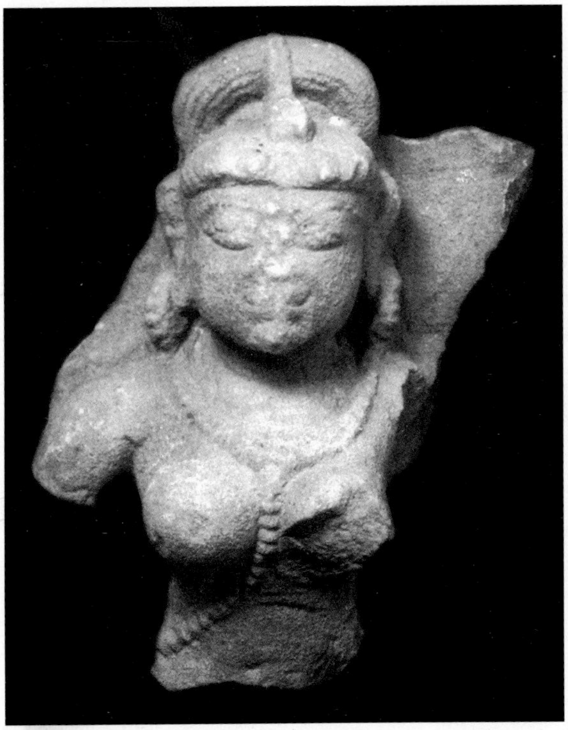

Pl. 197. Bust of Pārvatī, Pinjore.

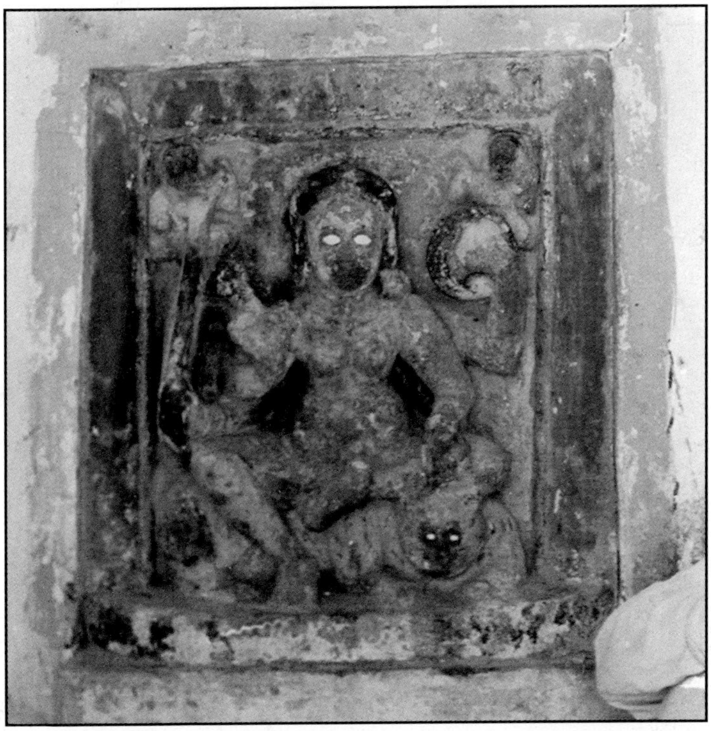

Pl. 198. Durgā, Kapālamochana.

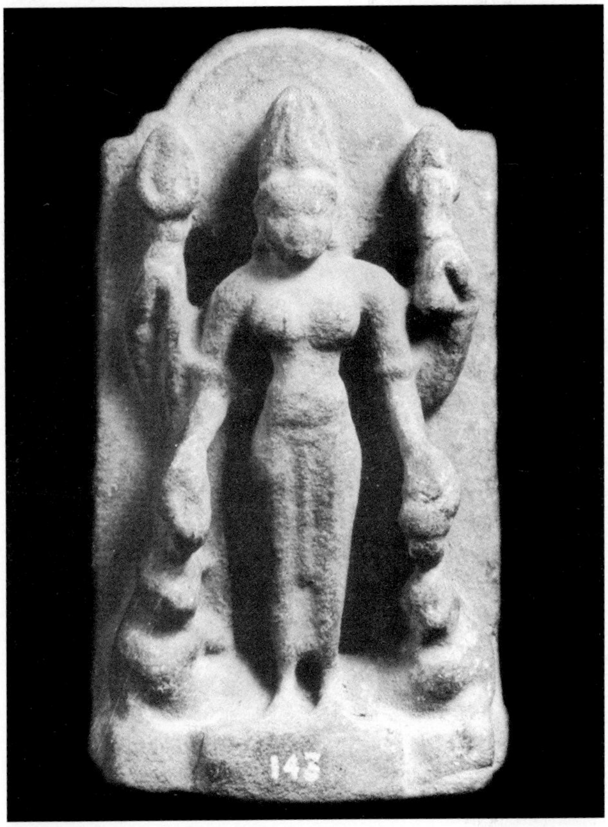

Pl. 199. Durgā, Mandhna.

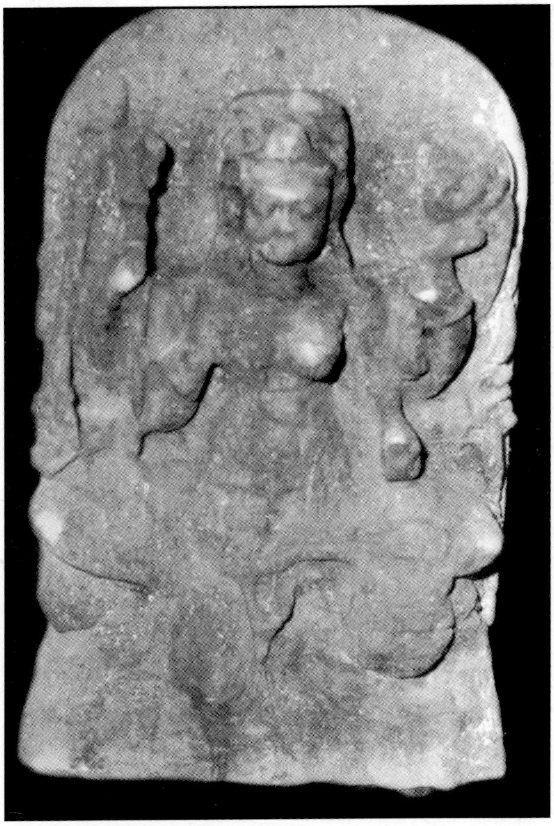

Pl. 200. Kshemaṅkarī Durgā, Rohtak.

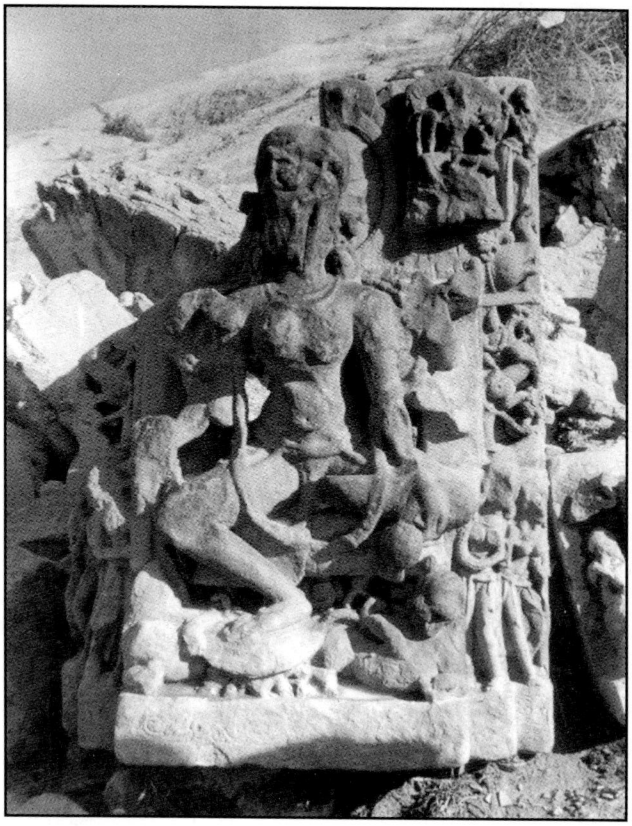

Pl. 201. Kshemaṅkarī Durgā, Sondh.

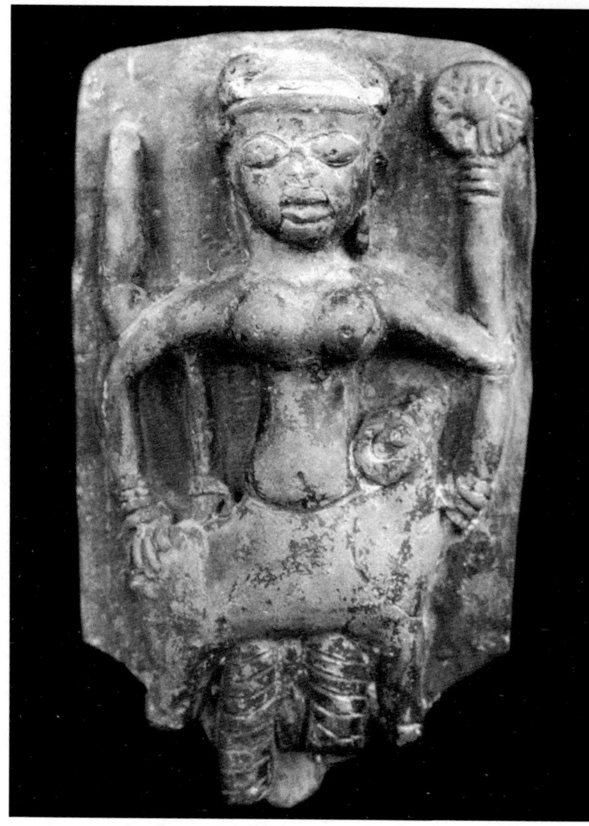

Pl. 202. Mahishamardinī, terracotta, Vara.

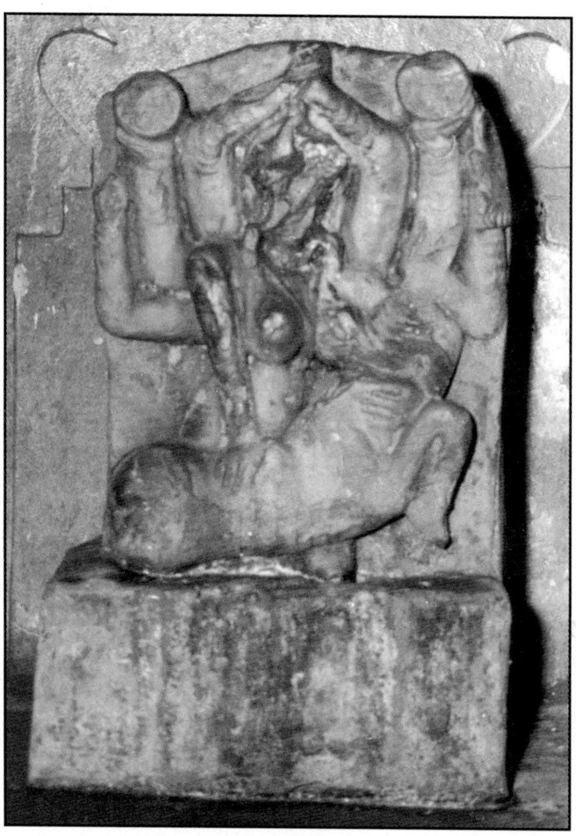

Pl. 203. Mahishamardinī, Rukhi.

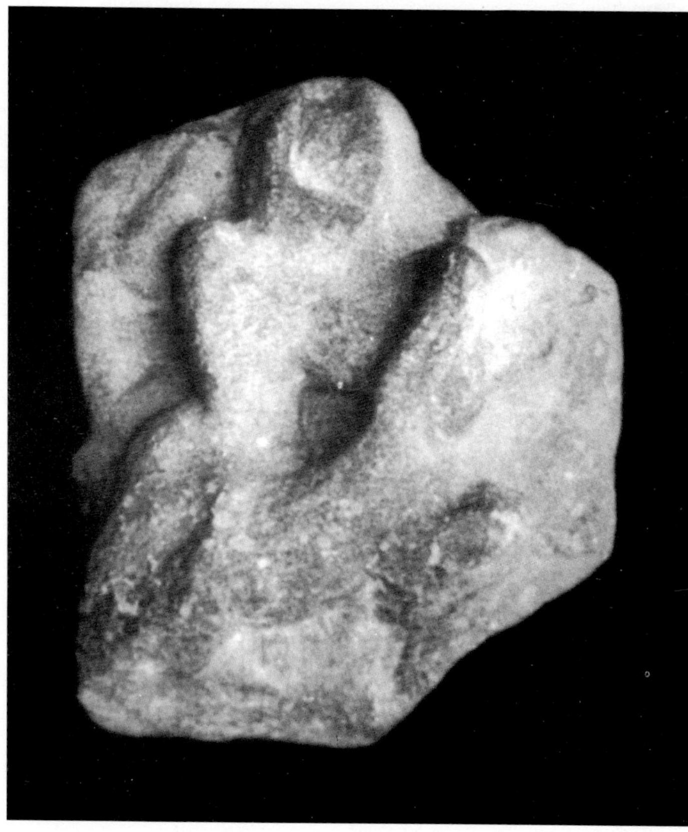

Pl. 204. Mahishamardinī, Sanghel.

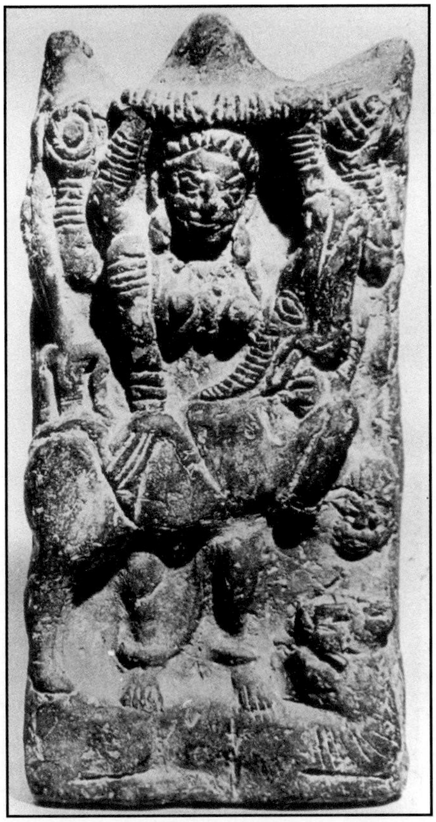

Pl. 205. Mahishamardinī, terracotta plaque, Gurukula Museum, Jhajjar.

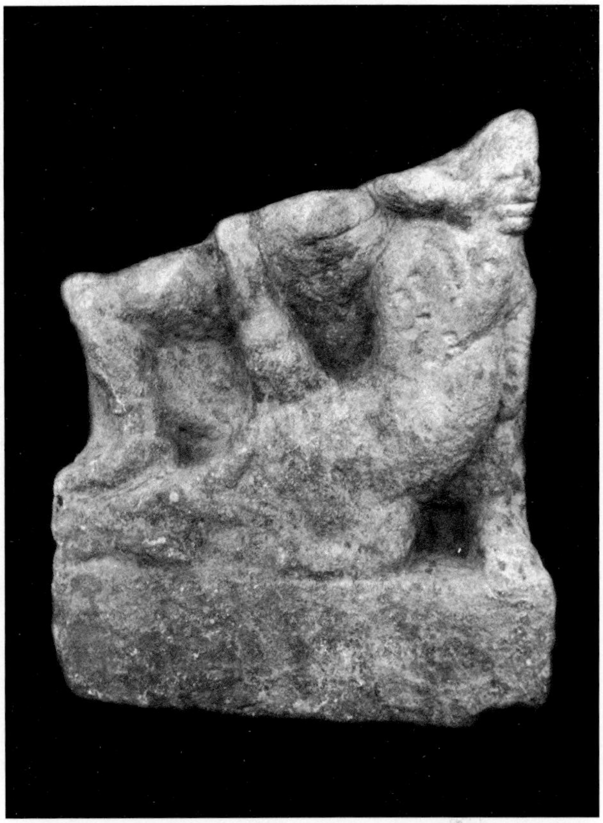

Pl. 206. Mahishamardinī, Sanghel.

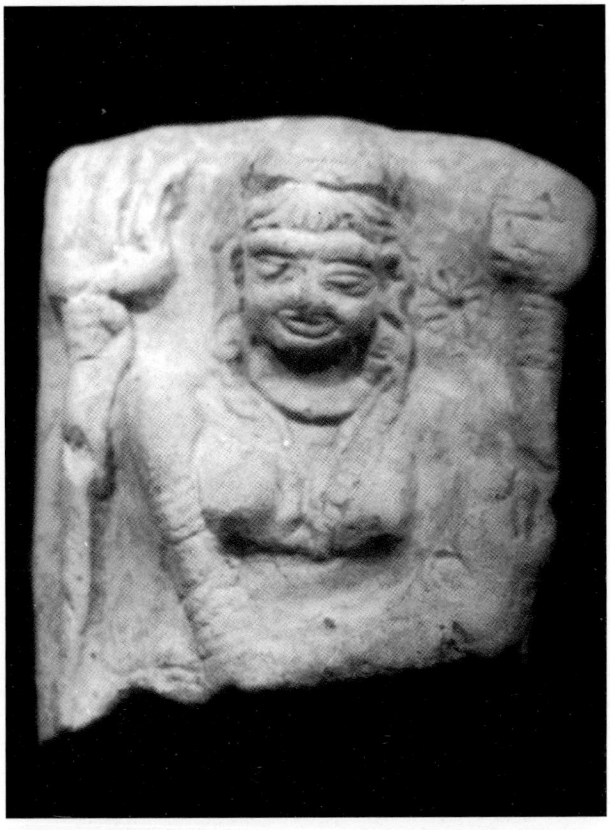

Pl. 207. Mahishamardinī, terracotta, Patlikhurd.

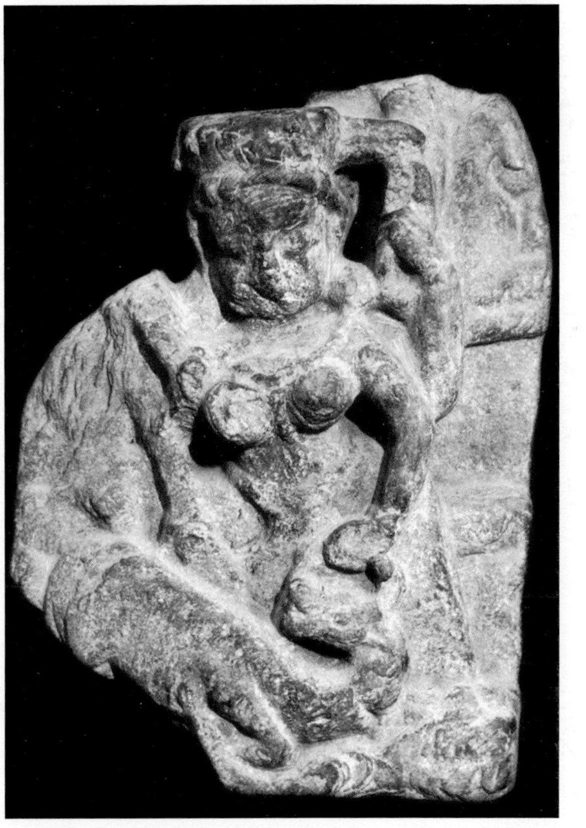

Pl. 208. Mahishamardinī, Baroli.

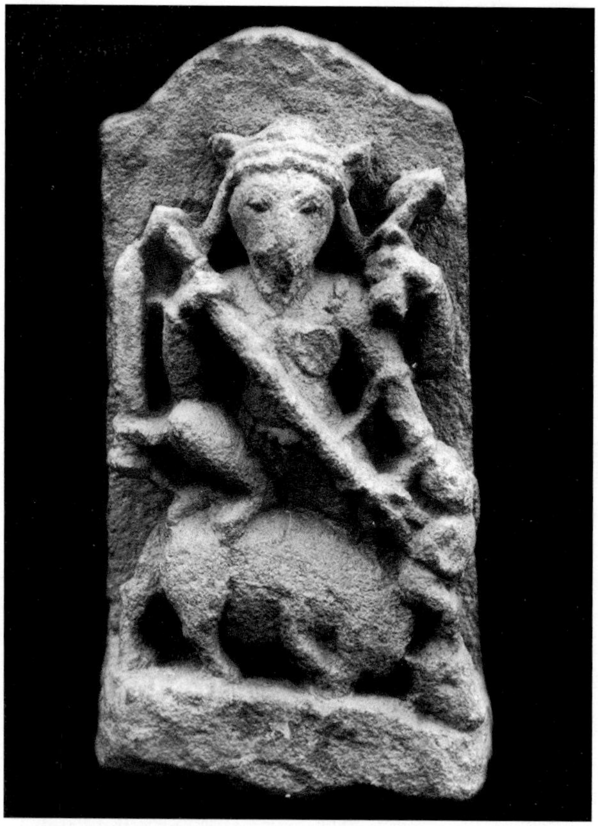

Pl. 209. Mahishamardinī, Gujjar Kheri.

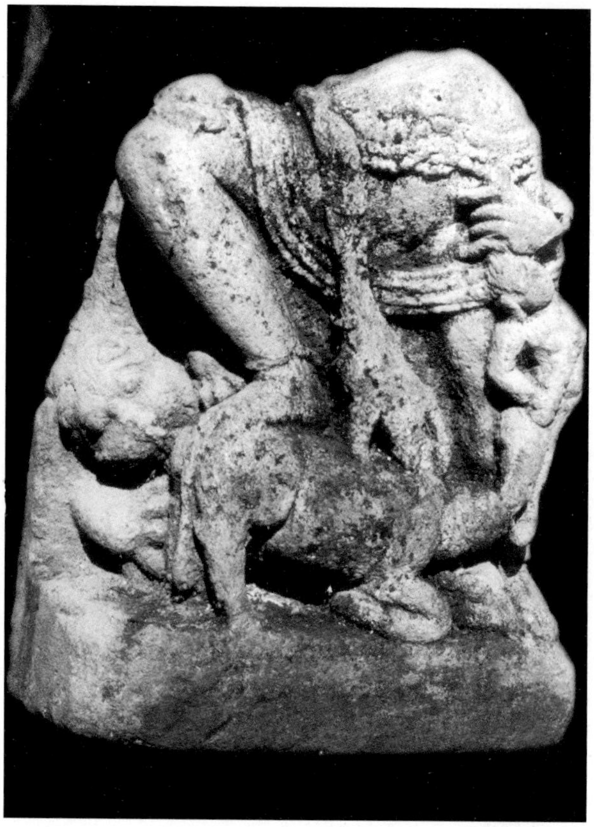

Pl. 210. Mahishamardinī, lower portion, Rohtak.

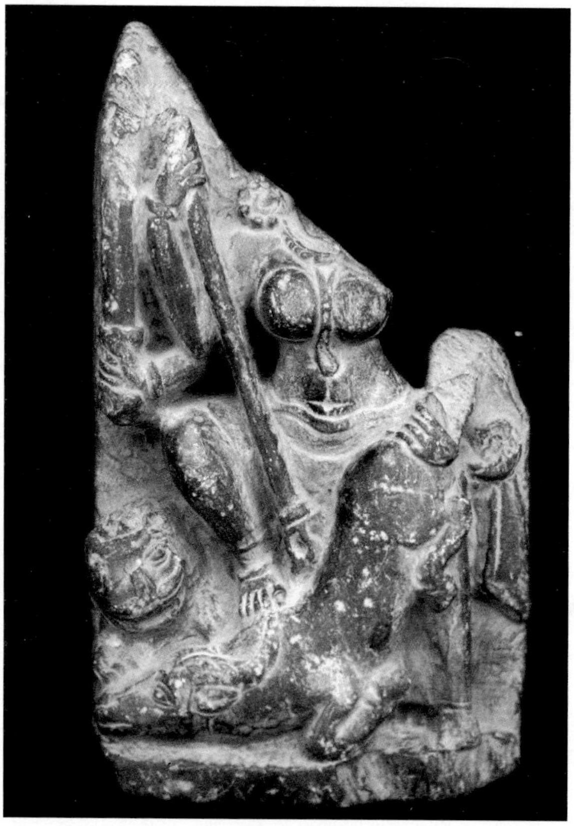

Pl. 211. Mahishamardinī, Sadhaura.

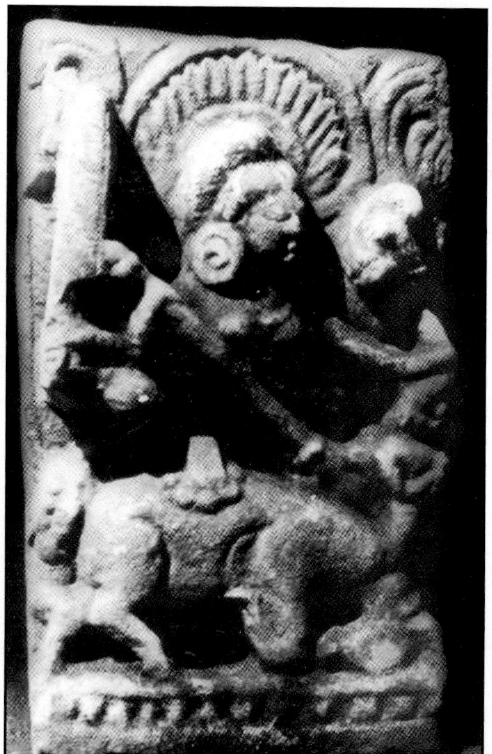

Pl. 212. Mahishamardinī, Hansi.

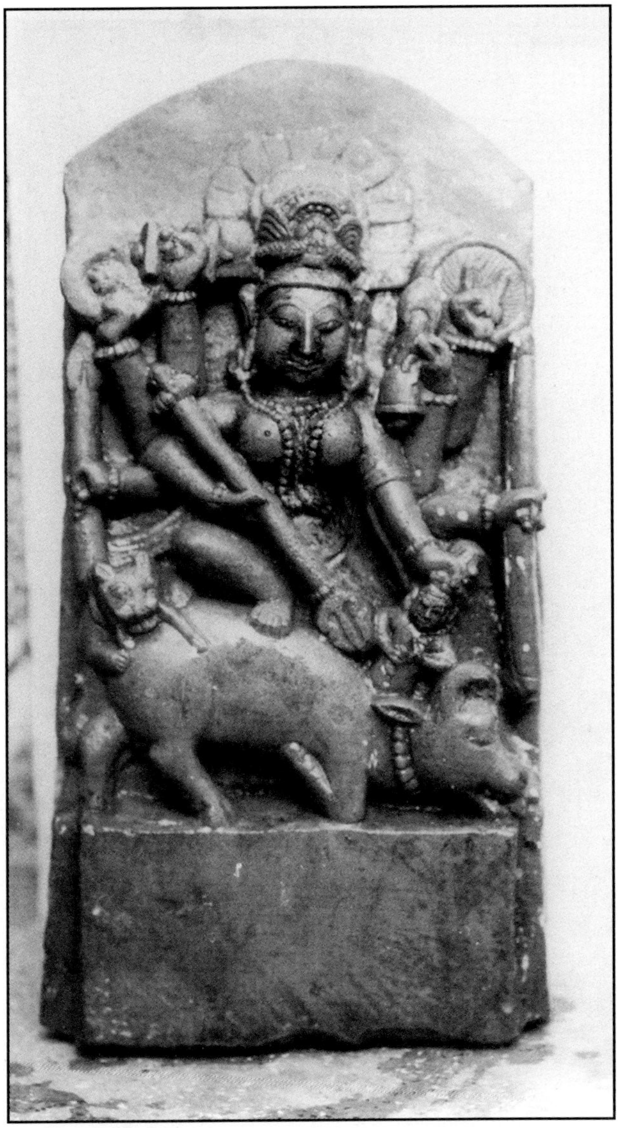

Pl. 213. Mahishamardinī, Hansi.

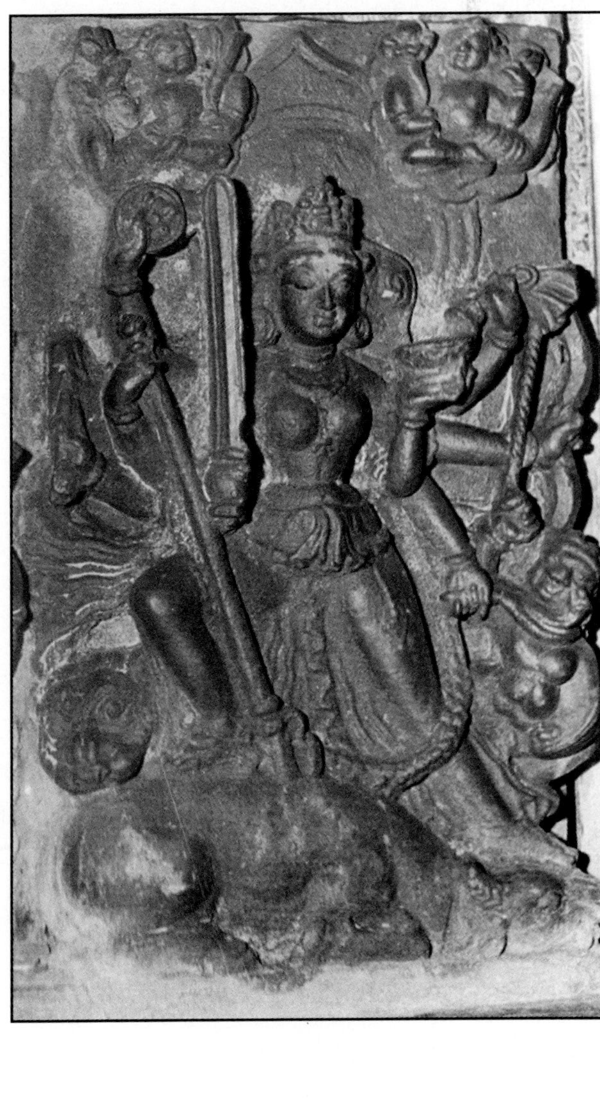

Pl. 214. Mahishamardinī, Kalayat.

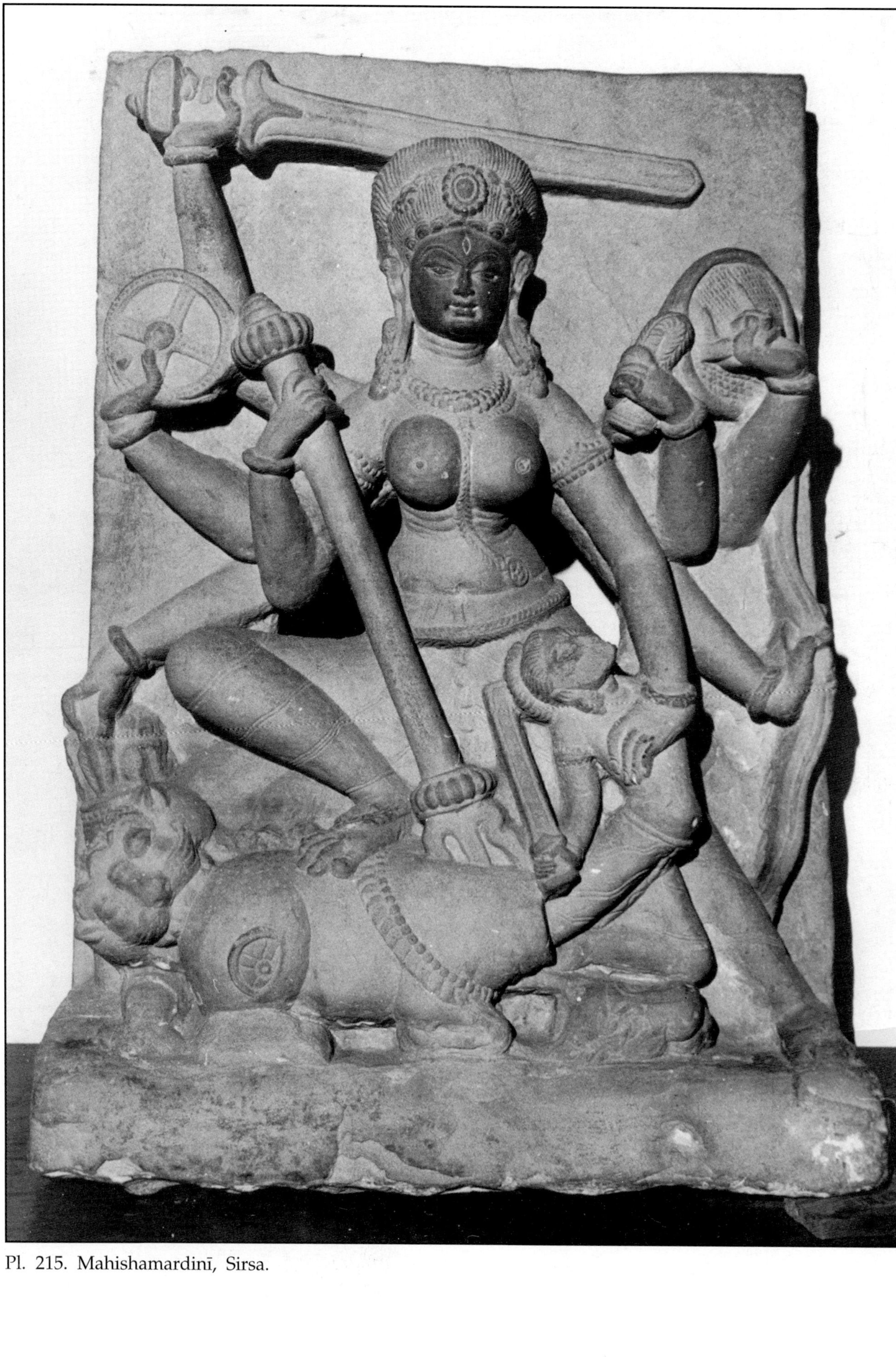

Pl. 215. Mahishamardinī, Sirsa.

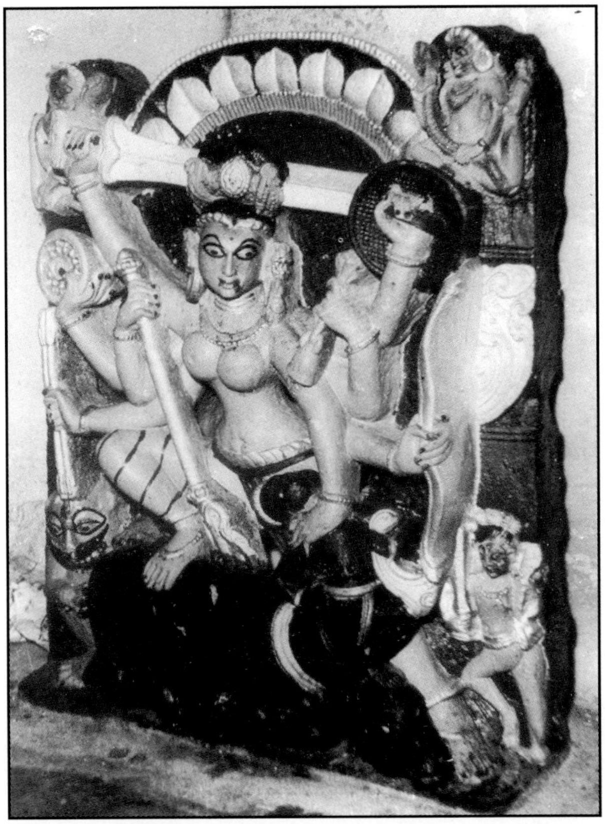

Pl. 216. Mahishamardinī, Pehowa.

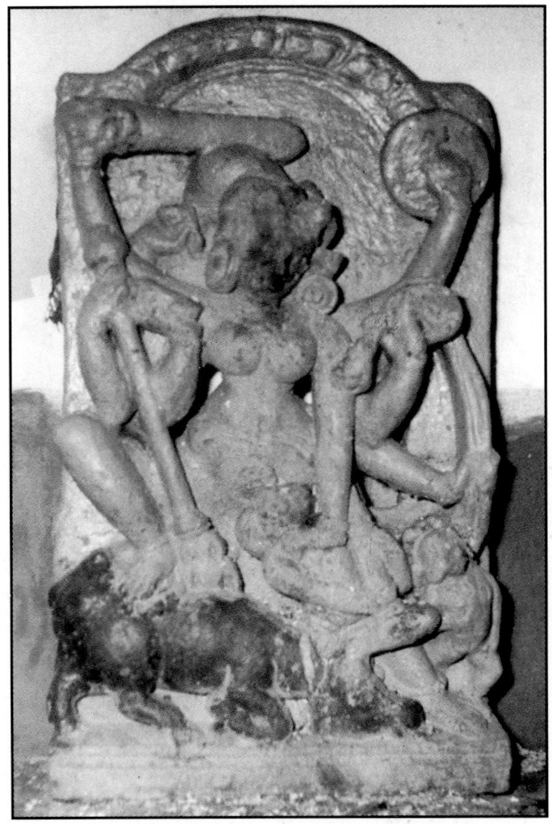

Pl. 217. Mahishamardinī, Tandwal.

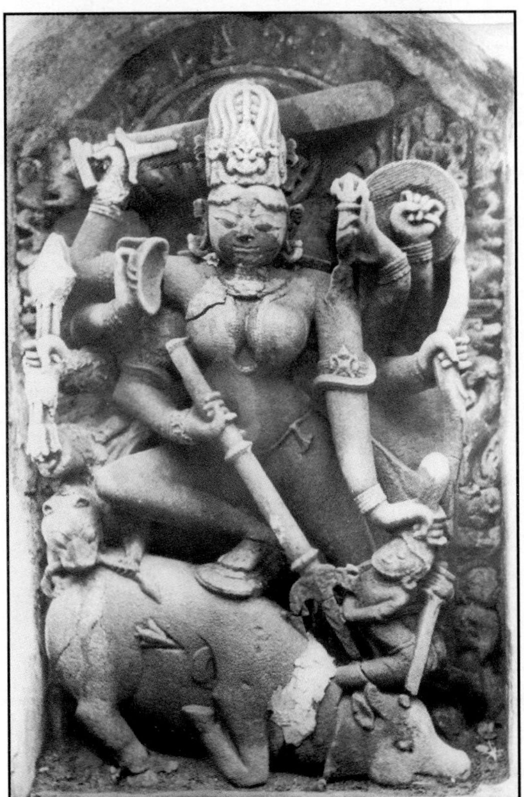

Pl. 218. Mahishamardinī, Chandimandir.

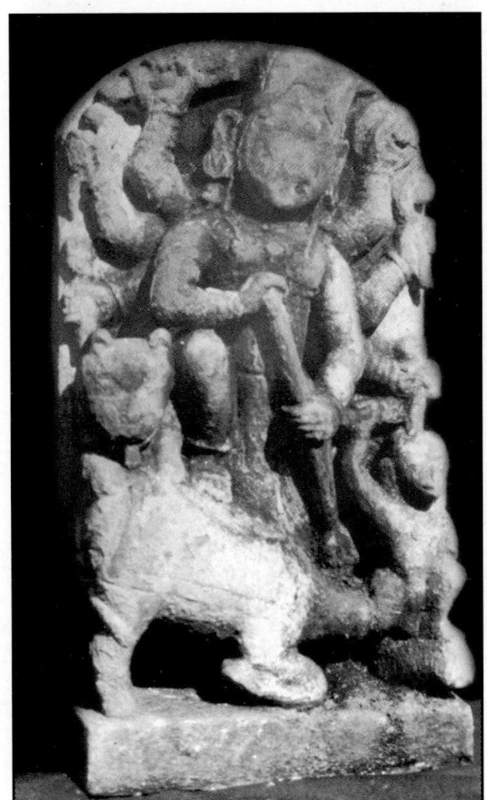

Pl. 219. Mahishamardinī, Gharaunda.

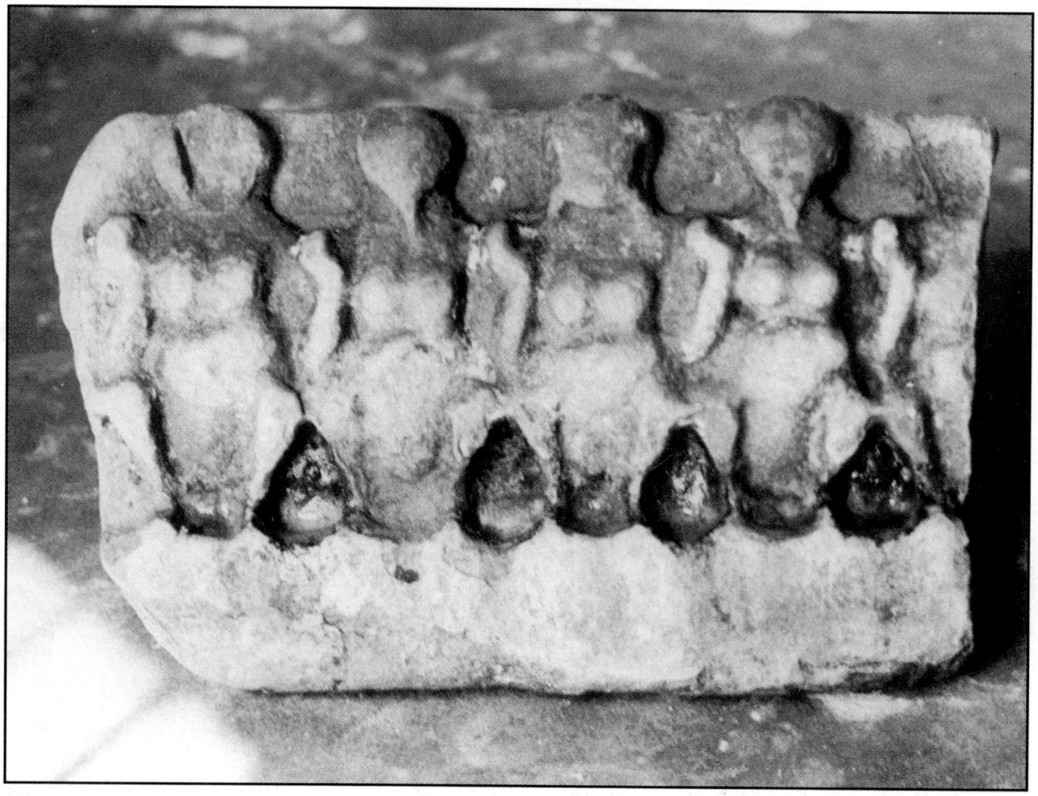

Pl. 220. Sapta-Mātṛikās, Rohtak.

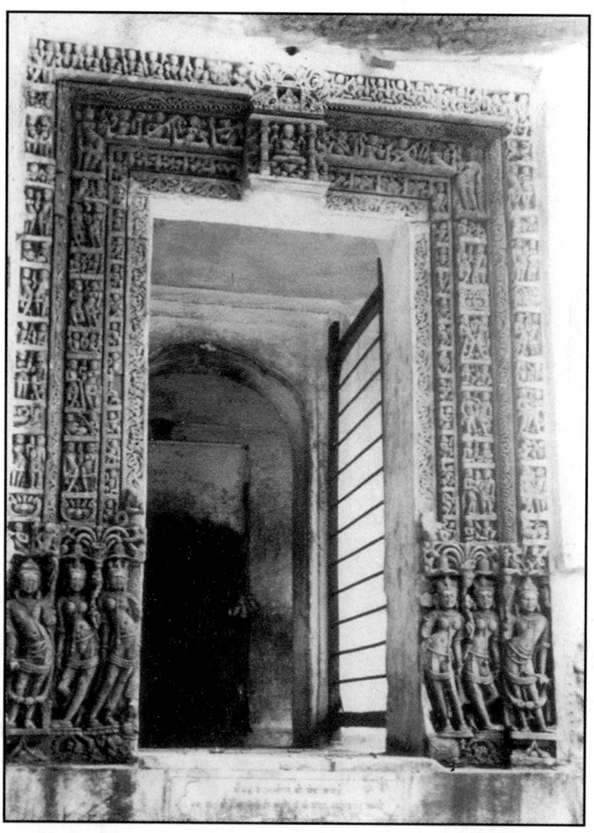

Pl. 221. Sapta-Mātṛikās on the lintel of the doorframe, Pehowa.

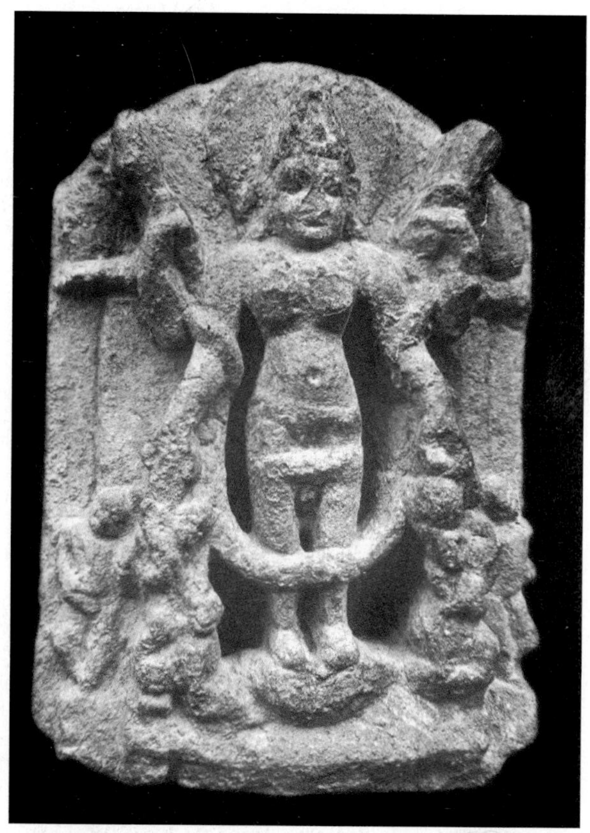

Pl. 222. Unfinished Brahmāṇī, Gujjar Kheri.

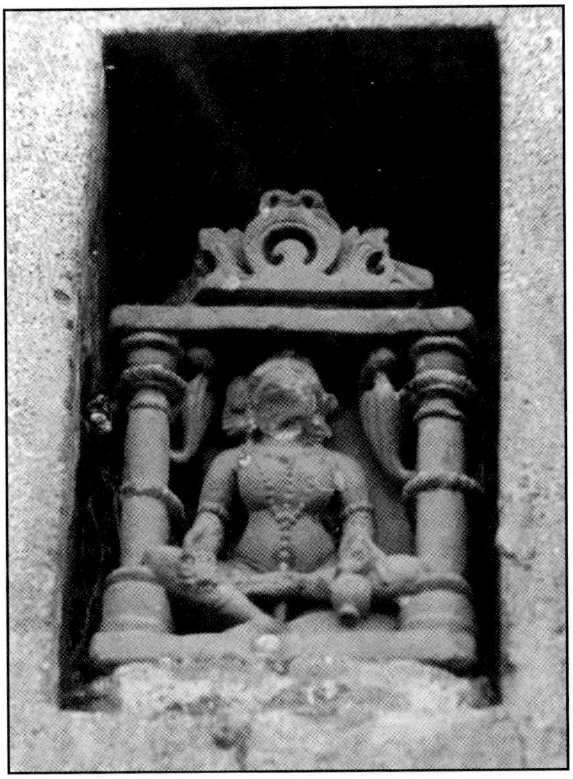

Pl. 223. Brahmāṇī, provenance unknown.

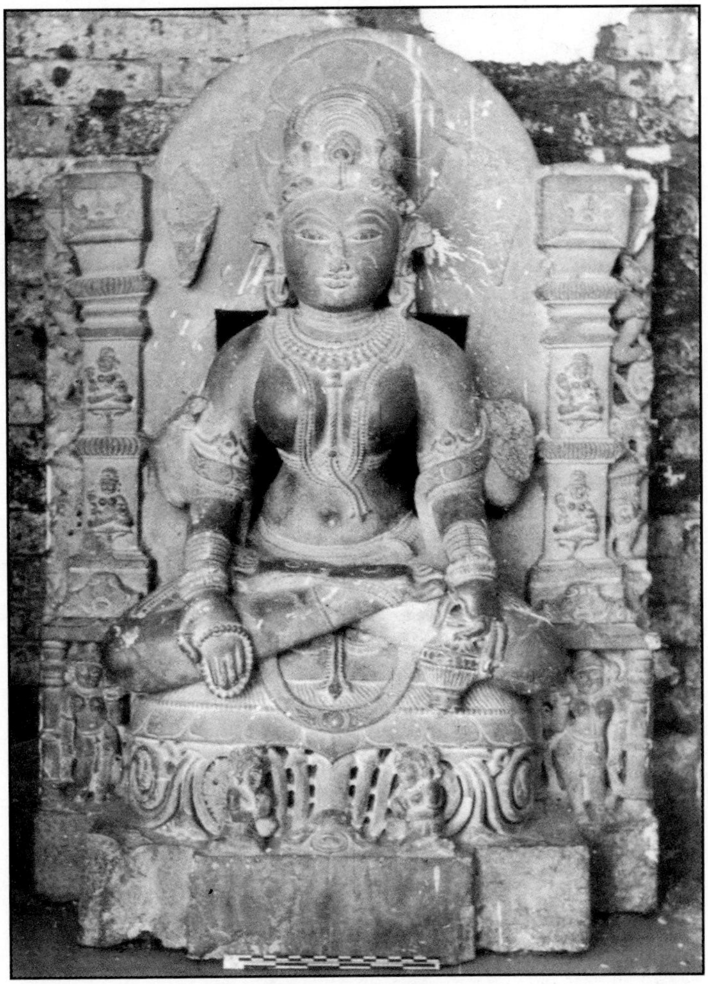

Pl. 224. Brahmāṇī, Asthal Bohr, Rohtak.

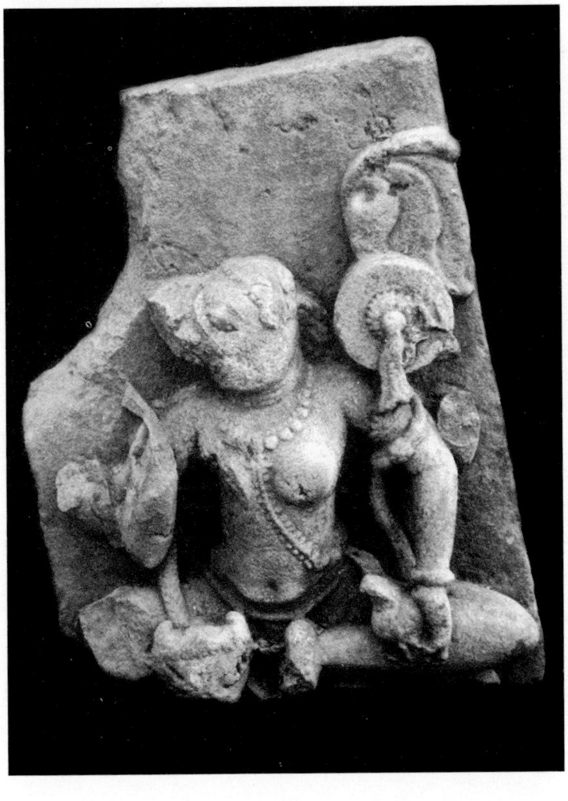

Pl. 225. Vārāhī, Pinjore.

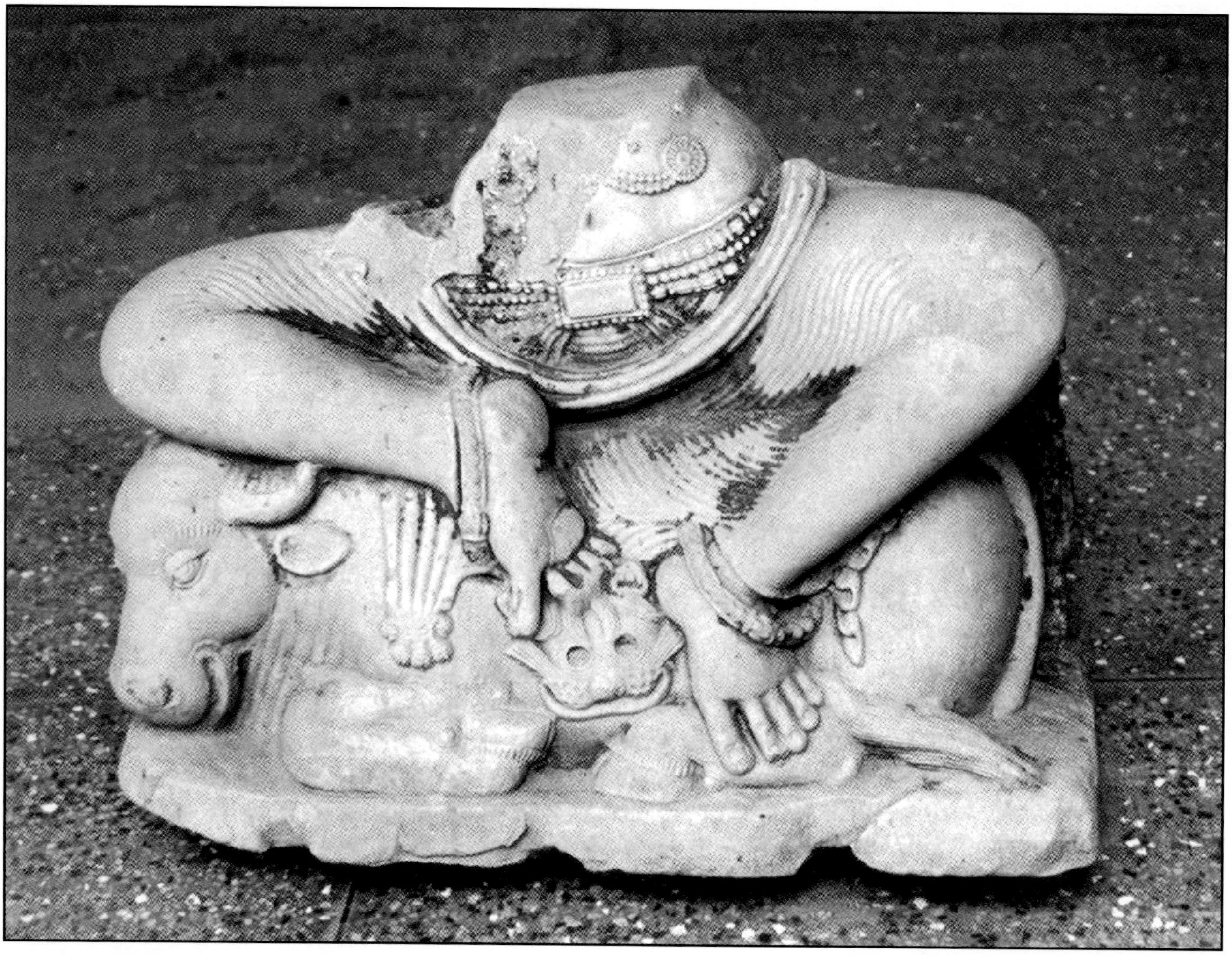

Pl. 227. Vārāhī, lower portion, Asthal Bohr, Rohtak.

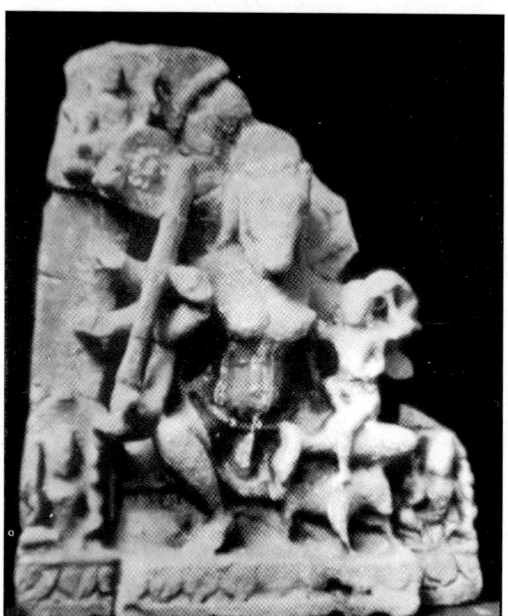

Pl. 226. Vārāhī, Jhajjar Museum.

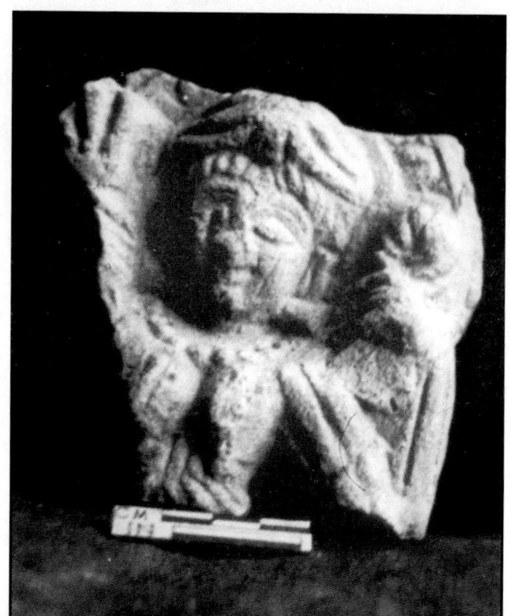

Pl. 228. Chāmuṇḍā, fragmentary, Mohanbari.

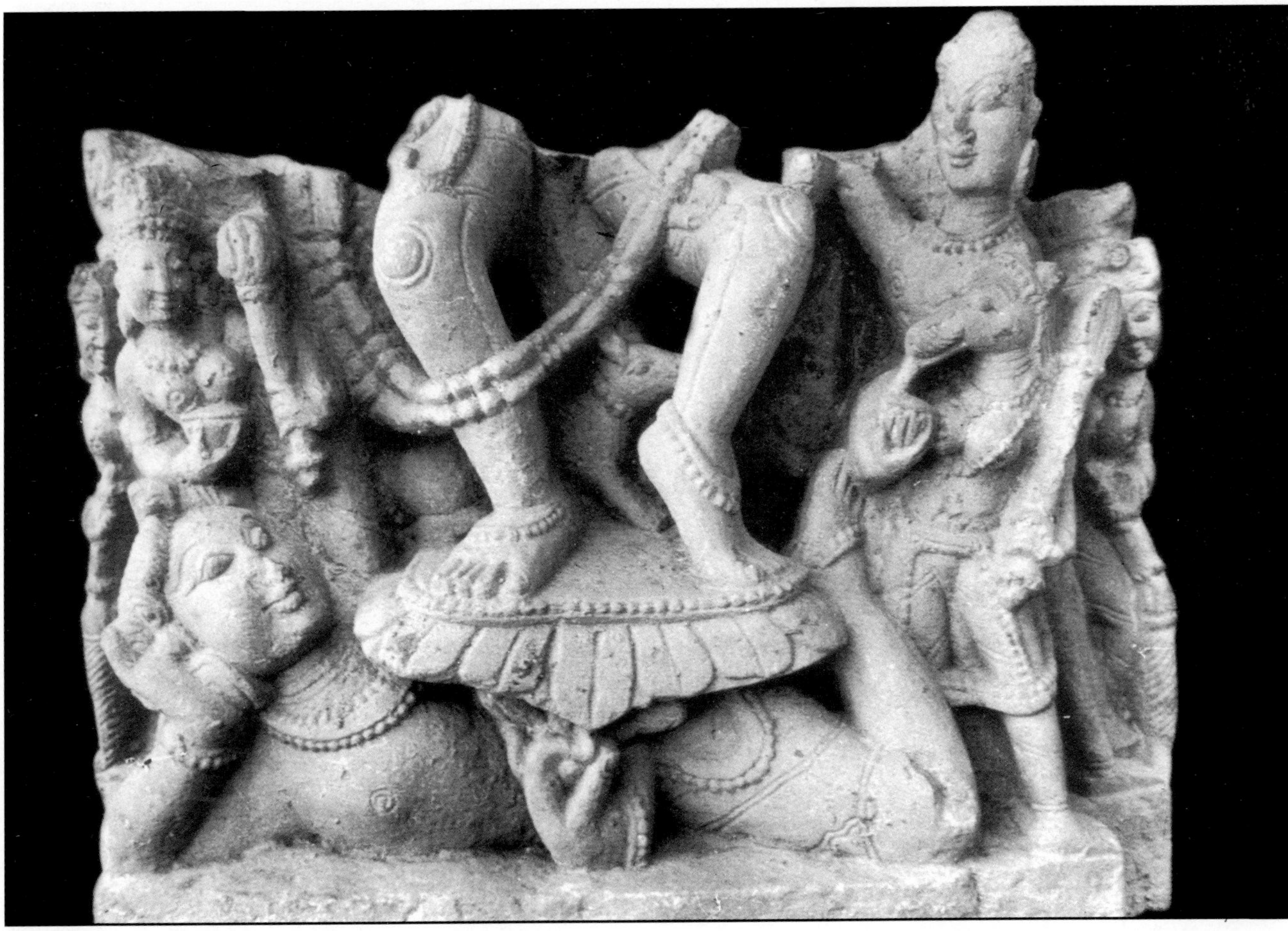

Pl. 229. Chāmuṇḍā, lower portion, Gujjar Kheri.

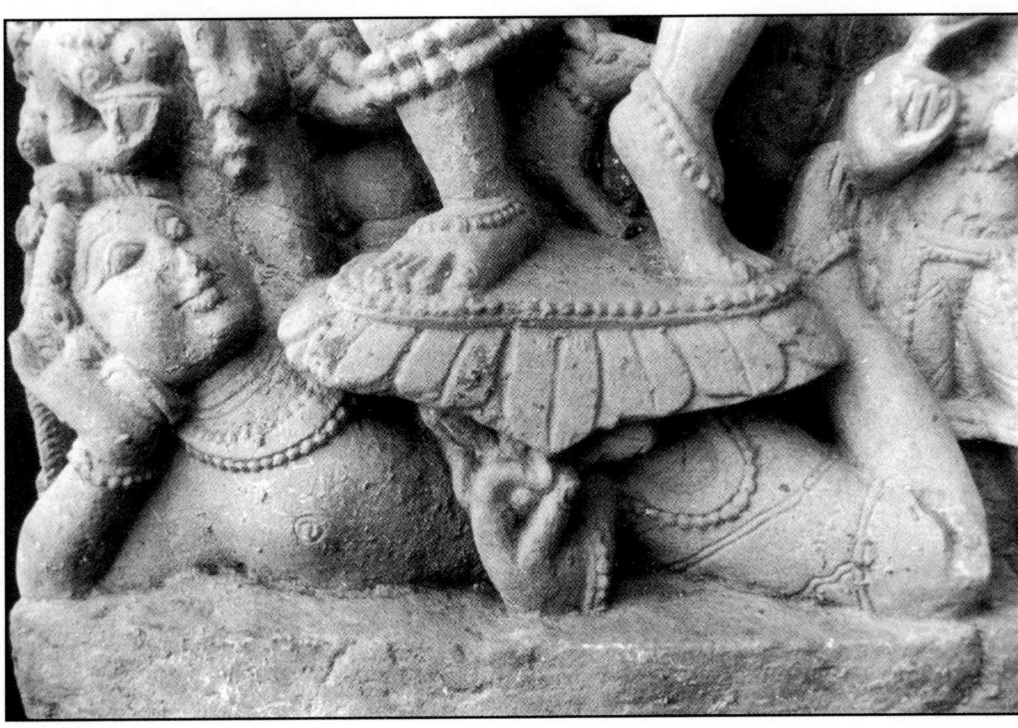

Pl. 230. Same, closer view.

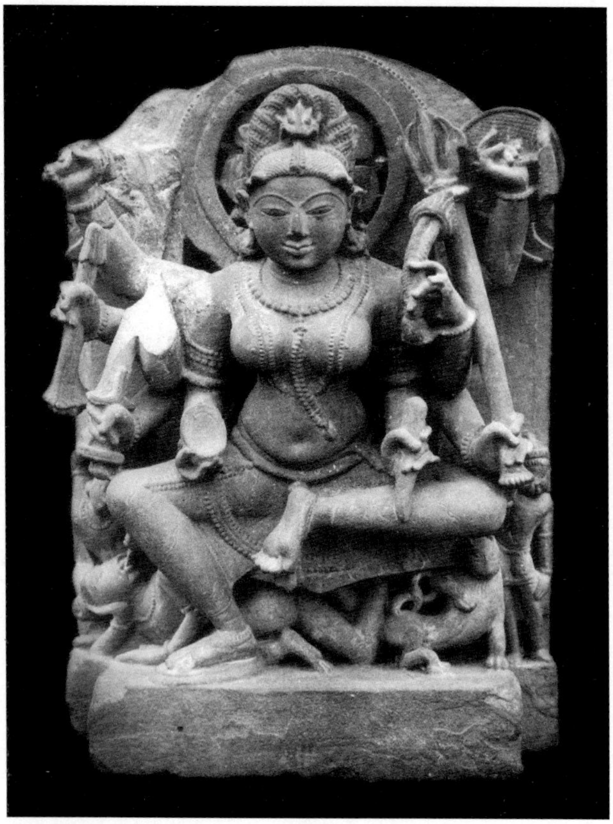

Pl. 231. Devī, Muradnagar.

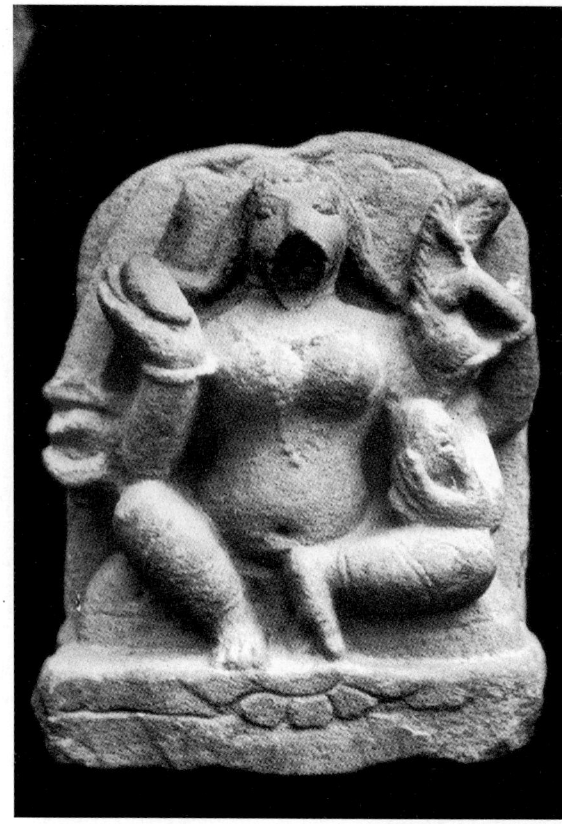

Pl. 232. Nārasiṃhī, Gujjar Kheri.

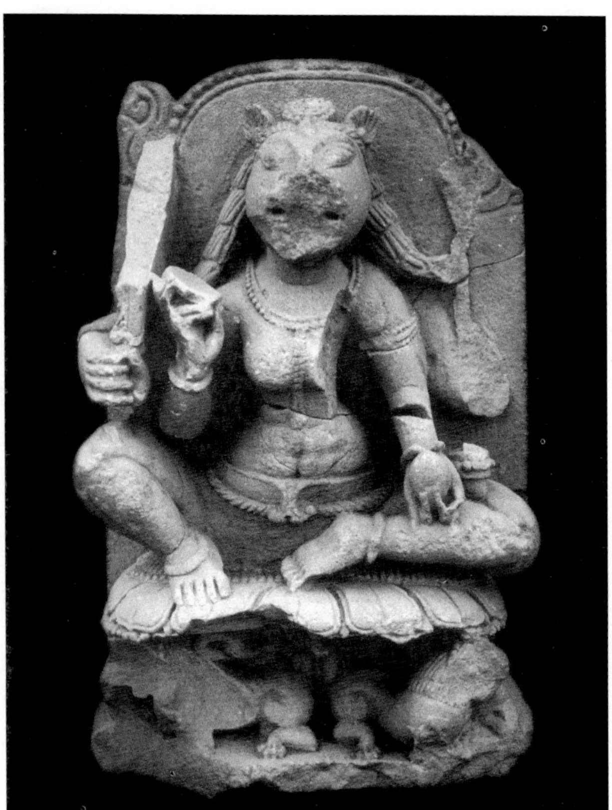

Pl. 233. Nārasiṃhī, Agroha.

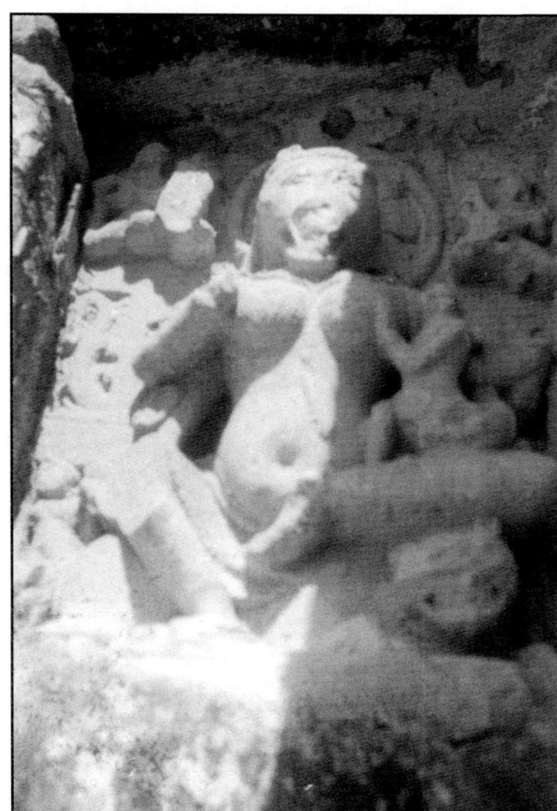

Pl. 234. Nārasiṃhī, Pehowa.

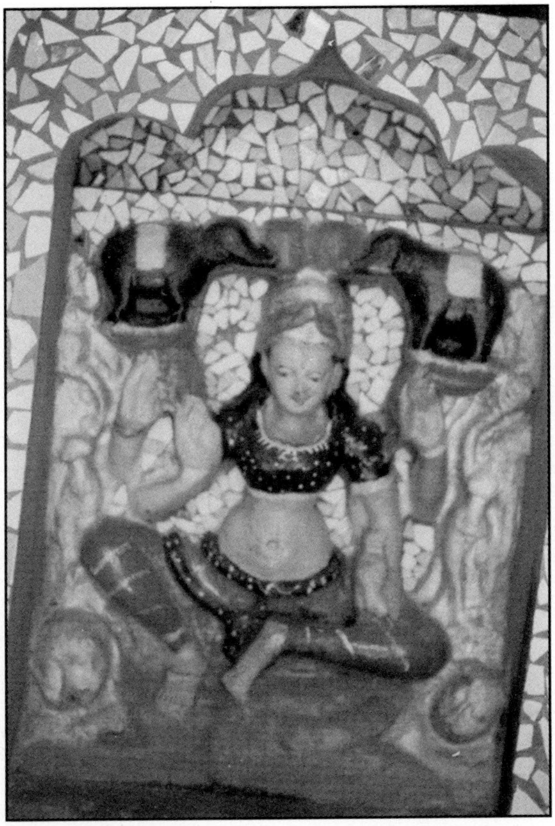

Pl. 235. Gaja-Lakshmī, Kapālamochana.

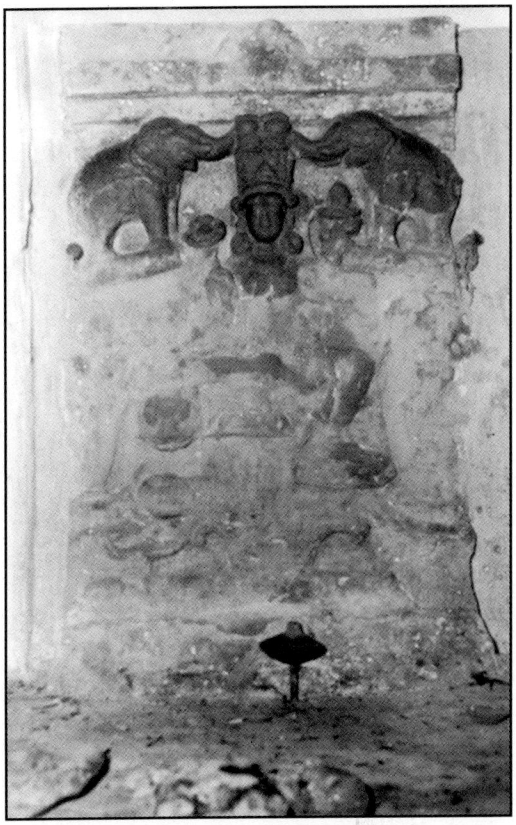

Pl. 236. Gaja-Lakshmī, Jaintipur.

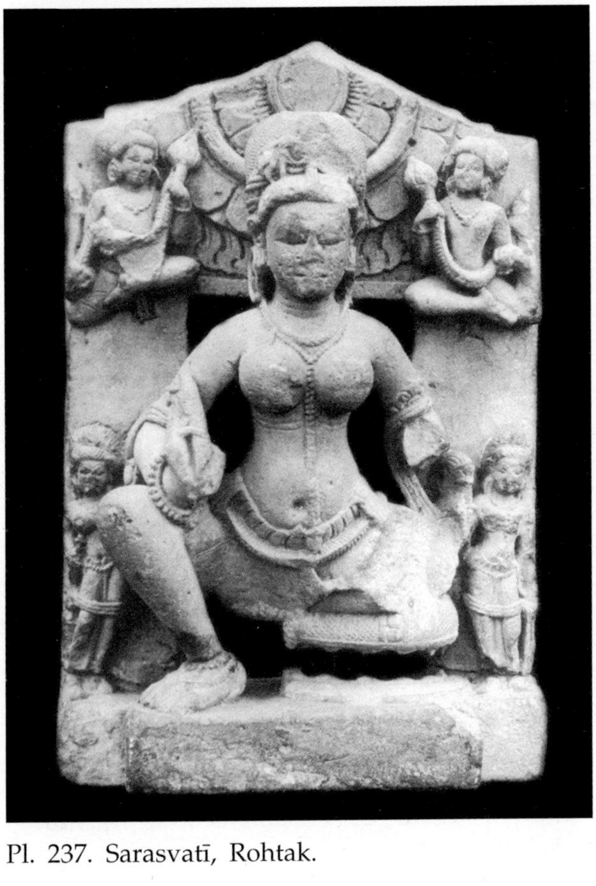

Pl. 237. Sarasvatī, Rohtak.

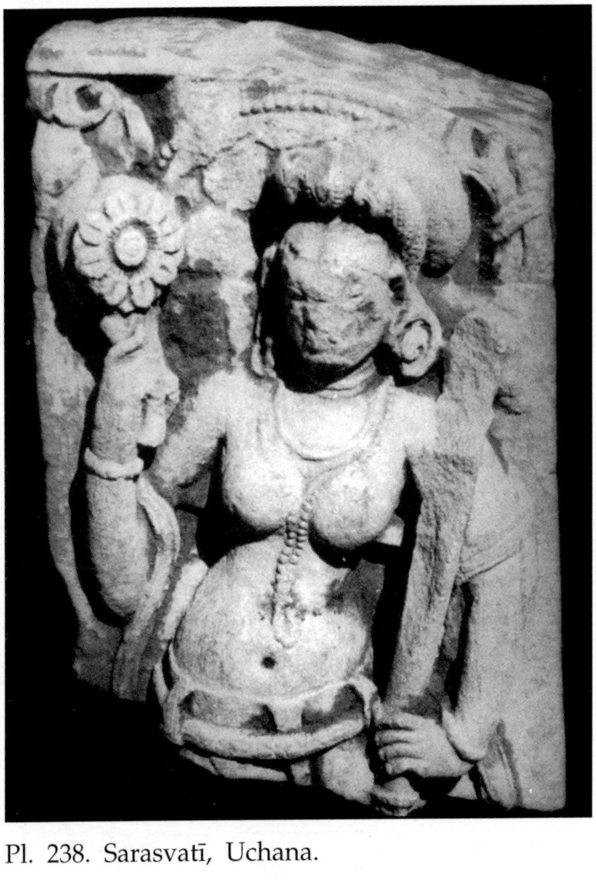

Pl. 238. Sarasvatī, Uchana.

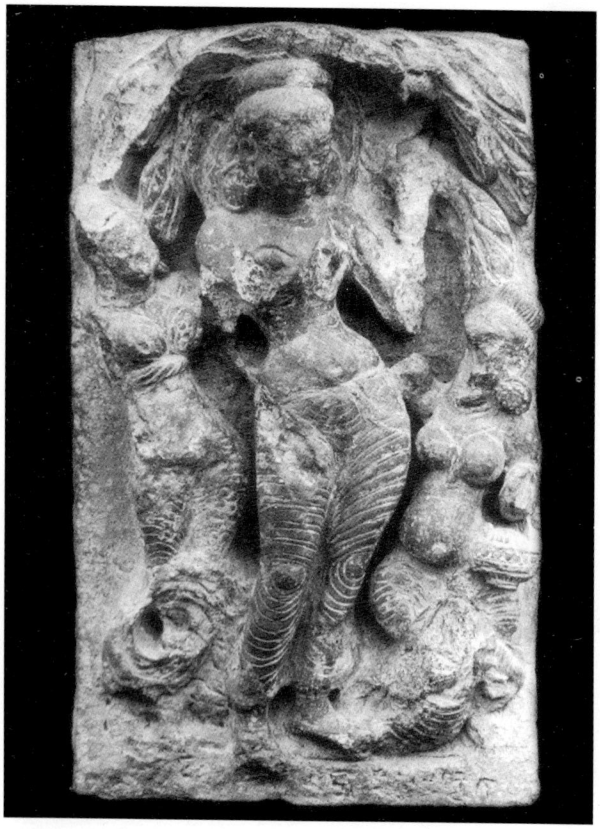

Pl. 239. Gaṅgā, terracotta, Kariwala.

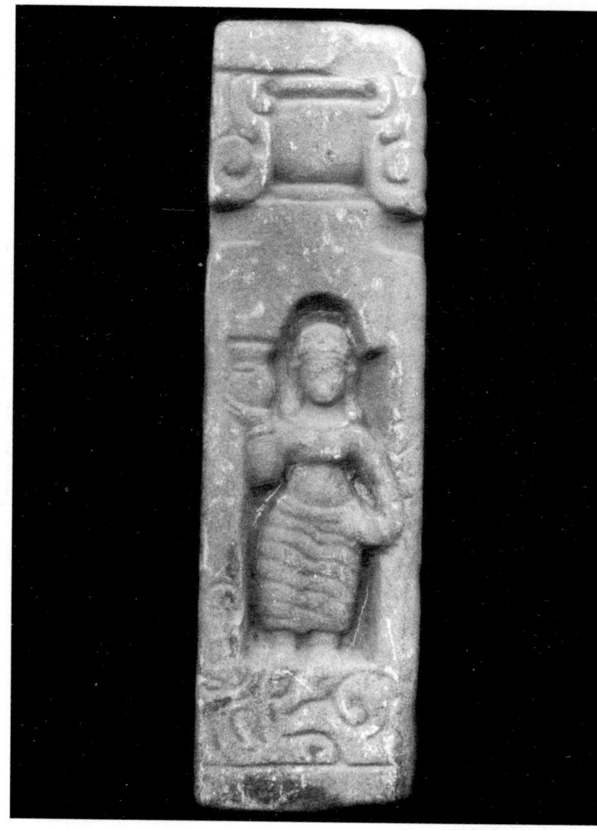

Pl. 240. Gaṅgā on a pillar, Kapālamochana.

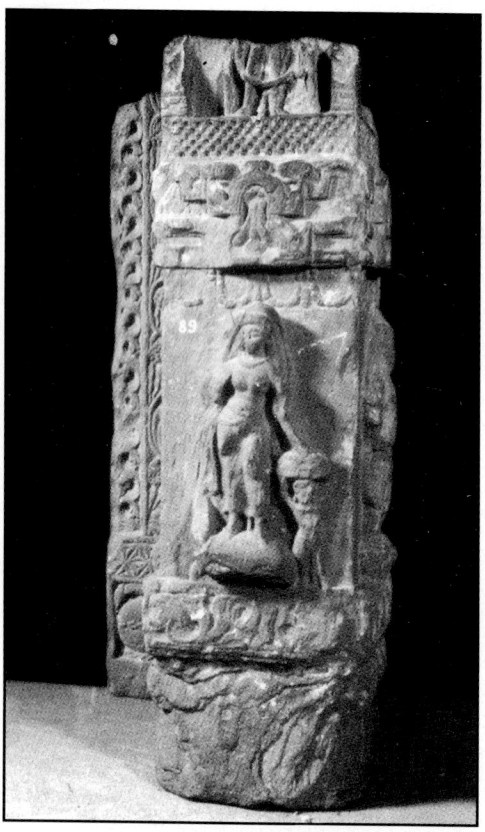

Pl. 241. Yamunā on tortoise on a pillar, Pinjore.

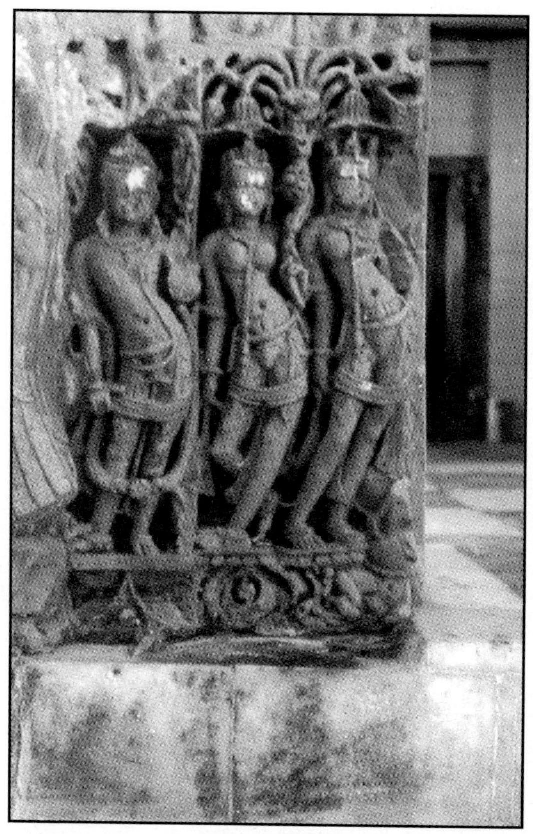

Pl. 242. Gaṅgā with attendants on doorjamb, Pehowa.

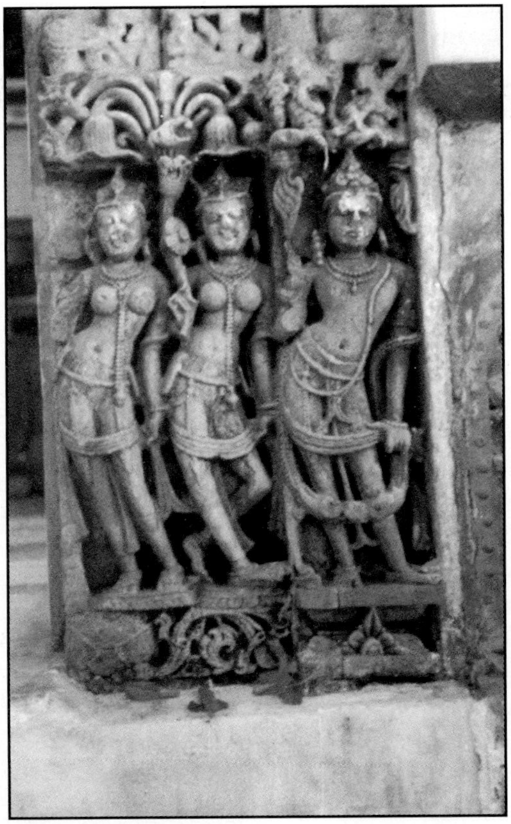

Pl. 243. Yamunā with attendants on doorjamb, Pehowa.

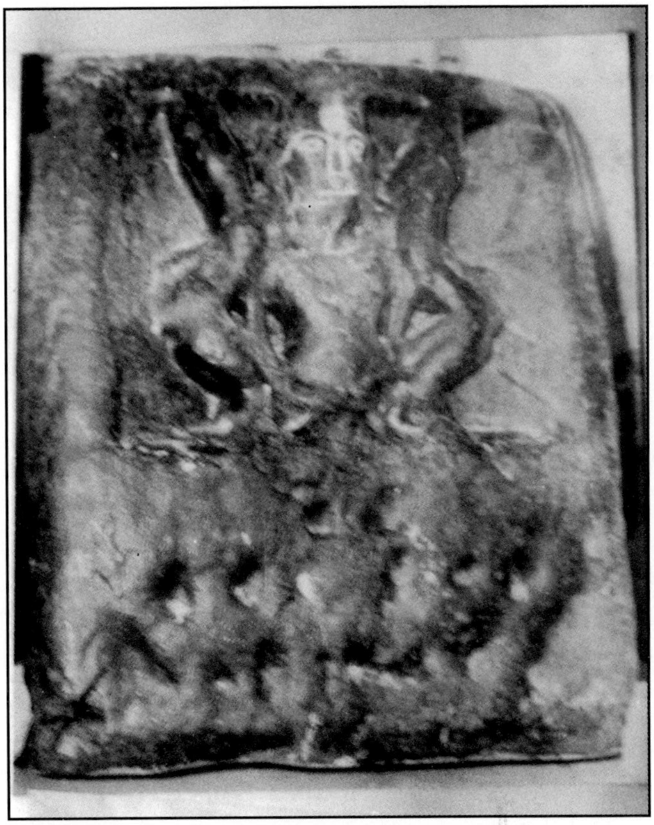

Pl. 244. Sūrya?, Kapālamochana.

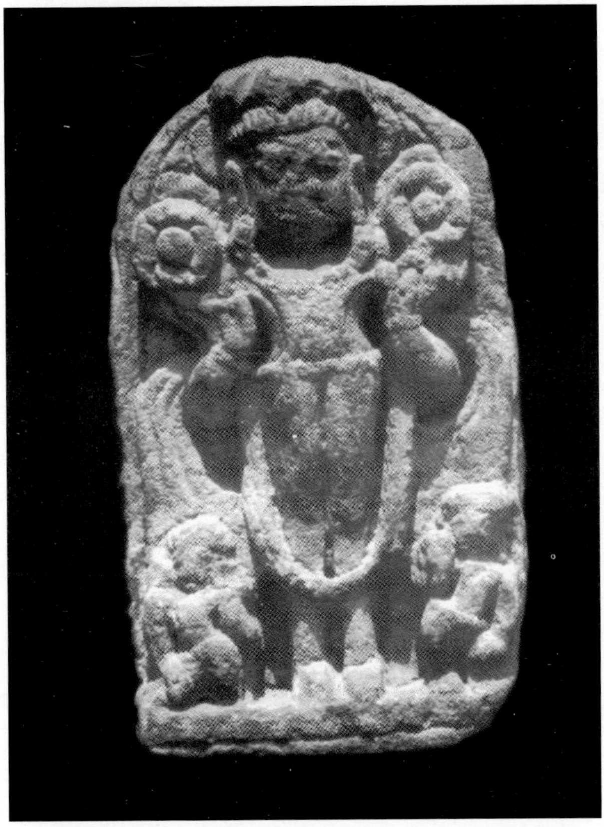

Pl. 245. Sūrya, Dhurand Khera.

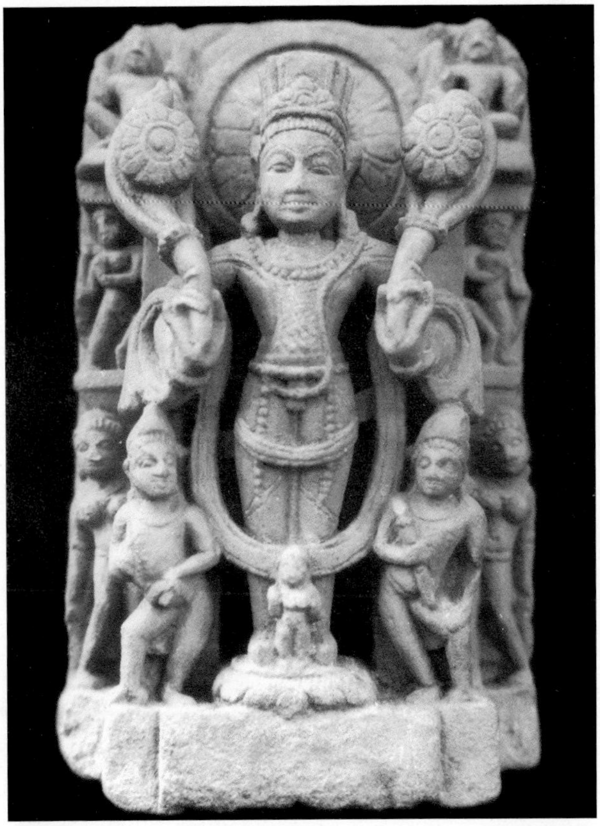

Pl. 246. Sūrya, Gujjar Kheri.

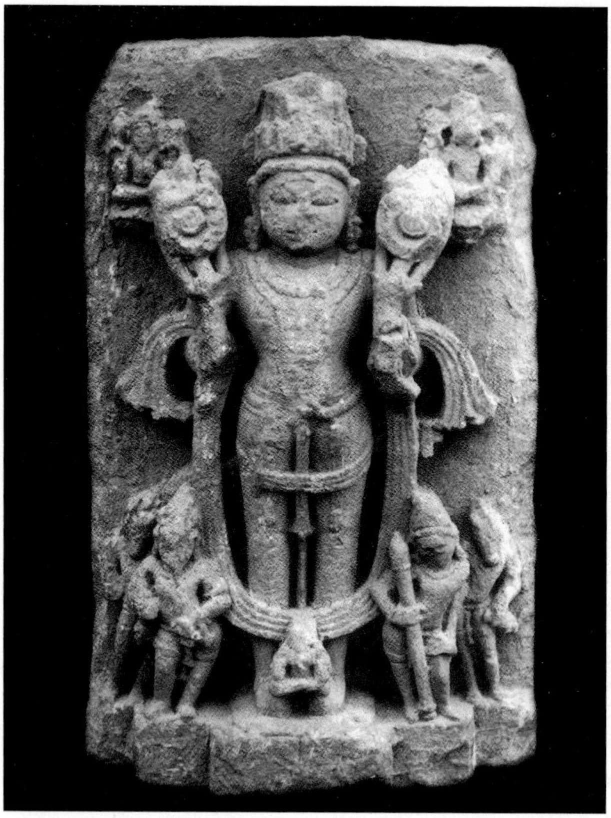

Pl. 247. Sūrya, Khokhrakot, Rohtak.

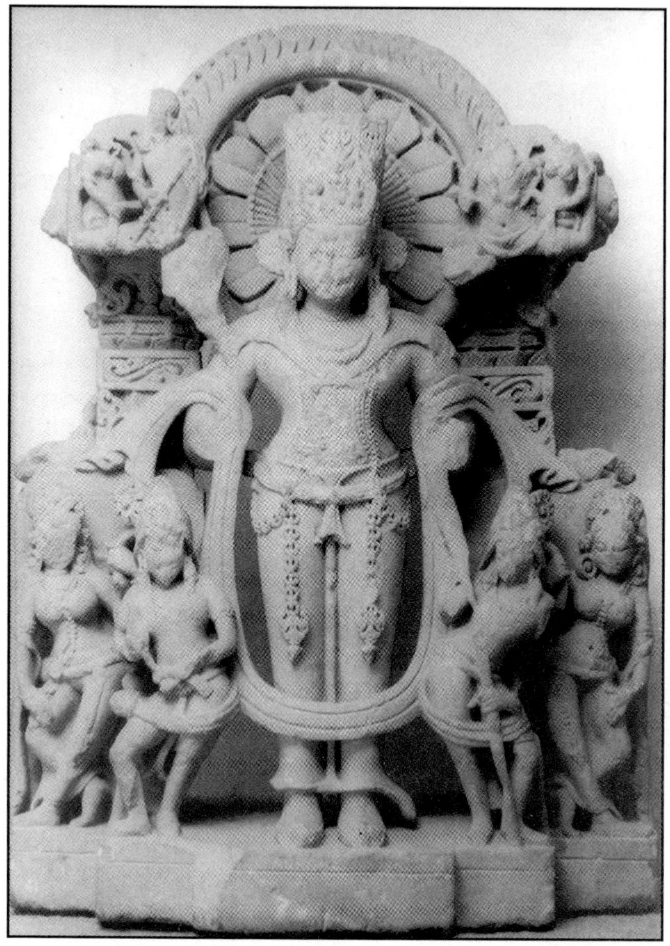

Pl. 249. Sūrya, Agroha.

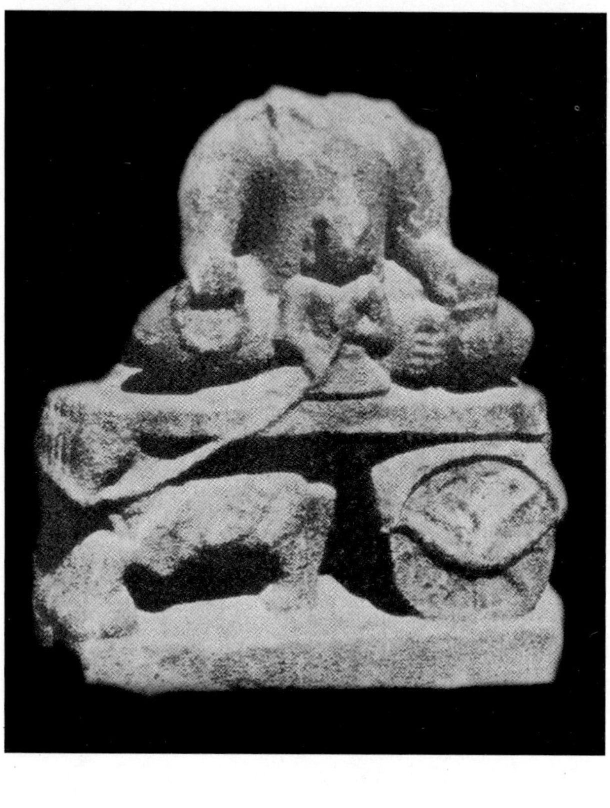

Pl. 248. Āditya-Sūrya from Thanesar.

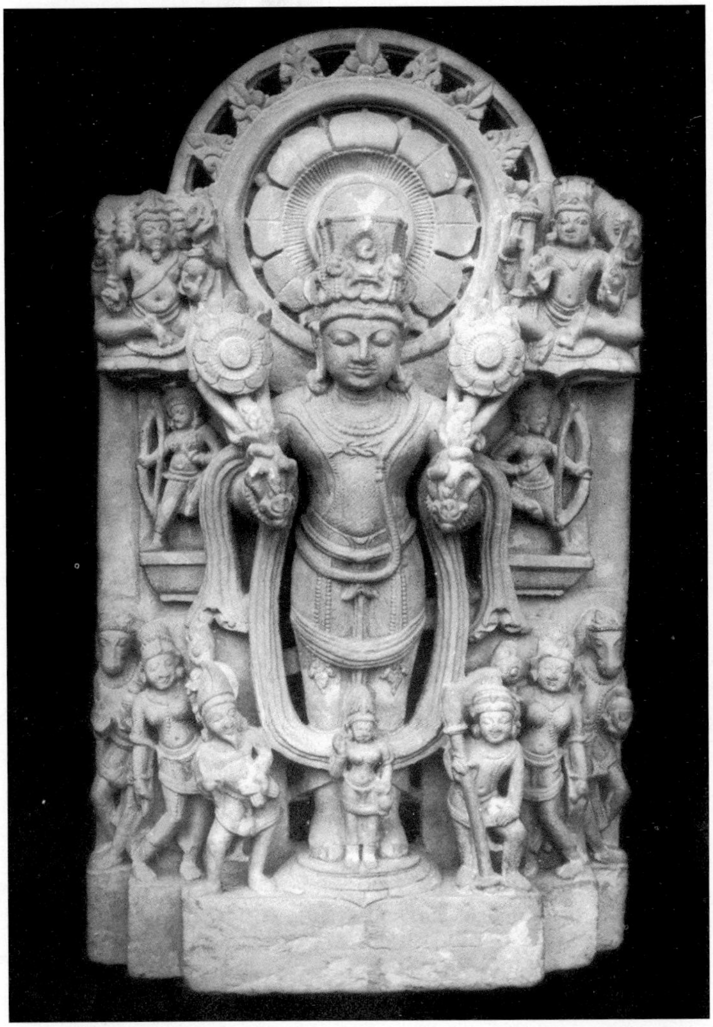

Pl. 250. Sūrya, Beri.

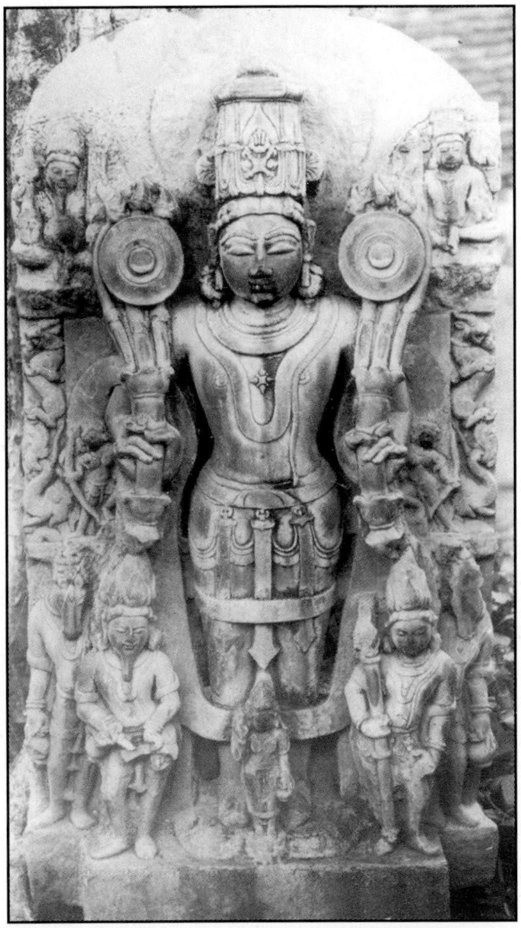

Pl. 252. Sūrya, Badali.

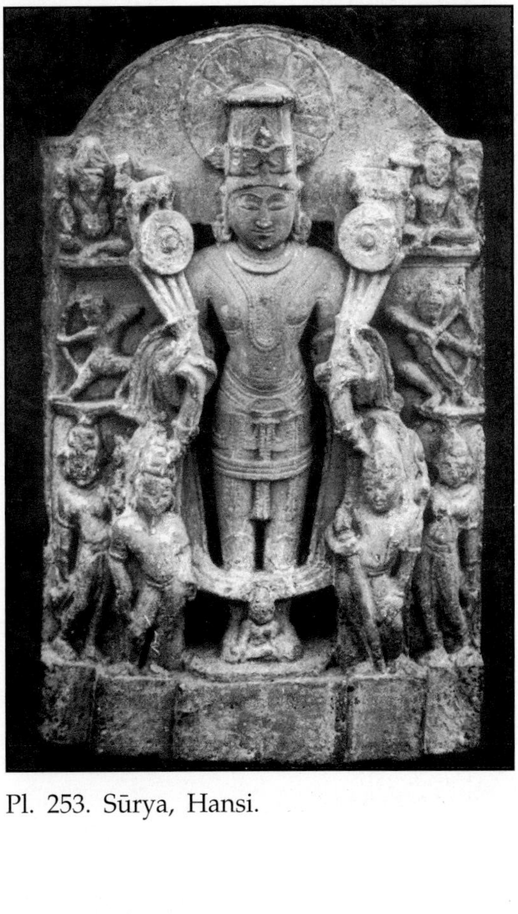

Pl. 253. Sūrya, Hansi.

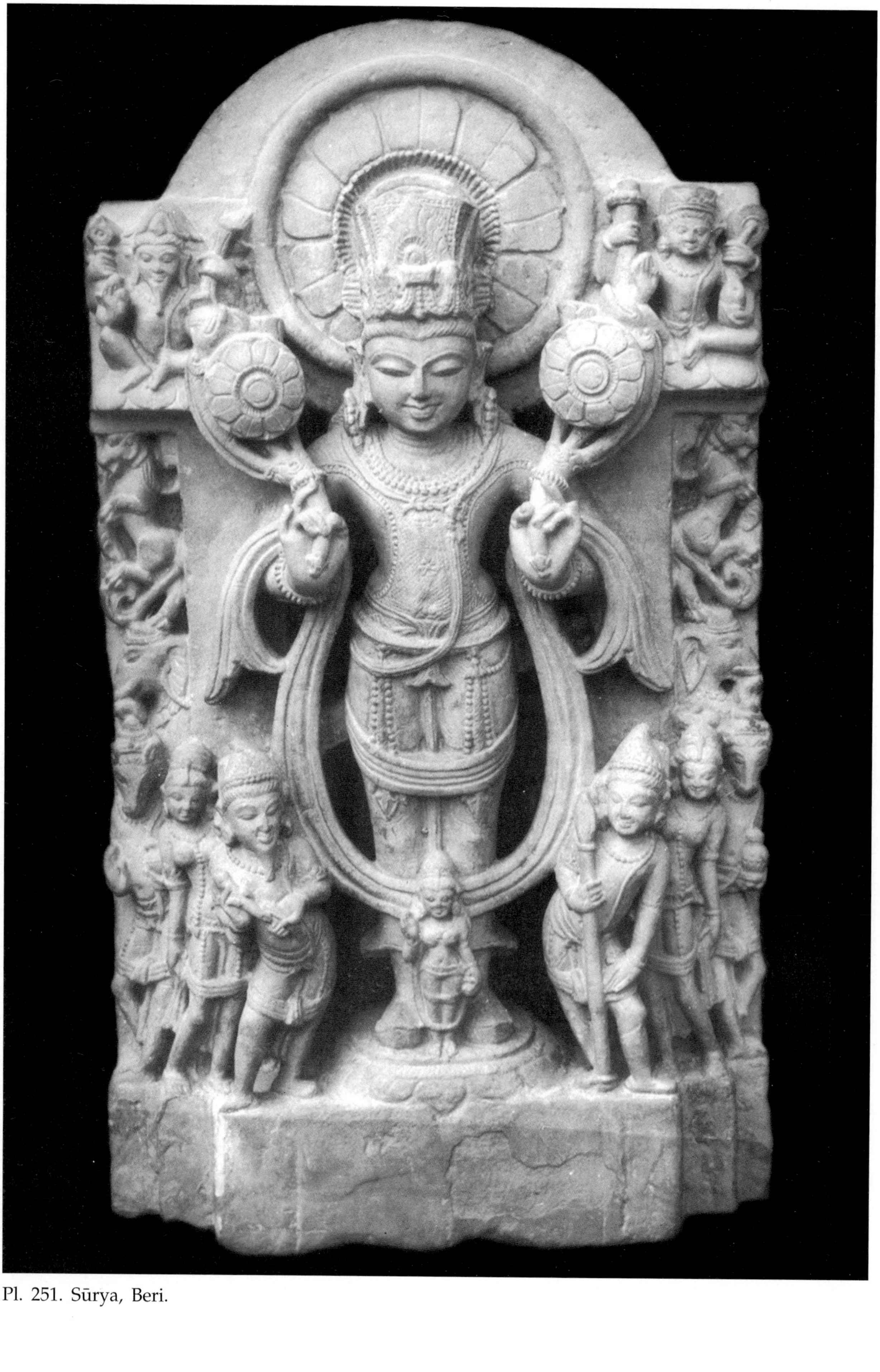

Pl. 251. Sūrya, Beri.

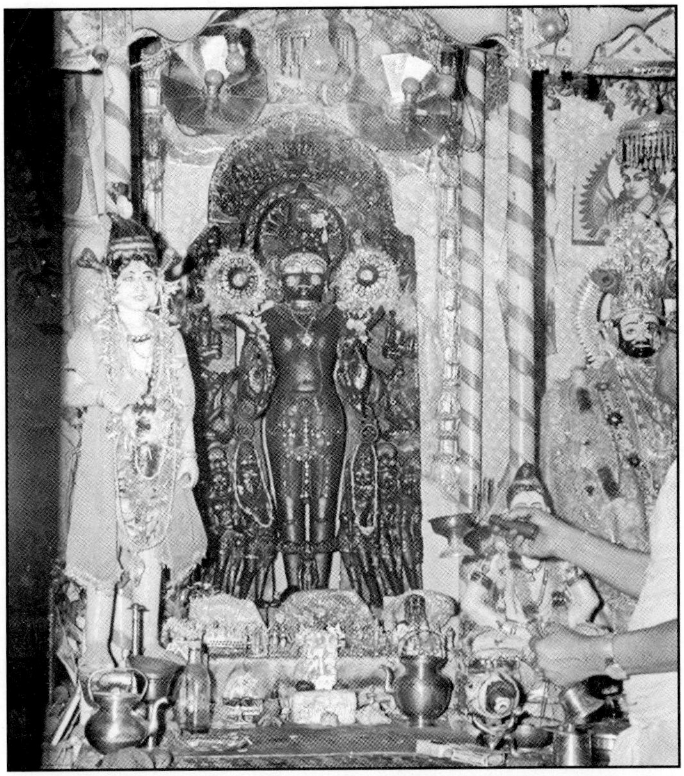

Pl. 254. Sūrya, Hansi.

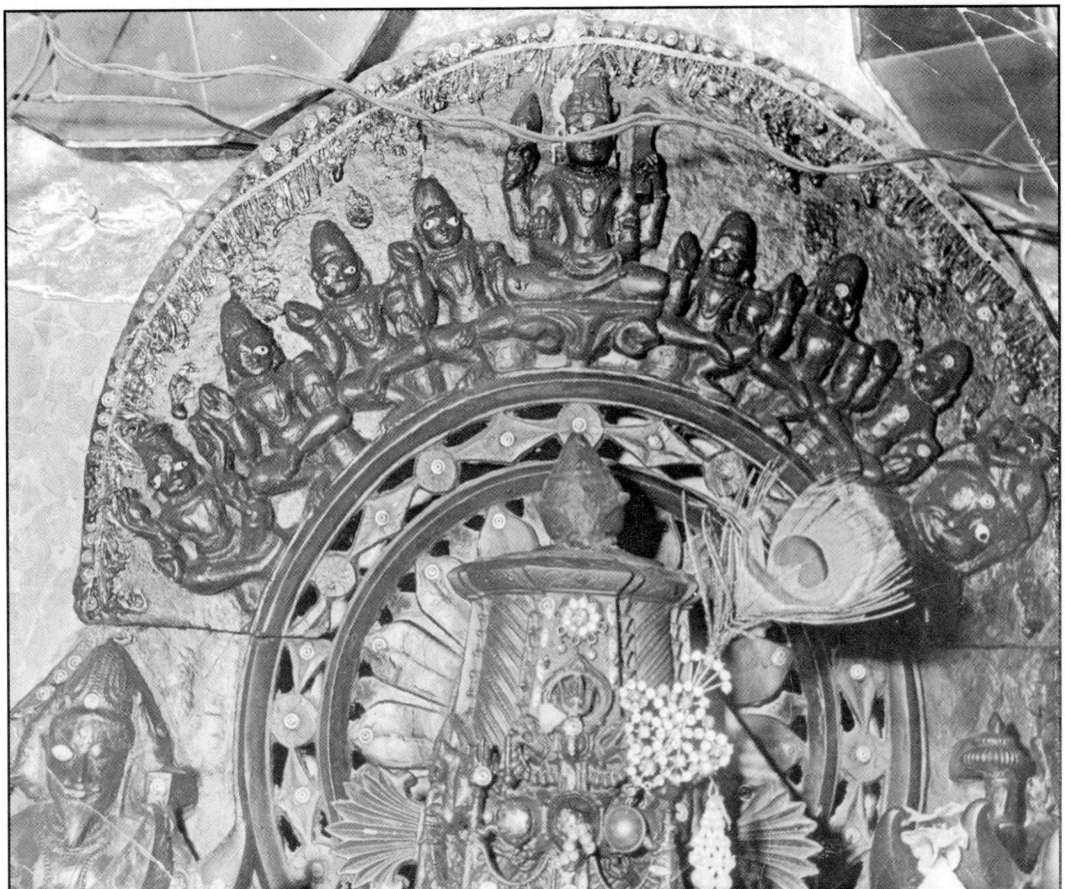

Pl. 255. Same, closer view of the *parikara*.

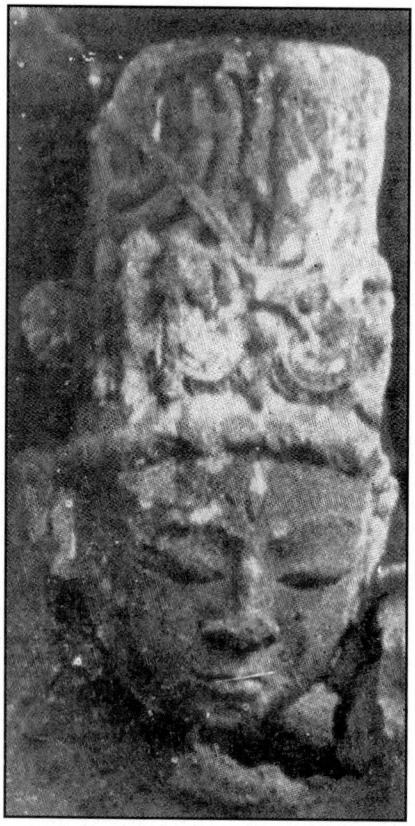

Pl. 256. Head of Harihara.

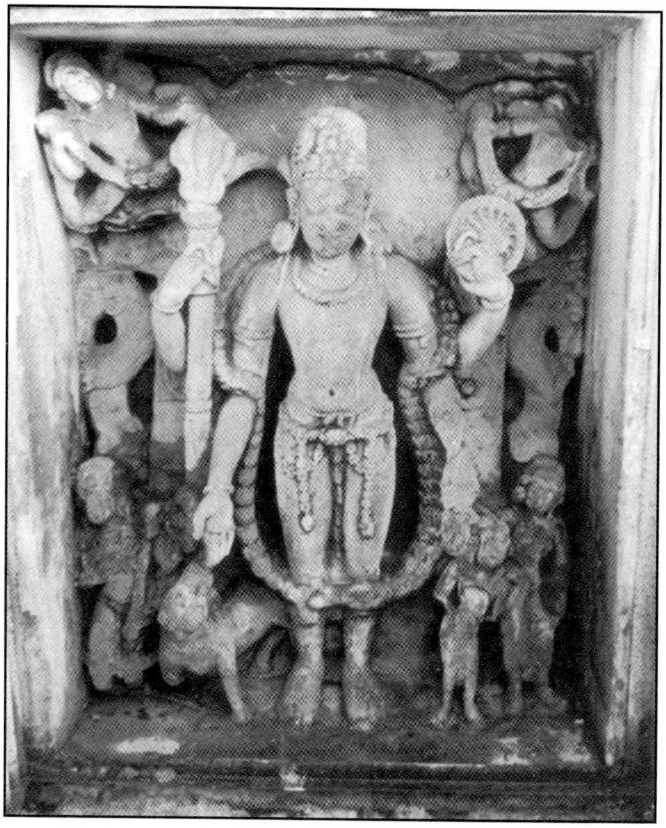

Pl. 257. Harihara, Punahana (Siddheśvara Temple, Gurgaon).

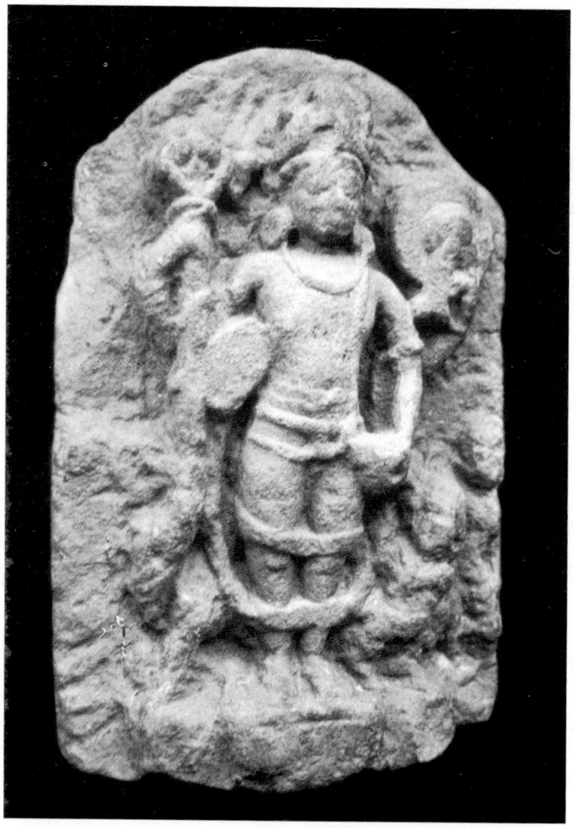

Pl. 258. Harihara, Gujjar Kheri.

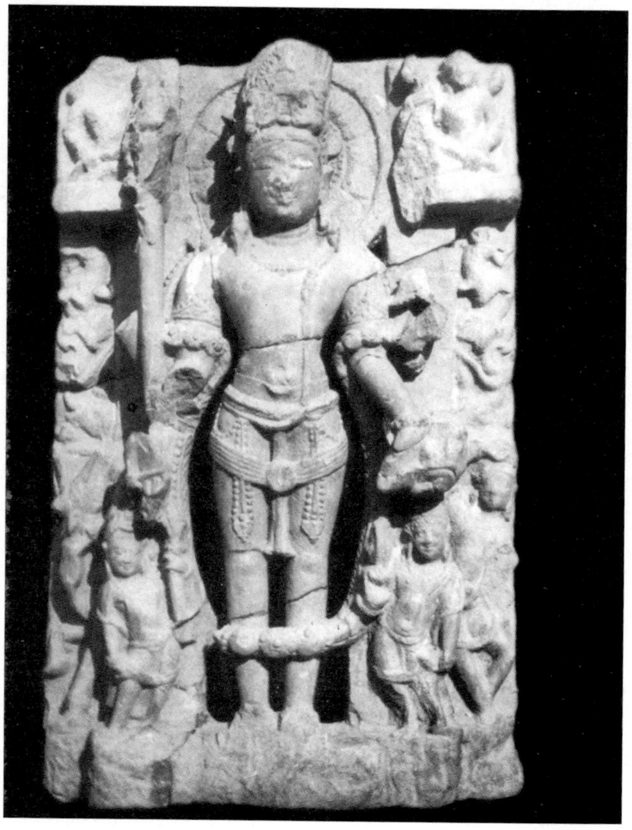

Pl. 259. Harihara, Chandimandir.

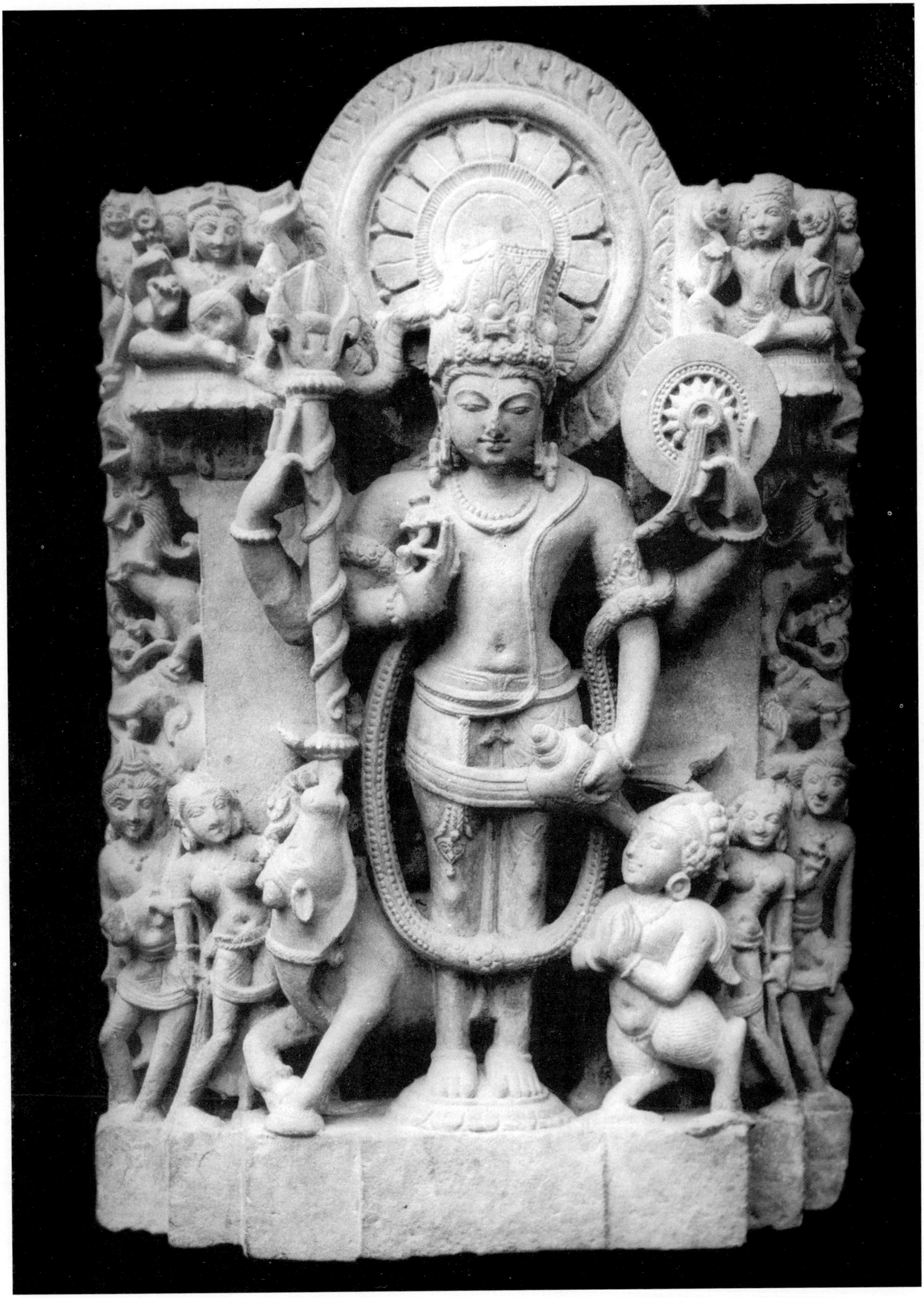

Pl. 260. Harihara, Beri.

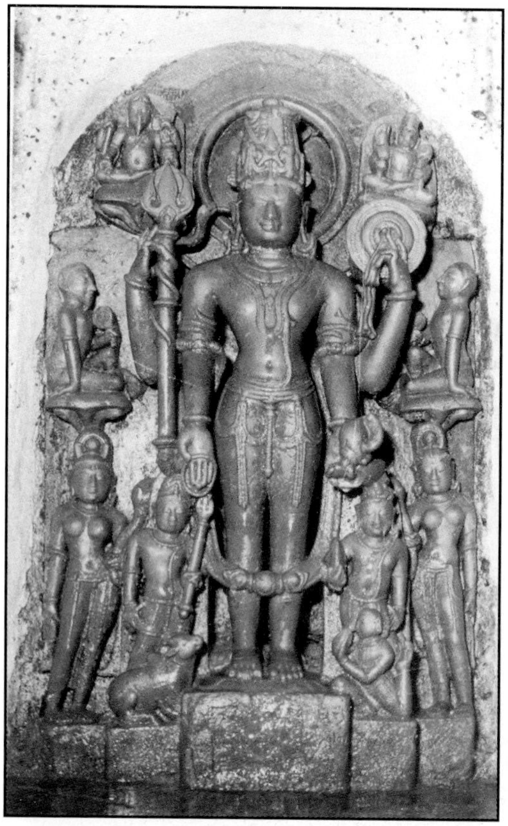

Pl. 261. Harihara, Panipat.

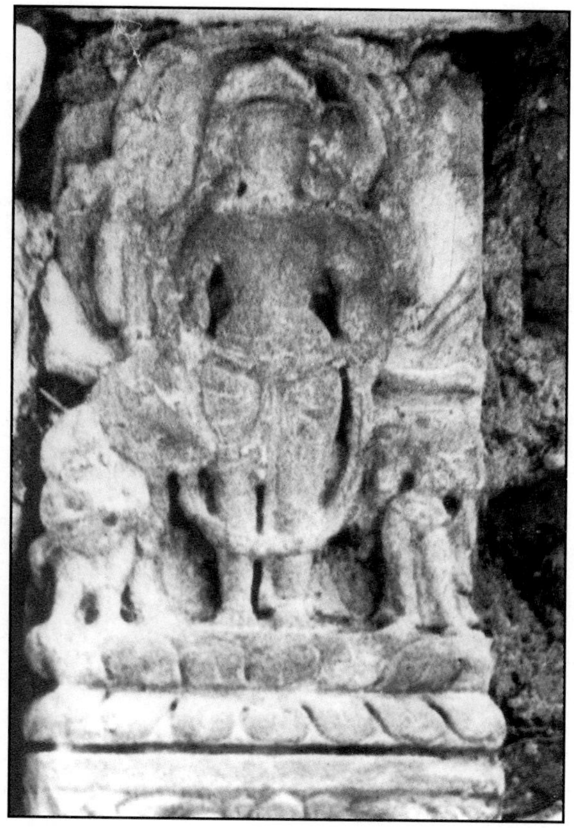

Pl. 262. Ardhanārīśvara, Pinjore.

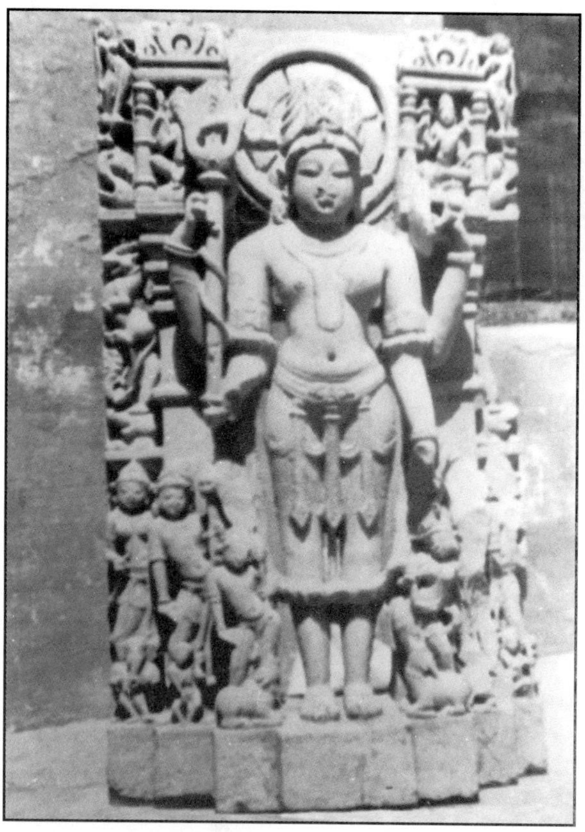

Pl. 263. Ardhanārīśvara, Palwal.

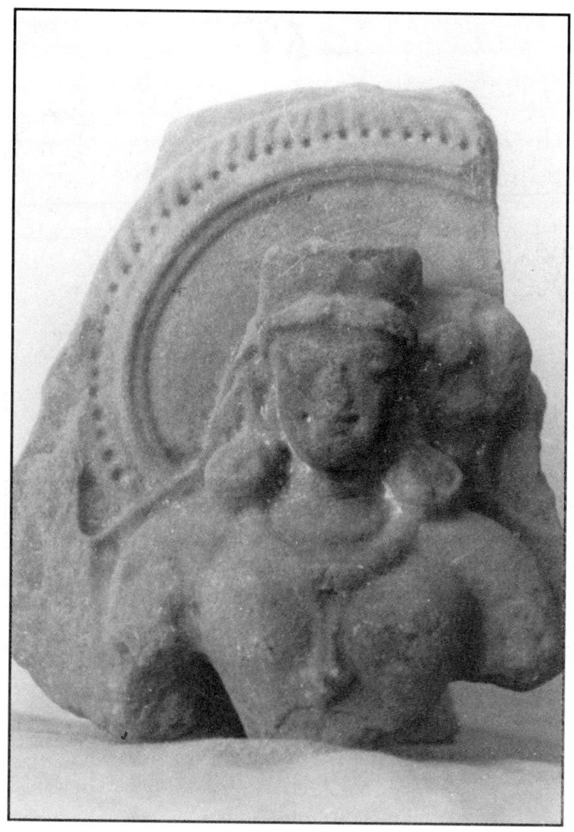

Pl. 264. Ardhanārī-Vishṇu, Jaintipur.

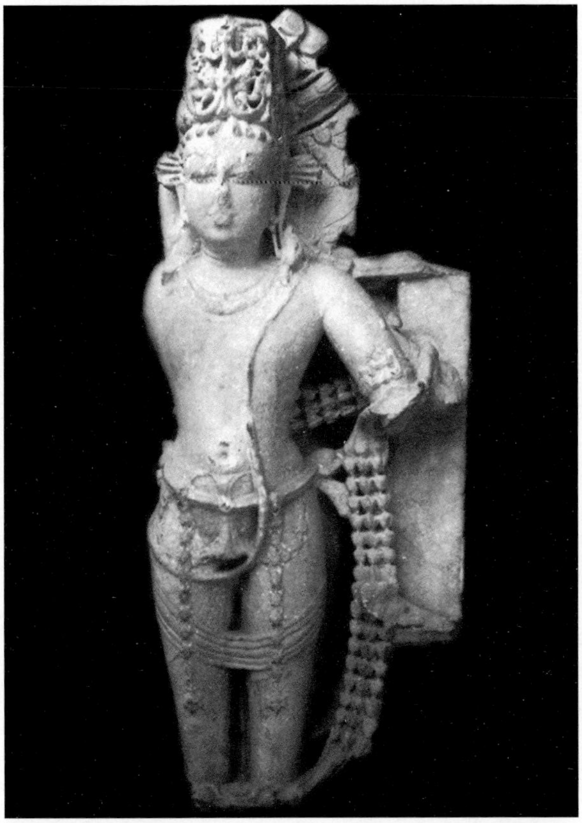

Pl. 265. Hari-Brahmā, Purkhas, Vishṇu's side.

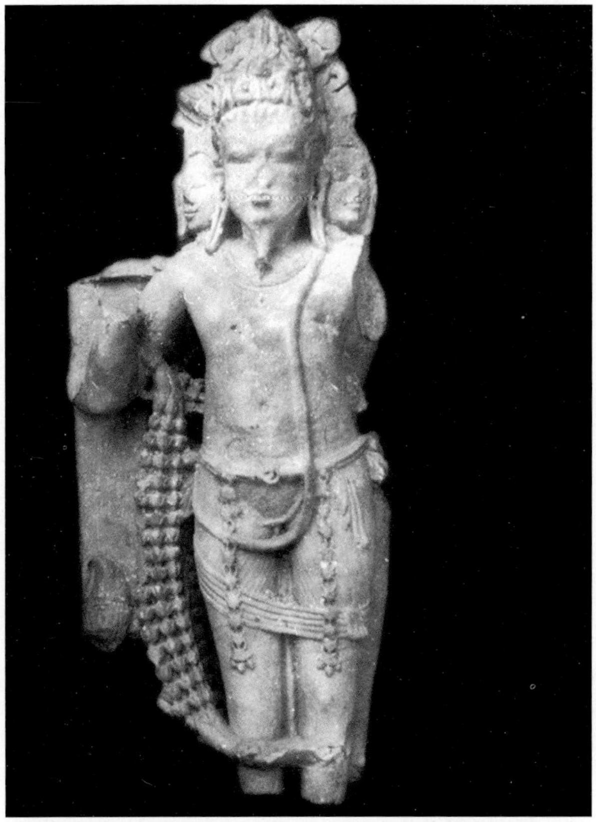

Pl. 266. Same, Brahmā's side.

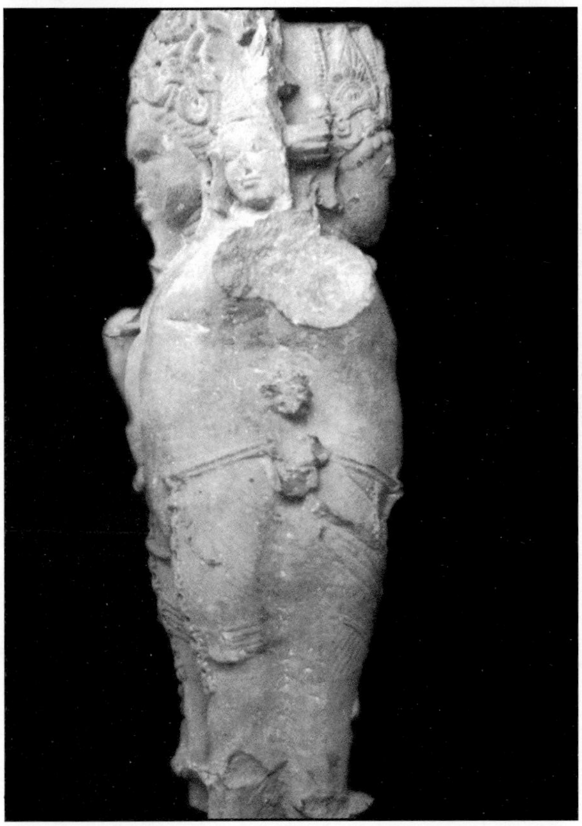

Pl. 267. Same, side view.

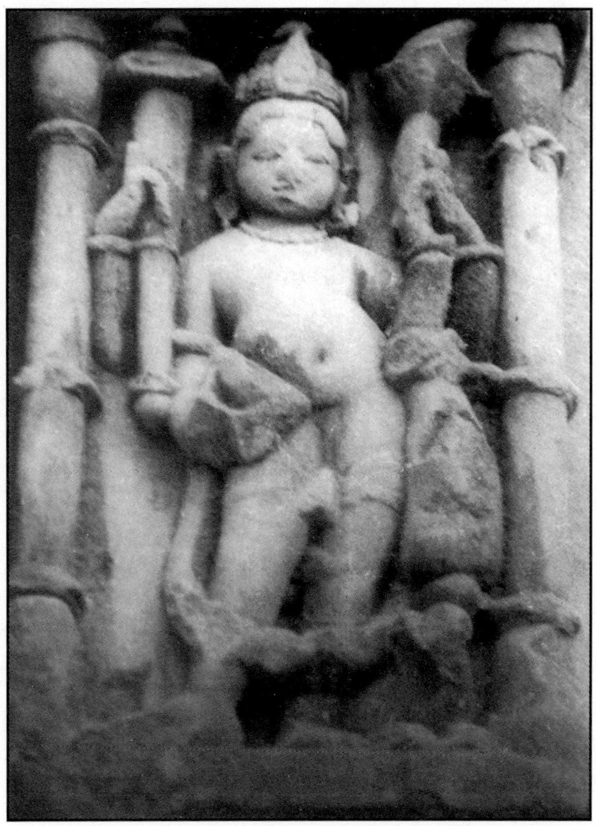

Pl. 268. Vishṇu-Kubera, Pinjore.

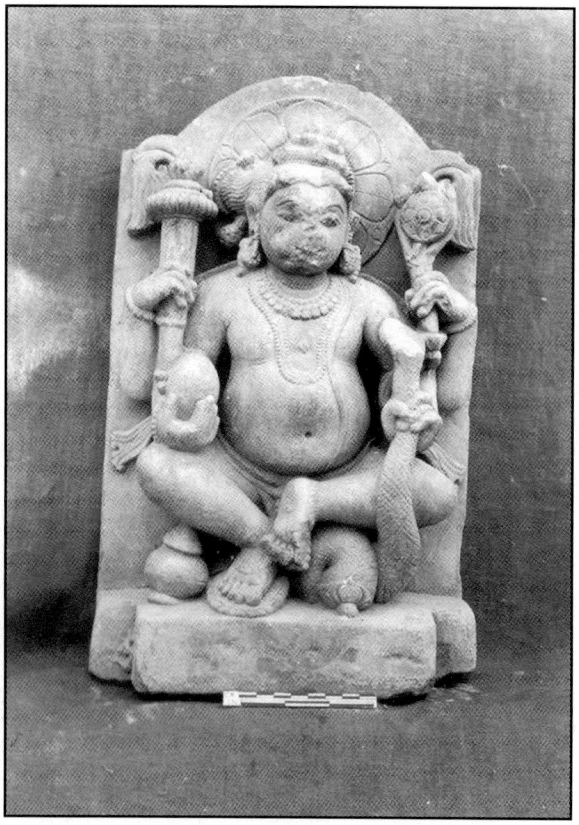

Pl. 269. Vishṇu-Kuḅera, Gurukula, Jhajjar.

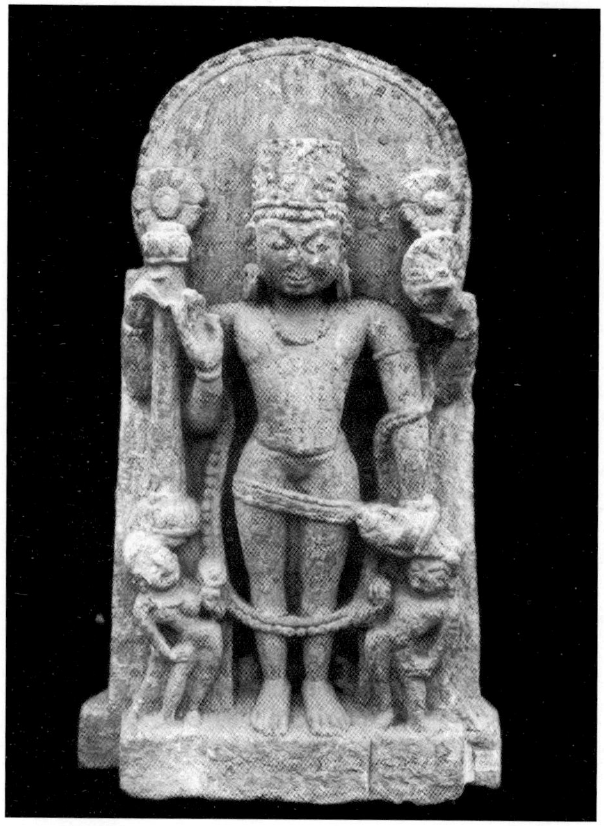

Pl. 270. Sūrya-Nārāyaṇa, Khokhrakot, Rohtak.

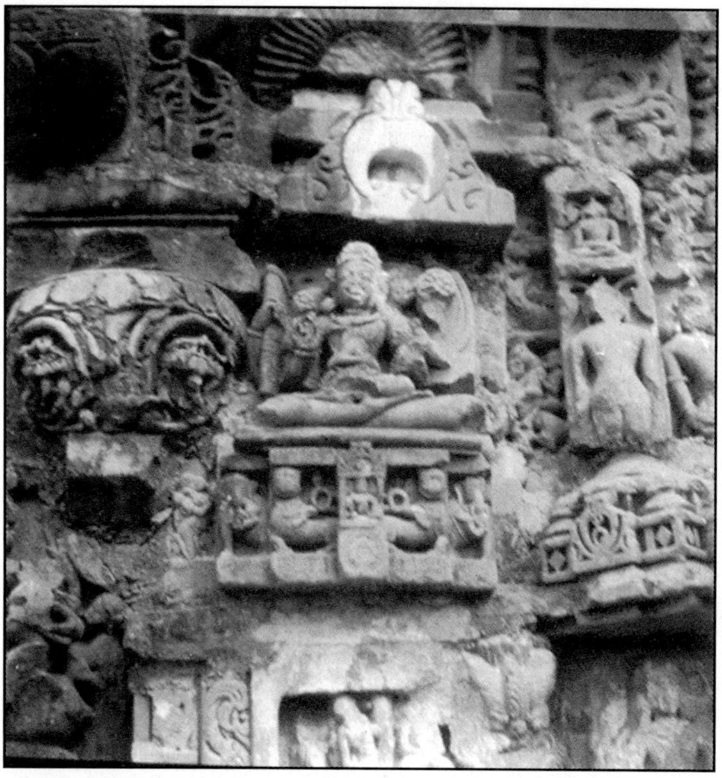

Pl. 271. Sūrya-Nārāyaṇa, Pinjore.

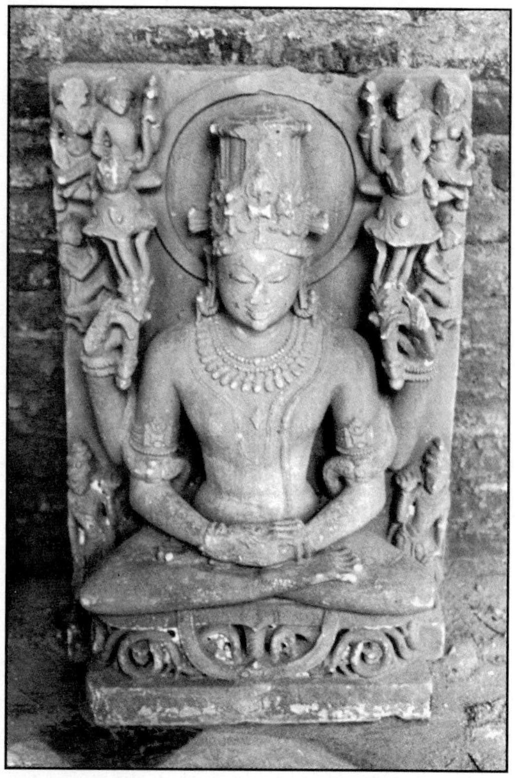

Pl. 272. Sūrya-Nārāyaṇa, Asthal Bohr, Rohtak.

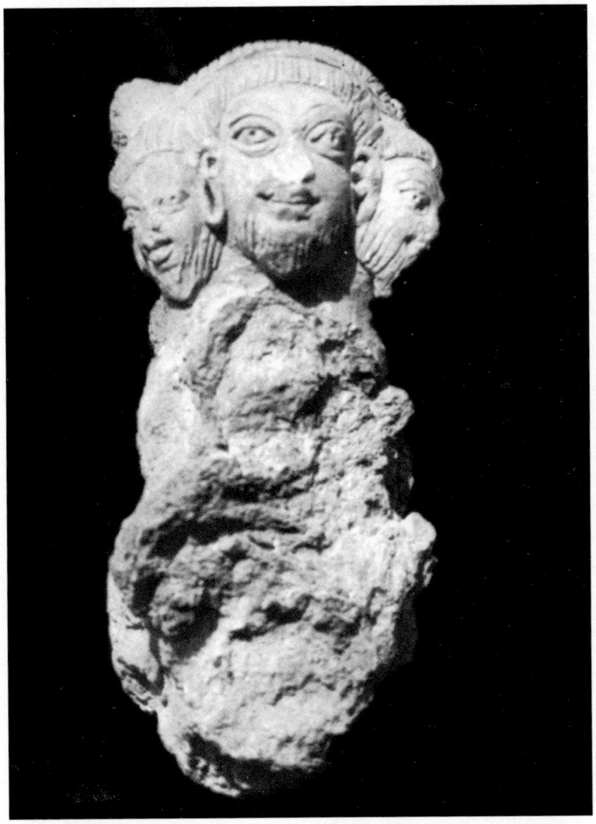

Pl. 273. Brahmā, terracotta, Agroha.

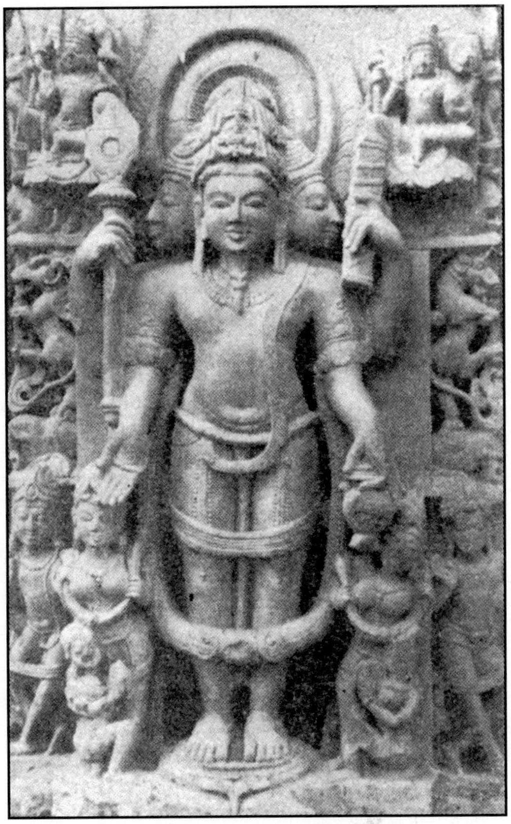

Pl. 274. Brahmā, Sirsa.

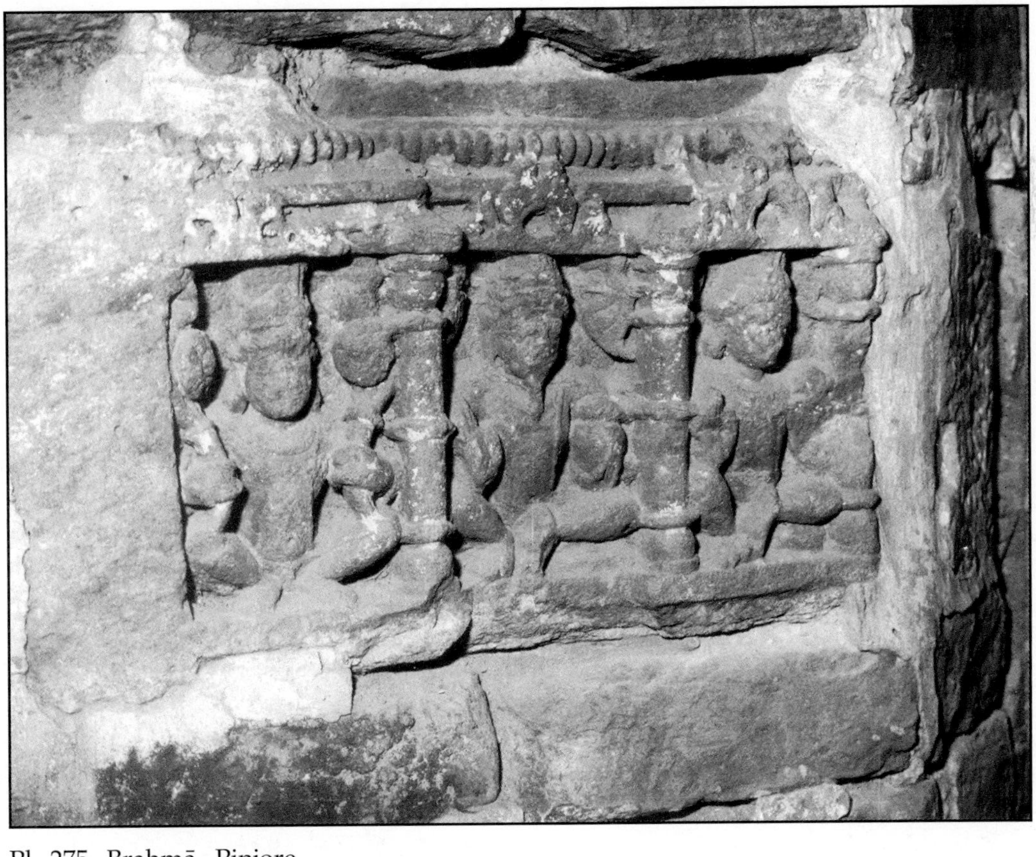

Pl. 275. Brahmā, Pinjore.

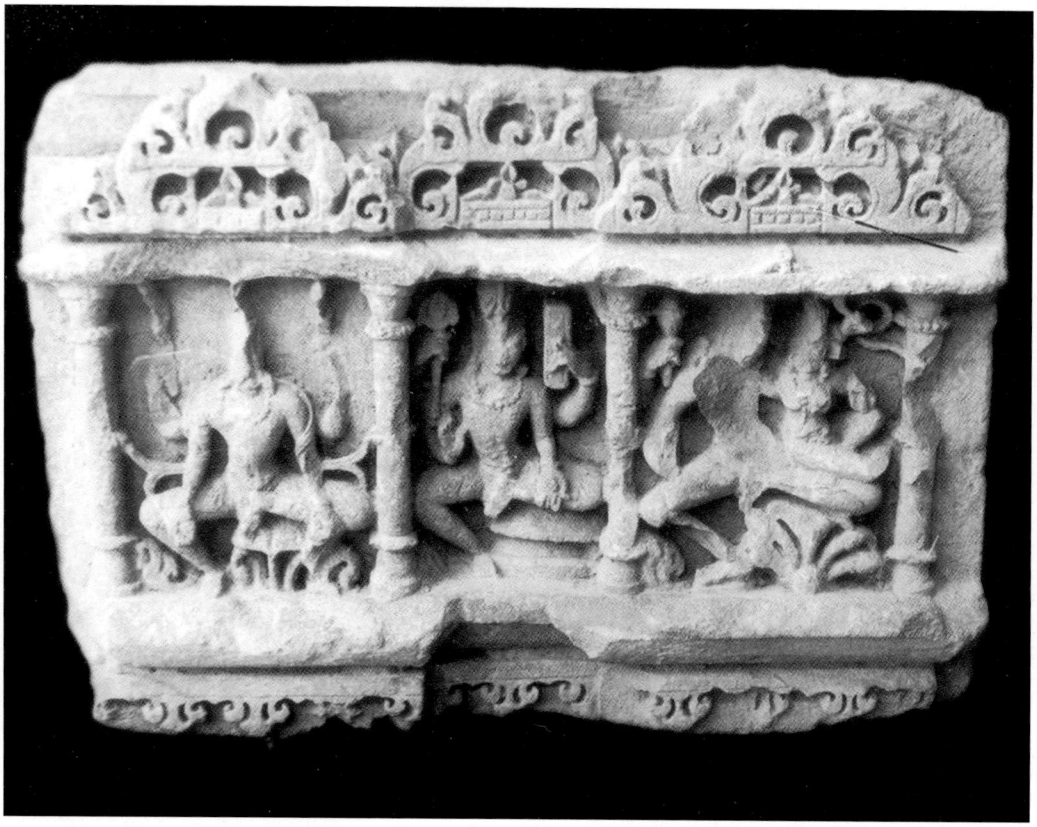

Pl. 276. Brahmā, Thanesar.

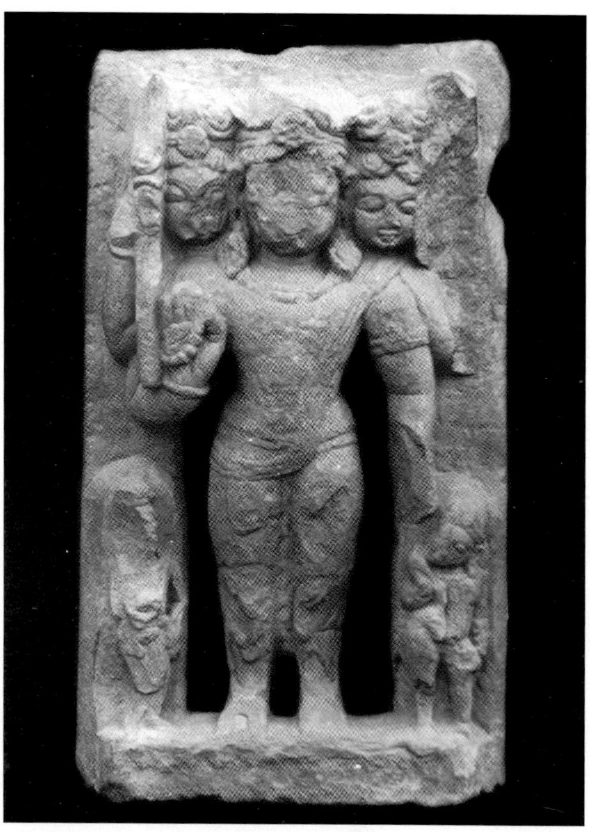

Pl. 277. Brahmā, Pehowa.

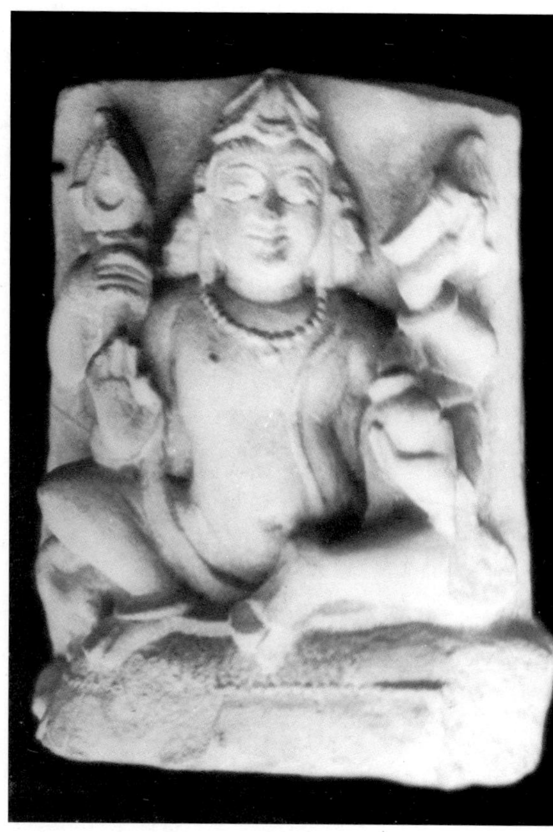

Pl. 278. Brahmā, Pehowa.

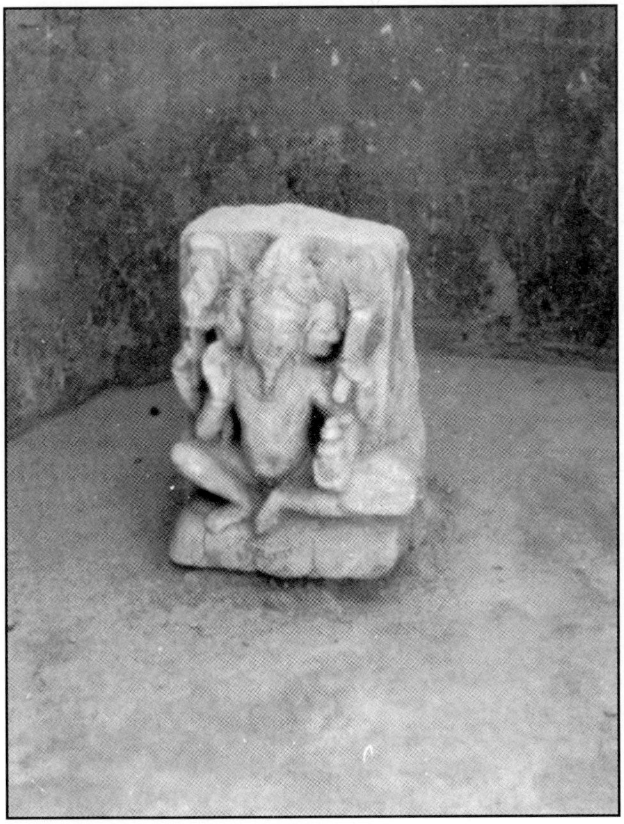

Pl. 279. Brahmā, Pehowa.

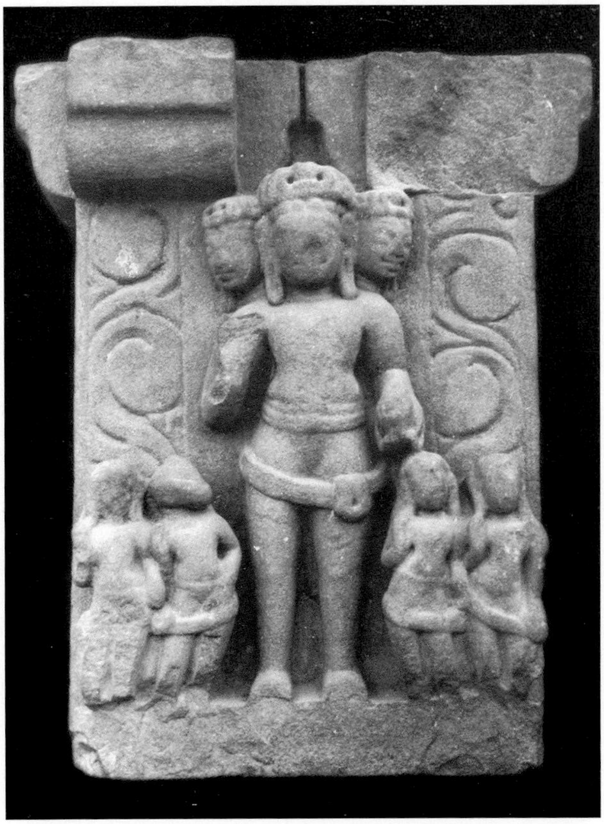

Pl. 280. Brahmā, Morni-ka-Tal.

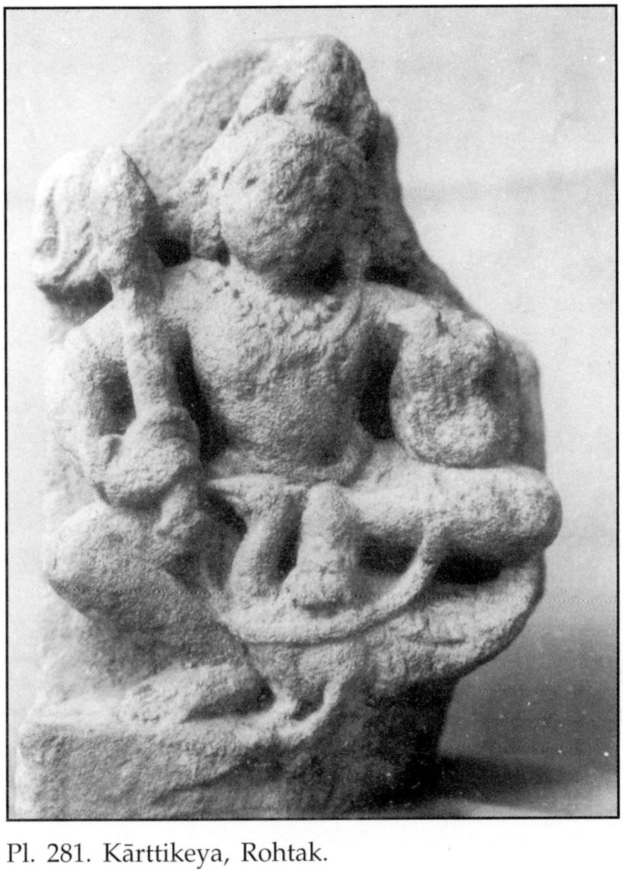

Pl. 281. Kārttikeya, Rohtak.

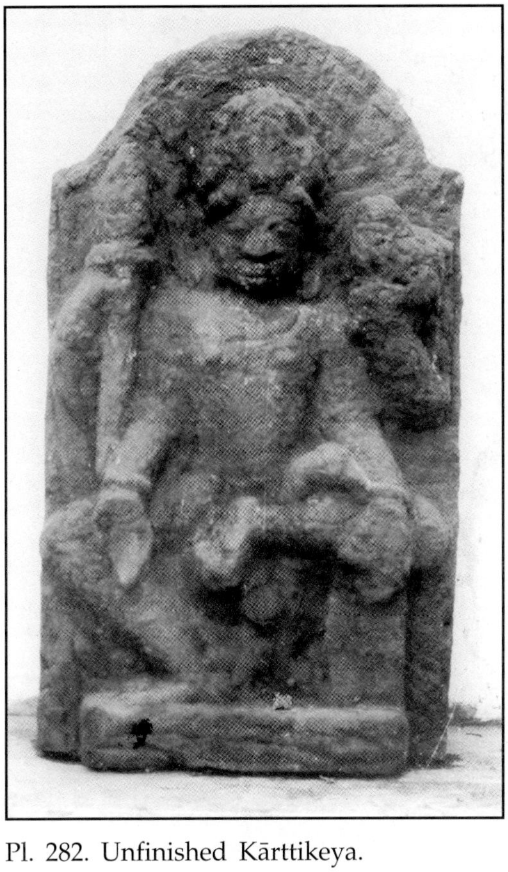

Pl. 282. Unfinished Kārttikeya.

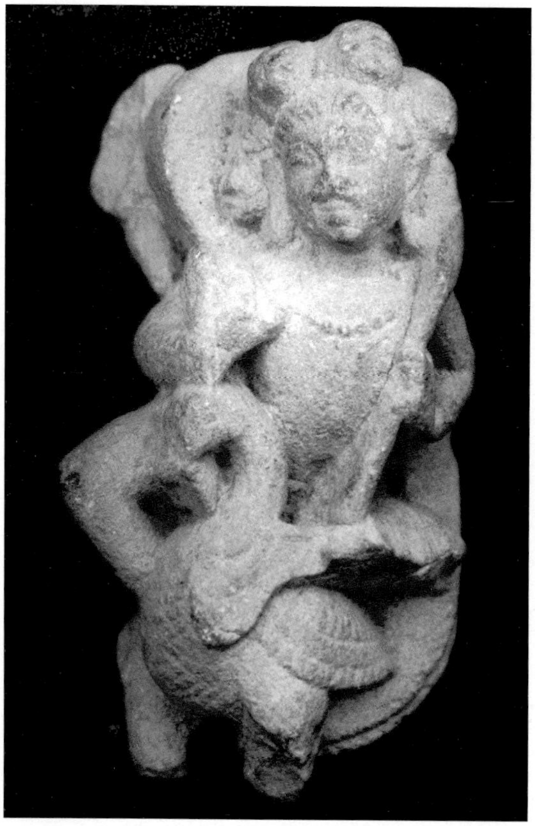

Pl. 283. Kārttikeya, Gujjar Kheri.

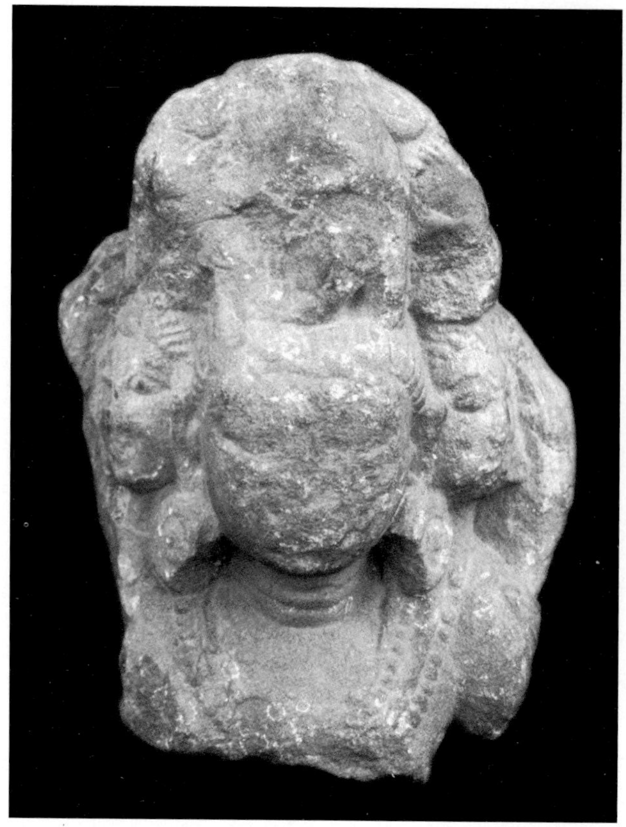

Pl. 284. Kārttikeya, Ratpur.

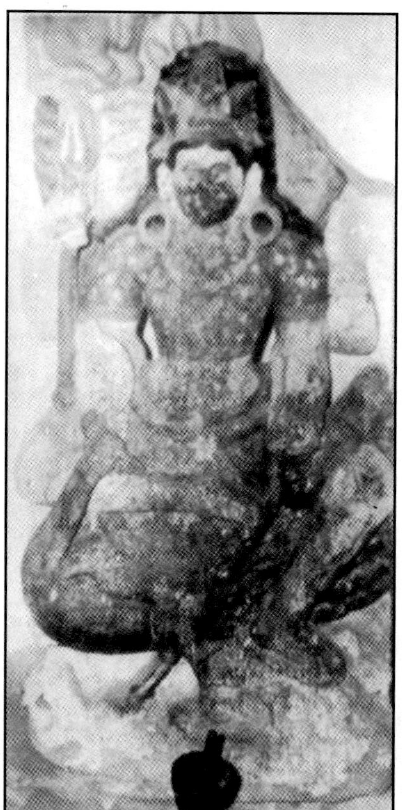

Pl. 285. Kārttikeya, Muradnagar.

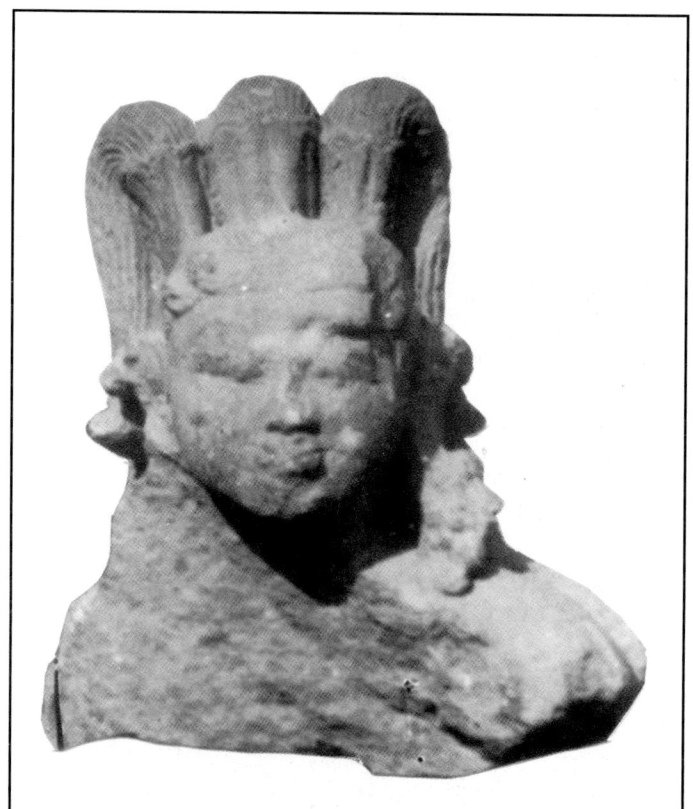

Pl. 286. Kārttikeya head, Jind.

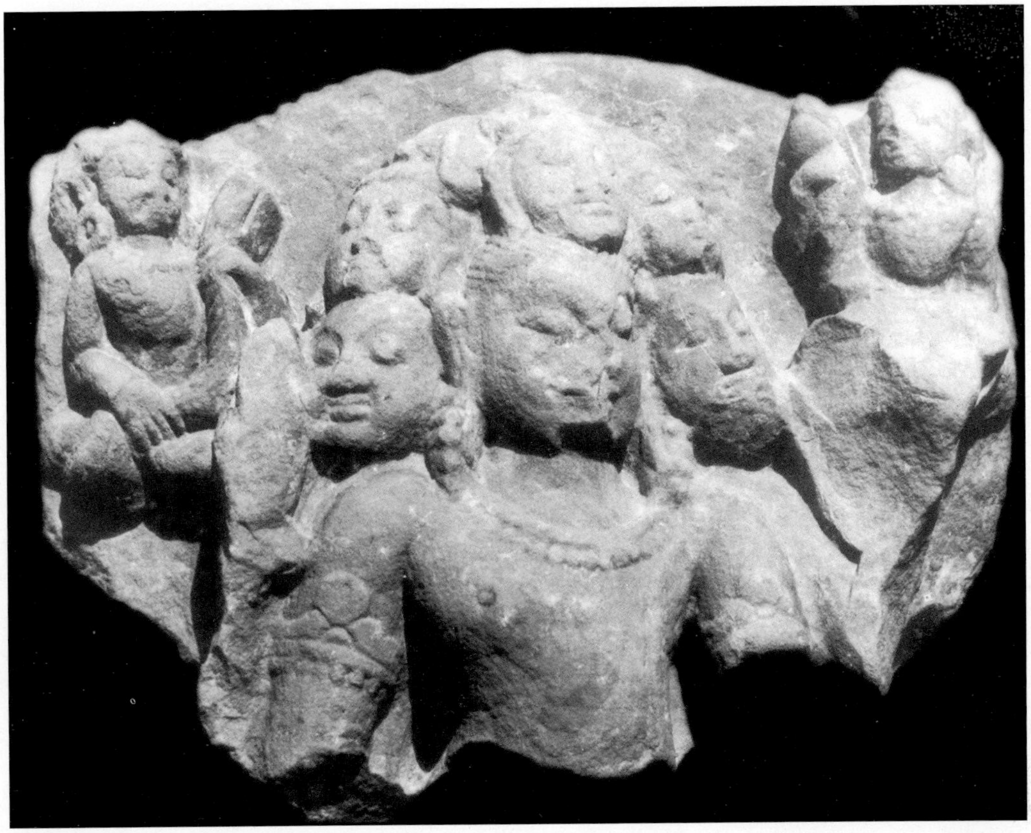

Pl. 287. Bust of Kārttikeya, Thanesar.

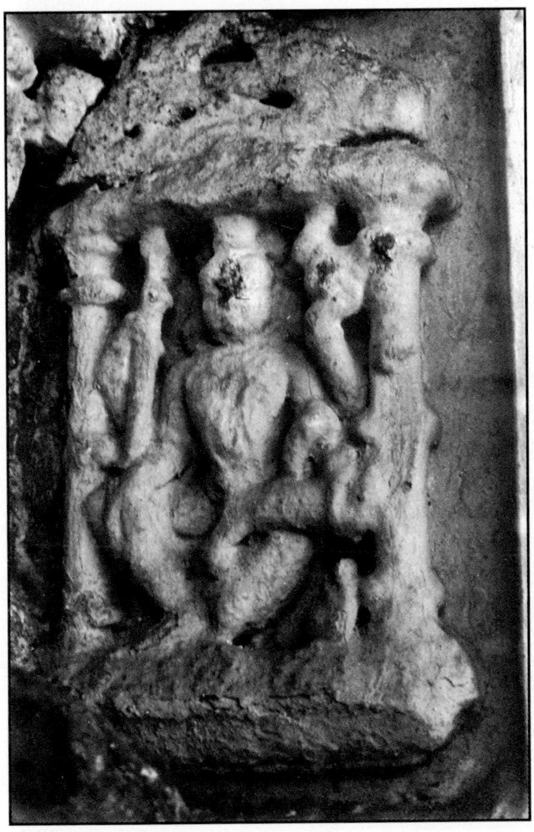

Pl. 288. Kārttikeya, Pinjore.

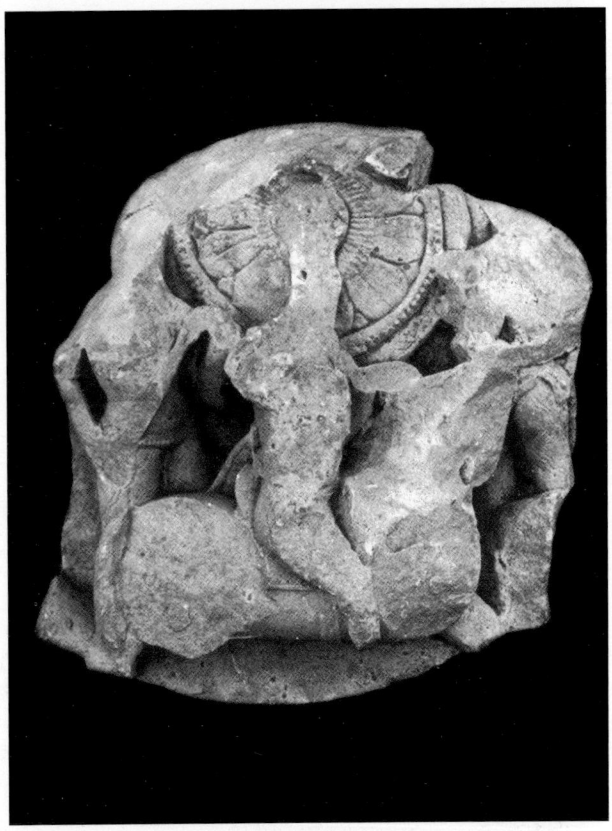

Pl. 289. Revanta, Gujjar Kheri.

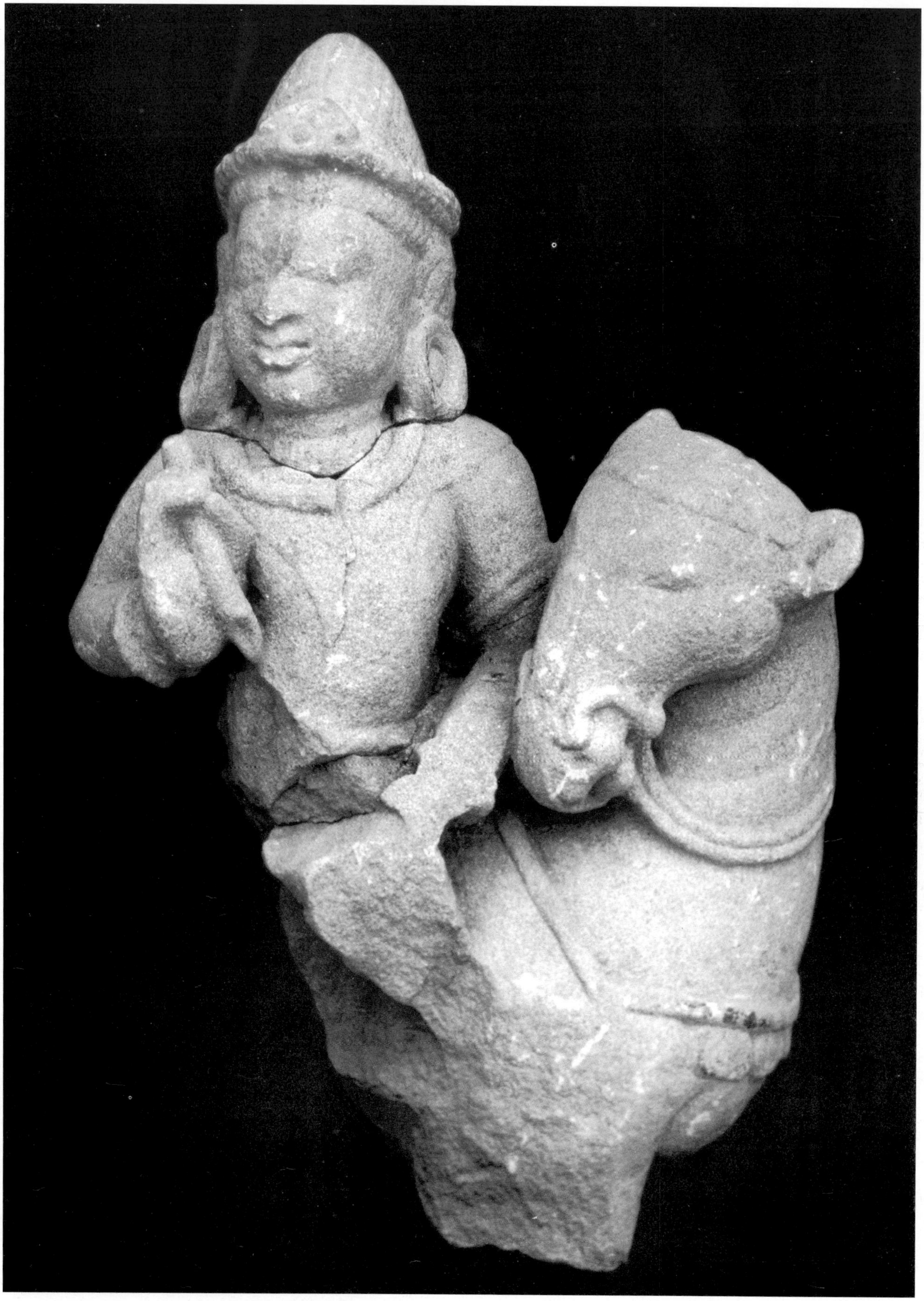

Pl. 291. Piṅgala, Rāma Mandira, Chandimandir.

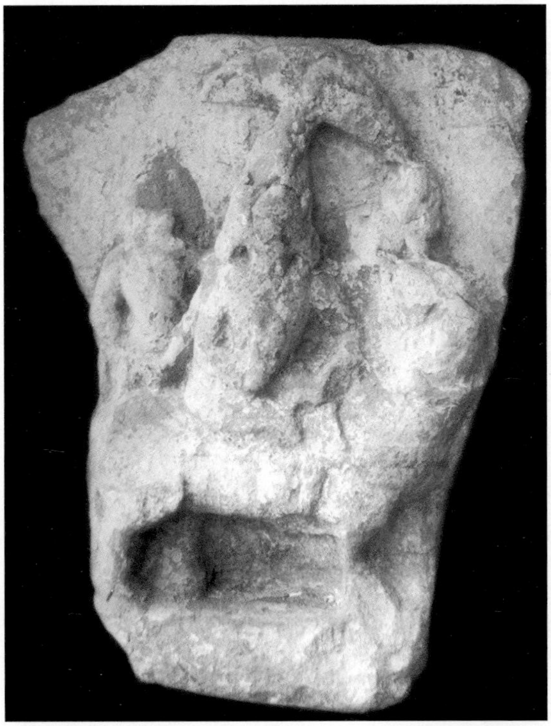

Pl. 290. Revanta, fragment, Chandimandir.

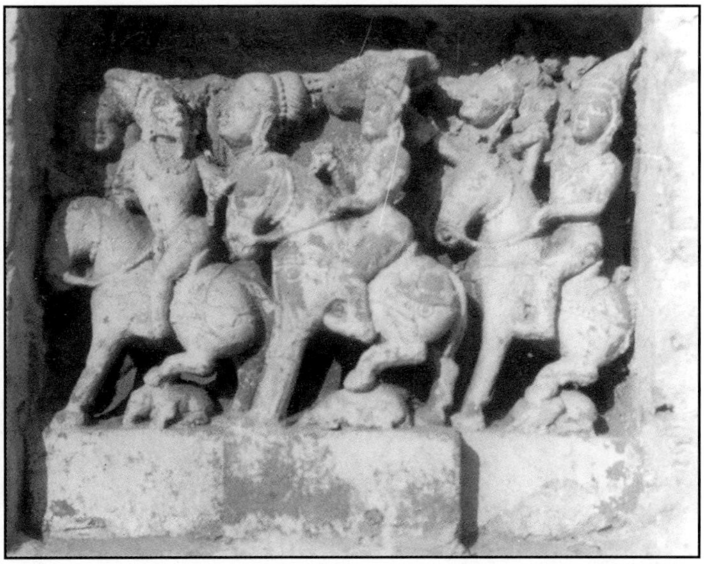

Pl. 292. Revanta, Kanwari.

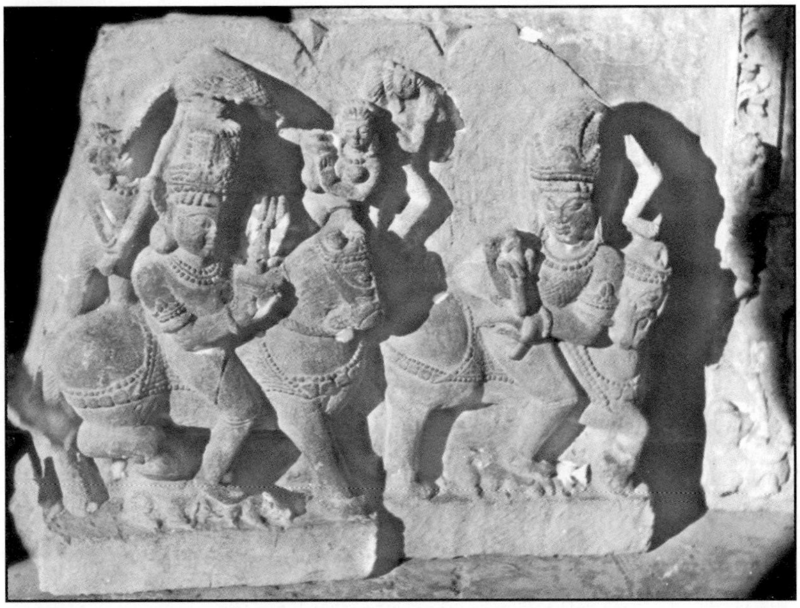

Pl. 293. Revanta, Pehowa.

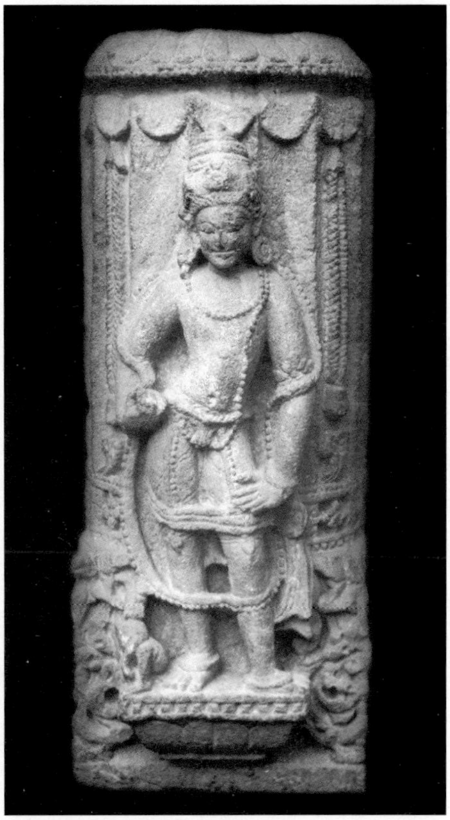

Pl. 294. Indra, Sagwan.

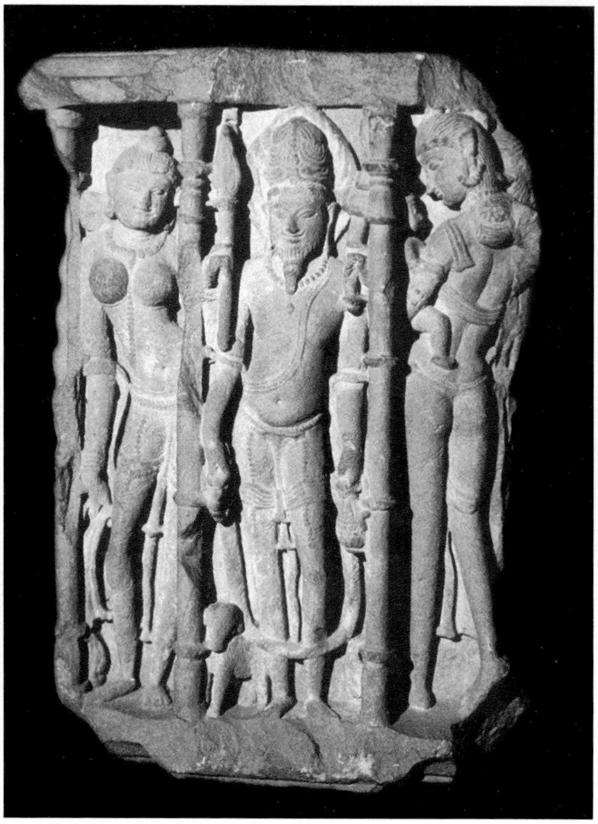

Pl. 295. Agni, Pinjore.

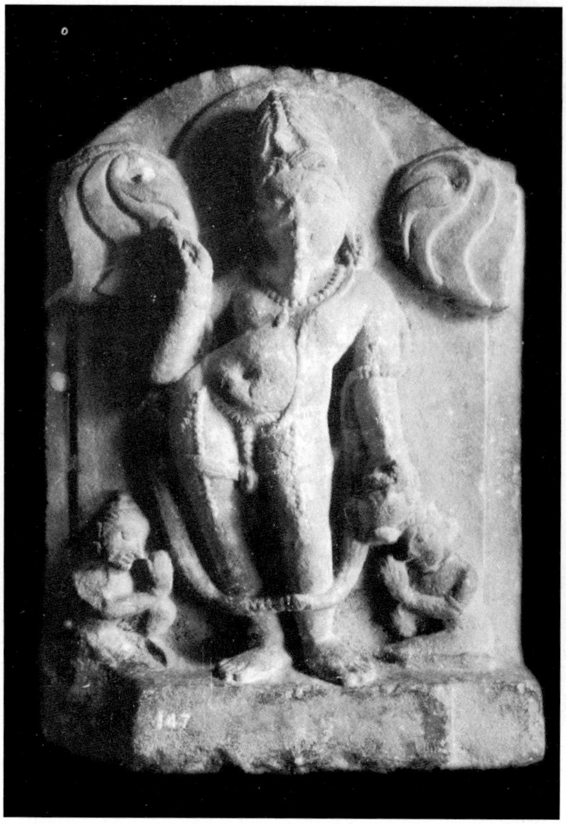

Pl. 296. Agni, Pinjore (Chandigarh Museum).

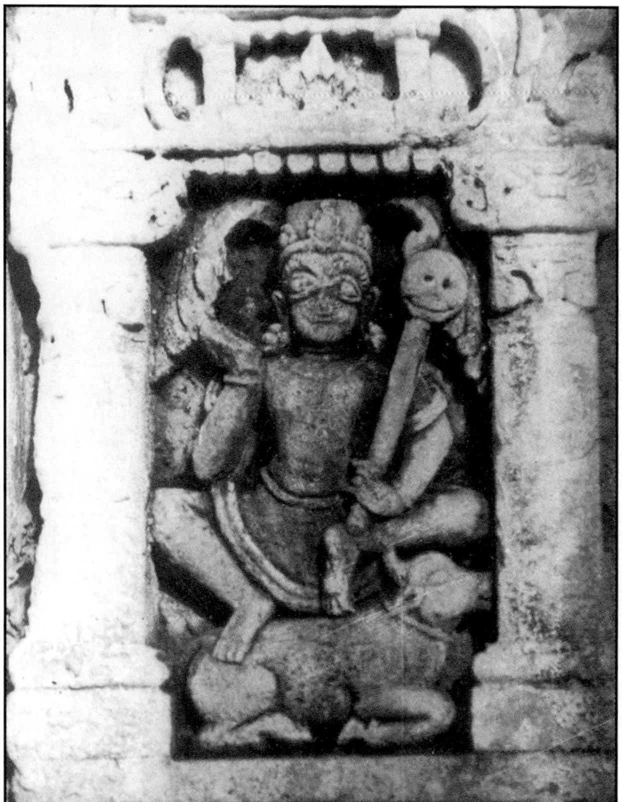

Pl. 297. Yama, Pehowa.

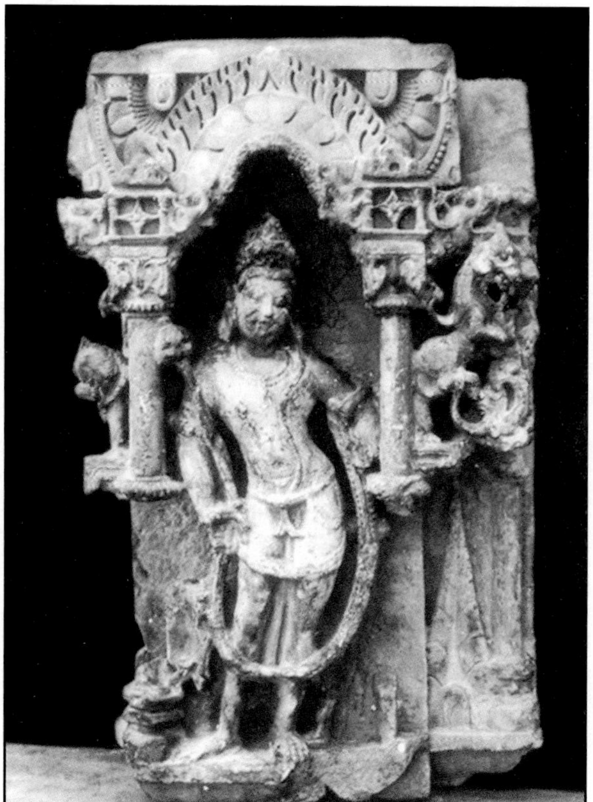

Pl. 298. Yama, Sagwan.

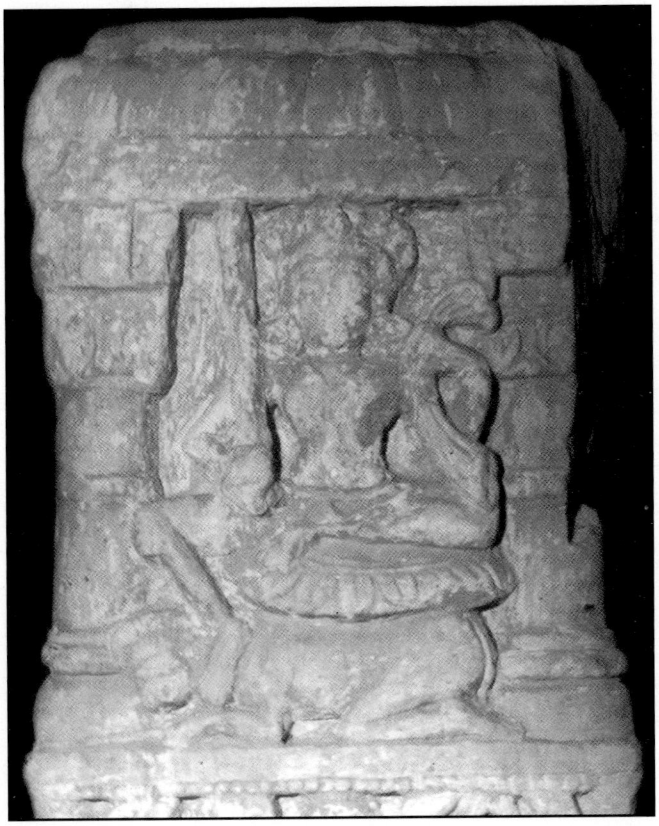

Pl. 299. Nirṛiti, Bulandpur Mustarka.

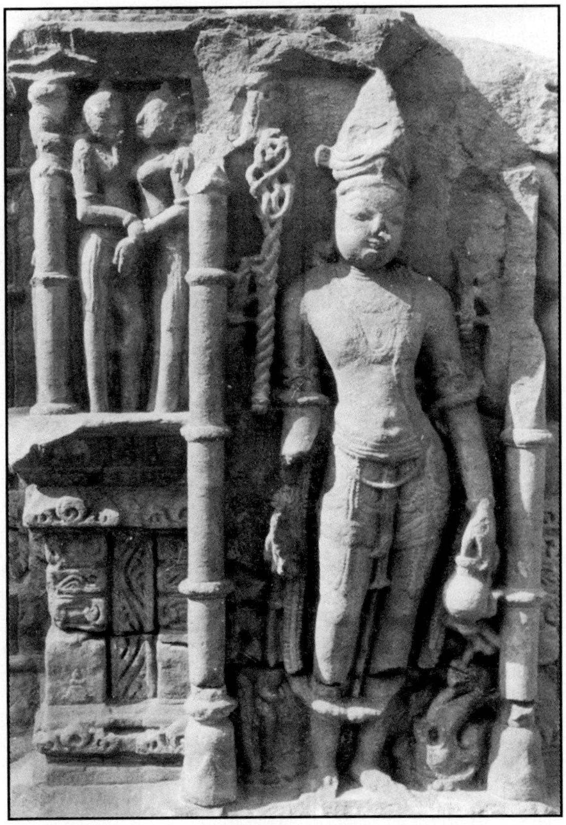

Pl. 300. Varuṇa, Bhīmādevī Temple, Pinjore.

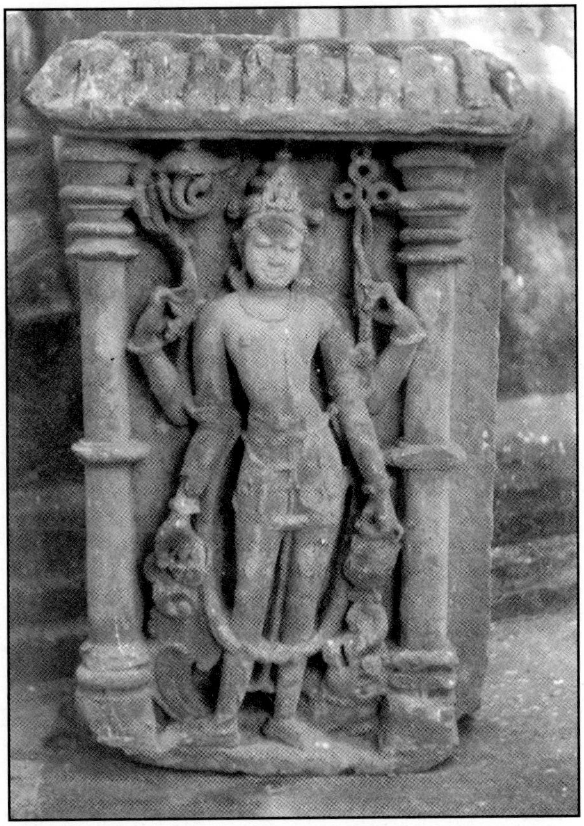

Pl. 301. Varuṇa, Topanātha kā Mandira, Pinjore.

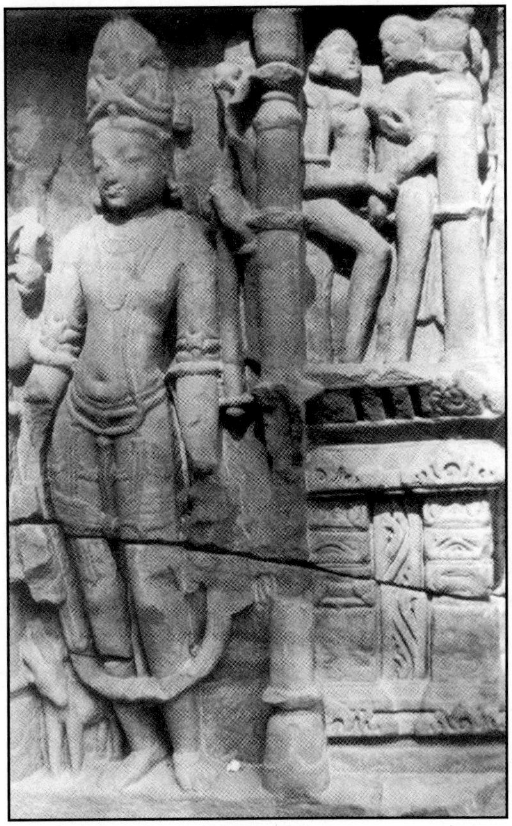

Pl. 302. Vāyu, Pinjore.

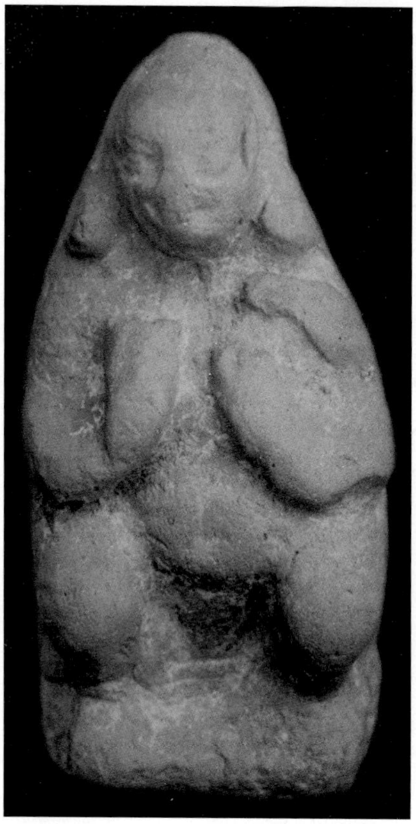

Pl. 303. Kubera, terracotta, Agroha.

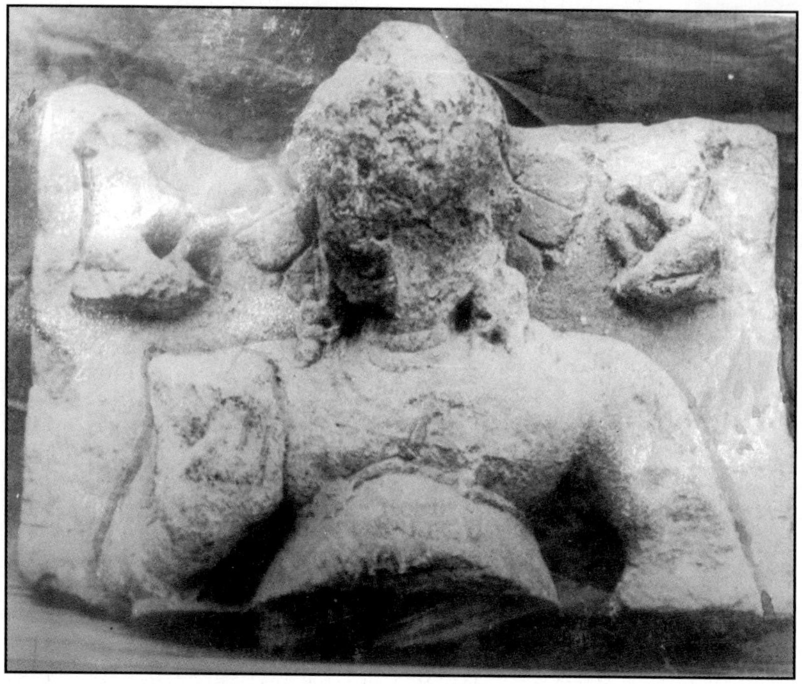

Pl. 304. Kubera, Lalkot.

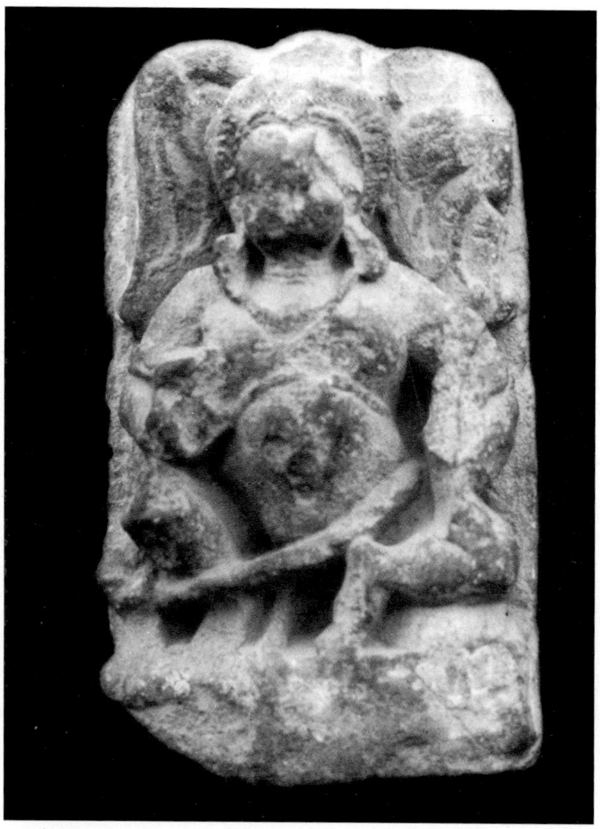

Pl. 305. Kubera, Chhichhrana.

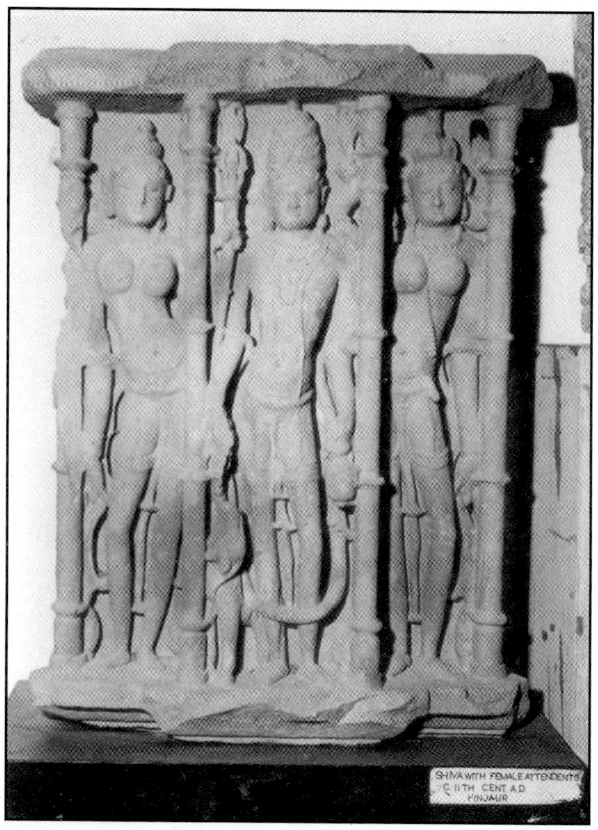

Pl. 306. Īśāna, Pinjore.

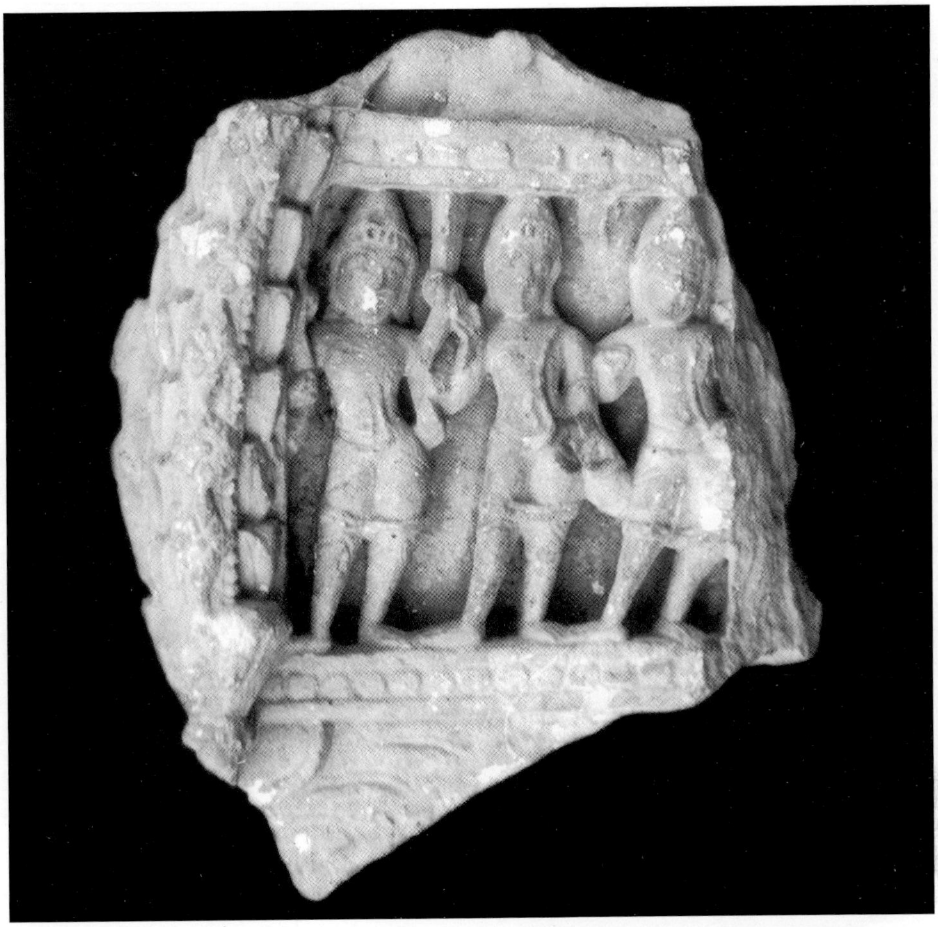

Pl. 307. Fragmentary *navagraha* panel, Kurukshetra.

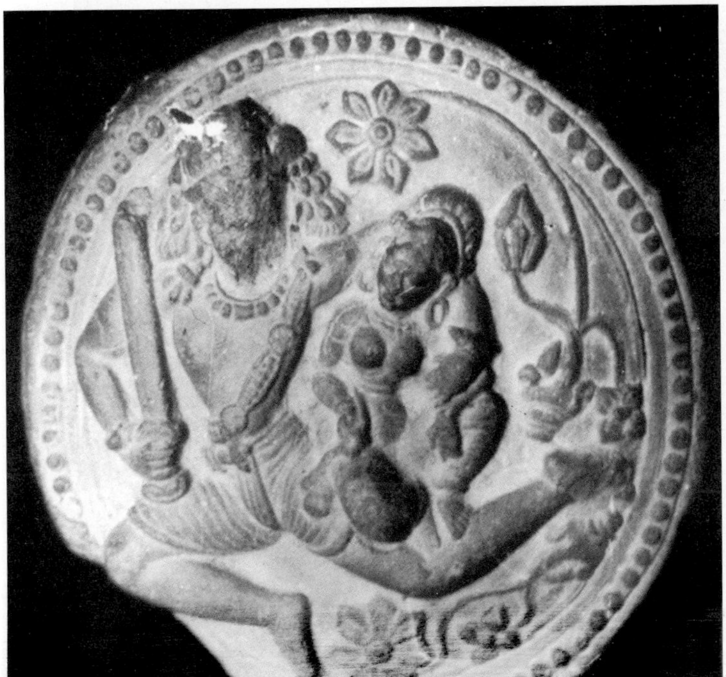

Pl. 308. *Gandharva-yugala*, terracotta, Sirsa.

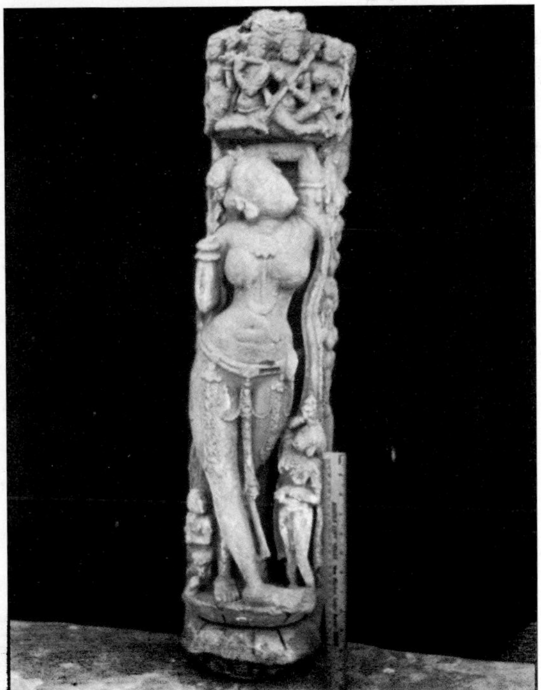

Pl. 309. Yawning beauty with a *andharva* couple above, Pinjore.

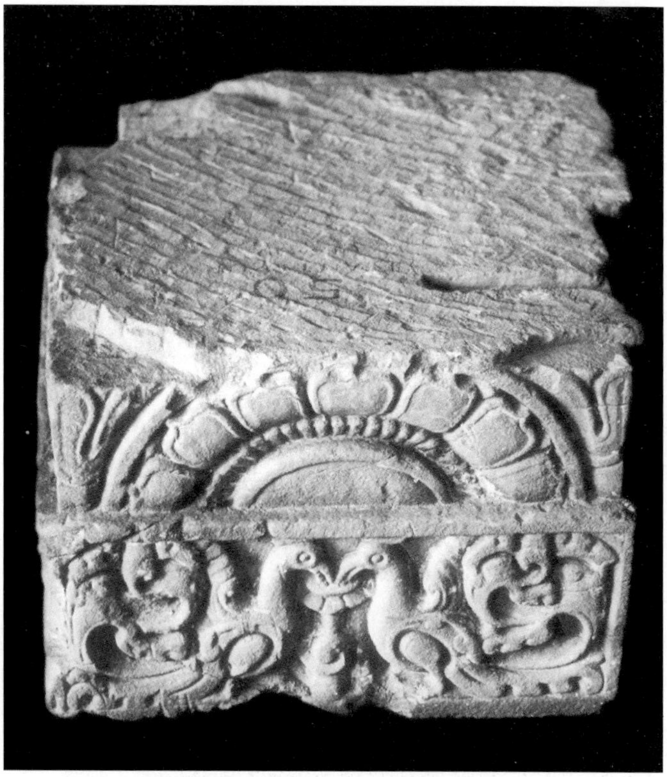

Pl. 315. Birds, provenance unknown.

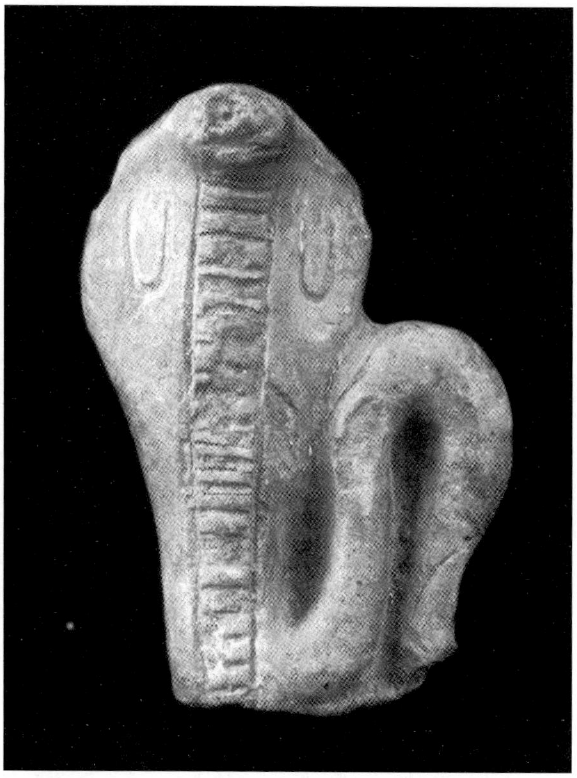

Pl. 316. Nāga, terracotta, Sugh.

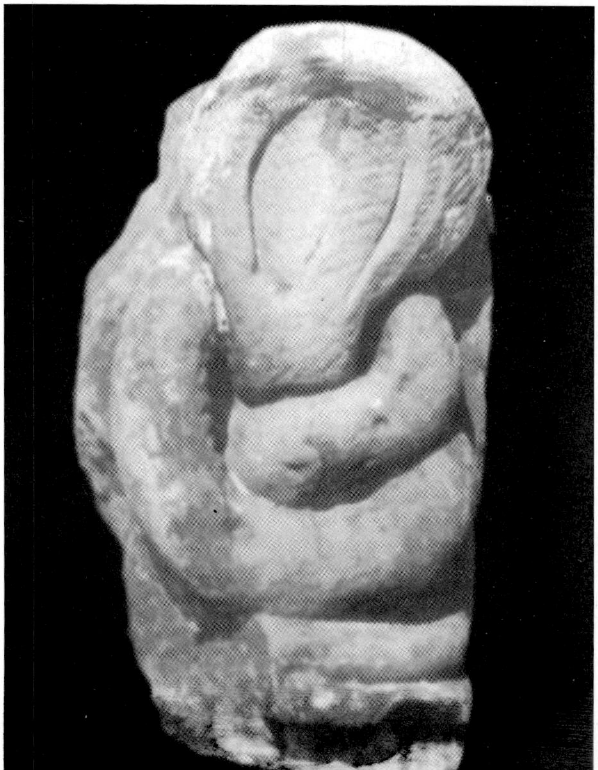

Pl. 317. Nāga, Ratpur.

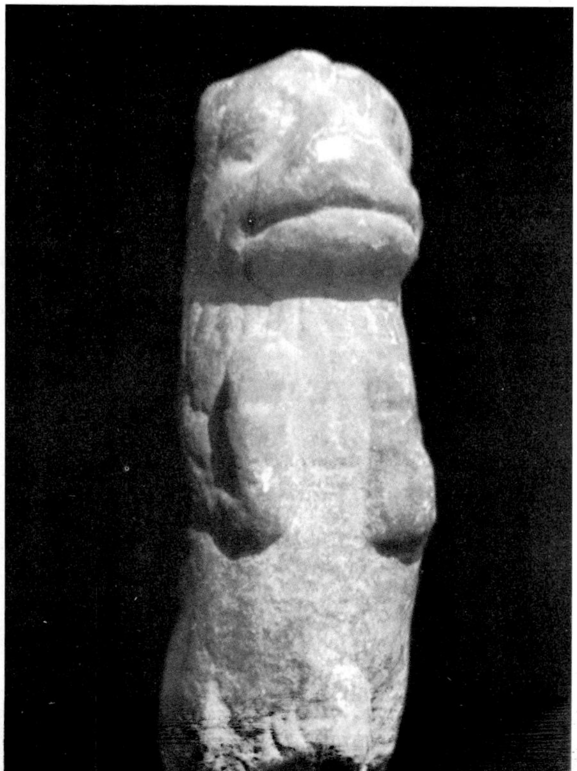

Pl. 318. Mythical lion, Ahirwan.

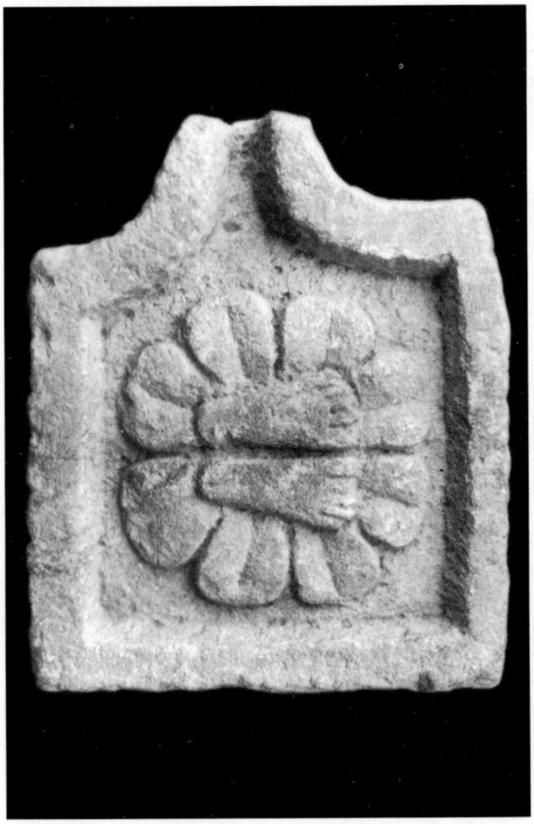

Pl. 319. *Charaṇa-pādukā*, Gujjar Kheri.

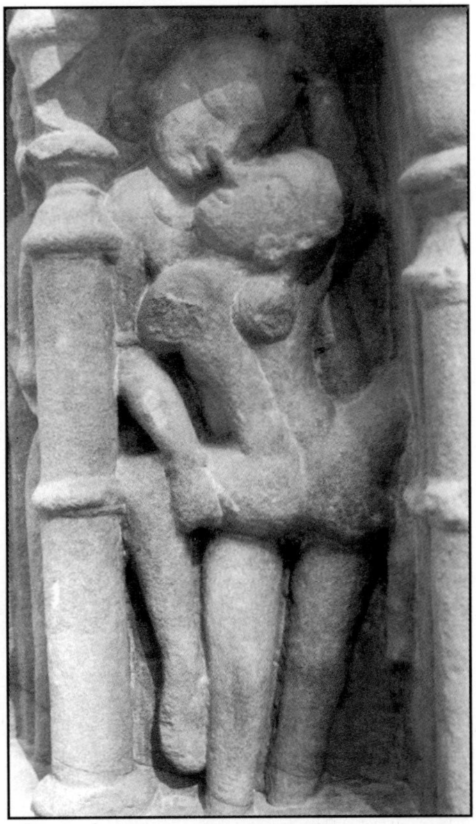

Pl. 320. Erotic couple, Pinjore.

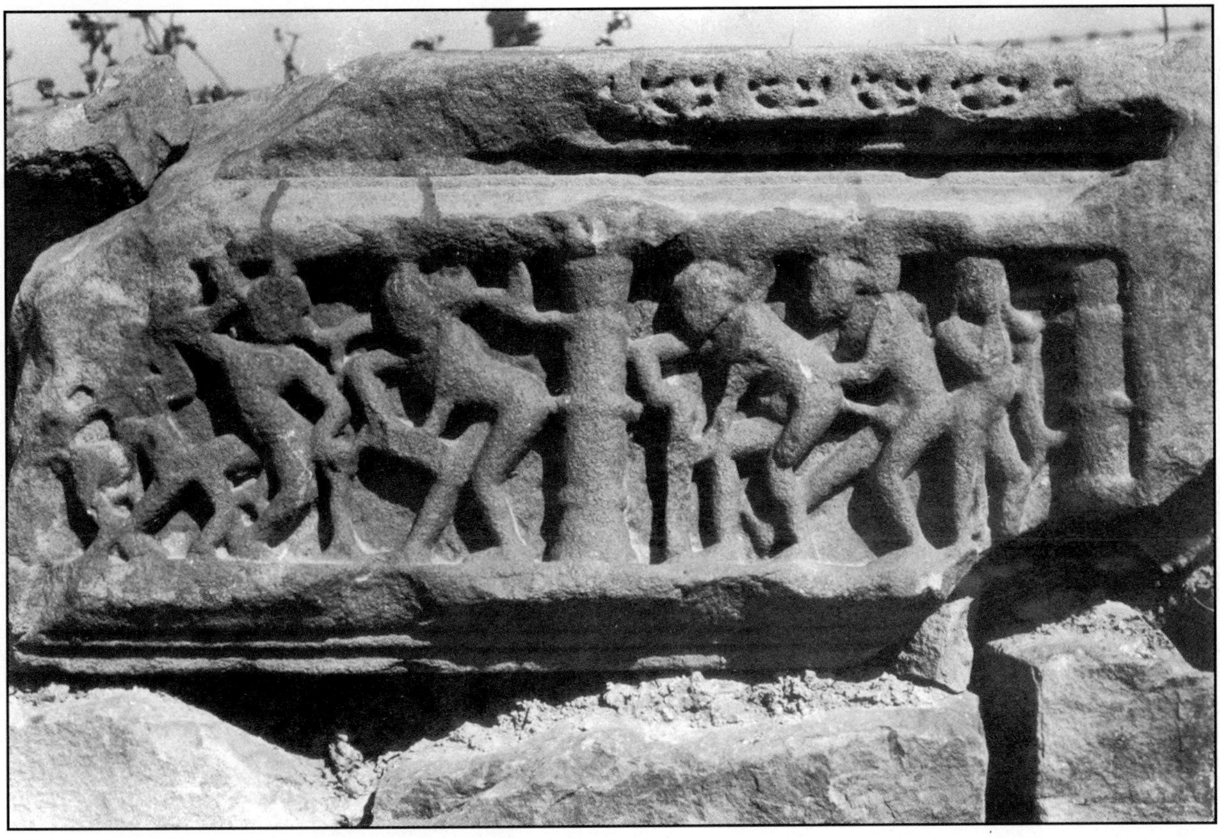

Pl. 321. Orgiastic group, Pinjore.

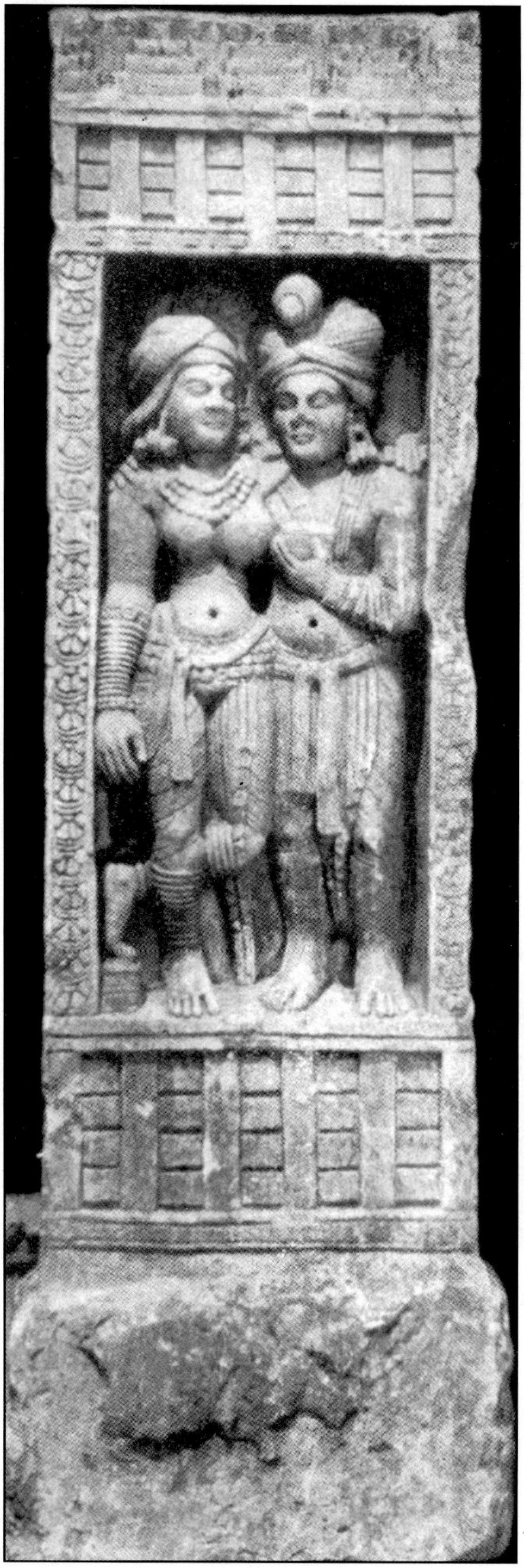

Pl. 322. Yaksha couple on Pillar No. 1, Amin.

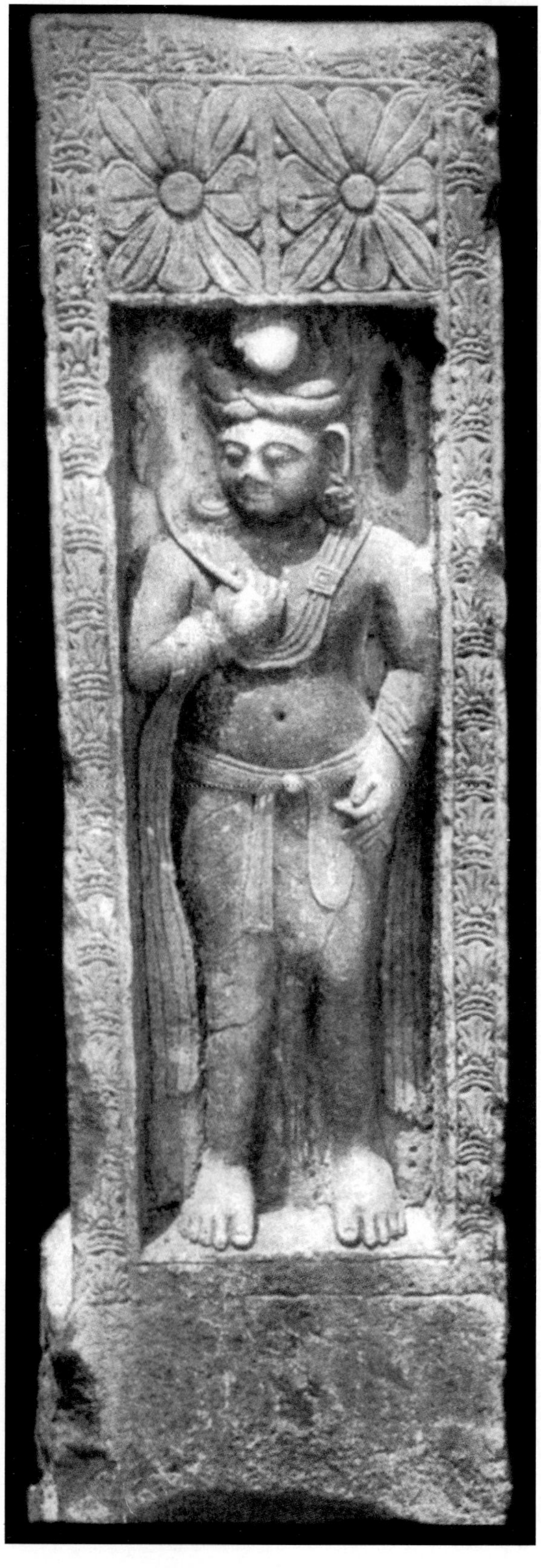

Pl. 323. Yaksha, Pillar No. 2, Amịn.

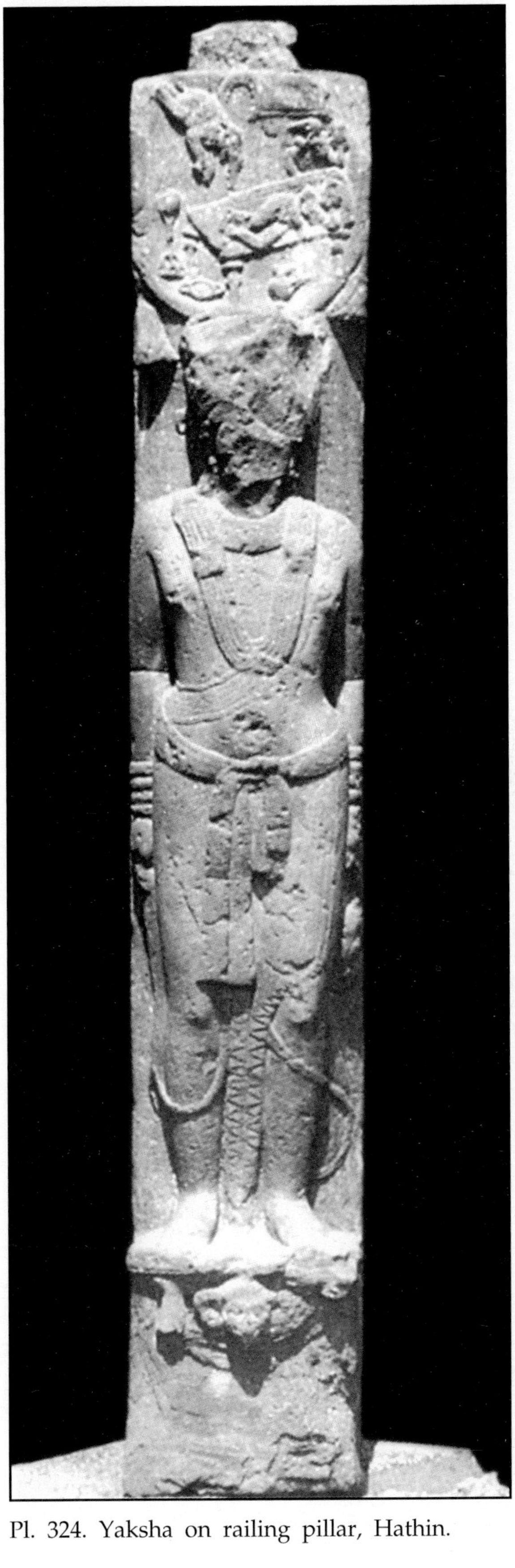

Pl. 324. Yaksha on railing pillar, Hathin.

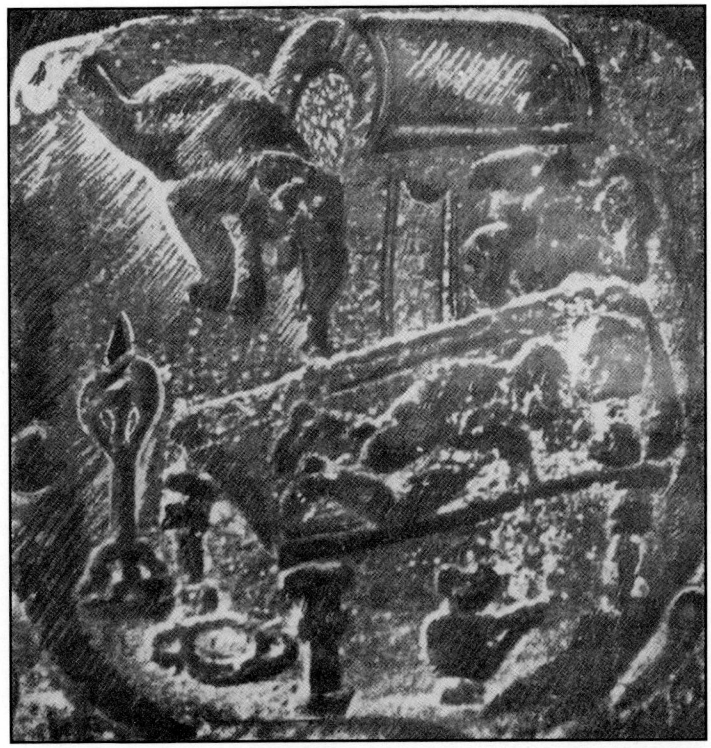

Pl. 325. Māyā's dream, Hathin pillar.

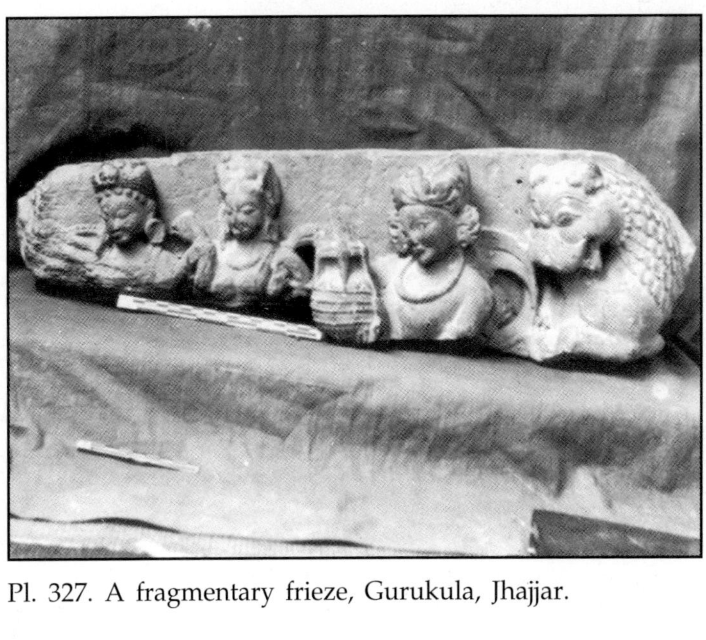

Pl. 327. A fragmentary frieze, Gurukula, Jhajjar.

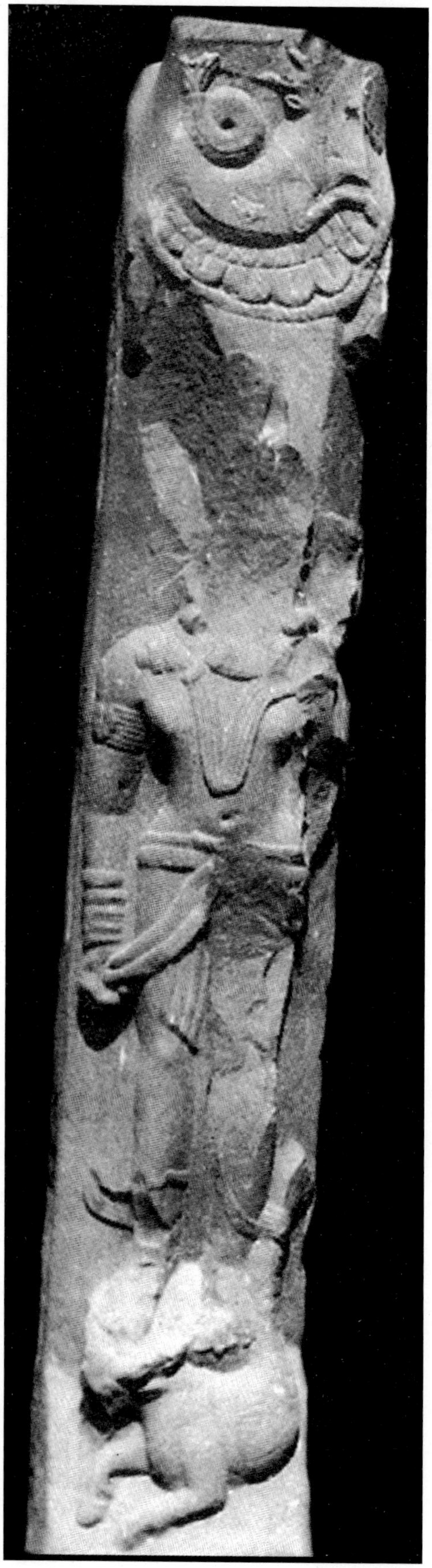

Pl. 326. Yaksha on railing pillar, Bhadas.

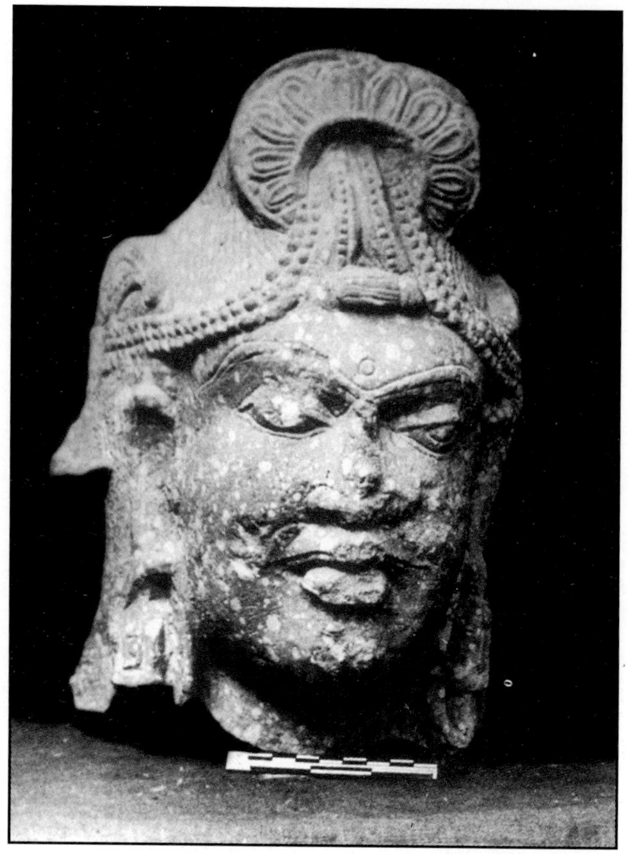

Pl. 328. Head of Bodhisattva, Mahmudpur.

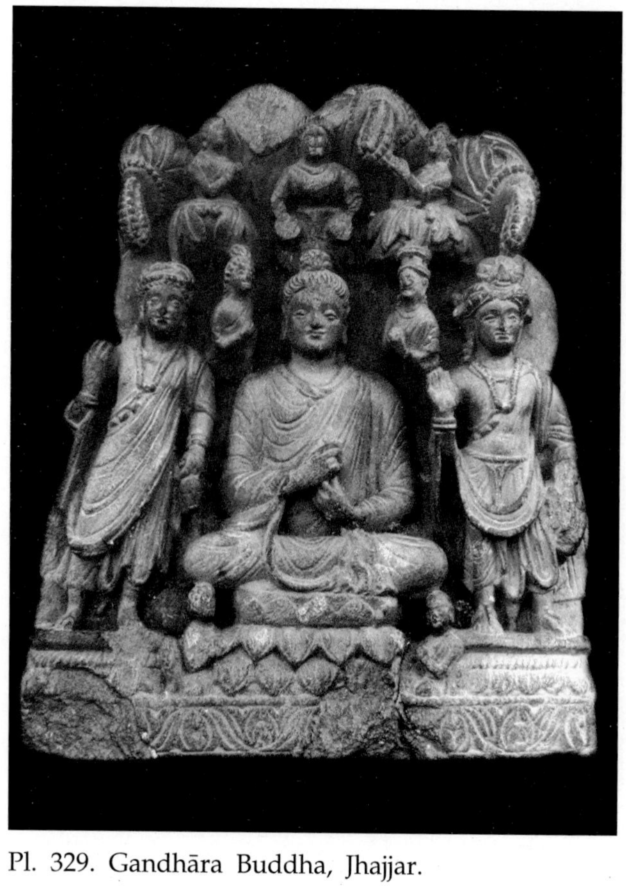

Pl. 329. Gandhāra Buddha, Jhajjar.

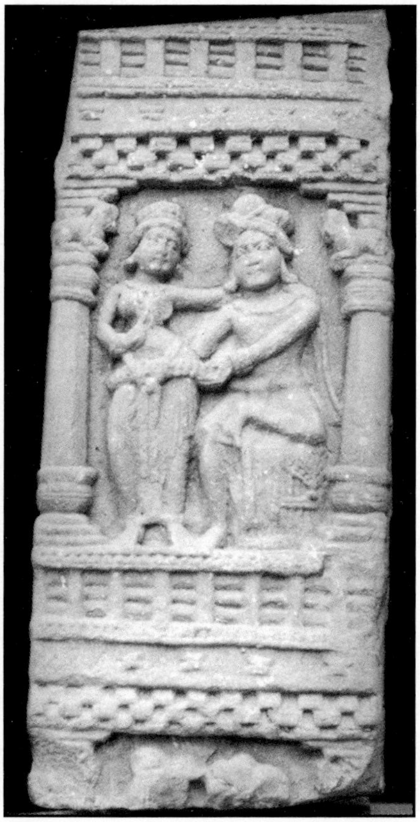

Pl. 330. Railing pillar, Bhuna.

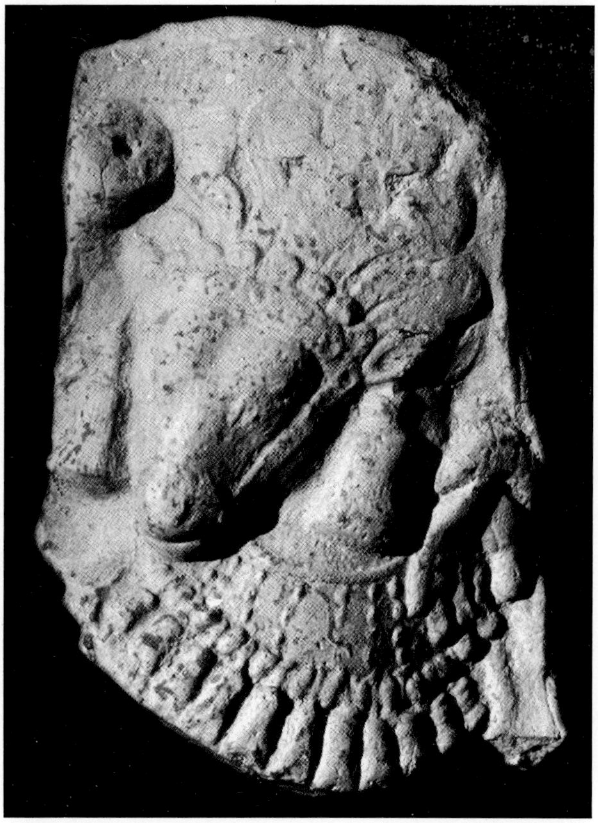

Pl. 331. Aśvamukhī Yakshī, terracotta, Sugh.

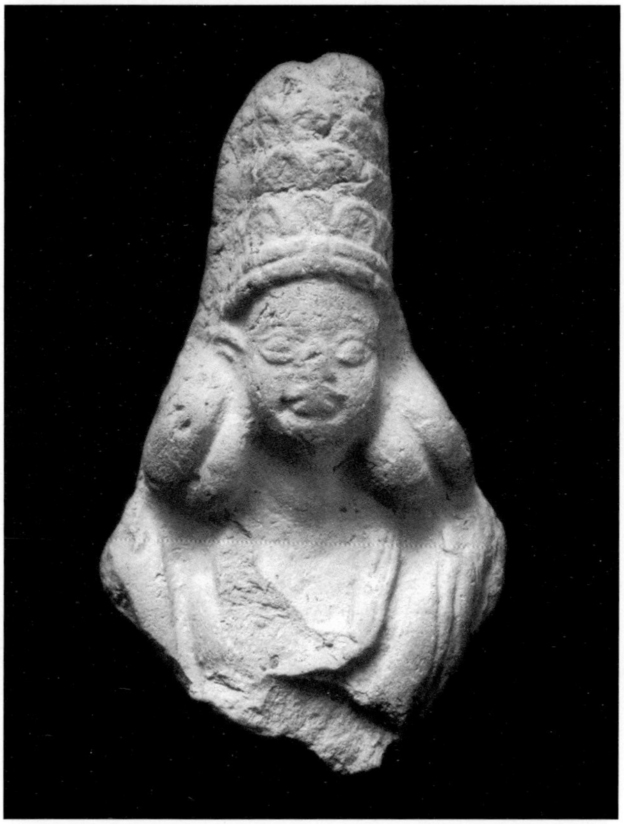

Pl. 332. Bust of Bodhisattva, terracotta, Sugh.

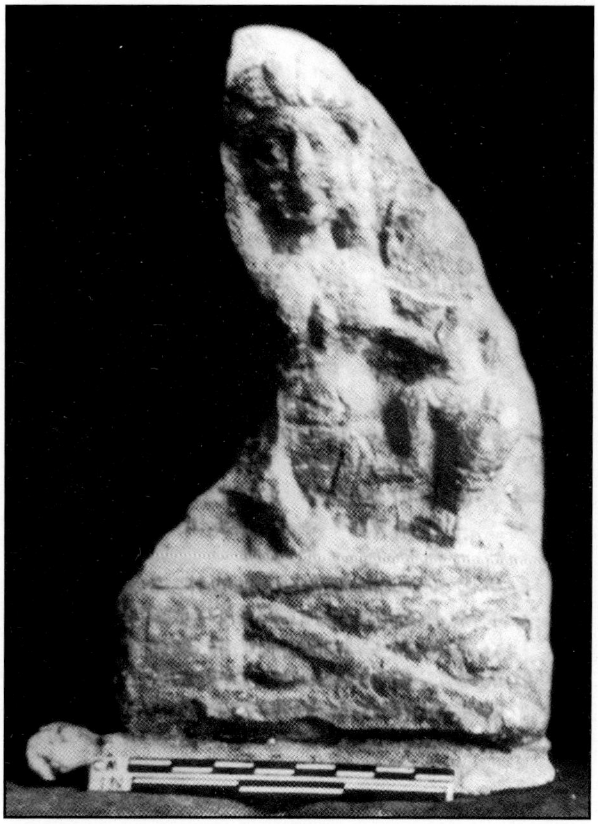

Pl. 333. Hārītī, Mohanbari.

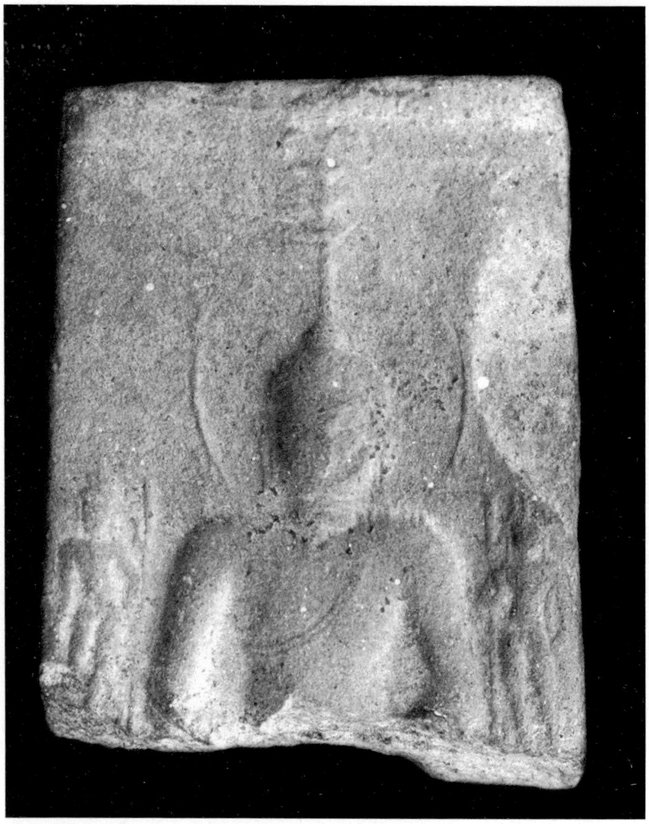

Pl. 334. Buddha, terracotta, Sugh.

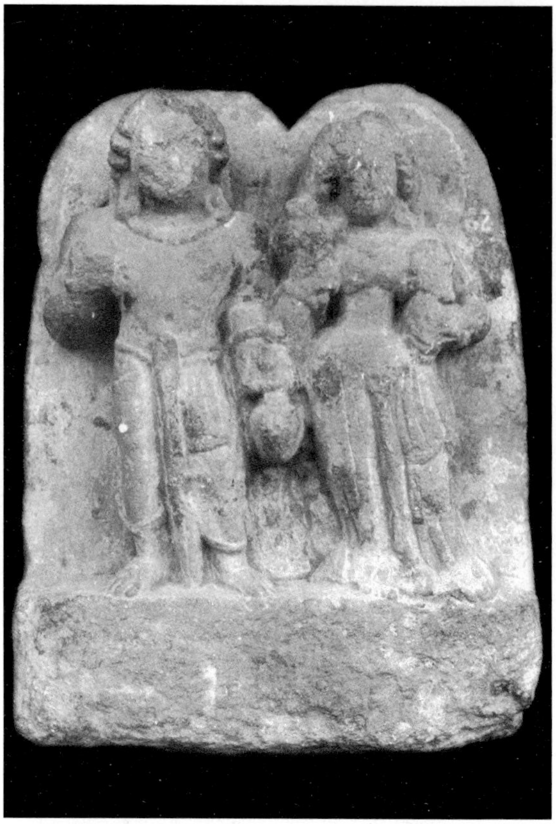

Pl. 335. Pañchika and Hārītī?, Rohtak.

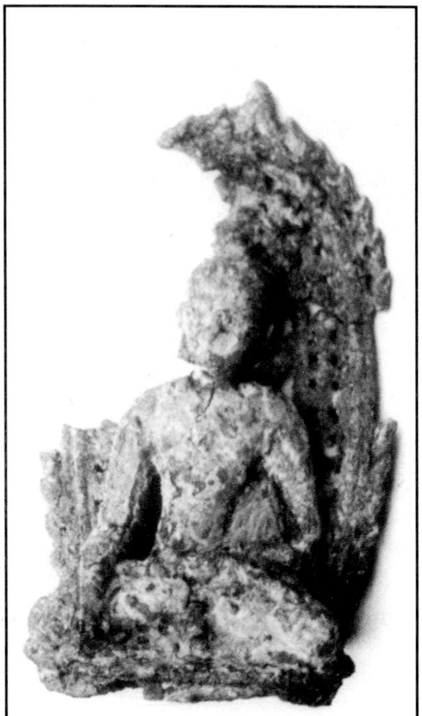

Pl. 336. *Bhūmisparśa*-Buddha, bronze, Hansi.

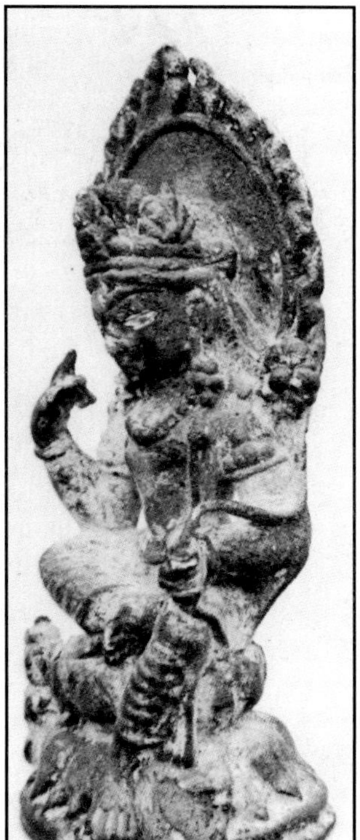

Pl. 337. Avalokiteśvara Padmapāṇi, bronze, Hansi.

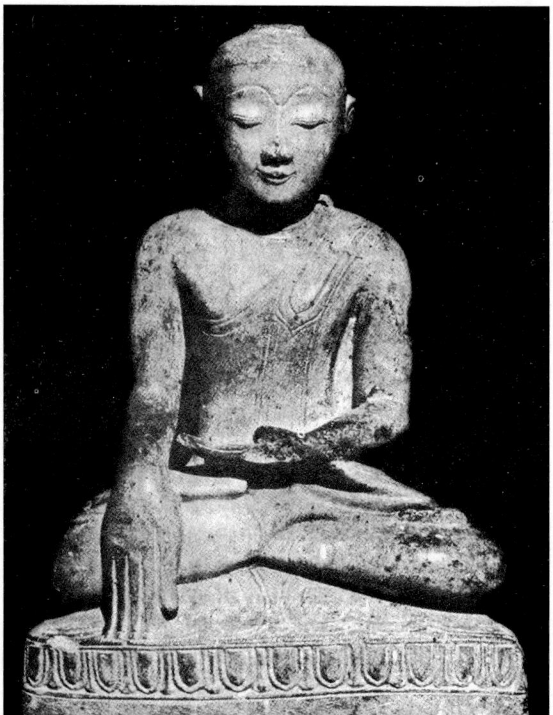

Pl. 340. *Bhūmisparśa*-Buddha, Taraori.

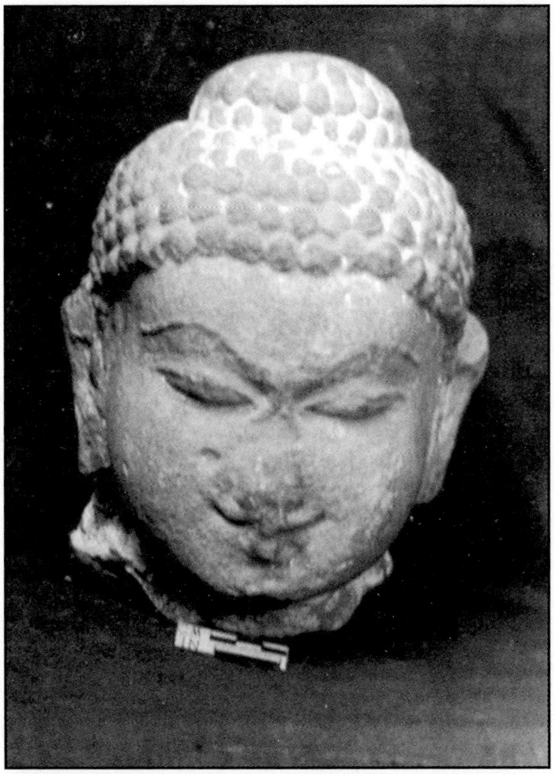

Pl. 338. Buddha head, Sanghi.

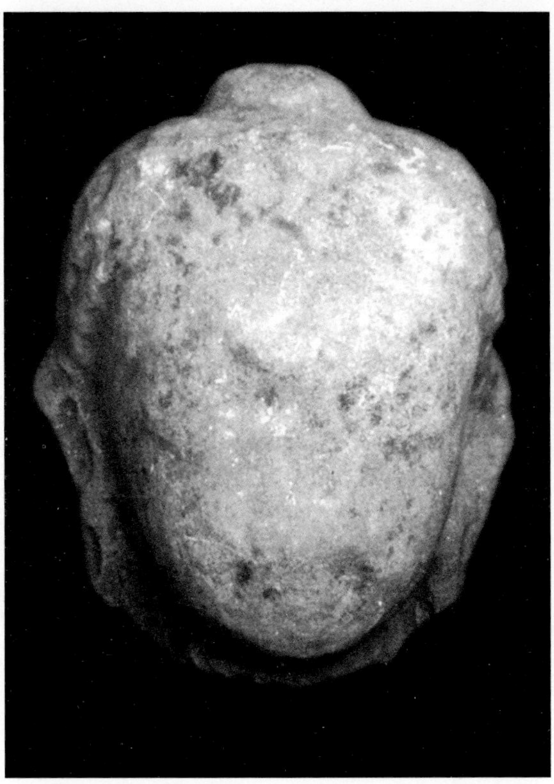

Pl. 339. Buddha head, Ad Badri.

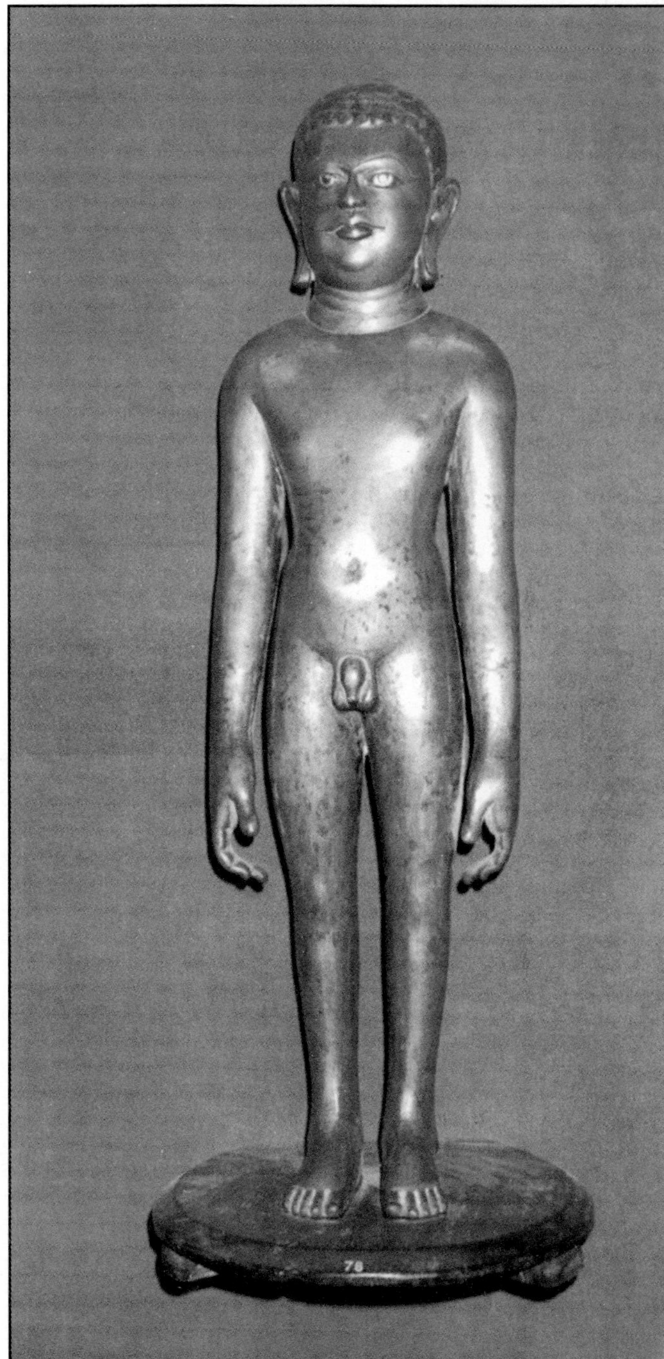

Pl. 341. Tīrthaṅkara, bronze, Hansi or Rohtak (Lahore Museum).

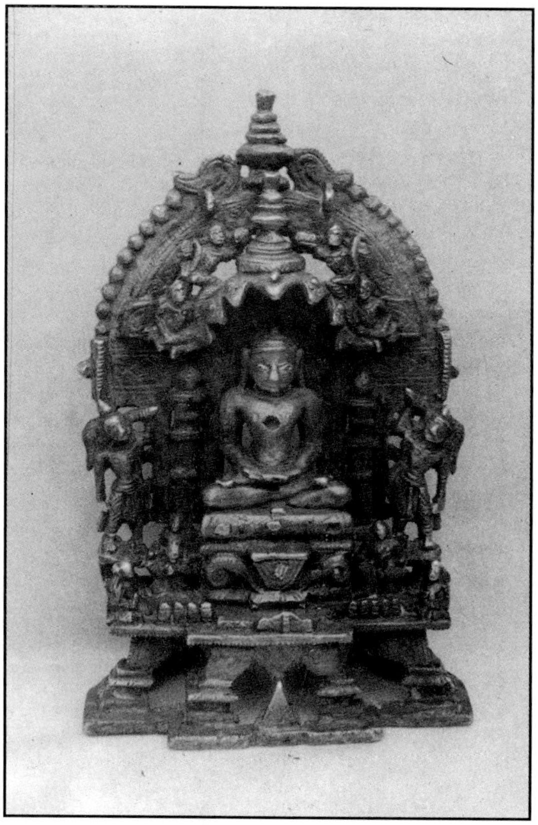

Pl. 342. Pārśvanātha, bronze, Badhara.

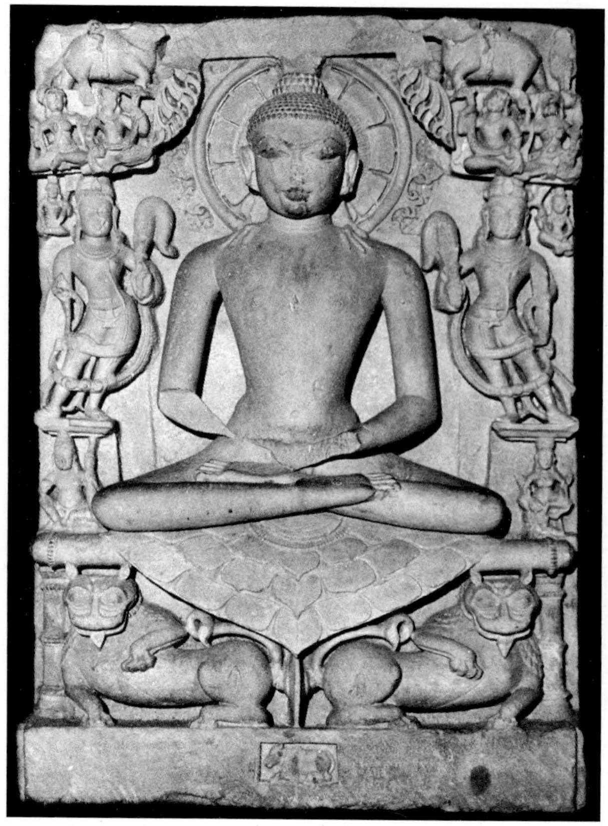

Pl. 343. Ādinātha, Jind.

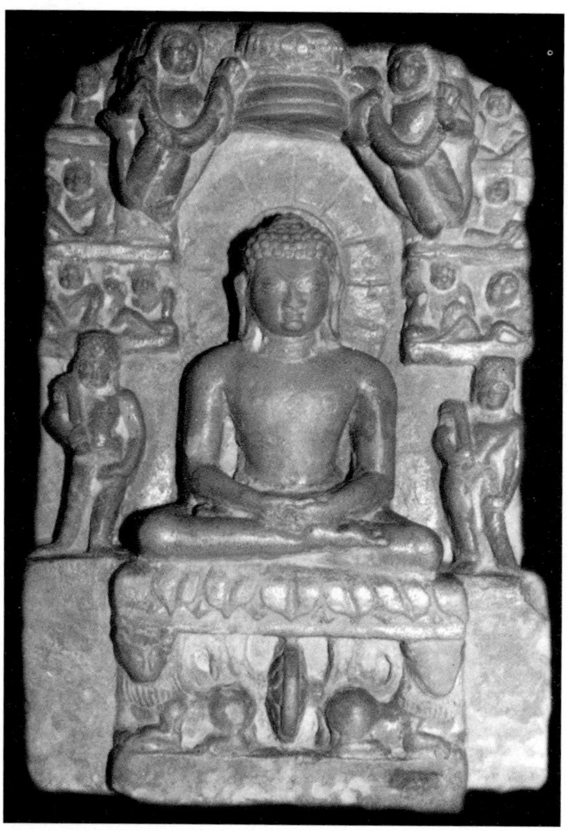

Pl. 344. Ādinātha, Narnaul.

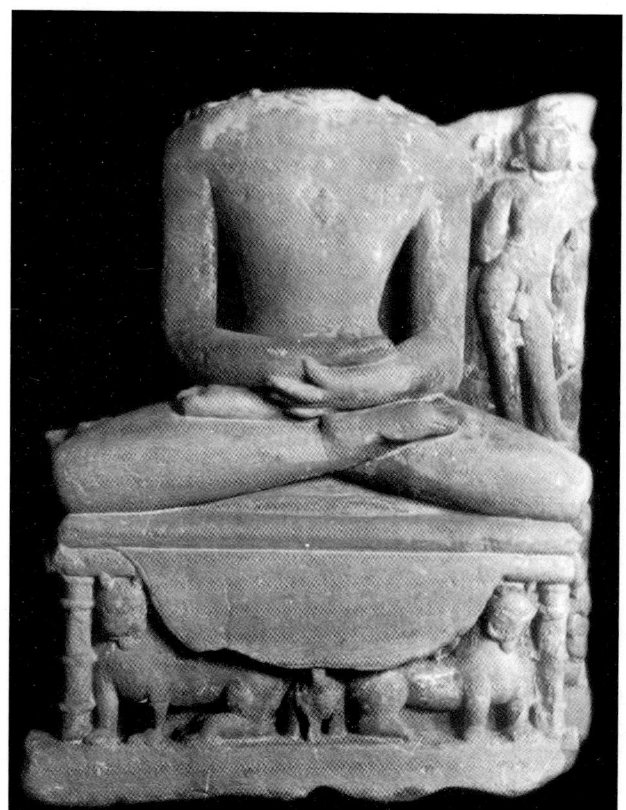

Pl. 345. Ādinātha, Pinjore.

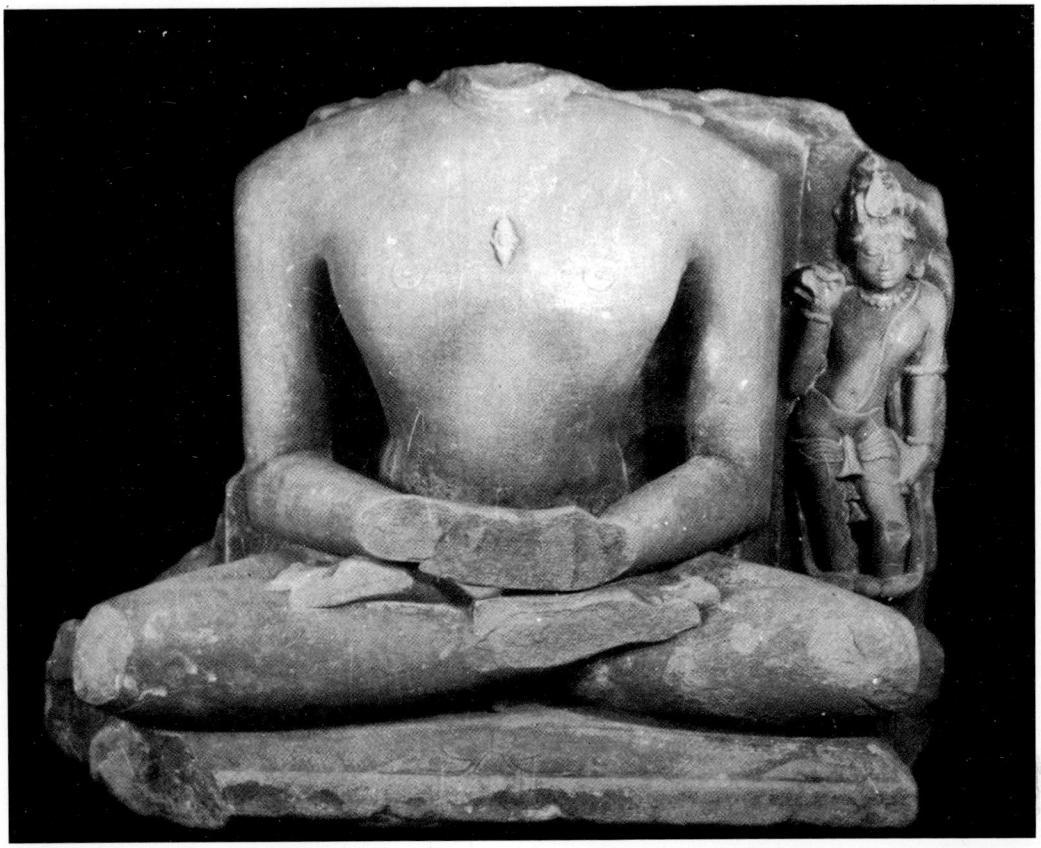

Pl. 346. Ādinātha, Pinjore.

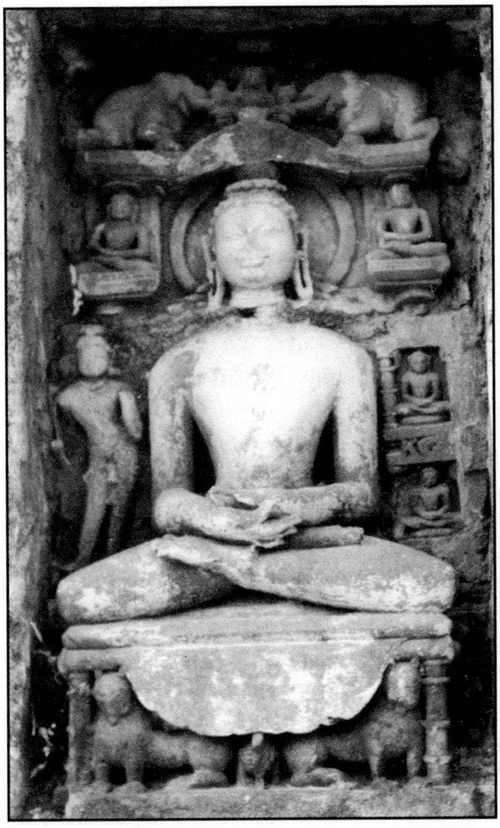

Pl. 347. Ādinātha, Pinjore.

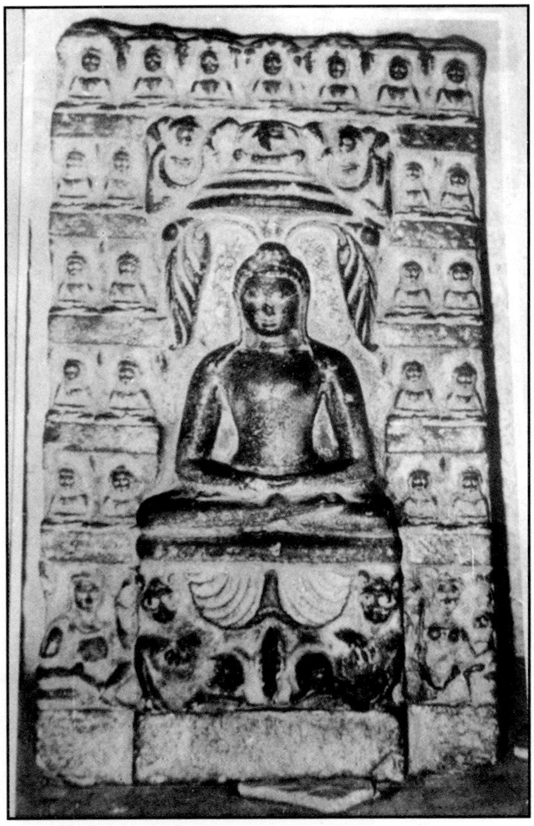

Pl. 348. Ādinātha *chaturviṃśati*, Narnaul.

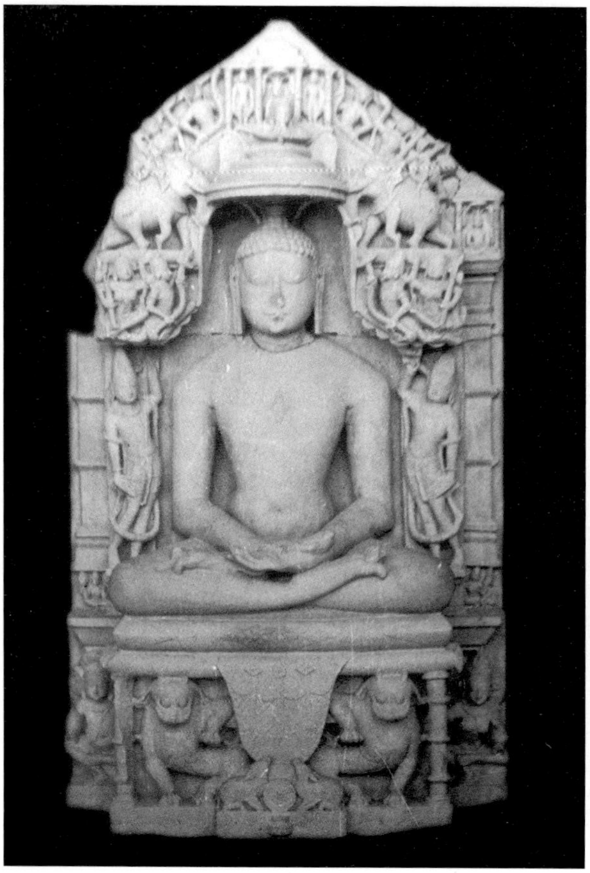

Pl. 356. Mallinātha, Narnaul.

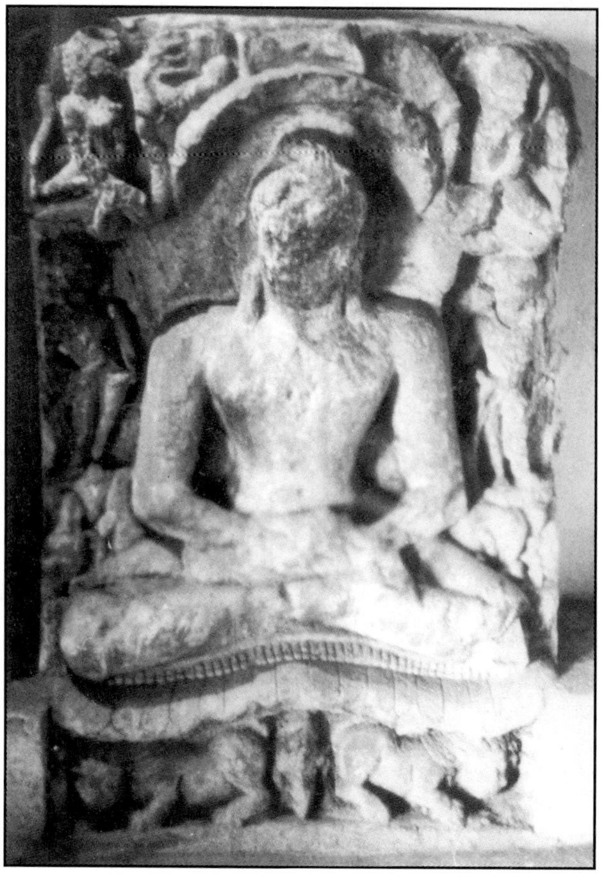

Pl. 358. Pārśvanātha, Ata.

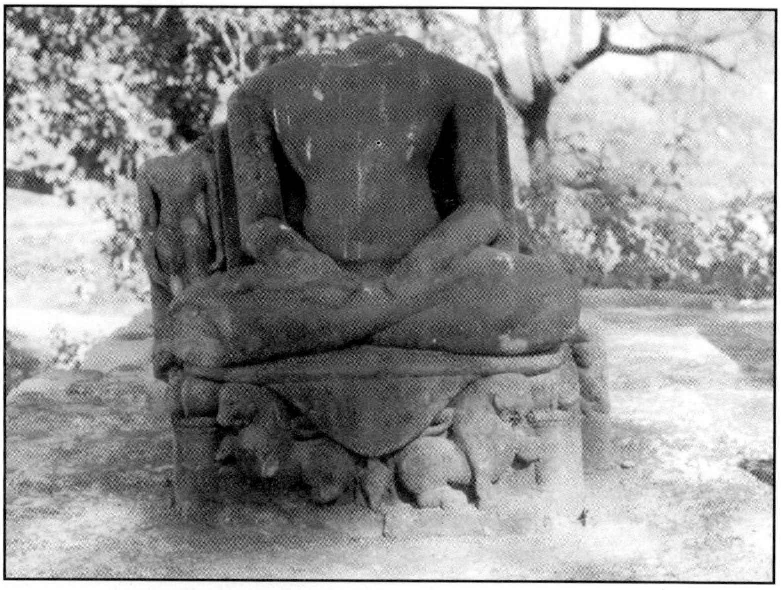

Pl. 357. Neminātha, headless, Ratpur.

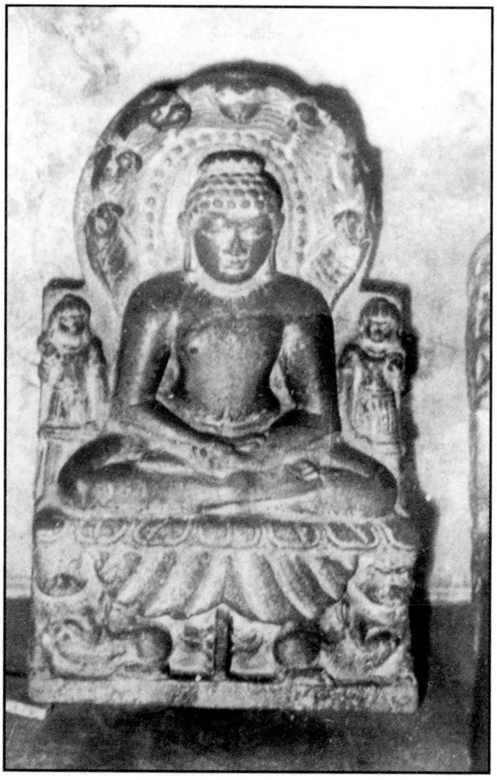

Pl. 359. Pārśvanātha, Narnaul.

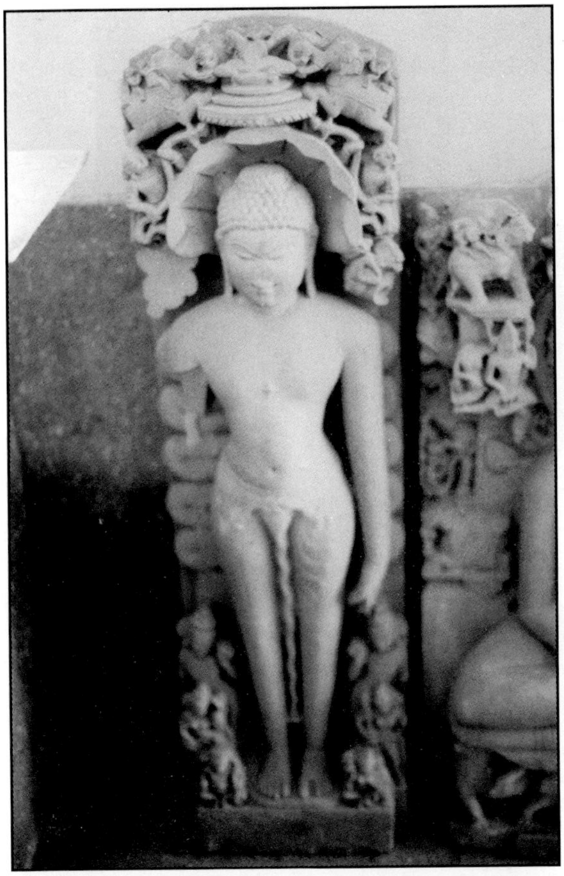

Pl. 360. Pārśvanātha, Asthal Bohr, Rohtak.

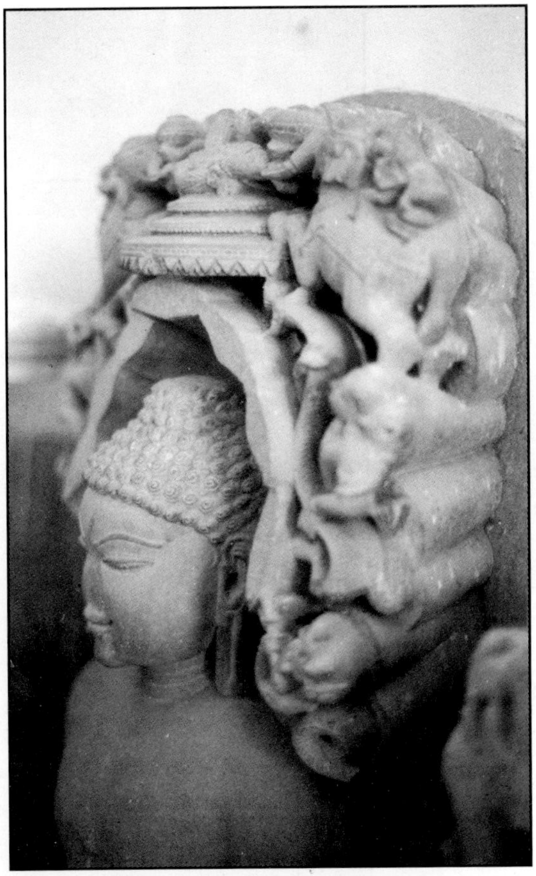

Pl. 361. Same, closer view of the head.

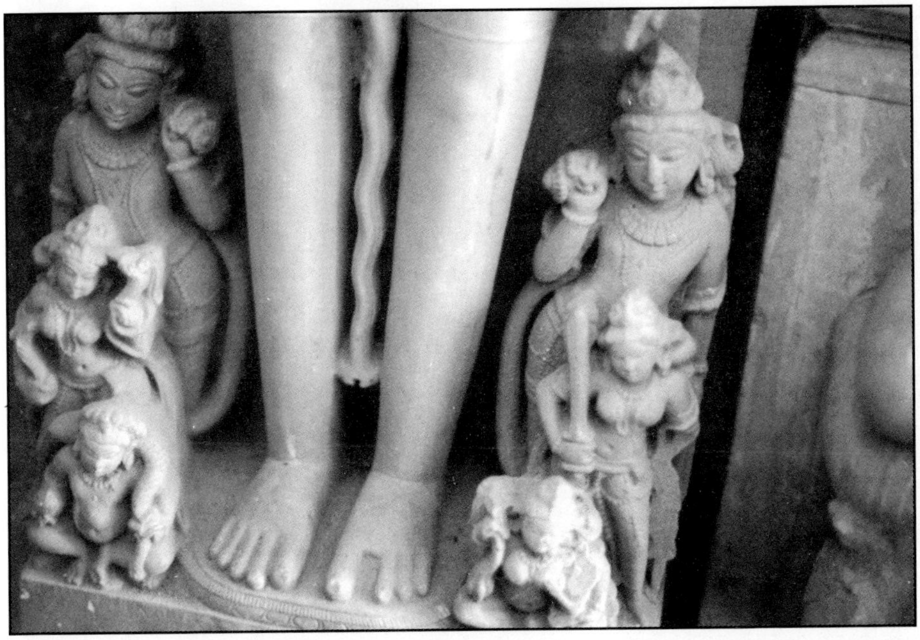

Pl. 362. Same, attendant figures.

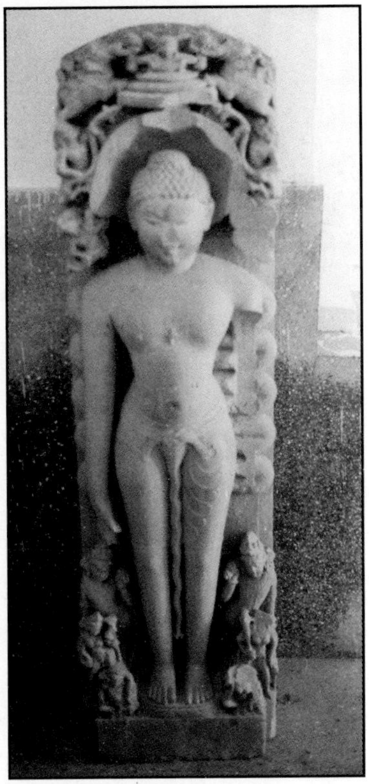

Pl. 363. Pārśvanātha, Asthal Bohr, Rohtak.

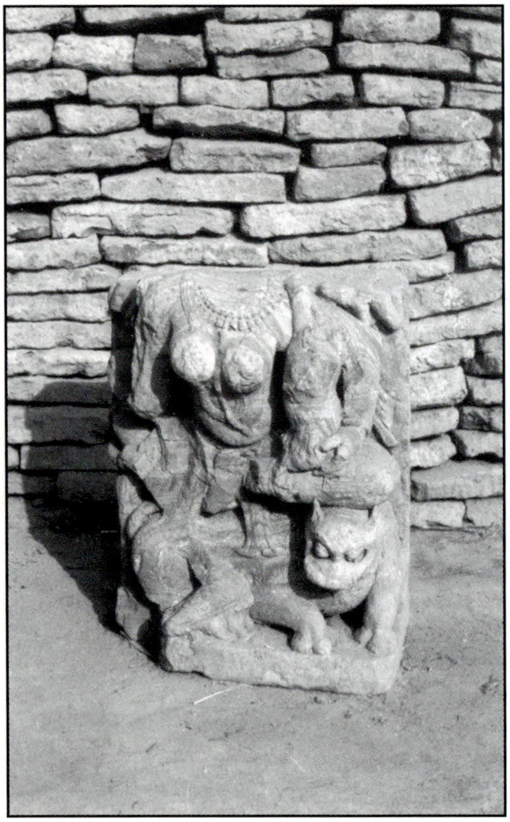

Pl. 377. Ambikā, Majra

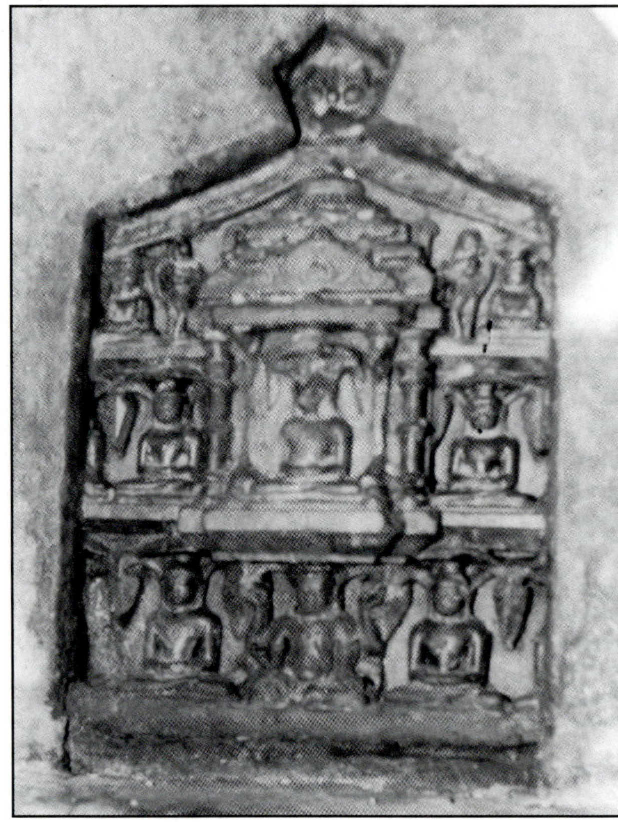

Pl. 378. A *takhtī*-shaped Jaina frieze, Bhatla.

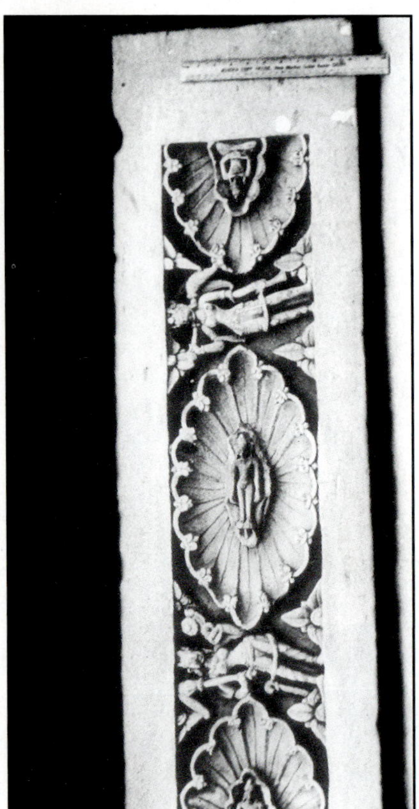

Pl. 379. Part of the ceiling, Rohtak.

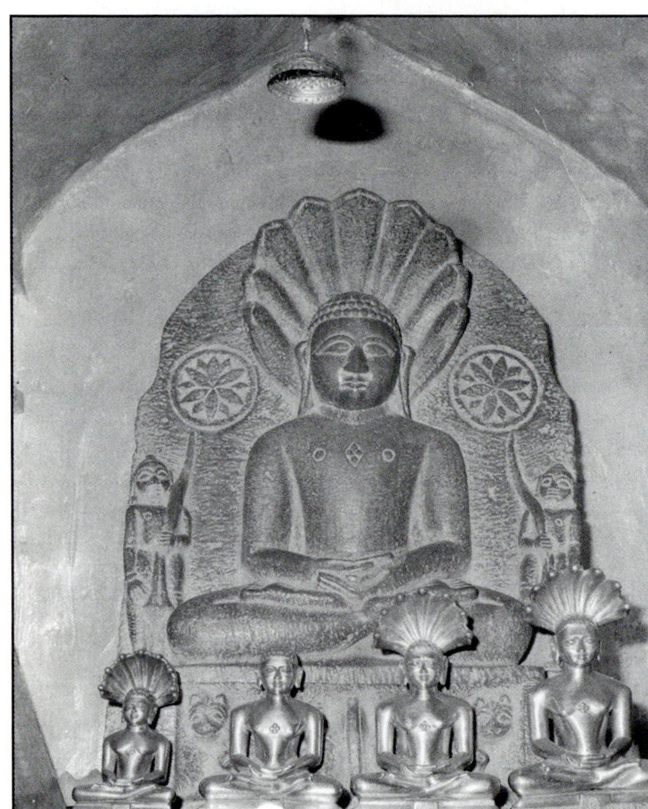

Pl. 380. Jaina images, Ambala.

Select Bibliography

ORIGINAL SOURCES

Agni Purāṇa, ASS, Poona, 1900.
Ahirbudhnya Saṃhitā, (ed.) Schrader O.F., Madras, 1916.
Aitareya Brāhmaṇa (tr.), Keith, A.B., Cambrige, 1920.
Amarakosha (ed.), Shastri, Raghunandan Prasad, Banaras, 1941.
Aṃśumadbhedāgama, ASS, Poona, 1900 and *EHI* by Gopinath Rao
Aparājitapṛichchhā, GOS, Baroda, 1950.
Arthaśāstra (tr.), Shamasastri, R., Mysore, 1956.
Ashṭādhyāyī (ed.), Vasu, S.C., Allahabad, 1891-97.
Atharvaveda, (tr.) Whitney, W.D., Cambridge, 1905; Pandit, S.P., Bombay, 1895-98.
Avadānaśataka (ed. Vaidya, P.L.), Darbhanga, 1958.
Bhāgavata Purāṇa, NSP, Bombay, 1916; Gita Press, Gorakhpur.
Brahmāṇḍa Purāṇa, Veṅkaṭeśvara Press, Bombay, 1923.
Brahma Purāṇa, ASS, Poona, 1895.
Bṛihatsaṃhitā, (tr.) Sastri, V.S., Bangalore, 1947; in *DHI* by Banerjea.
Buddhacharita (ed. with Hindi tr. Chaudhuri, S.N., Purnea, 1955).
Chaturvarga-Chintāmaṇi, Bibliotheca Indica Series, Calcutta, 1878.
Devatāmūrti Prakaraṇa and *Rūpamaṇḍana*, (ed.) Sankhya Tirtha V.M., Calcutta, 1936.
Devī Bhāgavata Purāṇa, Śrī Veṅkaṭeśvara Steam Press, Bombay, V.S. 1982.
Dīpavaṃsa (ed. Oldenberg, H.), London, 1879.
Divyāvadāna (ed. Vaidya, P.L., Darbhanga, 1959).
Harivaṃśa Purāṇa, Gita Press, Gorakhpur.
Garuḍa Purāṇa (Bareli, 1970).
Jayākhya Saṃhitā, GOS, Baroda, 1931.
Kālikā Purāṇa, Veṅkaṭeśvara Press.
Kapishṭhala-Kaṭha Saṃhitā, (ed.) Dr. Raghuvir, Lahore, 1932.
Kharatara-Gachchha-Bṛihad-Gurvāvali (edited by Acharya Jina Vijaya Muni), Bombay, 1956.
Kūrma Purāṇa, Veṅkaṭeśvara Press, Bombay, 1927; All India Kashiraj Trust, Varanasi, 1972.
Kurukshetra Māhātmya, Kurukshetra, 1973.
Kuvalayamālā, (ed.) Upadhye, A.N., Bombay, 1959.
Liṅga Purāṇa, Veṅkaṭeśvara Press, Bombay.
Mādhyandina Saṃhitā
Mahābhārata, BORI, Poona, 1927-64; Gita Press, Gorakhpur.
Mahābhāshya of Patañjali, ed. by Kielhorn, F.
Mahāmāyūrī (ed. Sylvan Levi, *Journal Asiatique*, 1915).

Mahāvaṃśa (tr. Bhadant Anand Kausalyayan), Prayag, VS 2014.
Majjhima Nikāya (ed. Jagdish Kashyap, Nalanda, 1952).
Mānasollāsa, GOS, Baroda, 1939.
Manusmṛiti
Mārkaṇḍeya Purāṇa, (ed.) More, M.R., Calcutta, 1962; (tr.) Pargiter, F.E., Calcutta, 1904; ed. Panchanan Tarkaratna, Calcutta, Śaka 1812.
Matsya Purāṇa, ASS, Poona, 1907.
Merutantra, Bombay, 1904.
Padma Purāṇa, ASS, Poona, 1893-94.
Rājataraṅgiṇī of Kalhaṇa, Eng. tr. by Pandit, R.S., Sahitya Academi, New Delhi, 1977 (reprint).
Rāmāyaṇa, Gita Press, Gorakhpur; Critical edition, Lahore, 1938.
Ṛigveda, Vedic Saṃśodhana Maṇḍala, 4 Vols., Poona, 1933-46; (tr.) Griffith, R.T.H., 2 Vols., Banaras, 1896-97.
Śatapatha Brāhmaṇa, (tr.) Eggeling, J., SBE, Oxford, 1882-1900 (Reprint, Delhi).
Śilparatna, (ed.) Śātrī, S. Sambasiva. Appendix in Rao's *EHI*.
Skanda Purāṇa, Veṅkaṭeśvara Press, Bombay, V.S. 1965.
Śrī-Tattvanidhi, Veṅkaṭeśvara Press, Bombay, V.S. 1923.
Suprabhedāgama, Appendix in Rao's *EHI*.
Therīgāthā, (ed.) Bhagwat, N.K., Bombay, 1956.
Taittirīya Brāhmaṇa, (ed.) Mitra, R., Calcutta, 1885.
Vājasaneyī Saṃhitā, NSS, Bombay, 1921.
Vāmana Purāṇa, Veṅkaṭeśvara Press, Bombay, 1929.
Vāyu Purāṇa, (tr.) Śāstrī, R.P. Tripathi, Prayāga, Saṃvat 2007.
Vishṇudharmottara Purāṇa, GOS, Baroda, 1958.
Vishṇu Purāṇa, (tr.) Wilson, H.H., London, 1840.
Yājñavalkya Smṛiti
Yajurveda Saṃhitā, (ed.) Weber, A.

MODERN BOOKS

Agrawal, Jagannath (2001), *Inscriptions of Haryana, Punjab, Himachal & Kashmir*, New Delhi.
Agrawala, P.K. (1967), *Skanda-Kārttikeya*, Varanasi.
——, (1994), *Studies in Indian Iconography*, Jaipur.
Agrawal, Urmila (1964), *Khajuraho Sculptures and their Significance*, Delhi.
Agrawala, V.S. (VS 2016), *Mahābhārata kī Nāmānukramaṇikā* (Hindi), Gorakhpur
Agrawala, V.S. (1963), *India as Known to Pāṇini*, Varanasi.
——, (1963), *Solar Symbolism of the Boar (Yajña-Varāha, an Interpretation)*, Banaras.
——, (1964), *Vāmana Purāṇa: A Study*, Varanasi.
——, (1964), *Harshacharita: Eka Sāṃskṛitika Adhyayana* (Hindi), 2nd ed., Patna.
——, (1965), *Studies in Indian Art*, Varanasi
——, (1966), *Śiva-Mahādeva*, Varanasi.
——, (1951), *A Catalogue of the Brahmanical Images in Mathura Museum*, Lucknow.
Ahir, D.C. (1971), *Buddhism in the Punjab, Haryana and Himachal Pradesh*, New Delhi.
Allan, John (1914), *Catalogue of the Coins of the Gupta Dynasties and of Śaśāṅka, king of Gauḍa*, London.
——, (1936), *Catalogue of the Coins of Ancient India in the British Museum*, London.
Altekar, A.S. (1957), *Coinage of the Gupta Empire*, Varanasi.
(Anonymous) (1986), *Indian Sculpture, A Catalogue of the Los Angeles County Museum of Art Collection*, Vol. I, University of California Press, Berkeley, Los Angeles, and London.
Apte, V.S. (1959), *Sanskrit-English Dictionary*, Delhi-Varanasi-Patna.
Arora, U.P. (ed.) (1991), *India's Cultural Contacts with Greek World (In the memory of Demetrius Galanose, 1760-1833, A Greek Sanskritist of Benaras)*, Delhi.
Awasthi, A.B. (1965), *Studies in the Skanda-Purāṇa*, Part I, Lucknow.

Awasthi, Ramashray (1967), *Khajurāho kī Deva Pratimāyeṃ*, Agra.
Bajpai, K.D. and Pandey, S.K. (1978), *Malhar*, Sagar.
Bajpai, K.D. (1964), *Sagar through the Ages*, Sagar.
——, (1976), *Indian Numismatic Studies*, New Delhi.
Bajpai, K.D. et al. (eds.), (2000), *Gleanings of Indian Archaeology History & Culture (Prof. Dr. R.N. Mehta Felicitation Volume)*, Jaipur.
Banerjea, J.N. (1956), *The Development of Hindu Iconography*, 2nd ed., Calcutta.
Banerjee, P. (1981), *Life of Krishna in Indian Art*, New Delhi, 1978; *Blue God*, New Delhi.
——, (1986), *Rāma in Indian Literature Art and Thought*, Delhi.
Beal, Samuel (1906), *Si-Yu-Ki: Buddhist Records of the Western World*, Vol. I, London.
Begley, W.E. (1973), *Viṣṇu's Flaming Wheel: The Iconography of the Sudarśana Cakra*, New York.
Bhadani, B.L. and Tripathi, Dwijendra (eds.), (1996), *Facets of A Marwar Historian*, Jaipur.
Bhandarkar, R.G. (1929), *Vaiṣṇavism, Śaivism and Minor Religious Systems*, Pune.
Bharadwaj, O.P. (1986), *Studies in the Historical Geography of Ancient India*, Delhi.
Bhattacharya, B.C. (1939), *The Jaina Iconography*, Lahore (2nd revised edition, Delhi-Varanasi-Patna, 1974).
——, (1954), *Indian Images*, Calcutta.
Bhattacharyya, Benoytosh (1968), *The Indian Buddhist Iconography*, Calcutta (reprint).
Bhattacharyya, D.C. (1981), *Medieval Indian Sculpture (In the Government Museum and Art Gallery, Chandigarh)*, Chandigarh.
——, (1982), *Iconology of Composite Images*, Delhi
Bhattacharyya, D.C. and Handa, Devendra (eds.) (1989), *Prācī-Prabhā: Perspectives in Indology (Essays in Honour of Prof. B.N. Mukherjee)*, New Delhi.
Bhattasali, N.K. (1972), *Iconography of Buddhist and Brahmanical Sculptures in the Dacca Museum*, Varanasi-Delhi.
Bhavnani, E. (1965), *The Dance in India*, Bombay.
Briggs, John (1910), *Tārīkh-i-Firishta* (Eng. Tr.), Calcutta.
Burgess, J. (1904), *Archaeological Survey of Western India*, VIII (NIS).
Chakravarti, Mahadev (1986), *The Concept of Rudra-Śiva Through the Ages*, Delhi.
Champakalakshmi, R. (1981), *Vaiṣṇava Iconography in the Tamil Country*, New Delhi.
Chandra, Rai Govinda (1964), *Prāchīna Bhārata meṃ Lakshmī Pratimā - Eka Adhyayana*, Varanasi.
Chandra, Lokesh and Gupta, S.P. (eds.) (1970), *India's Contribution to World Thought and Culture*, Madras.
Chandra, Lokesh and Jain, Jyotindra (eds.) (1986), *Dimensions of Indian Art (Pupul Jayakar Seventy)*, Delhi.
Chandra, Pramod (1970), *Stone Sculpture in the Allahabad Museum*, Poona.
Chatterjee, Asim Kumar (1970), *The Cult of Skanda-Kārttikeya in Ancient India*, Calcutta.
Choudhary, R.D. and Singh, Shri Bhagwan (eds.) (1990), *Aspects of History and Culture*, Delhi.
Coomaraswamy, A.K. (1948), *The Dance of Siva*, Bombay.
——, (1969), *Introduction to Indian Art*, Delhi.
——, (1971), *Yakṣas*, Part I, Delhi.
——, (1927), *History of Indian and Indonesian Art*, London.
Cunningham, Alexander, *Archaeological Survey Reports*, Vols. II and XIV.
——, (1962), *Stūpa of Bharhut*, Varanasi, (Reprint).
Czuma, S. (1985), *Kushana Sculpture - Images from Early India*, Cleveland.
Dallapiccola, A.L. et al. (eds.) (1982), *Krishna-the Divine Lover: Myth and Legend through Indian Art*, Bombay.
Dasgupta, K.K. (1974), *Tribal History of Ancient India – A Numismatic Approach*, Calcutta.
Datta, V.N. & Phadke, H.A. (1984), *History of Kurukshetra*, Kurukshetra.
Davidson, J. Leroy (1968), *Art of The Indian Subcontinent From Los Angeles Collections*, University of California, Los Angeles.
Dehejia, Vidya (1972), *Early Buddhist Rock Temples*, London.
Desai, Kalpana (1973), *Iconography of Viṣṇu*, New Delhi.
Desai, Devangana (1996), *The Religious Imagery of Khajuraho*, Mumbai.
Desai, Nileshvari Y. (1968), *Ancient Indian Society, Reliogion and Mythology as depicted in the Markandeya Purana: A Critical Study*, Baroda.

Dev, Acharya Bhagwan, (1965), *Vīra-bhūmi Hariyānā* (Hindi), Jhajjar..

Dey, Nundo Lal (1971), *The Geographical Dictionary of Ancient and Medieval India*, 3rd ed., New Delhi.

Dikshit, R.K. (1955), *Kannauj*, Lucknow.

Dubost, Paul Martin (1997), *Gaṇeśa the Enchanter of the Three Worlds*, Mumbai.

Elliot, H.M. and Dowson, J., *History of India as told by its own Historians.*

Fleet, J.F. (1888), *Inscriptions of the Early Gupta Kinga and Their Successors*, Corpus Inscriptionum Indicarum, Vol. III (Reprint, Varanasi, 1970).

Frauwallner, E. (1956), *The Earliest Vinaya and the Beginnings of Buddhist Literature*, Rome.

Ganguli, K.K. and Biswas, S.S. (eds.) (1986), *Rupanjali in memory of O.C. Gangoly*, Calcutta.

Gardner, Percy (1966), *The Coins of the Greek and Scythic Kings of Bactria and India in the British Museum*, Chicago.

Gaston, A-M. (1982), *Śiva in Dance, Myth and Iconography*, Delhi.

Gautam, Chamanlal (1967), *Devavāda kā Vaijñānika Svarūpa* (Hindi) I, Vishṇu-Rahasya, Bareilly.

Getty, Alice (1936), *Gaṇeśa*, Oxford.

Ghosh, A. (ed.) (1974), *Jaina Art and Architecture*, New Delhi.

Gonda, J. (1954), *Aspects of Early Viṣṇuism*, Utrecht.

Gupta, P.L. and Hardarkar, T.R. (1985), *Ancient Indian Silver Punchmarked Coins of the Magadha-Maurya Karshapana Series*, Anjaneri.

Gurney, O.R. (1961), *The Hittites*, Pelican.

Guy, John (ed.) (1995), *Indian Art & Connoisseurship Essays in Honour of Douglas Barret*, Indira Gandhi National Center for the Arts in association with Mapin Publishing Pvt. Ltd., New Delhi and Ahmedabad.

Handa, Devendra (1984), *Osian: History, Archaeology, Art & Architecture*, Delhi.

——, (1985), *Studies in Indian Coins and Seals*, Delhi.

——, (ed.) (1987), *Indological Studies (in memory of S.P. Singhal)*, Delhi.

——, (ed.) (1989), *Ajaya-Śrī: Recent Studies in Indology (Prof. Ajay Mitra Shastri Felicitation Volume)*, 2 vols., Delhi.

——, (2002), *Jaina Bronzes From Hansi*, Shimla-New Delhi.

——, (2004), *An Epic Pilgrimage – History and Antiquity of Pehowa: The Ancient Pṛithūdaka*, New Delhi.

——, (2004), *Buddhist Remains from Haryana*, New Delhi.

——, (2006), *Early Indian Coins from Sugh*, New Delhi.

Harle, J.C. (1974), *Gupta Sculpture*, Oxford.

Haertel, H. (1960), *Indische Sculpturen*, 1 (*Berlin Museum für Volkerkunde*), Berlin.

——, (1971), *Catalogue Museum für Indische Kunst Berlin*, Berlin.

Hastings, James (ed.), (1967), *Encyclopaedia of Religion and Ethics*, New York.

Hopkins, E.W. (1895), *The Religion of India*, Boston.

——, (1915), *Epic Mythology*, Strassburg (Indian Reprint, 1968).

Ingholt, Herald (1947), *Gandharan Art in Pakistan*, New York.

Jain, Jyoti Prasad (1964), *The Jaina Sources of The History of Ancient India*, Delhi.

Jash, P. (1974), *History of Śaivism*, Calcutta.

Jayaswal, Suvira (1967), *The Origin and Development of Vaiṣṇavism*, Delhi.

Joshi, Jagat Pati (ed.) (1997), *Facets of Indian Civilization: Recent Perspectives – Essays I Honour of Prof. B.B. Lal*, 3 vols., New Delhi.

Joshi, N.P. (1965), *Mathurā kī Kalā* (Hindi), Mathura.

(1966), *Mathura Sculpture*, Mathura.

——, (1972) *Catalogue of the Brahmanical Sculptures in the State Museum, Lucknow*, Part I, Lucknow.

——, (1979), *Iconography of Balarāma*, New Delhi.

——, (1996), *Tapasvinī Pārvatī - Iconographic Study of Pārvatī in Penance*, New Delhi.

Kala, S.C. (1980), *Terracottas in the Allahabad Museum*, New Delhi.

Kanta, Surya (1961), *Vaidika Devaśāstra* (Hindi), Delhi.

Karmarkar, A.P. (1950), *The Vrātya or Dravidian Systems*, Lonavala.

Keith, A.B. (1964), *Indian Mythology*, New York (Reprint).

Konow, S. Sten (1929), *Corpus Inscriptionum Indicarum*, Vol. II (I), Calcutta.
Kramrisch, Stella (1933), *Indian Sculpture*, Calcutta.
Krishna, Brajesh (1989), *The Art under the Gurjara-Pratihāras*, New Delhi.
Lal, B.B. and Gupta, S.P. (eds.), (1984), *Frontiers of the Indus Civilisation: Mortimer Wheeler Commemoration Volume*), New Delhi.
Law, B.C. (1954), *Historical Geography of Ancient India*, Paris.
——, (1973), *Tribes in Ancient India*, 2nd ed., Poona.
Macdonell, A.A. (1963), *Vedic Mythology*, Varanasi (Reprint).
Marshall, Sir John (1931), *Mohenjodaro and the Indus Civilization*, Vol. I, London.
Maxwell, T.S. (1988), *Viśvarūpa*, Delhi (OUP).
Mishra, Phanikanta (ed.), (1995), *Researches in Indian Archaeology, Art, Architecture, Culture and Tradition (Vijayakanta Mishra Commemoration Volume)*, Delhi.
Misra, O.P. (1989), *Iconography of the Saptamātrikās*, Delhi.
Mitra, Debala (1978), *Bronzes From Achutrajpur, Orissa*, Delhi.
Mookerji, R.K. (1959), *The Gupta Empire*, Bombay.
Munshi, K.M. (1957), *Saga of Indian Sculpture*, Bombay.
Nagar, Shanti Lal (1992), *Garuḍa : The Celestial Bird*, New Delhi.
——, (1989), *Composite Deities in Indian Art and Literature*, New Delhi.
——, (2000), *Jaina Sculptures in Indian and World Museums*, New Delhi.
Nagaswami, R. (1982), *Tantric Cult of South India*, Delhi.
Navaratnam, R. (1973), *Kārttikeya : The Divine Child*, Bombay.
Nazim, M. (1971), *The Life and Times of Sultan Mahmud of Ghazna*, Delhi.
Ohri, V.C. (ed.) (1975), *Arts of Himachal Pradesh*, Simla.
——, (1991), *Sculpture of Western Himalayas*, Delhi.
Ojha, G.H. (1938), *History of the Jodhpur State*, Part I, Ajmer.
Pal, Pratapaditya (1985), *Vaiṣṇava Iconology in Nepal – A Study in Art and Religion*, Calcutta.
——, (1975), *Bronzes of Kashmir*, New Delhi.
Pandey, Lalta Prasad (1971), *Sun-Worship in Ancient India*, Delhi-Patna-Varanasi.
Pillai, J.M. Somasudaram (1970), *Śiva Naṭarāja – The Cosmic Dancer in Cidambaram*, Chidambaram.
Panikkar, Shivaji K. (1997), *Sapta Mātṛkā Worship and Sculptures*, New Delhi.
Buddha Prakash (no date), *Haryana Through The Ages*, Kurukshetra.
——, (1966), *Glimpses of Ancient Punjab*, Patiala.
Prinsep, James (1858), *Essays on Indian Antiquities* (edited by Edward Thomas), London.
Przyluski, J. (1962), *Ancient Peoples of the Punjab* (Eng. Tr. By Chitrabhanu Sen, Calcutta, Reprint).
Pusalkar, A.D. (1955), *Studies in the Epics and Puranas*, Bombay.
Raghavan, V. (ed.) (1980), *The Ramayana Tradition in Asia*, Madras.
Rao, M.S. Nagaraja (ed.) (1987), *Kusumāñjali: New Interpretation of Indian Art & Culture – Sh. C. Sivaramamurti Commemoration Volume*, Delhi.
Rao, T.A. Gopinath (1914-16), *Elements of Hindu Iconography*, 2 Vols., Madras (Reprint, Indological Book House, Delhi-Varanasi, 1971).
Ray, Amita et al. (eds.) (1984), *India Studies (Essays Presented in Memory or Prof. Niharranjan Ray)* Delhi.
Ray, Niharranjan (1975), *Maurya and Post-Maurya Art*, New Delhi.
Rodgers, C.J. (1891), *Report of the Panjab Circle of the Archaeological Survey For 1888-89*, Calcutta, 1891.
——, (1891), *Revised List of Objects of Archaeological Interest in the Panjab, Lahore.*
Rosenfield, J.M. (1967), *The Dynastic Arts of the Kushans*, University of California Press, Barkeley and Los Angles.
Roy, Udai Narain (1979), *Śālabhañjikā in Art, Philosophy and Literature*, Allahabad.
Sahai, Bhagwant (1975), *Iconography of Some Important Minor Hindu Deities*, New Delhi.
Sampurnananda (VS 2001), *Gaṇeśa* (Hindi), Varanasi.
——, (1964), *Hindu Deva Parivāra kā Vikāsa* (Hindi), Allahabad.
Sarasvati, Swami Omanand (VS 2031), *Ancient Seals of Haryana*, Jhajjar.
Saraswati, S.K. (1957), *A Survey of Indian Sculpture*, Calcutta.

Sarma, I.K. (1982), *The Development of Early Saiva Art and Architecture (with special reference to Andhra Pradesh)*, Delhi.
Sashtry, H.K. (1986), *South Indian Images of Gods and Goddesses*, New Delhi (reprint).
Schrader, Otto E. (1916) *Introduction to the Pañcarātra and the Ahirbudhnya Saṃhitā*, Madras.
Shah, Umakant P. (1955), *Studies in Jaina Art*, Banaras.
——, (1959), *Akota Bronzes*, Bombay.
——, (1987), *Jaina Rūpa-Maṇḍana*, Vol. I, New Delhi.
Sharma, B.N. (1975), *Iconography of Revanta*, New Delhi.
——, (1976), *Iconography of Sadāśiva*, Delhi.
——, (1979), *Iconography of Vaināyakī*, New Delhi.
Sharma, Dasharatha (1959), *Early Chauhan Dynasties*, Delhi.
——, (Gen. ed.) (1985), *Rajasthan through the Ages*, Vol. I, Bikaner.
Sharma, R.K. and Handa, Devendra (Eds.) (2004), *Revealing India's Past – Recent Trends in Art and Archaeology*: Prof. Ajay Mitra Shastri Commemoration Volume, 2 vols., New Delhi.
Shastri, Yoganand (1999), *Prāchīna Bhārata meṃ Yaudheya Gaṇarājya*, New Delhi.
Shukla, D.N., *Bhāratīya Vāstuśāstra (Pratimā Vijñāna)*, Vol. IV. Lucknow.
Shukla, S.P. (1983), *Sculptures and Terracottas in the Archaeological Museum Kurukshetra University*, Kurukshetra.
Siddhantashastree, R.K. (1975), *Śaivism Through the Ages*, Delhi.
Singer, Milton (ed.) (1966), *Krishna Myths, Rites and Attitudes*, Honolulu.
Singh, J.P. and Ahmad, Nisar (1977), *Seminar Papers on Tribal Coins of Ancient India (C. 200 B.C. to 400 A.D.)*, Varanasi.
Singh, S.B. (1977), *Brahmanical Icons in Northern India*, New Delhi.
Singh, Udai Vir (1977), *Pinjore Sculptures*, Kurukshetra, 1977.
Sinha, Kachan (1979), *Kārttikeya in Indian Art & Literature*, Delhi.
Sircar, D.C. (1965), *Select Inscriptions*, Vol. I, Calcutta.
——, (ed.) (1970), *Foreigners in Ancient India and Lakṣmī and Sarasvatī in Art and Literature* Calcutta.
——, (1971), *Studies in the Religious Life of Ancient and Medieval India*, Delhi.
Sivaramamurti, C. and Bussagli, M. (1971), *5000 Years of the Art of India*, Harry N. Abrahams Inc. Publishers, New York.
Sivaramamurti, C. (1966), *Indian Epigraphy and South Indian Scripts*, Madras.
——, (1966), *Indian Epigraphy and South Indian Scripts*, Madras.
——, (1975), *Naṭarāja in Art, Thought and Literature*, New Delhi.
——, (1977), *The Art of India*, Harry N. Abrahams Inc. Publishers, New York.
——, (1978), *Chitrasūtra of the Vishṇudharmottara*, New Delhi.
Smith, H. Daniel (1975 & 1980), *A Descriptive Bibliography of the Pāñcharātrāgama*, 2 Vols., GOS Nos. 25 and 168, Baroda.
Smith, Vincent A. (1906), *Catalogue of the Coins in the Indian Museum, Calcutta*, Vol. I, Oxford.
Sorensen, S. (1963), *An Index to the Names in the Mahābhārata*, Delhi (reprint).
Srinivasan, K.R. (1964), *Cave Temples of the Pallavas*, New Delhi.
Srivastava, H.L. (1952), *Excavations at Agroha, Punjab*, Memoirs of the Archaeological Survey of India, no. 61.
Srivastava, V.C. (1971), *Sun-Worship in Ancient India*, Delhi.
Srivastava, V.S. (1960-61), *Catalogue and Guide to Ganga Golden Jubilee Museum, Bikaner*, Jaipur.
——, (1960-61), *Catalogue and Guide to Rajputana Museum, Ajmer*, Jaipur.
——, (ed.) (1981), *Cultural Contours of India*, New Delhi.
Stein, M.A. (1937), *Archaeological Reconnaissances in North-Western India and South-Eastern Iran*, London.
Thapar, D.R. (1961), *Icons in Bronze*, Bombay.
Tiwari, M.N.P. (1981), *Jaina Pratimāvijñāna*, Varanasi.
Trivedi, R.D. (1981), *Iconography of Pārvatī*, Delhi.
Vatsyayana, Kapila (1975), *Rāmāyaṇa in the Arts of Asia*, Teheran.
Vogel, J. Ph. (1910), *Catalogue of the Archaeological Museum at Mathura*, Allahabad.

Yadav, Nirmala (1997), *Gaṇeśa in Indian Art and Literature*, Jaipur.

Watters, Thomas (1961), *On Yuang Chwang's Travels in India*, Delhi (First Indian ed.).

Westropp and Wake, C. S. (1979), *Symbol Worship: Influence of the Phallic Ideas in the Religions of Antiquity*, New Delhi.

Wilkins, W.J. (1972), *Hindu Mythology: Vedic and Puranic* (Indian reprint).

Winternitz, M. (1933), *A History of Indian Literature*, Vol. II, Calcutta.

GAZETTEERS

Gazetteer Delhi District, 1883-84.

Gazetteer of the Gurgaon District (Lahore, 1884).

Imperial Gazetteer of India.

Punjab District Gazetteer: Jhelum District, Lahore, 1907.

UNPUBLISHED THESES AND DISSERTATIONS

Silak Ram, *Archaeology of Rohtak and Hissar Districts (Haryana)*, Ph. D. Thesis, Kurukshetra University, Kurukshetra, 1972.

Sheela Devi, *Art Tradition in Haryana*, Ph. D. Thesis, K.U., Kurukshetra, 1975.

Manmohan Kumar, *Archaeology of Ambala and Kurukshetra Districts (Haryana)*, Ph. D. Thesis, Kurukshetra University, Kurukshetra, 1976.

Punia, D.P.S., *Archaeology of Mahendragarh and Gurgaon Districts (Haryana)*, Ph. D. Thesis, Kurukshetra University, Kurukshetra, 1976.

Dhattarwal, Dhup Singh (1978), *Archaeology of Safidon Tehsil (Dist. Jind)*, M. Phil, Dissertation, K.U., Kurukshetra.

Sat Deva, *History and Archaeology of Jind*, M. Phil. Dissertation, K.U., Kurukshetra, 1981.

Amar Singh, *Archaeology of Karnal and Jind Districts (Haryana)*, Thesis, Kurukshetra University, Kurukshetra, 1981.

Yogeshwar Kumar, *Archaeology of Naraingarh and Its Neighbourhood (District Ambala)*, M. Phil. Dissertation, Kurukshetra University, Kurukshetra, 1987.

Lamba, Mani Ram, *Archaeology and History of Kalanaur Block, District Rohtak*, M. Phil. Dissertation, M.D. University, Rohtak, 1987-88.

Sneh Lata, *Archaeology and History of Sampla Block, District Rohtak (Haryana)*, M. Phil. Dissertation, M.D. University, Rohtak, 1987-88.

Lohan, Aditya, *A Historical Cultural Study of the Hansi Region (From the Earliest Times to* A.D. *1526)*, Ph. D. Thesis, K.U., Kurukshetra, 1988.

Ranbir Singh, *History and Archaeology of Tehsil Palwal (District Faridabad), Haryana*, M. Phil, Dissertation, Kurukshetra University, Kurukshetra, 1995.

Rahar, Jagdish Singh, *Archaeological Settlement Pattern of Mahemdragarh and Rewari Districts (Haryana)*, Ph. D. Thesis, M.D. University, Rohtak, 2001.

JOURNALS

Ājakala (Hindi), New Delhi

Ancient India, Bulletin of the Archaeological Survey of India, New Delhi

Annali

Annual Report of the Archaeological Survey of India

Archives of Asian Art

Artibus Asiae

Bhāratī

Bhāratīya Vidyā
Brahma Vidya, New Series, Adyar
Bulletin of the Ancient Indian History and Archaeology
Bulletin of Museums and Archaeology, U.P., Lucknow
Bulletin National Museum
Bulletin of the School of Oriental and African Studies, London
East and West
Epigraphia Indica
Half-Yearly Journal of the Mysore University, Mysore
Hariyāṇā Śodha Patrikā, Rewari
Haryana Sahitya Akademi Journal of Indological Studies
Indian Antiquary
Indian Express
Indo-Iranica
Indologica Jaipurensia
Indologica Taurinensia
Jana Sāhitya, Patiala
Journal of the Andhra Historical Research Society
Journal of the American Oriental Society
Journal of the Asiatic Society of Bangladesh, Dhaka
Journal of the Asiatic Society of Bengal
Journal of the Bihar Research Society
Journal of Haryana Studies
Journal of the Ganganatha Jha Kendriya Sanskrit Vidyapeetha, Allahabad
Journal of Indian History
Journal of the Madhya Pradesh Itihāsa Parishad, Bhopal
Journal of the Numismatic Society of India
Journal of the University of Bombay
Journal of the U.P. Historical Society
Journal of the Varendra Research Museum, Dhaka
Kalā
Kurukshetra University Research Journal
Lalit-Kala
Mārg
Memoirs of the Archaeological Survey of India
New Indian Antiquary
Numismatic Digest
Pañchāla
Prāchya-Pratibhā, Bhopal
Purāṇa, Varanasi
Purāvṛitta, Lucknow University, Lucknow
Report of the Rajputana Museum, 1913-14
Report of the Working of the Central Museum of Lahore
Roopa-Lekhā
The Researcher
The Tribune, Chandigarh
Zeitschrift der Deutschen Morgenlandischen Gesellschaft

Index

[The following abbreviations have been used: a – author; b – book or ancient text; c – city, town; d – deity; dyn – dynasty; eh – epic hero; i – image; k – king; p – place; pd – period; r – river or rivulet; s – style, T - temple. Important references have been underlined.]